EUROPEAN CAPITAL MARKETS LAW

This user-friendly, fully updated new edition continues to systematise the European law governing capital markets and examines the underlying concepts from a broadly interdisciplinary perspective. The third edition deals with three central developments: the project of the capital markets union; sustainable finance; and the further digitalisation of financial instruments and securities markets.

The first chapter deals with the foundations of capital markets law in Europe, the second explains the basics, and the third examines the regime on market abuse. Chapter four explores the disclosure system and chapter five the roles of intermediaries, such as financial analysts, rating agencies and proxy advisers. Short selling and high frequency trading is described in chapter six. Chapter seven deals with financial services and compliance requirements for investment firms. Chapter eight illustrates the regulation of benchmarks. Finally, chapter nine deals with public takeovers.

Throughout the book emphasis is placed on legal practice, and frequent reference is made to the key decisions of supervisory authorities and courts. This book is essential reading for students involved in the study of capital markets law and financial law.

European Capital Markets Law

Third Edition

Edited by
Rüdiger Veil

·HART·
OXFORD · LONDON · NEW YORK · NEW DELHI · SYDNEY

HART PUBLISHING

Bloomsbury Publishing Plc

Kemp House, Chawley Park, Cumnor Hill, Oxford, OX2 9PH, UK

1385 Broadway, New York, NY 10018, USA

29 Earlsfort Terrace, Dublin 2, Ireland

HART PUBLISHING, the Hart/Stag logo, BLOOMSBURY and the Diana logo are
trademarks of Bloomsbury Publishing Plc

First published in Great Britain 2022

Copyright © The editor and contributors severally 2022

The editor and contributors have asserted their right under the Copyright, Designs and
Patents Act 1988 to be identified as Authors of this work.

All rights reserved. No part of this publication may be reproduced or transmitted in any form or by any means,
electronic or mechanical, including photocopying, recording, or any information storage or retrieval system,
without prior permission in writing from the publishers.

While every care has been taken to ensure the accuracy of this work, no responsibility for loss or damage
occasioned to any person acting or refraining from action as a result of any statement in it can be
accepted by the authors, editors or publishers.

All UK Government legislation and other public sector information used in the work is Crown Copyright ©.
All House of Lords and House of Commons information used in the work is Parliamentary Copyright ©.
This information is reused under the terms of the Open Government Licence v3.0 (http://www.
nationalarchives.gov.uk/doc/open-government-licence/version/3) except where otherwise stated.

All Eur-lex material used in the work is © European Union, http://eur-lex.europa.eu/, 1998–2022.

A catalogue record for this book is available from the British Library.

Library of Congress Cataloging-in-Publication data

Names: Veil, Rüdiger, 1966-, editor.
Title: European capital markets law / edited by Rüdiger Veil. Other titles: Europäisches Kapitalmarktrecht. English
Description: Third edition. | Oxford, UK ; New York, NY : Hart Publishing, an imprint of
Bloomsbury Publishing, 2022. | Includes bibliographical references and index.
Identifiers: LCCN 2021059531 (print) | LCCN 2021059532 (ebook) | ISBN 9781509958481 (hardback) |
ISBN 9781509942114 (paperback) | ISBN 9781509942121 (pdf) | ISBN 9781509942138 (EPub)
Subjects: LCSH: Capital market—Law and legislation—European Union countries. | Financial institutions—Law
and legislation—European Union countries.
Classification: LCC KJE2245 .E9213 2022 (print) | LCC KJE2245 (ebook) | DDC 346.24/09—c23/eng/20220131
LC record available at https://lccn.loc.gov/2021059531
LC ebook record available at https://lccn.loc.gov/2021059532

ISBN: PB: 978-1-50994-211-4
ePDF: 978-1-50994-212-1
ePub: 978-1-50994-213-8

Typeset by Compuscript Ltd, Shannon
Printed and bound in Great Britain by CPI Group (UK) Ltd, Croydon CR0 4YY

To find out more about our authors and books visit www.hartpublishing.co.uk.
Here you will find extracts, author information, details of forthcoming events
and the option to sign up for our newsletters.

PREFACE

The first two editions of the textbook aimed to make the fragmentation of European capital markets law visible. At that time, capital markets in the EU were largely governed by minimum harmonising directives. This has since changed. Today, the European legal acts are regulations and fully harmonising directives. As a result, supervisory law is largely unified at the European level. In addition, the body of law has grown enormously. The EU has learned lessons from the financial market crisis. There is no longer any unregulated trading of financial instruments. Furthermore, benchmarks and securitisations are covered by European law for the first time. Another meta-theme is the transformation of finance in the direction of environmentally sustainable investments. Sustainable finance now permeates much of financial markets regulation. The digitalisation of investment services and the use of blockchain for the distribution and trading of financial products have also led to far-reaching reforms that are intended to provide market participants with a reliable legal framework, but also to enable innovation.

The third edition of this book aims to address these developments. It looks at the principles of European capital markets law, which is currently scattered across eight single rulebooks, each consisting of numerous legal acts, thereby aiming to reduce the complexity of the regimes and present the larger picture of capital markets regulation in Europe. The focus is on the market abuse regime, the disclosure obligations for both issuers and investors and the regulation of financial intermediaries, such as investment firms. Furthermore, important trading activities are dealt with, such as short selling and high frequency trading.

The third edition includes new sections on objectives of capital markets law (§ 2), DLT-based financial instruments and their trading on the blockchain (§ 10), on investment objectives (§ 23), proxy advisors (§ 28) and the prudential regulation of investment firms (§§ 29–31). The EU's goal of promoting sustainable investments is addressed in several sections of the book (§ 1 on the history of European capital markets law, § 2 on regulatory objectives and strategies, § 8 on financial instruments, §§ 16 and 18 on corporate disclosure, § 22 on disclosure of corporate governance issues, § 24 on investment objectives and § 35 on benchmarks).

This book is valuable for a wide audience. It offers students the possibility to examine European capital markets law from a dogmatic and interdisciplinary point of view. At the same time, it offers insights equally relevant to research and practice. National particularities, such as the different understanding of the role of private enforcement, are depicted through examples chosen from various European countries, including Austria, France, Germany, Italy, Spain, Sweden and the United Kingdom. The book places a strong emphasis on legal practice, presenting more than 30 decisions by Belgian, Danish, English, French, German and Swedish supervisory authorities and courts and the European Court of Justice, in order to improve understanding of how interpretational questions are being dealt with in legal practice.

I would like to thank the co-authors Hendrik Brinckmann, Marcus P. Lerch, Fabian Walla and Malte Wundenberg for their contributions to this book. Their chapters are inspired by their academic work and profit from the experiences they have gathered in listed companies, law firms and the Ministry of Finance.

I am grateful to Koray Cavusoglu, Tristan Denis, Jasmin Gärth, Gabriele Groß, Julian Heyermann, Lorena Meyer, Pia Richter, Evgenia Sardeli, Nadja Weber and Marc Wiesner for their great assistance in editing the manuscript.

The book is based on European legislation as of October 2021.

Suggestions regarding the book are welcome and can be submitted to me at ruediger.veil@jura.uni-muenchen.de.

Rüdiger Veil
Munich, October 2021

SUMMARY CONTENTS

Preface v
List of Contributors xxxi
List of Abbreviations xxxiii

1
Foundations of Capital Markets Legislature in Europe

§ 1. History (*Rüdiger Veil*) 3
§ 2. Concept and Aims of Capital Markets Regulation (*Rüdiger Veil*) 27
§ 3. Legislative Powers for Regulating and Harmonising Capital Markets
      in Europe (*Rüdiger Veil*) 43
§ 4. Rule-Making Process (*Fabian Walla*) 53
§ 5. Sources of Law and Principles of Interpretation (*Rüdiger Veil*) 65
§ 6. Intra- and Interdisciplinarity (*Rüdiger Veil*) 85

2
Basics of Capital Markets Law

§ 7. Capital Markets (*Rüdiger Veil*) 99
§ 8. Financial Instruments (*Rüdiger Veil*) 113
§ 9. Market Participants (*Rüdiger Veil*) 123
§ 10. Cryptoassets and DLT Market Infrastructures (*Rüdiger Veil*) 133
§ 11. Capital Markets Supervision (*Fabian Walla*) 143
§ 12. Sanctions (*Rüdiger Veil*) 171

3
Market Abuse

§ 13. Foundations (*Rüdiger Veil*) 183
§ 14. Insider Dealing (*Rüdiger Veil*) 189
§ 15. Market Manipulation (*Rüdiger Veil*) 227

4
Disclosure System

§ 16. Foundations (*Hendrik Brinckmann*) 259
§ 17. Prospectus Disclosure (*Rüdiger Veil*) 281
§ 18. Periodic Disclosure (*Hendrik Brinckmann*) 309
§ 19. Disclosure of Inside Information (*Rüdiger Veil*) 341
§ 20. Disclosure of Major Holdings (*Rüdiger Veil*) 373
§ 21. Directors' Dealings (*Rüdiger Veil*) 409
§ 22. Corporate Governance and Shareholder Rights (*Rüdiger Veil*) 419

5
Trading Activities

§ 23	Investment Objectives (*Rüdiger Veil*)	431
§ 24	Short Sales and Credit Default Swaps (*Fabian Walla*)	439
§ 25	Algorithmic Trading and High-Frequency Trading (*Marcus Lerch*)	457

6
Intermediaries

§ 26	Financial Analysts (*Rüdiger Veil*)	499
§ 27	Rating Agencies (*Rüdiger Veil*)	521
§ 28	Proxy Advisors (*Rüdiger Veil*)	547

7
Investment Firms

§ 29	Foundations (*Rüdiger Veil*)	555
§ 30	Investment Services (*Rüdiger Veil*)	559
§ 31	Product Intervention (*Rüdiger Veil*)	579
§ 32	Foundations of Compliance (*Malte Wundenberg*)	585
§ 33	Compliance Requirements (*Malte Wundenberg*)	591
§ 34	Governance (*Malte Wundenberg*)	623

8
Regulation of Benchmarks

§ 35	Foundations (*Malte Wundenberg*)	645
§ 36	Market Supervision and Organisational Requirements (*Malte Wundenberg*)	651

9
Takeover Law

§ 37	Foundations (*Rüdiger Veil*)	673
§ 38	Public Takeovers (*Rüdiger Veil*)	683
§ 39	Mandatory Bid (*Rüdiger Veil*)	687
§ 40	Defence against Takeover Bids (*Rüdiger Veil*)	697

Bibliography	701
Subject Index	705
Index of National Laws	719
Index of National Laws by Country	727
Index of European Laws	733
Index of Supervisory and Court Rulings	735

DETAILED CONTENTS

Preface v
List of Contributors xxxi
List of Abbreviations xxxiii

1
Foundations of Capital Markets Legislature in Europe

§ 1. History 3
    I. Introduction 4
    II. Segré Report (1966) 4
    III. Phase 1: Coordination of Stock Exchange and Prospectus
        Laws (1979–1982) 5
    IV. White Paper on Completing the Internal Market (1985) 6
    V. Phase 2: Harmonisation of the Laws on Securities Markets
        (1988–1993) 6
    VI. Financial Services Action Plan (1999) 7
    VII. Lamfalussy Report (2000) 8
    VIII. Phase 3: Reorganisation of the Laws on Prospectuses and Securities
        (2003–2007) 9
    IX. Continuation of Phase 3: Harmonisation of Takeover Law (2004) 12
    X. White Paper on Financial Services Policy (2005) 13
    XI. Phase 4: Overcoming the Financial Market Crisis through Unification
        of European Law and a European Supervisory Architecture
        (2009–2016) 14
    XII. Phase 4: European System of Financial Supervision (2009) 14
    XIII. Regulation of Credit Rating Agencies (2009–2013) 15
    XIV. Revision of the Framework Directives—from Minimum to Full
        Harmonisation and Unification of Union Law (2009–2014) 16
    XV. Regulation on Short Sales (2012) 18
    XVI. Continuation of Phase 4: Regulation on OTC Derivatives (2012) 19
    XVII. End of Phase 4: Regulation of Benchmarks (2016) 19
    XVIII. Phase 5: Capital Markets Union (since 2015) 20
    XIX. Prospectus Regulation 20
    XX. Securitisation 21
    XXI. ESA Review 22
    XXII. Improving Start-up and SME Financing 22
    XXIII. Sustainable Finance 23

	XXIV.	Action Plan 2020	24
	XXV.	Conclusion	25

§ 2. Concept and Aims of Capital Markets Regulation 27
    I. Concept 28
    II. Regulatory Aims 29
        1. Efficiency of Capital Markets and Investor Protection 29
        2. Financial Stability 32
        3. Sustainability 33
    III. Regulatory Strategies and Instruments 35
        1. Disclosure 35
            (a) Information Function 35
            (b) Regulatory Function 39
            (c) Monitoring Function 40
        2. Prohibition 40
        3. Enforcement 41

§ 3. Legislative Powers for Regulating and Harmonising Capital Markets in Europe 43
    I. Legal Foundations of the European Union 43
    II. Rules on Competence 44
        1. Coordination of Provisions on the Protection of Shareholders and Creditors 44
        2. Coordination of Start-Up and Pursuit of Self-Employment ... 45
        3. Establishing an Internal Market 45
        4. Cross-border Crimes 46
    III. Legislative Instruments 46
        1. Overview 46
        2. Regulation 47
        3. Directive 48
    IV. Harmonisation 49
        1. Concepts 49
        2. Tendency towards Full Harmonisation 49

§ 4. Rule-Making Process 53
    I. Historical Development 54
    II. The Lamfalussy II Process 55
        1. Framework Acts 55
            (a) Concept 55
            (b) Trialogue Procedure 56
        2. Delegated Acts and Implementing Measures 57
        3. Guidelines and Recommendations 60
        4. Supervisory Convergence 61
        5. Stakeholder Involvement 62
        6. Graph: Lamfalussy II Process 63
    III. Evaluation of the Lamfalussy II Process 63

§ 5. Sources of Law and Principles of Interpretation 65
I. Introduction 66
II. European Law 66
1. Sources of Law 66
(a) Single Rulebooks of EU Securities Regulation 67
(b) Regulations on the European Supervisory Authorities 69
(c) Further Relevant EU Law 69
2. Interpretation 70
(a) Autonomous Interpretation 70
(b) The Role of ESMA in the Development of Uniform Standards of Interpretation 71
(c) Methods of Interpretation 73
  (aa) Textual Interpretation 74
  (bb) Contextual Interpretation 74
  (cc) Historical Interpretation 75
  (dd) Teleological Interpretation 76
III. National Law of the Member States 78
1. Austria 78
2. France 79
3. Germany 80
4. Greece 81
5. Italy 81
6. Spain 82
7. Sweden 82
8. United Kingdom 83

§ 6. Intra- and Interdisciplinarity 85
I. Introduction 86
II. Intradisciplinarity 87
1. Legal Nature 87
(a) Interaction of Supervisory and Private Law 87
(b) Interpretation 88
2. Relations with Accounting, Corporate and Insolvency Law 89
III. Interdisciplinarity 91
1. The model of *homo oeconomicus* 91
2. Behavioural Finance 92
(a) Bounded Rationality 92
(b) Overconfidence 92
(c) Fairness 92
(d) Prospect Theory/Framing/Risk Aversity 93
(e) Hindsight Bias 93
(f) Representativeness/Availability/Salience 93
3. Relevance of Behavioural Finance for Capital Markets Law 94

2
Basics of Capital Markets Law

§ 7. Capital Markets 99
    I. Overview 100
        1. Trading Venue 100
        2. Primary and Secondary Markets 101
        3. Stock Exchanges 102
    II. Trading Venues under MiFID II 102
        1. Regulated Market (RM) 102
        2. Multilateral Trading Facility (MTF) 104
        3. Organised Trading Facility (OTF) 104
    III. SME Growth Markets 105
    IV. OTC Trade 108
    V. Access to Markets and Market Exit 108
        1. IPO and Listing 109
        2. Delisting 110

§ 8. Financial Instruments 113
    I. Introduction 113
    II. Securities 114
        1. Definitions in MiFID II 114
        2. Shares 116
        3. Bonds 117
        4. Other Investment Products 117
    III. Derivatives 118
    IV. ESG Financial Products 120

§ 9. Market Participants 123
    I. Introduction 123
    II. Providers of Market Infrastructures 124
    III. Issuers 126
    IV. Investors 127
        1. Types 127
        2. Level of Protection 129

§ 10. Cryptoassets and DLT Market Infrastructures 133
    I. Foundations 134
        1. Tokenisation of Securities on the Blockchain 135
        2. Transfer of Token 136
        3. Public Offer of Token 137
        4. Trade 137
    II. Requirements under MiFID II 138
        1. Types of Trading Platforms 138
        2. Advantages and Disadvantages of Decentralised Trading Platforms 138
    III. Commission Proposal for Regulation of Cryptoassets 139
        1. Pilot Regime 140
        2. Regime for Cryptoassets 141
        3. Evaluation 141

§ 11. Capital Markets Supervision 143
I. Introduction 145
II. European Law Requirements 145
1. Institutional Organisation 145
2. Powers 146
   (a) Administrative and Investigation Powers 146
   (b) Administrative Fines 147
   (c) Other Administrative Sanctions 148
   (d) Choice of Sanctions/Administrative Measures 148
III. Supervision by the NCAs 149
1. Institutional Design 149
   (a) Model of Integrated Supervision 149
   (b) Model of Sectoral Supervision 150
   (c) Hybrid Models 151
   (d) Twin Peaks Model 151
   (e) Direct Banking Supervision by the European Central Bank (ECB) 152
   (f) Generally Preferable Supervisory Model? 152
2. Internal Organisation and Independence 152
3. Administrative and Criminal Powers 153
4. Liability of Supervisory Authorities 153
5. Use of Resources and Sanctioning Activity 154
IV. Cooperation between the NCAs 154
1. Cooperation within the European Union 155
2. Cooperation with Third Countries' Authorities 155
V. Competition between the National Supervisory Institutions 156
VI. The European System of Financial Supervision (ESFS) 157
1. Institutional Design 158
   (a) Macro-prudential Level 158
   (b) Micro-prudential Level 158
   (c) European Banking Union 159
2. The European Securities and Markets Authority (ESMA) 160
   (a) Foundations 160
   (b) Independence and Budget 162
   (c) Powers of Intervention vis-à-vis the NCAs 163
      (aa) Breaches of EU Law by the National Supervisory Authorities 163
      (bb) Decisions on Emergency Situations and Disagreements between NCAs 164
         (1) Emergency Situations 164
         (2) Disagreements between Competent Authorities in Cross-Border Situations 164
         (3) National Fiscal Responsibilities Limit ESMA Powers 164
   (d) Direct Supervision of Market Participants 165
      (aa) Warnings and Prohibition of Financial Activities 165

                (bb) Supervision of Credit Rating Agencies (CRA) and
                     Trade Repositories (TR)/Security Repositories (SR) 166
                (cc) Supervision of Benchmarks and Data Services
                     Providers 167
           (e) Rule-making Powers and Supervisory Convergence 167
           (f) Compliance of ESMA's Powers with the TFEU 167
           (g) Judicial Review 168
           (h) Liability of ESMA 168
           (i) Access to Information 168
      3. Conclusion 169

§ 12. Sanctions 171
   I. Introduction 172
   II. Sanctioning Systems in the Pre-Crisis Era 173
      1. Public Enforcement (Criminal and Administrative Sanctions) 173
      2. Private Enforcement 173
   III. Reforms after the Financial Crisis 174
      1. Need for Reforms 174
      2. Public Enforcement 175
         (a) Provisions on the Detection and Exposure of Legal
             Infringements 176
         (b) Supervisory Measures 176
         (c) Sanctions 177
      3. Development of a Private Enforcement 178
   IV. Conclusion 179

3
Market Abuse

§ 13. Foundations 183
   I. Introduction 183
   II. Legal Foundations 184
      1. MAR 184
      2. CRIM-MAD 186
   III. Level of Harmonisation 186
      1. Minimum versus Maximum Harmonisation 186
      2. Evaluation 187
   IV. Scope of Application 187
   V. Presentation of Market Abuse Law in this Book 188

§ 14. Insider Dealing 189
   I. Introduction 191
   II. Regulatory Concepts 194
      1. Overview of the Market Abuse Regime 194
      2. Accompanying Rules 195
      3. Insider Compliance 195
   III. Regulatory Goals 196

Detailed Contents

- IV. Concept of Inside Information 197
  - 1. Definition and Interpretation of Inside Information under the MAD 2003 Regime 197
  - 2. Implementation in the MAR 200
    - (a) Information which has Not been Made Public 201
    - (b) Information of a Precise Nature 202
      - (aa) Circumstances and Events 202
      - (bb) Specific 204
      - (cc) Reference to an Issuer or to Financial Instruments 206
    - (c) Price Relevance 207
- V. Prohibitions 210
  - 1. Overview 210
  - 2. Prohibition of the Acquisition or Disposal of Financial Instruments 211
    - (a) Foundations 211
    - (b) Acquisition and Disposal of Financial Instruments 211
    - (c) Use of Inside Information and Legitimate Behaviours ... 212
  - 3. Unlawful Disclosure of Inside Information 214
    - (a) Disclosure 215
    - (b) Market Sounding 217
  - 4. Recommending or Inducing 218
  - 5. Exemptions 219
- VI. Supervision 219
  - 1. Tasks and Powers of National Authorities (NCAs) 219
    - (a) Insider Lists 221
    - (b) Notification Obligations and Whistleblowing 222
  - 2. Supervisory Convergence 223
- VII. Sanctions 223
  - 1. Overview 223
  - 2. Administrative Measures and Pecuniary Sanctions 224
  - 3. Criminal Sanctions 225
  - 4. Investor Protection through Civil Liability 225
- VIII. Conclusion 225

§ 15. Market Manipulation 227
- I. Introduction 228
- II. Foundations 229
  - 1. Regulatory System 229
  - 2. Direct Effect in the Member States 230
- III. Scope of Application of the MAR 231
  - 1. Personal Scope 231
  - 2. Material Scope 231
- IV. Prohibitions 232
  - 1. Regulatory System 232
  - 2. Information-based Market Manipulation 233
    - (a) Dogmatics 234
    - (b) Legal Practice 236
    - (c) Digression: Behavioural Finance 237

　　　　3. Transaction-based Market Manipulation 238
　　　　　　(a) Definition and Indicators 238
　　　　　　(b) Exceptions 240
　　　　4. Other Forms of Market Manipulation 241
　　　　5. Benchmark Manipulation 242
　　　　6. Specific Types of Market Manipulation 243
　　　　　　(a) Dominant Market Position 243
　　　　　　(b) Transactions at the Close of the Market 244
　　　　　　(c) Certain Means of Algorithmic and High-Frequency
　　　　　　　　Trading (HFT) 244
　　　　　　(d) Abusing Access to the Media 244
　　　　　　(e) Emission Allowances 245
　　V. Safe-Harbour Rules 245
　　　　1. Introduction 245
　　　　2. Buy-Back Programmes 246
　　　　　　(a) Aim of the Programme 246
　　　　　　(b) Disclosure Obligations 247
　　　　　　(c) Trading Conditions 247
　　　　　　(d) Restrictions 248
　　　　3. Price Stabilisation 248
　　　　　　(a) Scope of Application 249
　　　　　　(b) Period of Stabilisation 249
　　　　　　(c) Disclosure and Organisational Obligations 250
　　　　　　(d) Ancillary Stabilisation 250
　　VI. Supervision 251
　　　　1. Supervisory Mechanisms 251
　　　　2. Investigatory Powers 252
　　VII. Sanctions 252
　　　　1. Administrative and Criminal Sanctions 252
　　　　　　(a) Administrative Sanctions 252
　　　　　　(b) Criminal Sanctions 253
　　　　　　(c) Enforcement Practices 254
　　　　2. Private Enforcement 255
　　VIII. Conclusion 255

4
Disclosure System

§ 16. Foundations 259
　　I. Introduction 260
　　II. Transparency and Capital Market Efficiency 261
　　　　1. Allocational Efficiency 262
　　　　　　(a) Akerlof and the 'Market for Lemons' 262
　　　　　　(b) Fama and the Efficient Capital Market Hypothesis (ECMH) 262
　　　　　　(c) Discussion on the Scope of a Legal Reception of the ECMH 263
　　　　2. Institutional Efficiency 264
　　　　3. Operational Efficiency 265

III. Disclosure Provisions as Part of the Regulation of Capital Markets............ 266
 1. The Importance of Legal Disclosure Provisions from an Economic Point of View 266
  (a) Reduction of Information Asymmetries to Prevent Market Failure.. 266
   (aa) Social Value of Public Information.. 266
   (bb) Reduction of Agency Costs and Signal Theory..................... 267
  (b) Information and the Public Good Problem..................................... 267
  (c) Mandatory Disclosure and the Theory of Transaction Costs 268
  (d) Conclusion.. 269
 2. Disclosure Provisions as Part of Investor Protection 269
  (a) Principle of Investor Protection through Information Disclosure... 270
  (b) Discussion on the Scope of Investor Protection 271
  (c) Criticism of the Information Paradigm and Complementing Measures for Investor Protection.. 271
 3. Disclosure Provisions as an Instrument to Foster Sustainable Finance 272
IV. Development of a Disclosure System in European Capital Markets Law 274
V. Dissemination Procedure and Access to Regulated Information 275
 1. Development of Harmonised Requirements for the Access to Regulated Information 276
  (a) Requirements on the Dissemination of Regulated Information.... 277
  (b) Officially Appointed Mechanism (OAM) 278
  (c) Implementation in the Member States.. 278
  (d) European Electronic Access Point (EEAP) and European Single Access Point (ESAP) 278
 2. Conclusion 279

§ 17. Prospectus Disclosure 281
 I. Introduction.. 282
 II. Foundations 283
  1. Disclosure Obligation 283
  2. Accompanying Regimes... 284
  3. Legal Sources.. 284
   (a) European Level 284
   (b) National Level... 286
 III. Prospectus Requirement According to the Prospectus Regulation 286
  1. Scope of Application.. 286
  2. Exemptions from the Obligation to Publish a Prospectus..................... 287
   (a) Exceptions for Offers of Securities 287
   (b) Exemptions for Certain Issuances for the Admission to the Regulated Market... 288
  3. Format and Structure of a Prospectus.. 289
   (a) Single or Separate Documents and Base Prospectus 289
   (b) Preparation, Content and Presentation.. 290

			(c)	Structure	293
				(aa) Summary	293
				(bb) Risk Factors	294
			(d)	Incorporation by Reference	295
			(e)	Language	295
		4.	Approval and Publication		296
			(a)	Foundations	296
			(b)	European Passport	297
			(c)	Supplement to the Prospectus	298
		5.	Special Regimes		298
	IV.	Supervision			299
	V.	Administrative and Criminal Sanctions			300
	VI.	Private Enforcement			300
		1.	Requirements under European Law		300
		2.	National Law		301
			(a)	Deficiencies of the Prospectus	302
			(b)	Claimant and Opposing Party	304
			(c)	Causation	304
			(d)	Responsibility (Fault)	305
			(e)	Legal Consequences	305
	VII.	Conclusion			306

§ 18. Periodic Disclosure 309

	I.	Introduction			310
		1.	Development of a System of Periodic Disclosure		310
		2.	Financial Accounting Information as the Basis of Financial Reporting		313
		3.	The Growing Importance of Non-financial Information within the System of Periodic Disclosure		314
			(a)	The Disclosure of Environmental Issues as the Beginning of Non-financial Reporting	314
			(b)	Development of Non-financial Reporting by Initiatives on Corporate Social Responsibility	315
			(c)	Upcoming Developments of Non-financial Reporting by its Integration into the Sustainable Finance Agenda	317
			(d)	Conclusion	317
	II.	Regulatory Concepts			318
		1.	Requirements under European Law		318
			(a)	The Financial Report as a Unified Reporting Standard for Periodic Disclosure	318
			(b)	Correlation with European Accounting Law as a Reflection of the Dualistic Regulatory Concept	319
			(c)	Addressee of the Disclosure Obligation	320
		2.	Implementation in the Member States		321
	III.	Annual Financial Report			321
		1.	Overview		321

		2.	Financial Accounting Information 322
			(a) Consolidated and Individual Accounts 322
			(b) Management Report.. 324
			(c) Auditing of the Annual Financial Report....................................... 325
			(d) Single Electronic Reporting Format (ESEF) 325
	IV.	Half-yearly Financial Reports 326
		1.	Overview 326
		2.	Financial Accounting Information 326
			(a) Consolidated and Individual Accounts 326
			(b) Interim Management Report 327
			(c) Auditing of the Half-yearly Financial Report 328
	V.	Quarterly Periodic Financial Reports 328
		1.	The Question of a Sufficient Supply of Capital Markets with Information on Issuers 328
			(a) Concept of a Quarterly Reporting Obligation in the TD 2004 328
			(b) Content of Interim Management Statements 329
			(c) Quarterly Financial Reports under the TD of 2004 330
		2.	Concept of Additional Periodic Disclosure after the Reform of 2013 330
	VI.	Disclosure Procedures 332
		1.	Requirements under European Law 332
		2.	Transposition in the Member States 332
		3.	Outlook: Access to Financial Reports via a Central European Access Point 333
	VII.	Enforcement of Financial Information 334
		1.	Dual-enforcement in Germany and Austria 335
		2.	Enforcement in Ireland by the Financial Reporting Supervision Unit (FRSU) 336
	VIII.	Sanctions 337
		1.	Liability for Incorrect Financial Reporting 337
		2.	Sanctions under Criminal and Administrative Law 338
	IX.	Conclusion 339
§ 19.	Disclosure of Inside Information 341
	I.	Introduction 343
		1.	Regulatory Goals 343
		2.	Practical Relevance 346
		3.	Empirical Studies 347
	II.	Regulatory Concepts 348
		1.	Requirements under European Law 348
			(a) Disclosure Obligations under the MAR 348
			(b) Relationship to Other Disclosure Rules 349
		2.	National Regulation 350
	III.	Obligation to Disclose Inside Information (Article 17(1) MAR) 350
		1.	Issuers of Financial Instruments 350

		2.	Inside Information	352
			(a) Foundations	352
			(b) Information Directly Concerning the Issuer	352
			(c) Attribution of Knowledge	353
		3.	No Offsetting of Information	353
		4.	No Combination of Disclosure with Marketing Activities	354
		5.	Publication Procedure	354
	IV.	Delay in Disclosure		355
		1.	Foundations	355
		2.	Delay Pursuant to Article 17(4) MAR	357
			(a) Legitimate Interests	357
			(b) No Misleading the Public	360
			(c) Ensuring Confidentiality	360
			(d) Decision by the Issuer	362
		3.	Delay Pursuant to Article 17(5) MAR	363
	V.	Obligation to Disclose Inside Information (Article 17 (8) MAR)		363
	VI.	Supervision		364
	VII.	Sanctions		364
		1.	Administrative and Criminal Measures and Sanctions	364
		2.	Civil Liability	366
			(a) Germany	367
			(b) Austria	369
			(c) United Kingdom	370
			(d) Other Member States	371
	VIII.	Conclusion		372
§ 20.	Disclosure of Major Holdings			373
	I.	Introduction		375
		1.	Regulatory Aims	375
		2.	Degree of Harmonisation	377
		3.	Practical Relevance	378
	II.	European Concepts of Regulation		379
		1.	Legal Sources	379
		2.	Scope of Application	380
		3.	Disclosure Obligations under the TD	380
		4.	Further Disclosure Obligations	381
	III.	Disclosure Obligations on Changes in Voting Rights		382
		1.	Notification	382
			(a) Prerequisites	382
			(b) Thresholds	382
			(c) Exemptions from the Notification Obligation	384
			(d) Procedures Subject to Notification	385
		2.	Publication	386
		3.	Attribution of Voting Rights	386
			(a) Regulatory Concepts	386

		(b)	Cases of an Attribution of Voting Rights 387

- (b) Cases of an Attribution of Voting Rights 387
  - (aa) Acting in Concert 387
    - (1) Legal Practice in France 388
    - (2) Legal Practice in Germany 389
    - (3) Legal Practice in Italy 391
    - (4) Legal Practice in Spain 392
  - (bb) Temporary Transfer of Voting Rights 392
  - (cc) Notification Obligations of the Secured Party 392
  - (dd) Life Interest 393
  - (ee) Voting Rights Held or Exercised by a Controlled Undertaking 393
  - (ff) Deposited Shares 395
  - (gg) Shares Held on Behalf of Another Person 395
  - (hh) Voting Rights Exercised by Proxy 396
- IV. Disclosure of Financial Instruments 397
  - 1. Foundations 397
    - (a) Requirements under the TD 2004 397
    - (b) Deficits 398
    - (c) Reform of the Transparency Directive 2014 399
  - 2. Notification 399
    - (a) Prerequisites 399
    - (b) Attribution of Voting Rights 400
    - (c) Procedures Subject to Notification 400
  - 3. Publication 400
- V. Disclosure of the Intents of Investors 401
  - 1. France 401
  - 2. Germany 402
- VI. Supervision 403
  - 1. Requirements under European Law 403
  - 2. Supervisory Practices in the Member States 403
- VII. Sanctions 404
  - 1. Requirements under European Law 404
  - 2. Investor Protection by means of Civil Liability 405
- VIII. Conclusion 406

§ 21. Directors' Dealings 409
- I. Introduction 409
- II. Regulatory Concepts and Sources of Law 411
  - 1. MAR Regime 411
  - 2. Further Disclosure Rules in Union Law 412
- III. Disclosure Obligations 413
  - 1. Notification Requirements 413
    - (a) Persons Subject to the Notification Obligation 413
    - (b) Transactions Subject to the Notification Requirements 414
    - (c) Content of the Notification and Notification Period 414
  - 2. Publication 414

	IV.	Closed Period	415
	V.	Supervision and Sanctions	416
		1. Requirements under European Law	416
		2. Disgorgement of Profits	416
		3. Civil Liability	417
	VI.	Conclusion	418

§ 22. Corporate Governance and Shareholder Rights 419
    I.   Introduction 419
    II. Corporate Governance 420
          1. Introduction 420
          2. Corporate Governance Statement 421
          3. Sustainable Corporate Governance 422
    III. Shareholders' Rights 423
          1. Introduction 423
          2. Information Necessary to Exercise Shareholders' Rights 424
               (a) Disclosure of Changes in the Rights Attached to Shares 424
               (b) Disclosure of Information Necessary for Exercising Rights ... 425
                     (aa) Information Necessary for Shareholders 425
                     (bb) Information Necessary for the Holders of Debt Securities 425
          3. Institutional Investors 426
          4. Related Party Transactions 427
    IV. Conclusion 428

5
Trading Activities

§ 23. Investment Objectives 431
    I.   Foundations 431
          1. Return 431
          2. ESG Investments 433
          3. Investments in Accordance with Religious Principles 434
    II. Restrictions 434
          1. Private Investors 434
          2. Institutional Investors 436

§ 24. Short Sales and Credit Default Swaps 439
    I.   Introduction 441
    II. Terminology 441
    III. Need for Regulation 442
          1. Potential for Market Manipulation (Article 12 MAR) 443
               (a) Possible Means of Market Manipulation 443
               (b) Short Selling Attacks and Market Manipulation 444
          2. Short Sales as a Means for Destabilising the Financial System 445
    IV. EU Regulation on Short Selling and Credit Default Swaps (SSR) 445
          1. Scope of the SSR 446

Detailed Contents

		2.	Compliance of the SSR with the EU Treaty	447
		3.	Rules on Short Selling	447
			(a) Prohibited Transactions	448
			(b) Transparency Obligations	449
		4.	Rules on Sovereign Credit Default Swap Agreements (CDS)	451
		5.	Powers of the NCAs and ESMA	452
		6.	Sanctions	454
		7.	The *Wirecard* Case—a Prime Example of the Pros and Cons of Short Selling	454
	V.	Conclusion		455

§ 25. Algorithmic Trading and High-Frequency Trading 457
- I. Introduction 459
- II. Defining AT and HFT/Technical Aspects and Trading Strategies 461
  1. Definitions and Important Terms 461
  2. Trading Strategies 463
     - (a) AT and HFT as a Technical Means for Implementing Trading Strategies 463
     - (b) Overview of Concepts Behind Particular AT and HFT Strategies 464
- III. Potential Risks and Benefits of AT and HFT 469
  1. Potential Risks of AT and HFT 469
     - (a) Systemic Risk and Market Stability 469
     - (b) Market Quality and Market Integrity 470
  2. Potential Benefits of AT and HFT 474
     - (a) Increased Liquidity and Superior Intermediation 474
     - (b) Increased Market Efficiency and Market Quality 474
  3. Risk-Benefit Assessment and Consequences 475
- IV. Regulatory Measures with Regard to AT and HFT 478
  1. European Approach 478
     - (a) MiFID, MAD and ESMA Guidelines 478
     - (b) Level 1 regime: MiFID II 479
        - (aa) Provisions Concerning AT and HFT Firms and Investment Firms that Provide DMA/SA 480
        - (bb) Provisions Concerning Trade Venues with Particular Relevance for AT and HFT 481
     - (c) Level 2: ESMA's Technical Advice and Regulatory Technical Standards 483
        - (aa) Technical Advice 483
        - (bb) Regulatory Technical Standards 485
     - (d) Action Taken by Selected Member States/Gold Plating 488
     - (e) Assessment of the European Union Regime 489
  2. Some Thoughts on HFT Regulation in Other Jurisdictions 495
- V. Conclusion 495

6
Intermediaries

§ 26. Financial Analysts 499
    I.   Introduction 500
    II. Foundations 501
        1. Types of Financial Analysts 501
        2. Methods of Financial Analysis 502
    III. Regulatory Concepts 503
        1. Market Conduct 503
        2. Organisational Requirements 504
    IV. Investment Recommendations 505
        1. Objectives 505
        2. Scope 505
            (a) Material Scope 505
            (b) Personal Scope 507
        3. Production of Research 507
            (a) Objective Presentation of Investment Recommendations 508
                (aa) General Requirements 508
                (bb) Special Requirements for Qualified Persons and Experts 508
            (b) Disclosure Obligations 510
                (aa) Identity of the Producer of Investment Recommendations 510
                (bb) Conflicts of Interest 510
                      (1) General Provisions 510
                      (2) Additional Requirements for Qualified Persons and Experts 511
                      (3) Additional Requirements for Investment Firms, Credit Institutions and Other Persons 513
        4. Dissemination of Investment Recommendations Produced by Third Parties 513
        5. Principle of Proportionality—Non-written Recommendations 514
        6. Sanctions 515
    V. Relevance of the General Rules of Conduct for Financial Analysts 515
        1. Market Manipulation 515
            (a) Information-Based Manipulation 515
            (b) Fictitious Devices or Any Other Form of Deception or Contrivance 516
            (c) Scalping 517
            (d) Effects of Commission Delegated Regulation (EU) No. 2016/958 on the Prohibition of Market Manipulation 518
        2. Prohibition of Insider Dealings 518
        3. Research as an Inducement under MiFID II 519
    VI. Conclusion 520

§ 27. Rating Agencies 521
- I. Foundations 522
  1. The Role of Credit Rating Agencies 522
  2. Effects of a Rating 523
  3. Market Structure and Remuneration.. 524
  4. Development of Regulation in Europe 525
  5. Legal Sources 525
- II. Scope of Application and Regulatory Aims...................................... 527
  1. Foundations 527
  2. Aims.. 527
  3. Scope of Application 528
  4. Concepts and Definitions.. 528
- III. Regulatory Strategies 529
  1. Overview... 529
  2. Avoidance of Conflicts of Interest... 530
     (a) Independence of Credit Rating Agencies 530
     (b) Persons Involved in the Rating Procedure........................... 533
  3. Improvement of the Quality of Ratings.. 533
  4. Disclosure Obligations 535
     (a) Disclosure and Presentation of Credit Ratings 535
     (b) Transparency Report 535
  5. Registration 536
  6. The Problem of Over-Reliance 537
- IV. Supervision and Sanctions 538
  1. Foundations 538
  2. Procedure 539
  3. Administrative Measures and Sanctions...................................... 540
  4. Criminal Measures 541
- V. Private Enforcement 541
  1. Relevance.. 541
  2. National Laws... 541
  3. Liability under European Law 542
- VI. Conclusion 544

§ 28. Proxy Advisors.. 547
- I. Introduction... 547
- II. Regulatory Concepts... 548
  1. Transparency 549
  2. Liability under Private Law 550
  3. Public Enforcement 550
- III. Conclusion 550

7
Investment Firms

§ 29. Foundations 555
- I. Introduction... 555

  II. Legal Framework 556
    1. Supervisory Law 556
     (a) The MiFID II Regime 556
     (b) PRIIPs 557
     (c) IFR/IFD Regime 558
    2. Enforcement Mechanisms 558

§ 30. Investment Services 559
  I. Introduction 559
  II. Regulatory Concept of the MiFID II Regime 560
    1. Overview 560
    2. Investment Firms 560
    3. Market Operators (Regulated Market) 561
    4. Supervision and Sanctions 562
  III. General Rules of Conduct for Investment Firms 562
    1. Due Diligence Obligations 562
    2. Obligations in Cases of Conflict of Interest 563
  IV. Product Approval Process (Product Governance) 564
    1. Overview 564
    2. Scope 565
    3. Manufacturers 565
    4. Distributors 567
  V. Investment Advice 568
    1. Terminology 568
    2. Rules of Conduct 569
     (a) Exploration 570
     (b) Information 570
     (c) Assessment of Suitability 572
     (d) Execution Only 572
    3. Obligations under Private Law 573
  VI. Asset Management 575
    1. Terminology 575
    2. Rules of Conduct 576
  VII. Conclusion 577

§ 31. Product Intervention 579
  I. Introduction 579
  II. Legal Sources 580
  III. Product Intervention Pursuant to Article 42 MiFIR 581
    1. Premises 581
    2. Legal Consequences 582
  IV. Conclusion 583

§ 32. Foundations of Compliance 585
  I. Compliance 586
  II. Relationship between Compliance, Risk Management
    and Other Internal Control Functions 587
  III. Developments and Legal Foundations 588

§ 33. Compliance Requirements ... 591
I. Regulatory Concepts in European Law ... 593
1. Overview ... 593
2. Principles-based Approach to Regulation ... 594
3. Regulatory Aim ... 596
II. Regulatory Objectives and Scope of Compliance Obligations ... 597
1. Mitigation of Compliance Risk and Risk-Based Approach ... 597
2. Scope of the Compliance Obligations ... 599
III. Elements of a Compliance Organisation ... 600
1. Compliance Function ... 600
   (a) Requirements ... 600
      (aa) Independence ... 600
         (1) Operational and Financial Independence ... 601
         (2) Organisational Independence ... 602
      (bb) Permanence and Effectiveness ... 604
   (b) Responsibilities ... 604
      (aa) Monitoring and Assessment ... 604
      (bb) Advice and Assistance ... 605
2. Compliance Officer ... 606
   (a) Appointment ... 606
      (aa) Registration and Qualification Requirements ... 606
      (bb) Appointment of Members of Senior Management as Compliance Officers ... 607
   (b) Legal Status ... 608
      (aa) Independence Towards Senior Management ... 608
      (bb) Disciplinarian Independence and Protection against Dismissal ... 609
   (c) Responsibilities and Powers ... 610
      (aa) Right to Issue Instructions and Obtain Information ... 610
      (bb) Compliance Reporting ... 611
         (1) Internal Reporting ... 611
         (2) External Reports ... 612
3. Informational Barriers ('Chinese Walls') ... 613
   (a) Legal Foundations ... 614
   (b) Elements ... 614
      (aa) Segregation of Confidential Areas ... 615
      (bb) Watch Lists and Restricted Lists ... 616
   (c) Legal Effects ... 617
IV. Sanctions ... 618
1. Sanctions against Investment Firms ... 619
2. Sanctions against the Senior Management and the Compliance Officer ... 620
V. Conclusion ... 621

§ 34. Governance ... 623
I. Introduction ... 624
II. 'Governance-based' Regulation of Investment Firms ... 625

III. Regulatory Framework 626
   1. Overview 626
   2. Board Structure and Composition 628
      (a) One-tier vs. Two-tier Board Structures 628
      (b) Separation of Functions; Establishment of Board Committees for 'Significant' Firms 629
      (c) Diversity Requirements 630
      (d) Independent Board Members 631
   3. Personal Requirements of the Board Members 633
      (a) Fit and Properness 633
      (b) Limitation of Directorships 634
      (c) Collective Suitability 635
   4. Board Members' Duties 636
   5. Procedural Aspects 638
      (a) Assessment by the Institution 638
      (b) Assessment by Competent Authorities 639
IV. Sanctions 640
   1. Administrative Sanctions 640
   2. Civil Sanctions 640
V. Conclusions 641

8
Regulation of Benchmarks

§ 35. Foundations 645
   I. Introduction 645
   II. Legal Background and Regulatory Initiatives 647
   III. Functions of Benchmarks 649

§ 36. Market Supervision and Organisational Requirements 651
   I. Regulatory Concept of the Benchmark Regulation 651
      1. Regulatory Aim and Structure 651
      2. Scope and Definitions 652
      3. Concepts 654
      4. Legal Requirements 656
         (a) Governance Requirements Relating to the Benchmark Administrator 656
         (b) Input Data and Calculation Methodology 657
         (c) Governance and Control Requirements for Contributors ... 659
         (d) Investor Protection (Assessment Obligations) 660
         (e) ESG Disclosure Requirements; Specific Requirements for Climate Benchmarks 661
         (f) Power to Replace References in Contracts 662
      5. Restrictions on Use and Third-Country Benchmarks 662
      6. Authorisation, Supervision and Sanctions 663
         (a) Authorisation and Registration 663

	(b)	Supervisory Powers and Sanctions 664
	(aa)	Supervisory Powers of the National Supervisory Authorities 664
	(bb)	ESMA's Role 664
	(cc)	Civil Law Liability 666

II. Conclusion 666

9
Takeover Law

§ 37. Foundations 673
    I. Legal Sources 673
   II. Implications of Takeover Bids 675
  III. Administration and Supervision 676
  IV. Disclosure of Defensive Structures and Mechanisms 676
     1. Structure of the Capital 677
     2. Transfer of Shares 677
     3. Significant Shareholdings 678
     4. Holders of Special Rights 678
     5. System of Control for Employee Share Schemes 679
     6. Voting Rights 679
     7. Agreements between Shareholders 680
     8. Appointment and Replacement of Board Members 680
     9. Issue and Buyback of Shares 680
    10. Change of Control Clauses 681
    11. Compensation Agreements 681
    12. Conclusion 682

§ 38. Public Takeovers 683
    I. Introduction 683
   II. Types of Bids 684
  III. Decision to Launch a Bid 684
  IV. Offer Document 685

§ 39. Mandatory Bid 687
    I. Introduction 687
   II. Prerequisites 688
  III. Exemptions from the Mandatory Bid 689
  IV. Creeping-in 691
   V. Gaining Control by Acting in Concert 691
     1. Legal Foundations 691
     2. Legal Practice in the Member States 692
        (a) Sacyr/Eiffage (France) 692
        (b) WMF (Germany) 694
     3. Attempts to Further Harmonise the Concept 694
  VI. Conclusion 695

§ 40. Defence against Takeover Bids 697
    I. Board Members... 697
    II. Breakthrough 699

Bibliography 701
Subject Index 705
Index of National Laws 719
Index of National Laws by Country 727
Index of European Laws 733
Index of Supervisory and Court Rulings 735

LIST OF CONTRIBUTORS

Rüdiger Veil is a professor at the law faculty of Ludwig Maximilians-University (LMU), Munich and director of the Munich Center for Capital Markets Law (MuCCML) at LMU. His research focuses on corporate law and European capital markets law. He was a member of the ESMA Securities and Markets Stakeholder Group (SMSG) from 2014 to 2018. Rüdiger Veil also advises the German Federal Ministry of Finance on reforms of EU financial markets law. He has acted as an expert for the German, European, Chinese and Russian Parliaments.

Hendrik Brinckmann studied law at Bucerius Law School, Hamburg, and at the University of Sydney. He obtained his doctoral degree (Dr. iur.) in 2009. His doctoral thesis deals with financial reporting in capital markets law. He worked as an attorney in the area of corporate and capital markets law and as an executive officer at the German Federal Ministry of Finance. Currently, he is working as an advisor to the working group on finance of the CDU/CSU parliamentary group in the German Bundestag.

Marcus P. Lerch studied law at Bucerius Law School, Hamburg, Columbia University in the City of New York, and at the University of Cambridge (LL.M.). He received his doctoral degree (Dr. iur.) from Bucerius Law School in 2015 with a thesis on 'Investment advisers as financial intermediaries. The financial service provider's duty to declare vested interests'. Marcus is a Hamburg-based Principal Associate in the dispute resolution practice group of Freshfields Bruckhaus Deringer.

Fabian Walla is an inhouse legal counsel (*Syndikusrechtsanwalt*) and the head of corporate legal at adidas AG, Herzogenaurach. Before joining adidas AG he held various inhouse roles and was a corporate law associate with the law firm Gleiss Lutz. Fabian Walla studied law at Bucerius Law School, Hamburg, and Cornell Law School, USA; he received his doctoral degree (Dr. iur.) from Bucerius Law School in 2011 with a thesis on German and European capital markets supervision. He is also a lecturer at Bucerius Law School.

Malte Wundenberg studied law at Bucerius Law School, Hamburg, and NYU Law School; he holds a Dipl. Kfm. degree ('Master') in business administration and a doctoral degree (Dr. iur.) from Bucerius Law School. His thesis is entitled 'Compliance and the Principles-based Supervision of Banking Groups'. He is currently a capital markets and banking supervision law attorney at the Frankfurt office of Hengeler Mueller. He is also a lecturer at Bucerius Law School.

LIST OF ABBREVIATIONS

AB	Aktiebolag (Swedish stock corporation)
ABGB	Allgemeines Bürgerliches Gesetzbuch (Austrian Civil Code)
ABL	Aktiebolagslag (Swedish Stock Corporation Act)
Abl.	Amtsblatt (Official Journal)
AC	Appeal Cases (law reports)
Acad. Acc. Fin. Stud. J.	Academy of Accounting and Financial Studies Journal (journal)
AcP	Archiv für die civilistische Praxis (journal)
AG	Aktiengesellschaft (German stock corporation)/Die Aktiengesellschaft—Zeitschrift für das gesamte Aktienwesen, für deutsches, europäisches und internationales Unternehmens- und Kapitalmarktrecht (journal)
AIFMD	Alternative Investment Fund Manager Directive
AIM	Alternative Investment Market
AktG	Aktiengesetz (German Stock Corporation Act)
All ER	All England Law Reports (journal)
a.m.	ante meridiem
Am. Bus. Law J.	American Business Law Journal (journal)
Am. Econ. Rev.	American Economic Review (journal)
AMF	Autorité des marchés financiers (French Financial Markets Authority)
Analisi giur. Ec.	Analisi Giuridica dell'Economia (journal)
AnSVG	Anlegerschutzverbesserungsgesetz (German Investor Protection Improvement Act)
AO	Abgabenordnung (German Act on the Administrative Procedures in Taxation)
AOR	Automated Order Router
APER	Code of Practice of Approved Persons (FCA Handbook)
APRR	Autoroutes Paris-Rhin-Rhône
Ariz. L. Rev.	Arizona Law Review (journal)
ÅRL	Årsredovisningslag (Swedish Annual Report Act)
Art.	Article(s)

ASB	Accounting Standards Board
AT	Algorithmic Trading
ATF	Alternative Trading Facility
avr.	Avril (French: April)
BaFin	Bundesanstalt für Finanzdienstleistungsaufsicht (German Federal Financial Supervisory Authority)
BAKred	Bundesaufsichtsamt für Kreditwesen (German Federal Banking Supervisory Office)
Banca Borsa tit. Cred.	Banca, borsa e titoli di credito (journal)
Banking & Fin. Serv. Pol's Rep.	Banking and Financial Services Politics Report
BAV	Bundesaufsichtsamt für das Versicherungswesen (German Federal Agency for Financial Services Supervision); former agency
BAWe	Bundesaufsichtsamt für den Wertpapierhandel (German Federal Supervisory Office for Securities Trading); former agency
BB	Betriebs-Berater (journal)
BBC	British Broadcasting Corporation
BBLJ	Berkeley Business Law Journal (journal)
Begr.	Begründung (explanatory notes on German statutes)
BEHV—EBK	Verordnung der Eidgenössischen Finanzmarktaufsicht über die Börsen und den Effektenhandel (Swiss Regulation on Stock Exchanges and Securities Trading)
BFuP	Betriebswirtschaftliche Forschung und Praxis (journal)
BGB	Bürgerliches Gesetzbuch (German Civil Code)
BGBl.	Bundesgesetzblatt (German Federal Law Gazette)
BGH	Bundesgerichtshof (German Federal Court of Justice)
BGHSt	Entscheidungen des Bundesgerichtshofs in Strafsachen (Cases of the German Federal Court of Justice for Criminal Cases)
BGHZ	Entscheidungen des Bundesgerichtshofs in Zivilsachen (Cases of the German Federal Court of Justice for Civil Law Cases)
BilMoG	Gesetz zur Modernisierung des Bilanzrechts (German Accounting Law Modernisation Act)
BIS	Bank for International Settlements
BKR	Zeitschrift für Bank- und Kapitalmarktrecht (journal)
bn	billion(s)
BörseG	Börsengesetz (Austrian Stock Exchange Act)
BörsG	Börsengesetz (German Stock Exchange Act)

BörsO FWB	Börsenordnung (German Stock Exchange Rules for the Frankfurter Wertpapierbörse)
BörsZulVO	Börsenzulassungs-Verordnung (German Stock Exchange Admission Regulation)
BoS	Board of Supervisors
BR	Benchmark Regulation
BrB	Brottsbalk (Swedish Criminal Code)
BR-Drucks.	Bundesrats-Drucksache (printed papers of the German Bundesrat)
Brook. J. Corp. Fin. & Comm. L.	Brooklyn Journal of Corporate, Financial & Commercial Law (journal)
BT-Drucks.	Bundestags-Drucksache (printed papers of the German Bundestag)
Bull. Civ.	Bulletin civil (journal)
Bull. Joly Bourse	Bulletin Joly Bourse (journal)
Bull. Joly Soc.	Bulletin Joly Sociétés
BuM	Beton- und Monierbau AG
BVerfG	Bundesverfassungsgericht (German Federal Constitutional Court)
c/	Contre (French: v.)
CA	Competent Authority
CA/C.A.	Cour d'appel (French Court of Appeal)
CAC	Cotation assistée en continu (French benchmark stock market index)
Cal. L. Rev.	California Law Review (journal)
CAR	Contemporary Accounting Research (journal)
Cardozo L. Rev.	Cardozo Law Review (journal)
CASS	Client Asset Sourcebook (FCA Handbook)
Cass. Com.	Cour de cassation, chambre commerciale (French Supreme Court of Judicature, Commercial Chamber)
CBFA	Commission bancaire, financière et des assurances (Belgian Banking, Finance and Insurance Commissio)
Cc	Code civil (French Civil Code)
CC	Código Civil (Spanish Civil Code)
C. com.	Code de commerce (French Commercial Code)
CCZ	Corporate Compliance Zeitschrift (journal)
CDS	Credit Default Swaps
CEO	Chief executive officer
CEPR	Centre for Economic Policy Research Policy Insight
cert. denied	Certiorari Denied

CESR	Committee of European Securities Regulators
CESR Recommendation	Recommendations of the Committee of European Securities Regulators
CEX	Centralised Exchange
Cf.	confer
CFO	Chief Financial Officer
CFTC	Commodity Futures Trading Commission
ch./Chapt.	chapter/chamber (French: chamber)
ChD	Chancery Division (law reports)
Cir.	Circuit
CJA	Criminal Justice Act
CML	Capital Market Law Review (journal)
CMLJ	Capital Markets Law Journal (journal)
CML Rev.	Common Market Law Review (journal)
C. mon. fin.	Code monétaire et financier (French Monetary and Financial Code)
CMU	Capital Markets Union
CNMV	Comisión Nacional del Mercado de Valores (Spanish National Stock Market Commission)
COB	Commission des opérations de bourse (French Stock Exchange Commission)
COB	Compliance Officer Bulletin (journal)
COBS	Conduct of Business Sourcebook (FCA Handbook)
Colum. Bus. L. Rev.	Columbia Business Law Review (journal)
Colum. J. Transnat'l L.	Columbia Journal of Transnational Law (journal)
COM	Commission
Conn. Ins. L. Rev.	Connecticut Insurance Law Review (journal)
Consob	Commissione Nazionale per le Società e la Borsa (Italian Securities and Exchange Commission)
CP	Código Penal (Spanish Criminal Code)
CRA	Credit Rating Agency
CRAR I, II, III	Credit Rating Agencies Regulation I, II, III
CRDIV	Capital Requirements Directive IV
CRIM-MAD	Directive for Criminal Sanctions on Market Abuse
CRR	Capital Requirements Regulation
CSC	Carr Sheppards Crosthwaite Ltd.

CSDR	Central Securities Depositories Regulation
CSRD	Corporate Sustainability Reporting Directive
CSSF	Commission de Surveillance du Secteur Financier (Luxembourg Financial Supervisory Authority)
D. Lgs	Decreto legislativo (Spanish legislative decree)
D. Lgs	Decreto legislativo (Italian legislative decree)
DAI	Deutsches Aktieninstitut (German Equities Institute)
DAX	Deutscher Aktienindex (German stock market index)
DB	Der Betrieb (journal)
DEA	Direct Electronic Access
Dec	December
DEPP	Decision Procedure and Penalties (manual)
DEX	Decentralised Exchange
Die Bank	Die Bank—Zeitschrift für Bankpolitik und Praxis (journal)
Dir.	Directive
DiskE	Diskussionsentwurf (discussion papers for German statutes)
DL	decreto-legge (Italian legislative decree)
DLT	Distributed Ledger Technology
DM	Deutsche Mark (former German Currency)
DMA	Direct Market Access
DÖV	Die Öffentliche Verwaltung (journal)
Dr. soc.	Droit de sociétés (journal)
DRS	Draft Regulatory Standards
DRS	Deutsche Rechnungslegungsstandards (German Accounting Standards)
DRSC	Deutsches Rechnungslegungs Standards Committee e. V. (German Accounting Standards Committee)
DStR	Deutsches Steuerrecht (journal)
DTR	Disclosure Guidance and Transparency Rules sourcebook
Duke L. J.	Duke Law Journal (journal)
EAEC	European Atomic Energy Community
EAG	Europäische Atomgemeinschaft
EBA	European Banking Authority
EBK	Eidgenössische Bankenkommission (Swiss Federal Banking Commission)
EBLR	European Business Law Review (journal)

EBOR	European Business Organization Law Review (journal)
EC	European Community
EC Treaty	Treaty establishing the European Community
ECAI	External Credit Assessment Institution
ECB	European Central Bank
ECFR	European Company and Financial Law Review (journal)
ECJ	European Court of Justice
ECL	European Company Law (journal)
ECMH	Efficient Capital Market Hypothesis
ECMI	European Capital Markets Institute
ECOFIN	Economic and Financial Affairs Council
ECR	European Court Reports
ECSC	European Coal and Steel Community
ECSP	European Crowdfunding Service Providers Regulation
ECV	Emittenten-Compliance-Verordnung of 2007 (Austrian Issuer Compliance Regulation)
ed.	editor
eds.	editors
EEAP	European Electronic Access Point
EEC	European Economic Community
EEC Treaty	Treaty establishing the European Economic Community
EFSF	European Financial Stability Facility
EFTA	European Free Trade Association
EHA	Ministerio de Economía y Hacienda (Spanish Ministry of Economy and Finance)
Eidg.	Eidgenössisch (Swiss federal)
Einl.	Einleitung (introduction)
EIOPA	European Insurance and Occupational Pensions Authority
EMIR	European Market Infrastructure Regulation
EMMI	European Money Markets Institute
Emory Int'l L. Rev.	Emory International Law Review (journal)
Emory L.J.	Emory Law Journal
EOB	execution-only-business
ERT	Europarättslig Tidskrift (journal)
ESC	European Securities Committee

ESCB	European System of Central Banks
ESFS	European System of Financial Supervision
ESG	Environmental, Social, Governance
ESMA	European Securities and Markets Authority
ESMA Regulation	Regulation (EU) No. 1095/2010 of the European Parliament and of the Council of 24 November 2010 establishing a European Supervisory Authority (European Securities and Markets Authority), amending Decision No. 716/2009/EC and repealing Commission Decision 2009/77/EC)
ESME	European Securities Markets Expert Group
ESRB	European Systemic Risk Board
et al.	et alii/et aliae
et seq.	and the following page(s)/article(s)/section(s)
ETF	Exchange Traded Fund
EU	European Union
EuR	Europarecht (journal)
EUV/EU-Vertrag	Vertrag über die Europäische Union (TEU)
EuZW	Europäische Zeitschrift für Wirtschaftsrecht (journal)
EWCA Crim	England and Wales Court of Appeal Criminal
EWS	Europäisches Wirtschafts- und Steuerrecht (journal)
f.	and the following page/article/section
FCA	Financial Conduct Authority
FCA Handbook	Handbook of Rules and Guidance
Feb.	February
FESCO	Forum of European Securities Commission
ff.	and the following pages/articles/sections
FFFS	Författningssamling (Official Journal of Swedish Regulations)
FG	Festgabe (German commemorative publication)
FI	Finansinspektionen (Swedish Financial Supervisory Authority)
Fin. Analysts J.	Financial Analysts Journal
FinDAG	Gesetz über die Bundesanstalt für Finanzdienstleistungsaufsicht (German Law on the Financial Services Supervisory Authority)
Fin. L. Rev.	Financial Law Review
FMA	Finanzmarktaufsichtsbehörde (Austrian Financial Market Authority)
FMABG	Finanzmarktaufsichtsbehördengesetz (Austrian Financial Markets Supervisory Authorities Act)

FMG	Financial Markets Group
Fn.	Footnote
Frankfurter Kommentar zum WpÜG	Frankfurter Kommentar zum Wertpapiererwerbs- und Übernahmegesetz, see Haarmann/Schüppen, Frankfurter Kommentar zum Wertpapiererwerbs- und Übernahmegesetz (commentary)
FRUG	Finanzmarktrichtlinie-Umsetzungsgesetz (German Financial Market Directive Implementation Act)
FS	Festschrift (German commemorative publication)
FSA	Financial Services Authority
FSAP	Financial Services Action Plan
FSB	Financial Stability Board
FSMA	Financial Services and Markets Act 2000
FSMT	Financial Services and Markets Tribunal
FTD	Financial Times Deutschland
FTT	Financial Transaction Tax
FWB	Frankfurter Wertpapierbörse (Frankfurt Stock Exchange)
GBP	Pound sterling
Geo. Wash. L.R.	The George Washington Law Review
GesRZ	Der Gesellschafter (journal)
GG	Grundgesetz (German Constitution)
GLJ	German Law Journal (journal)
GmbH	Gesellschaft mit beschränkter Haftung (German limited liability company)
GmbH & Co. KG	Gesellschaft mit beschränkter Haftung & Compagnie Kommanditgesellschaft (German Limited Partnership with a Limited Liability Company as General Partner)
GRC	Governance, Risk-Management und Compliance
GWR	Gesellschafts- und Wirtschaftsrecht (journal)
Harv. Bus. L. Rev.	Harvard Business Law Review
Hdb.	Handbuch (handbook)
HFT	High-Frequency Trading
HGB	Handelsgesetzbuch (German Commcercial Code)
HM Treasury	Her Majesty's Treasury
IAS	International Accounting Standards
ibid.	ibidem

ICCLR	International Company and Commercial Law Review (journal)
ICO	Initial Coin Offering
ie	id est
IFD	Investment Firm Directive
IFLR	International Financial Law Review (journal)
IFR	Investment Firm Regulation
IFRS	International Financial Reporting Standards
IIMG	Inter-Institutional Monitoring Group
IKB	IKB Deutsche Industriebank AG
IMFS	Institute for Monetary and Financial Stability
Int'l J. Discl. & Gov.	International Journal of Disclosure and Governance (journal)
IOI	Indication of Interest
IOSCO	International Organization of Securities Commissions
IPO	Initial Public Offering
ISS	Institutional Shareholder Services
IT	Information Technology
ITS	Implementing Technical Standards
J. Acc., Aud. Finance	Journal of Accounting, Auditing and Finance (journal)
J. Acc. Econ.	Journal of Accounting and Economics (journal)
J. Acc. Res.	Journal of Accounting Research (journal)
Jan.	January
janv.	Janvier (French: January)
JBFA	Journal of Business Finance & Accounting (journal)
J. Bus.	Journal of Business (journal)
J. Comp. Econ.	Journal of Comparative Economics (journal)
J. Corp. L. Stud.	Journal of Corporate Law Studies (journal)
J. Corp. Law	Journal of Corporation Law (journal)
J. Exp. Psych., Hum. Perception & Performance	Journal of Experimental Psychology: Human Perception and Performance (journal)
J. Fin.	Journal of Finance (journal)
J. Fin. Econ.	Journal of Financial Economics (journal)
J. Fin. Quant. Analysis	Journal of Financial and Quantitative Analysis (journal)

J. Fin. Reg. & Comp.	Journal of Financial Regulation and Compliance (journal)
JIBFL	Journal of International Banking and Financial Law (journal)
JIBLR	Journal of International Banking Law and Regulation (journal)
J. Int. Bank. Law	Journal of International Banking Law (journal)
J. Invest. Comp.	Journal of Investment Compliance (journal)
JLE	Journal of Law and Economics (journal)
J. Mon. Econ.	Journal of Monetary Economics (journal)
JOA	Journal of Accountancy (journal)
J. Pol. Econ.	Journal of Political Economy (journal)
JST	Joint Supervisory Team
JT	Juridisk Tidskrift vid Stockholms Universitet (journal)
juill.	Juillet (French: July)
JuS	Juristische Schulung (journal)
JZ	Juristenzeitung (journal)
KapInHaG	Kapitalmarktinformationshaftungsgesetz (German Capital Markets Information Liability Act)
KapMuG	Gesetz über Musterverfahren in kapitalmarktrechtlichen Streitigkeiten (German Capital Markets Model Case Act)
KG	Kommanditgesellschaft (German limited partnership)
KMG	Kapitalmarktgesetz (Austrian Capital Market Act)
Kölner Kommentar zum AktG	Kölner Kommentar zum Aktiengesetz, see Zöllner/Noack, Kölner Kommentar zum Aktiengesetz (commentary)
Kölner Kommentar zum KapMuG	Kölner Kommentar zum KapMuG, see Hess/Reuschle/Rimmelspacher (eds.), Kölner Kommentar zum KapMuG (commentary)
Kölner Kommentar zum WpHG	Kölner Kommentar zum WpHG, see Hirte/Möllers (eds.), Kölner Kommentar zum WpHG (commentary)
Kölner Kommentar zum WpÜG	Kölner Kommentar zum Wertpapiererwerbs- und Übernahmegesetz, see Zöllner/Noack, Kölner Kommentar zum Wertpapiererwerbs- und Übernahmegesetz (commentary)
Kreditwesen	Zeitschrift für das gesamte Kreditwesen (journal)
KWG	Gesetz über das Kreditwesen (German Banking Act)
L. & Pol'y Int'l Bus.	Law and Policy in International Business (journal)
Law & Hum Beh.	Law and Human Behavior Law (journal)
Law & Soc'y Rev.	Law and Society Review (journal)

Lewis & Clark L. Rev.	Lewis & Clark Law Review (journal)
LG	Landgericht (German regional court)
LHF	Lag om handel med finansiella instrument (Swedish Act on Trading in Financial Instruments)
lit.	litera (letter)
Lit.	literature
LLP	Limited Liability Partnership
LMV	Ley del Mercado de Valores (Spanish Securities Market Act)
LR	Listing Rules
LSA	Ley de Sociedades Anónimas (Spanish Stock Corporation Act)
LSE	London Stock Exchange
LTF	Legal Theory of Finance
LVM	Lag om värdepappersmarknaden (Swedish Securities Market Act)
M&A	Mergers and Acquisitions
MaComp	Mindestanforderungen an Compliance (BaFin's Minimum Requirements for Compliance)
MAD 2003	Market Abuse Directive 2003
MAR	Code of Market Conduct (FCA Handbook)
MAR	Market Abuse Regulation
MaRisk	Mindestanforderungen an das Risikomanagement (German Minimum Requirements for Risk Management)
MDax	Mid-Cap-Deutscher Aktienindex (German Mid-cap Stock Index)
Mica	Markets in Crypto Assets Regulation
Mich. L. Rev.	Michigan Law Review (journal)
Mich. Telecomm. & Tech. L. Rev.	Michigan Telecommunications and Technology Law Review (journal)
Mich. YBI Legal Stud.	Michigan Yearbook of International Legal Studies (journal)
MIF	Marchés d'Instruments Financiers (Markets in Financial Instruments)
MiFID I, II	Markets in Financial Instruments Directive I, II
MiFIR	Markets in Financial Instruments Regulation
MoU	Memoranda of Understanding
ms	Millisecond
MTF	Multilateral Trading Facility

MTN	Medium Term Notes
Münchener Kommentar zum AktG	Münchener Kommentar zum Aktiengesetz, see Götte/Habersack, Münchener Kommentar zum Aktiengesetz (commentary on the German Stock Corporation Act)
Münchener Kommentar zum HGB	Münchener Kommentar zum Handelsgesetzbuch, see Schmidt, Münchener Kommentar zum Handelsgesetzbuch (commentary on the German Trade Act)
MVSV	Mindestinhalts-, Veröffentlichungs- und Sprachenverordnung (Austrian Ordinance on Minimum Contents, Publication and Language)
n.	Numero (Spanish: number)
NASDAQ	National Association of Securities Dealers Automated Quotations
NBER	National Bureau of Economic Research
NCA	National Competent Authority
NJW	Neue Juristische Wochenschrift (journal)
Notre Dame L. Rev.	Notre Dame Law Review (journal)
Nov.	November
nov.	Novembre (French: November)
Nr./Nr	Nummer (German: number)
NSM	National Storage Mechanism
NV	naamloze vennootschap (Dutch limited liability company)
Nw. U. L. Rev.	Northwestern University Law Review (journal)
NYSE	New York Stock Exchange
N.Y.L. Sch. L. Rev.	New York Law School Law Review (journal)
N.Y.U. L. Rev.	New York University Law Review (journal)
NZG	Neue Zeitschrift für Gesellschaftsrecht (journal)
öAktG	österreichisches Aktiengesetz (Austrian Stock Corporation Act)
ÖBA	Zeitschrift für das gesamte Bank- und Börsenwesen (journal)
Oct.	October
OGAW	Organismus für gemeinsame Anlagen in Wertpapieren (Undertakings for Collective Investment in Transferable Securities (UCITS))
OJ	Official Journal
OLG	Oberlandesgericht (German higher regional court)
OMX	Aktiebolaget Optionsmäklarna (Swedish Stock Broker Association)
OPA	Oferta pública de adquisición/Offre publique d'achat (public acquisition offer)

OPE	offre publique d'échange (public exchange offer)
OTC	Over-the-counter
OTF	Organised Trading Facility
OTR	Order-to-trade-ratio
öUWG	Unlauterer-Wettbewerbs-Gesetz (Austrian Act against Unfair Practices)
OWiG	Gesetz über Ordnungswidrigkeiten (German Administrative Offences Act)
ÖZW	Österreichische Zeitschrift für Wirtschaftsrecht (journal)
p.	page(s)
Pa. J. Bus. & Emp. L.	University of Pennsylvania Journal of Business and Employment Law (journal)
para.	paragraph(s)
PD	Prospectus Directive
PDG	Président-directeur général (Chief Executive Officer)
PDMR	Person discharging managerial responsibilities
plc.	public limited company
PR	Prospectus Regulation
PRA	Prudential Regulation Authority
PRIIPS	Packaged Retail and Insurance-based Investment Products
PRIN	Principles for Businesses (FCA Handbook)
Prop.	Regeringens proposition (explanatory notes)
PS	Policy Statements
pseud.	pseudonym
Q. J. Econ.	Quarterly Journal of Economics (journal)
RD	Real Decreto (royal decree)
RDBB	Revista de Derecho bancario y bursátil (journal)
RDBF	Revue de droit bancaire et financier (journal)
RDC	Regulatory Decisions Committee
RdS	Revista de Derecho Social (journal)
RE	Regolamento Emittenti (Italian Issuers' Regulation)
Reg.	Regulation(s)
Reg. NMS	Regulation National Market System
Reg. SCI	Regulation Systems Compliance and Integrity
RegE	Regierungsentwurf (German government drafts of statutes)

Rev. Fin. Studies	Review of Financial Studies (journal)
Rev. soc.	Revue des sociétés (journal)
RG AMF	Règlement général Autorité des Marchés Financiers (General Regulations of the French Stock Market Authority)
RIE	Recognised Investment Exchange
RINGA	Relevant information not generally available
RIS	Regulated Information Service
Riv. Dir. Civ.	Rivista di diritto civile (journal)
Riv. soc.	Rivista delle società (journal)
RIW	Recht der Internationalen Wirtschaft (journal)
RL-KG	Rechnungslegungkontrollgesetz
RM	Regulated Market
RMV	Revista de derecho del mercado de valores (journal)
RNS	Regulatory News Service
RRM	Regolamento del Registro Mercantil (Spanish regulation on Company Registries)
RTDcom.	La Revue trimestrielle de droit commercial (journal)
RTDF	La Revue trimestrielle de droit financier (journal)
RTS	Regulatory Technical Standards
SA	Sponsored Access
SA	Société Anonyme (French stock corporation)
Sanct.	Sanction
SDAX	Small-Cap-Deutscher Aktienindex (small-cap German stock index)
SE	Societas Europaea
SEA	Securities Exchange Act
SEC	Securities and Exchange Commission
Sec./sec./sect.	section
SEK	Swedish Krona (Swedish Currency)
Sept.	September
SETS	Stock Exchange Electronic Trading Service
SFDR	Sustainable Finance Disclosure Regulation
SFS	Svensk författningssamling (Swedish law gazette)
SFTR	Securities Financing Transactions Regulation
SFTaxR	Sustainable Finance Taxonomy Regulation
SI	Statutory Instruments
SIM	Società di Intermediazione Mobiliare

SME	Small and Medium Enterprises
SMSG	Securities and Markets Stakeholders Group
SOR	Smart Order Router
SOU	Statens offentliga utredningar (Swedish government reports)
S.p.A.	Società per azioni (Italian stock corporation)
SR	Securitisation Regulation
SRD I, II	Shareholder Rights Directive I, II
SRI	Socially Responsible Investing
SSM	Single Supervisory Mechanism
SSR	Short Selling Regulation
SSRN	Social Science Research Network
Stan. J. L. Bus. & Fin.	Stanford Journal of Law, Business and Finance (journal)
Stan. L. Rev.	Stanford Law Review (journal)
StGB	Strafgesetzbuch (German Criminal Code)
subsec.	subsection
SUP	Supervision
SvJT	Svensk Juristtidning (journal)
SYSC	Senior Management Arrangements, Systems and Controls (FCA Handbook)
SZW	Schweizerische Zeitschrift für Wirtschafts- und Finanzmarktrecht (journal)
TA	Technical Advice
TAR	The Accounting Review (journal)
TCI	The Children's Investment Fund Management
T. corr.	Tribunal correctionnel (French criminal court)
TD	Transparency Directive
TecDAX	Stock index for the technology sector (Frankfurt
Temp. Int'l & Comp. L.J.	Temple International and Comparative Law Journal
TEU	Treaty on European Union
TFEU	Treaty on the Functioning of the European Union
TGI	Tribunal de grande instance (French regional court)
TOD	Takeover Bids Directive
Trinity C.L. Rev.	Trinity College Law Review (journal)
TUF	Testo Unico della Finanza (Italian Consolidated Laws on Finance)

TUG	Transparenzrichtlinie-Umsetzungsgesetz (German Implementing Act on the Transparency Directive)
ÜbG	Übernahmegesetz (Austrian Takeover Act)
U Chi. L. Rev.	University of Chicago Law Review (journal)
U. Cin. L. Rev.	University of Cincinnati Law Review
UCITS	Undertakings for Collective Investments in Transferable Securities
U. Pa. J. Bus. L.	University of Pennsylvania Journal of Business Law (journal)
U. Pa. L. Rev.	University of Pennsylvania Law Review (journal)
URD	Universal Registration Document
U. Rich. L. Rev.	University of Richmond Law Review (journal)
USD	US dollar
UWG	Unlauterer-Wettbewerbs-Gesetz (German Law against Unfair Competition)
v/v.	versus
VAG	Versicherungsaufsichtsgesetz (German Law on Insurance Supervision)
Va. L. Rev.	Virginia Law Review (journal)
VMV	Veröffentlichungs- und Meldeverordnung (Austrian Disclosure and Notification Regulation)
vol.	volume
VW	Volkswagen AG
WA	Wertpapieraufsicht (capital markets supervison)
WAG	Wertpapieraufsichtsgesetz (Austrian Securities Supervision Act)
Wash. U. L. Q.	Washington University Law Quarterly (journal)
WEP	West European Politics (journal)
wistra	Zeitschrift für Wirtschafts- und Steuerstrafrecht (journal)
WM	Wertpapier-Mitteilungen Zeitschrift für Wirtschafts- und Bankrecht (journal)
Wm. & Mary Bus. L. Rev.	William and Mary Business Law Review
WMF	WMF Württembergische Metallwarenfabrik AG
WpAV	Verordnung zur Konkretisierung von Anzeige-, Mitteilungs- und Veröffentlichungspflichten nach dem Wertpapierhandelsgesetz (German Regulation on Security Trading Notification and Insider Lists)
WpDVerOV	Verordnung zur Konkretisierung der Verhaltensregeln und Organisationsanforderungen für Wertpapierdienstleistungsunternehmen (German Regulation Implementing the Rules of Conduct and Organisational Requirements for Investment Firms)

WpHG	Gesetz über den Wertpapierhandel (German Securities Trading Act)
WpHG-E	Gesetzesentwurf zum WpHG (draft proposal for WpHG)
WpHMV	Verordnung über die Meldepflichten beim Handel mit Wertpapieren und Derivaten (German Regulation on the Notification Obligations when Trading with Securities and Derivatives)
WpPG	Wertpapierprospektgesetz (German Securities Prospectus Act)
WpÜG	Wertpapiererwerbs- und –übernahmegesetz (German Securities Acquisition and Takeover Act)
WpÜG-AngebV	Verordnung über den Inhalt der Angebotsunterlage, die Gegenleistung bei Übernahmeangeboten und Pflichtangeboten und die Befreiung von der Verpflichtung zur Veröffentlichung und zur Abgabe eines Angebots (German WpÜG Offer Ordinance)
XETRA	Exchange Electronic Trading
Yale J. on Reg.	Yale Journal on Regulation (journal)
Yale Law J.	Yale Law Journal (journal)
ZBB	Zeitschrift für Bankrecht und Bankwirtschaft (journal)
ZEuP	Zeitschrift für Europäisches Privatrecht (journal)
ZEuS	Zeitschrift für europarechtliche Studien (journal)
Zfbf	Schmalenbachs Zeitschrift für betriebswirtschaftliche Forschung (journal)
ZfV	Zeitschrift für Verwaltung (journal)
ZgesKredW	Zeitschrift für das gesamte Kreditwesen (journal)
ZGR	Zeitschrift für Unternehmens- und Gesellschaftsrecht (journal)
ZHR	Zeitschrift für das gesamte Handels- und Wirtschaftsrecht (journal)
ZInsO	Zeitschrift für das gesamte Insolvenzrecht (journal)
ZIP	Zeitschrift für Wirtschaftsrecht (journal)
ZIS	Zeitschrift für Internationale Strafrechtsdogmatik (journal)
ZJapanR	Zeitschrift für Japanisches Recht (journal)
ZPO	Zivilprozessordnung (German Civil Procedure Code)
ZRP	Zeitschrift für Rechtspolitik (journal)
ZSR	Zeitschrift für Schweizerisches Recht (journal)

1

Foundations of Capital Markets Legislature in Europe

§ 1
History

Bibliography

Anschütz, David H., *Regelungskonzepte im neuen europäischen Verbriefungsrecht. Kapitalmarktregulierung zur Wiederherstellung von Vertrauen in Verbriefungen* (2020); Armour, John and Ringe, Wolf-Georg, *European Company Law 1999–2010: Renaissance and Crisis*, 48 CMLRev. (2011), 125–174; Avgouleas, Emilios, *The Global Financial Crisis and the Disclosure Paradigm in European Financial Regulation: The Case for Reform*, 6 ECFR (2009), 440–475; Bréhier, Bertrand and Pailler, Pauline, *La régulation du marché des materières premières*, Bull. Joly Bourse (2012), 122–128; Casper, Matthias, *Der Compliancebeauftragte – unternehmensinternes Aktienamt, Unternehmensbeauftragter oder einfacher Angestellter*, in: Bitter, Georg et al. (eds.), *Festschrift für Karsten Schmidt zum 70. Geburtstag* (2009), 199–216; Edwards, Vanessa, *EC Company Law* (1999); Ferran, Eilís and Goodhart, Charles A., *Regulating Financial Services and Markets in the 21st Century* (2001); Ferran, Eilís, *Building an EU Securities Market* (2004); Ferran, Eilís et al. (eds.), *The Regulatory Aftermath of the Global Financial Crisis* (2012); G30, *Financial Reform: A Framework for Financial Stability* (2009); Heinemann, Friedrich, *The Benefits of Creating an Integrated EU Market for Investment Funds*, 19 ZEW Economic Studies (2003), 89–93; Horn, Norbert, *Europäisches Finanzmarktrecht* (2003); Lannoo, Karel, *Emerging Framework for Disclosure in the EU*, 3 J. Corp. L. Stud. (2003), 329–358; Moloney, Niamh, *Confidence and Competence: The Conundrum of EC Capital Markets Law*, 4 J. Corp. L. Stud. (2004), 1–50; Moloney, Niamh, *Institutional Governance and Capital Markets Union: Incrementalism or a 'Big Bang'?*, 13 ECFR (2016), 376–423; Panasar, Raj and Boeckman, Philip (eds.), *European Securities Law*, 2nd edn. (2014); Papadopoulos, Thomas, *EU Law and the Harmonization of Takeovers in the Internal Market* (2010); Parmentier, Miriam, *Capital Markets Union – One Year On From the Action Plan*, 14 ECFR (2017), 242–251; Ringe, Wolf-Georg, *Capital Markets Union for Europe – A Political Message to the UK*, 9 LFMR (2015), 5–7; Rontchevsky, Nicolas, *L'harmonisation des sanctions pénales*, Bull. Joly Bourse (2012), 139–142; Sasso, Lorenzo and Kost de Sevres, Nicolette, *The New European Financial Markets Legal Framework: A Real Improvement? An analysis of Financial Law and Governance in European Capital Markets from a micro and macro economic perspective*, 7 CMLJ (2012), 30–54; Schammo, Pierre, *Market Building and the Capital Markets Union: Addressing Information Barriers in the SME Funding Market*, 14 ECFR (2017), 271–313; Segarkis, Konstantinos, *Le renforcement des pouvoirs des autorités compétentes*, Bull. Joly Bourse (2012), 118–121; Skeel, David A., *The New Financial Deal: Understanding the Dodd-Frank Act and its (Unintended) Consequences* (2010); Siems, Mathias M., *The Foundations of Securities Law*, 20 EBLR (2009), 141–171; Veil, Rüdiger and Lerch, Marcus P., *Auf dem Weg zu einem Europäischen Finanzmarktrecht: die Vorschläge der Kommission zur Neuregelung der Märkte für Finanzinstrumente*, 66 WM (2012), 1557–1565 (Part I); Veil, Rüdiger, *Europäische Kapitalmarktunion – Verordnungsgesetzgebung, Instrumente der europäischen Marktaufsicht und die Idee eines „Single Rulebook"*, 43 ZGR (2014), 544–607; Veil, Rüdiger, *Kapitalmarktzugang für Wachstumsunternehmen* (2016); Wheatley, Martin, *Review of LIBOR: final report* (2012).

I. Introduction

1   The former Treaty establishing the European Community (EC) did not contain any provisions regarding a European capital markets law. It did not take long after the foundation of the EC, however, for the European Commission and the Council of the European Union, seeking to fulfil the **aim** of an **internal market,** to claim to be competent for the harmonisation of the national laws. The first legislation was nevertheless not enacted until 20 years later. Its main purpose was to coordinate stock exchange and prospectus law of the Member States (phase 1). This was followed by a wide-ranging harmonisation of securities trading law, first by means of general provisions in directives, which gave Member States a wide scope for implementation (phase 2), and then by means of detailed provisions in directives (phase 3). The financial market crisis led to fundamental reforms of the supervisory architecture and a far-reaching unification of EU securities regulation (phase 4). This was followed by the Capital Markets Union project (phase 5). Its main aim is to promote growth and employment in the EU. This chapter describes the five phases of regulation and points out that European capital markets law has developed into an independent field of law.

II. Segré Report (1966)

2   The development of a European Capital Markets Law commenced in 1966, when a group of independent experts,[1] commissioned by the EEC Commission, published its report on a European capital market. The Committee, chaired by *Claudio Segré*, was 'to establish and specify what needs to be done to develop a European capital market, having regard [...] to the aims of the Treaty of Rome'.[2] The 350-page report, named after the committee's chair, brought to light significant structural problems on the national capital markets and criticised the disequilibrium between availability of capital and demand as well as limited markets. It recommended a variety of measures as solutions to these problems. The report emphasised the importance of integrating the securities markets and harmonising the access to the European capital market.

3   The **recommendations** on '**structure of equity markets**'[3] and the '**conditions for the development of a capital market integrated at European level**'[4] occupied an important place in the report. It found clear words in stating that disclosure of information to the public would be one of the main aims.[5] An information policy' would have to consider three aspects: firstly 'campaigns to familiarize the public with security investment and stock-exchange machinery'; secondly 'a permanent flow of information on the operations of companies in

---

[1] The members of the group were A. Batenburg, J. Blondeel, G. Della Porta, A. Ferrari, R. Franck, L. Gleske, J. Guyot, A. Lamfalussy, H. Möller, G. Plescoff, C. Segré and P. Tabatoni.
[2] Commission, The Development of a European Capital Market, Report of a Group of experts appointed by the EEC Commission, November 2006 ('Segré Report'), p. 11.
[3] Ibid. 203 ff.
[4] Ibid. 238–239.
[5] Ibid. 237.

addition to the annual publication of their accounts'; and thirdly 'especially comprehensive information whenever an appeal is made for the public's savings—that is, on the occasion of a security issue or the introduction of securities on a stock exchange'.[6]

While the Segré Report further contained information regarding legal enforcement, the Committee's recommendations on this point remained vague. The report regarded an external information control as necessary in order to enforce observation of certain 'minimum requirements concerning the scope and quality of information',[7] for example. It then, however, went no further than to demand that the systems for external information control be developed and harmonised. So far control had been exercised by banks and stock exchange authorities and only in some EEC countries by independent administrative bodies. The Committee did at least formulate the solution of 'an agency at Community level, to be competent for issues floated within the territory of the Community and to be endowed with powers similar to those of the Securities and Exchange Commission in the United States, the Banking Commission in Belgium or the Bank Control Commissariat in Luxembourg'.[8] However, it would take 43 years for this aim to be accomplished.

III. Phase 1: Coordination of Stock Exchange and Prospectus Laws (1979–1982)

The Segré Report contained detailed suggestions on the introduction of securities on the national stock markets and their trading.[9] It even presented a model prospectus adapted to the specific circumstances of different categories of securities and issuers.[10] In view of this, it is not surprising that the **first legislative measures** concerned the **law on stock exchanges** and **prospectuses**. However, it took thirteen years before legislature enacted the first laws.

The first steps the Council took on the way to a harmonisation of the Member States' statutory provisions were Directive 79/279/EEC[11] on securities admitted to official stock exchange listing, Directive 80/390/EEC[12] on the requirements for the drawing up, scrutiny and distribution of the listing, and Directive 82/121/EEC[13] on information to be published. All three directives were based on the Treaty establishing the European Economic Community, especially Article 54(3)(g) and Article 100.[14] Their aim was to eliminate the

---

[6] Ibid. 238.
[7] Ibid. 238.
[8] Ibid. 235.
[9] Ibid. 250–251.
[10] Ibid. 238, 252 ff.
[11] Council Directive 79/279/EEC of 5 March 1979 coordinating the conditions for the admission of securities to official stock exchange listing, OJ L 66, 16 March 1979, p. 21–32.
[12] Council Directive 80/390/EEC of 17 March 1980 coordinating the requirements for the drawing up, scrutiny and distribution of the listing particulars to be published for the admission of securities to official stock exchange listing, OJ L 100, 17 April 1980, p. 1–26.
[13] Council Directive 82/121/EEC of 15 February 1982 on information to be published on a regular basis by companies the shares of which have been admitted to official stock exchange listing, OJ L 48, 20 February 1982, p. 26–29.
[14] On the legal basis in the TFEU for the adoption of capital markets law, cf. R. Veil § 3 para. 4–12.

considerable differences in the Member States' provisions. The Council hoped to achieve this through minimum harmonisation of national laws: 'These differences should be eliminated by coordinating the rules and regulations without necessarily making them completely uniform, in order to achieve an adequate degree of equivalence in the safeguards required in each Member State to ensure the provision of information which is sufficient and as objective as possible for actual or potential security holders.'[15]

IV. White Paper on Completing the Internal Market (1985)

7   In 1985 the White Paper from the Commission to the European Council on 'Completing the Internal Market' was published. It can be seen as the next key moment in the development of a European capital markets law.[16] According to the Commission, the liberalisation of financial services represented a major step towards Community financial integration and the widening of the Internal Market.[17] The liberalisation of capital movements in the Community was also regarded as of utmost importance.[18]

8   Whilst the Commission only cited the UCITS Directive 85/611/EEC,[19] which became effective a few months later, but no other specific future legislative measures, it did, however, unequivocally highlight the parameters which, in its opinion, were relevant for the further legislation on capital markets law in Europe. The Commission pointed out, for example, that the **supervision** of ongoing activities of financial institutions should be guided **by** the **principle** of '**home country control**'[20] and that the barriers between stock exchanges needed to be removed in order to increase the stock exchanges' liquidity.[21]

V. Phase 2: Harmonisation of the Laws on Securities Markets (1988–1993)

9   A few years later, the harmonisation of the laws on securities markets began with the enactment of **Directive** 88/627/EEC[22] on **transparency**. The directive is inspired by the idea that a policy of adequate information for investors in the field of transferrable securities is likely to improve investor protection, to increase investors' confidence in securities markets and

---

[15] Cf. recitals of the Directive 80/390/EEC (fn. 12).
[16] Commission, Completing the Internal Market, White Paper from the Commission to the European Council (Milan, 28–29 June 1985), COM(85) 310 final, 14 June 1985.
[17] Ibid. para. 101.
[18] Ibid. para. 124.
[19] Council Directive 85/611/EEC of 20 December 1985 on the coordination of laws, regulations and administrative provisions relating to undertakings for collective investment in transferrable securities (UCITS), OJ L 375, 31 December 1985, p. 3–18.
[20] Commission, Completing the Internal Market, White Paper from the Commission to the European Council (Milan, 28–29 June 1985), 14 June 1985, COM(85) 310 final, para. 103.
[21] Ibid. para. 107.
[22] Council Directive 88/627/EEC of 12 December 1988 on the information to be published when a major holding in a listed company is acquired or disposed of, OJ L 348, 17 December 1988, p. 62–65.

thus to ensure that securities markets function correctly. Coordination at Community level should enhance the level of investor protection in order to foster the integration of Member States' securities markets and contribute to establish a true European capital market.

Directive 89/298/EEC[23] on the **issue of prospectuses**, which was enacted a few months later on the same legal basis, was to contribute to the 'Community information policy relating to transferrable securities'[24] for investors. The directive required that a prospectus containing information of this nature must be made available to investors when transferrable securities are offered to the public for the first time in a Member State, regardless of whether or not they are to be subsequently listed.[25]   10

Directive 89/592/EEC[26] **on insider dealing** was based on Article 100a of the former Treaty establishing the European Economic Community. It applied to secondary markets for securities and required Member States to introduce provisions prohibiting insider dealings as these are likely to undermine the investors' confidence and may therefore prejudice the smooth operation of the market. The directive contained only general provisions as to how compliance with these rules should be supervised by authorities. Also, the rights conferred on the competent national authorities were only outlined. The directive only stated that 'the competent authorities must be given all supervisory and investigatory powers that are necessary for the exercise of their functions, where appropriate in collaboration with other authorities'.[27]   11

The developments in this field ended with the enactment of **Directive** 93/22/EEC[28] **on investment services.** The Council regarded this directive as an essential instrument to achieving the aim of completing the Internal Market as described in the Commission's 1986 White Paper. The directive was to ensure the freedom of establishment and the free movement of services regarding investment firms. One of its main aims was investor protection. It demanded the introduction of 'prudential rules' on records to be kept of transactions executed and the companies' organisation (Article 10) alongside the enactment of provisions obliging investment firms to inform clients (Article 11).   12

VI. Financial Services Action Plan (1999)

The next step for the development of a European capital markets law was the Commission's presentation of a Financial Services Action Plan (FSAP) in 1999.[29] The Commission aimed   13

---

[23] Council Directive 89/298/EEC of 17 April 1989 coordinating the requirements for the drawing up, scrutiny and distribution of the prospectus to be published when transferrable securities are offered to the public, OJ L 124, 5 May 1989, p. 8–15.

[24] Cf. recitals of the Directive 89/298/EEC (fn. 23).

[25] Directive 80/390/EEC (fn. 12) only coordinated the information to be published for the admission of securities to official stock exchange listing.

[26] Council Directive 89/592/EEC of 13 November 1989 coordinating regulations on insider dealing, OJ L 334, 18 November 1989, p. 30–32; concerning its history, see V. Edwards, *EC Company Law*, 309 ff.

[27] See Art. 8(2) Directive 89/592/EEC (fn. 26).

[28] Council Directive 93/22/EEC of 10 May 1993 on investment services in the securities field, OJ L 141, 11 June 1993, p. 27–46.

[29] Communication from the Commission of 11 May 1999 entitled 'Implementing the Framework for Financial Markets: Action Plan', COM(1999) 232 final (hereafter FSAP).

to use the introduction of the Euro in order to supply the European Community with a **modern financial system**.[30] The idea was to reduce costs of capital for issuers and of intermediation.

14 The FSAP emphasised various priorities of a standardised Europe-wide financial market. These included joint provisions for integrated markets for securities and derivative instruments as well as for an EU-wide raising of capital. Several measures of varying priority were to achieve these aims. Some referred to existing directives—such as Directive 79/279/EEC on securities admitted to official stock exchange listing, Directive 80/390/EEC on the requirements for the drawing up, scrutiny and distribution of the listing, and Directive 82/121/EEC on Regular Reporting—and were to amend these.[31] Additionally, new directives were to be adopted, addressing, for example, market manipulation.[32]

15 Ultimately, in order to be able to keep up with the rapid development of capital markets and implement new regulatory measures, the FSAP recommended the introduction of suitable mechanisms of EU legislation.[33] Above all, the FSAP proposed the introduction of a securities committee, which should participate in the development of European provisions on securities.[34]

VII. Lamfalussy Report (2000)

16 Only a year later the Economic and Financial Affairs Council (ECOFIN) appointed a committee chaired by *Alexandre Lamfalussy*, who was already a member of the Segré Group.[35] The committee was to evaluate the developments of European capital markets and devise a new legislative procedure in order to guarantee a more rapid implementation of new directives and their uniform application through national authorities. Furthermore, the committee was to determine the key priorities for further legislation.

17 On 9 November 2000 the Lamfalussy committee published an interim report.[36] This report criticised the following: the 'EU passport for issuers' was still not a reality; rules on disclosure differed greatly between Member States; and there was no agreed definition of market manipulation.[37] In order to eliminate these deficits the Committee suggested that the transposition of the key priorities of the FSAP should be completed by 2003, rather than by the initial completion date in 2005.[38] The Committee saw the greatest difficulty in developing a European capital markets law as being the cumbersome nature of legislation and the inconsistency in the interpretation and application of existing regulations.[39] These problems were

---

[30] FSAP (fn. 29), p. 3.
[31] Cf. FSAP (fn. 29), p. 22.
[32] Cf. FSAP (fn. 29), p. 23.
[33] FSAP (fn. 29), p. 16 ff.
[34] FSAP (fn. 29), p. 30.
[35] Further members were C. Herkströter, L. Rojo, B. Ryden, L. Spaventa, N. Walter and N. Wicks.
[36] The Committee of Wise Men, Initial Report of the Committee of Wise Men on the Regulation of European Securities Markets, 9 November 2000.
[37] Ibid. 16.
[38] Ibid. 22 ff.
[39] Ibid. 18 ff.

to be countered by a four-step procedure of legislation and enforcement, based on the comitology procedure in the EU.[40]

On 15 February 2001, the Committee published its final report.[41] It recommended a **procedure** consisting of four levels, as had been outlined in the interim report, in order to help **accelerate** the **legislative process** for **securities markets**.[42] The details of this process, named the Lamfalussy process after the chair of the Committee, are described in the chapter on the regulation of capital markets in this book.[43] A short description of the first two levels (regarding legislation) has to suffice here.[44] The so-called framework directives and regulations are enacted by the European Parliament and the Council (first level). Subsequently, the European Commission adopts measures such as delegated acts or technical standards, which put the principles laid down in the framework directives into more concrete terms (level 2). In addition, a special Committee of European Securities Regulators (CESR) was created—in accordance with the recommendations of the Lamfalussy Group. It had advisory functions in the legislative process on level 2 where the Commission adopted technical implementing measures for the level 1 measures. Furthermore, it was the CESR's responsibility to improve the cooperation between the national supervisory authorities, to solve disputes between them and to evaluate the implementation of European law (level 3). Today the European Securities and Markets Authority (ESMA) carries out the tasks of CESR.

VIII. Phase 3: Reorganisation of the Laws on Prospectuses and Securities (2003–2007)

The three directives enacted between 1979 and 1982 and Directive 88/627/EEC were repeatedly subject to considerable amendments after their enactment. The European legislature therefore decided in 2001 to combine and newly codify the directives for reasons of clarity and efficiency. This resulted in Directive EC/2001/34[45] of 28 May 2001 on the admission of securities to official stock exchange listing and on information to be published on those securities. However, no relevant changes to the law were made by this directive.

In November 2002, British economists and auditors published a report, assigned to them by the European Commission. It provided economic proof[46] of the FSAP's legal understanding that the achievement of a European internal market would significantly reduce financing costs, thus paving the way for future developments. The level 1 measures announced

---

[40] Ibid. 24 ff.
[41] The Committee of Wise Men, Final Report of the Committee of Wise Men on the Regulation of European Securities Markets, 15 February 2001.
[42] Final Report (fn. 41), 27 ff.
[43] Cf. F. Walla § 4 para. 5–24.
[44] The two other levels relate to the application and enforcement of EU law. Cf. F. Walla § 4 para. 36.
[45] Directive 2001/34/EC of the European Parliament and of the Council of 28 May 2001 on the admission of securities to official stock exchange listing and on information to be published on those securities, OJ L 184, 6 July 2001, p. 1–66. Most of the provisions of the directive have now been repealed. However, Articles 5 to 19, 42 to 69 and 78 to 84 are still applicable.
[46] Cf. L. Burn, in: Panasar and Boeckman (eds.), *European Securities Law*, para. 1.08.

by the FSAP for the implementation of a European internal market were taken in 2003 and 2004. In these two years four framework directives were enacted, which are essentially still the core of regulation today: the Market Abuse Directive (MAD 2003), the Prospectus Directive (PD 2003), the Markets in Financial Instruments Directive (MiFID 2004) and the Transparency Directive (TD 2004). By 2007 the European Commission adopted so-called implementing measures, mainly directives, but partly regulations. These implementing measures followed the proceedings of level 2 of the Lamfalussy process.

21 The first directive was the **Market Abuse Directive**.[47] It was the European legislator's reaction to the fact that the Member States' legal framework regarding the protection of market integrity was incomplete at this time. Legal requirements varied from one Member State to another, often leaving economic actors uncertain over concepts, definitions and enforcement. The MAD was further intended to fill loopholes in Community legislation which could be used for wrongful conduct and which would have undermined public confidence and prejudiced the smooth functioning of the markets.[48] In some Member States there was no legislation addressing the issues of price manipulation and the dissemination of misleading price-relevant information.[49]

22 The MAD was the first European directive to contain provisions on market manipulation. It further requested the Member States to forbid insider dealings. These provisions were far more detailed than those of the former Directive 89/592/EEC on insider dealing. The reform of the rules on ad hoc disclosure obligations were a further important step.[50] These obligations were not restricted to insider *facts*, but rather covered all inside *information*, ie also a prognosis on possible future facts, such as profit forecasts. In other words, disclosure of inside information by issuers now had to take place sooner—a deliberate step by the legislature in order to prevent the abuse of insider knowledge.[51] Additionally, the directive introduced the obligation to disclose directors' dealings, which likewise intended to prevent the abuse of inside information and market manipulation. Furthermore, the MAD was the first directive to provide prudential rules for financial analysts. Last but not least, the directive dealt in depth with supervision by national authorities. The Member States were called upon to designate one single competent authority responsible for supervising compliance with the provisions adopted pursuant to the MAD, as well as international collaboration. The national authority was to be of an administrative nature, guaranteeing its independence of market participants and avoiding conflicts of interest.[52] The directive further requested a common minimum set of effective tools and powers for the competent authority of each Member State in order to guarantee supervisory effectiveness.[53]

23 Many of the directives' provisions were in need of concretisation. Thus, in order to provide the necessary legal certainty and guarantee a uniform application, the European

---

[47] Directive 2003/6/EC of the European Parliament and of the Council of 28 January 2003 on insider dealing and market manipulation (Market Abuse), OJ L 96, 12 April 2003, p. 16–25.
[48] Recitals 11, 13 MAD.
[49] Cf. recital 11 MAD.
[50] The former Directives 79/279/EEC (fn. 11) and 2001/34/EC (fn. 45) confined themselves to require the obligation to publish new facts, which would be likely to have a significant effect on the prices of financial instruments.
[51] Cf. N. Horn, *Europäisches Finanzmarktrecht*, 47.
[52] Recital 36 MAD.
[53] Recital 37 MAD.

Commission enacted various implementing measures, after a consultation with the CESR: Directive 2003/124/EC[54] on definitions, Directive 2003/125/EC[55] on investment recommendations and the disclosure of conflicts of interest, and Directive 2004/72/EC[56] with further specifications on insider legislation. Finally, the Commission enacted Regulation (EC) No. 2273/2003[57] on exemptions for buy-back programmes and stabilisation of financial instruments.

The **Prospectus Directive** 2003/71/EC[58] from 2003 was a further landmark in European capital markets legislation because it made cross-border securities offers in the EU possible for the first time. The Directive coordinated the requirements for the drawing up, scrutiny and distribution of the prospectus to be published for offers to the public or the admission of securities for trading on regulated markets. The aim of the Directive was once more to ensure investor protection and market efficiency.[59] The European Commission enacted further implementing measures to this directive: Prospectus Regulation (EC) No. 809/2004[60] contained details regarding the content of the prospectus and was directly applicable in the Member States.[61]

24

The third framework directive was the **Directive** 2004/39/EC[62] **on markets in financial instruments (MiFID)** from 2004. It mainly covered aspects of market organisation and prudential rules for investment firms. This also included compliance requirements for investment firms. Again, the principles laid down in the level 1 act were implemented by level 2 measures, such as the Directive 2006/73[63] and Regulation (EC) No. 1287/2006.[64]

25

---

[54] Commission Directive 2003/124/EC of 22 December 2003 implementing Directive 2003/6/EC of the European Parliament and of the Council as regards the definition and public disclosure of inside information and the definition of market manipulation, OJ L 339, 24 December 2003, p. 70–72.

[55] Commission Directive 2003/125/EC of 22 December 2003 implementing Directive 2003/6/EC of the European Parliament and of the Council as regards the fair presentation of investment recommendations and the disclosure of conflicts of interest, OJ L 339, 24 December 2003, p. 73–77.

[56] Commission Directive 2004/72/EC of 29 April 2004 implementing Directive 2003/6/EC of the European Parliament and of the Council as regards accepted market practices, the definition of inside information in relation to derivatives on commodities, the drawing up of lists of insiders, the notification of managers' transactions and the notification of suspicious transactions, OJ L 162, 30 April 2004, p. 70–75.

[57] Commission Regulation (EC) No. 2273/2003 of 22 December 2003 implementing Directive 2003/6/EC of the European Parliament and of the Council as regards exemptions for buy-back programmes and stabilisation of financial instruments, OJ L 336, 23 December 2003, p. 33–38.

[58] Directive 2003/71/EC of the European Parliament and of the Council of 4 November 2003 on the prospectus to be published when securities are offered to the public or admitted to trading and amending Directive 2001/34/EC, OJ L 345, 31 December 2003, p. 64–89.

[59] Recital 10 PD.

[60] Commission Regulation (EC) No. 809/2004 of 29 April 2004 implementing Directive 2003/71/EC of the European Parliament and of the Council as regards information contained in prospectuses as well as the format, incorporation by reference and publication of such prospectuses and dissemination of advertisements, OJ L 149, 30 April 2004, p. 3–143.

[61] On the legal effects of regulations cf. R. Veil § 3 para. 15.

[62] Directive 2004/39/EC of the European Parliament and of the Council of 21 April 2004 on markets in financial instruments amending Council Directives 85/611/EEC and 93/6/EEC and Directive 2000/12/EC of the European Parliament and of the Council and repealing Council Directive 93/22/EEC, OJ L 145, 30 April 2004, p. 1–44.

[63] Commission Directive 2006/73/EC of 10 August 2006 implementing Directive 2004/39/EC of the European Parliament and of the Council as regards organisational requirements and operating conditions for investment firms and defined terms for the purposes of that Directive, OJ L 241, 2 September 2006, p. 26–58.

[64] Commission Regulation (EC) No. 1287/2006 of 10 August 2006 implementing Directive 2004/39/EC of the European Parliament and of the Council as regards recordkeeping obligations for investment firms, transaction reporting, market transparency, admission of financial instruments to trading, and defined terms for the purposes of that Directive, OJ L 241, 2 September 2006, p. 1–25.

26 The fourth measure is the **Transparency Directive** from 2004.[65] This framework directive is still in force today. It concerns the harmonisation of transparency requirements in relation to information about issuers whose securities are admitted to trading on a regulated market. The legislature advanced the idea that the accurate, comprehensive and timely disclosure of information about security issuers builds sustained investor confidence and allows an informed assessment of their business performance and assets, thus enhancing both investor protection and market efficiency.[66]

27 The TD provides detailed provisions on the 'regular flow of information' in the shape of annual and half-yearly financial reports. Furthermore, it requires Member States to introduce disclosure obligations about 'ongoing information'. This is defined as information about major holdings and the information for holders of securities admitted to trading on a regulated market. In order to guarantee the uniform application of the TD's provisions, the European Commission enacted a directive with implementing measures, all of which concern procedural issues.[67]

IX. Continuation of Phase 3: Harmonisation of Takeover Law (2004)

28 In the 1980s, legislative attempts to regulate takeovers at a European level became apparent. A proposal for a 13th directive on takeover bids presented by the Commission in 1989, however, did not find the approval of the Member States, due to differences in their interests and views on regulatory approaches. In 1997, the Commission presented an amended proposal. This took into account the dissenting opinions and enabled the Council to adopt a common position on 19 July 2000. The European Parliament, however, raised objections, resulting in the involvement of the Conciliation Committee. On 5 July 2001 it presented a common draft which, however, did not win the recognition of the Parliament. A new proposal for a directive, presented in October 2002, once again threatened to fail due to the opposing views based on traditions in the corporate laws of some Member States. However, a compromise presented by Portugal enabled a political agreement, which led to the adoption of the **Takeover Directive (TOD)**[68] on 30 April 2004.

29 The directive has a number of aims. The first is to coordinate certain safeguards in the interests of shareholders and other stakeholders.[69] In this respect, the TOD contains corporate

---

[65] Directive 2004/109/EC of the European Parliament and of the Council of 15 December 2004 on the harmonisation of transparency requirements in relation to information about issuers whose securities are admitted to trading on a regulated market and amending Directive 2001/34/EC, OJ L 390, 31 December 2004, p. 38–57.

[66] Recital 1 Directive 2004/109/EC.

[67] Commission Directive 2007/14/EC of 8 March 2007 laying down detailed rules for the implementation of certain provisions of Directive 2004/109/EC on the harmonisation of transparency requirements in relation to information about issuers whose securities are admitted to trading on a regulated market.

[68] Directive 2004/25/EC of the European Parliament and of the Council of 21 April 2004 on takeover bids, OJ L 142, 30 April 2004, p. 12–23.

[69] Cf. recital 1 TOD.

law. One such provision is, for example, the prohibition for the management board to thwart takeover bids. However, the TOD also deals with important subjects of capital market law. The offeror's obligation to announce his decision to launch a bid, for example, is supposed to reduce the possibilities of insider dealings.[70] The offeror's obligation to submit an offer document is also part of capital markets law because it aims to overcome information asymmetries between the bidder and shareholders of the target company. The same must be said of the mandatory bid in cases of a change of control of the company. The TOD is limited to a core harmonisation. Essential aspects, such as the control threshold, are subject to Member States' regulatory autonomy. Due to disparate protective provisions in the national laws for the benefit of shareholders, there is still no level playing field for public takeover bids.

X. White Paper on Financial Services Policy (2005)

The reorganisation of the laws on prospectuses and securities and the enactment of the Takeover Directive meant that the European legislature had fulfilled the obligations put out by the FSAP. In its Green Paper on Financial Services Policy 2005–2010[71] the Commission could therefore restrict itself to recapitulating its achievements. For future legislation, it recommended an attempt at '**better regulation**'.[72] It was the Commission's opinion that the whole process of law-making and application had to be transparent, based on an impact assessment aimed at showing the economic benefits of the proposed measures. The legislative procedure was to take place with the participation of all affected groups.[73]   30

In the White Paper published a few months later, the Commission picked up on this approach and underlined the fact that in the future it would act in accordance with the principle of 'better regulation'. The continual assessment and evaluation of all new legislative measures was regarded a key component thereof.[74] Additionally, the Commission announced its plan to ensure a transposition of the directives by the Member States within the agreed deadlines.[75] International supervisory structures played a central role in the White Paper. The Commission planned to further harmonise the supervisory standards and practices. The development of a common European supervisory practice was to be facilitated through an informal cooperation of the national supervisory authorities, eg through joint inspections or staff exchanges.[76]   31

The Commission explicitly did not plan new provisions regarding rating agencies.[77] However, shortly afterwards the financial crisis required a change of thinking.   32

---

[70] Cf. recital 12 TOD.
[71] Commission, Green Paper on Financial Services policy (2005–2010), 3 May 2005, COM(2005) 177 final.
[72] Ibid. 5.
[73] Ibid. 5, 8 ff., 21 ff.
[74] Commission, White Paper on Financial Services Policy (2005–2010), 1 December 2005, COM(2005) 629 final, p. 5 ff.
[75] Ibid. 6–7.
[76] Ibid. 12.
[77] Ibid. 14.

XI. Phase 4: Overcoming the Financial Market Crisis through Unification of European Law and a European Supervisory Architecture (2009–2016)

33 The **financial crisis** revealed serious **deficiencies** of **global financial markets law**. In Europe, regulatory deficiencies and deficiencies in the implementation of existing provisions became apparent.[78] In October 2008 the European Commission therefore asked a group of outstanding experts to submit recommendations on the future regulation and supervision of the European capital markets. On 29 February 2009, this group, chaired by *Jacques de Larosière*,[79] published a report of close to 100 pages.[80]

34 Most of their recommendations, such as those for the reinforcement of financial stability on a global level, refer to topics this book does not cover. However, the Group's recommendations for a European financial supervisory system are of special interest for the securities markets. The de Larosière Group suggested replacing the previous level 3 committees of the Lamfalussy process, especially the CESR, by independent public authorities.[81] The existing national supervisory authorities were to continue the current supervision, keeping most of their powers, while the new European authorities (ESMA, EBA and EIOPA) would coordinate the application of high supervisory standards and guarantee intensive cooperation with the other supervisory authorities.

35 Furthermore, the de Larosière Group advocated a 'coherent regulatory framework for Europe'. The experts criticised the Member States' discretion in the implementation of European directives and the divergent interpretation of the transposed law,[82] and urged that the problem of legal inconsistencies also be taken into account at the European level: 'In the future, legal acts should be adopted as often as possible in the form of regulations (since they are directly applicable). If directives are used, the [...] legislator should make every effort to achieve maximum harmonisation of the central points'.[83] These recommendations led to the EU's strategy to unify financial markets law.

XII. Phase 4: European System of Financial Supervision (2009)

36 On 23 September 2009 the Commission communicated a comprehensive bundle of legislative measures on the basis of the de Larosière Report. It contained measures for recognising

---

[78] The legislative response to the financial crisis in the USA is the Dodd-Frank Wall Street Reform and Consumer Protection Act; on this reform cf. D. Skeel, *The New Financial Deal. Understanding the Dodd-Frank Act and its (Unintended) Consequences*; J. Coffee, in: Ferran et al. (eds.), *The Regulatory Aftermath of the Global Financial Crisis*, 301, 332.
[79] Further members of the group were L. Balcerowicz, O. Issing, R. Masera, C. McCarthy, L. Nyberg, J. Pérez and O. Ruding.
[80] Cf. The High-Level Group on Financial Supervision in the EU (de Larosière Group), Report, 25 February 2009 (de Larosière Report).
[81] Cf. ibid. 53.
[82] Cf. ibid. 31.
[83] Cf. ibid. 33.

and preventing systematic risks for Europe's entire financial system ('macro-prudential supervision') as well as measures to improve the supervision of individual financial service providers and capital market participants ('micro-prudential supervision').[84] The latter was intended to create a European System of Financial Supervision (ESFS), consisting of three European authorities with legal personality.[85]

These plans were accomplished in 2010, when the European Banking Authority (EBA), the European Insurance and Occupational Pensions Authority (EIOPA) and the **European Securities and Markets Authority** (ESMA) were established.[86] Since 1 January 2011, ESMA has participated in the legislative procedures. However, ESMA is not responsible for supervising the securities markets. This task generally continues to lie with the national supervisory authorities (so-called National Competent Authorities—NCAs), except with regard to rating agencies and trade repositories which are supervised by ESMA. However, ESMA has the task of ensuring the coherent, efficient and effective application of European legal acts (**supervisory convergence**). To this end, it may issue guidelines and recommendations addressed to national supervisory authorities and financial market participants. ESMA's primary task is therefore coordination. The ESA Review 2019 has not fundamentally changed this concept, but has further strengthened the respective powers of ESMA. Thus, ESMA's primary task continues to be to achieve supervisory convergence.

XIII. Regulation of Credit Rating Agencies (2009–2013)

An important step in the development of European Capital Markets Law was the regulation of credit rating agencies. The European Commission first addressed this issue in April 2002. However, in April 2006 it reached the conclusion that no legislative initiatives were needed.[87] It was suggested by the International Organization of Securities Commissions (IOSCO) that rating agencies should regulate themselves—and many regarded this as sufficient. The European Commission supported this understanding. It was only the outbreak of the financial crisis that lead to a change of thinking as people realised that the credit rating agencies were partly to blame for the incorrect evaluation of credit risks. Due to their important role on global securities and banking markets, in particular for financial stability, the European legislature now wanted to ensure that credit rating activities were conducted in accordance with the principles of integrity, transparency, responsibility and good governance in order to ensure that credit ratings used in the Community are independent, objective and of adequate quality.[88]

On 16 September 2009 the European Parliament and the Council enacted **Regulation (EC) No. 1060/2009 on credit rating agencies (CRAR-I)**. It primarily establishes disclosure

---

[84] Cf. Communication from the Commission on European financial supervision, 27 May 2009, COM(2009) 252 final.
[85] Commission, Proposal for a Regulation of the European Parliament and of the Council establishing a European Securities and Markets Authority, 23 September 2009, COM(2009) 503 final, Art. 3(1).
[86] See in more detail F. Walla § 11 para. 55–105.
[87] Cf. Communication from the Commission on Credit Rating Agencies, OJ C59, 11 March 2006, p. 2.
[88] Cf. recital 1 Regulation (EC) No. 1060/2009 of the European Parliament and of the Council of 16 September 2009 on credit rating agencies, OJ L 302, 17 November 2009, p. 1–31.

requirements and counters conflicts of interest, which mainly result from the so-called issuer pays model. In June 2010, in the course of its plans for preventing a future financial crisis and strengthening the financial system, the European Commission presented amendments to the Regulation. These aimed at attaining a more effective and centralised supervision of the agencies at a European level by ESMA and more transparency regarding issuers. The European Parliament and the Council adopted the Commission's proposal (**CRAR-II**),[89] thereby placing rating agencies under the supervision of ESMA. In May 2013, the European legislature adopted further amendments of the level 1 act (**CRAR-III**).[90] The new provisions contain stricter rules on transparency and specify when rating agencies are permitted to rate national debts. For the first time, Union law also provides for a civil liability of rating agencies vis-à-vis investors and issuers.

XIV. Revision of the Framework Directives—from Minimum to Full Harmonisation and Unification of Union Law (2009–2014)

40 Only a few years after the enactment of the four framework directives the European Commission initiated several consultations in order to assess the implementation of the directives and evaluate them. It addressed the consultations to all financial market participants as well as the governments and supervisory authorities in the Member States and other interested persons. The main aspects were regulatory deficiencies and the investigative and sanctioning powers of the supervisory authorities, which continued to differ greatly between the Member States. The consultations were preceded by talks between the Commission, CESR and the European Securities Markets Expert Group (ESME). The Expert Group was created by the European Commission to analyse legal coherence of the EU securities framework, to identify points of legal uncertainty, which impair the functioning of securities markets from the perspective of the regulated community and users of these markets. It should also provide the Commission with input for the reports on the application of various provisions of the framework directives.[91]

41 The consultations soon led to first results: In 2010 the European Parliament and the Council of the European Union enacted Directive 2010/73/EU on amendments to the **Prospectus Directive**.[92] The main aim of the amendments was to improve investor protection.

42 On 20 October 2011, the Commission presented a new strategy to fight against market abuse. Market abuse should for the first time be prohibited by a (directly applicable!)

---

[89] Regulation (EU) No. 513/2011 of the European Parliament and of the Council of 11 May 2011 amending Regulation (EC) No. 1060/2009 on credit rating agencies, OJ L 145, 31 May 2011, p. 30–56.
[90] Regulation (EU) No. 462/2013 of the European Parliament and of the Council of 21 May 2013 amending Regulation (EC) No. 1060/2009 on credit rating agencies, OJ L 146, 31 May 2013, p. 1–33.
[91] Cf. Commission, Securities markets: Commission encourages applications for new expert group, IP/06/403, Brussels, 30 March 2006.
[92] Directive 2010/73/EU of the European Parliament and of the Council of 24 November 2010 amending Directives 2003/71/EC on the prospectus to be published when securities are offered to the public or admitted to trading and 2004/109/EC on the harmonisation of transparency requirements in relation to information about issuers whose securities are admitted to trading on a regulated market, OJ L 327, 11 December 2010, p. 1–12.

regulation of the European Parliament and the Council to prevent regulatory arbitrage within the EU. An additional directive was to harmonise the criminal sanctions for insider dealings and market manipulation in Europe,[93] none of the four framework legislative acts on capital markets law having required the Member States to enact criminal provisions until then. The Commission's regulatory advance in this regard must therefore be seen as the start of a new era in European capital markets legislation. It reflects the recommendations by the High Level Group chaired by *Jacques de Larosière* to base 'future legislation [...] wherever possible, on regulations (which are of direct application). When directives are used, the co-legislator should strive to achieve maximum harmonisation of the core issues.'[94] The new approach was also to 'send a message to the public and potential offenders that these [manipulative behaviours] are taken very seriously'.[95] It took several years until Council, Parliament and Commission reached a consensus in the trialogue. The **Market Abuse Regulation** 596/2014/EU (MAR) of 16 April 2014[96] and **Directive** 2014/57/EU of 16 April 2014 on **Criminal Sanctions for Market Abuse** (CRIM-MAD)[97] are now at the heart of European capital market law. The two level 1 acts pursue the goal of ensuring the smooth functioning of securities markets and public confidence in these markets. They are based on the idea that market abuse violates the integrity of financial markets and undermines public confidence in securities and derivatives.[98] Both legislative acts create a legal framework for the trading of financial instruments on capital markets. This is done by prohibiting insider trading and the unlawful disclosure of inside information, by prohibiting market manipulation and by imposing disclosure obligations on issuers of inside information and on directors' dealings.[99]

A further reform proposed in 2001 concerned the **Transparency Directive.** It reduced the administrative burden for small and medium-sized issuers (SMEs) by abolishing the obligation to publish quarterly financial reports. Furthermore, the European legislature expanded the regime for disclosure of major holdings.[100] The main amendments concerned disclosure obligations for holders of financial instruments. This was the European legislator's reaction to spectacular cases in which investors had 'crept into' issuers through certain financial instruments not subject to disclosure. In this respect, the reformed TD provides for fully harmonising requirements for the Member States. Furthermore, the amending directive introduced stricter requirements for the Member States regarding the supervisory and sanctioning powers of the national supervisory authorities.[101]

43

---

[93] For further information see Commission, Commission Staff Working Paper Impact Assessment, 20 October 2011, SEC(2011) 1217 final.
[94] Cf. de Larosière Report (fn. 80), p. 29.
[95] Recital 6 Proposal for a Directive of the European Parliament and of the Council on Criminal Sanctions for Insider Dealing and Market Manipulation of 20 October 2011, COM(2011) 654 final.
[96] Cf. Explanatory Memorandum, Proposal for a Directive of the European Parliament and of the Council on Criminal Sanctions for Insider Dealing and Market Manipulation of 20 October 2011, COM(2011) 654 final, p. 3.
[97] Directive 2014/57/EU of the European Parliament and of the Council of 16 April 2014 on criminal sanctions for market abuse (market abuse directive), OJ L 173, 12 June 2014, p. 179–189.
[98] Cf. recital 2 MAR and recital 1 CRIM-MAD.
[99] Cf. Art. 1 MAR and Art. 1(1) CRIM-MAD
[100] Directive 2013/50/EU of the European Parliament and of the Council of 22 October 2013 amending Directive 2004/109/EC on the harmonization of transparency requirements in relation to information about issuers whose securities are admitted to trading on a regulated market and Commission Directive 2007/14/EC, OJ L 294, 6 November 2013, p. 13–27.
[101] For further information see Commission, Commission Staff Working Paper Impact Assessment, 25 October 2011, SEC(2011) 1279 final.

44 In 2012, the Commission proposed to reform the Markets in Financial Instruments Directive. It justified its initiative for a Directive on Markets in Financial Instruments repealing Directive 2004/39/EC (**MiFID II**) and for a Regulation on Markets in Financial Instruments (**MiFIR**) largely with the argument that the financial crisis had revealed weaknesses regarding the regulation of instruments other than shares. Financial innovation and the increasing complexity of financial instruments would require an increased investor protection. The Commission further claimed reforms to be necessary due to the fact that developments on the markets and in technology had led to a number of provisions in the MiFID no longer being up to date.[102] The new MiFID II[103] and MiFIR[104] were enacted on 15 May 2014 after two-year-long negotiations between Council, European Parliament and Commission. Whereas MiFID II requires implementation into the Member States' national laws, MiFIR is directly applicable. Both are complemented by numerous supplementary regulations of the Commission. The legal texts (including the level 3 measures) comprise more than 20,000 pages!

45 The so-called MiFID II regime regulates market infrastructures, investment services and ancillary services, and provides for governance and compliance requirements for investment firms and market operators. Furthermore, MiFID II defines the different trading venues (regulated market, multilateral trading facility (MTF) and organised trading facility (OTF), taking into account the decision of the G20 after the financial market crisis that no trading venue, no financial market participant and no financial product should be unregulated. Furthermore, MiFID II introduced the so-called SME growth market to improve the financing of SMEs. Finally, MiFID II requires transparency of prices and costs of securities transactions.

46 Another important measure to restore the confidence of investors in the financial market took place in 2014 with the adoption of the so-called **PRIPPS** regulation.[105] The level 1 act concerns packaged retail and insurance-based investment products (PRIIP). The main regulatory approach consists of uniform disclosure obligations for all participants in the PRIIP market. In particular, the regulation creates a common standard for the format and content of basic information sheets.

XV. Regulation on Short Sales (2012)

47 Legislative activity also became apparent regarding the topic of short sales. On 15 September 2010 the European Commission accepted a draft proposal for a Regulation on **short sales**

---

[102] Explanatory Memorandum, Proposal for a Directive of the European Parliament and of the Council on markets in financial instruments repealing Directive 2004/39/EC of the European Parliament and of the Council, 20 October 2011, COM(2011) 656 final, p. 2.

[103] Cf. Directive 2014/65/EU of the European Parliament and of the Council of 15 May 2014 on markets in financial instruments and amending Directive 2002/92/EC and Directive 2011/61/EU, OJ L 173, 12 June 2014, p. 349–496.

[104] Cf. Regulation (EU) No. 600/2014 of the European Parliament and of the Council of 15 May 2014 on markets in financial instruments and amending Regulation (EU) No. 648/2012, OJ L 173, 12 June 2014, p. 84–148.

[105] Regulation (EU) No 1286/2014 of the European Parliament and of the Council of 26 November 2014 on key information documents for packaged retail and insurance-based investment products (PRIIPs), OJ L 352, 9 December 2014, p. 1–23.

and certain aspects of **credit default swaps** (CDSs).[106] It was the experience gained from the financial crisis that led to these measures. The new regulation[107] entered into force in November 2012. Its main aim is to prevent the development of systemic risks. The level 1 act (known as Short Selling Regulation = SSR) applies to financial instruments, derivatives and debt instruments issued by a Member State. The SSR prohibits uncovered short sales of financial instruments and provides for disclosure obligations with regard to covered short sales of financial instruments. These regulatory approaches take into account the experience that short sales and credit default swaps can be used for market manipulation. It is particularly dangerous for the functioning of the markets if an investor sells shares short while spreading false rumours about the issuer (bear raids). Furthermore, short sales can result in a misleading signal to the capital market (abusive naked short sales).

XVI. Continuation of Phase 4: Regulation on OTC Derivatives (2012)

Derivatives play an increasingly important role on financial markets. They can be used for speculation or serve to hedge risks. According to the European Commission, over-the-counter (OTC) derivatives accounted for about 80% of all traded derivatives before the financial crisis. The nominal value of the entire OTC derivative market was almost US$ 615 billion in December 2009.[108] The financial crisis in general, and especially the insolvency of Lehman Brothers and the bail-out of AIG, revealed a number of deficiencies in the markets for OTC derivatives that led the Commission to propose a number of regulatory measures. The MiFID II,[109] for example, aims to subject derivatives to the rules of trading on a regulated market.[110] In addition, the Regulation on OTC derivatives[111] aims to make the European derivatives markets safer and more transparent, particularly by addressing counterparty credit risks. All transactions with OTC derivatives in the EU are now to be registered. Standardised OTC derivatives are further to be cleared by central counterparties.

48

XVII. End of Phase 4: Regulation of Benchmarks (2016)

The manipulation of the Libor and Euribor reference interest rates by banks[112] caused the Commission to propose a regulation in September 2013, which lays down requirements

49

---

[106] See F. Walla § 24 para. 7–11.
[107] Regulation (EU) No. 236/2012 of the European Parliament and of the Council of 14 March 2012 on short selling and certain aspects of credit default swaps, OJ L 86, 24 March 2012, p. 1–24.
[108] Commission, Press Release, Making Derivatives Markets in Europe Safer and More Transparent, 15 September 2010, IP/10/1125.
[109] See para. 44.
[110] Cf. R. Veil and M. Lerch, 66 WM (2012), 1557, 1561–1565.
[111] Regulation (EU) No. 648/2012 of the European Parliament and of the Council of 4 July 2012 on OTC derivatives, central counterparties and trade repositories, OJ L 201, 27 July 2012, p. 1–59.
[112] Cf. on the Libor scandal M. Wheatley, *Review of LIBOR: final report.*

for the provision of indices. The regulation[113] aims primarily to ensure the integrity and reliability of benchmarks. The legislature has also provided in MAR and CRIM-MAD for a prohibition of benchmark manipulation, which complements the framework of the Benchmark Regulation to ensure the accuracy and integrity of indices.

XVIII. Phase 5: Capital Markets Union (since 2015)

50   On 30 September 2015, the Commission adopted an Action Plan setting out 20 key measures to achieve a true single market for capital in Europe (Capital Markets Union Action Plan).[114] Stronger capital markets should (i) unlock more investment from the EU and the rest of the world, (ii) improve the connection between financing and investment projects throughout the EU, (iii) make the financial system more stable and (iv) deepen financial integration and increase competition.[115] The European Commission wants to achieve a 'real internal market'. Thus, the Action Plan aims to (i) develop new sources of finance for businesses, especially small and medium-sized enterprises; (ii) reduce the cost of raising capital; (iii) increase the supply of savings throughout the EU; (iv) facilitate cross-border investment and attract more foreign investment to the EU; (v) support long-term projects and (vi) make the EU financial system more stable, resilient and competitive.[116]

51   In Europe, capital markets play a less relevant role than in the US. The Action Plan wants to change this.[117] The Action Plan also aims to address the problem that capital markets are developed differently in the Union. Under the Juncker administration, the EU has therefore taken a number of legislative and non-legislative measures to improve access to capital markets.

XIX. Prospectus Regulation

52   The reform of the prospectus law can be seen as one of the most important measures to achieve the Capital Markets Union. The European legislature has replaced the Prospectus Directive, which was adopted in 2003 and reformed in 2011, by a regulation,[118] thus creating a uniform legal situation for the public offer and admission of securities to trading on

---

[113] Regulation (EU) 2016/1011 of the European Parliament and of the Council of 8 June 2016 on indices used as benchmarks in financial instruments and financial contracts or to measure the performance of investment funds and amending Directives 2008/48/EC and 2014/17/EU and Regulation (EU) No 596/2014, OJ L 171, 29 June 2016, p. 1–65.
[114] Cf. Commission, Action Plan Building a Capital Markets Union, 30 September 2015, COM(2015) 468 final.
[115] Cf. COM(2015) 468 final, p. 3.
[116] Cf. Commission, Action Plan Building a Capital Markets Union, 30 September 2015, COM(2015) 468 final, p. 3.
[117] Cf. M. Parmentier, 14 ECFR (2017), 242, 244.
[118] Regulation (EU) 2017/1129 of the European Parliament and of the Council of 14 June 2017 on the prospectus to be published when securities are offered to the public or admitted to trading on a regulated market, and repealing Directive 2003/71/EC, OJ L 168, 30 June 2017, p. 12–82.

a regulated market. Regulation (EU) 2017/1129 is directly applicable in all Member States. The new rules are to enable investors to make informed investment decisions, simplify the rules for companies that wish to issue shares or debt and foster cross-border investments in the single market.

Recital 4 of the Prospectus Regulation explains the **unification of prospectus law** by the fact that diverging approaches would result in a fragmentation of the internal market. Without a harmonised framework, 'it is likely that differences in Member States' laws would create obstacles to the smooth functioning of the internal market for securities. Therefore, to ensure the proper functioning of the internal market and improve the conditions of its functioning [...] and to guarantee a high level of consumer and investor protection, it is appropriate to lay down a regulatory framework for prospectuses at Union level.'[119] The use of a regulation should also 'reduce the possibility of divergent measures being taken at national level, and should ensure a consistent approach, greater legal certainty and prevent such significant impediments. The use of a regulation will also strengthen confidence in the transparency of markets across the Union, and reduce regulatory complexity as well as search and compliance costs for companies.'[120] This is likely to be particularly true for cross-border offerings. However, a large number of level 2 regulations increases regulatory complexity and can result in considerable capital costs.

XX. Securitisation

The Regulation (EU) 2017/2402 (Securitisation Regulation)[121] is an important measure of the investment offensive for Europe. It should contribute to a revival of the securitisation market in Europe, which had collapsed due to the financial market crisis. Securitisation of debt fulfils important functions. It enables broad risk management in the financial system and can help to ease the burden on the originator's balance sheet (company that grants loans, securitises them and then sells them in a bundle).

The Securitisation Regulation introduces a risk-based supervisory **framework** for **simple, transparent and standardised securitisations** (so-called STS securitisation).[122] A key regulatory approach is to address the risks for investors. The financial market crisis has shown impressively that securitised credit risks (so-called subprime loans) result primarily in default risks for investors. Agency risks, operational risks, liquidity and concentration risks may also exist.[123] An important instrument of investor protection is the disclosure of relevant information in so-called STS reports. The Securitisation Regulation also establishes due diligence obligations for institutional investors.

---

[119] Cf. recital 4 Prospectus Regulation.
[120] Cf. recital 5 Prospectus Regulation.
[121] Regulation (EU) 2017/2402 of the European Parliament and of the Council of 12 December 2017 laying down a general framework for securitisation and creating a specific framework for simple, transparent and standardised securitisation, and amending Directives 2009/65/EC, 2009/138/EC and 2011/61/EU and Regulations (EC) No 1060/2009 and (EU) No 648/2012, OJ L 347, 28 December 2017, p. 35–80.
[122] Cf. analysis by D. Anschütz, *Regelungskonzepte im neuen europäischen Verbriefungsrecht. Kapitalmarktregulierung zur Wiederherstellung von Vertrauen in Verbriefungen.*
[123] Cf. recital 9 Securitisation Regulation.

XXI. ESA Review

56 The reform of the ESAs established in 2009 (EBA, EIOPA, ESMA)[124] has not led to any fundamental changes in the tasks and governance of the agencies in the founding regulations. Admittedly, their mandates have been expanded, as the ESAs are now also to consider ESG concerns. The legislature has also strengthened the ESAs' powers to promote supervisory convergence.[125] From the perspective of financial market participants, it is important that the legislature has improved the democratic legitimacy of guidelines and recommendations as well as Q&A of the ESAs (level 3 measures). Furthermore, it has assigned ESMA the task of supervising certain data provision services, administrators of critical benchmarks and third country benchmarks.

XXII. Improving Start-up and SME Financing

57 Crowdfunding is the process of raising money for a specific purpose over the internet on a platform. Usually a start-up approaches a large number of investors, each of whom is expected to make only small amounts available. Crowdfunding has proven to be a cost-effective financing alternative for start-up companies, especially for companies that are still in the early stages of their projects and are interested in an alternative to bank financing. The market has grown considerably since 2011. Regulatory approaches in the Member States are disparate and reflect different ideas about the needs for investor protection achieved through supervisory law and private enforcement. The **Regulation on European Crowdfunding Service Providers (ECSP) for Business**[126] does not aim to harmonise Member States' laws, but rather to create an optional regulatory regime to complement national regulations on crowdfunding. If a platform applies the European regime for crowdfunding services, it does not need to comply with the national regulations. It should be able to operate throughout the EU and should only require approval by the competent national supervisory authority.[127] The regulatory approach can lead to productive competition between the laws of Member States and European law.

---

[124] Regulation (EU) 2019/2175 of the European Parliament and of the Council of 18 December 2019 amending Regulation (EU) No 1093/2010 establishing a European Supervisory Authority (European Banking Authority), Regulation (EU) No 1094/2010 establishing a European Supervisory Authority (European Insurance and Occupational Pensions Authority), Regulation (EU) No 1095/2010 establishing a European Supervisory Authority (European Securities and Markets Authority), Regulation (EU) No 600/2014 on markets in financial instruments, Regulation (EU) 2016/1011 on indices used as benchmarks in financial instruments and financial contracts or to measure the performance of investment funds, and Regulation (EU) 2015/847 on information accompanying transfers of funds, OJ L 334, 27 December 2019, p. 1–145.

[125] Cf. on the relevance of supervisory convergence N. Moloney, 13 ECFR (2016), 376, 410–420.

[126] Regulation (EU) 2020/1503 of the European Parliament and the Council on European Crowdfunding Service Providers (ECSP) for Business, OJ L347, 20. October 2020, p. 1–49.

[127] According to the Commission proposal COM(2018) 113 final, the authorisation should be granted by ESMA. Cf. M. Casper, in: FS Schmidt, 197, 200–211.

With the so-called JOBS Act, the US legislator had pursued the goal of facilitating and promoting access to capital markets for emerging growth companies.[128] The EU is also pursuing this goal. With Directive 2014/65/EU (MiFID II), the European legislature introduced the category of '**SME growth market**' in EU law. This category is intended as a 'seal of quality' for the alternative trading venues already operated by almost all European exchanges. The quality label shall raise the profile and reputation of existing markets and contribute to the development of common EU-wide regulatory standards for such markets. However, it became apparent early on that market operators did not see any major advantages in the new label. The European Commission therefore submitted a proposal to amend Regulations (EU) No. 596/2014 and (EU) 2017/1129 to promote the use of SME growth markets already on 24 May 2018. Regulation (EU) 2019/2115 was adopted on 27 November 2019. It is a 'small reform' that aims to reduce the administrative burden and thus ensure greater liquidity in SME growth markets. The problem that hardly any research is available for the listed SMEs[129] remains unsolved, however. Moreover, only issuers listed on SME growth markets benefit from the fact that the administrative burden is reduced by lower regulatory requirements. This market-based approach is criticised, as registration of the segment as an SME growth market by the competent supervisory authority is a prerequisite for the facilitations. If a market operator does not submit an application for registration, the facilitations for SMEs will be in vain.

XXIII. Sustainable Finance

The participants of the UN Climate Change Conference in Paris[130] agreed in 2015 that financial flows should be made consistent with a shift to low greenhouse gas emissions and climate-resilient developments. The EU has since been redesigning financial market legislation. Sustainable Finance has become a high priority within the project of a Capital Markets Union. The High Level Expert Group (HLEG) set up by the European Commission proposed a package of measures in 2018. The European legislator has already implemented the most important ones. The **Regulation** (EU) 2019/2088 on **sustainability-related disclosure requirements** in the financial services sector (SFDR – Disclosure Regulation)[131] establishes various disclosure requirements for institutional investors on sustainability risks of a financial product and on the sustainability of investments. Furthermore, the EU **Regulation** on the **Establishment** of a **Framework for Facilitating Sustainable Investments** (SFTaxR –Taxonomy Regulation)[132] determines how the environmental sustainability of

---

[128] Detailed comparative legal analysis by R. Veil, *Kapitalmarktzugang für Wachstumsunternehmen*.
[129] Cf. on information problems with the SME financing P. Schammo, 14 ECFR (2017), 271–313.
[130] Paris Agreement under the United Nations Framework Convention on Climate Change of 12 December 2015.
[131] Regulation (EU) 2019/2088 of the European Parliament and of the Council of 27 November 2019 on sustainability-related disclosures in the financial services sector, OJ L 317, 9 December 2019, p. 1–16.
[132] Regulation (EU) 2020/852 of the European Parliament and of the Council of 18 June 2020 on the establishment of a framework to facilitate sustainable investment, and amending Regulation (EU) 2019/2088, OJ L 198, 22 June 2020, p. 13–43.

investments can be assessed in a legally binding manner. It provides for six environmental goals and specifies under which conditions an economic activity contributes significantly to these goals.

60 The new regimes pursue the goal of environmental protection through financial markets law. However, European legislation does not pursue any strategies that are not in line with traditional regulatory objectives. Financial products are so-called credence goods. The disclosure regimes in European capital markets law for the primary and secondary markets have not yet been designed to balance information asymmetries between issuers and providers of capital investments on the one hand and investors on the other with regard to sustainability risks and green features of financial products. In addition, given the dazzling concept of environmental sustainability, it makes sense for the legislature to define the information to be disclosed.

XXIV. Action Plan 2020

61 The European Commission, under the presidency of *Ursula von der Leyen*, is continuing to pursue the Capital Markets Union project, which began in 2015. However, it still uses the term Capital Markets Union (CMU) in a misleading way.[133] The Commission is not interested in codifying securities regulation in a separate code based on coherent principles, thereby reducing regulatory complexity and discrepancies. Rather, its aim is to deepen the internal market for capital through a bundle of individual legislative and non-legislative measures in order to promote **growth** and **employment in the EU**. Once again, the focus is on attracting investment.[134]

62 A central theme of the second phase of the CMU is the digitalisation of the financial markets. The European Commission had already presented a Fintech Action Plan in 2018. The financial sector should be enabled 'to take advantage of advances in new technologies such as blockchain, artificial intelligence and cloud services. At the same time, the markets should become more secure and more accessible for new market participants.'[135] The proposal for a Crowdfunding Regulation, adopted in 2020 by the EU legislature[136] was one of the Commission's first initiatives.

63 The other measures listed in the Action Plan 2020 to harmonise insolvency law and promote cross-border investments take up proposals from the High Level Forum[137] set up by the European Commission in 2019. An essential element of the European Commission's **Digital Finance Strategy**, announced at the same time as the Action Plan, is the introduction of a legal framework by 2024 that allows the use of Distributed Ledger Technology

---

[133] Similarly on the CMU 2015 W.-G. Ringe, 9 LFMR (2015), 5, 7: 'The name is more symbolic than real, as the substance falls short of achieving a fully unified capital market across the EU.'

[134] European Commission, A Capital Markets Union for people and businesses-new action plan, 24.9.2020, COM(2020) 590 final.

[135] Communication from the Commission: FinTech Action plan: For a more competitive and innovative European financial sector, 8 March 2018, COM(2018) 109 final.

[136] See para. 57.

[137] A new Vision for Europe's Capital Markets, Final Report of the High Level Forum on the Capital Markets Union, June 2020.

(DLT) for crypto assets.[138] No less relevant are the European Commission's other initiatives on **Sustainable Finance** published in April 2021, which complement the already established regulatory framework on Sustainable Finance (see para. 59). A Delegated Regulation on EU climate taxonomy aims to promote investment in sustainable economic activities. In addition, six delegated acts are to help ensure that investment firms, asset managers and insurers take the issue of sustainability into account when selling financial products and advising clients. Finally, companies are to publish a sustainability report in the future. The Commission proposes to provide for this obligation in the CSR Directive (which it also calls Non Financial Reporting Directive – NFRD).[139]

XXV. Conclusion

Looking back at the development of European capital markets law, it is striking that all relevant stages of legislation were prepared by reports from independent high-ranking experts who identified regulatory deficits. The 1966 Segré report complained shortcomings and narrow and illiquid markets. The Lamfalussy report of 2000 criticised serious shortcomings in the supervisory system and the de Larosière report of 2009 drew attention to regulatory and supervisory arbitrage, which was at the root of the financial market crisis for various reasons. The Capital Markets Union project is also a reaction to regulatory deficits that European legislation is addressing in an exchange with experts and the financial industry. The reforms, which have always aimed at integrating capital markets, have led to an almost unmanageable number of regulations and directives. The enormous complexity of regulation makes access to the law more difficult even for experts and leads to redundancies and inconsistencies. Ultimately, this problem can only be countered by **codifying the EU securities laws**, which are spread across numerous so-called single rulebooks.

The harmonisation of capital markets law at the European level is limited to supervisory law. The relevant private law is still largely a national regulatory matter. The importance of these regimes should not be underestimated. The conditions under which securities can be created and transferred are determined by national private law. The rights of investors vis-à-vis issuers result from national private law rules on the issuance of bonds and other debt instruments as well as from corporate law on the issuance of shares. Issuers and investors usually have contractual relationships with intermediaries (especially banks and investment service providers), so that national private law governs the rights of the parties. Tort law can also offer investors protection and enable investors to claim damages in addition to special legal provisions. None of these private law matters is harmonised by EU law. The EU is therefore still far from integrating securities markets. Achieving this goal will require more than the establishment of expert groups to advise the European Commission for the next legislative period on gaps and the modernisation of the regulatory framework. What is required is a far-sighted approach that extends beyond the respective legislative period. The Commission should declare the possibilities of **harmonising** the respective **private law** to be a key issue for **the next decade**.

---

[138] See R. Veil § 10 para. 24.
[139] See R. Veil § 2 para. 23.

§ 2

Concept and Aims of Capital Markets Regulation

Bibliography

Andenas, Mads and Chiu, Iris H.-Y., *Financial Stability and Legal Integration in Financial Regulation*, 38 E.L. Rev. (2013), 335–359; Avgouleas, Emilios, *What Future for Disclosure as a Regulatory Technique? Lessons from Behavioural Decision Theory and the Global Financial Crisis*, in: MacNeil, Iain and O'Brian, Justin (eds.), *The Future of Financial Regulation* (2010), 205–225; Bachmann, Gregor, *Der Grundsatz der Gleichbehandlung im Kapitalmarktrecht*, 170 ZHR (2006), 144–177; Bauerschmidt, Jonathan, *Financial Stability as the Objective of the Banking Union*, 17 ECFR (2020), 155–183; Brinckmann, Hendrik, *Kapitalmarktrechtliche Finanzberichtserstattung* (2009); Brüggemeier, Alexander F.P., *Harmonisierungskonzepte im europäischen Kapitalmarktrecht* (2018); Bueren, Eckart, *Die EU-Taxonomie nachhaltiger Anlagen*, (WM 2020), 1611–1619, 1659–1663; Bumke, Christian, *Regulierung am Beispiel der Kapitalmärkte*, in: Hopt, Klaus J. et al. (eds.), *Kapitalmarktgesetzgebung im europäischen Binnenmarkt* (2008), 107–141; Coffee, John C. and Sale, Hillary, *Securities Regulation*, 12th edn. (2012); Fama, Eugene, *Efficient Capital Markets: A Review of Theory and Empirical Work*, 25 J. Fin. (1970), 383–417; Franke, Günter and Hax, Herbert, *Finanzwirtschaft des Unternehmens und Kapitalmarkt*, 6th edn. (2009); Gilson, Ronald J. and Kraakman, Reinier, *The Mechanisms of Market Efficiency*, 70 Va. L. Rev. (1984), 549–644; Habersack, Mathias, *Marktmissbrauchsrecht und Aktienrecht – Zielkonflikte im Zusammenhang mit der Ad hoc-Publizitätspflicht*, in: Klöhn, Lars and Mock, Sebastian (eds.), *Festschrift 25 Jahre WpHG* (2019), 217–235; Heinze, Stephan, *Europäisches Kapitalmarktrecht— Recht des Primärmarktes* (1999); Hell, Patrick A., *Offenlegung nichtfinanzieller Informationen* (2020); Hopt, Klaus J., *Der Kapitalanlegerschutz im Recht der Banken* (1996); Ipsen, Nils and Röh, Lars, *Mysterium Taxonomie*, ZIP (2020), 2001–2010; Klingenbrunn, Daniel, *Produktverbote zur Gewährleistung von Finanzmarktstabilität* (2018); Langevoort, Donald C., *Structuring Securities Regulation in the European Union: Lessons from the US Experience*, in: Ferrarini, Guido and Wymeersch, Eddy (eds.), *Investor Protection in Europe—Corporate Law Making, the MiFID and Beyond* (2006), 485–505; Loss, Louis and Seligman, Joel, *Securities Regulation*, vol I, 3rd edn. (1998); Lo, Andrew W., *The Adaptive Market Hypothesis*, 30 JPM (2004), 15–29; Luhmann, Niklas, *Vertrauen: Ein Mechanismus der Reduktion sozialer Komplexität*, 5th edn. (2014); Mattig Daniel, *Gleichbehandlung im europäischen Kapitalmarktrecht* (2019); Mehringer, Christoph, *Das allgemeine kapitalmarktrechtliche Gleichbehandlungsprinzip* (2007); Merkt, Hanno, *Unternehmenspublizität: Die Offenlegung von Unternehmensdaten als Korrelat der Marktteilnahme* (2009); Milgrom, Paul, *Good News and Bad News: Representation Theorems and Applications*, 12 Bell J. Econ. (1981), 380–391; Mülbert, Peter O., *Anlegerschutz und Finanzmarktregulierung – Grundlagen*, 177 ZHR (2013), 160–211; Mülbert, Peter O. and Sajnovits, Alexander, *Vertrauen und Finanzmarktrecht*, 2 ZfPW (2016), 1–51; Schinasi, Garry J., *Safeguarding Financial Stability: Theory and Practice* (2005); Stahl, Carolin, *Information Overload am Kapitalmarkt* (2013); Stark, Jürgen, *Das internationale Finanzsystem* (2004); Stumpp, Maximilian, *Die EU-Taxonomie für nachhaltige Finanzprodukte – Eine belastbare Grundlage für Sustainable Finance in Europa?*; ZBB (2019), 71–80; Tountopoulos, Vassilios, *Delineating Transparency for Stock Corporations and its Prospects*, in: Tountopoulos, Vassilios and Veil, Rüdiger (eds.), *Transparency of Stock Corporations in Europe* (2019), 353–363; Veil, Rüdiger, *Climate-related financial disclosure*, in: Tountopoulos, Vassilios and Veil, Rüdiger (eds.), *Transparency of Stock Corporations in Europe—Rationales, Limitations and Perspective* (2019), 129–141; Werner, Kai, *Ein Publizitätskonzept* (2011).

I. Concept

1 In academic literature, no clear definition of the term capital markets law has emerged. However, there is probably agreement that capital markets law deals with (i) the **organisation** of **capital markets**, (ii) **access** to them and (iii) the **trading** of **securities** both on **markets** and **bilaterally** (so-called over-the-counter transactions).

2 The first aspect (**organisation of markets**) has a long tradition in the legal systems of the Member States. Markets used to be organised as **stock exchanges.** The legislature of European countries reacted to manipulation and fraud by enacting stock exchange laws as early as the 19th century. Since the beginning of the 2000s, markets have also been operated by investment firms and there is competition between the different types of trading venues (regulated markets, MTFs and OTFs), which leads to better conditions and prices for investors. The term stock exchange no longer plays a role in European law. However, the market-based approach of European law does not exclude the possibility of markets being organised as stock exchanges. The operation and organisation of stock exchanges is governed by the national laws of the Member States.

3 Capital markets law also deals with **access to capital markets**. On the one hand, it deals with access of **issuers** to capital markets, especially as an alternative to bank financing and private equity (corporate finance). In order to be able to offer securities to the public or to admit securities to trading on a regulated market, an issuer is required by European law to provide investors with information on all relevant circumstances in a prospectus so that they can make an informed investment decision. An information document is required even if an issuer's securities are to be traded on a less regulated capital market (MTF or OTF) or if the issuer wishes to raise money through crowdfunding. On the other hand, European law regulates **investor** access to capital markets as well. Investors cannot, in principle, trade in securities on the exchange themselves, but must instead bring in securities dealers, as only these have the necessary expertise to trade on the exchange. Investors may also be limited in their ability to acquire particularly risky securities. In this context, the law on collective investment schemes also becomes relevant. It governs the acquisition of fund units, ie financial products by which investors are indirectly involved in a large number of issuers (whose securities are held in the fund assets).

4 Finally, capital markets law comprises the legal requirements for **trading in securities**. The rules were formerly provided for in the stock exchange laws of Member States and can now be found in the so-called Single Rulebooks of the EU. Securities trading law consists of two areas of regulation, which differ considerably with regard to the level of protection for investors. The first concerns the general **market conduct** regimes for **issuers** of securities and **investors**. Firstly, this includes the market abuse regime, which in Europe consists of a regulation directly applicable throughout the Union as well as of harmonised national criminal law provisions. Furthermore, securities trading law consists of disclosure requirements concerning price-sensitive circumstances that apply to issuers of securities as well as investors and that are designed to enable market participants to make informed investment decisions. This area of capital markets law is still largely based on the concept of a reasonable investor, who is basically able to understand all the information and draw conclusions from it for an investment decision. The second area of regulation concerns the **conduct** and **organisation** of **intermediaries**, in particular firms providing investment services such as investment advice and brokerage, asset management, investment research, etc. Other important information

intermediaries include rating agencies, proxy advisors and producers of benchmarks and securitisations. The regimes concerning intermediaries have developed into an independent area of capital markets law with increasingly paternalistic features. This applies in particular to the law on investment services, which no longer assumes that an investor can understand all information, but must be protected in a similar way to a consumer.

The legal sources of capital markets law consist of public law, private law and criminal law. A large part belongs to **public law**. Compliance with these regimes is supervised by public authorities. Therefore, the rules are also called **supervisory law**. These rules are almost entirely provided for in Union law. Furthermore, capital markets law consists of private law. The relevant **private law** is not harmonised throughout the Union. The purchase of securities is a purchase of rights, ownership is acquired in accordance with the private law of the respective Member State and, since investors on stock exchanges may not act for themselves but must involve banks as commission agents, in accordance with the rules of the applicable commercial law. There are often contractual relationships between intermediaries on the one hand and investors and issuers on the other. The rights and obligations of the parties arise primarily from the applicable private law. It is not yet clear whether the supervisory rules can determine the contractual obligations.[1] Finally, **criminal law** may be applicable. Violations of disclosure obligations and prohibition of market abuse are sanctioned by way of administrative penalties, and the prohibitions of market abuse can even be enforced by imprisonment.

II. Regulatory Aims

EU primary law does not contain any explicit provisions on the objectives of capital markets law. However, it clearly states that the EU is establishing a single market (Article 3(3) TEU). The capital market is part of the internal market. An integrated capital market results in a larger number of investments so that investors can better diversify their risks. A broader and larger investment in turn results in lower capital costs for issuers and lower transaction costs for investors.[2] The macro- and microeconomic effects of capital market integration are enormous.[3] This explains why the EU's Capital Markets Union project[4] aims to further unify regimes.

1. Efficiency of Capital Markets and Investor Protection

The level 1-acts aim to ensure the institutional **functioning** of **markets** in Europe.[5] The proper functioning of securities markets requires public confidence in the markets.[6]

---

[1] On the relevance of supervisory law for obligations under private law, see R. Veil § 30 para. 62.
[2] See A. Brüggemeier, *Harmonisierungskonzepte im europäischen Kapitalmarktrecht*, 79.
[3] Ibid. 81, with reference to studies according to which an internal capital market should reduce the capital costs of a listed company by an average of 0.467%.
[4] See R. Veil § 1 para. 50.
[5] This corresponds to ESMA's task of ensuring the integrity, transparency, efficiency and proper functioning of financial markets. Cf. Art. 1(5)(b) ESMA-Regulation.
[6] Recital 2 MAR; recital 7 PR.

A further regulatory objective is to ensure that efficient securities markets allow a better allocation of capital and a reduction in costs.[7]

8   The **allocation function** of capital markets means that the capital collected (from private households, institutional investors and investment-seeking companies) should flow to where the money is most urgently needed and where the highest return can be achieved with sufficient investment security. This requires investor confidence in the markets, which can be achieved by the disclosure of price relevant information and transparency concerning market participants' conflicts of interest.[8]

9   The aim of **ensuring the proper functioning** of capital markets concerns the basic requirements for an efficient mechanism of market segments. It requires access to the market to be as unhindered as possible, as well as for sufficient supply and demand by investors. A market that attracts a lot of capital is a liquid market, ie investors can expect to be able to sell their securities at a later date. Measures must therefore be taken to increase **investor confidence** and ensure the **integrity of the market**.[9]

10 Finally, capital markets law pursues the goal of optimising the **operational functioning** of capital markets by minimising the costs incurred by a transaction. On the one hand, issuers' efforts must be kept as low as possible; costs incur when securities are listed on the stock exchange (admission fees, costs of the prospectus, etc.) and for the subsequent publication of information and organisational arrangements. Secondly, the operational functioning of a market depends on the costs incurred by investors in investing in securities.[10] These costs can be reduced by imposing disclosure obligations on the issuer, who is usually the cheapest cost avoider.

11 The proper functioning of the markets and investor protection are two 'communicating vessels'[11] that support each other.[12] This explains why European legislature wants to achieve a 'high level of investor protection'.[13] What exactly the term **investor protection** encompasses, in particular whether even property interests of investors are protected,[14] is still an open question. In recent legislation, moreover, investor protection is repeatedly linked to the concept of consumer protection. The Prospectus Regulation 2017/1129, for example, intends to achieve a 'high level of consumer and investor protection'.[15] However, it is not apparent from the legislative act whether a higher level of protection should be associated with consumer protection than with investor protection. The European Commission and ESMA have not yet expressed their views on this either. For the interpretation of specific legal questions, the reference to consumer protection is unlikely to be helpful. The situation may be different in financial services law, where the focus is now on consumer protection, thereby implying that investors may be particularly vulnerable and in need of protection

---

[7] Recital 1 TD.
[8] For details on transparency and capital market efficiency, see H. Brinckmann § 16 para. 4–16.
[9] European legislature also assumes that market integrity serves to ensure investor confidence in the markets. See recital 2 MAR.
[10] In detail: G. Franke and H. Hax, *Finanzwirtschaft des Unternehmens und Kapitalmarkt*, 56.
[11] K. Hopt, *Der Kapitalanlegerschutz im Recht der Banken*, 52.
[12] C. Bumke, in: Hopt et al. (eds.), *Kapitalmarktgesetzgebung im europäischen Binnenmarkt*, 107, 119.
[13] Recitals 5 and 7 TD.
[14] This question becomes relevant in the context of investor protection under private law, ie the question of whether investors can claim damages for breach of disclosure requirements. See R. Veil § 19 para. 80 ff.
[15] Recital 4 PR.

because they are not capable of interpreting the information provided by issuers and intermediaries correctly.[16]

Understanding why **investor confidence** is protected, as well as identifying the subject of invertors' trust, is important for understanding capital market regulation. As a starting point, trust can be understood as an alternative mechanism for information in order to reduce complexity.[17] The trusting person refrains from exploring facts through information, but has trust in the (past, present or future) behaviour of persons or organisations. Thus, trust replaces an information deficit. A distinction can be made between personal trust (in a specific person, such as a bank advisor), organisational trust (in a legal entity, such as a public limited company with its management staff) and trust in a system (in institutions, such as the banking system or a market segment[18]). Trust in a system plays a major role in capital markets law, as capital markets are anonymous. Parties to a transaction do not usually know each other, so they cannot develop personal trust. In addition, investors cannot examine the financial products that are being traded. Therefore securities are also described as credence goods, as opposed to inspection goods. An investor who enters into securities transactions trusts that other investors will not cheat him and that all information relevant to his decisions will either be disclosed or kept secret from all market participants.

12

The **equal treatment** of **capital market participants** is a central **principle** of **European capital markets regulation.**[19] EU insider trading law is based on the idea of equal information opportunities for investors.[20] In addition, a large number of provisions can be identified that manage the equal treatment of intermediaries and investors. Issuers and investors should have equal access to markets. Furthermore, investors should have equal access to the information they need to acquire or dispose of securities. First of all, equal treatment means that market participants must not be discriminated against. The principle of equal treatment may require treating market participants equally. An unequal treatment may be justified if there is an objective reason and the unequal treatment is proportionate.[21] Whether the principle of equal treatment impacts the interpretation of legal provisions can only be assessed in individual cases.

13

Equal treatment of market participants is also a key principle for the further development of the regimes that strengthen investor confidence in the functioning of markets. However, other objectives of capital market regulation may justify unequal treatment. This will be illustrated by an example: The purpose of European law is to ensure that all investors can take note of new price-sensitive information at the same time. Article 2(1) of Regulation (EU) 2016/1055 requires that inside information be disseminated 'to as wide a public as possible on a non-discriminatory basis' and 'free of charge'. In addition, the issuer has to use 'electronic means that ensure that the completeness, integrity and confidentiality of the information is maintained during the transmission'. These procedural requirements are to ensure equal information opportunities for investors. However, European law allows high-frequency traders to exploit information before other investors, for

14

---

[16] Cf. recital 13 PRIIPS: 'Given the difficulties many retail investors have in understanding specialist financial terminology, particular attention should be paid to the vocabulary and style of writing used in the document'.
[17] P. Mülbert and A. Sajnovits, 2 ZfPW (2016), 1, 6, with reference to N. Luhmann, *Vertrauen*, 27 ff.
[18] P. Mülbert and A. Sajnovits, 2 ZfPW (2016), 1, 7–10.
[19] Cf. S. Heinze, *Europäisches Kapitalmarktrecht*, 7; G. Bachmann, 170 ZHR (2006), 144 ff.; C. Mehringer, *Das allgemeine kapitalmarktrechtliche Gleichbehandlungsprinzip*, passim; D. Mattig, *Gleichbehandlung im europäischen Kapitalmarktrecht*, passim.
[20] Cf. R. Veil § 14 para. 16.
[21] Cf. D. Mattig, *Gleichbehandlung im europäischen Kapitalmarktrecht*, 177–183, 288–300, 334–351, 376.

example by placing their computers directly in the trading computers' data centres (co-location).[22] This privilege can be justified by the positive aspects of high-frequency trading, in particular the improved liquidity of capital markets.

2. Financial Stability

15 Another regulatory objective of capital markets law is one that has only emerged in the last decade: financial stability. The financial market crisis 2007/08 demonstrated the importance that individual financial market participants, in particular systemically relevant banks, but also certain trading practices, such as short selling, can have for the stability of financial markets, and that financial markets are closely interlinked. Not all risks that endanger a financial system can be prevented solely by supervising banks. It has, rather, become apparent that the financial system must be regarded in its entire complexity. The European legislature has therefore created the European System of Financial Supervisors (ESFS).[23] The ESFS consists of three European supervisory authorities (EBA, EIOPA and ESMA), the European Systemic Risk Board (ESRB), the Joint Committee of European Supervisory Authorities and the supervisory authorities of the Member States.

16 Financial stability could also be understood as being a part of the regulatory objective of ensuring the proper functioning of markets. However, legislature considers financial stability as a separate regulatory objective. This applies above all to banking law.[24] One of the main goals of the CRD IV regime is to ensure financial stability, because the failure of large credit institutions has unfavourable consequences for payment systems and the real economy. Issuers and intermediaries on capital markets do not pose a comparable risk. Nevertheless, serious negative consequences for the financial system and the real economy may also arise on capital markets. According to Article 1(5) ESMA Regulation, the objective of **ESMA** is to '**protect** the public interest by contributing to the **short-, medium- and long-term stability** and effectiveness of the **financial system**, for the Union economy, its citizens and businesses.'[25] Financial stability is highlighted here as the second prominent objective of European capital markets law, alongside the proper functioning (effectiveness) of capital markets.

17 The regulations and directives adopted since 2009 are partly justified by the fact that they are intended to ensure financial stability in Europe. For example, the amendment to the Regulation on Credit Rating Agencies adopted in 2011 (CRAR-II) underlines the importance of these intermediaries for the stability of financial markets.[26] Furthermore, the regulation on short selling (SSR), which entered into force in 2012, also aims to ensure financial stability.[27] MiFID II and MiFIR are also supposed to help ensure stability of the financial markets.

---

[22] Cf. M. Lerch § 25 para. 42 on rules re. co-location.
[23] For more detail, see F. Walla § 11 para. 55 ff.
[24] Cf. J. Bauerschmidt, 17 ECFR (2020), 155, 158–178.
[25] See also recital 17 ESMA-Regulation.
[26] See recital 11 CRAR-II. The 2009 CRAR-I was still based exclusively on ensuring the functioning of the markets and the internal market.
[27] For more detail, see F. Walla § 24 para. 12.

For the interpretation of the respective supervisory rules, it may be necessary to specify the concept of financial stability, especially when the term 'financial stability' or 'stability of financial systems' is provided as a prerequisite for intervention by NCAs or the ESAs. For example, ESMA may prohibit or restrict certain financial activities if they threaten financial stability (Article 9(5) ESMA Regulation). In addition, the intervention powers of NCAs with regard to short selling and credit default swaps presuppose that financial stability is seriously threatened.[28] The product intervention powers of NCAs and ESAs under Articles 40–43 MiFIR also relate to the stability of the financial system.

18

> The concept of financial stability must therefore be put into more concrete terms. Garry Schinasi describes financial stability as follows: 'Financial Stability is a situation in which the financial system is capable of satisfactorily performing its three key functions simultaneously. First, the financial system is efficiently and smoothly facilitating the intertemporal allocation of resources from savers to investors and the allocation of economic resources generally. Second, forward-looking financial risks are being assessed and priced reasonably accurately and are being relatively well managed. Third, the financial system is in such condition that it can comfortably if not smoothly absorb financial and real economic surprises and shocks.'[29] So financial stability depends very much on whether **internal** and **external shocks** are **overcome** by **self-correction mechanisms** without the real economy suffering as a result. While external shocks have their origin outside the financial system, such as a sharp rise in commodity prices, terrorist attacks or natural disasters, internal shocks have their origin within the financial system. Banks are already unstable due to their business model. If they have to correct valuations significantly or even become insolvent, this can result in companies and other market participants losing confidence in the markets.[30] This shock poses a significant threat to the stability of the financial system. Self-correction mechanisms include the adjustment of market prices, the exit of failed market participants and the entry of new ones.[31]

19

These findings are helpful in a legal context.[32] However, for the application of the law, the concept of financial stability must be further developed.[33] This is done in the Single Rulebooks at Level 2. The regime on short selling, for example, provides a number of 'criteria and factors' that must be taken into account when a supervisory authority decides on its powers of intervention.[34] The authorities are given a wide margin of discretion in this respect.[35]

20

3. Sustainability

In Paris, the global community agreed on the goal of limiting global warming to well below 2°C compared to the pre-industrial era and also committed to a 1.5°C scenario with less dramatic effects. Since the Paris Climate Change Agreement 2015, the EU has been reshaping the financial system.[36] Following the UN General Assembly's 2030 agenda for sustainable

21

---

[28] For more detail, see F. Walla § 24 para. 52.
[29] G. Schinasi, *Safeguarding Financial Stability: Theory and Practice*, 82.
[30] D. Klingenbrunn, *Produktverbote zur Gewährleistung von Finanzmarktstabilität*, 15.
[31] Cf. J. Stark, *Das internationale Finanzsystem*, 7.
[32] Cf. D. Klingenbrunn, *Produktverbote zur Gewährleistung von Finanzmarktstabilität*, 17 ff.
[33] See J. Bauerschmidt, 17 ECFR (2020), 155, 180: 'interpretative function'.
[34] Cf. Art. 24 Delegated Regulation No. 918 of 5 July 2012, OJ L 274, 9 October 2012, p. 1 regarding unfavourable events or developments according to Art. 30 SSR.
[35] Cf. Art. 24 Delegated Regulation No. 918: 'which can reasonably be assumed or could reasonably be assumed'.
[36] See R. Veil § 1 para. 59.

development, sustainability has three dimensions for the EU: an **economic, social** and **environmental dimension**. The EU legislature is aligning the regimes for financial markets with these dimensions (Sustainable Finance). The main focus of European legislation so far has been on environmental sustainability.

22 Achieving the SDGs in the Union requires the channelling of capital flows towards sustainable investments.[37] A fundamental reorientation of capital markets law has not yet taken place. Rather, the measures to ensure sustainability introduced in European capital markets law are consistent with the traditional regulatory objectives. European legislation contributes to overcoming information asymmetries by requiring **financial market participants** (asset management companies; investment firms; insurance companies; etc.) to **disclose ecological risks** of **financial products**. In addition, financial market participants are to explain the ecological aspects of financial products distributed to their clients.[38] These **investor- and product-related disclosure requirements** of Regulation (EU) 2019/2088 (SFDR) have an informational and regulatory function.[39] Investors (in the terminology of European law: 'end clients') are encouraged to evaluate their investments with a view to environmentally sustainable economic activities and to take into account any (transitory or physical) sustainability risks of the financial product when making investment decisions.[40] Finally, it is also useful to define the concept of sustainability with as much certainty as possible. Regulation 2020/582 (SFTaxR)—also referred to as the Taxonomy Regulation—is necessary to develop a uniform understanding of environmental objectives throughout the Union.[41] This is particularly important when developing and distributing 'green' financial products.[42] The regime (consisting of numerous and extensive Level 2 legal acts) is dynamic[43] and will continue to develop in exchange with the Sustainable Finance.

23 Providers of financial products generally have no legal right to demand from companies the information they need to assess the environmental characteristics of a financial product. The European Commission's proposal to reform the CSR Directive (in future referred to as the **Non Financial Reporting Directive**)[44] therefore aims at improving access to information. In the future, **companies** should provide information on the sustainability aspects of their business activities in a **sustainability report** (which should be part of the management report). Furthermore, they are to state how they ensure that their business model and strategy is in line with the goal of a sustainable economy and the goal of limiting global warming, as agreed in the Paris Agreement in 2015.[45] This reporting obligation also has an information and regulatory function.

---

[37] Cf. recital 9 Regulation (EU) 2020/852.
[38] See R. Veil § 23 para. 8–11.
[39] Cf. R. Veil, in: Tountopoulos and Veil (eds.), *Transparency of Stock Corporations in Europe—Rationales, Limitations and Perspective* (2019), 129 ff. See also R. Veil § 23 para. 10.
[40] Cf. on these types of sustainability risks BaFin, *Fact sheet on dealing with sustainability risks*, p. 13: 'Events or conditions in the environmental, social or corporate governance fields […], the occurrence of which would have an actual or potential negative impact on the net assets, financial position and results of operations as well as on the reputation of a supervised entity.'
[41] Vgl. Cf. M. Stumpp, ZBB (2019), 71 ff.; E. Bueren, WM (2020), 1611 ff., 1659 ff.
[42] See on green bonds and ESG-funds R. Veil § 8 para. 28 ff.
[43] Vgl. N. Ipsen and L. Röh, ZIP (2020), 2001, 2010.
[44] Cf. European Commission, COM(2021) 189 final, 21.4.2021.
[45] See R. Veil § 7 para. 27.

Sustainable finance is a major challenge in its concrete implementation. The protection of the environment is not one of the established objectives of capital market law to ensure the institutional functioning of markets (see para. 11) and financial stability (see para. 15). Rather, it is traditionally realised in environmental, subvention and tax law. However, it is consistent with the traditional goals to enable sustainability-related investor decisions and to promote sustainable capital investments through disclosure obligations. This regulatory approach balances out information asymmetries between the issuer or provider of a green investment product on the one hand, and investors on the other. In contrast, the Commission's proposal for sustainability reporting by companies (see para. 23) can hardly be justified by the goals of accounting law. The disclosure requirements deeply interfere with entrepreneurial freedom. Finally, more far-reaching requirements on the consideration of ESG issues in investment decisions—for example, that asset managers would be obliged to invest a certain percentage in ecologically sustainable products—would lead to distortions with the traditional objectives of capital markets regulation.

III. Regulatory Strategies and Instruments

1. Disclosure

The regulatory objectives of European capital markets law are mainly pursued by the disclosure of price relevant information.[46] If **information is publicly available**, transparency exists. Anyone can then take note of the information.[47] Means for public disclosure used to be daily newspapers and financial newspapers in printed form. Today, information is transmitted via electronic information dissemination systems and the Internet, and in the future it will probably also be transmitted on the blockchain. Another traditional means of publicity are registers, which of course are now also kept in digital form.

(a) Information Function

Disclosure has various functions. The traditional and most established function is to enable investors to assess the **quality of an investment.** Securities are so-called credence goods. When purchasing a bond or share, an investor is not able to assess the expected return and the risks of the security without information about the issuer and the characteristics of the security (so-called *hidden information*). In the case of a derivative, information asymmetries exist with regard to the underlying and the structure of the derivative. One goal of capital markets regulation is to balance information asymmetries in order to enable investors to make an **informed decision** on the purchase and sale of the security or derivative (information function). But does this require disclosure obligations? The *market*

---

[46] Cf. E. Avgouleas, in: MacNeil and O'Brian (eds.), *The Future of Financial Regulation*, 205, 209; C. Bumke, in: Hopt et al. (eds.), *Kapitalmarktgesetzgebung im europäischen Binnenmarkt*, 107, 126.
[47] H. Merkt, *Unternehmenspublizität*, 11 f.; H. Brinckmann, *Kapitalmarktrechtliche Finanzberichterstattung*, 18.

for lemons[48] described by *Akerlof* suggests that an issuer that wants to sell its securities should have sufficient incentives to explain the quality of its security on its own initiative (*signaling*), otherwise there is a risk of market failure. The issuer should have sufficient incentive to disclose even unfavourable information, because otherwise market participants would give less weight to positive news in the future.[49] In addition, some argue that issuers are incentivised to disclose negative information to counteract the market's alleged worst-case assumptions ('*no news is bad news*').[50]

27 Nevertheless, European capital markets law provides for a large number of **disclosure obligations**. From an economic point of view, regulation can be justified by the fact that disclosure obligations best meet investors' information needs by focusing on 'relevant information' and therefore reduce transaction costs.[51] Statutory disclosure obligations are also suitable for standardising information. This makes it easier for investors to compare issuers with each other, which becomes particularly relevant in financial reporting. As an alternative to a mandatory statutory disclosure requirement, it may be appropriate to provide for a report-or-explain mechanism, so that the person required to disclose information can refrain from disclosing it, stating his or her reasons.

28 European capital markets regulation is based on the information paradigm. For example, the recitals to the Market Abuse Regulation state that 'immediate public **disclosure** of inside information is **essential**'.[52] The Transparency Directive also argues that the timely disclosure of reliable and comprehensive information on securities issuers strengthens investor confidence in the long term and enables a sound assessment of the company's business performance and financial position.[53] Finally, financial services legislation is based on the idea that investment firms must provide their clients with information about all relevant aspects of a security. MiFID II aims to ensure that clients receive 'all relevant information' about the financial service and the security.[54] It is not possible to give a general answer to the question of whether the disclosure obligations also serve as an instrument of **corporate governance**. According to the European legislature, the disclosure of major shareholdings in accordance with the Transparency Directive also improves the governance of listed companies.[55] In contrast, the European legislature understands ad hoc disclosure according to Article 17 MAR primarily as an instrument to prevent market abuse. Admittedly, the obligation of the issuer to disclose violations of law (to be qualified as inside information) can have a disciplinary effect on the management board.[56] However, the dislosure obligation does not serve purposes of corporate law and should therefore be interpreted in the light of its goal to improve market efficiency.[57]

---

[48] The *market for lemon* describes the danger of a race to the bottom if no information is available for high quality products. In the absence of demand, suppliers of such products withdraw from the market, with the result that the market collapses. See H. Brinckmann § 16 para. 7.
[49] K. Werner, *Publizitätskonzept*, 104.
[50] Cf. P. Milgrom, 12 Bell J. Econ. (1981), 380, 387.
[51] See H. Brinckmann § 16 para. 20.
[52] Recital 39 MAR.
[53] Recital 1 TD; also recital 3 and 7 PR.
[54] See for example recital 72 MiFID II.
[55] See R. Veil § 20 para. 4.
[56] See R. Veil § 19 para 8.
[57] Cf. M. Habersack, in: FS 25 Jahre WpHG, 217, 227.

According to the **Efficient Capital Market Hypothesis** (ECMH), securities prices reflect all publicly available information.[58] The theory distinguishes between weak, semi-strong and strong capital market efficiency. On a weak efficient market, securities prices reflect all (known) historical information. When a capital market is semi-strong efficient, securities prices reflect all generally available information, such as earnings estimates and securities analysis. A strong efficient market is characterised by the fact that prices are based on all relevant information, ie including non-publicly available inside information. In that case, investors cannot obtain any returns and insider trading is impossible. This form of efficiency has not yet been empirically proven.

29

> According to Eugene Fama, the ECMH is based on the assumption that no transaction costs are incurred in securities trading, all information is available to market participants free of charge and all market participants agree on the impact of the information.[59] Though the reality is different,[60] it is justified to assume for the purposes of capital market regulation that the market price behaves as if the publicly available information is known to all market participants. This means in particular that market prices reflect the entire level of information made public.[61]

30

> An explanation for the mechanisms of capital market efficiency is provided by Ronald Gilson and Reinier Kraakman.[62] Their academic work explains the central role of information costs. They distinguish between acquisition, processing and verification costs. Their central thesis is that the speed at which information is reflected in price is determined by the extent to which the information is disseminated. This depends very much on the costs of information incurred by investors. 'The lower the cost of particular information, the wider will be its distribution, the more effective will be the capital market mechanism operating to reflect it in prices, and the more efficient will be the market with respect to it.'[63]

31

The thesis developed by Gilson and Kraakman recognises that market prices do not necessarily reflect the **fundamental value** of a security.[64] This can have different reasons. Gilson and Kraakman assume four **market mechanisms of price formation**.[65] First, market prices can immediately reflect information that is known to all traders because this information has necessarily been made public to all market participants ('universally informed trading'). Second, information that is less well known but still public is incorporated into share prices almost as quickly as information that is known to everyone, through trading by professionally informed traders ('professionally informed trading'). Third, information known to very few traders would also find its way into prices (albeit more slowly), as uninformed traders learn of its content by observing activities of presumably informed traders or unusual price and volume movements ('derivative-informed trading'). Finally, information that is not known to anyone could be reflected in stock prices that aggregate the forecasts of numerous

32

---

[58] E. Fama, 25 J. Fin. (1970), 383 ff.
[59] E. Fama, 25 J. Fin. (1970), 383, 387.
[60] The Adaptive Markets Hypothesis (AMH), developed by A. Lo, 30 JPM (2004), 15–29, recognises that markets are not always efficient. It takes into account the limited rationality of market participants and their learning and adaptation behaviour. Cf. for a legal reception of the AMH, D. Klingenbrunn, *Produktverbote zur Gewährleistung von Finanzmarktstabilität*, 54–69.
[61] A. Brüggemeier, *Harmonisierungskonzepte im europäischen Kapitalmarktrecht*, 115.
[62] R. Gilson and R. Kraakman, 70 Va. L. Rev. (1984), 549–644: 'What makes the market efficient when it appears to be so?'.
[63] R. Gilson and R. Kraakman, 70 Va. L. Rev. (1984), 549, 593.
[64] See on the concept of the fundamental value R. Veil § 14 para. 56.
[65] *Gilson/Kraakman*, The Mechanisms of Market Efficiency, 70 Va. L. Rev. (1984), 549, 569.

33 market participants with heterogeneous information, albeit slowly and imperfectly ('uninformed trading', also called 'noise trading'). A proper functioning capital market is capable of recognising misjudgements, so that in the long run, at least, security prices are formed that reflect the fundamental value.

33 Against this background, the difficult question arises whether the ECMH can also be used for the interpretation of norms and further development of the law. It is assessed differently by the courts.

34 The famous decision of the US Supreme Court in the case *Basic v. Levinson* took the ECMH into account when developing principles for interpretation. Among other things, it dealt with the question of whether investors rely on information when buying securities. The court argued that this could be rebuttably presumed, because all publicly available information would be reflected in the prices of securities: 'The presumption is also supported by common sense and probability: an investor who trades stock at the price set by an impersonal market does so in reliance on the integrity of that price. Because most publicly available information is reflected in market price, an investor's reliance on any public material misrepresentations may be presumed for purposes of a Rule 10b-5 action.'[66] Interestingly two judges disagreed with these principles, also known as the fraud-on-the-market theory. Justice White, who was joined by Justice O'Connor, stated in his dissenting opinion: 'For while the economists' theories which underpin the fraud-on-the-market presumption may have the appeal of mathematical exactitude and scientific certainty, they are – in the end – nothing more than theories which may or may not prove accurate upon further consideration.'[67]

35 In Germany, the BGH refused in the Comroad IV decision to acknowledge a reversal of the burden of proof: The fraud-on-the-market theory would lead to a boundless extension of liability under torts law. If one were to follow the fraud-on-the-market theory, this would have the consequence of dispensing with the need to prove the concrete causal connection between the deception and the investor's decision to buy or sell securities.[68] The BGH did not even deal with the theoretical assumptions (at least not in the judgment), but in fact—unlike the US Supreme Court and unlike the two judges in their dissenting opinion—exclusively referred to the doctrines under German torts law.

36 Disclosure obligations should apply to those who can provide the information at the lowest costs. Usually the issuer is the *cheapest cost avoider*. The difficulty in **designing disclosure requirements** is to determine the content and scope of the information subject to disclosure. Firstly, 'too much' information results in higher capital costs for companies, although nowadays data is digitally recorded and processed in companies. However, the more complex disclosure obligations are, the more costly the processing of the information is. Secondly, too much information can also be disadvantageous for investors because they either cannot recognise the relevant information or can only recognise it in a time-consuming and therefore costly manner. The **information overload**[69] causes problems for private and institutional investors alike.

37 For the design of disclosure obligations it must also be clarified to whom information should be disclosed: an institutional investor or a private investor? Both categories cover a

---

[66] *Basic, Inc. v. Levinson*, 485 US 224, 225 (1988).
[67] *Basic, Inc. v. Levinson*, 485 US 224, 255 (1988).
[68] BGH of 4.06.2017 – II ZR 147/05, AG 2007, 620, 621.
[69] Cf. C. Stahl, *Information Overload auf dem Kapitalmarkt*, 2013.

wide range of investors that are difficult to define in more detail. It is today recognised that the private investor in particular does not act as *homo oeconomicus*, but behaves irrationally (herd behaviour, etc.)[70] and has disparate knowledge of financial markets. Investment services law increasingly takes account of these findings of Behavioural Finance and requires comprehensible information for retail investors.

Finally, the interests of issuers must be taken into account when designing disclosure obligations. They may have **secrecy interests** that outweigh the information interests of market participants.[71] This conflict can be solved by providing for exceptions or (temporary) exemptions under certain conditions. The most prominent example of a temporary exemption is the right of the issuer to delay the publication of inside information in case of a legitimate interest to keep the information confidential.[72]

(b) Regulatory Function

Disclosure requirements may also serve a regulatory function. This is well acknowledged in capital markets regulation in the context of **conflicts of interest** of intermediaries. Such conflicts arise from the remuneration system and business model of intermediaries. For example, credit rating agencies (CRAs) are paid by issuers to carry out ratings. This *issuer pays model* gives rise to concerns that the intermediary may not take due care in the rating. Conflicts of interest are even more serious when the intermediary provides other services to the issuer. For example, CRAs have provided additional advisory services to issuers that created (financial and economic) dependencies. A requirement to disclose the conflict of interest is a more proportionate solution to the problem than a prohibition, thus serving not only an information function, but also a regulatory function, as legislature requires that the intermediary behaves properly and makes best efforts to ensure that the conflict of interest does not become relevant.

When **designing disclosure obligations** about conflicts of interests, policymakers have to decide whether a conflict of interest is so serious that disclosure appears necessary. This depends on market conditions and the fairness perceptions of market participants. In addition, the obligation to ensure transparency entails costs for the intermediary, which the intermediary will ultimately shift to the investors via its remuneration. Moreover, disclosure requirements about conflicts of interest have a great potential for circumvention. European legislation considers this problem by generally defining conflicts of interest in an abstract way and then provide for precise examples in order to ensure legal certainty. Nevertheless, it is usually necessary to define the legal terms by soft law. This results in complex disclosure obligations, the usefulness of which is doubtful. In particular, investors often cannot draw reasonable conclusions from the conflicts of interest made public by the intermediary.

Disclosure requirements serve another regulatory function. They can be a more proportionate **alternative** to **substantive law.** For aspects of corporate governance, compliance and risk management, legislature has already implemented this regulatory strategy. Its application has now been extended to CSR reporting. Instead of introducing substantive

---

[70] See R. Veil § 6 para. 33.
[71] Cf. V. Tountopoulos, in: Tountopoulos and Veil (eds.), *Transparency of Stock Corporations in Europe*, 353, 359.
[72] Cf. Art. 17(4) MAR; see R. Veil § 19 para. 51.

legal requirements on the ecological and social behaviour of companies, legislature has introduced disclosure obligations concerning ESG issues, which indirectly affect companies' business strategies and policies. This mechanism for regulating corporate behaviour is the basis of the CSRD.[73] The disclosure obligations require companies to develop a policy on ESG issues (comply) or, if they fail to develop such a policy, to at least address that lack of policy (explain). Addressing its non-compliance with the disclosure requirements puts the company's reputation at risk of 'scrutiny' by consumers, investors, other companies, interest groups and other stakeholders.

(c) Monitoring Function

42   Finally, public disclosure requirements can improve the supervision of companies by public authorities. This is recognised for both financial and non-financial accounting information. Firstly, disclosure may serve to prepare possible substantive legislation.[74] Second, in the context of capital markets legislation, disclosure improves market supervision by NCAs as they have better access to information. The obligation to publish directors' dealings (Article 19 MAR) makes it easier for supervisory authorities to detect market abuse. The situation is similar with the disclosure requirements for short sales, which in some cases only exist vis-à-vis the national supervisory authorities.

2. Prohibition

43   A further key regulatory strategy is to prohibit certain behaviour on capital markets. Admittedly, bans have a negative impact on innovation. European capital markets law therefore only stipulates prohibitions if a certain conduct substantially undermines investor confidence and thus endangers the institutional functioning of the markets. The most prominent examples in European capital markets law are the **prohibitions of insider trading**[75] and **market manipulation**.[76] The regulatory objective of financial stability may also justify a prohibition. For example, **uncovered short selling** is prohibited without exception.[77]

44   The sale of financial products is generally permitted. However, national supervisory authorities and ESAs have **product intervention powers** under Articles 40-43 MiFIR. The NCAs and ESAs can restrict or prohibit the distribution of financial products if a financial instrument raises significant concerns for investor protection or represents a threat to the stability of the financial system.[78] However, this power of intervention may only be exercised if existing disclosure requirements fail to sufficiently address the risks to investor protection and financial stability.

45   In principle, European legislation is based on the idea that **transparency** through disclosure obligations (disclosure of information to the public) and reporting obligations (disclosure

---

[73] P. Hell, *Offenlegung nichtfinanzieller Informationen*, 98.
[74] P. Hell, *Offenlegung nichtfinanzieller Informationen*, 113.
[75] See R. Veil § 14 para. 65 ff.
[76] See R. Veil § 15 para. 12 ff.
[77] See R. Veil § 24 para. 6.
[78] See R. Veil § 31 para. 8.

of information to the supervisory authorities) are sufficient to achieve the regulatory objectives[79] and to counter conflicts of interest of market participants, in particular intermediaries. The legal policy question as to whether a particular matter should (only) be disclosed or rather be prohibited altogether usually resurfaces after scandals such as Enron, Worldcom, Parmalat and Wirecard. Whether behaviour on capital markets should be penalised under criminal law can only be assessed in the context of the established criminal law systems of the Member States.

Insofar as there are **exceptions** to prohibitions, European capital markets regulation aims to ensure through procedural requirements that the regulatory goals of the prohibition are not impaired. The Market Abuse Regulation, for example, provides for exceptions to the prohibition of the disclosure of inside information. In case of a so-called market sounding, the insider may be authorised to disclose inside information to another person.[80] However, the market abuse regime requires to record communications and make them available to the respective supervisory authority. 46

Prohibitions are typically enforced by **administrative** (fines) and **criminal sanctions** (imprisonment). In view of the seriousness of the sanctions, it is necessary to identify the behaviour penalised as clearly as possible. This explains the detailed regulation of the prohibitions of manipulation. 47

3. Enforcement

Finally, a central regulatory strategy is to introduce a system of enforcement.[81] It is supposed to prevent and avert the risk of market abuse and at the same time secure the quality of relevant information. Possible approaches to enforcement include private self-monitoring, private external monitoring and administrative supervision by public authorities. The European Union's legislative activities differ vastly between these three areas. Since they are described in detail in the disclosure obligations and in the market abuse law, only the essential aspects need to be described here. 48

Private self-monitoring is primarily articulated in specifications on the organisation of a company and on dealing with conflicts of interest (compliance).[82] It is legally required for investment firms and other financial intermediaries (financial analysts and rating agencies). Listed companies, on the other hand, are only required in certain cases to take organisational measures to ensure compliance with supervisory obligations.[83] 49

The **external private monitoring** by expert auditors is hardly to be found in European capital market law. An example of an external private control is the audit of annual and biannual financial reports. The audit is carried out by auditing companies that are subject to strict rules, the purpose of which is to avoid conflicts of interest. 50

---

[79] Cf. D. Klingenbrunn, *Produktverbote zur Gewährleistung von Finanzmarktstabilität*, 125–135.
[80] See R. Veil § 14 para. 86.
[81] C. Bumke, in: Hopt et al. (eds.), *Kapitalmarktgesetzgebung im europäischen Binnenmarkt*, 107, 126, 130 ff.
[82] See for financial analysts R. Veil § 26 para. 43 and for rating agencies R. Veil § 27 para. 30–33.
[83] On compliance requirements for the delay of the publication of inside information, see R. Veil § 19 para. 61.

51 **Supervision** of capital markets is carried out by the national supervisory authorities.[84] A European supervisory authority does not yet exist. ESMA's key role remains to coordinate national supervisors and develop common supervisory standards.[85] However, this could change in the future. ESMA has already been given some supervisory tasks.

---

[84] See F. Walla § 11 para. 7.
[85] See F. Walla § 11 para. 97.

§ 3

Legislative Powers for Regulating and Harmonising Capital Markets in Europe

Bibliography

Barnard, Catherine and Peers, Steve (eds.), *European Union Law*, 3rd edn. (2020); Brüggemeier, Alexander F.P., *Harmonisierungskonzepte im europäischen Kapitalmarktrecht* (2018); Dougan, Michael, *Minimum Harmonisation and the Internal Market*, 37 CML Rev. (2000), 853–885; Fleischer, Holger and Schmolke, Klaus-Ulrich, *Die Reform der Transparenzrichtlinie – Mindest- oder Vollharmonisierung der kapitalmarktrechtlichen Beteiligungspublizität?*, 13 NZG (2010), 1241–1248; Gerner-Beuerle, Carsten, *United in diversity: maximum versus minimum harmonization in EU securities regulation*, 7 CMLJ (2012), 317–342; Gruber, Michael, *Voll- oder Mindestharmonisierung?—Auf der Suche nach dem 'richtigen' Regelungskonzept im Europäischen Kapitalmarktrecht*, in: Braumüller, Peter et al. (eds.), *Die neue europäische Finanzmarktaufsicht—Band zur ZFR-Jahrestagung 2011* (2012), 1–15; Hartley, Trevor C., *The Foundations of European Union Law*, 8th edn. (2014); Mathijsen, Pierre and Dyrberg, Peter, *Guide to European Union Law*, 11th edn. (2013), Part III; Muhr, Eike, *Das Prinzip der Vollharmonisierung im Kapitalmarktrecht am Beispiel des Reformvorhabens zur Änderung der Transparenzrichtlinie* (2014); Veil, Rüdiger, *Auf dem Weg zu einem Europäischen Kapitalmarktrecht: die Vorschläge der Kommission zur Neuregelung des Transparenzregimes*, 40 WM (2012), 53–61; Veil, Rüdiger; *Europäische Kapitalmarktunion*, 43 ZGR (2014), 544–604; Woods, Lorna et al. (eds.), *EU Law*, 13th edn. (2017), Part III; Wymeersch, Eddy, *The Structure of Financial Supervision in Europe: About Single Financial Supervisors, Twin Peaks and Multiple Financial Supervisors*, 8 EBOR (2007), 237–306.

I. Legal Foundations of the European Union

Today's European Union is the result of many small and large steps of integration. The founding treaties of the EU were amended numerous times. For an understanding of the European legislation on capital markets, however, an overview of the European integration process and the treaties that contain legal foundations for legislative acts in capital markets law is sufficient.[1]

The European integration process commenced in 1957 with the enactment of the so-called **Treaties of Rome**, ie the Treaty establishing the European Economic Community (EEC) and the Treaty establishing the European Atomic Energy Community (EAEC or Euratom). The first legislative acts were thus based on the legal foundations that could be found in

---

[1] See in more detail P. Mathijsen and P. Dyrberg, *Guide to European Union Law*, para. 2.01–2.30.

the EEC Treaty.² The next turning point in the European integration process was the Treaty on European Union (EU) of 7 February 1992 (the so-called **Treaty of Maastricht**). This Treaty formed the 'roof' over the three pillars of the Communities, the first of which comprised the EC (former EEC), the EAEC and the ECSC.³ Therefore, the European legislature referred to the rules on competence laid down in the EC Treaty when it enacted the four framework directives in 2003 and 2004.⁴ Various small amendments of the Treaties ensued on the basis of the Treaty of Amsterdam⁵ (1995) and the Treaty of Nice (2003).

3   By 1995 the EU consisted of 15 Member States. Successive enlargements followed, leading to discussions as to whether a new constitution for the EU was necessary in order to secure the Union's ability to act. It took until 13 December 2007, however, for this Herculean task to be achieved. On this day, the Member States' governments signed the **Treaty of Lisbon**, which entered into effect on 1 December 2009, making the Treaty on the Functioning of the European Union (TFEU)⁶ and the Treaty on European Union (TEU) the new legal foundations of the EU. As of 2013, the EU consists of 28 Member States. Post-Brexit, the EU consists of 27 Member States.

II. Rules on Competence

1. Coordination of Provisions on the Protection of Shareholders and Creditors

4   Most of the capital market directives enacted in 2003 and 2004 were based on the European legislator's competence to ensure the **freedom of establishment** by coordinating the national provisions on the **protection of creditors, shareholders** and **investors**.⁷ This competence was originally defined in Article 54(3)(g) EEC Treaty, then implemented into Article 44(2)(g) EC Treaty by the Treaty of Amsterdam and can now be found in the identical Article 50(2)(g) TFEU. It provides the European Parliament, the Council and the Commission with the task to coordinate 'to the necessary extent the safeguards which, for the protection of the interests of members and others, are required by Member States of companies or firms [...] with a view to making such safeguards equivalent throughout the Union', thus fulfilling the freedom of establishment.

5   The provision only allows a *coordination* of national rules, ie an approximation of the national laws as opposed to a full unification. This can be achieved in two ways—either by reducing national protective provisions by regulating a maximum level of shareholder and third-party protection, or by increasing the level of protection provided by the national laws. The latter requires that the approximation takes place by defining a minimum level of

---

² Cf. R. Veil § 1 para. 6.
³ In 2002 the Treaty of Paris, establishing the ECSC expired, and the ECSC's activities and resources were absorbed by the European Community.
⁴ Cf. R. Veil § 1 para. 20.
⁵ The Treaty of Amsterdam did not bring any fundamental changes to the structure of the European Union, cf. P. Craig, in: Barnard and Peers (eds.), *European Union Law*, 24.
⁶ The Treaty establishing the European Community (EC Treaty) was amended by the Treaty of Lisbon and renamed 'Treaty on the Functioning of the European Union' (TFEU), receiving a new structure.
⁷ It referred to the Community's competence to establish a European internal market, see below para. 9.

shareholder and third-party protection. In both approaches the relevant provisions must aim at shareholder and third-party protection.

The European legislator based two of the four framework directives enacted in 2003/2004 (the PD 2003/71/EC[8] and the TD 2004/109/EC[9]) on Article 44(2)(g) of the EC Treaty.[10] Use was made of the same rule on competence for the Takeover Directive (TOD) 2004/25/EC.[11] For the more recent legislation (post-crisis and CMU), however, the equivalent of this legal basis—Article 50(2)(g) TFEU—has no longer played a role.

2. Coordination of Start-Up and Pursuit of Self-Employment

Additionally, Article 53(1) TFEU (formerly Article 47(2) EC Treaty and prior to that Article 57(2) EEC Treaty), which allows the European Union to issue directives to make it easier for persons to take up and pursue activities as self-employed persons, has become increasingly important. Once again, the provision only allows a coordination of the rules laid down by law, regulation or administrative action. The coordination must aim at making it easier for persons to take up and pursue activities as self-employed persons in other Member States. This can only be achieved if the differences between the Member States' laws are reduced.

Directive 93/22/EEC[12] on investment services was enacted on the basis of Article 57(2) EEC Treaty. This provision, later adopted in Article 47(2) EC Treaty, also served as the legal basis for MiFID I with its implementing measures and for MiFID II, enacted in 2014.[13]

3. Establishing an Internal Market

The European legislature also enacted a number of provisions on capital markets law on the basis of Article 95 EC Treaty. This allowed the Council to 'adopt the measures for the approximation of the provisions laid down by law, regulation or administrative action in Member States which have as their **object** the **establishment** and **functioning** of the **internal market**', independent of the respective subject matter.[14] The European legislature may, however, only take measures necessary for improving the establishment and functioning of the European internal market.[15]

The framework directive 2003/6/EC[16] on Market Abuse was based on Article 95 EC Treaty, just as the PD 2003/71/EC[17] and the TD 2004/109/EC,[18] which, however, were additionally based on Article 44(2)(g) EC Treaty. The European Parliament and the Council also enacted

---

[8] See R. Veil § 1 para. 24.
[9] See R. Veil § 1 para. 26.
[10] Both directives were also based on Art. 95 EC Treaty.
[11] See R. Veil § 1 para. 28.
[12] See R. Veil § 1 para. 12.
[13] See R. Veil § 1 para. 25.
[14] Cf. J. Snell, in: Barnard and Peers (eds.), *European Union Law*, 355 ff.; P. Mathijsen and P. Dyrberg, *Guide to European Union Law*, para. 26–02.
[15] Settled case law of the ECJ, cf. Case C-376/98 *(Federal Republic of Germany)*, para. 106–107.
[16] See R. Veil § 1 para. 21.
[17] See R. Veil § 1 para. 24.
[18] See R. Veil § 1 para. 26.

Regulation (EC) No. 1060/2009[19] on credit rating agencies with reference to Article 95 EC Treaty.

11   Meanwhile the provision has been adopted into Article 114 TFEU, which has since become the most important legal basis for European capital markets law. MAR (EU) No. 596/2014, SSR (EU) No. 236/2012, MiFIR (EU) No. 648/2012, BR (EU) No. 2016/1011, PR (EU) No. 2017/1129 and SR (EU) No. 2017/2402 are based on Article 114 TFEU. The Commission's proposal from September 2020 for a pilot regime for crypto assets is also to be enacted on the basis of Article 114 TFEU.

4. Cross-border Crimes

12   Article 83(2) TFEU provides that if the approximation of criminal laws and regulations of the Member States proves essential to ensure the effective implementation of a union policy in an area which has been subject to harmonisation measures, directives may establish **minimum rules** with regard to the **definition** of **criminal offences** and **sanctions** in the area concerned. For a long time, this legal basis was not of any noteworthy practical relevance. This only changed in 2014 when CRIM-MAD 2014/57/EU was enacted. The European legislature justified the enactment with the following explanation: 'The adoption of administrative sanctions by Member States has, to date, proved to be insufficient to ensure compliance with the rules on preventing and fighting market abuse. It is essential that compliance with the rules on market abuse be strengthened by the availability of criminal sanctions which demonstrate a stronger form of social disapproval compared to administrative penalties. Establishing criminal offences for at least serious forms of market abuse sets clear boundaries for types of behaviour that are considered to be particularly unacceptable and sends a message to the public and to potential offenders that competent authorities take such behaviour very seriously.'[20] The European legislature further argues with the risk of regulatory arbitrage, resulting from the fact that not all Member States had criminal sanctions for all forms of serious breaches of rules on market abuse.[21] Nevertheless, the harmonisation of criminal sanctions remains one of the aspects of the reform of the market abuse regime subject to the most controversial legal debate. The UK and Denmark have not opted into the CRIM-MAD, with the result that they were not obliged to adapt their criminal sanctions to the requirements of European law.

III. Legislative Instruments

1. Overview

13   The institutions of the European Union can make use of a number of legislative instruments under the TFEU. In order to carry out their task, they may adopt regulations, directives or

---
[19] See R. Veil § 1 para. 38.
[20] Cf. recital 5 and 6 CRIM-MAD.
[21] Cf. recital 7 CRIM-MAD.

decisions, make recommendations or deliver opinions.[22] The TFEU defines this type of legislation as legal acts.[23] Legal acts adopted in a legislative procedure are defined as legislative acts.[24] The distinction between **legislative** and **non-legislative acts** thus does not result from the nature of the legal act (regulation, directive, etc.) but rather from the procedure to be followed for its adoption according to the legal basis.

The ordinary legislative procedure consists of a joint adoption of a regulation, directive or decision by the European Parliament and the Council, following the proposal of the Commission.[25] While a legislative act may delegate the power to adopt non-legislative acts of general application, supplementing or amending certain non-essential elements of the legislative act, to the Commission, the essential elements of a field of law shall remain reserved for the legislative act itself.[26] 14

2. Regulation

A regulation is described by the TFEU in two short sentences: 'A regulation shall have general application. It shall be **binding** in its entirety and **directly applicable** in all **Member States**.'[27] Hence, the regulation need not be implemented into the Member States' national laws in order to become effective, but will rather become immediately enforceable as law. When a regulation comes into force, it overrides all national laws dealing with the same subject matter, ie the conflicting national provisions are not applicable—but not, however, void.[28] A characteristic feature of a regulation is that it contains abstract and general provisions.[29] 15

In capital markets law, regulations have not played much of a role until the financial crisis, European legislation mainly making use of directives until 2010. Meanwhile, the approach has changed entirely: The first regulation to be enacted by the European Parliament and the Council and becoming directly applicable in the Member States related to rating agencies.[30] Subsequently further regulations were enacted with regard to short sellings[31] and in order to combat market abuse.[32] The provisions of the MiFID were also partially transferred into a regulation.[33] A similar process was employed with regard to the regulation of benchmarks.[34] In 2015, the Prospectus Directive was replaced by a regulation.[35] 16

This **shift from directives** to **regulations** can be explained by the proposals of the High-Level Group on Financial Supervision in the EU, which, in its report on regulatory measures in 17

---

[22] Cf. Art. 288(1) TFEU.
[23] Cf. Art. 289(3) TFEU.
[24] Cf. Art. 289(3) TFEU.
[25] Cf. Art. 289(1) in conjunction with Art. 294 TFEU.
[26] Cf. Art. 290 TFEU.
[27] Cf. Art. 288(2) TFEU.
[28] Cf. P. Mathijsen and P. Dyrberg, *Guide to European Union Law*, para. 4–12.
[29] Cf. T. Hartley, *The Foundations of European Union Law*, 108.
[30] See R. Veil § 1 para. 38.
[31] Cf. R. Veil § 1 para. 47.
[32] Cf. R. Veil § 1 para. 42.
[33] Cf. R. Veil § 1 para. 42.
[34] Cf. R. Veil § 1 para. 49.
[35] Cf. R. Veil § 1 para. 52.

connection with the financial crisis, criticised the existing leeway of the Member States with regard to the implementation of directives and the diverging construction of the respective national laws.[36] The Group proposed enacting legislation in the form of regulations in the future whenever possible. Should the legislator nevertheless opt for a directive, it should at least endeavour to ensure that a maximum harmonisation is achieved in the central aspects of the provisions.[37] In view of this, it comes as no surprise that almost all level 2 measures are enacted as regulations, resulting in a 'single rulebook on European capital markets law'.[38]

3. Directive

18 A directive is defined as '**binding**, as to the **result** to be achieved, upon each Member State to which it is addressed, but [leaving] to the **national authorities** the **choice** of **form** and **methods**'.[39] This definition, which already existed in the former EC Treaty and has been adopted in the TFEU, suggests that a directive is a measure to harmonise the national laws. It fits more 'smoothly' into national law than a regulation, which is aimed at a full unification of the national laws. At the same time, a directive can also contain precise and detailed provisions, thus depriving the Member States of the possibility of choice of form and methods. Meanwhile, this is, for example, the case with regard to the directives on capital markets law. Whereas the first directives in this field[40] contained only few, abstract, provisions, the four framework directives[41] and their most recent amendments,[42] are far more specific. Only the provisions on enforcement remained imprecise for a long time, leaving the national legislators with a large margin of appreciation.[43] Meanwhile, however, this has also changed and both the amendments to the TD from 2013 and the fundamental revision of the MiFID II in 2014 aim to harmonise the administrative powers and sanctions by laying down detailed rules thereon.

19 **Directives** are **addressed to** the **Member States** and not to individuals. For the Member States the regulatory aims as laid down in the recitals or the introductory articles are binding. They can be achieved most effectively as described in the further provisions of the directive, as a consequence making these binding for the national legislatures too. The Member States must therefore ensure that their national laws are adapted to correspond with the legal situation laid out by the directive. If this is already the case in individual Member States no further implementing measures need to be taken.

20 Generally, the provisions of a directive do not have a direct effect. However, the European Court of Justice has developed the doctrine of direct effect which states that directives can have direct legal force should they not have been implemented correctly by the

---

[36] Cf. J. de Larosière, *The High-Level Group on Financial Supervision in the EU*, Report, 25 February 2009 (de Larosière Report), p. 31.
[37] Cf. de Larosière Report (fn. 36), p. 33.
[38] Cf. R. Veil § 1 para. 64.
[39] Cf. Art. 288(3) TFEU and ex Art. 249(3) EC Treaty.
[40] Cf. R. Veil § 1 para. 6.
[41] Cf. R. Veil § 1 para. 20–27.
[42] Cf. R. Veil § 1 para. 40–45.
[43] On the reform of the sanctions in European capital markets law see R. Veil § 12 para. 10.

transposition date.[44] This doctrine of direct effect has not yet been applied in capital markets law. This is mainly due to the fact that the framework directives only aim at structuring capital markets by providing supervisory rules without conveying rights to the investors, should capital market duties have been breached.

IV. Harmonisation

1. Concepts

The European legislature can limit itself to minimum harmonisation of national regulations or achieve full harmonisation. In case of **minimum harmonisation**, the Member States must at least align their laws with the requirements of European law. However, they are entitled to provide for more far-reaching, in particular stricter provisions (so-called **gold plating**). Minimum harmonisation facilitates the **competition** between the different legal systems in the Member States,[45] thus providing incentives for regulatory **innovations** and preventing the law from stagnation.[46] A minimum harmonisation also ensures that the Member States preserve their '**national identity**' to a certain degree.[47] This complies with the principle of subsidiarity.[48]

21

In contrast, **full harmonisation** (also referred to as maximum harmonisation) pursues the goal of achieving a uniform legal situation in the EU (so-called level playing field). The European legal act then conclusively regulates the matter in question—the subject matter of the legal act, which is usually described in the first article—throughout the Union. In particular, the Member States are then prohibited from providing for deviating or stricter regulations. The strategy of full harmonisation is the best way to **prevent regulatory arbitrage**. A uniform legal situation also reduces transaction costs, especially for market participants operating across borders.[49] It contributes most effectively to the integration of capital markets, which is essential for the completion of the internal market.[50]

22

2. Tendency towards Full Harmonisation

The European legislator can use both the instrument of a directive and the instrument of a regulation to implement the level of harmonisation. Although regulations usually aim at full harmonisation, it is also conceivable to have a regulation that only brings about minimum

23

---

[44] On this see L. Woods et al. (eds.), *EU Law*, 119 ff.
[45] N. Moloney, *EU Securities and Financial Markets Regulation*, 19 ff.
[46] H. Fleischer and K.-U. Schmolke, 13 NZG (2010), 1241, 1245–1246.
[47] Cf. M. Gruber, in: Braumüller et al. (eds.), *Die neue europäische Finanzmarktaufsicht—Band zur ZFR-Jahrestagung 2011*, 1, 14.
[48] Cf. M. Gruber, in: Braumüller et al. (eds.), *Die neue europäische Finanzmarktaufsicht—Band zur ZFR-Jahrestagung 2011*, 1, 13.
[49] Cf. A. Brüggemeier, *Harmonisierungskonzepte*, 88; C. Gerner-Beuerle, 7 CMLJ (2012) 317, 326 f.; E. Muhr, *Prinzip der Vollharmonisierung*, 45.
[50] See R. Veil § 2 para. 6.

standards. Directives are open to both regulatory strategies. However, measures under Article 50(2)(g) TFEU can only require minimum harmonisation of national legal systems, whereas Article 114(1) TFEU permits the adoption of fully harmonising legal acts.[51]

24   In the last decade, a new trend has become established in European capital markets law: Regulations replace directives.[52] The European legislature wants to create a level playing field. This strategy goes back to recommendations of the 'High-Level Group on Financial Supervision in the EU' chaired by Jacques de Larosière. In their report on regulatory measures in connection with the financial market crisis, the experts criticised the discretion of the Member States in transposing directives and the divergent interpretation of the transposed law.[53] The Group urged that the problem of legal inconsistencies should be taken into account at the European level: 'Future legislation should be based, wherever possible, on regulations (which are of direct application). When directives are used, the co-legislator should strive to achieve maximum harmonisation of the core issues.'[54] The European legislator has consistently followed these recommendations.

25   The legislative acts in European capital markets law are generally characterised by a mix of full and minimum harmonising rules. Most Level 1 regulations (MiFIR; PR; MAR; SSR; CRAR; BR; STSR) provide, on the one hand, directly applicable provisions that require full harmonisation. These provisions govern disclosure obligations, provide for prohibitions and establish rules of conduct. On the other hand, the sanctions provided for in the regulations aim at minimum harmonisation of the national rules.

26   Furthermore, even in a fully harmonised area of an EU regulation, Member States may be allowed to provide for stricter rules (**hybrid concepts of harmonisation**). This can be illustrated at the example of the TD. The European legislature introduced rules which follow the concept of a limited maximum harmonisation and a limited minimum harmonisation. Limited maximum harmonisation means that the Member States' leeway is extended by explicit exemptions from the principle of maximum harmonisation. Limited minimum harmonisation, *vice versa*, means that the Members States' legislative power is reduced explicitly although the concept of minimum harmonisation is generally applicable.

27   *Examples*: (i) The disclosure of major holding regime is generally subject to maximum harmonisation as Article 3(1)(a) TD states that a holder of shares, or a natural person or legal entity may not be made subject to requirements more stringent than those laid down in the TD. However, Article 3(1)(a) TD stipulates that this principle shall not apply (a) for setting lower or additional notification thresholds, (b) requiring equivalent notifications in relation to thresholds based on capital holdings or (c) more stringent procedural requirements and for Member States' provisions in relation to takeover bids, merger transactions and other transactions affecting the ownership or control of companies. Thus, maximum harmonisation is limited.[55] (ii) Regarding periodic disclosure the TD generally follows the concept of minimum harmonisation as Article 3(1) TD states that the home Member State may make an issuer subject to requirements more stringent than those laid down in the TD.[56] However, the TD explicitly excludes the Member States' right to require issuers

---

[51] Cf. A. Brüggemeier, *Harmonisierungskonzepte*, 43 ff.
[52] Cf. R. Veil, 43 ZGR (2014), 544, 564 ff.
[53] Cf. J. de Larosière, *The High-Level Group on Financial Supervision in the EU*, Report, 25. 2. 2009, p. 29.
[54] Cf. J. de Larosière, *The High-Level Group on Financial Supervision in the EU*, Report, 25. 2. 2009, p. 29: Recommendation 10.
[55] Cf. R. Veil, 43 ZGR (2014), 544, 570 ff.; E. Muhr, *Prinzip der Vollharmonisierung*, 70 ff.
[56] Also cf. on this R. Veil, 40 WM (2012), 53, 54.

to publish periodic financial information on a more frequent basis than with the annual and the half-yearly financial reports from this general rule. Thus, minimum harmonisation is limited.

The reasons for limited full harmonisation, which grants the Member States partial regulatory autonomy, are numerous. These can be the specific circumstances of national markets (high proportion of institutional investors on the one hand; high proportion of major shareholders on the other). It is also conceivable that the European legislator takes into account traditional legal concepts of some Member States or particularities of national company law (one-tier or two-tier system of a stock corporation) and therefore allows for deviating (usually stricter) regulations.

In order to determine whether a provision is minimally or maximally harmonising, one must **interpret** the provision, thus determining the underlying interests of the European legislator.[57] If a conclusion cannot be reached simply by interpretation of the legislative act's provisions, reference can often be made to the **recitals**. For example, the regulatory aim of avoiding regulatory arbitrage indicates maximum harmonisation.[58] Sometimes also the aim of protecting the integrity of financial markets is considered as an indication for maximum harmonisation.[59]

---

[57] Cf. Case 278/85 (*Commission/Denmark*) para. 16–17. On the methods of interpretation applied in European law see R. Veil § 5 para. 28; EFTA Court of 16 July 2012, Case E 9/11 (*EFTA Surveillance Authority/Norway*).
[58] R. Veil, 43 ZGR (2014), 544, 569 ff.
[59] Opinion of Advocate General Kokott, delivered on 10 September 2009, Case C-45/08 (*Spector*) para. 82 ff.; opposing view: C. Gerner-Beuerle, 7 CMLJ (2012), 317, 330.

§ 4

Rule-Making Process

Bibliography

Achtelik, Olaf and Mohn, Alexandra, *Die Reform der europäischen Finanzaufsichtsstruktur: Auswirkungen auf die Europäischen Aufsichtsbehörden im Banken- und Kapitalmarktbereich*, 50 WM (2019), 2339–2345; Anzinger, Heribert, *Rechtskontrolle informeller Verlautbarungen der europäischen Finanzaufsichtsagenturen*, 3 RdF (2018), 181–188; Binder, Jens-Hinrich, *Verbesserte Krisenprävention durch paneuropäische Aufsicht? Zur neuen Aufsichtsinfrastruktur auf EU-Ebene*, 1 GPR (2011), 34–40; Buck-Heeb, Petra, *Aufsichts- und zivilrechtliche Normen im Bank- und Kapitalmarktrecht: einheitliche oder gespaltene Auslegung?*, 4 WM (2020), 157–164; de Ruiter, Rik and Christine Neuhold, *Why Is Fast Track the Way to Go? Justifications for Early Agreement in the Co-Decision Procedure and Their Effects*, 18 European Law Journal (2012), 536–554; Fabricius, Constantin, *Der Technische Regulierungsstandard für Finanzdienstleistungen – Eine kritische Würdigung unter besonderer Berücksichtigung des Art. 290 AEUV* (2013), available at: http://telc.jura.uni-halle.de/sites/default/files/BeitraegeTWR/Heft124_0.pdf; Frank, Alexander, *Die Level-3-Verlautbarungen der ESMA – ein sicherer Hafen für den Rechtsanwender?*, 4 ZBB (2015), 213–220; Giersdorf, Fabian, *Der informelle Trilog* (2019); Hertig, Gerard and Lee, Ruben, *Four Predictions about the Future of EU Securities Regulation*, 3 J. Corp. L. Stud. (2003), 359–363; Hupka, Jan, *Kapitalmarktaufsicht im Wandel—Rechtswirkungen der Empfehlungen des Committee of European Securities Regulators (CESR) im deutschen Kapitalmarktrecht*, 29 WM (2009), 1351–1359; Kahl, Arno, *Europäische Aufsichtsbehörden und technische Regulierungsstandards*, in: Braumüller, Peter et al. (eds.), *Die neue europäische Finanzmarktaufsicht—Band zur ZFR-Jahrestagung 2011* (2012), 55–75; Kalss, Susanne, *Kapitalmarktrecht – bis es implodiert...*, 26 EuZW (2015), 569–570; Kämmerer, Jörn A., *Selbstregulierung am Beispiel des Kapitalmarktrechts – Eine normativ-institutionelle Positionsbestimmung*, in: Hopt, Klaus J. et al. (eds.), *Kapitalmarktgesetzgebung im europäischen Binnenmarkt* (2008), 145–163; Klöhn, Lars, *Kapitalmarktrecht*, in: Langenbucher, Katja (ed.), *Europäisches Privat- und Wirtschaftsrecht* (2017); Kröll, Thomas, *Artikel 290 und 291 AEUV*, in: Debus, Alfred G. et al. (eds.), *Verwaltungsrechtsraum Europa—51. Assistententagung Öffentliches Recht Speyer 2011* (2011), 195–211; Langenbucher, Katja, *Zur Zulässigkeit parlamentsersetzender Normgebungsverfahren im Europarecht*, 2 ZEuP (2002), 265–286; Leixner, Iris, *Komitologie und Lamfalussyverfahren im Finanzdienstleistungsbereich im Lichte der jüngsten Reformen* (2010); Lutter, Marcus et al. (eds.), *Europäisches Unternehmens- und Kapitalmarktrecht—Grundlagen, Stand und Entwicklung nebst Texten und Materialien* (2012); Möller, Andreas, *Kapitalmarktaufsicht—Wandel und Neubestimmung der nationalen und europäischen Kapitalmarktaufsicht anhand des Beispiels der Aufsicht über die Börsen und den Börsenhandel* (2006); Möllers, Thomas M.J., *Europäische Methoden- und Gesetzgebungslehre im Kapitalmarktrecht – Vollharmonisierung, Generalklauseln und soft law im Rahmen des Lamfalussy-Verfahrens als Mittel zur Etablierung von Standards*, 3 ZEuP (2008), 480–505; Möllers, Thomas M.J., *Auf dem Weg zu einer neuen europäischen Finanzmarktaufsichtsstruktur*, 8 NZG (2010), 285–290; Möllers, Thomas M.J., *European Legislative Practice 2.0: Dynamic Harmonisation of Capital Markets Law — MiFID II and PRIIP*, 31 BFLR (2015), 141–176; Möllers, Thomas M.J., *Vollharmonisierung im Kapitalmarktrecht—Zur Regelungskompetenz nationaler Gerichte und Parlamente*, in: Gsell, Beate and Herresthal, Carsten (eds.), *Vollharmonisierung im Privatrecht* (2010),

247–272; Moloney, Niamh, *The Committee of European Securities Regulators and Level 3 of the Lamfalussy Process*, in: Tison, Michel et al. (eds.), *Perspectives in Company Law and Financial Regulation, Essays in Honour of Eddy Wymeersch* (2009), 449–476; Moloney, Niamh, *The Financial Crisis and EU Securities Law-Making: A Challenge Met?*, in: Grundmann, Stefan et al. (eds.), *Festschrift für Klaus J. Hopt zum 70. Geburtstag, Vol. II* (2010), 2265–2282; Parmentier, Miriam, *Die Verhandlung eines Rechtssetzungsvorschlags*, 4 BKR (2013), 133–141; Riesenhuber, Karl (ed.), *Europäische Methodenlehre*, 4th edn. (2021); Roederer-Rynning, Christilla and Greenwood, Justin, *The culture of trilogues*, 22 JEPP (2015), 1148–1165; Scheel, Benedikt, *Die Neuregelungen der Komitologie und das europäische Demokratiedefizit*, 9 ZEuS (2006), 521–554; Schmolke, Klaus-Ulrich, *Der Lamfalussy-Prozess im Europäischen Kapitalmarktrecht—Eine Zwischenbilanz*, 22 NZG (2005), 912–919; Schmolke, Klaus-Ulrich, *Die Einbeziehung des Komitologieverfahrens in den Lamfalussy-Prozess – Zur Forderung des Europäischen Parlaments nach mehr Entscheidungsteilhabe*, 41 EuR (2006), 432–448; Seibt, Christoph H., *Europäische Finanzmarktregulierung zu Insiderrecht und Ad hoc-Publizität*, 2–3 ZHR 177 (2013), 388–426; Spindler, Gerald and Hupka, Jan, *Bindungswirkung von Standards im Kapitalmarktrecht*, in: Möllers, Thomas M.J. (ed.), *Geltung und Faktizität von Standards* (2009), 117–141; Stelkens, Ulrich, *Art. 291 AEUV, das Unionsverwaltungsrecht und die Verwaltungsautonomie der Mitgliedstaaten—zugleich zur Abgrenzung der Anwendungsbereiche von Art. 290 und Art. 291 AEUV*, 47 EuR (2012), 511–545; Stöbener de Mora, Patricia S., *Mehr Transparenz im EU-Trilog-Verfahren – Reichen die Vorschläge der Europäischen Bürgerbeauftragten für mehr Demokratie?*, 27 EuZW (2016), 721–722; Veil, Rüdiger, *Europäische Kapitalmarktunion—Verordnungsgesetzgebung, Instrumente der europäischen Marktaufsicht und die Idee eines „Single Rulebook"*, 43 ZGR (2014), 544–607; Veil, Rüdiger, *Aufsichtskonvergenz durch „Questions and Answers" der ESMA*, 1 ZBB (2018), 151–166; Walla, Fabian, *Die Konzeption der Kapitalmarktaufsicht in Deutschland* (2012); von Wogau, Karl, *Modernisierung der Europäischen Gesetzgebung*, 4 ZEuP (2002), 695–700; Wymeersch, Eddy, *The Future of Financial Regulation and Supervision in Europe*, 42 CML Rev. (2005), 987–1010.

I. Historical Development

1 Since the year 2002, rule-making in European capital markets law has been conducted via the so-called **Lamfalussy Process**.[1] The Lamfalussy Process is a **comitology process** based on Article 202 of the former EC Treaty which established four layers of regulation. Whilst it was originally restricted to the regulation of capital markets it was later applied in all areas of financial market regulation.[2]

2 The Lamfalussy Process was introduced to effectively fulfil the **Financial Services Action Plan (FSAP)**.[3] The measures referred to in the FSAP were to be achieved through a more efficient, flexible and faster legislative process and with the help of external expert knowledge.[4]

---

[1] The process is named after Baron Alexandre Lamfalussy († 9 May 2015), chair of the expert committee whose draft propositions are the basis for the present legislative procedure. See R. Veil § 1 para. 16.

[2] Commission Decision of 5 November 2003 (2004/5/EC) establishing the Committee of European Banking Supervisors, OJ L 3, 5 November 2003. This extension was initiated by the German and the British governments; cf. A. Möller, *Kapitalmarktaufsicht*, 149. On the comitology procedure in general see M. Horspool and M. Humphreys, *European Law*, para. 5.33 ff.

[3] Communication from the Commission implementing the framework for financial markets: action plan, 11 May 1999, COM(1999) 232 final. See in more detail R. Veil § 1 para. 13.

[4] N. Moloney, *EU Securities and Financial Markets Regulation*, 862 ff.

The creation of two pan-European committees who were to participate in the process of law making was a fundamental component: The **European Securities Committee (ESC)**,[5] a body composed of high-ranking officials of the Member States and chaired by a representative of the Commission, and the **Committee of European Securities Regulators (CESR)** as a committee of representatives of all national supervisory authorities plus their counterparts from Norway, Liechtenstein and Iceland as well as the Commission. CESR was the nucleus of the **European Securities Markets Authority (ESMA)**.

The Lamfalussy Process has been modified significantly due to the enactment of the **Treaty of Lisbon** on 1 December 2009 and the formation of **ESMA**.[6] ESMA assumed an important role within the European regulatory process.[7] The procedural requirements for the post-Lisbon process were laid down in the Comitology Regulation, enacted in 2011.[8] The legislative procedure based on these amendments can be referred to as the **Lamfalussy II Process**.[9]

II. The Lamfalussy II Process

The Lamfalussy II Process is based on **four layers** of regulation.

1. Framework Acts

(a) Concept

Level 1 of the process concerns the enactment of broad but sufficiently precise **framework directives or regulations** which have been developed in the legislative process (Article 294 TFEU), ie under participation of the European Parliament and the Council, based on proposals by the Commission.[10]

The Level 1 acts should in theory only contain **basic principles**, to be put into more concrete terms on Level 2 and Level 3 of the Lamfalussy Process. In reality, however, the four initial Lamfalussy directives—especially MiFID I—were in parts already very precise in their specifications for the Member States.[11] In the course of the latest round of reform

---

[5] See Commission Decision of 6 June 2001 establishing the European Securities Committee (ESC) and the Committee of European Securities Regulators, OJ L 191, 13 July 2001, p. 45.
[6] For more details on the concept of European supervision see F. Walla § 11.
[7] See below para. 24 and F. Walla § 11 para. 67.
[8] Regulation (EU) No. 182/2011 of the European Parliament and of the Council of 16 February 2011 laying down the rules and general principles concerning mechanisms for control by Member States of the Commission's exercise of implementing powers, OJ L 55, 16 February 2011, p. 13–18.
[9] The same terminology is used by J. Schmidt, in: Lutter et al. (eds.), *Europäisches Unternehmensrecht*, 252; L. Klöhn, in: Langenbucher (ed.), *Europäisches Privat- und Wirtschaftsrecht*, § 6 para. 21 ff.; T. Möllers, 31 BFLR (2015), 141, 143; other scholars still refer to the process as the Lamfalussy procedure or the revised Lamfalussy procedure, cf. eg R. Veil, 43 ZGR (2014), 544, 551 ff.; S. Kalss, 26 EuZW (2015), 569, 570.
[10] See on this N. Moloney, *EU Securities and Financial Markets Regulation*, 888 ff.
[11] E. Wymeersch, 42 CML Rev. (2005), 987, 991.

for European capital markets law Level 1 acts have become more and more concrete.[12] In particular, they provide for **annexes** that include important substantiations of the rules.[13]

7 Example: Under the initial Lamfalussy directive MAD the key term '**inside information**' was defined as '*information of a precise nature, which has not been made public, relating, directly or indirectly, to one or more issuers or to one or more financial instruments, and which, if it were made public, would be likely to have a significant effect on the prices of those financial instruments or on the price of related derivative financial instrument*' (Article 1(1) MAD). The MAD Level 2 Directive 2003/124/EC substantiated this broad definition in Article 1(1) and defined '*precise information*' as an information '*that indicates a set of circumstances which exists or may reasonably be expected to come into existence or an event which has occurred or may reasonably be expected to do so and if it is specific enough to enable a conclusion to be drawn as to the possible effect of that set of circumstances or event on the prices of financial instruments or related derivative*'. Article 7 MAR (as the currently in force Level 1 act) provides for the aforementioned basic definition in Article 7(1),(2) MAR. It is, however, complemented by various substantiations, inter alia, the aforementioned definition of 'precise' in Article 7 para. 2–4 MAR. The Level 1 prerequisites are now to be put into further concrete terms by ESMA guidelines as Level 3 (and ESMA Q&A on Level 4) as soft law and not by a Level 2 act.[14]

8 However, the basic approach of the Lamfalussy II procedure still is to have broad principles on Level 1. *Example*: A prime case for such interaction between Level 1 and Level 2 is Article 19(1) MAR. Under this provision persons discharging managerial responsibilities (PDMR), as well as persons closely associated with them, shall notify the issuer and the NCA about the existence of every '*transaction*' conducted on their own account relating to the shares or debt instruments of that issuer. A non-exhaustive but rather detailed list of transaction types is provided by Article 10 Delegated Regulation (EU) 2016/522 as a Level 2 measures on the basis of Article 19(14) MAR.

(b) Trialogue Procedure

9 In practice, the design of a Level 1 act is elaborated in extensive informal consultations between the three key European institutions, ie the European Parliament, the Council and the Commission. This informal procedure is commonly referred to as the '**Trialogue**'. Whereas the TFEU requires a Trialogue for matters related to the budgeting (Article 324 TFEU), pursuing a Trialogue procedure has become standard practice for rule-making on the European level.[15]

10 The aim of the Trialogue procedure is to reach an **early-stage consensus** between the institutions so that a legislative act can be approved in the first reading of the European Parliament ('early agreement' or 'first reading agreement').[16] The Trialogue should, in particular, avoid

---

[12] R. Veil, 43 ZGR (2014), 544, 577.
[13] See for example the indications of market manipulation provided for in Annex I of the MAR.
[14] Art. 7(4) MAR. Cf. on the European regulatory approach regarding inside information R. Veil § 14 para. 52.
[15] Cf. for empirical data on recent Trialogues in European law-making F. Giersdorf, *Der informelle Trilog*, 163 ff.; T. Wischmeyer, in: Dauses and Ludwigs (eds.), *Handbuch des EU-Wirtschaftsrechts*, A. II. para. 274; according to P. Stöbener de Mora, 27 EuZW (2016), 721, 722 around 85% of the legislative processes in the EU level are currently conducted with the help of an informal Trialogue procedure.
[16] T. Wischmeyer, in: Dauses and Ludwigs (eds.), *Handbuch des EU-Wirtschaftsrechts*, A. II. para. 273; on the reasoning for the implementation of the Trialogue R. de Ruiter and C. Neuhold, 18 European Law Journal (2012), 536 ff.

the formal legislative conciliation procedure between the European Parliament and the Council required by Article 294 TFEU.

The Trialogue is informal but not a legal vacuum. It is governed by **inter-institutional agreements**[17] and the respective **rules of procedures** of the institutions involved. In the course of a Trialogue, representatives of the three institutions try to reach an agreement on the substance matter of legislative proposal. All institutions have created specific guidelines to structure their involvement in the process.[18] In practice, the Trialogue discussions are typically divided between issues with **political relevance** and those of a rather **technical nature**.[19] The Trialogue procedure in general is subject criticism with regards to a **lack of transparency**[20] and **democratic legitimation**.[21]   11

The key importance of the Trialogue in European capital markets was illustrated by the revision of the core Lamfalussy acts (PR, MAR, TD, MiFID II/MiFIR):[22] In each case, the final design of the revised basic act was subject to intense discussion in the Trialogue procedure.   12

Example: During the Trialogue procedure for the revision of the MAR the question if the term *'inside information'* should be relevant for insider trading rules as well as for ad hoc disclosure was intensely discussed. Whereas in the beginning of the Trialogue a distinction between 'inside information' and 'relevant information not generally available' (following the UK's *'RINGA concept'*[23]) was favoured, a final compromise was achieved which sustained that status quo under the MAD, ie with the term 'inside information' as the key term for insider trading and ad hoc disclosure.[24]   13

2. Delegated Acts and Implementing Measures

Already under the initial Lamfalussy I scheme Level 2 enabled the Commission to enact so-called **implementing measures** regarding the framework directives without having to adhere to the usual legislative procedure.[25] The Commission may enact implementing regulations or directives,[26] depending on the aim of the framework provision. The Commission made use of both regulatory instruments.[27] Both former committees—the ESC and CESR—held advisory functions for the Commission in this process. The implementing measures led to a further harmonisation in the European Union due to their very   14

---

[17] See Joint Declaration on Practical Arrangements for the Codecision Procedure, OJ C 145, 30 June 2007, p. 5; Interinstitutional Agreement of 13 April 2016 on better law-making, OJ L 123, 12 May 2016, p. 1.
[18] Cf. F. Giersdorf, *Der informelle Trilog*, 70 ff.
[19] Cf. C. Roederer-Rynning and J. Greenwood, 22 Journal of European Public Policy (2015), 1148, 1153 ff.; F. Giersdorf, *Der informelle Trilog*, 72.
[20] Cf. European Ombudsman, Decision of the European Ombudsman setting out proposals following her strategic inquiry OI/8/2015/JAS concerning the transparency of Trilogues, 12 July 2016, para. 15 ff.
[21] Cf. T. Wischmeyer, in: Dauses and Ludwigs (eds.), *Handbuch des EU-Wirtschaftsrechts*, A. II. para. 278 ff.
[22] N. Moloney, *EU Securities and Financial Markets Regulation*, 856; M. Parmentier, 4 BKR (2013), 133 ff. (on the MAR revision).
[23] See on this C. Seibt, 2-3 ZHR 177 (2013), 388, 402 ff.
[24] See for more details on the term 'inside information' R. Veil § 14 para. 19.
[25] Scholars are critical regarding the lack of certainty regarding the Commission's competences, cf. eg S. Kalss et al., *Kapitalmarktrecht I*, § 1 para. 43.
[26] On the legislative instruments in general see R. Veil § 3 para. 13.
[27] Under the Lamfalussy I scheme five implementing directives and five implementing regulations have been enacted on the basis of the framework directives.

specific provisions. The downside to this was the fact that the autonomy of Member States was restricted significantly.[28]

15 As a consequence of the Treaty of Lisbon and ESMA's formation Level 2 became significantly more complex. One now has to distinguish between **delegated acts** under Article 290 TFEU and **implementing acts** under Article 291 TFEU.[29]

16 Regarding delegated acts under **Article 290 TFEU** one again has to distinguish between delegated acts enacted by the Commission after consultation of ESMA[30] and the Expert Group of the European Securities Committee (EGESC)[31] and **Regulatory Technical Standards (RTS)**. The latter are delegated acts drafted by ESMA under Article 10 ESMA Regulation which have to be endorsed by the Commission to become effective.[32] Regarding regulatory technical standards ESMA, in practice, is the body determining the content of such acts as the Commission can only object to ESMA's drafts under exceptional circumstances.[33]

17 Delegated acts can in theory be directives or regulations. However, regulations are most recommendable to achieve the harmonisation intended by Level 2 measures to the largest possible extent. As yet, most delegated acts on Level 2 of the Lamfalussy II procedure are designed as regulations.[34] ESMA submits the drafts of its RTS to the European Parliament and the Council, respectively, for their information (Article 10(1) ESMA Regulation). Both institutions have a veto right against each RTS under Article 13 ESMA Regulation. They are also competent to completely revoke ESMA's mandate to draft RTS (Article 12 ESMA Regulation) in case they generally disapprove the rule-making by ESMA. The design of the Level 1 acts is not consistent as to the use of delegated acts and RTS. In practice, the Commission frequently requests the **technical advice** of ESMA in case it is supposed to create a delegated act. In the course of the latest revision of the ESMA Regulation, a legal basis for such technical advice was added to the ESMA Regulation (Article 16a(4)). Thus, ESMA is influencing most Level 2 rules regardless of the nature of the delegation of set forth on Level 1.

18 *Examples*: (i) The MAR empowers the Commission to adopt a delegated act specifying the circumstances under which trading of PDMR during a closed period may be permitted by the issuer (Article 19(13) MAR).[35] The Commission requested ESMA to prepare the regulation by

---

[28] This is pointed out by W. Groß, *Kapitalmarktrecht*, Vorb. BörsG para. 18.

[29] The scope and distinction between these two provisions of the Treaty of Lisbon is still not completely clear, cf. R. Streinz et al., *Vertrag von Lissabon*, § 10 para. 3; A. Kahl, in: Braumüller et al. (eds.), *Die neue Europäische Finanzmarktaufsicht—Band zur ZFR-Jahrestagung 2011*, 55, 71; J. Kämmerer, in: Kämmerer and Veil (eds.), *Übernahme- und Kapitalmarktrecht in der Reformdiskussion*, 45, 58; U. Stelkens, 47 EuR (2012), 511 ff.; T. Kröll, in: Debus et al. (eds.), *Verwaltungsrechtsraum Europa—51. Assistententagung Öffentliches Recht Speyer 2011*, 195 ff.

[30] ESMA usually delivers so-called *technical advice* upon the request of the Commission during the drafting process for a Level 2 act, cf. F. Walla § 11 para. 97.

[31] See under http://ec.europa.eu/finance/securities/egesc/index_en.htm.

[32] Cf. also N. Moloney, in: FS Hopt, 2265, 2271–2272. A list of all regulatory technical standards in force can be found under www.esma.europa.eu/system/files/technical_standards_in_force.pdf. The list is updated on an ongoing basis.

[33] Regulation (EU) No. 1095/2010 of the European Parliament and of the Council of 24 November 2010 establishing a European Supervisory Authority (ESMA), recital 23; cf. also R. Veil, 43 ZGR (2014), 544, 553 ff. As yet, the Commission declined to endorse a draft technical standards only on very rare occasions, see eg Commission, Letter of 4 July 2013 (on an RTS under the AIFM Directive), Commission, Letter of 24 August 2018 (on an RTS under the Securities Financing Transactions Regulation).

[34] See R. Veil, 43 ZGR (2014), 544, 549.

[35] Commission Delegated Regulation (EU) 2016/522 of 17 December 2015 supplementing Regulation (EU) No 596/2014 of the European Parliament and of the Council as regards an exemption for certain third countries

technical advice.[36] (ii) At the same time, the MAR empowers ESMA to draft an RTS on the conditions that buy-back programmes and stabilisation measures (Article 5(6) MAR),[37] ie conferring a rule-making power to ESMA which is at least as important (and far-reaching) as the Commission's power under Article 19(13) MAR.

Delegated acts are complimented by **implementing acts** as described in **Article 291 TFEU**. Such implementing acts only define the conditions for the application of the law. Again, one has to distinguish between implementing acts adopted by the Commission and **Technical Implementing Standards (ITS)** drafted by ESMA that require endorsement by the Commission. Implementing acts by the Commission and ITS by ESMA mainly concern procedural requirements and put the requirements for the applicability of a provision into more concrete terms. The European Parliament and the Council do not have a veto right with regards to ITS. Both institutions are, however, informed by ESMA when a draft ITS is submitted to the Commission (Article 15(1)(3) ESMA Regulation). The Member States are competent to control ESMA and the Commission under the procedural rules stipulated in Regulation (EU) No. 182/2011.[38]

19

> *Examples*: (i) The Commission adopted implementing measures regarding the specific procedures for report of breaches of the market abuse regime (Article 32(5) MAR).[39] (ii) ESMA drafted technical implementing standards with regard to the disclosure procedure for inside information (Article 17(10) MAR) adopted by the Commission.[40]

20

This variety of legal sources on Level 2 of the Lamfalussy II Process can be structured as a **continuum with regard to the policy implications** of the respective legislative acts: The Commission's delegated acts put the framework provisions on Level 1 into more concrete terms. Whilst Article 290 TFEU only allows them to 'supplement or amend certain non-essential elements of the legislative act', the Commission is granted a creative power in fact, allowing it to exert significant influence through its delegated acts.[41] ESMA's leeway for policy decisions expressed via RTS is supposed to be narrower than the Commission's discretion with regard to delegated acts.[42] Under Article 15 ESMA Regulation regulatory technical standards may not 'imply strategic decisions or policy choices'. Implementing acts, finally, serve as the layer below two kinds of delegated acts. They should only substantiate the application of the law, ie primarily contain procedural rules without policy implications.

21

---

public bodies and central banks, the indicators of market manipulation, the disclosure thresholds, the competent authority for notifications of delays, the permission for trading during closed periods and types of notifiable managers' transactions, OJ L 88, 5 April 2016, p. 1.

[36] ESMA, Final Report, Technical advice on possible delegated acts concerning the Market Abuse Regulation, 3 February 2015, ESMA/2015/224.
[37] ESMA, Final Report, Draft technical standards on the Market Abuse Regulation, 28 September 2015, ESMA/2015/1455.
[38] Regulation (EU) No. 182/2011 on the European Parliament and the Council of 16 February 2011 laying down the rules and general principles concerning mechanisms for control by Member States of the Commission's exercise of implementing powers, OJ L 55, 28 February 2011, p.13–18.
[39] See ESMA/2015/224 (fn. 36).
[40] ESMA, Final Report, Draft technical standards on the Market Abuse Regulation, 28 September 2015, ESMA/2015/1455.
[41] Cf. N. Moloney, in: FS Hopt, 2265, 2271 ff.; N. Moloney, *EU Securities and Financial Markets Regulation*, 902 ff.; C. Fabricius, *Der Technische Regulierungsstandard für Finanzdienstleistungen—Eine kritische Würdigung unter besonderer Berücksichtigung des Art. 290 AEUV*, 23 ff.
[42] C. Fabricius, *Der Technische Regulierungsstandard für Finanzdienstleistungen—Eine kritische Würdigung unter besonderer Berücksichtigung des Art. 290 AEUV*, 70 ff.

22 It is doubtful if this theoretical system suffices to ascertain whether a substantiation of a Level 1 rule has to be made via a delegated act by the Commission or if a RTS drafted by ESMA can be sufficient.[43] The latest Level 1 regulations at least do not show a consistent system: It is, for example, highly questionable if the power to specify the criteria for an accepted market practice under Article 12 MAR (market manipulation) can be de facto deferred to ESMA (Article 13(7) MAR) considering the importance of the safe harbour rules for legal practice.[44]

23 In the course of the latest round of reforms of European capital market law Level 2 became more important. For example, the MAR empowers the Commission to adopt seven delegated acts and 15 technical standards. Legal practitioners thus have to consider a wide range of Level 2 acts. Such detailed Level 2 rules are a core part of the **ESMA Single Rulebook**.[45]

3. Guidelines and Recommendations

24 Level 3 is concerned with ESMA's task of developing guidelines and recommendations for a consistent interpretation of capital markets law throughout Europe in order to ensure a level playing field of all European capital markets.[46] Recommendations and Guidelines find their legal basis in Article 16 ESMA Regulation. They can be directed to the national supervisory authorities or to market participants.[47] ESMA has taken over this role and issued guidelines for a number of fields of law.[48] The guidelines and recommendations are not binding,[49] but rather a significant **interpretational help** for the national supervisory authorities and the market participants.[50] They are **soft law**, ie non-binding rules which have a high impact on legal practice.[51]

25 *Examples*: (i) The MAR requires ESMA to develop a non-exhaustive indicative list of information which is reasonably expected to be disclosed as inside information (Article 7(5) MAR); (ii) and to provide guidelines on the legitimate interests of issuers to delay the disclosure of inside information as well as on situations which are likely to mislead the public (Article 17(11) MAR). These terms to be substantiated by ESMA are vital for legal practice.

26 Under Article 16(3) ESMA Regulation Member States have to confirm that they comply with a guideline or recommendation or state the reasons why they refused to comply. This **comply or explain-mechanism** should ensure compliance with these acts despite their non-binding character. In practice, ESMA's guidelines and recommendations are generally

---

[43] Cf. also N. Moloney, *EU Securities and Financial Markets Regulation*, 923 ff.
[44] See R. Veil § 15 para. 39 on the legal implications of an accepted market practice under the MAR.
[45] Cf. on the scope and implications of the single rulebook R. Veil, 43 ZGR (2014), 544, 601 ff.; since 2018 an interactive version of the Single Rulebook can be found under https://www.esma.europa.eu/rules-databases-library/interactive-single-rulebook-isrb.
[46] S. Kalss et al., *Kapitalmarktrecht I*, § 1 para. 48.
[47] R. Veil, 43 ZGR (2014), 544, 589 ff.; S. Kalss et al., *Kapitalmarktrecht I*, § 1 para. 63.
[48] See for an updated overview https://www.esma.europa.eu/system/files/guidelines_list_of_final_guidelines.pdf.
[49] Lamfalussy Report, p. 47; cf. also T. Möllers, 3 ZEuP (2008), 480, 491 ff.
[50] See R. Veil § 5 para. 22.
[51] Cf. N. Moloney, *EU Securities and Financial Markets Regulation*, 874 ff., R. Veil, 1 ZBB (2018), 151, 159 f.; O. Achtelik and A. Mohn, 50 WM (2019), 2339, 2342.

complied with by national authorities. However, in a few cases national supervisory authorities have declared non-compliance or partial non-compliance.[52]

Although non-binding, other indirect legal effect may ensue from these measures. In German legal literature, for example, it is argued that the disregard of the ESMA's recommendations may facilitate the **proof of liability** for private law liability claims.[53] Furthermore, the German Federal Supreme Administrative Court held that the opinion of ESMA's predecessor CESR results in a presumption of a correct interpretation of the law.[54] Also a criminal offence may be classed as an unavoidable mistake of law if ESMA recommendations were adhered.[55]

The ECJ has not yet had the opportunity to decide on the implications of ESMA/CESR's soft law. Regarding other fields of law the ECJ, however, held that a deviation from soft law might lead to a violation of the principles of equality and legitimate expectations of the law.[56] The Member States' authorities have to at least consider EU soft law.[57] In German legal literature it is argued that a national court has to submit a case to the ECJ if it would like to deviate from ESMA's interpretation laid down in a guideline or recommendation.[58]

4. Supervisory Convergence

On the last level of the Lamfalussy II Process the Commission and ESMA monitor and evaluate the enforcement of the European rules on capital markets law by the Member States. Article 29 ESMA Regulation sets forth that ESMA should achieve **supervisory convergence** among the NCAs.[59] Enhancing supervisory convergence across the EU was defined as one of the core strategic aims of ESMA after in the ESA review that was completed in 2019. ESMA will start to develop an **EU Supervisory Handbook** for this purpose.[60]

Supervisory convergence should, for example, be achieved by **peer reviews** pursuant to Article 30 ESMA Regulation. Such Article 30 stipulates detailed rules for the peer review procedure which were included as a result of the latest ESA review; in particular, the ESMA

---

[52] Four Member States (Denmark, France, Germany and Sweden) and the former Member State United Kingdom, for example, expressed full or partial non-compliance with ESMA's guidelines on the interpretation of the SSR, cf. N. Moloney, *EU Securities and Financial Markets Regulation*, 934 f.; R. Veil, 43 ZGR (2014), 544, 591.
[53] G. Spindler and J. Hupka, in: Möllers (ed.), *Geltung und Faktizität von Standards*, 117, 135 ff.
[54] BVerwG of 24.05.2011 – 7 C 6.10, 32 ZIP (2011), 1313, 1316.
[55] J. Hupka, 29 WM (2009), 1351, 1355 ff.; T. Möllers, 8 NZG (2010), 285, 286; A. Frank, 4 ZBB (2015), 213, 218. For a more general approach see S. Kalss, in: Riesenhuber (ed.), *Europäische Methodenlehre*, 606. Opposing view (no exculpation) P. Buck-Heeb, 4 WM (2020), 157, 162.
[56] See eg ECJ Case C-189/02 (*Dansk Rørindustri et al./Commission*), para. 211 ff.; see on the applicability of the existing ECJ case law to ESMA's soft law R. Veil, 43 ZGR (2014), 544, 593; A. Frank, 4 ZBB (2015), 213, 217 ff.
[57] Case C-207/01 (*Altair Chimica/ENEL Distribuzione SpA*); Case C-188/91 (*Deutsche Shell AG/Hauptzollamt Hamburg-Harburg*), para. 18; Cases C-317/08 (*Rosalba Alassini/Telecom Italia SpA*); C-318/08 (*Filomena Califano/Wind SpA*); C-319/08 (*Lucia Anna Giorgia Iacono/Telecom Italia SpA*) and C-320/08 (*Multiservice Srl/Telecom Italia SpA*).
[58] J. Hupka, 29 WM (2009), 1351, 1355 ff.; T. Möllers, 8 NZG (2010), 285, 286; on the private law effects see G. Spindler and J. Hupka, in: Möllers (ed.), *Geltung und Faktizität von Standards*, 117, 135 ff.; on ESMA's soft law A. Frank, 4 ZBB (2015), 213, 218; R. Veil, 1 ZBB (2018), 151, 160; for a more general approach see S. Kalss, in: Riesenhuber (ed.), *Europäische Methodenlehre*, 606.
[59] See for details: N. Moloney, *EU Securities and Financial Markets Regulation*, 935 ff. and 989 ff.
[60] See ESMA, Strategic Orientation 2020-22, 9 January 2020, ESMA22-106-194.

Regulation now calls for special committees at ESMA level that conduct peer reviews (Article 30(2) ESMA-Regulation). Peer reviews are conducted on a regular basis. However, they can also be initiated on an ad hoc basis via a so-called **fast track procedure**.

31   *Example*: As a result of the *Wirecard* case,[61] ESMA recently reviewed the supervisory practice in Germany. It identified a number of deficiencies in the national supervision of Wirecard's financial reporting.[62]

32   As a last resort, the Commission is to commence an infringement proceeding against a Member State when a breach of European law becomes apparent. In order to facilitate the supervision, the Member States have to report on the progress of implementation vis-à-vis ESMA (Article 35 ESMA Regulation).

33   Over the last years, a tool to ensure supervisory convergence became more and more important: ESMA so far issued over 30 **Question and Answer-Lists (Q&A-Lists)** which are in part continuously updated.[63] ESMA's Q&As were initially designed as measures to ensure a common supervisory culture under Article 29(2) ESMA Regulation. As a result of the latest ESA review,[64] a distinct legal basis was enacted (Article 16b ESMA Regulation). This provision also includes details on the Q&A process. Inter alia, it requires ESMA to sustain a **web-based system** to process questions submitted by market participants.

34   As opposed to guidelines and recommendations, they do not trigger a comply or explain obligation for the NCAs. However, some NCAs (eg. the German BaFin) have issued a policy that they comply with Q&A unless they indicate the opposite. ESMA's Q&As are of high practical importance. Market participants rely on ESMA's Q&As de facto the same way they rely on Level 3 acts. Thus, complying with them should have the same legal consequences as adhering to ESMA's guidelines and recommendations.[65] In particular, after the Q&A's recognition in the ESMA Regulation there is no reason to make a distinction between Q&A and guidelines with regards to the legal consequences of such measures.

5. Stakeholder Involvement

35   One of the main original objectives of the Lamfalussy procedure was to include **stakeholder expert knowledge** in the law-making process. To achieve this goal the Lamfalussy II scheme includes a number of groups which deliver advice to European institutions: The Commission regularly asks relevant stakeholders (in particular: market participants) for their opinions in a formal consultation process in the very beginning of the legislative process for reforms on Level 1. Furthermore, ESMA has various committees where market participants and other stakeholders are represented. The most important

---

[61] See for other aspects of this case F. Walla § 24 para. 65 (short selling).
[62] ESMA, Fast Track Peer Review on the Application of the Guidelines on the Enforcement of Financial Information by BaFin and FREP in Context of Wirecard, 3 November 2020, ESMA42-111-5349; cf. also the ESMA, Q&A on the Fast Track Peer Review on the Wirecard Case, 3 November 2020, ESMA71-99-1423.
[63] See eg ESMA, Q&A on the Market Abuse Regulation (MAR), ESMA70-145-111, Version 15, last update on 6 August 2021; ESMA, Q&A on MiFIR data reporting, 16 July 2021, ESMA70-1861941480-56; ESMA, Q&A Transparency Directive (2004/109/EC), 9 November 2020, ESMA31-67-127; ESMA, Q&A on the Prospectus Regulation, ESMA/2020/ESMA31-62-1258, Version 10, last update on 27 July 2021.
[64] Cf. F. Walla § 11 para 57.
[65] Opposing view R. Veil, 1 ZBB (2018), 151, 165; concurring H. Anzinger, 3 RdF (2018), 181, 184.

committee is the **Securities and Markets Stakeholder Group (SMSG)** established pursuant to Article 37 ESMA Regulation.[66] Moreover, ESMA's various Standing Committees have created Consultative Working Groups which, respectively, provide a forum for stakeholders to share their views on the regulatory development in the relevant fields of capital markets law with ESMA, such as market abuse, corporate finance, etc.[67]

6. Graph: Lamfalussy II Process

EUROPEAN CAPITAL MARKETS LAW'S REGULATORY PROCESS

Levels	Sources of law	
Level 1	Legal Acts of the European Parliament and the Council (Articles 294 et seq. TFEU)	
Level 2	Delegated Acts by the Commission (Article 290 TFEU)	Regulatory Technical Standards developed by ESMA and endorsed by the Commission (Article 290 TFEU; Article 10 ESMA-Regulation)
	Implementing Acts by the Commission (Article 291 TFEU)	Implementing Technical Standards developed by ESMA and endorsed by the Commission (Article 291 TFEU; Article 15 ESMA-Regulation)
Level 3	Guidelines and Recommendations by ESMA (Article 16 ESMA-Regulation)	
Level 4	Supervisory Convergence via ESMA measures (Articles 16b, 29, 30 ESMA-Regulation)	Control of the Member States by ESMA (Article 17 ESMA-Regulation) and by the Commission (Article 258 TFEU)

Figure 1 shows a schematic of the Lamfalussy II process.

III. Evaluation of the Lamfalussy II Process

The Lamfalussy Process was revised and officially evaluated in 2007[68] and found not to be in urgent need of reform.[69] The aim of a **more efficient, flexible and faster legislative** process largely appears to have been achieved.[70] The use of expert knowledge and a faster and

---

[66] Statements and advice by the SMSG can be downloaded under www.esma.europa.edu/page/SMSG-Documents.
[67] See also F. Walla § 11 para. 72.
[68] Commission, Review of the Lamfalussy process strengthening supervisory convergence, 20 November 2007, COM(2007) 727 final; Inter-Institutional Monitoring Group, *Final Report Monitoring the Lamfalussy Process*, 15 October 2007, available at: http://ec.europa.eu/internal_market/finances/docs/committees/071015_final_report_en.pdf.
[69] N. Moloney, in: Tison et al. (eds.), *Perspectives in Company Law and Financial Regulation*, 449, 472; similarly N. Moloney, in: FS Hopt, 2264, 2281; N. Moloney, *EU Securities and Financial Markets Regulation*, 866 ff. For an overview of the points of criticism, especially of the work of the committees on Level 3, see I. Leixner, *Komitologie und Lamfalussyverfahren im Finanzdienstleistungsbereich*, 24 ff.
[70] T. Möllers, 3 ZEuP (2008), 480, 502 ff.; K.-U. Schmolke, 22 NZG (2005), 912, 918. See also the various reports published by the Inter-Institutional Monitoring Group, established by the Commission. With regard to this, the

more flexible legislative process are essential in an area subject to such continual changes as capital markets.

38   One may argue that the downside of this is that the legislative process in capital markets law lacks **democratic legitimacy and transparency.** However, the European Parliament and the Council are still competent for basic policy decisions on Level 1 and have comprehensive participation rights on Level 2.[71] Thus, at least the conformity of the Lamfalussy II Process with European primary law cannot be doubted.[72] The rapidly changing capital markets environment and the complexity of the issues to be solved,[73] require strong expert participation which justifies a well-balanced reduction of the European Parliament's and the Council's involvement in the rule-making process.

39   In particular, ESMA's involvement in the process has to be welcomed as it contributes to a higher degree of harmonisation within a short period of time and it provides the necessary expertise to the law-making process. Thus, an even stronger integration of ESMA into the law-making process would be recommendable.[74]

40   It also has to be admitted that another side of the coin is that Lamfalussy II has turned European capital market law into a **highly complex field of law**. It thus has been argued that legal practice can hardly comply with the current set of rules provided by European and national law.[75] This criticism is certainly true to a certain extent, in particular for market participants without pan-European operations.[76] However, it should not give rise to doubts with regards to the general Lamfalussy II approach but should rather lead to a more thorough choice of the measures used by the law-making authorities involved.

---

criticism expressed in the literature at the outset of this procedure is unsubstantiated. On this see G. Hertig and R. Lee, 3 J. Corp. L. Stud. (2003), 359, 364 ff.

[71] S. Kalss et al., *Kapitalmarktrecht I*, § 1 para. 50; regarding the Lamfalussy I procedure already K. Langenbucher, 2 ZEuP (2002), 265, 283 ff.; B. Scheel, 9 ZEuS (2006), 521 ff.; K.-U. Schmolke, 41 EuR (2006), 432, 443. Cf. also K. von Wogau, 4 ZEuP (2002), 695, 699–700 for a summary of the European Parliament's doubt at this time.

[72] Cf. K.-U. Schmolke, 41 EuR (2006), 432, 441. The ECJ explicitly confirmed that ESMA's rule-making powers are in compliance with the TFEU, see Case C-270/12 (*UK/Council and Parliament*), see on this case F. Walla § 24 para. 25.

[73] Cf. F. Walla, *Die Konzeption der Kapitalmarktaufsicht in Deutschland*, 39 ff.

[74] From a policy standpoint it would be advisable to allow ESMA to enact delegated acts without an involvement of the Commission, cf. the letter of ESMA's chairman Steven Maijoor to the Commission of 31 October 2013, Review of the European System on Financial Supervision (ESFS), 31 October 2013, ESMA/2013/1561. However, such delegation of powers to ESMA is currently not feasible as the 'Meroni Doctrine' of the ECJ prohibits any delegation of rule-making to European authorities apart from the Commission, cf. J. Kämmerer, in: Kämmerer and Veil (eds.), *Übernahme- und Kapitalmarktrecht in der Reformdiskussion*, 45, 65; N. Moloney, *EU Securities and Financial Markets Regulation*, 909 ff. and 921 ff.

[75] See S. Kalss, 26 EuZW (2015), 569, 570.

[76] J.-H. Binder, 1 GPR (2011), 34, 38.

§ 5

Sources of Law and Principles of Interpretation

Bibliography

Amorosino, Sandro, *Manuale Di Diritto Del Mercato Finanziario*, 3rd edn. (2014); Annunziata, Filippo, *La Disciplina del Mercato Mobiliare*, 10th edn. (2020); Assmann, Heinz-Dieter et al. (eds.), *Kommentar zum Wertpapierhandelsrecht*, 7th edn. (2019); Blair, Michael et al. (eds.), *Blackstone's Guide to the Financial Services and Markets Act 2000* (2001); Bonneau, Thierry et al. (eds.), *Droit Financier*, 2nd edn. (2019); Bieber, Roland et al. (eds.), *Die Europäische Union: Europarecht und Politik*, 14th edn. (2020); Capriglione, Francesco, *Manuale di Diritto Bancario e Finanziario*, 2nd edn. (2019); Carlson, Laura, *Fundamentals of Swedish Law* (2012); Costi, Renzo, *Il Mercato Mobiliare*, 11th edn. (2018); Frank, Alexander, *Die Level-3-Verlautbarung der ESMA – ein sicherer Hafen für den Rechtsanwender?*, 28 ZBB (2015), 213–220; Frank, Alexander, *Die Rechtswirkung der Leitlinien und Empfehlungen der Europäischen Wertpapier- und Marktaufsichtsbehörde* (2012); Fuchs, Andreas et al. (eds.), *Kommentar zum Wertpapierhandelsrecht*, 2nd edn. (2016); Klass, Susanne et al. (eds.), *Kapitalmarktrecht*, 2nd edn. (2015); Kümpel, Siegfried et al. (eds.), *Bank- und Kapitalmarktrecht*, 5th edn. (2019); Langenbucher, Katja, *Europarechtliche Bezüge des Privatrechts*, 2nd edn. (2008); Langenbucher, Katja (ed.), *Europäisches Privat- und Wirtschaftsrecht*, 4th edn. (2017); Langenbucher, Katja, *Zur Zulässigkeit parlamentsersetzender Normgebungsverfahren im Europarecht*, 10 ZEuP (2002), 265–286; Merville, Anne-Dominique, *Droit Financier*, 4th edn. (2018); Möllers, Thomas M. J., *Auf dem Weg zu einer neuen europäischen Finanzmarktaufsichtsstruktur*, 13 NZG (2010), 285–290; Möllers, Thomas M. J., *Europäische Methoden- und Gesetzgebungslehre im Kapitalmarktrecht—Vollharmonisierung, Generalklauseln und soft law im Rahmen des Lamfalussy-Verfahrens als Mittel zur Etablierung von Standards*, 16 ZEuP (2008), 480–505; Moloney, Niamh, *The Committee of European Securities Regulators and Level 3 of the Lamfalussy Process*, in: Tison, Michel et al. (eds.), *Perspectives in Company Law and Financial Regulation—Essays in Honour of Eddy Wymeersch* (2009), 449–476; Oppermann, Thomas et al. (eds.), *Europarecht*, 8th edn. (2018); Riesenhuber, Karl (ed.), *Europäische Methodenlehre*, 4th edn. (2021); Schulze, Reiner et al. (eds.), *Europarecht: Handbuch für die deutsche Rechtspraxis*, 4th edn. (2020); Spindler, Gerald and Hupka, Jan, *Bindungswirkung von Standards im Kapitalmarktrecht*, in: Möllers, Thomas M. J. (ed.), *Geltung und Faktizität von Standards* (2009), 117–142; Tapia Hermida, Alberto J., *Derecho del Mercado de Valores* (2000); Veil, Rüdiger and Walla, Fabian, *Schwedisches Kapitalmarktrecht: eine rechtsvergleichende Studie aus der Perspektive des Gemeinschaftsrechts* (2010); Veil, Rüdiger, *Europäische Kapitalmarktunion—Verordnungsgesetzgebung, Instrumente der europäischen Marktaufsicht und die Idee eines „Single Rulebook"*, 43 ZGR (2014), 544–607; Veil, Rüdiger, *Aufsichtskonvergenz durch „Questions and Answers" der ESMA*, 30 ZBB (2018), 151–166; Walker, Georg et al. (eds.), *Financial Service Law*, 3rd edn. (2014).

I. Introduction

1 The sources of capital markets law in Europe display the struggle between centralised European legislation and Member States' regulatory autonomy. With a few exceptions, European capital markets law is supervisory law.[1] The European sources of law can be divided in directly applicable regulations and directives, which generally have no direct effect in the Member States but rather have to be transposed into national laws of the Member State.[2] In the last decade there has been a trend towards regulations instead of directives.[3] The basic idea behind this is to create a level playing field in Europe thus preventing regulatory arbitrage and contributing to the creation of a single market. Nonetheless there are still directives in force and thus 27 different national legal systems have to be taken into account to some extent. In addition, private law is not harmonised.[4] For this reason, capital markets law in Europe is also still national law, even though it is characterised by a large number of EU legal acts. It is therefore necessary to provide an overview of the national sources of capital markets law in the Member States, ie parliamentary acts and regulations enacted by ministries and supervisory authorities. This chapter lists the most important national laws and regulations in Austria, France, Germany, Greece, Italy, Spain, Sweden and the United Kingdom, though having left the EU. It also looks at whether national supervisory authorities publish guidelines and recommendations on the application of the law. First, however, the relevant European legal acts shall be listed, without closer details to their content. In addition, methods of interpretation of EU capital markets law are explained.

II. European Law

1 Sources of Law

2 The most important sources of European capital markets law have been the four framework directives (2003/2004-regime) and their respective implementing measures (directives and regulations). In the last years they have been reformed and replaced (post-crisis regulation). Furthermore, a number of further regulations have been enacted on issues formerly subject to national legislation or self-regulation. Thus, the term 'framework directives or regulations' (established for the PD, TD, MAD and MiFID) may therefore be misleading today. Instead European capital markets law should be rather considered as an accumulation of Level 1 regulations and Level 1 directives, their implementing measures on Level 2 mostly in the form of regulations and further instruments on Level 3, such as guidelines

---

[1] See R. Veil § 2 para. 5.
[2] See in more detail R. Veil § 3 para. 13–20.
[3] R. Veil, 43 ZGR (2014), 544, 564 ff.
[4] See on the relevance of private law R. Veil § 2 para. 5.

and recommendations, Q&As etc.[5] All these acts and instruments build so-called **single rulebooks**.[6] EU securities regulation currently consists of eight single rulebooks.

(a) Single Rulebooks of EU Securities Regulation

The MiFID II regime plays a central role in European capital markets law. It consists of a directive (**MiFID II**)[7] and a regulation (**MiFIR**)[8] as well as numerous Level 2 and 3 measures. The two Level 1 legislative acts regulate the market infrastructure, lay down requirements for market operators and investment firms when providing investment services and govern the distribution of financial products. In addition, MiFID-II contains a number of definitions referred to in other EU legislative acts, such as the concept of trading venues, financial instruments, investment services, etc. The disparate regulatory content can only be explained historically. MiFID II and MiFIR are derived from the former Investment Services Directive,[9] which already defined key concepts. The MiFID II regime is complemented by the **PRIIP Regulation**.[10] This Level 1 legislative act regulates the distribution of packaged investment products and insurance investment products. 3

The law of primary markets is largely governed by the **Prospectus Regulation** (PR).[11] The Level 1 legislative act provides for disclosure requirements for the public offering of securities and their admission to trading on a regulated market. Issuers are in principle obliged in these two cases to publish a securities prospectus approved by the national supervisory authority. Admission of securities to trading on an MTF or OTF is not subject to the PR. 4

The market abuse law consists of two Level 1 EU legislative acts: the **Market Abuse Regulation** (MAR)[12] and the Directive on criminal sanctions (CRIM-MAD).[13] In addition to prohibitions on insider dealing and market manipulation, which are sanctioned under harmonised national administrative and criminal law, the regime provides for a wide range of disclosure obligations which, according to the European legislator, are primarily intended to prevent market abuse. 5

---

[5] R. Veil, 43 ZGR (2014), 544, 582.

[6] ESMA publishes on its website an interactive Single Rulebook, which contains the provisions of the Level 1 act, the respective provisions of the Level 2 acts and ESMA's guidance, Q&A papers and opinions. See www.esma.europa.eu/rules-databases-library/interactive-single-rulebook-isrb.

[7] Directive 2014/65/EU of the European Parliament and of the Council of 15 May 2014 on markets in financial instruments and amending Directive 2002/927/EC and Directive 2011/61/EU (MiFID II).

[8] Regulation (EU) No 600/2014 of the European Parliament and of the Council of 15 May 2014 on markets in financial instruments and amending Regulations (EU) No 648/2012, OJ L 173, 12 June 2014, p. 84 ff. (MiFIR).

[9] See R. Veil § 1 para. 12.

[10] Regulation (EU) No 1286/2014 of the European Parliament and of the Council of 26 November 2014 on key information documents for packaged retail and insurance-based investment products (PRIIPs), OJ L 352, 9 December 2014, p. 1.

[11] Regulation (EU) 2017/1129 of the European Parliament and of the Council of 14 June 2017 on the prospectus to be published when securities are offered to the public or admitted to trading on a regulated market, and repealing Directive 2003/71/EC, OJ L 168, 30 June 2017, p. 12.

[12] Regulation (EU) No 596/2014 of the European Parliament and of the Council of 16 April 2014 on market abuse (market abuse regulation) and repealing Directive 2003/6/EC of the European Parliament and the Council and Commission Directive 2003/124/EC, 2003/125/EC and 2004/72/EC (MAR).

[13] Directive 2014/57/EU of the European Parliament and of the Council of 16 April 2014 on criminal sanctions for market abuse (market abuse directive), OJ L 173, 12 June 2014, p. 179 ff. (CRIM-MAD).

6   The **Transparency Directive** (TD)[14] aims to harmonise disclosure requirements with regard to information about issuers whose securities are admitted to trading on a regulated market (corporate disclosure). It lays down disclosure obligations for issuers (financial reports and half-yearly financial reports; information on the exercise of voting rights at general meetings) and for investors (changes in voting rights; holding of financial instruments). The content of financial reporting is governed by Regulation (EC) No 1606/2002 on the application of international accounting standards.[15]

7   The **Regulation** on **short selling** and certain aspects of **credit default swaps** (SSR)[16] deals with certain trading practices and can largely be considered as market abuse law. In particular, it imposes disclosure obligations on net short selling positions and prohibits uncovered short sales of shares and public debt.

8   The **Regulation** on **Credit Rating Agencies** (CRAR)[17] applies to credit ratings issued by credit rating agencies registered in the EU and disclosed to the public or distributed to subscribers. It aims to promote integrity, transparency, responsibility, good corporate governance and independence of credit rating activities. The main goal is to improve the quality of credit ratings issued in the Union and ensure the smooth functioning of the internal market. The CRAR therefore provides requirements for issuing credit ratings and lays down rules on the organisation of credit rating agencies, including their shareholders and members, to promote the independence of credit rating agencies, the avoidance of conflicts of interest and the protection of consumers and investors.

9   The **Benchmark Regulation**[18] concerns indices which are used as a benchmark for financial instruments and financial contracts or to measure the performance of an investment fund. It establishes a common framework to ensure the accuracy and integrity of indices.

10 The **Securitisation Regulation**[19] establishes a framework for securitisations. This is done through due diligence requirements, rules on risk retention and disclosure obligations for parties involved in securitisations, lending criteria, requirements for the sale of securitisations to retail investors, a prohibition on resecuritisation, requirements for special purpose vehicles and conditions and procedures for securitisation registers. Finally, it establishes a specific framework for simple, transparent and standardised (STS) securitisations.

---

[14] Directive 2004/109/EC of the European Parliament and of the Council of 15 December 2004 on the harmonisation of transparency requirements in relation to information about issuers whose securities are admitted to trading on a regulated market and amending Directive 2001/34/EC (TD).

[15] Regulation (EC) No 1606/2002 of the European Parliament and of the council of 19 July 2002 on the application of international accounting standards.

[16] Regulation (EU) No 236/2012 of the European Parliament and of the council of 14 March 2012 on short selling and certain aspects of credit default swaps (SSR).

[17] Regulation (EC) No 1060/2009 of the European Parliament and of the Council of 16 September 2009 on credit rating agencies (CRAR).

[18] Regulation (EU) 2016/1011 of the European Parliament and of the Council of 8 June 2016 on indices used as benchmarks in financial contracts or to measure the performance of investments funds and amending Directives 2008/48/EC and 2014/17/EU and Regulation (EU) No 596/2014 (BR).

[19] Regulation (EU) 2017/2402 of the European Parliament and of the Council of 12 December 2017 laying down a general framework for securitisation, and amending Directives 2009/65/EC, 2009/138/EC and 2011/61/EU and Regulations (EC) No. 1060/2009 and (EU) No. 648/2012 (SR).

(b) Regulations on the European Supervisory Authorities

Since 1 January 2011 three European authorities are responsible for the coordination of national authorities and, to some extent, supervision of financial market participants. EBA, EIOPA and ESMA were established by three Regulations based on Article 114 TFEU. Regulation (EU) No 1093/2010 established the European Banking Authority (EBA);[20] Regulation (EU) No 1094/2010 established the European Insurance and Occupational Pensions Authority (EIOPA);[21] and Regulation (EU) No 1095/2010 established the European Securities and Markets Authority (ESMA).[22]

11

(c) Further Relevant EU Law

The European Union has adopted several directives, mainly concerning Member States' corporate law, but also covering capital market aspects. These directives *apply only to listed companies.*[23] **Directive** 2004/25/EC on **takeover bids** (TOD)[24] also regulates capital market issues relating to public takeover bids (disclosure requirements and supervision of takeovers by national authorities and bodies). The (amended) **Shareholders' Rights Directive** (SRD II)[25] lays down requirements for the exercise of certain rights of shareholders attached to voting shares in relation to general meetings of companies whose shares are admitted to trading on a regulated market situated or operating within a Member State. The requirements on the disclosure of related party transactions and consultants of share voting rights relate to capital markets legislation.

12

The law on collective investment schemes is governed by two directives, which aim at a far-reaching full harmonisation of the national regimes. The **UCITS Directive**[26] coordinates the laws, regulations and administrative provisions of the Member States concerning certain undertakings for collective investment in transferable securities. It is complemented by the **AIFM Directive**, which applies to managers of alternative investment funds. **Regulation (EU) 2019/2088** on **sustainability** related **disclosure requirements** in the financial services

13

---

[20] Regulation (EU) No 1093/2010 of the European Parliament and of the Council of 24 November 2010 establishing a European Supervisory Authority (European Banking Authority), amending Decision No 716/2009/EC and repealing Commission Decision 209/78/EC.

[21] Regulation (EU) No 1094/2010 of the European Parliament and of the Council of 24 November 2010 establishing a European Supervisory Authority (European Insurance and Occupational Pensions Authority), amending Decision No 716/2009/EC and repealing Commission Decision 2009/79/EC.

[22] Regulation (EU) No 1095/2010 of the European Parliament and of the Council of 24 November 2010 establishing a European Supervisory Authority (European Securities and Markets Authority), amending Decision No 716/2009/EC and repealing Commission Decision 2009/77/EC.

[23] These are companies whose securities are admitted to trading on a regulated market. The rules therefore do not apply to companies whose securities are traded on an MTF or OTF. See on the different trading venues R. Veil § 7 para. 2.

[24] Directive 2004/25/EC of the European Parliament and of the Council of 21 April 2004 on takeover bids (TOD).

[25] Directive (EU) 2017/828 of the Council of 17 May 2017 amending Directive 2007/36/EC as regards the encouragement of long-term shareholder engagement (SRD II).

[26] Directive 2009/65/EC of the European Parliament and of the Council of 13 July 2009 on the coordination of laws, regulations and administrative provisions relating to undertakings for collective investment in transferable securities (UCITS).

sector (SFDR)[27] establishes various disclosure requirements for UCITS, AIFM and other financial market participants regarding sustainability risks and the sustainability of financial products.

2 Interpretation

(a) Autonomous Interpretation

14 **Regulations** enacted by the European legislature are directly applicable in all Member States.[28] National courts and national supervisory authorities must therefore interpret a regulation's provisions when applying them. They may not refer to the national methods of interpretation but must rather apply the European doctrine of interpretation (autonomous interpretation).

15 *Example*: Regulation (EU) No. 596/2014 (MAR) prohibits insider dealing and the unlawful disclosure of inside information (Article 14). The term inside information is defined in Article 7 MAR. However, a number of interpretational questions arise with regard to elements of the notion of inside information. A French, German or Spanish court would have to interpret these aspects, such as the price relevance of an information (Article 7(4) MAR) or the term 'intermediate step' (Article 7(1) MAR) in accordance with the European doctrine of interpretation.

16 Exceptionally, the methods of interpretation established in the Member States may have to be taken into account when interpreting EU regulatory law. This is the case when European law declares these principles to be relevant.

17 Example: Regulation (EC) 462/2013 (CRAR-III) introduced a liability of credit rating agencies towards investors and issuers.[29] The Regulation does not define the individual elements of liability, such as the concepts of 'damage', 'intentional', 'gross negligence', 'reasonable' or 'appropriate'. Instead, the Regulation refers to national law: the terms must be interpreted and applied in accordance with the national law applicable under the relevant rules of private international law. This is because there are no definitions of terms in European private law and Member States have different ideas about these concepts.

18 **Directives**, on the other hand, have to be transposed into the Member States' national laws, thus allowing the national civil, criminal and administrative courts to apply national laws in accordance with national methods of interpretation. However, interpretation must be consistent with the directive's requirements and purposes (**interpretation in conformity with the directive**). The supreme body for deciding this question is the European Court of Justice (ECJ) which will generally be called upon by a national court for a binding[30] preliminary ruling on the interpretation of Union law.[31] The ECJ does not refer to national law or interpretational methods but rather adopts an autonomous European approach.[32]

---

[27] Regulation (EU) 2019/2088, OJ L 317, 9 December 2019, p. 1.
[28] See R. Veil § 3 para. 15.
[29] See R. Veil § 27 para. 78.
[30] Cf. Art. 19(1) EU Treaty.
[31] Cf. Art. 19(3)(b) EU Treaty.
[32] Cf. Case 26/62 (*van Gend & Loos*).

§ 5   Sources of Law and Principles of Interpretation

Example: The Belgian supervisory authority (CBFA) imposed fines on the Belgian issuer Spector and its board member van Raemdonck, finding that they had committed insider dealings as prohibited by the MAD 2003 and its Belgian national implementing provisions. The respondents brought an appeal before a higher court in Belgium, which had to decide on questions regarding the interpretation of Belgian law whilst considering the MAD 2003, and in this context referred a number of questions to the ECJ.[33] One of the questions referred was regarding the requirements for a 'use' of information for a transaction to be classed as insider dealing. In its ruling,[34] the ECJ had to interpret the respective provisions of the MAD 2003.

Facts: In the case *Geltl/Daimler*[35] the BGH presented the ECJ with two questions on the interpretation of the term 'inside information' regarding the ad hoc disclosure rules for a preliminary ruling.[36] The German court was of the opinion that its decision depended on the correct interpretation of the European provisions. The ECJ had to decide on the questions referred to it by interpreting the respective provisions in the MAD 2003 and the implementing Directive 2003/124/EC.

(b) The Role of ESMA in the Development of Uniform Standards of Interpretation

The Single Rulebooks contain detailed rules. Nevertheless, many terms require interpretation. As the ECJ has so far interpreted only a few terms, the interpretations by the supervisory authorities are of great importance. This soft law already existed at the time of the former **CESR**. The CESR could not make binding statements on the interpretation of European law. However, national authorities generally followed CESR's interpretative guidance.[37]

Since 2011, **ESMA** (replacing CESR) has the task of coordinating supervisory practices in the Member States. To that end, the Union legislator has granted ESMA the power to issue guidelines and recommendations to the competent authorities and financial market participants (Article 16 ESMA Regulation). ESMA can act on its own initiative; no special authorisation in a legislative act is required.

ESMA may issue guidelines and recommendations to establish **consistent, efficient** and **effective supervisory practices** within the ESFS and to ensure the **common, uniform** and **consistent application of Union law**. The competent authorities (AMF, BaFin, CNMV, Consob, etc.) and financial market participants shall make every effort to comply with the guidelines and recommendations.[38] As regards national supervisory authorities, a comply-or-explain mechanism is established: A national supervisory authority must confirm, within two months of the issuance of a guideline or recommendation, whether it complies or intends to comply with the guideline or recommendation. If a competent authority does not comply or does not intend to comply with the guideline or recommendation, it must notify ESMA, stating its reasons.[39] In the case of

---

[33] See R. Veil § 14 para. 70.
[34] Case C-45/08 (*Spector*).
[35] Case C-19/11 (*Geltl/Daimler*).
[36] BGH of 22.11.2010 – II ZB 7/09, 32 ZIP (2011), 72.
[37] Cf. BVerwG of 24.05.2011 - 7 C 6.10, 32 ZIP (2011), 1313, 1316 on Frequently asked questions regarding Prospectuses: Common positions agreed by CESR Members, 12th Updated Version – November 2010: They reflect a common view of the authorities concerned with this legal issue, which can claim a presumption of correctness.
[38] Art. 16(3) ESMA-Regulation.
[39] Art. 16(3) ESMA-Regulation.

non-compliance, ESMA will make that information public.[40] This shaming is intended to ensure greater compliance with the guidelines and recommendations.[41]

24 Guidelines cannot establish rights that individuals can rely on before national courts. In particular, guidelines issued by the ESAs (EBA, ESMA, EIOPA) 'cannot be regarded as producing binding **legal effects** vis-à-vis the competent authorities'.[42] However, this does not mean that they are legally ineffective. This has already been recognised by the ECJ in the *Grimaldi* case concerning recommendations of the European Commission, where the ECJ stated that national courts are obliged to take account of recommendations: 'The national courts are bound to take recommendations into consideration in order to decide disputes submitted to them, in particular where they cast light on the interpretation of national measures adopted in order to implement them or where they are designed to supplement binding Community provisions.'[43] Guidelines under Article 16 ESMA Regulation are ESMA's instruments which define the application of provisions of capital markets law and coordinate the supervisory culture of the Member State authorities.[44] Both **national supervisory authorities** and **financial market participants** are **obliged** to **take the guidelines into account**.[45] Moreover, national supervisors are not entirely free to decide whether they comply with the guidelines. They may only deviate from guidelines and recommendations for legitimate reasons due to the harmonisation objective of the guidelines and recommendations.[46] This may be the case, for example, where guidelines do not take sufficient account of national market conditions. A court must also consider a guideline. In doing so, it must take into account the secondary legislation's mandate to ESMA to ensure the common, uniform and consistent application of Union law.[47] If it assesses the legal issue differently from the ESMA guidelines, the national court is obliged to refer the matter to the ECJ. Finally, for **financial market participants**, guidelines and recommendations may provide a **safe harbour** provided they have relied on the guidelines to interpret Union law correctly.[48] Where an issuer, investor or financial intermediary acts in accordance with a guideline addressed to it by ESMA and a court comes to a different interpretation, it will in any case have to recognise an excusable error of law by the financial market participant. It is therefore difficult to imagine a court imposing sanctions on a capital market participant if the latter has acted in accordance with ESMA's interpretative recommendations. The ECJ has jurisdiction under Article 267 TFEU to assess the validity of guidelines.[49]

25 ESMA also regularly publishes **Q&A papers** in order to establish common, uniform and consistent supervisory practices with regard to the application of capital markets legislation. ESMA's documents provide answers to questions raised by the public (stakeholders) and national supervisory authorities on the application of European law. ESMA sees the Q&A mechanism as a practical tool and instrument within the meaning of Article 29(2)

---

[40] Art. 16(3) ESMA-Regulation.
[41] Cf. recital 26 ESMA-Regulation.
[42] ECJ of 15.7.2021 – C-911/19, para. 45.
[43] Case C-322/88 (*Grimaldi*), para. 18.
[44] Cf. R. Veil, 43 ZGR (2014), 544 (594).
[45] Cf. A. Frank, *Die Rechtswirkung der Leitlinien und Empfehlungen der Europäischen Wertpapier- und Marktaufsichtsbehörde*, 121 ff.; T. Möllers, 13 NZG (2010), 285, 289; R. Veil, 43 ZGR (2014), 544, 592 ff.
[46] Cf. R. Veil, 43 ZGR (2014), 544, 596.
[47] Cf. A. Frank, *Die Rechtswirkung der Leitlinien und Empfehlungen der Europäischen Wertpapier- und Marktaufsichtsbehörde*, 168; R. Veil, 43 ZGR (2014), 544, 599.
[48] Cf. A. Frank, 28 ZBB (2015), 213, 217 ff.
[49] ECJ of 15.7.2021 – C-911/19, para. 52.

ESMA Regulation to promote common supervisory concepts and practices. It has not considered a formal consultation to be necessary so far. Since the ESA Review, however, it has to conduct 'open public consultations where appropriate'.[50] There is also a formalised process for the publication of Q&A within ESMA: Q&A are decided by ESMA's Board of Supervisors. They therefore reflect the (at least majority) view of EU supervisors on the application of European legislation.[51]

> The question of whether Q&A, as well as guidelines and recommendations under Article 16 ESMA Regulation, establish an obligation for national supervisory authorities and financial market participants to take them into account has not been clarified by the courts. To answer this question, it should be noted that Q&A are not legally binding. In the absence of a comply-or-explain mechanism, an obligation for national supervisory authorities and financial market participants to consider Q&A must be rejected.[52] Q&A can, however, become relevant from a legal perspective in favour of a market participant. A court must take them into account, similar to guidelines and recommendations, when determining the level of due diligence of market participants and their bodies. This may be the case, for example, where a market participant or its board acts in accordance with a response published by ESMA under its Q&A mechanism.

26

The **Board of Appeal** of the ESAs (BoA) has commented in its decision-making practice on a whole range of methodological issues of Union law. The CESR Guidelines are of 'strong persuasive force' for the BoA.[53] This correlates with the BVerwG's interpretation (see para. 21) that the guidelines carry a presumption of correctness. According to the BoA, a Level 2 regulation is a 'tool of interpretation' of a Level 1 regulation.[54] This also seems convincing, admittedly with the proviso that the meaning of the Level 1 provision cannot be judged solely on the basis of the Level 2 provision. Finally, the BoA holds that a market participant can be reproached for not having asked the supervisory authority to comment on an unresolved legal question. According to the BoA, this should be taken into account in determining whether a credit rating agency has acted negligently.[55] This interpretation must be rejected. Neither the CRAR nor the ESMA Regulation provide that market participants have an obligation to provide information. This cannot be derived from a 'supervisory relationship' between the credit rating agency and ESMA.

27

(c) Methods of Interpretation

Based on the ECJ's case law, legal literature has developed principles for the interpretation of European Union law, ensuring its independence from the national laws and its uniform application within the Member States.[56] It consists mainly of the interpretational methods

28

---

[50] Cf. Art. 29(2)(3) ESMA-Regulation.
[51] R. Veil, 30 ZBB (2018), 151, 163.
[52] R. Veil, 30 ZBB (2018), 151, 164.
[53] ESA Board of Appeal, Ref. 2020-D-03, para. 106.
[54] ESA Board of Appeal, Ref. 2020-D-03, para. 125.
[55] ESA Board of Appeal, Ref. 2020-D-03, para. 148.
[56] K. Langenbucher, in: Langenbucher (ed.), *Europäisches Privat- und Wirtschaftsrecht*, § 1 para. 5 ff.; M. Pechstein and C. Drechsler, in: Riesenhuber (ed.), *Europäische Methodenlehre*, § 7 para. 9 ff.

known in the Member States, adapting these, however, to the particularities of the European legal system.[57] A specific order of importance of the different methods of interpretation cannot be deduced from the ECJ's decisions.[58]

(aa) Textual Interpretation

29 Starting point for any statutory interpretation is usually the so-called textual interpretation which examines the language and wording of a provision. The ECJ does not refer to the respective terms in national law,[59] rather developing an independent European understanding.[60] As all legislative acts of the EU are equally authentic in all languages, it is not sufficient to examine a single version of the respective provision. Rather, a representative number of versions will have to be taken into account.[61] Often this will lead to the problem that no definite answer can be found with the help of the textual approach.

(bb) Contextual Interpretation

30 The contextual approach to interpretation examines the structure and position of a provision in the statute as a whole in order to deduce the meaning of the provision therefrom. It is closely connected to teleological interpretation.[62] The contextual approach can aim at confirming a result determined through the literal interpretation by referring to a different provision which is based on similar concepts.[63] Contextual arguments, can, on the other hand, also enable rejection of a certain understanding of a provision.[64] If the result is contrary to the underlying concepts of law a different understanding may be favourable.

31 In the ECJ's case law, contextual arguments play an important role in the interpretation of the fundamental freedoms.[65] As opposed to this, the contextual approach to interpretation has played no great role in the field of capital markets law so far. This may change in the future, since meanwhile most fields of capital markets law are subject to European regulations and directives, resulting in a number of Single Rulebooks, where the underlying concepts are largely comparable.

32 *Example*: The Takeover Directive (TOD) requires that the decision to make a bid be made public without delay. Yet the directive contains no definition of the term 'decision'. However, the recitals of the Takeover Directive indicate that the European legislature understands the decision to make a bid as a price-sensitive information, thus requiring disclosure in order to prevent insider dealings.[66]

---

[57] See in detail: K. Langenbucher, in: Langenbucher (ed.), *Europäisches Privat- und Wirtschaftsrecht*, § 1 para. 5 ff.; M. Pechstein and C. Drechsler, in: Riesenhuber (ed.), *Europäische Methodenlehre*, § 7 para. 9 ff.
[58] Cf. M. Pechstein and C. Drechsler, in: Riesenhuber (ed.), *Europäische Methodenlehre*, § 7 para. 13.
[59] Cf. Case 43/77 (*Industrial Diamond Supplies/Riva*), para. 15 ff.; Case C-296/95 (*EMU Tabac and Others*), para. 30.
[60] K. Langenbucher, in: Langenbucher (ed.), *Europäisches Privat- und Wirtschaftsrecht*, § 1 para. 8.
[61] K.-D. Borchardt, in: Schulze et al. (eds.), *Europarecht*, § 15 para. 36.
[62] Therefore contextual and teleological interpretation are not always treated as different approaches, but seen as one (contextual-teleological interpretation). In this sense: K.-D. Borchardt, in: Schulze et al. (eds.), *Europarecht*, § 15 para. 45.
[63] R. Bieber et al.(eds.), *Die Europäische Union*, § 9 para. 16; T. Oppermann et al., *Europarecht*, § 9 para. 172.
[64] T. Oppermann et al. (eds.), *Europarecht*, § 9 para. 172.
[65] Cf. Case 155/73 (*Sacchi*), para. 7–8; Case 22/70 (*Commission/Council*), para. 12; cf. also M. Pechstein and C. Drechsler, in: Riesenhuber (ed.), *Europäische Methodenlehre*, § 7 para. 22 ff.
[66] In more detail below R. Veil § 38 para. 5.

For the interpretation of the term 'decision', it is therefore appropriate to take into account the interpretations of the market abuse regime regarding the obligation to publish inside information in accordance with Article 17 MAR. It must be taken into account that a circumstance which may occur in the future may also be subject to disclosure.[67] The conclusion regarding the contextual interpretation of the term 'decision' would be that a decision to make a bid within the meaning of the Takeover Directive may already exist if it has not yet been made in a legally binding manner due to the lack of approval by a company body, provided that it is sufficiently probable.[68]

A contextual interpretation can also be of help when a directive or a regulation makes use of a certain term without defining it. Whilst the Commission now mostly defines the relevant terms in the implementing measures on Level 2 of the Lamfalussy Process, it is not possible to provide accompanying definitions for every term. In these cases, a reference to another directive may be of help. Ideally, it may contain a definition itself or at least one may refer to the academic discussion regarding the interpretation of the term.

33

Example: According to the TD, notification requirements concerning the acquisition or disposal of major holdings of voting rights also depend on the voting rights attached to shares which are held by a 'controlled undertaking'. The 'controlled undertaking' is defined in Article 2(1)(f) of the TD, which, however, does not clarify what is to be classed as an 'undertaking'. Therefore, the interpretation of the term 'undertaking' in European accounting law can be evaluated on how to interpret the term in the TD.[69]

34

(cc) Historical Interpretation

For various reasons the interpretation of a provision according to its history is less important in primary law.[70] The main problem is that it will often be difficult to determine the underlying concept the legislature followed.[71] With regard to secondary legislation, historical interpretation is more fruitful.[72] The intentions of the legislative bodies involved in the legislative procedure can be deduced from the **recitals** of the **legislative act**.[73]

35

Example: In the judgment regarding the above-mentioned *Spector* case the ECJ justified its interpretation of the prohibition on insider dealing with the fact that the European legislature's aim in enacting the MAD 2003 was to fill gaps left by the old Directive on insider dealing. Because the Commission had originally submitted a different proposal during the legislative process, the ECJ assumed that the European Parliament favoured an objective approach regarding the notion of insider dealing without any element of purpose or intent.[74]

36

Historical interpretation is facilitated by the fact that the **European Commission** publishes **proposals** and impact assessments by its staff (**Commissions Staff Working**

37

---

[67] See R. Veil § 14 para. 37 and R. Veil § 19 para. 30.
[68] This does not, however, mean that the application will be based on this interpretation of the provision, as historical or teleological aspects may lead to a different result.
[69] On the problems of interpretation see R. Veil § 20 para. 78.
[70] Cf. T. Oppermann et al., *Europarecht*, § 9 para. 174.
[71] Cf. K. Langenbucher, in: Langenbucher (ed.), *Europarechtliche Bezüge des Privatrechts*, § 1 para. 12.
[72] Cf. Case C-540/03 (*Parliament/Council*), para. 38; Case C-104/01 (*Libertel/Benelux-Merkenbureau*).
[73] Cf. the ECJ's legislation in other areas of law: Case C-355/95P (*TWD*). Cf. K.-D. Borchardt, in: Schulze et al. (eds.), *Europarecht*, § 15 para. 44; and specifically on capital markets law: S. Kalss et al., *Kapitalmarktrecht I*, § 1 para. 99.
[74] Cf. Case C-45/08 (*Spector*), para. 33–34.

Documents) on the legislative acts. These contain general remarks, explain the underlying concepts regarding individual provisions and discuss regulatory alternatives (**Impact Assessments**). The **European Parliament** submits its opinion on these drafts, thus provides insights in its positions.

38 In addition, ESMA publishes various papers (Discussion Papers and Consultation Papers) and reports to the Commission on the proposed RTS/ITS which can also help with the interpretation. ESMA's **Technical Advice** to the Commission on the implementing measures answers questions that may arise when applying the draft's provisions. However, it depends on the individual case whether the technical advice can be used for the interpretation of the provisions enacted by the Commission. It may indicate why an original draft or individual provisions of such were later rejected and replaced by a different provision.

39 *Example*: In the Lafonta case, the ECJ ruled that in order for information to be classified as precise, it need not be possible to infer from that information, with a sufficient degree of probability, that, once it is made public, its potential effect on the prices of the financial instruments concerned will be in a particular direction. In order to substantiate this interpretation, the ECJ relied, inter alia, on the genesis of MAD 2003 and analysed a paper by CESR: 'It should also be noted in that context that the travaux préparatoires for Directive 2003/124 disclose that a reference to the possibility of drawing a conclusion as regards the "direction" of the effect of the information on the price of the financial instruments concerned, made in the version, subject to public consultation, of technical advice CESR/02-089d issued in December 2002 by the Committee of European Securities Regulators (CESR), for the European Commission and entitled "CESR's Advice on Level 2 Implementing Measures for the proposed Market Abuse Directive", was later deleted precisely in order to avoid such a reference being used as a pretext for not making information public.'[75]

(dd) Teleological Interpretation

40 The teleological approach has a central role in the principles of statutory interpretation in Europe. Determining the **spirit** and **purpose** of **a provision** is often facilitated by the **recitals** preceding directives and regulations, even in level 2 acts. Whilst most legislation in the field of capital markets law simply sums up the general aims of market efficiency and investor protection,[76] in some cases the purpose of the legislative act is actually described in more detail, enabling a clear teleological answer to the question of interpretation.[77]

41 *Example*: In the aforementioned *Spector* case the ECJ deducted from recitals 2 and 12 that the directive prohibited insider dealings in order to ensure the integrity of Community financial markets and enhancing investor confidence in those markets, a confidence which depends, inter alia, on investors being placed on an equal footing and protected against the improper use of inside information (para. 47). The Court then explained that recitals 18, 19 and 30 of the directive provided several examples of situations in which the fact that a primary insider in possession of inside information entered into a transaction on the market could not in itself constitute 'use of inside information' for the purposes of Article 2(1) of the Directive (para. 56).

---

[75] Cf. Case C-628/13 (*Lafonta*), para. 37.
[76] See R. Veil § 2 para. 9.
[77] Cf. also S. Kalss et al., *Kapitalmarktrecht I*, § 1 para. 100.

Example: In the *Geltl/Daimler* case, the ECJ concluded that information concerning an 42
intermediate step in a protracted process could constitute precise information under Union law.
The Court argued that it would follow from recitals 2 and 12 of the MAD 2003 that the directive
is intended to ensure the integrity of financial markets and to strengthen investor confidence in
those markets. That confidence depends on, inter alia, investors being placed on an equal footing and protected against the improper use of insider information. These regulatory objectives
are jeopardised if intermediate steps in a protracted process cannot constitute inside information
(para. 35). Certain parties who possessed inside information could be in an advantageous position
vis-à-vis other investors and be able to profit from that information, to the detriment of those
who are unaware of it (para. 36).

For teleological interpretation, two further aspects are important. Firstly, it must be taken 43
into account that capital market regulation is based on findings of **capital market theory**.
The regimes for secondary markets are based on the Efficient Capital Market Hypothesis
(ECMH). Thus, information is price-relevant if it concerns the fundamental value of a
security. Findings of capital market theory can be used in particular for the interpretation
of undefined legal terms, such as the concept of the reasonable investor. Secondly, for the
teleological interpretation, it should be considered that European capitals market law also
aims at ensuring legal certainty. This explains why the legal acts adopted at Level 1 of the
Lamfalussy procedure are put into concrete terms by numerous legal acts adopted at Level 2.
The ECJ takes this regulatory objective into account in its interpretation.

Example: In the *Geltl/Daimler* case, the ECJ found that, according to its third recital, Directive 44
2003/124 was intended to increase legal certainty for participants in the financial markets
(para. 28). In order to ensure such legal certainty for market participants, including issuers, information on circumstances and events which are not likely to occur cannot be classified as precise
information. Otherwise, issuers could believe that they are obliged to disclose information which
is not precise or which is not likely to influence the price of their financial instruments (para. 48).

Finally, the ECJ, when interpreting a provision in accordance with its spirit and purpose, 45
takes into account the *effet utile*.[78] This principle describes the obligation to interpret a provision in such a way that it unfolds the largest possible effectiveness and benefit. The *effet
utile* has the function of optimising the interpretation of the Treaties and all other European
provisions.[79] In its decisions on capital markets law issues, the ECJ has not yet explicitly
applied the *effet utile* principle. However, the ECJ could rely on it if the court is confronted
with the question whether the regulations under capital markets law grant investors the
right to claim damages from other financial market participants.

Example: In the *Muñoz* case, the ECJ considered whether provisions of a regulation of the EC on 46
quality standards for fruit and vegetables confer the right on an individual to bring an action to
compel another individual to comply with the obligations imposed on him by the Community
legislation.[80] The court argued, 'regulations have general application and are directly applicable in

---

[78] Cf. Case C-792/79 (*Camera Care*), para. 17–18; Case C-246/80 (*Broekmeulen*), para. 16; Cases C-6/90 and C-9/90 (*Francovich*), para. 32.
[79] K. Langenbucher, in: Langenbucher (ed.), *Europäisches Privat-und Wirtschaftsrecht*, § 1 para. 34; M. Pechstein and C. Drechsler, in: Riesenhuber (ed.), *Europäische Methodenlehre*, § 7 para 30.
[80] Case C-253/00.

all Member States. Accordingly, owing to their very nature and their place in the system of sources of Community law, regulations operate to confer rights on individuals which the national courts have a duty to protect' (para. 27). 'Accordingly, the full effectiveness of the rules on quality standards and, in particular, the practical effect of the obligation […] imply that it must be possible to enforce that obligation by means of civil proceedings instituted by a trader against a competitor' (para. 30). 'The possibility of bringing such proceedings strengthens the practical working of the Community rules on quality standards. As a supplement to the action of the authorities designated by the Member States to make the checks required by those rules it helps to discourage practices, often difficult to detect, which distort competition. In that context actions brought before the national courts by competing operators are particularly suited to contributing substantially to ensuring fair trading and transparency of markets in the Community' (para. 31).

47 Most of the Single Rulebooks do not contain provisions on the protection of investors through private enforcement. This applies in particular to the MAR rules on market manipulation and the incorrect publication of inside information. According to the regulatory concept of the MAR, the enforcement of prohibitions and disclosure obligations is to be carried out by national supervisory authorities and criminal courts. Nevertheless, it is discussed in literature that, according to the principles laid down in the *Muñoz* judgment, a right of action by investors should be recognised because it would strengthen the enforcement power of the MAR rules adopted in the interest of investors.[81]

III. National Law of the Member States

48 National law is still of great importance despite the extensive EU legislation. This can be explained, on the one hand, by the fact that EU regulations, too, do not always provide for prescriptive rules, but rather regulatory mandates to the Member States. These concern in particular the supervisory powers and sanctions imposed by supervisory authorities and criminal courts. Since the regulations and directives aim at minimum harmonisation in this respect, the legal situation may differ in the Member States. On the other hand, private law is not harmonised. The respective regimes in these Member States cannot be dealt with in this book. However, the national laws which implement European directives are mentioned. In addition, reference is made to interpretations by national supervisory authorities, as these guidelines continue to play an important role in practice alongside the guidelines and Q&A papers of ESMA.

1. Austria

49 The Austrian capital markets law is laid down in a number of statutes, the most important of which are the **Börsegesetz** (BörseG—Stock Exchange Act), the **Kapitalmarktgesetz** (KMG—Capital Market Act), **Wertpapieraufsichtsgesetz**

---

[81] See R. Veil § 12 para. 24.

(WAG—Securities Supervision Act), the **Übernahmegesetz** (ÜbG—Takeover Act) and the Finanzmarktaufsichtsbehördengesetz (FMABG—Financial Market Supervisory Authority Act). The main provisions on transparency, such as the disclosure of major holdings and the disclosure of financial reports can be found in the BörseG. The KMG mainly contains rules on the public offering of investments, to which European securities prospectus law does not apply. Statutes such as the Investmentfondsgesetz and the Beteiligungsfondsgesetz concern connected fields of law and also address a number of questions on capital markets law, especially on issuing, offering and managing financial instruments such as bonds and participation certificates.[82]

The supervisory authority FMA issues interpretative guidance to market participants.[83] These only aim to inform issuers, investors and other market participants of the interpretation of certain requirements, as can be deduced from the respective provisions of the statutes and regulations. They are therefore not legally binding.[84]

2. France

In France, the most important source of capital markets law can be found in the statutes, especially in the **Code monétaire et financier** (C. mon. fin., the French Monetary and Financial Code).[85] This law contains six chapters (*livres*) on money, products, services, markets, investment firms and banking and financial institutions.[86] Transparency of shareholdings, like all company law, is regulated by the Code de commerce, the French Commercial Code. In practice, the RG AMF (General Regulations of the French supervisory authority),[87] which were enacted by the Autorité des marchés financiers (AMF—French stock market supervisory authority) and countersigned by the Minister for Economic Affairs, is of particular importance.[88]

The statutes are supplemented by various regulations (*ordonnances*), which refer directly to the individual statutory provisions. If the statutory article is 'Art. L. ... C. mon. fin.', for example, the respective regulatory article will be named 'Art. R. ... C. mon. fin.'. These *ordonnances* play an important role in France. This is often seen critically, the provisions not always being of a technical nature and lacking the legislative materials which accompany statutory provisions and facilitate interpretation.[89] In an official procedure, the so-called *rescrit*, the AMF can present its interpretation of its *règlement général* and grant exemptions

---

[82] Cf. S. Kalss et al., *Kapitalmarktrecht I*, § 1 para. 94.
[83] These legal acts are available in English at: www.fma.gv.at/en/fma/fma-circulars/.
[84] Cf. S. Kalss et al., *Kapitalmarktrecht I*, § 2 para. 41.
[85] Cf. Couret et al., *Droit financier*, para. 29: 'source majeure'.
[86] Textbooks and handbooks for practitioners cover the entire spectrum of the act. Cf. Couret et al. (eds.), *Droit financier*; Bonneau et al. (eds.), *Droit financier*; Merville, *Droit Financier*.
[87] The French sources of law are available—partly in English—at: www.legifrance.gouv.fr. However, not all of the unofficial translations are up to date. The Règlement général can be found on the website of the AMF (www.amf-france.org) in French and in English.
[88] Cf. Art. L. 621-6 C. mon. fin.
[89] Cf. Y. Paclot, Bull. Joly Bourse (2009), 59.

from certain obligations.[90] The AMF also publishes instructions and recommendations which render the *règlement général* more precise.[91] Finally, the AMF publishes various forms of statements (*avis, principes généraux, notes, guides, vade-mecum, communiqués, recommendations, communications du collège ou des services, positions*).[92]

3. Germany

53 The main sources of capital markets law in Germany are the Börsengesetz (BörsG—Stock Exchange Act), the Wertpapierprospektgesetz (WpPG—Securities Prospectus Act), the Vermögensanlagegesetz (VermAnlG—Investment Act), the **Wertpapierhandelsgesetz** (WpHG—Securities Trading Act) and the Wertpapiererwerbs- und Übernahmegesetz (WpÜG—Securities Acquisition and Takeover Act).[93] Of these parliamentary acts, the WpHG continues to play a central role, it regulates the tasks and powers of BaFin, transposes MiFID II and the TD and contains administrative and criminal sanctions. The BörsG now only contains provisions on the organisation of stock exchanges, the admission of financial instruments to trading on the stock exchange and the determination of stock exchange prices. The BörsG previously also contained rules on the approval and publication of prospectuses for securities. These rules are now largely covered by the PR. The WpPG therefore only contains the rules on the liability for securities prospectuses and the powers of the supervisory authority. In addition, the Federal Ministry of Finance (BMF) has issued ordinances to concretise the legal provisions of parliamentary acts.

54 BaFin publishes notices on the application and interpretation of the most important provisions. These may take on the form of bulletins, newsletters or statements and have the legal nature of a simple administrative act without a regulatory content, only aiming to communicate the authority's understanding of certain provisions.[94] The objective of the *Emittentenleitfaden* (issuer guideline)[95] is to offer practical help with the provisions on securities trading law, without constituting a legal annotation. It is to aid the access to this field of law and clarify the BaFin's regulatory practice. The *Emittentenleitfaden* is legally non-binding and must be understood as an interpretative administrative provision[96] which may only have the effect of binding the BaFin internally.[97] The courts are not bound by

---

[90] Cf. Art. 121-1 ff. RG AMF; A. Couret et al., *Droit financier*, para. 356.

[91] A. Couret et al., *Droit financier*, para. 355: '*ces actes n'ont pas une pleine valeur juridique*'.

[92] Cf. Art. L. 621-6 C. mon. fin.

[93] The relevant versions of all statutes and regulations can be found on the website of the German Federal Ministry of Justice (www.gesetze-im-internet.de). English translations of the WpHG and the WpÜG are available on the BaFin's website (www.bafin.de).

[94] Cf. VGH Kassel of 31.05.2006 – 6 UE 3256/05, WM (2007), 382, 393; D. Döhmel, in: Assmann et al. (eds.), *Kommentar zum Wertpapierhandelsrecht*, § 6 WpHG para. 28.

[95] The *Emittentenleitfaden* (issuer guideline) is available on the BaFin's website (www.bafin.de). An English version is also available for information purposes.

[96] Cf. BGH of 25.02.2008 – II ZB 9/07, 29 ZIP (2008), 639, 641.

[97] P. Mennicke, in: Fuchs (ed.), *Kommentar zum WpHG*, Vor §§ 12–14 para. 40; A. Meyer, in: Kümpel et al. (eds.), *Bank- und Kapitalmarktrecht*, para. 12.131.

the BaFin's interpretation. The BaFin may exempt from certain obligations, which has particular relevance in takeover law where the BaFin can exempt the offeror from the duty to publish and make an offer.[98]

4. Greece

Capital market legislation in Greece is divided into several laws.[99] The most important are Law 4514/2018 (FEK A 14/30.01.2018), which implements MiFID II, Law 3556/2007 (FEK A 91/30.04.2007), which transposes the TD into Greek law, and Law 3461/2006 (FEK A 106/30.05.2006), which implements the TOD. Other aspects relating to listings are regulated by Law No 3371/2005 (FEK A 178/14.07.2005). Furthermore, Law No 4443/2016 (FEK A 232/9.12.2016) transposes the CRIM-MAD into Greek law and provides for administrative sanctions in relation to market abuse. Law No 3401/2005 on prospectuses for securities takes into account the unification of the regime through the PR and today mainly regulates the liability for prospectuses.

The Greek supervisory authority, the Hellenic Capital Markets Commission (HCMC), has the power to regulate certain aspects of capital markets legislation in a legally binding manner.[100] In addition, HCMC publishes circulars that comment on interpretative issues and explain the applicability of certain laws. HCMC also provides guidelines and recommendations (not legally binding) to intermediaries and listed companies.

5. Italy

Italy also enacted a statute for the most relevant provisions on capital markets law: the **Testo Unico della Finanza** (TUF—Italian Consolidated Laws on Finance).[101] The TUF contains six parts on (i) general provisions, (ii) intermediaries, (iii) systematic internalisers, (iv) issuers, (v) sanctions and (vi) transitional provisions, which mainly implement the European directives and regulatory mandates of the regulations. The TUF authorises the supervisory authority, Consob, to enact regulations (*regolamenti*) together with or without the Banca d'Italia. The three main regulations are the **Regolamento Emittenti** (Italian Issuers' Regulation) for issuers, the **Regolamento Dei Mercati E Relative Istruzioni** (Italian Financial Markets Regulation) for the markets and the **Regolamento Intermediari** (Italian Regulation on Intermediaries) for financial intermediaries.

The *comunicazione* (communications) published by the supervisory authority Consob constitute another level of regulation. They refer to specific legal problems which have

---

[98] BaFin may also, upon written application, permit voting rights from shares in the target company to remain unconsidered when calculating the percentage of voting rights, cf. § 36 WpÜG.
[99] The laws, regulations and ministerial decisions are published on the National Printing Office website, cf. http://www.et.gr/. The capital market regulations are also available on HCMC's website (http://www.hcmc.gr/).
[100] V. Tountopoulos, *Capital Market Law*, 148.
[101] Testo Unico della Finanza (TUF) Decreto legislativo (D.Lgs) del 24 febbraio 1998, n. 58. An English version is available at CONSOB's website (www.consob.it/mainen/index.html?mode=gfx under 'legal framework').

been presented to Consob by market participants. Whilst the *comunicazione* are not legally binding, it must generally be assumed that Consob will take enforcement measures if the provisions of the *comunicazione* are not abided by in a later, similar case. In reality, a *comunicazione* is therefore binding. The *comunicazione* will not, however, describe all the circumstances of the case to which it refers. Rather, it will often only contain the answers to the legal problem presented, making it difficult to determine whether the case at hand is sufficiently similar to the one treated in the *comunicazione*.

6. Spain

59 In Spain, parliamentary acts constitute the 'apex of the pyramid' concerning sources of capital markets law.[102] These are followed by the so-called RD (Royal Decree), a form of statutory regulation enacted by the government, and the *Orden*, enacted by the ministries and identifiable by their number and the abbreviation of the issuing ministry. In capital markets law this will mostly be the Ministerio de Economía y Hacienda (EHA), ie the Ministry of Economy and Finance. Circulars, enacted by the Spanish national securities markets commission—the CNMV—and published in the official gazette, constitute the base of this pyramid.

60 The **Ley 24/1988**, de 28 de julio, **del Mercado de Valores** (LMV) is the most important Spanish law on capital markets, which largely transposes EU directives. As a framework law it is restricted to the more general provisions, which are then substantiated by regulations. The LMV has priority over the Ley de Sociedades Anónimas (LSA—Spanish Stock Corporation Act), and the Reglamento del Registro Mercantil (RRM—Spanish Regulation on Company Registries).[103]

7. Sweden

61 In Sweden the main sources of capital markets law are parliamentary acts (*lagar*), government regulations (*förordningar*) and regulations enacted by the Finansinspektionen (*föreskrifter*).[104] All parliamentary statutes and governmental regulations since 1825[105] are compiled in the official Swedish Code of Statutes (SFS).[106] Statutes and regulations therein are sorted by the year of their enactment, followed by a consecutive numbering for all legislative acts of the respective year. The citation 'SFS 2005:551', for example, refers to legislative act 551 from 2005. Swedish statutes are divided into chapters which are then

---

[102] All Spanish statutes can be found in Spanish on the internet page of the official gazette, the Boletín Oficial del Estado, available at: www.boe.es and at www.noticias.juridicas.com. The internet page of the Spanish supervisory authority CNMV, available at: www.cnmv.es, which has English translations of some of the statutes, may also be of interest.
[103] Cf. A. Tapia Hermida, *Derecho del Mercado de Valores*, 64.
[104] In more detail R. Veil and F. Walla, *Schwedisches Kapitalmarktrecht*, 5 ff.
[105] L. Carlson, *Fundamentals of Swedish Law*, 38.
[106] All statutes and governmental regulations are available in Swedish on the website of the Swedish parliament (*Sveriges Riksdag*). Cf. www.riksdagen.se/.

subdivided into sections—shorter statutes only making use of the latter. In this book, the method of quotation for Swedish statutes has been adapted to the more common style, ie the section symbol (§) and the term for chapter (*kapitel*) precede the number, whereas Sweden generally uses the reverse order (eg Kapitel 29, § 1 ABL instead of the Swedish 29 Kapitel, 1 § ABL).

Most provisions on capital markets law can be found in the **Lag om handel med finansiella instrument** (LHF—Swedish Act on the Trading with Financial Instruments, SFS 1991:980) and in the **lag om värdepappersmarknaden** (LVM—Securities Market Act, SFS 2007:528) which as of 1 November 2007 replaced the Lag om börsoch clearingverksamhet (Act on Stock Markets and Clearing, SFS 1992:543) and the Lag om värdepappersrörelse (Act on Securities Transactions, SFS 1991:981). The LHF contains rules on public takeover bids, disclosure of shareholdings and supervisory powers of Finansinspektionen. The LVM provides for conduct of business rules for financial intermediaries and rule on the supervisory powers of Finansinspektionen with regard to operators of regulated markets and investment firms. An additional relevant statute in the field of capital markets law was (until the application of the MAR) the **Lag om straff för marknadsmissbruk vid handel med finansiella instrument** (Market Abuse Act, SFS 2005:377) which prohibited market manipulation and insider dealings. It now only provides for criminal penalties for market manipulation and insider dealing. The **lag om offentliga uppköpserbjudanden på aktiemarknaden** (SFS 2006:451; Takeover Act) regulates certain aspects of public takeover bids, such as obligations of the bidder and defensive measures. The parliamentary acts are often complemented by regulations enacted by the government or the supervisory authority. Recommendations published by the self-regulation committees also played an important role in Swedish capital markets law.[107]

8. United Kingdom

With Brexit, the United Kingdom is no longer part of the EU. This also has an impact on the legal sources for capital markets law. The United Kingdom no longer needs to apply European regulations and is no longer obliged to implement European directives. However, the national laws are largely in line with the European regimes.

The **Financial Services and Markets Act 2000** (FSMA) is the most important law for capital markets, although European post-crisis legislation had the effect that it no longer covered key aspects such as market abuse. Brexit has allowed the UK to take capital market regulation back into its own hands. However, this has not happened. Instead, the UK has created laws that declare the European legislative acts authoritative and provide for supplementary, largely technical provisions. Of particular importance for securities regulation are **The Market Abuse (Amendment) (EU Exit) Regulations 2019** and **The Official Listing of Securities, Prospectus and Transparency (Amendment etc.) (EU Exit) Regulations 2019**.

---

[107] See in detail R. Veil and F. Walla, *Schwedisches Kapitalmarktrecht*, 12 ff.

65 The rules issued by the supervisory authorities are also of outstanding importance for practice. Since the reorganisation of financial market supervision in 2013,[108] there are two handbooks with legally binding regulations: the Handbook of the Financial Conduct Authority (FCA Handbook) and the Handbook of the Prudential Regulation Authority (PRA Handbook).[109] The third source of law to be considered is common law. It is particularly important at the level of law.

66 The **FCA Handbook** is essential for legal practice. It is divided into 10 blocks and a glossary which defines several legal terms. It is preceded by the so-called 'High Level Standards', such as Principles for Business (PRIN), a Code of Conduct and Statements of Principle and Code of Practice for Approved Persons (APER). The seventh chapter contains (in implementation of European requirements) the Listing and Prospectus Rules. The PRA Handbook has a similar structure. It contains rules for CRR-firms, Non-CRR-firms, SII Firms, Non-SII Firms and non-authorised persons.

67 Legally binding rules are marked in the Handbook with an 'R', whilst sections marked with a 'G' are only a guidance to aid interpretation and indicate the FCA's legal understanding.[110] The FCA Handbook further contains a number of so-called evidential rules which provide a legal presumption on the interpretation of the respective provision. Provisions marked with a 'C' indicate safe-harbour rules.[111]

---

[108] See F. Walla § 11 para. 21.
[109] Cf. R. Purves, in: Walker/Purves/Blair (eds.), *Financial Services Law*, para. 5.01 ff.
[110] On the legal effects of this interpretational guidance cf. M. Threipland, in: Blair (ed.), *Blackstone's Guide to the Financial Services and Markets Act 2000*, 140–141.
[111] Cf. GEN 2.2 FCA Handbook.

§ 6

Intra- and Interdisciplinarity

Bibliography

Annunziata, Filippo, *Behavioural Finance and Market Efficiency: Is There a Dialogue? A preliminary Reflection on Regulation 596/2014/EU*, 5 Law and Economics Review (2016), 280–308; Barber, Brad and Odean, Terrance, *Boys Will Be Boys*, QJ Econ. (2001), 261–292; Becker, Gary S., *Der ökonomische Ansatz zur Erklärung menschlichen Verhaltens* (1982); Berle, Adolf A. and Means, Gardiner C., *The Modern Corporation and Private Property* (1933); Buck-Heeb, Petra, *Vom Kapitalanleger- zum Verbraucherschutz*, 176 ZHR (2012), 66–95; Bumke, Christian, *Regulierung am Beispiel der Kapitalmärkte*, in: Hopt, Klaus J. et al. (eds.), *Kapitalmarktgesetzgebung im Europäischen Binnenmarkt* (2008), 107–141; Cahn, Andreas, *Grenzen des Markt- und Anlegerschutzes durch das WpHG*, 162 ZHR (1998), 1–50; Choi, Stephen, *Regulating Investors not Issuers: A Market-Based Proposal*, 88 California Law Review (2000), 279–334; Choi, Stephen and Pritchard, Adam, *Behavioral Economics and the SEC*, 56 Stanford Law Review (2003), 1–74; Eidenmüller, Horst, *Der homo oeconomicus und das Schuldrecht: Herausforderungen durch Behavioral Law and Economics*, 60 JZ (2005), 216–224; Findeisen, Maximilian, *Über die Regulierung und die Rechtsfolgen von Interessenkonflikten in der Aktienanalyse von Investmentbanken* (2007); Fischhoff, Baruch, et al., *Knowing with Certainty: The Appropriateness of Extreme Confidence*, 3 J. Exp. Psychol., Hum. Perception & Performance (1977), 552–564; Fleischer, Holger, *Behavioral Law and Economics im Gesellschafts- und Kapitalmarktrecht—Ein Werkstattbericht*, in: Fuchs, Andreas et al. (eds.), *Festschrift für Ulrich Immenga* (2004), 575–588; Fleischer, Holger, *Empfiehlt es sich, im Interesse des Anlegerschutzes und zur Förderung des Finanzplatzes Deutschland, das Kapitalmarkt- und Börsenrecht neu zu regeln?*, Gutachten F zum 64. Deutschen Juristentag (2002); Fleischer, Holger et al., *Verhaltensökonomik als Forschungsinstrument für das Wirtschaftsrecht*, in: Fleischer, Holger and Zimmer, Daniel (eds.), *Beitrag der Verhaltensökonomie (Behavioral Economics) zum Handels- und Wirtschaftsrecht*, 75 ZHR Beiheft (2011), 10–62; Forschner, Julius, *Wechselwirkungen von Aufsichtsrecht und Zivilrecht* (2013); Furubotn, Eirik G. and Richter, Rudolf, *Neue Institutionsökonomik*, 4th edn. (2010); Göres, Ulrich L., *Interessenkonflikte von Wertpapierdienstleistern und -analysten bei der Wertpapieranalyse* (2004); Hackethal, Andreas and Meyer, Steffen, *Grenzen des Informationsmodells im Anlegerschutz — Lösungsansätze aus empirisch ökonomischer Sicht*, 113 ZVglRWiss (2014), 574–585; Hens, Thorsten and Rieger, Marc O., *Financial Economics*, 2nd edn. (2016); Kahneman, Daniel and Tversky, Amos, *Prospect Theory: An Analysis of Decision under Risk*, 47 Econometrica (1979), 263–292; Kahneman, Daniel, et al., *Fairness and the Assumptions of Economics*, 59 J. Bus. (1986), 285–300; Kalss, Susanne et al. (eds.), *Kapitalmarktrecht I: System*, 2nd edn. (2015); Kamin, Kim A. and Rachlinski, Jeffrey J., *Ex Post Ex Ante: Determining Liability in Hindsight*, 19 Law & Hum. Behav. (1995), 89–104; Kirchgässner, Gebhard, *Homo Oeconomicus*, 4th edn. (2013); Klöhn, Lars, *Der Beitrag der Verhaltensökonomik zum Kapitalmarktrecht*, in: Fleischer, Holger and Zimmer, Daniel (eds.), *Beitrag der Verhaltensökonomie (Behavioral Economics) zum Handels- und Wirtschaftsrecht*, 75 ZHR Beiheft (2011), 83–99; Klöhn, Lars, *Kapitalmarkt, Spekulation und Behavioral Finance* (2006); Klöhn, Lars, *Marktmissbrauchsverordnung: MAR* (2018); Link, Roger and Obst, Holger, *Finanzberichterstattung im Umbruch - vom Disclosure Overload zurück zur entscheidungsrelevanten Information?*, BB (2015),

2859–2863; MacNeil, Ian G., *An Introduction to The Law on Financial Investment*, 2nd edn. (2012); Meyer, Andreas et al. (eds.), *Handbuch zum Marktmissbrauchsrecht* (2018); Möllers, Thomas M. J. and Kernchen, Eva, *Information Overload am Kapitalmarkt*, 40 ZGR (2011), 1–26; Möllers, Thomas M. J., *Europäische Gesetzgebungslehre 2.0: Die dynamische Rechtsharmonisierung im Kapitalmarktrecht am Beispiel von MiFID II und PRIIP*, 24 ZEuP (2016), 325–357; Mülbert, Peter and Sajnovits, Alexander, *Insiderrecht und Ad-hoc-Publizität im anbrechenden ESG-Zeitalter*, 74 WM (2020), 1557–1567; Odean, Terrance, *Volume, Volatility, Price, and Profit. When All Traders Are Above Average*, 53 J. Fin. (1998), 1887–1934; Schwark, Eberhard et al. (eds.), *Kapitalmarktrechts-Kommentar*, 5th edn. (2020); Segna, Ulrich, *Die sog. gespaltene Rechtsanwendung im Kapitalmarktrecht*, 44 ZGR (2015), 84–123; Shefrin, Hersh, *Beyond Greed and Fear: Understanding Behavioral Finance and the Psychology of Investing* (2007); Shiller, Robert, *Irrational Exuberance*, 3rd edn. (2016); Shleifer, Andrei, *Inefficient Markets: An Introduction to Behavioral Finance* (2000); Skeel, David A., *The New Financial Deal: Understanding the Dodd-Frank Act and its (Unintended) Consequences* (2011); Stahl, Carolin, *Information Overload am Kapitalmarkt* (2013); Sunstein, Cass R., *What's Available? Social Influences and Behavioral Economics*, 97 Nw. Univ. L. Rev. (2003), 1295–1314; Sunstein, Cass R. and Thaler, Richard H., *Libertarian Paternalism is not an Oxymoron*, 70 The University of Chicago Law Review (2003), 1159–1202; Svenson, Ola, *Are We All Less Risky and More Skillful than Our Fellow Drivers?*, 77 Acta Psychologica (1981), 143–148; Teigelack, Lars, *Finanzanalysen und Behavioral Finance* (2009); Tversky, Amos and Kahneman, Daniel, *Judgement under Uncertainty: Heuristics and Biases*, 185 Science (1974), 1124–1131; Veil, Rüdiger, *Der Schutz des verständigen Anlegers durch Publizität und Haftung im europäischen und nationalen Kapitalmarktrecht*, 18 ZBB (2006), 162–171; Veil, Rüdiger, *Enforcement of Capital Markets Law in Europe—Observations from a Civil Law Country*, 11 EBOR (2010), 409–422; Veil, Rüdiger, *Regulierung von Finanzprodukten. Abschied vom Leitbild des verständigen Investors?*, in: Bumke, Christian and Röthel, Anne (eds.), *Autonomie im Recht* (2017), 185–200; Ventoruzzo, Marco and Mock Sebastian, *Market Abuse Regulation: Commentary and Annotated Guide* (2017); Zimmer, Daniel, *Vom Informationsmodell zu Behavioral Finance: Brauchen wir „Ampeln" oder Produktverbote für Finanzanlagen?*, 69 JZ (2014), 714–721.

I. Introduction

1   In most Member States, capital markets law only became an independent field of law with the implementation of European directives.[1] Subsequent EU regulations (instead of directives) have led to a high degree of harmonisation of supervisory law.[2] The European regimes are influenced by the **US Securities Regulation**. 30 years earlier than the European legislature made its first tentative steps the U.S. federal legislature regulated securities markets.[3] U.S. law continues to provide important impulses for reforms in Europe. The Level 1 directives enacted 2003/2004 are largely based on the example of the Securities Regulation in the United States. The post crisis regulatory efforts in the time between 2008 and 2015 also take into account the developments in the United States. Legal research in this area thus requires a comparative approach.

---

[1] On the history of European capital markets legislation see R. Veil § 1 para. 5 ff.
[2] See R. Veil § 1 para. 64.
[3] Cf. A. Berle and G. Means, *The Modern Corporation and Private Property*, 255 ff. (explaining already in 1933 the importance of capital markets for the economy and the necessity for a regulation).

International research is confronted with a number of difficulties resulting from the 2
intradisciplinary character of capital markets law. Whilst on the one hand it must be characterised as public law and is sanctioned by measures under administrative and **criminal law**, it also affects relationships between private parties (such as an issuer and an investor), thus also presenting the civil courts with the necessity to apply supervisory law or at least take it into account. The European regimes are therefore relevant in **private law**. In addition, capital markets law is closely linked to accounting, corporate and insolvency law.

Additionally, unlike any other field of law, capital markets law requires an **interdisciplinary** 3
view on legal concepts. The provisions regarding the disclosure of relevant information and the continuing legislative activities at both the European and national level, expanding disclosure obligations for issuers and financial intermediaries, could not be explained without the findings of economics, in particular the efficient capital market hypothesis (ECMH). The ECMH and the reasons for a mandatory disclosure regime are described in more detail in other sections of this book.[4] This chapter rather discusses the fundamental question whether capital markets regimes are based on the model of a *homo oeconomicus* or whether they should follow the findings of empirical research and behavioural finance.

II. Intradisciplinarity

1. Legal Nature

(a) Interaction of Supervisory and Private Law

One of the central goals of capital markets law is to ensure the proper functioning of capital 4
markets.[5] The regimes are established in the public interest. Public authorities supervise market participants and exercise sovereign powers. This can be seen, for example, in the national authorities' power to supervise compliance with rules provided in the national and European capital markets acts.[6] Thus, capital markets law is classed as an area of **public law**, the supervisory **authorities** being granted **administrative powers**: all Member States permit their supervisory authorities to adopt administrative measures, such as a correction of false or misleading disclosed information, a temporary prohibition of an unlawful activity, a suspension of trading of financial instruments or other acts, in order to ensure the proper functioning of markets.

The **sanctions** are of an **administrative** nature; most breaches of rules are sanctioned with 5
administrative fines and the most serious infringements even criminally with imprisonment. Whilst the European legislative acts initially did not require rules on criminal sanctions to

---

[4] See in detail R. Veil § 2 para. 29 and H. Brinckmann § 16 para. 4–13.
[5] See R. Veil § 2 para. 7.
[6] Capital markets law is therefore characterised as supervisory law. See R. Veil § 2 para. 5 and F. Walla. § 4 para. 1.

be introduced by the Member States,[7] the CRIM-MAD meanwhile harmonises the national laws by requiring the Member States to provide criminal sanctions for violations of the rules on insider dealings and market manipulation. Furthermore, the post crisis regulation in the EU has harmonised administrative sanctions. Thus all jurisdictions in the EU provide the imposition of a fine as a possible sanction.[8] Whether a fine will be imposed or not lies, however, with the discretion of the supervisory authorities.

6   The European legislative acts do not aim to regulate legal relationships under private law. The public nature of the provisions does not, however, prevent national legislatures and courts from referring to supervisory law requirements when determining the duties of the parties of a contract. In these cases, the provisions have a **dual nature**.[9] In many Member States prominent examples for this are the conduct of business rules for investment firms in MiFID II. The obligations of investment firms towards their clients regarding investment recommendations under MiFID/MiFID II,[10] for example, are also relevant in civil law. They put the contractual obligations of investment firms into more concrete terms.[11] Further examples include the rules of conduct in the European provisions on financial analysts[12] and rating agencies.[13]

7   The civil law courts may also be confronted with capital markets law by way of **private enforcement**. Different forms of private enforcement are common in numerous Member States.[14] In some jurisdictions the legislator included the possibility for investors to claim damages from the issuer or other responsible parties for breaches of disclosure obligations. Other Member States sanction breaches of the provisions on the notification of major shareholdings with a loss of voting and dividend rights that may become relevant in civil law proceedings.[15] All these forms of private enforcement allow civil law courts to take provisions of a public law nature into account.

(b) Interpretation

8   The legal nature of capital market legislation is important for the interpretation of the rules.[16] A public law provision must be interpreted in accordance with the rules of interpretation common for provisions of this nature.[17] At the same time, a criminal or civil law court will apply criminal or civil law methods of interpretation if the dual nature of the provisions allows this.[18] In some Member States criminal and civil law methods of interpretation have one important difference: the prohibition to draw an analogy to criminal

---

[7] This is in particular true for the four framework directives enacted in 2003/2004. See R. Veil § 12 para. 5.
[8] In more detail R. Veil § 12 para. 12 ff.
[9] J. Forschner, *Wechselwirkungen von Aufsichtsrecht und Zivilrecht*, 63 ff.
[10] See R. Veil § 31 para. 43 ff.
[11] It is unclear whether the provisions can be applied on a one-to-one basis in contract law or whether they merely have an indirect effect on civil law. See R. Veil § 31 para. 62, on private enforcement.
[12] See R. Veil § 26 para. 31 ff.
[13] See R. Veil § 27 para. 30 ff.
[14] Cf. R. Veil, 11 EBOR (2010), 409, 417 ff.
[15] See R. Veil § 20 para. 124.
[16] On the interpretation of European law see R. Veil § 5 para. 28–47.
[17] Cf. S. Kalss et al. (eds.), *Kapitalmarktrecht I*, § 1 para. 125.
[18] Cf. D. Zimmer, in: Schwark and Zimmer (eds.), *Kapitalmarktrechts-Kommentar*, § 1 WpHG para. 8.

and administrative penal provisions[19] does not apply in private law. This gives rise to the question whether in these Member States civil law courts are restricted in their methods of interpretation.

Some regard a **dual interpretation** of supervisory law as possible,[20] arguing that the interpretation of private law rules follows civil law principles, which allow gaps to be filled by way of analogy. The most important examples concern the disclosure of major shareholdings. In the past, by using new financial instruments, investors had exploited loopholes in the rules on the attribution of voting rights and could acquire shares in an issuer anonymously. An analogous application of the rules on the attribution of voting rights in the context of civil sanctions could help to achieve the objective of the disclosure obligations.

9

In practice, a dual interpretation has not yet become accepted. In the *Grøngaard/Bang* ruling, the ECJ has indicated that EU supervisory rules must be interpreted uniformly in the various areas of law (public law, criminal law, civil law).[21] In Germany, the BGH has expressed itself more clearly and excludes an analogy for constitutional reasons.[22] This argument is not convincing because there is no prohibition of analogy in private law. Nevertheless, a dual interpretation must be rejected. A different interpretation of capital markets law would result in legal uncertainty and higher transaction costs for capital market participants. The problem of circumvention of the law can be addressed by principle-based regulation.

10

2. Relations with Accounting, Corporate and Insolvency Law

Capital markets law is closely connected to other fields of law, the most important being accounting law, which is largely harmonised and partly even unified at a European level, and corporate law, which still falls mainly into the regulatory autonomy of the Member States. Insolvency law also plays a role regarding capital markets law and can lead to difficult legal questions.

11

Capital markets law and **accounting law** are closely connected: accounting law aims to ensure that investors are informed about the issuer's profitability and profit prospects. The content of a financial report is governed by the IAS regulation,[23] the TD simply referring to this regulation. EU rules on financial reporting are thus based on the European provisions on accounting law,[24] references thereto in capital markets law having informational purposes.[25]

12

---

[19] In Germany, the prohibition of analogy is of a constitutional nature. Cf. Art. 103(2) GG.
[20] On German law see A. Cahn, 162 ZHR (1998), 1, 8–9; U. Segna, 44 ZGR (2015), 84, 109–122; on Austrian law see S. Kalss et al. (eds.), *Kapitalmarktrecht I*, § 1 para. 127–128.
[21] Cf. Case C-384/02 (*Grøngard/Bang*), para. 28 (obiter dictum): 'the interpretation of a directive's scope cannot be dependent upon the civil, administrative or criminal nature of the proceedings in which it is invoked'.
[22] Cf. BGH of 19.07.2011 – II ZR 246/09, BGHZ 190, 291 para. 27; BGH of 18.09.2006 – II ZR 137/05 (WMF), BGHZ 169, 98, 106.
[23] Regulation (EC) No. 2002/1606 of the European Parliament and of the Council of 19 July 2002 on the application of international accounting standards (IAS Regulation), OJ L 243, 11 September 2002, p. 1–4.
[24] See H. Brinckmann § 18 para. 26.
[25] This function is the underlying concept for the principle of 'fair value', according to which assets and debts must be balanced according to their market value. An asset is recognised in the balance sheet if it is probable that there will be future economic benefits for the company.

13 **Corporate law** plays a role in a number of ways. Firstly, it is interesting to note that some obligations under capital markets law were originally regulated in Member States' corporate law and have been covered by capital markets legislation as European legislation has been implemented. One example is the obligation for investors to notify changes in voting rights to the issuer (disclosure of major shareholdings). In France, Germany and the United Kingdom, this obligation was previously part of corporate law. Its roots in corporate law can still be recognised under the current regime (obligation to notify the issuer, who is obliged to publish; right of the issuer to prove the notified shareholding; loss of rights under civil law).

14 Secondly, corporate law is important for the application of capital markets legislation. EU supervisory law is neutral as regards legal forms. The European Single Rulebooks do not use terms of corporate law but rather function-related concepts, such as 'issuer', 'members of an administrative, management or supervisory body' and 'investor'. This allows to take into account the specificities of different corporate governance structures in Europe.

15 Example a): An issuer is obliged to disclose inside information as soon as possible (Article 17 MAR). It may have legitimate reasons to delay the disclosure of the information. Under European law, an issuer is permitted to do delay the publication if immediate disclosure would be likely to prejudice the issuer's legitimate interests. What constitutes a 'legitimate interest' cannot be answered by an autonomous interpretation, but must be assessed in the light of the Member States' corporate laws. It is a matter of controversy in the Member States as to whether the company interest should be understood as the interests of shareholders in increasing the value of the company (shareholder value concept) or also the interests of creditors and employees (stakeholder value concept).[26] As a result, the disclosure obligation is handled differently across Europe. ESMA also takes into account the different corporate governance in Europe (monistic and dualistic system) and recognises a delay of publication when a price-sensitive event, such as a capital increase, in a dualistic company is subject to the vote of the supervisory board. Otherwise, its decision-making autonomy would not be respected.[27]

16 Example b): An insider may not disclose inside information to another person unless the disclosure is made in the normal exercise of an employment, a profession or duties (Article 10(1) MAR). Whether this is the case is determined by labour and corporate law. The ECJ recognises that these rules have not yet been harmonised at European level. The ECJ therefore respects the different regulatory frameworks of the Member States' law.[28] Consequently, disclosure may be legitimate in one Member State but not in another.

17 Example c): In the case of claims for damages by investors, rules of corporate law can interfere with capital markets law. If an investor has acquired shares on the basis of incorrect capital market information (stock exchange prospectus; ad hoc announcement) and claims damages, this could violate the principle of capital maintenance, as he is a shareholder of the company.[29] The relationship

---

[26] The goal of sustainability, which has found its way into European supervisory law (see R. Veil § 2 para. 21), could also be taken into account. Cf. P. Mülbert and A. Sajnovits, WM (2020), 1557, 1566 f.
[27] See R. Veil § 19 para. 58.
[28] See R. Veil § 14 para. 82.
[29] See R. Veil § 17 para. 93 and § 19 para. 97.

between the protection of investors under capital markets law and the protection of creditors under stock corporation law has been the subject of academic debate for more than 100 years. The European Court of Justice has rejected a priority of the capital maintenance requirement over the liability of stock exchange prospectuses.[30] This interpretation is convincing because the investor asserts claims as a creditor and not as a shareholder.

Insolvency law is in general not relevant for the interpretation of capital markets law. However, it plays a prominent role in the creation of financial instruments. The probability of default of a creditor is determined by the insolvency law of the Member States. The grounds for insolvency, the ranking of creditors' claims and the insolvency protection of collateral are regulated differently in the national jurisdictions. Europe is therefore far from having a uniform law on financial investments.

The European Commission is aware of the problem of divergent insolvency laws in the Member States: 'There are still significant barriers to a well-functioning CMU in many areas, including [...] insolvency laws. These barriers are driven by history, customs and culture. They are deep-rooted, and will take time to tackle.'[31] Nevertheless, the Commission intends to address the issue: 'To make the outcomes of insolvency proceedings more predictable, the Commission will take a legislative or non-legislative initiative for minimum harmonisation or increased convergence in targeted areas of non-bank insolvency law.'[32]

III. Interdisciplinarity

1. The model of *homo oeconomicus*

Capital market legislation intends to influence the market participants' behaviour. It must therefore apply certain concepts that predict the reactions of market participants to certain rules. The economic analysis of law refers to the concept of a *homo oeconomicus*,[33] thereby assuming that a **model person acts rationally** and **aims** to **maximise** its own **economic benefits**.[34] It will always choose the alternative most suited to its preferences, whilst the benefits for others will not play any role in its decision. The underlying premise of the economic analysis of law is that the *homo oeconomicus* can obtain and process all relevant information available.[35]

---

[30] See R. Veil § 17 para. 93.
[31] European Commission, Capital Markets Union for people and businesses – new action plan, 24.9.2020, COM (2020) 590 final, p. 2.
[32] European Commission, ibid, p. 13.
[33] G. Becker, *Der ökonomische Ansatz zur Erklärung menschlichen Verhaltens*, 15; on the criticsm regarding New Institutional Economics cf. R. Richter and E. Furubotn, *Neue Institutionenökonomik*, 3–4.
[34] According to the so-called 'expected utility theory' individuals will always opt for the alternative that maximises their expected utility. It can be determined by multiplication of the benefits of the option and its probability. Cf. L. Klöhn, *Kapitalmarkt, Spekulation und Behavioral Finance*, 86 ff., with further references.
[35] H. Eidenmüller, 60 JZ (2005), 216, 217.

2. Behavioural Finance

21 The assumption of rationality does not coincide with reality. The research on behavioural finance[36] of the past decades has shown numerous behavioural anomalies, which have unsettled the economic behavioural model. Even though these empirical studies do not always explicitly examine the behaviour of capital market participants, the conclusions must nonetheless lead to a critical evaluation of the concept of a *homo oeconomicus*.

(a) Bounded Rationality

22 The assumption of rationality assumes that man has unlimited possibilities to take in and process information. However, one will often be confronted with decisions that were made quickly, the affected person not having had the possibility to process all the information available. In these cases, man works with rules of thumb, so-called heuristics. In a complex situation that requires a decision, he will search for an anchor which he will use as a starting point to evaluate the possible alternatives. This anchor value will have a disproportionate influence on the decision.[37] Decisions can thus be manipulated by directing the decision-maker towards a certain anchor value.

(b) Overconfidence

23 A rational person should be able to determine correctly his knowledge and skills. Empirical studies have, however, proven that people systematically tend towards overconfidence. Most car drivers, for example, claim that they are better and safer drivers than their passengers.[38] Statistically, however, only 50% of all drivers can actually be better than average. Overconfidence is more pronounced with men than with women.[39] The problem of overconfidence must particularly be taken into account for provisions that aim to warn market participants, as an overconfident person will tend to ignore the warning.

(c) Fairness

24 According to the concept of rational behaviour a person will only be interested in maximising his own economic benefits. Numerous studies, however, revealed that the participants showed behaviour in which they were prepared to accept personal economic losses, in order to punish others for their behaviour if this was felt to be unfair (ultimatum game).[40]

---

[36] Cf. the literature listed in the bibliography and cited below: D. Kahneman and A. Tversky, *Prospect Theory: An Analysis of Decision under Risk*, 47 Econometrica (1979), 63–292; A. Shleifer, *Inefficient Markets. An Introduction to Behavioural Finance*; H. Shefrin, *Beyond Greed and Fear: Understanding Behavioural Finance and the Psychology of Investment*; R. Shiller, *Irrational Exuberance*.

[37] Cf. A. Tversky and D. Kahneman, 185 Science (1974), 1124.

[38] Cf. O. Svenson, 77 Acta Psychologica (1981), 143.

[39] B. Fischhoff/P. Slovic/S. Lichtenstein, 3 J. Exp. Psych., Hum. Perception & Performance (1977), 552; on the phenomenon of overconfidence on the capital market see T. Odean, *Volume, Volatility, Price and Profit When All Traders Are Above Average*, 53 J. Fin. (1998), 1887; on gender-specific overconfidence on the capital markets see B. Barber and T. Odean, *Boys Will Be Boys*, Q. J. Econ. (2001), 261.

[40] Cf. D. Kahneman/J. L. Knetsch/R. H. Thaler, 59 J. Bus. (1986), 285.

If a statute determines that certain facts are 'relevant' for human decisions, aspects of fairness may also play a role.

(d) Prospect Theory/Framing/Risk Aversity

The concept of rationality assumes that individuals will distinguish between alternatives according to the expected utility, the model person always choosing the alternative with the highest expected utility. As opposed to this, the *prospect theory* assumes that a decision will always depart from a certain reference point. Outcomes lower than this reference point will be considered as losses, higher outcomes as gains.

Framing means presenting an option with a certain expected utility in different formats to make it appear either as a loss or as a gain, thus proving that people's decisions can be influenced. Depending on the type of framing the participants of different study groups developed different risk attitudes. People usually prefer small but certain gains as opposed to the possibility of larger (or no) gains, showing a certain aversion to risk. As opposed to this, in the scenario of a certain loss or the possibility of an even higher (or no) loss, people will usually opt for the possibility of preventing the loss.[41] Thus, a person can influence decisions by manipulating the point of reference.

(e) Hindsight Bias

Events that have already occurred tend to be seen as more probable than before they took place. The evaluation of a certain decision depends on how the respective person processed the information available to him before the event. The actual result, not known at the time, plays a role in this process. However, for most people it is difficult to separate out actual developments, creating the impression the result had actually been foreseen. In these cases, the person who made the wrong decision is blamed for not having foreseen the result.

This behavioural anomaly is of legal relevance in cases where the question of a liability based on negligence arises,[42] the most prominent example being the introduction of the business judgment rule for management liability, in order to meet hindsight bias.

(f) Representativeness/Availability/Salience

Whether the occurrence of an event is regarded as probable depends strongly on the information that was available to the respective person. With information that is easily accessible or salient, such as newspaper reports on shark attacks and aeroplane crashes, the probability of an occurrence is overestimated.[43] Contrary to the model of the rationally acting person, people tend to not make use of all the information to which they would have access. Instead, they would rely only on the information easily available to them.[44]

---

[41] Cf. A. Tversky and D. Kahneman, 47 Econometrica (1979), 263.
[42] Cf. K. Kamin and J. Rachlinski, Law & Hum Behav. (1995), 89.
[43] Cf. C. Sunstein, 97 Nw. U. L. Rev. (2003), 1295 ff.
[44] Cf. A. Tversky and D. Kahneman, 185 Science (1974), 1124, 1127.

3. Relevance of Behavioural Finance for Capital Markets Law

30   The results of the research on behavioural finance can be of use on two levels. Firstly, it is possible to take the results into account when **interpreting the law**. This is particularly relevant in the case of vague legal concepts such as 'honestly', 'fairly' and 'professionally', which the legislator uses when regulating information intermediaries (investment firms, financial analysts and rating agencies).[45]

31   There is a controversial discussion whether findings from behavioural economics should be taken into account in **insider trading law**.[46] This regime is determined by the concept of a **reasonable investor**. According to Article 7(4) MAR, information is likely to have a significant influence on the price of a financial instrument which a reasonable investor would probably use as part of the basis for his investment decision. It is recognised that an informed investor bases his investment decisions on all available ex-ante information[47] The reasonable investor is to be understood as *homo oeconomicus* in the sense of the (semi-strong) Efficient Capital Market Hypothesis.[48] Information is therefore price-sensitive if it relates to the fundamental value of a security. A reasonable investor, understood as a *homo economicus*, does not take into account imprecise, vague and unfounded information.[49] It is conceivable, however, that the indefinite legal term could also be interpreted in the light of findings from Behavioural Finance research.[50] Courts have already taken up this idea. According to the BGH, a reasonable investor must also consider irrational reactions of other market participants, such as herd behaviour.[51] This interpretation is not convincing. It is not the purpose of market abuse law to ensure equal information opportunities for short-term speculative investors. Furthermore, the interpretation would exceed the limits of what is judiciable.

32   Secondly the results of behavioural economics could provide an incentive for a **reform** in order to take anomalies into account, thus providing a **higher level** of **investor protection**. When introducing and reforming disclosure requirements and rules of conduct for intermediaries, legislators should consider that recipients and clients of investment services act irrationally and have limited capacity to process information.

33   A fundamental problem of current capital market regulation is the limited capability of investors to process information (***information overload***).[52] When making investment decisions, investors, especially if they are swamped by the amount of information,[53] use rules of thumb or are guided by emotional motives such as the imperative of fairness. Regimes should therefore ensure the disclosure of information relevant to decision-making, ie material and meaningful information.[54]

---

[45] Cf. Art. 24(1) of MiFID II.
[46] Cf. L. Klöhn, *Kapitalmarkt, Spekulation und Behavioral Finance*, 210 f., 247 f.; L. Teigelack, *Finanzanalysen und Behavioral Finance*, 162 ff.; R. Veil, 18 ZBB (2006), 162, 163.
[47] Case C-19/11 (*Geltl/Daimler*), para. 55.
[48] H. Krause, in: Meyer and Veil et al. (eds.), *Handbuch Marktmissbrauchsrecht*, § 6 para. 116; L. Klöhn, in: Klöhn (ed.), *Kommentar zur MAR*, Art. 7 para. 271; M. Ventoruzzo, in: Ventoruzzo/Mock, *Market Abuse Regulation*, B.7.68.
[49] F. Annunziata, 5 Law and Economics Review (2016), 280, 305.
[50] F. Annunziata, 5 Law and Economics Review (2016), 280, 304 ff.
[51] BGH of 13.12.2011 – XI ZR 51/10 (IKB), BGHZ 192, 90, 107 f. para. 44. See R. Veil § 14 para. 55.
[52] Cf. J. Möllers and E. Kernchen, 40 ZGR (2011), 1, 9; P. Buck-Heeb, 176 ZHR (2012), 66, 70, 75; C. Stahl, *Information Overload am Kapitalmarkt*; J. Möllers, 24 ZEuP (2016), 325, 333.
[53] Cf. J. Möllers and E. Kernchen, 40 ZGR (2011), 1, 10.
[54] Cf. R. Link and H. Obst, BB (2015), 2859 ff.

In financial services law, information requirements on financial products should be based more on the findings of behavioural finance (*smart disclosure*).[55] When selling financial products, simple signs and colours can be used to draw attention to the complexity and risk of the product.[56]

Behavioural finance research can also be taken into account in the design of liability regimes. The PRIIPS Regulation provides for liability where irrational investors are misled.[57] Legislature could also adopt this approach in other regulatory areas. It could, for example, establish liability of financial analysts for bias in a financial analysis.[58] In addition, legislature may take special measures to protect investors. It could, for example, introduce trading restrictions, protecting investors of their own or the analyst's behavioural anomalies,[59] or introduce investment licence in order to raise investors' awareness of irrational behaviour and to enable them to make more rational decisions.[60] 34

The debate on taking the results of behavioural finance studies for legislation into account is still in its early stages.[61] The problem that anomalies do not occur with all market participants remains to be resolved. Their behaviour has furthermore not yet been studied in its entirety. One must further keep in mind that the main aim of capital markets law is to ensure the functioning of the markets as a whole. A financial analysis, for example, is made public to an unlimited number of people. In such a scenario it appears justifiable, or even necessary, to accept certain deviations from the model behaviour of a *homo economicus* without adapting the concept when developing rules on the presentation and distribution of a financial analysis. One will also have to ask the question as to how far legal rules on capital markets should be paternalistic.[62] The legal discussion has as yet not found an answer to this question.[63] 35

Rules should only be developed on the basis of robust research results. Since 2013, the **FCA** in the United Kingdom has been carrying out studies together with the London School of Economics on clients' behaviour when acquiring financial products.[64] Additionally, it has developed a **conceptual framework** determining how these **findings** may be **implemented into practice**,[65] thereby distinguishing between **hard** and **soft paternalism** as options for intervening. 36

---

[55] Cf. A. Hackethal and S. Meyer, 113 ZVglRWiss (2014), 574 ff.
[56] Cf. D. Zimmer, 69 JZ (2014), 714 ff.
[57] Cf. R. Veil, in: Bumke and Röthel, *Autonomie im Recht*, 185, 195.
[58] Cf. L. Teigelack, *Finanzanalysen und Behavioral Finance*, 287 ff.
[59] Cf. L. Teigelack, *Finanzanalysen und Behavioral Finance*, 294 ff.; on black out and quiet periods see M. Findeisen, *Regulierung und Rechtsfolgen von Interessenkonflikten in der Aktienanalyse*, 205; U. Göres, *Interessenkonflikte von Wertpapierdienstleistern*, 95.
[60] Dissenting opinion: L. Teigelack, *Finanzanalysen und Behavioral Finance*, 270 ff.; on investment licences S. Choi, 88 Cal. L. Rev. (2000), 279 ff.
[61] Cf. H. Fleischer, in: FS Ulrich Immenga, 575 ff.; L. Klöhn, *Kapitalmarkt, Spekulation und Behavioral Finance*, 153; L. Teigelack, *Finanzanalysen und Behavioral Finance*, 161 ff.; L. Klöhn, in: Fleischer and Zimmer (eds.), 75 ZHR Beiheft (2011), 83–99.
[62] On the different concepts of paternalism see C. Sunstein and R. Thaler, 70 U Chi. L. Rev. (2003), 1159 ff.; S. Choi and A. Pritchard, 56 Stan. L. Rev. (2003), 1 ff.; L. Klöhn, *Kapitalmarkt, Spekulation und Behavioral Finance*, 150 ff.
[63] For a solution following the principle of proportionality see L. Teigelack, *Finanzanalysen und Behavioral Finance*, 237 ff.
[64] The FCA publishes the studies in its *Occasional Papers Series* (see https://www.fca.org.uk/publications). 60 studies have been published so far (October 2021).
[65] Cf. FCA, Occasional Paper No. 1: Applying behavioural economics at the Financial Conduct Authority, April 2013, 42.

37 The results of behavioural finance are also taken into account at a European level, the PRIIPS-Regulation[66] aligning the disclosure obligations for financial products with the findings from behavioural finance (*smart disclosure*). Investment firms, credit institutions and insurance companies are obliged to inform retail investors on the investment product in a key information document. The disclosure obligations tackle the problem that retail investors have difficulties in understanding the financial terminology of a financial report. Therefore, particular attention shall be paid to the vocabulary and style of writing in the key information document.[67] Language should be clear and comprehensible and financial terminology is to be avoided. The requirements on the presentation of information in the document reflect the findings of the behavioural finance research on *framing*, according to which preferences can be influenced through certain wordings.

38 The European Commission justifies its increased attention to the findings of behavioural finance with the fact that the acquisition of financial products is often comparable to a life decision and the consumers' choices will often be driven by emotional aspects.[68]

---

[66] Regulation (EU) No. 1286/2014 of the European Parliament and of the Council of 26 November 2014 on key information documents for packaged retail and insurance-based investment products (PRIIPs), OJ L 352, 9 December 2014, p. 1–23.

[67] Cf. recital 13 PRIIPS-Regulation.

[68] Cf. Commission/European Economic and Social Committee, Emerging Challenges in Retail Finance and Consumer Policy, Conference Final Report, 18 November 2014.

2

Basics of Capital Markets Law

§ 7

Capital Markets

Bibliography

Arce, Óscar, López, Elias and Sanjuán, Lucio, *Access of SMEs with growth potential to the capital markets*, CNMV, Documentos de Trabajo No 52 (2011); Bashir, Imran, *Mastering-Blockchain*, 2nd edn. (2018); Blair QC, Michael et al. (eds.), *Financial Markets and Exchanges Law*, 2nd edn. (2012); Clausen, Nis J. and Sørensen, Karsten E., *Reforming the Regulation of Trading Venues in the EU under the Proposed MiFID II - Levelling the Playing Field and Overcoming Market Fragmentation?*, 9 ECFR (2012), 275–306; Cunningham, William M., *The JOBS Act* (2012); Di Noia, Carmine and Filippa, Luca, *Looking for New Lenses: How Regulation Should Cope with the Financial Market Infrastructures Evolution*, in: Binder, Jens-Hinrich and Saguato, Paolo (eds.), *Financial Market Infrastructure: Law and Regulation* (2022); Ferran, Eilís, *Building an EU Securities Market* (2004); Fleckner, Andreas M., *Stock Exchanges at the Crossroads*, 74 Fordham L. Rev. (2005–2006), 2541–2620; Fleischer, Holger, *Empfiehlt es sich, im Interesse des Anlegerschutzes und zur Förderung des Finanzplatzes Deutschland das Kapitalmarkt- und Börsenrecht neu zu regeln?*, Gutachten F zum 64. Deutschen Juristentag (2002); Fuller, Geoffrey, *The Law and Practice of International Capital Markets*, 3rd edn. (2012); Gomber, Peter and Nassauer, Frank, *Neuordnung der Finanzmärkte in Europa durch MiFID II/MiFIR*, 26 ZBB (2014), 250–260; Güllner, Mariam, *Die neue Handelsplatzarchitektur in der EU*, 71 WM (2017), 938–945; Habersack, Mathias et al. (eds.), *Unternehmensfinanzierung am Kapitalmarkt*, 4th edn. (2019); Harris, Larry, *Trading & Exchanges* (2003); Harwood, Alison and Konidaris, Tanya, *SME Exchanges in Emerging Market Economics*, World Bank Group, Policy Research Working Paper 7160 (2015); Marsch-Barner, Reinhard and Schäfer, Frank A. (eds.), *Handbuch börsennotierte AG*, 4th edn. (2017); Maume, Philipp, *The Parting of the Ways: Delisting under German and UK Law*, 16 EBOR (2015), 255–279; Panasar, Raj and Boeckman, Philip (eds.), *European Securities Law*, 2nd edn. (2014); Panasar, Raj and Boeckman, Philip (eds.), *European Securities Law*, 2nd edn. (2014); Rechtschaffen, Alan N., *Capital Markets, Derivatives and the Law* (2009); Schwartz, Robert and Francioni, Reto, *Equity Markets in Action* (2004); Storm, Philipp, *Alternative Freiverkehrssegmente im Kapitalmarktrecht* (2010); Veil, Rüdiger, *Marktregulierung durch privates Recht am Beispiel des Entry Standard der Frankfurter Wertpapierbörse*, in: Burgard, Ulrich et al. (eds.), *Festschrift für Uwe H. Schneider* (2011), 1313–1324; Veil, Rüdiger and Lerch, Marcus P., *Auf dem Weg zu einem Europäischen Finanzmarktrecht: die Vorschläge der Kommission zur Neuregelung der Märkte für Finanzinstrumente*, 66 WM (2012), 1557–1565 (Part I) and 1605–1613 (Part II); Veil, Rüdiger, *Kapitalmarktzugang für Wachstumsunternehmen* (2016); Veil, Rüdiger and Di Noia, Carmine, *SME Growth Markets*, in: Busch, Danny and Ferrarini, Guido (eds.), *Regulation of the EU Financial Markets—MiFID II and MiFIR* (2017), 345–362; von Berg, Catharina S., *Der Marktrückzug des Emittenten* (2018); Woepking, James, *International Capital Markets and Their Importance*, 9 Transnat'l L. & Contemp. Prob. (1999), 233–246.

I. Overview

1. Trading Venue

1 A market is a system in which supply and demand meet. A capital market is thus a market where companies can raise equity or borrow capital and where these financial instruments are publicly traded. Debt capital is generally raised by issuing bonds,[1] whilst equity is raised by issuing shares.[2] Secondary markets are also called cash markets in order to underline the fact that turnover transactions take place here. Generally, **stock transactions** have to be fulfilled within a period of **two days** (**settlement period**). Thus, the buyer is obliged to transfer cash to the seller and the seller must transfer ownership of the stock to the buyer within two days after the trade was made (T+2).[3] The largest stock markets are in the US, followed by Asia, Europe and Canada.[4] The same applies to the bond markets. The largest markets for sovereign bonds are in the US, China and Japan.[5] The market for sovereign bonds is larger than that for corporate bonds.[6]

2 European law defines a '**trading venue**' as a regulated market (RM), a multilateral trading facility (MTF) or an organised trading system (OTF).[7] MiFID II establishes transparent and non-discriminatory rules for all three trading venues that govern access to the system.[8] On the other hand, so-called OTC trading concerns trading that takes place directly between two or more investors, ie outside of regulated markets, MTFs or OTFs. The practical importance of OTC trading is significant. In 2019, it accounted for almost one-third of equity trading in the EEA.[9] ESMA has recorded a total of 430 trading venues for 2019.[10] The number of companies listed has declined steadily in recent years, from 5,414 (2010) to 5,024 (2018) in the EU 27.[11]

---

[1] See R. Veil § 8 para. 16–18.
[2] See R. Veil § 8 para. 11–15.
[3] Art. 7(2) Commission Delegated Regulation (EU) 2017/565 of 25 April 2016 supplementing Directive 2014/65/EU of the European Parliament and of the Council as regards organisational requirements and operating conditions for investment firms and defined terms for the purposes of that Directive, OJ L 87, 31 March 2017.
[4] Market capitalisation 2018 in trillions US-$: USA 68,65; Asia (Eastasia and Pacific) 23,82 (data for 2019); EU 5,768; Canada 1,938 (World Bank data, available at: https://data.worldbank.org/indicator/CM.MKT.LCAP.CD); cf. on market size of financial market infrastructures C. Di Noia and L. Filippa, in: Binder/Saguato, (eds.), *Financial Market Infrastructure: Law and Regulation* (2022).
[5] ICMA, Bond marke seize, available at: https://www.icmagroup.org/Regulatory-Policy-and-Market-Practice/Secondary-Markets/bond-market-size/: 'The SSA bond markets are dominated by the US ($22.4tn), China ($19.8tn), and Japan ($12.4tn). Between them they make up 62% of the global SSA market. Sovereign bonds constitute 73% ($63.7tn) of the global outstanding SSA market.'
[6] Cf. ICMA, ibid.: 'As of August 2020, ICMA estimates that the overall size of the global bond markets in terms of USD equivalent notional outstanding, is approximately $128.3tn. This consists of $87.5tn SSA bonds (68%) and $40.9tn corporate bonds (32%).'
[7] Cf. Art. 4(1)(24) MiFID II.
[8] Recital 14 MiFID II.
[9] Cf. ESMA, EU securities markets, ESMA Annual Statistic Report, 18 November 2020, ESMA-50-165-1355, p. 2.
[10] Cf. ESMA, EU securities markets, ESMA Annual Statistic Report, 18 November 2020, ESMA-50-165-1355, p. 10.
[11] Cf. European Commission, Primary and secondary equity markets, Final report, 2020, sub 2.3.2.

Capital markets must be distinguished from money markets, foreign exchange markets and futures and derivatives markets. The **money market** consists of banks procuring liquidity by borrowing and lending to each other, using short-term loans and credits. The **foreign exchange market** is where cheques and bills denominated in foreign currencies can be traded with foreign banks. It is usually an interbank market. The **derivatives markets**—closely connected to the capital markets[12]—trade in futures and options.[13]

In Europe, derivatives markets have been subject to considerable developments in the last decade.[14] Exchange traded derivatives are generally confined to more standard products such as options and futures, whilst OTC derivatives are not and may include products such as swaps and forward rate agreements.[15] This approach has been challenged by the devastating consequences of the opaque and highly systemic OTC derivatives markets during the financial crisis.[16] Therefore **MiFIR** introduced an **obligation** to **trade derivatives** on **trading venues**.[17] Whether a class of derivatives is subject to that obligation depends on ESMA's decision.[18] MiFIR also introduced the obligation to clear such derivatives via a Central Counterparty (CCP),[19] which accompanies the similar obligation in EMIR concerning OTC-traded derivatives.[20]

2. Primary and Secondary Markets

Two types of markets can be distinguished: primary and secondary capital markets. The **primary market** deals with issuing new securities (so-called initial public offering, **IPO**). Shares will generally be issued by stock corporations and acquired by investors. However, the shares may also be offered by a major shareholder.[21] In practice, both the stock corporation and the existing shareholders frequently put shares up for sale.[22] Unlike secondary markets, primary markets are not organised.

Shares can be issued by the issuer itself or through securities underwriting, the latter being predominant in practice. In these cases a syndicate of banks underwrites the transaction, subsequently selling the newly issued shares to the public.[23] The legal basis is an underwriting agreement between the stock corporation (and, if applicable, existing shareholders) and the bank consortium. A well-known example of a self-issuance is the IPO of the music streaming provider Spotify in 2018 (direct listing on the Nasdaq).

---

[12] Cf. G. Fuller, *The Law and Practice of International Capital Markets*, para. 1.214.
[13] Cf. A. Rechtschaffen, *Capital Markets, Derivatives and the Law*, 19.
[14] Cf. Commission, Commission Staff Working Paper, 20 October 2011, SEC(2011) 1217 final, p. 98 with reference to data on global OTC derivatives markets, mainly generated from statistics compiled by the Bank for International Settlements (BIS); cf. ECMI, *ECMI Statistical Package 2015*, Table 4.1.a, the notional amount outstanding of OTC Derivatives sums up to € 500.404,39 billion in December 2014.
[15] SEC(2011) 1217 final, ibid., p. 98.
[16] Recital 25 and 26 MiFIR.
[17] Art. 28 MIFIR.
[18] Art. 32 MiFIR.
[19] Art. 29 MiFIR.
[20] P. Gomber and F. Nassauer, 26 ZBB (2014), 250, 255 ff.
[21] This is also termed a secondary offer, the offer by the company being termed a primary offer, cf. R. Panasar et al., in: Panasar and Boeckman (eds.), *European Securities Law*, para. 2.32.
[22] Cf. ibid.
[23] See para 37.

7   Issuing shares through securities underwritings confers numerous advantages as opposed to issuing shares directly. Banks will generally have better business relations with institutional investors willing to buy shares. Banks are furthermore familiar with customs of capital markets and will thus be able to determine the best time to raise capital and the issuing price in a so-called bookbuilding procedure[24] more easily. This includes direct contact with the institutional investors. However, the underwriting fee the issuer must pay the bank for its services may be considerable.[25]

8   The **secondary market** is the market where previously issued securities and financial instruments are bought and sold. It allows investors to dispose of previously acquired securities, making these investments once again available to the public. The market participants of secondary markets are usually institutional investors, such as banks, pension funds, investment funds, hedge funds, but also private investors.[26]

3. Stock Exchanges

9   The large secondary markets are highly organised markets, operated by stock exchanges. What is meant by an exchange is not regulated in European capital markets law. Union law does not refer to the concept of an exchange, but to the concepts of RM, MTF and OTF. Consequently, the organisation of stock exchanges is subject to the laws of the Member States.

10 The details of national regulations for stock exchanges cannot be described here. It should be sufficient to present essential aspects of the role of stock exchanges, be it that they are organised in the legal form of a corporation (eg London Stock Exchange) or that they are institutions under public law with only partial legal capacity (eg Frankfurter Wertpapierbörse). Stock exchanges are subject to special rules intended to ensure the correct determination of stock prices, enabling them to represent the actual market situation. Additionally, the exchange prices must be made public. The stock exchange's management can suspend or prohibit trading if regulated stock exchange dealings are in its opinion endangered or no longer guaranteed.

II. Trading Venues under MiFID II

1. Regulated Market (RM)

11 A regulated market as defined in Article 4(1)(21) MiFID II 'means a **multilateral system** operated and/or managed **by** a **market operator**, which brings together or facilitates

---

[24] See para 38.
[25] Usually the issuer will owe a certain percentage of the volume of shares issued or its proceeds as commission. Cf. H. Haag, in: Habersack et al. (eds.) *Unternehmensfinanzierung am Kapitalmarkt*, para. 23.30: between 1% and 3%.
[26] See R. Veil § 9 para. 14 f.

the bringing together of multiple third-party buying and selling **interests** in **financial instruments**—in the system and in accordance with its non-discretionary rules—in a way that **results** in a **contract**, in respect of the **financial instruments** admitted to trading under its rules and/or systems, and which is **authorised** and functions regularly and in accordance with Title III' of the MiFID II.

This definition proves to be laborious. A regulated market must be authorised,[27] distinguishing it from an MTF.[28] However, the definition gives rise to a number of further questions: What is a 'system'? What does 'the bringing together of multiple third-party buying and selling interests' mean? What do the 'non-discretionary rules' refer to? And finally, when does a system not function 'regularly'? A 'multilateral system' is defined in Article 4(1)(19) MiFID II as 'any system or facility in which multiple third-party buying and selling trading interests in financial instruments are able to interact in the system'. The definition excludes bilateral systems.[29] However, the term system is not defined. Recital 6 of the former MiFID indicated that the notion of a system should encompass all those markets that are composed of a set of rules and a trading platform as well as those that only function on the basis of a set of rules, whilst the term buying and selling interests is to be understood in a broad sense and includes orders, quotes and indications of interest. Auction systems, traditional server-based trading platforms and peer-to-peer systems are examples of the organised matching of supply and demand.[30] Recital 6 further laid down that the interests be brought together in the system by means of non-discretionary rules set by the system operator, meaning that they are brought together under the system's rules or by means of the system's protocols or internal operating procedures (including procedures embodied in computer software). The term 'non-discretionary rules' means that these rules leave the investment firm operating an MTF with no discretion as to how interests may interact. These interpretations are still valid under the new regime though the MiFID II does not contain the former recital anymore.

The reference to Title III of the MiFID II finally indicates that a regulated market is subject to certain requirements regarding market management,[31] persons exercising significant influence over the management of the regulated market[32] and market organisation.[33] The operator of the regulated market must perform tasks relating to the organisation and operation of the regulated market under the supervision of the national competent authority (NCA).[34]

The list maintained by ESMA provides information on the regulated markets in the EU and the EEA states.[35] According to this list,[36] there are currently (in October 2021) a total of 128 regulated markets;[37] the most prominent are the regulated markets of Euronext (operated in France, Belgium, Portugal, the Netherlands, Ireland and the United Kingdom),

---

[27] Art. 54 MiFID II determines the requirements for a regulated market to be granted authorisation.
[28] See para. 16.
[29] Cf. ECJ of 16.11.2017 – Case C-658/15 (*Robeco Hollands Bezit*) para. 30.
[30] A. Fuchs, in: Fuchs (ed.), *Wertpapierhandelsgesetz, Kommentar*, § 2 para. 159.
[31] Cf. Art. 45 MiFID II.
[32] Cf. Art. 46 MiFID II.
[33] Cf. Art. 47 MiFID II.
[34] Cf. Art. 36(2) MiFID; Art. 44(2) MiFID II.
[35] Art. 56 MiFID II requires Member States to submit to ESMA a list of regulated markets, which shall publish a list of all regulated markets on its website and update it regularly.
[36] However, the registration of a market in this list is not a necessary condition for the qualification of the respective market as a regulated market. Cf. Case C-248/11 (*Nilaş*) guiding principle 2.
[37] Cf. ESMA, MiFID Database, available at: https://registers.esma.europa.eu/publication/searchRegister?core=esma_registers_upreg#.

15 Most important regulated markets are divided into segments.[38] The FWB, for example, distinguishes between Prime Standard and General Standard listing. The Prime Standard segment is a sub-segment of the regulated market segment, with a range of obligations that exceeds the rules provided for by the European legislative acts. These include the disclosure of corporate calendar and the organisation of annual analyst conferences. The admission to the Prime Standard listing is a prerequisite for the inclusion in one of the FWB indices, including DAX (large cap), MDAX (mid cap), TecDAX (technology issuers) and SDAX (small cap).

2. Multilateral Trading Facility (MTF)

16 A multilateral trading facility (MTF) means 'a **multilateral system** operated by an investment firm or a market operator, which **brings together multiple third-party** buying and selling **interests in financial instruments**—in the system and **in accordance with non-discretionary rules**—in a way that **results** in a **contract** in accordance with Title II of this Directive.'[39] Unlike a RM, an MTF is not subject to authorisation, but to supervision, which monitors compliance with organisational requirements and rules and procedure for fair and orderly trading.[40]

17 Like an RM and an OTF, an MTF requires a multilateral system.[41] However, the concept of RM is broader in that it includes a multilateral system that *promotes* the *pooling* of multiple third-party buying and selling *interests* in financial instruments.

18 The operation of an MTF constitutes an **investment service** under MiFID II[42] and a financial service under the CRD IV regime. The investment firm operating an MTF therefore requires a licence as an investment firm or financial services institution from the NCA.[43]

3. Organised Trading Facility (OTF)

19 The term 'organised trading facility' was introduced in the wake of the financial market crisis (MiFID II and MAR). The European legislature had observed that financial instruments had not been traded on an RM or MTF, but in other types of organised trading systems or over-the-counter. It was a declared aim of the European legislature to prevent market abuse for these transactions as well.[44]

---

[38] Cf. P. Storm, *Alternative Freiverkehrssegmente im Kapitalmarktrecht*, 149 ff.
[39] Art. 4(1)(22) MiFID II.
[40] Art. 16 and 18 MiFID II.
[41] See recital 13.
[42] Art. 4(1)(2) in conjunction with Section I Annex A No. 8 MiFID II.
[43] See R. Veil § 30 para. 4.
[44] Recital 8 MAR.

An OTF is defined as 'a **multilateral system** which is not a regulated market or an MTF and in which **multiple third-party buying** and **selling interests** in **bonds, structured finance products, emission allowances** or **derivatives** are able to **interact** in the system in a way that results in a contract in accordance with Title II of this Directive'.[45] The characteristic feature is therefore that the trading venue is a multilateral system.[46] This is the case with an electronic trading platform, but also for the systematic transmission of an investor's intention to trade with other investors, irrespective of the technical means used. However, it must be a multilateral system, which implies that an investor's intention to trade must interact with that of other investors (at least three market participants). The consequence of this broad definition is that a large proportion of the transactions in financial instruments that were previously carried out over-the-counter are now classified as OTF trading.[47]

20

It follows from the definition that no shares can be traded on an OTF, but only non-equity instruments,[48] and that **selling** and **buying interests** are **brought together on a discretionary basis** (which must not only be laid down in the rules of the investment firm operating an OTF but must also be in line with its daily practice). The operator of an OTF therefore has discretion as to how to execute a transaction (Article 20(6) MiFID II), but must observe certain rules of conduct (*best execution*).[49] This means that the OTF operator has discretion as to (i) whether to execute a client's order at all (it takes back an order already placed and executes it on another trading venue) or to execute it only partially (it executes the order only partially on the trading venue and forwards the remaining order to another trading venue) or (ii) whether, when and to what extent it matches two executable orders in the system.

21

The operation of an OTF represents both an investment service within the meaning of MiFID II[50] and a financial service under the CRD IV regime.

22

III. SME Growth Markets

With the so-called Jobs Act,[51] the US legislature aimed to facilitate and promote access to capital markets for emerging growth companies (EGCs). European legislature pursues a similar goal. MiFID II introduced a new category of MTF with the SME Growth Market. The SME Growth Market is intended as a **quality label** for **alternative trading venues**. The label should 'raise their visibility and profile and aid the development of common regulatory standards in the Union for those markets',[52] thus facilitating access to capital for SMEs.[53]

23

---

[45] Art. 4(1)(23) MiFID II.
[46] See recital 13.
[47] See N. Clausen and K. Sørensen, 9 ECFR (2012), 275, 285.
[48] P. Gomber and F. Nassauer, 26 ZBB (2014), 250, 253; M. Güllner, 71 WM (2017), 938, 943.
[49] N. Clausen and K. Sørensen, 9 ECFR (2012), 275, 292; see also recital 9 MiFIR.
[50] Art. 4(1)(2) in conjunction with Section I Annex A No. 9 MiFID II.
[51] Jumpstart Our Business Jobs Act of 5.4.2012; see also W. Cunningham, *The JOBS Act*; R. Veil, *Kapitalmarktzugang für Wachstumsunternehmen*, 3–34.
[52] Recital 132 MiFID II.
[53] See recital 132 MiFID II; for more details on this regulatory concept see R. Veil, *Kapitalmarktzugang für Wachstumsunternehmen*, 128 ff.

24 The term SME Growth Market describes an **MTF** that has been registered in accordance with Article 33 MiFID II.[54] Registration can be applied by the operator of an MTF at the NCA (AMF in France, Consob in Italy, CNMV in Spain, BaFin in Germany, etc.). It requires that at least 50% of the issuers whose financial instruments are admitted to trading on the MTF are SMEs at the time of registration of the MTF as an SME growth market and in each subsequent calendar year.[55] An **SME** is defined as a small and medium-sized enterprise whose **average market capitalisation**, based on year-end quotations, was **less** than € **200 million** in the last three calendar years.[56] The NCA registers the market, if the issuer complies with the requirements for an SME Growth Market. These are laid down in regulations adopted by the European Commission (level 2 regulation)[57] and the Member States under Article 33(3) MiFID II.

25 The requirements for an SME Growth Market are less stringent than for a RM. With regard to **admission to trading**, issuers benefit firstly from the fact that they do not have to publish a prospectus under the EU Prospectus Regulation. Instead, it is sufficient for them to publish an **information document** under the rules of the market operator, which is not subject to approval by the national supervisory authority.[58] Another important difference is that **issuers** are **not** obliged to publish **financial reports** in accordance with **IFRS** (but may apply national accounting law). They are also not required to publish half-yearly financial reports unless required by the rules of the market operator. Unlike the RM, the notification and disclosure requirements on changes in major shareholdings and financial instruments provided for under the Transparency Directive do not apply. This is also true for the requirements on corporate governance and related party transactions provided for listed companies by the Shareholder Rights Directive. In addition, issuers benefit from some facilitations in **market abuse law**.[59] However, these does not offer any significant cost advantages. The European legislature has not made any concessions to the obligation to publish inside information pursuant to Article 17(1) MAR, though recognising that the 'requirement to disclose inside information can be burdensome for small and medium-sized enterprises, whose financial instruments are admitted to trading on SME Growth Markets, given the costs of monitoring information in their possession and seeking legal advice about whether and when information needs to be disclosed.'[60] The European legislature argued that 'prompt disclosure of inside information is essential to ensure investor confidence in those issuers.'[61]

26 The concept of SME Growth Markets has so far had varying degrees of success in the Member States. There are 822 companies listed on the AIM London, 142 on the AIM Italia, 48 on Scale

---

[54] Art. 4(1)(12) MiFID II.
[55] Art. 33(3)(a) MiFID II.
[56] Art. 4(1)(13) MiFID II.
[57] Art. 77 Commission Delegated Regulation (EU) 2017/565, p. 1 ff.
[58] However, the rules of the market operator usually require the issuer to appoint an adviser to assist it in the admission of the securities (so-called nominated adviser). Cf. R. Veil, *Kapitalmarktzugang für Wachstumsunternehmen*, 44.
[59] Cf. Art. 17(9) MAR on the publication of inside information and Art. 18(6) MAR on the insider list.
[60] Recital 55 MAR.
[61] Recital 55 MAR. This is criticised in literature, cf. R. Veil and C. Di Noia, in: Busch and Ferrarini (eds.), *Regulation of the EU Financial Markets*, para 13.01.

of the Frankfurt Stock Exchange, 399 on Euronext Growth, 428 on the First North Growth Market and 120 on the Spanish BME Growth Market (as of July 2021). It is noteworthy that there were 68 listings in Italy between 2018 and 2019, which can be explained by tax incentives for investors.

Not all SME Growth Markets in the Member States have seen a significant increase in listings. On the AIM London there were even 1,694 companies listed in 2007 and 1,056 companies in 2015.[62] There are many reasons for the decrease in listings. Institutional investors are not interested in securities admitted to trading on SME growth markets because the investment volume and liquidity of the markets are too low.[63] In addition, there is a lack of *research* for small issuers. The high degree of regulatory complexity is also lamented. Finally, for some market operators the label SME growth market does not seem appropriate. The *m:access* segment (with 67 companies listed in July 2021) operated by the Munich Stock Exchange as an MTF, for example, sees itself as a trading center for SME financing and not primarily for growth companies. Börse München has therefore not applied for registration as an SME growth market.

27

With **Regulation (EU) 2019/2115** of 27.11.2019, the European legislator has attempted to take account of criticisms. The reform is based on the idea that only issuers admitted to trading on SME Growth Markets benefit from lower regulatory requirements. However, if a market operator does not apply for registration, SMEs do not benefit from reduced unnecessary administrative burdens.

28

The facilitations introduced by Regulation (EU) 2019/2115 are intended to reduce the administrative burden for SMEs and thus ensure greater liquidity on these markets. The Regulation addresses numerous regulatory requirements of the market abuse regime. An important issue is the obligation to draw up a list of all persons who have access to price-sensitive information (**insider lists**). Issuers on SME Growth Markets only have to put a limited number of persons on such a list, namely those who can access inside information at all times ('permanent insiders'). With regard to **directors' dealings**, the reform aims to ensure that issuers on SME Growth Markets have sufficient time to disclose transactions after notification by the manager. A further issue of the reform concerns the obligation to disclose inside information. If an issuer listed on a SME Growth Market decides to delay the disclosure of inside information (Article 17(4) MAR), it only has to justify such delay if requested by the competent national authority. In addition, the issuer is exempted from the obligation to keep continuous records of such justifications.

29

The success of the SME Growth Market can certainly not be assessed by the number of listed companies alone. Instead, it is more important that the SME Growth Market is associated with a high-quality listing.[64] Nevertheless, access to capital markets for SMEs can still be improved. The European Commission therefore continues to pursue the goal under the *von der Leyen* administration with a targeted consultation on the listing act (November 2021).

30

---

[62] R. Veil, *Kapitalmarktzugang für Wachstumsunternehmen*, 53 ff.
[63] A. Harwood and T. Konidaris, *WPS7160*, 20.
[64] R. Veil and C. Di Noia, in: Busch and Ferrarini (eds.), *Regulation of the EU Financial Markets*, para. 13.49.

IV. OTC Trade

31   The market structure established by MiFID I was characterised by intense competition between markets (regulated market, MTFs). In addition, for cost reasons and to ensure anonymity, a significant proportion of trading (in particular of derivatives) took place outside the trading venues[65] (so-called OTC trading - over-the-counter) and in so-called **dark pools** (such as broker-crossing systems),[66] where no pre-trade transparency existed and market participants therefore had no knowledge of existing orders and their volumes.[67] The aim of the reform of market infrastructures in Europe 2014 (MiFID II regime) and market abuse law (MAR/CRIM-MAD) was to direct this trading to (regulated) trading venues as far as possible and to prevent abusive behaviour.

32   To this end, the European legislature introduced the concept of an OTF and declared the regime on market abuse applicable to any multilateral trade (on RMs, MTFs and OTFs). It did not prohibit **bilateral trading**, but required **investment firms** to **ensure** the **trades** it undertakes in shares admitted to trading on an RM or traded on a trading venue generally **take place** on an **RM, MTF**, systematic internaliser or a third-country trading venue.[68]

33   Furthermore, legislature extended the scope of application of European market abuse law. The MAR regime also applies to transactions outside regulated trading venues (RM, MTF and OTF), ie to any transaction, order or behaviour concerning any financial instrument as referred to in Article 2(1) and (2) MAR, irrespective of whether or not such transaction, order or behaviour takes place on a trading venue (Article 2(3) MAR). According to the legislator, 'it is possible that certain financial instruments which are not traded on a trading venue are used for market abuse.'[69]

V. Access to Markets and Market Exit

34   Going public for the first time—also known as an Initial Public Offering (IPO)—is a complex transaction. On the one hand, it is necessary to make the company interested in accessing the capital market 'ready for the stock exchange'. This concerns in particular questions of corporate governance and accounting. On the other hand, numerous steps necessary for the capital market transaction must be taken. The focus is on the securities prospectus, which is required for the public offering, but in any case for the listing at a regulated market. An IPO can therefore take several months. This explains why alternative procedures have also become established in practice, which on the one hand promise a higher degree of transaction security, but on the other hand are particularly risky for investors. In recent years, the

---

[65] Cf. P. Gomber and F. Nassauer, 26 ZBB (2014), 250, 252.
[66] Cf. M. Güllner, 71 WM (2017), 938, 940.
[67] Cf. P. Gomber and F. Nassauer, 26 ZBB (2014), 250, 252; M. Güllner, 71 WM (2017), 938, 940.
[68] See Art. 23 MiFIR. This obligation also applies to proprietary trading, see P. Gomber and F. Nassauer, 26 ZBB (2014), 250, 255.
[69] See recital 10 MAR with specific examples.

IPO via Special Purpose Acquisition Companies (SPACs) has become attractive, especially in the USA. In this process, initiators raise money from investors via a shell company, which is then used to acquire a target company within two years.

1. IPO and Listing

A stock corporation must generally increase its capital in order to issue shares, unless the corporation holds own shares and wants to offer them publicly. On the other hand, the board of directors of a stock corporation does not need a resolution of the general meeting if the company wants to issue bonds. If an issuer wishes to offer mezzanine financial instruments, such as convertible bonds and profit participation rights, it may be necessary to obtain a resolution of the general meeting of shareholders. This is governed by corporate law of the Member States, which has not yet been harmonised in this respect. 35

Both the **increase in capital** and the issue of **bonds** usually require the **involvement of banks** that have the necessary business contacts to institutional investors and are familiar with the customs and expectations of the capital markets. Banks organise roadshows and conferences with analysts. Due to banks' expertise they are further able to judge the ideal time for the issuance better than the investor. They can further coordinate the cooperation with legal advisors, and together with these they correspond with the supervisory authorities.[70] Banks further fulfil a number of obligations after the issuance, including serving as the paying agency for the issued shares, ensuring trade for less liquid shares[71] and, if necessary, carrying out price-stabilising measures. 36

An issuer will generally assign a number of banks the task of carrying out the issuance,[72] the financial risk of larger transactions being too big for an individual bank. This association of banks is called a **banking syndicate** and is led by one of the participating banks (also referred to as lead manager, global coordinator or book runner).[73] A banking syndicate takes over all the shares from the capital increase and offers these to existing shareholders or interested third parties. The rights and obligations of the banks are laid down in an **underwriting agreement**.[74] This also contains provisions on the liability for the prospectus.[75] 37

One of the most difficult tasks is the determination of the issue price. In practice, three different procedures are known: the fixed price procedure, the auction procedure and the **book-building procedure**—the last one being the most important.[76] In book-building 38

---

[70] Cf. on the basic rules regarding communication with the supervisory authorities: R. Panasar et al., in: Panasar and Boeckman (eds.), *European Securities Regulation*, para. 2.60: 'There are three basic rules that market participants should follow when dealing with the regulator: (i) be nice to them; (ii) do not upset them; and (iii) do not be unpleasant to them. In addition, there is one overarching principle: tell the truth'.
[71] This function is also named Designated Sponsoring. See on market making R. Veil § 9 para. 8.
[72] Cf. R. Panasar et al., in: Panasar and Boeckman (eds.), *European Securities Regulation*, para. 2.04.
[73] Ibid.
[74] Cf. G. Fuller, *The Law and Practice of International Capital Markets*, para. 6.11–6.15; A. Meyer, in: Marsch-Barner and Schäfer (eds.), *Handbuch börsennotierte AG*, § 8 para. 104–191.
[75] On prospectus liability see R. Veil § 17 para. 75–93.
[76] Cf. G. Fuller, *The Law and Practice of International Capital Markets*, para. 6.17–6.18; A. Meyer, in: Marsch-Barner and Schäfer (eds.), *Handbuch börsennotierte AG*, § 8 para. 30–34.

procedures shares are not offered at a fixed price, the prospectus rather only containing a price range. During a so-called order-taking period the investors then have the opportunity to submit orders, listing the maximum number of shares they are willing to buy and the maximum share price they are prepared to pay. When the order-taking period is over, the banking syndicate will evaluate the information, allowing the management of the company to fix an issuing price.

39 The details of the underwriting are beyond the scope of this book, being a matter that is largely influenced by legal practice and varies widely between the Member States due to the different legal requirements in corporate law with regard to capital increases.

40 The success of an issue of securities usually requires that investors can sell the securities on a market. This is particularly important for the issuance of shares. It is not sufficient for a company to offer its shares publicly.[77] It must rather also apply to have its **shares traded** on a regulated **market**[78] or another market,[79] pursuant to the national stock exchange provisions in the Member States and the market operator's regulations. Some rules are harmonised by European law: Directive 2001/34/EC coordinates the rules of Member States on the admission of securities to official stock exchange listing (so-called listing directive).[80] Most of the provisions have been repealed in the meantime.[81] However, the rules on admission requirements for shares and bonds are still in force.

41 The Directive 2001/34/EC requires 'the provision of information which is sufficient and as objective as possible concerning the financial circumstances of the issuer and particulars of the securities for which admission to official listing is requested'.[82] Furthermore, issuers are to fulfil certain requirements, such as a minimum market capitalisation. In addition, the shares must be freely negotiable and a sufficient number of shares must be distributed to the public in one or more Member States not later than the time of admission. These requirements aim at protecting investors.

2. Delisting

42 Market exit is also termed '**delisting**' and constitutes the **revocation** of the **admission** of **shares** to **trading** on a regulated **market** or an MTF (going private). The transition from a regulated market to an MTF is called downgrading. The market operator revokes the admission either because an issuer failed to comply with the law or at the request of the issuer. The legal requirements can be found in the national laws of the Member States and the stock exchange operator's regulations. No provisions thereon exist at a European level as yet.

---

[77] On the term public offer see R. Veil § 17 para. 18.
[78] On the term regulated market see para. 11.
[79] On MTFs see para. 16.
[80] Directive 2001/34/EC of the European Parliament and of the Council of 28 May 2001 on the admission of securities to official stock exchange listing and on information to be published on those securities, OJ L 184, 6 July 2001, p. 1.
[81] This applies to the obligation to publish financial reports, the disclosure of major shareholdings (both requirements provided for by the Transparency Directive) and the obligation to publish a prospectus for the admission of securities to trading (regulated by the Prospectus Regulation).
[82] Recital 9.

There are numerous reasons for a delisting. The issuer may be interested in avoiding the costs resulting from the admission to the stock exchange due to numerous disclosure obligations and compliance requirements. The issuer can then either abstain from trading its shares on the stock exchange entirely or apply for the admission of its shares at a market with lowers requirements, such as the AIM in London, Scale in Frankfurt or Euronext Growth in Paris (downgrading).[83] The stock exchange operator may revoke the admission to the stock exchange, if the trade of the shares is no longer ensured or the issuer has breached important obligations.

For the **shareholders** of an issuer the delisting involves considerable disadvantages. Whilst they can legally still sell their shares, they have no market to operate over. This gives rise to the question of whether shareholders are protected in the event of a delisting. A uniform answer to this question for the whole of Europe is not possible as the European legislature has not addressed this question and the legal situation in the Member States is too disparate to be described in this book.[84]

---

[83] These alternative markets are organised as MTFs and registered as SME Growth Markets. See para. 23.
[84] Cf. for an analysis of the German and UK law P. Maume, 16 EBOR (2015), 255, 264–275; for the legal situation in Spain L. de Carlos and M. Rios, in: Panasar and Boeckman (eds.), *European Securities Regulation*, para. 20.305–20.307.

§ 8

Financial Instruments

Bibliography

Annunziata, Filippo, *Speak, If You Can: What Are You? An Alternative Approach to the Qualification of Tokens and Initial Coin Offerings*, 17 ECFR (2020), 129–154; Assmann, Heinz-Dieter et al. (eds.), *Kommentar zum Wertpapierhandelsgesetz*, 7th edn. (2019); Barsan, Iris M., *Legal Challenges of Initial Coin Offerings (ICO)*, RTDF (2017), 54–65; Brambring, Maximilian, *Zentrales Clearing von OTC-Derivaten unter EMIR (2017)*; Casper, Matthias, *Der Optionsvertrag* (2005); Choi, Stephen J., *A Framework for the Regulation of Securities Markets Intermediaries*, 45 BBLJ (2003), 45–81; Finck, Michèle, *Blockchain. Regulation and Governance in Europe* (2019); Fuller, Geoffrey and Collett, Elizabeth, *Structured Investment Vehicles—The Dullest Business on the Planet?*, 3 CMLJ (2008), 376–388; Fuller, Geoffrey, *The Law and Practice of International Capital Markets*, 3rd edn. (2013); Haisch, Martin L. and Helios, Marcus, *Rechtshandbuch Finanzinstrumente* (2011); Hu, Henry T., *Swaps, the Modern Process of Financial Innovation and the Vulnerability of a Regulatory Paradigm*, 138 U. Pa. L. Rev. (1989–1990), 333–436; Kalss, Susanne et al. (eds.), *Kapitalmarktrecht I*, 2nd edn. (2015); Klöhn, Lars et al., *Initial Coin Offerings (ICOs)*, 30 ZBB (2018), 89–106; Langenbucher, Katja, *European Securities Law – are we in need of a new definition? A thought inspired by initial coin offerings*, RTDF (2018), 40–48; Lenzi, Diletta, *Corporate Social Bonds: A Legal Analysis*, ECFR (2021), 291–319; Reiner, Günter, *Derivative Finanzinstrumente im Recht* (2002); Rechtschaffen, Alan N., *Capital Markets, Derivatives and the Law*, 3rd edn. (2013); Schmidt, Martin, *Derivative Finanzinstrumente*, 4th edn. (2014); Veil, Rüdiger, *Europa auf dem Weg zu einem Green Bond Standard*, WM (2020), 1093–1102; Veil, Rüdiger, *Climate-related financial disclosure*, in: Tountopoulos, Vassilios and Veil, Rüdiger (eds.), *Transparency of Stock Corporations in Europe—Rationales, Limitations and Perspective* (2019), 129–141; Werlauff, Erik, *EU Company Law*, 2nd edn. (2003); Zerey, Jean-Claude (ed.), *Finanzderivate*, 4th edn. (2016).

I. Introduction

The **Prospectus Regulation** (PR) harmonises the requirements for the drawing up, approval and distribution of the prospectus to be published when '**securities**' are offered to the public or admitted to trading on a regulated market.[1] The **Transparency Directive** (TD) establishes requirements in relation to the disclosure of periodic and ongoing information about issuers whose '**securities**' are already admitted to trading on a regulated market.[2]

1

---

[1] Cf. Art. 1(1) PR.
[2] Cf. Art. 1(1) TD.

Both legislative acts hence contain provisions on the disposal of and trade in securities. A precise definition of the term 'securities' is thus essential for determining the scope of application of both legal acts. However, it is not defined in the PR and TD. Instead, the two legislative acts refer to the concept of a security under MiFID II.[3]

2 The other level 1 regulations and directives operate largely with the term 'financial instruments'. The **MAR** and the **CRIM-MAD**, for example, demand from the Member States that they apply the prohibitions regarding insider dealings and market manipulation and the requirements on the disclosure of inside information and director's dealings to actions concerning '**financial instruments**'.[4] They do not define this term, but refer to Article 4(1)(5) MiFID II, which in turn refers to Annex I Section C MiFID II. Financial instruments are not only transferable **securities**, but inter alia also money market instruments, units in collective investment undertakings, physically or cash settled derivative contracts and financial contracts for difference.

3 The following section deals with **securities** as the key instrument for capital markets. However, it also examines other financial instruments in this context. Whilst this book places emphasis on the regulation of debt and equity capital markets, the derivatives markets are closely connected thereto and have been of increasing importance since 2008.[5] It is therefore necessary to make a few remarks to the concept of derivatives. Derivatives are used to limit risks from securities, currency risks or business risks. However, derivatives are also used to profit particularly strongly from the performance of a security (speculation).[6] Derivatives trading has grown enormously in importance in Europe over the last two decades. In recent years, financial instruments have been created and publicly offered for purchase on the blockchain, which are qualified as securities by national supervisory authorities (NCAs). This has led to an intensive discussion about the regulation of **DLT-based securities**. These instruments are explained in § 10 of this book.

II. Securities

1. Definitions in MiFID II

4 The MiFID II contains a definition of securities, which is referred to in the other Level 1 directives and regulations.[7]

'**Transferable securities**' means 'those classes of securities which are negotiable on the capital market, with the exception of instruments of payment, such as:

(a) **shares** in companies and other securities equivalent to shares in companies, partnerships or other entities, and depositary receipts in respect of shares;

---

[3] Cf. Art. 2(a) PR and Art. 2(1)(a) TD.
[4] Cf. Art. 2(1) MAR.
[5] Cf. R. Veil § 1 para. 48 and § 7 para. 3.
[6] See R. Veil § 23 para. 6.
[7] Cf. Art. 4(1)(44) MiFID II.

(b) **bonds** or other forms of securitised debt, including depositary receipts in respect of such securities;
(c) any **other securities** giving the right to acquire or sell any such transferable securities or giving rise to a cash settlement determined by reference to transferable securities, currencies, interest rates or yields, commodities or other indices or measures.'

This provision defines the concept of a security typologically by listing a number of instruments that qualify as securities, instead of providing an abstract definition of the term. This is the difference between the European and US concepts of securities.[8] It follows firstly that a security is characterised by three elements. After all, MiFID states that a security must be transferable, standardised and tradeable. 5

The requirement of **transferability** already follows from the wording of the provision. It means that there must be no legal obstacles to the disposal of the instruments. One such obstacle would be, for example, the requirement of a notarial certification of the transfer. 6

The **standardisation** of an instrument can also be derived from the wording of Article 4(1)(44) MiFID II ('categories' of securities). Consequently, securities may not be individually structured, but must have standardised (identical) features.[9] There must also be no personal liability of the owner of the instrument.[10] Otherwise, effective trading of the instrument would not be possible. It is sufficient if the rights vis-à-vis the issuer are standardised (issuer-related understanding). A bond issued by an issuer is therefore standardised if it gives all investors the same rights (for example, the right to repayment and interest). 7

Finally, the instrument must be '**negotiable** on the capital market'. The European concept of securities does not require tradability on a regulated market, MTF or OTF (trading venues under Article 4(1)(24) MiFID II). It is sufficient that the instrument can generally be negotiated on a market. Whether acquisition in good faith is possible is irrelevant under MiFID II.[11] 8

Secondly, qualification as a security requires that an **instrument** is functionally **comparable** to the examples of a security according to Article 4(1)(44) MiFID II (**shares** in companies, bonds or other forms of securitised debt, etc.).[12] In the absence of ECJ case law, there is no certainty about the characteristics of 'shares' (Article 4(1)(44)(a) MiFID II) and 'bonds' (Article 4(1)(44)(b) MiFID II).[13] 9

Whether the securities are securitised in (global) certificates is irrelevant according to the definition of MiFID II, which follows a technology-neutral approach. Thus, DLT-based instruments may also qualify as securities.[14] 10

---

[8] The US concept of securities is defined by the ruling of the US Supreme Court, *SEC v. W.J. Howey Co.*, 328 U.S. 293 (1946), also known as the Howey Test. The judgment concerns the term 'investment contract'. This is a 'contract, transaction or scheme whereby a person invests his money in a common enterprise and is led to expect profits solely from the efforts of the promoter or a third party.'
[9] Cf. H.-D. Assmann, in: Assmann et al. (eds.), *Kommentar zum Wertpapierhandelsrecht*, § 2 WpHG para. 11; S. Kalss et al. (eds.), *Kapitalmarktrecht I*, § 1 para. 4.
[10] Cf. S. Kalss et al. (eds.), *Kapitalmarktrecht I*, § 1 para. 4.
[11] P. Zickgraf, 63 AG (2018), 293, 302.
[12] Cf. recital 8 MiFID II.
[13] See para. 11 and 16.
[14] See R. Veil § 10 para. 7 f.

2. Shares

11 Shares are the prototype of negotiable securities on capital markets.[15] They are thus the first mentioned security in the MiFID's definition. Neither the understanding of shares nor that of shareholders is clearly described in European capital markets law. The TD merely defines the shareholder as any natural person or legal entity who holds shares of the issuer.[16]

12 In the absence of specifications in MiFID II the term must be construed in accordance with European corporate and accounting law. It follows from that: A share is a **participation** in the **company's capital** in **return** for a **contribution** in **cash** or in **kind**. Shares may confer different rights, including voting rights and profit-sharing rights. A shareholder is permanently associated with the company through the share[17] and has a residual claim on the company's assets after deduction of all debts.[18]

13 The rights and obligations of a shareholder are governed by national corporate laws. **Shares** can be issued as par shares or non-par shares.[19] For example, a stock corporation can issue shares with a nominal value of € 1 or higher or instead issue shares representing a fraction of ownership in a company. Non-par shares of a company must participate equally in its share capital. In many Member States, **preferred stocks** to which no voting rights are attributed are also commonly used. They are characterised by preferred share dividends which take precedent over common share dividends when an issuer allocates its profits. Preferred stocks normally carry no shareholder voting rights. They can also be traded on capital markets.

14 Generally, shares are **freely transferable**. Whether the transfer of shares can be restricted depends on the national corporate law of each Member State. In Germany, a restriction (*Vinkulierung*) is only possible for registered shares and has an immediate legal effect (in rem).[20] Therefore, the transfer of shares with restricted transferability is only possible with the consent of the issuer. This does not prevent registered shares with restricted transferability from being tradable on the capital markets. Smooth trade can, however, only be ensured if the company's consent can easily be obtained.[21]

15 If an issuer of shares from Europe wants access to the US capital market, this is usually done with **depositary receipts**. Such certificates securitise ownership rights in shares (or other securities). The depository receipts are issued by a custodian bank and can be traded on a capital market. The holder has the right vis-à-vis the depositary bank to exchange the depository receipt at any time for the underlying shares (deposited by the issuer). The most prominent example is American Depository Receipts (**ADRs**). To be traded on a US market, ADRs must be registered under the U.S. Securities Act.

---

[15] A. Rechtschaffen, *Capital Markets, Derivatives and the Law*, 43.
[16] Cf. Art. 2(1)(e) TD.
[17] Cf. Art. 2(2) Directive 2013/34/EU of 26 June 2013.
[18] Cf. R. Veil, 183 ZHR (2019), 346, 358 f.
[19] Cf. E. Werlauff, *EU Company Law*, chapter 9.3.
[20] Cf. § 68(2) AktG.
[21] H.-D. Assmann, in: Assmann/Schneider/Mülbert (eds.), *Kommentar zum Wertpapierhandelsrecht*, § 2 WpHG para. 184.

3. Bonds

Debt securities, especially bonds, play an important role in financing companies (**corporate bonds**) or states (**sovereign bonds**).[22] Similar to shares, they can also be traded on secondary markets.[23] The TD defines the term 'debt securities' as bonds or other forms of transferable securitised debts, with the exception of securities which are equivalent to shares in companies or which, if converted or if the rights conferred by them are exercised, give rise to a right to acquire shares or securities equivalent to shares.[24] Bonds may not be customised. The legal nature of a bond under civil law and the requirements for it to be effectively issued are to be determined pursuant to the national provisions of the respective Member State.

A debt instrument is any **tradable right** that entitles the **issuer** to **demand payment** of a specified **sum** of **money**, which the issuer must repay at maturity. Typical shareholders rights (voting rights, right to information, right to participate in a general meeting, right of appeal) as well as profit-sharing rights are not common to bonds and other debt instruments, although they can in principle be granted to the holder of the instrument, unless this is not permitted under national company law.

The holder (investor) of a debt instrument has a creditor stake as opposed to an equity stake in the company. In the case of the issuer's insolvency its claim is thus senior to the residual claims of the shareholders. The **interest rate** (coupon) the issuer has to pay to the bond holders is usually fixed throughout the life of the bond. The interest rate that the issuer of a bond must pay is influenced by a variety of factors, in particular the creditworthiness of the issuer, the length of the term and the mode of repayment. Due to the policy of the ECB, however, zero-interest bonds have now also become established, with sovereign bonds sometimes even yielding a negative return. Most bonds are annual, meaning that interest is paid at fixed yearly intervals. However, other agreements may also provide that the coupon is only paid on maturity of the bond. The terms of bonds vary, short-term bonds having an average maturity of four years, whilst long-term bonds have a maturity of more than eight years. On maturity, the issuer is obligated to repay the nominal amount to the investor.

The details of the term, in particular when the repayment claim is due, whether it is secured and whether the investor is entitled to a share of the issuer's profits (profit participation bond), are set out in the bond terms and conditions. These also govern protection against dilution. Whether the terms and condition are subject to a judicial control to ensure investor protection depends on the applicable national law.

4. Other Investment Products

The concept of financial instrument in EU capital markets law covers a wide range of instruments offered by issuers for the purpose of raising capital. However, there are debt instruments, which do not qualify as securities and do not fall under any other category of

---

[22] G. Fuller, *The Law and Practice of International Capital Markets*, para. 1.62; A. Rechtschaffen, *Capital Markets, Derivatives and the Law*, 18.
[23] See R. Veil § 7 para. 2.
[24] Art. 2(1)(b) TD. Cf. also Art. 4(1)(44)(b) MiFID II.

financial instrument. Thus, only national law of a Member State applies to the public offer of such assets. Examples are participatory loans and subordinated loans used in crowdfunding. Shares in partnerships are also not securities under Union law because they are not tradable.

III. Derivatives

21   Derivatives are **contracts** that are to be **fulfilled** at **fixed terms** and at a specific **future date**. This distinguishes them from normal (spot) transactions, which must be settled within two trading days.[25] **Futures** and **options** refer to a specific financial product (so-called underlying).[26] Underlying assets may be securities, currencies, interest rates, emission certificates or any other derivative instruments, financial indices or measures that can be effectively delivered or settled in cash. Futures are irrevocable for both parties. As opposed to this, an option grants the holder the right, but not the obligation, to buy (**call option**) respectively sell (**put option**) the underlying asset at a predetermined price. Certain options (premium deals) may require the buyer or seller to pay a premium (abandon) if it decides to withdraw from the contract.

22   Derivative contracts are transactions under uncertainty. In contrast to spot transactions, derivative transactions are not intended to transfer the underlying assets to the contracting party. For the purpose of derivatives, only the **market price** of the **underlying asset** and its further development is of interest. Thus, a small monetary investment promises a high profit (**leverage effect**). For example, with a call option for € 2 for a share at € 100, a profit of 50% can be achieved if the price rises to € 103 (3%). Derivative transactions are therefore mainly used for **speculation**.[27] The aim is then to make profits by correctly estimating future price developments or the intensity of price fluctuations. The risks of loss are therefore characterised by the price risks of the underlying asset. Furthermore, just as with securities, there is also a credit risk resulting from the creditworthiness of the issuer. Finally, derivatives can serve to **hedge** risks.

23   A bilateral OTC derivative construction proceeds in four steps. At the beginning (i) the parties conclude a master agreement that applies to a large number of transactions (**pre-trading phase**). This is followed by (ii) the trading phase (also called **matching**), which takes place either bilaterally or organised in a multilateral system. This is followed by the so-called clearing (iii). In this process, the outstanding claims between the parties are offset against each other (**netting**).[28] This has the advantage that the counterparty default risk is reduced.[29] Furthermore, open positions are collateralised. Finally, (iv) **settlement** takes place. In cash settlement, the parties owe money; in physical

---

[25] Art. 7(2) Delegated Regulation (EU) No. 2017/565 of 25 April 2016, OJ L 87, 31 March 2017, p. 1.
[26] A. Rechtschaffen, *Capital Markets, Derivatives and the Law*, 18.
[27] See on speculation R. Veil § 23 para. 7 f.
[28] In practice, different types of netting have emerged, namely payment netting, novation netting and liquidation netting. Cf. M. Brambring, *Zentrales Clearing von OTC-Derivaten unter EMIR*, 80 ff.
[29] Cf. M. Brambring, *Zentrales Clearing von OTC-Derivaten unter EMIR*, 71, 97.

settlement, they owe the transfer of the underlying asset. This process of a derivatives contract is being drastically changed by the regime the EU enacted in the aftermath of the financial market crisis of 2007/08 in order to counter the systemic risks of derivatives trading. EMIR[30] stipulates that standardised OTC derivative contracts must be cleared via central counterparties (CCPs) (clearing obligation). This means that the CCP joins as a contracting party and replaces one of the two contracting parties in each case. The CCP becomes the buyer on the one hand and the seller on the other.[31] This shifts the counterparty default risk to the CCP. As a consequence, the CCP requires collateral (so-called margins) from the parties. For non-standardised OTC derivative contracts, EMIR provides for risk mitigation obligations. Finally, EMIR requires all derivative contracts to be reported to trade repositories (supervised by ESMA).

The **variety** of **derivatives** is impressive. They can be divided into four categories:[32] (i) swaps; (ii) options; (iii) futures and forwards; (iv) stock loans and repos. Depending on the type of underlying, the MiFID II distinguishes between derivatives relating to securities and relating to commodities.[33]

Forwards and futures obligate the seller to deliver the underlying asset, eg shares, to the buyer at a specific time in the future (maturity) at a certain price (forward price).[34] The value of the forward on the settlement date is the difference between the agreed settlement price (forward price) and the current price of the security (underlyings). A future is a subtype of a forward. Unlike the forward, it is traded on stock exchanges.[35] As opposed to this, an **option** grants the buyer (beneficiary) the right but not the obligation to demand fulfilment by the other party (writer).[36] An option and a future can be either physically settled or cash settled. Under a cash settled option, physical delivery of the security is not required. The difference in price between the stock price and the fixed price in the option (strike price) is settled in cash.

With a swap, the contracting parties agree to exchange certain payments on future dates. The most prominent cases are interest rate and currency swaps. In the case of an **interest rate swap**, for example, one party may have a payment obligation that is fixed in the amount and the other party may have a payment obligation that is variable in the amount, depending on the current market interest rate. In contrast, a currency swap requires the parties to exchange payments in different currencies over a specified period of time.[37] A **cash settled swap** does not involve an exchange of payments. Instead, there is a cash settlement, for example between the price of the security on the financial market and the strike price specified in the warrant.

With a **total return swap** (TRS), the parties agree that one side must pass on the return on the reference asset and its increase in value to the other side, while the latter undertakes to compensate for any decrease in the value of the reference asset. Typically, a cash settlement is agreed. If the TRS

---

[30] Regulation (EU) No. 648/2012 of the European Parliament and the Council of 4. July 2012 on OTC derivatives, central counterparties and trade repositories, OJ EU L201 of 27. July 2012, p. 1.
[31] Cf. M. Brambring, *Zentrales Clearing von OTC-Derivaten unter EMIR*, 140.
[32] G. Fuller, *The Law and Practice of International Capital Markets*, para. 1.215.
[33] Cf. Annex I Sec. C (4), (5)–(7) MiFID II.
[34] Cf. G. Fuller, *The Law and Practice of International Capital Markets*, para. 1.226; C. Kumpan, in: Schwark and Zimmer (eds.), *Kapitalmarktrechts-Kommentar*, § 2 WpHG para. 37.
[35] Cf. C. Kumpan, in: Schwark and Zimmer (eds.), *Kapitalmarktrechts-Kommentar*, § 2 WpHG para. 40; U. Schüwer and S. Steffen, in: Zerey (ed.), *Finanzderivate*, § 1 para. 6.
[36] Cf. G. Fuller, *The Law and Practice of International Capital Markets*, para. 1.220; C. Kumpan, in: Schwark and Zimmer (eds.), *Kapitalmarktrechts-Kommentar*, § 2 WpHG para. 37.
[37] Cf. U. Schüwer and S. Steffen, in: Zerey (ed.), *Finanzderivate*, § 1 para. 7.

relates to a share, this means that the bank (writer) is obliged to pay the investor the difference between the value of the share at the beginning and end of the swap transaction plus any dividends; in return it receives interest and fees. If the share price rises, the investor is entitled to the difference; if the share price falls, the bank is entitled to the difference. Thus, both parties bear price risks of the share. The bank typically hedges against the risk by acquiring the shares of the company in question and holding them until the swap is terminated. The investor has no right to delivery of the shares. It is solely at the discretion of the writer whether to deliver the shares. In the end, the investor bears the economic consequences of the ownership of the shares.

IV. ESG Financial Products

28 The global community agreed at the UN Climate Change Conference in Paris that financial flows should be aligned with a pathway towards low greenhouse gas emissions and climate resilience.[38] The EU is reshaping financial markets law for this reason. The legal framework on sustainable finance has grown steadily over the past five years.[39] This also results in requirements for providers of financial products that pursue environmental goals and take social aspects into account (also referred to as ESG investments). In addition, the financial industry has developed best practices for financial market participants who distribute green financial products.[40] A characteristic feature of these financial products is that the financial means provided by investors are used to pursue specific environmental purposes.[41] The European regimes and non-binding best practices are primarily aimed at overcoming information asymmetries between providers of ESG financial products and investors. Above all, green washing is to be prevented. For providers, the information and disclosure requirements increase the cost of capital. However, the disclosure rules are essential to ensure investor confidence in environmentally sustainable financial products.

29 The range of ESG financial products is wide. The market for so-called impact investing is growing rapidly, **green bonds** being the most important ESG product. These bonds are usually designed in accordance with the ICMA's Green Bond Standards. A central element of these standards is the issuer's obligation to inform investors by means of a report on the appropriate use of funds (debt governance).[42] However, an expert group set up by the European Commission has proposed that the EU adopts a standard for green bonds.[43]

30 ESG fund units, when traded on the stock exchange, referred to as **Sustainability Screened ETFs**, play also a major role. These are shares in a UCITS that meet certain ESG criteria. France was the pioneer for this type of financial product with a detailed regime

---

[38] Art. 2 Abs. 1 lit. c) Paris Agreement.
[39] See R. Veil § 1 para. 59 und § 2 para. 22.
[40] Cf. ICMA, Green Bond Principles. Voluntary Process Guidelines, June 2021; Climate Bond Initiative, Climate Bonds Standard and Certification Scheme, Version 3.0.
[41] See on different objectives of investors R. Veil § 23 para. 8.
[42] Cf. R. Veil, WM (2020), 1093, 1098 ff.
[43] EU Technical Expert Group on Sustainable Finance, Report on EU Green Bond Standard, June 2019.

for the label Greenfin (originally named TEEC).[44] In addition, the financial industry has developed numerous labels to express that a fund meets minimum criteria and can therefore be considered ecologically and/or socially sustainable. Characteristically, a certain percentage (usually 50 or 75%) of the fund's assets consists of ecologically sustainable securities (stocks; bonds; etc.). The asset management company is obliged to disclose the sustainability risks to the investors and must explain the ecological sustainability of the fund, and also ensure that the companies in the portfolio act in an ESG-compliant manner (fund governance).

With green financial products, the question always arises as to the conditions under which the product may be called environmentally sustainable. To prevent **greenwashing**, the EU requires financial market participants to inform investors about the green characteristics of the financial product (disclosure obligations provided for by the SFDR). This requires classifying economic activities, ie whether nuclear power, for example, is 'green' or not. These aspects are regulated by the EU Taxonomy Regulation (SFTaxR). 31

---

[44] Cf. R. Veil, in: Tountopoulos/Veil (eds.), *Transparency of Stock Corporations in Europe* (2019), 129 ff.

§ 9

Market Participants

Bibliography

Audit, Mathias, *Les fonds souverains sont-ils des investisseurs étrangers comme les autres?*, 21 Recueil Dalloz (2008), 1424–1429; Bassan, Fabio, *Host States and Sovereign Wealth Funds, between National Security and International Law*, 21 EBLR (2010), 165–201; Beck, Roland and Fidora, Michael, *Sovereign Wealth Funds—Before and Since the Crisis*, 10 EBOR (2009), 353–367; de Meester, Bart, *International Legal Aspects of Sovereign Wealth Fund Investments: Reconciling International Economic Law and the Law of State Immunities with a New Role of the State*, 20 EBLR (2009), 779–817; Ferran, Eilís, *After the Crisis: The Regulation of Hedge Funds and Private Equity in the EU*, 12 EBOR (2011), 379–414; Gomber, Peter, *Elektronische Handelssysteme. Innovative Konzepte und Technologien im Wertpapierhandel* (2000); Goshen, Zohar and Parhomvsky, Gideon, *The Essential Role of Securities Regulation*, 55 Duke Law Journal (2006), 711–782; Gringel, Christoph, *Die Regulierung von Hedgefonds zwischen Anleger- und Fondsinteressen* (2009); Hofschroer, Josef, *Market Making und Betreuung im Börsenaktienhandel* (2011); Kahan, Marcel and Rock, Edward B., *Hedge Funds in Corporate Governance and Corporate Control*, 155 U. Pa. L. Rev. (2007), 1021–1094; Klein, April and Zur, Emanuel, *Entrepreneurial Shareholder Activism: Hedge Funds and other Private Investors*, 64 J. Fin. (2009), 182–229; Klöhn, Lars, *Wertpapierhandelsrecht diesseits und jenseits des Informationsparadigmas*, 177 ZHR (2013), 349–387; Kümpel, Siegfried et al. (eds.), *Bank- und Kapitalmarktrecht*, 5th edn. (2019); Kumpan, Christoph and Leyens, Patrick C., *Conflicts of Interest of Financial Intermediaries*, 5 ECFR (2008), 72–100; Markowitz, Harry M., *Portfolio Selection* (1952); Markowitz, Harry M., *Portfolio Selection, Efficient Diversification* (1991); Möllers, Thomas M. J., *Investor Protection in the System of Capital Markets Law: Legal Foundations and Outlook*, 36 N.C. J. Int'l L. & Com. Reg. (2010–2011), 57–84; Payne, Jennifer, *Private Equity and its Regulation in Europe*, 13 EBOR (2012), 559–585; Preißer, Maximilian M., *Sovereign Wealth Funds* (2013); Quaglia, Lucia, *The 'Old' and 'New' Political Economy of Hedge Fund Regulation in the European Union*, 34 WEP (2011), 665–682; Segna, Ulrich, *Die Rechtsform deutscher Wertpapierbörsen*, 11 ZBB (1999), 144–152; Schmidt, Reinhard H. and Spindler, Gerald, *Finanzinvestoren aus ökonomischer und juristischer Perspektive* (2008); Schmidt, Reinhard and Terberger, Eva H., *Investitions- und Finanzierungstheorie* (1999); Wentrup, Christian, *Die Kontrolle von Hedgefonds* (2009).

I. Introduction

Capital market participants can be divided into four categories: (i) **providers** of **market infrastructures**; (ii) **issuers** of **securities**; (iii) **investors**; (iv) **intermediaries**. On a primary market, investors act as buyers and **issuers** as sellers, whilst on a secondary market investors act both as buyers and sellers. Investors typically engage intermediaries because they do not have the expertise required for stock exchange transactions and rely on experts to evaluate the information (usually disclosed by the issuer). The financial intermediaries—primarily investment firms, financial analysts and rating agencies—play an important role, filtering the relevant information from the flood of information and submitting investment recommendations on its basis. Intermediaries are also in the interest of issuers whose costs for capital are reduced by letting financial analysts evaluate the information.[1] As opposed to this, rating agencies such as Standard & Poor's, Moody's and Fitch restrict themselves to evaluating the relative creditworthiness (solvency) of issuers of equity and debt in order to provide investors with the information necessary for well-informed investment decisions.[2]

2   This section deals with providers of market infrastructures, investors and issuers. It explains their role on capital markets and discusses whether they can be further categorised. The role of intermediaries and their specifics are not dealt with separately in this section, but are described in the sixth and seventh chapters of the book in the sections on the regulation of intermediaries.

II. Providers of Market Infrastructures

3   Market infrastructures are **trading venues** for **investors**. MiFID II provides for three types of trading venues (Regulated Market (RM)), Multilateral Trading Facility (MTF), Organised Trading Facility (OTF)) and thus aims to cover all types of multilateral trading of securities and derivatives.[3] The providers of market infrastructures are stock exchanges and investment firms. They operate trading venues and generate income from securities trading. Under MiFID II, a RM is operated by a market operator,[4] which may also operate MTFs and OTFs. MiFID II qualifies the operation of MTFs and OTFs as investment services.[5] The distinction is important because the governance and capital requirements for a market operator differ from those for investment firms.[6]

4   Turnover from stock trading is marginal today compared to other business of stock exchanges.[7] At Deutsche Börse AG, the 'Xetra' division (trading, clearing and listings) accounted for 7.58% of the turnover in 2019. In contrast, the financial derivatives business unit contributed 32.6% to the turnover. At the London Stock Exchange, Capital Market Formation and Trade (primary and secondary market for equity trading, excluding fixed income, derivatives and other) accounted for 14.5% of the turnover. In contrast, the division Financial Market Information contributed 39% to the turnover.

---

[1] See R. Veil § 26 para. 2.
[2] See R. Veil § 27 para. 1.
[3] See R. Veil § 7 para. 19.
[4] See Art. 4(1)(18) MiFID II.
[5] Cf. Art. 4(1)(2) in connection with Annex I Section A MiFID II.
[6] Market operators are subject to the rules of MiFID II. The capital requirements are laid down in Art. 47(1)(f) MiFID II. Investment firms were previously subject to the CRD IV-regime. This will not change for large investment firms. For others, Regulation (EU) 2019/2033 (Investment Firm Regulation – IFR) and Directive (EU) 2019/2034 (Investment Firm Directive – IFD) will apply from 26 June 2021.
[7] The information is taken from the Annual Reports 2019 of Deutsche Börse AG and the London Stock Exchange.

It is important for investors to be able to carry out transactions at the lowest possible cost on a trading venue. This implies, firstly, that they will find a buyer or seller at all and, secondly, that the transaction will have little impact, if any, on the price of the security. Investors therefore have an interest in a liquid capital market. The more frequently a share is traded, the greater the **liquidity** of the capital market.

Liquidity is a **term** from **financial market theory** that captures market quality.[8] The liquidity of capital markets can be considered from four points of view.[9] The first aspect of *market depth* concerns the possibility to execute transactions close to the existing market price (price continuity). Market depth is measured in terms of the number of orders whose price differs only slightly from the price at which the largest number of existing orders can be executed. *Market breadth* is the ability of the market to execute larger orders (so-called *block trades*).[10] Another aspect to describe liquidity is *market resiliency*. This refers to the ability of the market to offset price movements resulting solely from (large-volume) orders in the short term. If these lead to a fall in price and this fall is not due to new information, the market is resilient if the price moves quickly back to the original price. The *immediacy of orders* expresses the fact that an order can be executed promptly.

The term liquidity is also a **legal concept. Example a)** MiFID II allows investment firms to engage in **high frequency trading** under certain conditions,[11] because it has a **positive impact** on the **liquidity** of capital markets.[12] MiFID II therefore defines the concept of a liquid market in Article 4(1)(25). This is 'a market for a financial instrument [...], where there are ready and willing buyers and sellers on a continuous basis, assessed in accordance with [certain] criteria, taking into consideration the specific market structures of the particular financial instrument'. The criteria listed are: (i) the average frequency and size transactions over a range of market conditions, having regard to the nature and life cycle of products within the class of financial instrument; (ii) the number and type of market participants; (iii) the average size of spreads, where available. **Example b)** A national supervisory authority (NCA) may establish an **accepted market practice** (AMP) if the market practice has a **positive effect** on **market liquidity** and efficiency (Article 13(2) (c) MAR). Further specifications are laid down in Article 5 Regulation (EU) 2016/908. The NCA shall assess the impact the market practice has on at least the following elements: (i) volume traded; (ii) number of orders in the order book (order depth); (iii) speed of execution of the transactions; (iv) volume weighted average price of a single session, daily closing price; (v) bid/offer spread, price fluctuation and volatility; (vi) regularity of quotations or transactions. The definitions of MiFID II and MAR are based on financial market theory of liquidity, but also take into account the content and purpose of the rules.

The problem of illiquid markets is faced by **market makers.** According to the legal definition in European capital markets law, a market maker is a 'person who holds himself out on the financial markets on a continuous basis as being willing to deal on own account by buying and selling financial instruments against that person's proprietary capital at prices

---

[8] See on the information efficiency of markets as a further criterion of market quality R. Veil § 2 para. 29 ff.
[9] See on the four aspects P. Gomber, *Elektronische Handelssysteme*, 13 ff.; J. Hofschroer, *Market Making und Betreuung im Börsenaktienhandel*, 25 ff.
[10] What is meant by a block trade is not regulated by law and is understood differently in market practice. Cf. *Gomber*, Elektronische Handelssysteme, 43 with reference to the NYSE's practice of qualifying transactions involving more than 10,000 shares as block orders.
[11] See M. Lerch § 25.
[12] See recitals 62 and 113 MiFID II and Art. 17 MiFID II.

defined by that person'.[13] Thus, a market maker permanently indicates his willingness to trade on the financial markets for his own account. It makes a commitment to the market operator to place buy and sell orders for a certain quantity of securities, which may only differ by a certain percentage (so-called **spread**).[14] Investors can therefore rely on finding a buyer or seller, at least as long as the minimum volume promised by the market maker is not reached. Market makers do not receive a brokerage fee, but profit from the realised spread (difference between the price at which they sell and at which they buy securities), which represents the remuneration. Market makers improve liquidity and contribute to the institutional functioning of capital markets. For this reason, they also enjoy regulatory privileges in some areas.[15] Market makers are also known as designated sponsors. Stock exchanges are to ensure that a sufficient number of investment firms are admitted as market makers who post firm quotes at competitive prices with the result of providing liquidity to the market on a regular and predictable basis.[16]

9   The *spread* between buy and sell (bid and ask) prices is the difference between the bid and ask price. It is an important indicator of liquidity. For example, a small spread indicates a high market depth, whilst a high spread reflects different opinions of market participants about the fair price of the security and may reflect a high level of risk. An investor learns about the current bid and ask price on a market through his broker.

III. Issuers

10 In principle, anyone can be the issuer of a security, but only a stock corporation can issue shares. The European legislative acts waste few words on issuers. The PR defines the issuer as a **legal entity,** which **issues** or proposes to issue **securities**.[17] The TD extends this definition to 'a legal entity governed by private or public law, including a State, whose securities are admitted to trading on a regulated market, the issuer being, in the case of depository receipts representing securities, the issuer of the securities represented'.[18] The MAR provides for a similar definition.[19]

11 The PR refers to the situation of a securities issuer acting directly as a market participant by selling securities on the primary market.[20] Regarding securities traded on the secondary market, the issuer is no longer directly involved as the transaction takes place between investors, ie the individual seller and buyer. However, the issuer remains liable for the securitised claims. The issuer, for example, remains obligated to the buyer of bonds to repay the money

---

[13] Cf. Art. 2(1)(n) TD and Art. 4(1)(7) MiFID II.
[14] P. Gomber, *Elektronische Handelssysteme*, 51; J. Hofschroer, *Market Making und Betreuung im Börsenaktienhandel*, 34.
[15] Cf. Art. 9(2)(a) MAR and Art. 9(5) TD.
[16] Cf. Art. 48(2) MiFID II.
[17] Cf. Art. 2(1)(h) PR.
[18] Cf. Art. 2(1)(d) TD.
[19] Cf. Art. 1(1)(21) MAR.
[20] Shares can be issued by the issuer itself or through securities underwriting. See R. Veil § 7 para. 34 f.

on maturity.²¹ Trading in securities on the secondary market is ensured by subjecting the issuer to numerous disclosure obligations in the MAR and the TD. The issuer must therefore be regarded as an **indirect market participant** on the secondary market.²²

European capital markets law is limited to imposing obligations on issuers. However, market abuse law also imposes specific obligations on the issuer's executive bodies, such as the obligation to disclose directors' dealings. In this respect, **directors** and **members of** a **supervisory body** are indirect market participants. In addition, more stringent insider trading rules apply to members of executive bodies, as MAR considers them to be primary insiders.

IV. Investors

1. Types

Investors can be divided into **private investors** and **institutional investors**. Institutional investors encompass banks, insurance companies, investment funds, hedge funds, sovereign wealth funds and pension funds. They are indirect capital market participants,²³ as they are generally not permitted to participate directly in the conclusion of contracts on a regulated market.

The commonly used term '**financial investor**' is not a legal one. Financial investors are investors who do not pursue business policy strategies, but rather only pursue financial interests with their investments. Whilst a strategic investor will also follow financial aims, it must be distinguished from the financial investor who follows no long-term business strategy for making profits but rather aims at making profits from investment to investment.²⁴

Private equity companies and hedge funds are typical financial investors.²⁵ **Hedge funds** usually make use of certain types of financial instruments and certain trading practices, such as short selling, in order to attain leverage.²⁶ Activist hedge funds aim to improve the governance of companies and increase the value of the company. They are thus especially interested in publicly listed companies in which the principal-agent conflict is especially apparent. In order to achieve their aims, hedge funds must acquire a critical 3–10% of company shares. Generally, they will need, and search for, assistance by other investors to achieve this.

---

[21] On the duties of the issuer of a bond see R. Veil § 8 para. 17.
[22] Cf. M. Oulds, in: Kümpel et al. (eds.), *Bank- und Kapitalmarktrecht*, para. 10.68.
[23] Cf. M. Oulds, in: Kümpel et al. (eds.), *Bank- und Kapitalmarktrecht*, para. 10.79.
[24] R. Schmidt and G. Spindler, *Finanzinvestoren aus ökonomischer und juristischer Perspektive* (2008).
[25] In more detail M. Kahan and E. Rock, 155 U. Pa. L Rev. (2007), 1021–1094; A. Klein and E. Zur, 64 J. Fin. (2009), 182–229; C. Gringel, *Die Regulierung von Hedgefonds zwischen Anleger- und Fondsinteressen*; C. Wentrup, *Die Kontrolle von Hedgefonds*.
[26] Leverage means that an equity investor increases the return on equity by using debt (loans) or derivatives. Leverage depends on the debt ratio and can be positive, but also negative if the interest on the debt is greater than the return on total capital.

16 The **providers of collective investment schemes** are regulated by Union law. The regimes distinguish between Undertakings for Collective Investment in Transferable Securities (**UCITS**)[27] and Alternative Fund Managers (**AFM**).[28] There is no European regulation for sovereign wealth funds yet, although the European Commission has already started thinking about it.[29] The rules on the harmonisation of investment funds, which were introduced at a European level more than three decades ago,[30] constitute a separate regulatory area which cannot be described in detail here. However, three principles are to be examined in more detail.

17 The portfolio of a collective investment scheme typically comprises numerous assets (securities, derivatives, etc.). The large number of assets allows the **risks to be diversified**. This principle goes back to the **portfolio theory**[31] developed by Harry M. Markowitz. Among other things, portfolio theory deals with the fundamental question of how a portfolio should be rationally structured.[32] It is based on the assumption of a risk-averse investor who wants to achieve the highest possible return, but who only wants to take a certain risk that she considers appropriate. The investor best achieves the goal of an optimal return through diversification, which excludes a detrimental correlation of the investment securities as far as possible. The broader an investor invests in different asset classes (equities, bonds, derivatives), the more he reduces the risk of total loss.

18 The distinction between systematic risks (also called market risks) and unsystematic risks (also called specific risks) is one of the portfolio theory principles.[33] Systematic risk concerns external and uncontrollable variables related to the market or a market segment. It affects not only a single security, but a large number of securities. Examples include market risks, interest rate risks, currency risks and political risks. Protection can be achieved through asset allocation. This means that the assets are spread across various asset classes (shares, bonds, real estate, currencies, etc.). Unsystematic risks refer to the risks associated with a particular security or issuer. Examples are business risks and financial risks. Protection against these risks is achieved by diversifying the portfolio.

---

[27] Directive 2009/65/EC of the European Parliament and of the Council of 13 July 2009 on the coordination of laws, regulations and administrative provisions relating to undertakings for collective investment in transferable securities (UCITS), OJ L 302, 17 November 2009, p. 32.

[28] Directive 2011/61/EU of the European Parliament and of the Council of 8 June 2011 on Alternative Investment Fund Managers, OJ L 174, 1 July 2011, p. 1–73.

[29] Cf. Communication from the Commission to the European Parliament, the Council, the European Economic and Social Committee and the Committee of the Regions of 27 February 2008—a common European approach to Sovereign Wealth Funds, COM(2008), 115 final. For literature on sovereign wealth funds see M. Audit, *Les fonds souverains sont-ils des investisseurs étrangers comme les autres?*, 21 Recueil Dalloz (2008), 1424–1429; F. Bassan, *Host States and Sovereign Wealth Funds, between National Security and International Law*, 21 EBLR (2010), 165–201; R. Beck and M. Fidora, *Sovereign Wealth Funds—Before and Since the Crisis*, 10 EBOR (2009), 353–367; B. de Meester, *International Legal Aspects of Sovereign Wealth Fund Investments: Reconciling Economic Law and the Law of State Immunities with a New Role of the State*, 20 EBLR (2009), 779–817; M. Preisser, *Sovereign Wealth Funds*.

[30] Cf. Council Directive 85/611/EEC on the coordination of laws, regulations and administrative provisions relating to undertakings for collective investment in transferable securities (UCITS), OJ L 375, 31 December 1985, p. 3. Recast by Directive 2009/65/EC of the European Parliament and of the Council of 13 July 2009 on the coordination of laws, regulations and administrative provisions relating to undertakings for collective investment in transferable securities (UCITS), OJ L 302, 13 July 2009, p. 32–96.

[31] H. M. Markowitz, *Portfolio Selection* (1952); H. M. Markowitz, *Portfolio Selection, Efficient Diversification* (1991).

[32] R. A. Brealey, *Corporate Finance*, 178 ff., 198 ff.

[33] R. A. Brealey, *Corporate Finance*, 170.

The law on collective investment schemes is based on the portfolio theory. An efficient portfolio diversification takes into account not only the systematic risks but also the unsystematic risks. The principle of risk diversification is supplemented by the principle of risk avoidance by limiting the permissible assets.

The second principle of a collective investment scheme is the **principle of third-party management** of **portfolios**. A management company acts as fiduciary for investors. Third-party management results in principal-agent conflicts (information asymmetries between manager and investor; remuneration interests of the manager). Investors also have costs because they should control the manager. Investment law (UCITS and AIFM Directives) addresses these problems mainly through information obligations on the manager, in particular on its investment policy and strategy. It takes into account that professional investors and private investors need to be protected differently.

Finally, it is characteristic that a large number of investors with comparatively small amounts are enabled to invest in a diversified portfolio of assets. The concept of **collective investment** works best when there is no outflow of assets from the fund. In principle, investors have therefore no right of termination and no claim to repayment. However, it is basically possible to allow the trading of fund units on a secondary market (so-called exchange traded funds).[34]

2. Level of Protection

In academic discussion, a distinction is made between **information traders**, **liquidity traders** and **noise traders**.[35] According to *Goshen* and *Parchomovsky*, securities regulation should protect the interests of information traders, as they are best placed to ensure efficient and liquid capital markets.[36] They claim a core concern of securities regulation should be to ensure a competitive market for information traders.[37]

Goshen and *Parchomovsky* argue market participants be divided into four categories.[38] The first category consists of insiders who have access to inside information and the knowledge and ability to assess the information. The second group are information traders. These are experienced professional investors who have analytical models for their investment decisions, and analysts who act as buy-side or sell-side analysts or are independently. These information traders, like insiders, have the knowledge and ability to collect, evaluate and price company- and market-specific information. Thirdly, there are utility traders who do not collect and evaluate information, but buy securities according to a specific strategy independently of information (eg for pension purposes). Finally, there are noise traders who invest as if they were in possession of information. These may be irrational investors who invest based on rumours, or stock pickers who act in a similar way to information traders but are slower to gather and evaluate all relevant information.

---

[34] Although a fund unit does not qualify as a security, it has the same characteristics as a security (see R. Veil § 8 para. 6–8), so that it is justified to qualify it as a security *sui generis*.
[35] Z. Goshen and G. Parchomovsky, 55 Duke Law Journal (2006), 711; L. Klöhn, 177 ZHR (2013), 349 ff.
[36] Z. Goshen and G. Parchomovsky, 55 Duke Law Journal (2006), 711, 715.
[37] Z. Goshen and G. Parchomovsky, 55 Duke Law Journal (2006), 711, 716: 'Thus, the aggregate effect of securities regulation is to create and secure a competitive market for information traders.'
[38] Z. Goshen and G. Parchomovsky, 55 Duke Law Journal (2006), 711, 722 ff.

24 According to *Goshen* and *Parchomovsky*, disclosure obligations and market abuse prohibitions should ensure that information traders can fulfil their role in ensuring efficient securities markets. It would therefore be necessary, among other things, to reduce the information costs of information traders through mandatory disclosure requirements.[39] Furthermore, disclosure should not be limited to hard information, but should also encompass soft information, ie prognoses and other information about future circumstances. In addition, *Goshen* and *Parchomovsky* argue the Fraud-on-the-Market Theory[40] should also be applied as a presumption rule if the capital market is not efficient due to lack of liquidity.[41]

25 The concept of information traders is a typological classification of market participants, which reflects the observation that firstly investors invest money for different goals and with different strategies and secondly have limited access to information and limited abilities to evaluate information. This highlights the importance of information intermediaries and illustrates the concern of European capital markets regulation to ensure that intermediaries provide professional services in the interests of investors. However, no conclusions for the interpretation of standards can be drawn from the idea of a 'competitive market for information traders'.[42] The European legislature has not based securities regulation on this thesis. Problems of interpretation should be solved with regard to the declared regulatory objectives of market abuse and transparency law (market efficiency, equal information opportunities for investors, etc.).

26 The MAR does not differentiate between private and institutional investors. The disclosure requirements and prohibitions benefit all investors, the European legislature seeing **private** and **institutional investors** as **equally worthy of protection**.[43] In particular, the disclosure regimes of the MAR and TD for the secondary market assume that all investors are able to understand the information. This is clearly the idea of the obligation of an issuer to disclose inside information immediately to the public (Article 17 MAR). 'In order to guarantee at Union level equal access of investors to inside information, the inside information should be publicly disclosed free of charge, simultaneously and as fast as possible amongst all categories of investors throughout the Union'.[44] Consequently, ad hoc notifications are also addressed to private investors,[45] who must be able to assess the price relevance of the event disclosed. TD's disclosure requirements also aim at enabling all investors to make an investment decision.[46]

27 **Primary market disclosure** differentiates more between the two categories of investors because professional investors do not need to get the information in prospectuses. They either already have the information or they can obtain the information cheaply and reliably by talking to the issuer's management. The PR therefore provides for exemptions from the obligation to publish a prospectus when securities are offered to **qualified investors**, ie

---

[39] Z. Goshen and G. Parchomovsky, 55 Duke Law Journal (2006), 711, 738, 755 ff.
[40] See R. Veil § 2 para. 34.
[41] Z. Goshen and G. Parchomovsky, 55 Duke Law Journal (2006), 711, 738, 766 ff.
[42] Dissenting opinion: L. Klöhn, 177 ZHR (2013), 349 ff.
[43] See recitals 14 and 55 MAR.
[44] Recital 1 Regulation (EU) 2016/1055.
[45] Cf. R. Veil and A. Brüggemeier, in: Meyer et al. (eds.), *Handbuch Marktmissbrauchsrecht*, § 10 para. 168 ff.; critically H.-D. Assmann, in: Assmann et al. (eds.), *Kommentar zum Wertpapierhandelsrecht*, Art. 7 MAR para. 65 f.
[46] Cf. recital 5 and 7 TD: 'a high level of investor protection'.

credit institutions, investment firms, other authorised or regulated financial institutions and insurance companies.[47]

The MiFID II also distinguishes between different types of investors. Annex II lists who must be regarded as **professional clients** for the purpose of the directive. '**Retail clients**' are clients who are not professional clients.[48] The MiFID II assumes that professional clients require less protection, having sufficient experience, knowledge and expertise to make their own investor decisions and correctly assess the risks connected thereto. It thus abstains from protecting professional investors as recipients of investment advice or other investment services. The information obligations laid down in Articles 24(3)–(4), 25(2)–(3) MiFID II only apply to retail investors and potential retail investors.

MiFID II and PRIIPS are based on the premise that retail investors are particularly vulnerable.[49] This implies that retail investors have no experience with securities and do not understand the language of financial markets, or at least not sufficiently. Investment firms must take this into account when providing investment services

---

[47] Cf. Art. 2(e)(i) PR.
[48] Cf. Art. 4(1)(11) MiFID II.
[49] See R. Veil § 6 para. 36.

§ 10

Cryptoassets and DLT Market Infrastructures

Bibliography

Ammann, Thorsten, *Bitcoin als Zahlungsmittel im Internet*, CR (2018), 379–386; Annunziata, Filippo, *Speak, If You Can: What Are You? An Alternative Approach to the Qualification of Tokens and Initial Coin Offerings*, ECFR (2020), 129–154; Barsan, Iris M., *Legal Challenges of Initial Coin Offerings (ICO)*, RTDF N 3 (2017), 54–65; Bashir, Imran, *Mastering Blockchain*, 2nd edn. (2018); Braegelmann, Tom/Kaulartz, Markus, *Rechtshandbuch Smart Contracts* (2019); Brummer, Chris, *Cryptoassets. Legal, Regulatory, and Monetary Perspectives* (2019); Casper, Matthias, *Elektronische Schuldverschreibung: es ist Zeit für einen grundlegenden gesetzlichen Neustart – Anmerkungen zum Eckpunktepapier des BMJV und des BMF*, BKR (2019), 209–217; Ebers, Martin/Heinze, Christian/Krügel, Tina/Seinrötter, Björn, *Künstliche Intelligenz und Robotik, Rechtshandbuch* (2020); Finck, Michèle, *Blockchain. Regulation and Governance in Europe* (2019); Fischer, Marius, *Zur Regulierung dezentraler Sekundärmärkte*, ZBB (2020), 158–167; Geva, Benjamin, *Cryptocurrencies and the evolution of banking, money and payments*, in: Brummer, Chris (ed.), *Cryptoassets: Legal, Regulatory, and Monetary Perspectives* (2019), 11–38; Gurrea-Martinez, Aurelio/León, Nydia R., *The law and finance of Initial Coin Offerings*, in: Brummer, Chris (ed.), *Cryptoassets: Legal, Regulatory, and Monetary Perspectives* (2019), 117–156; Hacker, Philipp/Thomale, Chris, *Crypto-Securities Regulation: ICOs, Token Sales and Cryptocurrencies under EU Financial Law*, ECFR (2018), 645–696; Hahn, Christopher/Wilkens, Robert, *ICO vs. IPO – Prospektrechtliche Anforderungen bei Equity Token Offerings*, ZBB (2019), 10–26; Klöhn, Lars/Parhofer, Nicolas/Resas, Daniel, *Initial Coin Offerings (ICOs)*, ZBB (2018), 89–106; Koch, Philipp, *Die „Tokenisierung" von Rechtspositionen als digitale Verbriefung*, JBB (2018), 359–368; Kunschke, Dennis/Schaffelhuber, Kai A. (ed.), *FinTech* (2018); Langenbucher, Katja, *European Securities Law – Are we in need of a new definition? A thought inspired by initial coin offerings*, RTDF N 2/3 (2018), 40–48; Lerch, Marcus P., *Bitcoin als Evolution des Geldes: Herausforderungen, Risiken und Regulierungsfragen*, JBB (2015), 191–204; Lin, Lindsey X., *Deconstruction Decentralized Exchanges*, Stanford Journal of Blockchain Law & Policy (2019), 58–77; Maume, Philipp/Maute, Lena, *Rechtshandbuch Kryptowerte* (2020); Möslein, Florian/Omlor, Sebastian (eds.), *FinTech-Handbuch* (2019); Narayanan, Arvind/Bonneau, Joseph/Felten, Edward/Miller, Andrew/Goldfelder, Steven, *Bitcoin and Cryptocurrency Technologies* (2016); Pekler, Florian/Rirsch, Ralph/Tomanek, Stefan, *Kapitalmarktrechtliche Hindernisse für den Handel von Security Token*, ZFR (2020), 172–177; Schweizerische Eidgenossenschaft, *Rechtliche Grundlagen für Distributed Ledger Technologie und Blockchain in der Schweiz. Eine Auslegeordnung mit Fokus auf dem Finanzsektor*, Bericht des Bundesrats, 14.12.2018; Veil, Rüdiger, *Token-Emissionen im europäischen Kapitalmarktrecht*, ZHR 183 (2019), 346–387; von der Crone, Hans Caspar/Monsch, Martin/Meisser, Luzius, *Aktien Token. Eine privatrechtliche Analyse der Möglichkeit des Gebrauchs von DLT Systemen zur Abbildung und Übertragung von Aktien*, GesKR (2019), 1–17; Wolf, Nicolai, *Initial Coin Offerings* (2020); Zickgraf, Peter, *Initial Coin Offerings – Ein Fall für das Kapitalmarktrecht?*, AG (2018), 293–308.

I. Foundations

1 Securities markets are already largely digitalised. However, most of the securities traded on the markets are still securitised in (global) certificates, as this is required by national laws in many Member States. This is starting to change, as there are now also entirely digital securities which are generated on the blockchain.

2 A **blockchain** can be described as an **infrastructure** for **secure, decentralised** and **unchangeable data storage** (also called 'distributed ledger' - DLT),[1] which can generally be used by anyone—in the context of capital markets by investors and companies—to process transactions. All participants (also called nodes) have the blockchain stored simultaneously on their computers. There is no superordinate and identifiable person who has a regulatory function.[2] Rather, the nodes monitor transactions within the network.[3] If a transaction is to be made, a corresponding transaction message is distributed to all nodes via a peer-to-peer mechanism. The nodes have incentives to confirm transactions on the blockchain because they are remunerated for doing so.

3 The blockchain contains a list of data entries (blocks) that are linked together by a cryptographic procedure. A block contains a so-called hash of the previous block, a time stamp and certain transaction data. Transactions that have already been verified are bundled into new blocks. When a certain number of transactions is reached, a new block is added to the existing blockchain, which is thus constantly extended. To add a new block, a consensus mechanism is needed to ensure the security of the system. Such a mechanism should meet three requirements. It is necessary that (i) all nodes agree on the same blocks, (ii) the information contained in the blocks is correct, and (iii) the time required to confirm transactions is reasonable.[4]

4 The consensus mechanism determines which parties are involved in the operation of the blockchain.[5] With the proof of work mechanism, nodes (also called miners) verify and validate transactions. Nodes compete against each other to solve complex mathematical puzzles and are rewarded (through tokens) for solving them. The one who solves the puzzle first can generate the new block (so-called mining) and is rewarded (through tokens) for solving it. Nodes therefore have incentives to participate in the verification process. If everyone is free to participate in the operation of the infrastructure (in particular as a 'node'),[6] the **blockchain** is called **permissionless**. Otherwise, it is a so-called **permissioned blockchain**, which can be either **public** or **private**, depending on its accessibility.

---

[1] Cf. *Fromberger/Zimmermann*, in: Maume/Maute, Rechtshandbuch Kryptowerte, § 1 para. 1.
[2] Cf. KG of 25.9.2018 – (4) 161 Ss 28/18 (35/18), ZIP 2018, 2015, 2016.
[3] Cf. KG of 25.9.2018 – (4) 161 Ss 28/18 (35/18), ZIP 2018, 2015, 2016.
[4] *Roßbach*, in Möslein/Omlor, Fintech-Handbuch, § 4 para. 46.
[5] The two most prominent mechanisms are 'proof of work' and 'proof of stake'. In addition, a number of hybrid mechanisms exist. Cf. A. Narayanan et al., *Bitcoin and Cryptocurrency Technologies*, Chapter 8; I. Bashir, *Mastering blockchain*, 36–40.
[6] The 'proof of work' mechanism uses a process in which special nodes on the network verify and validate transactions. The nodes (also called miners) compete against each other to solve complex mathematical puzzles, and are rewarded for solving them. Cf., on the compensation of miners, A. Narayanan et al., *Bitcoin and Cryptocurrency Technologies*, 267; I. Bashir, *Mastering blockchain*, 171.

1. Tokenisation of Securities on the Blockchain

Tokens are software programs that lead to entries on a blockchain. They are created by a **smart contract** and digitally 'represent' claims and/or rights.[7] The blockchain uses asymmetric cryptography to authorise transactions. Asymmetric cryptography operates with two keys: the private key, a randomly generated number that is known only by the user, and the public key, which is freely accessible because it is published by the owner of the private key. With the private key, the owner declares her agreement with the transaction (transmission of a token). With the public key, anyone can find out that the owner has authorised the transaction.[8]

European supervisory authorities[9] and academic literature[10] distinguish between three types of tokens: (i) currency tokens, (ii) investment tokens (also called asset tokens, security tokens or equity tokens) and (iii) utility tokens. The distinction is made with regard to the different functions of the respective token. For example, **currency tokens** are used for payment purposes. The best-known examples for currency tokens are Bitcoin and Ether. They may qualify as (electronic) money.[11]

The situation is different with **investment tokens**. These represent ownership rights, rights to future profits of a company or other company-related rights, such as voting rights.[12] Supervisory authorities and legal literature qualify investment tokens as securities because they are functionally comparable to bonds or other debt instruments.

With other tokens, the qualification under European securities law is more difficult. This is particularly true for tokens that grant the holder the right to purchase a product or service.[13] Typically, the product does not exist at the time of the ICO because it is yet to be produced. Such types of tokens are called **utility tokens**, which is, however, not a legal concept. Among other things, utility tokens are granted as a reward for users who provide a service on a platform.[14] For example, a utility token can grant access to a communication network or enable data to be stored on other users' computers. In contrast to investment tokens, utility tokens do not represent profit claims against a company, but resemble a digital voucher.[15] In the legal discussion, however, some academics argue that utility tokens may

---

[7] Cf. Swiss Confederation, *Rechtliche Grundlagen für Distributed Ledger Technologie und Blockchain in der Schweiz. Eine Auslegeordnung mit Fokus auf dem Finanzsektor*, Bericht des Bundesrats, 14 December 2018, 34–36; P. Koch, 30 ZBB (2018), 359, 362.

[8] Cf. I. Bashir, *Mastering blockchain*, 85.

[9] Cf. EBA, *Report with advice for the European Commission on crypto-assets*, 9 January 2019, 7; ESMA, *Advice. Initial Coin Offerings and Crypto Assets*, ESMA50-157-1391, 9 January 2019, 8, 18 ff.; SMSG, *Own Initiative Report on Initial Coin Offerings and Crypto-Assets*, 19 October 2018, ESMA22-106-1338; Expert Group on Regulatory Obstacles to Financial Innovation (ROFIEG), *30 Recommendations on Regulation, Innovation and Finance, Final Report to the European Commission*, December 2019, 52–58 on the taxonomy of cryptoassets.

[10] Cf. P. Hacker and C. Thomale, 15 ECFR (2018), 645, 652.

[11] Cf. EBA (fn. 9), 13; B. Geva, in: Brummer (ed.), *Cryptoassets: Legal, Regulatory, and Monetary Perspectives*, 11, 30–36.

[12] Cf. P. Hacker and C. Thomale, 15 ECFR (2018), 645, 652.

[13] Cf. A. Gurrea-Martinez and N. Remolina León, in: Brummer (ed.), *Cryptoassets: Legal, Regulatory, and Monetary Perspectives*, 117, 119–123.

[14] Cf. L. Klöhn et al., 30 ZBB (2018), 89, 92; A. Gurrea-Martinez and N. Remolina León, in: Brummer (ed.), *Cryptoassets: Legal, Regulatory, and Monetary Perspectives*, 117, 120.

[15] Fromberger/Zimmermann, in: Maume/Maute, Rechtshandbuch Kryptowerte, § 1 para. 73.

qualify as securities within the meaning of MiFID II, provided that the investor does not merely use the token to purchase goods or services, but rather, as is characteristic of securities, to achieve a financial return.[16] This is supposed to be the case if there is the prospect that the token will be traded on a platform. However, this interpretation is not convincing because utility tokens are typically neither comparable to equity nor debt instruments,[17] which MiFID II qualifies as transferable securities.[18]

9 Tokens often cannot be assigned exclusively to one of the three categories—investment, utility or currency token—but have a hybrid character.[19] If they are intended to encourage users to provide services for and within the network, the tokens permit people to benefit from the network's increase in value and to monetise the positive network effects on a secondary market.[20] In this case, the utility tokens could be classified as a security.[21] However, it is also conceivable that a token could qualify as a collective investment scheme so that the UCITS or AIFMD would be applicable.[22]

10 The ECJ has not yet had the opportunity to comment on the legal qualification of tokens. There is a general lack of ECJ case law on the concept of securities under European law. This makes the application of EU law considerably difficult.[23] Likewise, ESMA has not yet issued any guidelines that would allow a uniform interpretation throughout the EU of what a security is. ESMA has so far only provided an Advice to the Commission on how different Member States' authorities classify digital instruments and what legal challenges the EU legislator will face in the future.[24] The Advice sets out, impressively, that supervisory authorities of the Member States have different views on the issue. The lack of legal clarity gives rise to the question of whether 'decentralization of trading platforms [...] is the poison pill that [could] make EU capital markets unable to capture the ICO phenomenon, when tokens are not per se transferable securities.'[25]

2. Transfer of Token

11 The blockchain uses asymmetric cryptography to identify accounts and authorise transactions (see para. 5). How ownership is transferred is determined by the national law of the Member States. In Germany, the legislature has regulated that ownership of an electronic bearer bond is transferred by agreement and registration in the crypto securities register.

---

[16] P. Hacker and C. Thomale, 15 ECFR (2018), 645, 652.
[17] R. Veil, 183 ZHR (2019), 346, 363 f.
[18] See R. Veil § 8 para. 11 ff.
[19] Detailed discussion of hybrid tokens in Annex 1 to ESMA's Advice (fn. 9), Legal qualification of crypto-assets - survey to NCAs, January 2019, ESMA50-157-1384.
[20] L. Klöhn et al., 30 JBB (2018), 89, 93.
[21] R. Veil, 183 ZHR (2019), 346, 360–364.
[22] P. Hacker and C. Thomale, 15 ECFR (2018), 645, 689.
[23] I. Barsan, RTDF (2017), 54, 62; K. Langenbucher, RTDF (2018), 40, 43 f.
[24] ESMA (fn. 9), ESMA50-157-1391, 9 January 2019, 4–6.
[25] F. Annunziata, 17 ECFR (2020), 129, 153.

3. Public Offer of Token

Tokens are publicly offered for purchase through **Initial Coin Offerings** (ICOs). The initiators usually make use of the Ethereum platform.[26] The participants of this platform take advantage of a peer-to-peer network. Consequently, there is no central institution. Instead, the individual transactions are confirmed by the participants (nodes), ie by the computers connected to the Ethereum network. Of course, only the miner who is the first to include the transaction in a block benefits.[27]

The ICO takes place through a smart contract. These are software programmes stored on the blockchain that coordinate the legal relationships between the initiator of the project and the investors. They independently ensure compliance with the agreements by automatic execution of a transaction. In the case of an ICO, the investors automatically receive the tokens generated in the network, provided that they have transferred the amount of Ether (the currency in the Ethereum network) determined by the company or have made another payment.

The ICO usually takes place via the internet and social media. The issuer typically explains the token in a white paper, ie an information document that mainly deals with the technical aspects. The white paper is usually less extensive than a securities prospectus and therefore less expensive, although it serves similar purposes. If the token qualifies as a security, however, the issuer has to publish a prospectus according to the Prospectus Regulation.

4. Trade

DLT-based instruments (tokens) can be transferred peer-to-peer. However, organised trading of tokens has not yet taken place. Issuers that have publicly offered tokenised securities in Europe so far are not seeking to trade their securities on the respective blockchain (Ethereum; Stellar). In particular, they do not intend to apply for admission to trading on an RM, MTF or OTF. Thus, there is currently no trading platform in Europe that lists DLT-based transferable securities.[28] The main reason is that the private laws of Member States do not allow for the creation of tradeable DLT-based securities. In a legal system that requires securitisation in order for a security to come into existence (such as Germany's), the trading of DLT-based instruments is not possible.[29] However, even if a jurisdiction recognises book-entry securities (such as the Swiss one), legal reforms of private law are needed to enable the trading of DLT-based instruments.[30]

---

[26] L. Klöhn et al., JBB 2018, 89, 92.
[27] Cf. A. Narayanan et al., *Bitcoin and Cryptocurrency Technologies*, 267.
[28] F. Pekler/R. Rirsch/S. Tomanek, ZFR (2020), 172, 173.
[29] For this reason, Germany has reformed the law governing bearer bonds. Cf. M. Casper, BKR (2019), 209–217.
[30] In Switzerland, a draft law has been introduced that will allow trading of DLT-based rights. For this purpose, the Swiss Code of Obligations introduces DLT book-entry securities. Cf. H. Caspar von der Crone/M. Monsch/L. Meisser, 1 GesKR (2019), 1–17.

II. Requirements under MiFID II

16   The requirements of the MiFID II regime for the operation of trading venues pose another regulatory obstacle to the trading of DLT-based securities. The MiFID II regime is technology-neutral.[31] Consequently, trading venues based on blockchain technology can also be trading venues as defined by MiFID II. But the requirements of MiFID II for the operation of trading venues are difficult to reconcile with the special characteristics of blockchain technology, especially the decentralised nature of the system.

1. Types of Trading Platforms

17   The applicability of MiFID II depends on the technical design of the platform and the way in which buying and selling interests are brought together. There are currently no platforms in Europe whose operators have admitted DLT-based securities to trading. However, platforms allow the trading of cryptocurrencies such as Bitcoin, Ether, etc. These platforms can be divided into central, decentral and hybrid trading platforms.

18   All three types of platform bring together supply and demand. A **central platform** (a so-called CEX) keeps an order book; supply and demand are therefore not brought together on the blockchain but only in the books of the platform (*off-chain*). Users' tokens are stored in wallets on the platform, the platform thus having access to each user's private key. In the case of a **decentralised platform** (a so-called DEX), supply and demand are brought together by means of smart contracts. The transactions take place on the blockchain (*on-chain*).[32] Users of decentralised platforms store their tokens at a separate address; the platform does not have access to the users' private keys.[33]

19   Furthermore, platforms can be distinguished by the way in which orders are brought together: (i) platforms that keep a central order book or that match orders according to a certain system (*on-chain* or *off-chain*), (ii) platforms whose operators trade on their own account, and (iii) platforms that are used to draw attention to buy/sell interests.[34]

2. Advantages and Disadvantages of Decentralised Trading Platforms

20   Decentralised trade of digital assets is multifaceted. For DEXs, however, a special feature can be highlighted: trading is per-to-peer and does not depend on an intermediary, such as a market operator or an investment firm.[35] From a regulatory perspective, a

---

[31] P. Hacker and C. Thomale, ECFR 2018, 645, 655 (referring to recital 13 MiFID II).
[32] Swiss Confederation, *Rechtliche Grundlagen für Distributed Ledger Technologie und Blockchain in der Schweiz. Eine Auslegeordnung mit Fokus auf dem Finanzsektor*, Bericht des Bundesrats, 14 December 2018, 29, 146; ESMA, *Advice. Initial Coin Offerings and Crypto Assets*, ESMA50-157-1391, 9 January 2019, para. 35, 54–57, 190 ff.
[33] Swiss Confederation (fn. 9), p. 28 f.
[34] ESMA (fn. 9), ESMA50-157-1391, para. 105, 195.
[35] Brooklyn Project, An Overview of Decentralized Trading of Digital Assets, 11.15.2018, sub 1: 'All of today's most popular DEXs are 'decentralized' when it comes to custody … However, when it comes to 'pricing' and 'execution' of trades, there is wide variation in approaches.'

decentralised platform (DEX) offers a number of advantages but also poses great challenges for rule-makers.[36]

First, it should be remembered that supply and demand are brought together by means of smart contracts. This may have some advantages for investors. Smart contracts create a fair and transparent market infrastructure, as investors do not have to trust a centralised entity to be an intermediary for the trade.[37] However, it is unclear by which mechanism prices are formed. DEXs generally do not keep a central order book. Instead, they either use a peer-to-peer system in which buyer and seller meet and negotiate the price, or they refer back to a smart contract or liquidity pool that fills submitted orders algorithmically.[38]

A further aspect concerns the fact that transactions take place on the blockchain. It is a common characteristic of DEXs that transactions are settled on-chain but users maintain custody of their assets. As users store their tokens at a separate address, the platform itself does not have access to the user's private key. This is a major advantage of DEXs.[39] There is less risk of a hack[40] than there is with CEXs. In addition, investors do not have any counterparty risk vis-à-vis the platform and are exposed to lower risks of insider trading. In the case of DEXs, transactions are executed by transparent, rule-based smart contracts. In contrast, CEXs are criticised due to a lack of transparency with regard to orders. This has caused concerns about insider trading, wash trading and other forms of market manipulation.[41]

Transactions need to be validated on the blockchain. Thus, executing transactions through DEXs can take longer depending on how the platform is structured. In addition, DEXs are vulnerable to unpredictable network congestion due to external factors that are beyond the control of the DEX as well as to higher gas fees for miners that depend on the congestion level and the complexity of the price calculation.[42] Furthermore, most DEXs operate only with tokens that are on the same platform, such as Ethereum, Stellar, etc.[43] In the future, cross-chain trading may be possible.

III. Commission Proposal for Regulation of Cryptoassets

An essential element of the European Commission's Digital Finance Strategy is the introduction of a legal framework by 2024 that allows the use of Distributed Ledger Technology (DLT) for cryptoassets. To this end, the Commission has proposed two regulations and a directive to provide legal certainty for the public offer and trading of cryptoassets, to ensure effective investor and consumer protection, market integrity and financial stability.

---

[36] Important DEXs are Ether Delta, Airswap, IDEX and 0x. Cf. L. X. Lin, Stanford Journal of Blockchain Law & Policy (2019), 58, 60.
[37] L. X. Lin, Stanford Journal of Blockchain Law & Policy (2019), 58.
[38] Cf. Brooklyn Project (fn. 35), sub. 3.3; L. X. Lin, Stanford Journal of Blockchain Law & Policy (2019), 58, 62–70; M. Fischer, JBB (2020), 158, 161.
[39] L. X. Lin, Stanford Journal of Blockchain Law & Policy (2019), 58, 76.
[40] The most prominent example is the 'The DAO' hack; cf. M. Finck, *Blockchain Regulation and Governance in Europe* (2019), 187.
[41] Brooklyn Project (fn. 35), sub. 2.3 on front-running and insider abuse.
[42] Brooklyn Project (fn. 35), sub. 3.2.
[43] Cf. L. X. Lin, Stanford Journal of Blockchain Law & Policy (2019), 58, 60.

25   Firstly, a legal **framework** for the **distribution** and **trading** of **DLT-based financial instruments** is to be created. This market infrastructure should be designed as far as possible in line with the MiFID II regime. The proposals are based on the distinction between investment tokens and utility tokens developed in academia and supervisory practice.[44] By amending MiFID II,[45] it is to be clarified that DLT-based instruments may qualify as financial instruments within the meaning of MiFID II.[46] In this case, the public offer and trading of DLT-based financial instruments is subject to Union capital markets law (to be partially adapted to the specifics of DLT). In addition, a **DLT pilot regime**[47]—a kind of regulatory sandbox—is to apply to MTF operators who want to establish a DLT market infrastructure.

26   Secondly, the Commission is pursuing the goal of creating a reliable market infrastructure for cryptoassets with the **Markets in Cryptoassets** (MiCa) **Regulation**. The term cryptoassets is intended to cover three categories of tokens: (i) utility tokens, (ii) stable coins ('asset-referenced tokens')[48] and (iii) tokens that have a payment function similar to e-money. The regimes are therefore distinct from each other. In practice, however, it is likely to be difficult to assess whether a token qualifies as a financial instrument or as a cryptoasset.

1. Pilot Regime

27   The proposal for a regulation on a pilot regime for market infrastructures based on distributed ledger technology (DLT Pilot Regime) aims to 'ensure an adequate level of consumer and investor protection, provide legal certainty for cryptoassets, enable innovative companies to use blockchain technology, distributed ledger technology and cryptoassets, and safeguard financial stability.'[49]

28   The DLT pilot regime would give investment firms and market participants the opportunity to test the use of DLT on a larger scale. The European Commission sees a central advantage of DLT in the fact that it allows settlement in near real-time and thus counterparty risk is reduced during the settlement process.[50] Furthermore, the decentralised structure of DLT could reduce cyber risks. The automated process through smart contracts means that less collateral has to be deposited, so that costs are reduced.

29   Conceptually, the pilot regime closely follows the MiFID II regime. A legal entity may only operate a DLT multilateral trading facility if it has received authorisation as an investment

---

[44] See para. 7–8.
[45] The European Commission also proposed a directive on 24.9.2020 to amend a number of directives, including MiFID II, cf. COM(2020) 593 final.
[46] Art. 4(1)(5) MiFID II shall be reformed as follows: 'financial instrument' means those instruments specified in Section C of Annex I, including such instruments issued by means of distributed ledger technology.
[47] Proposal for a Regulation of the European Parliament and of the Council on a pilot regime for market infrastructures based on distributed ledger technology, 24 September 2020, COM(2020) 594 final.
[48] This category of tokens is defined as 'a type of crypto-asset that purports to maintain a stable value by referring to the value of several fiat currencies that are legal tender, one or several commodities or one or several crypto-assets, or a combination of such assets'.
[49] European Commission, Explanatory Memorandum, Brussels, 24.9.2020, COM(2020) 594 final, p. 1.
[50] European Commission, Explanatory Memorandum, Brussels, 24.9.2020, COM(2020) 594 final, p. 7.

firm by the supervisory authority under the MiFID II rules and specific authorisation under the DLT Pilot Regulation. Only certain securities transferable by DLT shall be eligible for trading on a DLT MTF: (i) shares whose issuer has a market capitalisation or an expected market capitalisation of less than € 200 million; (ii) convertible bonds, covered bonds, corporate bonds, other public bonds and other bonds with an issue size of less than € 500 million.

2. Regime for Cryptoassets

In addition, the European commission has proposed to establish a **bespoke regime** for **cryptoassets**, as already proposed by ESMA. The scope of the proposed Regulation is defined by the concept of cryptoassets, which is conceivably broadly formulated: 'a digital representation of value or rights which may be transferred and stored electronically, using distributed ledger technology or similar technology.' The proposed Regulation for cryptoasset markets is not intended to apply to financial instruments as defined by MiFID II, so that DLT-based securities are subject to EU capital markets law. Instead, the regime is to apply to assets that currently qualify as utility tokens.[51]

30

The Regulation for MiCa provides different requirements for the issuance (**publication** of a **white paper**) and trading (**disclosure obligations** of the issuer) of tokens, depending on whether they are cryptoassets, asset-referenced tokens or e-money tokens. The requirements for the publication of a white paper makes sense against the background of information asymmetries between issuers and investors. Approval of the white paper by the national supervisory authority (NCA) is not required. However, the issuer must inform the NCA about the white paper so that the NCA can intervene if necessary. Finally, the **issuer** should be **liable** to **pay damages** to **investors** for incorrect information in the white paper.

31

3. Evaluation

The regulatory approach of creating a separate regime for utility tokens that is less stringent than the one EU legislation foresees for securities is convincing.[52] However, a fundamental problem remains unresolved: the concept of securities under MiFID II is unclear due to the lack of rulings by the European Court of Justice, so that the classification of DLT-based instruments as financial instruments or as cryptoassets will remain difficult in individual cases. It would therefore make sense to specify the characteristic elements of the concept of securities in more detail in MiFID II, than is currently the case.

32

Finally, the regime for cryptoassets should be even better designed. In particular, it is doubtful whether private enforcement of issuers' obligations under EU law constitutes effective

33

---

[51] Proposal for a Regulation of the European Parliament and of the Council on Markets in Crypto-assets, and amending Directive (EU) 2019/1937, 24 September 2020, COM(2020) 593 final.
[52] Cf. R. Veil, 183 ZHR (2019), 346, 367.

investor protection. At first glance, this regulatory approach is appealing. An *ex ante* supervisory approval process would cause considerable transaction costs. However, it is problematic whether a civil liability under Union law can be expected to have a deterrent effect. The example of the liability of credit-rating agencies according to Article 35a CRAR shows the weaknesses of the regulatory approach. Indeed, central questions of civil liability regarding causality and damage have not been clarified at the European level, yet. The legislature should not leave these questions to case law and ECJ jurisprudence, but should answer them in the Regulation for cryptoasset markets itself.

§ 11

Capital Markets Supervision

Bibliography

Abrams, Richard K. and Taylor, Michael W., *Assessing the Case for Unified Sector Supervision*, Financial Markets Group Special Papers No. 134, London (2002); Aoki, Hiroko, *The New Regulatory and Supervisory Architecture of Japan's Financial Markets*, 6 ZJapanR (2001), 101–115; Arnone, Marco and Gambini, Alessandro, *Architecture of Supervisory Authorities and Banking Supervision*, in: Masciandaro, Donato and Quintyn, Marc (eds.), *Designing Financial Supervision Institutions-Independence, Accountability and Governance* (2007), 262–308; Bebchuk, Lucian A. and Roe, Marc J., *A Theory of Path Dependence in Corporate Ownership and Governance*, 52 Stan. L. Rev. (1999–2000), 127–170; Buttlar, Julia von, *Stärkung der Aufsichts- und Sanktionsbefugnisse im EU-Kapitalmarktrecht*, 14 EuZW (2020), 598–603; Caspari, Karl-Burkhard, *Allfinanzaufsicht in Europa* (2003); Cihák, Martin and Podpiera, Richard, *Experience with Integrated Supervisors: Governance and Quality of Supervision*, in: Masciandaro, Donato and Quintyn, Marc (eds.), *Designing Financial Supervision Institutions-Independence, Accountability and Governance* (2007), 309–341; Coffee, John, *Law and the Market: The Impact of Enforcement*, 156 U. Pa. L. Rev. (2007), 230–308; Conac, Pierre-Henri, *The Reform of the French Financial Supervision Structure: 'Twin-Peaks' on the Menu*, in: Grundmann, Stefan et al. (eds.), *Festschrift für Klaus J. Hopt zum 70. Geburtstag* (2010), 3027–3042; de Kezel, Evelien, *The Liability of the Dutch Financial Supervisors in an International Perspective*, 6 ECL (2009), 211–216; Ferran, Eilís, *Capital Market Competitiveness and Enforcement*, SSRN Research Paper (2008), available at: http://papers.ssrn.com/sol3/papers.cfm?abstract_id=1127245; Ferran, Eilís, *Understanding the new institutional architecture of EU financial market supervision*, in: Wymeersch, Eddy, et al. (eds.), *Financial Regulation and Supervision* (2012), 111–158; Ferran, Eilís, *Crisis-Driven regulatory reform: where in the world is the EU going?*, in: Ferran, Eilís et al. (eds.), *The Aftermath of the Global Financial Crisis* (2012), 1–110; Frach, Lotte, *Finanzaufsicht in Deutschland und Großbritannien – Die BaFin und die FSA im Spannungsfeld der Politik* (2008); Gortos, Christos V. and Lagaria, Katerina, *The European Supervisory Authorities (ESAs) as 'direct' supervisors in the EU financial system*, EBI Working Paper Series 2020 No. 57; Gower, Laurence C.B., *Capital Market and Securities Regulation in the Light of the Recent British Experience*, in: Buxbaum, Richard M. et al. (eds.), *European Business Law-Legal and Economic Analysis of Integration and Harmonization* (1991), 307–325; Granner, Georg, *System und Organisation der neuen europäischen Finanzmarktaufsicht*, in: Braumüller Peter et al. (eds.), *Die neue europäische Finanzmarktaufsicht-ZFR-Jahrestagung 2011* (2012), 27–53; Hitzer, Martin and Hauser, Patrick, *ESMA – Ein Statusbericht*, 2 BKR (2015), 52–59; Hopt, Klaus J., *Auf dem Weg zu einer neuen europäischen und internationalen Finanzmarktarchitektur*, 36 NZG (2009), 1401–1408; Howell, Elizabeth, *The European Court of Justice: Selling Us Short?*, 11 ECFR (2014), 454–477; Jackson, Howell E., *Variation in the Intensity of Financial Regulation: Preliminary Evidence and Potential Implication*, 24 Yale J. on Reg. (2007), 253–290; Jackson, Howell E., *The Impact of Enforcement: A Reflection*, 156 U. Pa. L. Rev. (2007), 400–411, Jackson, Howell E. and Roe, Marc J., *Public and Private Enforcement of Securities Laws: Resource-based Evidence*, Public Law & Legal Theory Research Paper Series Paper No. 0-28 and John M. Olin Center for Law and Business Law & Economics Research Paper Series Paper No. 638 (2009); Karmel, Roberta, *The Case of a European Securities Commission*, 38 Colum. J. Transnat'l L. (1999), 9–44; Klingenbrunn, Daniel, *Produktintervention zugunsten des Anlegerschutzes—Zur Systematik innerhalb des Aufsichtsrechts, zum Anlegerleitbild und zivilrechtlichen Konsequenzen*, 7 WM (2015), 315–324; Krahnen, Jan Pieter and Langenbucher, Katja, *The Wirecard lessons: A reform proposal for the supervision of securities markets in Europe*, SAFE Policy Letter No. 88; Lamandini, Marco, *When More Is Needed: The European Financial Supervisory Reform and its Legal Basis*, 6 ECL (2009), 197–202; Lehmann, Matthias and Manger-Nestler, Cornelia, *Das neue Europäische Finanzaufsichtssystem*, 1 ZBB (2011), 2–24; Lehmann, Matthias and Manger-Nestler, Cornelia, *Die Vorschläge zur neuen Architektur der europäischen Finanzaufsicht*, 3 EuZW (2010), 87–92; Llewellyn, David T., *Institutional Structure of Financial Regulation and Supervision: The Basic Issues*, in: Carmichel, Jeffrey, Fleming, Alexander and Llewellyn, David T. (eds.), *Aligning Financial Supervisory Structures*, 2004, 17–92; Manger-Nestler, Cornelia, *Rechtsschutz in der europäischen Bankenaufsicht*, Kreditwesen (2012), 528–532; Manger-Nestler, Cornelia, *Lehren aus dem Leerverkauf?—Zum Verbot von Leerverkäufen durch ESMA*, 3 GPR (2014), 1410–1443; Masciandaro, Donato, *Regulating the Regulators: The Changing Face of Financial Architectures Before and After the Crisis*, 6 ECL (2009), 187–196; Masciandaro, Donato et al., *Will They Sing the Same Tune? Measuring Convergence in the New European System of Financial Supervisors*, Centre for Economic Policy Research Policy Insight No. 37 (2009); Masciandaro, Donato and Quintyn, Marc, *Reforming Financial Supervision and the Role of Central Banks: A Review of Global Trends, Causes and Effects* (1998–2008), Centre for Economic Policy Research Policy Insight No. 30 (2009); Möllers, Thomas M.J. et al., *Nationale Alleingänge und die europäische Reaktion auf ein Verbot ungedeckter Leerverkäufe*, 30 NZG (2010), 1167–1170; Moloney, Niamh, *The legacy effects of the financial crisis on regulatory design in the EU*, in: Ferran, Eilís et al. (eds.), *The Regulatory Aftermath of the Financial Crisis* (2012), 111–202; Moloney, Niamh, *Supervision in the Wake of the Financial Crisis: Achieving Effective 'Law in Action' – A Challenge for the EU*, in: Wymeersch, Eddy et al. (eds.), *Financial Regulation and Supervision – A post-crisis Analysis (2012)*, 71–109; Moloney, Niamh, *The Financial Crisis and EU Securities Law-Making: A Challenge Met?*, in: Grundmann, Stefan et al. (eds.), *Festschrift für Klaus J. Hopt zum 70. Geburtstag* (2010), 2265–2282; Nartowska, Urszula and Walla, Fabian, *Das Sanktionsregime für Verstöße gegen die Beteiligungstransparenz nach der Transparenzrichtlinie 2013*, 24 AG (2014), 891–905; Nartowska, Urszula and Walla, Fabian, *Die WpHG-Bußgeldleitlinien der BaFin*, 25 NZG (2015), 977–983; Nartowska, Urszula and Knierbein, Michael, *Ausgewählte Aspekte des, Naming and Shaming' nach § 40 c WpHG*, 7 NZG (2016), 256–261; Ogowewo, Tunde I., *Is Contract the Juridical Basis of the Takeover Panel?*, 12 J. Int. Bank. Law. (1997), 15–23; Pan, Eric J., *Harmonization of US-EU Securities Regulation: The Case for a Single European Securities Regulator*, 34 L. & Pol'y Int'l Bus. (2003), 499–536; Payne, Jennifer, *Institutional design for the EU Economic and Monetary Union: Financial Supervision and Financial Stability*, Oxford Legal Studies Research Paper No. 26/2017; Renner, Moritz, *Staatshaftungsrechtliche Implikationen des Wirecard-Skandals*, 1 ZBB (2021), 1–20; Romano, Roberta, *Empowering Investors: A Market Approach to Securities Regulation*, 107 Yale Law J. (1997–98), 2359–2430; Siekmann, Helmut, *Die Schaffung von Einrichtungen der Finanzaufsicht auf EU-Ebene – Stellungnahme zu dem Vorschlag der Sachverständigengruppe unter dem Vorsitz von Jacques de Larosière*, IMFS Working Paper No. 24 (2009); Sohn, Wook and Vyshnevskyi, Iegor, *The Effectiveness of Financial Supervision Frameworks*, 20 Journal of Accounting and Finance (2020), 81–92; Spindler, Gerald, *Informationsfreiheit und Finanzmarktaufsicht* (2012); Taylor, Michael, *Twin Peaks. A Regulation Structure for the New Century* (1995); Thieffry, Gilles, *Towards a European Securities Commission*, 18 Fin. L. Rev. (1999), 300–307; Thieffry, Gilles, *The Case for a European Securities Commission*, in: Ferran, Eilís and Goodhart, Charles A.E. (eds.), *Regulation Financial Services in the 21st Century* (2001), 211–234; Tröger, Tobias H., *Corporate Governance in a Viable Market for Secondary Listings*, 10 Pa. J. Bus. & Employ. L. (2007–08), 89–186; Veil, Rüdiger, *Enforcement of Capital Markets Law in Europe— Observations from a Civil Law Country*, 11 EBOR (2010), 408–422; Veil, Rüdiger, *Europäische Kapitalmarktunion – Verordnungsgesetzgebung, Instrumente der europäischen Marktaufsicht und die Idee eines 'Single Rulebook'*, 5 ZGR (2014), 544–607; Walla, Fabian, *Die Konzeption der Kapitalmarktaufsicht in Deutschland* (2012); Westrup, Jonathan, *Independence and Accountability: Why Politics Matters*, in: Masciandaro, Donato and Quintyn, Marc (eds.), *Designing financial supervision institutions-independence, accountability and governance* (2007), 117–150; Wittig, Arne, *Stärkung der Finanzaufsicht*, DB (2010) Standpunkte, 69–71; Wymeersch, Eddy, *Regulation European Markets: The Harmonisation of Securities Regulation in Europe in the new Trading Environment*, in: Ferran, Eilís and Goodhart, Charles A.E. (eds.), *Regulation Financial Services in the 21st Century* (2001), 189–210; Wymeersch, Eddy, *The future of financial regulation and supervision in Europe*, 42 CML Rev. (2005), 987–1010; Wymeersch, Eddy, *The Structure of Financial Supervision in Europe: About Single Financial Supervisors, Twin Peaks and Multiple Financial Supervisors*, 8 EBOR (2007), 237–306; Wymeersch, Eddy, *The European Financial Supervisory Authorities or ESA's*, in: Wymeersch, Eddy et al. (eds.), *Financial Regulation and Supervision* (2012), 232–317.

I. Introduction

The European and national supervisory authorities ensure the market participants' compliance with capital markets law. Capital markets law is therefore to a large extent **supervisory law**.[1] Notwithstanding the recent developments towards a further European harmonisation, the capital and financial markets supervision is **predominantly executed by the Member States** and its **National Competent Authorities (NCAs)**.[2] The mandate of the **European Securities and Markets Authority (ESMA)** is still rather limited.[3]

II. European Law Requirements

1. Institutional Organisation

European law only contains relatively few provisions on the structure of the Member States' NCAs. It hence comes as no surprise that the national supervisory concepts vary from one Member State to another, even though the recent reforms in European capital markets law resulted in a significant higher harmonisation of the NCAs' sanctioning powers.[4]

Regarding the institutional organisation of the national supervisory systems, European law merely requires that the Member States designate **a single administrative competent authority** competent to ensure that the provisions of the MAR (Market Abuse Regulation), the PR (Prospectus Regulation) and the TD (Transparency Directive) are complied with.[5] The regulatory approach of these Level 1 acts thus renounces the approach pursued in former European legislative acts and the revised Market in Financial Instruments Directive (MiFID II) which required only a *competent authority*.[6] The later

---

[1] Cf. on the scope of the term R. Veil, in: Grundmann et al. (eds.), in: FS Hopt, 2641, 2644 (fn. 19).
[2] N. Moloney, *EU Securities and Financial Markets Regulation*, 965.
[3] See below para. 89 ff.
[4] See R. Veil § 12 para. 10.
[5] Art. 31(1) PR; Art. 22 MAR; Art. 24(1) TD.
[6] See Art. 67(1) MiFID II; Art. 8(1) Directive on Insider Dealings; Art. 9(1) Council Directive 79/279/EEC of 5 March 1979 coordinating the conditions for the admission of securities to official stock exchange listing, OJ L66/21, 16 March 1979; Art. 18(1) Directive 94/18/EC of the European Parliament and of the Council of

wording is wider as it does not require a governmental (administrative) institution but also allows for bodies under private law entrusted with public powers.[7]

4   Even in the aftermath of the financial crisis of 2008 reforms for European capital markets law, no proposal has been brought forward to subject the Member States to coherent rules regarding the national supervisory structure. Considering the general tendency towards more harmonisation in European capital markets law this is surprising at first glimpse. However, the design of national institutions relates to the core of national sovereignty and will therefore remain one of the few elements of European capital markets law that are likely to be resistant to further harmonisation.

5   European law occasionally allows the Member States to delegate supervisory tasks of public authorities to other entities.[8] This is, nevertheless, only permitted under certain conditions, eg. that the entity to which the tasks are to be delegated is organised in such a manner as to avoid a conflict of interest.[9]

6   The Level 1 acts contain no further requirements regarding the institutional and internal organisation or the areas of responsibility of the national authorities. In particular, the decision whether the supervision of securities trading should be joined with bank and insurance supervision, resulting in one authority being responsible for the entire financial supervision, hence remains with the Member States.[10]

2. Powers

7   European law contains relatively detailed provisions with respect to the NCAs' powers. The Level 1 directives and regulations enumerate a **minimum of powers and sanctioning competences** with which the NCAs shall be provided. European law accordingly follows the concept of minimum harmonisation in this respect.[11] The minimum powers are, respectively, complemented by a **general clause requiring an effective enforcement** of the supervisory powers.

(a) Administrative and Investigation Powers

8   The core Level 1 acts (ie the MAR, PR, TD and MiFIR/MiFID II) contain a catalogue of minimum requirements regarding the administrative powers of the NCAs. They require,

---

30 May 1994 amending Directive 80/390/EEC coordinating the requirements for the drawing up, scrutiny and distribution of the listing particulars to be published for the admission of securities to official stock exchange listing, with regard to the obligation to publish listing particulars, OJ L135/1, 31 May 1994; Art. 9(1) Interim Report Directive; Art. 12(1) Council Directive 88/627/EEC on the information to be published when a major holding in a listed company is acquired or disposed of. Art. 22(1) Council Directive 93/22/EEC of 10 May 1993 on investment services in the securities field, OJ L 141/27, 11 June 1993, already used the term 'competent authorities'.

[7] S. Weber, in: Dauses (ed.), *Handbuch des EU-Wirtschaftsrechts*, F.III para. 101.
[8] In Germany, for example, a private body is supporting BaFin with the supervision of financial reporting under the TD. In the UK (as a former EU member state) the competence to oversee the EU law based takeover law were delegated to the Takeover Pane as private self-regulatory body. On the legal status of this body see T. Ogowewo, 12 J. Int. Bank Law (1997), 15 et seq.
[9] Art. 31(2) PR; cf. also Art. 67(2), 29(4) MiFID II.
[10] See in more detail below para. 18.
[11] See R. Veil § 3 para 21.

inter alia, that the NCAs must at least have the right to access any document and to receive a copy, demand information from any person involved, request existing telecommunication records, carry out on-site inspections or request the temporary prohibition of professional activity. The NCAs must further be empowered to require the cessation of any practice that is contrary to EU law and the freezing or sequestration of assets.[12] Notwithstanding their European determination, also such minimum powers are always to be used in accordance with the national administrative law. The NCAs, however, are under an obligation to consider the fundamental rights as set forth in the Charter of Fundamental Rights of the European Union.[13]

In particular, under the MiFID II the NCAs have received some remarkable additional powers: They may suspend the marketing or sale of financial instruments or structured deposits and suspend the marketing or sale of financial instruments if an investment firm has not developed or applied an effective product approval or require the removal of a natural person from the management board of an investment firm or market operator.[14]

9

In addition to these minimum powers the Level 1 acts contain general clauses ensuring that the competent authorities have the powers 'necessary'[15] for enforcement. Whether this is the case must be determined according to national law.[16] At the same time, general clauses must be understood as an expression of the legislator's aim to ensure effective enforcement,[17] hence constituting a form of the **effet-utile-principle** in secondary legislation.[18]

10

(b) Administrative Fines

All Member States provide for the possibility to impose administrative fines for non-compliance with capital markets law provisions. The post financial crisis reforms for the first time stipulated for fixed amounts of fines which the NCAs have to be at least able to levy on market participants (**minimum maximum fines**).

11

Under the new rules the NCAs must be in a position to impose fines of up to at least several million Euros.[19] The minimum maximum fines in the Level 1 acts vary: Breaches of the transparency obligations under the reformed TD must at least result in fines up to € 10,000,000 or up to 5% of the total **annual turnover** (or the double amount of profits gained/losses avoided, whichever is higher).[20] The bottom line of a national maximum

12

---

[12] Cf. Art. 38(2) PR; Art. 21(1) MAR; Art. 24(4) TD; Art. 69(2) MiFID II.
[13] See the recent judgment of the ECJ regarding the sanctioning powers of the Italian NCA (Consob) under Article 30(1)(b) MAR, Case C-481/19 (*DB v Commissione Nazionale per le Società e la Borsa (Consob)*).
[14] Art. 69(2)(s), (t), (u) MiFID II.
[15] Art. 32(3) PR; Art. 24(4) TD ('Each competent authority shall have all the powers necessary for the performance of its functions'); Art. 69(1) MiFID II ('Competent authorities shall be given all supervisory and investigatory powers that are necessary to fulfil their duties'). The MAR does not contain such explicit clause. However, under the *effet-utile*-principle an effective enforcement is also required.
[16] Case C-45/08 (*Spector*), para. 71.
[17] R. Veil, 11 EBOR (2010), 409, 411; R. Veil, in: Grundmann et al. (eds.), in: FS Hopt, 2641, 2642.
[18] The ECJ is entitled to put general clauses into more concrete terms, having, however, failed to make public its understanding of these terms as yet. In *Spector* the ECJ did, in fact, rule that when determining an administrative financial sanction, the general clauses in the former MAD cannot be interpreted as an obligation for the competent national authorities to take the possibility of a subsequent criminal sanction into account, cf. Case C-45/08 (*Spector*), para. 74.
[19] See for a comprehensive overview R. Veil § 12 para. 18.
[20] Art. 28(b)(1)(c)(i) TD.

fine for market manipulation or insider dealing (Articles 14 and 15 MAR) is fixed at € 15,000,000 or 15% of the total annual turnover of the legal person or the treble amount of profits gained or losses avoided because of the breach, where those can be determined.[21] The annual turnover is determined according to the last available accounts approved by the management body on a **group level**. MiFID II stipulates a maximum fine of at least € 5,000,000 or of up to 10% of the total annual turnover.[22]

13 Most national legislators have transposed these European requirements without any amendment to their national laws. However, other Members States (ie France, Italy, Hungary and the Czech Republic) included even higher maximum administrative fines in their national law.[23]

(c) Other Administrative Sanctions

14 In the course of the reforms of European capital markets law also administrative sanctions which can be imposed by the NCAs were harmonised. In particular, the Level 1 acts do not – as previously – only set forth that the NCAs may have the competence to publish a violation of the revised European law.[24] They rather oblige the Member States to publish any sanction imposed (**naming and shaming**).[25] The NCAs may only refrain from such publication regarding violations of the MAR and the MiFID II under narrow conditions.[26] In case of violations of the revised TD, they may even only delay (and not refrain from) the publication.[27]

15 Under Article 28b(2) TD the Member States shall ensure that their laws provide for the possibility of **suspending the exercise of voting rights** attached to shares in the event of breaches of the rules on transparency of major shareholdings. The Member States may provide that the suspension of voting rights is to apply only to the most serious breaches. Many Member States have equipped their NCAs with such a competence. However, other Member States such as Germany opted for **a loss of voting rights ex lege**.[28]

(d) Choice of Sanctions/Administrative Measures

16 Moreover, the MAR, the TD and the MiFID II now stipulate for criteria the NCAs have to consider when assessing which sanction is to be chosen and how the sanction is to be imposed; in particular, how the amount of possible fines shall be determined.

17 Under the new European laws the NCAs shall take into account the following criteria:

— gravity and duration of the infringement;
— the degree of responsibility;
— the financial strength;

---

[21] Art. 30(2)(h) MAR; Art. 30(2)(j)(i) MAR.
[22] Art. 70(6)(f) MiFID II.
[23] J. v. Buttlar, 14 EuZW (2020), 598, 601.
[24] Art. 29 TD; see on the relation between Art. 28b TD and Art. 29 TD U. Nartowska and F. Walla, 24 AG (2014), 891, 898; U. Nartowska and M. Knierbein, 7 NZG (2016), 256, 257 (as well on the German transposition of the TD).
[25] Art. 34 MAR; Art. 29 TD; Art. 71 MiFID II.
[26] Art. 34(1) subsec. 3(c) MAR; Art. 71(1) subsec. 1 MiFID II.
[27] Art. 29(1) subsec. 2 TD.
[28] See on this R. Veil § 20 para. 123.

— the profits gained or losses avoided;
— the level of cooperation with the competent authority;
— previous infringements; and
— measures taken by the person responsible to prevent a repetition of misconduct.[29]

Some NCAs have implemented these criteria with own enforcement guidelines or manuals (eg. the *Bußgeldleitlinien* of Germany's BaFin[30]).

III. Supervision by the NCAs

Taking into account the vague legal requirements of European law, the disparate nature of the supervisory structure, practice and culture throughout the European Union is hardly surprising.[31] A **comparative study** is indispensable in order to achieve an overview of capital markets supervision as practised in Europe. It must contain an examination of the different institutional concepts concerning supervision and the respective internal organisation. 18

1. Institutional Design

The various institutional concepts for the design of the national supervisory systems show the different understandings that are predominant in the Member States. The two 'classic' concepts are as follows: 19

— supervisory authorities with exclusive competence regarding capital markets supervision (**sectoral supervision**); and
— concentration of the entire financial markets supervision, ie securities trading, banking and insurance supervision, under the roof of one supervisory body (**integrated supervision**).

As a result of the financial and sovereign debt crisis of the past years, a number of jurisdictions have modified their concepts and separated **prudential supervision** and **conduct of business supervision** (**twin peak approach**).[32] 20

(a) Model of Integrated Supervision

In the first decade of the twenty-first century integrated supervision of securities trading appeared to prevail throughout Europe[33]—Sweden[34] and Denmark[35] being amongst the 21

---

[29] Art. 31 MAR; Art. 28c TD; Art. 72(2) MiFID II; Art. 39(1) PR; see on this J. v. Buttlar, 14 EuZW (2020), 598, 599.
[30] The guidelines can be downloaded at www.bafin.de; cf. on for further details U. Nartowska and F. Walla, 25 NZG (2015), 977 ff.
[31] N. Moloney, *EU Securities and Financial Markets Regulation*, 1104; E. Ferran, in: Wymeersch et al. (eds.), *Financial Regulation and Supervision*, 111 ('cluttered landscape').
[32] See para. 28.
[33] For example K.-B. Caspari, *Allfinanzaufsicht in Europa*, 5–6.
[34] The Swedish supervisory authority *Finansinspektionen* (FI) was established in 1991. On its organisation and functions see R. Veil and F. Walla, *Schwedisches Kapitalmarktrecht*, 8 ff.
[35] The Danish supervisory authority Finanstilsynet was established on 1 January 1988.

first to follow this concept. In 1997, also the United Kingdom established an integrated supervision and thus confirmed the tendency towards a single supervisory authority. The UK aggregated its supervision of the banking, insurance and securities sectors 'under one roof' by founding the **Financial Services Authority (FSA)**.[36]

22 After the formation of the FSA, Germany was the most prominent example of change towards integrated supervision. In 2002 the former *Bundesaufsichtsamt für den Wertpapierhandel* (BAWe), *Bundesaufsichtamt für das Kreditwesen* (BAKred) and *Bundesaufsichtamt für das Versicherungswesen* (BAV), ie the supervisory authorities for securities, banking and insurances, were combined in the **Bundesanstalt für Finanzdienstleistungsaufsicht (BaFin)**.[37] Austria followed suit and introduced a new supervisory authority, the **Finanzmarktaufsicht (FMA)**, in 2002.[38] Identical developments can be observed in Belgium, Finland and in the Eastern European Member States Poland, Slovenia, Hungary, Latvia, Estonia as well as in Malta and Cyprus.[39] Ireland, Slovakia and the Czech Republic concentrated their supervision with the respective national central bank.

23 States outside the European Union, such as Switzerland, Norway, Kazakhstan, Iceland and Lichtenstein, together with Australia, Columbia, South Korea, Ruanda, Nicaragua and Japan,[40] have also adopted this approach.[41] The degree to which the three supervisory sectors are integrated varies largely from state to state.[42]

24 The concept of integrated supervision was justified by the assumption that developments in the capital markets would make a distinction between the banking and insurance sector and the other financial services difficult in future,[43] as insurance companies, banks and other financial services companies increasingly compete for the sale of financial products.[44] A separation of the supervisory authorities could therefore lead to regulatory arbitrage.[45] Additionally, it was argued that the number of financial conglomerates active in all three economic sectors would increase.[46]

(b) Model of Sectoral Supervision

25 Other Member States, such as Spain with its **Comisión Nacional del Mercado de Valores (CNMV)** or Italy with its **Commissione Nazionale per le Società e la Borsa (Consob)**, have adhered to the concept of sectoral supervision. Similarly, Greece, Portugal, Slovenia, Lithuania and Romania all have an additional authority exclusively responsible for the supervision of capital markets. The European financial supervisory structure with its

---

[36] E. Wymeersch, 42 CML Rev. (2005), 987, 990.
[37] Cf. F. Walla, *Die Konzeption der Kapitalmarktaufsicht in Deutschland*, 19 ff.
[38] Finanzmarktaufsichtsgesetz (Financial Market Supervision Act), BGBl. I 2001/97.
[39] See table in E. Wymeersch, 8 EBOR (2007), 237, 256.
[40] For more details see H. Aoki, 6 ZJapanR (2001), 101, 106 ff.
[41] This enumeration is based on the research of D. Masciandaro, 6 ECL (2009), 187 and E. Wymeersch, 8 EBOR (2007), 237, 256–257.
[42] E. Wymeersch, 8 EBOR (2007), 237, 268.
[43] See the explanatory notes of the FinDAG, Allgemeiner Teil, 31, or the statements of HM Treasury regarding the establishment of the FSA as quoted in E. Wymeersch, 8 EBOR (2007), 237, 253.
[44] K.-B. Caspari, *Allfinanzaufsicht in Europa*, 7–8.
[45] K.-B. Caspari, *Allfinanzaufsicht in Europa*, 11–12.
[46] K.-B. Caspari, *Allfinanzaufsicht in Europa*, 7.

European Banking Authority (EBA), European Insurance and Occupational Pensions Authority (EIOPA) and ESMA also follows this approach.[47]

The main advantages of this concept are the possibility of referring to the expertise which has grown historically and preventing a single supervisory institution from becoming too powerful.[48] Additionally, one may assume that individual authorities will be in better position to specialise in their respective field of activity.

(c) Hybrid Models

Numerous Member States have developed hybrid forms of these two models. In Bulgaria, for example, capital markets supervision and insurance supervision are combined, whilst in Luxembourg, the local authority **Commission de Surveillance du Secteur Financier (CSSF)** is responsible for capital markets supervision as well as the for banking supervision.

(d) Twin Peaks Model

As a result of the financial crisis of 2008 there was a strong tendency among the Member States to reform the design of the national financial supervision by separating conduct of business supervision and prudential supervision. Prudential supervision covers the control of the financial institutions' solvency whereas conduct of business supervision monitors the financial institutions' compliance with rules of conduct and organisational requirements. Such a structure is referred to as a twin peaks scheme.[49] It was primarily initiated in order to prevent systemic risks in the field of prudential supervision.

This twin peak approach has been, for example, followed by the Netherlands since 2007. The **Autoriteit Financiële Markten (AFM)** assumed the conduct of business supervision over all sectors while the prudential supervision is executed by the national central bank. In 2010, France reformed its financial supervisory structure as well: It assigned the prudential supervision to the **Autorité de Contrôle Prudentiel (ACP)** and the conduct of business supervision to the **Autorité des Marchés Financiers (AMF)**.[50] Since 2011, Belgium likewise has adhered to the twin peaks model.[51]

Also the United Kingdom has meanwhile given up its integrated approach and abolished the former FSA. It instead divided its tasks between two new institutions:[52] The **Prudential Regulation Authority (PRA)**[53] and the **Financial Conduct Authority (FCA)**. The PRA is designed as a subsidiary of the Bank of England and carries out the prudential regulation of financial firms, including banks and significant investment firms and insurance companies. The conduct of business supervision of all market participants and the prudential

---

[47] See below para. 55.
[48] Cf. R. Romano, 107 Yale Law J. (1997–98), 2359 ff.
[49] See M. Taylor, *Twin Peaks: A Regulatory Structure for the New Century*, passim; N. Moloney, in: Ferran et al., *The Regulatory Aftermath of the Financial Crisis*, 111, 119.
[50] P.-H. Conac, in: Grundmann et al. (eds.), in: FS Hopt, 3027 ff.
[51] Cf. European Central Bank, *Recent development in supervisory structures in the EU member states (2007–10)*, p. 12 ff.
[52] Cf. E. Ferran, 31 Oxford J. Legal Studies (2011), 455 ff.
[53] Cf. Bank of England/FSA, *The Bank of England, Prudential Regulation Authority – Our Approach to Banking Supervision* (2011).

regulation over regulated firms not supervised by the PRA is now assigned to the FCA. The FCA is further supposed to ensure a high level of consumer protection.

(e) Direct Banking Supervision by the European Central Bank (ECB)

31　In 2014, the financial supervision scheme in Europe was (again) modified significantly with regards to the supervision of banks. The European Central Bank (ECB) assumed the direct supervision over all systemically significant banks of the Eurozone in cooperation with the national authorities via the **Single Supervisory Mechanism (SSM)**.[54] Currently, the ECB directly supervises 115 banking groups via the SSM.[55]

(f) Generally Preferable Supervisory Model?

32　Intensive economic and legal studies have not been able to prove the superiority of any one supervisory concept.[56] The German Scholar K.J. Hopt[57] therefore concludes that the decision regarding the institutional organisation of capital markets supervision is solely political, subject mainly to **national path dependence**.[58] The effectiveness of supervision is rather determined by the exact competencies of the respective supervisory authority.

33　Hopt's conclusions appear to be correct. Taking his conclusions into consideration, it can in particular not be assumed that the latest institutional reforms of the financial supervision structure (ie the establishment of the ESFS and SSM)[59] alone suffice in order to overcome the consequences of the financial crisis of 2007 and to prevent a further crisis.

2. Internal Organisation and Independence

34　There is a further diversity of methods with regard to the internal organisation of the national supervisory institutions. Most national authorities are managed by a collegiate body. The head of this body, however, has a very different function in each Member State. Germany, for instance, adheres to a concept in which the president of the managing body

---

[54] Cf. on the implications of the SSM for the supervision of financial markets N. Moloney, *EU Securities and Financial Markets Regulation*, 1019 ff.

[55] A continuously updated list of institutions supervised under the SSM can be downloaded under www.bankingsupervision.europa.eu.

[56] R. Abrams and M. Taylor, FMG Special Papers No. 134, passim; D. Llewellyn, in: Carmichel, Fleming and Llewellyn (eds.), *Aligning Financial Supervisory Structures*, 17 ff. According to M. Cihák and R. Podpiera, in: Masciandaro and Quintyn (eds.). *Designing Financial Supervision*, 309 ff., empirical studies have been able to prove the advantages of the model of integrated supervision. According to M. Arnone and A. Gambini, in: Masciandaro and Quintyn (eds.), *Designing Financial Supervision*, 262 ff., empirical studies have proven that an organisational connection between solvency supervision and organisational supervision is recommendable.

[57] K. Hopt, 36 NZG (2009), 1401, 1402. Nevertheless, empirical studies about the effectiveness of a certain supervisory design can deliver important findings for possible reforms, cf. eg W. Sohn and I. Vyshnevskyi, 20 Journal of Accounting and Finance (2020), 82 ff.

[58] D. Masciandaro and M. Quintyn, CEPR Policy Insight No. 30, 9; J. Westrup, in: Masciandaro and Quintyn, *Designing Financial Supervision*, 117 ff. Similarly E. Wymeersch, 8 EBOR (2007), 237, 264. On path dependence of legal systems L. Bebchuk and M. Roe, 52 Stan. L. Rev. (1999–2000), 127, 137 ff. With regard to the national supervisory systems the national central banks in particular have a certain path dependence, cf. D. Masciandaro et al., CEPR Policy Insight No. 37, 5.

[59] See para. 55.

holds a strong position.[60] The supervisory authorities' degree of **independence** towards the government moreover varies significantly.[61]

It must further be noted that in some Member States sanctions are imposed by an independent authority, eg by the **Commission des Sanctions** of the French AMF.

35

3. Administrative and Criminal Powers

As described above, the European capital markets law contains a catalogue of minimum powers for the NCAs combined with additional general clauses. In the past, the sanctions provided for in the various Member States differed widely.[62] The last reforms of the European capital markets law harmonised these national supervisory powers.

36

Some supervisory authorities – in particular the Irish supervisory authority[63] – also institute criminal proceedings against market participants. This once again demonstrates the differences that exist between the national systems of enforcement. The attribution of criminal powers to an administrative authority outside the rules on administrative offences is, for example, entirely unknown in other European legal systems.

37

4. Liability of Supervisory Authorities

Significant differences between the Member States are evident with respect to the liability of the NCAs.[64] Whilst in Germany, the BaFin is protected from any liability towards a third party under national law,[65] the Netherlands[66] and Sweden[67] have no rules limiting the liability of their supervisory authorities. In Ireland, France,[68] Belgium and Luxembourg certain restrictions on the liability for damages caused by their supervisory authorities apply.[69] Some legal scholars even argue that European law requires a state liability vis-à-vis market

38

---

[60] In 2002, when the German BaFin was established, it was organised as being managed solely by a president. This concept was, however, reorganised in 2008, newly introducing a managing body and giving the head of this body a strong position. On the background of these reforms see RegBegr. BR-Drucks. 671/07, 7–8 (explanatory notes).

[61] Cf. D. Masciandaro and M. Quintyn, CEPR Policy Insight No. 37, 7–8 who attempt to quantify the amount of independence of the national supervisory authorities.

[62] See 1st ed. (2013), F. Walla § 11 para. 20 ff.

[63] CESR, Report on administrative measures and sanctions as well as the criminal sanctions available in Member States under the Market Abuse Directive (MAD), CESR/08-099, February 2008, p. 13.

[64] According to D. Masciandaro and M. Quintyn, CEPR Policy Insight No. 37, 17 the immunity of the national supervisory authorities is an essential step for a further harmonisation of supervision in Europe.

[65] See § 4(4) *Gesetz über die Bundesanstalt für Finanzdienstleistungsaufsicht* (FinDAG). Despite this provision, claims for liability were recently brought forward against BaFin as a result of the *Wirecard* case. While BaFin has certainly made significant mistakes when supervising Wirecard, these claims are unlikely to be successful because of the FinDAG's statutory rule (dissenting: M. Renner, 1 ZBB (2021), 1 ff.). For more details on the Wirecard case cf. F. Walla § 24 para. 65.

[66] Cf. E. de Kezel, 6 ECL (2009), 211, 213.

[67] The liability of the Swedish supervisory authority is, however, not relevant in practice, cf. R. Veil and F. Walla, *Schwedisches Kapitalmarktrecht*, 18.

[68] On this R. Veil and P. Koch, *Französisches Kapitalmarktrecht*, 17.

[69] On the conflict of laws regarding liability of the supervisory authorities see E. de Kezel, 6 ECL (2009), 211, 214 ff.

participants in case of misconduct by the NCA.[70] However, considering that European law does not explicitly address this obvious issue, such interpretation seems to be an overstatement of the *effet-utile*-principle.

5. Use of Resources and Sanctioning Activity

39 Apart from these differences in the national legal concepts regarding the supervisory institutions, empirical studies have brought to light further differences regarding the resources used by the Member States in capital markets supervision and the activity of the supervisory authorities.

40 US scholar Howell E. Jackson, in particular, proved that large differences exist not only with regard to the financial and personal resources employed,[71] but also with regard to the supervisory activity measured by the frequency and severity of sanctions.[72] The most significant discrepancies can be found between legal systems adhering to common law rules and those based on civil law.[73]

41 Whilst such complex empirical studies are associated with a relatively high degree of uncertainty concerning their completeness, correctness and the comparability of data, this study does at least allow the definite conclusion that differences exist in the severity with which the supervisory institutions use their powers to enforce sanctions. The ensuing question, controversially discussed in the international legal literature,[74] is whether a high or rather a low level of supervision is recommendable.[75]

42 As a matter of fact, in the aftermath of the financial crisis of 2007 the supervisory activity and enforcement intensity has significantly increased throughout Europe.[76]

IV. Cooperation between the NCAs

43 Currently, capital markets are primarily supervised by the national authorities.[77] In order to adapt to the growing interaction between the European capital markets and the increasing number of cross-border cases resulting therefrom, cooperation between the supervisory authorities within the different Member States is therefore inevitable.

---

[70] M. Renner, 1 ZBB (2021), 1, 10 ff.
[71] H. Jackson, 24 Yale J. Reg. (2007), 253, 266 ff. Also see H. Jackson and M. Roe, Public Law & Legal Theory Research Paper Series Paper No. 0-28 and John M. Olin Center for Law and Business Law & Economics Research Paper Series Paper No. 638, 41 (table 2).
[72] H. Jackson, 24 Yale J. Reg. (2007), 253, 278 ff.
[73] Ibid., 272.
[74] Supporting a high intensity of supervision J. Coffee, 156 U. Pa. L. Rev. (2007), 229 ff.; T. Tröger, 10 U. Pa. J. Bus. & Emp. L. (2007–08), 89 ff. Dissenting: E. Ferran, *Capital Market Competitiveness and Enforcement*, passim; H. Jackson, 156 U. Pa. L. Rev. (2007), 400 ff.
[75] See on this also N. Moloney, *EU Securities and Financial Markets Regulation*, 946 ff.
[76] N. Moloney, *EU Securities and Financial Markets Regulation*, 967 ff.
[77] See para. 89 on the regulation directly supervised by ESMA.

1. Cooperation within the European Union

The Level 1 acts form the framework for the cooperation between the supervisory authorities. All contain an obligation for the national supervisory authorities to cooperate whenever necessary for the purpose of fulfilling their duties and a competence of **ESMA to coordinate and control the NCAs' cooperation**.[78]

44

A particularly high degree of cooperation is necessary in matters referring to the concept of a **single passport**, ie the supervision of investment firms and the admission of securities prospectuses. The single passport effects that securities prospectuses approved by one NCA are valid in all other Member States (Article 24 PR) and that an authorisation to provide investment services granted by the home Member State is valid for the entire EU (see eg Article 6(3) MiFID II). Yet, the host Member State of a branch of an investment firm is responsible for the authorisation and supervision of the respective branch.[79] In legal practice, this supervision over branches plays a major role in the day-to-day supervisory activities.[80]

45

European law also contains detailed rules on the cooperation among the NCAs as well as between the NCAs and ESMA: A competent authority may refuse to act on a request for cooperation only on very limited grounds specified in the Level 1 acts.[81] If a NCA is convinced that the European rules are being, or have been, breached on the **territory of another Member State**, it shall notify the NCA of the other Member State which must then take appropriate actions.[82] This NCA may then decide that an investigation is carried out by the competent authority of another Member State, on the latter's territory.[83] Such an investigation would, however, always be subject to the overall control of the Member State on whose territory it is conducted.

46

Despite the far-reaching obligations to cooperate all Level 1 acts of European law underline the importance of guarding **professional secrecy** with regard to information exchanged with other authorities.[84]

47

2. Cooperation with Third Countries' Authorities

The Level 1 acts, furthermore, contain rules on cooperation with third countries, leaving the Member States room to design their cooperation with non-EU members. Under European law, the NCAs are obliged to ensure an efficient exchange of information with competent authorities of third countries.[85] However, any exchange of information is subject to guarantees of professional secrecy at least equivalent to the European law standard.[86]

48

---

[78] Art. 25 MAR; Art. 25(2) TD; Art. 79 ff. MiFID II; Art. 34 PR.
[79] See Art. 35(8) MiFID II.
[80] N. Moloney, *EU Securities and Financial Markets Regulation*, 970 ff.
[81] Art. 25(2) MAR; Art. 83 MiFID II.
[82] Art. 25(5) MAR; Art. 79(4) MiFID II.
[83] Art. 25(6) MAR; Art. 80 MiFID II.
[84] Art. 27 MAR; Art. 35 PR; Art. 25(1), (3) TD; Art. 76 MiFID II.
[85] Art. 26(1)(2) MAR; Art. 25(4) TD; Art. 88(1) MiFID II; Art. 30(1) PR.
[86] Art. 88(1) subsec. 3 MiFID II; Art. 30(3) PR.

49 The cooperation with third countries is often carried out through so-called **memoranda of understanding (MoU)** concluded between the supervisory authorities of the Member State and the third country.[87] These agreements usually contain the obligation for both states to exchange information and consult each other before taking certain administrative measures.[88] In legal practice, such MoU are often constructed following the recommendations of the International Organisation of Securities Commissions (IOSCO) of 1991.[89]

50 The MoU between all Member States of the IOSCO from 2002 is especially relevant in practice, obligating the supervisory authorities of the IOSCO to pursue mutual cooperation. The last modifications of this MoU were agreed in 2012.[90] It must, however, be underlined that MoU can only legally obligate the supervisory authorities to cooperate but do not confer duties or powers or establish new powers.[91] MoU have no legally binding effect. They can, however, help to improve coordination and cooperation between the national supervisory authorities.[92]

51 After **Brexit** and the subsequent transition period on 1 January 2021 the UK (and in turn its supervisory authority FCA) is now to be considered such third country as well. To ensure a smooth cooperation, the FCA and ESMA[93] as well as the FCA and the NCAs[94] have, respectively, concluded comprehensive **MoUs** that outline the cooperation in the future. Notwithstanding such MoUs, it remains to be seen if and how ESMA and the NCAs will manage to sustain a co-operative relationship with their UK counterpart, in particular if the UK law should deviate from European capital markets law.[95]

V. Competition between the National Supervisory Institutions

52 The supervision of capital markets is subject to competition between the national supervisory authorities, especially within the European Union.[96] This is triggered by the options

---

[87] The conclusion of MoU between supervisory authorities within the European Union remains common practice even after the introduction of the new directives on cooperation, cf. M. Lamandini, 6 ECL (2009), 197, 198–199 (referring to banking supervision).

[88] E. Wymeersch, 42 CML Rev. (2005), 987, 995–996.

[89] IOSCO, Principles of Memoranda of Understanding, September 1991, available at: www.iosco.org/library/pubdocs/pdf/IOSCOPD17.pdf.

[90] IOSCO, Multilateral memorandum of understanding concerning consultation and cooperation and the exchange of information, May 2002 (revised May 2012), available at: www.iosco.org/library/pubdocs/pdf/IOSCOPD386.pdf.

[91] D. Döhmel, in: Assmann et al. (eds.), *Wertpapierhandelsrecht*, § 18 para. 58; J. v. Hein, in: Schwark and Zimmer (eds.), *Kapitalmarktrechts-Kommentar*, § 18 WpHG para. 17; F. Boehn, in: Park, Kapitalmarktstrafrecht, Chapter 1.2 para. 108; see already E. Wymeersch, 42 CML Rev. (2005), 987, 996.

[92] D. Döhmel, in: Assmann et al. (eds.), *Wertpapierhandelsrecht*, § 18 para. 57.

[93] Memorandum of Understanding concerning consultation, cooperation and the exchange of information between ESMA and the UK Financial Conduct Authority.

[94] Multilateral Memorandum of Understanding concerning consultation, cooperation and the exchange of information between each of the EEA competent authorities and the UK Financial Conduct Authority.

[95] As of 1 January 2021, the UK onboarded the substantive rules of European capital markets law in its entirety under the European Union (Withdrawal) Act 2018, as amended by the European Union (Withdrawal Agreement) Act 2020.

[96] E. Wymeersch, 42 CML (2005), 987, 1004 who assumes the existence of market for supervision in the European Union. Cf. for the impact of competition between NCAs F. Walla, *Die Konzeption der Kapitalmarktaufsicht in Deutschland*, 45 ff.

supervised institutions have as to which supervisory authority should be responsible. The concept of a **single passport** for security prospectuses and the admission of investment firms, as initially introduced by the PD and the MiFID I, grant a large amount of flexibility to investment firms and issuers. Said flexibility allows them to in fact choose which supervisory authority should approve their prospectus or decide on their admission as an investment firm. A prime example of the results of this competition is, for example, the fact that the Luxembourg supervisory authority CSSF has established a de facto position as the first port of call for the approval of bond prospectuses in the EU.

Whilst generally **no competitive atmosphere** between the supervisory institutions can as yet be observed, the NCAs are nevertheless aware of the continual competition.[97] This may either be greeted as a means for increasing their efficiency and innovation[98] or seen critically as hindering European integration.[99] The fact that some competition exists must at least be taken into consideration when analysing the European supervisory landscape.

53

VI. The European System of Financial Supervision (ESFS)

International legal literature has long been discussing whether a central European supervisory institution,[100] following the example of the US Securities and Exchange Commission (SEC), should be introduced. The financial crisis of 2007, finally, gave a strong incentive for introducing a **European System of Financial Supervision (ESFS)**.

54

The Commission laid down the cornerstones of the new supervisory system, based largely on the work of an expert group under the chair of **Jacques de Larosière**[101] in its legislative package of 2009.[102] In September 2010, the Parliament accepted the Commission's proposal, suggesting only few amendments.[103] The proposal was approved by the Council in November 2010 and the ESFS become operative 1 January 2011. The legal foundation for the ESFS is Article 114 TFEU.[104]

55

---

[97] Cf. BaFin's longtime President, Jochen Sanio, in the preface of L. Frach, *Finanzaufsicht in Deutschland und Großbritannien* (2008); further N. Moloney, in: Grundmann et al. (eds.), in: FS Hopt, 2264, 2274.

[98] Centre for European Policy Studies, *Financial Regulation and Supervision Beyond 2005*, p. 10.

[99] CESR, A proposed evolution of EU securities supervision beyond 2007, CESR/07-783, November 2007, p. 3 ('referees should not compete').

[100] L. Gower, in: Buxbaum et al. (eds.), *European Business Law*, 307, 315 ff.; E. Pan, 34 L. & Pol'y Int'l Bus. (2003), 499, 526 ff.; G. Thieffry, 18 Fin. L. Rev. (1999), 14 ff.; G. Thieffry, in: Ferran and Goodhart (eds.), *Regulation Financial Services in 21st Century*, 211, 220 ff.; R. Karmel, 38 Colum. J. Transnat'l L. Law (1999), 9, 32 ff.; E. Wymeersch, in: Ferran and Goodhart (eds.), *Regulation Financial Services in 21st Century*, 189, 193.

[101] See R. Veil § 1 para. 33.

[102] Commission Proposal for a regulation of the European Parliament of the Council on Community macro prudential oversight of the financial system and establishing a European Systemic Risk Board, 23 September 2009, COM(2009) 499 final; COM(2009) 500 final; COM(2009) 501 final; COM(2009) 502 final; COM(2009) 503 final. Cf. Communication from the Commission on European financial supervision, 27 May 2009, COM(2009), 252 final.

[103] On securities supervision: Legislative Proposal of the European Parliament of 22 September 2010 on the Proposal for a Regulation of the European Parliament and of the Council establishing a European Securities and Markets Authority, COM(2009) 0503, C7-0167/2009, 2009/0144(COD).

[104] See below para. 100 for details on this discussion on the scope of this legal basis.

56 A comprehensive legislative review was undertaken between 2017 and 2019 ('**ESA Review**').[105] The ESA Review included intense discussions between the European institutions on reforms for the ESFS. The result of the ESA review was a strengthening of ESMA's position, but without a paradigm shift with regard to the authority's powers. In particular, the voices calling for a far-reaching centralisation of capital market supervision in Europe at ESMA were not heard in the course of the ESA Review.[106]

1. Institutional Design

57 The European financial markets supervisory system consists of two pillars: The **macro-prudential level** aims to avoid systemic risks for the entire European financial system whilst the **micro-prudential level** is intended to develop a European system of supervision for the individual financial service providers and capital market participants.

(a) Macro-prudential Level

58 The **European Systemic Risk Board (ESRB)** is responsible for the macro-level supervision,[107] ensuring the general stability of Europe's financial system.[108] The ESRB, however, does not have its own legal personality.[109] It is rather a body for cooperation between members of the Commission, the European Central Bank, the European supervisory authorities on the micro-prudential level (ESAs) together with the national supervisory authorities and central banks. The ECB provides the secretariat for the ESRB. The President of the ECB is also the Chair of the ESRB. The ESRB has the power to issue warnings regarding systemic risks and recommendations for their prevention. The ESRB is not, however, to be equipped with legally binding legislative powers or powers of intervention.[110]

(b) Micro-prudential Level

59 At a micro-prudential level, the supervision of the individual financial actors is the responsibility of the three central European authorities: **the European Banking authority (EBA)**, the **European Insurance and Occupational Pensions Authority (EIOPA)** and the **European Securities and Market Authority (ESMA)**, all of which have their own legal personality.[111]

---

[105] Cf. on the discussion in the course of the ESA review eg C. Gortos and K. Lagaria, EBI Working Paper Series 2020 No. 57, 8.

[106] See eg J. Krahnen and K. Langenbucher, SAFE Policy Letter No. 88; J. Payne, Oxford Legal Studies Research Paper No. 26/2017.

[107] Regulation (EU) No. 1092/2010 of the European Parliament and of the Council of 24 November 2010 on European Union macro-prudential oversight of the financial system and establishing a European Systemic Risk Board, OJ L331, 15 December 2010, p. 1–11.

[108] See Commission Press Release of 23 September 2009, IP/09/1347.

[109] Cf. Recital 15 Regulation (EU) No. 1092/2010 of the European Parliament and of the Council of 24 November 2010 on European Union macro-prudential oversight of the financial system and establishing a European Systemic Risk Board, OJ L331, 15 December 2010, p. 1–11.

[110] Cf. Art. 15 ff. Regulation (EU) No. 1092/2010 of the European Parliament and of the Council of 24 November 2010 on European Union macro-prudential oversight of the financial system and establishing a European Systemic Risk Board, OJ L331, 15 December 2010, p. 1–11.

[111] COM(2009) 503 final (fn. 107), Art. 3(1). Cf. G. Granner, in: Braumüller et al. (eds.), *Die neue Europäische Finanzmarktaufsicht – ZFR Jahrestagung 2011*, 27, 31 ff.; H. Siekmann, IMFS Working Paper No. 24 (2009).

Together with the national supervisory authorities, these European authorities form a network responsible for the supervision of the financial markets.[112] As opposed to the macroprudential level, the European authorities of the ESFS all have **legally binding legislative powers and powers of intervention**.[113] Yet, the day-to-day supervision of market participants is in general to be carried out by the national supervisory authorities with narrow exceptions for ESMA. Hence, the national level remains the centre of supervision.[114] The ESA's function is, therefore, predominantly **watching-the-watchers**.[115]

A **Joint Committee** is to ensure a cooperation and coordination between the macro- and the micro-prudential level and between the individual authorities on the micro-prudential level.[116]

60

(c) European Banking Union

Since 2014 the ESFS's banking supervision has been complemented by a pan-European supervisory scheme.[117] The financial crisis demonstrated that simple coordination of financial supervision via the ESFS was not sufficient to effectively supervise the European banking sector and pre-empt a future financial crisis. In order to overcome this obstacle, a **European Banking Union** was established. In this course, the **Single Supervisory Mechanism (SSM)**, the **Single Resolution Mechanism (SRM)** and a **common deposit guarantee scheme** were created. Not all EU Member States participate in the Banking Union but only the Member States of the Eurozone. Non-euro area Member States are invited to join. In October 2020, Croatia and Bulgaria made use of this option and joined the SSM as first non-Eurozone countries.

61

The SSM is the heart of the European Banking Union. Based on the SSM Regulation[118] most tasks relating to the prudential supervision of credit institutions in the participating Member States are now conferred on the ECB. The ECB directly supervises **115 banks** of the participating countries which a considered 'Significant Institutions (SI)'. These banks hold almost **82% of the aggregate banking assets** in these countries. All other banks (so-called 'Less Significant Institutions (LSI)') are supervised by the national authorities with the ECB overseeing their supervisory practice.[119]

62

Notwithstanding, the direct supervisory powers of the ECB the spirit of the SSM is that the national authorities and the ECB cooperate closely and exchange information. For this

63

---

[112] Recital 9 Regulation EU No. 1095/2010 of the European Parliament and of the Council of 24 November 2010 establishing a European Supervisory Authority (European Securities and Markets Authority), OJ L331/84, 15 December 2010 (ESMA Regulation).

[113] See below para. 75.

[114] See A. Wittig, DB (2010) *Standpunkte*, 69.

[115] Cf. N. Moloney, *EU Securities and Financial Markets Regulation*, 973, for an analysis of ESMA's relation vis-à-vis the NCAs.

[116] E. Wymeersch, in: Wymeersch et al. (eds.), *Financial Regulation and Supervision*, 232, 288 ff.

[117] Cf. on the background N. Moloney, *EU Securities and Financial Markets Regulation*, 943 ff.

[118] Council Regulation (EU) No. 1024/2013 of 15 October 2013 conferring specific tasks on the European Central Bank concerning policies relating to the prudential supervision of credit institutions, OJ L287, 29 October 2013, p. 63–89; cf. also Regulation (EU) No. 468/2014 of the European Central Bank of 16 April 2014 establishing the framework for cooperation within the Single Supervisory Mechanism between the European Central Bank and national competent authorities and with national designated authorities, OJ L141, 14 May 2014, p. 1–50.

[119] A full list of all institutions currently qualified as SI and the allocation of the banking assets between SI and LSI can be found on www.ecb.eu.

purpose, they create **Joint Supervisory Teams (JSTs)** to execute the supervision over the significant institutions. The ECB is responsible for the effective and consistent functioning of the mechanism but is dependent on the support of the national authorities in order to execute the supervision. The SSM's mandate includes authorising credit institutions, ensuring compliance with prudential and other regulatory requirements, and carrying out supervisory reviews. Besides these micro-prudential tasks, the ECB also has a macro-prudential mandate. As a consequence, the ECB as well has macro-supervisory tools at its disposal, for example, in relation to capital buffers.

64   The SSM is closely linked with the SRM and the **Single Bank Resolution Fund (SBRF)**. Both institutions were founded on the basis of a European regulation.[120] The SRM provides tools for the recovery and resolution of credit institutions and certain investment firms in the Euro area and in other participating Member States. The SBRF serves as a financial backstop, ie should it become necessary to resolve a failed bank, in case a bank's shareholders and creditors prove insufficient to absorb a certain amount of losses, the SBRF can provide further funds. Some aspects of the SBRF, such as the transfer and mutualisation of national contributions, are not subject to an EU regulation but are covered by an intergovernmental agreement concluded between the participating Member States.

65   The last element of the European Banking Union is a common deposit protection mechanism. In 2015, the Commission published the proposal to establish a **European Deposit Insurance Scheme (EDIS)**.[121] However, no political agreement has yet been reached on the design of such a deposit protection scheme.

2. The European Securities and Markets Authority (ESMA)

(a) Foundations

66   ESMA was founded by the ESMA Regulation. It assumed all tasks and powers of the former CESR.[122] ESMA has its seat in **Paris**.[123] By the end of 2019, it had **233 full-time equivalent employees**.[124] The authority's mandate is to protect the public interest by contributing to the short-, medium- and long-term **stability and effectiveness of the financial system**.[125] The ESMA Regulation substantiates this mandate by point out that ESMA should ensure the functioning of the internal market and the supervisory convergence within the internal market. It should further protect the integrity, transparency and efficiency of the financial markets and support international supervisory cooperation. Finally, ESMA should

---

[120] See Regulation (EU) No. 806/2014 of the European Parliament and of the Council of 15 July 2014 establishing uniform rules and a uniform procedure for the resolution of credit institutions and certain investment firms in the framework of a Single Resolution Mechanism and a Single Resolution Fund and amending Regulation (EU) No. 1093/2010, OJ L225, 30 July 2014, p. 1–90.

[121] European Commission, A stronger Banking Union: New measures to reinforce deposit protection and further reduce banking risks, 24 November 2015.

[122] Recital 8 and 67 ESMA Regulation.

[123] Art. 7 ESMA Regulation.

[124] ESMA, 2019 Annual Report, ESMA20-95-1264, 15 June 2020, p. 73.

[125] Art. 1(5)(1) ESMA Regulation.

prevent regulatory arbitrage, regulate investment risks and strengthen investor as well as consumer protection.[126]

The authority's most important body is the **Board of Supervisors**.[127] Moreover, the authority's governance system includes a Management Board, a Chairperson, an Executive Director and a Board of Appeal.[128] In the course of the ESA Review the Board of Supervisors received the power to set up committees for specific tasks.[129]

67

The **Board of Supervisors** is composed of the heads of the NCAs and further non-voting members, namely the Chairperson, representatives of the Commission, the ESRB and one representative from each of the other two European Supervisory Authorities.[130] The Board of Supervisors appoints the **ESMA Chairperson**[131] who represents ESMA vis-à-vis third parties.[132] For up to one month after the selection, the European Parliament may, however, object to the designation of the selected person.[133] **Steven Maijoor** from the Netherlands was appointed the first Chairman and was re-appointment for a second five-year term.[134] The Chairperson's main task besides the representation of ESMA is chairing the meetings of the Board of Supervisors and the Management Board.[135] The Board of Supervisors must further elect an alternate to carry out the functions of the Chairperson in his absence and who may not be a member of the Management Board.[136]

68

After confirmation by the European Parliament, the Board of Supervisors must also appoint an **Executive Director** in charge of the management of ESMA and prepare the work of the Management Board,[137] which executes ESMA's day-to-day supervisory activities.[138] The Executive Director may participate in meetings of the Board of Supervisors but does not have the right to vote.[139] The first Executive Director was **Verena Ross**, a German national formerly working for the United Kingdom's supervisor. Verena Ross was also re-appointed for a second five-year term in 2015 before becoming Chair at ESMA in 2021.[140]

69

Besides the daily management the **Management Board** shall ensure that ESMA performs the tasks assigned to it and acts in accordance with its budgetary plan.[141] The Management Board is composed of the Chairperson and six other members of the Board of Supervisors,

70

---

[126] Art. 1(5) (2)(a-g) ESMA Regulation.
[127] Art. 43(1), (2) ESMA Regulation.
[128] Art. 6 ESMA Regulation.
[129] Art. 41 ESMA Regulation.
[130] Art. 40(1) ESMA Regulation. In general, decisions of the Board of Supervisors are taken by a simple majority of its members, each member having one vote, cf. Art. 44(1) ESMA Regulation. With regard to the acts specified in Art. 10–16 ESMA Regulation, however, the Board of Supervisors' decisions must be taken on the basis of a majority as defined in the Treaty of Lisbon, cf. Art. 44(1) subsec. 2 ESMA Regulation.
[131] Art. 43(3) ESMA Regulation.
[132] Art. 43(3) ESMA Regulation.
[133] Art. 48(2) ESMA Regulation.
[134] ESMA, Press Release of 24 September 2015, ESMA/2015/1425, 24 September 2015.
[135] Art. 48(1) ESMA Regulation.
[136] Art. 48(2) subsec. 3 ESMA Regulation. This position is currently held by Anneli Tuominen, Director-General of the Finnish Finanssivalvonta.
[137] Art. 51(2) ESMA Regulation.
[138] Cf. No. 6.3.3 COM(2009) 503 final (fn. 107).
[139] Art. 40(6) ESMA Regulation.
[140] ESMA/2015/1425 (fn. 145).
[141] Art. 47(1) ESMA Regulation.

elected by the voting members of the Board of Supervisors.[142] The Executive Director and a representative of the Commission participate in meetings of the Management Board but do not have the right to vote.[143]

71   In order to effectively fulfil its mandate ESMA makes use of advice by the NCAs and external experts.[144] The most important advisory body is the **Securities and Markets Stakeholders Group (SMSG)**.[145] Moreover, ESMA has created a number of committees that provide access to expertise in particular from market participants, consumers' and users of financial services' representatives as well as academics. In addition, ESMA has created several standing committees which draw together experts from the NCAs. Most standing committees have consultative working groups in which external stakeholders are represented.[146]

72   The Management Board further appoints the ESMA member of the **Board of Appeal**.[147] The Board of Appeal is a joint body of the three European Authorities providing legal protection against measures taken by ESMA, EIOPA or EBA.[148]

(b) Independence and Budget

73   According to the ESMA Regulation the authority is independent, acting **solely in the interest of the European Union**.[149] The autonomy of its bodies[150] and its budgetary autonomy do, in fact, provide such independence to a very large extent.[151] However, due to the fact that the members of ESMA's supervisory body stem from the NCAs, a certain adaptation towards the national interests might not be prevented.[152] Also, the involvement of the Commission in ESMA's bodies might give rise to a certain lack of independence.[153] This distinguishes ESMA from the ECB which is a fully independent institution.[154]

74   ESMA may decide autonomously over its budget. The authority's budget for 2020 amounts to **approx. € 58 million**.[155] This budget is financed by the NCAs (approx. 41%), by the EU (approx. 34%) and observers (below 1%) as well as by contributions and fees from directly supervised market participants (approx. 24%).[156] During the ESA Review, a direct contribution to ESMA by all market participants was discussed. This proposal, however, was rejected in the final negotiations between the European institutions.

---

[142] Art. 45(1) ESMA Regulation.
[143] Art. 45(2) ESMA Regulation.
[144] Cf. also R. Veil, 5 ZGR (2014), 544, 555 ff.
[145] See Art. 37 ESMA Regulation. The statements and recommendations of the SMSG can be downloaded under www.esma.europa.eu/about-esma/governance/smsg.
[146] A continuously updated overview over all committees of ESMA is available at www.esma.eu.
[147] Art. 47(8) ESMA Regulation.
[148] Cf. www.esma.europa.eu/about-esma/governance/board-appeal.
[149] Cf. Recital 59 ESMA Regulation.
[150] Art. 42, 46, 49, 52, 59 ESMA Regulation.
[151] Cf. M. Lehmann and C. Manger-Nestler, 3 EuZW (2010), 87, 89.
[152] Cf. also M. Hitzer and P. Hauser, 2 BKR (2015), 52, 53.
[153] Cf. N. Moloney, *EU Securities and Financial Markets Regulation*, 914 ff.
[154] Cf. M. Lehmann and C. Manger-Nestler, 3 EuZW (2010), 87, 89; M. Lehmann and C. Manger-Nestler, 1 ZBB (2011), 2, 8.
[155] ESMA, Budget for 2020, 13 January 2020, ESMA63-43-1444.
[156] ESMA, Budget for 2020, 13 January 2020, ESMA63-43-1444.

(c) Powers of Intervention vis-à-vis the NCAs

Generally, the concept of the European supervisory system does not provide for ESMA to have direct powers (of intervention) vis-à-vis issuers and market participants ('**watching the watchers**'-model). The continuous supervision of market developments is rather to remain a matter of the Member States' NCAs. The NCAs are coordinated by ESMA in order to ensure a consistent and coherent supervision of markets in the EU.[157]

To this end, peer reviews pursuant to Article 30 ESMA Regulation are an efficient and effective tool for analysing and comparing the national institutions' activities.[158] According to Article 35 of the regulation, ESMA further has the right to request information from the competent authorities within the Member States in order to perform its supervisory duties.

There are, nevertheless, three ways of intervening against national authorities or – in exceptional cases – even against market participants.[159]

(aa) Breaches of EU Law by the National Supervisory Authorities

When a NCA has incorrectly or insufficiently applied European Union law, Article 17 ESMA Regulation provides a **three-step mechanism**[160] for the authority as a proportionate response thereto.

ESMA itself, the Council, Parliament, Commission or the SMSG may initiate investigations regarding the incorrect or insufficient application of EU law obligations by national authorities in their supervisory practice. Within two months after commencement of the investigations, ESMA may issue a recommendation to the competent national authority on how to overcome the breach.

In the case that the respective NCA does not follow the recommendation within a one-month period, the ESMA is empowered on a second level to issue a formal opinion taking ESMA's recommendation into account and requiring the competent authority to take the actions necessary to ensure compliance with EU law.

To overcome situations in which these actions are not taken within the given time limit, ESMA may adopt **decisions addressed to individual participants** in the financial markets. These may obligate the respective participant to comply with its duties under EU law. This power, however, only exists where it is necessary to remedy such non-compliance in a timely manner in order to maintain or restore neutral conditions of competition on the market or ensure the orderly functioning and integrity of the financial system.[161] The breach must further affect directly applicable provisions of European law. ESMA is thus empowered to undertake a form of 'right of entry' in order to remedy breaches of EU law.[162]

During the first 10 years of its existence, ESMA has not yet made use of its powers in case of a breach of EU law at all.

---

[157] Art. 1(5)(c) and Art. 31 ESMA Regulation.
[158] Cf. Recital 41 ESMA Regulation; Cf. N. Moloney, in: Wymeersch et al. (eds.), *Financial Regulation and Supervision*, 71, 103 ff.; E. Wymeersch, in: Wymeersch et al. (eds.), *Financial Regulation and Supervision*, 232, 280 ff.
[159] See for an analysis also N. Moloney, *EU Securities and Financial Markets Regulation*, 976 ff.
[160] Recital 28 ESMA Regulation; cf. M. Lehmann and C. Manger-Nestler, 3 EuZW (2010), 87, 90.
[161] Art. 17(6) ESMA Regulation.
[162] M. Lehmann and C. Manger-Nestler, 3 EuZW (2010), 87, 91.

(bb) Decisions on Emergency Situations and Disagreements between NCAs

83 In cases of so-called **emergency situations**[163] and **disagreements between national supervisory authorities**[164] ESMA is permitted to address measures to individual national supervisory authorities. The measures must be necessary as a reaction to adverse developments which may seriously jeopardise the orderly functioning and integrity of financial markets or the stability of the whole or part of the financial system in the EU. Should the national authority not comply with the decision, ESMA may adopt an individual decision addressed to a financial market participant, requiring the necessary action to comply with its obligations.[165]

(1) Emergency Situations

84 The Council is empowered to determine the existence of so-called emergency situations in consultation with the Commission, the ESRB and, where appropriate, the ESAs.[166] The request for such a decision can be made by ESMA, the Commission or the ESRB. In an emergency situation ESMA **may issue decisions to the NCAs in order to overcome the thread for financial stability**. If a competent authority does not comply with the decision of ESMA, a decision addressed directly to a financial market participant requiring the necessary action to comply with its obligations under the directly applicable European law is only permitted under strict conditions: ESMA may only act if an urgent remedy is necessary in order to restore the orderly functioning and integrity of financial markets or the stability of the EU financial system.

(2) Disagreements between Competent Authorities in Cross-Border Situations

85 If permitted by a directive or regulation,[167] ESMA may adopt a decision in cases of disagreements between NCAs addressed to a financial markets participant. These decisions may include the action to be taken by the market participants to comply with its obligations under EU law. Prior to this, ESMA has, however, to act as a **mediator** between the authorities, setting a time limit for conciliation.[168] If a NCA does not comply with ESMA's decision, the latter may adopt an individual decision addressed to a financial markets participant requiring the necessary action to comply with its obligations under European law pursuant to Article 19(4) ESMA Regulation. Unlike in cases of emergency, this power is not subject to further conditions.

(3) National Fiscal Responsibilities Limit ESMA Powers

86 The limits to ESMA's powers are laid down in the **safeguard provision** in Article 38 ESMA Regulation, which prohibits any decisions adopted by ESMA from impinging on the fiscal

---

[163] Art. 18 ESMA Regulation.
[164] Art. 19 ESMA Regulation.
[165] M. Lehmann and C. Manger-Nestler, 3 EuZW (2010), 87, 91.
[166] Cf. Art. 18(2) ESMA Regulation.
[167] See eg Art. 13(6) MAR; Art 25(2a) TD; Art. 57(6) MiFID II; Art. 31(5) draft PR.
[168] Art. 19(2) ESMA Regulation.

responsibilities of Member States. In case a Member State argues that a decision impinges on its fiscal responsibilities, it may notify ESMA and the Commission within two weeks after it has been notified of ESMA's decision. As a result, this decision is suspended.

According to Article 38(2) ESMA Regulation, in cases of a disagreement being resolved by ESMA, the authority must then re-evaluate its decision. If it upholds it, the Council must take a decision according to the majority of the votes. It may then maintain the decision or revoke it (in which case the decision is terminated). 87

Should a Member State consider that an emergency decision taken under Article 38(3) impinges on its fiscal responsibilities, it may notify ESMA, the Commission and the Council that the decision will not be implemented by the competent authority. In this case, the Council is automatically responsible for deciding on the admissibility of the decision, without prior re-evaluation by ESMA. This requires a simple majority of its members. If the Council decides not to revoke the authority's decision relating to Article 18(3) ESMA Regulation and if the Member State concerned still considers that the decision of the authority impinges upon its fiscal responsibilities, it may again notify the Commission and the authority and request the Council to re-examine the matter, causing a suspension of ESMA's decision.[169] Article 38(5) ESMA Regulation clarifies that any abuse of this possibility is prohibited, as incompatible with the internal market. 88

(d) Direct Supervision of Market Participants

In some (still exceptional) cases ESMA regulation does not strictly abide by the concept of watching the watchers. In fact, the ESMA Regulation provides the authority with a limited number of direct powers of intervention towards individual market participants. In the course of the ESA Review further direct supervisory powers were granted to ESMA with effect from 1 January 2022 (supervision of benchmarks and data service providers).[170] 89

ESMA has such powers – as shown before[171] – in the exceptional emergency situations and in case of a disagreement between national supervisory authorities as well as a result of violations of EU law by a NCA; in each case provided the aforementioned strict conditions are all fulfilled and the respective NCA has not complied with the directions issued by ESMA. In addition, ESMA has a few further direct supervisory powers vis-à-vis market participant. 90

(aa) Warnings and Prohibition of Financial Activities

ESMA may also issue warnings in the event that a financial activity poses a serious threat to supervisory objectives.[172] In 2012, ESMA made use of this possibility for the first time, issuing a warning against dealing with unauthorised firms offering foreign exchange investments.[173] Pursuant to Article 9(5) ESMA Regulation the authority may furthermore temporarily prohibit or restrict certain financial activities if they threaten the orderly 91

---

[169] Cf. Art. 38(4) ESMA Regulation.
[170] The Commission was even advocating to confer the direct supervision on the approval of certain prospectuses and certain investment funds on ESMA. However, in the course of the Trialogue negotiations this position was dropped.
[171] See para. 84.
[172] Cf. Art. 9(3) ESMA Regulation.
[173] ESMA, Investor Warning against Trading in Foreign Exchange (Forex), ESMA/2011/412, 5 December 2011.

functioning and integrity of financial markets or the stability of the whole or part of the financial system in the EU. *Examples*: On this legal basis ESMA was assigned the right **to prohibit short sales** in emergency situations (Article 28 SSR)[174] or the **distribution, marketing or sale of certain financial products or financial services** (Article 40–42 MiFIR).[175]

92 An action of ESMA requires (i) either an emergency situation as laid down in Article 18 ESMA Regulation or (ii) that the respective special conditions laid down in another European legislative act (eg SSR, MiFIR) are fulfilled.

(bb) Supervision of Credit Rating Agencies (CRA) and Trade Repositories (TR)/ Security Repositories (SR)

93 As the only authority of the ESFS, ESMA has general and **direct supervisory powers** over entire groups of market participants. ESMA is responsible for registering and supervising **credit rating agencies (CRA)** and **trade repositories (TR)** as well as **security repositories (SR)**. It has the necessary sanctioning powers—such as withdrawal of registration, the suspension of ratings[176] and the ability to impose fines with a basic amount of up to € 750,000 (CRA) or € 20,000 (TR and SR)—as well as the accompanying investigatory powers for this task.[177]

94 The supervision of CRA is a key element of ESMA's mandate. In legal literature, this field of supervision was even regarded as a blueprint for the future developments of ESMA towards a '**European SEC**'.[178] Despite this, high importance, ESMA has made use of its sanctioning powers rather reluctantly in last years. It has only issued five public notices[179] and imposed six fines for breaches of the CRA Regulation.[180] The maximum fine was € 5.1 million.[181]

95 ESMA seems to follow this approach also when it comes to supervise TR under the EMIR[182] and SR under the Securitisation Regulation:[183] Until the end of 2020, ESMA has issued its two fines in this capacity.[184]

---

[174] The fact that this power of ESMA can have practical importance was demonstrated in the course of the COVID 19 pandemic for the first time: At the peak of the first pandemic wave in spring 2020, ESMA issued a EU-wide transparency requirement for short positions if these exceed the threshold of more than 0.1% of the share capital. Cf. on this F. Walla § 24 para. 32.

[175] See on this D. Klingenbrunn, 7 WM (2015), 315, 316.

[176] In particular, the powers laid down in Art. 23, 24 Rating Regulation are to be applied to the ESMA.

[177] Art. 36a CRA Regulation; Art. 65 EMIR (in conjunction with Art. 14 Securitisation Regulation). See also R. Veil § 27, for more details on the supervision of CRA.

[178] In this direction also E. Ferran, in: Ferran et al. (eds.), *The Regulatory Aftermath of the Financial Crisis*, 1, 48.

[179] See ESMA, Decision of the Board of Supervisors, ESMA/2014/544, 20 May 2014.

[180] See ESMA, Decision of the Board of Supervisors, ESMA/2015/1048, 24 June 2015.

[181] See ESMA, Public Notice of 28 March 2019, ESMA41-356-22, 28 March 2019 ('Fitch Ratings').

[182] Regulation (EU) No. 684/2012 of the European Parliament and of the Council of 4 July 2012 on OTC derivatives, central counterparties and trade repositories, OJ L201, 27 July 2012, p. 1–59.

[183] Regulation (EU) No. 2017/2402 of the European Parliament and of the Council of 12 December 2017 laying down a general framework for securitisation and creating a specific framework for simple, transparent and standardised securitisation, and amending Directives 2009/65/EC, 2009/138/EC and 2011/61/EU and Regulations (EC) No. 1060/2009 and (EU) No. 648/2012, OJ L347, 28 December 2017, p. 35–80.

[184] See ESMA, Press Release of 31 March 2016, ESMA/2016/468, 31 March 2016; ESMA, Public Notice of 15 July 2019, ESMA41-356-39, 15 July 2019.

(cc) Supervision of Benchmarks and Data Services Providers

Starting on 1 January 2022, ESMA will supervise EU critical benchmarks and their administrators. In addition, ESMA will be responsible for the recognition of third-country benchmarks. ESMA will also have the supervisory powers to authorise and supervise different types of Data Reporting Services Providers (DRSPs), ie Approved Publication Arrangements, Authorised Reporting Mechanisms and Consolidated Tape Providers under the MiFIR.

(e) Rule-making Powers and Supervisory Convergence

ESMA plays a major role in the European rule-making process.[185] The authority has an important function on Level 1, 2 and 3 of the Lamfalussy II Process.[186] Furthermore, it has assumed a further de facto rule-making power that are highly relevant for legal practice via its mandate to achieve supervisory convergence.[187]

(f) Compliance of ESMA's Powers with the TFEU

Since the formation of ESMA, compliance of the authority's supervisory and rule-making powers with the TFEU has been questioned by legal literature and by certain Member States.[188] The basis for these doubts was that under the ECJ's ***Romano***[189] judgment a conferral of legislative powers to bodies other than the EU institution is prohibited. Furthermore, under the ***Meroni***[190] ruling of the ECJ, powers involving a wide margin of discretion and policy decisions may not be delegated by EU institutions to other EU bodies.

The United Kingdom government challenged ESMA's powers to require market participants to notify the relevant NCA or disclose a net short position or to prohibit or impose conditions on short selling (Article 28(1) Short Selling Regulation)[191] arguing that the *Meroni* and the *Romano* rulings prohibit such delegation of powers. Moreover, it argued that ESMA's power to draft ITS and RTS violate Articles 290 and 291 TFEU[192] and that the EU could not even rely on Article 114 TFEU when establishing ESMA.

In 2014, the **ECJ dismissed the United Kingdom's actions** and ruled that ESMA's powers under the short selling regulation did not violate the TFEU.[193] In its decision the Court thoroughly analysed the framework of the ESMA Regulation and held it to be compliant with primary law and particularly concluded that ESMA's discretion is sufficiently limited.[194] The Court did not even follow the **concerns of Advocate-General Jääskinen** with regards to the compliance of ESMA's mandate with Article 114 TFEU.[195]

---

[185] See in detail F. Walla, § 4.
[186] Cf. N. Moloney, *EU Securities and Financial Markets Regulation*, 898 ff.; further F. Walla, § 4 para. 4.
[187] See F. Walla, § 4 para. 29.
[188] Cf. on this N. Moloney, *EU Securities and Financial Markets Regulation*, 994 ff.
[189] Case 89/90 (*Romano*).
[190] Case 9/56 (*Meroni/High Authority*).
[191] See on this provision F. Walla, § 24 para. 55.
[192] See on this F. Walla, § 4 para. 16.
[193] Case 270/15 (*UK v. Council and Parliament*).
[194] See for an analysis of the case C. Manger-Nestler, 3 GPR (2014), 141 ff.; N. Moloney, *EU Securities and Financial Markets Regulation*, 998 ff.; E. Howell, 11 ECFR (2014), 454 ff.
[195] Opinion of AG Jääskinen of 12 September 2013, Case 270/15 (*UK v. Council and Parliament*), para. 27 ff.

101   By dismissing the United Kingdom government's action the Court provided ESMA with legal certainty as to the compliance of its powers with primary law.[196] While this result is generally to be welcomed, the ECJ's ruling should nevertheless constantly remind ESMA that it is an independent body without direct democratic legitimation that should thus exercise its rule-making powers carefully.

(g) Judicial Review

102   The ESMA Regulation grants the market participants and national authorities legal protection against decisions made by ESMA on the grounds of Articles 17–19, providing them with the **right to make an appeal against any decision** addressed to them.[197] The Board of Appeal is a joint body of the ESAs and is composed of six members with a proven record of relevant knowledge and professional experience in the fields of finance and financial markets law.[198] The members of the Board of Appeal are to be independent in making their decisions and not bound by any instructions.[199]

103   Article 61 ESMA Regulation states that in order to contest a decision of the Board of Appeal, action may be brought before the ECJ in accordance with Article 263 TFEU.[200] In cases where there is no right to appeal laid down in the ESMA Regulation, proceedings may be brought before the ECJ directly. This particularly applies to proceedings against technical standards on the grounds of Article 263(4) TFEU.[201]

(h) Liability of ESMA

104   The ESMA Regulation clarifies in Article 69(1) that ESMA is to make good any damage caused by it or by its staff in the performance of duties according to the common general principles in the laws of the Member States. Respective claims for public liability are to be brought before the ECJ.

(i) Access to Information

105   Under Article 72 ESMA Regulation the public access to ESMA's documents is governed by the EU transparency regulation.[202] Under this regulation third persons are generally entitled to gain access to information. The access may, however, be denied because of public interests or to ensure the protection of personal data. Moreover, a request for information may be dismissed if an ongoing administrative of judicial proceedings might be affected or if the business interests of a third party are infringed.[203]

---

[196] Case C-270/15 (*UK v. Council and Parliament*).
[197] Art. 60(1) ESMA Regulation.
[198] Art. 58 ESMA Regulation.
[199] Art. 59 ESMA Regulation.
[200] Art. 47(1) ESMA Regulation.
[201] C. Manger-Nestler, *Kreditwesen* (2012), 528, 531.
[202] Regulation (EC) No. 1049/2001 of the European Parliament and of the Council of 30 May 2001 regarding public access to European Parliament, Council and Commission documents, OJ L145, 31 May 2001, p. 43–48.
[203] See on this exception G. Spindler, *Informationsfreiheit und Finanzmarktaufsicht*, 74.

3. Conclusion

During ESMA's formation numerous Member States did initially not agree with giving the European authorities the power to make decisions addressed directly to individual financial market participants.[204] The legal literature had **mixed opinions** on this matter: whilst some maintained the Commission's proposal did not go far enough,[205] not sufficiently ensuring the authority's independence and following the concept of sectoral supervision,[206] others claimed that the European Union ought to be more restrictive in introducing new harmonising provisions. They pointed out that difficulties in communication arise for the Member States when interacting with an authority at the European level.[207]

106

This criticism is certainly true to a certain extent. However, after the first years of its existence, one can already conclude that the European supervisory structure was **a step into the right direction**: increasing cross-border transactions and the growing unification of capital markets law at a European level make a European approach to supervision indispensable. Numerous questions of practical relevance are already decided by ESMA in Paris. ESMA's importance will continue to grow.[208] Legal practice is therefore well advised to continue to adjust to the European supervisory scheme.

107

Finally, one prediction of the first edition of this textbook[209] can be upheld: In the long run, ESMA has the potential to become the most important supervisory player in European capital markets law. The ESA Review was a further step into this direction. However, there is still a need to strengthen ESMA's role and mandate to build up a supervisor who is a true 'European SEC' in the long run. Further proposals for a partial extension of the mandate are made on an ongoing basis:[210] The European legislator should have the courage to take up these proposals and successively develop ESMA's powers.

108

---

[204] Cf. T. Möllers et al., 30 NZG (2010), 285, 290.
[205] K. Hopt, 36 NZG (2009), 1041, 1408; M. Lamandini, 6 ECL (2009), 197, 202.
[206] D. Masciandaro et al., CEPR Policy Insight No. 37, 16 ff.; T. Möllers et al., 30 NZG (2010), 285, 289.
[207] For example R. Veil, 11 EBOR (2010), 409, 422.
[208] See also E. Ferran, in: Wymeersch et al. (eds.), *Financial Regulation and Supervision*, 111, 156.
[209] 1st ed. (2013), F. Walla § 11 para. 79.
[210] See as an example the latest discussion on the supervision of the ESG ratings (cf. on this ESMA, Letter to the Commission of 28 January 2021, ESMA30-379-423).

§ 12

Sanctions

Bibliography

Af Sandeberg, Catarina, *Prospectus Liability in a Scandinavian Perspective*, 13 EBLR (2002), 323–334; Armour, John/Mayer, Colin/Polo, Andrea, *Regulatory Sanctions and Reputational Damage in Financial Markets*, 52 JFQA (2017), 1429–1448; Arsouze, Charles, *Réflexions sur les propositions du Rapport Coulon concernant le pouvoir de sanction de l'AMF*, Bull. Joly Bourse (2008), 246–257; Xi, Chao and Cao, Ning, *Greater Transparency, Better Regulation? Evidence from Securities Enforcement Actions*, 14(2) JCL (2020), 350–363; Coffee, John C., *Law and the Market: The Impact of Enforcement*, 156 U. Pa. L. Rev. (2007), 229–311; Conac, Pierre-Henri and Gelter, Martin (eds.), *Global Securities Litigation and Enforcement* (2019); Ferran, Eilís, *Are US-style Investor Suits Coming to the UK?*, 9 J. Corp. L. Stud. (2009), 315–348; Giudici, Paolo, *Private Enforcement of Transparency*, in: Tountopoulos, Vassilios D. and Veil, Rüdiger (eds.), *Transparency of Stock Corporations in Europe* (2019), 251–284; Gsell, Beate and Möllers, Thomas M.J. (eds.), *Enforcing Consumer and Capital Markets Law* (2020); Jackson, Howell E. and Roe, Mark J., *Public and Private Enforcement of Securities Laws: Resource-Based Evidence*, 93 J. Fin. Econ. (2009), 207–238; Kämmerer, Jörn A., *Bemessung von Geldbußen im Wettbewerbs- und Kapitalmarktrecht: Eine komparative Betrachtung*, in: Grundmann, Stefan et al. (eds.), *Festschrift für Klaus J. Hopt zum 70. Geburtstag* (2010), 2043–2060; Kämmerer, Axel J., *Transparency: Public Enforcement Strategies*, in: Tountopoulos, Vassilios D. and Veil, Rüdiger (eds.), *Transparency of Stock Corporations in Europe* (2019), 285–296; Kalss, Susanne and Oelkers, Janine, *Öffentliche Bekanntgabe—Ein wirksames Aufsichtsinstrument im Kapitalmarktrecht?*, ÖBA (2009), 123–143; Klöhn, Lars, *Die private Durchsetzung des Marktmanipulationsverbots*, in: Kalss, Susanne et al. (eds.), *Gesellschafts- und Kapitalmarktrecht in Deutschland, Österreich und der Schweiz 2013* (2014), 229–249; Koch, Philipp, *Naming and Shaming im Kapitalmarktrecht* (2019); La Porta, Rafael/Lopez-de-Silanes, Florencio/Shleifer, Andrei, *What Works in Securities Laws?*, 61 J. Fin. (2006), 1–32; Moloney, Niamh, *How to Protect Investors: Lessons from the EC and the UK* (2010); Pölzig, Dörte, *Private enforcement im deutschen und europäischen Kapitalmarktrecht*, 44 ZGR (2015), 801–848; Rontchevsky, Nicolas, *L'harmonisation des sanctions pénales*, Bull. Joly Bourse (2012), 139–142; Segarkis, Konstantinos, *Le renforcement des pouvoirs des autorités compétentes*, Bull. Joly Bourse (2012), 118–121; Stasiak, Frédéric, *Droit pénal des affaires* (2005); Tountopoulos, Vassilios D., *Market Abuse and Private Enforcement*, 11 ECFR (2014), 297–332; Veil, Rüdiger, *Concepts of Supervisory Legislation and Enforcement in European Capital Markets Law—Observations from a Civil Law Country*, 11 EBOR (2010), 409–422; Veil, Rüdiger and Brüggemeier, Alexander, *Kapitalmarktrecht zwischen öffentlich-rechtlicher und privatrechtlicher Normdurchsetzung*, in: Fleischer, Holger et al. (eds.), *Enforcement im Gesellschafts- und Kapitalmarktrecht* (2015), 277–309; Veil, Rüdiger, *Sanktionsrisiken im Kapitalmarktrecht*, 45 ZGR (2016), 305–328; Ventoruzzo, Marco, *When Market Abuse Rules Violate Human Rights: Grande Stevens v. Italy and the Different Approaches to Double Jeopardy in Europe and the US*, 16 EBOR (2015), 145–165; Werlauff, Erik, *Class Action and Class Settlement in a European Perspective*, 24 EBLR (2013), 173–186; Wundenberg, Malte, *Perspektiven der privaten Rechtsdurchsetzung im europäischen Kapitalmarktrecht*, 44 ZGR (2015), 124–160.

I. Introduction

1   Several approaches are applied in Europe to sanction misconduct under capital markets law, ranging from reprimands by self-regulatory bodies without legal consequences to damage claims under private law and administrative or criminal sanctions imposed by public bodies, such as supervisory authorities or courts. The most common administrative sanctions are fines and the disgorgement of profits, but the publication of breaches and imposed sanctions, so-called *naming and shaming*, is also an administrative sanction,[1] playing an important role in most Member States. Criminal sanctions consist of imprisonment, fines and the disgorgement of the profits the offender obtained through the offence. Under private law, the investors may claim damages. Furthermore, the loss of voting rights attached to shares is a common sanction in the Member States.[2]

2   Supervisory authorities have the task of preventing violations of the law. To this end, they can take administrative measures that prevent market participants from committing legal infringements, such as the suspension of trading of securities. **Administrative** and **criminal sanctions** not only have preventive purposes, in the sense that the perpetrator (**specific deterrence**) and the public (**general deterrence**) are deterred from committing legal violations in the future, but are also intended to have a repressive effect, ie to punish the offence committed (**repression**).[3] Private liability of market participants is a further enforcement mechanism. It influences the behaviour of market participants. In addition to this preventive function, it also has a compensatory function (compensation of damages).

3   The sanctions should take into account the insight from law and economics that individuals act in accordance with the goal of maximising individual benefits and take decisions based on a cost-benefit analysis. Individuals follow norms if the expected costs of a norm violation exceed the expected benefit from the norm violation. If the expected benefit resulting from the norm violation outweighs the expected costs, individuals will opt for the norm violation according to the model of *homo oeconomicus*. This cost-benefit assessment can be influenced by sanctions. The expected costs of a breach of the rules are determined by the amount of the sanction and the probability of sanctioning. The prerequisite is that both variables are rationally perceived by individuals.

4   Regarding the preventive effect, the total amount of the potential civil and public law sanctions is relevant. The probability of sanctioning, on the other hand, is subject to diverging imponderables depending on the sanctioning instrument, which are difficult to influence by the legislature. In addition to a knowledge problem that is central to both private and public authorities, there is often a suboptimal incentive to enforce the sanction. According to this model, a doubling of the probability of sanctions leads to a doubling of the expectation costs and thus to a significant strengthening of the preventive effect. The expected benefit of a breach of the law as the second factor in the above equation can be minimised through disgorgement of profits.

---

[1] Cf. S. Kalss and J. Oelkers, ÖBA 2009, 123 ff.; P. Koch, *Naming and Shaming*, 140 ff.
[2] Cf. R. Veil, 11 EBOR (2010), 409, 419–420.
[3] Cf. P. Koch, *Naming and Shaming*, 63 ff.

II. Sanctioning Systems in the Pre-Crisis Era

1. Public Enforcement (Criminal and Administrative Sanctions)

The four framework directives on capital markets law enacted in 2003 and 2004 contained only a few requirements regarding the sanctions to be introduced by the Member States. The directives contained the same provisions on sanctions: 'Without prejudice to the right of Member States to impose criminal sanctions and without prejudice to their civil liability regime, Member States shall ensure, in conformity with their national law, that the appropriate administrative measures can be taken or administrative sanctions be imposed against the persons responsible, where the provisions adopted in the implementation of this Directive have not been complied with. Member States shall ensure that these **measures** are **effective, proportionate** and **dissuasive**.'[4]

The Member States were therefore free to decide whether they wished to introduce criminal sanctions. According to the four framework directives, the Member States did not even need to introduce administrative sanctions. The directives did not contain provisions requiring any specific sanction or minimum fine—any measures that were effective, proportionate and dissuasive being sufficient.

The CESR's 'reports on administrative measures and sanctions and the criminal sanctions available in the Member States'[5] showed a number of differences in the national sanctioning regimes. The concepts differed greatly, especially regarding the severity of fines to be imposed. Yet the reports omitted to describe the legal practice in the Member States, although it is necessary to examine to the extent to which fines are imposed in order to determine how far they deter.[6] Finally, the CESR reports did not comment on sanctions under private law.[7]

2. Private Enforcement

Provisions on civil law sanctions were rare in the European directives enacted in 2003 and 2004. Neither the MAD nor the MiFID contained provisions on civil law liability for damages suffered by investors. The TD's requirements are only vague: 'Member States shall

---

[4] Art. 25 PD; Art. 14 MAD; Art. 28 TD; Art. 51 MiFID.

[5] CESR, Report on CESR Members' Powers under the PD and its Implementing Measures, June 2007, CESR/07-383; CESR, Report on administrative measures and sanctions as well as the criminal sanctions available in Member States under the market abuse directive (MAD), February 2008, CESR/08-099; CESR, Report on the mapping of supervisory powers, supervisory practices, administrative and criminal sanctioning regimes of Member States in relation to the Markets in Financial Instruments Directive (MiFID), February 2009, CESR/08-220; CESR, Report on the mapping of supervisory powers, administrative and criminal sanctioning regimes of Member States in relation to the Transparency Directive (TD), July 2009, CESR/09-058.

[6] ESMA has, however, meanwhile also begun to examine the legal practice. Cf. ESMA, Prospectus Directive: Peer Review Report on good practices in the approval Process, May 2012, ESMA/2012/300; ESMA, Actual use of sanctioning powers under MAD, 26 April 2012, ESMA/2012/270.

[7] One of ESMA's first reports on the sanctioning regimes under the PD 2003 also addressed civil liability for the first time. Cf. ESMA, Report: Comparison of liability regimes in Member States in relation to the Prospectus Directive, 30. Mai 2013, ESMA/2013/619, p. 12 ff.

ensure that responsibility for the information to be drawn up and made public in accordance with Articles 4, 5, 6 and 16 lies at least with the issuer or its administrative, management or supervisory bodies and shall ensure that their laws, regulations and administrative provisions on liability apply to the issuers, the bodies referred to in this Article or the persons responsible within the issuers.'[8]

9   The Member States were therefore free to decide who is to be held liable for incorrect financial reports, ie whether this be the issuer, the members of the administrative board, the supervisory board or the board of directors. They can also determine whether responsibility for breaches of the directive's provisions should require intent or also apply to cases of gross or ordinary negligence.[9] The PD 2003 only contained the following provisions on the civil law liability for incorrect information given in a prospectus: 'Member States shall ensure that responsibility for the information given in a prospectus attaches at least to the issuer or its administrative, management or supervisory bodies, the offeror, the person asking for the admission to trading on a regulated market or the guarantor, as the case may be.'[10] It did not, however, stipulate the conditions for such a liability, ie whether the issuer is only held liable for wrongful intent or also for negligence.[11] None of the four framework directives provided any further provisions on civil law liability. Furthermore, they did not require a loss of voting rights for breaches of the obligation to disclose major shareholdings.

III. Reforms after the Financial Crisis

1. Need for Reforms

10 The studies published by the former CESR showed that the criminal and administrative sanctions in the Member States differed considerably. This was criticised by the expert group under *Jacques de Larosière*[12] set up in reaction to the financial crisis, which requested 'sound prudential and conduct of business framework for the financial sector'. The **framework** '**must rest on strong supervisory and sanctioning regimes**'.[13] According to the experts it had proved to be very problematic during the financial crisis that 'there are substantial differences in the powers granted to national supervisors in different Member States, both in respect of what they can do by way of supervision and in respect of the enforcement actions (including sanctions) open to them when a firm is in breach of its duties.'[14] The High Level Experts deducted from this that the 'European Institutions should also set in motion a process which will lead to far more consistent sanctioning regimes across the Single Market. Supervision cannot be effective with weak, highly variant sanctioning regimes. It is essential

---

[8] Art. 7 TD.
[9] See H. Brinckmann § 18 para. 75.
[10] Cf. Art. 6(1) PD.
[11] See R. Veil § 17 para. 73–74.
[12] See R. Veil § 1 para. 33 ff.
[13] Cf. The High-Level Group on Financial Supervision in the EU (de Larosière Group), Report, 25 February 2009 (de Larosière Report), para. 83.
[14] Cf. de Larosière Report (fn. 13), para. 160.

that within the EU and elsewhere, all supervisors are able to deploy sanctions regimes that are sufficiently convergent, strict, resulting in deterrence.'[15]

The group of experts did not, however, present any specific proof for its findings that the deficits in the European sanctioning system had contributed to the financial crisis. The European Commission nevertheless implemented the expert group's recommendation and presented comprehensive reform proposals for an amendment of three of the four framework directives in autumn 2011.[16] The most considerable regulative initiative was taken concerning the directive on criminal sanctions for market abuse (CRIM-MAD), none of the four framework directives on capital markets law until then having required the Member States to enact criminal law provisions and the Commission's initiative in this regard therefore marking a new era. Criminal sanctions are to emphasise social disapproval of the infringements different from administrative sanctions or civil law compensation mechanisms.[17]

2. Public Enforcement

In amending the legislative acts on Level 1, the European legislature had the aim of improving the detection and exposure of legal infringements. A further intention was the Europe-wide minimum harmonisation and effectiveness of administrative measures and sanctioning powers. A central goal of the reform was the implementation of **stricter sanctions** to achieve a **better deterrence**. This will be illustrated below using the example of the reforms that have taken place in the field of market abuse law.[18] It should be noted that the European legal acts all require the national legislators to transpose the relevant provisions into national law. This also applies if the provisions are provided for in regulations. The provisions in EU regulations on administrative measures and sanctions have the legal nature of a directive.

European legislation does not intend to oblige Member States to provide for both administrative and criminal sanctions for the same infringements; Member States are 'entirely free' to do so.[19] It may be permissible under national law to sanction conduct both as a criminal offence and as an administrative offence. However, the ECHR limits the legislative powers of the Member States in this regard. The European Court of Human Rights has stated in the *Grande Stevens v. Italy* case[20] on the **prohibition** of **double jeopardy** under the ECHR that the fines imposed by Italy's public authority responsible for regulating the Italian financial markets ('Consob') for market abuse are to be regarded as a punishment in the sense of the 'ne bis in idem' principle.[21]

---

[15] Cf. de Larosière Report (fn. 22), para. 201.
[16] See R. Veil § 1 para. 40–42.
[17] Cf. Commission, Proposal for a Directive of the European Parliament and of the Council on criminal sanctions for insider dealing and market manipulation, 20 October 2011, COM(2011) 654 final, p.3 ff.
[18] The details of the sanctioning regimes are presented in chapters 3–9 of this book.
[19] Cf. recital 71 MAR and Art. 30(1) MAR.
[20] The prohibition of double jeopardy (ne bis in idem) is regulated in Art. 4 of the 7th Protocol to the ECHR.
[21] ECHR of 4.3.2014, Req. 18640/10, 18647/10, 18663/10, 18668/10, 18698/10; M. Ventoruzzo, 16 EBOR (2015), 145 ff.

(a) Provisions on the Detection and Exposure of Legal Infringements

14   The four legislative acts from 2003 and 2004 already contained some detailed provisions for the detection and exposure of legislative infringements by national supervisory authorities, the investigative and informative powers being particularly relevant. The new legislative acts contain concrete requirements for the Member States in this regard. In addition, the European legislator followed the US concept[22] and introduced rules on **whistleblowing**. Whistleblowing refers to a system in which private parties point out (potential) misconduct of individual market participants to the public supervisory authorities. This is seen controversially in particular with regard to the rewards for the whistleblower. The Commission originally planned to oblige the Member States to provide for respective provisions. However, it did not succeed with this proposal in the legislative procedure and the Member States are thus now free to decide whether they want to provide financial rewards to whistleblowers.

15   Directive (EU) 2019/1937 is another measure that takes into account the importance of whistleblowers and aims to ensure their protection: 'Common minimum standards ensuring that whistleblowers are protected effectively should apply as regards acts and policy areas where there is a need to strengthen enforcement, under-reporting by whistleblowers is a key factor affecting enforcement, and breaches of Union law can cause serious harm to the public interest.'[23] The Directive also applies to infringements of capital markets law.[24]

(b) Supervisory Measures

16   The new legislative acts further require the Member States to grant their supervisory authorities certain powers of intervention. Most measures in this regard are well-known from the former Level 1 measures and refer to the **disgorgement of profits**, trading suspensions, injunction measures and the **prohibition of further activities**, for example. The legislative acts thereby do not clarify whether these rules are to be understood as administrative measures or administrative sanctions. This aspect must therefore be clarified by way of interpretation. For example, Art. 30 of the MAR regulates both administrative sanctions and administrative measures. The provisions in lit. h), i) and j) concern 'financial sanctions'. In contrast, the measures in lit. a)-g) solely aim at preventing risks for security markets and investors. An order requiring the person responsible for the infringement to cease the conduct and to desist from a repetition of that conduct[25] is a typical administrative measure.

---

[22] Cf. Sec. 21F SEA 1934, which was introduced through the *Dodd-Frank Wall Street Reform and Consumer Protection Act*. According to this provision *whistleblowers*, whose voluntary information leads to the imposition of a fine of more than US$ 1 million, can expect a reward between 10% and 30%. Data from the *Office of the Whistleblower* of the SEC shows that numerous whistleblowers have submitted tips. Significant rewards of several million US$ have, however, only been granted in very few cases. See www.sec.gov/whistleblower.

[23] Recital 5 Directive (EU) 2019/1937 of the European Parliament and the Council of 23.10.2019 on the protection of persons who report breaches of Union law, OJ. EU No. L 305 of 26.11.2019, p. 17.

[24] Cf. Art. 2(1)(a)(ii): 'financial services, products and markets'.

[25] Cf. Art. 30(2)(a) MAR.

(c) Sanctions

All level 1 acts of the Single Rulebook aim to achieve stricter sanctions and an increased harmonisation at a European level in order to prevent supervisory arbitrage as described in the *de Larosière Report* and to achieve a higher degree of compliance.[26] Pecuniary sanctions (**fines**) are the most important instrument, for which the minimum rate of the maximum fines is to be determined uniformly across Europe. The Member States are thus required to fix the maximum fine at at least the height prescribed in the European legislative acts, but are permitted to exceed these amounts. One element that is to be taken into account when determining the height of a fine is the profit made or the loss prevented by the infringement. Fines are to be permissible up to at least three times the height of the profit made or the loss prevented.

The **minimum rates of the maximum fines** differ between the different legislative acts and legal infringements, the MAR, for example, providing for a nominal minimum rate of the maximum fine of € 5 million for natural persons in the case of breaches of the rules on inside information and market manipulation. For all other infringements of the MAR, the maximum fine provided for is € 1 million or € 500,000.[27] Legal persons are to be obliged to pay up to € 15 million or € 2.5 million for the same infringements.[28]

With regard to **legal persons**, the minimum rate of the maximum fines is further to be determined on the basis of the total annual turnover. Breaches of the rules on insider trading and market manipulation, for example, are to be sanctioned with fines of up to **15%** of the **total annual turnover** of the legal person according to the last available accounts. Other infringements (such as breaches of the obligations to disclose inside information) are still to be subject to fines of up to 2% of the total annual turnover. The regulatory concept stems from European competition law and is based on the understanding that the prohibited behaviour increased the respective market participant's turnover.[29] The new provisions under capital market law, however, go one step further and calculate the annual turnover not for the individual company but rather from a **group perspective**: Where the legal person is a parent undertaking or a subsidiary undertaking, the total annual turnover shall be the total annual turnover according to the last available consolidated accounts approved by the management body of the ultimate parent undertaking.[30] The link to the group's turnover increases the preventive effect, because it takes into account the calculation of a low probability of detection and reduces the incentive for legal infringements.[31]

> *Example*: Assuming a parent company had a total annual turnover of € 200 million and were sanctioned for market manipulation, the maximum administrative pecuniary sanction would amount to € 30 million (ie 15% of € 200 million). If the total annual turnover were to amount to € 50 million, the maximum fine would be € 15 million, based on the fact that a fine on the basis of the annual turnover could not exceed € 7.5 million (ie 15% of € 50 million). If the market manipulation was carried out by a subsidiary with an annual turnover of € 50 million, the maximum fine is

---

[26] Cf. on the deterrent effect of sanctions IOSCO, Credible deterrence in the enforcement of securities regulation, June 2015, available at: www.iosco.org/library/pubdocs/pdf/IOSCOPD490.pdf.
[27] Cf. Art. 30(2)(i) MAR.
[28] Cf. Art. 30(2)(j) MAR.
[29] Cf. R. Veil, 45 ZGR (2016), 305.
[30] Cf. Art. 30(2)(j) subsec. 3 MAR.
[31] See para. 3–4.

determined on the basis of the parent company's annual turnover (€ 200 million), with the result that the fine imposed against the subsidiary can amount to € 15 million.

21 The **disgorgement of profits** is a further administrative sanction that the Member States must include in the measures provided to the supervisory authorities. The Member States have to ensure that the NCAs have the power to impose maximum administrative pecuniary sanctions of at least three times the amount of the profits gained or losses avoided because of the infringement, where those can be determined.[32] This sanction is also known from European competition law. In capital markets law it plays a particularly important role with regard to infringements of the rules on insider trading. The calculation method for the profit gained or the loss prevented is not pre-determined by EU-law and must be regulated by national law. Member States thus have to determine whether courts are allowed to estimate profits or losses.

22 Furthermore, there are now to be uniform rules for **Naming and Shaming** throughout Europe. As a rule, the new provisions require the national authorities to publish the administrative measures and sanctions they have imposed, the publication having to contain at least the nature of the infringement. The publication of the authority's decision is to increase the deterring effect. It is the European legislator's understanding that the publication constitutes an important instrument in order to inform other market participants of the forms of behaviour that are regarded as impermissible. The publication is thus to be regarded as being of a general preventive nature and must therefore be classified as a sanction.

3. Development of a Private Enforcement

23 Private enforcement does not play the same prominent role in Europe as it does in the USA. US legislature regards private enforcement as an essential element of enforcement of market abuse and violation of disclosure obligations. This US approach is based on a number of empirical and comparative studies that have concluded that private enforcement is a far more effective means of capital markets regulation than a system relying mainly on public enforcement.[33] The introduction of substantive provisions granting investors the right to claim damages, however, does not suffice due to the generally high costs of civil liability claims, shared between a large number of injured parties. In capital markets law there is a high risk that the investors will not claim their damages, a phenomenon termed 'rational apathy'. The substantive provisions must, therefore, be accompanied by effective procedural provisions, which can, for example, provide for the possibility of class actions as in US law.[34]

---

[32] Cf. Art. 30(2)(h) MAR.

[33] R. La Porta et al., 61 J. Fin. (2006), 1, 27, argue that 'several aspects of public enforcement, such as having an independent and/or focused regulator or criminal sanctions, do not matter, and others matter in only some regressions. In contrast, both extensive disclosure requirements and standards of liability facilitation investor recovery of losses are associated with larger stock markets.' H.E. Jackson and M.J. Roe, 93 J. Fin. Econ. (2009), 207, 237, however come to different conclusions: 'Overall, and most importantly, we caution against using current views of the relative value of private and public enforcement to make public policy. Public enforcement as we measure it does well in the regressions.'

[34] The U.S. have, however, had bad experience with class actions, a main point of criticism being that the volume of securities class actions 'was increasing to epidemic proportions'. Furthermore, 'the benefits to individual class members were negligible, seldom exceeding a very small percentage of their losses'. Thirdly, class actions

As a result of the financial market crisis, European legislature has reformed only EU supervisory law. With a few exceptions, the reforms adopted since 2009 do not contain any provisions on private enforcement. Only the CRAR contains rules that grant investors and issuers the right to claim damages from a rating agency.[35] Investors may, however, nevertheless be entitled to claim damages for infringements under the new rules in the European regulations. Based on the ECJ's *Muñoz*-ruling it may be necessary to recognise a **right** to such **claims** for **investors**.[36] As is the case in competition law, the right to institute proceedings would increase the effectiveness of the MAR rules on insider dealings and market manipulations which were enacted in the interest of investors. However, this interpretation does not take into account that the European legislature has established an effective system of administrative and criminal sanctions, which not only has a repressive but also a deterrent effect.[37] It is therefore uncertain how the ECJ will decide these legal issues. The national courts will have to present these questions to the ECJ pursuant to the *acte claire-doctrine* as and when a case gives rise. Until then it remains a fact that investor protection in the shape of issuer liability remains subject to disparate regulations throughout Europe.[38]

Since the protection of investors under private law is still regulated disparately in Europe, the European legislature should counteract the fragmentation with a directive harmonising substantive liability law. An EU-wide harmonisation of the legal framework will reduce the transaction costs of market participants operating across borders. It also prevents fragmentation of the law that currently hinders competition.[39] An approximation of the right to compensation for losses incurred as a result of incorrect capital market information contributes to the completion of the internal market. Following the example of competition law, the European legislator should adopt a directive obliging the Member States to introduce liability for damages for all breaches of disclosure obligations provided for by the MAR and TD.[40]

IV. Conclusion

Both administrative and criminal sanctions and enforcement mechanisms under private law have specific deficits that impair their respective effectiveness. This entails the danger of under- and over-enforcement. In order to attenuate the latter, administrative, criminal and civil law sanctions should be carefully balanced. The development of hybrid forms of law enforcement can also be considered.[41]

were 'lawyer-driven'. Cf. J.C. Coffee and J. Seligman, *Securities Regulation*, ch. 15 A.1. ('The Dilemma of Private Securities Regulation').

[35] See R. Veil § 27 para.78.
[36] Cf. A. Hellgardt, 57 AG (2012), 154, 163; L. Klöhn, in: Kalss et al. (eds.), 129, 246–248; D. Pölzig, 45 ZGR (2015), 901, 805–838; V. Tountopoulos, 11 ECFR (2014), 297–332.
[37] Cf. R. Veil, in: Gsell and Möllers (eds.), *Enforcing Consumer and Capital Markets Law*, 405, 415.
[38] M. Wundenberg, 45 ZGR (2015), 124, 148–157.
[39] M. Wundenberg, 45 ZGR (2015), 124, 150.
[40] R. Veil, in: Gsell and Möllers (eds.), *Enforcing Consumer and Capital Markets Law*, 405, 417 ff.; P. Giudici, in: Tountopoulos and Veil (eds.), *Transparency of Stock Corporations in Europe*, 297, 308 ff.
[41] R. Veil and A. Brüggemeier, in: Fleischer et al. (eds.), *Enforcement im Gesellschafts- und Kapitalmarktrecht*, 277, 302 ff.

27 The reforms that have been implemented since the financial market crisis have considerably tightened administrative and criminal sanctions. The European legislature has therefore considerably increased the expected costs of a breach of the law. However, the low probability of sanctions remains problematic. To improve this, it will be necessary to further enhance access to information for the supervisory authorities and to provide them with better equipment.

28 Private enforcement is still underdeveloped in Europe. The incentive problems concerning claims for damages incurred as a result of a violation of disclosure obligations can only be solved via the introduction of a class action or other collective redress mechanisms. Another problem is that the EU still has no idea about the functions of private enforcement. The causality and damage prerequisites are regulated differently in Member States' laws. Legal basis in national laws do not permit effective enforcement of incorrect information on secondary markets under private law.

3
Market Abuse

§ 13

Foundations

Bibliography

Band, Christa and Hopper, Martyn, *Market Abuse—A Developing Jurisprudence*, JIBLR (2007), 231–239; Hauck, Pierre, *Europe's commitment to countering insider dealing and market manipulation on the basis of Art. 83 para. 2 TFEU*, 6 ZIS (2015), 336–347; Henderson, Andrew, *First Light: The Financial Services Authority's Enforcement of the Market Abuse Regime*, 20 JIBLR 2005, 494–500; Meyer, Andreas, et al. (eds.), Handbuch zum Marktmissbrauchsrecht (2018); Schimansky, Herbert and Bunte, Hermann-Josef, et al. (eds.), Bankrechts-Handbuch, 5th edn. (2017); Swan, Edward J. and Virgo, John, *Market Abuse Regulation*, 3rd edn. (2019); Tountopoulos, Vassilios D., *Market Abuse and Private Enforcement*, ECFR 2014, 297–332; Veil, Rüdiger, *Europäische Kapitalmarktunion*, ZGR (2014), 544–607; Ventoruzzo, Marco, *When Market Abuse Rules Violate Human Rights: Grande Stevens v. Italy and the Different Approaches to Double Jeopardy in Europe and the US*, 16 EBOR (2015), 145–165.

I. Introduction

The European Union has had a largely uniform legal framework to combat market abuse since 2003. The Market Abuse Directive 2003/6/EC (MAD 2003) from 22 December 2003[1] required the Member States to prohibit insider dealing and market manipulation. The Member States also had to ensure that inside information and directors' dealings were disclosed as soon as possible and recommendations published by financial analysts were subject to specific standards. However, the MAD 2003 only required a minimum harmonisation of the national laws. In 2008, the former CESR showed in a comprehensive study that, despite the harmonisation by the MAD 2003 and implementing directives, the market abuse law in the Member States differed and the existing administrative and criminal sanctions were disparate and not dissuasive.[2] The High Level Group, chaired by *Jacques de Larosière*, addressed this problem in the wake of the financial crisis and recommended the introduction of a coherent regulatory framework for Europe.[3] The European Commission responded to this recommendation with proposals for a Regulation and a Directive on market abuse (MAR and CRIM-MAD) published on 20 October 2011.

The **Market Abuse Regulation** (MAR) and the **Directive on criminal sanctions for insider dealing and market manipulation** (CRIM-MAD) were adopted on 16 April 2014 and

---

[1] See R. Veil § 1 para. 21.
[2] CESR, Report on Administrative Measures and Sanctions as well as Criminal Sanctions available in Member States under the Market Abuse Directive (MAD 2003), CESR/07-693, February 2008.
[3] Cf. The High-Level Group on Financial Supervision in the EU, 25.2.2009, 29.

published in the EU's Official Journal on 12 June 2014. The new regime has been applicable since 3 July 2016. The European legislator argued that the global economic and financial crisis had highlighted the importance of market integrity and it would be important to strengthen supervisory and sanctioning regimes in this regard. The legal framework established by the MAR and CRIM-MAD shall '**preserve market integrity, avoid regulatory arbitrage**' and 'provide more **legal certainty** and **less regulatory complexity** for market participants'.[4] It is based on the idea that 'an integrated, efficient and transparent financial market requires market integrity. The smooth functioning of securities markets and public confidence in markets are prerequisites for economic growth and wealth. Market abuse harms the integrity of financial markets and public confidence in securities and derivatives.'[5]

II. Legal Foundations

1. MAR

3   The main instrument for combating market abuse is the **Market Abuse Regulation** (MAR). It covers all regulatory areas of the MAD 2003 and is structured in a similar way. The first chapters set out the application of the Regulation, define important terms, establish prohibitions on insider trading and market manipulation and prescribe disclosure obligations for issuers and directors. As the rules are made in the form of a regulation, they have direct effect in the Member States (Article 288(2) TFEU). National legal provisions on insider trading and market manipulation are superfluous. Other chapters of the MAR include extensive new provisions on supervision by national authorities (NCAs) and administrative measures and sanctions to be introduced in the national laws of the Member States.

4   The legal instrument of a regulation is intended to achieve a **uniform interpretation** of the rules on market abuse. It also ensures that Member States no longer provide for divergent rules. The MAR implies that the same rules must be followed by all natural and legal persons throughout the Union. This helps to reduce compliance costs, especially for companies operating across borders, and to eliminate distortions of competition.[6] For these reasons, it can in principle be assumed that MAR aims at **full harmonisation of** the law on market abuse (with the exception of the rules on supervision in the Member States and the penalties to be provided for in the Member States).[7]

5   In order to achieve the objective of a single set of rules, the MAR empowers the Commission to adopt **delegated acts** (Art. 290 TFEU) and **implementing acts** (Art. 291 TFEU) (Level 2 acts). Furthermore, ESMA has to issue **guidelines** and recommendations, as set out in Art. 16 ESMA Regulation (Level 3 measures), to ensure uniform interpretation. The MAR and the national criminal legislation adopted in implementation of the CRIM-MAD, together with the Level 2 and Level 3 measures of the Commission and ESMA, form the '**Single Rulebook**

---

[4] Cf. Recital 4 MAR.
[5] Cf. Recital 2 MAR.
[6] See Recital 5 MAR.
[7] See para. 12.

on Market Abuse' (MAR regime). This is not a separate Securities Trading Act codifying the rules of market abuse law, but a compilation of Level 1, 2 and 3 acts and instruments.[8]

The European Commission has so far adopted 13 legal acts (Implementing Directives, Implementing Regulations and Delegated Regulations) on market abuse.[9] The following four measures should be listed here because they specify the prohibitions of insider dealing and market manipulation and the disclosure requirements for issuers and managers: **Delegated Regulation (EU) 2016/522** of 17 December 2015;[10] **Delegated Regulation (EU) 2016/958** of 9 March 2016;[11] **Delegated Regulation (EU) 2016/960** of 17 May 2016;[12] **Implementing Regulation (EU) 2016/1055** of 29 June 2016.[13]

So far, **ESMA** has issued **two guidelines** on the MAR[14] and a document on **'Q&As'** on market abuse law, which it regularly updates. The purpose of the Q&A document is to establish common, uniform and consistent supervisory practices with regard to the application of the MAR and its implementing acts.

Of even greater practical importance are **guidelines** and **circulars** by national supervisory authorities (**NCAs**) on their administrative practices. In Germany, the Issuer Guidelines of BaFin provides information on the administrative practice regarding market abuse law in Module C (5th ed. 2020). The Guidelines are designed as a hands-on guide to dealing with the requirements of securities trading legislation, albeit without constituting a legal commentary.[15] BaFin also publishes FAQs on its website. In France, the AMF has provided a guide explaining its administrative practices on the concept of inside information and obligations for issuers under MAR.[16] In Italy, Consob, the Italian supervisory authority, has also published guidelines on its administrative practices.[17]

The Single Rulebook aims at preventing harmful regulatory and supervisory arbitrage in Europe and creating legal certainty. Competition between Member States for the 'best market abuse law' is no longer possible due to the fully harmonising nature of the prohibitions and disclosure requirements. The 'price' is a highly **complex regulatory issue.** It was illusory from the outset to achieve the objective laid down in recital 4 of the MAR of creating 'less complex rules', because a uniform legal situation for all EU Member States can only

---

[8] Cf. R. Veil, ZGR (2014), 544, 601 ff.
[9] Cf. R. Veil, in: Meyer and Veil et al. (eds.), *Handbuch zum Marktmissbrauchsrecht*, § 2 para. 14.
[10] Delegated Regulation with regard to an exemption for certain public authorities and central banks of third countries, the indicators of market manipulation, the thresholds for disclosure, the competent authority to which a deferral has to be notified, the permission to trade during a closed period and the types of proprietary transactions to be reported by managers, OJ EU No. L88 v. 5.4.2016, p. 1 ff.
[11] Delegated Regulation as regards regulatory technical standards on the technical modalities for the objective presentation of investment recommendations or other information recommending or suggesting investment strategy and for the disclosure of certain interests or indications of conflict of interest, OJ EU No. L160 v. 17.6.2016, p. 15 ff.
[12] Delegated Regulation on appropriate rules, systems and procedures for market participants disclosing information for the purpose of carrying out market testing, OJ EU No. L160 v. 17.6.2016, p. 29 ff.
[13] Implementing Regulation laying down implementing technical standards as regards technical means for making adequate public disclosure of inside information and for the postponement of the public disclosure of inside information pursuant to Regulation (EU) No. 596/2014 of the European Parliament and of the Council, OJ EU No. L173 v. 30.6.2016, p. 47 ff.
[14] ESMA, MAR Guidelines Deferral of Inside Information Disclosure, 20.10.2016, ESMA/2016/1478; MAR Guidelines Information on commodity derivatives markets or related spot markets with regard to the definition of inside information on commodity derivatives, 17.1.2017, ESMA/2016/1480.
[15] BaFin, Issuer Guidelines, Introduction. See on the legal nature R. Veil § 5 para. 54.
[16] AMF, Guide de l'information permanente et de la gestion de l'information privilégiée, 26 October 2016.
[17] Consob, Gestione delle informazioni privilegiate, October 2017.

be achieved by making the obligations and prohibitions more concrete and by developing standards for the relevant questions of interpretation.

2. CRIM-MAD

10   The European legislator also enacted a Directive on criminal sanctions for insider dealing and market manipulation (CRIM-MAD).[18] Until this time, none of the Level 1 directives had required Member States to adopt criminal provisions. The CRIM-MAD thus marks the start of a new era in Union law.

11   The criminal sanctions are intended to demonstrate 'social disapproval of a qualitatively different nature compared to administrative sanctions or compensation mechanisms under civil law'.[19] The introduction of criminal sanctions for the most serious contraventions remains within the jurisdiction of Member States. However, the CRIM-MAD uses the most important definitions from the provisions of the MAR. In this way, EU law is 'incorporated' into national criminal laws.

III. Level of Harmonisation

1. Minimum versus Maximum Harmonisation

12   The **CRIM-MAD** establishes only 'minimum rules' for criminal sanctions.[20] It is expressly established as a minimum harmonisation legal instrument, so that Member States are allowed to impose or retain more stringent criminal sanctions.

13   It is more difficult to assess which strategy is followed by the **MAR**, which does not expressly address the issue of minimum or full harmonisation. Only the fifth chapter about administrative measures and sanctions explicitly allows for other sanctions or higher fines to be introduced by Member States.[21] The first argument in support of a fully harmonising approach is that the prohibitions are governed by a Regulation. In addition, the European Commission brought forward the effectiveness of the MAD 2003 was undermined by 'numerous options and discretions'.[22] The recitals therefore explain that a uniform legal framework be established.[23] Finally, the aim of the MAR to avoid potential regulatory arbitrage[24] is best achieved through maximum harmonisation.

---

[18] The CRIM-MAD is based on Art. 83(2) TFEU, which is seen critically in literature. Cf. P. Hauck, 6 ZIS (2015), 336, 346 ('disputable endeavor').

[19] See Commission, Proposal for a Directive of the European Parliament and of the Council on criminal sanctions for insider dealing and market manipulation, Explanatory Memorandum, 20 October 2011, COM(2011) 654 final, p. 3.

[20] Cf. Art. 1(1) CRIM-MAD.
[21] Cf. Art. 30(1) MAR.
[22] Cf. COM(2011) 654 final (fn. 19), p. 3.
[23] Cf. Recital 4 ('uniform framework'), Recital 5 ('more uniform interpretation' and 'uniform conditions') MAR.
[24] Cf. Recital 4 MAR.

2. Evaluation

The fully harmonising approach is convincing. In the past, many Member States 'gold plated' the provisions of the MAD 2003. Some had also retained some of their 'old' law. For example, insider dealing in the United Kingdom was covered by five different legislative provisions.[25] The disparate legal landscape lead to legal uncertainty and resulted in unnecessary costs for legal advice. In this respect, the MAR is an improvement. The limits of harmonisation are exposed in the area of criminal law: pursuant to Article 83(2) TFEU, minimum requirements for the determination of criminal offences and sanctions may only be implemented in the form of directives.

IV. Scope of Application

The MAR regime applies to all issuers whose financial instruments are traded on a regulated market (RM), MTF or OTF.[26] It does not differentiate between small, medium and large issuers. However, it provides for some (few) facilitations for issuers whose securities are traded on a SME growth market.[27] The concept of financial instrument and the listing of financial instruments are key elements determining the scope of the market abuse regime.

> The concept of a **financial instrument** is further defined in Art. 3(1) No. 1 MAR.[28] This provision refers to the concept of financial instruments under MiFID II. Thus, the MAR applies to shares, bonds, derivatives, etc.

> The listing requirement is laid down in Art. 2 MAR. The MAR applies firstly to financial instruments **admitted to trading** on a **regulated market** (RM) or for which an application for admission to trading on a regulated market has been made.[29] The admission of securities is carried out by the stock exchange or the market operator. In addition, the MAR applies to financial instruments traded on a **multilateral trading facility** (MTF), admitted to trading on an MTF or for which an application to trade on an MTF has been made.[30] The background to this extension of Union law is that financial instruments are increasingly traded on MTFs.[31] The European legislator explains that the MAR is already applicable when an application for authorisation has been made by stating that certain types of MTFs, like regulated markets, are designed to help companies raise capital. The applicability of the MAR improves investor protection, preserves the integrity of the markets and ensures that market manipulation is prohibited.[32] Finally, the MAR applies to (iii) financial instruments traded in an **organised trading system** (OTF).[33] This extension of the MAR also stems from the fact that financial instruments were traded on other types of organised trading systems in the past.[34]

---

[25] See 2nd edition of this book, R. Veil § 14 para. 55.
[26] See R. Veil § 7 para. 11, 16, 19.
[27] See R. Veil § 7 para. 23.
[28] See on the term R. Veil § 8 para. 2.
[29] See Art. 2(1)(a) MAR.
[30] Cf. Art. 2(1)(b) MAR.
[31] Recital 8 sentence 2 MAR.
[32] Recital 8 sentences 5–7 MAR.
[33] Cf. Art. 2(1)(c) MAR.
[34] Recital 8 sentence 3 MAR.

18 According to Art. 2(3), the MAR applies to all transactions, orders and actions concerning one of the financial instruments mentioned in Art. 2(1) and (2) MAR, regardless of whether such a transaction, order or action was carried out on a trading venue. It follows that the **place of action is** irrelevant. The MAR covers not only transactions, orders and actions on a RM, MTF and OTF, but also, according to Art. 2(3) MAR, transactions, orders and actions that take place elsewhere (**face-to-face transaction**).[35] However, this only applies if the financial instrument is admitted to trade on a RM, MTF or OTF. The European legislator has seen a need to ensure market integrity in order to prevent negative effects on investor confidence on the trading venues.

19 The prohibitions and requirements of the MAR shall apply to acts and omissions within the Union and in third countries in respect of the instruments referred to in Art. 2(1) and (2) MAR.[36] The **territorial scope** is therefore not limited to the Member States of the EU, but extends worldwide to acts and omissions relating to financial instruments traded on a RM, MTF or OTF[37] or to other financial instruments.[38] The European legislator has thus implemented the **principle of impact**. It depends on whether market manipulation or insider trading has had an impact on a market in the EU. The broad territorial scope ensures that the MAR cannot be circumvented. If the act is committed in a third country, the law of that country may also apply. This becomes particularly relevant in the case of multiple listings. Whether an equivalent prohibition of market abuse exists abroad is irrelevant for the application of Art. 2(4) MAR.[39]

V. Presentation of Market Abuse Law in this Book

20 European market abuse law consists of the insider trading prohibitions and the rules on market manipulation. Both regimes are described in the following paragraphs of this chapter, including a description of the powers of the supervisory authorities and the sanctions in this regard. The disclosure obligations (obligation to make public inside information and directors' dealings) will be examined more closely in Chapter 4, as their aim is not only to prevent market abuse but also to balance out information asymmetries. This justifies presenting these obligations in the context of the other rules on disclosure. As a consequence, the closed periods for directors will also be described in the paragraph on Directors' Dealings. Finally, the MAR contains directly applicable provisions on investment recommendations. These are described in the Chapter on financial intermediaries. This way, the additional organisational requirements for financial analysts can also be taken into account.

---

[35] K. Hopt and C. Kumpan, in: Schimansky and Bunte et al. (eds.), *Bankrechts-Handbuch*, § 107 para. 31.
[36] Cf. Art. 4 MAR.
[37] Cf. Art. 2(1) lit. a)–c) MAR.
[38] Cf. Art. 2(1)(d), second subparagraph and (2) MAR.
[39] K. Hopt and C. Kumpan, in: Schimansky and Bunte et al. (eds.), *Bankrechts-Handbuch*, § 107 para. 32.

§ 14

Insider Dealing

Bibliography

Anderson, John P., *Insider Trading. Law, Ethics, and Reform* (2018); Arden, Lady Justice, *Spector Photo Group and its Wider Implications*, 2 ECFR (2010), 342–346; Austin, Janet, *Insider Trading and Market Manipulation. Investigating and Prosecuting Across Borders* (2017); Bachmann, Gregor, *Ad-hoc Publizität nach 'Geltl'*, DB (2012), 2206–2211; Bachmann, Gregor, *Das Europäische Insiderhandelsverbot* (2015); Bainbridge, Stephen M., *Regulation insider trading in the post-fiduciary duty era: equal access or property rights?*, in: Bainbridge, Stephen M. (ed.), *Research Handbook on Insider Trading* (2013), 80–98; Bingel, Adrian, *Die „Insiderinformation" in zeitlich gestreckten Sachverhalten und die Folgen der jüngsten EuGH-Rechtsprechung für M&A-Transaktionen*, AG (2012), 685–700; Bonneau, Thierry, *L'information n'est-elle precise que s'il est possible de déterminer le sens, à la hausse ou à la baisse, de la -variation sur le cours du titre?*, Bull. Joly Bourse (2014), 15–18; Bühren, Lars, *Auswirkungen des Insiderhandelsverbots der EU-Marktmissbrauchsverordnung auf M&A-Transaktionen*, NZG (2017), 1172–1178; Di Noia, Carmine and Gargantini, Matteo, *Issuers at Midstream: Disclosure of Multistage Events in the Current and in the Proposed EU Market Abuse Regime*, 4 ECFR (2012), 484–529; Di Noia, Carmine/Milic, Mateja/Spatola, Paola, *Issuer obligations under the new Market Abuse Regulation and the proposed ESMA guideline regime: a brief overview*, 2 ZBB (2014), 96–108; Diekmann, Hans and Sustmann, Marco, *Gesetz zur Verbesserung des Anlegerschutzes (Anlegerschutzverbesserungsgesetz – AnSVG)*, NZG (2004), 929–939; Easterbrook, Frank H. and Fischel, Daniel, *The Economic Structure of Corporate Law* (1996); Fleischer, Holger, *Ad-hoc-Publizität beim einvernehmlichen vorzeitigen Ausscheiden des Vorstandsvorsitzenden—Der DaimlerChrysler-Musterentscheid des OLG Stuttgart*, 11 NZG (2007), 401–407; Gilotta, Sergio, *Disclosure in Securities Markets and the Firm's Need for Confidentiality: Theoretical Framework and Regulatory Analysis*, 13 EBOR (2012), 45–88; Hansen, Jesper L., *Market Abuse Case Law – Where Do We Stand With MAR?*, 14(2) ECFR (2017), 367–390; Hienzsch, André, *Das deutsche Insiderhandelsverbot in der Rechtswirklichkeit* (2006); Hilgard, Marc C. and Mock, Sebastian, *Stoneridge and its Impact on European Capital Market and Consumer Law*, 4 ECFR (2008), 453–466; Hopt, Klaus J. and Will, Michael R., *Europäisches Insiderrecht. Einführende Untersuchung, ausgewählte Materialien* (1973); Hopt, Klaus J. and Wymeersch, Eddy, *European Insider Dealing* (1991); Kiesewetter, Matthias and Parmentier, Miriam, *Verschärfung des Marktmissbrauchsrechts – ein Überblick über die neue EU-Verordnung über Insidergeschäfte und Marktmanipulation*, 40 BB (2013), 2371; Klöhn, Lars, *Der 'gestreckte Geschehensablauf' vor dem EUGH*, 5 NZG (2011), 166–171; Klöhn, Lars, *The European Insider Trading Regulation after Spector Photo Group*, 2 ECFR (2010), 347–366; Klöhn, Lars, *Das deutsche und europäische Insiderrecht nach dem Geltl-Urteil des EuGH*, 39 ZIP (2012), 1885–1895; Klöhn, Lars, *Die Haftung wegen fehlerhafter Ad-hoc-Publizität gem. §§ 37b, 37c WpHG nach dem IKB-Urteil des BGH*, 10 AG (2012), 345–358; Klöhn, Lars, *Wertpapierhandelsrecht diesseits und jenseits des Informationsparadigmas*, 177 ZHR (2013), 349–387; Klöhn, Lars, *Inside Information Without an Incentive to Trade? What's at stake in 'Lafonta v AMF'*, 10 CMLJ (2015), 162–180; Klöhn, Lars, *Ad-hoc-Publizität und Insiderverbot im neuen Marktmissbrauchsrecht*, 12 AG (2016), 423–434; Koch, Philipp, *Naming and shaming im Kapitalmarktrecht* (2019); Krause, Hartmut and Brellochs, Michael, *Insiderrecht und Ad-hoc-Publizität bei M&A- und Kapitalmarkttransaktionen im europäischen Rechtsvergleich*, AG (2013), 309–339; Krause, Hartmut and Brellochs, Michael, *Insider Trading and the Disclosure of Inside Information after Geltl v Daimler–A comparative analysis of the ECJ decision in the Geltl v Daimler case with a view to the future European Market Abuse Regulation*, 8 CMLJ (2013), 283–299; Kubesch, Nicholas, *Marktsondierung nach dem neuen Marktmissbrauchsrecht* (2018); Kumpan, Christoph and Misterek, Robin, *Der verständige Anleger in der Marktmissbrauchsverordnung*, 184(2) ZHR (2020), 180–221; Lahmann, Kai, *Insiderhandel. Ökonomische Analyse eines ordnungspolitischen Dilemmas* (1994); Langenbucher, Katja, *Zum Begriff der Insiderinformation nach dem Entwurf für eine Marktmissbrauchsverordnung*, NZG (2013), 1401–1406; Lasserre Capdeville, Jérôme, *Le délit de communication d'une information privilégiée: vingt ans après*, Bull. Joly Bourse (2009), 69–76; Loke, Alexander F., *From Fiduciary Theory to Information Abuse: The Changing Fabric of Insider Trading Law in the UK, Australia and Singapore*, 54(1) American Journal of Comparative Law (2006), 123–172; Madrazo, Regina, *Información no pública en las sociedades cotizadas españolas. Tipología y tratamiento en los reglamentos internos de conducta*, RMV No. 2 (2008), 471–481; Manne, Henry G., *Insider Trading and the Stock Market* (1966); Mayhew, David and Anderson, Karen, *Whither Market Abuse (in a More Principles-based Regulatory World)*, 22 JIBLR (2007), 515–531; Mehringer, Christoph, *Das allgemeine kapitalmarktrechtliche Gleichbehandlungsprinzip* (2007); Mennicke, Petra R., *Sanktionen gegen Insiderhandel—Eine rechtsvergleichende Untersuchung unter Berücksichtigung des US-amerikanischen und britischen Rechts* (1996); Moalem, David and Hansen, Jesper L., *Insider Dealing and Parity of Information—Is 'Georgakis' Still Valid?*, 19(5) EBLR (2008), 949–984; Mülbert, Peter O. and Sajnovits, Alexander, *The Inside Information Regime of the MAR and the Rise of the ESG Era*, ECFR (2021), 256–290; Perrone, Andrea, *EU Market Abuse Regulation: The Puzzle of Enforcement*, 21 EBOR (2020), 379–392; Pfeifle, Theresa, *Finanzielle Anreize für Whistleblower im Kapitalmarktrecht* (2016); Rider, Barry et al., *Market Abuse and Insider Dealing*, 3rd edn. (2016); Schall, Alexander, *Anmerkung*, ZIP (2012), 1286–1288; Sieder, Sebastian, *Legitime Handlungen nach der Marktmissbrauchsverordnung (MAR)*, ZFR (2017), 171–180; Snyder, Michael A., *United States v. O'Hagan, the Supreme Court and the Misappropriation Theory of Securities Fraud and Insider Trading: Clarification or Confusion?*, 27 Capital Univ. L. Rev. (1999), 419, 421; Seibt, Christoph H. and Wollenschläger, Bernward, *Revision des Marktmissbrauchsrechts durch Marktmissbrauchsverordnung und Richtlinie über strafrechtliche Sanktionen für Marktmanipulation*, AG (2014), 593–608; Singhof, Bernd, *Zur Weitergabe von Insiderinformationen im Unterordnungskonzern*, ZGR (2001), 146–174; Staikouras, Panagiotis K., *Four Years of MADness?—The New Market Abuse Prohibition Revisited: Integrated Implementation Through the Lens of a Critical, Comparative Analysis*, 9 EBLR (2008), 775–809; Steinberg, Marc I., *Insider Trading, Selective Disclosure and Prompt Disclosure: A Comparative Analysis*, 22(3) U. Pa. J. Int'l. Econ. Law (2001), 635–676; Sustmann, Marco, *Information und Vertraulichkeit im Vorfeld von Unternehmensübernahmen unter besonderer Berücksichtigung der EuGH-Entscheidung in Sachen Geltl./Daimler AG*, in: Kämmer, Jörn A. and Veil, Rüdiger (eds.), *Übernahme- und Kapitalmarktrecht in der Reformdiskussion* (2013), 230–259; Swan, Edward J. and Virgo, John, *Market Abuse Regulation*, 3rd edn. (2019); Tountopoulos, Vassilios D., *Market Abuse and Private Enforcement*, 11(3) ECFR (2014), 297–332; Veil, Rüdiger, *Weitergabe von Informationen durch den Aufsichtsrat an Aktionäre und Dritte. Ein Lehrstück zum Verhältnis zwischen Gesellschafts- und Kapitalmarktrecht*, 172(3) ZHR (2008), 239–273; Veil, Rüdiger, *Concepts of Supervisory Legislation and Enforcement in European Capital Markets Law—Observations from a Civil Law Country*, 11(3) EBOR (2010), 409–422; Veil, Rüdiger, *Europäisches Insiderrecht 2.0—Konzeption und Grundsatzfragen der Reform durch MAR und CRIM-MAD*, 2 ZBB (2014), 85–96; Ventoruzzo, Marco, *Comparing Insider Trading in the Unites States and in the European Union: History and Recent Developments*, 11(4) ECFR (2014), 554–593; Ventoruzzo, Marco, *When Market Abuse Rules Violate Human Rights: Grande Stevens v. Italy and the Different Approaches to Double Jeopardy in Europe and the US*, 16 EBOR (2015), 145–165; Vetter, Jochen et al., *Zwischenschritte als ad-hoc-veröffentlichungspflichtige Insiderinformation*, 5 AG (2019), 160–169; Villeda, Gisella V., *Prävention und Repression von Insiderhandel* (2010);

Voigt, Christian, *Konzernumsatzbezogene Verbandsgeldbußen im Marktmissbrauchsrecht* (2022); Wang, William K.S. and Steinberg, Marc I., *Insider Trading* 3rd edn. (2010); Ziehl, Katrin, *Kapitalmarktprognosen und Insider-Trading* (2006).

I. Introduction

In the **United States**, legislation on capital markets law, including aspects of market abuse, was already on the agenda in 1934, when the federal legislature enacted the Securities Exchange Act and the Securities and Exchange Commission laid down the SEC Rules. Both the US Supreme Court and lower courts extended the provisions—especially Rule 10b-5—thus developing a powerful regime, based on the notion that all insider dealings are disadvantageous for the market in the longer term.[1] In the 1960s and 1970s, however, debates flared up in the United States[2] and Europe[3] as to whether insider dealings might after all have a positive effect and ought therefore to be legalised. It was argued that an investor who concludes a securities transaction with an insider will generally not suffer any damage as the investor would in any case have carried out the transaction. It was furthermore claimed that insider dealings allow inside information to access the capital markets, thus ensuring an appropriate pricing of securities and market efficiency. Additionally, legalising insider dealings was assumed to solve conflicts arising between principals and agents. This theory was based on the understanding that the possibility of abusing inside information has to be seen as a form of manager remuneration.[4] Due to the fact that inside information is only produced when risks are taken, legalising insider dealings would encourage the managers' willingness to take such risks.

Yet these arguments purported by the critics of a regulation restricting insider dealings are not convincing. Whilst it is true that an investor concluding a security transaction will mostly not suffer any damage as he would also have concluded the same transaction with another person, market makers will react to a possible risk of losses with larger margins of sales and purchases. Thus, insiders cause higher transaction costs that must be carried by all market participants. Furthermore, an investor may well suffer a loss if he is induced to enter into a transaction as a result of insider trading (*induced selling*).[5] The second argument must also be rejected: it has been proven that an issuer's obligation to disclose information immediately[6] is more likely to ensure market efficiency than dealings on the basis of inside information.[7] The opinion that the legalisation of insider dealing would serve as an incentive for the management to take risks and thus be advantageous for the company

---

[1] Cf. S. Bainbridge, in: Bainbridge, *Research Handbook on Insider Trading*, 80 ff.; W. Wang and M. Steinberg, *Insider Trading*.
[2] Cf. H. Manne, *Insider Trading and the Stock Market*, 131 ff.
[3] Cf. K. Hopt and E. Wymeersch, *European Insider Dealing*.
[4] Cf. F. Easterbrook and D. Fischel, *The Economic Structure of Corporate Law*, 257 ff.
[5] Example: The share price is € 10. Due to insider trading, it rises to € 15. An investor sells his securities at this price. After the information becomes known, the price goes up to € 20.
[6] Cf. Art. 17 MAR. For more details on this obligation see R. Veil § 19 para. 24–71.
[7] Cf. K. Lahmann, *Insiderhandel*, 169.

and its shareholders can also not prevail. By using put options the management could easily gain financial advantages from negative information, thus not necessarily maximising company value. A further problem of legalised insider dealings is the fact that third parties would also be able to profit from inside information, resulting in the so-called 'free rider problem'.

3   Despite all these arguments various countries in the EU were sceptical towards regulations on insider dealings, some not introducing the first provisions until well into the 1980s. In Germany, the prevailing opinion was that voluntary rules were sufficient. The Federal Minister for Economics engaged an expert committee which published 'Recommendations on the Solution of the Insider Problem' in 1970. The report included guidelines on insider dealings, prohibiting members of the management board and supervisory board, major shareholders and employees of a stock corporation from dealing in shares and bonds of the corporation by using inside information.[8] This self-regulatory approach, however, did not prove successful.

4   The legal situation in Europe changed with the enactment of Directive 89/592/EEC of 13 November 1989 coordinating regulations on insider dealings.[9] The European legislature justified the introduction of a European directive with the fact that investor confidence was based mainly on the assurance that all investors are placed on an equal footing and are protected against the improper use of inside information. The smooth operation of markets depends to a large extent on the confidence it inspires in investors. By benefiting certain investors as opposed to others, insider dealing is likely to undermine that confidence and may therefore prejudice the smooth operation of the market.[10] In the mid-1990s insider dealings were thus prohibited in Europe.[11]

5   Only eleven years later the changes on the financial markets and in European Community law caused the European legislature to carry out fundamental reforms of the regime in order to be able to prevent insider dealings and market manipulations more effectively.[12] To this end the **Market Abuse Directive** (MAD)[13] was enacted, replacing the Insider Directive. The MAD's objective was to ensure the integrity of the Community's financial markets and to enhance investor confidence in those markets.[14] The directive conceived the prohibition of insider dealings as a prerequisite for achieving 'full and proper market transparency'.[15] The prohibition was thus justified by the necessity of organising markets and ensuring their proper functioning.[16] The underlying principle was that of informational equality of all investors,[17] whilst the aspect of managers breaching their duty of loyalty by taking

---

[8] For the last version of the recommendations see WM (1998), 1105. An analysis of the sanction for breaches of these obligations is made by G. Villeda, *Prävention und Repression im Insiderhandel*, 46 ff.
[9] See R. Veil § 1 para. 11.
[10] Recitals of Directive 89/592/EEC.
[11] Pursuant to Art. 14(1), the Insider Directive was to be transposed by 1 June 1992.
[12] A reason for the directive was also the aim of combating the financing of terrorist activities; cf. recital 14 MAD.
[13] See R. Veil § 1 para. 22.
[14] Cf. recital 12 MAD.
[15] Cf. recital 15 MAD.
[16] On this regulatory aim see R. Veil § 2 para. 7.
[17] Cf. L. Klöhn, ECFR (2010), 347, 354 ff.; N. Moloney, *EU Securities and Financial Markets Regulation*, 702; on the legitimacy of equal access in US capital market law cf. S. Bainbridge, in: Bainbridge, *Research Handbook on Insider Trading*, 80, 81 ff.

advantage of inside information, which plays an important role in the US discussion,[18] was not referred to by European capital markets law.

The next reform was initiated by the European Commission on 20 October 2011 when it made public two proposals regarding the market abuse regime.[19] The worldwide economic and financial crises made clear the importance of market integrity, and the CESR's study[20] and the *de Larosière* Report[21] underlined the fact that the legal situation in the Member States regarding criminal and administrative sanctions was disparate and hardly provided incentives to act lawfully.[22] The European Commission therefore regarded it as necessary to extend the rules on market abuse to other markets, to ensure that there are uniform rules in the EU in order to prevent supervisory arbitrage and to develop stricter rules on supervision and sanctions. 6

These proposals were implemented by the **Market Abuse Regulation** (MAR)[23] and the **Directive on Criminal Sanctions for Market Abuse** (CRIM-MAD).[24,25] Pursuant to Article 2(1)(b) and (c) MAR and Article 1(2)(a)–(c) CRIM-MAD, the rules on insider dealing also apply to financial instruments traded on multilateral trading facilities (MTFs) or organised trading facilities (OTFs).[26] Over-the-counter (OTC) trading has also been included in the scope of the new regime.[27] 7

The MAR further contains a number of provisions that have the aim to strengthen the powers of the national supervisory authorities (NCAs).[28] The unification and intensification of the sanctions are to increase the dissuasiveness of insider trading prohibitions in the future.[29] The MAR focuses on administrative measures and sanctions. In Chapter 5 it contains requirements for the Member States, obliging them to implement provisions on the imposition of administrative pecuniary sanctions into their national laws. The MAR's respective provisions are thus not to apply directly. According to the CRIM-MAD, the Member States are further to prohibit certain forms of behaviour by criminal law. Rules 8

---

[18] Cf. *Chiarella/US*, 445 US 222 (1980); F. Easterbrook and D. Fischel, *The Economic Structure of Corporate Law*, 269 ff.; H. Merkt, *US-amerikanisches Gesellschaftsrecht*, para. 1044; cf. on the misappropriation theory M. Snyder, 27 Capital Univ. L. Rev. (1999), 419–447.

[19] Commission, Proposal for a Regulation of the European Parliament and of the Council on Insider Dealing and Market Manipulation (Market Abuse), 20 October 2011, COM(2011) 651 final; Commission, Proposal for a Directive of the European Parliament and of the Council on Criminal Sanctions for Insider Dealing and Market Manipulation, 20 October 2011, COM(2011) 654 final.

[20] Cf. CESR, Report on administrative measures and sanctions as well as the criminal sanctions available in Member States under the market abuse directive (MAD), February 2008, CESR/08-099.

[21] Cf. The High-Level Group on Financial Supervision in the EU (de Larosière Group), Report, 25 February 2009 (de Larosière Report).

[22] Cf. recital 3 MAR and recital 3 and 4 CRIM-MAD.

[23] Regulation (EU) No 596/2014 of the European Parliament and of the Council of 16 April 2014 on market abuse (market abuse regulation) and repealing Directive 2003/6/EC of the European Parliament and of the Council and Commission Directives 2003/124/EC, 2003/125/EC and 2004/72/EC.

[24] Directive 2014/57/EU of the European Parliament and of the Council of 16 April 2014 on criminal sanctions for market abuse (market abuse directive)), OJ L 173 of 12 June 2014, p. 179 ff. (CRIM-MAD).

[25] See R. Veil § 13 para. 3 ff. for a detailed presentation of the sources of law and the conditions for the applicability of the provisions.

[26] See R. Veil § 7 para. 11 ff.

[27] Cf. Art. 2(3) MAR and Art. 1(5) CRIM-MAD.

[28] See in more detail below para. 96.

[29] Cf. recital 70 MAR: 'equal, strong and deterrent sanctions regimes'.

on criminal sanctions are assumed to demonstrate 'social disapproval of a qualitatively different nature compared to administrative sanctions or compensation mechanisms under civil law'.[30]

II. Regulatory Concepts

1. Overview of the Market Abuse Regime

9   The MAR and its corresponding Level 2 acts (the so-called single rulebook on market abuse)[31] contain **prohibitions** on **insider dealings** (Article 14 MAR). In addition, **issuers** are obliged to **disclose inside information** (Article 17 MAR). This duty also has the purpose of preventing insider trading: 'The public disclosure of inside information by an issuer is essential to avoid insider dealing and ensure that investors are not mislead.'[32] However, there are exceptions to the disclosure requirement because the publication of uncertain events can be detrimental to the issuer. These exceptions play a great role in practice.[33] The disclosure obligation can therefore only fulfil the purpose of combating insider trading to a limited extent.

10 The MAR provides **three types of prohibitions**. A person shall not (i) engage or attempt to engage in insider dealing, (ii) recommend that another person engage in insider dealing or induce another person to engage in insider dealing and (iii) unlawfully disclose inside information.[34] These rather abstract prohibitions are put into more concrete terms[35] thus providing legal certainty as to which kind of behaviour might be punished with severe sanctions. They apply to any person who possesses inside information, ie not only primary insiders,[36] but also to any person who knows or ought to know that they possess inside information.[37]

11 The prohibitions and the ad hoc disclosure obligation operate with the same concept of inside information.[38] Thus the notion of inside information is the core element of the insider trading regime. The MAR defines the term 'inside information' as 'information of a precise nature, which has not been made public, relating, directly or indirectly, to one or more issuers or to one or more financial instruments and which, if it were made public, would be likely to have a significant effect on the prices of those financial instruments or on the price of related derivative financial instruments'.[39] This concept which is further specified in Article 7(2)–(4) MAR is also relevant for criminal sanctions under the CRIM-MAD.[40]

---

[30] Cf. Commission, Explanatory Memorandum, 20 October 2011, COM(2011) 654 final, p. 3–4.
[31] See R. Veil § 13 para. 5.
[32] Recital 49 MAR.
[33] See R. Veil § 19 para. 51.
[34] Cf. Art. 14 MAR.
[35] Cf. Art. 8 and 10 MAR and Art. 3 and 4 CRIM-MAD.
[36] Cf. Art. 8(4) subsec. 1 MAR.
[37] Cf. Art. 8(4) subsec. 2 MAR.
[38] See on the different regulatory aims of the disclosure obligation R. Veil § 19 para. 1–9.
[39] Art. 7(1) MAR.
[40] Cf. Art. 2(4) CRIM-MAD.

2. Accompanying Rules

The prohibition of insider dealings is accompanied by numerous other rules in the MAR, the Transparency Directive (TD) and the Markets in Financial Instruments Directive (MiFID II), such as the issuer's obligation to make public inside information without delay.[41] The European legislature's aim was to ensure that all investors gain access to price-sensitive information as soon as possible and to counteract the dangers of insider dealings.

12

Other disclosure obligations, such as the obligation to notify and make public directors' dealings[42] and the TD's provisions on the notification and publication of changes in major shareholdings[43] are also aimed at preventing the misuse of inside information. The MiFID's rules of conduct for investment firms also pursue the goal of preventing prohibited insider dealings, especially by demanding the introduction of compliance structures,[44] such as Chinese walls.

13

3. Insider Compliance

European insider trading law provides some scattered rules on organisational requirements for market operators and issuers. **Market operators** and **investment firms** operating a trading venue under MiFID II are required to establish and maintain effective arrangements, systems and procedures for the prevention and detection of insider dealing.[45] The organisational requirements are supplemented by an obligation to **report suspicions** (regarding potential violations of the prohibition of insider trading).[46] Market operators and investment firms are required to train their staff on the regulatory requirements of MAR.[47] Finally, the compliance requirements of MiFID II (compliance function with compliance officer; Chinese walls; watch list and restricted list; etc.) aim to ensure that investment firms comply with the rules of MAR when providing investment services.[48]

14

With regard to issuers, the obligation to keep insider lists should be mentioned above all.[49] If an issuer decides to postpone the publication of inside information, it shall ensure the confidentiality of such information.[50] There are no further specific rules for issuers on insider compliance in European market abuse law. However, the board of directors of the issuer has duties (towards the company) regarding the management of inside information. Finally, effective compliance may become relevant if a supervisory authority imposes a fine on an issuer for violating Art. 17 MAR (fine-reducing effect).[51]

15

---

[41] Cf. Art. 17(4) MAR.
[42] Cf. Art. 19(1) MAR; see in more detail R. Veil § 21 para. 2.
[43] Cf. Art. 9 TD; see R. Veil § 20 para. 20.
[44] See M. Wundenberg § 33 para. 20 ff.
[45] Cf. Art. 16(1) MAR.
[46] Art. 16(2) MAR.
[47] Cf. Art. 4(1) Commission Delegated Regulation (EU) No. 2016/957 of 9 March 2016 supplementing Regulation (EU) No. 596/2014 of the European Parliament and of the Council with regard to regulatory technical standards for the appropriate arrangements, systems and procedures as well as notification templates to be used for preventing, detecting and reporting abusive practices or suspicious orders or transactions, OJ L 160, 17 June 2016.
[48] See M. Wundenberg § 33.
[49] Cf. Art. 18(1) MAR.
[50] Cf. Art. 17(4)(c) MAR.
[51] Cf. C. Voigt, *Konzernumsatzbezogene Verbandsgeldbußen im Marktmissbrauchsrecht*.

III. Regulatory Goals

16   European market abuse law is based on the idea that market abuse violates the integrity of financial markets and undermines public confidence in securities and derivatives.[52] This applies in particular to insider trading. European insider trading law aims to ensure **equal informational opportunities for investors** in order to strengthen their **confidence** in the proper functioning of **capital markets**.[53]

17   Recital 23 MAR explains this regulatory approach and purpose as follows: 'The essential characteristic of insider dealing consists in an **unfair advantage** being obtained from inside information to the **detriment of third parties** who are unaware of such information and, consequently, the **undermining** of the **integrity** of financial markets and **investor confidence**. Consequently, the prohibition against insider dealing should apply where a person who is in possession of inside information takes unfair advantage of the benefit gained from that information by entering into market transactions in accordance with that information by acquiring or disposing of, by attempting to acquire or dispose of, by cancelling or amending, or by attempting to cancel or amend, an order to acquire or dispose of, for his own account or for the account of a third party, directly or indirectly, financial instruments to which that information relates.'

18   The characteristic of the prohibition of trading on the basis of inside information is that the insider has an information advantage (inside information) and he profits from this advantage to the detriment of a third party.[54] The rationale for a strict insider trading law is to be seen in the goal of ensuring the functions of securities markets.[55] Insider bans are necessary to protect investor and market confidence, though there are no empirical studies to support the assumption that investors leave the capital market or are deterred from investing due to a loss of confidence.[56] However, there is at least anecdotal evidence that professional as well as private investors consider it unfair if individual investors can exploit their information advantages.[57] Loss of confidence results in a decline in investment[58] and in the worst case investors leave capital markets. Investor confidence[59] ensured by insider trading prohibitions is therefore a prerequisite for liquid and well-functioning capital markets.[60]

---

[52] Recital 1 MAR.
[53] J. Hansen, in: Ventoruzzo/Mock (eds.), *Market Abuse Regulation*, Art. 8 para. B.8.42: 'the essence of insider dealing as that of being in an advantageous position by possessing information that is not available to the counterparty of the relevant transaction, that is, the parties are not on an equal footing.'; ibid B.8.67 'informational advantage and that advantage is defined by the concept of inside information.'
[54] ECJ of 23 December 2009 – Case C-45/08 (Spector), ECR I-12073 para. 48, NZG (2010), 107; J. Hansen, ECFR (2017), 367, 378.
[55] Cf. K. Hopt and M. Will, *Europäisches Insiderrecht*, 49 ff.; P. Mennicke, *Sanktionen gegen Insiderhandel*, 98 ff.
[56] Cf. P. Mennicke, *Sanktionen gegen Insiderhandel*, 102.
[57] The First Quotation Board of the Frankfurt Stock Exchange was closed in 2012 due to numerous cases of fraud and manipulation. In Japan and Frankfurt, insider trading led to a massive drop in turnover on the stock exchanges in 1991. Cf. P. Mennicke, *Sanktionen gegen Insiderhandel*, 103.
[58] Cf. A. Hienzsch, *Das deutsche Insiderhandelsverbot in der Rechtswirklichkeit*, 41, 184; P. Mennicke, *Sanktionen gegen Insiderhandel*, 99 ff.
[59] See R. Veil § 2 para. 11 f.
[60] Cf. G. Bachmann, *Das europäische Insiderhandelsverbot*, 20 f.; L. Klöhn, 177 ZHR (2013), 349, 372 f.

IV. Concept of Inside Information

1. Definition and Interpretation of Inside Information under the MAD 2003 Regime

The concept of inside information is the key element of various rules in capital markets law. It constitutes a **requirement** for all three **prohibitions** of insider dealings described in the MAR and CRIM-MAD and for the **ad hoc disclosure obligation**, also provided for by the MAR. Issuers of financial instruments are required to inform the public as soon as possible of inside information which directly concerns said issuer.[61] The concept of inside information also plays an important role regarding the rules on market manipulation.[62]

The definition of the term inside information was one of the most strongly disputed issues during the reform of market abuse law. The European Commission originally wanted to define an inside information following the British definition for the prohibition of insider dealings (so-called RINGA concept).[63] It was, however, not able to assert itself with this proposal. The Council and the European Parliament agreed that the MAR should contain the same definition as the MAD 2003 had, the reason behind this being that the ECJ had based its decision in the case *Daimler/Geltl* on exactly this definition and interpreted the term in a convincing manner. The European legislator approved the ECJ's approach to this case and saw no need to introduce a different concept on inside information. An understanding of the ECJ's interpretative principles under the old MAD 2003 regime is therefore essential for an analysis of the term inside information provided for in Article 7 MAR.

> *Facts (abridged):*[64] In its meeting on 28 July 2005, the supervisory board of DaimlerChrysler AG decided at 9.50 a.m. that the CEO Schrempp should retire from the board as of 31 December 2005 and be replaced by board member Zetsche. A few minutes later DaimlerChrysler AG published an ad hoc notification with this information and its share price rose considerably. Schrempp had already discussed his retirement with the chairman of the supervisory board at length on 17 May 2005 and informed two other members of the supervisory board on 1 June 2005. DaimlerChrysler's communication manager and the executive secretary, who had been informed on 6 July 2005, had been working on the press release, an external statement and a letter to the employees since 10 July 2005. On 27 July 2005 the presiding committee of the supervisory board had decided to recommend a decision on the early retirement of Schrempp and his successor to the supervisory board the following day. Investors who had disposed of shares before the ad hoc information was published claimed a total of € 5,500,000 in damages from DaimlerChrysler AG for these events.

---

[61] Art. 17(1) MAR. See R. Veil § 19 para. 24.
[62] See R. Veil § 15 para. 18.
[63] Cf. Art. 6(1)(e) MAR-COM: 'information not falling within paragraphs (a), (b), (c) or (d) relating to one or more issuers of financial instruments or to one or more financial instruments, which is not generally available to the public, but which, if it were available to a reasonable investor, who regularly deals on the market and in the financial instrument or a related spot commodity contract concerned, would be regarded by that person as relevant when deciding the terms on which transactions in the financial instrument or a related spot commodity contract should be effected'. Cf. for a critical analysis H. Krause and M. Brellochs, 8 CMLJ (2013), 283, 295–299.
[64] Cf. OLG Stuttgart of 22.4.2009 – 20 Kap 1/08, ZIP (2009), 962 and BGH of 25.2.2008 – II ZB 9/07, ZIP (2008), 639.

22 In *Daimler/Geltl* the courts had to deal with the concept of inside information. The BGH first ruled that the intent or deliberation of a CEO to retire early from his position by mutual agreement with the supervisory board is price-sensitive information and could thus be subject to the provisions on inside information. Until the supervisory board has agreed to the retirement, the information will, however, only be classifiable as inside information if the board's consent is sufficiently probable. According to the BGH, such an overwhelming probability can be assumed if the chances of the supervisory board consenting are over 50%.[65] The Oberlandesgericht (OLG, higher regional court) Stuttgart, again presented with the case after the decision of the BGH,[66] ruled that the supervisory board's consent became sufficiently probable on 27 July 2005 when a committee of the supervisory board came to an unanimous agreement.[67] However, the plaintiffs appealed the decision and argued this interpretation did not comply with the regulatory aims of the MAD. The case was therefore submitted to the BGH a second time, the BGH now coming to a different conclusion and therefore presenting the question, whether in a multi-stage process an intermediate step can be classed as inside information, to the ECJ for a preliminary ruling.[68]

23 In **multi-stage processes**, such as capital increases or mergers, it is either possible to refer to the individual process—eg the process of fixing the stock's issue price in the case of a capital increase or fixing the share exchange ratio in merger cases—or to the process as a whole, ie the final result. The BGH reasoned that in a protracted set of facts, the individual steps that have taken place could also constitute 'precise information' in the sense of the MAD and Article 1(1) Directive 2003/124/EC.[69] A preliminary ruling was necessary as the two approaches (the intermediate step or the final event constitutes an inside information) do not necessarily come to the same results.[70]

24 The ECJ answered the question in the light of the aims of the MAD 2003:

> 'An interpretation of the terms 'set of circumstances' and 'event' which disregards the intermediate steps in a protracted process risks undermining the objectives [to protect the integrity of the European Union financial markets and to enhance investor confidence in those markets]. To rule out the possibility that information relating to such a step in a protracted process may be of a precise nature for the purposes of point 1 of Article 1 of Directive 2003/6 would remove the obligation, provided for in the first subparagraph of Article 6(1), to disclose that information, even if it were quite specific and even though the other elements making up inside information […] were also present. In such a situation, certain parties who possessed inside information could be in an advantageous position vis-à-vis other investors and be able to profit from that information, to the detriment of those who are unaware of it. The risk of such a situation occurring is all the greater given that it would be possible, in certain circumstances, to regard the outcome of a specific process as an intermediate step in another, larger process. Consequently, **information relating** to an **intermediate step** which is part of a protracted process may be **precise information**. It should be

---

[65] BGH ZIP of 25.2.2008 – II ZB 9/07, (2008), 639.
[66] The BGH reversed the OLG Stuttgart's decision and referred the case back to a different civil division of the court in Stuttgart.
[67] OLG Stuttgart of 22.4.2009 – 20 Kap 1/08, ZIP (2009), 962, 966 ff.
[68] BGH of 22.11.20210 – II ZB 7/09, ZIP (2011), 72.
[69] Ibid.
[70] Ibid, 72, 74.

noted that this interpretation does not hold true only for those steps which have already come into existence or have already occurred, but also concerns [...] steps which may reasonably be expected to come into existence or occur.'[71]

This interpretation is convincing. The wording of the resp. provisions permitted both interpretations. Particular note must therefore be taken of the regulatory aim. The prohibitions on insider dealings constituted the centrepiece of the MAD 2003 and it was the explicit aim of the European legislature to effectively prevent insider dealings.[72] The understanding of the concept of inside information must therefore also focus on this aim of ensuring that the prohibitions are as effective as possible.[73] This aim is most suitable attained if the individual steps are also regarded as possible inside information. It must then be determined from case to case whether an intermediate step—such as the decision to resign from the position of the chairman of the management, etc.—or the final event—such as the cancellation agreement as in the case *Daimler/Geltl*—is likely to have a significant effect on the prices of the financial instruments.[74]

The BGH further asked the ECJ to clarify how the requirement has to be interpreted that **'circumstances/events'** which **may reasonably** be **expected** to **come into existence'** may be considered as inside information. There are two possible approaches to interpretation. The first is to require a predominant probability, ie over 50%, the second a high probability.

The ECJ opted for a broad interpretation of the terms 'may reasonably be expected':

> 'Article 1(1) of Directive 2003/124, in using the terms 'may reasonably be expected', cannot be interpreted as requiring that proof be made out of a high probability of the circumstances or events in question coming into existence or occurring. To restrict the scope of [the provision] in respect of future circumstances and events to such a degree of probability would undermine the objectives [...] to protect the integrity of the European Union financial markets and to enhance investor confidence in those markets. In such a scenario, insiders would be able to derive undue benefit from certain information which, under such a restrictive interpretation, would be held not to be precise, to the detriment of others who are unaware of it. However, in order to ensure legal certainty for market participants, including issuers, [...] precise information is not to be considered as including information concerning circumstances and events the occurrence of which is implausible. Otherwise, issuers could believe that they are obliged to disclose information which is not specific or is unlikely to influence the prices of their financial instruments. It follows that, in using the terms 'may reasonably be expected', Article 1(1) of Directive 2003/124 refers to **future circumstances** or **events** from which it appears, on the basis of an overall assessment of the factors existing at the relevant time, that there is a **realistic prospect** that they will **come into existence or occur**.'[75]

A further possibility is to determine the degree of probability by the effects the event will have on the issuer: events that are particularly likely to have a significant effect on the security price need only be of slight probability,[76] whilst a higher probability is required for events less likely to have a significant effect. This second approach is also called **probability/magnitude-formula**.[77]

---

[71] ECJ of 28 June 2012, Case C-19/11 (*Daimler/Geltl*), para. 35–38.
[72] See para. 5.
[73] On the *effet utile* as a method of interpretation in European law see R. Veil § 5 para. 45.
[74] Cf. L. Klöhn, NZG (2011), 166, 170.
[75] ECJ of 28 June 2012, Case C-19/11 (*Daimler/Geltl*), para. 46–49.
[76] Cf. BGH of 22.11.20210 – II ZB 7/09, ZIP (2011), 72, second question referred for a preliminary ruling.
[77] Cf. L. Klöhn, NZG (2011), 166, 168.

29 The Advocate General argued for the second approach:

> 'It follows that, where the potential of that information for affecting share prices is significant, it is sufficient that the occurrence of the future set of circumstances or event, albeit uncertain, be not impossible or improbable. In making that assessment, the extent of the consequences for the issuer will be of relevance inasmuch as that will form part of the information available *ex ante*, given that a reasonable investor will base his decisions on the anticipated impact of the information in the light of the totality of the related issuer's activity, the reliability of the information source and every other market variable which might, in the circumstances, affect the financial instrument in question or the related derivative financial instrument.'[78]

30 The ECJ, however, did not follow the Advocate General in this regard: 'The question whether the required probability of occurrence of a set of circumstances or an event may vary depending on the magnitude of their effect on the prices of the financial instruments concerned must be answered in the negative.'[79] This interpretation appears favourable, the Advocate General's approach causing legal uncertainty for investors and issuers.

31 With its decision, the ECJ has provided clarity in some respects. The **'realistic prospect'** required by the ECJ for future circumstances is to be understood in the sense of an overwhelming probability (of more than 50%).[80] According to the ruling, both occurred and future intermediate steps of a protracted process can qualify as inside information. In the case *Daimler/Geltl* inside information could thus already have existed on 17 May 2005.[81] Whether this was actually the case depends on the possible effect of the information (the intermediate step) on the prices of the financial instruments.

2. Implementation in the MAR

32 The MAR provides for **four types** of **inside information** in Article 7(1). The first category under **lit. a)** covers information that relates to an issuer or a financial instrument. This term is essential for the securities markets and is therefore explained in more detail in this section. The category regulated in **lit. b)** concerns information relating to commodity derivatives and the category specified in **lit. c)** information relating to emission certificates. For example, in the case of derivatives on pigs, the fact of epidemics may qualify as inside information. The same applies to derivatives on potatoes with regard to changes in subsidy policy.[82] The European legislature further wanted to tackle the practice known as front running, ie stockbrokers executing orders on a security for their own account while taking advantage of advance knowledge of pending orders from its customers. Therefore, **lit. d)** MAR provides that 'for persons charged with the execution of orders concerning financial instruments', inside information should also mean 'information conveyed by a client and relating to the client's pending orders in financial instruments, which is of a precise nature, relating

---

[78] Cf. Opinion of Advocate General Mengozzi, delivered on 21 March 2012, Case C-19/11, para. 106–107.
[79] ECJ of 28 June 2012, Case C-19/11 (*Daimler/Geltl*), para. 50.
[80] Cf. G. Bachmann, DB (2012), 2206, 2209; L. Klöhn, ZIP (2012), 1885, 1889, 1892; H. Krause and M. Brellochs, AG (2013), 309, 313; M. Ventoruzzo and C. Picciau, in: Ventoruzzo/Mock (eds.), *Market Abuse Regulation*, Art. 7 para. B.7.38.
[81] Cf. BGH of 23.4.2013 – II ZB 7/09, ZIP (2013), 1165, 1168.
[82] BaFin, Issuer Guideline, Module C, p. 23.

directly or indirectly, to one or more issuers of financial instruments or to one or more financial instruments, and which, if it were made public, would be likely to have a significant effect on the prices of those financial instruments, the price of related spot commodity contracts, or on the price of related derivative financial instruments. Not every order of a client has a significant effect on the price. Front running must, however, be assumed, if the large volume of the client's order gave rise to an incentive for the person executing the order to acquire or dispose of the respective financial instruments, for example.[83]

Article 7(1)(a) MAR provides the same definition of inside information as the MAD 2003. The term is defined as 'information of a precise nature, which has not been made public, relating, directly or indirectly, to one or more issuers or to one or more financial instruments, and which, if it were made public, would be likely to have a significant effect on the prices of those financial instruments or on the price of related derivative financial instruments.'[84] The requirement of a precise information is defined in Article 7(2) MAR. It must be taken into account that, according to Article 7(3) MAR, an intermediate step can also be considered as inside information, provided that it fulfils the criteria for inside information in itself. A further specification is made in Article 7(4) MAR with regard to the price relevance of an information.

The individual elements are examined in more detail below. In particular, the supervisory practice in Europe is taken into account. **BaFin** has commented in detail on the interpretation of the concept of insider information in the issuer guide.[85] In France, **AMF** has provided information on its administrative practice in a guide.[86] **Consob** has also published guidelines on administrative practice in Italy.[87] These are legally non-binding interpretative guidelines. Nevertheless, they are of outstanding importance in practice for issuers.

(a) Information which has Not been Made Public

The information is considered to be non-public when the public at large could not have this knowledge. Thus, gathering public information is legal. It provides an incentive to create value via analysis, which is vital for the proper functioning of capital markets. It is irrelevant how the public at large became aware of the information. When interpreting the term 'non-public', it must be taken into account that European insider law aims to ensure equal informational opportunities for investors. Therefore, information is only publicly known if all investors can take note of it.[88] This is to be affirmed if the publication is made through an electronic information dissemination system, which is prescribed by law for ad hoc announcements.[89] This system ensures a Europe-wide dissemination of information. Information in the local press, through social media, at a general meeting or at a press conference of the issuer is not sufficient.[90]

---

[83] Cf. BaFin, Issuer Guideline, Module C, p. 24.
[84] Cf. Art. 7(1) MAR.
[85] Cf. BaFin, Issuer Guideline, Module C, p. 9 ff.
[86] Cf. AMF, Guide de l'information permanente et de la gestion de l'information privilégiée, 26 October 2016.
[87] Cf. Consob, Gestione delle informazioni privilegiate, October 2017.
[88] M. Ventoruzzo and C. Picciau, in: Ventoruzzo/Mock (eds.), *Market Abuse Regulation*, Art. 7 para. B.7.54.
[89] See R. Veil § 19 para. 41–43
[90] BaFin, Issuer Guideline, Module C, p. 10; Consob, Gestione delle informazioni privilegiate, October 2017, 4.3.2.

(b) Information of a Precise Nature

36 The 'information of a precise nature' is specified in the same way as under the former MAD 2003 regime. 'Information shall be deemed to be of a precise nature if it indicates a set of circumstances which exists or which may reasonably be expected to come into existence, or an event which has occurred or which may reasonably be expected to occur, where it is specific enough to enable a conclusion to be drawn as to the possible effect of that set of circumstances or event on the prices of the financial instruments or the related derivative financial instrument, the related spot commodity contracts, or the auctioned products based on the emission allowances.'[91]

(aa) Circumstances and Events

37 First of all, it should be noted that circumstances or events that have occurred as well as future circumstances or events can constitute inside information. This regulation was already provided for in the MAD 2003. In addition, Article 7(2) sentence 2 MAR now stipulates, following the ECJ ruling in *Daimler/Geltl*, that 'in the case of a **protracted process** that is intended to bring about, or that results in, particular circumstances or a particular event, those future circumstances or that future event, and also the intermediate steps of that process which are connected with bringing about or resulting in those future circumstances or that future event, may be deemed to be precise information.' Consequently, the (future) final event does not preclude an intermediate step from being examined as a possible inside information.[92]

38 Example: The merger of two listed stock corporations is a process that takes place over a long period of time and involves numerous intermediate steps, such as the agreement of the boards of directors on an exchange ratio of the shares, the amount of an additional cash payment, agreements of the boards of directors on the closure of locations, the signing of the merger agreement, the approval of the merger agreement by the supervisory board and, finally, the approval of the general meetings of both companies and the entry of the resolutions in the commercial registers. Under insider trading law, firstly, the final event, ie the merger, could qualify as inside information. For these purposes, it must be examined whether the entry of the merger in the commercial register (a future event) can reasonably be expected. Secondly, however, each individual intermediate step may also constitute inside information. Thus, it must be examined whether the negotiations on the exchange ratio (an event that has occurred and constitutes an intermediate step) 'in itself fulfils the criteria for inside information' (cf. Article 7(3) MAR).

39 There is no legal definition of what is meant by an intermediate step. Recital 17 MAR gives the following **examples**: 'the state of contract negotiations, terms provisionally agreed in contract negotiations, the possibility of the placement of financial instruments, conditions under which financial instruments will be marketed, provisional terms for the placement of financial instruments, or the consideration of the inclusion of a financial instrument in a major index or the deletion of a financial instrument from such an index.' Of course, these are not exhaustive examples. Strictly speaking, every event arises through numerous intermediate steps. This is also recognised by the BGH, which understands an intermediate step

---

[91] Cf. Art. 7(2) sentence 1 MAR.
[92] Cf. M. Kiesewetter and M. Parmentier, BB (2013), 2371, 2373; K. Langenbucher, NZG (2013), 1401, 1404.

as '**each individual event** on the **way** to an **intended event**'.[93] In addition, each individual intermediate step is initially a future one until it occurs and is followed by a further, future intermediate step that occurs until the final event has finally occurred. The ECJ explicitly recognised this in the *Daimler/Geltl* case[94] and the legislator has adopted this interpretation with the provision in Article 7(2) sentence 2 and (3) MAR.[95]

Circumstances can above all be defined as **facts**, ie past or present external procedures or situations that can be proven.[96] Whether knowledge of internal plans and intentions of a person can also be classed as inside information was discussed controversially at length in Germany, being of relevance especially for so-called cases of scalping.[97] The BGH ruled that the intention to later sell the recommended securities could not be classed as inside information.[98] The concept of information imperatively requires a connection to a third party. A person cannot therefore be regarded as informed about his own intentions.[99] Under MAR, scalping is still to be understood as market manipulation. However, it follows from Article 9(5) MAR that, in principle, internal facts, such as the decision to buy or sell securities, can also constitute inside information. This becomes particularly relevant in stakebuilding. The decision of an investor to acquire further shares can be inside information.[100]

40

Circumstances which may **reasonably be expected** to come into **existence**, might constitute inside information. This is the case, with the words of the ECJ, when 'it appears, on the basis of an overall assessment of the factors existing at the relevant time, that there is a realistic prospect that they will come into existence or occur.'[101] Where inside information concerns a process which occurs in stages, each stage of the process as well as the overall process could constitute inside information.[102] This is now explicitly clarified in the MAR: 'In the case of a protracted process that is intended to bring about, or that results in, particular circumstances or a particular event, those future circumstances or that future event, and also the **intermediate steps** of that process which are connected with bringing about or resulting in those future circumstances or that future event, may be deemed to be precise information'.[103]

41

The ECJ rejected the *probability/magnitude*-formula arguing it would lead to legal uncertainty. This is also the understanding of the European legislator. It follows from Recital 16 of the MAR, that the notion of inside information should not be interpreted as meaning that the magnitude of the effect of that set of circumstances or that event on the prices of the financial instruments concerned must be taken into consideration.[104] The European

42

---

[93] BGH of 23.4.2013 – II ZB 7/09, ZIP 2013, 1165.
[94] ECJ of 28 June 2012, Case C-19/11 (*Daimler/Geltl*), para. 15.
[95] H. Krause, in: Meyer et al. (eds.), *Handbuch Marktmissbrauchsrecht*, § 6 para. 71.
[96] Cf. H. Krause, in: Meyer et al. (eds.), *Handbuch Marktmissbrauchsrecht*, § 6 para. 31 f.
[97] See R. Veil § 15 para. 50.
[98] On *scalping* as a form of market manipulation see R. Veil § 15 para. 52.
[99] BGH of 6.11.2003 – 1 Str 24/04, BGHSt 48, 373.
[100] See on legitimate behaviours para. 74.
[101] See above para. 27.
[102] Cf. recital 16 MAR.
[103] Cf. Art. 7(2) sentence 2 MAR.
[104] However, the magnitude of the effect may be taken into account when determining the price relevance. See below para. 58.

legislator made clear that 'an intermediate step in a protracted process shall be deemed to be inside information if, by itself, it satisfies the criteria of inside information'.[105]

43 In the example (see para. 38), a probability of occurrence of at least 50% is to be used as a basis when examining whether the entry of the merger in the commercial register can reasonably be expected. The probability of occurrence cannot be determined with mathematical accuracy. In order to assess it, all known circumstances and information must be taken into account.[106] For the assessment of the probability, it must be considered, for example, how far the merger process has already progressed, ie whether the contract has already been concluded. BaFin also takes into account how the company has proceeded in similar cases.[107]

44 Value judgements, forecasts and recommendations can in any case be inside information if they have a factual element.[108] In addition, the judgement, forecast or recommendation must be specific enough to allow a conclusion to be drawn about the security price. It is conceivable that the factual element itself also qualifies as inside information.

(bb) Specific

45 A circumstance is precise if it is specific enough to allow a conclusion to be drawn about the possible effect of the circumstance on the price of the security. Strictly speaking, this requirement is superfluous because it is already covered by the requirement of price relevance. A reasonable investor does not buy or sell on the basis of non-specific information.[109] In practice, the requirement plays a role above all in the assessment of information that is ambiguous. Only vague or general information does not, according to the administrative practice of the supervisory authorities, allow a conclusion to be drawn regarding its possible impact on the price of the financial instruments in question.[110]

46 *Facts (abridged)*:[111] While working as an auditor, Mohammed obtained knowledge of the fact that an industrial enterprise which was being audited by his auditing company was planning to sell the electronics sector of the company. When this information was later disclosed, the shares prices rose about 19%. Mohammed, who had bought shares on the ground of this information, justified himself with the fact that before the notification of the sale rumours of this had already existed on the market and the information had therefore no longer been inside information. The Tribunal did not share this point of view, arguing that one must distinguish between information that has been made public and is sufficiently precise and information that exists only as a rumour.[112] Furthermore, the progression of the share prices after the disclosure of the information indicated that the rumours had not yet influenced the share prices and could therefore not be regarded as publicly available. The Tribunal did not support Mohammed in the point that the decision to sell

---

[105] Cf. Art. 7(3) MAR.
[106] BaFin, Issuer Guideline, Module C, p. 10.
[107] BaFin, Issuer Guideline, Module C, p. 10.
[108] H. Krause, in: Meyer et al. (eds.), *Handbuch Marktmissbrauchsrecht*, § 6 para. 35.
[109] See R. Veil § 6 para. 31.
[110] BaFin, Issuer Guideline, Module C, p. 10.
[111] *Arif Mohammed/Financial Services Authority* (2005), The Financial Services Markets Tribunal, para. 12. This is the first decision of the Tribunal regarding sec. 118 FSMA, which was, however, still based on the old insider rules which applied the 'relevant information not generally available test' now contained—as described above—in sec. 118(4) FSMA as a catch-all clause.
[112] Cf. *James Parker/Financial Services Authority* (2006), The Financial Services Markets Tribunal, para. 37.

had not been specific and precise information, as he had not had any information on the modalities of the sale.¹¹³ The Tribunal regarded an information as sufficiently precise once the insider has more or less certain knowledge of the future sale of the sector, independent of the fact whether the details of the transaction were known to him.

The former CESR stated in its Guidelines that it did not regard rumours to be sufficient to constitute inside information: 'CESR considers that in determining whether a set of circumstances exists or an event has occurred, a key issue is whether there is firm and objective evidence for this as opposed to rumours or speculation.'¹¹⁴ This interpretation is still valid under the current market abuse regime (cf. Article 17(7) MAR). A **rumour** is characterised by the fact that the truth of the information is uncertain. The subject matter can be an event that has occurred, but it can also refer to a future event. If the rumour is based on a factual element, a rumour can be inside information. If the rumour is based on an event that has occurred, the reliability of the information is important; if it refers to a future event, the probability of occurrence of this factual element is decisive.¹¹⁵ 47

The **Lafonta** case concerned **information** for which it had been **impossible** to **predict** whether it would have a **positive** or **negative effect** on the price of the shares. The ECJ held: 'in order for information to be regarded as being of a precise nature for the purposes of those provisions, it need not be possible to infer from that information, with a sufficient degree of probability, that, once it is made public, its potential effect on the prices of the financial instruments concerned will be in a particular direction.'¹¹⁶ 48

> The ECJ first justified this interpretation with the broad **wording** and then referred to the **systematic structure** of the **MAD 2003** regime. Lafonta argued 'that information is precise, for the purposes of that provision, only if it allows the person in possession of that information to anticipate how the price of the security concerned will change when that information is made public. He argued that only information that enables the person in possession of it to predict whether the price of the security concerned is going to increase or decrease allows that person to know whether he should buy or sell and, accordingly, grants him an advantage as compared with all the other actors on the market, who are unaware of that information.' The ECJ was not convinced by this interpretation. According to the court, the respective provision of the MAD 2003-regime 'does not require that the information make it possible to determine the direction of change in the prices of the financial instruments concerned. A particular item of information can be used by a reasonable investor as one of the grounds for his investment decision [...], even though it does not make it possible to determine the movement in a given direction of the prices of the financial instruments concerned' (para. 34). Finally, the ECJ argued with the purpose of insider trading law: „As regards the purpose of Directive 2003/6, it should be observed that [...] to confine the scope of point (1) of Article 1 of Directive 2003/6 and Article 1(1) of Directive 2003/124 solely to information which makes it possible to anticipate the direction of a change in the prices of those instruments risks undermining the objectives [the MAD 2003]. The increased complexity of the financial markets makes it particularly difficult to evaluate accurately the direction of a change in the prices of those instruments [...]. In those circumstances—which can lead to widely differing assessments, 49

---

¹¹³ Para. 73 ff. of the judgment.
¹¹⁴ CESR, Level 3—second set of CESR guidance and information on the common operation of the Directive to the market, July 2007, CESR/06-562b, No. 1.15.
¹¹⁵ H. Krause, in: Meyer et al. (eds.), *Handbuch Marktmissbrauchsrecht*, § 6 para. 55.
¹¹⁶ ECJ of 11 March 2015, Case C-628/13 (*Lafonta*), para. 38, ZIP (2015), 627.

depending on the investor—if it were accepted that information is to be regarded as precise only if it makes it possible to anticipate the direction of a change in the prices of the instruments concerned, it would follow that the holder of that information could use an uncertainty in that regard as a pretext for refraining from making certain information public and thus profit from that information to the detriment of the other actors on the market' (para. 35 and 36).

(cc) Reference to an Issuer or to Financial Instruments

50 The concept of inside information further requires that the information relates either to the *issuer* of a financial instrument or to a *financial instrument* itself. This requirement has no independent significance because information that does not relate to the issuer or financial instrument cannot be price-sensitive.

51 Most circumstances relevant for price developments, such as profit drops, the discovery of a new oilfield or the resignation of the management board's chairman, refer to the issuer. As opposed to this, the case *Georgakis* dealt with information relating to an issuer's financial instruments.[117]

> *Facts (abridged)*:[118] Georgakis and members of his family were major shareholders of Parnassos and Atemke, two stock corporations whose shares were admitted to trading on the Greek stock market. On recommendation of their financial consultant, Georgakis and further members of the family decided to support Parnassos' shares price when a decline in prices became apparent, by buying, selling and buying back Parnassos and Atemke shares amongst each other. The ECJ ruled that the decision of the members of the Georgakis group concerning the support of Parnassos shares established a common position within the group regarding the transactions to be effected between its members, with the aim of causing an artificial increase in the price of Parnassos' transferable securities. For those who participated in its adoption, knowledge of the existence of such a decision and of its content constitutes inside information, being information of a precise nature which has not been made public and relates to transferable securities.[119] Whilst the ECJ's decision was still based on the former Insider Directive, the Court's considerations can be applied analogously to the interpretation of the notion of inside information as defined in the former MAD[120] and in the existing MAR.

52 The MAR's definition of inside information also encompasses information which relates indirectly to issuers or financial instruments.[121] However, such information is not subject to the disclosure obligation under Article 17(1) MAR. Information diretly concerning the issuer is also descried as corporate information, in contrast to market information.[122] The former CESR had compiled a list of examples of such information, which includes inter alia future publications of rating agencies' reports and antitrust authority's decisions concerning a listed company.[123]

---

[117] The term financial instrument is defined in Art. 3(1)(1) MAR by referring to Art. 4(1)(15) MiFID II; see on the term 'financial instrument' R. Veil § 13 para. 16.
[118] Cf. ECJ of 10 May 2007, Case C-391/04 (*Georgakis*) [2007] ECR I-3741.
[119] Cf. ECJ of 10 May 2007, Case C-391/04 [2007] ECR I-3741, para. 33.
[120] Cf. D. Moalem and J. Hansen, 19(5) EBLR (2008), 949, 957 ff.
[121] The issuer is only required to disclose inside information that concerns the issuer directly. See R. Veil § 19 para. 32.
[122] Cf. C. Di Noia and M. Gargantini, 4 ECFR (2012), 484, 493; M. Ventoruzzo and C. Picciau, in: Ventoruzzo/Mock (eds.), *Market Abuse Regulation*, Art. 7 para. B.7.58.
[123] CESR/06-562b (fn. 114).

(c) Price Relevance

Article 7(4) MAR states that 'information which, if it were made public, would be likely to have a significant effect on the prices of financial instruments, derivative financial instruments, related spot commodity contracts, or auctioned products based on emission allowances shall mean **information a reasonable investor would be likely to use** as **part** of the basis of his or her **investment decisions.**' Recital 14 MAR sets out the principles according to which a reasonable investor makes his decisions: 'Reasonable investors base their investment decisions on information already available to them, that is to say, on ex ante available information. Therefore, the question whether, in making an investment decision, a reasonable investor would be likely to take into account a particular piece of information should be appraised on the basis of the ex ante available information.' Furthermore, recital 14, in line with the interpretative principles of the ECJ in *Daimler/Geltl*,[124] states that 'such an assessment has to take into consideration the anticipated impact of the information in light of the totality of the related issuer's activity, the reliability of the source of information and any other market variables likely to affect the financial instruments [...] in the given circumstances.'

Practice and academia debate above all whether the reasonable investor should be determined on the basis of characteristics (knowledge of the capital market, critical ability, investment motives, professionalism) or whether he should be understood as a collective, namely as a personification of the market.[125] The courts tend to determine a 'prototype investor'.[126] The BGH ruled on securities prospectus law that a reasonable investor is an attentive reader of a prospectus who understands a balance sheet but does not have above-average expertise.[127] He knows the conditions and practices of capital markets; however, he is not necessarily familiar with all the details of the relevant regimes, such as accounting law.[128] The XI Senate of the BGH followed up on these interpretations and held in the IKB case that a reasonable investor has to **take into account irrational reactions** of **other market participants**, such as herd behaviour.[129]

> *Example*: The OLG Düsseldorf[130] had to determine whether the IKB-Bank had been affected by the subprime mortgage crisis in the United States due to its investment history. The OLG Düsseldorf classed the information on subprime-based instruments held by the IKB-Bank and its special-purpose entities as a specific information. It ruled, however, that the information was not able to influence significantly the IKB-Bank's share price on 27 July 2007. According to the predominant understanding at the time, subprime-based instruments in the company's portfolio were not particularly significant for investment decisions, the ratings received by rating agencies being deemed far more relevant in determining credit risks.[131] The BGH came to a different conclusion, arguing that the potential of inside information to influence the share price must be determined by way of

---

[124] ECJ of 28 June 2012, Case C-19/11 (*Daimler/Geltl*), para. 55.
[125] Cf. M. Ventoruzzo and C. Picciau, in: Ventoruzzo/Mock (eds.), *Market Abuse Regulation*, Art. 7 para. B.7.66 ff.; C. Kumpan and R. Misterek, 184(2) ZHR (2020), 180 ff.
[126] Expression used by C. Kumpan and R. Misterek, 184(2) ZHR (2020), 180, 204.
[127] Cf. BGH of 12 July 1982 – II ZR 175/81, NJW (1982), 2823, 2824.
[128] See R. Veil § 17 para. 34.
[129] BGH of 13 December 2011 – XI ZR 51/10 (IKB), BGHZ 192, 90, 107 f. para. 44; dissenting opionion: L. Klöhn, AG (2012), 345, 349; id., 177 ZHR (2013), 349, 380 ff.
[130] OLG Düsseldorf of 4.3.2010 – I-6 U 94/09, 6 U 94/09, AG (2011), 31, 34.
[131] Ibid., 31, 35.

an ex ante prognosis.[132] The court determined that the subprimes were downgraded by the rating agencies in the middle of July 2007 and there were rumours according to which IKB was subject to a considerable risk due to its involvement with the US subprime market. Due to the fact that at the same time the share price of IKB had decreased considerably, a reasonable investor who is required to also take into account the irrational reactions of other market participants, would have associated a considerable influence on the share price on the highly sensitive market from the middle of July 2007 onwards, taking into account the subprime share of 38.5% IKB held in its own investments and the 90% subprime share in its special purpose vehicles.[133]

56 The concept of inside information should be interpreted with regard to the purpose of insider trading law. A reasonable investor acts behaves in rational way[134] on the basis of **fundamental value-related information**[135] and does not base his decision on irrational market reactions even if these are likely to be profitable.[136] The literature discusses whether a reasonable investor acts on the basis of ecologically sustainable information.[137] This interpretation is not convincing. Ecological aspects do not play a role for the reasonable investor unless they affect the fundamental value of the security, which can be the case with sustainability risks, for example.

57 BaFin refers to the fact whether the respective information will encourage an investor to acquire or dispose of shares and whether this appears profitable to a reasonable investor. A transaction is already profitable if the expected return minus transaction costs exceeds the opportunity costs, ie the return that an investment in financial instruments with comparable risk would achieve.[138] In a first step BaFin examines, from an ex ante point of view, whether the event itself could potentially be price sensitive in a significant way according to general experience.[139] This must be assumed, for example, for an important cooperation, the acquisition or disposal of major holdings and if the issuer has liquidity problems. In a second step the BaFin takes into account the existing or foreseeable specific aspects of the case at hand that may reduce or increase price sensitivity, paying special attention to the question whether the respective information was already known and taken into consideration on the capital market. Investors will, for example, often already have taken the issuer's results into account for their investment or divestment. The information in question may already have been assessed by market participants. For example, investors have often already taken the issuer's business performance into account in their investments and disinvestments. However, if the information is already reflected in the price of the security, it may not be likely to have a significant impact on the price of the financial instruments. Finally, the impact of information must also be measured in terms of the issuer's overall business, the reliability of the information source and other market variables. In particular, the volatility of the market, especially of comparable financial instruments (from issuers in the same industry), must be taken into account. The effects of information must also be considered in the light of the issuer's overall activity, the reliability of the information's source and other market variables,

---

[132] BGH of 13.12.2011 – XI ZR 51/10, BGHZ 192, 90, 106 para. 41.
[133] Ibid., 90, 107 ff. para. 44.
[134] M. Ventoruzzo and C. Picciau, in: Ventoruzzo/Mock (eds.), *Market Abuse Regulation*, Art. 7 para. B.7.67.
[135] L. Klöhn, 177 ZHR (2013), 349, 366 ff.; M. Ventoruzzo and C. Picciau, in: Ventoruzzo/Mock (eds.), *Market Abuse Regulation*, Art. 7 para. B.7.67; C. Kumpan and R. Misterek, 184(2) ZHR (2020), 180, 203 ff.
[136] Cf. also M. Sustmann, in: Kämmerer and Veil (eds.), *Übernahme- und Kapitalmarktrecht in der Reformdiskussion*, 230, 251: 'rational and non-speculative acting person'.
[137] The question is being raised by P. Mülbert and A. Sajnovits, ECFR (2021), 256, 287 f.
[138] Cf. BaFin, Issuer Guideline, Module C, p. 12.
[139] Cf. also OLG Düsseldorf of 4.3.2010 – I-6 U 94/09, 6 U 94/09, AG (2011), 31, 34.

such as the volatility of the market, especially with regard to comparable financial instruments of other issuers in the same industry.

According to the wording of Article 7 MAR, the reasonable investor is 'likely' to use the information as part of the basis of his investment decision. This means on the one hand that the mere possibility is not sufficient; and on the other hand that a degree of probability close to certainty is not required.[140] Theoretically, it is irrelevant for the price relevance whether an inside information actually has an effect on the price. Nevertheless, this aspect plays a major role in practice. The supervisory authorities attach indicative importance to an actual change in the share price after the inside information has become known.[141] According to Recital 15 MAR, **ex post information** can be used to check the presumption that the ex ante information was price sensitive, but should not be used to take action against persons who drew reasonable conclusions from ex ante information available to them. 58

In the case of intermediate steps, the price relevance shall be determined with regard to the principles of interpretation set out in the third sentence of Recital 14. Consequently, the potential to influence the price is to be determined with regard to, among other criteria, the relevance of the final event for the security price.[142] Intermediate steps may therefore be price-relevant (and constitute inside information) even if the final event is not predominantly likely, provided the final event has a particularly high impact on the issuer and thus on the share price. 59

In the example of the merger of two listed stock corporations (see para. 38), when examining whether the negotiations on the exchange ratio of the shares (an event that has occurred, which is precise and therefore constitutes an intermediate step) 'in itself fulfils the criteria for inside information' (cf. Article 7(3) MAR), it may have to be taken into account that the merger is likely to have tremendous synergy effects and therefore will have a particularly strong impact on the stock exchange price. Even if at the time of the occurrence of the intermediate step (agreement on the exchange ratio) the final event (entry of the merger in the commercial register) is not yet predominantly probable, the intermediate step may already be relevant to the share price because of the enormous impact of the final event. 60

BaFin distinguishes between intermediate steps that derive their quality as inside information from themselves and those intermediate steps that derive their price relevance from the future final event.[143] In the latter case, BaFin assumes that the more significant and probable the final event is, the more likely it is that the price will be influenced and that an overall consideration of the past and future circumstances, taking into account the respective market situation, suggests that a reasonable investor would already use this intermediate step for his own benefit.[144] 61

Ultimately, it will be a question of each individual case whether certain information may have a significant effect on the prices of financial instruments. There is currently no uniform European understanding in this regard with ESMA not yet having published any guidelines 62

---

[140] Consob, Gestione delle informazioni privilegiate, October 2017, 4.3.5.
[141] BaFin, Issuer Guideline, Module C, p. 12.
[142] Highly controversial; in line with the author L. Klöhn, ZIP (2012), 1885, 1891; A. Schall, ZIP (2012), 1286, 1288; A. Bingel, AG (2012), 685, 690 ff.; dissenting opinion: H. Krause and M. Brellochs, AG (2013), 309, 314.
[143] Cf. BaFin, Issuer Guideline, Module C, p. 13 f.; J. Vetter et al., AG (2019), 160, 164 ff.
[144] Cf. BaFin, Issuer Guideline, Module C, p.14.

on this topic.¹⁴⁵ It is thus only possible to present the approaches taken by individual supervisory authorities.

63   Some national supervisory authorities have published their administrative practice.¹⁴⁶ BaFin and Consob provide the most detailed information on how they assess the price relevance of forecasts, business figures, dividends, capital measures, significant extraordinary income or expenses, mergers & acquisitions, personnel decisions and insolvencies.¹⁴⁷ Furthermore, they explain numerous examples where there is usually a considerable potential to influence the share price.

64   The BaFin's interpretative notes on financial figures are particularly detailed. BaFin determines price relevance according to whether the information in question deviates materially from the relevant benchmark.¹⁴⁸ In the important case that the issuer in its forecast has indicated a corridor, a significant potential to influence the share price shall as a rule be affirmed if the business figures are outside the corridor. For business figures that lie within the corridor, the following principle applies: the narrower the corridor is defined, the more likely it is that there is no potential to significantly influence the share price. Conversely, this also means that the business figures can have a significant potential to influence the share price if the forecast corridor is very wide and the results are close to the upper or lower edge of the corridor. If, on the other hand, the issuer has only stated a minimum expectation in its forecast, this does not exclude the potential to influence the share price simply because the upper forecast range was formulated in an open manner. In such a case, the issuer has to determine how the forecast statement has been perceived in the market.¹⁴⁹

V. Prohibitions

1. Overview

65   The MAR 'establishes a common regulatory framework on insider dealing [and] the unlawful disclosure of inside information [...] to enhance investor protection and confidence in

---

[145] However, the former CESR had established guidelines how NCAs should determine the price relevance. It argued that the potential influence on the price of financial instruments should be determined ex ante. The CESR also commented on the difficult question of the degree of probability required for a significant price effect to be expected. Whilst the mere possibility that a piece of information will have a significant price effect is not enough to trigger a disclosure obligation, a degree of probability close to certainty could also not be required. Quantitative criteria alone, such as specific thresholds (2 or 5%), were not a suitable means for determining the significance of price movement, due to the fact that the volatility of 'blue-chip' securities of larger companies is typically less than that of smaller, less liquid stocks. The CESR named three criteria that should be taken into consideration when determining whether a significant effect is likely to occur: (i) whether the type of information is the same as information which has, in the past, had a significant effect on prices; (ii) whether pre-existing analyst research reports and opinions indicate that the type of information in question is price sensitive; and (iii) whether the company itself has ever treated similar events as inside information. Cf. CESR/06-562b (fn. 114), No. 1.12–1.14.

[146] Cf. AMF, Guide de l'information permanente et de la gestion de l'information privilégiée, 26 October 2016, 18 f. (*avertissement sur résultats*).

[147] Cf. BaFin, Issuer Guideline, Module C, p. 15 ff.; Consob, Gestione delle informazioni privilegiate, October 2017, 4.6.7.

[148] Cf. BaFin, Issuer Guideline, Module C, p. 16; equally Consob, Gestione delle informazioni privilegiate, October 2017, 4.6.7.5.

[149] Cf. BaFin, Issuer Guideline, Module C, p. 16 with numerous further interpretative notes on the assessment of financial figures under insider law.

those markets' (Art. 1 MAR). To that end, it prohibits insider dealing and the unlawful disclosure of inside information.[150] The prohibitions are further defined in Article 8 (insider dealing) and Article 10 (unlawful disclosure of inside information) MAR. The prohibitions correspond nearly entirely with the requirements the MAD 2003 laid down. It is therefore justified to refer to the interpretational principles developed by the ECJ with regard to the prohibitions in the former MAD, unless the specific provisions on legitimate behaviour (Article 9 MAR) and market soundings (Article 11 MAR) require otherwise.

2. Prohibition of the Acquisition or Disposal of Financial Instruments

(a) Foundations

A person may not engage or attempt to engage in insider dealing.[151] Insider dealing occurs, when a **person possesses inside information** and **uses** that **information** by directly or indirectly **acquiring** or **disposing of financial instruments** to which that information relates, for its own account or for the account of a third party.[152] The MAR has widened the scope of this prohibition, the use of inside information by cancelling or amending an order concerning a financial instrument to which the information relates and the order was placed before the person concerned possessed the inside information, also being considered an insider dealing.[153] If the insider trading is committed by a legal person, the prohibition applies 'to the natural persons who participate in the decision to carry out the acquisition, disposal, cancellation or amendment of an order for the account of the legal person concerned.'[154]

This prohibition is to ensure the integrity of the financial markets and enhance investor confidence, at the same time ensuring more equality between contracting parties in market transactions.[155] In the abovementioned case *Georgakis*[156] all contracting parties of the transactions had access to the same information and no one had been able to benefit from having more information than the others. The ECJ therefore correctly ruled that Georgakis and the members of his family had not breached the rules prohibiting the use of inside information by acquiring or disposing of financial instruments.[157]

(b) Acquisition and Disposal of Financial Instruments

The prohibition requires an **acquisition** or **disposal of financial instruments**.[158] An acquisition or a sale already takes place with the validly concluded legal transaction under the law

---

[150] Art. 14 MAR.
[151] Cf. Art. 14(a) MAR.
[152] Art. 8(1) MAR.
[153] Cf. Art. 8(1) sentence 2 MAR.
[154] Art. 8(5) MAR.
[155] Cf. ECJ of 10 May 2007, Case C-391/04 [2007] ECR I-3741 on Art. 2 of the former Insider Directive 89/592/EEC; J. Hansen, in: Ventoruzzo/Mock (eds.), *Market Abuse Regulation*, Art. 8 para. B.8.47 and B.8.50.
[156] See above para. 51.
[157] The aim was to fix artificially and simultaneously the prices of certain securities. This constitutes a type of market manipulation as prohibited by the MAR. See R. Veil § 15 para. 32 ff.
[158] Insider dealing must relate to financial instruments. The term is not defined in MAR. Rather, Art. 3(1) No. 1 MAR refers to Art. 4(1) No. 15 of Directive 2014/65/EU (MiFID II). This provision refers with regard to the term financial instrument to the instruments listed in Annex I Section C MiFID II, which in turn are partly defined in Art. 4(1) No. 17, No. 44, No. 45, No. 46, No. 47, No. 48, No. 49 and No. 50 MiFID II, partly by reference to Regulation (EU) No. 600/2014 (MiFIR).

of obligations.[159] This interpretation is required by the meaning and purpose of the norm, because an insider already engages in harmful arbitrage through the transaction under the law of obligations, ie obtains an unjustified advantage.[160] The typical case of an acquisition or sale is the purchase contract. Furthermore, an acquisition based on a donation may also be covered by the prohibition.[161] Furthermore, insider trading requires that a person **directly** or **indirectly acquires** or **sells** financial instruments for **his own account** or for the **account of a third party**. The offence is broadly defined in order to avoid any circumvention of the law. It covers the case that the insider himself is a party to the contract and concludes the transaction for his own account or for the account of a third party (eg as a commission agent), as well as the case that the insider acts as a proxy. Acting in another's name and for another's account occurs, for example, in the case of the repurchase of own shares by the executive board of the company, furthermore in the case of front running for the benefit of a customer or in the case of asset management for which the bank has a power of attorney.

(c) Use of Inside Information and Legitimate Behaviours

69   Under the MAD 2003 regime, literature and courts argued that there must—at least additionally to other factors—be a chain of causation between the acquisition or disposal of the financial instruments to the inside information. This can, for example, become relevant if the target company passes on inside information to an investor in the course of a due diligence proceeding. If the investor is only strengthened in her decision to acquire a financial instrument of the respective company a breach of the prohibition of acquisitions of financial instruments cannot be assumed.[162] As opposed to this, the rules prohibiting the use of inside information are breached if the investor makes additional purchases on the stock market.[163] These questions were also subject to the ECJ's ruling in *Spector*[164] in which the court examined the prohibition closely and gave concrete details on how the European rules are to be interpreted.

70   *Facts (abridged)*: Spector, a listed company under Belgian law, offered a programme via which employees could acquire shares in the company, which Spector planned to acquire on the market. On 21 May 2003 Spector informed Euronext Brussels of its plan to acquire a certain number of its own shares. On 11 and 13 August 2003 board member van Raemdonck acquired 19,773 shares at an average price of € 9.97 for Spector. The price for exercising the acquisition option laid at € 10.45. Subsequently Spector disclosed the company's business results and company policy, leading to a price increase up to € 12.50. The Belgian supervisory authority (CBFA) imposed fines of € 80,000 and € 20,000 on Spector and van Raemdonck, respectively, for the acquisition of the shares.

---

[159] K. Hopt and C. Kumpan, in: Schimansky et al. (eds.), *Bankrechts-Handbuch*, § 107 para. 63; F. Schäfer, in: Marsch-Barner and Schäfer (eds.), *Handbuch börsennotierte AG*, § 14 para. 39.
[160] Cf. J. Hansen, in: Ventoruzzo/Mock (eds.), *Market Abuse Regulation*, Art. 8 para. B.8.81: 'any transaction that may produce a detriment to third parties'.
[161] K. Hopt and C. Kumpan, in: Schimansky et al. (eds.), *Bankrechts-Handbuch*, § 107 para. 65.
[162] Cf. H. Assmann, in: Assmann and Schneider (eds.), *Kommentar zum WpHG*, § 14 para. 45; M. Kemnitz, *Due Diligence und neues Insiderrecht*, 67 ff.
[163] Cf. BaFin, Issuer Guideline, Module C, p.37–38; H. Diekmann and M. Sustmann, NZG (2004), 929, 931; on Austrian law S. Kalss et al., *Kapitalmarktrecht I*, § 21 para. 37; dissenting opinion: P. Mennicke, in: Fuchs (ed.), *Kommentar zum WpHG*, § 14 para. 75.
[164] ECJ of 23 December 2009, Case C-45/08 (*Spector*) [2009] ECR I-12073.

The court, having to decide on the legality of the fines, submitted a number of questions to the ECJ for a preliminary ruling, especially regarding the requirement of making use of inside information.

The ECJ ruled that the fact that a **primary insider** 'in **possession of inside information**, **acquires** or **disposes of**, or tries to acquire or dispose of, for his own account or for the account of a third party, either directly or indirectly, the **financial instruments** to which that information relates **implies** that that *person* has '**used that information**' within the meaning of that provision, but without prejudice to the rights of the defence and, in particular, to the right to be able to rebut that presumption. The question whether that person has infringed the prohibition on insider dealing must be analysed in the light of the purpose of that directive, which is to protect the integrity of the financial markets and to enhance investor confidence, which is based, in particular, on the assurance that investors will be placed on an equal footing and protected from the misuse of inside information.'[165]

71

The ECJ established a rebuttable presumption.[166] The court listed a number of examples for which the assumption does not apply—the most practically relevant being the circumstance of a public takeover bid and a merger proposal. In these cases, the use of the inside information 'should not in itself be deemed to constitute insider dealing. The operation whereby an undertaking, after obtaining inside information concerning a specific company, subsequently launches a public take-over bid for the capital of that company at a rate higher than the market rate cannot, in principle, be regarded as prohibited insider dealing since it does not infringe on the interests protected by that directive.'[167]

72

The **MAR** now provides detailed rules on 'legitimate behaviour'.[168] These provisions are **based on** the **assumption** that a **person** who **possesses inside information** and **acquires** or **disposes** of financial **instruments** to which that information relates **has used that information**.[169] This shall, however, 'not be deemed' to be a use of information and engagement in insider dealing, provided that the requirements laid down in Article 9(1)–(5) MAR are fulfilled. The European legislator has thus implemented into the MAR the examples developed by the ECJ in the *Spector* case, according to which the use of inside information can be refuted, rendering the rules developed by the ECJ more precise and extending them. It is important to underline the fact that it is now also recognised that adequate compliance measures can ensure that a legal person is not held liable for insider dealings of its employees (compliance as a defence measure).[170]

73

The ECJ has not yet had the opportunity to clarify the legal nature of Article 9. Correctly, it should not be seen as an exemption but as a **delineation** of **behaviour** that is **legitimate**.[171] Thus, Article 9 should not be subject to a narrow interpretation.[172] The provisions ensure legal certainty, whilst at the same time giving rise to a number of new questions. The first relates to Article 9 MAR according to which an infringement of the prohibition of insider

74

---

[165] Ibid., para. 62.
[166] J. Hansen, in: Ventoruzzo/Mock (eds.), *Market Abuse Regulation*, Art. 8 para. B.8.158.
[167] Ibid., para. 59.
[168] Cf. Art. 9 MAR.
[169] Cf. Recital 24 MAR.
[170] Cf. Art. 9(1) MAR.
[171] J. Hansen, in: Ventoruzzo/Mock (eds.), *Market Abuse Regulation*, Art. 8 para. B.9.07 and 9.09.
[172] Ibid., para. B.914.

dealing set out in Article 14 MAR may still be deemed to have occurred if the NCA establishes that there was an illegitimate reason for the orders to trade, transactions or behaviours concerned. This exception gives rises to legal uncertainty and it is doubtful whether it is sufficiently precise from a constitutional point of view. The scope of application of Article 9 MAR is also problematic, as there may be further situations in which it appears justified to refute the assumption that an insider made use of inside information. In cases in which the interests appear comparable, the provision should be applied by way of analogy, as it is not apparent that the legislator intended the definition of legitimate behaviour to be exhaustive.

75 The so-called master plan theory[173] concerns situations in which an insider (in possession of inside information) carries out a securities transaction after having obtained information through a due diligence. The theory states that the insider does not use the inside information if he has already taken the decision to enter into the transaction beforehand. If the investor obtains negative inside information and then refrains from acquiring the shareholding, he does not use the information either. If he obtains positive inside information and acquires securities as originally planned, he does not violate the prohibition because he had already decided to buy and does not use the inside information. The situation is different if the investor acquires the securities at a different price after obtaining the inside information. In this case, use of the inside information can be affirmed. The master plan theory does not apply if the insider makes changes to the previous plans, for example is only prepared to pay a lower price.[174] The same applies if the insider carries out additional securities transactions (not covered by the master plan), regardless of whether they take place on or off a market (so-called alongside purchases).

76 The trading prohibition does not apply if buyer and seller have the same level of knowledge, as equal informational opportunities of the investors are not impaired. The ECJ had already taken this into account in the Georgakis case: 'Thus, where, in a case such as that in the main proceedings, all of the contracting parties have the same information, they are on an equal footing and the information ceases to be inside information for them in the context of the implementation of the decision adopted within the group. Against this background, since none of them is in a position to derive an advantage over the others, the transactions effected between the members of the group on the basis of that information do not constitute taking advantage, with full knowledge of the facts, of inside information.'[175] These principles of interpretation can also be applied to insider trading law under the MAR.[176] In practice, this can be particularly relevant in face-to-face transactions, for example in the context of a capital increase, acquisition financing or a Stakebuilding prior to a public takeover.[177]

3. Unlawful Disclosure of Inside Information

77 A person shall not unlawfully disclose inside information.[178] Such disclosure arises where a person possesses inside information and discloses that information to any other person,

---

[173] Cf. BaFin, Issuer Guideline, Module C, p. 60.
[174] See also K. Hopt and C. Kumpan, in: Schimansky et al. (eds.), *Bankrechts-Handbuch*, § 107 para. 98.
[175] Cf. ECJ of 10 May 2007, Case C-391/04 (*Georgakis*) [2007] ECR I-3741, para. 39.
[176] C. Seibt and B. Wollenschläger, AG (2014), 593, 598; S. Sieder, ZFR (2017), 171, 178; L. Bühren, NZG (2017), 1172, 1175.
[177] See C. Seibt and B. Wollenschläger, AG (2014), 593, 598.
[178] Cf. Art. 14(c) MAR.

except where the disclosure is made in the normal exercise of an employment, a profession or duties.[179] This prohibition was already laid down in the former Insider Directive and the MAD 2003 and was refined by the ECJ's decision in *Grøngaard/Bang*.[180] It aims at preventing insider trading.[181]

(a) Disclosure

Inside information is disclosed if the recipient is enabled to obtain knowledge of the inside information without significant effort.[182] This can be done by action,[183] but also by omission. It follows from the reference to Article 8(4) MAR that the prohibition applies to both primary and secondary insiders. 78

The provision only prohibits the unlawful disclosure of inside information. The wording (unless it 'is made in the normal exercise of an employment, a profession or duties') has remained unchanged compared to the provisions of the Insider Dealing Directive and the MAD 2003, so that the ECJ jurisprudence in the Grøngaard/Bang case issued on the predecessor rules can be applied for the interpretation of Article 10 MAR.[184] 79

> *Facts (abridged)*: Bang was chairman of the Finansforbund, a trade union in the financial sector. Grøngaard, who had been appointed by the employees, was a member of the administrative board of the company RealDanmark, a relatively large listed financial institution. Subsequent to an extraordinary administrative board meeting of RealDanmark, Grøngaard passed on information to Bang on 28 August 2000, regarding the planned merger negotiations with the Danske Bank, another large Danish financial institution. Between 28 August and 4 September 2009 Bang consulted with his two deputies and one of his employees in the administration of the Finansforbund and passed the information he had received from Grøngaard on to them. On 2 October 2000 the merger between RealDanmark and Danske Bank was made public and RealDanmark's shares price rose by 65%. Grøngaard and Bang were criminally prosecuted under section 36(1) of the Danish Securities Trading Act (vædipapirhandelslov) for disclosing inside information. The Københavns Byret decided to stay the proceedings and made reference to the ECJ for a preliminary ruling. 80

> The ECJ examined in particular the fact that the prohibition of disclosing inside information does not apply unconditionally. The provision is not applicable if the insider passes on the information in the normal course of the exercise of his employment, profession or duties. According to the ECJ, this exemption clause must be treated restrictively, and can only be justified if there is a **close link between** the **disclosure** and the **exercise** of the **employment, profession** or duties and the **disclosure** of such information is **strictly necessary** for the **exercise thereof**.[185] Particular care is required with regard to sensitive information. In these cases, the disclosure is manifestly capable of 81

---

[179] Cf. Art. 10(1) MAR.
[180] ECJ of 22 November 2005, Case C-384/02 (*Grøngaard/Bang*) [2005] ECR I-9939.
[181] C. Mosca, in: Ventoruzzo/Mock (eds.), *Market Abuse Regulation*, Art. 10 para. B.10.27.
[182] BaFin, Issuer Guideline, Module C, p. 62; A. Meyer, in: Meyer et al. (eds.), *Handbuch Marktmissbrauchsrecht*, § 8 para. 4.
[183] Cf. C. Mosca, in: Ventoruzzo/Mock (eds.), *Market Abuse Regulation*, Art. 10 para. B.10.14: written message, sharing access codes or passwords that make inside information available to others.
[184] A. Meyer, in: Meyer et al. (eds.), *Handbuch Marktmissbrauchsrecht*, § 8 para. 11; C. Mosca, in: Ventoruzzo/Mock (eds.), *Market Abuse Regulation*, Art. 10 para. B.10.71 (the exemption should be applied narrowly).
[185] ECJ of 22 November 2005, Case C-384/02 (*Grøngaard/Bang*) [2005] ECR I-9939. The High Court of Denmark ruled that a member nominated by the employees has the possibility to discuss a merger that would have a considerable effect on the employees with the chair of his union. The defendants in *Grøngaard/Bang* were therefore exempted from liability. Cf. Højesteret Kopenhagen, ZIP (2009), 1526, 1527.

significantly affecting the price of the transferable securities in question. The ECJ stated that inside information relating to a merger between two companies quoted on the stock exchange is an example of such particularly sensitive information.

82 Whether the exception from the prohibition can be assumed must, according to the ECJ, be determined by the national court in the light of the applicable national laws. What is to be regarded as coming within the normal ambit of the exercise of an employment, profession or duties, depends to a large extent, in the absence of harmonisation in that respect, on the rules governing those questions in the various national legal systems.[186] In particular, the underlying legal concepts in national labour and company law must therefore be taken into account in order to determine whether a member of the board of directors or the supervisory board was permitted to pass on inside information on the company to a major shareholder or whether a representative of the employees on the supervisory board may pass on information to 'his' union. Under consideration of these facts, as part of its examination, 'a national court must, in the light of the applicable national rules, take particular account of: the fact that that exception to the prohibition of disclosure of inside information must be interpreted strictly, the fact that each additional disclosure is liable to increase the risk of that information being exploited for a purpose contrary to [the market abuse regime], and the sensitivity of the inside information'.[187]

83 For the question of whether the disclosure is strictly necessary, it may have to be taken into account whether the recipient makes a declaration of confidentiality or the insider points out to the recipient that the information is inside information (with the consequence that the recipient becomes a secondary insider and is therefore subject to the disclosure obligation pursuant to Article 10 MAR).[188] Irrespective of this, the issuer must include the recipient in the insider list (Article 18 MAR).

84 The prohibition of disclosure becomes relevant in the case of acquisitions of a **block of shares** if the board of directors grants the prospective buyer access to information in the course of a due diligence. The board of directors is authorised to pass on inside information if this is necessary to secure a concrete acquisition intention. Particularly in the case of the acquisition of significant shareholdings, both the economic interest of the issuer and that of the acquirer justify greater transparency than is the case with ordinary share purchases on the stock exchange. For this reason, disclosure by the issuer's management board is made in the normal exercise of a profession or duties, if the prospective buyer wants to acquire a block of shares of more than 3%.[189]

85 Examples for further cases, in which the disclosure is allowed, however, include the possibility for members of the supervisory board to disclose inside information to a major shareholder outside the general shareholders' meeting if this may heighten the chances of a certain measure, such as a capital increase, being adopted by the shareholders' meeting.[190] As opposed to this, the members of the supervisory board are not permitted to disclose inside information regarding upcoming business and personnel policy measures to individual

---

[186] ECJ of 22 November 2005, Case C-384/02 (*Grøngaard/Bang*) [2005] ECR I-9939, para. 39–40.
[187] Cf. ibid., para. 48.
[188] Cf. BaFin, Issuer Guideline, Module C, p. 63.
[189] A. Meyer, in: Meyer et al. (eds.), *Handbuch Marktmissbrauchsrecht*, § 8 para. 35.
[190] Cf. for a discussion of reasons to disclose C. Mosca, in: Ventoruzzo/Mock (eds.), *Market Abuse Regulation*, Art. 10 para. B.10.57 ff.

shareholders. These cases may again have to be treated differently when the issuer is a subsidiary of a parent company. The members of the supervisory board must in these circumstances take the controlling company's interest in a unified management of the whole group into consideration. The disclosure of inside information to the controlling company can therefore be permissible.[191]

(b) Market Sounding

MAR privileges market soundings (also called testing the waters in the US) because they are 'a highly valuable tool to gauge the opinion of potential investors, enhance shareholder dialogue, ensure that deals run smoothly, and that the views of issuers, existing shareholders and potential new investors are aligned. They may be particularly beneficial when markets lack confidence or a relevant benchmark, or are volatile. Thus the ability to conduct market soundings is important for the proper functioning of financial markets and market soundings should not in themselves be regarded as market abuse.'[192] It is a **widespread** market **practice** to **determine** the **interest of investors** in a capital markets transaction (such as an offer of securities) **prior to the transaction**, with the aim of assessing its prospects of success. The market sounding is usually not carried out by the issuer itself, but rather by lawyers or investment bankers retained by the issuer for carrying out the transaction. Prior to the enactment of the MAR, rules on market sounding only existed in France. The procedure is now laid down uniformly for the whole of Europe.

The persons involved in a market sounding are (i) the issuer, (ii) the disclosing market participant (DMP) and the person receiving the market sounding (market sounding beneficiaries = MSB). Disclosure of inside information made in the course of a market sounding is deemed to be made in the normal exercise of a person's employment, profession or duties where the DMP complies with Article 11(3) and (5) MAR (cf. Article 11(4) MAR).

Market sounding is defined in Article 11(1) MAR. It comprises the communication of information prior to the announcement of a transaction, in order to gauge the interest of potential investors[193] in a possible transaction and the conditions relating to it, such as its potential size or pricing, to one or more potential investors.[194] This is usually carried out only few hours before the publication of the transaction. The transaction may then be regarded as inside information—provided the intermediate steps are already price relevant. The feedback from the investors is important for the issuer, as it enables it to assess the transaction's prospects of success. The DMP informs potential investors (MSBs) of the key features of the planned capital market transaction if they agree to the transmission of the information (wall crossing). In most cases, this information does not yet qualify as inside information. However, there may already be an intermediate step which in itself fulfils the requirements of inside information.[195] The disclosure of other inside information, such as

---

[191] Cf. B. Singhof, ZGR (2001), 146, 162; R. Veil, 172 ZHR (2008), 239, 268.
[192] Recital 32 MAR.
[193] They are also described as market sounding recipients (MSR).
[194] Cf. also Art. 11(2) MAR about market sounding in the course of a takeover bid.
[195] See para. 37.

the decision of a board member to resign from the board, is generally not privileged under Article 11(4) MAR. Only such information may be communicated which, from the point of view of the DMP, is necessary to explore the interest of potential investors in the capital market transaction.[196]

89 Article 11(3)–(5) MAR provide numerous obligations for a DMP, which are put into more concrete terms by Commission Delegated Regulation (EU) No. 2016/960 of 17 May 2016.[197] ESMA has furthermore issued guidelines for persons receiving market soundings.[198] These need, however, not be covered in more detail herein. These rules are intended to facilitate the supervisory authority's monitoring of compliance with the prohibitions on insider trading. The prerequisite for the privileged treatment is merely that the DMP complies with the rules provided for in Article 11(3) and (5) MAR. In addition, the DMP is subject to further obligations, which, however, are not sanctioned. Of practical importance is above all the so-called **cleansing**: If information is disclosed in the course of a market sounding and, in the DMP's opinion, loses its status as inside information, the DMP must inform the recipient immediately.[199]

4. Recommending or Inducing

90 A person may not recommend to another person to engage in insider dealing or induce another person to engage in insider dealing.[200] This prohibition is a catch-all clause, to which the ECJ has not yet referred to. It has the aim of preventing an insider from using a third party or acting collusively with him, in order to circumvent the prohibitions applying to the insider dealing himself by recommending the deals to the third party.

91 The prohibition is further specified in Article 8(2) MAR. Recommending or inducing another person to engage in insider dealing occurs where the **person possesses inside information** and (i) **recommends**, on the basis of that information, **another person to acquire** or **dispose of financial instruments** to which that information relates, or induces that person to make such an acquisition or disposal. It further occurs (ii) where such a person recommends that **another person cancel** or amend an **order** concerning a financial instrument to which that information relates or induces that person to make such a cancellation or amendment.

92 'Induce' can be defined as any means of influencing the will of a third party. It is sufficient if the insider suggests a specific transaction to a third party, irrespective of whether or not it explicitly discloses the inside information. The prohibition requires causation between the insider's information and the offender's recommendation, ie the offender must recommend the acquisition or disposal of shares based on his/her inside knowledge.

---

[196] ESMA, Final Report, Draft technical standards on the Market Abuse Regulation, 28 September 2015, ESMA/2015/1455, p. 23; N. Kubesch, *Marktsondierung nach dem neuen Marktmissbrauchsrecht*, 196 ff.; A. Meyer, in: Meyer et al. (eds.), *Handbuch Marktmissbrauchsrecht*, § 8 para. 91.

[197] Cf. also ESMA, Final Report, Draft technical standards on the Market Abuse Regulation, 28 September 2015, ESMA/2015/1455, p. 21–33 with further interpretational remarks.

[198] Cf. ESMA, Final Report, Guidelines on the Market Abuse Regulation – market soundings and delay of disclosure of inside information, 13 July 2016, ESMA/2016/1130.

[199] Art. 11(6) MAR.

[200] Cf. Art. 14(b) MAR.

5. Exemptions

93 The European legislature admits that in certain circumstances and for economic reasons the stabilisation of financial instruments or trading in own shares in buy-back programmes can be legitimate, and therefore should not in itself be regarded as market abuse.[201] The prohibition should thus not apply to trading in own shares in 'buy-back' programmes or to the stabilisation of a financial instrument provided such trading is carried out in accordance with Article 5(1)–(5) and the RTS developed by ESMA and endorsed by the Commission.[202]

94 Trading in own shares under buy-back programmes is privileged if it has the purpose of reducing an issuer's capital, meeting obligations arising from a debt instrument that can be converted into equity capital (example: convertible bond) or meeting obligations arising from an employee share scheme. Certain procedural requirements must also be met. The details of the programme must be fully disclosed, trades must be reported to the regulator as part of the repurchase programme and subsequently publicly announced, appropriate limits on price and volume must be observed and trading must be conducted in accordance with the specified conditions.

95 Similar restrictions apply to price stabilisation transactions. This means any purchase or offer to purchase relevant securities and any transaction in comparable linked instruments that investment firms or credit institutions undertake as part of a significant offering of those securities for the sole purpose of supporting the market price of those securities when there is selling pressure on those securities. The insider trading prohibitions do not apply if the price stabilisation measures are limited in time, properly reported and subject to reasonable limits in relation to the price.[203]

VI. Supervision

1. Tasks and Powers of National Authorities (NCAs)

96 The prohibition on insider dealings must be supervised by the national authorities.[204] The European legislature regarded it as imperative that a single competent authority of an administrative nature, guaranteeing its independence of economic actors and avoiding conflicts of interest, be designated in each Member State to supervise compliance with the provisions. It further regarded a common minimum set of effective tools and powers for the competent authority of each Member State necessary in order to guarantee supervisory effectiveness. The national authorities' powers had differed greatly between the Member States,[205] which is why the European legislature approached this aspect in such detail.

---

[201] Cf. recital 12 MAR.
[202] Commission Delegated Regulation (EU) No. 2016/1052 of 8 March 2016 supplementing Regulation (EU) No. 596/2014 of the European Parliament and of the Council with regard to regulatory technical standards for the conditions applicable to buy-back programmes and stabilisation measures, OJ L 173, 30 June 2016, p. 34–41.
[203] Cf. Art. 5(4) MAR.
[204] Art. 22 ff. MAR.
[205] See R. Veil § 12 para. 6.

ESMA has no market surveillance powers. The law does not specify how national authorities are to exercise supervision.

97 The nature of supervision is rooted in national administrative law and culturally shaped by national administrative practice. Nevertheless, certain trends can be identified in Europe. In a more **risk-based approach**, the authority takes into account the significance of the matter for the integrity of the capital market and prioritises matters where there are clear indications of market abuse.[206] Challenges arise from the (digital) evolution of markets[207] and the difficulty of accessing information in cross-border transactions.[208] Empirically proven patterns of insider trading are helpful in analysing the vast data sets.[209]

98 In Article 23, the MAR lays down that the competent authorities must be given all supervisory and investigatory powers that are necessary for the exercise of their functions,[210] including at least the right to (a) have **access** to any **document** and **data** in any form, and to receive a copy of it; (b) **require** or demand **information** from any person, including those who are successively involved in the transmission of orders or conduct of the operations concerned, as well as their principals, and if necessary, to summon and question any such person with a view to obtain information; (c) in relation to commodity derivatives, to request information from market participants on related spot markets, obtain reports on transactions, and have direct access to traders' systems; (d) carry out **on-site inspections**; (e) **enter** the **premises** of natural and legal **persons** in order to seize documents and data; (f) to **refer matters** for **criminal investigations**; (g) require existing recordings of telephone conversations, electronic communications or data traffic records; (h) to require existing data traffic records held by a telecommunications operator; (i) to **request** the **freezing** or sequestration of **assets**; (j) **suspend trading** of the financial instruments concerned; (k) to require the temporary cessation of any practice that the NCA considers contrary to the MAR; (l) to impose a **temporary prohibition** on the exercise of **professional activity**; and (m) to take all necessary measures to ensure that the public is correctly informed, inter alia, by correcting false or misleading disclosed information etc.[211]

99 Additionally, the MAR provides detailed rules for the NCAs on cooperation with ESMA[212] and with each other,[213] obliging NCAs render assistance to NCAs of other Member States, especially by exchanging information and cooperating in investigation activities. In addition, there is a worldwide exchange of information and mutual assistance in cross-border cases on the basis of a 'Multilateral Memorandum of Understanding Concerning Consultation and Cooperation and the Exchange of Information'.[214]

---

[206] Cf. BaFin, Annual Report 2019, p. 92, 95.
[207] The FCA is addressing this challenge through a Digital Evidence Unit, where a team of technologically savvy specialists examine computers, smartphones and other electronic devices of suspected offenders. Cf. E. Swan and J. Virgo, *Market Abuse Regulation*, para. 1.45.
[208] Cf. J. Austin, *Insider Trading and Market Manipulation*, 255.
[209] Cf. K. Ziehl, *Kapitalmarktprognosen und Insider-Trading*, 48 ff.
[210] Cf. Art. 23(3) MAR.
[211] Art. 23(2)(a)–(m) MAR.
[212] Cf. Art. 24 MAR.
[213] Art. 25 MAR.
[214] Cf. J. Austin, *Insider Trading and Market Manipulation*, 184 ff.

(a) Insider Lists

Under the MAD 2003, the Member States had to ensure that issuers, or persons acting on their behalf or for their account, draw up a list of those persons working for them, under a contract of employment or otherwise, who have access to inside information.[215] Though former Commission Directive 2004/72/EC put these requirements into more concrete terms, national differences in regard to data to be included in those lists imposed unnecessary administrative burdens on issuers.[216] In order to reduce costs, the MAR unifies data fields required for insider lists.

100

Article 18 MAR requires issuers or other persons acting on their behalf or on their account to draw up a list of all **persons** who have **access** to **inside information** and who are **working for them** under a contract of employment, or otherwise performing tasks through which they have access to inside information, such as advisers, accountants or credit rating agencies.[217] They must provide the insider list to the NCA as soon as possible upon its request. The insider list must include at least the identity of any person having access to inside information, the reason for including that person in the list, the date and time at which that person obtained access to inside information and the date on which the insider list was drawn up.

101

The extensive content of insider lists is explained against the background that insider lists are considered an important tool for NCAs when investigating possible market abuse.[218] Moreover, insider lists may serve issuers to control the flow of inside information and thereby help manage their confidentiality duties.[219]

102

Issuers and persons acting on their behalf or for their account must regularly update this list and transmit it to the competent authority whenever the latter requests it.[220] There is thus no obligation for an issuer to spontaneously provide its insider list to the competent authority or inform it of updates to the list if the competent authority has not requested it from the issuer.[221] The lists of insiders must be promptly updated whenever there is a change in the reason why any person is already on the list, whenever any new person has to be added to the list or if any person already on the list no longer has access to inside information.[222]

103

A central element of the supervision of insiders through the use of insider lists is the **duty to inform insiders** of their obligations: the persons required to draw up lists of insiders shall take reasonable steps to ensure 'that any person on the insider list acknowledges the legal and regulatory duties entailed and is aware of the sanctions applicable to insider dealing and unlawful disclosure of inside information'.[223] This provision aims to make the respective person aware of its behaviour regarding the dissemination of inside information.

104

---

[215] Art. 6(3) MAD.
[216] Cf. Recital 56 MAR.
[217] Cf. BaFin, Issuer Guideline, Module C, p. 88 f.
[218] Cf. Recital 56 MAR.
[219] Cf. Recital 57 MAR.
[220] Art. 18(1)(b) and (c) MAR.
[221] CESR/06-562b (fn. 114).
[222] Art. 18(4)(a)–(c) MAR.
[223] Cf. Art. 18(2) MAR.

105 According to the former CESR, the supervision of insider lists has proven very successful.[224] This has, however, not hindered ESMA to examine national supervisory practices regarding the handling of insider lists. ESMA's peer review came to the conclusion that four Member States had to be considered as not applying sufficient supervisory practices.[225] Meanwhile, ESMA has found the NCAs fully compliant with the requirements regarding insider lists.[226]

(b) Notification Obligations and Whistleblowing

106 Further central elements regarding the prevention and detection of market abuse are organisational requirements and notification obligations. **Market operators** and **investment firms** that **operate a trading venue** are required to establish and maintain effective arrangements, systems and procedures aimed at preventing and detecting insider dealing, market manipulation and attempted insider dealing and market manipulation. They must further report orders and transactions, including any cancellation or modification thereof, that could constitute insider dealing, market manipulation or attempted insider dealing or market manipulation to the competent authority of the trading venue without delay.[227]

107 The same obligations apply to '**any person professionally arranging or executing transactions**'.[228] They are required to establish and maintain effective arrangements, systems and procedures to detect and report suspicious orders and transactions. Where such a person has a reasonable suspicion that an order or transaction in any financial instrument, whether placed or executed on or outside a trading venue, could constitute insider dealing, market manipulation or attempted insider dealing or market manipulation, the person must notify the competent authority without delay.[229]

108 These notification obligations constitute a central aspect of the supervision of insiders, enabling the supervisory authorities to examine cases of market abuse and strengthen the market participants' understanding of the fact that market integrity is essential for the functioning of capital markets. The European Commission has therefore laid down detailed rules on the arrangements, systems and procedures for persons to comply with requirements under Article 16(1) and (2) MAR and the content of such a notification and on the procedure to be followed when notifying the national authorities.[230]

109 Any other persons than those professionally arranging or executing transactions are not obliged to inform NCAs about possible insider trading and market manipulations.

---

[224] Cf. CESR, Level 3—Third Set of CESR Guidance and Information on the Common Operation of the Directive to the Market, May 2009, CESR/09-219.

[225] Cf. ESMA, Supervisory Practices under MAD. Peer Review and Good Practices, 1 July 2013, ESMA/2013/805, para. 14.

[226] Cf. ESMA, Peer Review on Supervisory Practices against Market Abuse. Follow-up Report, 22 December 2015, ESMA/2015/1905, p. 4.

[227] Cf. Art. 16(1) MAR.

[228] This category is defined in Art. 3(1)(28) MAR. See also ESMA, Question and Answers on the Market Abuse Regulation, 20 May 2016, ESMA/2016/738 Section 1 (regarding the definition of 'person professionally arranging or executing transactions').

[229] Cf. Art. 16(2) MAR.

[230] Cf. Commission Delegated Regulation (EU) No. 2016/957 of 9 March 2016 supplementing Regulation (EU) No. 596/2014 of the European Parliament and of the Council with regard to regulatory technical standards for the appropriate arrangements, systems and procedures as well as notification templates to be used for preventing, detecting and reporting abusive practices or suspicious orders or transactions, OJ L 160, 17 June 2016, p. 1–14.

Whistleblowers may, however, bring new information to the attention of competent authorities which assists them in detecting and imposing sanctions in cases of insider dealing and market manipulation.[231] The European legislature therefore considered measures regarding whistleblowing necessary to facilitate detection of market abuse and to ensure the protection and the respect of the rights of the whistleblower and the accused person.[232] The most important question, however, is subject to national legislation: Member States are free with regard to the question whether they provide for financial incentives to persons who offer relevant new information about potential infringements that results in the imposition of an administrative or criminal sanction.[233]

2. Supervisory Convergence

Little is known about the way in which the NCAs supervise the securities markets. The peer reviews published by ESMA,[234] however, show that the approaches vary considerably throughout Europe. This relates primarily to the question whether procedures are examined on a regular or a risk-based basis. The annual reports further show that some supervisory authorities, such as BaFin, follow empirically proven typical patterns of insider trading.[235] The exchange of information between NCAs plays a very important role.

VII. Sanctions

1. Overview

The MAD 2003 contained no provisions on possible sanctions for breaches of the prohibitions. The Member States could therefore decide individually whether they wished to impose criminal sanctions.[236] They had, however, to ensure that 'in conformity with their national law, the appropriate administrative measures can be taken or administrative sanctions be imposed'.[237] The details were once again left to the national legislatures: 'The Member States shall ensure that these measures are effective, proportionate and dissuasive.'[238] This demand, also to be found in the other framework directives enacted 2003 and 2004,[239] was to ensure that the European legal framework against market abuse was sufficient.[240]

---

[231] Cf. Recital 74 MAR.
[232] Cf. Recital 74 and Art. 32 MAR.
[233] Cf. Art. 32(4) MAR. Cf. on the US regulatory model T. Pfeifle, *Finanzielle Anreize für Whistleblower im Kapitalmarktrecht*.
[234] ESMA/2013/805 (fn. 225).
[235] Cf. K. Ziehl, *Kapitalmarktprognosen und Insider-Trading*, 48 ff.
[236] Cf. Art. 14(1) MAD: 'Without prejudice to the right of Member States to impose criminal sanctions [...]'.
[237] Art. 14(1) MAD.
[238] Art. 14(1) MAD.
[239] See R. Veil § 1 para. 21 ff.
[240] Recital 38 MAD.

112 The Market abuse regime under the MAR aims to achieve **further harmonisation** and requires **stricter sanctions** for infringements of the prohibitions laid down in Article 14 MAR. The possible sanctions are also described in detail and range from 'temporary prohibition of an activity' to 'administrative pecuniary sanctions' and 'suspend trading of the financial instrument'. The supervisory authorities are further required to make public any measures and sanctions unless such publication would seriously jeopardise the stability of the financial markets. The MAR then continues by listing the circumstances which the supervisory authority must take into account when determining the type of administrative measures and sanctions to be applied.[241] These requirements were introduced due to the insight that the national authorities made very different use of their sanctioning powers in the past.

2. Administrative Measures and Pecuniary Sanctions

113 The national supervisory authorities must be empowered to **impose fines** of at least **three times** the amount of **profits** obtained or **losses avoided** because of the infringement.[242] This can become relevant in particular in cases of prohibited insider trading. Pecuniary sanctions constitute the core of all administrative sanctions. The MAR provides for a nominal minimum rate of the maximum fine of **€ 5 million** for natural persons in case of breaches of the prohibitions on insider trading. With regard to legal persons, administrative pecuniary sanctions of up to **15%** of the **total annual turnover** in the preceding business year are possible.[243] In its report on sanctioning practices in the Member States for 2019, ESMA states that almost all NCAs did not impose administrative sanctions for a breach of MAR insider trading prohibitions.[244]

114 Competent supervisory authorities shall publish any decision to impose an administrative sanction or administrative measure in relation to a breach of MAR on their website without undue delay. At a minimum, the nature and character of the breach and the identity of the persons responsible shall be disclosed.[245] If disclosure would be disproportionate, or jeopardise ongoing investigations or the stability of financial markets, the NCA will defer publication, make it anonymous or refrain from it altogether.[246]

115 Naming and shaming has a repressive and general preventive effect, because the publication of violations makes it clear to market participants that violations will be sanctioned. Thus, the public announcement can be qualified as an administrative sanction.[247]

---

[241] Cf. Art. 32(1) MAR.
[242] See in more detail R. Veil § 12 para. 18–20.
[243] Cf. Art. 30(2)(j) subsec. 2 MAR; see in more detail R. Veil § 12 para. 20.
[244] Cf. ESMA, Annual Report on administrative and criminal sanctions and other administrative measures under MAR, ESMA70-156-2005, 12 December 2019. An exception is Belgium, where the supervisory authority imposed administrative sanctions in 7 cases.
[245] Art. 34(1) MAR.
[246] Art. 34(2) MAR.
[247] Cf. P. Koch, *Naming and shaming im Kapitalmarktrecht*, 140 ff.

3. Criminal Sanctions

According to the CRIM-MAD, the Member States are also required to introduce criminal sanctions for the most serious market abuse offences. They only have to sanction intentional offences.[248] Furthermore, Member States are obliged to ensure that legal persons can be held liable.[249] They are, however, not obliged to provide criminal sanctions. It follows from recital 18 CRIM-MAD, that 'non-criminal sanctions or other measures which are effective, proportionate and dissuasive, for example those provided for in' the MAR are sufficient.

4. Investor Protection through Civil Liability

The MAR contains no provisions requiring the introduction of a civil liability, leaving this to the choice of the Member States. In many Member States, such as France, Germany, Spain and Sweden, no specific provisions exist granting investors the right to claim damages from insiders. Such claims are therefore subject to the general civil law provisions. French courts see the possibility of an investor's damages being compensated in cases of insider dealings. In *Sidel*, shareholders claimed compensation in criminal proceedings which both the Tribunal correctionnel and the Cour d'appel awarded on the merits, based on Articles 1382 and 1384 Code civil (Cc, French Civil Code). However, the proof of actual damage was not possible, the insider dealing only affecting 30,000 shares, whilst during the relevant period a total of more than 3 million shares were being traded. The courts therefore concluded that the information was not price sensitive.[250]

VIII. Conclusion

Insider trading law has evolved in Europe over three decades. The unification of the law in 2014 was an important step to prevent harmful regulatory arbitrage. Moreover, legal unification helps to reduce transaction costs for investors and issuers. Nevertheless, the MAR is far from a comprehensive codification. This is mainly due to the fact that the legislator essentially limited itself to adopting the regulations of the MAD 2003, which aim at a minimum harmonisation, and the case law of the ECJ. The regimes are designed in a non-systematic way, so that regulatory gaps occur. Questions of interpretation are difficult to assess.

Another point of criticism concerns the notion of inside information. With the concept of intermediate steps as inside information, first the ECJ and then the European legislator have gone beyond the limits of what is justifiable. This concept raises numerous questions

---

[248] Cf. Art. 3(1), 4(1) and 6(1) CRIM-MAD.
[249] Cf. Art. 8 CRIM-MAD.
[250] T. corr. Paris, 11e ch., 1re sect., of 12 September 2006, no. 0018992026; CA Paris, 9e ch., sect. B, of 17 October 2008, no. 06/09036.

of interpretation that it can hardly be handled with legal certainty. The attempts of national supervisory authorities to provide more legal certainty through case groups are laudable. However, the guidelines are legally non-binding interpretations. In the absence of a uniform Europe-wide understanding of the concept of the reasonable investor, central legal questions are answered differently by supervisory authorities and courts. This problem arises with the insider trading prohibitions, but also with the ad hoc disclosure obligation under Article 17 MAR.

120 A central goal of the 2014 reform was to improve the sanctions regime. The stricter administrative sanctions should have a deterrent effect. However, it is still too early to assess this reliably, as only a few cases reach the courts. The probability of detection remains low. There is therefore a need to improve access to information by the supervisory authorities through a functioning whistleblower system. The supervisory authorities must also keep pace with new technologies.

§ 15

Market Manipulation

Bibliography

af Sandeberg, Catarina, *Marknadsmissbruk—insiderbrott och kursmanipulation?*, Ny Juridik (2002), 7–20; af Sandeberg, Catarina, *Strikt ansvar vid insiderbrott—administrativa- sanktioner för effektivare brottsbekämpning*, JT (2002–2003), 869–884; Aggarwal, Rajesh K. and Wu, Guijon, *Stock Market Manipulations*, 79 J. Bus. (2006), 1915–1953; Allen, Franklin and Gale, Douglas, *Stock Price Manipulation*, 5 Rev. Fin. Studies (1992), 503–529; Assmann, Heinz-Dieter et al. (eds.) *Kommentar zum Wertpapierhandelsrecht*, 7th edn. (2019); Avgouelas, Emilios, *The Mechanics and Regulation of Market Abuse* (2005); Barber, Brad M. and Odean, Terrance, *All that Glitters: The Effect of Attention and News on the Buying Behavior of Individual and Institutional Investors*, 21 Rev. Fin. Studies (2008), 785–818; Barber, Brad M. and Odean, Terrance, *Trading Is Hazardous to Your Wealth: The Common Investment Performance of Individual Investors*, 55 J. Fin. (2000), 773–806; Brammsen, Joerg, *Marktmanipulation (§ 38 Abs. 2 WpHG) 'über die Bande'—Das perfekte 'Delikt'?*, 66 WM (2012), 2134–2143; Chen, Qi and Jiang, Wei, *Analysts' Weighting of Public and Private Information*, 19 Rev. Fin. Studies (2006), 319–355; Deshmukh, Sanjay et al., *CEO Overconfidence and Dividend Policy*, 22 Journal of Financial Intermediation (2013), 440–463; Eichelberger, Jan, *Das Verbot der Marktmanipulation* (2006); Faure, Michael G. and Leger, Claire, *The Directive on Criminal Sanctions for Market Abuse: A Move Towards Harmonizing Inside Trading Criminal Law at the EU-Level*, 9 Brook. J. Corp., Fin. & Comm. Law (2015), 387–427; Fischel, Daniel R. and Ross, David J., *Should the Law Prohibit Manipulation in Financial Markets?*, 105 Harv. L. Rev. (1991), 503–553; Fleischer, Holger, *Stock Spams—Anlegerschutz und Marktmanipulation*, 20 ZBB (2008), 137–147; Fleischer, Holger and Bueren, Eckart, *Cornering zwischen Kapitalmarkt und Kartellrecht*, 34 ZIP (2013), 1253–1264; Friesen, Geoffrey C. and Weller, Paul A., *Quantifying Cognitive Biases in Analysts Earnings Forecasts*, 9 Journal of Financial Markets (2006), 333–365; Grüger, Tobias W., *Kurspflegemaßnahmen durch Banken—Zulässige Marktpraxis oder Verstoß gegen das Verbot der Marktmanipulation nach § 20a WpHG?*, 7 BKR (2007), 437–447; Hellgardt, Alexander, *Europarechtliche Vorgaben für die Kapitalmarktinformationshaftung de lege lata und nach Inkrafttreten der Marktmissbrauchsverordnung*, 57 AG (2012), 154–168; Herlin-Karnell, Ester and Ryder, Nicholas, *Market Manipulation and Insider Trading. Regulatory Challenges in the United States of America, the European Union and the United Kingdom* (2019); Huang, Jim Y. et al., *Starting points for a new researcher in behavioral finance*, 12 International Journal of Managerial Finance (2016), 92–103; Jacobson, Hans and Lycke, Johan, *Marknadsmissbruksdirektivet och dess genomförande i Sverige*, ERT (2005), 303–320; Kahneman, Daniel and Tversky, Amos, *Prospect Theory: An Analysis of Decision under Risk*, 47 Econometrica (1979), 263–291; Kalss, Susanne et al., *Kapitalmarktrecht I*, 2nd edn. (2015); Klöhn, Lars, *Kapitalmarkt, Spekulation und Behavioral Finance* (2006); Klöhn, Lars, *Marktmanipulation auch bei kurzfristiger Kursbeeinflussung—Das 'IMC Securities'-Urteil des EuGH*, 14 NZG (2011), 934–936; Langevoort, Donald C., *Taming the Animal Spirits of the Stock Market— A Behavioral Approach to Securities Regulation*, 97 Nw. U. L. Rev. (2002), 135–188; Malmendier, Ulrike and Tate, Geoffrey A., *Who Makes Acquisitions? CEO Overconfidence and the Market's Reaction*, 89 Journal of Financial Economics (2008), 20–43; Marsch-Barner, Reinhard and Schäfer,

Frank A., *Handbuch börsennotierte AG*, 4th edn. (2017); Meyer, Andreas et al. (eds.), *Handbuch Marktmissbrauchsrecht* (2018); Moloney, Niamh et al. (eds.), *The Oxford Handbook of Financial Regulation* (2015); Moloney, Niamh, *EU Securities and Financial Markets Regulation*, 3rd edn. (2016); Nietsch, Michael, *Kapitalmarkttransparenz und Marktmanipulation*, 74 WM (2020), 717–726; Rückert, Christian, *Marktmanipulation durch Unterlassen und Bestimmtheitsprinzip*, 40 NStZ (2020), 391–397; Sajnovits, Alexander, *Marktmanipulation durch Unterlassen? Untersuchung der Rechtslage nach MAR und FiMaNoG sowie deren Konsequenz für Alt-Taten*, 71 WM (2017), 1189–1199; Samuelsson, Per, *Nya regler om marknadsmissbruk*, JT (2004–2005), 256–268; de Schmidt, Sebastian, *Neufassung des Verbots der Marktmanipulation durch MAR und CRIM-MAD*, 6 RdF (2016), 4–12; Schultheiß, Tilman, *Die Neuerungen im Hochfrequenzhandel*, 67 WM (2013), 596–602; Stotz, Olaf and von Nitzsch, Rüdiger, *Warum sich Analysten überschätzen—Einfluss des Kontrollgefühls auf die Selbstüberschätzung*, 15 ZBB (2003), 106–113; Swan, Edward J. and Virgo, John, *Market Abuse Regulation*, 3rd edn. (2019); Teigelack, Lars, *Finanzanalysen und Behavioral Finance* (2009); Teigelack, Lars, *Insiderhandel und Marktmanipulation im Kommissionsentwurf einer Marktmissbrauchsverordnung*, 39 BB (2012), 1361–1365; Tountopoulos, Vassilios, *Market Abuse and Private Enforcement*, 11 ECFR (2014), 297–332; Tountopoulos, Vassilios, *Rückkaufprogramme und Safe-Harbor-Regelungen im Europäischen Kapitalmarktrecht*, 22 EWS (2012), 449–456; Tversky, Amos and Kahneman, Daniel, *Rational Choice and the Framing of Decisions*, 59 J. Bus. (1986), 251–278; Veil, Rüdiger, *Der Schutz des verständigen Anlegers durch Publizität und Haftung im europäischen Kapitalmarktrecht*, 18 ZBB (2006), 162–171; Veil, Rüdiger, *Sanktionsrisiken für Emittenten und Geschäftsleiter im Kapitalmarktrecht*, 45 ZGR (2016), 305–328; Ventoruzzo, Marco, *Do Market Abuse Rules Violate Human Rights? The Grande Stevens v. Italy Case*, 16 EBOR (2015), 145–165; Wiedemann, Herbert and Wank, Rolf, *Begrenzte Rationalität—gestörte Willensbildung im Privatrecht*, 68 JZ (2013), 340–345; Wesser, Erik, *Har du varit ute och shoppat, Jacob?—En studie av Finansinspektionens utredning av insiderbrott under 1990-talet* (2001).

I. Introduction

1 The aim of every market manipulation is to steer the present market price towards positive results for the manipulator, ie increasing the price before sales and lowering it before acquisitions. Prices can be influenced by information-based as well as transaction-based manipulations.[1] Manipulations most commonly occur on illiquid markets with only little regulation; these markets have the least stringent transparency rules and therefore the largest informational asymmetries between the manipulators and other market participants. In these cases, manipulators can exert particular influence on the amount of information available to the public regarding a certain financial instrument. Additionally, each individual order is potentially more likely to cause price movements on relatively illiquid markets.[2] This can particularly effect emerging markets, which do not yet have sufficient liquidity and efficiency.[3] Within the European Union, market segments below the threshold of regulated markets, eg the *Freiverkehr* (open market) in Germany or the *Alternative*

---

[1] R. Aggarwal and G. Wu, 79. J. Bus. (2006), 1915.
[2] R. Aggarwal and G. Wu, 79. J. Bus. (2006), 1915, 1917.
[3] R. Aggarwal and G. Wu, 79. J. Bus. (2006), 1915, 1918, quoted studies referring to China and Pakistan.

Investment Market (AIM) in the United Kingdom, remain most likely to be subject to manipulation.

Manipulated prices impair the proper **functioning of the market** and must therefore be prohibited.[4] Investors could lose confidence in a manipulated market and eventually exit the market, a move which would adversely affect the market mechanism. The United States, therefore, introduced comprehensive prohibitions on market manipulation as early as the 1930s. In Europe, a community-wide approach was only adopted in 2003. The former MAD 2003 was intended to ensure a uniform framework throughout the Community,[5] because some Member States had not prohibited such manipulations. The directive's rules for the Member States thus aimed to protect the reliability and accuracy of price formation.

2

The **MAR 2014 regime**,[6] consisting of a Regulation (**MAR**) and a Directive (**CRIM-MAD**), maintains the regulatory approach of the MAD 2003 to **prohibit** both **information-based** and **transaction-based manipulation**. The new rules fill gaps in relation to new trading platforms and OTC instruments, ie instruments traded over the counter, as well as benchmarks, and create a single regulatory framework to avoid regulatory arbitrage. CRIM-MAD also aims at providing greater deterrence and preventing misconduct through stricter sanctions. The objectives have remained unaltered.[7] Investors must be able to rely on a price that has evolved through supply and demand and not through manipulation.

3

II. Foundations

1. Regulatory System

A person shall not engage in or attempt to engage in market manipulation.[8] The concept of market manipulation is specified in Article 12 MAR. This provision provides **four definitions** of **market manipulation**[9] and also offers **five** practically relevant **examples** of these core definitions.[10] The fourth core definition (benchmark manipulation) is new and was introduced in reaction to the LIBOR scandal (cf. Recital 44 MAR). However, the MAR exempts certain activities from the ban on market manipulation. These include the trading in own shares in 'buy-back' programmes and the stabilisation of a financial instrument, provided such trading is carried out in accordance with certain requirements.[11] Secondly, the prohibition does not apply to activities if the person has legitimate reasons

4

---

[4] Recitals 2, 7 and 47 MAR; cf. H. McVea, in: Moloney et al. (eds.), *The Oxford Handbook of Financial Regulation*, 638; recital 14 of the MAD 2003 aimed to prevent terrorism financing but recitals of the MAR do not mention this purpose anymore.
[5] Recitals 11, 12 MAD 2003; cf. also Communication from the Commission on implementing the Financial Services Action Plan, 11 May 1999, COM(1999) 232 final.
[6] See R. Veil § 1 para. 42 und R. Veil § 13 para. 2.
[7] Recital 3 MAR.
[8] Art. 15 MAR.
[9] Art. 12(1)(a)–(d) MAR.
[10] Art. 12(2)(a)–(d) MAR.
[11] Art. 5 MAR.

and the transaction, order or activity is in accordance with accepted market practice.[12] The MAR additionally contains organisational requirements necessary for detecting market manipulation. Market operators and investment firms that operate a trading venue are required to 'establish and maintain effective arrangements, systems and procedures aimed at preventing and detecting insider dealing, market manipulation and attempted insider dealing and market manipulation'.[13] It also establishes a reporting obligation for securities transactions to enable national supervisors to better monitor compliance with the prohibitions.[14]

5   The broadly phrased prohibitions and exemptions were implemented under the former MAD 2003 regime through three Implementing Directives. These have been repealed by Commission Delegated Regulation (EU) No. 2016/908[15] on accepted market practices and Commission Delegated Regulation (EU) No. 2016/1052[16] on buy-back programmes and stabilisation measures. Annex I of the MAR also provides a list of indicators of prohibited practices.[17]

6   The former CESR had published guidelines that set out its views on the requirements for determining acceptable market practices[18] and explained various manipulative activities and the application of the safe harbour rules.[19] ESMA has not yet issued guidelines on the application of the prohibition of market manipulation. However, it has already issued several opinions on accepted market practices.[20] In addition, some national supervisory authorities (NCAs) have published guidance documents and circulars setting out their administrative practices to prohibit market manipulation.[21]

2. **Direct Effect in the Member States**

7   The direct effect of the MAR in all Member States makes most national substantive law obsolete. With the exception of the sanctioning regime, all prohibitions on market manipulation are now European law. Member States only need to pass or amend legislation with regard to the MAR's provisions on administrative sanctions and the CRIM-MAD's provisions on criminal sanctions.

---

[12] Art. 13 MAR.
[13] Art. 16(1) MAR.
[14] Art. 4 MAR.
[15] Commission Delegated Regulation (EU) No. 2016/908 supplementing Regulation (EU) No. 596/2014 of the European Parliament and of the Council laying down regulatory technical standards on the criteria, the procedure and the requirements for establishing an accepted market practice and the requirements for maintaining it, terminating it or modifying the conditions for its acceptance, OJ L153, 10 June 2016, p. 3–12.
[16] Commission Delegated Regulation (EU) No. 2016/1052 supplementing Regulation (EU) No. 596/2014 of the European Parliament and of the Council with regard to regulatory technical standards for the conditions applicable to buy-back programmes and stabilisation measures, OJ L173, 30 June 2016, p. 34–41.
[17] Art. 12(3) MAR.
[18] CESR, Level 3 – First Set of CESR Guidance and Information on the Common Operation of the Directive to the Market, CESR/04-505b, Oktober 2008.
[19] CESR, Level 3 – Third Set of CESR Guidance and Information on the Common Operation of the Directive to the Market, CESR/09-219, May 2009.
[20] Legal basis for such opinions is Art. 13(4) MAR. The opinions are available at ESMA's website.
[21] Cf. BaFin, Emittentenleitfaden (issuer guideline), Module C, Chapter Market Manipulation.

III. Scope of Application of the MAR

1. Personal Scope

The prohibition of market manipulation **generally applies to all market participants**, regardless of whether they are natural or legal persons.[22] If a member of a company issues a false press release, he or she may be the perpetrator, but also the board member who signed the press release. Where information is prepared, however, for the purpose of **journalism** or other form of expression in the media, the 'disclosure or dissemination of information shall be assessed taking into account the rules governing the freedom of the press and freedom of expression in other media and the rules or codes governing the journalist profession, unless those persons [...] derive, directly or indirectly, an advantage or profits from the disclosure dissemination of the information in question or the disclosure or the dissemination is made with the intention of misleading the market [...]'.[23]

2. Material Scope

The **MAR considerably extends** the material scope of the rules on market manipulation compared to the former MAD 2003. The scope is **no longer limited to financial instruments** traded on **regulated markets**.[24] The MAR also applies to financial instruments traded on **MTFs**, admitted to trading on an MTF or for which a request for admission to trading on an MTF has been made[25] and to financial instruments traded on an **OTF**.[26] Financial instruments include in particular shares, bonds and derivatives.[27]

The MAR also applies to any related financial instruments traded **OTC**, which depend on or can have an effect on the covered underlying market (eg credit default swaps [CDSs]).[28] The reasoning behind this extension is to avoid regulatory arbitrage among trading venues and to ensure investor protection throughout the European Union.[29] The prohibition of market manipulation in the MAR also covers the interlinkages between spot commodity markets and related financial markets, ie manipulative strategies which use financial instruments to influence spot commodity contracts and vice versa.[30] In this context, the regulation excludes monetary and public debt management as well as climate policy activities from its scope.[31] Emission allowances are classified as financial instruments, thus subjecting financial instruments relating to wholesale energy products to the provisions on market abuse.[32] The MAR

---

[22] Cf. Art. 12(4) MAR.
[23] Art. 21 MAR.
[24] Art. 2(1)(a) MAR; cf. H. McVea, in: Moloney et al. (eds.), *The Oxford Handbook of Financial Regulation*, 646.
[25] Art. 2(1)(b) MAR.
[26] Art. 2(1)(c) MAR.
[27] See R. Veil § 8 para. 2 ff.
[28] Recital 10 and Art. 2(1)(d) MAR.
[29] Recital 8 MAR.
[30] Recital 20 and Art. 2(2)(a)–(c) Commission Proposal for a Regulation of the European Parliament and of the Council on insider dealing and market manipulation (market abuse), 20 October 2011, COM 2011(651) final.
[31] Art. 6 MAR.
[32] Recital 15 and Art. 3(1)(2) MAR refer to Art. 4(1)(15) and Annex I Section C (11) of Directive 2014/65/EU.

further covers emission allowances that are auctioned on an auction platform pursuant to Regulation (EU) No. 1031/2010, even when auctioned products are not financial instruments. This ensures that the MAR constitutes a single rule book of market abuse measures for the entirety of primary and secondary markets in emission allowances.[33]

11 The market manipulation prohibitions also apply if the activity takes place outside the EU (**extraterritoriality**).[34] This applies irrespective of whether a similar prohibition exists in the third country.

IV. Prohibitions

1. Regulatory System

12 Market manipulation prevents the market from being fully and properly transparent. The European legislature is of the opinion that full and proper market transparency is a prerequisite for all economic actors to be able to participate in integrated financial markets.[35] The MAR and CRIM-MAD distinguish transaction-based and information-based manipulations as well as benchmark manipulations.[36]

13 *Transaction-based* manipulations[37] are based on the possibility of giving false or misleading signals as to the supply of, demand for or price of financial instruments through an actual order or transaction. *Information-based* manipulation requires the dissemination of false or misleading information.[38] The third type is a combination of both types of manipulation, which must be assumed if transactions or orders to trade employ fictitious devices or any other form of deception or contrivance.[39] Annex I to the MAR specifies the requirements of both (i) transaction-based manipulations and (ii) manipulations through fictitious devices by establishing non-exhaustive *indicators* that shall be taken into account when investigating manipulative behaviour.[40] However, these indicators do not allow the automatic conclusion that the behaviour in question constitutes market manipulation. *Benchmark manipulations*, a subset of information-based manipulations, occur when a person transmits false or misleading information or input to a benchmark and that person knows or ought to have known about that the information or input was false. The most prominent benchmarks are interest rate benchmarks such as LIBOR and EURIBOR, that determine interest payments under a very large number of financial instruments.[41]

---

[33] Recital 37 and Art. 2(1)(2) MAR.
[34] Cf. Art. 2(4) MAR and R. Veil § 13 para. 19.
[35] Cf. Recital 7 MAR.
[36] The distinction between 'trade-based' and 'information-based' was established by F. Allen and D. Gale, 5 Rev. Fin. Stud. (1992), 503.
[37] Art. 12(1)(a) MAR.
[38] Art. 12(1)(c) MAR.
[39] Art. 12(1)(b) MAR.
[40] Art. 12(3) MAR; Annex I is identical to the former Art. 4 and 5 of repealed Directive 2003/ 124/EC.
[41] Art. 12(1)(d) MAR.

The MAR further provides **specific types** of manipulative behaviour, which it derives from the core definitions.[42] These types are also non-exhaustive. Article 12(2)(c) MAR now specifically mentions algorithmic and high-frequency trading. Even if none of these provisions apply, the respective behaviour can still be considered manipulative if such behaviour meets the conditions set out in Article 12(1)(a), (b), (c) or (d) MAR.[43] If one of the instances does, however, apply, the respective behaviour definitely constitutes market manipulation; hence, the instances are not merely indicators within the meaning of Annex I MAR.

14

The MAR thus generally maintains the former MAD 2003 approach, but also prohibits attempted market manipulation; examples of attempted manipulations include all cases where 'the activity is started but is not completed, for example as a result of failed technology or an instruction to trade which is not acted upon.'[44] In prohibiting attempted market manipulation, the MAR considerably broadens the scope of the prohibition. The European legislator found this necessary to enable the supervisory authorities to impose sanctions for attempted manipulations.[45] This conclusion seems somewhat circular and the European legislator does not point to any empirical evidence that would render it necessary to prohibit attempted manipulations. One can safely predict an in-depth discussion and extensive case law on the threshold between 'regular', ie allowed, behaviour and 'prohibited' behaviour, ie attempts to manipulate. Often, inner circumstances, such as a person's intentions, will play a role in determining the exact contours of the prohibition. A more factual question is whether supervisory authorities will be able to reliably detect attempted manipulations and enforce the prohibition.

15

Manipulations are further no longer limited to transactions or orders to trade but also **include any other behaviour**.[46] The European legislature refers to 'behaviour which occurs outside of a trading venue'[47] but provides no specific examples. The MAR includes 'other behaviour' in an attempt to cover as many forms of manipulations as possible. This approach comes at a price—legal certainty for market participants suffers from the broader wording. This is even more important when criminal sanctions are at stake. Constitutional laws of some Member States require that behaviours leading to criminal sanctions are specifically outlined by the law before the act is committed.

16

2. Information-based Market Manipulation

The European legislature considers information-based market manipulation to be particularly dangerous for investors and the proper functioning of markets. It has made this impressively clear in Recital 47:

17

'The spreading of **false** or **misleading information** can have **a significant impact** on the **prices** of financial instruments in a relatively short period of time. It may consist in the

18

---

[42] Art. 12(2) MAR.
[43] Recital 38 of the MAR explicitly opens the MAR to 'new' forms of manipulation as they may arise in the future.
[44] Recital 41 and Art. 15 MAR.
[45] Recital 41 MAR.
[46] Art. 2(3) MAR.
[47] Recital 46 MAR.

invention of manifestly false information, but also the wilful omission of material facts, as well as the knowingly inaccurate reporting of information. That form of market manipulation is **particularly harmful to investors**, because it causes them to base their investment decisions on incorrect or distorted information. It is also harmful to issuers, because it reduces the trust in the available information related to them. A lack of market trust can in turn jeopardise an issuer's ability to issue new financial instruments or to secure credit from other market participants in order to finance its operations. Information spreads through the market place very quickly. As a result, the harm to investors and issuers may persist for a relatively long time until the information is found to be false or misleading, and can be corrected by the issuer or those responsible for its dissemination. It is therefore necessary to qualify the spreading of false or misleading information, including rumours and false or misleading news, as being an infringement of this Regulation.'

(a) Dogmatics

19   Information-based manipulation is the **dissemination** of '**information** through the **media**, including the Internet, or by any other means, which

— **gives**, or is likely to give, **false** or **misleading signals** as to the **supply** of, **demand** for, or **price**', or
— 'secures, or is likely to secure, the price at an abnormal or artificial level'

of **a financial instrument**, a related spot commodity contract or an auctioned product based on emission allowances. This includes the dissemination of rumours, where the person who made the dissemination knew, or ought to have known, that the information was false or misleading'.[48]

20   There are therefore two prerequisites for market manipulation: (i) the dissemination of false or misleading information, which (ii) gives false or misleading signals as to supply, demand or price of a financial instrument. The ECJ has not yet commented on these concepts. In the absence of coordinating guidelines from ESMA, it is quite conceivable that there are different interpretations in Europe, as national supervisory authorities and courts are likely to rely on the findings of the old market abuse law.

21   With regard to the first requirement, it should be noted that information does not only include facts, forecasts and prognosis, but also rumours. Where, how and to whom information is given is irrelevant for the application of the prohibition. In particular, it is not necessary for the information to be announced to a large audience, for example in a daily newspaper or in social media. The information can be disseminated via traditional communication channels and the Internet, but also in anonymous blogs, by email, etc. Information is incorrect if it does not correspond to the actual facts (because it is untrue or incomplete). Misleading information is correct in terms of content, but its presentation gives the recipient of the information a false idea of the facts described. Information-based manipulation may, among other ways, be achieved by publishing incorrect balance sheets, incorrect ad hoc notifications about inside information, incorrect notices about major shareholdings, or by incorrect statements in the media, eg during press conferences dealing with a company's financial statements or in internet chat rooms.

---

[48] Art. 12(1)(c) MAR.

The MAR requires that the **information** be **disseminated**. It is doubtful whether this can be done 22
by omission. This question arises for all disclosure obligations under capital markets law. Where an
investor is obliged to make a notification of changes in voting rights and fails to make such a notification, the failure to do so could also constitute market manipulation. The same applies to an issuer
who fails to disclose an inside information immediately. In implementing the MAD 2003, national
laws of Member States provided that market manipulation can also occur if someone withholds
information contrary to existing legal obligations. The MAR does not explicitly provide for such
an offence. However, some interpret the MAR in such a way that even an omission can constitute
a market manipulation.[49] The interpretation is based on the argument that under Article 2(4) the
MAR also applies to omissions. However, this provision only describes the territorial scope of the
MAR.[50] It is also argued that a criminal liability arises from the national criminal codes. However,
these rules cannot be applied because of the maximum harmonising character of the MAR. It is
therefore no longer possible to commit market manipulation by concealing information contrary
to existing legal obligations.[51] The European legislator should extend the ban on information-based
market manipulation accordingly in the course of the MAR review.

Significant problems of interpretation arise from the requirement that the information must be 23
relevant. In insider trading law, this is defined by the criterion of price relevance: information must
be likely to significantly influence the price of the financial instrument. In the case of information-
based market manipulation, on the other hand, it is stated that the information 'gives false or misleading signals as to the supply or price of a financial instrument or the demand for it'. It is even
sufficient if 'this is likely'. Finally, it suffices that the information 'will lead to an abnormal or artificial price level of a financial instrument' or that 'this is likely'. First it can be noted, that price
relevant information is subject to the information-based prohibition of market manipulation.[52] It
is sufficient, however, that the information is likely to give false or misleading signals about supply,
demand or price. A probability of more than 50% is generally sufficient—the suitability of the signal effect must be assessed from the perspective of a reasonable investor.[53] A price level is artificial
if it does not reflect the true economic circumstances or the market price.[54] Legal doctrine develops
groups of cases in which it can be assumed that they regularly give a signal with a suitability to
influence the price.[55] These include (i) significant cooperations, (ii) liquidity problems and indebtedness, (iii) significant inventions, (iv) important litigation, (v) changes in key personnel positions
and (vi) strategic corporate decisions.

BaFin determines false or misleading signals by an objective ex-post evaluation. A signal effect is to 24
be affirmed if a reasonable market participant would (probably) take the information into account
when making an investment decision because the information (probably) influences supply and
demand. It is irrelevant in which direction the supply and demand could be influenced, ie whether
the information was suitable to move the price up or down or to keep it.

---

[49] Cf. Begr. RegE, BT-Drucks. 18/7482, 64 (explanatory notes); H. Brinckmann, in: Meyer et al. (eds.), *Handbuch Marktmissbrauchsrecht*, § 15 para. 36; S. de Schmidt, 6 RdF (2016), 4, 5.
[50] See para. 11.
[51] Cf. P. Mülbert, in: Assmann et al. (eds.) *Kommentar zum Wertpapierhandelsrecht*, Art. 12 MAR para. 58, 180; M. Nietsch, 74 WM (2020), 717 ff.; A. Sajnovits, 71 WM (2017), 1189, 1193 ff.; L. Teigelack, in: Meyer et al. (eds.), *Handbuch Marktmissbrauchsrecht*, § 13 para. 28 ff.
[52] Cf. L. Teigelack, in: Meyer et al., (eds.) *Handbuch Marktmissbrauchsrecht*, § 13 para. 43.
[53] Cf. P. Mülbert, in: Assmann et al. (eds.), *Kommentar zum Wertpapierhandelsrecht*, Art. 12 MAR para. 187; L. Teigelack, in: Meyer et al. (eds.), *Handbuch Marktmissbrauchsrecht*, § 13 para. 46.
[54] Cf. P. Mülbert, in: Assmann et al., (eds.) *Kommentar zum Wertpapierhandelsrecht*, Art. 12 MAR para. 187.
[55] Cf. P. Mülbert, in: Assmann et al. (eds.), *Kommentar zum Wertpapierhandelsrecht*, Art. 12 MAR para. 192 ff.

(b) Legal Practice

25 The prohibition of information-based market manipulation is particularly important for issuers. It applies not only when issuers are legally obliged to provide information, but also becomes relevant in the case of voluntary reporting by issuers or by investors.

26 *Example*: In Germany the 'Porsche case' made headlines with the accusation of information-based market manipulation. **Porsche Automobil Holding SE** was accused of intentionally hiding its intent to take over Volkswagen AG (VW).[56] In September 2005 Porsche, which then held 20% of VW's shares, publicly denied any intention of taking over VW. In the following months, Porsche increased its stake in VW, resulting in a holding of more than 30% of the shares by March 2007. Porsche submitted a mandatory takeover offer pursuant to the WpÜG (German Takeover Act) and its supervisory board permitted the acquisition of a majority shareholding in March 2008. In a press release published a week later, Porsche publicly denied any intention of extending its shareholding to a total of 75%. In October 2008 Porsche's CEO announced the plan to acquire further shares to reach a total of 75% and thus cross the threshold needed to enter into a domination and profit/loss transfer agreement.[57] In November 2009 a letter by Porsche's General Counsel was published, stating that Porsche had already 'run through' the possibility of a complete takeover of VW during the first acquisition of VW shares in 2005. Several hedge funds filed claims against Porsche in the United States and in Germany demanding billions in damages, claiming information made public by Porsche would be false and misleading. The funds lost in the US and in Stuttgart and Braunschweig.[58]

27 *Example*: An already closed criminal case that received thorough media attention in Germany is that of the former CEO of **IKB Deutsche Industriebank AG**. In a press release of 20 July 2007, the defendant stated that the risks of dealing with US subprime mortgages would have 'practically no influence' on IKB. The depreciation would not exceed a seven-figure sum. On the day of publication, the price of IKB shares outperformed that of the MDAX,[59] where IKB was listed. One week later it became apparent that the depreciation would run to billions rather than millions. The court ruled that the former CEO had knowingly misled investors by creating the impression (through a press release) that IKB Bank AG had not been materially influenced by the subprime problems, although further analyses of banks and rating agencies showed that the opposite was true.[60]

28 *Example*: In the United Kingdom, the FCA fined the Canadian company formerly carrying on business as **Swift Trade Inc** £8 million for *layering*, a type of trade-based market manipulation.[61] The former FSA further imposed a fine of £17 million on Shell for continually having delivered

---

[56] Cf. OLG Stuttgart of 26.3.2015 – 2 U 102/14, 60 AG (2015), 404.

[57] This agreement (cf. § 291 AktG—German Stock Corporation Act) allows a parent company to give binding instructions to the board of the subsidiary and to obtain the profits gained by the subsidiary.

[58] OLG Stuttgart of 26.3.2015 – 2 U 102/14, 60 AG (2015), 404; LG Braunschweig of 9.6. 2013 – 5 O 552/12, 10 NZKart (2013), 380.

[59] The MDAX Index is part of the Prime Standard Segment of the Frankfurt Stock Exchange (FWB). It includes the 50 shares from classical sectors excluding technology that rank immediately below the companies included in the DAX index.

[60] BGH of 20.7.2011 – 3 StR 506/10, 56 AG (2011), 702.

[61] FCA, Final Notice, 7722656, Canada Inc formerly carrying on business as Swift Trade Inc, 24 January 2014; layering is the 'practice of entering relatively large orders on one side of an [...] order book without the genuine intention that the orders will be executed [...] while they nevertheless [move] the price of the relevant share as the market adjusts to the fact that there has been an apparent shift in the balance of supply and demand [...] The movement is followed by [...] a trade on the opposite side of the order book which takes advantage of [...] that movement. This trade is in turn followed by a rapid deletion of the large orders [...]', cf. the decision of the Upper Tribunal (Tax and Chancery Chamber) of 23 January 2013, ref. no. FS/2011/0017, 0018 (*Swift Trade*) 3.

incorrect information regarding the reserves of a certain natural resource, thus influencing the share price.[62]

Rumours and false information occur frequently and quickly lead to price changes, with the result that investors buy securities at artificial prices. *Examples*: Shares of the social network Twitter briefly gained 7 % following a fake Bloomberg article conveying takeover rumours in July 2015.[63] The same happened to Avon Products in June 2015 when the SEC's online database was abused to enter false filings for takeover bids.[64] In 2014, British security company G4S took a plunge following a false statement about accounting problems.[65] Shares of American car-maker Tesla rose by 0.75 % following an April fools' joke in 2015 announcing the release of a watch in a tweet.[66]

(c) Digression: Behavioural Finance

Any information-based manipulation aims to influence the perception of other market participants. Whether information potentially gives incorrect or misleading signals depends not only on the information itself, but also to a large extent on how the information is understood by the recipient. If investors have persistent problems understanding or processing certain information correctly, a clever manipulator can take advantage of this fact.[67] The literature on behavioural finance has proven that humans generally tend to overestimate their abilities. This phenomenon of **overconfidence** also arises on financial markets, as studies on financial analysts,[68] CEOs with regard to takeovers and dividend policies,[69] and private investors with online trading accounts[70] have shown. The result of such overconfidence can be that people do not fall for the manipulator because they believe him, but rather because they believe they can still control events.[71] The human assessment of risks furthermore changes, depending on whether information is framed as a possibility to make profits or prevent losses (**framing effect**), the inclination to take risks being larger when trying to prevent losses. Similarly, humans tend to choose safe profits over possible, but uncertain, higher profits, even if the expected utility in both cases is the same.[72] Finally, humans take in information more easily the more prominently it is presented (**availability bias**).

---

[62] FSA, Final Notice, Shell Transport and Trading Company, plc and The Royal Dutch Petroleum Company NV, 24 August 2004 (this judgment was made prior to the introduction of the new regime and is now viewed as a sanction for information-based manipulation).
[63] www.nytimes.com/2015/07/15/business/dealbook/twitter-shares-jump-after-fake-bloomberg-report.html?r=0.
[64] http://fortune.com/2015/05/15/sec-enables-avon-stock-scam-and-doesnt-seem-to-care/.
[65] www.wsj.com/articles/g4s-hit-by-elaborate-hoax-after-fake-statement-released-1415816334.
[66] http://blogs.wsj.com/moneybeat/2015/04/01/tesla-stock-moves-on-april-fools-joke/.
[67] L. Teigelack, *Finanzanalysen und Behavioral Finance*, 182, concerning the use of information resulting from a research report. For a recent overview of research in behavioural finance see J. Huang et al., 12 Int. J. of Managerial Finance (2016), 92; see also R. Veil § 6 para. 20–29.
[68] G. Friesen and P. Weller, 9 Journal of Financial Markets (2006), 14; O. Stotz and R. von Nitzsch, 15 ZBB (2003), 106 ff.; see also Q. Chen and W. Jiang, 19 Rev. Fin. Studies (2006), 319, 339, 350.
[69] U. Malmendier and G. Tate, 89 Journal of Financial Economics (2008), 20; S. Deshmukh et al., 22 Journal of Financial Intermediation (2013), 440.
[70] B. Barber and T. Odean, 21 Rev. Fin. Studies (2008), 785; B. Barber and T. Odean, 55 J. Fin. (2000), 773.
[71] Cf. L. Teigelack, *Finanzanalysen und Behavioral Finance*, 143.
[72] In general D. Kahneman and A. Tversky, 47 Econometrica (1979), 263, 268–269; A. Tversky and D. Kahneman, 59 J. Bus. (1986), 251, 260.

This can lead to the problem that certain information is not acknowledged, simply because of the way it is presented, eg disclaimers on possible conflicts of interest of the manipulator or information on particular risks.[73]

31 These examples show how much influence human weaknesses in processing information can have on investment decisions. However, the MAR-regime does not take behavioural finance into account. It rather builds on the concept of a *reasonable investor*[74] who bases his decision on all available information.[75] It has not yet been considered that this reasonable investor may make mistakes when coming to an investment decision. Accepting this danger would lead to new problems, as one can hardly predict which person will make which mistake in processing information in any given situation. The concept of a reasonable investor must therefore be regarded as a deliberate decision of the legislature not to want to protect incorrect investment decisions.[76]

3. Transaction-based Market Manipulation

(a) Definition and Indicators

32 The MAR further prohibits **transaction-based market manipulations**, ie any transactions or orders to trade

— which give, or are likely to give, false or misleading signals as to the supply of, demand for, or price of a financial instrument, a related spot commodity contract or an auctioned product based on emission allowances, or

— which secure the price of one or several financial instruments, a related spot commodity contract or an auctioned product based on emission allowances at an abnormal or artificial level.[77]

33 Annex I Section A of the MAR specifies these broadly phrased definitions. Certain non-exhaustive **indicators**, which do not necessarily in themselves constitute market manipulation, are taken into account when transactions or orders to trade are examined by market participants and competent authorities.

34 The indicators are, among other things:

— the extent to which orders to trade given or transactions undertaken represent a significant proportion of the daily volume of transactions in the relevant financial instrument, related spot commodity contract or auctioned product based on emission allowances in particular when those activities lead to a significant change in their prices;

— the extent to which orders to trade given or transactions undertaken by persons with a significant buying or selling position in a financial instrument, related spot commodity contract or auctioned product based on emission allowances lead to significant changes in the price of

---

[73] L. Teigelack, *Finanzanalysen und Behavioral Finance*, 131, 143–144.
[74] See R. Veil § 6 para. 31 and § 14 para. 53.
[75] Cf. Recital 14 MAR, recital 1 of the MAD 2003 and CESR, CESR's Advice on Level 2 Implementing Measures for the Proposed Market Abuse Directive, August 2003, CESR/02–89d, p. 10; overview in R. Veil, 18 ZBB (2006), 162 ff.; L. Teigelack, *Finanzanalysen und Behavioral Finance*, 83 ff.
[76] R. Veil, 18 ZBB (2006), 162, 171; L. Teigelack, *Finanzanalysen und Behavioral Finance*, 86–87.
[77] Art. 12(1)(a) MAR; the ECJ has ruled that 'securing' the price at an abnormal level requires no minimum time period. Even very short-lived distortions constitute trade-based manipulation (Case C-445/09 *(IMC Securities)*).

that financial instrument, related spot commodity contract or auctioned product based on emission allowances;
— whether transactions undertaken lead to no change in beneficial ownership of a financial instrument, related spot commodity contract or auctioned product based on emission allowances;[78]
— the extent to which orders to trade given or transactions undertaken or orders cancelled include position reversals in a short period and represent a significant proportion of the daily volume of transactions in the relevant financial instrument, related spot commodity contract or auctioned product based on emission allowances;
— the extent to which orders to trade given or transactions undertaken are concentrated within a short time span in the trading session and lead to a price change which is subsequently reversed;
— the extent to which orders to trade are given or transactions are undertaken at or around a specific time when reference prices, settlement prices and valuations are calculated and lead to price changes which have an effect on such prices and valuations.[79]

Annex II Sections 1 and 2 of Commission Delegated Regulation (EU) No. 2016/522 supplement MAR with regard to the indicators in Annex I.[80] Annex II section 1 gives a good overview of possible forms of trade-based market manipulations. **Wash sales** are a prominent example: if an investor sells shares to a company that it owns, the economic ownership of the security does not change and this may be considered trade-based manipulation. **Marking the close** can happen, if transactions are intentionally entered into at the close of the market, so that investors trading on the basis of the closing price pay a higher price. **Spoofing** describes the procedure in which a manipulator who holds a *long position* submits one or more orders to buy, thus achieving the incorrect impression of a high demand. Shortly thereafter (before executing the order) the manipulator cancels the order, hoping that other market participants submit buy orders due to the seemingly higher demand. The manipulator then sells his securities at this higher price. **Improper matched orders** are orders placed by different parties at basically identical conditions. However, the parties have previously agreed on placing these orders, so that an unnatural strike price can result. Market participants could be **colluding in the after-market of an Initial Public Offer** if they buy positions in the secondary market after a placement in the primary market to post the price to an artificial level and generate interest from other investors. The **creation of a floor/ceiling in the price pattern** means creating obstacles to prices falling below or rising above a certain level. **Ping orders** are small orders that are intended to ascertain the level of hidden orders and to assess what is resting on a hidden platform. Uncovering orders of other market participants through own transactions or orders and then taking advantage of this information is referred to as **phishing**. An **abusive squeeze** lies in taking advantage of the significant influence over supply of, or demand for, or the delivery mechanism of financial instruments etc. in order to distort prices. **Inter-trading venues manipulation** aims

---

[78] This refers to so-called wash sales; see para. 35.
[79] Annex I Section A MAR.
[80] Commission Delegated Regulation (EU) No. 2016/522 supplementing Regulation (EU) No. 596/2014 of the European Parliament and of the Council as regards an exemption for certain third countries public bodies and central banks, the indicators of market manipulation, the disclosure thresholds, the competent authority for notifications of delays, the permission for trading during closed periods and types of notifiable managers' transactions, OJ L88, 5 April 2016, p. 1–18.

to influence the price of financial instruments etc. on one trading venue through transactions or orders to trade on another venue. **Cross-product manipulation** aims to achieve the same goal through transactions or orders to trade in another product. **Concealing ownership** relates to breaches of disclosure obligations in order to conceal the true ownership of financial instruments etc. **Pump and dump** and **trash and cash** concern the dissemination of false or misleading positive or negative information to benefit a long or short position. **Quote stuffing** can create uncertainty among other market participants by entering a large number of trades, cancellations or updates. This can slow down other market participants or camouflage one's own trading strategy. **Momentum ignition** describes the orders or series of orders designed to start or exacerbate a trend in the behaviour of other market participants to move the price in a certain direction. **Layering and spoofing** means placing multiple or large orders to trade on one side of the order book to be able to execute a trade on the other side. Once the actual trade has taken place the unwanted orders are removed. **Placing orders with no intention of executing them** and then removing these orders before execution can mislead other market participants as to the actual supply or demand. **Excessive bid-offer spreads** are maintained if a market participant (ab)uses its power through orders that (likely) bypass trading safeguards such as price/volume limits and thus causes an artificial spread. **Advancing the bid** happens when orders are entered at prices that will increase the bid or decrease the offer and thus move prices. **Smoking** means attracting slower trades by posting orders and then rapidly reversing these orders in a less favourable direction for the slower traders. **Distorting costs associated with a commodity contract** (insurance or freight) can lead to the settlement price of a financial instrument to be set at an artificial level.

36 If the parties disclose the exceptional circumstances before the transaction, their behaviour does not constitute market manipulation. In these cases, the reliability of the price formation does not need to be protected, as the market is informed of the special circumstances beforehand, and thus cannot be misled.

(b) Exceptions

37 No trade-based manipulation within the meaning of Article 12(1)(a) MAR occurs if the person entering into a transaction or placing an order to trade or engaging in any other behaviour can establish that such transaction, order or behaviour has been carried out for **legitimate reasons** and conform with an **accepted market practice** established in accordance with Article 13 MAR.[81] The MAR phrases the exception as a reversal of the burden of proof. The behaviour is therefore prohibited, unless the person who entered into the transaction can submit a legitimate reason and show that the transaction conforms to an accepted market practice. There is an intensive discussion in the legal literature as to the legitimate reasons and accepted market practices; however, this largely remains *law in the books*.

38 The MAR contains no information as to what constitutes a **legitimate reason**. Additionally, ESMA has not made any statement in this respect. There does not appear to be any jurisprudence on this question as yet. Legitimate reasons can, for example, be assumed if the

---

[81] Cf. Recital 42 MAR.

transaction is based on a legal or supervisory obligation towards a third party. As opposed to this, a legitimate reason is less likely if the transaction was performed in order to give incorrect or misleading signals.

The MAR defines **Accepted Market Practices** (AMPs) as 'a specific market practice that is accepted by a competent authority in accordance with Article 13'.[82] Article 13 MAR has replaced Directive 2004/72/EC in setting forth the criteria that national supervisory authorities may take into account in establishing a market practice and outlines the consultation process for acceptance. ESMA drafted regulatory technical standards with regard to AMPs,[83] and the Commission passed Delegated Regulation (EU) No. 2016/908 on Level 2 signing ESMA's draft into law. The national competent authorities, such as AMF, BaFin, CNMV, CONSOB, etc., may take into account several aspects, such as the level of transparency of the relevant market practice to the market as a whole, the need to safeguard the operation of market forces and the proper interplay of the forces of supply and demand, the risk inherent in the relevant practice for the integrity of related markets, the structural characteristics of the relevant market (ie the type of market participants and the extent of retail investor participation), and the outcome of any investigation of the relevant market practice by any other competent authority.[84] Commission Delegated Regulation (EU) No. 2016/908 specifies these criteria.[85]

39

4. Other Forms of Market Manipulation

Entering into a transaction, placing an order to trade or any other activity or behaviour which affects or is likely to affect the price of one or several financial instruments, a related spot commodity contract or an auctioned product based on emission allowances, which employs **fictitious devices or any other form of deception** or contrivance is also prohibited.[86] This serves as a **catch-all clause** for all market manipulations that are not covered by the other two definitions, in order to prevent any behaviour that ought to be prohibited from remaining unsanctioned. Annex I Section B MAR provides for indicators that must be taken into account when trying to determine whether behaviour is to be considered manipulative:

40

— whether orders to trade given or transactions undertaken by persons are preceded or followed by dissemination of false or misleading information by the same persons or by persons linked to them;[87]
— whether orders to trade are given or transactions are undertaken by persons before or after the same persons or persons linked to them produce or disseminate research or investment recommendations which are erroneous or biased or demonstrably influenced by material interest.

---

[82] Art. 3(9) MAR; cf. N. Moloney, *EU Securities and Financial Markets Regulation*, 750 ff., for a detailed description of the AMP rules.
[83] According to Art. 13(7) MAR.
[84] Art. 13(2)(a)–(g) MAR.
[85] Art. 3–9 Commission Delegated Regulation (EU) No. 2016/908.
[86] Art. 12(1)(b) MAR.
[87] This can only refer to information that is not already likely to give false or misleading signals, as this form of information is already included in the core definition in Art. 12(1)(c) MAR.

41 Annex II Section 2 to Commission Delegated Regulation (EU) No. 2016/522 specifies these two indicators. With regard to the first indicator ESMA describes several forms of behaviour, such as disseminating false or misleading positive information after taking a long position and then selling out the position when the price is at an artificially high level (*pump and dump*) or vice-versa (*trash and cash*)[88] and moving empty cargo ships.[89] With regard to the second indicator ESMA also mentions *pump and dump* and *trash and cash*.[90]

5. Benchmark Manipulation

42 Following public reports on the manipulation of reference rates, such as LIBOR in particular, the Commission's proposal of the MAR (published in 2011) was amended in 2012 to prevent such behaviour in the future. The MAR aims to protect investor confidence and also mentions damages to individual investors and potential setbacks to the real economy.[91] It therefore prohibits '**transmitting false** or **misleading information** or providing false or misleading inputs in **relation to a benchmark** where the person who made the transmission or provided the input knew or ought to have known that it was false or misleading, or any other behaviour which manipulates the calculation of a benchmark.'[92]

43 The term benchmark is defined broadly and means 'any rate, index or figure, made available to the public or published that is periodically or regularly determined by the application of a formula to, or on the basis of the value of one or more underlying assets or prices, including estimated prices, actual or estimated interest rates or other values, or surveys, and by reference to which the amount payable under a financial instrument or the value of a financial instrument is determined.'[93] This could have also applied to the alleged influencing of the Foreign Exchange Rates. Several large banks are facing litigation in the US for allegedly distorting the WM/Reuters fix. The 'fix' is based on actual transactions occurring in a certain window of time and is used to determine the 'official' exchange rate between currencies. The allegations are that banks deferred customers' transactions into this window of time to distort the 'fix' in their own favour.[94] Another example could be the influencing of the settlement prices for gas futures on the European Energy Exchange that followed a similar pattern.[95]

44 The indicators in Annex I to the MAR **do not** apply **to benchmark manipulation**, and ESMA considers it premature to provide specific examples or practices of benchmark manipulation.[96]

---

[88] Annex II sec. 2(1)(c) Regulation (EU) No. 2016/522.
[89] Annex II sec. 2(1)(g) Regulation (EU) No. 2016/522.
[90] Annex II sec. 2(2)(b) Regulation (EU) No. 2016/522.
[91] Recital 44 MAR; cf. N. Moloney, *EU Securities and Financial Markets Regulation*, 744 ff., for a detailed description of benchmark measures.
[92] Art. 12(1)(d) MAR; see in more detail M. Wundenberg §§ 35, 36.
[93] Art. 3(1)(29) MAR.
[94] United States District Court for Southern District of New York, Case 1:13-cv-07789, In re Foreign Exchange Benchmark Rates Antitrust Litigation; UK and US regulators also took action, cf. FCA, Final Notice, Deutsche Bank, 23 April 2015.
[95] BaFin, Jahresbericht 2014 (annual report), p. 220.
[96] ESMA, Final Report, Technical Advice on possible delegated acts concerning the Market Abuse Regulation, 3 February 2015, ESMA/2015/224, para. 13.

6. Specific Types of Market Manipulation

(a) Dominant Market Position

The first example of market manipulation is conduct by a person, or persons acting in collaboration, to secure a dominant position over the supply of or demand for a financial instrument, related spot commodity contracts or auctioned products based on emission allowances which has or is likely to have the effect of fixing, directly or indirectly, purchase or sale prices or creates or is likely to create other unfair trading conditions.[97] Strictly speaking, this example does not refer to a manipulation on the ground of the information accessible for market participants. Having a dominant market position does not entail misleading other market participants. This is rather an **antitrust issue**, affecting market fairness.[98] The reason why the dominant market position was still introduced as part of the definition of market manipulation may be that monopolies are likely to weaken investors' trust in the market.

According to the MAR, **any conduct** to secure a dominant position is to be prohibited, irrespective of whether the person intends to abuse this position.[99] The dominant position must, however, have the effect of fixing, directly or indirectly, purchase or sale prices or creating other unfair trading conditions.[100] Such manipulation can occur if many uncovered short sales have taken place, and the securities of the respective company are thus in great demand on the market.[101]

> *Example*: In Germany, the case of VW shares, which briefly soared to a price of over € 1,000, making VW the world's most valuable company for a short time, has proven controversial. At the same time as declaring Porsche's intention to acquire a total of 75% of VW's shares,[102] Porsche's CEO had informed the public of already having raised its holdings to 43%, with an additional 31% in 'options' as a forward cover. These were *cash-settled equity swaps* that did not have to be disclosed at the time.[103] As a result, short sellers and index funds had to acquire further VW shares. However, the supply of ordinary VW shares was extremely low at this time, as large numbers of the available shares were held by Porsche itself or by its contractual counterparties via option contracts. The counterparties had acquired shares in order to hedge the risks resulting from the option contract. The federal state of Lower Saxony held a little more than 20% of the shares, so that a supply of merely 6% of available shares was met by 13% of shorted shares. However, the prohibition of cornering does not grant investors a claim under section 823(2) of the German Civil Code (Bürgerliches Gesetzbuch – BGB). The courts have therefore dismissed claims for damages.[104] Irrespective of this, Porsche is unlikely to have had a dominant position on the market.[105]

---

[97] Art. 12(2)(a) MAR.
[98] P. Mülbert, in: Assmann et al. (eds.), *Kommentar zum Wertpapierhandelsrecht*, Art. 12 MAR para. 226.
[99] Cf. H. Fleischer and E. Bueren, 34 ZIP (2013), 1253, 1256.
[100] Art. 1(2)(a) MAR.
[101] Cf. H. Fleischer and E. Bueren, 34 ZIP (2013), 1253, 1256.
[102] See para. 26.
[103] In more detail see R. Veil § 20 para. 93.
[104] OLG Braunschweig of 12.1.2016 – 7 U 59/14, 61 AG (2016), 290; OLG Stuttgart of 26.3.2015 – 2 U 102/14, 60 AG (2015), 404; H. Fleischer and E. Bueren, 34 ZIP (2013), 1253 f.
[105] Cf. A. Anschütz and M. Kunzelmann, in: Meyer et al. (eds.), *Handbuch Marktmissbrauchsrecht*, § 14 para. 30.

(b) Transactions at the Close of the Market

48   A second example of market manipulation is the so-called ***marking the close***.[106] The MAR defines this as 'the buying or selling of financial instruments at the opening or closing of the market which has or is likely to have the effect of misleading investors acting on the basis of the prices displayed, including the opening or closing prices.'[107] This can be especially profitable when further transactions are concluded on the basis of an upwards distorted closing price.

(c) Certain Means of Algorithmic and High-Frequency Trading (HFT)

49   Algorithmic trading and HFT are **not prohibited per se.** Certain forms are rather classified as *trade-based* market manipulations. In general, sending orders to a trading venue without an intention to trade is prohibited if the order is placed with the intention of disrupting or delaying the functioning of the venue's trading system, making it more difficult for others to identify genuine orders (so-called *layering* or *quote stuffing*) or creating a false or misleading impression about the supply and demand for a financial instrument.[108] The enumeration is non-exhaustive because the MAR **aims to provide adaptable measures against market manipulation in the face of rapidly changing forms of trading.**[109]

(d) Abusing Access to the Media

50   A further example of market manipulation refers to 'taking advantage of occasional or regular access to the traditional or electronic media by voicing an opinion about a financial instrument, related spot commodity contract or an auctioned product based on emission allowances (or indirectly about its issuer) while having previously taken positions on that financial instrument, related spot commodity contract or an auctioned product based on emission allowances and profiting subsequently from the impact of the opinions voiced on the price of that instrument, related spot commodity contract or an auctioned product based on emission allowances without having simultaneously disclosed that conflict of interest to the public in a proper and effective way'.[110] This is also called *scalping* and might, for example, involve spam e-mails, which promise considerable increases in the share price of specific issuers. Before sending the e-mail, the sender buys shares in the generally illiquid titles, enabling them to profit from the subsequent price movement. Successful *scalping* requires that the opinion of the scalper can influence the share price. It therefore usually happens with regard to illiquid shares for which even slight trading activities can lead to price movements.[111]

51   *Example*: In Germany the BGH had to deal with a criminal case on scalping in 2003. The defendant was the editor of a money magazine and appeared in stock market programmes on television

---

[106] See above para. 35.
[107] Art. 12(2)(b) MAR.
[108] Art. 12(2)(c) MAR; The FCA fine of £ 8 million mentioned in para. 19 was for layering.
[109] Recital 38 MAR.
[110] Art. 1(2)(d) MAR.
[111] Cf. R. Aggarwal and G. Wu, 79. J. Bus. (2006), 1915, 1917; one of the most commonly cited examples from the United States is the case *SEC v. Lebed*, 73 SEC Docket 741, 20 September 2000, in which a teenager earned a few hundred thousand dollars through scalping on the Internet.

issuing investment recommendations. He had obtained the reputation of being an opinion maker in the 'new market' (Neuer Markt) and had entered into consultancy contracts with two funds. These usually followed his recommendations without any further enquiries. The defendant and an accomplice raised funds, before acquiring new economy stock and then recommending these to the two funds without, however, indicating that he was holding respective shares himself. Due to the high order volume the prices of the securities rose and the defendant sold his shares at a higher price.

Before this case, the prevailing view in legal literature held that the acquisition of securities by a *scalper* prior to the public recommendation thereof violated the rules on insider dealings, the knowledge of the *scalper* of the ensuing recommendation being regarded as inside information. The BGH did not follow this understanding, arguing that personally created facts did not constitute inside information requiring that the information have a connection to a third party and not only exist in the mind of the *scalper*.[112] 52

Under the MAR regime, a self-generated fact can also be inside information.[113] However, European law understands scalping as market manipulation, so that insider trading law is not applicable. 'Positions' are not only securities, but also derivatives and short positions (of a short seller).[114] Ultimately, lack of transparency is penalised. For a 'proper and effective' disclosure of the conflict of interest, it is not necessary to disclose the size of the position.[115] The prohibition does not require that the scalper's statement is false or misleading or that the recommendation is factually untenable. However, statements of a scalper which contain false or misleading signals may constitute market manipulation according to Article 12(1)(c) MAR. The *scalper's* recommendation needs not in itself be incorrect or misleading. Recommendations of a *scalper* that give false or misleading signals in the sense of the core definition already constitute market manipulation for this reason. 53

(e) Emission Allowances

The acquisition or sale of emission allowances or related derivatives on the secondary market prior to the auction under Regulation (EU) No. 1031/2010 is to be considered market manipulation, if it has the effect that the auction clearing price is fixed at an abnormal or artificial level or if bidders are misled.[116] 54

V. Safe-Harbour Rules

1. Introduction

The MAR stipulates **two exceptions from the prohibition of market manipulation**. The prohibitions do not apply to trading in own shares in '**buy-back**' programmes and the 55

---

[112] BGH of 06.11.2003 – 1 StR 24/03, BGHSt 48 (2003), 373.
[113] See R. Veil § 14 para. 51.
[114] Cf. L. Teigelack, in: Meyer et al. (eds.), *Handbuch Marktmissbrauchsrecht*, § 13 para. 62 ff.
[115] Cf. L. Teigelack, in: Meyer et al. (eds.), *Handbuch Marktmissbrauchsrecht*, § 13 para. 74, 79; P. Mülbert, in: Assmann et al. (eds.), *Kommentar zum Wertpapierhandelsrecht*, Art. 12 MAR para. 249.
[116] Art. 12(2)(e) MAR.

stabilisation of a financial instrument, provided such trading is carried out in accordance with the procedure laid down in the MAR and the applicable RTS.[117] Buy-back programmes and stabilisation measures are of considerable practical importance. Commission Delegated Regulation (EU) No. 2016/1052 takes the place of repealed Regulation (EC) No. 2273/2003 in specifying conditions for buy-back programmes and stabilisation measures.

2. Buy-Back Programmes

56 The acquisition of own shares by a company can help signal to the market that the securities are not undervalued. The incentive to buy caused by the company can lead to a stabilisation or increase of the share price. A company may also buy back shares as currency for acquisitions, to prevent takeovers or to meet obligations arising from employee share option programmes or exchangeable bonds. Once the share price deviates from the securities' 'real value', one enters the realm of market manipulation, because the **price is no longer determined by the free interaction of market forces**, but rather by the company steering the market. Nevertheless, buy-back programmes for own shares (not bonds) are exempted from the prohibition of market manipulation under certain conditions due to their great importance for issuers.

57 The exemption applies only to outright trading in own **shares**, however. The issuer may not use derivatives anymore to acquire own shares. The MAR mentions the term 'associated instruments' in connection with stabilisation measures but not in the context of buy-back programmes.[118] Buy-back programmes that meet the requirements established by the regulation are exempt from the prohibition of market manipulation and insider dealing. However, the obligations to disclose inside information[119] and major shareholdings[120] remain applicable.[121] The issuer also has to meet the EU corporate law requirements regarding share buy-backs.[122]

(a) Aim of the Programme

58 **Legitimate objectives** for buy-back programmes **only** include the **reduction** of an **issuer's capital** (in value or in number of shares), **meeting obligations** arising from debt financial instruments exchangeable into equity instruments or employee share option programmes, or **other allocations** of **shares** to employees or to members of the administrative, management or supervisory bodies of the issuer or of an associate company.[123] Calls to include buy-back programmes for acquisition financing into the *safe harbour* can be heard regularly in legal practice. The former CESR rebuffed this demand, although not all supervisory

---

[117] Art. 5 MAR.
[118] Recital 2 Commission Delegated Regulation (EU) No. 2016/1052; using derivatives was explicitly allowed by former Regulation (EC) No. 2273/2003 (recital 8).
[119] Art. 17(1) MAR; see R. Veil § 19.
[120] Art. 9 and 10 TD; see R. Veil § 20.
[121] P. Mülbert, in: Assmann et al., *Kommentar zum Wertpapierhandelsrecht*, Art. 5 MAR para. 13, 14.
[122] A buy-back programme is defined as trading in own shares in accordance with Art. 21 to 27 of Directive 2012/30/EU.
[123] Art. 5(2)(a)–(c) MAR.

authorities of the Member States shared this opinion.[124] France, for example, has declared the acquisition of own shares to finance the acquisition of a company on Euronext an *accepted market practice*.[125] The Greek competent authority did not evaluate the aim of the programme at all as long as the trading conditions were met.[126] ESMA describes the purposes listed in the MAR as the 'sole legally allowed' purposes[127] thus making them factually binding outside of grandfathered Accepted Market Practices.

(b) Disclosure Obligations

In order to profit from the *safe-harbour* rule, an issuer must comply with certain disclosure obligations, both prior to and after implementing the buy-back. Full details of the programme must be adequately disclosed to the public, *prior* to the start of trading.[128] The 'adequate disclosure' of information is defined in Commission Delegated Regulation (EU) No. 2016/1052 and will not be described in any further detail herein.[129] Trades must be reported as being part of the buy-back programme to the competent authority of the trading venue and subsequently disclosed to the public.[130] The issuer must report each transaction relating to the buy-back programme to the competent authority of the trading venue on which the shares have been admitted to trading or are traded, including certain information specified in Regulation (EU) No. 600/2014.[131]

(c) Trading Conditions

The buy-back programme must follow the procedure laid down in the MAR and in Commission Delegated Regulation (EU) No. 2016/1052. The provisions on trading conditions are to ensure that the acquisition of own shares by the company does not lead to an artificial price increase by higher acquisition prices or a shortage of shares on the free market.[132] The MAR therefore calls for adequate limits with regard to price and volume to be complied with.[133] Commission Delegated Regulation (EU) 2016/1052 contains detailed provisions on trading conditions. Shares shall be purchased on a trading venue where the shares are admitted to trading or are traded.[134] The issuer may not pay a higher price for the shares than the highest price of the last independent trade/bid on the respective trading venue.[135] A shortage of shares on the market is to be prevented by the fact that

---

[124] CESR, CESR's response to the Commission call for evidence on the review of the Market Abuse Directive, July 2009, CESR/09-635, 7.
[125] Cf. www.cesr-eu.org/popup2.php?id=3379.
[126] V. Tountopoulos, 22 EWS (2012), 449, 454.
[127] ESMA, Final Report, Draft Technical Standards on the Market Abuse Regulation, 28 September 2015, ESMA/2015/1455, para. 12; cf. also N. Moloney, *EU Securities and Financial Markets Regulation*, 753.
[128] Art. 5(1)(a) MAR.
[129] Art. 1(b) Commission Delegated Regulation (EU) No. 2016/1052.
[130] Art. 5(1)(b) MAR.
[131] Art. 5(3) MAR refers to Art 25(1) and (2) Art 26(1), (2) and (3) of Regulation (EU) No. 600/2014; Art. 2 Commission Delegated Regulation (EU) No. 2016/1052 contains details on the disclosure obligations.
[132] P. Mülbert, in: Assmann et al. (eds.), *Kommentar zum Wertpapierhandelsgesetz*, Art. 5 MAR para. 52.
[133] Art. 5(1)(c) MAR.
[134] Recital 4 and Art. 3(1)(a) Commission Delegated Regulation (EU) No. 2016/1052.
[135] Art. 3(2) Commission Delegated Regulation (EU) No. 2016/1052.

'issuers shall not [...] purchase more than 25% of the average daily volume of the shares in any trading day on trading venue on which the purchase is carried out'.[136]

(d) Restrictions

61 Additionally, the issuer is subject to a number of restrictions, which are to ensure fairness and transparency of the buy-back programme.[137] The issuer may not sell own shares for the duration of the programme and may not trade at all during certain, so-called 'closed' periods, or where the issuer has decided to delay the public disclosure of inside information.[138] *Closed* in the sense of the MAR are periods during which the issuer's board members are prohibited to trade in the issuer's shares. The RTS point to the MAR's definition of closed periods in the context of managers' transactions (30 calendar days before the mandatory publication of a financial report).[139]

62 The restrictions on trading do not apply if the issuer is an investment firm or credit institution and has established effective information barriers (*Chinese walls*) between those responsible for the handling of inside information and those responsible for any decision relating to the trading of own shares.[140] They also do not apply if the issuer has a time-scheduled buy-back programme in place or the buy-back programme is managed by an investment firm or a credit institution with sole discretion as to the transactions.[141] A *time-scheduled* programme sets out the dates and quantities of securities to be traded during the period of the programme at the time of the public disclosure of the buy-back programme.[142] The disadvantage of these programmes is that the issuer can no longer react flexibly to the actual market conditions.[143] At the same time, they guarantee transparency and independence, thus exempting the issuer from the prohibitions.

3. Price Stabilisation

63 So-called stabilisation activities constitute a second safe harbour. The MAR defines stabilisation as a **purchase** or offer to purchase **securities**, or a transaction in associated instruments equivalent thereto, which is undertaken by a **credit institution** or an investment firm in the context of a significant distribution of such securities **exclusively for supporting** the **market price** of those securities for a **predetermined period of time**, due to a **selling pressure** in such securities.[144] These measures are privileged, because stock offerings are often accompanied by numerous disposals of shares by short-term traders. Some investors also subsequently sell as many shares as necessary to cover their costs of acquiring the newly issued shares (so-called *flipping*). The resulting selling pressure reduces the price of the

---

[136] Art. 3(3) Commission Delegated Regulation (EU) No. 2016/1052.
[137] P. Mülbert, in: Assmann et al. (eds.), *Kommentar zum Wertpapierhandelsrecht*, Art. 5 MAR para. 66.
[138] Art. 4(1)(c) Commission Delegated Regulation (EU) No. 2016/1052.
[139] Art. 4(1)(c) Commission Delegated Regulation (EU) No. 2016/1052.
[140] Art. 4(3) and (4) Commission Delegated Regulation (EU) No. 2016/1052.
[141] Art. 4(2) Commission Delegated Regulation (EU) No. 2016/1052.
[142] Art. 1(a) Commission Delegated Regulation (EU) No. 2016/1052.
[143] P. Mülbert, in: Assmann et al. (eds.), *Kommentar zum Wertpapierhandelsrecht*, Art. 5 MAR para. 69.
[144] Art. 3(2)(d) MAR.

financial instruments. This is regarded as contrary to market interests, and the regulation thus aims to prevent such price drops.[145] Since stabilisation activities lead to an artificial price level, adequate public disclosure is necessary in order to ensure the investors' trust in the market mechanisms.[146]

As with buy-back programmes, the safe harbour for stabilisation measures only exempts an issuer from the prohibition of market manipulation and insider trading. Ad hoc disclosure obligations and the general rules governing investment firms and credit institutions still apply, as only these institutions are allowed to carry out stabilisation measures. 64

(a) Scope of Application

Only investment firms and credit institutions are permitted to undertake stabilisation activities under the MAR.[147] The safe harbour is open to significant distributions defined as an *initial* and *secondary* offer of securities that is distinct from ordinary trading both in terms of the amount in value of the securities to be offered and the selling method to be employed.[148] This also includes the placement of shares after a capital increase.[149] So-called *block trades*, in which large shareholdings are traded between individual persons, generally do not fall within the scope of the exemption. The Commission, however, leaves a door open for 'negotiated transactions that do not contribute to price formation.'[150] 65

The *safe-harbour* rule further does not apply to a decline in stock prices resulting from the poor economic situation of an issuer. Additionally, stabilisation may under no circumstances 'be executed above the offering price'.[151] Stabilisation may only aim to stabilise the price, not, however, to increase it. According to ESMA, sales also do not fall within the scope of the directive, as only the purchase of shares can stabilise the price.[152] 66

(b) Period of Stabilisation

The MAR only exempts stabilisation activities from the market manipulation provisions if these activities were limited to a certain time period in advance.[153] The activities must furthermore have an immediate relation to an offering. In an **initial public offering** of shares and other securities equivalent to shares, the **period begins on the date of commencement of trading and ends no later than 30 calendar days thereafter.**[154] The *safe harbour* is therefore not open for transactions during the *bookbuilding* phase. In a secondary offering, the relevant period begins on the date of adequate public disclosure of the final price of the relevant securities and ends no later than 30 calendar days after the date of allotment.[155] 67

---

[145] Recital 6 Commission Delegated Regulation (EU) No. 2016/1052.
[146] Recital 8 Commission Delegated Regulation (EU) No. 2016/1052.
[147] Art. 3(2)(d) MAR.
[148] Art. 3(2)(c) MAR.
[149] P. Mülbert, in: Assmann et al. (eds.), *Kommentar zum Wertpapierhandelsrecht*, Art. 5 MAR para. 78.
[150] Recital 4 Commission Delegated Regulation (EU) No. 2016/1052.
[151] Art. 7(1) (shares or other securities equivalent to shares) and accordingly 7(2) (securitised debt convertible or exchangeable into shares) Commission Delegated Regulation (EU) No. 2016/1052.
[152] Recital 11 Commission Delegated Regulation (EU) No. 2016/1052.
[153] Art. 5(4) MAR.
[154] Art. 5(1)(a) Commission Delegated Regulation (EU) No. 2016/1052.
[155] Art. 5(1)(b) Commission Delegated Regulation (EU) No. 2016/1052.

Special rules exist for bonds and other forms of debt securities, because the quotation of prices usually does not begin immediately after the issuance of the securities.[156]

(c) Disclosure and Organisational Obligations

68 As for buy-back programmes, European law also demands disclosure of stabilisation activities. Before the opening of the offer period of the relevant securities, adequate public disclosure[157] is required. The person appointed to do so[158] must make public the fact that stabilisation may or may not be undertaken and that it may be stopped at any time. The disclosure must further contain information on the beginning and end of the period during which stabilisation may occur and on the conditions under which a so-called *greenshoe* option may be exercised.[159]

69 Within one week after the end of the stabilisation period, certain details of the transactions or the fact that no stabilisation was undertaken are to be adequately disclosed and the competent authority is to be informed.[160] The responsible person is additionally obligated to record each stabilisation order or transaction, ensuring a better supervision by the competent authority.[161]

(d) Ancillary Stabilisation

70 'Ancillary stabilisation' means 'the **exercise** of an **overallotment facility** or of a ***greenshoe* option** by investment firms or credit institutions, in the **context** of a **significant distribution of securities**, exclusively for **facilitating stabilisation activity**.'[162] In the offering, a greater number of securities is allotted than originally offered. This measure serves to mitigate any potential demand surplus. The additional securities are usually provided by one or more securities loans. If the market price of the instrument declines after the offering, the underwriting bank (or banks) acquires securities on the market in order to stabilise the instrument's price, and 'repays' the securities loans with these shares. If the market price increases or remains stable, the underwriting bank or banks can acquire the shares lent to it at the issue price and sell them with a profit in the market. A conflict of interest may occur if the bank acquires too many shares through the *greenshoe* option, and now wants to sell those shares.[163]

71 The former CESR and now ESMA are of the opinion that neither the disposal of securities that were acquired through stabilisation measures nor the subsequent purchase of such papers (*refreshing the greenshoe*) fall within the scope of the safe harbour. The MAR defines

---

[156] P. Mülbert, in: Assmann et al. (eds.), *Kommentar zum Wertpapierhandelsgesetz*, Art. 5 MAR para. 87; cf. Art. 5(2) and (3) Commission Delegated Regulation (EU) No. 2016/1052.
[157] Art. 6(1) Commission Delegated Regulation (EU) No. 2016/1052.
[158] Art. 6(3) Commission Delegated Regulation (EU) No. 2016/1052.
[159] Art. 6(1)(a)–(f) Commission Delegated Regulation (EU) No. 2016/1052.
[160] Art. 6(3), (4) Commission Delegated Regulation (EU) No. 2016/1052.
[161] Art. 6(4) Commission Delegated Regulation (EU) No. 2016/1052.
[162] Art. 1(e) Commission Delegated Regulation (EU) No. 2016/1052; on the concept of overallotment and *greenshoe* options see Art. 2(13), (14) Regulation (EC) No. 2273/2003 and A. Meyer, in: Marsch-Barner and Schäfer (eds.), *Handbuch börsennotierte AG*, § 8 para. 63 ff.
[163] P. Mülbert, in: Assmann et al. (eds.), *Kommentar zum Wertpapierhandelsgesetz*, Art. 5 MAR para. 101.

stabilisation measures as measures supporting the market price of securities due to selling pressure in such securities. This can only be achieved through buy orders.[164]

Ancillary stabilisation depends on additional prerequisites. An overallotment of securities is only permitted during the subscription period and only at the issue price. The *greenshoe* option can only be exercised in the context of an overallotment, it must be exercised during the stabilisation period, and it may not amount to more than 15% of the original offer. An overallotment of shares that is not covered by the *greenshoe* is only allowed up to 5% of the original offer. Further disclosure obligations apply after the completion of the offering.[165]

VI. Supervision

Even the best rules against market abuse require an effective level of supervision and enforcement. Market manipulation in particular has been said to be especially difficult to police.[166] However, enforcement activity seems to be on the rise across the EU and other continents.[167]

1. Supervisory Mechanisms

Each Member State shall designate a competent authority (NCA) for the purposes of the MAR.[168] The MAR makes supervision possible through general notification obligations for all transactions and special notification obligations for suspicious transactions.[169] The supervisory authorities employ increasingly sophisticated methods of IT monitoring to determine deviations from normal order behaviour with the help of algorithms and statistical tests.[170]

The MAR further introduces a whistleblowing mechanism.[171] Member states must 'ensure that competent authorities establish effective mechanisms that enable reporting of [...] infringements'.[172] The MAR outlines several key measures that Member States must introduce, such as data protection and employment protection for the whistleblower and the alleged perpetrator.[173]

---

[164] Recital 11 Commission Delegated Regulation (EU) 2016/1052; CESR, Level 3—Third Set of CESR Guidance and Information on the Common Operation of the Directive to the Market, May 2009, CESR/09-219, 12.

[165] Art. 8 Commission Delegated Regulation (EU) No. 2016/1052; ESMA, Final Report, Draft Technical Standards on the Market Abuse Regulation, 28 September 2015, ESMA/2015/1455, para. 53 ff.

[166] N. Moloney, *EU Securities and Financial Markets Regulation*, 754.

[167] H. McVea, in: Moloney et al. (eds.), *The Oxford Handbook of Financial Regulation*, 651.

[168] Art. 22 MAR; for a detailed account of supervisory mechanisms and cooperation cf. N. Moloney, *EU Securities and Financial Markets Regulation*, 755, 763.

[169] Art. 16 MAR for suspicious transaction reporting; Art. 26 MiFIR for general transaction reporting obligations; cf. N. Moloney, *EU Securities and Financial Markets Regulation*, 755 ff.

[170] Report on CESR Members' Powers Under The Market Abuse Directive and its Implementing Measures (07-380), 27 ff.; H. McVea, in: Moloney et al. (eds.), *The Oxford Handbook of Financial Regulation*, 653.

[171] Art. 32 MAR.

[172] Art. 32(1) MAR.

[173] Art. 32(2) MAR.

2. Investigatory Powers

76 The MAR contains detailed provisions on the minimum powers of supervisory authorities. These powers include the **right** to have **access** to any **document** and to receive copies, **demand information** from any person, and if necessary, to summon and hear any such person, to carry out **on-site inspections**, to require existing telephone and existing data traffic records, to require the cessation of any practice that is contrary to the MAR, to suspend trading in the respective financial instrument, to request the freezing and/or sequestration of assets, to request temporary prohibition of professional activity, and to enter the premises of natural or legal persons with prior judicial authorisation.[174] Member States must implement these powers into their national laws.

77 The MAR is open to Member States granting more powers to their NCA.[175] It further makes it clear that the provision of information to a competent authority will not breach any (data protection) law, any contractual non-disclosure obligation or any other restriction on the provision of information; no person will be held liable for providing information to the competent authority.[176] This clarification can be especially important for banks providing customer-related information (banking secrecy).

VII. Sanctions

1. Administrative and Criminal Sanctions

(a) Administrative Sanctions

78 The Commission had reached the conclusion that the framework under the former MAD 2003 was insufficient.[177] In a remarkable change from the former MAD 2003 regime, the MAR therefore now contains detailed requirements for the Member States to adhere to in developing their administrative sanctioning systems.[178] The MAR generally leaves it to the Member States to provide 'for competent authorities to have the power to take appropriate administrative sanctions or other administrative measures' for at least certain infringements, including market manipulation.[179] The Member States may only refrain from laying down administrative sanctions where, under national law, criminal sanctions already apply to the infringements in question.[180] This is partly relevant for market manipulation because the Member States had to impose criminal sanctions for several forms of severe market manipulation under the CRIM-MAD.

---

[174] Art. 23(2) MAR.
[175] Art. 23(3) MAR.
[176] Art. 23(4) MAR.
[177] See recital 70 MAR and recitals 3–5 CRIM-MAD; N. Moloney, *EU Securities and Financial Markets Regulation*, 762; M. Faure and C. Leger, 9 Brook. J. of Corp., Fin. & Comm. Law (2015), 417, criticise this approach as empirically unfounded.
[178] Art. 30(2) MAR.
[179] Art. 30(1)(1) MAR.
[180] Recital 72 and Art. 30(1)(2) MAR.

The MAR further describes measures and sanctions that can be imposed.[181] Member States must, among other measures, specify maximum pecuniary sanctions but the MAR establishes a floor for the maximum amounts. It calls for **pecuniary sanctions** of at least three times the amount of profits gained or losses avoided where these can be determined.[182] For natural persons, Member States must impose maximum pecuniary sanctions of at least € 5 million for market manipulation.[183] For legal persons, Member States must impose maximum pecuniary sanctions of at least € 15 million or 15% of last year's annual (consolidated, if applicable) turnover for market manipulation.[184]

Unlike the former MAD 2003 regime, the MAR now generally requires **supervisory authorities to publish** all **administrative sanctions** or **measures** imposed, excluding investigatory measures, and make the publications available on their website for at least five years.[185] This so-called naming and shaming can be considered an administrative sanction.[186] It can lead to considerable reputational damage[187] and enhance transparency by disclosing to the market all the sanctions imposed.

The MAR grants the NCAs a certain degree of discretion but non-publication is only the last resort. Rather, if a NCA considers publication disproportionate or hazardous to the stability of the financial markets, it shall choose between deferred or anonymous publication. Only if both of these options still jeopardised the stability of the financial markets or be disproportionate can the competent authority not publish the decision.[188]

(b) Criminal Sanctions

The Member States must also ensure that market manipulation is a **criminal offence at least in serious cases and when committed intentionally**.[189] The Commission was restricted to the instrument of a directive, as the European Union does not have the powers to harmonise criminal law by way of a regulation.[190] The scope of the directive is identical to the scope of the regulation with the exception that a transaction, order or other behaviour on a spot commodity market must have an actual effect on the price or value of a related financial instrument and vice-versa.[191] The CRIM-MAD excludes buy-back programmes, stabilisation measures and behaviour in pursuit of monetary and other public policies by reference to the MAR.[192]

Market manipulation is separately defined for the purposes of the CRIM-MAD.[193] The definition is almost identical to that of the MAR. However, the CRIM-MAD does not include

---

[181] Art. 30(2) MAD.
[182] Art. 30(2)(h) MAR.
[183] Art. 30(2)(i)(i) MAR.
[184] Art. 30(2)(j), 30(2)(3) MAR.
[185] Recital 73 and Art. 34(1) MAR.
[186] R. Veil, 45 ZGR (2016), 305, 308, 318 ff.
[187] CESR, Review Panel Report, MAD Options and Discretions, March 2010, CESR/09-1120, 115.
[188] Art. 34(1)(3) MAR.
[189] Recital 10 and Art. 5(1) CRIM-MAD.
[190] Art. 83(1) TFEU; cf. M. Faure and C. Leger, 9 Brook. J. Corp., Fin. & Comm. Law (2015), 389. See also R. Veil § 13 para. 12.
[191] Art. 1(4)(a), (b) CRIM-MAD.
[192] Art. 1(3) CRIM-MAD.
[193] Art. 5(2) CRIM-MAD.

auctioned products based on emission allowances and only applies if false signals are actually given and prices are actually secured or affected. Unlike under the MAR, it is not sufficient that false signals are likely to be given or prices are likely to be secured.[194] Like the MAR, the CRIM-MAD does not explicitly mention omissions but only applies to orders, etc. and other 'behaviour'.[195]

84 The CRIM-MAD considers cases of market manipulation to be serious where the impact on market integrity, the actual or potential profits gained or loss avoided, the level of damage caused to the market, the level of actual alteration of the value of a financial instrument etc. or the amounts of funds originally used is high. Cases are also serious where the manipulator comes from within the financial sector or a supervisory authority.[196] Member States must also impose criminal sanctions for inciting, aiding and abetting and attempting market manipulation as defined for the purposes of the CRIM-MAD.[197]

85 Criminal penalties for **natural persons** committing market manipulation must be 'effective, proportionate and dissuasive'. Member States must provide for a maximum term of imprisonment of at least four years for market manipulation.[198] Inciting, aiding and abetting and attempted market manipulation must only be punishable as a criminal offence. The Member States must also provide for **criminal penalties against legal persons** when market manipulation was committed for the benefit of a legal person by any person acting individually or as part of an organisation of the legal person. The acting person must have a leading position within the legal person based on certain defined criteria.[199] The Member states must also ensure that a legal person can be held liable where the lack of supervision or control by one of the persons in a leading position has made it possible for a subordinate to commit market manipulation for the benefit of the legal person.[200] Criminal sanctions against legal persons do not shield the acting natural persons from (parallel) criminal liability.[201]

86 Recently, the European Courts of Human Rights (ECHR) held that in an Italian case the possibility to accumulate criminal and administrative sanctions for the same behaviour (market manipulation) violates the European Convention of Human Rights because it creates a **double jeopardy**.[202]

(c) Enforcement Practices

87 In its report on sanctions practice in the Member States for 2019, ESMA states that almost all NCAs have imposed administrative sanctions for breach of the ban on market manipulation in very few cases.[203] No information on criminal sanctions is included in the report.

---

[194] Art. 5(2) CRIM-MAD.
[195] See para. 22.
[196] Recital 12 CRIM-MAD.
[197] Art. 6 CRIM-MAD.
[198] Art. 7(1) and (2) CRIM-MAD.
[199] Art. 8(1) CRIM-MAD.
[200] Art. 8(2) CRIM-MAD.
[201] Art. 8(3) CRIM-MAD.
[202] ECHR of 4 March 2014 (application No. 18640/10, 18647/10, 18663/10, 18668/10 and 18698/10), *Grande Stevens et. al. v. Italy*, cf. M. Ventoruzzo, 16 EBOR (2015), 145.
[203] Cf. ESMA, Annual Report on administrative and criminal sanctions and other administrative measures under MAR, ESMA70-156-2005, 12 December 2019. An exception is Sweden, where Finansinspektionen has imposed administrative sanctions in 29 cases.

Different experiences with enforcement practice by supervisory authorities are reported from Member States. The FCA in the UK has adopted a strategy of strict enforcement, 'if necessary', ie if the specific facts of a prohibition are not met, it reverts to the High Level Standards and Principles of the FCA Handbook, which enable it to impose drastic fines.[204]

2. Private Enforcement

Market manipulation results in investors buying or selling securities at distorted prices. This raises the question of whether investors can claim damages from the manipulator. Unlike the Prospectus Regulation[205] the MAR is silent on civil liability as a means of investor protection. Commentators have argued that the Member States are required to introduce civil liability to ensure the practical effectiveness of the market abuse prohibitions (*effet utile*).[206] Whether the ECJ follows this interpretation can, of course, hardly be assessed. One argument against this interpretation is that the European legislator has established a comprehensive system of supervision with extensive powers of investigation and administrative and criminal sanctions, thus providing an effective system of enforcement.

In Austria, the Supreme Court has recognised **liability for damages** in **favour of investors**. The court argues that the prohibition of information-based market manipulation is aimed at protecting the individual investor, who relies on information disseminated by professionals or through the media when making investment decisions.[207] Liability under private law is also possible in other jurisdictions. French, Greek and Italian law can be construed to allow private enforcement; Portuguese, Irish and Cyprus laws explicitly allow for it.[208] In Germany, on the other hand, the possibility of private enforcement has been denied by the courts, arguing that the aim of the prohibition of market manipulation is only to ensure the functioning of the markets at a macro-level.[209]

The recitals to the MAR emphasise that misinformation to capital markets harms investors and causes damages. A liability of the manipulator should therefore be recognised by that legislature. Ideally, this issue should be subject to a coordinating directive of the EU, ensuring liability also for grossly negligent misinformation of market participants.

88

89

90

VIII. Conclusion

The rules against market manipulation follow the same mechanism as under the former MAD 2003 regime. The MAR generally prohibits market manipulation and explains the prohibition through core definitions and a number of instances. Buy-back programmes and stabilisation measures are exempted under identical conditions as they were under the

91

---

[204] Cf. E. Swan and J. Virgo, *Market Abuse Regulation*, para. 5.37.
[205] See R. Veil § 17 para. 73.
[206] See R. Veil § 12 para. 24.
[207] Cf. OGH, 8 Ob 104/12b; OGH, 6 Ob 28/12d, 5.2 ff; S. Kalss et al., *Kapitalmarktrecht I*, § 22 para. 72.
[208] V. Tountopoulos, 11 ECFR (2014), 304.
[209] BGH of 19.07.2004 - II ZR 218/03, BGHZ 160, 134, 139–140; confirmed in BGH of 13.12.2011 - XI ZR 51/10 (*IKB*), BGHZ 192, 90; BVerfG of 24.09.2002 - 2 BvR 742/02, 23 ZIP (2002), 1986.

MAD 2003. The MAR's aim to expand the prohibition beyond the scope of the MAD 2003 is, however, clearly visible. More trading venues are included, manipulation is prohibited even across markets and products and attempts as well as 'any behaviour' not expressly mentioned in the MAR are covered. As a result of the Libor scandal, the European legislature has introduced a fourth extremely broad core example of market manipulation. However, the numerous technical provisions of the MAR and the Delegated Regulation reflect the difficulty of precisely describing manipulative behaviour that has a harmful effect.

92 After five years of practical experience with the MAR regime, it can be positively noted that hardly any relevant regulatory gaps have occurred. This is also due to the fact that the material scope of application of the prohibitions has been extended and the elements of the prohibitions are broadly defined. However, there is a need for reform in the case of information-based market manipulation. It should be expressly regulated that market manipulation can also take place by concealing information.

93 MAR and CRIM-MAD aim to ensure market integrity and a high level of investor protection. It is difficult to assess whether these regulatory objectives have been achieved. This is mainly because little is known about enforcement practices in the Member States. In particular, it is unclear whether NCAs and public prosecutors have the necessary expertise to judge and prosecute complex cases of market manipulation. In addition, the civil law liability for damages of manipulators is still terra incognita.

4
Disclosure System

§ 16

Foundations

Bibliography

Akerlof, George A., *The Market for 'Lemons': Quality Uncertainty and the Market Mechanism*, 84 Q. J. Econ. (1970), 488–500; Amihud, Yakov and Mendelson, Haim, *Liquidity, Volatility and Exchange Automation*, 3 J. Acc., Aud. Finance (1988), 369–395; Assmann, Heinz-Dieter, *Kapitalmarktrecht—Zur Formation eines Rechtsgebietes in der vierzigjährigen Rechtsentwicklung der Bundesrepublik Deutschland*, in: Nörr, Knut Wolfgang (ed.), *40 Jahre Bundesrepublik Deutschland—40 Jahre Rechtsentwicklung* (1989), 251–291; Beaver, William, *Financial Reporting: Accounting Revolution*, 3rd edn. (1998); Ben-Shahar, Omri and Schneider, Carl E., *The Failure of Mandated Disclosure*, U. Pa. L. Rev. (2011), 645–749; Bodie, Zvi et. al., *Investments and Portfolio Management*, 9th edn. (2011); Brandeis, Louis D., *Other People's Money and How the Bankers Use It* (1914); Brellochs, Michael, *Publizität und Haftung von Aktiengesellschaften im System des Europäischen Kapitalmarktrechts* (2005); Brinckmann, Hendrik, *Kapitalmarktrechtliche Finanzberichterstattung* (2009); Buck-Heeb, Petra, *Verhaltenspflichten beim Vertrieb—Zwischen Paternalismus und Schutzlosigkeit der Anleger—*, 177 ZHR (2013), 310–343; Daeniker, Daniel, *Fraud on the Market: ökonomische Theorien vor Gericht*, GesKR (2014), 396–404; Dauses, Manfred A. (ed.), *Handbuch des EU-Wirtschaftsrechts*, looseleaf, as of March 2020; Deckert, Martina and von Rüden, Jens, *Anlegerschutz durch Europäisches Kapitalmarktrecht*, EWS (1998), 46–54; Easterbrook, Frank H. and Fischel, Daniel R., *Mandatory Disclosure and the Protection of Investors*, 70 Va. L. Rev. (1984), 669–715; Enriques, Luca and Gilotta, Sergio, *Disclosure and Financial Market Regulation*, in: Moloney, Niamh et al. (eds.), The Oxford Handbook of Financial Regulation (2015), 511–535; Enriques, Luca et al., *Coporate Law and Securities Markets*, in: Kraakman, Reinier et al. (eds.), *The Anatomy of Corporate Law*, 3rd edn. (2017), 243–266; Ewert, Ralf, *Bilanzielle Publizität im Lichte der Theorie vom gesellschaftlichen Wert öffentlich verfügbarer Information*, BFuP (1989), 245–263; Fama, Eugene F., *Efficient Capital Markets: A Review of Theory and Empirical Work*, 25 J. Fin. (1970), 383–417; Fama, Eugene F. and Laffer, Arthur B., *Information and Capital Markets*, 44 J. Bus. (1971), 289–298; Fleischer, Holger, *Informationsasymmetrie im Vertragsrecht* (2001); Franck, Jens-Uwe and Purnhagen, Kai, *Homo Economicus, Behavioural Sciences, and Economic Regulation: On the Concept of Man in Internal Market Regulation and Its Normative Basis*, EUI Working Papers LAW No. 2012/26, available at SSRN: http://ssrn.com/abstract=2180895; Fülbier, Rolf U., *Regulierung der Ad-hoc-Publizität* (1998); Gilson, Ronald J. and Kraakman, Reinier H., *The Mechanisms of Market Efficiency*, 70 Va. L. Rev. (1984), 549–641; Gilson, Ronald J. and Kraakman, Reinier H., *Market Efficiency After the Financial Crisis: It's Still A Matter of Information Costs*, 100 Va. L. Rev. (2014), 313–375; Gonedes, Nicholas J., *The Capital Market, the Market for Information, and External Accounting*, 31 J. Fin. (1976), 611–630; Gonedes, Nicholas J. and Dopuch, Nicholas, *Capital Market Equilibrium, Information Production, and Selecting Accounting Techniques: Theoretical Framework and Review of Empirical Work*, Supplement to 12 J. Acc. Res. (1974), 48–129; Hennrichs, Joachim, *Die Grundkonzeption der CSR-Berichterstattung und ausgewählte Problemfelder*, ZGR (2018), 206–230; Hirshleifer, Jack, *The Private and Social Value of Information and the Reward to Inventive Activity*, 61 Am. Econ. Rev. (1971), 561–574; Hopt, Klaus J., *Inwieweit empfiehlt sich eine allgemeine gesetzliche Regelung des Anlegerschutzes?*, Gutachten G für den 51. Deutschen Juristentag (1976); Hopt, Klaus J.,

Vom Aktien- und Börsenrecht zum Kapitalmarktrecht?, Teil 1: Der international erreichte Stand des Kapitalmarktrechts, 140 ZHR (1976), 201–235, *Teil 2: Die deutsche Entwicklung im internationalen Vergleich,* 141 ZHR (1977), 389–441; Klöhn, Lars, *Wertpapierhandelsrecht diesseits und jenseits des Informationsparadigmas—Am Beispiel des „verständigen Anlegers" im Sinne des deutschen und europäischen Insiderrechts—,* 177 ZHR (2013), 349–388; Köndgen, Johannes, *Die Relevanz der ökonomischen Theorie der Unternehmung für rechtswissenschaftliche Fragestellungen—ein Problemkatalog,* in: Ott, Claus and Schäfer, Hans-Bernd (eds.), Ökonomische Analyse des Unternehmensrechts (1993), 128–155; Kohl, Helmut et al., *Abschreibungsgesellschaften, Kapitalmarkteffizienz und Publizitätszwang—Plädoyer für ein Vermögensanlagegesetz,* 138 ZHR (1974), 1–49; Kress, Sabine L., *Effizienzorientierte Kapitalmarktregulierung* (1996); Meier-Schatz, Christian J., *Wirtschaftsrecht und Unternehmenspublizität* (1989); Merkt, Hanno, *Unternehmenspublizität* (2001); Möslein, Florian and Mittwoch, Anne-Christin, *Der Europäische Aktionsplan zur Finanzierung nachhaltigen Wachstum,* WM (2019), 481–489; Moloney, Niamh, *How to Protect Investors: Lessons from the EC and the UK* (2010); Möllers, Thomas M.J., *Anlegerschutz durch Aktien- und Kapitalmarktrecht—Harmonisierungsmöglichkeiten nach geltendem und künftigem Recht,* ZGR (1997), 334–367; Möllers, Thomas M.J., *Effizienz als Maßstab des Kapitalmarktrechts: Die Verwendung empirischer und ökonomischer Argumente zur Begründung zivil-, straf-, und öffentlich-rechtlicher Sanktionen,* 208 AcP (2008), 1–36; Mülbert, Peter O., *Anlegerschutz und Finanzmarktregulierung—Grundlagen—,* 177 ZHR (2013), 160–212; Mülbert, Peter O., *Konzeption des europäischen Kapitalmarktrechts für Wertpapierdienstleistungen,* WM (2001), 2085–2102; Paredes, Troy A., *Blinded by the Light: Information Overload and its Consequences for Securities Regulation,* 81 Wash. U. L. Q. (2003), 417–485; Rehberg, Markus, *Der staatliche Umgang mit Information: Das europäische Informationsmodell im Lichte von Behavioral Economics,* in: Eger, Thomas and Schäfer, Hans-Bernd (eds.), Ökonomische Entwicklung der europäischen Zivilrechtsentwicklung (2007), 314–354; Schmidt, Reinhard H., *Rechnungslegung als Informationsproduktion auf nahezu effizienten Kapitalmärkten,* 34 Zfbf (1982), 728–748; Stout, Lynn A., *The Unimportance of Being Efficient: An Economic Analysis of Stock Market Pricing and Securities Regulation,* 87 Mich. L. Rev. (1988), 613–709; Veil, Rüdiger, *Die Ad-hoc-Publizitätshaftung im System kapitalmarktrechtlicher Informationshaftung,* 167 ZHR (2003), 365–402; Veil, Rüdiger, *Der Schutz des verständigen Anlegers durch Publizität und Haftung im europäischen und nationalen Kapitalmarktrecht,* ZBB (2006), 162–171; Veil, Rüdiger, *Climate-related financial disclosure,* in: Tountopoulos, Vassilios and Veil, Rüdiger (eds.), Transparency of Stock Corporations in Europe—Rationales, Limitations and Perspective (2019), 129–141; Veil, Rüdiger, *Transparenz über nachhaltige Investments und Nachhaltigkeitsrisiken—ist die europäische Gesetzgebung zu kurz gesprungen?,* in: Grundmann, Stefan et al. (eds.), Festschrift für Klaus J. Hopt zum 80. Geburtstag am 24. August 2020, 1321–1334; Verrecchia, Robert E., *Discretionary Disclosure,* 5 J. Acc. Econ. (1983), 179–194; Vokuhl, Nikolai, *Kapitalmarktrechtlicher Anlegerschutz und Kapitalerhaltung in der Aktiengesellschaft* (2007); West, Richard R., *On the Difference between Internal and External Market Efficiency,* 31 Fin. Analysts J. (1975), 30–34; Walz, Rainer, *Ökonomische Regulierungstheorien vor den Toren des Bilanzrechts,* ZfbF Sonderheft 32 (1993), 85–106; Wüstemann, Jens et al., *Regulierung durch Transparenz—Ökonomische Analysen, empirische Befunde und Empfehlungen für eine europäische Kapitalmarktregulierung,* in: Hopt, Klaus J. et al. (eds.), Kapitalmarktgesetzgebung im Europäischen Binnenmarkt (2008), 1–21.

I. Introduction

1   The legal framework for an efficient capital markets law essentially requires mandatory disclosure rules in order to supply the market with the necessary information on issuers. This was pointed out as early as 1966 by the Segré Committee in its Summary Report, thus

preparing the ground for the development of a disclosure system in the European Member States. The Segré Committee underlined the fact that disclosure is a necessary prerequisite for the viability of a harmonised European capital market. It considered a pan-European minimal framework of mandatory disclosure rules to be a fundamental measure in improving investor information through capital-seeking issuers.[1] Subsequently, disclosure provisions became one of the central regulatory instruments of European capital markets law. This regulatory concept was inspired by the US Securities Regulation which has always followed a disclosure philosophy for regulating capital markets.[2]

Justice *Louis D. Brandeis* described the disclosure philosophy applied by the US Securities Regulation as follows: 'Publicity is justly commended as a remedy for social and industrial diseases. Sunlight is said to be the best of disinfectants; electric light the most efficient policeman.'[3] *Louis Loss* and *Joel Seligman* highlighted the importance of mandatory disclosure rules in capital markets law in a similarly simple way: 'Then, too, there is the recurrent theme throughout these statutes of disclosure, again disclosure, and still more disclosure.'[4]

2

The recognition that mandatory disclosure rules play an important role in the viability of capital markets as proclaimed by the Segré Committee is not an exclusively legal one. The necessity for a mandatory system of disclosure can also be examined from an economic point of view. Theoretical studies on capital markets and economic models are of essential importance for the regulation of capital markets and are regarded as the justification for the disclosure philosophy in US capital markets law.[5] Therefore, the following short introduction into the underlying economic principles is necessary for understanding the disclosure system in European capital markets law.

3

II. Transparency and Capital Market Efficiency

The statements of *Louis D. Brandeis*, *Louis Loss* and *Joel Seligman* in the previous paragraphs emphasise the idea of mandatory disclosure being an instrument to manage a conflict of interests. But, furthermore, mandatory disclosure is also seen as essential for investors to make optimal investment decisions. In economics the connection between disclosure and its influence on the behaviour of investors on the one hand and capital markets on the other hand is examined under the benchmark of efficiency. In general, one distinguishes three different types of efficiency: allocational, institutional and operational.[6]

4

---

[1] European Commission, The Development of a European Capital Market, Report of a Group of experts appointed by the EEC Commission, November 2006 ('Segré Report'), p. 225 ff.
[2] L. Klöhn, 177 ZHR (2013), 349, 350–351; K. Hopt, 140 ZHR (1976), 201, 204 ff.; K. Hopt, 141 ZHR (1977), 389, 415.
[3] L. Brandeis, *Other People's Money and How the Bankers Use It*, 92.
[4] L. Loss and J. Seligman, *Securities Regulation*, 29.
[5] Cf. K. Hopt, 140 ZHR (1976), 201, 205; T. Möllers, 208 AcP (2008), 1, 5.
[6] Cf. H.-D. Assmann, in: Nörr (ed.), *Rechtsentwicklung*, 251, 263–264; H. Kohl et al., 138 ZHR (1974), 1, 16 ff.; M. Oulds, in: Kümpel et al. (eds.), *Bank- und Kapitalmarktrecht*, para. 11.57 ff.; N. Vokuhl, *Kapitalmarktrechtlicher Anlegerschutz*, 179 ff. See also R. Veil § 2 para. 8–10.

1. Allocational Efficiency

5   Allocational efficiency describes the main function of the capital markets as allocating scarce investable financial resources to investment opportunities.[7] Disclosure is regarded as having a positive influence on the reduction of information asymmetries between investors and issuers. Informational deficits of investors regarding important aspects of pricing and the quality of the issuers' investment offers can cause market failure or at least influence market efficiency decisively. The 'Market for Lemons' described by *Akerlof* is a well-cited model in this context.[8]

(a) Akerlof and the 'Market for Lemons'

6   *Akerlof* chose the market for used cars as an example of the problem of quality uncertainty.[9] If the quality of the product is uncertain, the customer can no longer distinguish between good and bad quality by looking at the price. In this case the buyers' behaviour is determined by 'adverse selection' and 'moral hazard'. In consequence sellers of good-quality products are at a disadvantage. They are unable to obtain a high enough price to make selling their products worthwhile. The higher costs of production cannot be passed on to the buyer as due to the uncertainty the buyer has to make deductions and will only be willing to pay an average price which therefore replaces the competitive price. These uncertainties are thus only advantageous for sellers of low-quality products, ie 'lemons'. Therefore, more and more sellers of products of above-average quality are squeezed out of the market. This finally leads to a complete market collapse.[10]

(b) Fama and the Efficient Capital Market Hypothesis (ECMH)

7   In addition to *Akerlof*'s 'Market for Lemons' the 'Theory of Informational Efficiency of Capital Markets'[11] proposed by *Fama* has also gained wide influence regarding the determination of the implications and effects of information on the markets. Originally this theory was developed for the securities analysis. It soon, however, also found its way into general theories on capital markets. Nevertheless the theory's informative value regarding the allocational mechanism is only indirect, as the theory of informational efficiency does not refer to the actual market processes but rather to procedures prior to these. It explores the relationship between information and market prices, or, in other words, the messages communicated by certain prices.[12] The main assertion of the theory of informational efficiency is that a capital market is efficient if the stock prices immediately and fully reflect the

---

[7] L. Enriques and S. Gilotta, in: Moloney and Ferran (eds.), *Financial Regulation*, 513; T. Möllers, 208 AcP (2008), 1, 7; P. Mülbert,177 ZHR (2013), 160, 172.
[8] G. Akerlof, 84 Q. J. Econ. (1970), 488 ff.
[9] See R. Veil § 2 para. 26.
[10] Cf. for this concept also H. Fleischer, *Informationsasymmetrie im Vertragsrecht*, 121 ff.; N. Moloney, *EU Securities and Financial Markets Regulation*, 56, argues with the 'Market for Lemons' model in favour of mandatory disclosure in the primary market.
[11] E. Fama, 25 J. Fin. (1970), 383 ff.
[12] W. Beaver, *Financial Reporting*, 127, 134–135.

available information.[13] The primary aim of the theory is to establish the actual degree of informational efficiency on the capital markets in order to be able to determine the amount of information already reflected in the prices. If, for example, the stock prices already reflect all existing information, trading decisions based solely on existing information do not yield abnormal returns as the relevant securities are not mispriced.[14]

The stipulations made by the theory of informational efficiency can only be proven for the very restrictive condition of market equilibrium as it is imperative that the adjustment process takes place immediately, that there are zero transaction costs, the market participants have homogeneous investor expectations and that they behave strictly rationally regarding all new information.[15] If the theory of informational efficiency requires such restrictive conditions in order to have a significant explanatory power, it is as such very imprecise and useless for empirical analysis. For this reason *Fama* amended his theory with the **efficient capital market hypothesis (ECMH)**.[16]

8

The ECMH describes three forms of informational efficiency on capital markets depending on the degree to which the market price ideally reflects different information: a weak informational efficiency means that the market price only reflects historical information, such as past prices or return sequences.[17] In a semi-strong form of informational efficiency, the market prices reflect all publicly available information. Strong informational efficiency implies that the market prices instantly reflect all price relevant information, ie not only all publicly available information, but also all hidden 'inside information'.[18]

9

(c) Discussion on the Scope of a Legal Reception of the ECMH

There are dissenting opinions as to what extent binding parameters for the development of a legal disclosure regime can be deduced from the ECMH.[19] In 1988 the US Supreme Court established the **fraud-on-the-market doctrine** by adopting the semi-strong form of the ECMH into its jurisprudence. In *Basic Inc. v Levinson* the court applied a presumption of reliance for investors who wanted to recover damages for misrepresentation from the issuer and who had to prove that they had relied on such misrepresentations. The court held that the investors could satisfy this reliance requirement by invoking a presumption that the price of stock traded in an efficient market reflects all public material information—including material misrepresentations.[20]

10

By justifying its fraud-on-the-market doctrine with the ECMH in *Basic* the US Supreme Court took an active part in the process of transforming the ECML from an academic

11

---

[13] E. Fama, 25 J. Fin. (1970), 383.
[14] S. Kress, *Effizienzorientierte Kapitalmarktregulierung*, 40; R. West, 31 Fin. Analysts J. (1975), 30. For a description of the market model which the ECMH is based on, cf. L. Klöhn, 177 ZHR (2013), 349, 354 ff.
[15] E. Fama, 25 J. Fin. (1970), 383, 387; R. West, 31 Fin. Analysts J. (1975), 30.
[16] E. Fama, 25 J. Fin. (1970), 383.
[17] E. Fama, 25 J. Fin. (1970), 383, 388, 414.
[18] Cf. also Z. Bodie et al., *Investments and Portfolio Management*, ch. 11 (p. 371 ff.).
[19] N. Moloney, *EU Securities and Financial Markets Regulation*, 57. See also H. Brinckmann, *Kapitalmarktrechtliche Finanzberichterstattung*, 61–62, in detail.
[20] *Basic Inc. v Levinson* [1988], 485 U.S., 224: 'Because most publicly available information is reflected in market price, an investor's reliance on any public material misrepresentations may be presumed […]'.

theory into a broad ideological justification for preferring market outcomes over regulation, beginning in the 1970s and influencing regulatory policy mainly in the United States for over thirty years since then.[21] Due to the overstatement of its implications the ECMH was always exposed to strong criticism, especially by insights derived from behavioural finance.[22] After the financial crisis some critics even went so far as to hold the ECMH responsible for this worldwide collapse of financial markets.[23] The increasing criticism also reached the jurisprudence of the US Supreme Court. In *Halliburton Co. v. Erica John Fund, Inc.* the court confirmed its presumption of reliance established in *Basic* by the conclusion that 'Halliburton has not identified the kind of fundamental shift in economic theory that could justify overruling a precedent on the ground that is misunderstood, or has since been overtaken, by economic realities'.[24] But three dissenting judges argued that *Basic* should be overruled by referring to new economic insights that called the implications of the ECMH for the fraud-on-the-market doctrine into question.[25]

12 The criticism on the ECMH makes clear that it should not be overstated by assuming a convergence of informational and fundamental efficiency. As fundamental efficiency means that investors get the 'correct price', informational efficiency only means that stock prices respond quickly to the release of new public information.[26] Having this in mind an essential observation that can be deduced from the semi-strong form of the ECMH is that if information is made public, the capital markets are capable of reflecting this publication in the prices[27] and informational efficiency and price accuracy are increased.[28]

2. Institutional Efficiency

13 Institutional efficiency outlines the criteria necessary for capital markets to function as markets. It is generally measured in terms of free market access for investors and traders, the range of products offered and the depth of financial capital available on the market.[29] Others consider investor confidence to be the main criteria for institutional efficiency. From this more politico-economic point of view, the main priority of capital markets law is to strengthen the level of investor confidence in the integrity and stability of the markets.[30] However, these diverging approaches only result in variations regarding terminology and

---

[21] Cf. R. Gilson and R. Kraakman, 100 Va. L. Rev. (2014), 313, 315 ff., state that the ECMH was 'hijacked by a powerful political cliente'.
[22] Cf. D. Daeniker, GesKR 2014, 396, 398; see also below para 31.
[23] Cf. D. Daeniker, GesKR 2014, 396, 398; R. Gilson and R. Kraakman, 100 Va. L. Rev. (2014), 313 ff. with further references.
[24] *Halliburton Co. v. Erica John Fund, Inc.* [2014], 573 U.S., Opinion of the Court, 10.
[25] *Halliburton Co. v. Erica John Fund, Inc.* [2014], 573 U.S., Thomas, J., concurring in judgment, 7 ff.
[26] Cf. R. Gilson and R. Kraakman, 100 Va. L. Rev. (2014), 313.
[27] M. Brellochs, *Publizität und Haftung*, 169–170.
[28] L. Enriques and S. Gilotta, in: Moloney and Ferran (eds.), *Financial Regulation*, 519; N. Moloney, *EU Securities and Financial Markets Regulation*, 57.
[29] Cf. K. Hopt, *Gutachten G 51. Dt. Juristentag*, G 49; M. Oulds, in: Kümpel et al. (eds.), *Bank- und Kapitalmarktrecht*, para. 11.58 ff.; N. Vokuhl, *Kapitalmarktrechtlicher Anlegerschutz*, 180.
[30] M. Oulds, in: Kümpel et al. (eds.), *Bank- und Kapitalmarktrecht*, para. 11.85; N. Vokuhl, *Kapitalmarktrechtlicher Anlegerschutz*, 180.

reasoning while the specifications concerning the content of institutional efficiency are the same. Institutional efficiency is measured in liquidity and volatility.[31]

Disclosure can positively or negatively influence an investor's decision to enter or exit the market and therefore have a direct impact on **liquidity**. If a market participant is uncertain about the accuracy of public information or is not able to compare investment possibilities sufficiently with the help of the disclosed information, this may restrain him from participating, thus resulting in a reduction of liquidity on the markets.[32] Disclosure can, if standardised and reliable, prevent this effect and thus have a positive effect on liquidity.[33] The influence of disclosure on the **volatility** of the market can be determined similarly. When new information is published, the market prices adapt accordingly, thus increasing volatility.[34] A certain volatility may even be seen as necessary with regard to informational efficiency in order for the prices to be able to adjust to the appearance of new information.[35] Similarly, when requesting an increase of liquidity one has to consider that in a situation of total liquidity, ie if an additional supply or demand will lead to no change in the equilibrium price, the price will not adjust to new information.[36] The market mechanisms can thus only function correctly if a certain level of volatility is accompanied by some degree of illiquidity.

3. Operational Efficiency

Operational efficiency describes a process-orientated examination of capital markets involving aspects of time and transaction costs.[37] Insufficient disclosure may not necessarily lead to market migration, but will certainly lead to higher costs for an investor to make an informed investment decision. The informational efficiency of capital markets depends on the extent to which the information has spread. The circulation of information will in turn be higher the lower the informational costs are and vice versa.[38]

One can distinguish between three types of **information costs**: costs of acquisition, verification and processing.[39] Disclosure primarily reduces the costs for investors to acquire information. Additionally, requiring a specific content of the information to be disclosed and effective quality control can reduce the costs of verification and processing. The auditor's certificate attained through the audit of financial statements, for example, can be seen as an instrument ensuring the quality of the information, enabling investors to rely on it and thus

---

[31] Cf. S. Kress, *Effizienzorientierte Kapitalmarktregulierung*, 59 ff.
[32] R. Schmidt, 34 ZfbF (1982), 728, 741.
[33] C. Meier-Schatz, *Wirtschaftsrecht und Unternehmenspublizität*, 216–217; H. Merkt, *Unternehmenspublizität*, 345.
[34] S. Kress, *Effizienzorientierte Kapitalmarktregulierung*, 65.
[35] Y. Amihud and H. Mendelson, 3 J. Acc., Aud. Finance (1988), 369, 374; S. Kress, *Effizienzorientierte Kapitalmarktregulierung*, 66.
[36] S. Kress, *Effizienzorientierte Kapitalmarktregulierung*, 64.
[37] S. Kress, *Effizienzorientierte Kapitalmarktregulierung*, 44; N. Vokuhl, *Kapitalmarktrechtlicher Anlegerschutz*, 181.
[38] R. Gilson and R. Kraakman, 70 Va. L. Rev. (1984), 549, 593.
[39] R. Gilson and R. Kraakman, 70 Va. L. Rev. (1984), 549, 593 ff.: 'The lower the cost of particular information, the wider will be its distribution, the more effective will be the capital market mechanism operating to reflect it in prices, and the more efficient will be the market with respect to it.'

reducing their costs of verification.[40] Operational efficiency can be increased if the effects of provisions on disclosure are seen as a whole: by burdening the issuers with mandatory disclosures instead of leaving the acquisition of information up to the investors the total transaction costs on the market are minimised.[41]

III. Disclosure Provisions as Part of the Regulation of Capital Markets

1. The Importance of Legal Disclosure Provisions from an Economic Point of View

17 Economics is often confronted with the task of having to find binding parameters for the development of legal disclosure provisions.[42] The benchmark of full market efficiency could work as such a standard for the regulation of capital markets,[43] but Economics does not provide clear parameters that can be used to design a system of mandatory disclosure and its necessary content for achieving full market efficiency.[44] Rather, the findings can only be understood in a model theoretical context giving no more than an indication for the legislator of how to shape the system of mandatory disclosure.[45] In Economics the reference model and benchmark is usually an allocationally efficient market and all deviations from this which occur in reality are immediately classed as market failure. Market failure thus becomes the criterion to describe a market that is unable to fulfil its allocational task. In order to counteract market failure, regulatory intervention is regarded necessary.[46]

(a) Reduction of Information Asymmetries to Prevent Market Failure

18 **Market failure** may result from an asymmetrical distribution of information[47] between market participants which can be prevented or reduced by legal disclosure provisions.[48]

(aa) Social Value of Public Information

19 The theory of the social value of public information, which can be traced back to *Fama/Laffer*[49] and *Hirshleifer*,[50] supports this concept, especially with regard to capital

---

[40] F. Easterbrook and D. Fischel, 70 Va. L. Rev. (1984), 669, 674–675; H. Merkt, *Unternehmenspublizität*, 470–471.
[41] Cf. R. Veil, 167 ZHR (2003), 365, 379–380.
[42] Cf. C. Meier-Schatz, *Wirtschaftsrecht und Unternehmenspublizität*, 161 ff.; H. Merkt, *Unternehmenspublizität*, 212 ff.
[43] Cf. J. Wüstemann et al., in: Hopt et al. (eds.), *Kapitalmarktgesetzgebung*, 11 and passim.
[44] L. Enriques and S. Gilotta, in: Moloney and Ferran (eds.), *Financial Regulation*, 525.
[45] L. Enriques and S. Gilotta, in: Moloney and Ferran (eds.), *Financial Regulation*, 525.
[46] L. Enriques and S. Gilotta, in: Moloney and Ferran, (eds.) *Financial Regulation*, 526.
[47] In more detail H. Fleischer, *Informationsasymmetrie im Vertragsrecht*, 121 ff.; R. Fülbier, *Regulierung der Ad-hoc-Publizität*, 176 ff.
[48] N. Moloney, *EU Securities and Financial Markets Regulation*, 54; R. Fülbier, *Regulierung der Ad-hoc-Publizität*, 179.
[49] E. Fama and A. Laffer, 44 J. Bus. (1971), 289 ff.
[50] J. Hirshleifer, 61 Am. Econ. Rev. (1971), 561 ff.

markets law. It shows that if information is merely obtained privately this can be disadvantageous for an allocationally efficient market mechanism. The costs of obtaining information constitute a use of resources by each market participant without any advantage for society as a whole. An excessive amount of information is produced as market participants generate the same information parallel to one another.[51] That is why the production of public information through a legal disclosure obligation is regarded as economically advantageous, substituting private procurement of information and reducing the loss of resources associated with an information surplus.[52] However, this cannot lead to the conclusion that mandatory legal regulation of disclosure is necessary. It must be noted that investors have collective means of forcing issuers to necessary disclosure measures. These means include risk surcharges, discounts[53] and influencing shareholder meetings.[54]

(bb) Reduction of Agency Costs and Signal Theory

Some argue that economic incentives are sufficient to provide the necessary level of disclosure. The asymmetric distribution of information between issuers and investors results in so-called **agency costs**. These describe the costs for the investors to minimise the information advantages of the issuers.[55] The issuer's management has a large interest in keeping the agency costs low. The reduction in share price and manager remuneration as a result of the asymmetry of information lead directly to economic disadvantages for the management. Thus, the necessary information is voluntarily disclosed in order to reduce asymmetries of information.[56]

The **signal theory** generalises this idea by stating that anyone having better information will signal this if he can gain economic advantages therefrom.[57] Similarly, there can be an incentive to disclose negative company data, as reluctance to do so will provoke scepticism in the investors. This scepticism may cause more of the investors to sell off their shares than would the disclosure of the negative information itself.[58] These incentives for voluntary disclosure resulting from agency costs and the signal theory are, however, put into perspective when compared to opposing incentive systems. In particular, *Verrecchia*'s concept of 'proprietary costs'[59] exemplifies how a company may be dissuaded from voluntary disclosure by the ensuing negative externalities.

(b) Information and the Public Good Problem

A different line of argumentation focuses on the nature of information as a public good. Public goods can lead to market failure due to the so-called **free-rider**

---

[51] E. Fama and A. Laffer, 44 J. Bus. (1971), 289, 292; J. Hirshleifer, 61 Am. Econ. Rev. (1971), 573.
[52] L. Enriques and S. Gilotta, in: Moloney and Ferran (eds.), *Financial Regulation*, 512.; R. Fülbier, *Regulierung der Ad-hoc-Publizität*, 177–178.
[53] R. Fülbier, *Regulierung der Ad-hoc-Publizität*, 178.
[54] R. Ewert, BFuP (1989), 245, 261.
[55] In more detail R. Richter and E. Furubotn, *Neue Institutionenökonomie*, 176–177.
[56] H. Merkt, *Unternehmenspublizität*, 212–213.
[57] C. Meier-Schatz, *Wirtschaftsrecht und Unternehmenspublizität*, 164; M. Rehberg, in: Eger and Schäfer (eds.), *Ökonomische Entwicklung*, 314.
[58] H. Merkt, *Unternehmenspublizität*, 213; J. Köndgen, in: Ott and Schäfer (eds.), *Ökonomische Analyse*, 128, 152, takes a more restrictive point of view by stating that disclosure provisions have to be at least partly mandatory.
[59] R. Verrecchia, 5 J. Acc. Econ. (1983), 179, 181.

effect.⁶⁰ The free-rider effect describes a situation in which anybody can gain access to public goods without costs so that the market price of these public goods is reduced to zero. As a result, there is no longer any incentive to offer public goods on the market and a shortage may occur.⁶¹ Yet whilst economic studies assume all information to be a public good,⁶² thereby enabling disclosure to prevent market failure, this approach is too general: the nature of information changes, taking on the characteristics of a private good during the period of production and developing the character of a mixed good during distribution. Only when fully distributed can information then be classed as a public good.⁶³ There is proof of this understanding with regard to the capital markets: according to the ECMH, additional returns can be attained on semi-strong capital markets by making use of inside information.⁶⁴ As a result share prices will adjust to the new level of information and no further returns will be attained by making use of the inside information— the information has been exhausted.⁶⁵ Information therefore must be classed as a hybrid good,⁶⁶ thus preventing a general statement on the necessity of mandatory disclosure.

23   Market failure can further result from the monopoly which exists regarding information. Corporate information in particular is usually subject to the monopoly of the issuer who will mostly be the only one with access to internal company data—or at least the one whose access involves the lowest costs.⁶⁷ A disclosure obligation could prevent the issuer from exploiting his monopoly.⁶⁸ However, once again the above-mentioned incentives of voluntary disclosure militate against the understanding that a regulatory intervention is inevitable. They are said to ensure sufficiently that the issuer will not abuse his monopoly on corporate information.⁶⁹

(c) Mandatory Disclosure and the Theory of Transaction Costs

24   By contrast, the **transaction cost theory** promises considerable insight,⁷⁰ stipulating that disclosure provisions are not absolutely but only relatively mandatory from an economic point of view, provided the legislative disclosure rules contribute to a reduction

---

⁶⁰ A public good is defined by two aspects: firstly, that no rivalry exists regarding its consumption—even when one consumer makes use of public information it remains available for others; secondly, the fact that one cannot be excluded from the use of the good when not paying for it, R. Fülbier, *Regulierung der Ad-hoc-Publizität*, 172.

⁶¹ Cf. L. Enriques and S. Gilotta, in: Moloney and Ferran (eds.), *Financial Regulation*, 521; Meier-Schatz, *Wirtschaftsrecht und Unternehmenspublizität*, 166–167; H. Merkt, *Unternehmenspublizität*, 219.

⁶² The immaterial nature of information proves that the amount of existing information cannot be reduced by the fact that an individual makes use of it, N. Gonedes and N. Dopuch, Supplement to 12 J. Acc. Res. (1974), 48, 65, ie the use of information by one person does not exclude others from using it, N. Gonedes, 31 J. Fin. (1976), 611, 617.

⁶³ C. Meier-Schatz, *Wirtschaftsrecht und Unternehmenspublizität*, 170 ff.

⁶⁴ Cf. L. Klöhn, 177 ZHR (2013), 349, 354 ff., on information traders who try to gain extra returns by comparing market prices with the fundamental value of the company.

⁶⁵ C. Meier-Schatz, *Wirtschaftsrecht und Unternehmenspublizität*, 171; R. Fülbier, *Regulierung der Ad-hoc-Publizität*, 175.

⁶⁶ C. Meier-Schatz, *Wirtschaftsrecht und Unternehmenspublizität*, 172; H. Merkt, *Unternehmenspublizität*, 219.

⁶⁷ E. Fama and A. Laffer, 44 J. Bus. (1971), 289, 292; N. Gonedes, 31 J. Fin. (1976), 611, 618; T. Möllers, 208 AcP (2008), 1, 8.

⁶⁸ R. Fülbier, *Regulierung der Ad-hoc-Publizität*, 181.

⁶⁹ Cf. R. Fülbier, *Regulierung der Ad-hoc-Publizität*, 182.

⁷⁰ For details cf. R. Richter and E. Furubotn, *Neue Institutionenökonomie*, 53 ff.

of transaction costs on the market. This can be determined by drawing up a balance in order to determine and compare the transaction costs with and without the respective disclosure provisions. A mandatory disclosure regime must be regarded as necessary if the overall level of the transaction costs improves under legislative disclosure provisions compared to without them.

In cases of information asymmetries regarding internal company data it must be kept in mind, that issuers have much easier and cheaper access to these than investors. The issuers can thus often be seen as the *cheapest cost avoiders*,[71] thus justifying placing them under the obligation of disclosure. Especially regarding capital markets, it has been suggested to lower transaction costs by introducing fixed standards that must be adhered to when providing information.[72] Legislative provisions which improve the content and quality of information and standardise the methods of disclosure hold many advantages over a concept relying on the market process.[73] It is less cost-intensive, improves the possibilities of comparing the information provided and reduces the processing costs.[74] Yet one must bear in mind that standardising the disclosure mechanisms requires a consensus. In order to achieve this, opposing interests have to be assessed.[75] This usually results in a compromise which entails that mostly only minimum standards will be achieved.[76]

25

(d) Conclusion

Altogether, various incentives can be found that may lead an issuer to disclose information voluntarily, thus reducing the lack of transparency. In other words: 'A world without mandatory disclosure would not be completely in the dark'.[77] But it has not been clearly determined to date whether voluntary disclosure is sufficient or whether legislative intervention remains necessary. Economic research findings remain unclear on this.[78]

26

2. **Disclosure Provisions as Part of Investor Protection**

Economic theories have produced only a few clear parameters that can be applied to the disclosure systems of European capital markets. Therefore the development of a disclosure system can be seen more as a reaction to regulatory concerns[79] that have occurred or been identified than as the implementation of economic theories guaranteeing ideal

27

---

[71] T. Möllers, 208 AcP (2008), 1, 10–11; L. Stout, 87 Mich. L. Rev (1988), 613, 705; R. Veil, 167 ZHR (2003) 365, 379–380; N. Vokuhl, *Kapitalmarktrechtlicher Anlegerschutz*, 181.
[72] See also, especially regarding the disclosure of accounting, J. Wüstemann et al., in: Hopt et al. (eds.), *Kapitalmarktgesetzgebung*, 11–12, 16.
[73] Cf. L. Enriques and S. Gilotta, in: Moloney and Ferran (eds.), *Financial Regulation*, 524–525, 531.
[74] L. Enriques et al., in: Kraakman et al. (eds.), *The Anatomy of Corporate Law*, 244, 246; R. Walz, ZfbF Sonderheft 32 (1993), 85, 94–95; R. Fülbier, *Regulierung der Ad-hoc-Publizität*, 192; M. Rehberg, in: Eger and Schäfer (eds.), *Ökonomische Entwicklung*, 314 ff.; N. Vokuhl, *Kapitalmarktrechtlicher Anlegerschutz*, 172.
[75] Cf. R. Walz, ZfbF Sonderheft 32 (1993), 85, 95.
[76] R. Fülbier, *Regulierung der Ad-hoc-Publizität*, 193.
[77] L. Enriques and S. Gilotta, in: Moloney and Ferran (eds.), *Financial Regulation*, 525.
[78] L. Enriques and S. Gilotta, in: Moloney and Ferran (eds.), *Financial Regulation*, 525.
[79] O. Ben-Shahar and and C. Schneider, U. Pa. L. Rev. (2011), 645, 680; L. Enriques and S. Gilotta, in: Moloney and Ferran (eds.), *Financial Regulation*, 512–513.

conditions for the functioning of the market. Legislative measures will usually be based on the justification that pan-European provisions are necessary to ensure **investor protection**.[80] It is generally argued that an adequate investor protection increases the investors' confidence in the market and deters them from withdrawing their financial capital from capital markets which would have a disastrous consequence for the entire economic system.[81]

(a) Principle of Investor Protection through Information Disclosure

28   Investor protection in capital markets law is generally based on the overall principle of an investor making its decisions autonomously, ie free of governmental paternalism.[82] This also includes an investor's freedom to act irrationally[83] even though such behaviour is not the benchmark for the legislator's regulation. Following this liberal approach, the European model of investor protection is like the US Securities Regulation based on the concept of a **reasonable investor** who makes rational decisions on the capital markets.[84]

29   Although Economic theory in general does not provide a precise guidance for the legislator and its task to regulate capital markets, the ECMH had a huge impact on this concept of investor protection in capital markets law, beginning with the US Securities Regulation and when the European capital markets law followed the US approach.[85] Deficits in the level of investor protection are countered with further information, helping investors to make reasonable decisions.[86] This approach can best be described as an '**information paradigm**'.[87] The core function of mandatory disclosure provisions is therefore to provide investors with information on the issuers to help them make better decisions,[88] meaning that such decisions shall be based on the disclosed information. According to the insights of the semi-strong form of the ECMH, informational efficiency and price accuracy shall be increased in respect to the disclosed information. Mandatory disclosure thereby has the effect of controlling investors' decisions and the reasonable investor works as a purely functional, normative model, making capital markets more informationally efficient.[89]

---

[80] Cf. M. Deckert and J. v. Rüden, EWS (1998), 46, 49 ff.; P. Mülbert, WM (2001), 2085, 2092, 2100.
[81] L. Enriques and S. Gilotta, in: Moloney and Ferran (eds.), *Financial Regulation*, 514.
[82] P. Buck-Heeb, ZHR 177 (2013), 310, 326–327; P. Mülbert, 177 ZHR (2013), 160, 206.
[83] P. Buck-Heeb, ZHR 177 (2013), 310, 327; P. Mülbert, 177 ZHR (2013), 160, 173.
[84] Cf. L. Klöhn, 177 ZHR (2013), 349, 369 ff.; R. Veil, ZBB (2006), 162 ff.
[85] Cf. N. Moloney, *EU Securities and Financial Markets Regulation*, 55; L. Klöhn, 177 ZHR (2013), 349, 350–351, 363 ff.
[86] P. Buck-Heeb, ZHR 177 (2013), 310, 326–327; J.-U. Franck and K. Purnhagen, *Homo Economicus, Behavioural Sciences, and Economic Regulation: On the Concept of Man in Internal Market Regulation and Its Normative Basis*, 5; N. Moloney, *EU Securities and Financial Markets Regulation*, 771.
[87] Cf. J.-U. Franck and K. Purnhagen, *Homo Economicus, Behavioural Sciences, and Economic Regulation: On the Concept of Man in Internal Market Regulation and Its Normative Basis*, 7, 9. In Germany, the notion of an 'information model' is used to describe this approach, cf. P. Buck-Heeb, 177 ZHR (2013), 310, 326; P. Mülbert,177 ZHR (2013), 160, 184; W.-G. Ringe, in: Lehmann and Kumpan, *European Financial Services Law*, Art. 1 TD para. 2.
[88] L. Enriques and S. Gilotta, in: Moloney and Ferran (eds.), *Financial Regulation*, 512; 515; see also N. Moloney, *How to Protect Investors*, 46.
[89] J.-U. Franck and K. Purnhagen, *Homo Economicus, Behavioural Sciences, and Economic Regulation: On the Concept of Man in Internal Market Regulation and Its Normative Basis*, 6 ff.; L. Klöhn, 177 ZHR (2013), 349, 383 ff.

(b) Discussion on the Scope of Investor Protection

The extent to which investor protection is achieved through disclosure provisions has been subject to extensive legal discussions.[90] Some argue that disclosure provisions are crucial for an efficient capital market, are based on economic insights and thus only aim to achieve a supra-individual level of investor protection.[91] Others purport that the disclosure provisions are rather orientated towards the protection of the individual investor.[92] The European provisions alone do not provide a clear answer to this dispute. Most disclosure provisions are laid down in directives which require implementation into the national laws of the Member States, granting them discretion with regard to the exact wording of the provisions. On an abstract level it can only be said that disclosure provisions are primarily based on economic parameters to control investors' decisions[93] as a whole.[94] The protection of an individual investor would be better achieved by information rights of the investors or notification obligations of the issuers.[95] The protection of the individual investor is also an objective of European capital markets law.[96] But, in general terms, it cannot be said that European disclosure provisions aim to achieve investor protection by ensuring that an individual investor can claim for civil liability.

30

(c) Criticism of the Information Paradigm and Complementing Measures for Investor Protection

The idea of a rational investor has more and more frequently been questioned due to new insights derived from **behavioural finance**.[97] Problems of bounded rationality and information overload[98] can impair the ability of individual investors to handle and correctly process the information available at the market and may keep them from making optimal decisions.[99] The insights from behavioural finance have therefore questioned the concept of investor protection being based on a system of 'disclosure, again disclosure, and still more disclosure'.[100],[101] As a consequence, the information paradigm and the principle of investor

31

---

[90] N. Moloney, *EU Securities and Financial Markets Regulation*, 55. For an overview on the German discussion cf. H. Brinckmann, *Kapitalmarktrechtliche Finanzberichterstattung*, 76 ff.; H. Merkt, *Unternehmenspublizität*, 301 ff.
[91] Cf. M. Deckert and J. v. Rüden, EWS (1998), 46, 49; L. Klöhn, 177 ZHR (2013), 349, 384; P. Mülbert, 177 ZHR (2013), 160, 172–173.
[92] Cf. T. Möllers, ZGR (1997), 334, 336 ff.
[93] For the idea of controlling people's decisions through disclosure provisions see L. Enriques and S. Gilotta, in: Moloney and Ferran (eds.), *Financial Regulation*, 512; C. Meier-Schatz, *Wirtschaftsrecht und Unternehmenspublizität*, 106–107; H. Merkt, *Unternehmenspublizität*, 338 ff.
[94] H. Brinckmann, *Kapitalmarktrechtliche Finanzberichterstattung*, 82 ff.
[95] H. Brinckmann, *Kapitalmarktrechtliche Finanzberichterstattung*, 86.
[96] See R. Veil § 2 para. 11, K. Follak, in: Dauses (ed.), *Handbuch des EU-Wirtschaftsrechts*, F.III para. 6.
[97] N. Moloney, *EU Securities and Financial Markets Regulation*, 57 ff. For an overview on the behavioural finance-research see R. Veil § 6 para. 20–29.
[98] Cf. T. Paredes, 81 Wash. U. L. Q. (2003), 417, 434 ff.
[99] P. Buck-Heeb, 177 ZHR (2013), 310, 327–328; L. Enriques and S. Gilotta, in: Moloney and Ferran (eds.), *Financial Regulation*, 515, 528; N. Moloney, *EU Securities and Financial Markets Regulation*, 773; P. Mülbert, 177 ZHR (2013), 160, 169 ff., 187 ff.
[100] Cf. L. Loss and J. Seligman, *Securities Regulation*, 29.
[101] Cf. L. Enriques and S. Gilotta, in: Moloney and Ferran (eds.), *Financial Regulation*, 528; N. Moloney, *EU Securities and Financial Markets Regulation*, 55; L. Klöhn, 177 ZHR (2013), 349, 358 ff. See also O. Ben-Shahar and C. Schneider, U. Pa. L. Rev. (2011), 645, 679 ff.

protection through mandatory disclosure are complemented by different, rather paternalistic regulative measures, such as the prohibition of an execution-only transaction for certain investment products[102] or even the prohibition of certain investment products[103] or forms of transactions[104] in general.[105] These measures follow the realisation that investors are unable to make rational—meaning optimal—decisions even if provided with sufficient information.[106] Investor protection is therefore adjusted through the principle of **consumer protection**[107] justifying a higher level of governmental paternalism und limited autonomy of the individual.

32   The critics of the information paradigm can rely on the accepted findings of behavioural finance. Nevertheless, other regulative measures for investor protection should only be applied very rarely in capital markets law.[108] The reason is that a renunciation of the information paradigm and a higher level of governmental paternalism would mean jeopardising the basic social approach of individual freedom and free capital markets.[109] The information paradigm accepts these premises and stems from the idea of free markets and the goal to reach market efficiency. Behavioural finance still describes and systemises irrational behaviour on the market more than actually presenting a comprehensive alternative model for capital markets regulation.[110] The information paradigm is therefore still without a viable alternative that could ensure better investor protection. In other words: The information paradigm is not without weaknesses but it still seems to be the best regulative approach for investor protection as long as other approaches have not been proven to be better than this second best choice.[111]

3. Disclosure Provisions as an Instrument to Foster Sustainable Finance

33   Since 2015, the Paris Agreement on climate change[112] and the UN 2030 Agenda for Sustainable Development[113] highly accelerated governmental measures for more sustainability. In the area of financial market regulation, the concept of **sustainable finance** summarises measures in this respect. The Commission's Action Plan 'Financing Sustainable

---

[102] Art. 25(4) MiFID II.
[103] Cf. Art. 40 ff. MiFIR.
[104] Cf. Art. 12 ff. Regulation (EU) No. 236/2012 of the European Parliament and of the Council of 14 March 2012 on short selling and certain aspects of credit default swaps, OJ L 86, 24 March 2012, 1–24.
[105] Cf. P. Buck-Heeb, 177 ZHR (2013), 310, 330; N. Moloney, *EU Securities and Financial Markets Regulation*, 771 ff.; P. Mülbert, 177 ZHR (2013), 160, 198 ff.
[106] With criticism P. Mülbert, 177 ZHR (2013), 160, 207.
[107] Cf. P. Buck-Heeb, ZHR 177 (2013), 310, 340; N. Moloney, *How to Protect Investors*, 40; N. Moloney, *EU Securities and Financial Markets Regulation*, 773; P. Mülbert, 177 ZHR (2013), 160, 178, 180–181.
[108] Cf. P. Buck-Heeb, 177 ZHR (2013), 310, 342.
[109] O. Ben-Shahar and C. Schneider, U. Pa. L. Rev. (2011), 645, 681; L. Enriques and S. Gilotta, in: Moloney and Ferran (eds.), *Financial Regulation*, 512, 513; P. Buck-Heeb, 177 ZHR (2013), 310, 328–329.
[110] P. Buck-Heeb, 177 ZHR (2013), 310, 329–330.
[111] Cf. N. Moloney, *EU Securities and Financial Markets Regulation*, 58; L. Klöhn, 177 ZHR (2013), 349, 363.
[112] Paris Agreement under the United Nations Framework Convention on Climate Change, 12 December 2015, available at: https://unfccc.int/sites/default/files/english_paris_agreement.pdf.
[113] Resolution adopted by the General Assembly of the United Nations, Transforming our world: the 2030 Agenda for Sustainable Development, 25 September 2015, available at: www.un.org/ga/search/view_doc.asp?symbol=A/RES/70/1&Lang=E.

Growth' of 2018[114] marked the starting point for a comprehensive set of European regulatory initiatives to implement this political agenda. The Commission pointed out that sustainability and the transition to a low-carbon, more resource-efficient and circular economy are key in ensuring long-term competitiveness of the European economy.[115] Thus, the sustainable finance framework aims to reorient capital flows towards sustainable investments meaning the provision of funding for economic activities taking longer-term interests on environmental, social and governance (ESG) considerations into account.[116]

In order to achieve these objectives, the European legislator focused its regulatory measures on two main aspects.[117] This is first the establishment of an European classification system for sustainable activities, so called '**EU Taxonomy**'.[118] Since 2020, the Taxonomy Regulation sets out the conditions an economic activity has to meet in order to qualify as environmentally sustainable.[119] Besides, the European legislator also identified **disclosure obligations on sustainability issues** as a key instrument to reorient capital flows towards sustainable investments.[120] In the Commission's view fostering corporate transparency on sustainability issues will enable investors and stakeholders to assess companies' long-term value creation and their sustainability risk exposure.[121] The legislative transposition took place (i) by Regulation (EU) 2019/2088[122] on sustainability-related disclosures in the financial services sector (SFDR), laying down sustainability disclosure obligations for manufacturers of financial products and financial advisers toward end-investors[123] and also (ii) by integrating the already existing non-financial reporting stipulated by Directive 2014/95/EU[124] amending the Accounting Directive as regards disclosure of non-financial and diversity information by certain large undertakings and groups (NFRD) into the sustainable finance agenda.[125]

34

By using mandatory disclosure for its strategy on sustainable finance, the European legislator refers again to the characteristics of disclosure provisions as a control instrument for the decisions of capital market participants.[126] The legislator justified its approach of fostering transparency on sustainability issues by deficits revealed in the existing framework of corporate disclosure.[127] Sustainable investments would require a long-term orientation

35

---

[114] Communication from the Commission to the European Parliament, the European Council, the Council, the European Central Bank, the European Economic and Social Committee and the Committee of the Regions, Action Plan: Financing Sustainable Growth, 8 March 2018, COM(2018) 97 final (Sustainable Finance Action Plan 2018).
[115] Commission, Sustainable Finance Action Plan 2018, p. 1.
[116] Commission, Sustainable Finance Action Plan 2018, p. 2.
[117] Cf. R. Veil, in: FS Hopt, 1321, 1322.
[118] European Commission, Sustainable Finance Action Plan 2018, p. 3 ff.
[119] See R. Veil § 1 para. 59 and § 2 para. 22.
[120] Cf. R. Veil, in: FS Hopt, 1321, 1322 ff.
[121] Commission, Sustainable Finance Action Plan 2018, p. 3 ff.
[122] Cf. Regulation (EU) 2019/2088 of the European Parliament and of the Council of 27 November 2019 on sustainability- related disclosures in the financial services sector, OJ L 317, 9 December 2019, p. 1–16 (SFDR).
[123] Cf. R. Veil, in: FS Hopt, 1321, 1327 ff.
[124] Directive 2014/95/EU of the European Parliament and of the Council of 22 October 2014 amending Directive 2013/34/EU as regards disclosure of non-financial and diversity information by certain large undertakings and groups, OJ L 330, 15 November 2014, p. 1–9 (NFRD).
[125] Cf. F. Möslein and A.-C. Mittwoch, WM (2019), 481, 487 ff. See also H. Brinckmann § 18 para. 16 ff. On problems with the connection between these two disclosure regimes cf. R. Veil, in: Tountopoulos and Veil (eds.), *Transparency of Stock Corporations in Europe*, 129, 138.
[126] See above para. 29.
[127] Cf. European Commission, Sustainable Finance Action Plan 2018, p. 4.

whereas the current framework was seen as focusing on the production of high returns over a short timeframe.[128] This can been explained by the increasing degree of uncertainty when it comes to predict a company's performance over a longer period of time. Although capital markets law refers to financial accounting information for its system of periodic disclosure assuming that such information provide the best instrument for a prognosis on future companies' performance business economics has developed so far,[129] nonetheless, the more the prognosis goes into the future even financial accounting information are losing their capacity as a prognosis tool. As the European legislator tries to reorient capital flows towards long-term (meaning sustainable) investments, disclosure provisions need to supply the market with information on these sustainability issues. As they are intended to open investment decisions for a long-term perspective, they bear a higher degree of uncertainty as eg financial accounting information. However, by requiring companies to report on sustainability issues these companies are forced to integrate environmental, social and governance concerns in their business operations and in their interaction with their stakeholders.[130] In this way disclosure obligations on sustainability issues act as an **instrument of permanent self-control**.[131]

IV. Development of a Disclosure System in European Capital Markets Law

36 In the beginning, the European legislator did not follow an overall concept for the development of a disclosure system. The first directives[132] referred to limited aspects of capital markets law[133] and only contained provisions for issuers whose securities were admitted to the official listing of a stock exchange. Meanwhile the European Union has enlarged its regulatory activity.[134] This led to the development of an overall disclosure regime.

---

[128] Cf. Commission, Sustainable Finance Action Plan 2018, p. 3, 10; R. Veil, in: Tountopoulos and Veil (eds.), *Transparency of Stock Corporations in Europe*, 129, 141.

[129] See H. Brinckmann § 18 para. 7 ff. with further references.

[130] Cf. Commission, Sustainable Finance Action Plan 2018, p. 3; R. Veil, in: Tountopoulos and Veil (eds.), *Transparency of Stock Corporations in Europe*, 129, 137 ff.

[131] Cf. J. Hennrichs, ZGR (2018), 206, 209.

[132] These were Council Directive 79/279/EEC of 5 March 1979 coordinating the conditions for the admission of securities to official stock exchange listing, OJ L 66, 16 March 1979, 21–32 (Securities Admission Directive); Council Directive 80/390/EEC of 17 March 1980 coordinating the requirements for the drawing up, scrutiny and distribution of the listing particulars to be published for the admission of securities to official stock exchange listing, OJ L 100, 17 April 1980, p. 1–26 (Securities Admission Prospectus Directive) and Council Directive 82/121/EEC of 15 February 1982 on information to be published on a regular basis by companies the shares of which have been admitted to official stock-exchange listing, OJ L 48, 20 February 1982, p. 26–29 (Half-Yearly Report Directive).

[133] M. Brellochs, *Publizität und Haftung*, 26.

[134] Initially, the European disclosure system which was based mainly on European directives followed a concept of a system of five concentric circles, P. Mülbert, WM (2001), 2085, 2094–2095. Since regulated and non-regulated markets have been consolidated, cf. M. Brellochs, *Publizität und Haftung*, 50–51, the distinction between the different market areas which used to be laid out in the legislative regulation has been reduced. For a systematic presentation of European capital markets law see M. Brellochs, *Publizität und Haftung*, 26 ff.; H. Merkt, *Unternehmenspublizität*, 140 ff.; P. Mülbert, WM (2001), 2085, 2094–2095.

A company's disclosure obligations can be divided into three categories, depending on the company's stages of market participation.[135] The first disclosure obligations arise when a company makes a public offering. According to the Prospectus Regulation the issuer then has to publish a prospectus.[136] Activities on secondary markets are accompanied by further periodic and ad hoc disclosure obligations. Periodic disclosure ensures that the market is continually supplied with the company's relevant financial accounting and—to some degree—non-financial information. The Transparency Directive requires the regular publication of financial reports to these means.[137] Additionally there are various obligations on disclosure for a company during market participation, the most important being the disclosure of inside information,[138] changes of major shareholdings,[139] control over a target company[140] and directors' dealings.[141] A mandatory disclosure upon market exit does not exist at a European level.

Studies trying to develop an overall concept of corporate disclosure[142] came to the conclusion that disclosure correlates with market participation: The more capital an issuer raises on the market, the more its disclosure obligations grow. The same applies with regard to the mandatory disclosure on capital markets. From the perspective of capital markets law, an issuer's relevance to the overall market increases with the amount of capital it raises on the market.[143] The more capital the issuer raises, the more important the issuer becomes regarding the protection of the investors and the institutional efficiency of the capital markets as a whole. It also increases its impact on the overall allocational efficiency of the markets, making an effective and correct pricing mechanism for the issuer's securities more important. The correct pricing conveys the allocational potential of an issuer. It becomes more important the more capital is bound to it. Economically a misallocation of large amounts of capital entails more ineffectual real investments of this issuer than would be the case for an issuer with a lower market capitalisation. The amount of capital bound by an issuer thus indicates its economic importance for the market.[144]

V. Dissemination Procedure and Access to Regulated Information

Economic insights have shown that legislative provisions standardising content and procedure for the information provision can have a positive effect for the regulation of capital

---

[135] Overview in: Brinckmann, *Kapitalmarktrechtliche Finanzberichterstattung*, 91 ff.; M. Brellochs, *Publizität und Haftung*, 30 ff.
[136] See R. Veil § 17 para. 5.
[137] See H. Brinckmann § 18 para. 32–47.
[138] See R. Veil § 19 para. 24.
[139] See R. Veil § 20 para. 23.
[140] See R. Veil § 28 para. 5, § 39 para. 2.
[141] See R. Veil § 21 para. 12.
[142] Cf. H. Merkt, *Unternehmenspublizität*, 332 ff. and passim; on the periodic disclosure system H. Brinckmann, *Kapitalmarktrechtliche Finanzberichterstattung*, 138 ff.
[143] H. Brinckmann, *Kapitalmarktrechtliche Finanzberichterstattung*, 139 ff.
[144] This approach is confirmed by the European law. Issuers are exempted from disclosure if certain capital related minimum thresholds are not reached by the issuer, cf. Art. 1(2)(h) PD, Art. 8(2) TD, or the issuer only affects a small group of investors due to a high denomination per unit set for the issued securities, cf. Art. 8(1)(b) TD.

markets.[145] With the legislative aim of mandatory disclosure provisions to increase capital markets informational efficiency,[146] legal requirements have to secure the investors' immediate and cost-efficient access to the relevant information.[147]

1. **Development of Harmonised Requirements for the Access to Regulated Information**

40   In the beginning European capital markets law followed a separate approach regarding the requirements on the disclosure procedure. Every single directive—meaning the Securities Admission Directive, Securities Admission Prospectus Directive and the Half-Yearly Report Directive and their successors[148]—laid down their own provisions on the disclosure procedure regarding the disclosure obligation contained in each directive. At that time the legislator mainly relied on a publication in printed newspapers in order to ensure fast access to such information throughout the relevant Member State.[149]

41   The European legislature realised the high importance of a harmonised access to information for the functioning of the capital markets and, therefore, follows a more integrated and unified approach since the TD of 2004. The TD contains more specific requirements regarding the (i) **disclosure procedure** and the (ii) **storage of information**. The TD and the Implementing Directive 2007/14/EC[150] laying down detailed rules for the implementation of certain provisions of Directive 2004/109/EC on the harmonisation of transparency requirements in relation to information about issuers whose securities are admitted to trading on a regulated market, require the disclosure and storage of '**regulated information**'. This term refers to all information which the issuer is required to disclose under the TD, ie notifications on major holdings[151] and financial reports,[152] and under any super-equivalent disclosure obligation adopted by the Member States under Article 3(1) TD.[153] But as far as issuers of financial instruments which are traded on a regulated market are concerned, the term also refers to inside information[154] and directors' dealings[155] under the MAR.[156] This shows the overarching approach of the European legislator in the respect.

---

[145] See above para. 25.
[146] See above para. 29.
[147] See above para. 25.
[148] See R. Veil § 1 para. 24.
[149] Cf. Art. 17 Securities Admission Directive; Art. 20 et. seq. Securities Admission Prospectus Directive; Art. 7 Half-Yearly Report Directive.
[150] Commission Directive 2007/14/EC of 8 March 2007 laying down detailed rules for the implementation of certain provisions of Directive 2004/109/EC on the harmonisation of transparency requirements in relation to information about issuers whose securities are admitted to trading on a regulated market, OJ L 69, 9 March 2007, p. 27–36.
[151] See R. Veil § 20 para. 39.
[152] See H. Brinckmann § 18 para. 58–60.
[153] Cf. Art. 2(1)(k) TD.
[154] See R. Veil § 19 para. 41–43.
[155] See R. Veil § 21 para. 19.
[156] Cf. Art. 2(1)(k) TD. References to the MAD in this provision shall be construed as references to the MAR in accordance with the correlation table set out in Annex II MAR: Art. 37 MAR. See also W.-G. Ringe, in: Lehmann and Kumpan (eds.), *European Financial Services Law*, Art. 21 TD para. 4.

(a) Requirements on the Dissemination of Regulated Information

Under the TD the Member States must ensure that an **issuer discloses regulated information** in a **manner** ensuring **prompt access** to such information on a **non-discriminatory basis**.[157] It must be disseminated in a manner that ensures it is capable of being disseminated to as wide a public as possible.[158] The issuer must refer to such media as may reasonably be relied upon for the effective dissemination of information to the public throughout the Community.[159] These requirement can realistically only be met by use of the Internet, which is why the European legislature explicitly allows the information to be published on the issuer's website, provided this publication is then announced to the media.[160] These requirements illustrate a development for the dissemination procedure in two areas. This is first that today issuers are required to use such media that ensure effective dissemination throughout the European Union and not only throughout the relevant Member State.[161] Secondly, the legislator respects past technical developments and opens the media to be used for dissemination from print to electronic means, primarily the Internet.

Although inside information and directors' dealings are covered by the term 'regulated information' in the TD, the disclosure of this information by issuers is also regulated by the MAR.[162] The reason for this is that the scope of the MAR is wider; Article 17(1) and Article 19(1) MAR also require issuers of financial instruments traded on MTFs and OTFs to make public the respective information. That is why the MAR empowers the Commission to endorse implementing technical standards submitted by ESMA[163] with regard to the public disclosure of inside information.[164] The provisions of the Commission Implementing Regulation (EU) No. 2016/1055 (ITS)[165] are directly applicable in the Member States, whilst the disclosure requirements of the TD (relevant for issuers whose securities are admitted to trading on a regulated market) have to be implemented into national law of the Member States.

Under the MAR the issuer must ensure fast access and a complete, correct and timely opportunity for assessment by the public.[166] These requirements are further specified in Article 2 ITS, which does not explicitly refer to the terms of the TD. Nevertheless, ESMA has developed compatible requirements and standards to those set out in the TD to establish a level playing field between regulated markets and MTFs and OTFs.[167]

---

[157] Cf. Art. 21(1) sentence 1 TD.
[158] Cf. Art. 12(2) Directive 2007/14/EC.
[159] Cf. Art. 21(1) sentence 3 TD.
[160] Art. 12(3) Directive 2007/14/EC.
[161] Cf. W.-G. Ringe, in: Lehmann and Kumpan (eds.), *European Financial Services Law*, Art. 21 TD para. 9.
[162] Cf. Art. 17(1) sentence 2 MAR; Art. 19(3) MAR.
[163] Cf. ESMA, Final Report, Draft technical standards on the Market Abuse Regulation, 28 September 2015, ESMA/2015/1455, Annex XII.
[164] Cf. Art. 17(10) MAR; Art. 19(3) sentence 1 MAR.
[165] Cf. Commission Implementing Regulation (EU) No. 2016/1055 of 29 June 2016 laying down implementing technical standards with regard to the technical means for appropriate public disclosure of inside information and for delaying the public disclosure of inside information in accordance with Regulation (EU) No. 596/2014 of the European Parliament and of the Council, OJ L 173, 30 June 2016, p. 47–51.
[166] Cf. Art. 17(1) sentence 2 MAR; Art. 19(3) MAR.
[167] Cf. ESMA/2015/1455 (fn. 163), p. 43.

(b) Officially Appointed Mechanism (OAM)

45 The Member States must further ensure that the issuer makes the regulated information available to an '**officially appointed mechanism**' (OAM),[168] ie to a database responsible for the central storage of the regulated information, which complies with minimum quality standards of security and certainty as to the information source and guarantees easy access by end users.[169] As a result, each Member State established or appointed an OAM.[170]

46 The storage of inside information and directors' dealings is also regulated by the MAR.[171] Only if the information disclosed under the MAR is also 'regulated information' as defined by the TD, the issuer has to make the information available to an OAM.[172] This means, that there is no obligation for issuers of financial instruments traded on an MTF and OTF to make the inside information and directors' dealings available to an OAM, unless the Member States establish such an obligation.

(c) Implementation in the Member States

47 Aside from the requirements concerning the OAMs, the requirements in the TD are limited to the general foundations of disclosure and storage of regulated information. Each Member State is responsible for the details thereof, such as the exact media to be employed. The individual Member State must determine whether a dissemination of the information in daily newspapers or via the Internet is sufficient. As a consequence, the European legal requirements for the access to regulated information have led to a strong divergence (i) in the disclosure procedures as well as (ii) to the central storage mechanisms within the Member States.[173] As a consequence access to regulated information still follows a national not a European approach.[174]

(d) European Electronic Access Point (EEAP) and European Single Access Point (ESAP)

48 Albeit the recommendation of the Actica Feasibility Study to replace all national OAMs and to establish one central OAM,[175] the reform of the Level 1 acts has not abolished the existence of national databases. Instead, after its revision in 2013,[176] the TD only requires

---

[168] Cf. Art. 21(1) sentence 1 TD.
[169] Cf. Art. 21(2) TD.
[170] ESMA provides a list of OAMs, available at: www.esma.europa.eu/access-regulated-information.
[171] Cf. Art. 17(1) sentence 2 MAR; Art. 19(3) MAR.
[172] Cf. Art. 17(1) sentence 2 MAR; Art. 19(3) sentence 2 MAR.
[173] For more details on the transposition in the Member States, see H. Brinckmann § 18 para. 58 ff. See also 2nd edn. (2017), R. Veil, § 22 para. 8 ff.
[174] Cf. W.-G. Ringe, in: Lehmann and Kumpan (eds.), *European Financial Services Law*, Art. 21a TD para. 2.
[175] Cf. Actica, Feasibility Study for a pan-European storage system for information disclosed by issuers of securities—Final Report, 18 October 2011, available at: https://ec.europa.eu/info/sites/info/files/report-storage-system-18102011_en.pdf, p. 53.
[176] Directive 2013/50/EU of the European Parliament and of the Council of 22 October 2013 amending Directive 2004/109/EC of the European Parliament and of the Council on the harmonisation of transparency requirements in relation to information about issuers whose securities are admitted to trading on a regulated market, Directive 2003/71/EC of the European Parliament and of the Council on the prospectus to be published when securities are offered to the public or admitted to trading and Commission Directive 2007/14/EC laying down detailed rules for the implementation of certain provisions of Directive 2004/109/EC, OJ L 294, 6 November 2013, p. 13–27 (ADTD).

ESMA to establish and operate a '**European electronic access point**' (EEAP) to connect the national OAMs.[177] The EEAP shall facilitate pan-European access to regulated information[178] by allowing to access and search the national databases centrally, using unique identifiers for each issuer. The technical requirements of the EEAP are specified by Level 2 legislation. The RTS on the EEAP have been developed by ESMA in 2015[179] and published in 2016.[180] However, ESMA realised at the end of 2016 that work on this project was more ambitious than initially planned, especially with respect to cost.[181]

Looking for a technical solution for the EEAP, the Commission started a pilot project for a European financial transparency gateway (EFTG)[182] that is based on the distributed ledger technology.[183] But before it even started, the EEAP seems to merge into the new project of a **European single access point (ESAP)**. In 2020, the Commission presented its new action plan for a capital markets union[184] based on the report of a high-level forum on the capital markets union.[185] In order to make companies more visible to cross-border investors, better integrate national capital markets and facilitate their access to market funding, the Commission wants to tackle the lack of accessible and comparable company data for investors. Therefore, the Commission aims to set up the ESAP as an EU-wide platform that provides investors with seamless access to financial and sustainability related company information.[186] The ESAP shall built on the EFTG pilot project but follow a broader approach than the EEAP as it shall also improve the availability and accessibility of sustainability-related data.[187] In this context, further amendments to the TD can be expected.[188]

49

2. Conclusion

The legal requirements on the access to regulated information under European capital markets law go in the right direction but, however, are still far away from the target. The TD contains harmonised requirements on the disclosure and central storage of regulated information under the TD as well as under the MAR. Thereby, the European legislator follows an overarching approach, releasing from focusing on separate legislative acts. It is also

50

---

[177] Cf. Art. 21a(1) TD.
[178] Recital 15 ADTD.
[179] ESMA, Final Report on Draft Regulatory Technical Standards on European Electronic Access Point (EEAP), 25 September 2015, ESMA/2015/1460.
[180] Commission Delegated Regulation (EU) 2016/1437 of 19 May 2016 supplementing Directive 2004/109/EC of the European Parliament and of the Council with regard to regulatory technical standards on access to regulated information at Union level, OJ L 234, 31 August 2016, p. 1–7.
[181] Cf. W.-G. Ringe, in: Lehmann and Kumpan (eds.), *European Financial Services Law*, Art. 21a, para. 9.
[182] The EFTG is available at: https://eftg.eu/.
[183] Commission, Governance for a DLT/Blockchain enabled European Electronic Access Point (EEAP), Final Report, available at: https://op.europa.eu/en/publication-detail/-/publication/98da7b74-38db-11ea-ba6e-01aa75ed71a1.
[184] Communication from the Commission to the European Parliament, the Council, the European Economic and Social Committee and the Committee of the Regions, A Capital Markets Union for people and businesses-new action plan, 24 September 2020, COM(2020) 590 final (New CMU Action Plan).
[185] Final Report of the High Level Forum on the Capital Markets Union 'A new vision for Europe's capital markets', available at: https://ec.europa.eu/info/sites/info/files/business_economy_euro/growth_and_investment/documents/200610-cmu-high-level-forum-final-report_en.pdf.
[186] Commission, New CMU Action Plan. p. 7.
[187] Commission, Annex to the New CMU Action Plan. p. 1.
[188] Commission, Annex to the New CMU Action Plan. p. 1.

important that the scope of the MAR includes MTFs and OTFs as it improves the internal market and facilitates the competition between regulated markets and MTFs/OTFs. But the approach to provide different legal sources for issuers whose financials instruments are admitted to trading on a regulated market on the one side and MTF/OTF-issuers on the other side is not convincing. This might lead to unnecessary differences in the disclosure and storage of information and thereby makes the access to price relevant information more difficult and costly. The same applies to other disclosure obligations, especially the obligation to disclose a prospectus[189] which is not available via OAM but via the website of the competent authority.[190] A unified system of access to information is necessary. The EEAP is on the starting block and will reduce the costs of information about issuers from other Member States, thereby improving the internal market and market efficiency.[191] To replace all national OAMs by a central European OAM would probably be the best but also most difficult solution. It remains to be hoped that a gateway based on distributed ledger technology will be able to operate the EEAP or ESAP in a way as if all national OAMs have been merged into one central European OAM.

---

[189] See. R. Veil § 17 para. 58.
[190] Cf. Art. 21(5) PR.
[191] Cf. W.-G. Ringe, in: Lehmann and Kumpan (eds.), *European Financial Services Law*, Art. 21a para. 8.

§ 17

Prospectus Disclosure

Bibliography

Assmann, Heinz-Dieter, *Prospekthaftung als Haftung für die Verletzung kapitalmarktbezogener Informationsverkehrspflichten nach deutschem und US-amerikanischem Recht* (1985); Berrar, Carsten et al., *Frankfurter Kommentar WpPG und EU-Prospekt-VO*, 2. edn. (2017); Crüwell, Christoph, *Die europäische Prospektrichtlinie*, AG (2003), 243–253; Di Noia, Carmine and Gargantini, Matteo, *The Approval of Prospectus: Competent Authorities, Notifications, and Sanctions*, in: Busch, Danny et al. (eds.), *Prospectus Regulation and Prospectus Liability* (2017), Chapter 16; Ferran, Eilis, *Cross-border Offers of Securities in the EU: The Standard Life Flotation*, 4 ECFR (2007), 461–490; Fleischer, Holger, *Empfiehlt es sich, im Interesse des Anlegerschutzes und zur Förderung des Finanzplatzes Deutschland das Kapitalmarkt- und Börsenrecht neu zu regeln?*, Gutachten F für den 64. Deutschen Juristentag (2002); Freitag, Robert, *Internationale Prospekthaftung revisited – Zur Auslegung des europäischen Kollisionsrechts vor dem Hintergrund der „Kolossa"-Entscheidung des EuGH*, WM (2015), 1165–1173; Gebauer, Stefan, *Börsenprospekthaftung und Kapitalerhaltungsgrundsatz in der Aktiengesellschaft* (1999); Gerner-Beuerle, Carsten, *The Market for Securities and its Regulation through Gatekeepers*, 23 Temp. Int'l & Comp. L.J. (2009), 317–377; Grimaldos García, María I., *Algunos apuntes acerca del desarrollo reglamentario del régimen de la responsabilidad civil derivada del contenido del folleto*, 102 RDBB (2006), 271–278; Groß, Wolfgang, *Kapitalmarktrecht*, 7th edn. (2020); Gruber, Michael, *EU-Prospektrecht* (2016); ten Have, Robert, *The Summary and Risk Factors*, in: Busch, Danny et al. (eds.), *Prospectus Regulation and Prospectus Liability* (2017), Chapter 12; Hellgardt, Alexander and Ringe, Wolf-Georg, *Internationale Kapitalmarkthaftung als Corporate Governance*, 173 ZHR (2009), 802–838; Horsten, Pim, *'Light' Disclosure Regimes: Secondary Issuances*, in: Busch, Danny et al. (eds.), *Prospectus Regulation and Prospectus Liability* (2017), Chapter 11; Iribarren Blanco, Miguel, *Responsabilidad civil por la información divulgada por las sociedades cotizadas* (2008); Kastelein, Gerard and Reutelingsperger, Tom, *The New Advertisement Regime: What a Difference a Word Makes?*, in: Busch, Danny et al. (eds.), *Prospectus Regulation and Prospectus Liability* (2017), Chapter 14; Kullmann, Walburga and Metzger, Jürgen, *Der Bericht der Expertengruppe 'Europäische Wertpapiermärkte' (ESME) zur Richtlinie 2003/71/EG ('Prospektrichtlinie')—Ausgewählte Aspekte des ESME-Berichts unter Berücksichtigung der Stellungnahme des Ausschusses der Europäischen Wertpapierregulierungsbehörden (CESR) zu 'Retail Cascades' und der inhaltlichen Abgrenzung von Basisprospekt und endgültigen Bedingungen*, WM (2008), 1292–1298; Lenz, Susanne and Heine, Maurice, *Incorporation by Reference*, NZG (2019), 766–771; Mülbert, Peter O., *EU-rechtliche Kapitalmarktinformationsvorschriften und mitgliedstaatliche Haftungsregeln*, in: Dreher, Meinrad et al. (eds.), *Festschrift zum 65. Geburtstag von Alfred Bergmann* (2019), 529–540; Moloney, Niamh, *EU Securities and Financial Markets Regulation* (2014); Panasar, Raj and Boeckmann, Philip (eds.), *European Securities Law*, 3rd edn. (2021); Perrone, Andrea, *'Light' Disclosure Regimes: The EU Growth Prospectus*, in: Busch, Danny et al. (eds.), *Prospectus Regulation and Prospectus Liability* (2017), Chapter 10; Schammo, Pierre, *EU Prospectus Law—New Perspectives on Regulatory Competition in Securities Markets* (2011); Schlitt, Michael et al., *Aktuelle Rechtsfragen und neue Entwicklungen im Zusammenhang mit Börsengängen*, BKR (2005), 251–264; Seibt, Christoph H. et al., *Prospektfreie Zulassung von Aktien bei internationalen Aktientausch-Transaktionen mit gleichwertigen Dokumentenangaben (§ 4 Abs. 2 Nr. 3 WpPG)*, AG (2008), 565–577; de Serière, Victor, *The Contents of the Prospectus: Non-Financial Information and Materiality*, in: Busch, Danny et al. (eds.), *Prospectus Regulation and Prospectus Liability* (2017), Chapter 9; Strampelli, Giovanni, *The Contents of the Prospectus: Rule for Financial Information*, in: Busch, Danny et al. (eds.), *Prospectus Regulation and Prospectus Liability* (2017), Chapter 8; Veil, Rüdiger and Walla, Fabian, *Schwedisches Kapitalmarktrecht* (2010); Veil, Rüdiger and Wundenberg, Malte, *Prospektpflichtbefreiung nach § 4 Abs. 2 Nr. 3 WpPG bei Unternehmensübernahmen*, WM (2008), 1285–1292; Vokuhl, Nikolai, *Kapitalmarktrechtlicher Anlegerschutz und Kapitalerhaltung in der Aktiengesellschaft* (2007); Wild, Eva-Maria, *Prospekthaftung einer Aktiengesellschaft unter deutschem und europäischem Kapitalschutz* (2007).

I. Introduction

1 The Prospectus Regulation (EU No. 2017/1129 – PR) aims to protect investors by providing information. Recital 3 expresses this concisely as follows: '**Disclosure** of **information** in cases of **offers** of securities to the public or **admission** of **securities** to **trading** on a regulated market is vital to **protect investors** by removing asymmetries of information between them and issuers. Harmonising such disclosure allows for the establishment of a cross-border passport mechanism which facilitates the effective functioning of the internal market in a wide variety of securities.' Recital 7 adds that the PR also intends to 'to ensure investor protection and market efficiency, while enhancing the internal market for capital.' The obligation to publish information about the issuer and the securities is based on the idea to enable all investors to make an informed investment decision. The appropriate way to make this information available is to publish a prospectus.

2 The rules on prospectus disclosure are based on the recognition that securities are so-called credence products.[1] Unlike with so-called search goods, an investor cannot reduce uncertainties by obtaining information about the product prior to acquisition, or realistically assess securities at acceptable information costs due to their complexity and the duration of capital investments. The investor must therefore rely upon the promised quality of the securities. This confidence can only be based on reliable information.[2] Primary markets do not bear the characteristics of strong-form efficiency in terms of the ECMH,[3] resulting in an asymmetric distribution of information between issuers and investing market participants.[4] These deficits are to be reduced through prospectus disclosure.

3 Professional investors usually do not need the information provided by a securities prospectus. They can obtain relevant information easily and cost-efficiently from the issuer, through individual discussions with the investor relations department and the management as well as in the context of roadshows. Prospectus disclosure is primarily intended to

---

[1] See R. Veil § 2 para. 12.
[2] Cf. L. Burn, in: Panasar and Boeckmann (eds.), *European Securities Law*, para. 1.39; H. Fleischer, *Gutachten F 64. Dt. Juristentag*, F 23; N. Moloney (ed.), *EU Securities and Financial Markets Regulation*, 55–56.
[3] See on the Efficient Capital Market Hypothesis R. Veil § 2 para. 29 and H. Brinckmann § 16 para. 8–9.
[4] Cf. H.-D. Assmann (ed.), *Prospekthaftung*, 292 ff.; N. Vokuhl, *Kapitalmarktrechtlicher Anlegerschutz*, 176.

enable **retail investors** to make an informed investment decision.[5] European prospectus law determines who is to be understood as a qualified investor. Conversely, it follows that information asymmetries are to be assumed for all other investors, which are to be countered by a securities prospectus. Information should be adapted to the level of knowledge and expertise of retail investors.[6]

For the issuer, the prospectus is not only the legal prerequisite for the offer of the securities and their admission to listing, but also a **sales document** with which it attracts investors (dual function of the prospectus).[7] The marketing function becomes particularly relevant when shares or bonds are offered to the public for the first time (IPO). An issuer will then have particular cause to highlight the advantages of the business strategy or the attractiveness of its products. The European prospectus regime takes account of the marketing aspect by imposing requirements on advertising that are intended to ensure the fairness and truthfulness of advertising in the prospectus in the interest of retail investors.[8]

II. Foundations

1. Disclosure Obligation

At the centre of the prospectus regime is the obligation to publish a prospectus. Securities may only be offered to the public after prior publication of a prospectus (also referred to as an **offering prospectus**).[9] Furthermore, a prospectus obligation also exists for the admission of securities to trading on a regulated market (also referred to as **admission prospectus**).[10] The regime (preparation, content and presentation) is identical for both prospectuses.

There are numerous exceptions to the prospectus requirement where there is no need for investors to be informed by means of prospectus publication because the information asymmetries are balanced out by market forces or other information documents. For example, if a public offer is directed exclusively at qualified investors, an offer prospectus does not need to be published.[11] If the securities are to be admitted to trading, however, a prospectus must be prepared and published because retail investors also acquire the securities via the secondary market.

The securities prospectus is subject to **ex ante control** by the **supervisory authority**. It may only be published after the competent authority has approved it.[12] The supervisory

---

[5] Cf. M. Gruber (ed.), *EU-Prospektrecht*, 16.
[6] Cf. recital 7 Regulation (EU) No. 2019/980.
[7] Cf. H.-D. Assmann, *Prospekthaftung*, 218; G. Kastelein and T. Reutelingsperger, in: Busch et al. (eds.), *Prospectus Regulation and Prospectus Liability*, 14.04; A. Meyer, in: Habersack et al. (eds.), *Unternehmensfinanzierung am Kapitalmarkt*, Rn. 36.13; M. Schlitt, in: Habersack et al. (eds.), *Handbuch der Kapitalmarktinformation*, § 3 Rn. 2.
[8] Cf. Art. 20 PR.
[9] Cf. Art. 3(1) PR.
[10] Cf. Art. 3(3) PR.
[11] Cf. Art. 1(4)(a) PR.
[12] Cf. Art. 20(1) PR.

authority shall verify that the prospectus is complete, comprehensive and consistent.[13] It does not check whether the content of the prospectus is correct. This could hardly be done by an authority and would prolong the procedure. Therefore, administrative sanctions and civil enforcement mechanisms in the form of prospectus liability are needed to ensure that the issuer provides correct information.

2. Accompanying Regimes

8   The disclosure obligations of the PR concern the primary market. The information of investors required on the secondary market is ensured by other disclosure obligations. The Market Abuse Regulation (MAR) requires issuers of financial instruments to **disclose inside information** without delay.[14] In addition, the Transparency Directive (TD)[15] requires Member States to provide for the publication of an **annual and half-yearly financial report**[16] and require investors to make public **changes** in **major holdings** in issuers.[17]

9   The dense regime of investor information on the secondary market justifies imposing lower requirements on the content of the securities prospectus in case of a secondary issuance.[18] The premise of the simplified disclosure rules is that, due to the secondary market obligations (on a Regulated Market and on the SME Growth Market), information-efficient securities prices are achieved, which make publication of the information already reflected in the securities price through a prospectus unnecessary.

3. Legal Sources

(a) European Level

10   The obligation to publish a prospectus was first introduced by the European legislature in 1979. Since then, it has been subject to a number of reforms.[19] For 'reasons of consistency', the legislature regrouped the provisions in 2003, making extensive amendments. The **Prospectus Directive** (PD 2003) constituted an instrument essential to the achievement of the internal market.[20] In 2010, the PD was amended by Directive 2010/73/EU,[21] ensuring

---

[13] Cf. Art. 20(4) PR.
[14] Cf. Art. 17 MAR. See R. Veil § 19.
[15] Directive 2004/109/EC of the European Parliament and of the Council of 15 December 2004 on the harmonisation of transparency requirements in relation to information about issuers whose securities are admitted to trading on a regulated market and amending Directive 2001/34/EC (TD), p. 38 ff. (TD).
[16] See H. Brinckmann § 18 Rn. 41 ff.
[17] See R. Veil § 20.
[18] Cf. Art. 14 PR.
[19] See R. Veil § 1 para. 5–6, 10 and 24; more details on historical aspects in N. Moloney, *EU Securities and Financial Markets Regulation*, 71 ff.; P. Schammo, *EU Prospectus Law*, 74 ff.
[20] Cf. recital 4 PD.
[21] Directive 2010/73/EU of the European Parliament and of the Council of 24 November 2010 amending Directives 2003/71/EC on the prospectus to be published when securities are offered to the public or admitted to trading and 2004/109/EC on the harmonisation of transparency requirements in relation to information about issuers whose securities are admitted to trading on a regulated market, OJ L327, 11 December 2010, p. 1–12.

a more effective investor protection and facilitating cross-border offers. The 2017 reform built on this and pursued the goal of reducing the administrative burden for companies on the one hand, and making the prospectus a more valuable source of information on the other hand.[22]

The Prospectus Regulation (PR)—a Level 1 measure of the European legislature—is an essential step towards the completion of the Capital Markets Union[23] and counters the divergent approaches of the PD 2003/2010, which resulted in a fragmentation of the internal market.[24] The choice of the form of a regulation (instead of a directive) is justified by the fact that in the 'absence of a harmonised framework to ensure uniformity of disclosure and the functioning of the passport in the Union it is therefore likely that differences in Member States' laws would create obstacles to the smooth functioning of the internal market for securities. Therefore, to ensure the proper functioning of the internal market and improve the conditions of its functioning, in particular with regard to capital markets, and to guarantee a high level of consumer and investor protection, it is appropriate to lay down a regulatory framework for prospectuses at Union level.'[25]

Most of the provisions of the PR aim at a **full harmonisation** of prospectus law. However, with regard to individual aspects, Member States have regulatory options (see para. 68). Moreover, the provisions on supervision and sanctions are directive-like regulatory mandates. Finally, the disclosure requirements of the PR do not affect the right of a Member State, a competent authority or a stock exchange (by means of its stock exchange rules) to lay down further specific requirements in connection with the admission of securities to trading on a regulated market, in particular in relation to corporate governance. Such requirements should not directly or indirectly restrict the drawing up, the content and the dissemination of a prospectus approved by a competent authority.[26] Of practical importance, for example, is the admission requirement to organise analyst conferences annually.

The PR is supplemented by a Level 2 regime developed by ESMA and endorsed by the Commission. **Delegated Regulation** (EU) No **2019/979** governs a number of technical aspects (key financial information in the summary of the prospectus, the publication and classification of prospectuses, the advertising of securities, supplements to the prospectus and the notification portal). **Delegated Regulation** (EU) No **2019/980** concerns the presentation, content, scrutiny and approval of the prospectus. It is a huge set of rules. The detailed provisions reflect the aim of the European legislator and the Commission to establish a uniform legal situation in the EU. The more detailed the European regulations are, the lower the risk of divergent interpretations by national supervisory authorities.

In order to promote consistent supervisory practice by national competent authorities, the former CESR published a document with recommendations on how to interpret the requirements of the European disclosure regimes and a document with questions

---

[22] Cf. M. Gruber (ed.), *EU-Prospektrecht*, 20.
[23] Cf. recital 1 PR.
[24] Cf. recital 4 PR.
[25] Cf. recital 4 PR.
[26] Cf. recital 8 PR.

and answers on the common positions agreed by CESR members. **ESMA** has continued this approach and publishes updates of these documents accordingly. The **guidelines**[27] are intended to ensure uniform interpretation and application of the rules. The **Q&A document**[28] is a practical convergence tool that provides interpretation and guidance to market participants. Finally, ESMA's guidelines on alternative performance measures (so-called APM guidelines)[29] are relevant for securities prospectuses.

(b) National Level

15   The provisions of the PR are directly applicable in the Member States; they therefore do not need to be transposed into national law. However, the PR provides for regulatory options for the Member States (see para. 68). Thus, Member States may facilitate the public offer of securities through crowd-funding. National laws also regulate prospectus liability and the powers of national supervisory authorities.

III. Prospectus Requirement According to the Prospectus Regulation

1. Scope of Application

16   Offers of securities to the public as well as the admission of securities to trading on a regulated market that fall within the PR's scope of application are generally subject to the publication of a prospectus.[30] The scope of application is thus defined through the terms '**admission of securities to a regulated market**' and '**offers of securities to the public**'.

17   In Article 2(1)(a), the PR defines 'securities' as all transferrable securities with the exception of money market instruments having a maturity of less than 12 months.[31] The definition of the term in MiFID II is applicable.[32] The term includes dividend-paying securities (especially shares, convertible bonds and bonds with warrants) and debt securities (especially bonds).[33] This distinction is important for the preparation and content of a prospectus. For lack of fungibility, registered bonds, time deposits, savings bonds, shares in a limited liability company or a limited partnership are not securities.[34] The PR also does not apply to unit certificates issued by an investment fund or a capital management company.[35]

---

[27] ESMA, Guidelines on Risk Factors under the Prospectus Regulation, 1. 10. 2019, ESMA31-62-1293.
[28] ESMA, Questions and Answers, Prospectuses, ESMA/2019/ESMA31-62-1258, Version 10, last updated on 27 July 2021.
[29] ESMA, Guidelines on Alternative Performance Measures (APM), 5.10.2015, ESMA 2015/1415.
[30] Cf. Art. 1 PR.
[31] See R. Veil § 8 para. 4.
[32] See R. Veil § 8 para. 9.
[33] Cf. Art. 2(b) and (c) PR.
[34] See R. Veil § 8 para. 20.
[35] Cf. Art. 1(2)(a) PR. The obligation to publish a prospectus results from UCITS/AIFMD.

The term '**offer** of **securities to** the **public**' means a communication to persons in any form and by any means, presenting sufficient information on the terms of the offer and the securities to be offered, in order to enable an investor to decide to purchase or subscribe to these securities.[36] This solves the problem that used to arise from the fact that the Member States had differing views on whether an offer requires a prospectus publication, resulting in a possible obligation to publish a prospectus in one Member State whilst the offer or the admission of the same security in a different Member State was possible without a prospectus.[37]

18

> An '**offer**' does not require a legally binding declaration of intent. Already the invitation to submit an offer (invitatio ad offerendum) is to be regarded as an offer. Whether an offer is **public** is not determined by whether it is addressed to a certain number of investors. According to the meaning and purpose of prospectus law, the requirement of publicity is not to be determined quantitatively, but qualitatively.[38] An offer is public if it is addressed to an indefinite group of investors. Private placements are not regarded as public. In doing so, the issuer specifically addresses investors who are known to it and who are not in need of protection due to their knowledge.[39]

19

The **admission** of **securities** to **trading** on an MTF does not give rise to an obligation to publish a prospectus under EU law. This is only the case for an admission to trading on a Regulated Market.[40] If an issuer offers shares only to qualified investors[41] and applies for admission of the shares to trading on an SME growth market (for example Scale of the FWB) which is not a Regulated Market but an MTF,[42] there is no obligation to publish a prospectus under the PR. However, the rules and regulations of the trading venue may provide that a prospectus or other information document must be published for admission to trading. With regard to the SME Growth Market Scale, the issuer shall prepare an 'inclusion document' which shall be published on the website of Deutsche Börse AG.[43]

20

2. Exemptions from the Obligation to Publish a Prospectus

(a) Exceptions for Offers of Securities

The PR exempts **offers** of securities addressed solely **to qualified investors** from the obligation to publish a prospectus.[44] The term 'qualified investors' primarily refers to all professional investors such as credit institutions, investment firms, financial institutions and insurance companies. These investors do not require protection due to their level of expertise and better access to information.[45]

21

---

[36] Art. 2(d)(1) PR. This definition also applies to the placement of securities by financial intermediaries (Art. 2(d)(2) PR).
[37] P. Schammo, *EU Prospectus Law*, 80.
[38] M. Schlitt, in: Habersack et al. (eds.), *Handbuch der Kapitalmarktinformation*, § 3 para. 32.
[39] A. Meyer, in: Habersack et al. (eds.), *Unternehmensfinanzierung am Kapitalmarkt*, para. 36.5.
[40] Cf. Art. 2(j) PR i.V.m. Art. 4(1) No. 21 MiFID II.
[41] An offer prospectus does not need to be published then, Art. 1(4)(a) PR.
[42] See R. Veil § 7 para. 11 and 16.
[43] Cf. § 17(1)(b),(3)(b), Annex 2, General Terms and Conditions of Deutsche Börse AG for the Open Market on the Frankfurt Stock Exchange, 9.12.2019.
[44] Art. 1(4) PR.
[45] Cf. P. Schammo, *EU Prospectus Law*, 126 ff.

22 The PR further contains an exception for an offer of securities addressed to fewer than 150 natural or legal persons per Member State, other than qualified investors, which is aimed at facilitating **private placements**. If the offer has a high minimum denomination or amount, it can be assumed that retail investors are either not addressees or have sufficient assets to bear the risks.

23 If the obligation to draw up a prospectus is to be avoided when submitting an offer for securities, use will generally be made of this last exemption in practice. Securities with a minimum consideration of € 100,000 per investor are offered publicly with a minimum denomination of € 100,000 (or full € 1,000 above € 100,000) or with a minimum denomination of € 1,000 (whereby only securities with a minimum consideration of € 100,000 or full € 1,000 above € 100,000) may be transferred. This exemption is of particular relevance in practice, as the issuer itself can assure adherence to the prerequisites, without having to rely on the banks. Nevertheless issuing banks will generally declare in their contract with the issuer to submit the offer only under the preconditions described above, ie only to qualified investors or less than 150 investors. In addition, the persons acquiring the securities must confirm that they are qualified in the sense of the PR. This so-called '*belt and suspenders*' strategy is of outstanding importance in practice.

24 The obligation to publish a prospectus does not apply to offers to the public for certain types of securities. The exemptions refer to cases in which the securities are offered as substitutes for existing securities or in connection with certain transactions. In these cases investors have already been supplied with the necessary information at an earlier point.[46] Shares issued as substitutes for shares of the same class already issued does not therefore need to be accompanied by a prospectus if the issuing of such new shares does not involve any increase in the issued capital. Similarly, securities offered in connection with a takeover or a merger by means of an exchange offer do not require a prospectus to be published provided that a document is available containing information which is regarded as being equivalent to that of a prospectus by the competent authority. This requirement will usually be fulfilled by the offer document in takeovers and the merger report.

(b) Exemptions for Certain Issuances for the Admission to the Regulated Market

25 The obligation to publish a prospectus is also not applicable to the admission to trading certain types of securities on a regulated market.[47] The cases are similar to those mentioned above, with the addition of exemptions, such as that for securities already admitted to trading on *another* regulated market, provided certain conditions ensuring investor protection are fulfilled. The admission of shares resulting from the conversion or exchange of other securities or from the exercise of the rights conferred by other securities to the regulated market is also not subject to the publication of a prospectus, provided that said shares are of the same class as the shares already admitted to trading on the same regulated market.

---

[46] C. Seibt et al., AG (2008), 565 ff.; R. Veil and M. Wundenberg, WM (2008), 1285 ff.
[47] Art. 1(5) PR.

3. Format and Structure of a Prospectus

(a) Single or Separate Documents and Base Prospectus

The PR provides the possibility to draw up the prospectus as a single document or separate documents. **Separate documents** must divide the required information into a **registration document** (including information on the issuer), a **securities note** and a **summary note** (which is divided into four sections). In these cases, the registration document can be published in advance and remains valid for 12 months after its publication (cf. Article 12 Abs. 1 PR) for numerous offers to the public or admissions to trading on a regulated market (of course, a securities note and a summary note have to be published for each offer). It is especially suited to the needs of issuers that regularly place offers of securities to the public, such as banks.[48] As opposed to this, the single document appears more suited to the issuance of shares.[49]

With the modernisation of prospectus law, the European legislature intended to give **frequent issuers** the opportunity to reduce their cost of compliance with the PR and enable them to swiftly react to market windows.[50] For this purpose, it has created a specific regime, inspired by the US shelf registration.[51] Every financial year, any issuer whose securities are admitted to trading on a regulated market or an MTF may draw up a registration document in the form of a **universal registration document** describing the company's organisation, business, financial position, earnings and prospects, governance and shareholding structure.[52] This form requires the approval of the authority. If it has been approved in two consecutive financial years (the issuer is then granted the status of a frequent issuer),[53] uniform registration forms can be filed in future without prior approval.[54] When market conditions are favourable for a public offer of securities, the issuer can use the universal registration document and draw up a prospectus by adding a securities note and a summary note. Finally, the issuer also benefits from shorter approval periods.[55]

For offers of certain non-equity securities (bonds) the prospectus can consist of a **base prospectus**[56] which must contain the same 'relevant information' on the issuer and the securities as a single or separate document, with the exception of the final terms of the offer.[57] The issuer announces the specific terms and conditions of each offer only immediately prior to the commencement of the relevant offer period. The base prospectus may also

---

[48] Cf. R. Panasar et al., in: Panasar and Boeckmann (eds.), *European Securities Law*, para. 2.72.
[49] Cf. M. Schlitt et al., BKR (2005), 251, 251; A. Meyer, in: Habersack et al. (eds.), *Unternehmensfinanzierung am Kapitalmarkt*, para. 36.17; M. Schlitt, in: Habersack et al. (eds.), *Handbuch der Kapitalmarktinformation*, § 4 para. 5.
[50] Cf. recital 39 PR.
[51] Cf. D. Fischer-Appelt, in: Busch et al. (eds.), *Prospectus Regulation and Prospectus Liability*, para. 13.67.
[52] Cf. Art. 9(1) PR.
[53] Cf. Art. 9(11) subsec. 2 PR.
[54] Cf. Art. 9(2) subsec. 2 PR.
[55] Cf. Art. 9(2) subsec. 2 PR.
[56] Cf. Art. 9(11) PR.
[57] Art. 2(s) PR.

be prepared as a single document or in several individual documents.[58] The final terms shall be published at the latest on the day of the respective public offer.

29 In practice, the base prospectus plays a major role. It is mainly used for offering programmes (such as Medium Term Notes – MTN programmes) or for structured products (such as certificates).[59] The final conditions shall be set out in a separate document.[60] If the final terms are neither included in the base prospectus nor in a supplement, the issuer shall make them available to the public and file them with the competent authority as soon as possible after the offer of securities to the public or the admission to trading on a regulated market.[61]

(b) Preparation, Content and Presentation

30 European prospectus law is characterised by the **principle** of **investor protection through information**. A prospectus shall 'contain the necessary information which is material to an investor for making an informed assessment of a) the assets and liabilities, profits and losses, financial position, and prospects of the issuer and of any guarantor; b) the rights attached to the securities; and c) the reasons for the issuance and its impact on the issuer.'[62]

31 The **materiality** of the information to an investor is central to the preparation of a prospectus.[63] However, the law does not explicitly specify which investor the EU prospectus law has in mind as the addressee of the prospectus. Is it a professional investor who has extensive specialist knowledge, a retail investor who has no specialist knowledge and is easily misled, or an average investor who can at least be said to have a minimum of expertise. Furthermore, what are the investment objectives of this investor? Is he profit-oriented or does he (also) make his decisions with regard to ecological and social concerns?

32 In a 1982 decision regarding a listing prospectus, the BGH focused on the attentive reader and average investor who understands a balance sheet but does not have above-average expert knowledge. An average investor does not necessarily need to be familiar with the key language used in professional circles.[64] With regard to an offering prospectus, the BGH came to a different interpretation 30 years later: 'The question of whether a securities prospectus is incorrect or incomplete must be based on the recipient's horizon, whereby the understanding of the interested parties addressed by the prospectus is decisive. If a sales prospectus for securities that are not to be traded on the stock exchange is explicitly addressed to the uninformed and stock market inexperienced public, the average (small) investor addressed cannot be expected to be able to read a balance sheet. In these cases, the recipient's horizon is therefore determined by the abilities and knowledge of an average (retail) investor who informs himself about the investment solely on the basis of the information in the prospectus and does not have any special knowledge.'[65]

---

[58] Art. 8(6) PR.
[59] Cf. R. Panasar et al. in: Panasar and Boeckmann (eds.), *European Securities Law*, para. 2.73; W. Kullmann and J. Metzger, WM (2008), 1292, 1296; P. Schammo (ed.), *EU Prospectus Law*, 96 ff.
[60] Art. 8(4) subsec. 1 PR.
[61] Art. 8(5) subsec. 1 PR.
[62] Art. 6(1) subsec. 1 PR.
[63] Cf. V. de Seriére, in: Busch et al. (eds.), *Prospectus Regulation and Prospectus Liability*, para. 9.13.
[64] BGH of 12. 7. 1982 – II ZR 175/81, NJW 1982, 2823, 2824.
[65] BGH of 18. 9. 2012 – XI ZR 344/11, BGHZ 195, 1.

The principles of interpretation concern prospectus liability, which is largely subject to the national laws of the Member States.[66] For the interpretation of Union supervisory law, the principles are nevertheless helpful because they shed light on the various facets of the potential addressees of a prospectus and the legal issues associated with the investor concept. Should it be an inexperienced and unsophisticated investor, particularly high demands are to be made on the scope and presentation of the information in a prospectus.

For an answer, it should first be noted that a prospectus is not exclusively aimed at institutional investors, because an issuer does not need to prepare a prospectus for an offer to them. The guiding principle is therefore a **retail investor**, both for the offering prospectus and for the admission prospectus. It must also be taken into account that prospectus law provides for requirements regarding the comprehensibility of the information contained in a securities prospectus. These requirements are based on the assumption of a reasonable investor who has knowledge of financial products and the capital market. This can in any case be derived from the requirement that the information in a prospectus must be written and presented in an easily analysable, concise and comprehensible form.[67] A special need for protection due to lack of knowledge does not come up in these requirements. The requirements for the summary are different: it must be 'easy to read', 'characters of readable size' must be used, and the language must be 'clear, non-technical, concise and comprehensible'. Thus, the guiding principle of an inexperienced, uninformed and easily misled investor is to be used as addressee of the summary. However, it cannot be applied to the entire EU securities prospectus law. For the remaining prospectus content, the guiding principle of the reasonable investor applies.[68] In this respect, an attentive reader with average professional knowledge is to be assumed for both offer and admission prospectuses.[69] This investor is profit-oriented. Prospectus law does not assume, as does financial services law, that retail investors pursue additional purposes, such as social or environmental objectives, in addition to the investment objective of financial returns.[70]

The **content** and **format** of a prospectus shall be determined pursuant to Article 13 PR in accordance with the provisions of Delegated Regulation 2019/980 of the European Commission. The Level 2 legal act requires that the prospectus has a certain structure. The schedules and modules of the Level 2 regime specify the information to be provided by the respective issuers and for the issuance of the securities concerned (so-called building block approach).

Schedule means a list of minimum disclosures tailored to the specific nature of the different securities and issuers, whereas a module means a list of additional disclosures not included in the schedules. By combining the relevant annexes in each case, the information necessary for the preparation of the prospectus can be identified for the specific securities offered by the issuer. The Delegated Regulation not only specifies the intended use of each schedule and module, but also determines the 'possible' combinations of the schedules and modules.

---

[66] Cf. Art. 11 PR.
[67] Cf. Art. 6(2) PR.
[68] Cf. V. de Seriére, in: Busch et al. (eds.), *Prospectus Regulation and Prospectus Liability*, para. 9.22–9.31.
[69] See para. 80 on the question of whether this guiding principle is also decisive for prospectus liability law.
[70] This aspect becomes particularly relevant in the case of prospectus liability. Whether a statement in the prospectus is material is determined by the decision-making preferences of a reasonable investor. See para. 81.

37 The **minimum information** to be included in a prospectus for certain securities is set out in the Annexes to Delegated Regulation 2019/980. For example, in the case of a **share issue**, Annex I (equity securities) provides for minimum information to be included in the share registration document and Annex XI provides for minimum information to be included in the share securities note. On the one hand, information must be provided about the issuer, such as risk factors, the business and financial position, the capital resources, the corporate bodies and senior management, the major shareholders, and the assets and liabilities, financial position and profit and loss of the issuer. On the other hand, specific information must be provided on the respective 'share', in particular on security-related risk factors, the issuer's capital, the securities, the terms and conditions of the offer as well as on the admission to trading and any dilution resulting from the offer.

38 A much quoted stock market saying is that the future is traded on the stock exchange. Therefore, two minimum disclosures of a prospectus in a share issue are of particular importance for investors. The first is the **Operating and Financial Review** (Annex I, Section 7; comparable to the Management's Discussion and Analysis of Financial Condition and Results of Operation (MD&A) in the US). The prospectus must include 'a fair review of the development and performance of the issuer's business and of its position for each year and interim period for which historical financial information is required, including the causes of material changes.' The review shall also give an indication of the issuer's likely future development and activities in the field of research and development.

39 Secondly, EU prospectus law seeks to counter the danger of unreliable statements about company profits.[71] The prospectus of a share issue must also contain trend information (section 10) and provide information on earnings forecasts or estimates (section 11) if the issuer has published one. Where an issuer chooses to include a new profit forecast or a new profit estimate, or a previously published profit forecast or a previously published profit estimate (which is often done for marketing reasons),[72] the profit forecast or estimate shall be clear and unambiguous and contain a statement setting out the principal assumptions upon which the issuer has based its forecast, or estimate. An audit of profit forecasts and estimates by an independent auditor with subsequent reporting (audit report on profit forecasts and estimates) is no longer required under the PR regime. This is the most controversial new provision of the 2017 reform, because the external audit can be valuable information for investors.[73] The European legislator has abolished it for cost reasons.

40 A prospectus contains the **terms** and **conditions** of the **offer**. As a rule, the final issue price and the final issue volume are not yet precisely determined when the prospectus is published. Both will be determined later if the issue takes place in the bookbuilding process.[74] It is then sufficient if the prospectus states either the maximum price and/or the maximum issue volume or the valuation methods and criteria.[75] The final price and the final issue volume shall be filed with the competent authority and published.[76]

---

[71] Cf. G. Strampelli, in: Busch et al. (eds.), *Prospectus Regulation and Prospectus Liability*, para. 8.64.
[72] Cf. M. Schlitt and C. Landschein, 31 ZBB (2019), 103, 106.
[73] Cf. G. Strampelli, in: Busch et al. (eds.), *Prospectus Regulation and Prospectus Liability*, para. 8.78.
[74] See R. Veil § 7 para. 38.
[75] Art. 17(1) PR.
[76] Art. 17(2) PR.

(c) Structure

A prospectus must contain a table of contents, a summary, the risk factors and the contents of the schedules and modules of Regulation 2019/980. The requirements for the summary and risk factors are discussed below. The requirements for the schedules and modules are not presented here (for an overview of the minimum disclosures for a share issue, see para. 37–39). 41

(aa) Summary

The prospectus shall include a summary that provides the key information investors need in order to understand the nature and the risks of the issuer, the guarantor and the securities that are being offered or admitted to trading on a regulated market.[77] It should 'aid investors when considering whether to invest in such securities'.[78] The summary takes into account the limited knowledge of retail investors who are often overwhelmed by reading the financial information of a prospectus.[79] In addition, the sometimes-daunting size of the prospectus discourages retail investors from reading it.[80] 42

The summary must be prepared in a uniform format to facilitate comparison with similar securities. European law prescribes a detailed structure and gives clear instructions on how the document is to be drafted. In formal terms, the summary must be concise and presented in a manner that is easily understandable. In terms of language and style, it must be drawn up in such a way as to facilitate the understanding of the information, in particular by using language that is clear, precise and generally understandable to investors. 43

The summary must be divided into **four sections**: a) an introduction, containing warnings; b) key information on the issuer; c) key information on the securities; d) key information on the offer of securities to the public and/or the admission to trading on a regulated market.[81] Further content requirements are also provided for each section. Of particular importance are the warnings which, among other things, inform the investor that the summary is to be understood as an introduction to the prospectus and that the investor should rely on the prospectus as a whole when deciding to invest in the securities.[82] 44

The regime on the summary of a prospectus has undergone a fundamental change through the 2003, 2010 and 2017 reforms. The guiding principle of the summary is an inexperienced, uninformed and easily misled investor (see para. 34). In terms of content, the summary now covers all aspects that an investor needs for an investment decision. The summary has become a 'prospectus within a prospectus', even if it is expressly provided that it is written as a short document and printed out in a maximum length of seven A4 pages.[83] However, the legislature still maintains that an investor should make his decision 45

---

[77] Art. 7(1) subsec. 1 hs. 1 PR.
[78] Art. 7(1) subsec. 1 hs. 2 PR.
[79] Cf. R. ten Have, in: Busch et al. (eds.), *Prospectus Regulation and Prospectus Liability*, para. 12.06.
[80] Cf. M. Gruber (ed.), *EU-Prospektrecht*, 99.
[81] Art. 7(3) PR.
[82] Art. 7(5)(2)(a) and (b) PR.
[83] Art. 7(3)(1) PR.

on the basis of the entire prospectus. This is made clear to investors in the warning notices. In addition, liability under civil law due to incorrect information exclusively in the summary is generally excluded.[84]

(bb) Risk Factors

46 Risk factors are an essential element of a securities prospectus. The risks of a capital investment are explained by the peculiarities of a security and the difficulty to forecast issuer's earnings. The issuer is in the best and most cost-effective position to counter such information asymmetries. However, given the liability risks arising from a prospectus, an issuer may be inclined to provide too much information that is ultimately irrelevant to the investment. The regime on risk factors (consisting of the requirements set out in Article 16 PR and standards issued by ESMA in guidelines)[85] seeks to address this problem through quantitative and qualitative requirements.

47 The **qualitative requirements** aim to ensure that the reader learns about the specific and material risks. Thus, Article 16(1) PR stipulates that the risk factors featured in a prospectus shall be limited to **risks** which are **specific** to the **issuer** and/or to the **securities** and which are **material** for taking an informed investment decision, as corroborated by the content of the registration document and the securities note. Recital 54 PR adds that a prospectus should not contain risk factors which are generic and only serve as disclaimers, as those could obscure more specific risk factors that investors should be aware of, thereby preventing the prospectus from presenting information in an easily analysable, concise and comprehensible form. To determine materiality, the PR follows a procedural approach. An issuer has to assess the likelihood of the risk factor occurring and the expected magnitude of the negative impact.

48 The ESMA guidelines divide the risk factors into categories.[86] With regard to risk factors which are **specific** and **material** to the **issuer**/guarantor, ESMA recommends the following categories (Guidelines para. 35): Risks related to the issuer's financial situation; risks related to the issuer's business activities and industry; legal and regulatory risk; internal control risk; environmental, social and governance risks. Risk factors which are **specific** and **material** to the **securities** could be divided into the following categories (Guidelines para. 36): risks related to the nature of the securities; risks related to the underlying; risks related to the guarantor and the guarantee; risks related to the offer to the public and/or admission of the securities to trading on a regulated market.

49 The **quantitative requirement** aims at not letting the section of the prospectus get out of hand. An absolute number would be too schematic a requirement. It is therefore foreseen that the risk factors shall be presented in a limited number of categories depending on their nature. In each category the most material risk factors shall be mentioned first.[87] This restriction articulates the concern that investors could be overwhelmed with too much information (information overload).[88] ESMA Guideline 9 requires that the number of

---

[84] Art. 11(2) subsec. 2 PR.
[85] ESMA, Guidelines on risk factors under the Prospectus Regulation, 1.10.2019, ESMA31-62-1293.
[86] Cf. R. ten Have, in: Busch et al. (eds.), *Prospectus Regulation and Prospectus Liability*, para. 12.41: 'useful, but still are (and can only be) generic in nature'.
[87] Art. 16(1) subsec. 4 PR.
[88] See on the problem of information overload R. Veil § 6 para. 33.

categories and subcategories included in the prospectus should not be disproportionate to the size/complexity of the transaction and risk to the issuer/guarantor.

The guiding principle for the section on risk factors is the **reasonable investor**.[89] Each risk factor shall be adequately described, explaining how it affects the issuer or the securities being offered or to be admitted to trading. The assessment of the materiality of the risk factors provided for in the second subparagraph may also be disclosed by using a qualitative scale of low, medium or high.[90]

(d) Incorporation by Reference

Information may be incorporated by reference in a prospectus where it has been previously or simultaneously published electronically, drawn up in a language fulfilling the requirements of Article 27 and where it is contained in one of the documents, specified in Article 19(1) PR. In practice, the reference is mainly used for information from balance sheets, transaction documents (eg in the case of a merger), audit opinions and financial statements, the company's articles of association or from already approved prospectuses, but predominantly for the issuance of debt instruments. The incorporation of information by reference is intended to facilitate the issuer's preparation of the prospectus; however, with this technique it is not intended to reduce the information.[91]

(e) Language

The need to translate the prospectus into the language of the host Member State for mutual recognition had previously proved to be a serious obstacle.[92] In order to facilitate the cross-border raising of capital, the European legislature amended this requirement in the PD. Article 19 PD distinguished between four scenarios, the cross-border cases being of particular practical relevance. Where an offer to the public was made or admission to trading on a regulated market was sought in one or more Member States excluding the home Member State, the prospectus could be drawn up 'in a language customary in the sphere of international finance'.[93] The competent authority of each host Member State could only require that the summary be translated into its official language.[94] With the reform of prospectus law in 2017, the legislator adopted these requirements in Art. 27 PR.

Where an **offer** of securities to the public is made or **admission** to **trading** on a regulated market is sought only in the **home Member State**, the prospectus shall be drawn up in a language accepted by the competent authority of the home Member State.[95] Where an offer of securities to the public is made or admission to trading on a regulated market is sought

---

[89] Cf. V. de Serière in: Busch et al. (eds.), *Prospectus Regulation and Prospectus Liability*, para. 9.26.
[90] Art. 16(1) subsec. 3 PR.
[91] Cf. S. Lenz and M. Heine, NZG 2019, 766, 767.
[92] Cf. C. Crüwell, AG (2003), 243, 248; U. Kunold and M. Schlitt, BB (2004), 501, 508.
[93] For a list of the languages accepted for prospectus review and the translation of the summary in case of passporting, cf. R. Panasar et al., in: Panasar and Boeckmann (eds.), *European Securities Law*, para. 2.124.
[94] Art. 19(2) PD.
[95] Cf. Art. 27(1) PR.

in one or more Member States excluding the home Member State, the prospectus shall be drawn up either in a language accepted by the competent authorities of those Member States or in a language customary in the sphere of international finance, at the choice of the issuer, the offeror or the person asking for admission to trading on a regulated market.[96] As a rule, such a prospectus will be drawn up in the English language.[97]

4. Approval and Publication

(a) Foundations

54 A prospectus shall not be published unless the relevant competent authority has approved it.[98] European law provides for an **ex ante control mechanism**. In this respect, it is stricter than US law, which allows so-called well-known seasoned issuers to make a public offering of securities without prior approval of a securities prospectus in order to take advantage of favourable times for an offering as quickly as possible. In the USA, a strict prospectus liability regime and an effective enforcement mechanism in the form of class action ensue a high level of investor protection. Such a system does not exist in Europe. Therefore, it makes sense for Europe to stick to ex ante approval by NCAs.

55 'Approval' means the positive act at the outcome of the scrutiny by the home Member State's competent authority of the completeness, the consistency and the comprehensibility of the information given in the prospectus.[99] It follows that the national authorities do not merely check completeness of a prospectus.[100] By coherence is meant that the prospectus has no inconsistencies. The requirements for comprehensibility differ, depending on whether it is the summary (see paras. 25, 43) or the other parts of the prospectus (see paras. 36 ff.). An authority does not check the accuracy of the content or the issuer's business model.

56 A variety of competent authorities in Member States, with different responsibilities, might create unnecessary costs and overlapping of responsibilities without providing any additional benefit. In each Member State, a single competent authority should be designated to approve prospectuses and to assume responsibility for supervising compliance with this Regulation.[101] The competent authority shall be the authority in the issuer's home Member State.[102] It shall be independent from market participants.[103]

57 For the approval, the Authority shall have a maximum period of 10 working days after receipt of the draft prospectus;[104] in the case of an initial offer of securities, the time limit shall be 20 working days.[105] If information is submitted subsequently, the deadlines shall

---

[96] Cf. Art. 27 (2) subsec. 1 PR.
[97] R. Panasar et al. in: Panasar and Boeckmann (eds.), *European Securities Law*, para. 2.121.
[98] Art. 20(1) PR.
[99] Art. 2(r) PR.
[100] Cf. C. Crüwell, AG (2003), 243, 250; U. Kunold and M. Schlitt, BB (2004), 501, 509; C. Sandberger, EWS (2004), 297, 300; L. Burn, in: Panasar and Boeckmann (eds.), *European Securities Law*, para. 1.100 f.
[101] Recital 71 PR.
[102] Cf. on the concept of home Member State, the legal definition in Art. 2(m) PR.
[103] Art. 31(1) PR.
[104] Art. 20(2) PR.
[105] Art. 20(2) PR.

only apply from that point in time.[106] The timing of a public offering of securities may become unpredictable for the issuer or offeror.[107] In legal practice it is therefore not uncommon to agree on a time plan with a number of dates for the submission of documents with the supervisory authority. The supervisory authority can then comment on the documents that have been provided and notify the issuer as to what further information is required. The issuer will often submit multiple drafts of the prospectus to the authority.[108]

Once approved, the prospectus shall be made available to the public by the issuer, the offeror or the person asking for admission to trading on a regulated market at a reasonable time in advance of, and at the latest at the beginning of, the offer to the public or the admission to trading of the securities involved.[109] **Publication** on a **website** of the **issuer**, the offeror or the person asking for admission to trading shall be sufficient.[110] A prospectus shall be valid for 12 months after its approval for offers to the public or admissions to trading on a regulated market, provided that it is completed by any supplement.[111]

58

(b) European Passport

The introduction of the European passport for cross-border offerings and a multiple listing was an important milestone in European capital markets legislation in 2010. The regime has basically proven its worth, although a significant increase in pan-European offerings cannot be observed to date.[112]

59

From a legal point of view, a cross-border public offer or admission to trading in a Member State other than the home Member State requires that the competent authority of the host Member State is informed by means of a 'certificate of approval' pursuant to Article 25 PR (so-called notification).[113] The notification may be accompanied by a translation of the summary.[114] The competent authorities of the host Member States[115] may not carry out their own approval procedure.[116]

60

Passporting allows issuers to offer or admit to trading securities in any Member State without the need for multiple approvals of the prospectus.[117] It replaces the previous concept of mutual recognition, which had proven to be incomplete and too complex. The European Passport Mechanism aims to ensure the widest possible access to investment capital on a Community-wide basis.[118]

61

---

[106] Art. 20(4)(2) PR.
[107] Cf. C. Crüwell, AG 2003, 243, 251; U. Kunold and M. Schlitt, BB 2004, 501, 509.
[108] Cf. M. Schlitt, in: Habersack et al. (eds.), *Handbuch der Kapitalmarktinformation*, § 5 para. 18.
[109] Cf. Art. 21(1) PR; L. Burn, in: Panasar and Boeckmann (eds.), *European Securities Law*, para. 1.114.
[110] Cf. Art. 21(2) PR.
[111] Cf. Art. 12(1) PR.
[112] Cf. M. Schlitt, in: Habersack et al. (eds.), *Handbuch der Kapitalmarktinformation*, § 5 para. 36.
[113] Cf. Art. 24 PR.
[114] Cf. Art. 24(1) subsec. 2 PR.
[115] Art. 2(n) PR.
[116] Art. 24(1)(2) PR.
[117] L. Burn, in: Panasar and Boeckmann (eds.), *European Securities Law*, para. 1.106 f.
[118] Cf. recital 3 PR.

(c) Supplement to the Prospectus

62　A prospectus, whether a single document or consisting of separate documents, shall be valid for 12 months after its approval for offers to the public or admissions to trading on a regulated market, provided that it is completed by any supplement.[119] The obligation to update by means of supplements is provided for in Article 23 (1) PR: 'Every **significant new factor**, **material mistake** or **material inaccuracy** relating to the information included in a prospectus which may affect the assessment of the securities and which arises or is noted between the time when the prospectus is approved and the closing of the offer period or the time when trading on a regulated market begins, whichever occurs later, shall be mentioned in a supplement to the prospectus without undue delay.' The duty to supplement also includes updating the summary and any translations.[120]

63　The supplement shall not be published until it has been approved by the competent authority. The approval period shall not exceed five working days.[121] The supplement to an offering prospectus is associated with a right of withdrawal for investors. Investors who have already committed to purchase or subscribe for the securities before the supplement is published have the right to withdraw their commitments within two days of the publication of the supplement.[122] In practice, this right has not played a major role so far.

64　The provision has been criticised many times,[123] especially with regard to the period within which an investor can revoke his commitment.[124] In this respect, the European legislator has already taken the criticism into account by amending the Prospectus Directive 2010. At the time, he did not address the criticism that investors are entitled to a right of revocation even if the subsequently provided information does not have a negative impact on the investment decision.[125] Neither did the PR established in 2017 change the legal situation. An investor can therefore withdraw from the investment if he comes to the conclusion that he has made a 'bad' deal due to negative market developments.[126]

5. Special Regimes

65　Issuers can make use of the simplified disclosure rules for **secondary issuances** under certain conditions.[127] The simplified prospectus requires that securities of the issuer have been admitted to trading on a regulated market or SME growth market for at least 18 continuous months. Under these conditions, the issuer is obliged to disclose periodic financial reports and ad hoc price-sensitive information. Due to secondary market disclosure, lower requirements may be imposed on primary market disclosure. However, the securities

---

[119] Cf. Art. 12(1) PR.
[120] Art. 23(1) subsec. 2(2) PR.
[121] Art. 23(1) subsec. 2(1) PR.
[122] Art. 23(2) subsec. 1 PR.
[123] Cf. U. Kunold and M. Schlitt, BB (2004), 501, 510; W. Kullmann and J. Metzger, WM (2008), 1292, 1297.
[124] Cf. P. Schammo, *EU Prospectus Law*, 105.
[125] Cf. P. Schammo, *EU Prospectus Law*, 104.
[126] Cf. W. Kullmann and J. Metzger, WM (2008), 1292, 1297; M. Schlitt, in: Habersack et al. (eds.), *Handbuch der Kapitalmarktinformation*, § 5 para. 30.
[127] Cf. Art. 14 PR in connection with Art. 4 and Annex 3 and 12 Delegated Regulation 2019/980.

have to be fungible with existing securities which were previously issued. The regime of a simplified prospectus is used in particular for the issue of subscription rights.[128] It is based on the idea of the ECMH that security prices reflect publicly available information. However, it is yet unclear whether the new simplified regime will play a role in practice.[129]

A proportionate regime is also provided for **small and medium-sized enterprises** (SMEs) and for issuers listed on a SME growth market in the form of the EU growth prospectus.[130] The regime is intended to facilitate SMEs' access to the capital market.[131] It lies 'in the middle ground' between exemption from disclosure obligations under the PR and the 'fully fledged application of the standard regime'.[132] Some interesting privileges are provided, such as limiting the obligation to include historical financial information to the last two financial years.[133]   66

Member States may exempt small offers of securities from the obligation to publish a prospectus.[134] For **micro-issues** with a total consideration of less than € 1 million, there is generally no prospectus requirement under EU law. Member States may also not provide for such a requirement.[135] Prospectus disclosure is disproportionate in these cases, as it is costly and a high level of investor protection through supervision is not strictly necessary.   67

IV. Supervision

The Prospectus Regulation requires a competent administrative authority to be responsible for supervising the adherence to the prospectus obligations.[136] These competent authorities (NCAs) are to be completely independent from all market participants.[137] The most important task of an NCA is to review and approve the prospectus. In addition, it has to detect and sanction violations of the law. ESMA limits itself to coordinating the practices of NCAs and determining best practices in prospectus approval.   68

Ideally, national supervisory authorities have the same practices and apply the law consistently. However, the authorities of the Member States are still far from having an essentially consistent supervisory culture. The peer reviews conducted by ESMA reveal different approaches among supervisors, ranging from the question of how many authority staff are involved in the approval process, to the fundamental question of whether a risk-based approach is followed.[138] Divergences are explained by different financial resources of the authorities, but may also reflect supervisory arbitrage. Finally, national   69

---

[128] Cf. M. Schlitt, in: Habersack et al. (eds.), *Handbuch der Kapitalmarktinformation*, § 4 para. 118; M. Gruber, *EU-Prospektrecht*, 180 ff.
[129] Cf. P. Horsten, in: Busch et al. (eds.), *Prospectus Regulation and Prospectus Liability*, 11.59.
[130] Cf. Art. 15 PR in connection with Art. 28 ff. Delegated Regulation 2019/980.
[131] See R. Veil § 1 para. 58 und § 7 para. 23.
[132] Cf. A. Perrone, in: Busch et al. (eds.), *Prospectus Regulation and Prospectus Liability*, 10.17.
[133] Cf. M. Schlitt, in: Habersack et al. (eds.), *Handbuch der Kapitalmarktinformation*, § 4 para. 122.
[134] Cf. Art. 3(2) PR.
[135] Cf. Art. 1(3) PR.
[136] Art. 21(1) PD.
[137] Cf. Art. 31 PR.
[138] Cf. ESMA, Peer Review on Prospectus Approval Process. Peer Review Report, 30 June 2016, ESMA/2016/1055.

supervisory practice always reflects the jurisprudence of national administrative courts and national courts.[139] Finally, any liability of supervisory staff may also lead to a bureaucratic approach.[140]

70 Each competent authority shall have all the powers necessary for the performance of its functions, the powers upon receipt of an application for approving a prospectus and in connection with the securities admitted to trading on a regulated market being described in detail.

V. Administrative and Criminal Sanctions

71 Under the regime of the Prospectus Directive 2003/2010, the legal situation and practice in Europe was disparate. In particular, there were considerable differences in the administrative sanctions.[141] Most Member States had maximum amounts for fines. The amounts varied; in Denmark, fines could be imposed up to € 1,350, while the maximum amount in France was € 2.5 million and the United Kingdom had no upper limit.[142] Criminal sanctions played a minor role. However, a considerable number of 20 states had established special legal offences.[143] In addition, the general provisions of criminal law were applicable, which were quite important in practice.[144]

72 The reform of prospectus law in 2017—as well as the reforms of transparency and market abuse law—harmonised the sanction regimes of the Member States and strengthened them.[145] Recital 74 PR emphasises that the sanctions should have a deterrent effect. The administrative pecuniary sanctions to be provided for by the Member States are high and are based on the models of the TD and MAR.[146] Member States do not need to introduce criminal sanctions.

VI. Private Enforcement

1. Requirements under European Law

73 The PR requires Member States to provide for liability under private law: 'Member States shall ensure that **responsibility** for the information given in a prospectus, and any

---

[139] Cf. C. Di Noia and M. Gargantini, in: Busch et al. (eds.), *Prospectus Regulation and Prospectus Liability*, 16.88.
[140] Cf. C. Di Noia and M. Gargantini, in: Busch et al. (eds.), *Prospectus Regulation and Prospectus Liability*, 16.88.
[141] Cf. CESR, Report on Members' Powers under the Prospectus Directive and its Implementing Measures, CESR/07-383, Juni 2007, p. 65 ff.; ESMA, Report: Comparison of liability regimes in Member States in relation to the Prospectus Directive, 30 May 2013, ESMA/2013/619, p. 17 ff.
[142] Sec. 91 (1A) FSMA; R. Veil and M. Wundenberg, *Englisches Kapitalmarktrecht*, 37 f.
[143] Cf. ESMA, Report: Comparison of liability regimes in Member States in relation to the Prospectus Directive, 30 May 2013, ESMA/2013/619, p. 22.
[144] Cf. about Sweden: *Högsta domstolen*, NJA 1992, 691 ff. (Leasing Consult).
[145] See R. Veil § 12 para. 10 ff. on the EU's sanctions strategy.
[146] Art. 38(1) PR.

supplement thereto, attaches to at least the **issuer** or its **administrative, management or supervisory bodies**, the **offeror**, the **person asking for the admission to trading** on a regulated market or the guarantor, as the case may be. The persons responsible for the prospectus, and any supplement thereto, shall be clearly identified in the prospectus by their names and functions or, in the case of legal persons, their names and registered offices, as well as declarations by them that, to the best of their knowledge, the information contained in the prospectus is in accordance with the facts and that the prospectus makes no omission likely to affect its import.'[147] Thus, liability is not imposed on any particular person. However, Member States must ensure that their laws, regulations and administrative provisions apply to the persons responsible for the information contained in a prospectus.[148] Finally, liability for incorrect information in a summary is limited.[149] The conditions for prospectus liability are, moreover, left to the discretion of the Member States.

The **applicability** of **national law** governing prospectus liability in **cross-border situations** has not yet been clarified by the courts. The ECJ has so far only commented on the international jurisdiction in a prospectus liability action.[150] It can at least be deduced from this that the ECJ qualifies a prospectus liability claim as a non-contractual claim.[151] As a consequence, the Rome II Regulation is applicable. According to Article 4(2) Rome II Regulation, the law of the state in which the damage occurred applies. Academics argue this would be the place of the market (so-called market principle). They put forward that prospectus disclosure would aim at ensuring the proper functioning of capital markets. Thus, the law of the market at which the securities are listed is to be applied.[152] This means that French prospectus liability law is applicable to the issue of a security in France. This also applies to investors domiciled abroad and whose securities account is located abroad.

74

2. National Law

The civil liability for the publication of an incorrect prospectus could not differ more throughout the EU. Some European Member States have introduced special provisions thereon, and may additionally apply general civil law provisions, other Member States rely solely on their general concepts under torts law. Whilst Germany,[153] Spain,[154] Italy[155] and Austria,[156] for example, have introduced special provisions thereon, and may additionally apply general civil law provisions, other Member States, such as France[157] and Sweden,[158] rely

75

---

[147] Cf. Art. 11(1) PR.
[148] Cf. Art. 11(2) subsec. 1 PR.
[149] Cf. Art. 11(2) subsec. 2 PR.
[150] Cf. EuGH of 28. 1. 2015 – Rs. C-375/13 (Kolassa), NJW (2015), 1581, 1583.
[151] Cf. B. Singhof and O. Seiler, in: Berrar et al.(eds.), *WpPG*, Vor § 21 ff. para. 17.
[152] Cf. R. Freitag, WM (2015), 1165; W. Groß, *Kapitalmarktrecht*, § 9 WpPG para. 72b; M. Habersack, in: Habersack et al. (eds.), *Handbuch der Kapitalmarktinformation*, § 28 para. 57; B. Singhof and O. Seiler, in: Berrar et al., *WpPG*, Vor § 21 ff. para. 26. Dissenting opinion A. Hellgardt and W.-G. Ringe, 173 ZHR (2009), 802, 826 ff.
[153] Cf. §§ 8 ff. WpPG.
[154] Cf. Art. 38(3) LMV.
[155] Cf. Art. 94(8) and (9) TUF.
[156] Cf. § 22 KMG.
[157] Cf. Art. 1382 Cc.
[158] An issuer may be held liable on the legal basis of the Kapitel 29, § 1(1)(2), (2)(2) ABL and the general rules of tort law, cf. R. Veil and F. Walla, *Schwedisches Kapitalmarktrecht*, 25 ff.

solely on their general civil law liability concepts. The national regimes are well researched in comparative literature.[159] The details in the European jurisdictions will not be discussed here. Some central problems regarding prospectus liability should, however, be examined more closely at the example of German law: which deficiencies result in prospectus liability? What must be considered regarding the other requirements of a prospectus liability, such as causation between the incorrect publication and the transaction, responsibility, the capacity to sue and the legal consequences of prospectus liability?

(a) Deficiencies of the Prospectus

76 A prospectus is regarded as deficient if it contains **incorrect** or **insufficient information**. Information is incorrect if it does not relate to the facts. A prospectus contains insufficient information if it does not include all the information required by the Prospectus Regulation. Common examples are the reference to an incorrect or manipulated balance sheet in the prospectus or the omission of the fact that an action for annulment is pending against the capital increase resolution. A prospectus can further be deficient if it **reflects** an **unrealistic picture** of the **issuer** or his financial situation or **profit expectations**.[160]

77 *Facts (abridged and simplified):*[161] The Beton- und Monierbau AG (BuM) was experiencing liquidity problems that could only be cleared with the help of a loan, guaranteed by the federal state of North Rhine-Westphalia. When new financial difficulties arose a short time later the company applied for a federal guarantee which was granted under the premise of a capital increase. After the prospectus was published, an investor acquired new shares from the capital increase. Less than six months later, bankruptcy proceedings were instituted against BuM. The Bundesgerichtshof (BGH—German Federal Court of Justice) ruled that when determining whether a prospectus contains incorrect or insufficient information it is not sufficient to examine the presented facts individually. One must rather also take into account the impression these facts give as a whole. In the case at hand, the general picture conveyed did not sufficiently indicate that the shares had to be classed as high-risk investments of a highly speculative nature. The prospectus rather attempted to give the impression that the difficulties were merely temporary and the capital increase was intended to consolidate the company's budget, indicating that the financial results would improve compared with those of previous year.

78 In Germany, Italy and Austria the rules on liability require that the prospectus has to be **incorrect** in an aspect **material** for the **evaluation** of the **security**. This can be assumed, if the relevant aspect is taken into account for an investment decision of a **reasonable investor**. The prevalent understanding in Germany is that a reasonable investor must be

---

[159] Cf. the country reports on France, Germany, Italy, Spain, the Netherlands, Luxembourg and the United Kingdom. in: Busch et al. (eds.), *Prospectus Regulation and Prospectus Liability*, sec. III; see also: K. Hopt and H.-C. Voigt (eds.), *Prospekt- und Kapitalmarktinformationshaftung*, 2004; R. Veil and M. Wundenberg, *Englisches Kapitalmarktrecht*, 24 ff.; R. Veil and P. Koch, *Französisches Kapitalmarktrecht*, 29 ff.; R. Veil and F. Walla, *Schwedisches Kapitalmarktrecht*, 20 ff.; C. Gerner-Beuerle, 23 Temp. Int'l & Comp. L. J. (2009), 317, 344–372.

[160] BGH of 06.05.1982 – III ZR 18/91, NJW (1982), 2823 ff. (described in further detail in the example below); cf., however, OLG Frankfurt of 15.05.2012 – 23 Kap 1/26, ZIP (2012), 1240 ff., which held that a prospectus is not incorrect, if the valuation of the real estate owned by the issuer is overstated by 12%, as such deviation still ranges within the acceptable margin.

[161] BGH of 06.05.1982 – III ZR 18/91, NJW (1982), 2823 ff.

able to read and understand a balance sheet without, however, having above-average expert knowledge.[162]

Example: In the case *Beton- und Monierbau AG (BuM)* the prospectus contained the information that the company's financial results would improve considerably in 1978, compared to 1977 when the company suffered severe losses. The BGH ruled that no reasonable investor would have got the overall impression that this improvement could still mean overall losses—albeit reduced compared to the year before. An average investor need not understand the terminology common to insiders.

The BGH developed the principles of interpretation at a time when the European legislature had issued minimum harmonising directives for the first time. In the meantime, prospectus law has been unified by the Prospectus Regulation. This raises the question (already intensively discussed in financial services law)[163] whether national liability law is determined by the requirements of EU prospectus law: Is the reasonable investor the one under the Prospectus Regulation 2017/1129?[164] This interpretation is supported by the fact that stricter liability law requirements for the content and design of a prospectus would lead to legal uncertainty and would result in considerable transaction costs for issuers.

The concept of the reasonable investor under EU law (see para. 33) is important in two respects. Firstly, it is relevant for the way in which the prospectus is presented: What level of knowledge of the investor can be assumed? Can he be easily misled (see para. 34)? Secondly, the guiding principle of a reasonable investor also determines the content of a prospectus, in particular the question of which facts must be included in the prospectus. In this context, it is also significant whether the reasonable investor is profit-oriented and/or makes his decisions according to ESG criteria.

It is particularly difficult to determine whether a prospectus is incorrect with regard to statements referring to future events and prognoses. In Germany, incorrect statements are also subject to prospectus liability. **Statements** on **future events** are regarded as **incorrect** if they are **not** reasonable or are **not based** on actual **facts**.[165] France treats the problem of a liability for an incorrect prognosis similarly, all statements on future developments requiring a verifiable foundation.[166] If this is not the case and the prognosis is based on intentions (eg future acquisition of a company) or estimations (eg future profits), this must be made clear in the prospectus. A prognosis based on facts must be accompanied by information on how it was established. A number of examples put the content of prognoses into more concrete terms.[167]

Example: In *BuM* the BGH ruled that the wording of the provisions on prospectus liability did not include facts in the term 'information' but also evaluative statements on the economic situation of the company and its future developments, as these could not always be clearly distinguished.

---

[162] Cf. BGH of 06.05.1982 – III ZR 18/91, NJW (1982), 2823, 2824; OLG Frankfurt am Main of 10.07.2005 – 5 U 182/03, AG (2005), 851, 852; OLG Frankfurt am Main of 01.02.1994 – 5 U 213/92, WM (1994), 294, 295; OLG Stuttgart of 07.08.1984 – 6 U 51/84, WM (1984), 586, 592.
[163] See R. Veil § 30 para 62.
[164] P. Mülbert, in: FS Bergmann, 529, 539; M. Habersack, in: Habersack et al. (eds.), *Handbuch der Kapitalmarktinformation*, § 28 para. 15.
[165] BGH of 06.05.1982 – III ZR 18/91, NJW (1982), 2823, 2824; OLG Frankfurt am Main of 01.02.1994 – 5 U 213/92, WM (1994), 291, 295; LG Frankfurt am Main of 10.10.1997 – 3/11 O 77/97, WM (1998), 1181, 1184.
[166] Cf. Art. 212-14–212-16 RG AMF.
[167] Cf. H.-J. Puttfarken and A. Schrader, in: Hopt and Voigt (eds.), *Prospekt- und Kapitalmarktinformationshaftung*, 600–601.

An investor must therefore be able to rely on the evaluative statements to be conclusions deduced from the facts on the basis of a thorough analysis. Accordingly, the issuer of the prospectus could not be held liable for the incorrectness of the statements, his liability rather depending on whether the prognosis is commercially justifiable on the basis of the underlying facts.

(b) Claimant and Opposing Party

84 In Germany, France and Austria it is not only **investors** still holding securities who are **entitled** to assert **claims**, but also investors who have already disposed of the respective securities. Under German law this right exists for the acquisition of securities within six months of the prospectus publication, irrespective of whether the securities were acquired on the primary or secondary market.[168] Spain[169] also provides for compensation claims for investors who have acquired respective securities on the secondary market within a certain time frame after the prospectus was published.

85 The PR does not specify against whom the claim is to be brought. It is thus hardly surprising that the Member States have not answered this question uniformly. In general it can be said that Germany, France, Italy, Austria and Spain all assume the **issuer** to be **held liable**.

86 In **Germany**, the action for prospectus liability can further be brought against any person responsible for the drawing up and publication of the prospectus,[170] ie the **issuer** and the **banks** issuing the securities, as well as against any person upon whose initiative the publication is based.[171] The latter is any person with an economic interest in the issuance, such as **major shareholders** or banks participating in the issuance of shares by a smaller and less solvent issuing company. German legal literature does not assume any liability of lawyers who only participate in drawing up parts of the prospectus without any personal economic interest in the issuance.[172]

(c) Causation

87 An essential element of prospectus liability is the question as to whether the claimant actually based his investment decision on the incorrect information. Germany has eased the **burden** of **proof of causation**,[173] whilst France, Italy and Sweden do not provide any rules easing the burden of proof for the investor.

88 In Germany, the courts formerly ruled that a general disposition towards the acquisition of shares, initiated through publications in the media or investment consulting, was sufficient for the assumption of causation between the prospectus and the investor's decision to acquire the securities (so-called *Anlagestimmung*).[174] The investor was assumed to have

---

[168] Cf. § 9(1) WpPG.
[169] Cf. M. Iribarren Blanco, *Responsabilidad civil por la información divulgada por las sociedades cotizadas*, 47 ff.; M. Grimaldos García, 102 RDBB (2006), 271, 278–279.
[170] § 9(1) No. 1 WpPG.
[171] § 9(1) No. 2 WpPG.
[172] M. Habersack, in: Habersack et al. (eds.), *Handbuch der Kapitalmarktinformation*, § 28 para. 30.
[173] Cf. on the legal situation in Austria S. Kalss et al., *Kapitalmarktrecht I*, § 12 para. 79.
[174] Cf. BGH of 14.07.1998 – XI ZR 173/97, BGHZ 139, 225, 233; BGH of 06.05.1982 – III ZR 18/91, NJW (1982), 2827, 2828.

indirectly gained knowledge of the content of the prospectus through information that was publicly available. The BGH ruled that the investor need not have read the prospectus or gained knowledge of it, ruling that it was sufficient if the report was decisive for the assessment of the security amongst experts and had thus helped to create a general disposition towards its acquisition.[175] The legislature finally adopted this understanding in § 12(2) no. 1 WpPG, which now contains a **legal assumption of causation**: The claim is unsubstantiated if the decision to acquire the respective securities was not based on the information in the prospectus. The defendant must prove this missing causation. It depends on the investor's individual motives that are decisive for the acquisition decision.[176]

(d) Responsibility (Fault)

All jurisdictions require responsibility for prospectus liability, **negligence** sufficing in Spain, France, Italy and Sweden, whilst in Austria the required standard of fault depends on the person who is to be held liable.[177] Germany has the most restrictive rules concerning responsibility.[178] Pursuant to § 12(1) WpPG, a person is exempt from liability if he can prove that he did not know that the prospectus contained incorrect or insufficient information and that his lack of knowledge was not based on gross negligence. Burden of proof is thus reversed: The opposing party must exculpate himself. A person acts with gross negligence if he fails to exercise reasonable care in a particularly serious way,[179] ie if he failed to make the most obvious deliberations.[180] The standard can vary, as the personal and expert knowledge of a person must be taken into consideration when determining whether it acted with gross negligence. The **issuer** has particularly high due diligence responsibilities because it has the relevant information at its disposal, has the legal means to obtain it (also from subsidiaries) and is in a position to assess its accuracy. In contrast, the banks managing the issue of securities usually do not have the necessary information from their own knowledge. Their due diligence obligations concern the verification of the information provided by the issuer.[181] This includes a plausibility check of the completeness and consistency of the information. In principle, the banks do not have to check the accuracy of the information. However, this is to be assessed differently if there are any indications that the information is incorrect or incomplete.[182]

89

(e) Legal Consequences

The Member States attach different legal consequences to the liability for incorrect prospectus information which can be divided into two categories. In some jurisdictions, investors may claim the **difference** between the **acquisition price** and **disposal price** for

90

---

[175] BGH of 14.07.1998 – XI ZR 173/97, BGHZ 139, 225, 233.
[176] Cf. BGH of 15.12.2020 – XI ZB 24/16, ZIP 2021, 508, 515 para. 87.
[177] Cf. § 22 (1) KMG.
[178] Cf. C. Gerner-Beuerle, 23 Temp. Int'l & Comp. L.J. (2009), 317, 374.
[179] Cf. BGH of 11. 5. 1953 – IV ZR 170/52, BGHZ 10, 14, 17; BGH of 5. 2. 1983 – II ZR 252/82, BGHZ 89, 153, 161.
[180] Cf. OLG Düsseldorf of 5. 4. 1984 – 6 U 239/82, WM (1984), 586, 595.
[181] Cf. M. Habersack, in: Habersack et al. (eds.), *Handbuch der Kapitalmarktinformation*, § 28 para. 41; O. Mülbert and B. Steup, in: Habersack et al. (eds.), *Unternehmensfinanzierung am Kapitalmarkt*, para. 41.113.
[182] Cf. O. Mülbert and B. Steup, in: Habersack et al. (eds.), *Unternehmensfinanzierung am Kapitalmarkt*, para. 41.111.

the shares or the actual value of the security as damages. Other Member States additionally provide the possibility to rescind the contract or claim compensation by restoration of the previous situation (**restitution in kind**).

91 In Germany, an investor can demand specific performance, ie the return of the securities against reimbursement of the acquisition price, pursuant to § 9(1) WpPG. If an investor has meanwhile disposed of the securities he can alternatively demand the difference in price between the acquisition and disposal, including all costs related thereto, such as the broker's commission paid to the issuing bank or a stockbroker and all costs attached to the exercise of subscription rights.

92 It has been discussed controversially whether **payments** the **issuer** must **make** to the investors based on the rules of prospectus liability **comply with** the (European) **capital maintenance regime**. Literature and courts tend to purport that the rules on prospectus liability comply with the principles on capital maintenance,[183] arguing that the respective stock exchange law provisions came into force after the rules on capital maintenance (*lex posterior* rule). The highest civil court in Austria (Oberste Gerichtshof) also ruled that the provisions on prospectus liability would override the rules on capital maintenance.[184] It appears doubtful, however, whether this interpretation complies with European company law.[185]

93 The ECJ, however, rejected this argument: 'In those circumstances, a payment made by a company to a shareholder because of irregular conduct on the part of that company prior to or at the time of the purchase of its shares does not constitute a distribution of capital within the meaning of Article 15 of the Second Directive and, consequently, such a payment ought not to be subject to the conditions stated in that article.'[186] The Court argued that 'liability of the company concerned to investors, who are also its shareholders, by reason of irregular conduct on the part of that company prior to or at the time of the purchase of its shares, does not derive from the memorandum and articles of association and is not directed solely at the internal relations of that company. The source of the liability at issue in such a case is the share purchase contract.'[187] According to the ECJ, the 'establishment of [...] a liability regime is therefore within the discretion conferred on the Member States and is not contrary to European Union law.'[188]

VII. Conclusion

94 With the enactment of the PD in 2003, the European legislature aimed to ensure the largest possible access to investment capital at a European level. The aims of the provisions further

---

[183] Cf. W. Bayer, WM (2013), 961, 966; S. Gebauer, *Börsenprospekthaftung und Kapitalerhaltungsgrundsatz*, 190 ff.; distinguishing between acquisition on the primary markets (liability is restricted to free assets) and acquisitions on the secondary markets (no restriction on liability, cf. § 57 AktG); cf. also BGH of 09.05.2005 – II ZR 287/02 NZG (2005), 672; OLG Frankfurt am Main of 11.10.2000 – 7 U 203/98, AG (2000), 132, 134.
[184] Cf. OGH of 30.03.2011 – 7 Ob 77/10i, GesRZ (2011), 193.
[185] Cf. N. Vokuhl (ed.), *Kapitalmarktrechtlicher Anlegerschutz*, 46 ff.; E.-M. Wild (ed.), *Prospekthaftung einer Aktiengesellschaft unter deutschem und europäischem Kapitalschutz*, 183 ff.
[186] ECJ of 19 December 2013, Case C 174/12 (*Hirmann*), para. 32.
[187] ECJ of 19 December 2013, Case C 174/12 (*Hirmann*), para. 29.
[188] ECJ of 19 December 2013, Case C 174/12 (*Hirmann*), para. 44.

include investor protection and market efficiency. These aims have largely been achieved. The reform of the Prospectus Directive in 2010 brought about further harmonisation of the requirements for the preparation and content of a prospectus when securities are offered to the public or admitted to trading. Nevertheless, the EU was still far from a level playing field. The 2017 reform was therefore an important step in the context of the Capital Markets Union project.

Since European prospectus law has undergone a high degree of maturity within four decades, the European legislator could simply transfer a large part of the regime of the EU directive into a EU regulation. Modernisations on Level 1 were implemented within the existing framework. The European legislature has not adopted completely new regulatory approaches, such as the transition from ex ante to ex post supervision by NCAs for well-known seasoned issuers. Though flexibilisation of EU prospectus law is inspired by reforms of the US Securities Regulation, it is plausible that the EU has not taken more ambitious steps for a reform. In the USA, flexibility in supervisory law can be provided for because the federal law on securities regulation provides for strict prospectus liability and, as an accompanying measure, effective mechanisms of collective redress in the form of class action. The legal situation in the EU is fundamentally different. Prospectus liability is regulated differently in the EU, a preventive effect of private enforcement being doubtful in all EU countries. Class actions or other types of action are only recognised in some Member States and have not been tested there either. Whether representative actions in the sense of Directive 2020/1828 will enable effective collective protection cannot yet be assessed. Against this background, it is not surprising that EU supervisory law is developing in small steps. 95

A fundamental question of European capital markets regulation also arises in prospectus law: Who is the addressee of capital market information? In market abuse law, the reasonable investor is protected. This figure is also found in prospectus law. Since the 2017 reform, European supervisory law has been characterised by a dichotomy. On the one hand, the summary of a prospectus must be oriented towards the inexperienced and easily misled investor; on the other hand, the other contents are directed towards a self-responsible investor with average knowledge of the capital market. The Member States may not apply stricter standards in this respect. Although the 2017 reform has infiltrated EU supervisory law with consumer protection considerations in a central area, the traditional figure of the reasonable investor continues to determine civil liability. 96

§ 18

Periodic Disclosure

Bibliography

Alibhai, Salim et al. (eds.), *Wiley 2020: Interpretation and Application of International Financial Reporting Standards* (2020); Assmann, Heinz-Dieter et al. (eds.), *Kommentar zum WpHG*, 7th edn. (2017); Beaver, William H., *What Should Be the FASB's Objectives?*, 136 JOA (1973), 49–56; Beaver, William H. and Demski, Joel S., *The Nature of Financial Accounting Objectives: A Summary and Synthesis*, 12 J. Acc. Res. (1974), 170–187; Böcking, Hans-Joachim, *Zum Verhältnis von Rechnungslegung und Kapitalmarkt: Vom 'financial accounting' zum 'business reporting'*, 50 ZfbF Sonderheft 40 (1998), 17–53; Brellochs, Michael, *Publizität und Haftung von Aktiengesellschaften im System des Europäischen Kapitalmarktrechts* (2005); Brinckmann, Hendrik, *Periodische Kapitalmarktpublizität durch Finanzberichte*, IUKR Working Paper (2008), available at: http://iukr.de/tl_files/iukr/pdf/1.arbeitspapieriukr.pdf; Brinckmann, Hendrik, *Kapitalmarktrechtliche Finanzberichterstattung* (2009); Brinckmann, Hendrik, *Die geplante Reform der Transparenz-RL: Veränderungen bei der Regelpublizität und der Beteiligungstransparenz*, 67 BB (2012), 1370–1373; Bushman, Robert M. and Smith, Abbie J., *Transparency, Financial Accounting Information, and Corporate Governance*, 9 Economic Policy Review (2003), 65–87; Busse von Colbe, Walther, *Die Entwicklung des Jahresabschlusses als Informationsinstrument*, 45 ZfbF Sonderheft 32 (1993), 11–29; Campbell, John Y. and Shiller, Robert J., *Stock Prices, Earnings, and Expected Dividends*, 43 J. Fin (1988), 661–676; Chang, Hsihui et al., *CEOs'/CFOs' Swearing by the Numbers: Does It Impact Share Price of the Firm?*, 81 TAR (2006), 1–27; Eidenmüller, Horst (ed.), *Ausländische Kapitalgesellschaften im deutschen Recht* (2004); Ekkenga, Jens, *Anlegerschutz, Rechnungslegung und Kapitalmarkt* (1998); Enriques, Luca et al., *Coporate Law and Securities Markets*, in: Kraakman, Reinier et al. (eds.), *The Anatomy of Corporate Law*, 3rd edn. (2017), 243–266; Fleischer, Holger, *Prognoseberichterstattung im Kapitalmarktrecht und Haftung für fehlerhafte Prognosen*, 45 AG (2006), 2–16; Fleischer, Holger, *Buchführungsverantwortung des Vorstands und Haftung der Vorstandsmitglieder für fehlerhafte Buchführung*, 60 WM (2006), 2021–2029; Fleischer, Holger, *Der deutsche 'Bilanzeid' nach § 264 Abs. 2 S. 3 HGB*, 28 ZIP (2007), 97–106; Franke, Günter and Hax, Herbert, *Finanzwirtschaft des Unternehmens und Kapitalmarkt* (2009); Fuchs, Andreas (ed.), *Kommentar zum WpHG*, 2nd edn. (2016); Habersack, Mathias et al. (eds.), *Handbuch der Kapitalmarktinformation* (2020); Hazen, Thomas L., *The Law of Securities Regulation* (2009); Henn, Harry G. and Alexander, John R., *Laws of Corporations*, 3rd edn. (1983); Hennrichs, Joachim, *Die Grundkonzeption der CSR-Berichterstattung und ausgewählte Problemfelder*, 47 ZGR (2018), 206–230; Hirte, Heribert and Möllers, Thomas M. J. (eds.), *Kölner Kommentar zum WpHG*, 2nd edn. (2014); Iordache, Irina D., *Information Transparency on Financial Markets, an International View*, 18 Audit Financiar (2020), 568–577; Kalss, Susanne et al. (eds.), *Kapitalmarktrecht I*, 2nd edn. (2015); Kumm, Nina, *Praxisfragen bei der Regelpublizität nach Inkrafttreten des TUG*, 64 BB (2009), 1118–1122; Lehmann, Matthias and Kumpan, Christoph (eds.), *European Financial Services Law* (2019); Levy, Robert A., *Random Walks: Reality or Myth*, 32 Fin. Analysts J. (1967), 69–77; Merkt, Hanno and Göthel, Stephan, *US-amerikanisches Gesellschaftsrecht* (2013);

Moloney, Niamh, *EU Securities and Financial Markets Regulation*, 3rd edn. (2014); Mülbert, Peter O. and Steup, Steffen, *Emittentenhaftung für fehlerhafte Kapitalmarktinformation am Beispiel der fehlerhaften Regelpublizität—das System der Kapitalmarktinformationshaftung nach AnSVG und WpPG mit Ausblick auf die Transparenzrichtlinie*, 59 WM (2005), 1633–1655; Mülbert, Peter O. and Steup, Steffen, *Das zweispurige Regime der Regelpublizität nach Inkrafttreten des TUG—Nachbesserungsbedarf aus Sicht von EU- und nationalem Recht*, 10 NZG (2007), 761–770; Paredes, Troy A., *Blinded by the Light: Information Overload and Its Consequences for Securities Regulation*, 81 Washington University Law Quarterly (2003), 417–485; Ronen, Joshua, *The Dual Role of Accounting: A Financial Economic Perspective*, in: Bicksler, James L. (ed.), Handbook of Financial Economics (1979), 415–454; Schüppen, Matthias, *Der Regierungsentwurf des Gesetzes zur Stärkung der Finanzmarktintegrität (FISG)—Hart, bissig, unausgegoren*, 56 DStR (2021), 246–254; Sehgal, Sanjay and Gupta, Meenakshi, *Technical Analysis in the Indian Capital Market ... A Survey*; 32 Decision (2005), 91–122; Seibt, Christoph H. and Wollenschläger, Bernward, *Europäisierung des Transparenzregimes: Der Vorschlag der Europäischen Kommission zur Revision der Transparenzrichtlinie*, 51 AG (2012), 305–315; Strieder, Thomas and Ammedick, Oliver, *Der Zwischenlagebericht als neues Instrument der Zwischenberichterstattung*, 60 DB (2007), 1368–1372; Veil, Rüdiger, *Prognosen im Kapitalmarktrecht*, 45 AG (2006), 690–698; Veil, Rüdiger, *Der Schutz des verständigen Anlegers durch Publizität und Haftung im europäischen und nationalen Kapitalmarktrecht*, 18 ZBB (2006), 162–171; Veil, Rüdiger, *Auf dem Weg zu einem Europäischen Kapitalmarktrecht: die Vorschläge der Kommission zur Neuregelung des Transparenzregimes*, 66 WM (2012), 53–61; Veil, Rüdiger, *Climate-related financial disclosure*, in: Tountopoulos, Vassilios and Veil, Rüdiger (eds.), *Transparency of Stock Corporations in Europe—Rationales, Limitations and Perspective* (2019), 129–141; Wagner, Franz W., *Zur Informations- und Ausschüttungsbemessungsfunktion des Jahresabschlusses auf einem organisierten Kapitalmarkt*, 34 ZfbF (1982), 749–773; Walz, Rainer, *Ökonomische Regulierungstheorien vor den Toren des Bilanzrechts*, 45 ZfbF Sonderheft 32 (1993), 85–106.

I. Introduction

1. Development of a System of Periodic Disclosure

1 Periodic disclosure is defined as the continual supply of the capital market with information on the issuer. The concept can first be found in the Directive 79/279/EEC[1] coordinating the conditions for the admission of securities to official stock exchange listing (Securities Admission Directive) of 1979.[2] It required companies and undertakings, whose shares and debt securities, respectively, were admitted to a stock exchange's official listing, to immediately make their annual accounts and annual report available to the public. The directive provided the possibility for group companies to publish additionally or alternatively

---

[1] Council Directive 79/279/EEC of 5 March 1979 coordinating the conditions for the admission of securities to official stock exchange listing, OJ L 66, 16 March 1979, p. 21–32 (Securities Admission Directive).
[2] See R. Veil § 1 para. 6. For the legislative history of the TD cf. W.-G. Ringe, in: Lehmann and Kumpan (eds.), *European Financial Services Law*, Art. 1 TD para. 12 ff.

a consolidated account.³ This marked the beginning of an annual mandatory disclosure under stock exchange law.

The disclosure obligation provided for by the European legislature with the Securities Admission Directive was restricted to annual accounts and annual reports which had already been harmonised with the Fourth Directive 78/660/EEC⁴ on the annual accounts of certain types of companies (Fourth Directive) and which were thus already subject to disclosure requirements.⁵ The provisions of the Securities Admission Directive thus built upon the already existing structures and stipulated an additional disclosure obligation. This resulted in a **dualistic regulatory concept**, in which the obligation to disclose and the content thereof were regulated separately.

In 1982, the Securities Admission Directive was complemented by the Directive 82/121/EEC⁶ on information to be published on a regular basis (Half-Yearly Report Directive) which required companies, whose shares were admitted to official listing on a stock exchange, to publish a half-yearly report on the activities, profits and losses of the company during the first six months of each financial year.⁷ The directive constituted the European legislature's reaction to the recommendations in the Segré Report for the introduction of the requirement for a continuous flow of information for companies on capital markets.⁸ Unlike the commonly known methods of annual accounts and annual reports that could be referred to in the Securities Admission Directive, the half-yearly reports were until then an unknown reporting format. Therefore, the Half-Yearly Report Directive had to contain provisions on the content of the half-yearly report, in addition to laying down the disclosure obligation for it.⁹

In 1999, the Commission defined the measures necessary to fulfil the aim of a single market for financial services in its Financial Services Action Plan and underlined the importance of a directive to improve the rules on transparency.¹⁰ In trying to comply with its time scale for the legislative reforms of the financial market, the Commission adhered to the Lamfalussy Report,¹¹ which recommended a more effective legislative process on four levels.

---

³ Art. 4(2) in conjunction with Annex III Schedule C 4, Annex IV Schedule D A. 3 Securities Admission Directive. These provisions were later adopted, without amendments in Art. 67, 80 Directive 2001/34/EC of the European Parliament and of the Council of 28 May 2001 on the admission of securities to official stock exchange listing and on information to be published on those securities, OJ L 184, 6 July 2001, p. 1–66 (New Securities Admission Directive).
⁴ Fourth Council Directive 78/660/EEC of 25 June 1978 based on Art. 54 (3) (g) of the Treaty on the annual accounts of certain types of companies, OJ L 222, 14 August 1978, p. 11–31 (Fourth Directive).
⁵ Art. 47(1) Fourth Directive.
⁶ Council Directive 82/121/EEC of 15 February 1982 on information to be published on a regular basis by companies the shares of which have been admitted to official stock-exchange listing, OJ L 48, 20 February 1982, p. 26–29 (Half-Yearly Report Directive).
⁷ Art. 1(1), Art. 2 Half-Yearly Report Directive, later adopted without amendments in Art. 70 New Securities Admission Directive.
⁸ Commission, The Development of a European Capital Market, Report of a Group of experts appointed by the EEC Commission, November 2006 ('Segré Report'), p. 228–229.
⁹ Art. 5 Half-Yearly Report Directive, later adopted without amendments in Art. 73 New Securities Admission Directive.
¹⁰ Cf. recital 3 TD.
¹¹ Final Report of the Committee of Wise Men on Securities Markets Regulation, 15 February 2001, available at: https://www.esma.europa.eu/sites/default/files/library/2015/11/lamfalussy_report.pdf; see R. Veil § 1 para. 18.

Based on this, the **Transparency Directive (TD)** was enacted as the fourth framework directive in 2004. It contains framework measures and general principles on the transparency requirements regarding information about issuers whose securities are admitted to trading on a regulated market. In 2007, the TD was followed by the Level 2 Directive 2007/14/EC[12] laying down detailed rules for the implementation of certain provisions of Directive 2004/109/EC on the harmonisation of transparency requirements in relation to information about issuers whose securities are admitted to trading on a regulated market, containing more detailed rules on the requirements described in the TD.

5   The TD essentially refined the system of periodic disclosure on the basis of financial reporting. It revoked existing provisions[13] and, at first, introduced a total of four reporting formats: the annual financial report, the half-yearly financial report, the quarterly financial report and the interim management statement. But already at the time of its adoption, the TD provided for a critical review and required the Commission to present a report to the European Parliament and to the Council until 30 June 2009 on the operation of the TD.[14] As a result of this review, Directive 2013/50/EU[15] amending the TD (ADTD) was enacted in 2013. Member States had to implement the new rules into their national laws until the end of November 2015.[16] The ADTD provided for substantial changes to the original concept of the TD: The interim management statement has been abolished only a few years after its introduction[17] and the annual and half-yearly financial report became largely subject to the concept of maximum harmonisation.[18] As a consequence, today Member States may only require issuers to publish additional periodic financial information besides annual and half-yearly financial reports under very limited conditions.[19]

6   All financial reports are based on financial accounting information and subject the latter to a capital markets law disclosure obligation. This, however, did not apply to the former interim management statement. The interim management statement had a pure narrative content and, therefore, presented a disruptive factor within the system of financial reporting. It is thus to be welcomed that the interim management statement has been abolished.

---

[12] Commission Directive 2007/14/EC of 8 March 2007 laying down detailed rules for the implementation of certain provisions of Directive 2004/109/EC on the harmonisation of transparency requirements in relation to information about issuers whose securities are admitted to trading on a regulated market, OJ L 69, 9 March 2007, p. 27–36.

[13] Art. 32(5) TD.

[14] Cf. Art. 33 TD. Pursuant to Art. 33 TD, Commission published the Report on the Operation of Directive 2004/109/EC on the harmonisation of transparency requirements in relation to information about issuers whose securities are admitted to trading on a regulated market, 27 May 2017, COM(2010) 243 final, and the Commission Staff Working Document, 27 May 2010, SEC(2010) 611.

[15] Directive 2013/50/EU of the European Parliament and of the Council of 22 October 2013 amending Directive 2004/109/EC of the European Parliament and of the Council on the harmonisation of transparency requirements in relation to information about issuers whose securities are admitted to trading on a regulated market, Directive 2003/71/EC of the European Parliament and of the Council on the prospectus to be published when securities are offered to the public or admitted to trading and Commission Directive 2007/14/EC laying down detailed rules for the implementation of certain provisions of Directive 2004/109/EC, OJ L 294, 6 November 2013, p. 13–27 (ADTD); see R. Veil § 1 para 43. On the Commission's proposal for the ADTD, 25 October 2011, COM(2011) 683 final, cf. H. Brinckmann, 67 BB (2012), 1370 ff.

[16] Cf. Art. 4(1) ADTD.

[17] Cf. Art. 1(5) ADTD replacing former Art. 6 TD.

[18] Cf. Art. 1(2) ADTD amending former Art. 3 TD; cf. also H. Brinckmann, 67 BB (2012), 1370, 1371 ff.

[19] See below para 54 ff. Cf. also R. Veil, 66 WM (2012), 53, 54.

2. Financial Accounting Information as the Basis of Financial Reporting

Periodic disclosure meets the capital market's continual need for information. Yet the determination of the exact need for information is difficult. An empirical study on all information required or used by investors for their investment decisions would probably bring to light a very complex picture: whilst professional investors mainly rely on economic data and indicators, such as sales figures, sales revenues and profits, as well as the analysis of charts and past share prices,[20] other investors will often only rely on the recommendations of investment advisors or follow investment decisions or insider tips of supposed stock market gurus.[21] All these methods have in common that they give a basis for a prognosis[22] on future market developments,[23] which will, however, always be accompanied by a certain amount of uncertainty.[24]

Whilst no method can completely eliminate this uncertainty, it can nevertheless be assumed that some information will be more suitable than others as the basis for predicting future market developments. Financial accounting information is an established[25] and well-tried prognosis instrument and has been proven at least to reduce the uncertainties regarding future developments.[26] Although market reactions resulting from natural disasters or terrorist attacks cannot be taken into account, information on capital reserves, liabilities and pension provisions will give an insight into the future chances and risks of a company.[27] Therefore financial accounting information must be regarded as the best prognosis instrument business economics has so far developed.[28]

---

[20] On the two different approaches of securities analysis—the fundamental and the technical one—and information processing through investors cf. S. Sehgal and M. Gupta, 32 Decision (2005), 91, 93; R. Levy, 23 FAJ (1967), 69; G. Franke and H. Hax, *Finanzwirtschaft des Unternehmens und Kapitalmarkt*, 402 ff.

[21] The high importance of future-oriented information for investors describes the US Court of Appeals in *Wielgos v. Commonwealth Edison Company*, 892 F.2d 509 (7th Cir. 1989): 'Investors value securities because of beliefs about how firms will do tomorrow, not because of how they did yesterday. If enterprises cannot make predictions about themselves, then securities analysts, newspaper columnists, and charlatans have protected turf'; cf. also H. Fleischer, 45 AG (2006), 2.

[22] On the importance of prognosis by management cf. L. Enriques et al., in: Kraakman et al. (eds.), *The Anatomy of Corporate Law*, 244, 250; T. Hazen, *The Law of Securities Regulation*, § 3.8[4], 147 ff.; on prognosis in capital markets law in general cf. R. Veil, 45 AG (2006), 690 ff.

[23] Cf. W. Beaver and J. Demski, 12 J. Acc. Res. (1974), 170, 171. Before an investor makes a decision regarding an investment or divestment it must make a prognosis as to which investments promise the highest returns in the future. If it decided correctly the price will adapt accordingly and thus correctly reflect where there is a scarcity of capital, cf. J. Ronen, in: Bicksler (ed.), *Handbook of Financial Economics*, 415, 431 ff.; L. Enriques et al., in: Kraakman et al. (eds.), *The Anatomy of Corporate Law*, 244, 249 ff.; R. Walz, 45 ZfbF Sonderheft 32 (1993), 85, 102.

[24] H. Brinckmann, *Kapitalmarktrechtliche Finanzberichterstattung*, 197.

[25] Cf. L. Enriques et al., in: Kraakman et al. (eds.), *The Anatomy of Corporate Law*, 244, 252; W. Beaver, 136 JOA (1973), 49, 51; W. Busse von Colbe, 45 ZfbF Sonderheft 32 (1993), 11, 15; J. Ronen, in: Bicksler (ed.), *Handbook of Financial Economics*, 415, 437 ff. On the problem of 'information overload' cf. T. Paredes, 81 Washington University Law Quarterly (2003), 417, 448–449.

[26] Cf. W. Beaver, 136 JOA (1973), 49, 50 ff.; J. Campbell and R. Shiller, 43 J. Fin. (1988), 661, 675; J. Ekkenga, *Anlegerschutz, Rechnungslegung und Kapitalmarkt*, 75–76; H. Brinckmann, *Kapitalmarktrechtliche Finanzberichterstattung*, 194 ff. On the relationship between capital markets and financial accounting information cf. also H.-J. Böcking, 50 Zfbf Sonderheft 40 (1998), 17, 23 ff.

[27] Cf. J. Ronen, in: Bicksler (ed.), *Handbook of Financial Economics*, 415, 435 ff.

[28] On the reporting obligations of financial accounting information in the United States cf. T. Hazen, *The Law of Securities Regulation*, § 9.3, 328 ff.

9   The European legislature's recourse to financial accounting information for a periodic disclosure to the capital markets can be justified by the fact that it is a common prognosis instrument and is, in general, price sensitive.[29] For this reason, **financial accounting information** is the **substantial part** of financial reporting regarding **periodic capital market information**. Although investors may continually demand information not contained in the financial reports,[30] the European legislature's aim is still to control the investors' market behaviour mainly by supplying them with information gained from corporate accounting.

10 The fact that the information is to be used on the capital market influences the evaluation of the financial accounting information itself, as its primary aim is to inform investors.[31] This requires the most exact description possible of the issuer's economic situation. Thus, the European regime on disclosure of financial accounting information results in investor control based on real economic performance indicators. It ensures that share prices can periodically adjust to the company's fundamental value, limiting the effects speculations had on the share price.

3. The Growing Importance of Non-financial Information within the System of Periodic Disclosure

11 Even though the predominance of financial accounting information for the system of periodic disclosure is not called into question, however, it can be seen that non-financial information became constantly of more importance within this regime. This development has probably not reached its end as it is part of the still very active discussion on **sustainable finance**.[32] By integrating non-financial information into the system of periodic disclosure the legislator follows the same aim as for financial accounting information: investors' market behaviour shall be controlled and the allocation of capital guided to those companies that are preferable in the legislator's view.

(a) The Disclosure of Environmental Issues as the Beginning of Non-financial Reporting

12 First approaches to supplement the disclosure of financial accounting information by a non-financial reporting go back to the early 1990s. Resulting from the growing importance of the environmental protection movement in the second half of the twentieth century, the

---

[29] Empirical studies have proved that financial accounting information has influence on the share price, cf. W. Beaver, 136 JOA (1973), 49, 51; W. Busse von Colbe, 45 ZfbF Sonderheft 32 (1993), 11, 16; F. Wagner, 34 ZfbF (1982), 749, 758 ff.; cf. also L. Enriques et al., in: Kraakman et al. (eds.), *The Anatomy of Corporate Law*, 244, 246 ff.

[30] The German Bundesgerichtshof (BGH—German Federal Court of Justice) underlined that apart from stock exchanges it cannot be expected that investors are able to fully understand and interpret a company's financial statement, BGH of 18.9.2012 – XI ZR 344/11, BGHZ 195, 1.

[31] Therefore, investors get better information under a reporting regime that consequently follows a 'fair-value-approach' like the 'Anglo-Saxon' model or the IFRS, L. Enriques et al., in: Kraakman et al. (eds.), *The Anatomy of Corporate Law*, 244, 252 ff.; H. Brinckmann, *Kapitalmarktrechtliche Finanzberichterstattung*, 190 ff. and passim. On the development of the different financial reporting models cf. Alibhai, Salim et al., *Wiley 2020: Interpretation and Application of International Financial Reporting Standards*, 1 ff.

[32] See H. Brinckmann § 16 para 33 ff.

concept of environmental protection also became part of European policies. In 1993, the Commission published its strategy and policy for the environment and sustainable development within the European Community.[33] In that analysis, the Commission identified a failure in companies' accounting information to fully reflect their environmental impact. To improve awareness of environmental issues, the Commission provides for an initiative in the area of company accounting to foster reporting on financial aspects relating to the environment.[34]

The implantation of this initiative took place in 2001 when the Commission adopted a recommendation on European accounting law[35] to strengthen a better recognition and measurement of environmental issues in annual accounts and—as well—better disclosure of environmental issues in annual reports.[36] The European legislator had recognised a very low level of voluntary disclosure on environmental issues by the companies, notwithstanding an increasing demand by investors and other stakeholders for such information.[37] The environmental information disclosed by companies was often seen inadequate or unreliable for investors.[38] Therefore, the legislator wanted to allow for higher comparability and consistency of the environmental information presented and recommended the disclosure of environmental issues with the annual and consolidated annual reports or in the notes to the annual and consolidated accounts.[39]

13

This marked the beginning of a non-financial reporting becoming part of European accounting law and—due to its regulatory concept—also of the system of periodic disclosure. At this early stage, non-financial reporting was based on a Commission's recommendation and, therefore, a non-binding, **purely descriptive element** that was limited in frequency to annual reports and in its content to **environmental issues**.

14

(b) Development of Non-financial Reporting by Initiatives on Corporate Social Responsibility

Already two years later, the legally non-binding recommendation has been transferred into binding European law. Directive 2003/51/EC amending Directives 78/660/EEC, 83/349/EEC, 86/635/EEC and 91/674/EEC on the annual and consolidated accounts of certain types of

15

---

[33] Commission, Towards Sustainability—European Community programme of policy and action in relation to the environment and sustainable development, COM(1992) 23, OJ C 138, 17 May 1993, p. 5–98 (Towards Sustainability 1993).

[34] Commission, Towards Sustainability 1993, p. 71.

[35] Commission Recommendation of 30 May 2001 on the recognition, measurement and disclosure of environmental issues in the annual accounts and annual reports of companies, OJ L 156, 13 June 2001, p. 33–42 (Recommendation 30 May 2001).

[36] The 'annual report' has later been renamed into 'management report' when Art. 46 Fourth Directive and Art. 36 Seventh Council Directive 83/349/EEC of 13 June 1983 based on the Art. 54 (3) (g) of the Treaty on consolidated accounts, OJ L 193, 18 July 1983, p. 1–17 (Seventh Directive), have both been consolidated in Art. 19 and 29 Directive 2013/34/EU of the European Parliament and of the Council of 26 June 2013 on the annual financial statements, consolidated financial statements and related reports of certain types of undertakings, amending Directive 2006/43/EC of the European Parliament and of the Council and repealing Council Directives 78/660/EEC and 83/349/EEC, OJ L 182, 26 June 2013, p. 19–76 (Accounting Directive).

[37] Cf. recital 4 Recommendation 30 May 2001.

[38] Cf. recital 4 Recommendation 30 May 2001.

[39] Annex 4 Recommendation 30 May 2001.

companies, banks and other financial institutions and insurance undertakings[40] amended the European accounting law and integrated the obligation to report on non-financial information relating to **environmental and some social (employee) matters** into the company's annual report.[41] Directive 2003/51/EC stipulated for the first time the obligation to report on environmental as well as social (employee) matters.

16 The reason for the extension of environmental by social matters can be explained by the debate on **corporate social responsibility (CSR)** that included ideas on environmental protection and sustainability towards the end of the twentieth century.[42] When the Commission presented its first CSR-initiative in 2001 by the Green Paper on promoting a European framework for CSR,[43] it already specified CSR as concept whereby companies integrate social and environmental concerns in their business operations.[44] With respect to the disclosure of non-financial information in companies' annual reports, the Green Paper referred to the existing disclosure of environmental issues based on the Commission's recommendation and empathised the development of further environmental and social reporting.[45]

17 In 2011, the Commission presented a renewed strategy on CSR.[46] In it, the Commission concluded that the economic crisis has damaged confidence in enterprises and focused public attention on their social and ethical performance. Therefore, the Commission aimed to create conditions favourable to sustainable growth, responsible business behaviour and durable employment generation by a renewed strategy on CSR.[47] And although progress was made, the Commission observed many companies in the EU had not sufficiently integrated social and environmental concerns into their operations.[48] The Commission therefore extended the scope of CSR by a new definition meaning, very broadly, the responsibility of enterprises for their impacts on society,[49] and announced new legislative action to improve company disclosure of social and environmental information.[50]

18 As a result, Directive 2014/95/EU[51] amended the Accounting Directive as regards disclosure of non-financial and diversity information by certain large undertakings and groups (NFRD). The NFRD introduced an **independent reporting element** for non-financial

---

[40] Directive 2003/51/EC of the European Parliament and of the Council of 18 June 2003 amending Directives 78/660/EEC, 83/349/EEC, 86/635/EEC and 91/674/EEC on the annual and consolidated accounts of certain types of companies, banks and other financial institutions and insurance undertakings, OJ L 178, 17 July 2003, p. 16–22.
[41] Recital 9, Art. 1(14)(a), Art. 2(10)(a) Directive 2003/51/EC.
[42] Cf. J. Hennrichs, 47 ZGR (2018), 206, 208.
[43] Commission, Green Paper—Promoting a European framework for corporate social responsibility, 18 July 2001, COM(2001) 366 final (Green Paper CSR).
[44] Commission, Green Paper CSR, p. 6.
[45] Commission, Green Paper CSR, p. 17.
[46] Communication from the Commission to the European Parliament, the Council, the European Economic and Social Committee of the Regions—A renewed EU strategy 2011–14 for Corporate Social Responsibility, 25 October 2011, COM(2011) 681 final (CSR Strategy 2011).
[47] Commission, CSR Strategy 2011, p. 4.
[48] Commission, CSR Strategy 2011, p. 5.
[49] Commission, CSR Strategy 2011, p. 6.
[50] Commission, CSR Strategy 2011, p. 11.
[51] Directive 2014/95/EU of the European Parliament and of the Council of 22 October 2014 amending Directive 2013/34/EU as regards disclosure of non-financial and diversity information by certain large undertakings and groups, OJ L 330, 15 November 2014, p. 1–9 (NFRD).

information within the management report and the consolidated management report in the form of the non-financial statement and the consolidated non-financial statement, but limits their application to large public-interest companies (eg listed companies, banks, insurance companies)[52] with more than 500 employees.[53] To help companies disclose relevant non-financial information in a more consistent and more comparable manner, the Commission published Guidelines on non-financial reporting[54] and Supplementing Guidelines on reporting climate-related information.[55]

(c) Upcoming Developments of Non-financial Reporting by its Integration into the Sustainable Finance Agenda

The upcoming awareness of climate change in recent years has highly accelerated governmental measures for more sustainability with the objective of combating further consequences of climate change. In the area of financial market regulation, the concept of sustainable finance summarises measures in this respect. The Commission's Action Plan 'Financing Sustainable Growth' of 2018[56] took up the existing level of non-financial reporting reached by the NFRD und integrated it into further initiatives under its sustainable finance strategy. In this regard, the Commission acknowledged that the NFRD already requires large public interest entities to disclose material information on key environmental, social and governance aspects and announced an evaluation of the non-financial reporting according to sustainability aspects.[57] In 2019, the Commission finally committed to a review of the NFRD in its Communication on the European Green Deal.[58] This review will be aimed at increasing companies' and financial institutions' disclosure on climate and environmental data so that investors are fully informed about the sustainability of their investments.[59]

(d) Conclusion

Non-financial information became continuously of more importance within the system of periodic disclosure and developed into an **important supplement** to financial accounting information. Currently, it is still limited in frequency to the annual financial report in so far as only the management report and the consolidated management report contain a

---

[52] Art. 2(1) Accounting Directive.
[53] Art. 1(1) and (3) NFRD. This covers approximately 6,000 large companies and groups across the European Union, cf. J. Hennrichs, 47 ZGR (2018), 206, 209; this figure is also mentioned by the Commission, cf. https://ec.europa.eu/info/business-economy-euro/company-reporting-and-auditing/company-reporting/non-financial-reporting_de.
[54] Communication from the Commission, Guidelines on non-financial reporting methodology for reporting non-financial information, OJ C 215, 5 July 2017, p. 1–20.
[55] Communication from the Commission, Guidelines on non-financial reporting: Supplement on reporting climate-related information, OJ C 209, 20 June 2019, p. 1–30.
[56] Communication from the Commission to the European Parliament, the European Council, the Council, the European Central Bank, the European Economic and Social Committee and the Committee of the Regions, Action Plan: Financing Sustainable Growth, 8 March 2018, COM(2018) 97 final (Sustainable Finance Action Plan 2018).
[57] Commission, Sustainable Finance Action Plan 2018, p. 9 ff.
[58] Communication from the Commission to the European Parliament, the European Council, the Council, the European Central Bank, the European Economic and Social Committee and the Committee of the Regions, The European Green Deal, 11 December 2019, COM(2019) 640 final (The Green Deal).
[59] Commission, The Green Deal, p. 17.

disclosure obligation for non-financial information;[60] the interim management report of the half-yearly financial report does not contain the requirement to disclose non-financial information.[61] Together with the corporate governance statement, which is also an element of the management report and the consolidated management report,[62] the content of non-financial reporting refers to **environmental, social and governance matters** relevant to the reporting entity.

21 As it is a pure **descriptive element** withing the annual financial report, non-financial information can be presented in a less integrated and less consistent way compared to financial accounting information. As a result, issuers are less comparable on matters included in their non-financial reporting. Investors focusing on non-financial information for their investment decisions will, therefore, have to accept greater uncertainty when it comes to predict future performance and market valuation of that issuer. For a legal framework of the integration of non-financial information within the system of periodic disclosure it should be observed that due to their greater scope of interpretation, the extent of non-financial information within financial reports has to remain low and should only supplement financial accounting information where necessary.

II. Regulatory Concepts

1. Requirements under European Law

(a) The Financial Report as a Unified Reporting Standard for Periodic Disclosure

22 Since the enactment of the TD, the periodic supply of the capital market with information is ensured by an obligation for the issuer to publish financial reports. All reporting formats—annual financial report and half-yearly financial report—are referred to as 'financial reports', showing the European legislature's efforts to introduce a unified standard of reporting for periodic information about the capital market. The TD of 2004 also contained references to the quarterly financial report by comparing it with the interim management statement.[63] But since the interim management statement has been abolished[64] the quarterly financial report is no longer subject of the TD. Nevertheless, the history of the quarterly financial report as a former additional reporting format within the system of financial reporting supports the European approach of having 'financial reports' as a unified reporting standard for the periodic supply of the capital market with information on the issuers.

23 Financial reporting can be regarded as the disclosure of financial accounting under capital markets law. **Periodic statements** by the **issuer** are a central element of this—a

---

[60] Cf. Art. 19(1) and 29(1) Accounting Directive.
[61] Cf. Art. 5(4) TD.
[62] Cf. Art. 20 and 29 Accounting Directive.
[63] Cf. recital 16, Art. 6(2) TD of 2004.
[64] The former interim management statement, which was introduced by the TD of 2004, stood outside the periodic disclosure system based on financial reports. Therefore, the abolishment of the interim management statement in 2013 has also removed a disruptive factor out of the system of periodic disclosure.

financial statement is contained in the annual financial report and a condensed financial statement is included in the half-yearly financial report.[65]

The reason why the European legislator recourses to financial accounting information for the periodic disclosure can directly be deduced from the functions connected to financial accounting.[66] Financial accounting has the role of a monitoring mechanism by which the company's stockholder can control and the company's management have to account for the management of the entrusted resources.[67] Financial reporting addresses the disclosure of financial accounting information to investors on capital markets, who shall process the financial accounting information and orientate their investment decisions respectively. The underlying legal and political objective behind this concept is that the investors shall be in a position to control the issuer's economic activities by their investment decisions. Additionally, financial reporting improves transparency of, and thereby confidence in, the capital markets. 24

Additionally, the annual financial report also contains—to some extent—non-financial information as a supplement to financial accounting information.[68] The European legislator integrates this non-financial reporting into periodic disclosure mainly to follow a political agenda and foster **sustainable investments**.[69] This follows the rationale that pure financial accounting information have deficits when it comes to predict a company's long-term performance.[70] Therefore, non-financial reporting within the system of periodic disclosure aims at strengthening investors' long-term perspective as it is much too focused on short-term financial performance.[71] By the disclosure of environmental, social and governance matters within annual financial reports, the European legislator tries to control the investors' market behaviour and guide financial resources to issuers with a more sustainable business than others. 25

(b) Correlation with European Accounting Law as a Reflection of the Dualistic Regulatory Concept

The dualistic regulatory concept first addressed in the Securities Admission Directive[72] has since intensified in the European law about financial reports. Whilst originally elements of accounting law were only referred to regarding the annual disclosure obligations of annual accounts and reports, leaving the half-yearly report largely independent of these rules, the 26

---

[65] Art. 4(2)(a), 5(2)(a) TD. Although the TD of 2004 did not stipulate any detail regarding the elements of a quarterly financial report, referring to it as a 'financial report', much can be said for subjecting the quarterly report to the same requirements as the annual and half-yearly financial reports, especially requiring it typically to have a structure characteristic of a (condensed) financial statement, cf. H. Brinckmann, *Kapitalmarktrechtliche Finanzberichterstattung*, 179–180.
[66] Cf. H. Brinckmann, *Kapitalmarktrechtliche Finanzberichterstattung*, 181 ff.; J. Ronen, in: Bicksler (ed.), *Handbook of Financial Economics*, 415, 417 ff.
[67] Cf. R. Bushman and A. Smith, 9 Economic Policy Review (2003), 65, 67 ff.; J. Ronen, in: Bicksler (ed.), *Handbook of Financial Economics*, 415, 417.
[68] See above para. 11 ff.
[69] Commission, The Green Deal, p. 17.
[70] Cf. R. Veil, in: Tountopoulos and Veil (eds.), *Transparency of Stock Corporations in Europe*, 129, 141.
[71] Commission, The Green Deal, p. 17.
[72] See above para. 1.

European legislature now refers to accounting law more extensively.[73] Hence, the obligation to disclose is an element of capital markets law, whilst the content of the disclosure takes into consideration the objects of accounting law.

27   Similar can be said of the auditing obligation regarding financial statements. It is also subject to the provisions of European accounting law,[74] whilst the obligation to declare a balance sheet oath is an element related to the content developed by the European legislature exclusively for the area of financial reporting, based on the similar provision in the US *Sarbanes-Oxley Act*.[75] The balance sheet oath is an instrument to strengthen the personal responsibility for the financial accounting within the issuer. This character of the balance sheet oath also becomes apparent in the fact that the persons responsible within the issuer must submit a statement containing their name and function in which they declare that the financial statement and management report comply with the 'true and fair view principle' as laid down in the applicable set of accounting standards.[76] A balance sheet oath must be made for all annual and half-yearly financial reports.[77]

28   The references to accounting law in the financial reporting framework still provide scope for an individual design of the financial reporting information presented by an issuer. Depending on different sectors or a special economic situation of the issuers it might be necessary to adjust the information of a financial report as far as this is permitted by the applicable accounting law and as long as this is without giving the financial report a misleading character. One example for the possible adjustment of financial reporting information are **Alternative Performance Measures (APM)**. An APM can be described as a financial measure of historical or future financial performance, financial position, or cash flows, other than a financial measure defined or specified in the applicable financial reporting framework.[78] APMs like, eg the EBITDA are very common and can be very useful to present a better description of the issuer than financial measures contained in the applicable accounting law framework. Since 2015 a European harmonisation of APMs has been reached by ESMA Guidelines.[79]

(c) Addressee of the Disclosure Obligation

29   The annual financial report must be made public by all issuers[80] and the half-yearly report by all issuers of shares and debt securities.[81] The TD defines the term 'issuer' as a natural person or a legal entity governed by private or public law, including a state, whose securities

---

[73] Only the former interim management statements had no connection to accounting provisions.

[74] Cf. Art. 4(4) TD. The TD refers in Art. 4(4) to provisions of the former Fourth Directive and the Seventh Directive, which have both been consolidated in Art. 34 and 35 Accounting Directive.

[75] Sec. 302(a) Sarbanes-Oxley Act 2002, cf. H. Chang et al., 81 TAR (2006), 1, 3–4; T. Hazen, *The Law of Securities Regulation*, § 9.3[1], 333–335; H. Fleischer, 28 ZIP (2007), 97–98.

[76] Art. 4(2)(c), 5(2)(c) TD explicitly refers to the concept of true and fair view in its English version; cf. also N.-C. Wunderlich, in: Habersack et al. (eds.), *Handbuch der Kapitalmarktinformation*, § 9 para. 88; W.-G. Ringe, in: Lehmann and Kumpan (eds.), *European Financial Services Law*, Art. 4 TD para. 14.

[77] Art. 4(2)(c), 5(2)(c) TD.

[78] Cf. ESMA, Guideline on Alternative Performance Measures, 5 October 2015, ESMA/2015/1415en, para. 17.

[79] ESMA/2015/1415en (fn. 78).

[80] Art. 4(1) TD.

[81] Art. 5(1) TD.

are admitted to trading on a regulated market.[82] The provisions thus exempt certain public bodies, especially states, regional or local authorities of a state, the ECB, EFSF and the Member States' national central banks, from the rules on financial reporting.[83] Legal entities governed by public law are therefore only partly required to oblige with the rules on financial reporting. The TD also exempts an issuer of debt securities admitted to trading on a regulated market, the denomination per unit of which is at least € 100.000, from the obligation to publish a financial report.[84]

The addressees of the provisions are further defined by the criteria 'regulated market' and 'securities'. Both terms are defined in MiFID II.[85] Put briefly, this entails that annual reports are required on all regulated securities markets and half-yearly reports are additionally necessary on all regulated markets for shares and debt securities.

2. Implementation in the Member States

The disclosure obligation for financial reports is part of the Members States' national laws. The Commission monitors the transposition measures taken by each Member State.[86] The requirements on financial reporting stipulated by the TD have mostly been adopted by the Member States one-to-one into their national law so that the national provisions comply with the European requirements.[87] Thus, the national provisions on financial reporting shall not be presented in detail at this point.

III. Annual Financial Report

1. Overview

The TD requires the issuer to make public its annual financial report at the latest four months after the end of each financial year.[88] The annual financial report comprises the **audited financial statement** (lit. a) and **management report** (lit. b) as well as a **statement** made by the **persons responsible** within the issuer whose names and functions shall be clearly indicated to the effect that, to the best of their knowledge, the financial statements prepared in accordance with the applicable set of accounting standards give a true and fair view of the assets, liabilities, financial position and profit or loss of the issuer and the undertakings included in the consolidation taken as a whole. The management report must

---

[82] Art. 2(1)(d) TD.
[83] Art. 8(1)(a) TD.
[84] Art. 8(1)(b) TD.
[85] See R. Veil § 1 para 44. For more details on the concept of a regulated market see R. Veil § 7 para. 11–15 and on the term 'security' R. Veil § 8 para. 4–5.
[86] An overview is available at: https://eur-lex.europa.eu/legal-content/DE/NIM/?uri=CELEX:32004L0109.
[87] Cf. W.-G. Ringe, in: Lehmann and Kumpan (eds.), *European Financial Services Law*, Art. 1 TD para. 14.
[88] Art. 4(1) TD.

include a fair review of the development and performance of the business and the position of the issuer and the undertakings included in the consolidation taken as a whole, together with a description of the principal risks and uncertainties that they face (lit. c).[89]

33   This statement by the persons responsible within the issuer is termed the '**balance sheet oath**'. The TD does not make sufficiently clear who the 'persons responsible' are, this being a problem that has transferred itself to the Member States' implementations. Those Member States that adopted the directive's provisions one-to-one must therefore deal with this question in their national laws.

34   A particularity can be found in German law where the TD's provisions on the balance sheet oath are connected with the provisions in the HGB (German Commercial Code) on accounting law[90] by making reference to the latter.[91] As a consequence of this, the obligation to make the respective statement is addressed to the legal representatives of a corporation, in a German stock corporation this being the board members (and not the members of the supervisory board). This only appears consistent when one considers that the accounting law in the German HGB generally calls upon all legal representatives regarding the obligation to compile annual accounts and annual reports,[92] thus expressing the principle of joint responsibility which underlies all German corporate law.[93] This connection between the balance sheet oath and the HGB accounting provisions, however, leads to problems with regard to foreign companies[94] if their home countries follow other principles regarding legal responsibility than that of joint responsibility.[95] Countries that follow the concept of a single-tier system for the board of a stock corporation will often provide for differing competencies of the directors.[96] In the United States, for example, only the CEO and CFO are obliged to make a balance sheet oath.[97]

2. Financial Accounting Information

(a) Consolidated and Individual Accounts

35   The information to be made public in the annual financial report was not developed by the European legislature specifically for the TD. The TD rather refers to the harmonised provisions on accounting law which require a distinction between consolidated and

---

[89] Art. 4(2) TD.
[90] § 264(2), § 289(1), § 297(2) and § 315(1) HGB.
[91] For annual reports § 114(2)(3) WpHG and for half-yearly reports § 115(2)(3) WpHG state that the reports must contain a statement as described in § 264(2), § 289(1) HGB. For corporate group companies these provisions are referred to in § 117(1) WpHG.
[92] Cf. § 264(1) HGB.
[93] H. Fleischer, 28 ZIP (2007), 97, 100, with further references.
[94] The German concept of so-called domestic issuers may also subject foreign issuers to the German rules on financial reporting.
[95] In more detail H. Brinckmann, *Kapitalmarktrechtliche Finanzberichterstattung*, 273 ff.
[96] Cf. § 141(a) Delaware General Corporation Law (DGCL); on the legal situation in the United States cf. G. Henn and J. Alexander, *Laws of Corporations*, 564, 593 ff.; H. Merkt and S. Göthel, *US-amerikanisches Gesellschaftsrecht*, 327 ff.; G. Rehm, in: Eidenmüller (ed.), *Ausländische Kapitalgesellschaften im deutschen Recht*, § 11 para. 41.
[97] Sec. 302(a) Sarbanes-Oxley Act 2002. On the impact of the balance sheet oath in the United States cf. H. Chang et al., 81 TAR (2006), 1, 5 ff.

individual accounts. Where the issuer is required to prepare consolidated accounts according to the Accounting Directive,[98] the audited financial statements must comprise a consolidated account drawn up in accordance with the Regulation (EC) No. 1606/2002[99] on international accounting standards[100] (IAS/IFRS Regulation) as well as an annual account of the parent company drawn up in accordance with the national law of the Member State in which the parent company is incorporated.[101] Where the issuer is not required to prepare consolidated accounts, the audited financial statement must comprise the accounts prepared in accordance with the national law of the Member State in which the company is incorporated.[102]

The accounting standards regarding annual financial accounts differ greatly between the Member States. In Ireland the issuer has the option to prepare not only the consolidated account but also the annual financial account in accordance with the IAS/IFRS.[103] In Austria,[104] France, Germany, Spain and Sweden, on the other hand, the annual financial account must be prepared in accordance with national accounting law.

> *Example*: The home Member State of issuer A is Ireland. Issuer A is required to prepare consolidated accounts. Issuer B is also required to prepare consolidated accounts. Its home Member State is Germany. Issuer A has to prepare his consolidated account in accordance with IAS/IFRS and—to save costs—will probably also prepare his annual financial account in accordance with IAS/IFRS, which is permitted in Ireland. Hence, the information made public by issuer A in his annual financial report is developed on a consistent accounting standard. Issuer B also has to prepare his consolidated account in accordance with IAS/IFRS, but will prepare his annual financial account in accordance with German accounting law, Germany not allowing annual financial accounts to be based solely on IAS/IFRS. Accounts compiled on this basis must rather simultaneously comply with German accounting law. As a consequence, the information disclosed by issuer B in his annual financial report will be based on two different accounting standards and will therefore not be consistent.

The European requirements regarding annual financial reports depend strongly on whether the report refers to an individual company or a group company, the respective provisions being from different legal fields.[105] This dualistic regulatory concept depends strongly on accounting law. A uniform standard of accounting throughout Europe has so far only been achieved by the IAS/IFRS Regulation[106] for consolidated accounts.[107] The regulation is

---

[98] With respect to the obligation to prepare consolidated accounts, Art. 4(3) TD still refers to the Seventh Directive. After the Seventh Directive has been repealed and consolidated in the Accounting Directive, Art. 4(3) TD has to be read as reference to the obligation to prepare consolidated accounts according to the Accounting Directive.
[99] Regulation (EC) No. 1606/2002 of the European Parliament and of the Council of 19 July 2002 on the application of international accounting standards, OJ L 243, 11 September 2002, p. 1–4 (IAS/IFRS Regulation).
[100] On the process of IFRS standard setting cf. Alibhai, Salim et al., *Wiley 2020: Interpretation and Application of International Financial Reporting Standards*, 4–5.
[101] Art. 4(3) TD.
[102] Art. 4(3) TD.
[103] Sec. 272(2) Companies Act 2014.
[104] Cf. S. Kalss et al. (eds.), *Kapitalmarktrecht I*, § 15 para. 25.
[105] Cf. W.-G. Ringe, in: Lehmann and Kumpan (eds.), *European Financial Services Law*, Art. 4 TD para. 9.
[106] On the road to the IAS/IFRS Regulation cf. N. Moloney, *EU Securities and Financial Markets Regulation*, 153 ff.
[107] On the international distribution of IAS/IFRS cf. I. Iordache, 18 Audit Financiar (2020), 568, 571 ff.

applicable to the consolidated accounts of publicly traded companies since the financial year starting 1 January 2005.[108] The annual accounts are still subject to the Member States' national provisions, a uniform level only being attained within the limits of the Accounting Directive. So far it is not foreseeable when and if the IAS/IFRS must also be made applicable to annual accounts Europe-wide. Annual accounts have further reaching functions in the Member States than solely informational purposes: they play an important role for determining the dividend payout[109] and as the basis for tax assessment, thus preventing a stronger unification at a European level. In consequence, the provisions on annual financial reports contain different requirements for individual companies and group companies, resulting in difficulties when trying to compare the different annual financial reports.

(b) Management Report

38 The management report contained in annual financial reports is also subject to the accounting laws. It is governed by Article 19 of the Accounting Directive and, should the issuer be required to prepare consolidated accounts, also by Article 29 of the Accounting Directive.[110] It is a descriptive reporting element in order to provide further analysis of both, financial and also non-financial information relevant for an understanding of the issuer's development, performance or position.[111]

39 The management report of issuers with more than 500 employees is also subject to the provisions of the NFRD stipulating higher reporting requirements for non-financial information by a '**non-financial statement**'.[112] The non-financial statement creates an independent reporting element of the management report and requires non-financial reporting in more detail as the issuer shall report on the undertaking's development, performance, position and impact of its activity, relating to, as a minimum, environmental, social and employee matters, respect for human rights, anti-corruption and bribery matters.[113] By requiring issuers that do not pursue policies in relation to these matters to provide a clear

---

[108] Art. 4 IAS/IFRS Regulation.

[109] When calculating the dividends the annual accounts are taken as the basis for determining the company's profits that can be distributed. According to Art. 17 and 18 of Directive 2012/30/EU of the European Parliament and of the Council of 25 October 2012 on coordination of safeguards which, for the protection of the interests of members and others, are required by Member States of companies within the meaning of the second paragraph of Art. 54 of the Treaty on the Functioning of the European Union, in respect of the formation of public limited liability companies and the maintenance and alteration of their capital, with a view to making such safeguards equivalent, OJ L 315, 14 November 2012, p. 74–97, the distribution of profits is limited by the purpose of capital maintenance. A study published by KMPG on behalf of the European Union in 2008 showed that IAS/IFRS annual accounts were used as the basis for profit distribution in 17 of the 27 Member States in 10 of which the IFRS accounting profits are not modified for this, cf. KPMG, *Feasibility study on an alternative to the capital maintenance regime established by the Second Company Law Directive 77/91/EEC of 13 December 1976 and an examination of the impact on profit distribution of the new EU accounting regime*, available at: https://ec.europa.eu/docsroom/documents/42762/attachments/1/translations/en/renditions/native, 1.

[110] Cf. Art. 4(5) TD, which refers to the repealed Art. 46 Fourth Directive and Art. 36 Seventh Directive for the content of the management report. But pursuant to Art. 52 Accounting Directive references to the repealed Fourth and Seventh Directives shall be construed as references to the Accounting Directive and shall be read in accordance with the correlation table in Annex VII of the Accounting Directive.

[111] Cf. Art. 19(1) Accounting Directive.

[112] Cf. Art. 19a Accounting Directive.

[113] Cf. Art. 19a(a) Accounting Directive.

and reasoned explanation for not doing so ('comply or explain') the European legislator tries to force the relevant issuers to take care and to create a greater awareness of these matters.[114]

(c) Auditing of the Annual Financial Report

European law stipulates an obligation that annual financial reports have to be audited in accordance with Article 34, 35 Accounting Directive.[115] The TD refers to the harmonised European accounting law for the requirements on auditing annual financial reports. The auditing has to be completed by an audit report,[116] which has to be disclosed in full to the public together with the annual financial report.[117] The audit reports therefore proofs the reliability of the—financial as well as non-financial—information disclosed in the annual financial report. 40

(d) Single Electronic Reporting Format (ESEF)

Since its revision in 2013, the TD provided for a greater harmonisation of the format of annual financial reports. Since 1 January 2020 all annual financial reports shall be prepared in a **single electronic reporting format (ESEF)**.[118] The European legislator is of the opinion that a harmonised electronic format for reporting is very beneficial for issuers, investors and supervisory authorities, since it makes reporting easier and facilitate accessibility, analysis and comparability of annual financial reports.[119] Following preparations by ESMA[120] the Commission laid down further details and technical specifications of the ESEF by Level 2 Delegated Regulation (EU) 2019/815[121] supplementing the TD with regard to regulatory technical standards on the specification of a single electronic reporting format (ESEF DR). From 1 January 2020, issuers on EU regulated markets shall prepare their entire annual financial reports in Extensible Hyper Text Markup Language (XHTML) format.[122] Where annual financial reports contain IAS/IFRS consolidated financial statements, these shall be labelled by using the Inline XBRL markup language, which makes the labelled disclosures structured and machine-readable.[123] 41

---

[114] Cf. J. Hennrichs, 47 ZGR (2018), 206, 209.
[115] Cf. Art. 4(4) TD, which refers to the repealed Art. 51, 51a Fourth Directive and Art. 37 Seventh Directive. But pursuant to Art. 52 Accounting Directive references to the repealed Fourth and Seventh Directives shall be construed as references to the Accounting Directive and shall be read in accordance with the correlation table in Annex VII of the Accounting Directive.
[116] Cf. Art. 35 Accounting Directive.
[117] Art. 4(4) TD.
[118] Art. 4(7) TD.
[119] Recital 26 ADTD. Cf. W.-G. Ringe, in: Lehmann and Kumpan (eds.), *European Financial Services Law*, Art. 4 TD para. 27.
[120] ESMA, Final Report on the RTS on the European Single Electronic Format, 18 December 2017, ESMA32-60-204.
[121] Commission Delegated Regulation (EU) 2019/815 of 17 December 2018 supplementing Directive 2004/109/EC of the European Parliament and of the Council with regard to regulatory technical standards on the specification of a single electronic reporting format, OJ L 143, 29 May 2019, p. 1–792 (ESEF DR).
[122] Art. 3 ESEF DR. Cf. W.-G. Ringe, in: Lehmann and Kumpan (eds.), *European Financial Services Law*, Art. 4 TD para. 26.
[123] Art. 4(4) and 6 ESEF DR.

IV. Half-yearly Financial Reports

1. Overview

42 The half-yearly financial report is structured parallel to the annual financial report and covers the first six months of the financial year. An issuer of shares or debt securities shall make public a half-yearly financial report covering the first six months of the financial year as soon as possible after the end of the relevant period, but at the latest three months thereafter.[124] The half-yearly financial report must comprise a **condensed set of financial statements** (lit. a), an **interim management report** (lit. b) and a **balance sheet oath** comparable to that of the annual financial report (lit. c).[125]

2. Financial Accounting Information

(a) Consolidated and Individual Accounts

43 The condensed set of financial statements is not a question of harmonised European accounting law. Rather, its content was first defined by the TD and follows the concept of the annual financial report. Once again one must distinguish between consolidated and individual accounts.

44 Where the issuer is required to prepare consolidated accounts, the TD requires that the condensed set of financial statements must be prepared in accordance with the IAS/IFRS applicable to **interim financial reports**.[126] The relevant standard for interim reports is described in IAS 34.[127] According to IAS 34, a condensed set of financial statements must include, at a minimum, a statement of financial position, income statement, statement showing all changes in equity, cash flow statement—all in condensed form—and selected explanatory notes.[128] For publicly traded companies the explanatory notes must contain segment information.[129]

45 Where the issuer is not required to prepare consolidated accounts, the TD stipulates own requirements for the condensed set of financial statements. It must at least contain (i) a condensed balance sheet, (ii) a condensed profit and loss account and (iii) explanatory

---

[124] Art. 5(1) TD. The TD of 2004 provided for a deadline of two months for publishing half-yearly financial reports. In 2013 the ADTD extended this deadline to three months in order to provide additional flexibility and thereby reduce administrative burdens. By the extension of the deadline, small and medium-sized issuers' reports were expected to receive more attention from and become more visible for the market participants, cf. recital 6, Art. 4 ADTD.

[125] Art. 5(2) TD.

[126] Art. 5(3) TD.

[127] On the objectives of interim financial reporting under IAS 34 cf. Alibhai, Salim et al., *Wiley 2020: Interpretation and Application of International Financial Reporting Standards*, 899 ff.

[128] IAS 34.8; Alibhai, Salim et al., *Wiley 2020: Interpretation and Application of International Financial Reporting Standards*, 903 ff.

[129] IAS 34.16A(g), IFRS8.2.

notes on these accounts.[130] However, about half of the Member States require all condensed financial statements to be prepared in line with IAS/IFRS which permitted under Article 3(1) TD.[131] In preparing the condensed balance sheet and profit and loss account, the issuer must follow the same principles for recognising and measuring as when preparing annual financial reports.[132] Further minimum requirements regarding the content of the condensed set of financial statements can be found in the Directive 2007/14/EC. According to this, the condensed balance sheet and profit and loss account must show each of the headings and subtotals included in the most recent annual financial statements of the issuer.[133] Additional line items shall be included if, as a result of their omission, the half-yearly financial statements would give a misleading view of the assets, liabilities, financial position and profit or loss of the issuer.[134] In addition, the condensed account must include a comparative balance sheet and a comparative profit and loss account of the preceding financial year.[135] The explanatory notes must include sufficient information to ensure the comparability of the condensed half-yearly financial statements with the annual financial statements and sufficient information and explanations to ensure a user's proper understanding of any material changes in amounts and of any developments in the half-year period concerned, which are reflected in the balance sheet and the profit and loss account.[136]

(b) Interim Management Report

The interim management report must include at least an indication of **important events** that have occurred during the first six months of the financial year, and their impact on the condensed set of financial statements, together with a description of the principal risks and uncertainties for the remaining six months of the financial year. For issuers of shares, the interim management report must also include major **transactions** of **related parties**.[137] This includes related parties' transactions that have taken place in the first six months of the current financial year and that have materially affected the financial position or the performance of the enterprise during that period and any changes in the related parties' transactions described in the last annual report that could have a material effect on the financial position or performance of the enterprise in the first six months of the current financial year.[138] Thus, the interim management report must be regarded as an independent part of the half-yearly financial report which was developed without any reference to accounting law.[139] A reporting of non-financial information is no mandatory element of the interim management report.

46

---

[130] Art. 5(3) TD.
[131] Cf. W.-G. Ringe, in: Lehmann and Kumpan (eds.), *European Financial Services Law*, Art. 5 TD para. 19.
[132] Art. 5(3) TD.
[133] Art. 3(2) Directive 2007/14/EC (fn. 12).
[134] Art. 3(2) Directive 2007/14/EC (fn. 12).
[135] Art. 3(2) Directive 2007/14/EC (fn. 12).
[136] Art. 3(3) Directive 2007/14/EC (fn. 12).
[137] Art. 5(4) TD.
[138] Cf. Art. 4 Directive 2007/14/EC (fn. 12).
[139] For companies subject to the German accounting standards of the DRSC, DRS 16 contains further information on the interim report. Cf. T. Strieder and O. Ammedick, 60 DB (2007), 1368 ff.

(c) Auditing of the Half-yearly Financial Report

47 Unlike for the annual financial report, European law contains no obligation regarding the auditing of the half-yearly financial report. If the half-yearly financial report has been audited by choice, however, the audit report must be reproduced in full. The same must apply in the case of an auditors' review.[140] If the half-yearly financial report has not been audited or reviewed by auditors, the issuer must make a statement to that effect in its report.[141] The Member States national laws mostly provide that the auditing of half-yearly reports is optional.[142]

V. Quarterly Periodic Financial Reports

1. The Question of a Sufficient Supply of Capital Markets with Information on Issuers

48 One of the most controversial issues for the system of periodic disclosure is the frequency for an obligation to publish information on issuers. Currently, it is the opinion of the European legislator that an obligation to publish annual and half-yearly financial reports with information on the assets, financial positions and profit and losses is sufficient for the continual supply of the capital market.[143] For that reason, Member States may require issuers to publish **additional periodic financial information** on a more frequent basis than annual and half-yearly financial reports only under **very limited conditions**.[144] But at this point, the TD has passed through a significant change since its enactment in 2004.

(a) Concept of a Quarterly Reporting Obligation in the TD 2004

49 In its initial proposal for the TD in 2003, the Commission followed the idea that the key data required under former Community law for half-yearly reporting should in future be published as quarterly financial information.[145] The Commission's proposal for the TD therefore contained the provision that for issuers whose shares are admitted to trading on the regulated market quarterly financial information should be mandatory for the first and third quarter of a financial year.[146] As with the former half-yearly reports, the quarterly financial information was to contain the consolidated figures, presented in table form, indicating the net turnover and the profit or loss before or after deduction of tax as well as an

---

[140] Art. 5(5) TD.
[141] Art. 5(5) TD.
[142] Germany merely provides that the condensed set of financial statements and the interim management report *may* be reviewed by auditors, cf. § 115(5) WpHG.
[143] Cf. Art. 3(1) TD.
[144] Cf. Art. 3(1a) TD.
[145] Cf. Commission, Proposal for a Directive of the European Parliament and of the Council on the harmonisation of transparency requirements with regard to information about issuers whose securities are admitted to trading on a regulated market and amending Directive 2001/34/EC, 26 March 2003, COM(2003) 138 final, p. 16 ff.
[146] COM(2003) 138 final (fn. 145), Art. 6 TD-Proposal, p. 12 ff.

explanatory statement relating to the issuer's activities and profits and losses during the relevant three-month period. Furthermore, the issuer was to choose whether it wanted to publish an indication of the likely future development for itself and its subsidiaries.

The Commission justified the shorter intervals with a comparison of the information standards in the Member States and the necessity to strengthen the European stock markets as compared with the US market where such quarterly financial reporting has been required since 1946.[147] In this context the Commission explained that quarterly financial information would provide more structured and reliable information thus enhancing the stock market performance and investor protection.[148] Before the TD was enacted in 2004, only eight Member States, including Austria, France, Italy and Spain, required the publication of quarterly financial reports. In other Member States, such as Germany, quarterly financial reporting rules existed only on the basis of stock exchange rules.[149]

The Commission's suggestion on quarterly financial reporting as the new concept regarding periodic disclosure in Europe was not greeted warmly. After the report of the Committee on Economic and Monetary Affairs[150] the concept of quarterly financial reports threatened to be deleted altogether until a Council compromise proposal was accepted by the European Parliament. The negative attitude towards the requirement to disclose quarterly reports was mainly justified by the substantial additional costs for issuers and the danger of a focus on short-term earnings performance rather than on a company's longer-term strategy.[151] As a result the Commission's proposal was reduced to the format of so-called **interim management statements** which had lower requirements regarding their content than the quarterly financial information.

(b) Content of Interim Management Statements

The TD of 2004 stipulated that issuers whose shares are admitted to trading on a regulated market must make public a statement by its management during the first six-month period of the financial year and another one during the second six-month period of the financial year.[152] It had to contain an explanation of material events and transactions that have taken place during the relevant period and their impact on the financial position of the issuer and its controlled undertakings; and a general description of the financial position and performance of the issuer and its controlled undertakings during the relevant period.[153] The interim management statements as such had no relation to the financial statements, rather constituting an independent reporting format in the TD of 2004. Their content was very similar to that of management reports.

---

[147] Cf. COM(2003) 138 final (fn. 145), p. 14 ff.
[148] Cf. COM(2003) 138 final (fn. 145), p. 14 ff.
[149] Cf. COM(2003) 138 final (fn. 145), p. 14 ff.
[150] Cf. Report by the Committee on Economic and Monetary Affairs on the proposal for a European Parliament and Council directive on the harmonisation of transparency requirements, A5/2004/79 final, available at: PreLex COD/2003/45, p. 38 ff.
[151] Explanatory Statement of the European Committee on Economic and Social Affairs on the Proposal for a TD, OJ C 80, 30 March 2004, p. 87–88. Also seen critically by the European Central Bank, OJ C 242, 9 October 2003, p. 6, 8, that favours minimum disclosure obligations for issuers.
[152] Art. 6(1) TD of 2004.
[153] Art. 6(1) TD of 2004.

(c) Quarterly Financial Reports under the TD of 2004

53 The TD of 2004 also introduced the **non-binding** format of a **quarterly financial report** by stating that issuers which, under either national legislation or the rules of the regulated market or of their own initiative, publish quarterly financial reports in accordance with such legislation or rules are not required to make public the aforementioned interim management statements.[154] The European legislature did not make any statements on the structure and content of the quarterly financial reports, rather referring to the fact that the requirements can be dictated and defined by national regulation or the rules of the stock exchange. The quality requirements to be met were also not defined in the directive. But the quarterly financial report was approximated to the annual and half-yearly financial report by the term 'financial report', making it seem only logical that the quarterly financial report had to contain the same periodic statement that is essential in the other two reports.[155] The transposition of the TD of 2004 confirmed this point of view, showing similarities in the quarterly and half-yearly financial reports in many Member States, although most of the Member States did not introduce a legal obligation to make public quarterly financial reports.[156]

2. Concept of Additional Periodic Disclosure after the Reform of 2013

54 During the **revision** of the TD[157] the provisions on interim management statements as well as any reference to quarterly financial reports have been abolished in the TD.[158] Instead of the interim management statement the Commission introduced a new report on payments to governments into the TD.[159] But this report on payments to governments follows a different approach compared to financial reporting and is therefore not part of the system of periodic disclosure.[160] The Commission justified its rethinking for interim management statements with the argument that the administrative burden linked to the preparation of such statements is too high especially for small and medium-sized issuers. Additionally, interim management statements foster pressure on issuers to focus on short term results instead of encouraging long-term investments. Therefore and unlike at the time of the initial enactment of the TD in 2004 the publication of quarterly information is no longer considered necessary by the European legislator for investor protection.[161]

55 After the revision of the TD, Member States are exceptionally permitted to require issuers to publish additional periodic financial information other than annual and half-yearly

---

[154] Art. 6(2) TD of 2004.
[155] H. Brinckmann, *Kapitalmarktrechtliche Finanzberichterstattung*, 127–128.
[156] Cf. 1st edn. (2013), H. Brinckmann, § 18 para. 54.
[157] Cf. R. Veil § 1 para. 43.
[158] Art. 1(5) ADTD.
[159] The new Art. 6 TD contains an obligation for issuers active in the extractive or logging of primary forest industries to prepare annual reports on payments made to governments.
[160] The report pursuant to Art. 6 TD intends to make governments accountable for the use of their resources and to promote good governance, cf. Commission, Proposal for a Directive of the European Parliament and of the Council amending Directive 2004/109/EC on the harmonisation of transparency requirements in relation to information about issuers whose securities are admitted to trading on a regulated market and Commission Directive 2007/14/EC, 25 October 2011, COM(2011) 683 final (TD-II-COM), p. 8 ff.
[161] TD-II-COM, p. 5, 7, 11 (recital 4).

financial reports if (i) such a disclosure obligation does not constitute a disproportionate financial burden, in particular for the small and medium-sized issuers concerned, and (ii) the content of the additional periodic financial information required is proportionate to the factors that contribute to investment decisions by the investors in the Member State concerned.[162] Before taking a decision requiring issuers to publish additional periodic financial information (or keeping a requirement already in place after the revision of the TD), Member States have to examine (i) whether such additional requirements may lead to an excessive focus on the issuers' short-term results and performance and (ii) whether they may impact negatively on the ability of small and medium-sized issuers to have access to the regulated markets.[163] With these restrictions for the Member States the revision of the TD in 2013 implemented the concept of maximum harmonisation at least for the annual and half-yearly financial reporting of small and medium-sized issuers.[164]

Originally, the Commission intended to go even further and completely prohibit Member States from requiring issuers to publish periodic information other than annual and half-yearly financial reports.[165] This would have led to a maximum harmonisation of annual and half-yearly financial reporting and Member States would have been prohibited from introducing (or keeping) any quarterly reporting obligation into their national law.[166] But this very strict approach of the Commission has been significantly moderated during the legislative process. Within the limits laid down in Article 3(1a) TD, Member States are permitted to have additional periodic disclosure obligations beside annual and half-yearly financial reports in their national law. But Member States hardly make use of this scope for implementation. When implementing the ADTD most of the Member States abolished the legal obligation to publish interim management statements so that most of the Member States do no longer contain any quarterly reporting obligation in their national legislation. But the limits for additional periodic disclosure set by the TD do not apply to stock exchanges or market operators who are able to require issuers to publish periodic financial information on a more frequent basis than annual and half-yearly financial reports.[167] The additional periodic disclosure beside the requirements set by the TD is therefore part of the self-regulation by the markets. 56

As an example, the German stock exchange in Frankfurt requires issuers listed in the sub-segment 'Prime Standard' to disclose quarterly statements beside annual and half-yearly financial reports.[168] These quarterly statements are very similar to the former interim management statements as required by the TD of 2004 and do therefore not provide the same quality of financial information as annual and half-yearly financial reports. 57

---

[162] Art. 3(1a) TD.
[163] Art. 3(1a) TD.
[164] W.-G. Ringe, in: Lehmann and Kumpan (eds.), *European Financial Services Law*, Art. 3 TD para. 6.
[165] TD-II-COM, p. 7, 16 (Art. 1(2)).
[166] H. Brinckmann, 67 BB (2012), 1370 ff.; R. Veil, 66 WM (2012), 53, 54.
[167] Recital 5 ADTD; TD-II-COM, p. 7; H. Brinckmann, 67 BB (2012), 1370 ff.; R. Veil, 66 WM (2012), 53, 54; W.-G. Ringe, in: Lehmann and Kumpan (eds.), *European Financial Services Law*, Art. 5 TD para. 41; dissenting opinion: C. Seibt and B. Wollenschläger, 51 AG (2012), 305, 308.
[168] § 53 Exchange Rules for the Frankfurter Wertpapierbörse (effective as of 18 March 2016), available at: https://www.xetra.com/resource/blob/31802/c5112b158d9f72e3fb6c2b9405d63a27/data/2020-11-23-Exchange-Rules-for-the-Frankfurter-Wertpapierb-rse.pdf.

VI. Disclosure Procedures

1. Requirements under European Law

58 European law only stipulates two requirements regarding the disclosure of financial reports. The first being that the disclosure must take place through media ensuring that financial reports will be disseminated to as wide a public as possible in all Member States.[169] This can realistically only be met by use of the Internet.[170] The European legislature explicitly allows the information to be published on the issuer's website, provided this publication is then announced to the media.[171] The Internet is therefore the primary publication medium for financial reports. The second requirement is that the Member States must supply an **officially appointed mechanism (OAM)** for the central storage of financial reports.[172]

2. Transposition in the Member States

59 These very general rules under European law have led to a strong divergence in the disclosure procedures within the Member States. In Germany, prior to making the financial reports publicly available for the first time, any company which issues securities as a domestic issuer must make a pan-European publication concerning when and on which website the financial reports will be publicly available in addition to their availability in the company register. Simultaneously with the publication of such announcement, the company must notify the supervisory authority thereof.[173] Only after the publication of the announcement is the actual financial report disclosed—usually on the issuer's website[174]—and transmitted to the company register in order to be stored there.[175] German law partially deviates from the TD's provisions and exempts issuers that are already subject to the obligation to disclose the respective accounting documents under commercial law from the obligation to disclose an annual financial report.[176] This exemption only applies to German corporations,[177] whilst foreign companies must still make public an annual financial report.[178] The German legislature sought to relieve the German corporation from a double burden.[179] The result of this exemption is, however, that the disclosure procedure regarding annual financial reports differs for national and foreign issuers.[180]

---

[169] Art. 21(1) TD, Art. 12(2) Directive 2007/14/EC (fn. 12).
[170] See H. Brinckmann § 16 para. 42.
[171] Art. 12(3) Directive 2007/14/EC (fn. 12).
[172] Art. 21(2) TD. See also H. Brinckmann § 16 para. 43 ff.
[173] § 114(1), § 115(1) WpHG, § 8b(3)(2) HGB.
[174] § 114(1), § 115(1) WpHG, This is not, however, mandatory, cf. N. Kumm, 64 BB (2009), 1118, 1119.
[175] § 114(1), § 115(1) WpHG, § 8b(3)(2) HGB.
[176] § 114(1) WpHG.
[177] Cf. § 325 HGB.
[178] H. Hönsch, in: Assmann et al. (eds.), *Kommentar zum WpHG*, § 114 para. 14; M. Zimmermann, in: Fuchs (ed.), *Kommentar zum WpHG*, § 37v para. 7.
[179] Begr. RegE TUG, BT-Drucks. 16/2498 (explanatory notes), p. 43.
[180] For more details cf. H. Brinckmann, *Kapitalmarktrechtliche Finanzberichterstattung*, 283 ff. On possible conflicts resulting from this, cf. P. Mülbert and S. Steup, 10 NZG (2007), 761, 763 ff.

The information requested by the TD is so-called 'regulated information', which, in Ireland shall be made public by means of a Regulatory Information Service (RIS).[181] Such a RIS is provided by the Irish stock exchange.[182] The Central Bank of Ireland has to be notified simultaneously when a financial report has been send to a RIS for its dissemination and publication.[183] If no RIS is open for business, the issuer shall without delay disseminate and make public regulated information through two newswire services or other media that ensure dissemination and making public of regulated information, and a RIS, for release, as soon as one reopens.[184] The Irish stock exchange also operates the OAM for the central storage of financial reports. In Sweden, the FI's website gives access to a database in which all financial reports are stored.[185]

3. Outlook: Access to Financial Reports via a Central European Access Point

The strong divergence in the disclosure procedures within the Member States also applies to the central storage mechanisms of regulated information. As a result of the TD 2004, each Member State established or appointed an OAM.[186] But access to these information still follows a national not a European approach.

> *Example:* An institutional investor from the US is interested in investing into different European insurance companies. It shall be his first investment in Europe. So far, he only has some names of potential companies, but he wants to deeper analyse and compare the performance of the companies by going through their last financial reports. To find the relevant financial reports, first, he must find out the home state of the company. Then, second, he must find out the relevant OAM of that Member State to search for the information he is looking for. To compare with the other companies he has to repeat the same procedure for every company.

During the revision of the TD in 2013, the Commission concluded that the access to financial information on listed companies on a pan-European basis is burdensome because interested parties have to go through 27 different national databases in order to search for information.[187] This leads to the fact that cross-border access to financial reporting information is highly limited across the European Union. To facilitate pan-European access to regulated information, the network of the Member State's appointed storage mechanisms shall be enhanced and greater harmonised.[188] A web portal shall be developed and operated by ESMA serving as a **European electronic access point (EEAP)**. Interested parties shall have access to information in the central storage mechanisms of every Member State via the EEAP.[189] Currently, the Commission is

---

[181] Regulation 6(1) S.I. No. 366 of 2019, Central Bank (Investment Market Conduct) Rules 2019.
[182] Available at: https://direct.euronext.com/#/rispublication.
[183] Regulation 6(2)(3) S.I. No. 366 of 2019, Central Bank (Investment Market Conduct) Rules 2019.
[184] Regulation 7(1) S.I. No. 366 of 2019, Central Bank (Investment Market Conduct) Rules 2019.
[185] The information is available at: https://fiapplfinanscentralen.fi.se/FinansCentralen/search/Search.aspx.
[186] ESMA provides a list of OAM, available at: https://www.esma.europa.eu/access-regulated-information.
[187] TD-II-COM, p. 8.
[188] Recital 15 ADTD.
[189] Cf. Art. 21a(1) TD.

looking for a technical solution for the EEAP and envisages to merge the EEAP into the new project of a '**European single access point (ESAP)**' which shall follow a broader approach than the EEAP as it shall also improve the availability and accessibility of sustainability-related data.[190]

VII. Enforcement of Financial Information

63   After the occurrence of numerous major corporate accounting scandals since the 1990s the Member States as well as the European Union have gradually become convinced that a system of sanctions and civil liability alone does not provide for issuers' consistent compliance with the relevant financial reporting framework. This conclusion might result from the fact that provisions on criminal and administrative sanctions or civil liability in the Member States (still) need further development until they force issuers to comply with the relevant accounting law. But the reason may also lie in the financial reporting itself. Any misstatement published by an issuer in its financial report has spread in the capital market long before a system based on sanctions and liability will be able to force the issuer to publish a revised statement and to correct its misleading financial report.

64   Member States have taken different measures and established new mechanisms to ensure the compliance of financial statements with the relevant legal framework.[191] These measures and mechanisms are generally defined as the '**enforcement**' of financial information, meaning (i) examining the compliance of financial information with the relevant financial reporting framework and (ii) taking appropriate measure where infringements are discovered.[192]

65   The European requirements on enforcement are very limited. The IAS/IFRS Regulation states in its recitals that '*a proper and rigorous enforcement regime is key to underpinning investors' confidence in financial markets*' and requires Member States '*to take appropriate measures to ensure compliance with international accounting standards*'.[193] The TD stipulates that Member States shall ensure the competent authority being empowered (i) to examine that information referred to in the TD is drawn up in accordance with the relevant reporting framework and (ii) to take appropriate measures in case of discovered infringements.[194] Thus, under European law Member States are required to establish an enforcement regime[195] but the European legislator has not set any parameters for the specific organisation of such a regime so that the Member States are free to establish their enforcement system based on self-regulation, supervision or a mixture of both.

---

[190] See H. Brinckmann § 16 para. 49.
[191] For an overview of models in different countries cf. H. Hirte and S. Mock, in: Hirte and Möllers (eds.), *Kölner Kommentar zum WpHG*, § 37n para. 26 ff.
[192] Cf. ESMA, Guidelines on enforcement of financial information, 4 February 2020, ESMA32-50-218, p. 11 (Enforcement Guidelines).
[193] Recital 16 IAS/IFRS Regulation.
[194] Recitals 28, Art. 24(4)(h) TD.
[195] S. Kalss et al. (eds.), *Kapitalmarktrecht I*, § 15 para. 47.

A European harmonisation of enforcement exists in the form of a coordination of European enforcement institutions.[196] European enforcers coordinate a consistent application of the European IAS/IFRS accounting framework through the European Enforcers Coordination Session (EECS), a network advising ESMA on accounting matters. In 2020 ESMA has also published new Guidelines on enforcement to ensure effective and consistent enforcement within the European Union.[197]

Almost all Member States have given a supervising authority the responsibility of enforcement of financial information. An exception can be found in Germany and Austria where a procedure of dual enforcement has been established. To exemplify the Member State's different approaches in the area of enforcement the dual-enforcement as it only exists in Germany and Austria[198] as well as the enforcement in Ireland shall be presented.

1. Dual-enforcement in Germany and Austria

In 2005 Germany, followed by Austria in 2013, established a system of dual-enforcement. The characteristic of the dual-enforcement can best be described as a two-tier enforcement regime involving a private and a supervisory enforcement institution.[199] The first tier involves the private enforcement institution, in Germany the **Financial Reporting Enforcement Panel (FREP)** and in Austria the **Austrian Financial Reporting Enforcement Panel (AFREP)**. FREP or AFREP will initiate an examination (i) with cause if there are concrete indications of an infringement of financial reporting requirements or (ii) on a random sampling basis.[200] In Germany the FREP also has to initiate proceedings on request of BaFin.[201]

Subject to examination is the most recently adopted annual or half-yearly financial report of capital market oriented companies.[202] The examination procedure of FREP and AFREP is based on cooperation. If a company is not willing to cooperate, FREP or AFREP will notify the supervisory authority (BaFin resp. FMA) to initiate a formal examination proceeding.

Basically, the supervisory authority participates in the enforcement proceedings at the second tier level only if a company does not participate willingly in the examination or does not agree with the findings of FREP or AFREP or has substantial doubts about whether the findings of FREP or AFREP are correct or whether the examination was conducted properly. The relevant supervisory authority, the BaFin in Germany and the FMA in Austria, is entitled to decide on the infringement of financial reporting requirements by order and also to order the publication that the financial statement was incorrect.

---

[196] For a list of European enforcers see: ESMA, Report Enforcement and regulatory activities of European enforcers in 2019, 2 April 2020, ESMA32-63-846, p. 64 (Annex 2).
[197] ESMA, Enforecment Guidelines, p. 8.
[198] Cf. European Parliament, Study Requested by the ECON committee [external authors K. Langenbucher et al.]— What are the wider supervisory implications of the Wirecard case?, November 2020, PE 651.385, 20, available at: https://www.europarl.europa.eu/RegData/etudes/STUD/2020/651385/IPOL_STU(2020)651385_EN.pdf (Wirecard Study).
[199] Cf. N.-C. Wunderlich, in: Habersack et al. (eds.), *Handbuch der Kapitalmarktinformation*, § 9 para. 104.
[200] § 342b(2) HGB, § 2(1) RL-KG.
[201] § 342b(2) HGB.
[202] § 342b(2) HGB, § 1(1), § 2 RL-KG.

70 The supervisory authorities in Germany and Austria are only entitled to decide on the infringement of financial reporting requirements by order in cases of *material* infringement. In Germany the OLG Frankfurt ruled that the BaFin is only entitled to decide on the infringement by order if accounting law provisions have been *materially* infringed.[203] Relevant for the question whether infringements reach the level of materiality shall be the perspective of an investor on the capital markets.[204] The same criteria also apply in Austria although they have not been confirmed by a court decision so far.[205]

71 Recently, the potential accounting fraud of the German **Wirecard AG** called the German dual-enforcement regime into question. Over years, neither the auditors nor examinations of FREP were able to reveal that financial accounting information have possibly been manipulated although concrete indications had been made public and brought to the attention of BaFin.[206] The modifications of the German system of dual-enforcement are still under discussion. As one consequence, German government terminated the contractual relationship with FREP. The termination becomes effective as of the end of 2021.[207] ESMA conducted a fast-track peer review focusing on the application of the ESMA Guidelines on enforcement by BaFin and FREP and on impediments to the effectiveness of the German system of dual-enforcement in the specific context of the Wirecard case. In its report[208] ESMA identified, among other, various deficiencies in the effectiveness of the German enforcement system, mainly with respect to the cooperation of BaFin and FREP regarding the exchange of information, competences and speed.[209] Due to a first legal proposal[210] for improvements of the German enforcement system, the BaFin shall obtain more powers for own examinations and investigations in cases of suspected infringements of financial reporting requirements.[211]

2. Enforcement in Ireland by the Financial Reporting Supervision Unit (FRSU)

72 In Ireland, the Irish Auditing and Accounting Supervisory Authority (IAASA) has been designated as the competent authority for the purposes of Article 24(4)(h) TD[212] and is therefore responsible for examining affected issuers' compliance with the financial reporting framework requirements and for taking appropriate action where non-compliance is

---

[203] OLG Frankfurt of 22.01.2009—WpÜG 1/08 and 3/08, 30 ZIP (2009), 368, 369.
[204] OLG Frankfurt of 22.01.2009—WpÜG 1/08 and 3/08, 30 ZIP (2009), 368, 371.
[205] S. Kalss et al. (eds.), *Kapitalmarktrecht I*, § 15 para. 65.
[206] An overview on the facts and the timeline of the Wirecard case can be found in: European Parliament, Wirecard Study, 30 ff. (Appendix A).
[207] Cf. European Parliament, Wirecard Study, 32 (Appendix A).
[208] ESMA, Fast Track Peer Review on the Application of the Guidelines on the Enforcement of Financial Information (ESMA/2014/1293) by BaFin and FREP in the Context of Wirecard, Peer Review Report, 2 November 2020, ESMA42-111-5349 (Wirecard Report).
[209] ESMA, Wirecard Report, p. 13 ff.
[210] Draft legislation for a Gesetz zur Stärkung der Finanzmarktintegrität (Finanzmarktintegritätsstärkungsgesetz—FISG), BR-Drucks. 9/21.
[211] Cf. M. Schüppen, 56 DStR (2021), 246, 251 ff.
[212] Regulation 36(2) and 42(2) S.I. No. 277 of 2007, Transparency (Directive 2004/109/EC) Regulations 2007.

identified. At the IAASA its **Financial Reporting Supervision Unit (FRSU)** has taken over this task.

FRSU follows a risk-based approach to the selection of financial reports for examination. This risk-based approach considers (i) the risk of material misstatement in issuers' financial reports and (ii) the potential impact of such a misstatement on the users of financial reports.[213] The FRSU tries to find out in cooperation with the examined issuer whether relevant accounting or reporting requirements have been breached and—if this is the case— tries to reach an agreement with the company on the corrective or clarificatory action.[214] There is considerable pressure on the issuers to cooperate with the FRSU during the examination. Since the amendment of the IASSA's competences in 2015,[215] it has wider discretion in terms of publication of its financial reporting enforcement findings than heretofore and may even bring its examination to the attention of the public.[216] Nevertheless, the FRSU enjoys substantial rights on information vis-à-vis the issuer, its directors, managers, employees or the auditors.[217] It may also appoint authorised officers with substantial powers to carry out an investigation.[218]

73

VIII. Sanctions

The TD originally did not lay down a well-differentiated concept regarding the sanction for breaches of financial reporting duties. The revision of the TD in 2013 led to more detailed requirements for administrative sanctions but it is still in the power of the Member States to take the necessary measures.

74

1. Liability for Incorrect Financial Reporting

The TD requires Member States to ensure the necessary penalties for breaches of financial reporting duties. In this context the Member States must ensure that responsibility for drawing up the information and making this public lies at least with the issuer or its administrative, management or supervisory bodies, and that the national laws, regulations and administrative provisions on liability are applicable to the issuers, their bodies or the persons responsible within the issuers.[219] Whilst the European regulations remain vague and leave a large margin of appreciation to the Member States in the transposition

75

---

[213] Cf. IAASA FAQs in financial reporting supervision, available at: http://www.iaasa.ie/FAQs/FRS.
[214] Cf. IAASA FAQs in financial reporting supervision, available at: http://www.iaasa.ie/FAQs/FRS.
[215] Regulation 43(3) S.I. No. 277 of 2007, Transparency (Directive 2004/109/EC) Regulations 2007, as amended by Regulation 2(d) S.I. No. 44 of 2015, Transparency (Directive 2004/109/EC) (Amendments) Regulations 2015.
[216] IAASA, Policy Paper on Publication of IAASA's Financial Reporting Enforcement Findings, 17 July 2015, p. 2, available at: http://www.iaasa.ie/getmedia/815203c6-a917-4ee6-985e-036508400053/IAASA_FRSU_Publications_July2015.pdf.
[217] Regulation 43(1) S.I. No. 277 of 2007, Transparency (Directive 2004/109/EC) Regulations 2007.
[218] Regulation 53 and 54 S.I. No. 277 of 2007, Transparency (Directive 2004/109/EC) Regulations 2007.
[219] Art. 7 TD.

of the directive,[220] it still becomes clear that a specific liability for incorrect financial reporting is required;[221] otherwise, the European legislature would not try to ensure that Member States take the necessary measures. General rules on liability will often be insufficient, as they do not achieve the specific level of protection required in financial reporting; in particular, the liability may not be restricted to cases of wilful action.[222] The European concept allows the liability rules to be addressed either solely to the issuer or also to the responsible bodies within the issuer.[223]

76 Due to the very restrictive European requirements, the civil liability for incorrect financial reporting is still very inconsistent between the Member States.[224] Most Member States, such as Austria, German and Sweden, even have by no means implemented the requirements of Article 7 TD into their national rules on civil liability. As a result, no specific liability for incorrect financial reporting exists and the question arises (i) as to whether incorrect financial reporting is subject to the general rules on civil liability of that Member State and (ii) whether these rules comply with the requirements of Article 7 TD.[225]

2. Sanctions under Criminal and Administrative Law

77 The TD requires Member States to lay down rules on sanctions only with respect to administrative measures and sanctions. They shall be effective, proportionate and dissuasive.[226] The TD clarifies that this requirement is without prejudice to the right of Member States to provide for and impose criminal sanctions,[227] but the TD does not lay down any further requirements for criminal sanctions. Where obligations apply to legal entities, Member States shall ensure that in the event of a breach, sanctions can be applied to the members of administrative, management or supervisory bodies of that legal entity and to other individuals who are responsible for the breach under national law.[228]

78 After the reform in 2013, the TD stipulates requirements for administrative measures and sanctions in much more detail. If an issuer fails to make public its annual or half-yearly financial report, the competent authority shall have the power to impose a whole range of sanctions, in particular, a public statement indicating the natural or the legal entity responsible and the nature of the breach, in case of a legal entity fines (i) up to € 10,000,000 or 5% of the total annual turnover or (ii) up to twice the amount of the profits gained or losses avoided because of the breach, whichever is higher.[229] The new European rules also lay

---

[220] Cf. recital 17 TD.
[221] Cf. also P. Mülbert and S. Steup, 59 WM (2005), 1633, 1653; R. Veil, 18 ZBB (2006), 162, 168–169.
[222] R. Veil, 18 ZBB (2006), 162, 169.
[223] M. Brellochs, *Publizität und Haftung*, 95; H. Fleischer, 60 WM (2006), 2021, 2027; R. Veil, 18 ZBB (2006), 162, 168.
[224] For more details on different concepts of civil liability rules in the Member States, cf. 2nd edn. (2017), H. Brinckmann, § 18 para. 68 ff.
[225] Cf. 2nd edn. (2017), H. Brinckmann, § 18 para. 70 ff., for examples presented in more detail.
[226] Art. 28(1) TD.
[227] Art. 28(1) TD.
[228] Art. 28(2) TD.
[229] Art. 28b(1)(c) TD.

down criteria for the determination of the type and the level of administrative measures and sanctions.[230]

Even though the requirements of the TD for sanctions under criminal or administrative law have reached a higher level of harmonisation with the ADTD, Member States still follow very different approaches as to whether incorrect financial reporting shall be subject to criminal and/or administrative law and to what extend sanctions apply.[231]

IX. Conclusion

The capital markets must continually be supplied with information on the issuers in order to ensure an adequate price formation for securities. Capital market regulation must enable investors to compare different issuers and allow them to trust the information disclosed. The European legislature had this in mind when it enacted the TD. This Directive also takes into account that according to economic studies, only the company's accounting can provide a regular informational basis for investors. It therefore integrates the rules on company accounting into the regulatory concept of capital markets law. The rules on company accounting include financial accounting information and—as a necessary complement—non-financial information regarding environmental, social and governance matters.

Legal developments in the area of periodic disclosure are not yet complete. It can be expected that shaping the precise concept for non-financial reporting within the system of periodic disclosure will soon become even more important for the European legislator as it is decisive for an efficient implementation of sustainable finance.

Further improvement is also necessary with regard to the fact that financial reports are not the only possible format for periodic disclosure. Although the former interim management statement has been abolished with the revision of the TD in 2013 and thereby a disruptive factor within the system of European periodic disclosure has been eliminated, the Commission's original target of a maximum harmonisation of annual and half-yearly financial reports has not been reached. As a consequence, Member States are under certain conditions[232] still permitted to establish additional periodic disclosure obligations beside annual and half-yearly financial reports in their national law and there are no requirements of the European law on these additional reporting formats. This may result in a serious fragmentation of reporting obligations in the Member States and a pan-European harmonisation of periodic disclosure regime is far from being established.

Another open task can be found when looking at the investors' access to financial reporting information. The TD only provides for general standards and requires the Member States to establish one OAM for the central storage of this information.[233] From an investor's perspective, the current pan-European access to financial reporting information requires searching

---

[230] Art. 28c(1) TD.
[231] See 2nd edn. (2017), H. Brinckmann, § 18 para. 74 ff., for examples presented in more detail.
[232] Cf. Art. 3(1) TD.
[233] Art. 21(2) TD.

through 27 different national databases and therefore forms a significant barrier to the investors' access to this information. A first step to increase harmonisation in this respect is in sight: The European access point (EEAP) will provide much easier access and searching through different databases in form of the OAMs. This alone will improve comparability of the financial reports of issuers from different Member States. The same applies to the ESEF for annual financial reports which increases comparability of the reports covered.

84 A solution must also be found for the fact that financial reports rely on accounting law which is still mainly in the hands of the Member States. The information in the financial reports is thus not subject to any uniform accounting standards, although it is becoming increasingly apparent that the IAS/IFRS may become such internationally accepted standards.[234]

85 The requirements of the TD on sanctions and liability in cases of an incorrect financial reporting are probably the last essential part within the system of periodic disclosure that needs to be revised in order to achieve a better harmonisation in the future. The revision of the TD by the ADTD already led to more detailed requirements for administrative sanction but, however, this does not seem to be enough to ensure an equally high quality of financial reports in all Member States. For the next revision of the TD, more detailed requirements for civil liability are vitally necessary as well as minimum standards for the Member States' enforcement systems. Only an effective law enforcement regime that includes public and private measures will be able to safeguard that issuers fully comply with the rules on financial reporting and supply investors with reliable information.

---

[234] IFRS are the dominant global financial reporting standard, N. Moloney, *EU Securities and Financial Markets Regulation*, 152.

§ 19

Disclosure of Inside Information

Bibliography

Bachmann, Gregor, *Kapitalmarktrechtliche Probleme bei der Zusammenführung von Unternehmen*, 172 ZHR (2008), 597–634; Bachmann, Gregor, *Ad-hoc-Publizität nach 'Geltl'*, DB (2012), 2206–2211; Bank, Mathias/Baumann, Ralf H., *Market efficiency under ad hoc informaion: evidence from Germany*, 29 Financ. Mark. Portf Manag (2015), 173–206; Baule, Rainer and Tallau, Christian, *Market Response to Ad Hoc Disclosures and Periodic Financial Statements: Evidence from Germany*, SSRN Working Paper (2010), available at: http://ssrn.com/abstract=1660679; Behn, Lars, *Ad-hoc-Publizität und Unternehmensverbindungen. Informationszugang des Emittenten im faktischen Aktienkonzern* (2012); Bonneau, Thierry, *L'information n'est-elle precise que s'il est possible de determiner le sens, à la hausse ou à la baisse, de la variation sur le cours du titre?*, Bull. Joly Bourse (2014), 15–18; Brellochs, Michael, *Publizität und Haftung von Aktiengesellschaften im System des Europäischen Kapitalmarktrechts* (2005); Bruno, Ferdinando and Ravasio, Nicoletta, *Ambito soggettivo ed oggettivo dell'informazione privilegiata post Market Abuse directive*, 8 Le società (2007), 1026–1033; Buck-Heeb, Petra, *Wissenszurechnung, Informationsorganisation und Ad-hoc-Mitteilungspflicht bei Kenntnis eines Aufsichtsratsmitglieds*, AG (2015), 801–812; Chiu, Iris H.-Y., *United Kingdom: A Confidence Trick: Es Ante versus Ex Post Frameworks in Minority Investor Protection*, in: Conac, Pierre-Henri and Gelter, Martin (eds.), *Global Securities Litigation and Enforcement*, 627–654; Conac, Pierre-Henri, *La pratique de la publicité des décisions de sanctions et d'absence de sanction par la commission des sanctions de l'AMF*, 1 RTDF (2006), 128–130; Conac, Pierre Henri/Gelter, Martin, *Global Securities Litigation and Enforcement* (2019); Conac, Pierre-Henri, *France: The Compensation of Investors' Losses for Misrepresentation on Financial Markets*, in: P.-H. Conac and M. Gelter (eds.), *Global Securities Litigation and Enforcement* (2019), 331–362; Dettenrieder, Dominik/Theissen, Erik, *The Market Reaction to Corporate Disclosure: Evidence from Germany*, available at https://papers.ssrn.com/sol3/papers.cfm?abstract_id=2146816; Di Noia, Carmine and Gargantini, Matteo, *Issuers at Midstream: Disclosure of Multistage Events in the Current and in the Proposed EU Market Abuse Regime*, ECFR (2012), 484–529; Di Noia, Carmine/Milic, Mateja/Spatola, Paola, *Issuers obligations under the new Market Abuse Regulation and the proposed ESMA guideline regime: a brief overview*, ZBB (2014), 96–108; Entrena Ruiz, Daniel, *El empleo de información privilegiada en el mercado de valores: un estudio de su régimen administrativo sancionador* (2006); Ferrarrini, Guido and Giudici, Paolo, Italy: The Protection of Minority Investors and the Compensation of their Losses, in: Conac/Gelter (eds.), *Global Securities Litigation and Enforcement*, 446–468; Fleischer, Holger, *Ad-hoc-Publizität beim einvernehmlichen vorzeitigen Ausscheiden des Vorstandsvorsitzenden*, NZG (2007), 401–407; Fox, Merritt B., *Civil Liability and Mandatory Disclosure*, 109 Colum. L. Rev. (2009), 237–308; Gilotta, Sergio, *Disclosure in Securities Markets and the Firm's Need for Confidentiality: Theoretical Framework and Regulatory Analysis*, 13 EBOR (2012), 46–88; Hansen, Jesper L., *Say when: When must an issuer disclose inside information?*, SSRN Research Paper (2016), available at: http://ssrn.com/abstract=2795993; Habersack, Mathias, *Marktmissbrauchsrecht und Aktienrecht – Zielkonflikte im Zusammenhang mit der Ad hoc-Publizitätspflicht*, in: Klöhn, Lars/Mock, Sebastian (eds.), *Festschrift 25 Jahre WpHG* (2019), 217–235; Hellgardt, Alexander, *Kapitalmarktdeliktsrecht* (2008); Hellgardt, Alexander/Ringe, Wolf-Georg, *Internationale*

Kapitalmarkthaftung als Corporate Governance, 173 ZHR (2009), 802–838; Hössl-Neumann, Mario, *Informationsregulierung durch Insiderrecht* (2020); Hopt, Klaus J., *Die Haftung für Kapitalmarktinformationen—Rechtsvergleichende, rechtsdogmatische und rechtspolitische Überlegungen*, WM (2013), 101–112; Ihrig, Hans-Christoph and Kranz, Christopher, *EuGH-Entscheidung Geltl/ Daimler: 'Selbstbefreiung' von der Ad-hoc-Publizität*, BB (2013), 451–458; Ihrig, Hans-Christoph, *Wissenszurechnung im Kapitalmarktrecht – untersucht anhand der Pflicht zur Ad-hoc-Publizität gemäß Art. 17 MAR*, 181 ZHR (2017), 381–415; Iribarren Blanco, Miguel, *Responsabilidad civil por la información divulgada por las sociedades cotizadas* (2008); Kalss, Susanne, *Anlegerinteressen: Der Anleger im Handlungsdreieck von Vertrag, Verband und Markt* (2000); Karpoff, Jonathan M./Lee, D. Scott/Martin, Gerald S., *The Cost to Firms of Cooking the Books*, 43(3) Journal of Financial and Quantitative Analysis (2008), 581–611; Klöhn, Lars, *Optimistische Prognosen in der bürgerlich-rechtlichen Prospekthaftung*, WM (2010), 298–296; Klöhn, Lars, *Der Aufschub der Ad-hoc-Publizität wegen überwiegender Geheimhaltungsinteressen des Emittenten (§ 15 Abs. 3 WpHG)*, 178 ZHR (2014), 55–97; Klöhn, Lars, *Kollateralschaden und Haftung wegen fehlerhafter Ad-hoc-Publizität*, ZIP (2015), 53–60; Klöhn, Lars, *Ad-hoc-Publizität und Insiderverbot im neuen Marktmissbrauchsrecht*, AG (2016), 423–434; Klöhn, Lars, *Der Aufschub der Ad-hoc-Publizität zum Schutz der Finanzstabilität (Art. 17 Abs. 5 MAR)*, 181 ZHR (2017), 746–780; Klöhn, Lars/Rothermund, Marius, *Haftung wegen fehlerhafter Ad-hoc-Publizität–Die Tücken der Rückwärtsinduktion bei der Schadensberechnung in sechs Fallgruppen*, JBB (2015), 73–83; Klöhn, Lars/Schmolke, Ulrich, *Der Aufschub der Ad-hoc-Publizität nach Art. 17 Abs. 4 MAR zum Schutz der Unternehmensreputation*, ZGR (2016), 866–896; Klöhn, Lars, *Die (Ir-)Relevanz der Wissenszurechnung im neuen Recht der Ad-hoc-Publizität und des Insiderhandelsverbots*, NZG (2017), 1285–1292; Koch, Jens, *Wissenszurechnung aus dem Aufsichtsrat*, ZIP (2015), 1757–1767; Koch, Philipp, *Die Ad-hoc-Publizität nach dem Kommissionsentwurf einer Marktmissbrauchsverordnung. Nicht ad-hoc-pflichtige Insiderinformationen und Aufschub der Veröffentlichung bei systemrelevanten Insiderinformationen*, BB (2012), 1365–1369; Krämer, Lutz, and Teigelack, Lars, *Gestaffelte Selbstbefreiungen bei gegenläufigen Insiderinformationen? Publizitätsanforderungen beim Zusammentreffen von unterjährigen Ergebniszahlen mit Kapitalmaßnahmen*, AG (2012), 20–28; Krause, Hartmut and Brellochs, Michael, *Insiderrecht und Ad-hoc-Publizität bei M&A—und Kapitalmarkttransaktionen im europäischen Rechtsvergleich*, AG (2013), 309–339; Kumpan, Christoph, *Ad-hoc-Publizität nach der Marktmissbrauchsverordnung–Untersuchung wesentlicher Neuerungen und deren Auswirkungen auf Emittenten*, DB (2016) 2039–2046; Lerman, Alina/Livnat, Joshua, *The New Form 8-K Disclosures*, 15 Review of Accounting Studies (2010), 752–778; Markworth, David, *Marktmissbrauchsverordnung und effet utile*, 183 ZHR (2019), 46–72; McDonnell, Brian, *Handling and Disclosing Inside Information: A Guide to the Discloure Rules*, 88 COB (2011), 1–33; Mülbert, Peter O./Sajnovits, Alexander, *Der Aufschub der Ad-hoc-Publizitätspflicht bei Internal Investigations*, WM (2017), 2001–2006, 2041–2047; André Muntermann/Jan Güttler, *Intraday Stock Price Effects of Ad Hoc Disclosures: The German Case*, 17 Journal of International Financial Markets, Institutions and Money 17(1) 2007, 1 ff.; Nietsch, Michael, *Emittentenwissen, Wissenszurechnung und Ad-hoc-Publizitätspflicht*, ZIP (2018), 1421–1429; Nowak, Eric, *Eignung von Sachverhalten in Ad-hoc-Mitteilungen zur erheblichen Kursbeeinflussung*, JBB (2001), 449–465; Payne, Jennifer, *Disclosure of Inside Information*, in: Tountopoulos, Vassilios/Veil, Rüdiger (eds.), *Transparency of Stock Corporations in Europe* (2019), 89–107; Poelzig, Doerte, *Die Neuregelung der Offenlegungsvorschriften durch die Marktmissbrauchsverordnung*, NZG (2016), 761–773; Pisani, Hervé, *L'information financière: les responsables*, 3 RTDF (2007), 18–20; Puttfarken, Hans-Jürgen and Schrader, Anne, *Frankreich*, in: Hopt, Klaus J. and Voigt, Hans-Christoph (eds.), *Prospekt—und Kapitalmarktinformationshaftung* (2005), 595–620; Richter, Stefan, *Schadenszurechnung bei deliktischer Haftung für fehlerhafte Sekundärmarktinformation* (2012); Roch, Géraldine, *Annotation to CA Paris, 1re ch., sect. H, 3 July 2007, No. 2006/19083, X. et autres c/ AMF*, Bull. Joly Bourse (2008), 204–209; Rontchevsky, Nicolas, *Annotation to AMF Commission des sanctions, 28.9.2006 and CA Paris, 3 July 2007*, 1 RTDF (2008), 86–88; Sajnovits, Alexander, *Ad-hoc-Publizität und Wissenszurechnung*, WM (2016), 765–774; Sastre

Corchado, Galo J., *La Directiva de Abuso de Mercado—un nuevo marco en Europa*, 1 RMV (2007), 253–302; Sauer, Knut, *Haftung für Falschinformation des Sekundärmarktes* (2004); Seibt, Christoph H., *Empirische Betrachtungen zur Ad-hoc-Publizität in Deutschland*, CFL (2013), 41–48; Seibt, Christoph H. and Wollenschläger, Bernward, *Revision des Marktmissbrauchsrechts durch Marktmissbrauchsverordnung und Richtlinie über strafrechtliche Sanktionen für Marktmanipulation*, AG (2014), 593–608; Tomasi, Martin, *L'imputation des manquements aux règles de l'Autorité des marchés financiers*, 109 Banque & Droit (2006), 35–43; Veil, Rüdiger, *Die Ad-hoc-Publizitätshaftung im System kapitalmarktrechtlicher Informationshaftung*, 167 ZHR (2003), 365–402; Veil, Rüdiger, *Die Haftung des Emittenten für fehlerhafte Information des Kapitalmarkts nach dem geplanten KapInHaG*, BKR (2005), 91–98; Veil, Rüdiger, *Marktregulierung durch privates Recht am Beispiel des Entry Standard der Frankfurter Wertpapierbörse*, in: Burgard, Ulrich et al. (eds.), *Festschrift für Uwe H. Schneider* (2011), 1313–1324; Veil, Rüdiger, *Private Enforcement in European Capital Markets Law. Perspectives for a Reform at the Example of the Obligation to Disclose Inside Information*, in: Gsell, Beate/Möllers, Thomas M. J. (eds.), *Enforcing Consumer and Capital Markets Law*, 2020, 405–422; Veil, Rüdiger/Gumpp, Tobias/Templer, Lena/Voigt, Christian, *Personalbezogene Ad-hoc-Meldungen nach Art. 17 MAR: eine rechtstatsächliche und rechtsdogmatische Analyse*, ZGR (2020), 2–34; Vokuhl, Nikolai, *Kapitalmarktrechtlicher Anlegerschutz und Kapitalerhaltung in der Aktiengesellschaft* (2007); Wundenberg, Malte, *Perspektiven der privaten Rechtsdurchsetzung im europäischen Kapitalmarktrecht, Möglichkeiten und Grenzen der kapitalmarktrechtlichen Informationshaftung*, ZGR (2015), 124–160.

I. Introduction

1. Regulatory Goals

The obligation to publish inside information has a long tradition in European capital markets law.[1] Directive 79/279/EEC already stipulated that an issuer must make such information available to the public. These were 'any major new developments in [the] sphere of activity [of the issuer] which are not public knowledge and which may, by virtue of their effect on its assets and liabilities or financial position or on the general course of its business, lead to substantial movements in the prices of its shares.'[2] The purpose of this requirement was to improve the **efficiency** of **markets**.

The next reform was the Insider Dealing Directive 89/592/EEC of 13.11.1989.[3] The legislative act provided that the ad hoc disclosure obligation also applied to companies and undertakings the transferable securities of which are admitted to trading on a market which is regulated and supervised by authorities, operates regularly and is accessible directly oder indirectly to the public. More importantly, ad hoc disclosure of inside information could for the first time be understood as a **preventive measure** under **insider trading law**. The European legislature consistently continued this approach in 2003. The legal basis for the ad

---

[1] A. Pietrancosta, in: Ventoruzzo/Mock (eds.), *Market Abuse Regulation*, Art. 17 para. B.17.16 points to the 1966 Segré Report.

[2] Art. 17 (1), Schedule C no. 5 a Council Directive 79/279/EEC of 5 March 1979 coordinating the conditions for the admission of securities to official stock exchange listing, OJ L66, 16. March 1997, p. 21 ff.

[3] Council Directive 89/592/EEC of 13 November 1989 coordinating regulations on insider dealing of 13. 11. 1989, OJ. L334, 18. November 1989, p. 30 ff.

hoc disclosure obligation was now to be found in the Market Abuse Directive (MAD 2003).[4] Both regimes—the **insider trading prohibitions** and the **disclosure obligation**—provided for the **same concept** of **inside information**. Consequently, the legislature understood the duty to disclose inside information as an important instrument to combat insider trading. This was also reflected in recital 24 MAD 2003: 'Prompt and fair disclosure of information to the public enhances market integrity'.

3   On the other hand, it must be recognised that the publication of price-sensitive information improves the information efficiency of the markets. In interaction with the **periodic disclosures**, market participants obtain the **information** necessary to **evaluate** the **fundamental value** of the issuer. Thus, the disclosure obligation has a dual function.[5] The ad hoc disclosure obligation is not only intended to counter insider trading, but also to protect the pecuniary interest of investors with regard to achieving 'correct' prices as well as their freedom of decision.[6]

4   If one focuses on the preventive nature of disclosure obligations regarding insider dealings, it appears reasonable to require the same conditions when prohibiting insider trading and when requiring disclosure. Both concepts can then apply the same notion of inside information. This was taken into account by the European legislator who understood the disclosure obligations as a complement to the prohibitions on insider trading (MAD 2003 regime).

5   From the perspective of transparency and efficient price formation on markets, the close link of the disclosure obligation with the insider trading prohibition is not strictly necessary, as disclosure can have a detrimental effect on the issuer.[7] The issuer may have a legitimate interest in not disclosing inside information without delay. This had already been recognised by Directive 79/279/EEC. At the time, the 'competent authorities' could exempt an issuer from the disclosure obligation, if the disclosure of particular information is such as to prejudice the legitimate interests of the company. Now the issuer itself decides on the delay of publication. This right is of great importance in practice because the ECJ has interpreted the concept of inside information of the MAD 2003 regime broadly (with an insider law justification) and the European legislator has taken up these principles with the Market Absue Regulation (MAR) 2014.[8] This means that—to put it briefly—uncertain events must also be disclosed. However, an issuer may have a variety of legitimate interests in keeping such information secret.

6   With the proposal for a Market Abuse Regulation published in 2011, the European Commission pursued the aim of decoupling the prohibitions on insider trading and the ad hoc disclosure obligation. This should be done with a new category of inside information that should not be subject to disclosure. However, the Commission was not able to assert itself with this proposal in the trialogue. Yet the proposal made perfect sense, as current practice shows that the one-tier concept (synchronisation of insider trading prohibitions and ad hoc dislosure) has not proven its worth

---

[4] Directive 2003/6/EC of the European Parliament and of the Council of 28 January 2003 on insider dealing and market manipulation (market abuse), OJ L96, 12 April 2003, p. 16 (MAD 2003).

[5] Cf. H.-D. Assmann, in: Assmann/Schneider/Mülbert (eds.), *Kommentar zum Wertpapierhandelsrecht*, Art. 17 MAR para. 7–9; P. Buck-Heeb, *Kapitalmarktrecht*, para. 459; Kalss/Hasenauer, in: Kalss et al. (eds.), *BörseG/MAR*, Art. 17 MAR para. 5.

[6] BGH of 23.4.2013 – II ZB 7/09, ZIP 2013, 1165, 1170 para. 34.

[7] Cf. J. Payne, in: Tountopoulos/Veil (eds.), *Transparency of Stock Corporations in Europe*, 89, 106.

[8] See R. Veil § 14 para. 19–31.

(see para. 44). This gives rise to the research question whether the ad hoc disclosure obligation should be redesigned.

A reform should be discussed with a view to the US Securities Regulation, which does not provide for a similar ad hoc disclosure obligation of inside information.[9] Instead, an issuer in the U.S. has to report on current events according to section 13(a)(1) SEA. This disclosure obligation is supplemented by numerous specific disclosure obligations and the disclose-or-abstain rule. The SEC's detailed disclosure requirements on current events (Rule 13a-11 and Form 8-K) relate to circumstances described in abstract terms, such as 'financial information', 'matters related to accountants and financial statements' or 'corporate governance and management', which the SEC has defined in very precise terms. The circumstances are characterised by the fact that they have already occurred. Consequently, an issuer is not obliged to publicly announce uncertain events, such as in the case of Geltl/Daimler the intention of the chairman of the board to resign from office.[10] There is therefore far greater legal certainty for issuers, and disclosure costs are likely to be considerably lower for issuers compared to the European regime. Empirical capital market research also teaches that the disclosure requirement makes a significant contribution to overcoming information asymmetries.[11] Not every piece of information that can be used for insider trading must also be disclosed.

The US Securities Regulation also pursues **corporate governance purposes** with disclosure requirements. It is sometimes argued that this is even one of the main goals of mandatory disclosure rules.[12] The recitals of MAR do not comment on this.[13] However, some scholars in Europe qualify ad hoc publicity of inside information (also) as a norm under company law that contributes to effective corporate governance.[14] It is true that issuers may be obliged to immediately disclose legal violations within the company, provided that this information is relevant to the share price. The capital markets react to such compliance-relevant information with price reductions. The obligation of ad hoc disclosure can therefore have a disciplinary effect on business managers and reduce agency costs. In addition, shareholders are enabled to assert shareholder rights through access to compliance-relevant information. However, these interdependencies do not justify qualifying Article 17 MAR as a norm under company law and making this aspect useful for questions of interpretation. According to the recitals of MAR, the European legislature pursues other purposes with the obligation to disclose inside information.[15] The interpretation of Article 17 MAR should be based on the two traditional purposes.

---

[9] Comparative analyses of both regimes by J. Payne, in: Tountopoulos/Veil (eds.), *Transparency of Stock Corporations in Europe*, 89, 91 ff.

[10] See R. Veil § 14 para. 21.

[11] Empirical research indicates abnormal returns of 8-K notices. Cf. A. Lerman and J. Livnat, 15 Review of Accounting Studies (2010), 752 ff.

[12] Cf. L. Gullifer and J. Payne, Corporate Finance Law, 548 with reference to US-American literature; M. B. Fox, 109 Colum. L. Rev. (2009), 237, 253 ff.

[13] A. Hellgardt, in: Assmann/Schneider/Mülbert (eds.), *Wertpapierhandelsrecht*, §§ 97, 98 WpHG para. 34 argues, it would follow from recital 55 MAR that the disclosure obligation would also have a corporate governance function. However, recital 55 only stipulates that the disclosure requirement would increase investor confidence in SME issuers.

[14] Cf. A. Hellgardt, *Kapitalmarktdeliktsrecht*, 407 ff.; L. Klöhn, in: Klöhn (ed.), MAR, Art. 17 para. 11; A. Hellgardt, in: Assmann/Schneider/Mülbert (eds.), *Wertpapierhandelsrecht*, §§ 97, 98 WpHG para. 34. Dissenting opinion M. Habersack, in: Klöhn/Mock (eds.), Festschrift 25 Jahre WpHG, 217, 226 f.; L. Gullifer and J. Payne, *Corporate Finance Law*, 548, 580 (acknowledging a governance function for periodic disclosure, rejecting it for ad hoc disclosure of inside information).

[15] This is different for transparency of major shareholdings (see R. Veil § 20 para. 4) and disclosure of related party transactions (see R. Veil § 22 para. 33).

9   In summary, the MAR 2014 pursues two goals with the obligation to publish inside information. Firstly, the disclosure obligation is intended to prevent insider trading and, secondly, to improve price efficiency. The overall objective is to protect investors and their confidence in issuers. Private investors, in particular, also benefit from immediate publication, because they benefit in any case from the fact that professional market participants (analysts, brokers, portfolio managers and other arbitrageurs) evaluate the information without delay, so that the information is immediately reflected in the prices of securities.[16] However, the addressee of the notification is not only the professional market participant: the issuer must ensure that the inside information is published in a way that allows the public, ie investors of any kind to access it quickly and to make a complete, accurate and timely assessment of it.[17]

2. Practical Relevance

10 Little is known about how many **inside information** issuers admitted to the regulated market or on an MTF **discloses** each year. Most supervisory authorities in the Member States do not provide information about this in their activity reports and on their websites. Figures are known for Germany. The number of publications rose to 5,421 in the early 2000s.[18] Thereafter, the number decreased steadily (2008: 3,037; 2009: 2,657; 2010: 2,207; 2011:2,002; 2012 1,818).[19] It remains at this level today (2018: 2,069; 2019: 1,977).[20] At first glance, these facts about a decline in ad hoc disclosures[21] do not reflect the fact that the ECJ's case law (taken up with MAR) on the concept of inside information has not only extended the prohibitions on insider trading, but also the disclosure requirements. However, to evaluate the figures, it must be taken into account that issuers used ad hoc notifications as a marketing tool in the early 2000s until the legislature banned this practice. Furthermore, there were far more listed companies than today.

11 **Delay** of **disclosure** has become increasingly important over the past 20 years. Prior to the implementation of MAD in 2003, delay hardly played a role. In Germany, only 26 requests for approval of a delay were submitted in 2002, of which 18 were granted.[22] This changed with the MAD 2003 regime. In Germany, there were a total of 244 delays in 2012 (2011:202; 2010: 177; 2009: 240; 2008: 209), often in multi-stage decision-making processes, for example when a decision still required the approval of the supervisory board.[23] The number has nearly tripled to date (2018: 532; 2019: 557).[24] The delay is of great practical significance primarily because the ECJ has interpreted the concept of inside information in a broader

---

[16] Cf. J. Payne, in: Tountopoulos/Veil (eds.), *Transparency of Stock Corporations in Europe*, 89, 91.
[17] See para. 42.
[18] BaFin, *Annual Report* 2002, p. 75.
[19] BaFin, *Annual Report* 2012, p. 189; BaFin, *Annual Report* 2011, p. 211.
[20] BaFin, *Annual Report* 2019, p. 96.
[21] The development in Austria is similar, cf. S. Kalss and C. Hasenauer, in: Kalss et al. (eds.), BörseG/MAR, Art. 17 MAR para. 8. In 2019, 373 ad hoc notifications were published, cf. FMA, Annual Report 2019, p. 100.
[22] Cf. BaFin, Annual Report 2002, p. 75.
[23] Cf. BaFin, Annual Report 2012, p. 189; BaFin, Annual Report 2011, p. 210; BaFin, Annual Report 2009, p. 189.
[24] BaFin, Annual Report 2019, 96.

way, with the consequence that uncertain events must also be disclosed.[25] In its report on the MAR Review, ESMA states that national supervisors were notified of a delay in publication in approximately 14,000 cases between July 2016 and June 2019. Significant differences can be observed in the Member States.[26]

3. Empirical Studies

Empirical research makes use of event studies to determine the influence of unanticipated price-relevant events on the value of companies with the help of security prices.[27] These financial statistical methods are based on the assumption that capital markets are semi-strong information efficient in the sense of the ECMH.[28] Accordingly, liquid capital markets reflect all publicly available price-relevant information at all times. Under this assumption, all public information, such as news published ad hoc by companies, is immediately reflected in the prices of securities. Event studies can be used to determine how strongly and in which direction company share prices react to published events. The influence of an event is called abnormal return. To determine this, an event window is defined. For each day of this period, the normal (ie expected) return corrected for market influences is subtracted from the actual return. Then, the calculated abnormal returns are aggregated over the period of the event window. This cumulative abnormal return indicates the influence of the event under investigation with respect to the entire event window. Finally, the statistical significance of the abnormal return is determined using appropriate tests.

12

Empirical research already exists on the early phase of European securities regulation. A study published in 2001 came to the conclusion that even with highly statistically significant average stock market reactions, never more than one-third of the individual announcements in a sample proved to be statistically price-sensitive.[29] A few years later, an article suggested that security prices had responded within 30 minutes to ad hoc published inside information. The larger the company, the smaller the statistically significant abnormal returns.[30]

13

Empirical research on the MAD 2003 regime is limited, but agrees on the basic finding that there are statistically significant abnormal returns on the day of publication of ad hoc announcements. One paper demonstrates this for earnings.[31] Two recent research papers show post-release adjustments in security prices.[32] One of these papers concludes that the ad hoc disclosure requirement is an effective means of improving market efficiency, whilst the other finds that investors would view ad hoc disclosures as valuable.[33] Event studies on the MAR regime have not been published to date.

14

---

[25] See R. Veil § 14 para. 39 ff.
[26] ESMA, MAR Review Report, ESMA70-156-2391, 23 September 2020, para. 192.
[27] Cf. for an explanation of event studies J. Y. Campbell/A. W. Lo/A. C. MacKinley, *Econometrics of Financial Markets* (1997), Chapter 4.
[28] See on the ECMH R. Veil § 2 para. 29 and H. Brinckmann § 16 para. 7.
[29] Cf. E. Nowak, JBB (2001), 449, 465.
[30] Cf. A. Muntermann and J. Güttler, 17 Journal of International Financial Markets, Institutions and Money (1) 2007, 1 ff. (Analysis of 2,705 notifications in the period from 1. 8. 2003 to 31. 8. 2004).
[31] R. Baule and C. Tallau, *Market Response to Ad Hoc Disclosures and Periodic Financial Statements*, Chapter 4.
[32] M. Bank and R. Baumann, 29 Financ Mark Portf Manag (2015), 173, 196; D. Dettenrieder and E. Theissen, *The Market Reaction to Corporate Disclosure*, Chapter 4.
[33] D. Dettenrieder and E. Theissen, *The Market Reaction to Corporate Disclosure*, Chapter 4.

15 None of the aforementioned research differentiates between certain and uncertain information. This would require analysing every ad hoc disclosure. A legal analysis of 244 personnel-related ad hoc announcements in 2017 has shouldered this task.[34] Only 13.52% of the notifications disclosed uncertain information. In many cases, notifications were made after multiple transactions and the market was thus only informed about transactions that had been completed (from the issuer's point of view). The information content of a relevant portion of ad hoc announcements was at least doubtful, so that it may have been difficult for investors to recognise the inside information at all. A conclusion on the price relevance is often made difficult by the fact that either no information is given on the subject or the ad hoc announcement contains various information.

II. Regulatory Concepts

1. Requirements under European Law

(a) Disclosure Obligations under the MAR

16 The obligation to disclose inside information is laid down in Article 17(1) MAR. The European legislature primarily understands this obligation as an instrument to **prevent insider dealings** (see para. 9), the MAR's (as the former MAD's) aim being to ensure the integrity of EU financial markets.[35] The obligation to disclose inside information is essential to avoid insider dealing and ensure that investors are not misled.[36] This is also the ECJ's view.[37]

17 Article 17(1) MAR requires **issuers** to **disclose** as soon as possible **inside information** which **directly concerns** that **issuer**. The term 'inside information' is defined in Article 7 MAR,[38] the definition applying both to the rules prohibiting insider dealings and to those requiring the disclosure of inside information. The European Commission's plans to introduce a new category of inside information that would not have been subject to the disclosure obligations have been abandoned.[39]

18 Article 17(4) MAR allows an issuer to **delay** the public **disclosure** of inside information at its own responsibility, provided that (i) immediate disclosure is likely to prejudice his legitimate interests, (ii) the delay of disclosure is not likely to mislead the public and (iii) the issuer is able to ensure the confidentiality of that information. In the case of a protracted

---

[34] Cf. R. Veil et al., ZGR (2020), 2 ff.
[35] Cf. Recital 2–4 MAR.
[36] Cf. Recital 49 MAR.
[37] ECJ of 28 June 2012, Case C-19/11 (*Daimler/Geltl*), para. 33. The ECJ also highlighted the importance of legal certainty and systematic coherence, see ibid., para. 48, 52. Confirmed in ECJ of 11 March 2015, Case C-628/13 (*Lafonta*), EuZW (2015), 387 ff. On the foregoing ruling of the Cour de cassation, see T. Bonneau, Bull. Joly Bourse (2014), 15 ff.
[38] See R. Veil § 14 para. 32.
[39] Cf. Art. 6(1)(e) and Art. 12(3) Proposal for a Regulation of the European Parliament and of the Council on Insider Dealing and Market Manipulation (Market Abuse), 20 October 2011, COM(2011) 651 final; on these plans P. Koch, BB (2012), 1365 ff.; see also para. 6.

process that occurs in stages and that is intended to bring about, or that results in, a particular circumstance or a particular event, an issuer may on its own responsibility delay the disclosure of inside information relating to this process.[40] As a lesson of the financial crisis, Article 17(5) and (6) MAR provide a second possibility to delay the disclosure of inside information if the issuer is a credit or financial institution and the disclosure of the inside information entails a risk of undermining the financial stability of the issuer and of the financial system. Unlike the 'general delay' (under Article 17 (4) MAR), this delay is granted in the public interest and is subject to the competent authority's prior consent.

Article 17 MAR is supplemented by the Implementing Regulation (EU) 2016/1055[41] and the Delegated Regulation (EU) 2016/522[42] (Level 2 legal acts). Furthermore, ESMA has issued MAR guidelines to ensure a uniform application of certain rules.[43]

19

(b) Relationship to Other Disclosure Rules

The MAR does not determine the relationship between the disclosure obligation for inside information and other disclosure obligations under EU und national law. This question is of outstanding importance. In particular, this is true for the relationship between the TD rules on **periodic disclosure** (financial reports) and those on the disclosure of inside information. Generally speaking, both regimes are **simultaneously applicable and independent** from each another, the disclosure of inside information not only being an addition to the rules on periodic disclosure but also an independent instrument aimed at combating insider dealing.[44] Information subject to the rules on periodic disclosure may thus also have to be made public as inside information prior to its disclosure in the financial reports if it is publicly unknown and price-relevant. The upcoming publication of a financial report does not release the issuer from its duty to disclose inside information as soon as possible and does not constitute a legitimate interest for the issuer to delay the disclosure of the inside information.[45]

20

In general, the obligation to disclose inside information is also independent from all other rules of transparency and the time limits for their disclosure. This especially refers to the rules on disclosure regarding major shareholdings under Article 9 and 10 TD, for example.[46] Changes in the structure of shareholdings can have a direct effect on the issuer even before the thresholds regarding control have been reached. If the investor intends to intervene in

21

---

[40] Art. 17(4) subsec. 2 MAR.
[41] Commission Implementing Regulation (EU) 2016/1055 of 29.6.2016 laying down implementing technical standards with regard to the technical means for appropriate public disclosure of inside information and for delaying the public disclosure of inside information in accordance with Regulation (EU) No 596/2014 of the European Parliament and of the Council, OJ L173, 30. June 2016, p. 47 ff.
[42] Commission Delegated Regulation (EU) 2016/522 of 17 December 2015 supplementing Regulation (EU) No 596/2014 of the European Parliament and of the Council as regards an exemption for certain third countries public bodies and central banks, the indicators of market manipulation, the disclosure thresholds, the competent authority for notifications of delays, the permission for trading during closed periods and types of notifiable managers' transactions, OJ L88, 05 April 2016, p. 1 ff.
[43] ESMA, MAR-Guidelines – Delay in the Disclosure of Inside Information, 20.10.2016, ESMA/2016/1478.
[44] See above para. 2–3.
[45] BaFin, Emittentenleitfaden (issuer guideline), Module C, p. 35; H.-D. Assmann, in: Assmann et al. (eds.), *Kommentar zum Wertpapierhandelsrecht*, Art. 17 MAR para. 9; S. Kalss et al. (eds.), *Kapitalmarktrecht I*, § 16 para. 6. Dissenting opinion: J.L. Hansen, *Say when: When must an issuer disclose inside information?*, p. 27.
[46] See also R. Veil § 20 para. 20.

the business policy, the information about the acquisition of the shareholding may be price relevant.[47] The same applies with regard to the disclosure obligations for managers' transactions (formerly directors' dealings), although these will generally be of indirect concern to the issuer.

2. National Regulation

22 As the European market abuse framework is now laid down in a regulation, the **MAR rules** are **directly applicable** and need no implementation into the Member States' national laws. The unification of the disclosure obligations raises the question if and to what extent the Member States may also adopt further rules under the MAR. Under the MAD 2003 regime, the ECJ had left the question unanswered.[48] As the instrument of the regulation has been chosen to prevent diverging national requirements as a result of the transposition of a directive[49] and the MAR heavily relies on ESMA for further implementation and guidelines, the Member States' room for manoeuvre should be very limited. Even where national rules only specify the applicable European requirements, these national interpretations will be subject to the ECJ's review.[50]

23 Yet, these restrictions do not apply to national provisions on supervision and sanctions,[51] special rules on the liability for incorrect or omitted publications of inside information (see para. 81 ff.) not being affected. Also, the national supervisory authorities may continue to publish further **guidance** as the French (**AMF**),[52] German (**BaFin**)[53] and Italian (**Consob**)[54] authorities do. The NCAs interpretation is not legally binding on the courts. It nevertheless has a large practical relevance for the market participants, the NCA being the competent supervisory authority and as such permitted to impose administrative sanctions.

III. Obligation to Disclose Inside Information (Article 17(1) MAR)

1. Issuers of Financial Instruments

24 The obligation to disclose inside information as laid down in Article 17 MAR is addressed primarily to the issuers (of financial instruments).[55] Article 17(1) subsec. 3 MAR specifies

---

[47] L. Klöhn in: Klöhn (ed.), *MAR*, Art. 17 para. 406; S. Kalss et al. (eds.), *Kapitalmarktrecht*, § 16 para. 7.
[48] ECJ of 23 December 2009, Case C-45/08 (*Spector*) [2009] ECR I-12073, para. 63–64; also OLG Stuttgart, ZIP (2009), 962, 970.
[49] Cf. Recital 5 MAR.
[50] For more detail see also R. Veil § 5 para. 18.
[51] Cf. Art. 23(2), 30(1) and (2) MAR ('at least').
[52] AMF, Guide de l'information permanente et de la gestion de l'information privilégiée, 26.10.2016.
[53] BaFin, Emittentenleitfaden (issuer guideline), 5th ed. 25.3.2020 (Module C); on the legal nature and practical relevance of the issuer guideline see R. Veil § 5 para. 59.
[54] Consob, Gestione delle informazioni privilegiate, October 2017.
[55] On the term 'financial instrument' see R. Veil § 8 para. 2.

that the obligation applies to all **issuers** who have requested or approved **admission** of their **financial instruments** to trading on a **regulated market** in a Member State or, in the case of instruments only traded on an **MTF** or on an **OTF**, issuers who have approved trading of their financial instruments on an MTF or an OTF or have requested admission to trading of their financial instruments on an MTF in a Member State.

The question as to in which Member State an issuer is subject to disclosure proves technical and difficult to answer but essential for legal practice. Pursuant to Article 21(1) in conjunction with Article 2(1)(i) TD, an issuer is subject to the disclosure provisions in its home Member State. Article 21(3) TD modifies this home Member State rule for cases in which securities are admitted to trading on a regulated market in only one host Member State and not in the home Member State.

Situations in which subsidiaries of a company are involved lead to a number of problems with regard to the disclosure of inside information. The MAR and most national laws provide no solution to these problems. Companies in a **corporate group** can then only be subject to disclosure obligations individually, and the parent company, for example, cannot be obliged to disclose information on the listed financial instruments of a subsidiary.

> Facts (Dieselgate): Volkswagen AG (VW) had provided defeat devices in its vehicles in order to pretend on the test bench that the vehicles complied with the respective emission regulations and standards. VW made this publicly known with the following ad hoc announcement dated 22. 9. 2015: 'Volkswagen is pressing ahead with the clarification of irregularities in the software used in diesel engines. [...] Further internal checks to date have shown that the control software in question is also used in other diesel vehicles of the Volkswagen Group. In the majority of these engines, the software has no effect whatsoever. Vehicles with engines of type EA 189 with a total volume of around eleven million vehicles worldwide are in question. Only in the case of this engine type was a conspicuous deviation between test bench values and real driving operation detected. Volkswagen is working at full speed to eliminate these deviations with technical measures. The company is currently in contact with the responsible authorities and the German Federal Motor Transport Authority. To cover necessary service measures and further efforts to regain the trust of our customers, Volkswagen intends to set aside around €6.5 billion in the 3rd quarter of the current financial year, with an impact on earnings. [...] The Group's earnings targets for 2015 will be adjusted accordingly.'[56]
>
> VW and (also listed) Porsche SE (Porsche), VW's majority shareholder, were sued by investors for compensation. The investors argue that VW had published the inside information too late. This would also apply to Porsche, which had also been obliged to issue an ad hoc announcement because of the event.
>
> The court decisions are not yet legally binding. However, the Stuttgart Regional Court has already partially upheld an action against Porsche SE for failure to publish inside information. It assumed that Porsche itself had an obligation to disclose inside information due to the manipulation in its subsidiary. In the case of groups of companies, there would be a double obligation on the part of the parent company and the subsidiary. The court argued that both companies were legally independent persons and that the respective ad hoc notifications addressed different groups of shareholders.[57]

---

[56] The ad hoc announcement was published in German. This translation does not originate from VW.
[57] LG Stuttgart v. 24.10.2018 – 22 O 101/16, JBB (2020), 59 ff. para. 187.

2. Inside Information

(a) Foundations

30 Pursuant to Article 17(1) MAR, issuers must disclose all inside information directly concerning them. In both this context and in the prohibitions on insider dealings the same definition of the term 'inside information' applies.[58] The application of this term had caused difficulties particularly with regard to disclosure obligations in protracted processes, such as multi-stage decision-making processes. This has led the European legislator to clarify the rules for protracted processes in Articles 7(2), (3) and 17(4) subsec. 2 MAR. However, inside information subject to disclosure will always be less than the inside information resulting in prohibitions of insider dealings, as information that only refers to the financial instruments and information only concerning the issuer indirectly need not be made public.[59]

31 In its decision on the investor lawsuit against Porsche (see para. 27),[60] the Regional Court of Stuttgart referred to several intermediate steps, including (i) the decision by an executive of VW to approve the installation of manipulation software in order to activate the defeat device, (ii) the notification of an executive of VW on 28 April 2014 about the financial consequences of the manipulation (penalties and damages) and (iii) the written notification of Prof. Winterkorn, Chairman of the board of directors of VW, by memoranda about the events in the USA in May 2014. The court examined whether these intermediate steps in themselves fulfil the criteria for inside information. This is now expressly regulated in Article 7(3) MAR. The Stuttgart Regional Court affirmed the relevance to the share price, arguing, among other things, that the implementation of the manipulation software had resulted in risks that threatened the existence of the company.

(b) Information Directly Concerning the Issuer

32 The MAR does not offer a definition as to when information 'directly concerns the issuer'. This causes problems in legal practice, where the term needs to be put into more concrete terms in order to be applied correctly. Fulfilling its former role on Level 3 of the Lamfalussy Process,[61] the CESR published a positive list of circumstances which generally directly concern the issuer and a negative list of circumstances that will generally only concern an issuer indirectly.[62] The BaFin's issuer guideline contains a further, more detailed list, although none of these lists can be regarded as final. They must rather be understood as listing the most common cases, the given examples having, however, to be interpreted in the light of the respective situation. Under certain circumstances, a case may thus have to be regarded as concerning the issuer directly although it is listed as generally not doing so, and vice versa.[63]

33 General economic and market data do not fall within the direct concern of the issuer and are therefore not subject to the disclosure obligation. The distinction may, however, prove

---

[58] On the term 'inside information' see R. Veil § 14 para. 32–64.
[59] See R. Veil § 14 para. 50.
[60] LG Stuttgart of. 24.10.2018 – 22 O 101/16, JBB (2020), 59 ff. para. 227 ff.
[61] See F. Walla § 4 para. 4.
[62] CESR, Market Abuse Directive Level 3—second set of CESR guidance and information on the common operation of the Directive to the market, July 2007, CESR/06-562b, p. 7 ff.; CESR, (amended version of) CESR's Advice on Level 2 Implementing Measures for the proposed Market Abuse Directive, December 2002, CESR/02-089d, p. 12 f.
[63] BaFin, Emittentenleitfaden (issuer guideline), Module C, p. 33.

difficult in individual cases. Similarly, the issuer generally need not disclose changes concerning competitors and the development of commodity prices.

As opposed to this, **circumstances** in the **issuer's sphere of activity** are always **subject to disclosure**. These generally constitute the most important group of relevant information to be published and usually refer to measures taken by the management or other bodies of the issuer, business-related activities undertaken by employees and any developments originating within the issuer's business. 34

Yet, the disclosure obligation is not restricted to developments and activities in the issuer's sphere of activity.[64] Takeover offers made by another company, for example, also directly concern the issuer, control over the company not only having an effect on the financial instruments of the company but also on the decision-making process in the general meeting of the target company.[65] The same applies to squeeze-out procedures or to changes in an agency's rating of the company. 35

(c) Attribution of Knowledge

According to the wording of Article 17 MAR, the ad hoc disclosure obligation exists irrespective of whether the issuer is aware of the existence of inside information. The duty could therefore already exist if inside information objectively exists. This interpretation is criticised with the argument that something impossible would be required of the issuer (ultra posse nemo obligatur).[66] However, according to the wording and purpose of Article 17(1) MAR, the disclosure obligation does not require the issuer's knowledge.[67] Knowledge of the existence of inside information becomes relevant at the level of sanctions and legal consequences.[68] In particular, liability for damages on the part of the issuer requires fault. In this context, not only the knowledge of the board members is to be attributed to the issuer, but also the knowledge of employees if the issuer violated its duties to organise knowledge within the company.[69] 36

3. **No Offsetting of Information**

In the United Kingdom issuers have occasionally argued that negative information could be cancelled out by positive information. If the market's expectations are not changed by the information as a whole, disclosure should not be necessary. The FCA/FSA has repeatedly refuted this approach, eg in its ruling in the case of *Wolfson Microelectronics plc*: 37

> *Facts (abridged):*[70] Wolfson Microelectronics plc was a listed company that produced semiconductors for consumer electronics. On 10 March 2008 a major customer, formerly generating 38

---

[64] BaFin, Emittentenleitfaden (issuer guideline), Module C, p. 33.
[65] M. Pfüller, in: Fuchs (ed.), *Kommentar zum WpHG*, § 15 para. 245 f.
[66] H.-C. Ihrig, 181 ZHR (2017), 381, 389.
[67] M. Nietsch, ZIP (2018), 1421, 1427.
[68] M. Nietsch, ZIP (2018), 1421, 1427 ff.
[69] H.-C. Ihrig, 181 ZHR (2017), 381, 388.
[70] FSA, Final Notice, 19 January 2009; cf. B. McDonnell, 88 COB (2011), 1, 13–14; R. Veil and M. Wundenberg, *Englisches Kapitalmarktrecht*, 117–118. The FSA also fined *Entertainment Rights plc* on the same day for not disclosing inside information in the mere hope to be able to compensate a loss of profits in the course of the financial year, cf. FSA, Final Notice, 19 January 2009.

approximately 18% of Wolfson's revenue, told Wolfson that they would not be ordering parts for future editions of products A and B, two of the major customer's products. For Wolfson this represented a loss of 8% of its forecast revenue for the year. At the same time, Wolfson was informed that the same major customer would increase its demand for the supply of parts for product C, making Wolfson's overall revenues from the major customer in 2008 equivalent to those of the previous year. On the recommendation of external consultants, Wolfson disclosed the information on the loss of the order for products A and B on 27 March 2008, subsequently suffering an 18% fall in its share price.

39 The FSA ruled that the delay in disclosing information breached the obligation to disclose inside information as soon as possible to conform with DTR 2.2.1 and Listing Principle 4. Offsetting negative and positive news—or cancelling out negative by positive news—is not acceptable. Rather, companies should disclose both types of information and allow the market to determine whether, and to what degree, the positive information compensates for the negative information. Additionally, Wolfson's calculations failed to take the implications for revenues post 2008 into account although the previously anticipated level of 2008 revenues could be achieved. The information was significant for investors with regard to its implications for Wolfson's future status vis-à-vis the major customer.

4. No Combination of Disclosure with Marketing Activities

40 Transparency can be affected not only by price-sensitive information which remains undisclosed but also by a flood of information, impairing the processing of information important for investment decisions. In Spain, the disclosure of future circumstances, which are not yet entirely certain, had been regarded as the most severe risk to transparency regarding inside information. In addition, issuers might use the disclosure as an instrument towards investor relations. Replacing former Article 2(1) subsec. 1 of Directive 2003/124/EC, Article 17(1) subsec. 2 sentence 2 MAR now expressly prohibits to combine the disclosure of inside information with marketing activities.

5. Publication Procedure

41 The issuer must make the **publication 'as soon as possible'**. Thus, the information must be published immediately (see para. 46). An issuer may, however, take a reasonable period of time to investigate the facts and decide on an exemption, if necessary.[71]

42 Ad hoc announcements must be formulated in such a way that they eliminate information asymmetries with regard to inside information. According to Article 17(1) MAR, the ad hoc notification shall enable **fast access** and **complete, correct** and **timely assessment** of the information by the public. Specific requirements on the means of disclosure of inside information are provided for in Article 2 Implementing Regulation (EU) 2016/1055. It must be made unambiguously clear in the announcement that the information communicated is inside information and what the subject matter of the inside information is.[72] The concept

---

[71] Cf. BGH of 17.12.2020 – II ZB 31/14, ZIP 2021, 346, 361 (*Hypo Real Estate*).
[72] BaFin, Emittentenleitfaden (issuer guideline), Module C, p. 43 ff.

of the public used in Article 17 MAR is not further defined in the Implementing Regulation (EU) 2016/1055. However, recital 1 of Regulation (EC) 2016/1055 states that the 'inside information should be publicly disclosed free of charge, simultaneously and as fast as possible amongst **all categories of investors** throughout the Union'. It can be concluded from this that a private investor is also an addressee of ad hoc notifications.[73] It must be possible for him to assess the price relevance of the disclosed event.[74]

How the publication is to be made is determined by Article 2(1) Implementing Regulation (EU) 2016/1055. Inside information is disseminated (i) to as wide a public as possible on a non-discriminatory basis, (ii) free of charge and (iii) simultaneously throughout the Union. In addition, inside information shall be communicated, directly or through a third party, to the media which are reasonably relied upon by the public to ensure its effective dissemination. The issuer also has to post and maintain on its website for a period of at least five years all inside information.

IV. Delay in Disclosure

1. Foundations

The far-reaching disclosure obligation laid down in Article 17(1) MAR, which is based on the ECJ's wide interpretation of the term inside information,[75] requires correction.[76] In some cases, such as mergers or squeeze-outs, the early disclosure of this intent may endanger its success. Article 17(4) MAR therefore provides for a 'general delay' and permits the **issuer** to **delay** the public **disclosure** of inside information under its own responsibility, if (i) immediate disclosure is likely to **prejudice the legitimate interests** of the issuer, (ii) the delay is **not likely to mislead the public** and (iii) the issuer is able to ensure the **confidentiality** of the information. The importance of this possibility of delay in the disclosure regime for inside information cannot be emphasised enough.

While Article 17(4) subsec. 2 MAR clarifies that issuers may delay the disclosure of inside information relating to a protracted process that occurs in stages, Article 17(4) subsec. 3 MAR requires an issuer who had delayed the disclosure of inside information to **inform** the **competent authority** of this **delay** immediately after the disclosure. It also has to provide—although not necessarily simultaneously[77]—a written[78] **explanation** unless the Member

---

[73] Cf. R. Veil and A. Brüggemeier, in: Meyer/Veil/Rönnau (eds.), *Handbuch Marktmissbrauchsrecht*, § 10 para. 168 ff.; L. Klöhn, in: Klöhn (ed.), *MAR*, Art. 17 para. 515 ff.
[74] L. Klöhn, in: Klöhn (ed.), *MAR*, Art. 17 para. 523 f.; R. Veil and A. Brüggemeier, in: Meyer/Veil/Rönnau (eds.), *Handbuch Marktmissbrauchsrecht*, § 10 para. 174.
[75] See ECJ of 28 June 2012, Case C-19/11 (*Daimler/Geltl*); ECJ of 11 March 2015, Case C-628/13 (*Lafonta*), EuZW (2015), 387 ff.
[76] Cf. BGH of 23.4.2013 – II ZB 7/09, ZIP (2013), 1165, 1168; G. Bachmann, 172 ZHR (2008), 597, 608. See also S. Gilotta, 13 EBOR (2012), 45 ff. emphasising the issuer's need for secrecy.
[77] Cf. ESMA, Final Report. Draft Technical Standards on the Market Abuse Regulation, ESMA/2015/1455, 28 September 2015, para. 230.
[78] According to Recital 4 Commission Implementing Regulation (EU) 2016/1055, written form means the use of electronic means of transmission accepted by the relevant competent authority.

State has chosen that the explanation depends on a request of the competent authority. Some Member States have made use of this in order to achieve deregulation and reduce the supervisory authority's audit burden.[79]

46   The short period necessary for determining whether a disclosure obligation exists is not regarded as a delay as in these cases the disclosure takes place '**as soon as possible**'.[80] This is all but trivial when the issuer's management itself is surprised by the possible inside information, as may be the case with compliance irregularities (eg in the case of *Volkswagen*) or in corporate groups. It may be tricky to determine to what extent an issuer needs to organise its internal chains of information in order to ensure timely disclosure, and when information which is not available to or even hidden from the management is still attributed to the issuer.

47   After this period a delay is only possible provided the prerequisites under Article 17(4) or (5) MAR are given; in the case that a requirement ceases to exist, the information must be disclosed immediately. The issuer must therefore check continually whether all the requirements for the delay are still given.[81] This means that disclosure may in some cases be delayed indefinitely, as the MAR contains no maximum duration for the delay. In these cases, there is no obligation to inform the competent authority, either.

48   The issuer will then have to disclose the information without undue delay. The relevant date for assessing which information must be disclosed is the time at which the requirements for the delay cease to exist. If by this time the information has lost its character as inside information, it need not be disclosed. This is, for example, conceivable if the issuer has meanwhile abandoned its plans to take certain measures. In these cases, there is no obligation to inform the competent authority of the delay and explain it. According to the unambiguous wording of Article 17(4) subsec. 3 MAR, such obligations are only triggered when inside information is actually disclosed. This has to be seen critically: The information and explanation requirements are conceived as tools to be used in potential insider-dealing investigations[82] and are equally, if not even more important when the inside information is never disclosed.

49   In the wake of the financial crisis, financial institutions (eg Northern Rock and Société Générale) have repeatedly been faced with the duty to disclose inside information where this disclosure risked leading to a bank run and thereby endanger the stability of the financial system. The disclosure regime did not provide a clear legal base to delay disclosure in these cases, however, since it was rather the public interest than a legitimate interest of the issuer which required the delay. Articles 17(5) and (6) MAR therefore provide for a new and **separate**[83] possibility to **delay** the **disclosure** of inside information to preserve the **stability**

---

[79] Cf. ESMA, MAR Review Report, 23 September 2020, ESMA70-156-2391, para. 195: Austria, Denmark, Finland, France, Greece, Italy, Luxembourg, the Netherlands, Spain, Sweden and the United Kingdom.

[80] Cf. L. Klöhn, AG (2016), 423, 430; S. Kalss et al. (eds.), *Kapitalmarktrecht I*, § 16 para. 48; C. Di Noia and M. Gargantini, ECFR (2012), 484, 507.

[81] Cf. CESR, Market Abuse Directive Level 3—second set of CESR guidance and information on the common operation of the Directive to the market, July 2007, CESR/06–562b, p. 11.

[82] Cf. ESMA/2015/1455 (fn. 77), para. 232 ff.

[83] As Art. 17(6) subsec. 4 MAR clarifies, issuers that are credit or financial institutions are free to choose the 'general' delay mechanism in these cases. It appears doubtful if the requirement of the issuer's legitimate interests can be met, however.

of the financial system, especially for inside information concerning a temporary liquidity problem or the need to receive temporary liquidity assistance.[84] It applies only to issuers which are **credit** or **financial institutions**. The following conditions, which according to ESMA are to be interpreted narrowly,[85] have to be met: (i) the disclosure risks to undermine the financial stability of the issuer and of the financial system, (ii) it is in the public interest to delay the disclosure, (iii) the confidentiality of the information can be ensured, and (iv) the competent authority has consented to the delay. Article 17(6) MAR specifies the procedure for these delays.

Confidentiality may also exist for other legal reasons. The **obligation** to **publish** inside information is **excluded by law** if the **personal rights** of a natural person **outweigh** the **interest** of the **capital markets** in publishing the information. The legal basis is the general right of personality pursuant to Article 7 and 8 of the Charter of Fundamental Rights of the European Union.[86] In practice, this has so far mainly become relevant in the case of a serious illness of a football player. The disclosure can be omitted without the issuer taking a delay decision pursuant to Article 17(4) MAR.[87] Furthermore, the exclusion of the obligation to publish is justified in literature by the principle of **nemo tenetur**.[88] If internal investigations revealed suspicions of compliance violations, the issuer could refer to the principle that no one was obliged to incriminate himself. This prohibition of self-incrimination is based on Article 6(1) of the European Convention on Human Rights.

50

2. Delay Pursuant to Article 17(4) MAR

(a) Legitimate Interests

The issuer's 'legitimate interests' that may justify a delay in disclosure are a key element of the disclosure regime. It is therefore essential to put this abstract concept into more concrete terms. Whilst the European legislator did not define the term 'legitimate interests', it assigned ESMA to issue a guideline to establish a non-exhaustive indicative list of such legitimate interests[89] and included two examples of legitimate interests in Recital 50 of the MAR which mirror former Article 3(1) of Directive 2003/124/EC. These are:

51

— ongoing negotiations, or related elements, where the outcome or normal pattern of those negotiations would be likely to be affected by public disclosure. In particular, in the event that the financial viability of the issuer is in grave and imminent danger, although not within the scope of the applicable insolvency law, public disclosure of information may be delayed for a limited period where such a public disclosure would seriously jeopardise the interest of

---

[84] On this delay cf. L. Klöhn, AG (2016), 423, 432; P. Koch, BB (2012), 1365, 1367; N. Moloney, *EU Securities and Financial Markets Regulation*, 731, 734.
[85] Cf. ESMA/2015/1455 (fn. 77), para. 251; L. Klöhn, AG (2016), 423, 432.
[86] Cf. H.-D. Assmann, in: Assmann/Schneider/Mülbert (eds.), *Kommentar zum Wertpapierhandelsrecht*, Art. 17 MAR para. 74; *Klöhn*, in: Klöhn (ed.), *MAR*, Art. 17 para. 379 ff.
[87] Cf. H.-D. Assmann, in: Assmann/Schneider/Mülbert (eds.), *Kommentar zum Wertpapierhandelsrecht*, Art. 17 MAR para. 75.
[88] Cf. H.-D. Assmann, in: Assmann/Schneider/Mülbert (eds.), *Kommentar zum Wertpapierhandelsrecht*, Art. 17 MAR para. 76 ff.
[89] Art. 17(11) MAR.

existing and potential shareholders by undermining the conclusion of specific negotiations designed to ensure the long-term financial recovery of the issuer;
— decisions taken or contracts made by the management body of an issuer which need the approval of another body of the issuer in order to become effective, where the organisation of such an issuer requires the separation between those bodies, provided that public disclosure of the information before such approval, together with the simultaneous announcement that the approval remains pending, would jeopardise the correct assessment of the information by the public.

52 In its guidelines, ESMA has put both cases into more concrete terms and split the first case into the two independent examples of **ongoing negotiations** and a **danger** to the **financial viability** to an **issuer**. The guidelines comprise three further situations which largely perpetuate the CESR's examples.[90] These are (i) the development of a product or an invention; (ii) plans to buy or sell a major holding in another entity (but negotiations have not yet started); and (iii) deals or transactions previously announced and subject to a public authority's approval. The former case of impending developments that could be jeopardised by premature disclosure is suppressed for being too generic.[91] The listed examples are non-exhaustive; even in the listed cases the issuer has to carry out a case-by-case assessment whether its interests are legitimate.[92]

53 It is highly controversial if the term 'legitimate interests' has to be construed generously or narrowly. While the SMSG suggested a generous interpretation, ESMA expressly refused this approach and calls for a narrow interpretation.[93] This reflects the discussion on the scope of the disclosure duty. Since the legislator embraced a far-reaching understanding of the term inside information, opponents of an extensive duty to disclose argue for an enhanced need for possibilities to delay disclosure—mostly from a transparency-oriented perspective. Supporters fear that the delay could be abused to thwart the disclosure obligation and argue from both a transparency-oriented and a insider trading preventive point of view.[94] Whilst the legislator's decision may obviously not be reversed by admitting legitimate interests too extensively, there is **no need for a narrow interpretation**, either.[95] Article 17(4) MAR recognises the need for delay and provides for confidentiality in order to prevent insider dealing during the delay. In particular, Article 17(4) subsec. 2 MAR expressly allows delay to the disclosure of intermediate steps subject to the same conditions as any other inside information, but does not generally justify the delay. In any event, an issuer may not delay the disclosure of 'uncertain' inside information based on an alleged risk of misleading the public by this disclosure.[96]

54 An abstract specification of the legitimate interests causes problems because there is no '**interest of a company**' or 'interest of an issuer'. Moreover, this concept is probably

---

[90] Cf. CESR, Market Abuse Directive, Level 3 – second set of CESR guidance and information on the common operation of the Directive to the market, July 2007, CESR/06-562b.
[91] ESMA, Final Report. Guidelines on the Market Abuse Regulation – market soundings and delay of disclosure of inside information, ESMA/2016/1130, 13 July 2016, para. 50.
[92] Cf. Recital 50 MAR; ESMA/2016/1130 (fn. 91), para 52 ff.; Annex IV, para. 113; Annex V, para. 88, 94.
[93] ESMA/2016/1130 (fn. 91), para. 52; Annex III, para. 24 (SMSG's response to ESMA's CP).
[94] Cf. G. Bachmann, DB (2012), 2206, 2210.
[95] C. Kumpan, DB (2016), 2039, 2043.
[96] Dissenting opinion: J.L. Hansen, *Say when: When must an issuer disclose inside information?*, 26, 28: 'Correctness and completeness trumps haste'.

understood differently among Member States.⁹⁷ In order to ensure a common understanding in the EU, the interests of the company should be interpreted on the basis of what interests shareholders typically have.⁹⁸ This interpretation is supported by the 50th recital of MAR, which refers to the interests of existing and potential shareholders.

A legitimate interest of the issuer exists in principle if the shareholders are threatened with disadvantage by the publication. This disadvantage manifests itself in expected negative effects on the fundamental value of the share.⁹⁹ Even if the wording of Article 17(4) MAR does not contain any further requirements, the purpose of ad hoc disclosure requires that the disadvantage is of such intensity that the capital market's interest in information is to be assessed as lower. The issuer has no discretion as to the existence of legitimate interests.¹⁰⁰ 55

> Legitimate interests of the issuer may exist in negotiations the outcome of which would likely be jeopardised by immediate public disclosure.¹⁰¹ ESMA gives the following non-exhaustive examples: mergers, acquisitions, splits and spin-offs, purchases or disposals of major assets or branches of corporate activity, restructurings and reorganisations. 56

> Recital 50 MAR addresses financial problems of the issuer: 'In the event that the financial viability of the issuer is in grave and imminent danger [...], public disclosure of information may be delayed for a limited period where such a public disclosure would seriously jeopardise the interest of existing and potential shareholders by undermining the conclusion of specific negotiations designed to ensure the long-term financial recovery of the issuer'. The wording of ESMA's guideline is almost identical: 'the financial viability of the issuer is in grave and imminent danger, although not within the scope of the applicable insolvency law, and immediate public disclosure of the inside information would seriously prejudice the interests of existing and potential shareholders by jeopardising the conclusion of the negotiations designed to ensure the financial recovery of the issue.' 57

> In the context of multi-stage decision-making processes, the individual intermediate steps may already constitute inside information subject to publication (see para. 30). In particular, if a decision taken by the board of directors or the conclusion of a contract is still dependent on the approval of the supervisory board, this may constitute a legitimate interest for a delay. However, waiting for the further necessary decision should not constitute an automatism.¹⁰² According to ESMA's guidance, an issuer may have 'legitimate interests in a delay if the inside information relates to decisions taken or contracts entered into by the management body of an issuer which need, pursuant to national law or the issuer's bylaws, the approval of another body of the issuer, other than the shareholders' general assembly, in order to become effective, provided that (i) immediate public disclosure of that information before such a definitive decision would jeopardise the correct assessment of the information by the public; and (ii) the issuer arranged for the definitive decision to be taken as soon as possible.'¹⁰³ 58

---

⁹⁷ A. Pietrancosta, in: Ventoruzzo/Mock (eds.), *Market Abuse Regulation*, Art. 17 para. B.17.81.
⁹⁸ BaFin, Emittentenleitfaden (issuer guideline), Module C, p. 38; H.D. Assmann, in: Assmann/Schneider/Mülbert (eds.), *Kommentar zum Wertpapierhandelsrecht*, Art. 17 MAR para. 101; L. Klöhn, 178 ZHR (2014), 55, 73 ff.; L. Klöhn and U. Schmolke, ZGR (2016), 866, 875 f.; P. *Mülbert and A. Sajnovits*, WM (2017), 2001, 2004.
⁹⁹ L. Klöhn, 178 ZHR (2014), 55, 80 f. See on the concept of the fundamental value R. Veil § 14 para. 56 and R. Veil § 26 para. 11 f.
¹⁰⁰ Dissenting opinion: L. Klöhn, in: Klöhn (ed.), *MAR*, Art. 17 para. 157 ff.
¹⁰¹ ESMA/2016/1478 para. 8 lit. a., 4; ESMA/2016/1130 para. 55 f.
¹⁰² ESMA/2016/1130 para. 68.
¹⁰³ ESMA/2016/1478 para. 8 lit. c); recital 50 lit. b) MAR.

(b) No Misleading the Public

59 Whether the public may be misled by the delay in disclosure is difficult to determine.[104] Generally speaking, any delay leads to a pricing that does not reflect all the relevant information, the price-sensitive nature of the information being a defining element of the concept of information and therefore a necessary prerequisite for any disclosure obligation. Applying this understanding of the term 'misleading the public' would, however, be absurd.[105] Misleading the public is therefore only to be assumed if the information available to the market gives an impression that is contrary to the actual situation under consideration of the inside information and the issuer's behaviour.[106]

60 ESMA has identified the following three sets of circumstances when the delay is likely to mislead the public; the list is non-exhaustive:[107]

— the inside information whose disclosure the issuer intends to delay is materially different from the[108] previous public announcement of the issuer on the matter to which the inside information refers to;
— the inside information whose disclosure the issuer intends to delay regards the fact that the issuer's financial objectives are likely not to be met, where such objectives were previously publicly announced;
— the inside information whose disclosure the issuer intends to delay is in contrast with the **market's expectations**, where such expectations are based on signals that the issuer has previously sent to the market, such as interviews, roadshows or any other type of communication organized by the issuer or with its approval.

Especially the last example with its reference to the market's expectations was highly controversial.[109] However, it reflects the importance ESMA gives to the disclosure obligation.

(c) Ensuring Confidentiality

61 Article 17 MAR does not specify when an issuer is able to ensure the confidentiality of the information. Two of the three specific duties for issuers formerly contained in Article 3(2) Directive 2003/124/EC[110] can be deduced from Article 4(1)(c) Commission Implementing Regulation (EU) No. 2016/1055 which implicitly requires: (i) **information barriers** to be put in place internally and with regard to third parties to prevent access to inside information by persons other than those who require it for the normal exercise of their functions within the issuer; (ii) **arrangements** to be put in place **to disclose** the relevant **inside information**

---

[104] Remarkably, Art. 17(5) MAR does not rely on this condition.
[105] Cf. CESR, Market Abuse Directive Level 3—second set of CESR guidance and information on the common operation of the Directive to the market, July 2007, CESR/06-562b, p. 11; OLG Stuttgart of 22.4.2009 – 20 Kap 1/08, ZIP (2009), 962, 970; C. Di Noia and M. Gargantini, ECFR (2012), 484, 506.
[106] OLG Stuttgart of 22.4.2009 – 20 Kap 1/08, ZIP (2009), 962, 970.
[107] ESMA/2016/1130 (fn. 91).
[108] In the draft guidelines, reference was made to 'a' previous public announcement. Now, only the last public announcement concerning the relevant matter is referred to, cf. ESMA/2016/1130 (fn. 91), Annex IV, para. 141.
[109] Cf. C. Di Noia et al., ZBB (2014), 96, 101.
[110] Repealed by Art. 37 MAR.

as soon as possible where the confidentiality is no longer ensured. Furthermore, the issuer needs to appoint persons responsible for ensuring the ongoing monitoring of the conditions for the delay according to Article 4(1)(b)(ii). The third duty under Article 3(2) Directive 2003/124/EC—to take the necessary measures to ensure that any person with access to such information acknowledges the legal and regulatory duties entailed and is aware of the sanctions attached to the misuse or improper circulation of such information—can be found in Article 18(2) MAR.

Under the former regime, any breach of these duties made the delay unlawful—even if the inside information was not leaked. This is still true for the duties implied in Article 4(1)(c) Commission Implementing Regulation (EU) No. 2016/1055 as they are referred to as serving to fulfil the conditions for delay according to Article 17(4) MAR. Issuers must also comply with these duties to make a delay according to Article 17(5) MAR lawful. As the obligation to take all reasonable steps to ensure that the duties ensuing from inside information are acknowledged by any person involved is no longer designed as a part of the delay mechanism, breaches do not result in a breach of confidentiality (but are subject to sanctions under the rules for insider lists). 62

> The BGH and the OLG Stuttgart had to examine the obligation to take measures to ensure that the duties ensuing from inside information are acknowledged by any person involved in the case of *Geltl*.[111] The OLG Stuttgart ruled that this obligation also existed towards members of the board even though these were bound to confidentiality through their position. It argued that only persons with a general obligation to confidentiality are allowed access to inside information. The required instruction takes this into account and aims at further information in order to ensure that the insider is reminded of his obligations as an insider and the sanctions for breaches of these obligations. In case the insider is not instructed duly, the issuer may entail **civil liability**, as the BGH—dissenting from the OLG Stuttgart—does not allow the issuer to refer to the fact that even if it had acted correctly, it would only have instructed the respective person, but would not have disclosed the respective information sooner. 63

If inside information is leaked to the public and confidentiality is therefore no longer ensured, the issuer must promptly make a complete disclosure of that information. Although there may be other indicators for a leak, such as unusual developments of the stock exchange price or trade volume, the focus lies on **rumours**. While Article 6 MAD 2003 did not directly address this issue, Article 17(7) subsec. 2 MAR obliges issuers to disclose the inside information immediately—both in cases of a general delay or a delay to preserve the stability of the financial system—where a rumour explicitly relates to that inside information and is sufficiently accurate to indicate that the confidentiality is no longer ensured.[112] ESMA has specified that the disclosure obligation is triggered whether the leak comes from the sphere of the issuer or not. Otherwise, disclosure might be delayed further due to the potentially time-consuming search for the source of the leak.[113] 64

---

[111] BGH of 23.4.2013 – II ZB 7/09, ZIP (2013), 1165, 1170; OLG Stuttgart of 22.4.2009 – 20 Kap 1/08, ZIP (2009), 962, 969, 972.
[112] On the reform proposal see C. Di Noia and M. Gargantini, ECFR (2012), 484, 521 ff.
[113] ESMA/2015/1455 (fn. 77), para. 243.

65 This puts an end to a long discussion on this point and to the practice in some Member States, such as Germany where the BaFin[114] had a more generous approach towards rumours. When such rumours arise, the issuer can no longer rely on a 'no comment policy' as was widely accepted before.[115] Issuers should therefore reconsider their communication strategy with a view to potential upcoming inside information. As neither the European legislator nor ESMA[116] specify when a rumour fulfils these requirements, especially when it is 'sufficiently accurate', there is a risk that divergent national practices will persist.

(d) Decision by the Issuer

66 Under the MAD 2003 regime, literature discussed the question of whether it was sufficient if the requirements for a delay were given,[117] or whether the issuer additionally had to make a conscious decision to this end.[118] The issuer might in particular fail to make a conscious decision in a protracted process that occurs in stages if it realises too late that certain information qualifies as inside information. In the civil proceedings in *Geltl* the OLG Stuttgart ruled[119] that a delay in disclosure did not necessarily require the issuer's conscious decision. However, the BGH, in its appeal decision, and the OLG Frankfurt, entrusted with the supervisory proceedings in the same case, left the question unanswered.[120]

67 Under the MAR regime, the question must be decided unambiguously. The wording of Article 17(4) subsec. 1 MAR indicates that European law requires a conscious decision: If 'an issuer *may* [...] delay' disclosure, this constitutes an action which necessitates an underlying decision.[121] Article 17(4) subsec. 3 MAR also implies a conscious decision: an issuer who is unaware of the fact that it has been delaying disclosure cannot inform the competent authority of the delay and explain it. Article 4(3)(e) Commission Implementing Regulation (EU) No. 2016/1055 now even explicitly requires the issuer to make a conscious decision and inform the competent authority of its date and time. The reason for this is that ESMA considers this information crucial for potential insider-dealing investigations.[122] As European law requires the conscious decision,[123] national laws cannot free issuers from it.

68 The requirements this decision must meet remain somewhat unclear, although ESMA and the Commission provide orientation through their technical standards which specify which information on the delay has to be given to the competent authority—and which further information has to be maintained as evidence in proceedings.[124] While ESMA apparently

---

[114] Cf. BaFin, Emittentenleitfaden 2013 (issuer guideline), p. 61. In the 5th edition of its issuer guideline, BaFin now confirms this change of practice.

[115] Cf. CESR, Market abuse Directive Level 3—third set of CESR guidance and information on the common operation of the Directive to the market, May 2009, CESR/09-219, p. 14 ff.

[116] ESMA expressly refused to provide more explanation in the draft technical standard (para. 244) and did not come back on the issue in the guidelines.

[117] OLG Stuttgart of 22.4.2009 – 20 Kap 1/08, ZIP (2009), 962, 973.

[118] BaFin, Emittentenleitfaden 2009 (issuer guideline), p. 59.

[119] OLG Stuttgart of 22.4.2009 – 20 Kap 1/08, ZIP (2009), 962 ff.

[120] BGH of 23.4.2013 – II ZB 7/09, ZIP (2013), 1165, 1169.

[121] Cf. C.H. Seibt and B. Wollenschläger, AG (2014), 593, 600.

[122] ESMA/2015/1455 (fn. 77), para. 232, 239. Dissenting opinion: L. Klöhn, AG (2016), 423, 431 (no clear statement from ESMA).

[123] BaFin, Emittentenleitfaden (issuer guideline), Module C, p. 36; R. Veil, JBB (2014), 85, 93; D. Poelzig, NZG (2016), 762, 765.

[124] Cf. Art. 4 Commission Implementing Regulation (EU) 2016/1055.

sees no obligation under European law that the decision be taken by the management board itself,[125] it does not address global or preventive authorisations to this effect.[126] As Article 17(4) subsec. 2 MAR recognises the particular difficulties in the case of a protracted process which occurs in stages, it should be legitimate at least here to **decide preventively** on the **delay** when the issuer itself does not yet consider the information concerned as inside information. Whilst a separate decision is required for each intermediate step, the issuer may make the decision for several intermediate steps at the same time.

3. Delay Pursuant to Article 17(5) MAR

Certain issuers have another option to delay the publication of inside information. The regulation in Article 17(5) MAR goes back to experiences from the financial market crisis (see para. 49). Ad hoc announcements by banks sometimes resulted in drastic share price losses, triggering a bank run and threatening the stability of the financial system.[127] **Credit institutions** and other **financial institutions** may now postpone the publication of inside information if there is a **risk** that the **financial stability** of the **financial system** and the **issuer** will be undermined by disclosure, the delay is in the public interest, confidentiality can be ensured and the competent authority agrees to the postponement.

A credit or financial institution has the choice whether to delay disclosure under Article 17(4) or (5) MAR. In the latter case, unlike Article 17(4) MAR, it does not matter whether the postponement of disclosure would be likely to mislead the public. According to the European legislature, efficient price formation is less important than the goal of the stability of the financial system.

The right to delay publication pursuant to Article 17(5) MAR exists in the case of inside information entailing a risk of undermining the financial stability of the issuer and of the financial system. Recital 52 MAR gives the following examples: 'information pertinent to temporary liquidity problems, where they need to receive central banking lending including emergency liquidity assistance from a central bank where disclosure of the information would have a systemic impact'. In this context, BaFin considers significant outflows of liquid funds or a significant decrease in equity capital.[128] With regard to the threat to the financial stability of the financial system, BaFin takes into account whether the institution is (globally) systemically important.[129]

V. Obligation to Disclose Inside Information (Article 17 (8) MAR)

Article 17(8) MAR extends the disclosure obligation to persons acting on behalf or on account of the issuer and who disclose inside information to third parties in the normal

---

[125] ESMA/2015/1455 (fn. 77), para. 239 ('eg a managing board member or a senior executive director').
[126] Cf. M. Pfüller, in: Fuchs (ed.), *Kommentar zum WpHG*, § 15 para. 474 ff.
[127] Cf. P. Koch, BB (2012), 1365, 1367 f.; L. Klöhn, 181 ZHR (2017), 746, 753 ff.
[128] BaFin, Emittentenleitfaden (issuer guideline), Module C, p. 41.
[129] BaFin, Emittentenleitfaden (issuer guideline), Module C, p. 41.

course of the exercise of their employment, profession or duties. In legal practice, this provision is of little importance.[130] In general, the issuer will in these cases also be subject to a disclosure obligation due to the fact that it can no longer ensure that the information remains confidential.[131] This disclosure obligation is intended to ensure equal access to information for all capital market participants.[132] It may become relevant if the issuer has delayed disclosure due to the existence of legitimate interests pursuant to Article 17(4) or (5) MAR or Article 17(1) MAR is not applicable because the inside information does not directly relate to the issuer.

VI. Supervision

73 One of the main novelties of the MAR regime when compared to the former MAD 2003 are the much more detailed and stricter rules on supervision and sanctions. According to Articles 22 ff. MAR, it is still the national supervisory authorities who are responsible for ensuring that the regulation's provisions are applied correctly. They must follow the same rules as for insider trading.[133]

VII. Sanctions

1. Administrative and Criminal Measures and Sanctions

74 Unlike under Article 14(1) MAD 2003 when Member States were only required to 'ensure, in conformity with their national law, that the appropriate administrative measures can be taken or administrative sanctions be imposed against the persons responsible where the provisions adopted in the implementation of this Directive have not been complied with', Articles 30 ff. MAR contain very detailed rules on administrative sanctions. Uncommonly within a regulation, these rules need to be implemented into national law.

75 Pursuant to Article 30(2)(i)(ii) MAR, the maximum fine for an infringement of Article 17 MAR must be at least € **1 million** in respect of a natural person. For a legal person, the maximum fine must be at least € **2.5 million or 2% of its total annual turnover** according to Article 30(2)(j)(ii) MAR. In the case of corporate groups, the relevant turnover is that of the ultimate parent undertaking, pursuant to Article 30(2) subsec. 3 MAR. Although the level of fines may still vary considerably amongst the different Member States, these rules have brought about major changes for some European countries: In 2008, maximum

---

[130] Cf. L. Klöhn, WM (2010), 1869 ff.
[131] See para. 61.
[132] L. Klöhn, WM (2010), 1869; H.-D. Assmann, in: Assmann/Schneider/Mülbert, *Kommentar zum Wertpapierhandelsrecht*, Art. 17 MAR para. 285.
[133] See R. Veil § 14 para. 96–110.

sanctions ranged from € 100 in Bulgaria and Finland to € 2.5 million in Ireland, Portugal and Belgium, whilst the United Kingdom[134] did not restrict the level of fines.[135]

Article 34(1) MAR requires the competent authorities to **publish** any **decision** imposing an **administrative sanction** or other administrative measure in relation to an infringement of the MAR on their website immediately after the sanctioned person has been informed of the decision. When the decision is subject to an appeal, it must still be published immediately, as Article 34(2) MAR explicitly addresses this case and limits the sanctioned person's rights to having information on the appeal and its outcome published in the same way. The European legislator put remarkable emphasis on this instrument known as 'naming and shaming'. Under the MAD 2003 regime, such disclosure was left to the competent authorities' discretion—and rarely applied in some Member States. After long debates, the publication of any sanction is now **mandatory** and has to be carried out **immediately**. Due to concerns regarding the proportionality of the publication, especially if natural persons are being sanctioned, Article 34 MAR allows for several exceptions including a delay of the publication and a publication on an anonymous basis. 76

> Article 34 MAR does not explain why a decision should be made public. Recital 73 MAR mentions the dissuasive effect and the information of market participants of behaviour which is considered an infringement. This seems to follow the French concept: In France, all sanctions were made public on the AMF's website pursuant to Article L. 621–15-V C. mon. fin., even before the MAD 2003 was enacted. The publication of sanctions has also been recommended with regard to the directives based on the Financial Services Action Plan.[136] In 2007 the Conseil d'État ruled that the disclosure of imposed sanctions constitutes a sanction in itself. It does not require the decision to have full legal effect before it is made public in order to comply with the presumption of innocence.[137] The publication must, however, follow the principles of legality and proportionality. The AMF regards naming and shaming as particularly effective, as a deterrent to others and because it helps market participants understand which behaviour is seen critically. This is exactly the MAR's position. 77

Criminal sanctions and civil liability are not directly addressed.[138] **Member States** are therefore **free** not to sanction breaches by criminal or civil law at all.[139] However, Member States are free to impose stricter sanctions.[140] This means that they may choose to sanction breaches of the disclosure obligations for inside information also by **criminal law**.[141] But criminal sanctions for breaches of the disclosure obligations for inside information play a subordinated role in Europe. Under the MAD 2003 regime, breaches were only sanctioned under criminal law in 9 out of 29 CESR Member States, possible penalties reaching from 78

---

[134] For examples of FSA enforcement action see B. McDonnell, 88 COB (2011), 1, 15 ff.
[135] Cf. CESR, Executive Summary to the Report on Administrative Measures and Sanctions and the Criminal Sanctions available in Member States under the Market Abuse Directive (MAD), February 2008, CESR/08-099, p. 5, 10; see also the individual descriptions on p. 34 ff.
[136] Cf. P.-H. Conac, 1 RTDF (2006), 128 ff.
[137] Cf. G. Roch, Bull. Joly Bourse (2008), 204, 207. Seen critically by N. Rontchevsky, 1 RTDF (2008), 86 ff.
[138] The CRIM-MAD does not prescribe to implement criminal sanctions for breaches of the disclosure obligations, either.
[139] Dissenting opinion: A. Hellgardt, AG (2012), 154, 162 ff.; sceptically (as herein) K.J. Hopt, WM (2013), 101, 111. See also R. Veil § 12 para. 23–25.
[140] See R. Veil § 12 para. 12.
[141] Cf. D. Verse, RabelsZ 76 (2012), 893, 896.

fines of € 5,000 in Ireland to a maximum prison sentence of eight years in Italy.[142] Whilst criminal liability does not require a special provision but can rather be based on the general provisions for pecuniary offences, it appears of little importance in legal practice. As the CRIM-MAD does not address breaches of the obligation to disclose inside information according to Article 17 MAR, no major changes are to be expected concerning criminal sanctions.

79   As the (implementing) rules on sanctions and their application into practice continue to fall within the Member States' responsibility, sanctioning breaches of disclosure obligations for inside information is still largely a matter of national law. Member States are able to pursue their national approaches to enforcement which make use of and combine various sanctions under civil, administrative and criminal law in very different ways.

2. Civil Liability

80   The MAR does not provide for any rules on liability for damages on the part of the issuer and/or members of management due to breaches of the ad hoc disclosure obligation. The legal situation in Europe is therefore different.[143] This is also due to the fact that Member States have different traditions and ideas about the purpose of private enforcement. It is seen as problematic, above all, that ultimately the existing shareholders bear the financial burden of incorrect ad hoc disclosure, as they bear the financial disadvantages of a liability claim against the issuer. If liability for damages is to pursue preventive purposes, it should be possible to bring claims against the members of the management. Liability for damages would then have the greatest possible preventive effect. Addressing the claims for damages to the managers would also have the advantage that the existing shareholders, who are typically uninvolved in the breach of the ad hoc obligation, would not suffer any financial damage. However, national legislators are reluctant to do so because external liability could have prohibitive effects and managers could find the office of managing director in listed companies unattractive. Finally, the concept of issuer liability would have to address the risk of over-deterrence. In view of the difficulty in determining ex ante the duties of conduct for issuers, liability for negligence bears the risk of over-enforcement, which would be detrimental to information efficiency. In the United Kingdom, the legislature has therefore set high requirements for issuer liability. Keeping this in mind, it may not be surprising that tort law plays a dominant role in the judicial practice of the Member States.[144]

---

[142] Cf. CESR, Report on administrative measures and sanctions as well as the criminal sanctions available in Member States under the market abuse directive (MAD), February 2008, CESR/08-099, p. 5, 10; see also the individual descriptions on p. 34 ff.

[143] See on the discussion of whether the principle of effet utile requires recognition of a private right of action by investors, R. Veil § 12 para. 25.

[144] In the Netherlands, a trend has developed to claim damages from issuers and managers. The legal basis lies in tort law. Cf. L. Lennarts and J. Roest, in: Conac/Gelter (eds.), *Global Securities Litigation and Enforcement*, 491 f. In France, courts also apply tort law, cf. P.-H. Conac, in: Conac/Gelter (eds.), *Global Securities Litigation and Enforcement*, 346. Cf. on Italy G. Ferrarini and P. Giudici, in: Conac/Gelter (eds.), *Global Securities Litigation and Enforcement*, 455.

(a) Germany

As there will generally be no contractual relationship between the investor and the issuer or its management, liability for breaches of the obligation to disclose inside information will usually be based on tort law or the special provisions in §§ 119, 120 WpHG. In **tort law**, liability is attached either to the violation of a protected right or interest in § 823(1) BGB, the infringement of a protective law in § 823(2) BGB or an intentional damage contrary to public policy in § 826 BGB. As breaches of the disclosure obligation result in pure economic losses and § 26(3) sentence 1 WpHG excludes the applicability of § 823(2) BGB, tortious liability for incorrect or omitted publications of inside information is usually restricted to § 826 BGB.[145] This provision prescribes compensation for intentional damages: A person who, in a manner contrary to public policy, intentionally inflicts damage on another person is liable to the other person to make compensation for the damage. The case of *Infomatec* is one of the BGH's leading cases on § 826 BGB in which the court set out the basic requirements for a tortious liability for incorrect information.

81

> *Facts (abridged):*[146] Infomatec AG published the information that a mobile telephone network provider had placed an order for wifi hubs and their licences with a total order volume of more than DM 55 million as inside information. In fact, the binding order the customer had placed only had an order volume of DM 9.8 million. Immediately after the publication the share price rose by 20%. Two months later an investor acquired shares at this high share price, which dropped considerably in value after it became public that the information was incorrect.

82

The BGH held the **members** of the **board of directors** liable for the damage suffered, arguing that the **conscious publication** of **incorrect information** was **contrary to public policy** and immoral. The BGH was of the opinion that management had published the information intentionally in order to induce investors to acquire shares at an extortionate price. The BGH justified the immorality on the grounds that the board members had intentionally deceived investors by issuing a grossly inaccurate ad hoc announcement.

83

The BGH developed this line of argumentation towards a tort liability for the publication of incorrect information further in *EM.TV*[147] and *Comroad*.[148] Both the issuer (§§ 826, 31 BGB) and the members of the management board responsible for the disclosure (§ 826 BGB) can be held liable. In legal practice, the personal liability of the members of the management will be more relevant for investors, as the issuer itself will often be insolvent—as in *Infomatec*.

84

Requiring full **proof of causation** between the incorrect information and the investor's decision to acquire the shares is seen particularly critically, as this is usually nearly impossible

85

---

[145] Cf. M. Brellochs, *Publizität und Haftung*, 109 ff., 144 ff.; A. Hellgardt, *Kapitalmarktdeliktsrecht*; S. Richter, *Schadenszurechnung bei deliktischer Haftung für fehlerhafte Sekundärmarktinformation*; K. Sauer, *Haftung für Falschinformation des Sekundärmarktes*.
[146] BGH of 19.7.2004 – II ZR 218/03, BGHZ 160, 134 ff. (*Infomatec I*); BGH of 19.7.2004 – II ZR 402/02, BGHZ 160, 149 ff. (*Infomatec II*).
[147] BGH of 9.5.2005 – II ZR 287/02, NZG (2005), 672 ff. (*EM.TV*).
[148] BGH of 28.11.2005 – II ZR 80/04, NZG (2007), 345 f.; BGH of 28.11.2005 – II ZR 246/04, NZG (2007), 346 f.; BGH of 26.6.2006 – II ZR 153/05, NZG (2007), 269 ff.; BGH of 4.6.2007 – II ZR 147/05, NZG (2007), 708 ff.; BGH of 4.6.2007 – II ZR 173/05, NZG (2007), 711 ff.; BGH of 7.1.2008 – II ZR 229/05, NZG (2008), 382 ff.; BGH of 7.1.2008 – II ZR 68/06, NZG (2008), 385 f.; BGH of 3.3.2008 – II ZR 310/06, NZG (2008), 386 ff.(*Comroad I-VIII*).

for the investor. The BGH nonetheless grants no alleviation of the burden of proof, arguing that the decision to acquire shares requires the decision of an individual person and cannot be generalised.[149] The BGH further does not accept the US 'fraud on the market theory', according to which the general deception of investor confidence in the integrity of market prices constitutes liability, purporting that this would lead to an interminable applicability of § 826 BGB.[150] As opposed to this, the issuer may be held liable if an investor has abstained from disposing of his shares on the basis of incorrect information resulting from a breach of the disclosure obligation.[151]

86   The nature of claimable damages was also unclear. Specific performance pursuant to § 249 BGB, ie the reimbursement of the acquisition price and the return of the shares or—should the shares meanwhile have been disposed of—payment of the difference between the acquisition and disposal price, subjects the defendant to the risk of all price fluctuations. It would therefore appear more reasonable to restrict the damages to the difference between the acquisition price and the price that would have developed if the information had been disclosed correctly. The BGH, however, sees the damage in any detriment to a legitimate interest or exposure to an undesired legal obligation, allowing restitution and therefore not restricting the investor's claims to the difference between the actual and the hypothetical acquisition price. If the investor only claims the latter, the exact amount of damages must be determined according to the methods of modern finance. In this procedure the damages are determined on the basis of the difference in price after the true facts have become known. According to the BGH, the judge will in certain cases have to estimate the damages on the legal basis of § 287 Zivilprozessordnung (ZPO—German Civil Procedure Code).[152]

87   Restitution must further be seen critically with regard to the provisions on capital maintenance in §§ 57 ff. AktG and the restricted possibilities of an issuer to acquire his own shares, pursuant to § 71 AktG. Yet the BGH has given restitution priority over the special rules on company law in cases of intentional damage contrary to public policy, arguing that the investor may not be treated differently from a third-party creditor of the issuer if it acquired the shares on the secondary market. The issuer's liability could therefore not be restricted to the issuer's free assets. The acquisition of the shares by the issuer only takes place more or less by chance if the issuer decides not to dispose of the shares to a third party and claim the difference in price from the issuer, but rather to claim the full amount from the issuer.[153] Equally, the ECJ has stated that such priority to restitution is compatible with the Capital Maintenance Directive 77/91/EEC.[154]

88   In 2002 the German legislator further introduced **special rules** on the **liability** for **incorrect or omitted inside information** in §§ 37b, 37c WpHG (later transferred into §§ 119, 120 WpHG), which have meanwhile led to a number of proceedings.[155] § 119 WpHG constitutes a liability for the omission to disclose inside information, whilst § 120 WpHG applies to the publication of incorrect inside information. The provisions only concern the issuers

---

[149] Cf. BGH of 19.7.2004 – II ZR 218/03, BGHZ 160, 134, 144 (*Infomatec I*).
[150] BGH of 26.6.2006 – II ZR 153/05, NZG (2007), 269 (*Comroad III*).
[151] BGH of 9.5.2005 – II ZR 287/02, NZG (2005), 672, 675 (*EM.TV*).
[152] BGH of 9.5.2005 – II ZR 287/02, NZG (2005), 672 ff. (*EM.TV*); BGH of 19.7.2004 – II ZR 218/03, BGHZ 160, 134 et ff. (*Infomatec I*).
[153] BGH of 9.5.2005 – II ZR 287/02, NZG (2005), 672, 674 (*EM.TV*); BGH of 26.6.2006 – II ZR 153/05, NZG (2007), 269, 270 (*Comroad III*).
[154] ECJ of 19 December 2013, Case C-174/12 (*Hirmann*), ZIP (2014), 121 ff. with regard to the prospectus disclosure obligations. See R. Veil § 17 para. 93.
[155] Cf. BGH of 17.12.2020 – II ZB 31/14, ZIP 2021, 346, 366; BGH of 13.12.2011 – XI ZR 51/10 (IKB), BGHZ 192, 90 ff. (*IKB*).

of financial instruments that have been admitted to trading on a domestic stock exchange. The management can be held responsible by the company pursuant to § 93 AktG.

According to § 119 WpHG the **issuer** is to be held **liable** if the investor bought the financial instruments after the omission and still owns the financial instruments upon disclosure of the information, ie paid too high a price due to the omission to disclose the negative information. The issuer is further to be held liable if the investor bought the financial instruments before the existence of the relevant inside information and sells them after the omission at too low a price due to the omission to disclose the positive information. § 119 WpHG declares the issuer to be held liable if the investor made the investment decision because it relied on the false information, if the issuer acted with intent or gross negligence and the investor has incurred damages. This can be the case if the investor bought the financial instruments after publication due to the overly positive impression given and still owns the financial instruments at the point in time at which it becomes publicly known that the information was inaccurate. Such is also the case if it bought the financial instruments before publication and sold them at too low a price before it became clear that the information was inaccurate because of the unduly negative impression the information gives. 89

§§ 119(2), 120(2) WpHG exempt the issuer from liability if it can prove that it acted neither with intent nor with gross negligence. A similar reversal of the burden of proof concerning causation[156] between the breach of the disclosure obligation and the investment decision does not, however, exist.[157] As in § 826 BGB, the BGH allows the investor to claim restitution and does not restrict claims to the difference between the actual and the hypothetical acquisition price.[158] 90

During the subprime crisis investors argued that the issuer's involvement in certain securities—directly or via special-purpose vehicles—should have been disclosed as inside information. The BGH[159] shared this view and ruled that the issuer had to reimburse the acquisition price if the investors could prove that they would not have purchased the shares if the issuer had disclosed his involvement in the usual way. If the investors could not prove causation, they could still claim the difference between the actual and the hypothetical acquisition price. At the same time, the BGH argued that §§ 119, 120 WpHG could not be applied analogously to simple press releases as no gap in the law in this respect existed.[160] 91

(b) Austria

The Austrian OGH—unlike the German legislator—regards the obligation to disclose inside information as a **protective rule**, aimed directly at the protection of investors, thereby enabling claims based on § 1311 ABGB (Austrian General Civil Code) in cases of negligence.[161] Damages for the intentional publication of incorrect information can be claimed on the 92

---

[156] Cf. on this discussion R. Veil, ZHR 167 (2003), 365, 370 with further references.
[157] BGH of 13.12.2011 – XI ZR 51/10, BGHZ 192, 90, 115 f. (*IKB*).
[158] BGH of 13.12.2011 – XI ZR 51/10, BGHZ 192, 90, 109 ff. (*IKB*).
[159] BGH of 13.12.2011 – XI ZR 51/10, BGHZ 192, 90 ff. (*IKB*).
[160] Confirmed in OLG Braunschweig of 12.1.2016 – 7 U 59/14, ZIP (2016), 414 ff. (*Porsche*); OLG Stuttgart of 26.3.2015 – 2 U 102/14, WM (2015), 875 ff. (*Porsche/Volkswagen*).
[161] OGH of 15.3.2012 – 6 Ob 28/12d, ÖBA 2012, 548, 550; OGH of. 24.1.2013 – 8 Ob 104/12w, ÖBA 2013, 438; S. Kalss et al. (eds.), *Kapitalmarktrecht I*, § 16 para. 99, § 20 para. 16; S. Kalss, ZBB (2013), 126, 131.

basis of § 1300 ABGB and § 1295(2) ABGB, the latter applying to intentional behaviour contrary to public policy.[162] The Austrian approach further understands the obligation to disclose inside information as a special legal relationship between issuer and investor that may lead to a liability for negligent breaches of this obligation on the basis of the concept of *culpa in contrahendo*.[163] Austrian law also accepts the possibility of damages pursuant to § 2 öUWG (Austrian Act against Unfair Practices). Generally, damages cannot be claimed from the issuer's bodies directly; rather the issuer itself is held liable for their behaviour pursuant to § 26 ABGB.[164]

93   Damages may be claimed not only by investors who have acquired of disposed of shares to their detriment, but in some cases also by investors who simply still hold the respective shares.[165] Potential investors that abstained from acquiring the shares due to an incorrect or omitted ad hoc notification only lose the opportunity to make profits. This opportunity is not recoverable.[166]

94   Although the proof of causation in the case of breaches of a protective law is generally facilitated under Austrian law, the breach of the obligation to disclose inside information does not entail any particular alleviation for the investor's proof of causation.[167] Generally, breaches of the modalities of disclosure can also entitle the investor to damages. In these cases causation will, however, be particularly difficult to prove.[168]

95   As in Germany, investors may generally claim specific performance, meaning the reimbursement of the acquisition price in exchange for the return of the shares. Yet, this principle is watered down considerably as the OGH also sees the risk of overcompensation if the general market risk is shifted to the issuer. The OGH therefore deducts any advantages resulting from the contract's unwinding.[169] As in Germany, these claims are not regarded as being contrary to the principle of equal treatment (§ 47a öAktG (Austrian Stock Corporation Act), § 83 BörseG), the prohibition to retransfer capital contributions (§ 52 öAktG) or the prohibition for the issuer to buy back its own shares (§ 65 öAktG).[170]

(c) United Kingdom

96   In the United Kingdom, a legal foundation for investors' claims for damages was introduced into the FSMA on 1 October 2010.[171] Section 90A in conjunction with Schedule 10A establishes a liability of the issuer for any incorrect, misleading or delayed information or the

---

[162] S. Kalss et al. (eds.), *Kapitalmarktrecht I*, § 20 para. 15.
[163] S. Kalss et al. (eds.), *Kapitalmarktrecht I*, § 16 para. 99.
[164] S. Kalss et al. (eds.), *Kapitalmarktrecht I*, § 20 para. 10; on court decisions in the wake of the financial crisis, cf. S. Kalss, ZBB (2013), 126 ff.
[165] S. Kalss et al. (eds.), *Kapitalmarktrecht I*, § 19 para. 24–25.
[166] S. Kalss et al. (eds.), *Kapitalmarktrecht I*, § 19 para. 27.
[167] S. Kalss et al. (eds.), *Kapitalmarktrecht I*, § 20 para. 23 ff.
[168] S. Kalss et al. (eds.), *Kapitalmarktrecht I*, § 20 para. 11.
[169] OGH of 15.3.2012 – 6 Ob 28/12d, ÖBA (2012), 548, 552; on this see K.J. Hopt, WM (2013), 101, 107; S. Kalss, ZBB (2013), 126, 131 ff.
[170] OGH, ÖBA (2012), 548, 549, 552.
[171] The amendments were implemented by the Financial Services and Markets Act 2000 (Liability of Issuers) Regulations 2010; for more detail see L. Gullifer and J. Payne, *Corporate Finance Law*, 586–592; K.J. Hopt, WM (2013), 101, 105; D. Verse, RabelsZ 76 (2012), 893 ff.

omission to publish the information.[172] Any person who possesses, acquired or disposed of shares based on the belief that the published information was complete and correct is entitled to claim damages pursuant to this provision.[173] The burden of proof has not been facilitated for investors—in particular the US 'fraud on the market theory' is not applicable. A further requirement in cases of incorrect or incomplete information is that the issuer intentionally or recklessly failed to disclose the information correctly. If the publication was omitted entirely, the issuer is only held liable for intent.[174]

As a result, the hurdles for civil liability are high, which is justified by the trust in effective enforcement through the public authorities.[175] The reservations about private enforcement can also be explained by concerns about opportunistic lawsuits and disruptive developments for companies, as well as the observation that secondary market liability would ultimately only mean a transfer of wealth from the company to the shareholders bringing the lawsuit (pocket shifting).[176] 97

(d) Other Member States

In other Member States civil liability towards investors appears to play a less important role.[177] None of the other Member States seems to provide a special legal foundation for damages based on a breach of disclosure obligations or to have published court decisions on this matter. The legal literature gives little attention to this question, although in general the possibility to claim damages under tort law appears to be accepted.[178] 98

In Spain, a liability under tort law is possible pursuant to Article 1902 CC (Spanish Civil Code), although in legal practice the claim will be met by strict requirements and the outcome will usually be uncertain.[179] Whilst the general rule on a liability for torts in France, Article 1382 C. civ. (French Civil Code), would also be applicable to these circumstances, it has not as yet played any role in legal practice.[180] In both states the discussion is mostly combined with that on a liability for breaches of the periodic disclosure obligations, ie under the generic term of a liability for incorrect information on the secondary market.[181] Whilst 99

---

[172] Cf. L. Gullifer and J. Payne, *Corporate Finance Law*, 587; R. Veil and M. Wundenberg, *Englisches Kapitalmarktrecht*, 112. The scope of application is much larger, though, cf. D. Verse, RabelsZ 76 (2012), 893, 902 ff.; M. Wundenberg, ZGR (2015), 124, 145.
[173] Sec. 90A schedule 10A(3) and (5) FSMA.
[174] Sec. 90A schedule 10A(3) FSMA states: 'The issuer is liable in respect of the omission of any matter required to be included in published information only if a person discharging managerial responsibilities within the issuer knew the omission to be a dishonest concealment of a material fact.'
[175] Cf. I. Chiu, in: Conac/Gelter (eds.), *Global Securities Litigation and Enforcement*, 627, 643; D. Verse, RabelsZ 76 (2012), 893, 919; M. Wundenberg, ZGR (2015), 124, 146.
[176] Cf. I. Chiu, in: Conac/Gelter (eds.), *Global Securities Litigation and Enforcement*, 627, 643; L. Gullifer and J. Payne, *Corporate Finance Law*, 591.
[177] The legal situation in the European Union is described in P.-H. Conac and M. Gelter (eds.), *Global Securities Litigation and Enforcement* (2019), Part III.
[178] Cf. on court decisions in France P.-H. Conac, in: Conac/Gelter (eds.), *Global Securities Litigation and Enforcement* (2019), 331, 346.
[179] Cf. G.J. Sastre Corchado, 1 RMV (2007), 253, 254.
[180] Cf. P.-H. Conac, in: Conac/Gelter (eds.), *Global Securities Litigation and Enforcement* (2019), 331, 346 on claims against issuers and 347 ff. on claims against third parties.
[181] Cf. M. Iribarren Blanco, *Responsabilidad civil por la información divulgada por las sociedades cotizadas*, passim.

Italian legal literature also discusses the tort liability of issuers and the management, no legal practice to this regard is apparent.[182] Similarly, Swedish legal literature acknowledges the applicability of the general provisions of tort law, although legal practice has not yet adopted this approach.[183]

VIII. Conclusion

100 Ad hoc disclosure of inside information has had a dual function since the 1989 reform. Conceptually, the unified approach for the prohibitions on insider trading and the disclosure of inside information, orientated towards the term 'inside information', remains critical, not all information relevant for insider trading prohibitions necessarily requiring disclosure obligations. The European legislator missed the chance to extract the disclosure obligation from the market abuse regime and regulate it together with the other transparency obligations. Thus, the link to the insider trading prohibition via the uniform basic concept of inside information remains a weak point of the MAR regime. The expansion of the concept of inside information subject to disclosure has led to issuers increasingly making use of the right to delay publication due to legitimate interests. This gives rise to a fundamental reform of ad hoc disclosure.

101 De lege lata, the concept of inside information requires further clarification. This is already of central importance for the application of insider prohibitions, but also becomes relevant in the case of ad hoc disclsoure. If one accepts that a reasonable investor is willing to take irrational behaviour into account (as jurisprudence does!), the fulfillment of the ad hoc disclosure obligation becomes an almost impossible task for issuers. Furthermore, the right of the issuer to delay disclosure should be put into more concrete terms. In order to achieve more legal certainty, it will be essential to develop an accurate understanding of the issuer's interest. The consequence of diverging interpretations of the basic terms is that a uniform practice throughout Europe is a distant prospect. ESMA's MAR guidelines are in need of improvement and should be further developed.

102 In Europe, ad hoc disclosure is mainly enforced by administrative sanctions imposed by the national supervisory authorities. It is still too early to evaluate the more stringent MAR regime. Whilst private enforcement plays a major role in the US, this is not the case in Europe. Indeed, most Member States do not pursue any particular strategies in this respect, but rely on the general rules of tort law. However, in Austria and Germany private liability of an issuer due to incorrect or omitted publication of inside information is not only inspired by the idea of compensation, but also has a deterrent effect. It is advisable to harmonise the divergent approaches of the Member States and develop a common understanding of private enforcement throughout Europe.[184]

---

[182] Cf. G. Ferrarini and M. Leonardi, in: Hopt and Voigt (eds.), *Prospekt- und Kapitalmarktinformationshaftung*, 720; on the legal basis G. Ferrarini and P. Giudici, in: Conac/Gelter (eds.), *Global Securities Litigation and Enforcement*, 446, 454 and 464 on the SCI case, establishing a 'disclose or abstain' obligation, based on principles of Italian civil law and European capital markets law.

[183] Cf. R. Veil and F. Walla, *Schwedisches Kapitalmarktrecht*, 87.

[184] Cf. R. Veil, in: Gsell/Möllers, *Enforcing Consumer and Capital Markets Law*, 405 ff.

§ 20

Disclosure of Major Holdings

Bibliography

Baj, Claude, *Action de concert et dépôt d'une offre publique obligatoire: réflexions à la lumière de l'affaire Gecina*, RDBF (2008), 57–66; Baums, Theodor and Sauter, Maike, *Anschleichen an Übernahmeziele mit Hilfe von Aktienderivaten*, 173 ZHR (2009), 454–503; Biard, Jean-François, *Comment on Consultations publiques*, RDBF (2009), 70–73; Bethel, Jennifer E. et al., *Block Share Purchases and Corporate Performance*, 53 J. Fin. (1998), 605–634; Bonneau, Thierry and Pietrancosta, Alain, *Acting in Concert in French Capital Markets and Takeover Law*, 1 RTDF (2013), 37–43; Brav, Alon et al., *Hedge Fund Activism, Corporate Governance, and Firm Performance*, 63 J. Fin. (2008), 1729–1775; von Bülow, Christoph, *Acting in Concert: Anwendungsprobleme des neuen Zurechnungstatbestands*, in: Veil, Rüdiger (ed.), *Übernahmerecht in Praxis und Wissenschaft* (2009), 137–162; von Bülow, Christoph and Petersen, Sven, *Stimmrechtszurechnung zum Treuhänder?*, 35 NZG (2009), 1373–1378; von Bülow, Christoph and Stephanblome, Markus, *Acting in Concert und neue Offenlegungspflichten nach dem Risikobegrenzungsgesetz*, 39 ZIP (2008), 1797–1806; Burgard, Ulrich, *Die Berechnung des Stimmrechtsanteils nach §§ 21–23 Wertpapierhandelsgesetz*, 41 BB (1995), 2069–2078; Carbonetti, Francesco, *I patti parasociale nelle società non quotate alla luce del Testo Unico della Finanza*, 43 Riv soc. (1998), 909–917; Choi, Dosoung, *Toehold Acquisitions, Shareholder Wealth, and the Market for Corporate Control*, 26 J. Fin. Quant. Analysis (1991), 391–407; Conac, Pierre-Henri, *Le nouveau régime des franchissements de seuils issu de l'ordonnance no 2009–105 du 30 janvier 2009 et du Règlement général de l'AMF*, Revue des sociétés (2009), 477–501; Conac, Pierre-Henri, *Cash-Settled Derivates as a Takeover Instrument and the Reform of the EU Transparency Directive*, in: Birkmose, Hanne S. et al. (ed.), *The European Financial Market in Transition* (2012), 49–68; Elster, Nico, *Europäisches Kapitalmarktrecht. Recht des Sekundärmarktes* (2002); Ferrarini, Guido, *Equity Derivatives and Transparency: When Should Substance Prevail*, in: Grundmann, Stefan et al. (eds.), *Festschrift für Klaus J. Hopt zum 70. Geburtstag* (2010), 1803–1822; Fidler, Phillipp, *Beteiligungspublizität zwischen Vollharmonisierung und Übernahmerecht*, 12 ZFR (2017), 222–229; Fleischer, Holger, *Finanzinvestoren im ordnungspolitischen Gesamtgefüge von Aktien-, Bankaufsichts- und Kapitalmarktrecht*, 37 ZGR (2008), 185–224; Fleischer, Holger, *Mitteilungspflichten für Inhaber wesentlicher Beteiligungen (§ 27a WpHG)*, 24 AG (2008), 873–883; Fleischer, Holger and Bedkowski, Dorothea, *Stimmrechtszurechnung zum Treuhänder gemäß § 22 I 1 Nr. 2 WpHG: Ein zivilgerichtlicher Fehlgriff und seine kapitalmarktrechtlichen Folgen*, 48 DStR (2010), 933–938; Fleischer, Holger and Schmolke, Klaus U., *Das Anschleichen an eine börsennotierte Aktiengesellschaft*, 12 NZG (2009), 401–409; Fleischer, Holger and Schmolke, Klaus U., *Kapitalmarktrechtliche Beteiligungstransparenz nach §§ 21 ff. WpHG und 'Hidden Ownership'*, 33 ZIP (2008), 1501–1512; Fleischer, Holger and Schmolke, Klaus U., *Zum beabsichtigten Ausbau der kapitalmarktrechtlichen Beteiligungstransparenz bei modernen Finanzinstrumenten (§§ 25, 25a DiskE-WpHG)*, 13 NZG (2010), 846–854; Fleischer, Holger and Schmolke, Klaus U., *Die Reform der Transparenzrichtlinie: Mindest- oder Vollharmonisierung der kapitalmarktrechtlichen Beteiligungspublizität?*, 13 NZG (2010), 1241–1248; Funck-Brentano, François and Mason, Alan, *La dérive des produits dérivés. Considérations pratiques sur les produits dérivés et les franchissements de seuils*, RTDF (2009), 31–36; Fusi, Alessandra, *I patti parasociali alla luce della nuova disciplina societaria e le possibili applicazioni dei voting trust*, 6 Le Società (2007), 689–694; Goyet, Charles, *Action de concert*, in: *Dictionnaire Joly Bourse et produits financiers*, Vol. I, looseleaf, as of 30 November 2008; Grillier, Frédéric and Segain, Hubert, *Franchissements de seuils: Réglementation applicable et évolutions souhaitables*, RTDF (2007), 20–44; Hazen, Thomas L., *The Law of Securities Regulation* (2017); Kalss, Susanne, *Creeping-in und Beteiligungspublizität nach österreichischem Recht*, in: Kämmerer, J. Axel and Veil, Rüdiger (eds.), *Übernahme- und Kapitalmarktrecht in der Reformdiskussion* (2013), 139–162; König, Wolfgang, *Das Risikobegrenzungsgesetz – offene und gelöste Fragen*, 36 BB (2008), 1910–1914; Krause, Hartmut, *Stakebuilding im Kapitalmarkt- und Übernahmerecht*, in: Kämmerer, J. Axel and Veil, Rüdiger (eds.), *Übernahme- und Kapitalmarktrecht in der Reformdiskussion* (2013), 163–197; Le Cannu, Paul, *Les silences d'un concert espagnol, note sous Cour d'appel de Paris, 1re ch., sect. H, 2 avril 2008, SA Sacyr Vallehermoso et autre c/ SA Eiffage*, Revue des sociétés (2008), 394–404; Maison-Blanche, Catherine and Lecat, Dimitri, *Essai de synthèse sur les sanctions en cas de violation de l'obligation de declarations des franchissements de seuils dans le capital et les droits de vote des sociétés dont les actions sont admises sur un marché réglementé*, RTDF (2007), 146–151; Merkner, Andreas and Sustmann, Marco, *Vorbei mit dem unbemerkten Anschleichen an börsennotierte Unternehmen?*, 13 NZG (2010), 681–688; Meo, Giorgo, in: Bessone, Mario (ed.), *Trattato di diritto privato*, Vol. XVII, Le Società di capitali (2008); Mikkelson, Wayne H. and Ruback, Richard S., *An Empirical Analysis of the Interfirm Equity Investment Process*, 14 J. Fin. Econ. (1985), 523–553; Möllers, Thomas M.J. and Holzner, Florian, *Die Offenlegungspflichten des Risikobegrenzungsgesetzes (§ 27 II WpHG-E)*, 11 NZG (2008), 166–172; Muñoz Pérez, Ana F., *El concierto como presupuesto de la OPA obligatoria*, La Ley, (2007); Neye, Hans-Werner, *Gemeinschaftsrecht und Recht der verbundenen Unternehmen*, 24 ZGR (1995), 191–207; Omaggio, Alexandre, *Ordonnance du 30 janvier 2009: regard critique sur la réforme relative aux déclarations de franchissement de seuils et aux déclarations d'intentions*, Dr. sociétés April (2009), 49–53; Pietrancosta, Alain, *Disclosure of Major Holdings in Listed Companies*, in: Tountopoulos, Vassilios and Veil, Rüdiger (eds.), Transparency of Stock Corporations in Europe (2019), 109–128; Piselli, Diego, *La validità e l`efficacia dei patti parasociali dopo la riforma societaria*, 2 Le Società (2009), 197–204; Prechtl, Felix, *Kapitalmarktrechtliche Beteiligungspublizität* (2010); Querfurth, Jan, *§ 27a WpHG und die Folgen eines Verstoßes*, 42 WM (2008), 1957–1963; Reburn, James P., *A Note on Firm Size, Information Availability and Market Reactions to US Stock Ownership Reporting Announcements*, 21 J. Bus. Fin. & Account (1994), 445–455; Rechtschaffen, Alan N., *Capital Markets, Derivatives and the Law* (2019); Ringe, Wolf-Georg, *Die Neuregelung des Internationalen Kapitalmarktpublizitätsrechts durch die Neufassung der Transparenz-RL*, 22 AG (2007), 809–815; Schanz, Kay-Michael, *Schaeffler/Continental: Umgehung von Meldepflichten bei öffentlichen Übernahmen durch Einsatz von derivativen Finanzinstrumenten*, 35 DB (2008), 1899–1905; Scherr, Frederick C. et al., *Returns to Target Shareholders from Initial Purchases of Common Shares: A Multivariate Analysis*, 32 Q. J. Bus. & Econ. (1993), 66–78; Schiessl, Maximilian, *Beteiligungsaufbau mittels Cash-settled Total Return Equity Swaps—Neue Modelle und Einführung von Meldepflichten*, Der Konzern (2009), 291–299; Schmidt, Dominique, *Action de concert et dépôt d'une offre publique obligatoire*, RDBF (2008), 56–70; Schneider, Uwe H., *Der kapitalmarktrechtliche Strategie- und Mittelherkunftsbericht—oder: wem dient das Kapitalmarktrecht?*, in: Habersack, Mathias et al. (eds.), Festschrift für Gerd Nobbe zum 65. Geburtstag (2009), 741–754; Schneider, Uwe H. and Anzinger, Heribert M., *Umgehung und missbräuchliche Gestaltungen im Kapitalmarktrecht oder: Brauchen wir eine § 42 AO entsprechende Vorschrift im Kapitalmarktrecht?*, 1 ZIP (2009), 1–10; Schockenhoff, Martin and Schumann, Alexander, *Acting in Concert—Geklärte und ungeklärte Fragen*, 34 ZGR (2005), 568–610; Schockenhoff, Martin and Wagner, Eric, *Zum Begriff des 'acting in concert'*, 10 NZG (2008), 361–368; Schouten, Michael C., *The Case for Mandatory Ownership Disclosure*, 15 Stan. J. L. Bus. & Fin. (2009), 127–182; Segain, Hubert, *Les franchissements de seuil: évolutions récentes*, RTDF (2008), 7; Seibt, Christoph and Wollenschläger, Bernd, *Europäisierung des Transparenzregimes: Der Vorschlag der Europäischen Kommission zur Revision der Transparenzrichtlinie*, 9 AG (2012), 305–315; Seligman, Joel, *The Historical Need for a Mandatory Corporate Disclosure System*, 9 J. Corp. Law (1983), 1–61; Tautges, Marco, *Empty Voting und Hidden (Morphable) Ownership* (2015);

Teichmann, Christoph and Epe, Daniel, *Neuer Regelungsansatz in der kapitalmarktrechtlichen Beteiligungstransparenz: Generalklauseln statt Fallgruppen-Lösung*, 32 WM (2010), 1477–1483; Uzan, Carole, *Des projets de réforme en matière de franchissement de seuils, de déclarations d'intention et d'offre obligatoire*, Bull. Joly Bourse (2008), 530–536; Veil, Rüdiger, *Der Schutz des verständigen Anlegers durch Publizität und Haftung im europäischen und nationalen Kapitalmarktrecht*, 18 ZBB (2006), 162–171; Veil, Rüdiger, *Stimmrechtszurechnungen aufgrund von Abstimmungsvereinbarungen gemäß § 22 Abs. 2 WpHG und § 30 Abs. 2 WpÜG*, in: Bitter, Georg et al. (eds.), *Festschrift für Karsten Schmidt zum 70. Geburtstag* (2009), 1645–1664; Veil, Rüdiger and Dolff, Christian, *Kapitalmarktrechtliche Mitteilungspflichten des Treuhänders. Grundsätze und Grenzen der Zurechnung von Stimmrechtsanteilen nach § 22 WpHG*, 11 AG (2010), 385–391; Veil, Rüdiger, *Enforcement of Capital Markets Law in Europe—Observations from a Civil Law Country*, 11 EBOR (2010), 409–422; Veil, Rüdiger, *Wie viel 'Enforcement' ist notwendig? Zur Reform des Instrumentenmix bei der Sanktionierung kapitalmarktrechtlicher Mitteilungspflichten gemäß §§ 21 ff. WpHG*, 175 ZHR (2011), 83–109; Veil, Rüdiger, *Acting in Concert in Capital Markets and Takeover Law—Need for a Further Harmonisation?*, 1 RTDF (2013), 33–37; Veil, Rüdiger, *The Reform of the Transparency Regime in European Capital Markets Laws*, 10 ECFR 2013, 18–44; Veil, Rüdiger, *Beteiligungstransparenz im Kapitalmarktrecht. Rechtsentwicklungen und Reformperspektiven*, 177 ZHR (2013), 427–446; Veil, Rüdiger et al., *Today's or yesterday's news? Eine empirische Analyse von Stimmrechtsmitteilungen gemäß §§ 21 ff. WpHG und Schlussfolgerungen für die Kapitalmarktregulierung*, 44 ZGR (2015), 709–753; Witt, Carl-Heinz, *Übernahmen von Aktiengesellschaften und Transparenz der Beteiligungsverhältnisse* (1998); Zabala, Erasun, *Urteilsanmerkung zu CA Paris, 1re ch., sect. H, 24 juin 2008, no 2007/21048, Gecina SA*, Bull. Joly Bourse (2008), 389–397; Zetzsche, Dirk A., *Hidden Ownership in Europe: BAFin's Decision in Schaeffler v. Continental*, 10 EBOR (2009), 115–147; Zetzsche, Dirk A., *Against Mandatory Disclosure of Economic—Only Positions Referenced to Shares of European Issuers—Twenty Arguments against CESR Proposal*, 11 EBOR (2010), 231–252; Zimmermann, Martin, *Die kapitalmarktrechtliche Beteiligungstransparenz nach dem Risikobegrenzungsgesetz*, 2 ZIP (2009), 57–64.

I. Introduction

1. Regulatory Aims

The transparency regarding major holdings was high on the agenda of the European legislature from a very early point in time. It was regarded as necessary in order to ensure an equal level of investor protection throughout the Community and to make for greater interpenetration of the Member States' transferrable securities markets, thus helping to establish a true European capital market.[1] The **Transparency Directive** (TD) from 1988 therefore obliged Member States to develop rules on disclosure and information to be published when a major holding in a listed company is acquired or disposed of.[2] However, it only

---

[1] Cf. Recitals of Council Directive 88/627/EEC of 12 December 1988 on the information to be published when a major holding in a listed company is acquired or disposed of, OJ L 348/62, 17 December 1988 (Transparency Directive I); on its historical background see R. Veil § 1 para. 9.

[2] The first directive to contain provisions on this was the Council Directive 79/279/EEC of 5 March 1979 coordinating the conditions for the admission of securities to official stock exchange listing, OJ L 66/21, 16 March 1979 coordinating the conditions for the admission of securities to an official stock exchange listing (cf. R. Veil § 1 para. 6), obligating companies to inform the public by including information in the prospectus on changes in the structure of major holdings (ownership and shares) of its capital compared to former publications.

contained a non-cohesive collection of thresholds, obliging the Member States to ensure that a person or legal entity notifies the company and the competent authority if, following the acquisition or disposal of a holding in a company, the proportion of voting rights held by them reaches, exceeds or falls below the thresholds of 10%, 20%, 1/3, 50% and 2/3.

2 Most of the Member States at that time did not regard this level of information as sufficient and provided additional thresholds in their national laws.[3] It was therefore not surprising that the European legislature saw the need to amend the former European provisions by adopting Directive 2004/106/EC[4] and establishing a 'more securities market directed transparency regime'.[5] The directive obliged Member States to introduce additional thresholds and to provide transparency rules for financial instruments resulting in an entitlement to acquire shares to which voting rights are attached. These rules were intended to **enhance investor protection** and **market efficiency** by enabling shareholders to have full knowledge of changes in the voting structure when acquiring or disposing of shares.[6] The background to this is the importance of the criteria of shareholder composition and the changes regarding major holdings for the investors' decisions, especially for domestic and foreign institutional investors, and the large influence these criteria have on the price of shares. Knowing the identity of major shareholders provides investors with important information, such as allowing them to assess the possibility of conflicts of interest.[7] Furthermore, the reform 2004 was to 'enhance effective control of share issuers and overall market transparency of important capital movements'.[8]

3 Additionally, offering market participants, and especially investors, the latest and the most extensive information provides a **transparency** that **counteracts** the **abuse** of (potential) **inside information**. The general knowledge of the volume of shares freely negotiable and the identity of major shareholders reduces information asymmetries. Thus, the system of disclosure of major shareholdings—similar to the obligation of disclosure of inside information[9]—reinforces the provisions on market abuse.[10]

4 However, only a few years after the TD was transposed in the Member States, it became apparent that the disclosure obligations were being circumvented by market participants. Financial innovation led to the creation of new types of financial instruments that gave investors economic exposure to companies, the disclosure of which was not provided for in the TD 2004: 'Those instruments could be used to secretly acquire stocks in companies,

---

[3] Cf. Commission, Proposal for a Directive of the European Parliament and of the Council of 26 March 2003 on the harmonisation of transparency requirements with regard to information about issuers whose securities are admitted to trading on a regulated market and amending Directive 2001/34/EC, 26 March 2003, COM(2003) 138 final, p. 18 (only three out of 15 Member States limited themselves to the level of transparency provided for by the Transparency Directive I).

[4] Directive 2004/109/EC of the European Parliament and of the Council of 15 December 2004 on the harmonisation of transparency requirements in relation to information about issuers whose securities are admitted to trading in a regulated market and amending Directive 2001/34/EC, OJ L 390, 31 December 2004, p. 38–57 (Transparency Directive II), hereafter simply referred to as Transparency Directive (TD).

[5] Cf. COM(2003) 138 final (fn. 3), p. 18.

[6] Cf. Recital 1 TD.

[7] COM(2003) 138 final (fn. 3), p. 21; also F. Prechtl, *Kapitalmarktrechtliche Beteiligungspublizität*, 31.

[8] Cf. Recital 18 TD.

[9] See R. Veil § 19 para. 1–6.

[10] F. Prechtl, *Kapitalmarktrechtliche Beteiligungspublizität*, 32.

which could result in market abuse and give a false and misleading picture of economic ownership of publicly listed companies.'[11] The European legislator therefore reformed the TD in 2013[12] by, inter alia, extending the disclosure obligations to all instruments with similar economic effect to holding shares and entitlements to acquire shares. This was to ensure that **issuers** and **investors** have **full knowledge** of the **structure** of **corporate ownership**.

Today, the regime is mainly shaped by purposes of capital markets law.[13] The disclosure of changes in voting rights is justified by the assumption that shareholders exert influence on business policy from a certain shareholding. The information on changes in the shareholder base is therefore indirectly relevant for the fundamental value of the company.

> This is impressively confirmed by empirical research.[14] For US law,[15] several research papers show that statistically significant abnormal returns can be observed when changes in shareholdings are published.[16] Similar results can be found for the German capital market. The evaluation of 3,645 notifications on exceeding thresholds shows statistically significant abnormal returns of 0.42% on the day of the event. In the case of the 116 notifications on exceeding the 15% threshold, statistically significant abnormal returns of 1.09% are observed on the event day, and in the case of 46 notifications on exceeding the 30% threshold, a statistically significant effect of 3.16% is recorded.[17]

The extension of disclosure obligations is also viewed critically in literature. If investors have to announce stakebuilding at an early stage, this will be reflected in securities prices, with the consequence that the acquisition of further voting rights and therefore company takeovers will become more expensive. The expansion of transparency rules may therefore have the effect of reducing the incentive for investors to identify undervalued companies. This affects the market for corporate control.[18]

2. Degree of Harmonisation

The TD 2004 only required a **minimum harmonisation**[19] regarding the disclosure of major shareholdings.[20] The Member States could therefore enact provisions that were more strict

---

[11] Cf. Recital 18 TD 2013.
[12] Directive 2013/50/EU of the European Parliament and of the Council of 22 October 2013 amending Directive 2004/109/EC of the European Parliament and of the Council on the harmonisation of transparency requirements in relation to information about issuers whose securities are admitted to trading on a regulated market, Directive 2003/71/EC of the European Parliament and of the Council on the prospectus to be published when securities are offered to the public or admitted to trading and Commission Directive 2007/14/EC laying down detailed rules for the implementation of certain provisions of Directive 2004/109/EC, OJ L 294/13, 6 November 2013, hereafter simply referred to as Transparency Directive 2013 (TD 2013).
[13] Cf. R. Veil, 177 ZHR (2013), 427, 428 ff.; A. Pietrancosta, in: Tountopoulos and Veil (eds.), Transparency of Stock Corporations in Europe, 109, 112 f.
[14] See on the methodology of event studies R. Veil § 19 para. 12.
[15] See para. 106.
[16] Cf. W. Mikkelson and R. Ruback, 14 J. Fin. Econ. (1985), 523, 532–543: price increase of 2.88% after the disclosure of Schedule 13D; J. Reburn, 21 J. Bus. Fin. & Account (1994), 445: 2.46%; F. Scherr et al., 32(4) Quarterly J. Bus. & Econ. (1993), 66, 72–73: 2.49%; D. Choi, 26 J. Fin. Quant. Analysis (1991), 391, 396: 2.2%; J. Brav et al., 63 J. Fin. (2008), 1729, 1755: 2%.
[17] Cf. R. Veil et al., 44 ZGR (2015), 709, 717–733.
[18] Cf. N. Elster, Europäisches Kapitalmarktrecht, 22.
[19] On the concept of minimum harmonisation see R. Veil § 3 para. 21.
[20] Cf. F. Prechtl, *Kapitalmarktrechtliche Beteiligungspublizität*, 22; R. Veil, in: FS Schmidt, 1645, 1664.

than those provided for in the TD.²¹ Some Member States took advantage of this possibility, introducing thresholds as low as 2% and reducing the intervals between the thresholds provided for by the TD. They also developed stricter provisions on the attribution of voting rights attached to shares belonging to a third party. Some of these measures, such as the introduction of stricter national provisions on acting in concert, were aimed in particular at disclosing the influence of financial investors. These measures were criticised by some as they raise the price of takeovers, thus allegedly restricting the market for corporate control.²²

9   In fact, a harmonised regime for notification of major holdings of voting rights, especially regarding the aggregation of holdings of shares with holdings of financial instruments, improves legal certainty, enhances transparency and reduces the administrative burden for cross-border investors. The TD 2013 therefore introduced the concept of **maximum harmonisation**. Member States are no longer 'allowed to adopt more stringent rules than those provided for in Directive 2004/109/EC regarding the calculation of notification thresholds, aggregation of holdings of voting rights attaching to shares with holdings of voting rights relating to financial instruments, and exemptions from the notification requirements.'²³

10 However, the TD 2013 does not strictly adhere to the concept of maximum harmonisation due to 'existing differences in ownership concentration in the Union, and the differences in company laws in the Union'. Member States therefore 'continue to be allowed to set both lower and additional thresholds for notification of holdings of voting rights, and to require equivalent notifications in relation to thresholds based on capital holdings. Moreover, Member States [...] continue to be allowed to set stricter obligations than those provided for in Directive 2004/109/EC with regard to the content (such as disclosure of shareholders' intentions), the process and the timing for notification, and to be able to require additional information regarding major holdings not provided for by Directive 2004/109/EC. In particular, Member States [are] able to continue to apply laws, regulations or administrative provisions adopted in relation to takeover bids, merger transactions and other transactions affecting the ownership or control of companies supervised by the authorities.'²⁴

3. Practical Relevance

11 In legal practice, the obligation to publish changes in major shareholdings plays an important role. The numbers of publications in the different Member States, however, vary considerably. The number of notifications has declined in Germany in recent years, despite the extension of disclosure obligations. This is probably also due to the fact that the number of issuers has decreased (from 1,075 in 2007 to 873 in 2011 and to 513 in 2019).²⁵ In Germany, BaFin received 5,929 notifications in 2011 (2010: 5,439; 2009: 5,711; 2008: 8,242;

---

[21] Cf. Art. 3(1) TD 2004. H. Fleischer and K. Schmolke, 13 NZG (2010), 1241, 1244 ff. recommend a maximum harmonisation of the disclosure regime de lege ferenda.

[22] Cf. N. Elster, *Europäisches Kapitalmarktrecht*, 22.

[23] Cf. Recital 12 TD 2013.

[24] Cf. Recital 12 TD. The 'laws, regulations or administrative provisions' are mainly the national provisions on acting in concert. See para. 41–64.

[25] Data according to BaFin annual reports. The figures relate to companies that were listed on a domestic regulated market.

2007: 9,134);²⁶ in 2019, investors notified only 3,840 changes of voting rights. In other countries, the number has increased. In Austria, a total of 107 notifications of significant participations were submitted in 2011 (2010: 124; 2009: 139; 2008: 177; 2007: 123).²⁷ In 2019, the number increased to 373 notifications.²⁸ In Spain, 638 notifications were issued in 2011, 13% more than in 2010; they concerned 111 listed companies.²⁹ In 2019, 1591 notifications were filed for 107 listed companies.³⁰ In France, 866 notifications were filed in 2011 (747 in 2010).³¹ The AMF's annual report does not provide any information for 2019.

II. European Concepts of Regulation

1. Legal Sources

The **Transparency Directive** (TD)—the basic Level 1-act—defines the general principles underlying the harmonisation of transparency obligations and requires the Member States to introduce disclosure obligations. The European Commission enacted an implementing directive on Level 2 of the Lamfalussy Process in order to ensure a uniform application of these provisions, mainly containing procedural rules.³² Furthermore, it enacted the Delegated Regulation (EU) No. 2015/761 of 17 December 2014 with regard to certain regulatory technical standards on major holdings as a further Level 2 act.³³ 12

So far, ESMA has not published 'Guidelines' in accordance with Article 16 ESMA Regulation that could be used as a necessary interpretational help regarding abstract legal concepts. In particular, the provisions on the attribution of voting rights attached to shares belonging to a third party contain various problems regarding their interpretation. As several Member States have adopted some of the attribution rules one-to-one in their national laws, recommendations on the interpretation would prove very helpful. ESMA has, however, only issued an indicative list of financial instruments that are subject to notification requirements according to the TD (ESMA/2015/1598).³⁴ Furthermore, ESMA's Q&A Transparency Directive of 22.10.2015 (ESMA/2015/1595) plays an important role in establishing supervisory convergence. Both papers are legally non-binding instruments of ESMA. 13

---

²⁶ Cf. BaFin, Annual Report 2011, p. 213; W. Bayer and T. Hoffmann, AG (2013), R 143 ff.
²⁷ Cf. FMA, Annual Report 2011, p. 113.
²⁸ Cf. FMA, Annual Report 2019, p. 100.
²⁹ Cf. CNMV, Annual Report 2011, p. 133.
³⁰ Cf. CNMV, Annual Report 2011, p. 154.
³¹ Cf. AMF, Annual Report 2011, p. 103.
³² Commission Directive 2007/14/EC of 8 March 2007 laying down detailed rules for the implementation of certain provisions of Directive 2004/109/EC on the harmonisation of transparency requirements in relation to information about issuers whose securities are admitted to trading on a regulated market, OJ L 69, 9 March 2007, p. 27–36; amended by Directive 2013/50/EU.
³³ Commission Delegated Regulation (EU) No. 2015/761 of 17 December 2014 supplementing Directive 2004/109/EC of the European Parliament and of the Council with regard to certain regulatory technical standards on major holdings, OJ L 120, 13 May 2015, p. 2–5.
³⁴ ESMA, Indicative list of financial instruments that are subject to notification requirements according to Art. 13(1b) of the revised Transparency Directive, 22 October 2015, ESMA/2015/1598.

2. Scope of Application

14 The TD 'establishes requirements in relation to the disclosure of periodic and ongoing information about issuers whose securities are already admitted to trading on a regulated market situated or operating within a Member State'.[35] It follows that the directive's scope of application is restricted to **securities trading** on **regulated markets**.[36] The Member States need not apply these provisions to their non-regulated markets, an example being the Open Market in Germany or the Alternative Investment Market in Italy, both organised as an MTF.[37]

15 The TD is addressed to the '**home Member States**'. These must ensure that a notification on the acquisition or disposal of major holdings takes place and the information contained in the notification is then published. The term 'home Member State' is defined in the directive. For issuers of shares incorporated in the Community the term refers to the Member State in which the issuer has its registered office.[38] The location of the head office is irrelevant.[39] The notification obligations regarding changes in major holdings also apply to third-country investors as the TD makes no restrictions regarding the origin of the person acquiring or disposing of shares with voting rights.[40] An investor from China or the United States must therefore notify the issuer as must an investor from an EU Member State.

16 *Example*: For a French public limited company (*Société Anonyme*) that has its registered office in France the home Member State is therefore France. Any shareholder thus has to fulfil the French provisions on disclosure when acquiring or disposing of shares—irrespective of from where it may come. These will even apply if the issuer has transferred its administrative head office to Belgium—provided this is permissible under French company law.

17 Where the issuer is incorporated in a third country, the issuer may choose the Member State where its securities are to be admitted to trading on a regulated market. This choice remains valid until the issuer chooses a new home Member State and has disclosed the choice.[41]

3. Disclosure Obligations under the TD

18 The TD requires 'information about major holdings', such as the provision on the '**notification of the acquisition or disposal of major holdings**' in Article 9 which can be regarded as the core of the disclosure system for major holdings. The provision defines to whom the notification obligation applies and which procedures are subject to notification. Article 10 TD extends the notification obligations of Article 9 to further cases in which the obligation 'shall apply', ie cases in which someone is not owner of the shares but is nonetheless entitled to acquire or to dispose of the shares or may exercise voting rights belonging to a third party.

---

[35] Cf. Art. 1(1) TD.
[36] The term 'regulated market' is defined in Art. 2(1)(c) TD by referring to the MiFID. For more details on this concept see R. Veil § 7 para. 11–15.
[37] See R. Veil § 7 para. 16–18.
[38] Cf. Art. 2(1)(i) first indent TD.
[39] Cf. W.-G. Ringe, 22 AG (2007), 810–811; F. Prechtl, *Kapitalmarktrechtliche Beteiligungspublizität*, 20–21.
[40] Cf. F. Prechtl, *Kapitalmarktrechtliche Beteiligungspublizität*, 19.
[41] Cf. Art. 2(1)(i) second indent TD.

Without this addition the general rules on notification could easily be avoided. Hereafter, the provisions in Articles 9 and 10 will therefore be regarded as an entity. Both articles aim to ensure transparency regarding any changes in major holdings (voting rights).

A further notification obligation required by the TD concerns situations in which a person has only the possibility of influencing voting rights. According to Article 13 TD, the obligation to **notify** the **issuer** applies to such **financial instruments** (i) that **give** the **holder** a **right to acquire** or the **discretion** as to his right to **acquire shares** and (ii) to **financial instruments with similar economic effect**. 19

4. Further Disclosure Obligations

The rules regarding changes of major shareholding are based on the understanding that changes in the voting rights are of relevance for the shareholders' decisions to invest or divest. Therefore, the issuer must be notified of this information in order that it can make it public. This can also be required by other provisions, such as the provisions of the MAR, which oblige the issuers of financial instruments to inform the public as soon as possible of inside information which directly concerns them.[42] Whether this **ad hoc disclosure obligation** also applies to changes in major holdings was not decided by the European legislature. The TD does not define its relationship to the MAR. With respect to their divergent purposes, it is assumed that neither the regime on transparency of major holdings nor the regime on ad hoc disclosure generally has priority over the other.[43] An issuer can therefore be obliged to publish immediately the acquisition or disposal of major shareholdings if this fact should be regarded as price relevant and therefore has to be considered as inside information in accordance with Article 7(1) MAR.[44] The disclosure obligation pursuant to Article 17 MAR may also arise in the case of changes in shareholdings,[45] as information only indirectly related to the fundamental value of the company may also be likely to have a significant effect on the price of the security.[46] 20

Furthermore, in the case of an acquisition of a shareholding, the requirements of a notification obligation according to Article 19 MAR (**directors' dealings**) may be fulfilled. In principle, every acquisition of shares is subject to notification. However, the obligation only applies to managers and their relatives. 21

France and Germany, following the example of the United States (see para. 106), provide for a further disclosure obligation about the intent of certain investors. Both Member States require an investor to **disclose** her **intentions** underlying the **purchase of voting rights**, such as the plan to acquire control or at least further shares or whether she intends to exert influence on the appointment or removal of board members. The issuer then has to publish this information. European law so far does not oblige the Member States to introduce such provisions. 22

---

[42] Art. 17(1) MAR. See R. Veil § 19 para. 24 ff.
[43] Cf. H. Hirte, in: Hirte and von Bülow (eds.), *Kölner Kommentar zum WpHG*, § 21 para. 56 ff.
[44] On this aspect of inside information see R. Veil § 14 para. 53 ff.
[45] See R. Veil § 19 para. 21.
[46] Cf. Klöhn, in Klöhn (ed.), MAR, Art. 7 para. 372.

III. Disclosure Obligations on Changes in Voting Rights

1. Notification

23 The TD prescribes the introduction of notification obligations toward the issuer on changes in voting rights. The home Member States[47] must ensure that a shareholder notifies the issuer of the proportion of voting rights it holds as a result of an acquisition or disposal where that proportion reaches, exceeds or falls below the thresholds of 5, 10, 15, 20, 25, 30, 50 and 75% (cf. Article 9(1) TD). These thresholds are binding for the Member States. A Member State can, however, refrain from applying the 30%, respectively the 75% threshold, if a threshold of one-third, respectively two-thirds, of all voting rights is applied in lieu (cf. Article 9(3) TD). Member States may provide for further notification thresholds. As a result, the legal situation in the EU is disparate.

(a) Prerequisites

24 Any **person** with **legal capacity**, ie natural persons and legal entities as well as partnerships with legal capacity, may be required to file a notification. As a rule, it can be stated that a notification obligation not only ensues from the **acquisition** but also from the **disposal** of **shares**. The TD restricts the obligation to transactions that are effective. As to when this is the case is not defined in the TD and must therefore be determined in accordance with the civil law of the respective Member State.

25 Shareholders are also required to 'notify the issuer of the proportion of voting rights, where that proportion reaches, exceeds or falls below the thresholds [...] as a result of events changing the breakdown of voting rights' (Article 9(2) TD). This provision refers in particular to preference shares without voting rights. In a number of Member States, shares which carry the benefit of a cumulative preference right with respect to the distribution of profits may be issued without voting rights. If the preference dividend is not paid or not paid in full in any given year and the shortfall is not made up within the following year, the preference shareholders are given a voting right until payment of the shortfall. If the preference shareholder reaches or exceeds one of the thresholds of the directive due to this exceptional voting right, it must also notify the issuer thereof. Furthermore, a disclosure obligation exists if **shares** are **transferred** to another person by way of **universal succession** (inheritance, merger, demerger). Mere changes in the composition of the share of voting rights (example: voting rights were previously attributed to the person obliged to notify pursuant to Article 10 TD; the shares are transferred to her, so that she is entitled to voting rights from her own shares) do not trigger a duty to file a notification.[48]

(b) Thresholds

26 Since the reform in 2004 the European law provides a non-cohesive system of notification obligations. The first notification threshold only begins at 5% of the voting rights, thereafter

---

[47] On the concept of 'home Member States' see above para. 15.
[48] BaFin, Emittentenleitfaden (issuer guideline), Module B, p. 18; OLG Hamburg of 14.6.2012 – 11 AktG 1/12, AG 2012, 639, 642.

rising at 5% intervals up to 30% of the voting rights. The interval between 30% and 50% was further broken down by many Member States as this was considered too large an interval.

Several Member States, whose national company laws allow for corporate restructuring with a two-thirds majority vote, have made use of the possibility to provide alternative thresholds as described in Article 9(3) TD. This is, for *example*, the case in Sweden. Additionally, some Member States—notably Germany,[49] Spain,[50] Italy[51]—and the United Kingdom,[52] but not, however, Austria and Sweden—have introduced an initial threshold at 3% of all voting rights.[53] This reflects the influence institutional investors do have in companies with dispersed ownership structures.[54] 27

Yet most Member States have not only reduced the lowest threshold level, but also provided for additional thresholds in their national capital markets laws. The most stringent rules can be found in the former Member State United Kingdom where any changes in voting rights of more than 1% (acquisition or disposal) must be disclosed from a level of 3% upwards.[55] Italy and Spain have also developed a cohesive system of notification thresholds. The notification obligations in these states begin at 5% and continue in 5% steps up to the threshold of 50%. Furthermore, most Member States—amongst others France, Italy, Austria, Sweden and Spain, though not, however, Germany—require notification should 90% or 95% of all voting rights or shares be held. This results from the fact that in these states such shareholdings enable a squeeze-out of small shareholders and these should be notified thereof. 28

Furthermore, it is noteworthy that France and Sweden, with other Member States, refer not only to changes in the voting rights but also to the proportion of capital,[56] since the stock corporation laws in these countries permit multiple voting rights.[57] 29

As the TD only requires a minimum harmonisation regarding the thresholds triggering the notification obligations on acquisition or disposal of major holdings,[58] so-called 'gold plating' is legally permissible and widespread throughout the European Union. France[59] and Austria[60] follow the concept that an **issuer** must have the possibility to define **further thresholds** regarding voting rights or the proportion of capital in its **articles of association**. This concept is also consistent with the TD which gives Member States freedom regarding the implementation. In France, the possibility of providing thresholds in 30

---

[49] Cf. § 33(1) WpHG.
[50] Cf. Art. 23(1) RD 1362/2007.
[51] Cf. Art. 120(2) TUF. Moreover, Art. 120(2-bis) TUF allows Consob temporarily to reduce this threshold should this be necessary for protection of the investor and the market for corporate control. However, this only applies to companies with a wide circle of investors.
[52] Cf. DTR 5.1.2 FCA Handbook. However, in the case of a non-UK issuer, other thresholds apply.
[53] In Austria the initial threshold is at 4% of the voting rights. Cf. § 130(1) BoerseG. In Sweden, the initial threshold is at 5% of the voting rights or the proportion of capital. Cf. Kapitel 4, § 5(1)(1) LHF.
[54] Cf. Begr. RegE Transparenzrichtlinie-Umsetzungsgesetz (TUG), BT-Drucks. 16/2498, p. 34 (explanatory notes); on ownership structures in Italy cf. Consob, Report on corporate governance of Italian listed companies, 2020.
[55] The thresholds only applies to 'UK Issuers'. Cf. R. Veil and M. Wundenberg, *Englisches Kapitalmarktrecht*, 125.
[56] Cf. for France Art. 233-7.1 C. com. and for Sweden Kapitel 4, § 5(1)(1) LHF.
[57] Cf. R. Veil and F. Walla, *Schwedisches Kapitalmarktrecht*, 90.
[58] See above para. 8–10.
[59] Cf. Art. 233-7.3 C. com.
[60] Cf. § 130(1) BörseG.

the articles of association plays an important role: Most of the companies listed in the CAC 40, ie the French stock market index, have provided specific thresholds in their articles of associations, the lowest of which start at 0.5%.[61] And even beyond the 5% threshold defined by European law several French issuers have set down further thresholds in their articles of association.[62] Should these additional thresholds defined in the articles of association be exceeded, only the company itself needs to be notified, not, however, the capital market.[63]

31 Determining the exact proportion of the voting rights may be difficult due to various technical questions in this context. The most important of these has been decided upon by the European legislature in the TD: the voting rights shall be calculated on the basis of all the shares to which voting rights are attached[64] even if the exercise thereof is suspended.[65] Thus, even a suspension of voting rights will not prevent them from being taken into consideration when determining the total amount of voting rights.[66]

(c) Exemptions from the Notification Obligation

32 The notification on changes in major holdings is not always necessary. In cases in which the acquirer or the transferor does not exercise her voting rights such notification is superfluous. For this reason, the obligations described in the TD are not applicable (i) to **shares acquired** for the **sole purpose of clearing and settling** within the usual short settlement cycle of a maximum length of three trading days,[67] and (ii) to **custodians** holding shares in their custodian capacity provided such custodians can only exercise the voting rights attached to such shares under instructions given in writing or by electronic means.[68]

33 A further exemption has been provided for so-called **market makers**, ie persons 'holding themselves out on the financial markets on a continuous basis as being willing to deal on own account by buying and selling financial instruments against their proprietary capital at prices defined by them'.[69] Market makers ensure the markets' liquidity and in general are not interested in exercising their voting rights, thus justifying their in many ways privileged position: a market maker's acquisition or disposal of a major holding which reaches or crosses the 5% threshold is not subject to the notification obligation of Article 9 TD provided the market maker is authorised by his home Member State.[70] Furthermore, the exemption only

---

[61] Cf. F. Grillier and H. Segain, RTDF (2007), 20, 24.
[62] Cf. R. Veil and P. Koch, *Französisches Kapitalmarktrecht*, 81–82.
[63] Seen critically by P.-H. Conac, Rev. soc. (2009), 477, 485, 499–500.
[64] At the end of each calendar month during which an increase or decrease of the total number of voting rights has occurred the issuer is required to disclose to the public the total number of voting rights and capital (cf. Art. 15 TD).
[65] Art. 9(1) TD.
[66] The reasons for this can be multiple, for example a shareholding losing the rights attributed to his shares due to the failure to comply with his notification duties. On this sanction see below para. 123 f.
[67] Cf. Art. 9(4) TD.
[68] Art. 9(4) TD.
[69] Cf. Art. 2(1)(n) TD. On this see also R. Veil § 9 para. 8.
[70] Those Member States that have introduced lower thresholds (of 2% or 3%) have extended these exceptions to these initial thresholds.

applies if the market maker does not intervene in the management of the issuer concerned or exert influence on the issuer to buy such shares or back the share price.[71]

> *Example*: A market maker acquires 6% of an issuer's voting rights. If the conditions of the exempting provision are fulfilled, it is not obliged to notify the issuer about the fact that it has exceeded the 5% threshold. It must, however, immediately inform the supervisory authority that regarding the respective shares it is acting as a market maker. If it acquires another 5% of the voting rights, it must notify the issuer, as it then exceeds the 10% threshold.

34

Finally, a disclosure obligation does not apply to voting rights held in the **trading book** of a credit institution or investment firm, provided that (i) the voting rights held in the trading book do not exceed 5% and (ii) the voting right attached to shares held in the trading book are not exercised or otherwise used to intervene in the management of the issuer.[72]

35

In practice, the calculation of the thresholds for the market making and trading book exemptions give rise to a number of difficult interpretational question. In order to ensure consistent application of the principle of aggregation of all holdings of financial instruments subject to notification requirements and to prevent a misleading representation of how many financial instruments related to an issuer are held by an entity benefiting from those exemptions, Commission Delegated Regulation (EU) No. 2015/761 requires to aggregate voting rights relating to shares with voting rights related to financial instruments. Furthermore, the Delegated Regulation stipulates that in the case of a group of companies the thresholds should be calculated at group level.

36

(d) Procedures Subject to Notification

The notification to the issuer must be effected **promptly**, but not later than within **four trading days**.[73] Germany and Spain adopted this time limit, whilst Austria reduced it to only two days.[74] The notification must contain the resulting situation in terms of voting rights, the date on which the threshold was reached or crossed and the identity of the shareholder.[75] If the voting rights attributed are attached to shares held by another member of the same corporate group,[76] the notification must also contain the chain of controlled undertakings through which voting rights are effectively held.[77]

37

In practice, it is especially important that the TD allows the notification to be made by the parent undertaking (P). In these cases, an undertaking is exempt from making the required notification.[78] If, for example, the subsidiary company (S) holds 5% of the voting rights, P can make the notification, thus releasing S from its legal obligation.

38

---

[71] Art. 9(5) TD and Art. 6 Commission Directive 2007/14/EC of 8 March 2007 laying down detailed rules for the implementation of certain provisions of Directive 2004/109/EC on the harmonisation of transparency requirements in relation to information about issuers whose securities are admitted to trading on a regulated market, OJ L 69/27, 9 March 2007.
[72] Cf. Art. 9(6) TD.
[73] Art. 12(2) TD. Transparency Directive I of 12 December 1988 still prescribed the notification to take place within seven calendar days.
[74] Cf. § 131(1) BoerseG.
[75] Art. 12(1)(a), (c) and (d) TD.
[76] On this see below para. 75–80.
[77] Art. 12(1)(b) TD.
[78] Art. 12(3) TD.

2. Publication

39 Upon receipt of the notification, but no later than three trading days thereafter, the **issuer** is obligated to **make public** all the **information** contained in the notification.[79] The home Member State may exempt issuers from this requirement if the information contained in the notification is made public by its competent supervisory authority.[80] France has exercised this possibility, now requiring that the information on changes of major holdings be filed with the AMF no later than four days after the shareholding threshold has been crossed.[81] The AMF must ensure that the information is made public within an additional three trading days.[82]

40 The disclosure must take place in a manner that guarantees **fast access** to the information on **a non-discriminatory basis**. In particular, the home Member State must ensure that the issuer uses such media as may reasonably be relied upon for the effective dissemination of information to the public throughout the EU,[83] such as news agencies, print media and Internet pages regarding the financial market.[84]

3. Attribution of Voting Rights

(a) Regulatory Concepts

41 In accordance with Article 10 TD the notification requirements defined in Article 9 also apply to a **natural person** or **legal entity** to the extent it is **entitled** to **acquire**, to **dispose of**, or to **exercise voting rights** in any of the cases laid out in lit. a to lit. h. These cases are described relatively precisely.[85] They are not all based on common ground but rather constitute borderline cases, such as voting rights attached to shares in which that person or entity has the life interest (usufruct), where it is unclear who holds the voting rights and who is thus required to notify the issuer. Other circumstances described refer to cases in which a person has a legally secured influence on the voting rights.

42 Most of the circumstances described in Article 10 TD refer to cases in which a **person** is **attributed** the **voting rights** attached to **shares** belonging to a **third party**.[86]

43 *Example*: If a person holds 5% of the shares with voting rights attached to them and is additionally entitled to exercise voting rights as described in Article 10(a) TD to the extent of 5%, both voting rights have to be totalled, thus obliging the person to notify the issuer that his proportion of the

---

[79] Art. 12(6) TD.
[80] Art. 12(7) TD.
[81] Cf. Art. R. 233-1 C. com. and Art. 223-14.I RG AMF.
[82] Cf. Art. 223-14.VI (3) RG AMF.
[83] Art. 21(1) TD.
[84] See in more detail H. Brinckmann § 16 para. 39 ff.
[85] The TD does not contain a general clause, comparable to the US-American Rule 13d-3(b) SEA on 'the determination of beneficial ownership', preventing forms of circumvention of the provisions. Therefore, a number of interpretational questions arise in legal practice. It remains to be seen whether ESMA will issue guidelines dealing with this topic in order to ensure a consistent application across the EU.
[86] This was laid down more explicitly in the former TD of 1988 in Art. 7, which declared that 'the following voting rights shall be regarded as voting rights held by that person or entity'. Cf. N. Elster, *Europäisches Kapitalmarktrecht*, 26–27.

voting rights has reached the 10% threshold. The German legislature clarified this by making the notification requirement dependent on whether a shareholder reaches, exceeds or falls below the thresholds by purchase, sale or '*by any other means*'. The threshold is affected '*by any other means*' if voting rights of third party shares are attributed to the shareholder. Therefore, a person can also be required to notify the issuer if he holds nothing but voting rights attributed to him through third-party shares.

According to the concept of the TD the attribution of voting rights leads to a multiple notification and disclosure of voting rights. The third party remains obligated to notify the issuer on the voting rights of his shares. There is no provision according to which voting rights attributed to someone else do not have to be taken into account for the shareholder himself.[87] The capital markets are not likely to be misled, as in the case of an attribution of voting rights in a corporate group the notification must contain the chain of controlled companies.[88]

(b) Cases of an Attribution of Voting Rights

The TD lists **eight cases** in which notification requirements regarding the attribution of voting rights attached to third-party shares exist. The European Commission adopted most of these from the first TD in 1988 and the Directive 2001/34/EC,[89] taking only a few of the consultations regarding the reform into account.[90] This already indicates that it is probably now necessary to revise some of the provisions.

In the following the various cases of an attribution of voting rights will be examined in terms of the legal practice in the different Member States, who may extend some of the provisions and provide further cases of an attribution of voting rights.[91] Some Member States have made use of these regulatory powers.

(aa) Acting in Concert

Notification is required for voting rights held by a third party with whom a person or entity has concluded an agreement, which obliges them to adopt, by concerted exercise of their voting rights, a lasting common policy towards the management of the issuer in question.[92] The Commission's original proposal for a new TD from 2003 still required the parties to conclude an *effective* agreement, obliging them to adopt, by concerted exercise of the voting rights they hold, a lasting common policy towards the management of the issuer in question.[93] However, the case of 'acting in concert' was nevertheless adopted as in the Directive 2001/34/EC. An effective agreement is therefore not explicitly required.[94]

---

[87] Cf. N. Elster, *Europäisches Kapitalmarktrecht*, 27, on TD I.
[88] See para. 75.
[89] On this directive see R. Veil § 1 para. 19.
[90] Cf. COM(2003) 138 final (fn. 3), p. 25.
[91] On the mix of maximum and minimum harmonisation provided for by the TD see above para. 8–10. It is difficult to assess in which cases Member States may provide stricter rules than required by the TD. Cf. C. Seibt and B. Wollenschläger, 9 AG (2012), 305, 309–312 (arguing this would be the case for the provisions requiring the attribution of voting rights in a group of companies and for persons acting in concert).
[92] Art. 10(a) TD.
[93] Cf. COM(2003) 138 final (fn. 3), p. 25.
[94] The TD 2013 defines the term 'formal agreement' as an 'agreement which is binding under the applicable law' (cf. Art. 2(1)(q) TD. However, Art. 9(a) TD only requires an 'agreement'.

48 It needs first to be clarified which types of agreements fulfil the definition of acting in concert. The starting point for this is the wording of the provisions according to which the concerted exercise of the voting rights has to have the **aim** of **ensuring a lasting common policy regarding** the **management** of the issuer. Shareholders of stock companies incorporated in the Member States usually have no power to issue instructions addressed to the directors. However, acting in concert in the sense of the TD does not presuppose such means of influence.[95] The definition reaches further, encompassing all questions on which the shareholder has influence—albeit indirectly—eg the election of board of directors (one-tier-system) or the supervisory board (two-tier-system).[96] The requirement of a 'lasting' common policy expresses that an ad hoc coalition does not suffice.[97]

49 Furthermore, acting in concert with respect to the TD can only be assumed if the respective parties reach a **contractual agreement**. For this a minimum of two persons is required, ie an attribution of voting rights can also take place regarding an agreement between more than two people. The agreement has to refer to the concerted exercise of the voting rights.

50 An attribution of voting rights due to acting in concert results in a **reciprocal attribution of voting rights**. If, for example, A (5% of the shares) and B (10% of the shares) act in concert, A is attributed the voting rights attached to B's shares in accordance with Article 10(a) TD. At the same time, however, B is also subject to Article 10(a) TD and is attributed the voting rights attached to A's shares, thus obliging both A and B to notify the issuer that they hold voting rights of 15%.

51 The legal ground for this attribution is the influence the contracting party has over the pooled voting rights. Whilst neither of the two contracting parties will be able to prevail over the other, both have the legally ensured possibility to influence the other party's voting. This community of interest justifies the attribution of voting rights to the respective other party.[98]

(1) Legal Practice in France

52 In French law acting in concert is defined as any agreement (*accord*) on the acquisition, transfer or exercise of voting rights with the aim of a common policy regarding the management of the issuer.[99] Acting in concert has gained great attention in France on account of a few spectacular cases, the most famous being *Sacyr/Eiffage* and *Gecina*. These contain questions of takeover law and will therefore be examined in a different section of this book.[100] It is especially noteworthy that even a person who holds no shares himself must fulfil the disclosure requirements for voting rights attributed to him, as it can potentially influence the exercising of these voting rights.[101]

53 This leads to two aspects of the French rules which will be examined in more detail. The discussion centres on the question whether an agreement necessarily has to have the nature

---

[95] Cf. U. Burgard, 41 BB (1995), 2069, 2075; N. Elster, *Europäisches Kapitalmarktrecht*, 33.
[96] Cf. N. Elster, *Europäisches Kapitalmarktrecht*, 33.
[97] Cf. U. Burgard, 41 BB (1995), 2069, 2075; N. Elster, *Europäisches Kapitalmarktrecht*, 33.
[98] Cf. N. Elster, *Europäisches Kapitalmarktrecht*, 32; R. Veil, in: FS Schmidt, 1645, 1648 ff.
[99] Cf. Art. L. 233-10 C. com. and Art. L. 233-9.I.3 C. com. The provisions were amended in October 2010.
[100] See R. Veil § 39 para. 15 ff.
[101] Cf. F. Grillier and H. Segain, RTDF (2007), 20, 29.

of a contract under civil law or whether other types of agreements are also sufficient for assuming acting in concert.[102] In *Eiffage*[103] the court appears to adopt a wide understanding of the term 'agreement'.[104] The French legal literature on this question, however, claims that this statement cannot be regarded as a renunciation of the requirement of a contract.[105]

A further characteristic of French law is the wide understanding of a common company policy, including not only the company policy which the shareholders aim at influencing by making use of their voting rights in the shareholders meeting and which is defined in the TD, but also the strategy which the shareholders acting in concert pursue with the acquisition and exercise of their voting rights. The French understanding is thus that the concepts of a 'common policy' and 'control' merge.[106] Therefore, it comes as no surprise that the term 'acting in concert' is described in French as *flou*, ie vague.[107] Thus, it can only be welcomed that French law clearly defines a few cases in which an *accord* is statutorily presumed.[108]

54

(2) Legal Practice in Germany

The concept of acting in concert has attracted a lot of attention in Germany due to the fact that shareholder agreements are widespread and Germany has exceeded the European legislature's provisions, introducing much stricter rules regarding the notification requirements for acting in concert.

55

One of the main issues with respect to acting in concert is the attribution of voting rights in cases of **pooling agreements** in which certain parties of the agreement prevail over others. This can occur if the parties of the pooling agreement adopt resolutions concerning the exercise of the pooled voting rights in the issuer's general meeting by majority vote. This form of agreement raises the question whether voting rights may have to be attributed reciprocally.

56

> *Facts*:[109] A, B, C and D conclude a pooling agreement. A holds 9.0% and B 4.0% of the voting rights, C is attributed 0.5% of the voting rights attached to shares held by a subsidiary company and D has no voting rights. The BaFin is of the opinion that the voting rights must be attributed reciprocally in this case, ie all four persons must notify the company that they hold 13.5% of the voting rights, A being attributed 4.5%, B 9.5%, C 13.0% and D 13.5% of the voting rights. This understanding does not convince.[110] The purpose of the provisions on disclosure of major holdings requires an attribution of voting rights if the person is in the position to influence the voting rights attached to the shares. This is generally the case if all of the shareholders involved in the pooling agreement have the same legal possibility to exert influence on the voting rights of the other participating

57

---

[102] Cf. E. Zabala, Bull. Joly Bourse (2008), 389, 395; C. Baj, RDBF (2008), 57, 59.
[103] CA Paris, 1re ch., sect. H, 18 décembre 2008, no. 2008/07645, *Adam c/ société Sacyr Vallehermoso SA*, Bull. Joly Bourse (2009), 185 ff.
[104] Cf. Les dispositions de l'article L. 233–10 du code de commerce n'exigent pas que l'accord résulte d'un écrit, ni qu'il revête un caractère contraignant.
[105] Cf. P. Le Cannu, Rev. soc. (2008), 394, 403–404.
[106] Cf. D. Schmidt, RDBF (2008), 56.
[107] Cf. C. Goyet, *Action de concert*, 9.
[108] Cf. Art. L233-10 C. com. (presuming an acting in concert in five situations). The CA Paris ch. 5–7, 15 septembre 2011, No. 2011/00690, *Adam et al. c/ SARL Émile Hermès et al.*, concluded from the behaviour of family members that they acted in concert ('family concerted action').
[109] Cf. BaFin, Emittentenleitfaden (issuer guideline), Module B, p. 29.
[110] In more detail R. Veil, in: FS Schmidt, 1645 ff.

shareholders. However, if one or more of the shareholders of the pooling agreement can prevail over the others, the latter need not be attributed its voting rights as they do not have the legal possibility of influencing the exercise of the voting rights.

58 The provision regarding the attribution of voting rights in cases of acting in concert reaches even farther in Germany: voting rights of a third party are not only attributed to a person or legal entity with a notification obligation on the grounds of a binding voting or pooling agreement but also if the parties coordinate their behaviour with regard to the issuer, based on an agreement or in another manner, with the exception of an agreement in individual cases.[111] A person or a legal entity is also attributed the voting rights of a third party if the **parties coordinate** their **behaviour** with regard to the issuer '*in another manner*'.

59 By extending the provision to '*coordinations in another manner*' the German legislature aimed to achieve transparency regarding the influence of financial investors on issuers. Supervisory practice has shown that it is not always easy to prove that financial investors have coordinated their behaviour. The term '*coordination in another manner*', however, leads to difficulties, especially regarding the question as to how much contact between the shareholders is necessary in order to be able to assume such coordination. Legal practice generally requires a wilful cooperation with the aim of continually exercising and coordinating the rights attached to the shares. Simply following parallel business strategies, such as the restructuring of the company through a certain concept, does not suffice.[112]

60 The person with the notification obligation must coordinate her behaviour with that of the third party. This is defined in § 34(2) WpHG: Coordinated conduct requires that the notifying party or its subsidiary and the third party reach a consensus on the exercise of voting rights or collaborate in another manner with the aim of bringing about a permanent and material change in the issuer's business strategy.[113]

61 The reform of the provision in 2008 has caused many discussions.[114] Even non-binding agreements *outside* the *general shareholder meeting* can be classed as acting in concert under the new rule. However, the agreement must have the aim of bringing about a permanent and material change in the issuer's business strategy and the shareholders must follow a joint strategy, such as is the case in one-on-one consultations.[115] These describe situations in which the shareholders collaborate with the aim of exerting pressure on the management of the company to change the company's strategy.[116]

62 Other forms of collaboration outside the general meeting do not lead to an attribution of voting rights in Germany. In particular, a collaborative acquisition of shares does not suffice because it is not covered by the wording of the provision.[117]

---

[111] Cf. § 34(2) WpHG.
[112] OLG Frankfurt/Main of 25.06.2004 – WpÜG 5/03, ZIP (2004), 1309.
[113] Cf. § 34(2) WpHG.
[114] Cf. H. Fleischer, 37 ZGR (2008), 185, 196; W. König, 36 BB (2008), 1910; T. Möllers and F. Holzner, 11 NZG (2008), 166; M. Schockenhoff and E. Wagner, 10 NZG (2008), 361.
[115] Bericht Finanzausschuss (Report Finance Committee) Risikobegrenzungsgesetz, BT-Drucks. 16/9821, p. 16.
[116] Cf. C. von Bülow, in: Veil (ed.), *Übernahmerecht in Praxis und Wissenschaft*, 141, 164.
[117] Cf. E. Schockenhoff and A. Schumann, 34 ZGR (2005), 568, 582; R. Veil, in: Schmidt and Lutter (eds.), *Kommentar zum AktG*, § 34 WpHG para. 41.

(3) Legal Practice in Italy

The Italian provisions on acting in concert differ greatly from those in the TD. Shareholder agreements are defined as agreements whose object is the exercise of voting rights in a company with listed shares or in a company that controls it.[118] Italian law provides that any person with a shareholding of less than 3% partaking in a shareholder agreement is attributed the voting rights of the other parties to the agreement at thresholds of 5, 10, 15, 20, 25, 30, 50 and 66.6%.[119] The notification must contain information on the total amount of shares to which the agreement refers and also on the shares held by that person but not included in the shareholder agreement.

In practice, shareholder agreements are of great importance in Italy due to the fact that most listed companies are companies with a long tradition and still family owned, the most famous example being Fiat. For the families a shareholder agreement can be a means of ensuring their influence on the company and will thus mostly deal with questions of company policy and pre-emption rights for shares.[120]

The decisive element of the provisions on notification and publication is the concept of the shareholder agreement, which under Italian law is understood in a wide sense. Article 120 RE (Regulation for Issuers) on the attribution of voting rights refers to Article 122 TUF with regard to the meaning of a shareholder agreement. It must therefore be an agreement whose object is the exercise of voting rights. Additionally, Article 122(5) TUF also applies to an agreement that creates obligations of consultation prior to the exercise of voting rights or that has as its object or effect the exercise, jointly or otherwise, of a dominant influence on the company.

Consob must be notified of any agreement regarding the exercise of voting rights within five days of its conclusion. In addition, the agreement must be published in abridged form in the daily press within five days of the date of its conclusion and entered in the Company Register where the company has its registered office within 15 days from the date of their conclusion.[121] These measures are intended to improve the transparency of the markets.[122]

Italy's sanctions in the case of non-compliance with these provisions are harsh. If the shareholder agreement is not made public, it is null and void. Breaches of disclosure obligations may also lead to a loss of voting rights.[123] If the voting rights are exercised, Consob can challenge any resolution made in the shareholder meeting. The challenge will, however, only be successful if the required majority would not have been reached without the votes attached to the challenged agreement.[124] In practice this possibility of appeal does not appear to have played an important role so far.

---

[118] Art. 122 TUF.
[119] Art. 120 RE.
[120] Cf. G. Meo, in: Bessone (ed.), *Trattato di diritto privato*, 81 ff.; A. Fusi, 6 Le Società (2007), 689.
[121] Cf. Art. 122(1) TUF.
[122] Cf. F. Carbonetti, Riv. soc. (1998), 909, 911; D. Piselli, 2 Le Società (2009), 199, 200.
[123] Cf. Art. 122(4)(1) TUF.
[124] Cf. Art. 122(4)(2) TUF in conjunction with Art. 14(6) TUF.

(4) Legal Practice in Spain

68 Spanish law defines acting in concert similarly to the TD, requiring the conclusion of an agreement between a person or legal entity and a third party obligating them to adopt a lasting common policy towards the management of the issuer or with the aim of influencing the management through a concerted exercise of voting rights.[125] This definition is more restrictive than that of Spanish takeover law,[126] which also applies to agreements that refer to the exercise of voting rights in the company's administrative board or executive committee (*comisión ejecutiva o delegada de la sociedad*).[127] The notification requirement is addressed to all parties of the contract together and can only be fulfilled by a joint notification.

69 Shareholder agreements that affect the exercise of voting rights in the shareholders' meeting or restrict the free transferability of shares immediately have to be communicated to the company and the Spanish national supervisory authority, the CNMV. The respective document has to be deposited at the trade register. The shareholder agreement also has to be published as an ad hoc notification,[128] otherwise it does not become effective.[129]

(bb) Temporary Transfer of Voting Rights

70 A **person** or **legal entity** is also required to notify the company of **voting rights** held by them due to an **agreement** providing for the **temporary transfer** of voting rights as consideration.[130] In the TD from 1988 and the Directive 2001/34/EC this obligation still required a written agreement. This is no longer necessary. The wording of the TD now states more clearly than before that the voting rights are only held by the person or entity temporarily, ie will eventually be transferred back to the original owner.

71 The provision refers to those cases to which Article 10(g) TD is not applicable as the voting rights are not held 'on behalf of' the other person or entity. Its objective is to prevent a shareholder from 'parking' her funds with a third party whilst secretly increasing her holding, thus justifying the attribution of the third-party's voting rights. In contrast to the case described by Article 10(g) TD, the shareholder holds the voting rights on her own behalf in these cases.[131]

(cc) Notification Obligations of the Secured Party

72 The TD also requires notification for voting rights attached to shares which are lodged as collateral with a person or entity provided that person or entity controls the voting rights and declares its intention of exercising them.[132] A notification requirement in such cases stands to reason as voting rights will automatically ensue if the shares are transferred by way of security. However, regarding the internal relationship with the collateral provider

---

[125] Cf. Art. 24 1.a) RD 1362/2007.
[126] Cf. Art. 5.1.b) RD 1066/2007.
[127] Cf. A. Muñoz Pérez, *El concierto como presupuesto de la OPA obligatoria*, 267–268.
[128] Cf. Art. 531 3. LSC.
[129] Cf. Art. 533 LSC.
[130] Art. 10(b) TD.
[131] Cf. N. Elster, *Europäisches Kapitalmarktrecht*, 35.
[132] Art. 10(c) TD.

the secured party will usually not exercise these voting rights. The provision creates legal certainty by laying down a notification obligation in the event that the secured party plans on exercising its voting rights.

It is questionable whether the collateral provider must notify the company in these cases. 73 When answering this, it must be taken into account that the collateral provider may be entitled to instruct the secured party on how to exercise the voting right. In this case the voting rights may be attributed pursuant to Article 10(g) TD.[133] The question whether the secured party should also notify the company about voting rights attributed to it if the collateral provider has not made specific instructions on the exercise of the voting rights is answered by Article 10(f) TD.[134]

(dd) Life Interest

A life interest awards the beneficiary with the benefits of the shares. In particular, it receives 74 the dividend. It is, however, unclear whether the beneficiary is also permitted to exercise the voting rights, this question being answered inconsistently in the different Member States' civil laws. The TD appears to attribute the voting right to the beneficial owner, at least regarding the notification requirements: for **voting rights** attached to **shares** in which a **person** or an **entity** has the **life interest**, this person or entity is subject to the notification requirement described in Article 9 TD.[135]

(ee) Voting Rights Held or Exercised by a Controlled Undertaking

Further notification requirements are laid down for a **person** or a **legal entity** with **voting rights** held or exercised within the meaning of Article 10 points (a)–(d), **by an undertaking controlled by that person or entity**.[136] The voting rights attached to shares held by the subsidiary company are therefore attributed to the parent undertaking. Furthermore, voting rights that are attributed to the subsidiary company must also in a chain of attribution be attributed to the parent undertaking. The practical relevance has grown enormously compared to the precursory provision due to its wider scope of application.[137]

> *Example*: Assuming M held 10% of the voting rights of issuer I and subsidiary S acquired 5%, M 76 would have a notification obligation regarding 15% of I's voting rights and S would have an additional notification obligation regarding 5% of the voting rights. There would be no absorption of the voting rights with M. If further 5% of the voting rights are attributed to S due to acting in concert with D, these voting rights would also be attributed to M, who would then have to submit a notification regarding 20% of the voting rights, whilst S would have to publish the fact that it holds 10% of the voting rights.

---

[133] See below para. 83.
[134] See below para. 81.
[135] Art. 10(d) TD.
[136] Art. 10(e) TD.
[137] 'Following numerous requests' the European Commission developed a 'determination of situations in which voting rights which may be exercised on behalf of controlled undertakings [that] is much wider' than in the former provisions. 'This [was] possible due to a wider definition laid down in the proposed Art. 2(f).' Cf. COM(2003) 138 final (fn. 3), p. 25.

77 Examining the attribution of voting rights in a corporate group requires definition of a 'controlled undertaking'. According to the TD this is:

> 'any undertaking (i) in which a natural person or legal entity has a majority of the voting rights; or (ii) of which a natural person or legal entity has the right to appoint or remove a majority of the members of the administrative, management or supervisory body and is at the same time a shareholder in, or member of, the undertaking in question; or (iii) of which a natural person or legal entity is a shareholder or member and alone controls a majority of the shareholders' or members' voting rights, respectively, pursuant to an agreement entered into with other shareholders or members of the undertaking in question; or (iv) over which a natural person or legal entity has the power to exercise, or actually exercises, dominant influence or control'.[138]

78 The first three criteria are defined very precisely and do not lead to any relevant difficulties in their application. As opposed to this, the TD does not provide a definition of when a **person** or a legal entity has the **power to exercise**, or actually exercises, **dominant influence or control over an issuer**. Whilst these terms were also contained in Directive 83/349/EEC, they served a different aim, which was to extend the obligation to consolidate accounts to a wide range of subsidiaries.[139]

79 The question becomes relevant when a shareholder only has a minority stake but the usual attendance at the shareholders' general meeting may allow this to suffice for resolutions to be made. The Member States do not appear to have answered this question of interpretation in their national capital markets laws, rather adopting the legal definition contained in the TD into their national laws one-to-one. The FCA Handbook refers to the national company law in this context,[140] and defines the concepts of 'parent undertaking' and 'controlled undertaking' in accordance with the provisions of the Directive 83/349/EEC on annual accounts of corporate groups.[141] In contrast, German capital markets law refers to the accounting provisions for the definition of a controlled undertaking[142] and to the stock corporation provisions regarding the definition of a controlling influence.[143] The latter is given a broad meaning by the BGH. If a minority shareholding can have the same influence on the general meeting as a major holding, the holder of the minority shareholding must be regarded as a controlling enterprise.[144]

80 The present legal situation is unsatisfactory. The problems of interpretation described here are not mere trivialities but must be regarded as topics of a very general nature which should ideally be treated uniformly by the capital markets laws of all Member States. This need not necessarily mean an amendment of the TD by the European legislature, rather being a possible task for ESMA as part of its supervisory convergence work programme, which could define the concept of a controlled undertaking more clearly.

---

[138] Art. 2(1)(f) TD.
[139] Cf. H.-W. Neye, 24 ZGR (1995), 191, 197.
[140] Sec. 1162 Companies Act 2006.
[141] Cf. R. Veil and M. Wundenberg, *Englisches Kapitalmarktrecht*, 130–131.
[142] Cf. § 35 No1 WpHG in conjunction with § 290 HGB.
[143] Cf. § 35 No 2 WpHG in conjunction with § 17 AktG.
[144] Cf. for German law BGH of 13.10.1977 - II ZR 123/76, BGHZ 69, 334; BGH of 17.03.1997 – II ZB 3/96, BGHZ 135, 107.

(ff) Deposited Shares

A **person** or **legal entity** must furthermore notify the company of **voting rights** attached 81
to **shares** which have been **deposited** with them and which they can **exercise** at their **discretion** in the absence of specific instructions from the shareholders.[145] The person with
whom the shares are deposited is not the owner of the shares, thus necessitating a rule on
the attribution of the voting rights attached to third-party shares.

A deposition of the shares does not require the respective person physically to hold the 82
shares, rather allowing any management of the shares for a third party to suffice.[146] For the
application of the provision the important question is whether the depositary can exercise the voting rights at its own discretion.[147] This is still the case even if the depositary
has to take into account the shareholder's interest. Article 10(d) TD can become relevant
for credit institutions and other persons that have been empowered to exercise voting
rights of the shareholders. Voting rights exercised by proxy are, however, also covered by
Article 10(h) TD.[148]

(gg) Shares Held on Behalf of Another Person

A **person** or legal entity must also notify the company if it is entitled to acquire, to dispose 83
of, or to **exercise voting rights held** by **a third party in its own name** but **on behalf of that
person** or entity.[149] This provision especially envisages the trust in the United Kingdom and
the *Treuhand* in Germany[150] in which a trustor, respectively *Treugeber*, is attributed the voting rights attached to shares which are held for him by a trustee/*Treuhänder*. In Germany,
the legal literature supports the point of view that the *Treugeber* (trustor) must be permitted to instruct the *Treuhänder* (trustee), otherwise there is no guarantee that the trustor can
influence the trustee's vote. If the trustee is only subject to the trustor's instructions de facto
and not in a legally binding way an attribution of voting rights is not justified.[151]

> *Example (abridged and simplified)*: Three shareholders, L (5%), T (5%) and S (5%), acted in concert regarding the issuer, resulting in a reciprocal attribution of the voting rights attached to their shares. L had further transferred an additional 5% of its shares to a trustee (*Treuhänder*). The OLG Munich[152] decided that all voting rights attributed to trustor (*Treugeber*) L, due to acting in concert, would also have to be attributed to *Treuhänder* H. The court justified its decision by describing the need to prevent investors from avoiding the provision and emphasising the fact that the *Treugeber* who was entitled to instruct the *Treuhänder* was bound by the acting in concert. This explanation is not convincing when one considers that the *Treuhänder* had no influence whatsoever on 84

---

[145] Art. 10(f) TD.
[146] Cf. U. Burgard, 41 BB (1995), 2069, 2076; N. Elster, *Europäisches Kapitalmarktrecht*, 40.
[147] Cf. N. Elster, *Europäisches Kapitalmarktrecht*, 40.
[148] See below para. 88.
[149] Art. 10(g) TD.
[150] Cf. European Parliament, Report on the proposal for a European Parliament and Council directive on the harmonisation of transparency requirements with regard to information about issuers whose securities are admitted to trading on a regulated market and amending Directive 2001/34/EC, 25 February 2004, A5-0079/2004, Amendment 85.
[151] Cf. C. von Bülow, in: Hirte and Möllers (eds.), *Kölner Kommentar zum WpHG*, § 22 para. 71; R. Veil, in: Schmidt and Lutter (eds.), *Kommentar zum AktG*, § 34 WpHG para. 16.
[152] OLG München of 09.09.2009 – 7 U 1997/09, 21 AG (2009), 793.

how the *Treugeber* exercises its voting rights in the pool with the other shareholders.[153] The BGH therefore ruled in favour of the appellant and against the OLG Munich, stating that voting rights held by a third party acting in concert with the *Treugeber* (trustor) could not be attributed to the *Treuhänder* (trustee).[154]

85 Article 10(g) TD further gains practical relevance for **securities lending agreements**. These exist for multiple reasons and play an especially important role regarding short sellings. The following case concerns a shareholder who had increased its shareholdings to 95% of the shares with the help of stock lending agreements. Its aim was to squeeze out the remaining minority shareholders, this being possible in Germany from this proportion upwards.[155]

86 *Example (abridged and simplified):*[156] A shareholder (A) had transferred shares with voting rights of 12% to a different shareholder (B). The contract was concluded for an indefinite period and contained the provision that for the duration of the loan the cash dividends relating to the loan would belong to A. On termination of the contract B was to transfer shares of the same type and number back to A. The BGH saw B as the owner of the shares since a 'second-class' shareholding does not exist. Thus, shareholder B was held responsible for the notification. B was required to notify the issuer that it had exceeded the threshold of 10%. Furthermore, the BGH ruled that the voting rights attached to the shares referred to in the stock lending agreement could not be attributed to the lender (A) pursuant to § 22(1) sentence 1(2) WpHG which constitutes the German implementation of Article 10(g) TD. Therefore, lender A had to notify the issuer that it had fallen below the threshold of 10%.[157]

87 The attribution of voting rights is also discussed controversially with regard to so-called **cash-settled equity swaps**,[158] a type of contract where a bank promises to pay an investor the difference between the price of certain shares at the beginning and the end of the contractual period plus dividends, that may have been paid by the issuer, in exchange for interest and fees payable by the investor. Under the TD it has been argued that shares acquired by the bank as collateral may not be attributed to the investor because it typically has no influence on the voting rights attached to these shares.[159] First some Member States and thereafter the EU have reacted to the TD's deficit in transparency by providing additional disclosure rules.[160]

(hh) Voting Rights Exercised by Proxy

88 Voting rights that a person or a legal entity may exercise by proxy, at its discretion and without specific instructions, are also subject to the notification requirements.[161] The TD

---

[153] Cf. C. von Bülow and S. Petersen, 35 NZG (2009), 1373; H. Fleischer and D. Bedkowski, DStR (2010), 933; R. Veil and C. Dolff, 11 AG (2010), 385.
[154] BGH of 19.07.2011 – II ZR 246/09, ZIP (2011), 1862.
[155] The legal basis for squeeze-outs is § 327a AktG.
[156] BGH of 16.03.2009 – II ZR 302/06, BGHZ 180, 154.
[157] However, in this case lender A may be subject to a notification obligation pursuant to Art. 13 TD.
[158] Cf. on this type of derivatives A. Rechtschaffen, *Capital Markets, Derivatives and the Law*, 178–180.
[159] Cf. T. Baums and M. Sauter, 173 ZHR (2009), 454, 467; H. Fleischer and K. Schmolke, 33 ZIP (2008), 1501, 1506. Dissenting opinion: D. Zetzsche, 10 EBOR (2009), 115, 132.
[160] See below para. 92 ff.
[161] Art. 10(h) TD.

from 1988 and Directive 2001/34/EC did not contain such a provision. The European Commission's justification for the new disclosure obligation was that since proxy participation across Member States is usually allowed in general meetings, a company should be duly informed about major shareholdings for which a proxy received common instructions from a number of shareholders.[162] The TD adopting this provision, does not, however, require a common instruction of the proxy by the shareholders.

It is unclear if voting rights exercised by a credit institution as a proxy are also covered by Article 10(h) TD. In Germany a financial institution may, with the exception of explicit instructions received from the shareholder, only exercise its proxy voting rights in accordance with its own proposal or the proposal of the management or supervisory board for the exercising of the voting rights.[163] It has no discretion in this. Therefore, voting rights exercised by a credit institution as a proxy are not attributed. · 89

IV. Disclosure of Financial Instruments

1. Foundations

(a) Requirements under the TD 2004

The TD 2004 demanded the inclusion of financial instruments from the Member States into their transparency systems, as can be deduced from the TD's goal of 'moving towards more capital market-oriented thinking'.[164] This ensures that investors are informed if a holder of financial instruments has the right to acquire shares and thus may exercise the voting rights resulting therefrom. The obligation introduced in 2004 concerned a natural **person** or legal entity that **holds financial instruments** that result in an **entitlement to acquire**, on such holder's own initiative alone, under a formal agreement, **shares** to which voting rights are attached, already issued, of an issuer whose shares are admitted to trading on a regulated market.[165] 90

The reference to Article 9 indicated that the notification requirement only existed if through the acquisition or disposal of financial instruments a person reaches, exceeds or falls below a threshold of 5, 10, 15, 20, 25, 30, 50 or 75% of the voting rights. Whilst the Member States were entitled to provide a lower threshold, here they did not make use of this possibility, unlike in the case of notifications regarding major holdings. They justified this by wanting to reduce the obligations for the parties involved to the extent necessary for transparency. 91

---

[162] Cf. COM(2003) 138 final (fn. 3), p. 28.
[163] Cf. § 135 AktG.
[164] Cf. COM(2003) 138 final (fn. 3), p. 19.
[165] Art. 13(1) TD 2004.

(b) Deficits

92 However, in recent years after the transposition of the TD, investors were able to use financial instruments with no notification requirements, in particular cash-settled equity swaps,[166] in order to creep in on a listed company and achieve a takeover.[167]

93 *Example*: When announcing its takeover offer regarding shares of Continental AG, the Schaeffler-Group held 2.97% shares with voting rights. It also held financial instruments which entitled it to acquire a further 4.95% of Continental's shares. The Schaeffler- Group concluded contracts for difference with various banks, providing them with another 28% of the shares. A notification was necessary neither based on proportion of the shares owned directly by it, nor based on the financial instruments due to the fact that the initial threshold for notification requirements in Germany was 3% for shares and 5% for financial instruments at that time. Contracts for difference were not subject to any notification requirements, according to the BaFin's point of view, as generally they will not give an investor any influence on voting rights.[168]

94 The *Continental/Schaeffler* case and others triggered an intense discussion on the question of whether the provisions on notification requirements should be amended. The **United Kingdom** established notification requirements for so-called contracts for difference as early as 1 June 2009. Which financial instruments with 'similar economic effects' were affected by this was specified in detail.[169] However, the instruments were not listed explicitly, the former FSA rather having defined clearly when 'similar economic effects' to the financial instruments already subject to notification duties can be assumed. In doing so, the FSA adopted a principles-based approach. The notification duty did not require that an instrument holder influences the exercising of voting rights or aims to achieve such an influence.[170]

95 Germany also enacted a law to enhance investor protection and improve the functioning of the capital markets,[171] which introduced new rules regarding the notification requirements for holders of financial and other instruments in the WpHG. The aim was to prevent further major holdings being built unknown to the company, and to ensure market integrity.[172] German legal literature mostly welcomed these amendments,[173] reasoning that the abuse of loopholes in the law by individual investors undermines the confidence in the functioning of the markets.[174] However, care should be taken that this does not result in an *information overload*.[175]

---

[166] See above para. 87.
[167] The cases are described briefly in CESR's Consultation Paper, CESR Proposal to extend major shareholding notifications to instruments of similar economic effect to holding shares and entitlements to acquire shares, January 2010, CESR/09-1215b. Cf. also T. Baums and M. Sauter, 173 ZHR (2009), 454.
[168] Cf. BaFin, Press Release, 21 August 2008; T. Baums and M. Sauter, 173 ZHR (2009), 454, 467; M. Schiessl, Der Konzern (2009), 291, 295; H. Fleischer and K. Schmolke, 33 ZIP (2008), 1501, 1506; dissenting opinion: K.-M. Schanz, 35 DB (2008), 1899, 1903.
[169] On this see R. Veil and M. Wundenberg, *Englisches Kapitalmarktrecht*, 127.
[170] Cf. R. Veil and M. Wundenberg, *Englisches Kapitalmarktrecht*, 127–128.
[171] Gesetz zur Stärkung des Anlegerschutzes und Verbesserung der Funktionsfähigkeit des Kapitalmarkts vom 7. April 2011, BGBl. I, p. 538 (German Investor Protection Enhancement and Improvement of the Functioning of the Capital Markets Act).
[172] In *Porsche/VW* the use of financial instruments led to a low free float. As a consequence, short sellers suffered significant losses (see R. Veil § 15 para. 26).
[173] Cf. H. Fleischer and K. Schmolke, 13 NZG (2010), 846, 852; A. Merkner and M. Sustmann, 13 NZG (2010), 681, 683 ff.; C. Teichmann and D. Epe, 32 WM (2010), 1477, 1480 ff.
[174] Cf. H. Fleischer and K. Schmolke, 13 NZG (2010), 846, 852.
[175] Cf. C. Teichmann and D. Epe, 32 WM (2010), 1477, 1480 ff.

(c) Reform of the Transparency Directive 2014

The introduction of provisions on transparency regarding financial instruments has been discussed at European level since 2010 when the former CESR submitted a recommendation to introduce notification requirements regarding financial instruments conveying an economic interest,[176] as it must be assumed that the investor in these cases will try and influence the issuer. This recommendation was not with universal approval.[177] The main argument against notification requirements was the considerable costs for investors.[178] Furthermore, the obligations would increase the price of company takeovers, thus interfering with the market for corporate control.

Nevertheless, the European Commission was right to attend to this question.[179] It cannot be regarded as desirable for the European capital markets if strong variations in notification requirements exist between the Member States. Thus, the Transparency Directive was amended by Directive 2013/50/EU on 22 October 2013, arguing that 'new types of financial instruments [...] could be used to secretly acquire stocks in companies, which could result in market abuse and give a false and misleading picture of economic ownership of publicly listed companies. In order to ensure that issuers and investors have full knowledge of the structure of corporate ownership, the definition of financial instruments [...] should cover all instruments with similar economic effect to holding shares and entitlements to acquire shares.'[180]

2. Notification

(a) Prerequisites

The notification obligation also applies to financial instruments that, on maturity, give the holder either the unconditional right to acquire or the discretion to acquire, shares to which voting rights are attached of an issuer whose shares are admitted to trading on a regulated market.[181] Furthermore a notification obligation arises if a person holds financial instruments which are not covered by the aforementioned definition but which refer to shares and have a similar economic effect, irrespective of the right to a physical settlement.[182]

The **TD** further **lists** which **financial instruments** may result in disclosure obligations: transferrable securities, options, futures, swaps, forward rate agreements, contracts for differences; any other contracts or agreements with similar economic effects which may be settled physically or in cash.[183]

---

[176] Cf. CESR/09-1215b (fn. 167).
[177] Seen critically by D. Zetzsche, 11 EBOR (2010), 231 ff.
[178] Cf. C. Teichmann and D. Epe, 32 WM (2010) 1477, 1481.
[179] Cf. Report from the Commission to the Council, the European Parliament, The European Economic and Social Committee and the Committee of the Regions, 27 May 2010, COM(2010)243 final.
[180] Cf. Recital 9 TD 2013.
[181] Cf. Art. 13(1)(a) TD.
[182] Cf. Art. 13(1)(b) TD.
[183] Cf. Art. 13(1)(b) TD.

100 In order to ensure legal certainty, **ESMA** has published an **indicative list** of financial instruments that are subject to notification obligations.[184] It first explains that 'options' should be read as including calls, puts or any combination thereof. Furthermore, ESMA considers the following to be financial instruments, provided they reference shares to which voting rights are attached: irrevocable convertible and exchangeable bonds referring to already issued shares; financial instruments referred to a basket of shares; warrants; repurchase agreements; rights to recall lent shares; contractual buying pre-emption rights; other conditional contracts or agreements than options and futures; hybrid financial instruments; combinations of financial instruments; shareholder agreements.

101 ESMA's list is helpful for market participants to assess whether they have to fulfil disclosure obligations. However, some of the instruments mentioned should have been explained in more depth. ESMA should, for example, clarify 'hybrid financial instruments' and 'combinations of financial instruments'.

(b) Attribution of Voting Rights

102 A central question is in what way the potential influence on voting rights resulting from financial instruments has to be communicated to the market. The European legislature opted for an **aggregation** of the number of **voting rights** held under Articles 9 and 10 with the **number** of **voting rights relating** to **financial instruments** held under Article 13,[185] thus leading to the initial threshold of 5% being reached sooner and increasing the number of notifications.

103 *Example*: An investor holds 4% of the voting share capital and acquires financial instruments that grant him the right to acquire further 3% of the voting share capital. The investor must then publish a notification regarding the fact that he has exceeded the 5%-threshold.

(c) Procedures Subject to Notification

104 The **holder** of an instrument must make a **notification to** the **issuer** that includes a number of data, such as 'the resulting situation in terms of voting rights' and the date on which the threshold was reached or crossed. For instruments with an exercise period, the notification must contain an indication of the date or time period when the shares will or can be acquired. The instrument holder must also inform the issuer on the date of maturity or expiration of the instrument and the identity of the holder together with the name of the underlying issuer.[186]

3. Publication

105 The notification should be made as soon as possible, within a maximum period of four trading days,[187] to the competent authority of the home Member State of the issuer and

---

[184] ESMA/2015/1598 (fn. 34).
[185] Art. 13a(1) TD.
[186] Art. 11(3)(a)–(g) Directive 2007/14/EC.
[187] Art. 11(4) Directive 2007/14/EC in conjunction with Art. 12(2) TD.

the issuer of the underlying shares itself.[188] The latter must then disclose the information contained in the notification.[189]

V. Disclosure of the Intents of Investors

US capital markets law introduced provisions requiring a **person** to **disclose** his **purposes** regarding the **future developments** of the **issuer** in 1968.[190] The obligation applies to all investors acquiring at least 5% of the company's shares and constitutes the centrepiece of the rules on investor transparency. The disclosure of the intent of investors is regarded as having a high informational value. Empirical studies have proven that the reaction of investors depends not only on the disclosure of an acquisition of a major shareholding but rather also on the aims the respective issuer pursued with the acquisition.[191]

Neither the TD nor the other directives on capital markets law request that EU Member States introduce provisions that would obligate investors to disclose their intent regarding the acquisition or disposal of shares. France and Germany, however, introduced such provisions nonetheless. These shall be described below, taking into account the possibility of addressing this question at EU level.

1. France

France has far-reaching rules on the investor's notification of intent,[192] which were originally based on section 13d of the US Securities Exchange Act. The provisions were enacted in 1988 and introduced a notification obligation for exactly these cases. They have the primary aim of making it transparent at an early stage, if a company takeover is under way. This is not only relevant for investor protection but also in order to inform the company of a potential new shareholder with control over the company. However, the disclosure regime did not prove very successful in France, the notifications submitted often being formulaic and of little informative value. Examples of the investor notifications were: 'We retain the option of acquiring or disposing of further shares in the future, depending on the opportunities on the market.' Or: 'We declare that we momentarily do not have the intention of appointing one or more members to the board. However, we retain the option of doing so in the future.'[193]

These problems were the reason for the reforms of the French rules in 2009.[194] The amendments ensured that investors must now give precise **information** about their **strategy**, their

---

[188] Art. 11(5) Directive 2007/14/EC.
[189] Cf. Art. 21 TD.
[190] See above para. 6.
[191] Cf. W. Mikkelson and R. Ruback, 14 J. Fin. Econ. (1985), 532, 536; J. Bethel et al., 53 J. Fin. (1998), 605, 628; F. Scherr et al., 32(4) Quarterly J. Bus & Econ. (1993), 66, 70, 73.
[192] Defined in Art. L233-VII C. com. and Art. 223-14 RG AMF.
[193] C. Uzan, Bull. Joly Bourse, (2008), 530, 533.
[194] Cf. P.-H. Conac, Rev. Soc. (2009), 477, 495 ff.

methods of financing the acquisition of shares and the measures planned regarding the issuer—ie mergers, restructuring, the assignment of assets and changes in the dividend policy, the company structure, the capitalisation, the area of business, the articles of association and any agreements on regarding shares and voting rights. The investor must further notify the company whether it intends to acquire control of the company.[195]

110 The notification (to be made public by the issuer) is restricted to **aims** in the **next six months**. The investor is not bound by this declaration; it can change its intentions any time, provided it notifies the company of this. The thresholds at which the notification must be made are 10, 15, 20 and 25% of the voting rights. Since the reform, the notification must be made within ten trading days. Failure to comply with the obligation results in a loss of voting rights for two years after the notification is completed.[196] Additionally, appropriate regulatory measures may be taken by the AMF, which tends to impose fines.

2. Germany

111 In 2008 Germany introduced provisions on the notification duties for major holdings, reasoning that German capital markets law provisions fell short of rules on notification provided for in France and the US.[197] Therefore, § 27a WpHG now determines that a **shareholder** must **notify** the **issuer** of the **aims underlying the purchase** of the **voting rights** when it reaches or exceeds a threshold of 10% or one of the further thresholds.[198] The company must also be informed about any changes to the aims.[199]

112 The word 'aim' is ambiguous. Therefore, § 27a(1) sentence 3 WpHG defines more closely which aims the issuer has to notify the company of: these are whether (1) the investment is aimed at implementing strategic objectives or at generating a trading profit; (2) it plans to acquire further voting rights within the next twelve months by means of a purchase or by any other means; (3) it intends to exert an influence on the appointment or removal of members of the issuer's administrative, managing and supervisory bodies and (4) it intends to achieve a material change in the company's capital structure, in particular as regards the ratio between own funds and external funds and the dividend policy.[200]

113 The notification obligations have been criticised.[201] The information content of some of the data required in a notification of intent remains unclear. This especially refers to the fact that the investor has to reveal the origin of the funds, ie whether these are own funds or external funds raised by the notifying party in order to finance the purchase of the voting rights. It has also been criticised that no notification requirement applies for the question as

---

[195] In detail J.-F. Biard, RDBF (2009), 70 ff.
[196] Cf. on this R. Veil and P. Koch, *Französisches Kapitalmarktrecht*, 102–103.
[197] Begr. RegE Risikobegrenzungsgesetz, BT-Drucks. 16/7438, p. 8 (explanatory notes).
[198] The thresholds are laid out in § 33(1) WpHG which is referred to in § 43(1) WpHG with the result that a notification under § 43 WpHG is necessary when reaching or crossing the thresholds of 10, 15, 20, 25, 30, 50 and 75% of the voting rights.
[199] Cf. § 43a(1) WpHG.
[200] Cf. § 43(1) WpHG.
[201] H. Fleischer, 24 AG (2008), 873; J. Querfurth, 42 WM (2008), 1957; U. Schneider, in: FS Nobbe, 741; M. Zimmermann, 2 ZIP (2009), 57.

to whether the investor intends to acquire control of the company. The fact that the articles of association of an issuer may exempt the company from the notification requirements[202] is also seen critically, as it is in the public interest that the investor notifies the issuer of his intents.

Legal practice in Germany shows that the investors' notifications of intent often contain reservations or are formulated restrictively. Others contain explanatory details, in which an investor may, for example, describe itself as a 'long-term investor'.[203]

114

The notification must follow within 20 trading days of reaching or exceeding the threshold (§ 27a(1) WpHG). This rule is not convincing. There is no reason why an investor should be granted such a long period of time to disclose its aims. The publication of the information is up to the issuer and must take place within three trading days of receiving the notification or discovering the failure to comply with the requirements.

115

Failure to comply with § 43 WpHG does not—unlike in France—entail any sanctions. The BaFin is not entitled to impose fines on the investor who breached his notification duties and the investor is not subject to a loss of rights. The question whether a civil liability of the investor towards shareholders must be assumed in these cases remains unclear.[204]

116

VI. Supervision

1. Requirements under European Law

Each Member State must designate a central competent administrative authority[205] responsible for ensuring that the provisions adopted pursuant to the TD are applied by market participants. This administrative authority must be equipped with all the powers necessary for the performance of this function.[206] It must be empowered to require holders of shares or other financial instruments to submit information and documents[207] and to notify it on changes in major holdings.[208] It must also be empowered to take appropriate action should the issuer not disclose in a timely fashion the required information in order to ensure that the public has effective and equal access to this information in all Member States.[209]

117

2. Supervisory Practices in the Member States

The NCAs (in France: AMF; in Germany: BaFin; in Italy: Consob; in Spain: CNMV; etc.) are entitled to prescribe when a person must make a notification, correct a former notification

118

---

[202] Cf. § 43(3) WpHG.
[203] Cf. R. Veil, in: Schmidt and Lutter (eds.), *Kommentar zum AktG*, § 43 WpHG para. 7.
[204] Cf. ibid, § 43 WpHG para. 24.
[205] Art. 24(1) TD.
[206] Art. 24(4) TD.
[207] Art. 24(4)(a) TD.
[208] Art. 24(4)(c) TD.
[209] Art. 24(4)(f) TD.

or refrain from making a notification in order to fulfil his notification duties. They may even notify the respective company itself.

119 There is little knowledge on the way in which the NCAs exercise their supervisory tasks. Due to the multitude of notifications it is practically not possible to verify the correctness of each individual notification. It must therefore be assumed that the NCAs only carry out random checks.

120 The notification obligations give rise to a number of problems that are not as yet solved in a uniform way throughout the EU: This starts with the question of who is actually subject to the notification obligation. In cases of foreign investors— for example a Massachusetts Business Trust (MBT)—it must be determined on the basis of this foreign law, whether the investor itself has legal capacity. The trustees behind the trust can also be subject to notification obligations. It must be seen positively that the NCAs are prepared to clarify numerous questions with the investors at short notice, for example via e-mail. It is, however, important that these questions are solved on the basis of uniform principles throughout the EU. It will therefore be the task of ESMA to ensure a uniform handling of such issues by the NCAs. This also applies with regard to the provisions on an attribution of voting rights, which give rise to numerous questions on their interpretation.

VII. Sanctions

1. Requirements under European Law

121 The **TD 2004** only vaguely described what sanctions were to be introduced by the Member States. It did not include any instructions on criminal penalties, merely stipulating that Member States had to ensure that the appropriate administrative measures were taken or civil and/or administrative penalties were imposed.[210] It was thus for each Member State to decide whether it introduced administrative fines or sanctions under civil law,[211] provided it ensured that the chosen measures were effective, proportionate and dissuasive.[212]

122 As Member States had much room for discretion it was hardly surprising that their sanctioning regimes differed greatly.[213] Whilst some Member States relied on a combination of administrative sanctions, etc., under civil law, others adopted a regime of criminal penalties.

123 This legal situation was highly unsatisfactory. The European Commission therefore aimed to enhance the sanctioning powers of the competent authorities, making the system more effective.[214] The European legislature completed the **reform** in 2013 by enacting the Directive 2013/50/EU, thus amending the TD. The amended TD contains detailed

---

[210] Art. 28(1) TD 2004.
[211] Cf. R. Veil, 18 ZBB (2006), 162.
[212] Art. 28(1) TD 2004.
[213] Cf. CESR, Report on the mapping of supervisory powers, administrative and criminal sanctioning regimes of Member States in relation to the Transparency Directive (TD), July 2009, CESR/09-058, p. 8.
[214] Cf. Commission Staff Working Paper, Impact Assesment, 25 October 2011, SEC(2011) 1279 final, p. 84–85.

rules on the sanctions to be introduced into the national laws of the Member States. The Member States are obliged to empower the **NCAs** to **suspend** the **exercise** of **voting rights** for **holders** of **shares** and **financial instruments** who do not comply with the notification requirements.[215] It is further possible to impose pecuniary sanctions. According to Article 28b(1)(c) TD, **administrative pecuniary sanctions** against legal persons of up to 5% of the total annual turnover in the preceding business year may be imposed; administrative pecuniary sanctions in the case of a natural person are limited to € 2,000,000.[216] The amended TD also includes precise criteria for the national supervisory authorities to take into account when imposing sanctions.[217] This is supposed to ensure a more uniform sanctioning practice than was common in the past.

The loss of voting rights has a strong preventive effect. This explains why Directive 2013/50/EU (TD 2013) requires Member States to ensure that their laws, regulations and administrative provisions provide for the possibility of suspending the exercise of voting rights attached to shares in the event of a breach of the obligation of disclosure of shareholdings. Member States may provide that voting rights are suspended only in the case of the most serious breaches. These are minimum harmonising requirements. It is therefore permissible, for example, as in Germany, to provide for the loss of all share rights (right to participate in the general meeting; dividend rights; right to information; right to bring an action for annulment; etc.). Furthermore, a Member State can also provide that the loss of voting rights takes place *ex lege*, ie does not have to be ordered by the supervisory authority. In this case, the preventive effect is particularly strong. This is why France and Germany provide for a loss of (voting) rights *ex lege*. 124

2. Investor Protection by means of Civil Liability

A further means of enforcing the provisions on notification is the possibility of a civil law liability for damages caused to the investors. This possibility does not, however, appear to be at the top of the legislatures' agendas in Europe. Whilst in all Member States the **general provisions** on civil law liability—especially of the **law of torts**—are applicable to the failure to comply with notification and disclosure, so far no investors have applied these rules to claim damages from shareholders or issuers for non-compliance. 125

Investor protection through rules on civil liability has also not attracted much interest in the legal literature. In Germany, some maintain that an investor can demand compensation of damages under tort law, reasoning that the capital markets law provisions on the transparency regarding major holdings are protective laws in terms of tort law.[218] An argument against this is, however, that the aim of the notification and publication requirements is 126

---

[215] A loss of voting rights *ex lege* already existed in France and Germany and is regarded as a very effective sanction due to its preventative nature. The legal practice in Italy also realises the effectiveness of this sanction, however, in judicial practice it has not so far been widely applied and Consob also has not yet set aside any resolution of a general meeting upon the grounds of it being based on lost voting rights.
[216] Cf. Art. 28b(1)(c)(ii) TD.
[217] Cf. Art. 28c TD.
[218] Cf. W. Bayer, in: Goette and Habersack (eds.), *Münchener Kommentar zum AktG*, § 33 WpHG para. 2; H. Hirte, in: Hirte and Möllers (eds.), *Kölner Kommentar zum WpHG*, § 21 para. 4.

primarily to ensure the functioning of the capital markets. The legislature did not specifically aim to ensure individual investor protection.[219]

127 The situation in the other EU Member States is similar. In the laws of the United Kingdom, France, Italy and Sweden there are no specific regulations regarding claims for investors against shareholders or issuers not fulfilling their notification or publication duties. Once again, only the general civil law provisions, especially those under the law of torts, may apply, although it remains unclear whether their requirements are met if a shareholder breaches its notification requirements.

VIII. Conclusion

128 The European legislature attributes great importance to the transparency of major holdings for the proper functioning of capital markets and the corporate governance of listed companies. It has largely reached these regulatory goals. Since the reform in 2013, no relevant cases have emerged in which investors managed to creep up on an issuer through hidden acquisitions of shareholdings. It is hard to imagine that an investor secretly builds up its stake under the current regime. However, it is yet unclear whether the extended disclosure requirements on financial instruments have had an adverse effect on institutional investors.

129 It is a problem that Member States are still entitled to provide for additional thresholds triggering the obligation to make a notification to the issuer. The TD only provides a few non-cohesive thresholds. Whilst some Member States restricted themselves to implementing these provisions into their national capital markets laws, the majority opted for the introduction of additional thresholds or for provision allowing the issuers to stipulate additional thresholds in their articles of association. In France the latter has, however, proved not to provide market efficiency but rather to be employed when trying to prevent hostile takeovers. Today, the different legal situation can hardly be justified by a different concentration of ownership in listed companies. It causes unnecessary transaction costs for global investors.

130 Another cause for concern are the provisions on the attribution of voting rights attached to third-party shares which vary greatly between the Member States, some Member States once again having adopted stricter provisions. Acting in concert, for example, is defined very differently in France, Germany, Italy and Spain. Furthermore a unified European level of information cannot be assumed when one considers how far France and Germany have gone in their requirements for a notification of intent. A mix of fully harmonising and minimum harmonising rules results in legal fragmentation. Therefore, the task remains to develop an effective and consistent system of disclosure of shareholdings.

131 The harmonisation of administrative sanctions was an important measure of the 2013 reform. In addition, the European legislator has tightened sanctions across Europe. However, the level of sanctions is not aligned with market abuse law. It is not

---

[219] Cf. R. Veil, 175 ZHR (2011), 83, 88–89.

consistent that minimum fines for violations of the obligation to disclose inside information (Article 17 MAR) is lower than for violations of disclosure of shareholdings (Article 9 TD). Finally, the interaction with the other sanctioning instruments, in particular the loss of voting rights, does not seem well thought-out.

For the time being, a future topic is the question of whether the regime of shareholding transparency will become superfluous if shares can be traded on the blockchain.[220] As things stand, the legal basis for the tokenisation of shares is already lacking. This will change in future! 132

---

[220] Cf. A. Pietrancosta, in: Tountopoulos and Veil (eds.), *Transparency of Stock Corporations in Europe*, 109, 128.

§ 21

Directors' Dealings

Bibliography

Cox, James D. and Hazen, Thomas L., *Corporations* (2003), § 12.08; Diekgräf, Moritz B., *Directors' Dealings* (2017); Dymke, Björn M., *Directors' Dealings am deutschen Kapitalmarkt—eine empirische Bestandsaufnahme*, Finanz-Betrieb (2007), 450–460; Friederich, Sylvain et al. (eds.), *Short-run Returns around the Trades of Corporate Insiders on the London Stock Exchange*, 8 EFM (2002), 7–30; Fuchs Andreas, *Kommentar zum Wertpapierhandelsrecht*, 2nd edn., (2016); Grimberg, Julia and Herberger, Tim A., *Industry Effects in Directors' Dealings and Abnormal Stock Returns: Results from the German Stock Market*, 18 Corporate Ownership & Control (2020), 310–330; Gregory, Alan et al. (eds.), *UK Directors' Trading—The Impact of Dealings in Smaller Firms*, 104 EJ (1994), 37–53; Heidorn, Thomas, Meyer, Bernd and Pietrowiak, Alexander, *Performance-Effekte nach Directors' Dealings in Deutschland, Italien und den Niederlanden*, in: Hochschule für Bankwirtschaft (eds.), *Arbeitsberichte 57* (2004); Hower-Knobloch, Christian, *Directors' Dealings gem. § 15a WpHG. Eine ökonomische Analyse einer Mitteilungspflicht über Wertpapiergeschäfte von Personen mit Führungsaufgaben* (2007); Jacobs, Arnold S., *An Analysis of Section 16 of the Securities Exchange Act of 1934*, 32 N.Y.L. Sch. L. Rev. (1987), 209–700; Kumpan, Christoph, *Die neuen Regelungen zu Directors' Dealings in der Marktmissbrauchsverordnung*, 61 AG (2016), 446–459; Maume, Philipp and Keller, Martin, *Directors' Dealings unter der EU-Marktmissbrauchsverordnung*, 46 ZGR (2017), 273–311; Osterloh, Falk, *Directors' Dealings* (2007); Rau, Michael, *Directors' Dealings am deutschen Aktienmarkt. Empirische Analyse meldepflichtiger Wertpapiergeschäfte* (2004); Riedl, Albert M., *Transparenz- und Anlegerschutz am deutschen Kapitalmarkt. Eine empirische Analyse am Beispiel meldepflichtiger Wertpapiergeschäfte nach § 15a WpHG (Directors' Dealings)* (2008); Rüttenauer, Frank, *Directors' Dealings. Untersuchung von Performanceeffekten nach meldepflichtigen Aktiengeschäften* (2007); Schuster, Gunnar, *Kapitalmarktrechtliche Verhaltenspflichten von Organmitgliedern am Beispiel des § 15a WpHG*, 167 ZHR (2003), 193–215; Steinberg, Marc I. and Landsdale, Daryl L., *The Judicial and Regulatory Constriction of Section 16(b) of the Secuities Exchange Act of 1934*, 68 Notre Dame L. Rev. (1992), 33–79; Veil, Rüdiger, *Europäisches Insiderrecht 2.0 – Konzeption von Grundsatzfragen der Reform durch MAR und CRIM-MAD*, 26 ZBB (2014), 85–95; Veil, Rüdiger, *Gewinnabschöpfung im Kapitalmarktrecht*, 34 ZGR (2005), 155–199; Wang, William and Steinberg, Marc, *Insider Trading* (2010).

I. Introduction

The necessity for transparency regarding dealings executed by the management of a company was not discovered by the European legislature until surprisingly late. The first directives on capital markets law[1] did not yet contain provisions thereon. It was not until the

---

[1] See R. Veil § 1 para. 5–6.

MAD was enacted in 2003 that notification and disclosure obligations for directors' dealings were required to be introduced into the Member States' national laws. The provisions followed the example of US capital markets law.[2]

2   The obligation was intended as a **preventive measure against market abuse**.[3] Disclosure prevents the suspicion of the directors taking advantage of their insider knowledge—such may arise if the dealing only becomes publicly known at a later time. The notification of transactions conducted by persons discharging managerial responsibilities on their own account within an issuer also constitutes an additional means for competent authorities to supervise markets. The MAD 2003 regime was further based on the idea that disclosure of directors' dealings would provide a better informational basis for investment decisions (so-called signalling effect). The publication of individual transactions could be a highly valuable source of information for investors.[4] The **disclosure obligations** should therefore be regarded as an **additional instrument** for **ensuring** the **proper functioning** of **capital markets**.[5]

3   The **Market Abuse Regulation 2014** (MAR) builds on the MAD 2003 regime and considers 'greater transparency of transactions conducted by persons discharging managerial responsibilities at the issuer level and, where applicable, persons closely associated with them, [as a] a preventive measure against market abuse, particularly insider dealing.'[6] The disclosure obligation is also justified as improving the level of information for investors: 'The publication of those transactions on at least an individual basis can also be a highly valuable source of information to investors.'[7] Finally, the European legislator reiterates that the reporting of transactions gives supervisory authorities an additional possibility to monitor the markets.[8]

4   Whether directors' dealings that have been made public can be an indication of the future prospects of the company is, however, doubtful. The reasons why the directors (PDMRs) performed the specific transaction need not be made public and will therefore usually remain unknown. The underlying motives for the share transaction will often be entirely irrelevant for the assessment of the profit expectations of the company. The publication of transactions for the directors' own accounts also bears the additional risk of so-called noise trading, ie investors basing their investment decisions on unfounded, alleged information.[9]

5   These disadvantages have not prevented the majority of the literature from viewing the disclosure obligations for directors' dealings generally positively. Various empirical studies on German,[10] English[11] and other European[12] capital markets have confirmed the legislature's

---

[2] Sec. 16(a) Securities Exchange Act. A detailed analysis of the obligations can be found in A. Jacobs, 32 N.Y.L. Sch. L. Rev. (1987), 209.
[3] Cf. recital 26 MAD 2003.
[4] Cf. recital 26 MAD 2003.
[5] See on this regulatory aim R. Veil § 2 para. 7–11.
[6] Cf. recital 58 sentence 1 MAR.
[7] Cf. recital 58 sentence 2 MAR.
[8] Cf. recital 59 MAR.
[9] Cf. G. Schuster, 167 ZHR (2003), 193, 200.
[10] Cf. B. Dymke, Finanz-Betrieb (2007), 450, 452 ff.; M. Rau, *Directors' Dealings am deutschen Aktienmarkt*, 153 ff.; A Riedl, *Transparenz und Anlegerschutz am deutschen Kapitalmarkt*, 123 ff.; for a summary of the empirical studies on US-American and German stock markets see F. Rüttenauer, *Directors' Dealings*, 37 ff.
[11] Cf. S. Friederich et al., 8 EFM (2002), 7, 16 ff.; A. Gregory et al., 104 EJ (1994), 37, 46 ff.
[12] On Germany, Italy and the Netherlands see T. Heidorn et al., *Performance-Effekte nach Directors' Dealings in Deutschland, Italien und den Niederlanden*, in: Hochschule für Bankwirtschaft (eds.), Arbeitsberichte 57, 15 ff.

reasons for their introduction, concluding that members of the management of the supervisory board generally achieve excess return from up to 5% with their transactions,[13] thus justifying the provisions on the transparency of directors' dealings.[14] Studies on the German capital market after MAR 2014 confirm the findings obtained on the previous legal situation of the MAD 2003.[15] Furthermore, it is indisputable that greater transparency facilitates supervision of markets by public authorities.

The disclosure obligations are supplemented by a **closed period** for **PDMRs**. In general, PDMRs are not allowed to trade before the announcement of an interim financial report or a year-end report. The European legislature first introduced this closed period throughout the Union with the MAR 2014. Some Member States already had statutory regulations in place, while in others it was common practice to provide for trading bans on a voluntary basis. Recital 61 of the MAR claims that PDMRs should be prohibited from trading before the announcement of an interim financial report or a year-end report, unless specific and restricted circumstances exist which would justify a permission by the issuer allowing a PDMR to trade. The trading ban aims at strengthening the confidence of investors that members of the management do not exploit information advantages during a particularly sensitive period. The closed periods reinforces the insider trading prohibition, thus ensuring equal informational opportunities for investors and protecting the proper functioning of the capital markets.[16]

II. Regulatory Concepts and Sources of Law

1. MAR Regime

The MAD 2003 required the Member States to introduce provisions obligating persons discharging managerial responsibilities within an issuer (PDMRs) to notify the competent authority of the existence of transactions conducted on their own account. The Member States had further to ensure that public access to information concerning such transactions was available.[17] These national provisions were replaced by the provision of the MAR on 3 July 2016. The overall concept has largely remained the same, the new rules also containing (more extensive) ex post disclosure obligations and no provisions on pre-trading disclosure. It would not be recommendable to oblige

---

[13] Cf. M. Rau, *Directors' Dealings am deutschen Aktienmarkt*, 219 ff.; A. Riedl, *Transparenz und Anlegerschutz am deutschen Kapitalmarkt*, 233 ff.; seen more restrictively by A. Gregory et al., 104 EJ (1994), 37, 52 (above-average returns can especially occur in small and medium-sized firms); seen sceptically by B. Dymke, Finanz-Betrieb (2007), 450, 460.
[14] Cf. F. Osterloh, *Directors' Dealings*, 68–69; seen critically on the basis of a legal economic analysis C. Hower-Knobloch, *Directors' Dealings gem. § 15a WpHG*, passim.
[15] Cf. J. Grimberg and T. Herberger, 18 Corporate Ownership & Control (2020), 310, 328 (abnormal returns mainly in companies with small market capitalisation and more on sales than on purchases).
[16] Cf. M. Diekgräf, *Directors' Dealings*, 160; R. Veil, 26 ZBB (2014), 85, 95.
[17] Cf. Art. 6(4) MAD.

PDMRs to disclose their transactions in shares to the capital markets prior to the conclusion of the deal as this would be likely to mislead the other market participants. As opposed to this, a (limited) closed period for PDMRs appears recommendable and the European legislature now contains uniform rules in this regard for all Member States for a certain time period prior to the announcement of an interim financial report or a year-end report.

8   The legal basis for the disclosure obligations is to be found in Article 19(1)–(10) MAR (**level 1 regime**). The closed periods for PDMRs are laid down in Article 19(11) and (12) MAR. The provisions are rendered more precise by Article 7–10 Commission Delegated Regulation (EU) No. 2016/522 (**level 2 regime**). In addition, ESMA has published a Q&A document on market abuse law, which also comments on questions about the application of the rules on directors' dealings (**level 3 guidance**).[18] The document is legally non-binding for market participants.[19]

9   The disclosure obligations and the MAR rules on a closed period aim at **full harmonisation** within the EU. Member States are therefore not entitled to provide for stricter rules. With regard to individual aspects, however, the MAR recognises a legislative competence of the Member States.[20]

2. Further Disclosure Rules in Union Law

10   The notification obligations for directors conducting transactions on their own account coexist with the **ad hoc disclosure obligations** for **inside information** (Article 17(1) MAR)[21] and for changes in major holdings (Article 9 TD).[22] Therefore, the obligation to disclose the acquisition of shares by a director may be accompanied by the obligation to notify the issuer that a certain threshold[23] has been reached or exceeded. This will, however, only rarely happen, the first threshold lying at 5% of the voting rights under European law.

11   A PDMR only has to disclose *transactions* with shares of the issuer or financial instruments relating to them. The MAR does not require managers to disclose shareholdings. However, information on this must be provided in the prospectus under the regime of the Prospectus Regulation (PR).[24] Furthermore, such disclosure may be required under the company law of the Member States.

---

[18] ESMA, Questions and Answers on the Market Abuse Regulation, Chapter 7, ESMA70-145-111, Version 14, 29 Mach 2019.
[19] See R. Veil § 5 para. 25 f.
[20] Cf. Art. 19(2) MAR: 'and without prejudice to the right of Member States to provide for notification obligations other than those referred to in this Article'.
[21] See R. Veil § 19.
[22] See R. Veil § 20.
[23] On the numerous different thresholds see R. Veil § 20 para. 27–30.
[24] Cf. Art. 2 PR in conjunction with Annex I, 15.2 (Registration Document for Equity Securities) Commission Delegated Regulation (EU) 2019/980 of 14 March 2019.

III. Disclosure Obligations

1. Notification Requirements

(a) Persons Subject to the Notification Obligation

The obligation to disclose directors' dealings as defined in the MAR is addressed to **persons discharging managerial responsibilities** (PDMRs) within an issuer. Article 3(1)(25) MAR puts this concept into more concrete terms, defining such a person as a member of the administrative, management or supervisory bodies of the issuer. Additionally, any senior executive, who is not a member of one of these bodies but has regular access to inside information relating directly or indirectly to the issuer, and the power to make managerial decisions affecting the future developments and business prospects of the issuer, is also subject to this obligation. It can only be determined in each individual case who belongs to this second management level. According to the former CESR this especially refers to so-called 'Top Executives'.[25]

A further practically relevant question under the MAD 2003 regime was whether the members of the body of a subsidiary that deal in the parent company's financial instruments must be defined as such a 'senior executive'. Generally, this was assumed if the subsidiary is the only operationally active subsidiary of a holding company.[26] It also remained unclear whether the bodies of the parent company were subject to the notification requirements if they deal in the issuing subsidiary's shares. Whilst the MAD 2003 contained no provisions hereon, literature confirmed a notification obligation if the parent company had access to the subsidiary's information.[27] The wording of the provision speaks against this interpretation. Instead, it must be determined whether the person in question is a member of the issuer's board.

The MAR further provides that the notification obligation also refers to '**persons closely associated**' with PDMRs. Thus, these persons are also obliged to disclose their transactions. The extension of the notification obligation is necessary in order to prevent the rule from being circumvented. Article 3(1)(26) MAR especially refers to spouses or any partners considered by national law as equivalent to a spouse, dependent children and other relatives of the person discharging managerial responsibilities. The provision further subjects any legal person, trust or partnership to these obligations, if their managerial responsibilities are discharged by a person who is regarded as discharging managerial responsibilities with the issuer.[28]

---

[25] Cf. CESR, Advice on the Second Set of Level 2 Implementing Measures for a Market Abuse Directive, August 2003, CESR/03/212c, No. 42.
[26] Cf. M. Pfüller, in: Fuchs (ed.), *Kommentar zum WpHG*, § 15a para. 76; R. Sethe and A. Hellgardt, in: Assmann et al. (eds.), *Kommentar zum Wertpapierhandelsrecht*, Art. 19 VO Nr. 596/2014 Rn. 32. Dissenting opinion: BaFin, Emittentenleitfaden, Modul C, p. 67.
[27] Cf. M. Pfüller, in: Fuchs (ed.), *Kommentar zum WpHG*, § 15a para. 77.
[28] Cf. in more detail C. Kumpan, 61 AG (2016), 446, 450–451.

(b) Transactions Subject to the Notification Requirements

15 The MAR defines **'every transaction conducted** on [a persons'] **own account** relating to the **shares** or **debt instruments** of that issuer, or to **derivatives** or **other financial instruments** linked to them' as subject to the notification requirement.[29] However, no notification is required or notification may be delayed until the total amount of transactions has reached € 5,000 at the end of a calendar year.[30] This exemption is to prevent a flood of notifications and an 'information overload' regarding irrelevant transactions. If the threshold of € 5,000 is exceeded in the course of the year, all prior transactions must subsequently be reported to the competent authorities.

16 Article 10 Delegated Regulation (EU) No. 2016/522 specifies notified transactions as including, inter alia, (a) acquisition, disposal, short sale, subscription or exchange and (b) acceptance or exercise of a stock option. Under the MAD 2003 regime, the acquisition of shares through gifts/donations or inheritances was not subject to notification requirements. This has changed since 3 July 2016. Article 10(2)(k) defines gifts and donations made or received and inheritances received as notified transactions.

17 The disclosure obligations under the MAD 2003 were limited to **financial instruments admitted** to **trading** on a **regulated market**. The European legislator has expanded the regime to financial instruments, which are only traded on an MTF or an OTF, provided the issuer has approved trading or requested admission to trading of their financial instrument on an MTF.[31] This is in line with other reforms of the market abuse regime, which aim at ensuring a high level of investor protection also on the less regulated markets, such as the AIM Italia, Euronext Growth in Paris, First North in the Nordic Countries or Scale in Frankfurt.[32]

(c) Content of the Notification and Notification Period

18 Delegated Regulation 2016/523 provides a **template** for **notification** that is to be used by the PDMR and persons closely associated with them. The template must in particular contain information on the **name** of the **person**, the **reason** for **notification** and **details** of the **transaction**, such as a description of the financial instrument and the price and volume of the transaction. The MAR requires that the **notification** be made **promptly** and no later than three business days after the transaction.[33] It shall be submitted to the national supervisory authority and the issuer.

2. Publication

19 The **issuer** then has to ensure that the notified **information** is **made public promptly** and no later than three business days after the transaction in a manner which enables fast access

---

[29] Cf. Art. 19(1)(a) MAR.
[30] Cf. Art. 19(8) MAR.
[31] Cf. Art. 19(4) MAR.
[32] See on the so-called SME Growth Markets R. Veil § 7 para. 23 ff.
[33] Cf. Art. 19(1)subsec(2) MAR.

to this information on a non-discriminatory basis.[34] Member States may, however, provide that the NCA may itself make public the information.

IV. Closed Period

According to Article 19(11) MAR, **PDMRs** shall **not conduct** any **transactions** on their own account or for the account of a third party relating to the shares or debt instruments of the issuer or to derivatives or other financial instruments linked to them during a closed period of **30 calendar days before the announcement** of an **interim financial report** or a **year-end report** which the issuer is obliged to make public according to the rules of the trading venue or national law. PDMRs are thus usually prevented from carrying out transactions twice a year. If the respective issuer publishes quarterly financial reports on the basis of the applicable listing rules or national laws,[35] its PDMRs are prevented from trading in these shares for a total of four months per year. 20

The closed periods constitute a considerable interference with a manager's rights. Exceptions from this general rule are thus necessary in order to avoid disproportionate results. Transactions are, however, not permitted ex lege, the respective approval rather having to be granted by the issuer: The issuer may allow a PDMR to trade either (i) on a case-by-case basis due to the existence of exceptional circumstances, such as severe financial difficulty, which require the immediate sale of shares,[36] or (ii) due to characteristics or the trading involved for transactions made under an employee share or saving scheme, qualification or entitlement of shares, or transactions where the beneficial interest in the relevant security does not change.[37] 21

The details of the prerequisites for an exemption are laid down in Article 8 and 9 of Regulation 2016/522. Interestingly, the requirements are considerably stricter than those provided for in the Model Code of the United Kingdom, which served as a regulatory model for Union law.[38] In a stock corporation with a two-tier system, the supervisory board is competent for granting the permission regarding share transactions of a member of the board of directors. 22

Comparable to the insider trading prohibitions, the underlying notion of the new provisions is to ensure an equal treatment of investors with regard to the information relevant for an investment decision. There are, however, numerous reasons against such a trading prohibition. Firstly, it can not *per se* be regarded as inappropriate if a manager carries out certain transactions based on his general knowledge of the issuer's business development. It is rather sufficient to prohibit managers from making use of inside information in order to ensure investor confidence in the functioning of the markets. Secondly, 23

---

[34] Cf. Art. 19(3) MAR. See in more detail H. Brinckmann § 16 para. 39 ff.
[35] See H. Brinckmann § 18 para. 54 ff.
[36] The term 'exceptional circumstances' is defined in Art. 8 Delegated Regulation (EU) No. 2016/522: Circumstances shall be considered to be exceptional when they are extremely urgent, unforeseen and compelling and where their cause is external to the PDMR and the PDMR has no control over them.
[37] Cf. Art. 19(12) MAR.
[38] Cf. M. Diekgräf, *Directors' Dealings*, 171 ff. and 185 ff. on former rules in Sweden and Poland.

prohibiting all transactions runs contrary to the regulatory aim of improving informational efficiency of the markets by making public directors' dealings. Thirdly, for managers, the closed periods interfere with their constitutional ownership rights. Fourthly, the possible exceptions from the general prohibition lead to difficult questions in their practical application.

V. Supervision and Sanctions

1. Requirements under European Law

24 The compliance with the provisions on directors' dealings is supervised by the national supervisory authorities (NCAs) which have the supervisory and investigatory powers laid down in the MAR.[39]

25 The MAR also requires Member States to introduce sanctions that can be imposed for breaches of the notification and publication duties.[40] These must not only apply to PDMRs and persons associated with them, but also to the issuer with regard to his obligation to publish the information. In respect of a natural person, Member States have to provide maximum **administrative pecuniary sanctions** of at least € 500,000 and in respect of legal persons of at least € 1 million.[41]

2. Disgorgement of Profits

26 In the **United States**, the cradle of capital markets law, the phenomenon of directors having an informational advantage and using this unfairly is countered by strict rules on the recovery of profit by the issuer. The issuer, and under certain conditions also the shareholders, are in these cases permitted to recover so-called 'short swing trading profits'.[42] The disgorgement of profits does not require that the director breached his notification obligation regarding security tradings on his own account.[43] It rather encompasses all profits that were attained by the acquisition or disposal of the issuer's shares during a six-month-period ('**short-swing trading profits**'). These profits can be recovered by the issuer irrespective of whether the offender had access to inside information, had possession thereof, intended to make use of the information or to make profits.[44] It is irrefutably assumed that the respective person possessed inside information during the six-month-period.[45] The length of the

---

[39] See R. Veil § 14 para. 96 ff.
[40] Cf. Art. 30(1)(a) MAR.
[41] Cf. Art. 30(2)(i)(iii) and (j)(iii) MAR.
[42] Cf. sec. 16(b) SEA.
[43] This notification obligation is laid down in sec. 16(a) SEA.
[44] Cf. W. Wang and M. Steinberg, *Insider Trading*, § 15.1.
[45] J. Cox and T. Hazen, *Corporations*, § 12.08; M. Steinberg and D. Landsdale, 68 Notre Dame L. Rev. (1992), 33, 35.

period was chosen due to the fact that insider dealings usually take place during a relatively short time.[46] The strict liability was already described as a 'crude rule of thumb' during the legislative procedure.[47]

In **Europe**, a similarly strict sanction does not exist. The MAR requires Member States to provide the disgorgement of the profits gained or losses avoided due to the infringement insofar as they can be determined.[48] Whether this general provision is applicable in case of an infringement of the obligation to disclose directors' dealings is, however, doubtful. The director does not obtain the economic advantage through the failure to notify the issuer on the transaction, as would be required for a liability under the MAR, but rather through the transaction itself.[49]

3. Civil Liability

In the case of a violation of the closed period provided for in Article 19(11) MAR, the transaction could be null and void. The question is to be assessed in the same way as in insider trading law. The protection of investors and proper functioning of markets do not require nullity.

The question as to whether individual investors may claim damages from members of the company's bodies or other persons obligated to notification for a breach of their duties regarding directors' dealings remains as yet largely unclear. This question can arise especially if a member of the administrative or supervisory board makes an incorrect notification and the issuer publishes this information. The courts have not as yet examined this question and it is also hardly discussed in the Member States. The predominant opinion in Germany is that the provisions on directors' dealings do not constitute 'protective rules' in the sense of the law of torts, granting the right to claim damages.[50] The legislature's aim was, however, not the protection of the individual investor's financial interests but rather ensuring the functioning of the capital markets.[51] Therefore, the only applicable legal basis for damage claims is § 826 BGB which is, however, hardly likely to be of practical relevance due to its strict prerequisite of an intentional damage contrary to public policy. Investors would further have to prove that their transaction was based on incorrect notification—a requirement that is already difficult to prove in cases of incorrect ad hoc notifications.[52]

---

[46] Cf. *Blau v. Max Factor & Co.*, 342 F.2d 304, 308 (9th Cir.), cert. denied, 382 U.p. 892 (1965).
[47] Thomas Corcoran (principal spokesman of the Congress), as cited in A. Jacobs, 32 N.Y.L. Sch. L. Rev. (1987), 209, 345 fn. 1533.
[48] Cf. Art. 30(2)(b) MAR.
[49] Cf. R. Veil, 34 ZGR (2005), 155, 168.
[50] Cf. R. Sethe and A. Hellgardt, in: Assmann et al. (eds.), *Kommentar zum Wertpapierhandelsrecht*, Art. 19 MAR para. 185, § 15a para. 140; G. Schuster, 167 ZHR (2003), 193, 215; F. Osterloh, *Directors' Dealings*, 202–203. Dissenting opinion: P. Maume and M. Keller, 46 ZGR (2017), 273, 298.
[51] On the regulatory aims see above para. 2.
[52] See R. Veil § 19 para. 85.

VI. Conclusion

30 The disclosure obligation regarding directors' dealings is meanwhile a central element of European capital markets law. Whilst market participants may not be able to draw reliable conclusions regarding the future profits of an issuer from every transaction by a PDMR, empirical studies show that publication of directors' dealings does allow certain conclusions to be drawn. The disclosure obligations additionally facilitate supervision by the national authorities in uncovering insider dealings. It is therefore legitimate that the rules apply to all issuers whose financial instruments are traded on a regulated market, an MTF or an OTF, provided they have approved trading or requested admission to trading of their financial instrument on an MTF.

31 The further changes established by the MAR are only partially convincing. The fact that the European legislator extended the disclosure obligations, thereby enabling a better supervision of the markets by the NCAs, is to be welcomed. It is unlikely that market participants will experience an information overload through too many notifications. At the same time, however, the closed periods must be criticised as counteracting the concept of informational efficiency pursued by the disclosure obligations. It is furthermore highly unlikely that the predetermined period of four weeks prior to the announcement of interim financial reports and year-end reports really covers the entire relevant time during which managers should be prohibited from exploiting an information advantage.

§ 22

Corporate Governance and Shareholder Rights

Bibliography

Bachmann, Gregor, *Disclosure of Corporate Governance by Codes*, in: Tountopoulos, Vassilios and Veil, Rüdiger (eds.), *Transparency of Stock Corporations in Europe* (2019), 57–70; Bachmann, Gregor, *Der 'Europäische Corporate Governance-Rahmen'—Zum Grünbuch 2011 der Europäischen Kommission*, 28 WM (2011), 1301–1310; Dauner-Lieb, Barbara, *Siegeszug der Technokraten?—Der Kampf der Bits und Bytes gegen das Papier bei Börseninformationen am Beispiel von Art. 17 des Entwurfs der Transparenzrichtlinie*, 9 DStR (2004), 361–366; Enriques, Luca and Tröger, Tobias H., *The Law and Finance of Related Party Transactions* (2019); Faure, Anna, *Verantwortung institutioneller Aktionäre im deutschen Aktienrecht* (2019); Fleischer, Holger and Strothotte, Christian, *Ein Stewardship Code für institutionelle Investoren: Wohlverhaltensregeln und Offenlegung der Abstimmungspolitik als Vorbild für Deutschland und Europa?*, 7 AG (2011), 221–233; Habersack, Mathias, *Europäisches Gesellschaftsrecht im Wandel—Bemerkungen zum Aktionsplan der EG-Kommission betreffend die Modernisierung des Gesellschaftsrechts und die Verbesserung der Corporate Governance in der Europäischen Union*, 1 NZG (2004), 1–9; Katsas, Theodoros, *Disclosure as a Legal Instrument against Potential Abusive Behaviour in the Case of Related Party Transactions*, in: Tountopoulos, Vassilios and Veil, Rüdiger (eds.), *Transparency of Stock Corporations in Europe* (2019), 71–86; Klene, Victor, *Related Party Transactions* (2017); Sørensen, Karsten E., *Access to Information in Company Registers*, in: Tountopoulos, Vassilios and Veil, Rüdiger (eds.), *Transparency of Stock Corporations in Europe* (2019), 7–28; Veil, Rüdiger and Sauter, Bettina, *Corporate Governance-Berichterstattung nach dem BilMoG—eine empirische Analyse der Publizitätspflichten und Reformvorschläge*, in: Veil, Rüdiger (ed.), *Unternehmensrecht in der Reformdiskussion* (2013), 19–34; Velte, Patrick and Weber, Stefan C., *Prüfung von Corporate Governance Statements post BilMoG*, 7 StuB (2011), 256–261; Weber, Stefan C. and Velte, Patrick, *Die Bedeutung von Corporate Governance Reports aus Investorensicht. Eine empirische Untersuchung im DAX*, 24 DStR (2011), 1141–1147.

I. Introduction

A European concept on the organisational structure of companies has been under discussion for the last 50 years. The European Commission's first proposal for a respective directive restricted to stock corporations in 1972 was unsuccessful. The main reasons for this are presumably the two different organisational structures for companies—*one tier-* and *two tier-*systems—in the Member States, the fact that managerial codetermination—in the *one tier-*system in the board of directors and in the *two tier-*systems in the supervisory board—is not equally established in all Member States and codified laws on company groups are unknown to most jurisdictions in the Member States. The Commission has since restricted itself to regulating individual organisational aspects or developing non-binding recommendations.[1] The conceptual basis for its measures at a European level can be found in the **Action Plan** of 23 May 2003 relating to the **modernisation of company law** and the enhancement of **corporate governance**.[2]

2 The European legislature has implemented the Commission's proposals in accounting law. The disclosure obligations not only pursue the goal of overcoming informational asymmetries (between the company and the public), but also have a regulatory function, incentivising the management of the company to take into account the respective ESG aspects in its business policy.[3] They are presented in this section insofar as they are not already dealt with in § 18 of this book on periodic dislosure. In this context, the recent initiative of the European Commission to align corporate governance more strongly with the idea of sustainability (**sustainable corporate governance**) is also addressed. Subsequently, the disclosure obligations concerning shareholders' rights are examined. The latter are a plethora of rules under company and capital markets law, which have the purpose of making it easier for shareholders to exercise their rights.

3 The **transparency** of corporations provided by the **commercial register** is not dealt with, as it is a matter of commercial and company law. Directive (EU) 2017/1132 of the European Parliament and of the Council of 14 June 2017 relating to certain aspects of company law coordinates the relevant legislation of the Member States. However, there is no European register so far; instead, each Member State has its own register subject to different filing and verification obligations. Access to information by third parties and the legal effects of a registration are also regulated disparately.[4] Nonetheless, the national registers are interconnected through the Business Registers Interconnection System (BRIS).[5]

II. Corporate Governance

1. Introduction

4 The Action Plan closely examined the question in which way the corporate governance of companies can be effectively regulated at a European level. The European Commission determined that most Member States had implemented rules for improving corporate governance and corporate control at the beginning of the millennium. It nevertheless refused to develop a **European Corporate Governance Codex**, referring to the OECD's measures in this regard and to the fact that the national codices in the Member States on this topic

---

[1] Cf. M. Habersack, 1 NZG (2004), 1, 3.
[2] Cf. Commission, Modernising Company Law and Enhancing Corporate Governance in the European Union—A Plan to Move Forward, 21 May 2003, COM(2003) 284 final.
[3] See on the different functions of disclosure obligations R. Veil § 2 para. 26 ff., 39 ff.
[4] Cf. K. Sørensen, in: Tountopoulos and Veil (eds.), *Transparency of Stock Corporations in Europe*, 7, 12 ff.
[5] Cf. Art. 22 Directive (EU) 2017/1132 of the European Parliament and of the Council of 14 June 2017 relating to certain aspects of company law.

were to a high degree comparable. The Commission therefore did not regard a European Codex as particularly recommendable. In its Action Plan the Commission instead focused on increasing the disclosure obligations with regard to the rules on corporate governance and supervision of publicly listed companies. This approach was realised with the Directive of 14 June 2006.[6] Companies of which the securities are admitted to trading on a regulated market are obliged to include a corporate governance statement in their annual report.[7] The statement about key information constitutes a separate section of the management report.

2. Corporate Governance Statement

Companies whose securities are admitted to trading on a regulated market shall include a **corporate governance statement** in the **management report**.[8] This duty applies to listed companies because such companies may play a prominent role in the economies in which they operate.[9] The corporate governance statement has an important information function. According to empirical studies, market participants attach great importance above all to the way in which the board of directors and the supervisory board work together.[10]

The corporate governance statement should at least contain the following information: (i) the **corporate governance code** to which the company is subject; (ii) an explanation by the company as to which **parts** of the corporate governance **code it departs from** and the reasons for doing so; (iii) a description of the main features of the company's internal control and **risk management systems** in relation to the financial reporting process; (iv) a description of the operation of the **shareholder meeting** and its key powers and a description of shareholders' rights and how they can be exercised (unless the information is already fully provided for in national law); (v) the **composition** and **operation** of the administrative, management and supervisory **bodies** and their committees (vi) information on the **diversity concept** pursued by the company in connection with the administrative, management and supervisory bodies of the company with regard to aspects such as age, gender, or educational and professional experience.

Member States are not obliged to adopt a corporate governance code. However, Directive 2013/34/EU assumes that a code exists in most Member States.[11] The requirements regarding the content of the corporate governance statement are based on the fact that the Member States provide so-called *comply or explain*-mechanisms. The board of directors (*one tier*-system) or, respectively, the managing board and the supervisory board (*two tier*-system)

---

[6] Directive 2006/46/EG of the European Parliament and of the Council of 14 June 2006, OJ L 224, 16 August 2006, p. 1–7. The Directive was repealed by Directive 2013/34/EU of the European Parliament and of the Council of 26 June 2013, on the annual financial statements, consolidated financial statements and related reports of certain types of undertakings, amending Directive 2006/43/EC of the European Parliament and of the Council and repealing Council Directives 78/660/EEC and 83/349/EEC, OJ L 182, 29 June 2013, p. 19–76.
[7] Cf. Art. 20(1) Directive 2013/34/EU.
[8] Cf. Art. 20(1) Directive 2013/34/EU.
[9] Cf. Recital 28 Directive 2013/34/EU.
[10] Cf. S. Weber and P. Velte, 24 DStR (2011), 1141, 1146.
[11] Cf. G. Bachmann, in: Tountopoulos and Veil (eds.), *Transparency of Stock Corporations in Europe*, 57, 62 f.

must explain whether they comply with the recommendations of the Corporate Governance Codex applicable in the respective Member State. The **comply-or-explain mechanism** can be regarded as a key feature of European company law.[12] In practice, the information submitted by different companies varies considerably. A lot of reports focus on compliance programs, others on labour and social standards. Some companies further provide specifics of their legal form (eg SE) or describe their co-determination and participation agreement (SE).[13]

8   The requirements regarding the description of the composition and operation of the administrative, management and supervisory bodies and their committees are easier for the companies to follow. Some provide very detailed information in this regard, including information on the agreed and actual frequency of meetings, and partially also on committees and the number of participants.[14]

9   It can be recommendable to inform investors on certain aspects of corporate governance. Empirical studies have shown that market participants place particular importance on the way in which management and supervisory board cooperate.[15] The European legislator should therefore amend these rules and put the respective reporting obligations into more concrete terms.

10 It must further be regarded as problematic that European law does not make any specific requirements for the Member States on the enforcement of the rules on the corporate governance statements, ie in particular which sanction they should foresee for breaches of these rules.

3. Sustainable Corporate Governance

11 Under the presidency of *Ursula von der Leyen*, the European Commission has set itself the task of improving the European legal framework for corporate governance. The aim is to enable companies to focus on long-term, sustainable value creation rather than on short-term benefits. The initiative aims to better align the interests of companies, their shareholders, managers, stakeholders and society. A reform of corporate governance is an essential element of the 'European Green'.[16]

12 In July 2020, the European Commission published a study it had commissioned from the auditing firm EY (Study on directors' duties and sustainable corporate governance), which reveals a multitude of reform topics. The study claims that short-term thinking by directors is detrimental to companies and society, and that in order to counter this problem, fundamental reforms of company law should be considered. The study does not make any

---

[12] Cf. G. Bachmann, in: Tountopoulos and Veil (eds.), *Transparency of Stock Corporations in Europe*, 57, 69.
[13] Cf. evaluation of an empirical analysis by R. Veil and B. Sauter in: Veil (ed.), *Unternehmensrecht in der Diskussion*, 19, 28.
[14] R. Veil and B. Sauter, in: Veil (ed.), *Unternehmensrecht in der Diskussion*, 19, 29.
[15] The survey amongst investors carried out by S. Weber and P. Velte, 24 DStR (2011), 1141, 1146 comes to comparable results, the participants in the survey placing great importance on reports relating to the way in which managing board and supervisory board cooperate.
[16] The European Green Deal is the European Commission's plan to make the European economy more sustainable. See https://ec.europa.eu/info/strategy/priorities-2019-2024/european-green-deal_en.

concrete proposals, but points out various possibilities for action. These include directives of company law aimed at harmonising national laws.

Of particular interest in the context of the European disclosure regimes on corporate governance is that one of the measures could be to oblige **companies** to **integrate sustainability aspects** into their **business strategies**. The study discusses the idea that companies could also be obliged to set sustainability targets. A reform could also, according to the study, require companies to **disclose** their sustainability strategy and targets to the public.[17] These reform proposals would perfectly fit into the company, accounting and capital markets law of the Member States. This does not apply to other reform proposals, such as the alignment of the corporate purpose with social and environmental concerns (ESG) and the involvement of stakeholders in the enforcement of duties of the board of directors. However, the disclosure obligations should be aligned with CSR reporting, which is already harmonised across the Union.

III. Shareholders' Rights

1. Introduction

When the European legislature enacted the TD in 2004, its aim was to ensure that the holders of shares traded on the regulated market could exercise their rights. This presents a particular problem for investors not situated in the issuer's home Member State[18] as obtaining information on the general meeting and the procedures for exercising voting rights is more difficult from abroad. The TD aims at ensuring **access** to **information** about the investor and **facilitating** the **use of proxies**.[19] It merely establishes requirements concerning the information necessary for shareholders to be able to exercise their rights.

In contrast, aspects of company law are covered by the directive on the exercise of certain rights of shareholders in listed companies (Shareholder Rights Directive).[20] The SRD contains provisions on proxy voting: every shareholder has the right to appoint any other natural or legal person as a proxy holder to attend and vote at a general meeting in his name.[21]

With the reform of this directive (SRD II), the European legislator has taken into account the increasing importance of institutional investors and asset managers. On the one hand, this group of investors is to be encouraged to exercise the voting rights from shares they

---

[17] Commission, Study on directors' duties and sustainable corporate governance, Final Report, July 2020, p. 104.
[18] Cf. Recital 25 TD.
[19] Cf. Commission, Proposal for a Directive of the European Parliament and of the Council on the harmonisation of transparency requirements with regard to information about issuers whose securities are admitted to trading on a regulated market and amending Directive 2001/34/EC, 26 March 2003, COM(2003) 138 final, p. 22.
[20] Directive 2007/36/EC of the European Parliament and of the Council of 11 July 2007 on the exercise of certain rights of shareholders in listed companies, OJ L 184, 14 July 2007, p. 17.
[21] Cf. Art. 10(1) SRD.

have in their portfolio. In doing so, the legislator wants to corporate governance of listed companies. On the other hand, institutional investors and asset managers shall be transparent towards their clients. Finally, transparency can counter conflicts of interest. This is a traditional approach of capital markets law, which the SRD II takes up with regard to related party transactions. Therefore, this book looks at these disclosure requirements in the context of the European transparency regimes.

2. Information Necessary to Exercise Shareholders' Rights

17 The TD centres around two different concepts regarding the information of shareholders: firstly, it requires issuers to make public without delay any change in the rights attached to the various classes of shares;[22] secondly, it requires that issuers of shares[23] and debt securities[24] admitted to trading on a regulated market ensure that all information necessary to enable the holders to exercise their rights is publicly available. In both cases the requirements are thus addressed to the issuer.[25] The provisions are therefore to be classed as regulatory disclosure obligations.[26] The TD does not only contain disclosure obligations but also demands that all shareholders in the same position be treated as equal.[27] A corresponding right of equal treatment exists for the holders of debt securities.[28]

(a) Disclosure of Changes in the Rights Attached to Shares

18 According to Article 16 TD, the Member States must introduce two disclosure obligations. The first applies to issuers whose shares are admitted to trading on a regulated market. They must disclose all changes in the rights attached to the various classes of shares, including changes in the rights attached to derivative securities issued by the issuer itself and giving access to the shares of that issuer. The rights referred to will mostly be voting and dividend rights.

19 The second disclosure obligation applies to issuers of securities other than shares admitted to trading on a regulated market, such as loans,[29] especially convertible bonds and warrant bonds.[30] Issuers of such financial instruments are also required to make public without delay any changes in the rights of holders which could indirectly affect the rights, in particular resulting from a change in loan terms or in interest rates.[31]

---

[22] Cf. Art. 16 TD.
[23] Cf. Art. 17 TD.
[24] Cf. Art. 18 TD.
[25] Defined in Art. 2(1)(d) TD.
[26] Cf. P. Mülbert, in: Assmann et al. (eds.), *Kommentar zum Wertpapierhandelsrecht*, vor § 48 WpHG para. 11.
[27] Cf. Art. 17(1) TD.
[28] Cf. Art. 18(1) TD.
[29] Cf. the definition of the term securities in Art. 2(1)(a) TD; in more detail see R. Veil § 8 para. 4.
[30] Cf. P. Mülbert, in: Assmann et al. (eds.), *Kommentar zum Wertpapierhandelsrecht*, § 50 para. 10.
[31] Cf. Art. 16(2) TD.

(b) Disclosure of Information Necessary for Exercising Rights

(aa) Information Necessary for Shareholders

An issuer of shares admitted to trading on the regulated market must ensure that all the facilities and information necessary to enable holders of shares to exercise their rights are available in the home Member State and that the integrity of data is preserved.[32] The directive divides this general requirement into four more specific obligations for the issuer.

The issuer must provide **information** on the place, time and agenda of **meetings**, the total number of shares and voting rights and the rights of holders to participate in meetings in order to facilitate the correct participation in the general meetings for the investors.[33] This information is particularly helpful to foreign investors.

The issuer must further make a **proxy form** available to each person entitled to vote at a shareholders' meeting, either on paper or, where applicable, by electronic means, together with the notice concerning the meeting or, on request, after an announcement of the meeting.[34] This provision aims to facilitate the use of proxies for the general meeting.

The provision according to which the issuer must designate a financial institution through which shareholders may exercise their financial rights as its **agent**[35] has the same aim. The legal foundations for proxy voting through agents of financial institutions can be found in the company laws of the Member States.

An issuer must further publish notices or distribute circulars concerning the allocation and **payment** of **dividends** and the issue of new shares, including information on any arrangements for allotment, subscription, cancellation or conversion.[36]

(bb) Information Necessary for the Holders of Debt Securities

Issuers of debt securities admitted to trading on a regulated market are also subject to extensive disclosure requirements. 'Debt securities' include bonds or other forms of transferable securitised debts, with the exception of securities which are equivalent to shares in companies or which, if converted or if the rights conferred by them are exercised, give rise to a right to acquire shares or securities equivalent to shares.[37]

Issuers of debt securities must also ensure that all the facilities and information necessary to enable debt securities holders to exercise their rights are publicly available in the home Member State and that the integrity of data is preserved.[38] This general obligation is defined more precisely by numerous more detailed disclosure requirements which largely coincide with those binding for issuers of shares admitted to trading on a regulated market.

The issuer of debt securities must, for example, publish notices, or distribute circulars, concerning the place, time and agenda of meetings of debt securities holders, the payment of interest, the exercise of any conversion, exchange, subscription or cancellation rights, and

---

[32] Cf. Art. 17(2) TD.
[33] Cf. Art. 17(2)(a) TD.
[34] Cf. Art. 17(2)(b) TD.
[35] Cf. Art. 17(2)(c) TD.
[36] Cf. Art. 17(2)(d) TD.
[37] Cf. Art. 2(1)(b) TD.
[38] Cf. Art. 18(2) TD.

repayment, as well as the right of those holders to participate therein.[39] It must further make a proxy form available either on paper or, where applicable, by electronic means, to each person entitled to vote at a meeting of debt securities holders, together with the notice concerning the meeting or, on request, after an announcement of the meeting.[40] Finally, the issuer is required to designate a financial institution as its agent through which debt securities holders may exercise their financial rights.[41]

3. Institutional Investors

28   The SRD II recognises that **institutional investors** (life insurance companies and institutions for occupational retirement provision) and **asset managers** (asset managers as defined by MiFID II, AIFM, UCITS management companies and UCITS investment companies) are **significant shareholders of listed companies** and play an important role in corporate governance as well as in the long-term success of listed companies.[42] However, experience shows that they often do not involve themselves in the companies in which they hold shares and also lack transparency regarding their investment strategy, their engagement policy and its implementation.[43]

29   The SRD II addresses these problems using two **disclosure requirements** based on a **comply-or-explain mechanism**. Thus, institutional investors and asset managers are to publish the relevant information or publicly disclose a reasoned explanation as to why they have chosen not to comply with one or more of these requirements. The FRC Stewardship Code from the United Kingdom serves as a model in this respect.[44] The European regime attempts to counter the investors' apathy to take a closer look at the portfolio company. However, this apathy may well be rational if a manager has invested in numerous companies, possibly with comparatively small sums.

30   The first disclosure obligation concerns the **engagement policy**.[45] Institutional investors and asset managers have to describe their participation in the portfolio companies. This includes, among other things, the exercise of shareholder rights, the monitoring of important matters of the portfolio companies, the exchange of opinions with the corporate bodies, the cooperation with other shareholders and the handling of conflicts of interest. The implementation of the policy (including the description of voting behaviour) must be publicly disclosed annually. The disclosure obligation has an information function (informing the end customers of the institutional investor and asset manager) and a regulatory function under company law (incentives to exercise shareholder rights and thereby improve the corporate governance of listed companies).[46]

---

[39] Cf. Art. 18(2)(a) TD.
[40] Cf. Art. 18(2)(b) TD.
[41] Cf. Art. 18(2)(c) TD.
[42] Cf. Recital 15 SRD II; for further details regarding the institutional investors' influence see A. Faure, *Verantwortung institutioneller Aktionäre*, 103 ff.
[43] Cf. Recital 15 SRD II.
[44] Cf. H. Fleischer and C. Strothotte, 7 AG (2011), 221 ff.; A. Faure, *Verantwortung institutioneller Aktionäre*, 124 ff.
[45] Cf. Art. 3g SRD II; according to A. Faure, *Verantwortung institutioneller Aktionäre*, 170, almost word-for-word adoption of the principles of the Stewardship Code.
[46] See regarding these functions R. Veil § 2 para. 39.

The second disclosure obligation concerns the **investment strategy** of institutional investors. The extent to which the main elements of the investment strategy match the profile and maturity of the liabilities and how they contribute to the medium-to-long-term performance of the institutional investor's assets shall be made public.[47] If the institutional investor mandates an asset manager for the investment, the institutional investor shall disclose certain aspects of the underlying arrangement, namely how the arrangement incentivises the asset manager to align its investment strategy and investment decisions with the profile and maturity of the institutional investor's liabilities.[48] Ultimately, the asset manager is also subject to disclosure obligations vis-à-vis the institutional investor.[49]

The Stewardship Code has found wide acceptance in the UK in practice.[50] Issuers report that institutional investors' behaviour has changed due to the Code.[51] This is anecdotal evidence of the regulatory function of the disclosure requirement. It remains to be seen whether the European regime will be as successful.

4. Related Party Transactions

The TD is limited to requiring the publication of information that is significant for the exercise of shareholders' rights (see para. 18). The corporate law aspects of the exercise of shareholders' rights are regulated by the SRD. The SRD I, adopted in 2007, already addressed the issue and provided rules for proxy voting: every shareholder has the right to appoint another person as a proxy to attend the general meeting on his or her behalf and exercise his or her voting right.[52]

The SRD II of 2017 took up another topic under company law: transactions of the company with related parties. The problem of these transactions, also referred to as related party transactions, is well illustrated in recital 42 of the SRD II: '**Transactions with related parties** may cause prejudice to companies and their shareholders, as they may give the related party the opportunity to **appropriate value belonging to the company**.'

The SRD II seeks to counter the dangers of so-called *tunnelling*—hidden transfer of assets (mostly by means of sales transactions at non-market prices) of the company to its major shareholder—in two ways. One regulatory approach is to make transactions with related parties above a certain size subject to **shareholder or supervisory board approval**. In this way, the related party can be prevented from exploiting its position to the detriment of minority shareholders. Another regulatory approach is the **disclosure of transactions**. The SRD II stipulates that material transactions must be publicly disclosed at the latest at the time of their conclusion.[53]

---

[47] Cf. Art. 3h(1) SRD II.
[48] Cf. Art. 3h(2) SRD II.
[49] Cf. Art. 3i SRD II.
[50] Cf. FRC Annual Reports.
[51] Cf. A. Faure, *Verantwortung institutioneller Aktionäre*, 133.
[52] Cf. Art. 10(1) SRD.
[53] Cf. Art. 9c(2) SRD II.

36　The requirements of SRD II are limited to a minimum harmonisation of national rules. In addition, the Member States have numerous regulatory options. In particular, they are largely free to determine the conditions under which a transaction is to be considered material. This is explained by the different regulatory concepts that Member States have traditionally used to deal with conflicts of interest in related party transactions.[54] In Germany, for example, the statutory capital maintenance requirement is of central importance, as it prohibits hidden contributions of assets to shareholders.[55] Besides, non-competition obligations and fiduciary duties of directors and officers play an important role. Against this background, it is not surprising that individual Member States have not attached great importance to the harmonisation requirements of SRD II. The consequence of the harmonisation of core areas is that the legal landscape in the EU is fragmented.[56]

IV. Conclusion

37　Transparency on the corporate governance of publicly listed stock corporations developed slowly in Europe. The legislature has not followed any specific plan. It therefore comes as no surprise that there is as yet no consistent transparency regime. The approach implemented in accounting law to make the legal and actual structures of corporate management and control visible via disclosure requirements is convincing. The duty of disclosure has primarily the goal to overcome information asymmetries between the company on the one hand, and investors, creditors, customers on the other hand. In particular, the information can be valuable for shareholders and investors to better assess the development and the situation of the company and the functioning of the company's internal supervision. The content of the report is only prescribed in key words. However, it is not strictly necessary to ensure coherent reporting through extensive and detailed requirements, as is the case in other areas of European capital markets law.

38　The further regulatory approach of strengthening shareholder rights through information obligations under capital markets law is to be assessed positively. The TD's disclosure requirements ensure that proxy voting is not subject to excessive administrative requirements and cannot be restricted unnecessarily. Further disclosure obligations for institutional investors and asset managers take into account the increased importance of these investors. Investors are enabled to better assess the investment strategy. In addition, the obligation to publish an engagement policy has a regulatory function that should not be underestimated.

39　The harmonisation of the transparency of related party transactions, on the other hand, has proven unsuccessful. The EU is far from a uniform legal landscape because the SRD II grants the Member States numerous regulatory options that cannot be justified even taking into account the divergent regulatory approaches already existing in the national legal systems.

---

[54] Cf. T. Katsas, in: Tountopoulos and Veil (eds.), *Transparency of Stock Corporations in Europe*, 71, 86.
[55] For a detailed analysis of the protective provisions see V. Klene, *Related Party Transactions*, 117 ff.
[56] Cf. regarding regional- and country-specific insights the contributions in L. Enriques and T. Tröger, *The Law and Finance of Related Party Transactions*, Chapters 11–17.

5

Trading Activities

§ 23

Investment Objectives

Bibliography

Alamad, Samir, *Financial and Accounting Principles in Islamic Finance* (2017); Bauer, Rob et al., *The Ethical Mutual Fund Performance Debate: New Evidence from Canada*, 70 JBE (2007), 111–124; Casper, Matthias et al., *Was vom Wucher übrig bleibt – Zinsverbote im historischen und kulturellen Vergleich* (2014); Dresig, Tilo, *Handelbarkeit von Risiken* (2000); Häuser, Franz, *Außerbörsliche Optionsgeschäfte (OTC-Optionen) aus der Sicht des novellierten Börsengesetzes*, 4 ZBB (1992), 249–266; Ekkenga, Jens, *Investmentfonds als neue Kontrollagenten einer „nachhaltigen" Realwirtschaft*, 36 WM (2020), 1664–1674; Ekkenga, Jens and Posch, Peter, *Die Klassifizierung umweltnützlicher „Wirtschaftstätigkeiten" und ihrer Finanzierung nach neuem Unionsrecht und das Problem des Greenwashing*, 5 WM (2021), 205–213; Heukamp, Wessel, *§ 8: Solvabilität, Kapitalanlage und Rechnungslegung*, in: Bürkle, Jürgen (ed.), *Compliance in Versicherungsunternehmen*, 3rd edn. (2020); Klöhn, Lars, *Kapitalmarkt, Spekulation und Behavioral Finance* (2006); Köndgen, Johannes, *Sustainable Finance: Wirtschaftsethik – Ökonomik – Regulierung*, in: Boele-Woelki, Katharina et al. (eds.), *Festschrift für Karsten Schmidt zum 80. Geburtstag* (2019), 671–700; Kreander, Niklas et al., *Evaluating the Performance of Ethical and Non-ethical Funds: A Matched Pair Analysis*, 32 JBFA, 7 (2005), 1465–1493; Langlois, Hugues and Lussier, Jacques, *Rational Investing* (2017); Lötscher, Marcel, *Prinzipien der katholischen Vermögensanlage* (2020); Perridon, Louis et al., *Finanzwirtschaft der Unternehmung*, 17th edn. (2017); Renneboog, Luc et al., *The price of ethics and stakeholder governance: The performance of socially responsible mutual funds*, 14 Journal of Corporate Finance (2008), 302–322; Röh, Lars and Scherber, Nina, *Nachhaltige Finanzinstrumente – ein neuer Produkttyp für den europäischen Finanzmarkt*, 4 RdF (2020), 250–257; Veil, Rüdiger et al., *Nachhaltige Kapitalanlagen durch Finanzmarktregulierung* (2019); Veil, Rüdiger, *Europa auf dem Weg zu einem Green Bond Standard*, 24 WM (2020), 1093–1102; Veil, Rüdiger, *Transparenz über nachhaltige Investments und Nachhaltigkeitsrisiken – ist die europäische Gesetzgebung zu kurz gesprungen?*, in: Grundmann, Stefan et al. (eds.), *Festschrift für Klaus J. Hopt zum 80. Geburtstag* (2020), 1321–1334; Veil, Rüdiger and Templer, Lena, *GameStop, Reddit und die Hedgefonds. Betrachtungen aus der Perspektive des europäischen Kapitalmarktrechts*, 19 ZIP (2021), 981–989; Wentrup, Christian, *Die Kontrolle von Hedgefonds* (2009).

I. Foundations

1. Return

When investing capital, an investor pursues the goal of generating a high return, ideally in the long term. In doing so, investors want to minimise the risk of capital loss and are interested in high liquidity of the assets. These three objectives are also referred to as the **magic triangle** of **financial investments**. However, as this term indicates, not all three objectives can be met at the same time. High returns typically imply high risk and low levels of liquidity; conversely, low-risk investments typically do not lead to high returns. The interconnection between the three objectives can be illustrated using the following two examples of traditional financial instruments.

2   In the case of a **bond**, the yield results from the interest rate promised by the issuer (also referred to as 'coupon'), which can be fixed or variable. The investment risk is determined by the creditworthiness of the issuer. Liquidity depends to a large extent on whether the bond is traded on a secondary market. An issuer whose credit rating is particularly high does not need to promise high interest rates in order to successfully place a bond nor will it necessarily apply for a listing of the bond. Yield, risk and liquidity are each low in this example of a bond issuer with the best rating.

3   In the case of a **share**, the issuer does not promise any interest payment. Instead, the return is received from the dividend and any other monetary benefits under the articles of association. In addition, there is the prospect of price increases of the shares, which also explains why shares are traded more frequently than bonds.[1] The flip side is that the risks are complex. The price change risk can be broken down into a general market risk and a company-specific risk. The return prospects are greater in the case of an issuer of listed shares than in the case of a bond issuer, but at the same time, the risks of the capital investment are greater as well.

4   The motives and reasons for investing capital (investment objectives) are very different. A private investor may be concerned with securing his retirement provision or building up assets; he then pursues a long-term investment horizon. If he is prepared to take high risks in order to achieve the greatest possible monetary advantage, he has short-term investment goals.

5   The investment objectives of institutional investors are determined by their business model. Insurance companies must be in a position to provide services to their customers in the long term. The legislature therefore requires them to invest their assets in accordance with the principle of prudence (see on the prudent person para. 21). Asset management companies distribute different funds in order to attract investors. These can be active and speculative (hedge funds) or passive and conservative (index funds).[2]

6   **Speculation** is characterised by the investor seeking to make a profit through a short-term capital investment.[3] This can happen in many different ways, for example via the purchase of a security and its sale shortly afterwards (speculation on a rising price) or the sale of a security and its purchase shortly afterwards (speculation on a falling price, in particular through short selling). Furthermore, an investor can use derivative financial products in order to profit disproportionately from price developments with a small capital investment. An investor speculates because he believes he can anticipate the development of the price of the security. If he assesses the price development with regard to the fundamental value of the security, he is also referred to as an information arbitrageur.[4] A short seller expects the price of the security to fall and sells it with the idea of being able to buy it later at a lower price. In terms of legal policy, this type of speculation is generally desirable because it contributes to the formation of information-efficient prices of securities.[5]

---

[1] Cf. L. Perridon et al., *Finanzwirtschaft der Unternehmung*, 229.
[2] Cf. regarding the active management of funds H. Langlois and J. Lussier, *Rational Investing*, 36 ff.
[3] Cf. L. Klöhn, *Kapitalmarkt, Spekulation und Behavioral Finance*, 23.
[4] Cf. L. Klöhn, *Kapitalmarkt, Spekulation und Behavioral Finance*, 26.
[5] See F. Walla § 24 para. 7.

The situation is different for investors who want to make a profit from the future trading of other investors. The *Gamestop* case attracted a lot of attention.[6] Private investors bought shares in this company in order to put short sellers at risk of a short squeeze. They managed to drive up the share price just by trading. In any case, the price increase was not driven by fundamental value-related information. As a result, short sellers had to buy the shares at inflated prices in order not to become liable to pay damages to their contractual partners with whom they had concluded lending transactions (danger of *short squeeze* or *market cornering*). This resulted in a further rise in the price of the shares. The speculation of small investors is harmful and can constitute market manipulation. Such investors are also known as parasitic traders.[7]

2. **ESG Investments**

Private and institutional investors are increasingly pursuing environmental and social objectives in their investments (also known as **Impact Investing** or Socially Responsible Investment (SRI)). The magic triangle becomes a magic square because the criterion of an ESG investment potentially conflicts with the other three criteria. The market for green investments is diverse.[8] Green bonds[9] and green funds[10] have the greatest practical importance.

Whether ESG investments generate higher or lower returns than conventional investments is subject to differing assessments. Empirical studies on SRI portfolios do not come to any clear conclusions. The majority of studies claim that statistically significant differences cannot be found.[11] However, it is not the EU's aim to improve investors' return prospects with the regulatory initiatives on sustainable finance. Instead, an economic and socio-political concern is being pursued. Private capital is to be mobilised so that the economy can be transformed in a climate-neutral way.[12]

ESG capital investments refer to people's ecological and social conscience. Investors are willing to achieve lower returns, if necessary, if their capital is used to promote ecologically meaningful projects. EU capital market regulation aims to prevent *greenwashing*—a product is described as being 'green' but is not—through **disclosure requirements** and to ensure that investors are able to assess the green quality of a financial product. The EU Regulation 2019/2088 provides for various disclosure obligations for insurance companies, managers of an AIF or UCITS, etc. (financial market participants in the terminology of the Regulation 2019/2088). These obligations are intended to **balance out information asymmetries**. A financial market participant that distributes sustainable financial products must inform investors about how the product is designed to achieve sustainability goals, such as the goals of the Paris Agreement (product-related transparency of sustainable investments).[13]

---

[6] The share price rose from approx. $ 30 to approx. $ 350 due to purchases by private investors. Cf. R. Veil and L. Templer, 19 ZIP (2021), 981.
[7] Cf. L. Klöhn, *Kapitalmarkt, Spekulation und Behavioral Finance*, 52.
[8] See R. Veil § 8 para. 29.
[9] Cf. R. Veil, 24 WM (2020), 1093 ff.
[10] Cf. R. Veil, in: FS Hopt, 1321 ff.
[11] Cf. amongst others N. Kreander et al., 32 JBFA, 7 (2005), 1465; L. Renneboog et al., 14 Journal of Corporate Finance (2008), 302; R. Bauer et al., 70 JBE (2007), 111.
[12] See R. Veil § 1 para. 59, R. Veil § 2 para. 21 ff. and H. Brinckmann § 16 para. 33 ff.
[13] Cf. R. Veil, in: FS Hopt, 1321, 1331.

11 The disclosure obligations set out in Regulation 2019/2088 also have a **regulatory function**.[14] They are intended to encourage institutional investors to consider **sustainability risks**. A financial market participant must disclose how it takes sustainability risks into account when making investment decisions. This applies irrespective of whether it offers a financial product with sustainability relevance or not. However, a financial market participant may not disclose by stating the reasons (*report-or-explain* mechanism).[15] French law provides for more extensive disclosure obligations for funds, which have a stronger regulatory effect. In France, an asset management company must declare how environmentally sustainable the managed funds are and how the portfolio (the fund's assets—shares, loans, derivatives, etc.) contributes to compliance with international climate protection targets. These disclosure obligations are also designed in accordance with the *report-or-explain* mechanism.[16]

3. Investments in Accordance with Religious Principles

12 Closely related to ESG investments is investment according to religious principles. **Islamic finance** has developed into a discipline of its own. The background to this is that Islam is opposed to traditional banking transactions. Islamic law provides for a ban on interest and prohibits speculation and gambling. Nevertheless, compliant financial instruments could be developed. More recently, scholars have also discovered the **investment of assets** according to **Catholic principles** as a separate sub-discipline of the law of capital investment. They are developing on which governance mechanisms best ensure that the respective investment objectives are met.[17]

II. Restrictions

13 Private and institutional investors can pursue their investment objectives using a wide range of financial instruments.[18] Nevertheless, there are certain restrictions, especially for retail investors, in pursuing their investment goals. This applies in particular to financial products that are suitable for speculation and are particularly risky or complex and therefore difficult to assess.

1. Private Investors

14 A simple approach to discourage private investors from making a risky investment is to set a **high minimum amount**. Shares used to have high minimum nominal amounts—in Germany it amounted to 1,000 marks at the end of the 20th century—with the consequence

---

[14] See regarding this function R. Veil § 2 para. 39.
[15] Cf. R. Veil, in: FS Hopt, 1321, 1327 ff.
[16] Cf. R. Veil, in: FS Hopt, 1321, 1324 ff.; R. Veil et al., *Nachhaltige Kapitalanlagen durch Finanzmarktregulierung*, 66.
[17] Cf. M. Lötscher, *Prinzipien der katholischen Vermögensanlage*, 43 ff. including an analysis of the foundations of Catholic social doctrine.
[18] See R. Veil § 8.

of even higher stock market prices for a single share, so that even the purchase of a single share required a large monetary investment and was only a possibility for the wealthy.[19] Nowadays, however, there are only a few shares that have such a high stock market price that they are hardly affordable for retail investors (examples: Lindt approx. SFR 80,000; voting shares of Berkshire Hathawy approx. $ 200,000). With the successive reduction of the nominal amount to € 1, the German legislature has pursued the goal of making the share market accessible to small investors in particular.[20] In addition, numerous models of acquiring fractions of a share (fractional shares; trusteeships) have emerged in practice, so that even small amounts can now be invested in shares (mostly via digital brokers).

In other areas of law, the regulatory approach of **thresholds** for minimum investment amounts is still relevant. The public offering of securities can be made without a prospectus if the offering has a minimum amount of € 100,000 or a minimum denomination of € 100,000.[21] In these cases, issuers exclusively address professional investors. Conversely, certain privileges do not apply to *crowdinvesting* if investors' investments exceed certain amounts.[22] The legislator then considers it necessary for investors to receive further information in order to be able to make informed decisions.

With regard to **futures** and **forward contracts**,[23] private investors experienced a paradigm shift in the period from 1990 to the early 2000s. Originally, they could only enter into such transactions in a legally binding manner if they were eligible to enter into forward transactions on a stock exchange. Merchants fulfilled this requirement, as well as traders on the stock exchange (eligibility to enter into futures transactions by virtue of status). The strictly formalistic approach kept large groups of investors away from the derivatives market. In order to increase the liquidity and attractiveness of these markets, the legislature also granted non-merchants the ability to enter into futures transactions if they had been sufficiently informed by their credit institution beforehand (eligibility to enter into futures transactions by virtue of information). Furthermore, the clients had to sign an information document. However, this paternalistic approach remained subject to criticism,[24] which was also due to the unconvincing regime of legal consequences.[25] The German legislature therefore abolished the model of forward transaction eligibility, arguing it was internationally unusual and also highly complicated.[26] Since then, anyone with legal capacity can conclude futures transactions. The necessary protection of inexperienced persons from the particular danger of futures transactions is achieved through **information obligations** (information model of MiFID II).[27]

---

[19] Cf. S. Vatter, in: Spindler and Stilz (eds.), *Kommentar zum AktG*, § 8 para. 2.
[20] With the Second Financial Market Promotion Act (*Finanzmarktförderungsgesetz*), the nominal amount was reduced to DM 5 to facilitate access to the capital market for small investors. Cf. Begr. RegE, BT-Drucks. 12/6679 of 27 January1994, 82 f. At that time, the weighted average market price of the ordinary shares was approximately nine times the nominal amount.
[21] Cf. Art. 1(4)(c) and (d) PR.
[22] Cf. § 2a(3) VermAnlG (German Investment Act).
[23] See regarding the term R. Veil § 8 para. 21.
[24] Cf. F. Häuser, 4 ZBB (1992), 249, 264.
[25] If the parties had concluded a non-binding forward transaction (due to a lack of eligibility to enter into forward transactions), they had, on the one hand, created an imperfect, non-enforceable obligation. On the other hand, § 55 BörsG (old version) excluded the recovery of performance under the law of unjust enrichment.
[26] Cf. Begr. RegE 4. Finanzmarktförderungsgesetz, BT-Drucks. 14/8017, 64.
[27] See R. Veil § 30 para. 46 ff.

17 **Securitisations** are subject to stricter requirements for distribution to retail investors.[28] The information model of MiFID II (suitability assessment; retail investor information)[29] is complemented by a limit on investment amounts. If the retail investor's portfolio of financial instruments does not exceed € 500,000, the seller shall ensure that the retail investor does not invest a total amount exceeding 10% of his financial instrument portfolio in securitisation positions and that the minimum initial amount invested in one or more securitisation positions is € 10,000.

18 Today, an even stricter control in the form of **prohibitions** hardly ever exists. One remaining example is the UCITS regime, which does not allow private investors to acquire units of a single hedge fund.[30] Public distribution is only possible for a fund of a hedge fund, as this type of collective investment ensures a broader risk diversification than single hedge funds.

19 To sum it up, investors are enabled via information to carry out even highly risky transactions in financial instruments. The information model is based on the idea of a self-reliant investor who is able, if necessary, to put together an optimal portfolio for himself on the basis of advice by intermediaries.[31] Financial products are no longer generally prohibited for retail investors. However, supervisory authorities have the power to restrict or prohibit the marketing, distribution and sale of financial products and practices.[32] The case-by-case **product intervention power** complements the information model.[33] It has proven to be necessary in the wake of the financial market crisis to ensure investor protection and to counter threats to financial stability.

2. Institutional Investors

20 Institutional investors can be insurance companies and pension funds, credit institutions, asset managers and investment funds.[34] They want to generate returns with an investment, but are also incentivised by European legislation to make ESG investments.[35] Restrictions regarding their investment objectives result from the CRR/CRD IV regime for credit institutions, Solvency II regime for insurance companies and UCITS/AIFMD regime for investment funds. They are firstly motivated by the goal of ensuring financial stability, and secondly serve to protect depositors, customers and investors.

21 To date, scholars and practitioners have not presented a cross-jurisdictional systematic analysis of investment freedoms.[36] Instead, the respective regimes are examined. In **insurance law**, a paradigm shift towards freedom of investment can be observed. This principle

---

[28] Cf. Art. 3 STSR.
[29] See R. Veil § 30 para. 50.
[30] Cf. §§ 1(6) in connection with (19) n° 33 KAGB. The purchase is intended for professional and semi-professional investors only.
[31] See regarding the 'portfolio-theory' R. Veil § 9 para. 17.
[32] Cf. Art. 40 ff. MiFIR.
[33] See R. Veil § 31 para. 1.
[34] See R. Veil § 9 para. 13 ff.
[35] See R. Veil § 2 para. 22.
[36] Cf. for an analysis of institutional investors' freedom to invest in hedge funds C. Wentrup, *Die Kontrolle von Hedge-Fonds*, 242 ff.

is explicitly recognised and is concretised by the principle of prudent person.[37] Instead of rigid requirements on permissible and impermissible capital investments, principle-like specifications are provided for, which are based on the insurance company's own responsibility and are intended to ensure a risk-adequate investment.[38] The prudent person principle determines capital investments by insurance companies.[39]

The law of **collective investment** does not provide for such a principle. It is even more strongly characterised by the idea of investment freedom, although it also relies on procedural approaches to risk management. In contrast to insurance law, the regimes doe no provide for capital requirements.

As a starting point, it should be noted that an investment fund is characterised by the fact that the undertaking for collective investment invests the capital in accordance with a **defined investment strategy** for the **benefit of the investors**.[40] An 'investment strategy' consists of investment objectives and concepts with which the investment objectives are to be achieved (acquisition, disposal and holding of securities, derivatives and other assets, etc.).[41] The 'benefit to investors' is typically that a return is to be generated for the investors.[42] The fund manager must explain the investment strategy (laid down in the articles of association or the investment conditions) in the sales prospectus.[43] The investment strategy also limits the scope of action of the fund manager (asset management company).[44] The company must make investments for the investment fund in accordance with the investment strategy.[45] The investment strategy also determines the **risk profiles** of the assets.[46] Again, investment law does not set any material criteria, but follows a procedural approach. This is impressively demonstrated by leverage requirements.[47] Taking into account the investment strategy, the capital management company determines the maximum amount of leverage it can use for each of the investment assets it manages.[48]

Consequently, collective investment law is characterised by **extensive freedom of investment** on the part of fund managers. The premise is that the fund manager informs the investors about the investment strategy and manages the risks from financial products and trading activities. However, there are also legal restrictions for certain funds, depending on whether or not they may also be publicly marketed to retail investors. This is paradigmatically evident in the case of **hedge funds**. Leverage, with the exception of borrowing and short selling, may not be carried out for funds of hedge funds (which may be marketed

---

[37] Cf. Art. 132 and 133 Solvency II Directive, implementation of the principle of prudence in § 124 VAG; W. Heukamp, in: Bürkle (ed.), *Compliance in Versicherungsunternehmen*, § 8 para. 48.
[38] Cf. W. Heukamp, in: Bürkle (ed.), *Compliance in Versicherungsunternehmen*, § 8 para. 42 ff.
[39] Cf. W. Heukamp, in: Bürkle (ed.), *Compliance in Versicherungsunternehmen*, § 8 para. 85.
[40] Cf. § 1(1) KAGB.
[41] Cf. T. Eckhold and P. Balzer, in: Assmann et al. (eds.), *Handbuch des Kapitalanlagerechts*, § 22 para. 21.
[42] Cf. T. Eckhold and P. Balzer, in: Assmann et al. (eds.), *Handbuch des Kapitalanlagerechts*, § 22 para. 21.
[43] Cf. §§ 165, 173 KAGB.
[44] Cf. L. Verfürth and E. Emde, in: Emde et al. (eds.), *KAGB*, § 1 para. 59.
[45] Cf. § 29 (3) n° 1 KAGB.
[46] Cf. § 29 (3) n° 3 KAGB.
[47] Pursuant to § 1(19) n° 25 KAGB this shall be understood as a method by which the management company increases the investment degree of an investment fund managed by it through borrowing, securities loans, leverage financing embedded in derivatives or in some other manner.
[48] Cf. § 29(4) KAGB.

publicly to retail investors).⁴⁹ However, this does not apply to single hedge funds (which may not be offered to the public).⁵⁰ Hedge funds can engage in high-risk transactions without the risks (eg from short selling) being covered by own funds.

25 Disclosure of investment strategy has also emerged as a cross-jurisdictional regulatory approach for institutional investors who invest their clients' or investors' money. The SRD II prescribes the disclosure of the investment strategy for companies in the life insurance industry and for institutions for company pension schemes.⁵¹

---

⁴⁹ Cf. § 225(1) s. 3 KAGB.
⁵⁰ Cf. § 238(1) KAGB; cf. also C. Wentrup, *Die Kontrolle von Hedge-Fonds*, 244 ff.
⁵¹ Cf. Art. 3h SRD II and the corresponding duty of transparency for asset managers pursuant to Art. 3i SRD; see on this already R. Veil § 22 para. 31.

§ 24
Short Sales and Credit Default Swaps

Bibliography
Ashcraft, Adam B. and Santos, Joao A. C., *Has the CDS Market Lowered the Cost of Corporate Debt?*, 56 J. Mon. Econ. (2009), 514–523; Assmann, Heinz-Dieter, et al. (eds.), *Wertpapierhandelsrecht: Kommentar*, 7th edn. (2019); Avgouleas, Emilios, *A New Framework for the Global Regulation of Short Sales*, 15 Stan. J. L. Bus. & Fin. (2010), 376–425; Battalio, Robert et al., *Market Declines: Is Banning Short Selling the Solution?*, Federal Reserve Bank of New York Staff Report No. 518, September 2011; Bayram, Milian and Meier, Dominik, *Marktmanipulation durch Leerverkaufsattacken*, 18 BKR (2018), 55–61; Beber, Alessandro and Pagano, Marco, *Short-Selling Bans around the World: Evidence from the 2007–09 Crisis*, 68 J. Fin. (2013), 343–381; Berges, Nino and Kiesel, Florian, *Werteffekte bei Einführung der EU-Verordnung über Leerverkäufe und Credit Default Swaps*, 6 CFL (2015), 354–361; Boehmer, Ekkehart and Wu, Juan (Julie), *Short Selling and the Informational Efficiency of Prices*, Working Paper (2012), available at SSRN: http://papers.ssrn.com/sol3/papers.cfm?abstract_id=972620; Boehmer, Ekkehart and Wu, Juan (Julie), *Short Selling and the Price Discovery Process*, 26 Review of Financial Studies (2013), 287–322; Boehmer, Ekkehart et al., *Which Shorts Are Informed?*, 63 J. Fin. (2008), 491–527; Brenner, Menachem and Subrahmanyam, Marti G., *Short Selling*, in: Acharya, Viral and Richardson, Matthew (eds.), *Restoring Financial Stability*, (2009); Bris, Arturo, et al., *Efficiency and the Bear: Short Sales and Markets Around the World*, 62 J. Fin. (2007), 1029–1079; Chamon, Merjin, *Granting powers to EU decentralised agencies, three years following Short-selling*, 18 ERA Forum (2019), 597–609; Commandeur, Marcus, *Short-Attacken aktivistischer Leerverkäufer*, 65 AG (2020), 575–583; Das, Sanjiv et al., *Did CDS Trading Improve the Market for Corporate Bonds?*, 111 J. Fin. Econ. (2014), 495–525; Da Fonseca, José and Wang, Peming, *A Joint Analysis of Market Indexes in Credit Default Swap, volatility and stock markets*, 48 Applied Economics, 1767–1784; Dörge, Andreas, *Rechtliche Aspekte der Wertpapierleihe* (1992); Elineau, Rodolphe B., *Regulating Short Selling in Europe after the Crisis*, 8 Intl. L. & Mgmt. Rev. (2012), 61–86; Fleckner, Andreas M., *Regulating Trading Practices*, in: Moloney, Niamh et al. (eds.), *Oxford Handbook of Financial Regulation* (2015), 596–630; Gilson, Ronald J. and Kraakman, Reinier H., *The Mechanisms of Market Efficiency*, 70 Va. L. Rev. (1984), 549–644; Grünewald, Sereina N. et al., *Short Selling Regulation after the Financial Crisis—First Principles Revisited*, 7 International Journal of Disclosure and Regulation (2009), 108–135; Hull, John C., *Options, Futures, and other Derivatives*, 7th edn. (2009); Howell, Elizabeth, *Short Selling Reporting Rules: A Greenfield Area*, 12 ECL (2015), 79–88; Howell, Elizabeth, *The European Court of Justice: Selling Us Short?*, 11 ECFR (2014), 454–477; Howell, Elizabeth, *Regulatory Intervention in the European Sovereign Credit Default Swap Market*, 17 EBOR (2016), 319–353; Howell, Elizabeth, *The regulation of short sales: a politicised topic*, 12 Law and Financial Markets Review (2018), 203–209; Juurikkala, Oskari, *Credit Default Swaps and the EU Short Selling Regulation: A Critical Analysis*, 9 ECFR (2012), 307–341; Kimball-Stanley, Arthur, *Insurance and Credit Default Swaps: Should Things Be Treated Alike?*, 10 Conn. Ins. L. Rev. (2008), 241–266; Klingenbrunn, Daniel, *Produktverbote zur Gewährleistung von Finanzmarktstabilität* (2018); Klöhn, Lars, *Kapitalmarkt, Spekulation und Behavioral Finance* (2006); Krüger, Harmut and Ludewig, Verena, *Leerverkaufsregulierung—aktueller Stand in Deutschland und Ausblick auf die europäische Regulierung unter besonderer Berücksichtigung der aktuellen Vorschläge zu*

den ausgestaltenden Rechtsakten, 66 WM (2012), 1942–1951; Langenbucher, Katja et al., *What are the wider supervisory implications of the Wirecard case?, Study requested by the ECON committee* (November 2020); Laurer, Thomas, *Der Leerverkauf von Aktien—Abgrenzung, Formen und aufsichtsrechtliche Implikationen*, 61 ZgesKredW (2008), 980–984; Lehmann, Matthias and Kumpan, Christoph, *European Financial Services Law* (2019); Lorenz, Manuel, *Regulierung von Leerverkäufen als Dauerbaustelle*, 55 AG (2010), R511–R512; Lübke, Julia, *Kapitalverkehrsfreiheit in der Finanzkrise—Zur Renaissance staatlicher Sonderrechte an Unternehmen*, 21 EWS (2010), 407–416; Ludewig, Verena and Geilfus, Marie C., *EU-Leerverkaufsregulierung: ESMA-Guidelines bestimmen neuen Rahmen der Ausnahmeregelungen für Market-Maker und Primärhändler—Betrachtung unter besonderer Berücksichtigung der BaFin-Erklärung, dem Großteil der Regelungen nachzukommen (Partially-Comply-Erklärung)*, 67 WM (2013), 1533–1540; Mattarocci, Gianluca and Sampagnaro, Gabriele, *Financial Crisis and Short Selling: Do Regulatory Bans Really Work? Evidence from the Italian Market*, 15 Acad. Acc. Fin. Stud. J. (2011), 115–140; Miller, Edward M., *Risk, Uncertainty and Divergence of Opinion*, 32 J. Fin. (1977), 1151–1168; Mock, Sebastian, *Das Gesetz zur Vorbeugung gegen missbräuchliche Wertpapier- und Derivategeschäfte*, 84 WM (2010), 2248–2256; Mittermeier, Martin, *Grundlagen und Regulierungsperspektiven von Leerverkäufen*, 22 ZBB (2010), 139–149; Möllers, Thomas M.J. et al., *Nationale Alleingänge und die europäische Reaktion auf ein Verbot ungedeckter Leerverkäufe*, 13 NZG (2010), 1167–1170; Möllers, Thomas M.J., *Marktmanipulationen durch Leerverkaufsattacken und irreführende Finanzanalysen*, 21 NZG (2018), 649–658; Mülbert, Peter O., *Rechtsschutzlücken bei Short Seller-Attacken – und wenn ja, welche?*, 182 ZHR (2018), 105–113; Mülbert, Peter O. and Sajnovits, Alexander, *Das künftige Regime für Leerverkäufe und Credit Default Swaps nach der VO (EU) Nr. 236/2012*, 24 ZBB (2012), 266–285; Mülbert, Peter O. and Sajnovits, Alexander, *Short-Seller-Attacken 2.0: Der Fall Wirecard*, 19 BKR (2019), 313–323; Payne, Jennifer, *The Regulation of Short Selling and Its Reform in Europe*, 13 EBOR (2012), 413–440; Poelzig, Dörte, *Shortseller-Attacken im Aufsichts- und Zivilrecht*, 184 ZHR (2020), 697–760; Sajnovits, Alexander and Weick-Ludewig, Verena, *Europäische Leerverkaufsregulierung in der praktischen Anwendung: Anforderungen an die Deckung von Leerverkäufen von Aktien nach Artikel 12 und 13 der Verordnung (EU) Nr. 236/2012 (EU-LVVO)*, 69 WM (2015), 2226–2233; Poelzig, Dörte, *Shortseller-Attacken im Aufsichts- und Zivilrecht*, ZHR 184 (2020), 697–760; Saunders, Benjamin B., *Should Credit Default Swap Issuers Be Subject to Prudential Regulation?*, 10 J. Corp. L. Stud. (2010), 427–450; Schimansky, Herbert et al. (eds.), *Bankrechts-Handbuch*, 5th edn. (2017); Schlimbach, Friedrich, *Leerverkäufe—Die Regulierung des gedeckten und ungedeckten Leerverkaufs in der Europäischen Union* (2015); Schmidt, Karsten et al. (eds.), *Münchner Kommentar zum Handelsgesetzbuch: Bankvertragsrecht*, 4th edn. Bd. 6 (2019); Schneider, Uwe H., *Auf dem Weg in die europäische Kapitalmarktunion—Die Vertreibung aus dem Paradies—oder auf dem Weg ins kapitalmarktrechtliche Arkadien?*, 57 AG (2012), 823–826; Schmolke, Klaus U., *„Leerverkaufsattacken" und Marktmissbrauch*, 49 ZGR (2020), 291–318; Schockenhoff, Martin, *Schutzlos gegen Short-Seller-Attacken?*, 74 WM (2020), 1349–1356; Sieder, Sebastian, *Short-Selling-Regulierung in Europa und den USA* (2019); Sieder, Sebastian, *Anwendungsschwierigkeiten mit den Eingriffsbefugnissen der Short Selling Regulation (SSR)*, 31 ZBB (2019), 179–189; Sieder, Sebastian, *COVID-19 bringt Short-Selling-Verbot*, 15 ZFR (2020), 40–43; Splinter, Christopher and Gansmeier, Johannes, *Leerverkaufsbeschränkungen nach der Leerverkaufs-Verordnung*, 184 ZHR (2020), 761–792; Trüg, Gerson, *Ist der Leerverkauf von Wertpapieren strafbar?*, 62 NJW (2009), 3202–3206; Tyrolt, Jochen and Bingel, Adrian, *Short Selling—Neue Vorschriften zur Regulierung von Leerverkäufen*, 62 BB (2010), 1419–1426; Veil, Rüdiger, *Europäische Kapitalmarktunion—Verordnungsgesetzgebung, Instrumente der europäischen Marktaufsicht und die Idee eines „Single Rulebook"*, 43 ZGR (2014), 544–607; Voß, Thorsten, *Leerverkäufe*, in: Klöhn, Lars and Mock, Sebastian (eds.), *Festschrift 25 Jahre WpHG* (2019), 715–755; Walla, Fabian, *Kapitalmarktrechtliche Normsetzung durch Allgemeinverfügung?—Hat die BaFin mit den Verboten für ungedeckte Leerverkäufe und bestimmte Kreditderivate vom 18. Mai 2010 ihre Kompetenzen überschritten?*, 63 DÖV (2010), 853–857; Wandsleben, Till and Weick-Ludewig, Verena, *'Unvollkommene Deckung' von Leerverkäufen nach der VO (EU) Nr. 236/2012*, 27 ZBB (2015), 395–407; Wentz, Jasper, *Shortseller-Attacken - ökonomische und* *juristische Bewertung eines ambivalenten Geschäftsmodells*, 73 WM (2019), 196–204; Wilken, Oliver and Bertus, Jana, *Professionelle Leerverkaufsattacken – rechtliche Grundlagen und Grenzen*, 71 BB (2019), 2754–2760; Zimmer, Daniel and Beisken, Thomas, *Die Regulierung von Leerverkäufen de lege lata und de lege ferenda*, 64 WM (2010), 485–491.

I. Introduction

Short selling and Credit Default Swaps regularly reappear on the public and the political agenda[1] in the course of a **crisis hitting the financial markets** and in the context of **short selling attacks** on certain issuers (having true or alleged compliance problems) on a regular basis. Just recently, the *Wirecard* case[2] in Germany demonstrated the implications of short selling on modern capital markets.

Short selling and Credit Default Swaps allow investors to profit from decreasing prices of financial instruments or a reduced creditworthiness of an issuer. As a result, such transactions have frequently been the reason for political critics against certain investors. A reaction to this was the first pan-European regulation of short selling and credit default swaps in the aftermath of the financial market and **sovereign debt crisis in the mid-2000s**.

The regulatory framework, which was created with great effort at that time, has since been gradually developed further. In the course of the **COVID-19 pandemic**, it faced its latest, and so far heaviest, test when numerous national supervisory authorities (and ultimately also ESMA) restricted and in some cases even completely banned short sales and credit default swaps.[3]

II. Terminology

A short sale is a transaction in which a party sells financial instruments for a fixed price while having an obligation to deliver the respective financial instruments to a third party at a later point in time without a fixed price.[4] Commonly, the definition is restricted to cases in which the seller does not yet own[5] or possess[6] the financial instruments at the time of entering into the sales agreement. This definition does, however, not include covered short sales where the cover transaction was already completed.[7] In this respect, the common definition falls short of the mark.[8]

---

[1] See E. Howell, 12 Law and Financial Markets Review (2018), 203 ff.
[2] See for the details of the case below para. 65.
[3] For more detail see below at para. 54.
[4] T. Laurer, 61 ZGesKredW (2008), 980, 982; in line with this: G. Trüg, 62 NJW (2009), 3202, 3203; J. Tyrolt and A. Bingel, 62 BB (2010), 1419; see para. 23 ff. for the definition of short sales established by the SSR.
[5] Cf. A. Dörge, *Rechtliche Aspekte der Wertpapierleihe*, 28; F. Schlimbach, *Leerverkäufe*, 8 ff.
[6] C. Kienle, in: Schimansky et al. (eds.), *Bankrechts-Handbuch*, § 105 para. 54; M. Lorenz, 35 AG (2010), 511.
[7] On this term see para. 28.
[8] J. Tyrolt and A. Bingel, 62 BB (2010), 1419.

5   Short sales can be divided into two types: **covered short sellings** describe constellations in which a seller has a claim for the sold financial instruments or possesses it already, ie when he has borrowed the financial instruments or made other arrangements to ensure it can be obtained before the short sale, thereby ensuring that it will be able to fulfil his obligation.

6   In contrast, there are **uncovered** or **'naked' short sales**. These terms refer to a scheme where at the time of the short sale the seller has not yet borrowed the financial instruments sold or ensured they can be borrowed.[9] The short seller hence has to acquire the financial instruments between the sale agreement and the execution of the transaction. He must ensure that he obtains the financial instruments he owes within the performance period. The seller can do so either by acquiring or borrowing the financial instruments.[10] Uncovered short sales can result in any number of transactions regarding the respective financial instruments. In extreme cases, they may even result in more financial instruments being traded than have actually been issued.[11]

7   For the seller, the economic intention behind short sales is to make profits because of falling prices, enabling him to buy the financial instruments it owes at a lower price than the price it made with his sale. It will, however, suffer a loss if the price of the financial instruments rises higher than the price the buyer has the obligation to pay, before the seller has had the opportunity to acquire the financial instruments it owes. Profits made through short sales are primarily used for **hedging**[12] losses of other investments or for **speculation**[13] on falling prices.[14]

8   **Credit default swap agreements (CDS)** have similar effects as short sales. CDS are derivative contracts under which one party is obliged to make a payment to the other party in case a certain credit event (in particular a default of the creditor) occurs.[15] Accordingly, CDS have the same economic function as credit default insurance agreements.[16]

III. Need for Regulation

9   Notwithstanding all criticism against short sales and CDS, short sales and CDS without doubt have positive effects. In particular, they provide the possibility to **hedge risks**, thereby securing investors against losses. Short sales can furthermore contribute to the efficiency of

---

[9] J. Ekkenga, in: Schmidt et al. (eds.), *Münchener Kommentar HGB*, Effektengeschäft para. 74; G. Trüg, 62 NJW (2009), 3202, 3203; D. Zimmer and T. Beisken, 64 WM (2010), 485, 486; F. Walla, 63 DÖV (2010), 853. The concept of uncovered short selling was first described at the outset of the 17th century in the Netherlands, cf. for further details A. Bris et al., 62 J. Fin. (2007), 1029.
[10] Cf. G. Trüg, 62 NJW (2009), 3202, 3203.
[11] M. Lorenz, 55 AG (2010), R 511. Cf. R. Veil § 15 para. 26 on the effects of short selling in the case *Porsche v. VW*.
[12] IOSCO, Regulation on Short Selling Final Report, June 2009, available at: www.iosco.org/library/pubdocs/pdf/IOSCOPD292.pdf, 5.
[13] See on the term 'speculation' and its legal implications L. Klöhn, *Kapitalmarkt, Spekulaltion und Behavioural Finance*, 22.
[14] See on the different types of investors R. Veil § 9 para. 13 ff.
[15] See J. Hull, *Options, Futures, and other Derivatives*, 528.
[16] O. Juurikkala, 9 ECFR (2012), 307, 310. As a result, some scholars argue that CDS' regulatory treatment should follow insurance contracts, see A. Kimball-Stanley, 15 Conn. Ins. L. Rev. (2008), 241 ff.; B. Saunders, 10 J. Corp. Stud. (2010), 427 ff.

the capital markets by allowing investors to act when they believe a financial instrument is overvalued, thereby leading to increased market liquidity which, in turn, leads to a **more efficient pricing**[17] as a result of a reduced **bid-ask-spread**. Some legal scholars thus conclude that there is no need to regulate short sellings.[18]

In addition, short selling helps to correct **overvaluations** efficiently. Authors advocating short selling therefore refer to recent cases where known short sellers have been successful in exposing serious compliance violations by issuers.[19] In principle, this reference is indeed correct: Short sellers also contribute to the control of issuers—they can therefore also be regarded as an element of **external corporate governance**.

On the other hand, short sales and credit default swaps also have negative effects: Uncovered short sales, furthermore, are particularly dangerous as they are accompanied by the risk of **settlement failures**.[20] The option of short selling can also provide an incentive for market manipulation, for example by spreading market rumours or artificially influencing prices. Further, short selling may lead to **higher market volatility** and a **downward spiral** in prices.[21]

These risks only become legally relevant when short selling or CDS are used as part of an abusive strategy, ie to conduct market manipulation, or if they contribute to a destabilisation of the entire financial system.[22]

1. Potential for Market Manipulation (Article 12 MAR)

(a) Possible Means of Market Manipulation

Short sales and CDS can be used as a means for market manipulation in the sense of Article 12 MAR.[23] In particular, it constitutes market manipulation if a short position is accompanied by the spreading of false adverse rumours.[24] Short selling can also play a role in **scalping**.[25] This is the case when a short seller makes recommendations to sell without disclosing a conflict of interest. Furthermore, short selling is classified as market

---

[17] Cf. E. Boehmer and J. Wu, *Short Selling and the informational efficiency of prices*, 1 ff.; E. Boehmer et al., 63 J. Fin. (2008), 491 ff.; M. Mittermeier, 22 ZBB (2010), 139, 141; D. Zimmer and T. Beisken, 64 WM (2010), 485, 486. Also R. Gilson and R. Kraakman, 70 Va. L. Rev. (1984), 549 ff.

[18] For example A. Fleckner, in: Moloney et al. (eds.), *Oxford Handbook of Financial Regulation*, 596, 624 ff.

[19] P. Mülbert and A. Sajnovits, in: Assmann et al. (eds.), *Wertpapierhandelsrecht*, Vor Art 1-41 SSR para. 50; U. Sorgenfrei and F. Saliger, in: Park (ed.), *Kapitalmarktstrafrecht*, § 39 Abs. 2d Nr. 3, 4 WpHG para. 5; M. Schockenhoff, 74 WM (2020), 1350.

[20] IOSCO, Regulation on Short Selling (fn. 12), 22; M. Mittermeier, 22 ZBB (2010), 139, 142; E. Howell, 12 ECL (2015), 79, 80.

[21] IOSCO, Regulation on Short Selling (fn. 12), 21–22; cf. M. Mittermeier, 22 ZBB (2010), 139, 141–142 on the dangers of short selling for market integrity and O. Juurikkala, 9 ECFR (2012), 307, 312 ff. for the risks associated with CDS.

[22] See Recital 1 SSR.

[23] J. Payne, 13 EBOR (2012), 413, 416 ff.

[24] G. Trüg, 62 NJW (2009), 3202, 3206; D. Zimmer and T. Beisken, 64 WM (2010), 485, 488; M. Bayram and D. Meier, 18 BKR (2018), 55, 57.

[25] M. Bayram and D. Meier, 18 BKR (2018), 55, 57; O. Wilken and J. Bertus, 71 BB (2019), 2754, 2756 ff.; J. Wentz, 73 WM (2019), 196, 198 f.

manipulation if the seller lacks the intention to fulfil the cover transaction and merely wants to send a misleading signal to the market (*abusive naked short selling*).[26]

(b) Short Selling Attacks and Market Manipulation

14 Recently, the discussion about market manipulation through short selling has focused on so-called **short seller attacks**.[27] According to recent studies, up to one hundred such 'attacks' can be observed annually.[28] In the course of the revision of the MAR, the ESMA Securities and Markets Stakeholder Group noted an increase in the number of such cases as well.[29]

15 Such 'attacks' refer to a common strategy of certain investors to (co-)cause a price drop of an issuer's shares in order profit from short selling. In practice, a typical *modus operandi* is as follows: Investors known as short sellers sell certain shares short and publish information about an issuer either via so-called **research reports** or in other ways (for example via the financial press or social media),[30] which contain a negative assessment of an issuer's business model and/or compliance (in particular, accounting practice). If the price falls, as expected, the short seller settles out his position by buying the shares at a lower price.

16 A key driver for the expansion of this business model is the digitalisation of stock market trading. These days, negative information about issuers is immediately recognised by **algorithm-based** computers and translated into sales of the shares concerned at very short notice.[31] This accelerates the rapid decline in the price of the 'attacked' shares as intended by the short seller.[32]

17 Notwithstanding the political and economic implications of such a business model, 'short selling attacks' are legal, provided that all legal regulations are complied with: This includes first and foremost the prohibitions of insider trading and unlawful disclosure of inside information. Moreover, research reports typically constitute **investment recommendations** or information **recommending or suggesting an investment strategy** under Article 3(1) (34) (35) MAR. The authors of such studies must therefore disclose that they have made short sales.[33] Furthermore, Article 20(1) MAR requires to objectively present the published information. If a short seller exceeds these legal limits—which are, of course, difficult to determine in individual cases—market manipulation is likely.[34] This also applies if negative information about an issuer are not disclosed by means of a research report, but rather by deliberately disseminating the information via (social) media.

18 As a result of recent cases, there is a lively discussion in the capital markets literature about adequate **means of defence for issuers** in the event of a 'short selling attack': First and

---

[26] G. Trüg, 62 NJW (2009), 3202, 3204; T. Möllers et al., 13 NZG (2010), 1167, 1168.
[27] See for a detailed overview S. Sieder, *Short-Selling-Regulierung in Europa und den USA*, 210 ff.
[28] T. Möllers, 21 NZG (2018), 649, 650 citing a study by the law firm Schulte, Roth & Zabel LLP.
[29] ESMA, MAR Review Report, 23 September 2020, ESMA70-156-2391, para. 1028, 1030.
[30] Cf. the intense discussion this approach in German legal literature P. Mülbert, 182 ZHR (2018), 105 f.; T. Voß, in: Klöhn and Mock (eds.), *Festschrift 25 Jahre WpHG*, 715, 745 ff.; D. Poelzig, 184 ZHR (2020), 696, 700; M. Schockenhoff, 74 WM (2020), 1349, 1351.
[31] See M. Lerch § 25 para. 10 ff.
[32] M. Schockenhoff, 74 WM (2020), 1349, 1350; T. Möllers, 21 NZG (2018), 649 f.
[33] On the scope of the disclosure see ESMA, Final Report, Draft technical standards on the Market Abuse Regulation, 28 September 2015, ESMA/2015/1455, p. 80 (para. 379); K. Schmolke, 49 ZGR (2020), 291, 302.
[34] This legal framework is criticised by leading scholars, cf. T. Möllers, 21 NZG (2018), 649, 654 ff.

foremost, issuers are of course protected by transparent business model and strategy[35] as well as careful investor relations work. However, further preventive measures have also been developed to prepare issuers for an attack scenario:[36] These include, inter alia, a distinct **risk analysis**,[37] on the basis of which a **defence team** of internal and external functions is defined and a plan of procedure is drafted. Depending on the individual case, it may also be advisable to prepare a **preventive communication** for a negative research report or market rumours. Moreover, it could be helpful to obtain expert opinions from external advisors. Furthermore, it should be examined at an early stage whether, when and, if so, which price-stabilising measures can be taken by the issuer. Depending on the jurisdiction of the issuer, it could also be an option to **contact to the relevant NCA** to assess the probability of an intervention against short sellers.[38]

2. Short Sales as a Means for Destabilising the Financial System

Under extreme market conditions with falling prices, short selling and CDS can also lead to further and excessive downward spirals in prices, causing the entire financial system to become destabilised. As a consequence, efforts were taken worldwide during the **financial and sovereign debt crisis** to adopt regulatory measures restricting or banning short sales and/or CDS. The predominant political agenda was to prevent speculation on falling prices of sovereign bonds and shares/bonds of financial institutions.[39] These measures were the result of the broad political consensus at that point in time that investors should be prohibited from profiting from an instability of the financial system.[40]

IV. EU Regulation on Short Selling and Credit Default Swaps (SSR)

The **Regulation on Short Selling and Credit Default Swaps (SSR)**[41] entered into force in 2012 and has rendered the previous national regulations on short selling obsolete. The Commission has since then endorsed **two Regulatory Technical Standards (RTS)** and one **Implementing Technical Standard (ITS)** drafted by ESMA[42] and enacted the **Delegated**

---

[35] See eg M. Schockenhoff, 74 WM (2020), 1350, 1355.
[36] See for more details on this M. Commandeur, 65 AG (2020), 575, 580 f.; P. Mülbert and A. Sajnovits, 19 BKR (2019), 313, 321 f.
[37] See M. Schockenhoff, 74 WM (2020), 1350, 1355 f.
[38] The German NCA (BaFin) acted against short sellers in the *Wirecard* case. See on this below para. 65.
[39] See the overview provided by A. Beber and M. Pagano, 68 J. Fin. (2013), 343, 354. See on the various measures taken by EU Member States 1st edn. of this textbook, § 15 para. 8.
[40] See eg J. Payne, 13 EBOR (2012), 413, 415.
[41] Regulation (EU) No. 236/2012 of the European Parliament and of the Council of 14 March 2012 on short selling and certain aspects of credit default swaps, OJ L 86, 24 March 2012, p. 1–24. Cf. for a detailed analysis of the SSR P. Mülbert and A. Sajnovits, 24 ZBB (2012), 2 ff.
[42] Commission Delegated Regulation (EU) No. 826/2012 of 29 June 2012 supplementing Regulation (EU) No. 236/2012 of the European Parliament and of the Council with regard to regulatory technical standards on notification and disclosure requirements with regard to net short positions, the details of the information to be provided to the European Securities and Markets Authority in relation to net short positions and the method for

Regulation No. 918.[43] All these measures put the provisions of the SSR into more concrete terms.

21 The EU framework for the regulation of short selling and CDS thus consists of one Level 1 regulation and our Level 2 regulations. ESMA has additionally issued a 'Q&A list' regarding the interpretation of the SSR[44] and guidelines for exemptions of market makers and primary market operators under the SSR.[45] The SSR aims on **maximum harmonisation** within its scope.[46] Nevertheless, the European framework is complemented by national laws and guidelines by the NCAs[47] which govern the administration and the enforcement of the SSR as well as the sanctions for violations of the SSR. The SSR and its delegated acts are currently subject to review by ESMA.[48]

22 This **multi-layer regulatory framework** was a blueprint for modern European capital markets law, ie a regulatory design that is characterised by a complex interaction of rules made by the European legislator, the Commission and ESMA. These rules are applied and enforced by the NCAs on the basis of further national legislation. This regulatory approach has a direct impact for legal practice: The **depth of regulation** within the short selling regime has led to a genuine harmonisation in Europe—which is to be welcomed considering the aim of a true European capital market union.

1. Scope of the SSR

23 According to its Article 1(1), the SRR applies to all financial instruments that are **admitted to trading in the EU** and to all derivatives relating to such instruments. The SSR thus also

---

calculating turnover to determine exempted shares, OJ L 251, 18 September 2012, p. 1–10; Commission Delegated Regulation (EU) No. 919/2012 of 5 July 2012 supplementing Regulation (EU) No. 236/2012 of the European Parliament and of the Council on short selling and certain aspects of credit default swaps with regard to regulatory technical standards for the method of calculation of the fall in value for liquid shares and other financial instruments, OJ L 274, 9 October 2012, p. 16–17; Commission Implementing Regulation (EU) No. 827/2012 of 29 June 2012 laying down implementing technical standards with regard to the means for public disclosure of net position in shares, the format of the information to be provided to the European Securities and Markets Authority in relation to net short positions, the types of agreements, arrangements and measures to adequately ensure that shares or sovereign debt instruments are available for settlement and the dates and period for the determination of the principal venue for a share according to Regulation (EU) No. 236/2012 of the European Parliament and of the Council on short selling and certain aspects of credit default swaps, OJ L 251, 18 September 2012, p. 11–18. See under F. Walla § 4 para. 14 ff. for an analysis of the function and legal classification of ITS and RTS.

[43] Commission Delegated Regulation (EU) No. 918/2012 of 5 July 2012 supplementing Regulation (EU) No. 236/2012 of the European Parliament and of the Council on short selling and certain aspects of credit default swaps with regard to definitions, the calculation of net short positions, covered sovereign credit default swaps, notification thresholds, liquidity thresholds for suspending restrictions, significant falls in the value of financial instruments and adverse events, OJ L 274, 9 October 2012, p. 1–15.

[44] ESMA, Questions and Answers—Implementation of the Regulation on short selling and certain aspects of credit default swaps (2nd Update), 29 January 2013, ESMA/2013/159.

[45] ESMA, Guidelines Exemption for market making activities and primary market operations under Regulation (EU) No. 236/2012 of the European Parliament and the Council on short selling and certain aspects of Credit Default Swaps, 2 April 2013, ESMA/2013/74.

[46] D. Poelzig, 184 ZHR (2020), 697, 743 f.; cf. on the principle of maximum harmonisation see R. Veil § 3 para. 21 ff.

[47] See eg the FAQ issued by the German NCA BaFin, available at: www.bafin.de or the guidelines by the Swedish NCA Finanzinspektionen, Guidelines for determining a special fine for certain breaches of the EU Short Selling Regulation, November 2014, FI Ref. 14-13923.

[48] ESMA, Review of certain aspects of the Short Selling Regulation, 21 September 2021, ESMA70-156-3914.

applies to transactions outside EU trading venues. The SSR thus has extraterritorial effect in this respect.[49] Moreover, the SSR is applicable to debt instruments issued by the EU or a Member State as well as derivatives relating thereto.

The SSR is not applicable to financial instruments which are only traded on MTFs.[50] According to Article 16 SSR it furthermore does not apply to shares which have their main place of trading (Article 2(1)(o) SSR) outside the EU.[51] Pursuant to Article 17 SSR, certain market participants, ie market makers, primary market operators and certain entities whose sole purpose is the protection of the stability of the EU financial system (ie the ESM/ESFS and equivalent national institutions), are to a large extent exempt from complying with the rules of the SSR.[52] ESMA has issued guidelines on the interpretation of Article 17 SSR.[53] However, various Member States (Denmark, Germany, France and Sweden) have decided to only partially comply with ESMA's guidelines.

2. Compliance of the SSR with the EU Treaty

The United Kingdom questioned the SSR's compliance with the EU Treaty shortly after its entry into force and submitted it to the ECJ for review in an **action for annulment**. Specifically, the UK argued that ESMA's powers of intervention under the SSR to regulate or prohibit short selling (Article 28 SSR[54]) were not covered by the competence title on which the SSR was based (ie Article 114 TFEU). However, the ECJ did not agree with this argumentation—contrary to the opinion of Advocate General *Jääskinen*[55]—and ruled that the SSR was in fact compliant with European primary law.[56]

3. Rules on Short Selling

The SSR in principle stipulates a two-fold approach on the regulation of short sales. It (i) **prohibits uncovered short sales** and (ii) introduces **specific transparency requirements** for all other (ie covered) short sales. The legal rationale behind this approach is that uncovered short sales might result in delivery failures and in a particularly strong decrease of market prices. As opposed to this, covered short sales are not as critical for the market, it thereby being sufficient for the NCAs and/or the market to be aware of the existence of certain net short positions.

---

[49] K. Schmolke, in: Lehmann and Kumpan (eds.), *European Financial Services Law*, Art. 1 SSR para. 3.
[50] P. Mülbert and A. Sajnovits, 24 ZBB (2012), 266, 269; H. Krüger and V. Ludewig, 66 WM (2012), 1492, 1946.
[51] The NCAs create a list of shares that qualify for a main place of trading outside the EU for the trading venues under their supervision. The NCAs have to consider the criteria of Art. 6 RTS No. 826 (method of calculation) and Art. 9 ITS No. 827 (period of time to be used for the calculation) when creating such list. Under Art. 10 and 11 ITS No. 827 these lists are to be submitted to ESMA which publishes them. The current consolidated list for all Member States can be downloaded under www.esma.europa.eu.
[52] See on this V. Ludewig and M. Geilfus, 67 WM (2013), 1533 ff.
[53] ESMA/2013/74 (fn. 31). Cf. ESMA's overview on the Member States' compliance with these guidelines, 2 February 2016, ESMA/2016/205.
[54] Cf. para. 55 for more details on this provision.
[55] Opinion of GA Jääskinen of 12 September 2013, Case C-270/12.
[56] ECJ (Grand Chamber), Case C-270/12 (United Kingdom v Parliament and Council); see on this E. Howell, 11 ECFR (2014), 454 ff.; U. Chamon, 18 ERA Forum (2018), 597, 599 ff.

(a) Prohibited Transactions

27 Pursuant to Article 12 SSR, **uncovered short sales** in shares are generally prohibited.[57] The prohibition also refers to **intraday transactions**.[58] The scope of this prohibition is first determined by Article 2(1)(b) SSR. Under this provision, a short sale is **defined** as a sale where the seller does not own the instrument sold at the time of entering into the sales agreement including a sale seller where has borrowed or agreed to borrow the instrument for delivery at settlement. Article 3 Delegated Regulation No. 918 clarifies that the ownership may also result from an **economic attribution** of financial instruments. Article 2(1)(b) SSR excludes (i) sales by either party under a repurchase agreement where one party has agreed to sell the other a security at a specified price with a commitment by the other party to sell the security back at a later date at another specified price; (ii) transfers of securities under a securities lending agreement; and (iii) future contract or other derivative contracts where it is agreed to sell securities at a specified price at a future date from being considered a short sale under the SSR.

28 According to Article 12 SSR short sales of **shares** under said definition are only legal if they qualify as covered short sales. A transaction can be qualified as a covered short sale if the seller has ensured that he actually holds the shares at the time of the transaction settlement. According to Article 12(a)–(c) SSR this can be achieved if the short seller (i) has borrowed the shares or has made alternative provisions resulting in a similar legal effect, (ii) has entered into an agreement to borrow shares or has another enforceable claim[59] under contract or property law to be transferred ownership of a corresponding number of securities of the same class so that settlement can be effected when it is due or (iii) has made an arrangement with a third party under which that third party has confirmed that the share has been located and has taken measures vis-à-vis third parties necessary for the natural or legal person to have a reasonable expectation that settlement can be effected when it is due (**locate agreement**). Detailed rules that substantiate the types of agreements, arrangements and measures that adequately ensure that shares will be available for settlement are laid down in Articles 5–8 of Implementing Technical Standard No. 827.[60]

29 Moreover, Article 13 SSR prohibits uncovered short sales of **sovereign debt**, ie in particular in bonds issued by state entities of the Member States or the EU. All issuers whose debt instruments are affected by this prohibition are defined by Article 2(1)(d)(f) SSR. Accordingly, debt instruments issued by the EU itself, a Member State (or its respective governmental departments, agencies or special purpose entities), in the case of a federal Member State, any member of the federation (such as the German and Austrian *Länder* or the Belgian *Gewesten/Régions*) as well as debt issued by the ESM/EFSF or the European Investment Bank fall within the scope of Article 13 SSR. Debt instruments issued by municipalities are, however, not covered by the prohibition.

---

[57] It remains unclear whether this also applies to intraday transactions. Consenting opinion M. Lorenz, 55 AG (2010), R 511, R 512; dissenting opinion T. Möllers et al., 13 NZG (2010), 1167, 1170.
[58] Before the SSR came into force some Member States (eg Germany) excluded intraday transactions from their ban of uncovered short sales.
[59] See on the details of this requirement T. Wandsleben and V. Weick-Ludewig, 27 ZBB (2015), 395 ff.
[60] See on the scope of these exemptions A. Sajnovits and V. Weick-Ludewig, 69 WM (2015), 2266 ff.

The prohibition of short sales relating to sovereign debt under Article 13 SSR is subject to the same exceptions as the short selling of shares. In addition, under Article 13(2) SSR the prohibition does not apply if a transaction serves to hedge a long position[61] in debt instruments of an issuer whose pricing has a **high correlation** with the pricing of the relevant bond. 30

Under Article 13(3) SSR and Article 22(2) Delegated Regulation No. 918 the prohibition of uncovered short sales of sovereign debt instruments may be **temporarily suspended** for up to six months by a NCA if the liquidity of a sovereign debt instrument has decreased significantly. This is deemed to be the case if the monthly turnover of a sovereign debt instrument is lower than the fifth percentile of the monthly volume traded during the previous twelve months provided the NCA notifies the ESMA and the other NCAs prior to the suspension. Such a suspension may be renewed multiple times with a maximum duration of further six months. 31

(b) Transparency Obligations

The SSR includes **transparency obligations** for persons holding **net short positions**. The rules for disclosure of short positions for **shares** follow the model of German law at the time before the SSR became effective.[62] Under Article 5(1)(2) SSR a market participant must notify the relevant NCA of any net short position that reaches, exceeds or falls below a percentage that equals 0.2% of the value of the issued share capital of the company concerned and any 0.1% above that. If the net short position reaches, exceeds or falls below a threshold of 0.5% of the issued share capital, Article 6(1)(2) SSR requires that this fact is disclosed to the public. 32

Accordingly, the SSR stipulates for a **two-fold disclosure system,** following the rationale that a short position of more than 0.5% is so important that the market should be informed, whereas short positions of 0.2%–0.5% do not have such a severe impact on the market. Hence, a disclosure vis-à-vis the NCAs on such short positions is sufficient. The Commission is empowered to modify the aforementioned thresholds by means of a delegated act should the financial markets require such adjustments.[63] 33

Under Article 7 SSR **net short positions in sovereign debt** are to be disclosed to the NCAs only. Unlike with regard to short sales of shares, the SSR does not stipulate any duties of disclose to the public with regard to such short positions.[64] Article 21 Delegated Regulation No. 918 includes the relevant thresholds for the notification duty vis-à-vis the NCAs. 34

The applicable **initial threshold** depends on the total volume of all debt issued by a sovereign issuer: For issuers with an outstanding debt of less than € 500 billion the threshold is fixed at 0.1%, while the relevant figure for all other issuers is 0.5% (Article 21(7) Delegated Regulation No. 918). ESMA releases a continuously updated list which gathers the respective applicable thresholds for all sovereign issuers.[65] Article 21(8) Delegated Regulation No. 918 introduces **incremental notification thresholds** at each 0.05% above the initial notification 35

---

[61] See para. 37 on the definition of a long position under the SSR.
[62] See the (meanwhile repealed) §§ 30h ff. of the German *Wertpapierhandelsgesetz* (WpHG).
[63] Art. 5(4) SSR; Art. 6(4) SSR.
[64] Critical on this O. Juurikkala, 9 ECFR (2012), 307, 317.
[65] The list is available at: www.esma.europa.eu/net-short-position-notification-thresholds-sovereign-issuers.

threshold of 0.1%, starting at 0.15%, and at each 0.25% above the initial threshold of 0.5%, starting at 0.75%.

36 The key term of the transparency obligations under the SSR is the term **net short position**. Article 3(4) SSR defines this term as the balance between a short position under Article 3(1) SSR and a long position under Article 3(2) SSR.

37 A **long position** under Article 3(1) SSR equals the aggregate amount of all shares/sovereign debt instruments held and all financial instruments held by which the holder profits from a price increase of the underlying share/debt instrument. According to Article 5(2) SSR in connection with Annex I Delegated Regulation No. 918 such financial instruments can be, inter alia, derivatives, futures, index instruments or stakes in packaged retail or professional investment products. This means the rules also encompass short positions accumulated over-the-counter (OTC). Under Article 3(5) SSR also positions in debt instruments of a sovereign issuer whose pricing is **highly correlated** to the pricing of another sovereign debtor shall be considered as if they were a long position. Article 8(5)–(7) Delegated Regulation No. 918 contains detailed rules for determining such high correlation.

38 A **short position** can either result from a short sale of a share/debt instrument issued by a sovereign issuer or a transaction which creates or relates to a financial instrument where the effect of the transaction is to confer a financial advantage in the event of a decrease in the price of the share or debt instrument upon the market participant. The rules for the calculation of short positions, again, also encompass short positions accumulated OTC.[66] The aggregate amount of the aforementioned positions equals the short position of a market participant under Article 3(2) SSR.

39 Article 7 Delegated Regulation No. 918 further clarifies that it is irrelevant for the purpose of determining a net short position whether a cash settlement or physical delivery of underlying assets is agreed and that short positions on financial instruments that give rise to a claim to unissued shares, subscription rights, convertible bonds and other comparable instruments shall not be considered as short positions when calculating a net short position. All relevant positions for determining the long or short position are to be considered with their **delta-adjusted value** under Articles 10, 11 and Annex II Delegated Regulation No. 918. The delta value describes the impact a price change of a financial instrument has in relation to a direct investment in a share or debt instrument (which respectively have a delta value of one). As a consequence, all financial instruments are considered in accordance with their economic impact.[67]

40 Finally, under Article 3(4), (5) SSR the long position is subtracted from the short position. The result is divided through the total amount of issued shares/the nominal value of all outstanding debt. The final net short position is expressed as a **percentage rate**. The following **formula** can be used to calculate a net short position:

41 The disclosure procedure for net short positions is governed by Article 9 SSR and Articles 2 and 3 Regulatory Technical Standard No. 826 as well as Article 2 Implementing Technical Standard No. 827. The Annexes of the two latter legal acts contain templates for the public

---

[66] E. Howell, 12 ECL (2015), 79, 81; R. Elineau, 8 Intl. L. & Mgmt. Rev. (2012), 61, 72.
[67] Cf. J. Hull, *Options, Futures, and other Derivatives*, 247 ff., 360 ff.; P. Mülbert and A. Sajnovits, 24 ZBB (2012), 266, 277 f.

disclosure and the notification of a net short position vis-à-vis the NCAs. The relevant time for the calculation of a net short position is at midnight at the end of the trading day on which the person holds the relevant position. Any disclosure necessary is required to be made not later than at 15:30 on the following trading day.

The disclosure rules of the SSR are complemented by Article 26(3)–(8) MiFIR. Under this provision, investment firms are under an obligation to notify transactions that qualify as a short sale under the SSR to the relevant NCA after the execution of such transactions. Based on these notifications, each NCA learns at an early stage about the number of short sales currently taking place in the market, without, however, being able to allocate short positions to individual market participants.

4. Rules on Sovereign Credit Default Swap Agreements (CDS)

Under the SSR similar rules as to short selling apply to **Credit Default Swap Agreements (CDS)** relating to sovereign debt.[68] This equation of short selling and CDS is justified by the fact that entering into CDSs without having a long position in underlying sovereign debt can be used to secure a position economically equivalent to a short position in the sovereign debt instruments. The holder of an uncovered CDS benefits from the deterioration of the creditworthiness of the issuer in a very similar way as the short seller of a debt instrument profits from decreasing market prices of the instrument.

Article 2(1)(c) SSR defines CDS as derivative contracts in which one party pays a fee to another party in return for a payment or other benefit in the case of a credit event relating to a reference entity and of any other default, relating to that derivative contract, which has a similar economic effect.

Article 14 SSR **prohibits all transactions in uncovered sovereign CDSs**, eg CDSs that do not serve to hedge against the risk of long positions to which the swap relates or the risk of a decline of the value of the sovereign debt for which the person holds assets or is subject to liabilities, such as financial contracts, a portfolio of assets or financial obligations whose value is correlated to the value of the sovereign debt (Article 4 SSR). The restrictions thus reach farther than with regard to the short sale of shares.

The Commission substantiated these rules in its Delegated Regulation No. 918. Articles 14–15 list examples for transactions which fall under the definition of an uncovered CDS. Articles 17–19 stipulate detailed rules on transactions which have a hedging purpose. Article 18, finally, includes a **correlation test** by which one can determine whether an asset or a debt position has a sufficient correlation to the price of a sovereign debt instrument.

The NCAs may **temporarily suspend the restrictions** on transactions in uncovered CDSs, if, based on objective elements, they believe that their sovereign debt market is not functioning properly and that the restrictions might have a negative impact on the sovereign CDS market, especially by increasing the cost of borrowing for sovereign issuers or affecting the sovereign issuers' ability to issue new debt. Article 14(2)(a)–(e) SSR contains a non-exhaustive list of indicators for a non-functioning market.

---

[68] Critical on this E. Howell, 17 EBOR (2016), 319, 333 ff.

48 If a NCA exercises its power to suspend the prohibitions of sovereign CDSs, Article 8 SSR subjects these CDSs to the same notification obligations as short sales in sovereign debt instruments.[69] Unlike with regard to short selling, the SSR does not contain further disclosure requirements for 'covered' CDS.

5. Powers of the NCAs and ESMA

49 The NCAs are supposed to enforce the rules of the SSR. The SSR is directly applicable in the Member States so that the NCAs may act on its basis und do not need to rely on any national transformation act.

50 The SSR grants the NCAs far-reaching powers of intervention in emergency situations. Pursuant to Article 18 SSR, the NCAs can **order market participants to reveal their net short positions** in financial instruments not covered by the scope of the SSR. For example, the NCAs could order market participants to reveal short positions in certain corporate bonds.[70]

51 Article 19 SSR empowers the NCAs to require market participants engaged in the lending of a specific financial instrument or class of financial instruments to notify any significant change in the fees requested for such lending. Article 20 SSR allows the NCAs to individually prohibit a natural or legal person from engaging in short selling or similar transactions. Article 21 SSR additionally enables the NCAs to ban transactions in CDS which are not already prohibited by the SSR.

52 All measures imposed on the basis of the said Articles 18–21 SSR require adverse events or developments which constitute a serious threat **to financial stability** or **to market confidence** in the Member State or other Member States. Both requirements are to be assessed separately and may form a legal basis for an action by a NCA.[71] These prerequisites are substantiated by Article 24 Delegated Regulation No. 918. This provision contains a detailed catalogue of indicators for a threat for the financial stability. It specifies, for example, budgetary problems of a Member State, a bank or other financial institution important for the global financial system as an indication for a threat for the financial stability. The catalogue provided is non-exhaustive.[72]

53 The respective measure must further be necessary to address the threat and may not have a detrimental effect on the efficiency of financial markets **disproportionate** to its benefits. This means that the measure must be necessary to address the threat and must not disproportionately affect the efficiency of the financial markets compared to the benefits of the measure.[73]

54 *Example:* During the first wave of the **COVID-19 pandemic** in spring 2020, the NCAs of Austria,[74] Belgium, France, Greece, Italy, and Spain issued a short-selling ban because they believed that the pandemic, respectively, amounted to a threat to the national financial stability.[75]

---

[69] On the regulation in Germany, cf. S. Mock, 64 WM (2010), 2248, 2252.
[70] Cf. O. Juurikkala, 9 ECFR (2012), 307, 320.
[71] See C. Splinter and J. Gansmeier, ZHR 184 (2020), 761, 779 ff.
[72] K. Schmolke, in: Lehmann and Kumpan (eds.), *European Financial Services Law*, Arts. 18-26 SSR para. 3.
[73] See C. Splinter and J. Gansmeier, ZHR 184 (2020), 761, 787 ff. (on the assessment of proportionality required).
[74] See on this situation in Austria S. Sieder, 15 ZFR (2020), 240 ff.
[75] See ESMA, Press Release of 15 April 2020, ESMA71-99-1318.

Measures under Articles 18–21 SSR are valid for an initial period not exceeding **three months** from the date of publication. They can be renewed for further three months after review (Article 24 SSR). ESMA is supposed to issue an opinion on any NCA measure within 24 hours. A dissenting opinion results in a duty of the NCA to repeal the measure or to explain it within another 24 hours (Article 27(2) SSR).

> *Example*: In the aftermath of the 2010 sovereign debt crisis, the Greek NCA, Hellenic Capital Market Commission (HCMC), imposed comprehensive short selling bans on shares traded on Greek stock exchanges several times. ESMA approved these measures on each occasion.[76] However, towards the end of the crisis, HSMC banned short selling in *Attica Bank* shares. ESMA for the first time disagreed with an NCA's measure.[77] HCMC maintained its measure and explained this in a statement.[78]

Article 23(1) SSR further provides the NCAs with the power to temporarily restrict or prohibit short sales of financial instruments in case of **a significant decrease in price** on a particular trading venue. Such a **circuit breaker** rule exists in most capital market hubs.[79] The NCAs have made use of this power several times in the recent years.[80]

A decrease of liquid shares[81] is considered significant at a loss of at least 10% (Article 23(5) SSR). According to Article 23(1) Delegated Regulation No. 918 this 10% threshold is also relevant for non-liquid shares that are included in the relevant major national equity index (ie the German *DAX 40* or the French *CAC 40*) and which are the underlying financial instrument for a derivative admitted to trading. A 20% threshold applies to non-liquid shares of which the share price is higher than € 0.50. The threshold is fixed at 40% for all other non-liquid shares. Rules for the calculation of a significant price decrease are laid down in the Regulatory Technical Standard No. 919.

The NCAs may only intervene to prevent a **disorderly decline** in the price of a financial instrument. This is only the case if the price drop is not fundamentally justified.[82] However, the national authority has a wide margin of judgment in this assessment.[83]

A measure based on Article 23 SSR may last until the trading day after the trading day on which the significant price decrease occurred. It may, however, be extended for further two trading days given that the decrease in price continues at a level of at least half of the initial threshold for a significant price decrease.

---

[76] ESMA, Opinion of 1 September 2015, ESMA/2015/1304; ESMA, Opinion of 30 September 2015, ESMA/2015/1489; ESMA, Opinion of 9 November 2015, ESMA/2015/1638; ESMA, Opinion of 7 December 2015, ESMA/2015/1854; ESMA, Opinion of 21 December 2015, ESMA/2015/1900.
[77] ESMA, Opinion of 11 January 2016, ESMA/2016/28.
[78] HSMC, Opinion of 12 January 2016, available at www.hcmc.gr.
[79] See the comparative overview by S. Sieder, 31 ZBB (2019), 179, 181 ff.
[80] K. Schmolke, in: Lehmann and Kumpan (eds.), *European Financial Services Law*, Arts. 18–26 SSR para. 15.
[81] The term is defined by Article 22 of Commission Regulation (EC) No. 1287/2006 of 10 August 2006 implementing Directive 2004/39/EC of the European Parliament and of the Council as regards record-keeping obligations for investment firms, transaction reporting, market transparency, admission of financial instruments to trading, and defined terms for the purposes of that Directive, OJ, 2 September 2006, p. L241, p. 1–25.
[82] S. Sieder, 31 ZBB (2019), 179, 184.
[83] D. Klingenbrunn, *Produktverbote zur Gewährleistung von Finanzmarktstabilität*, 249; S. Sieder, 31 ZBB (2019), 179, 185.

61 As opposed to the NCAs, ESMA **generally has no direct supervisory powers** over market participants under the SSR. It should rather only coordinate its national counterparts. However, Articles 28 and 29 SSR deviate from this principle and convey the power to ESMA to intervene vis-à-vis market participants in certain situations. Under Article 28(1) SSR in conjunction with Article 9(5) ESMA Regulation[84] ESMA may require market participants to notify a NCA or to disclose to the public details of any such position or prohibit or impose conditions on short sales. ESMA may, however, only act (i) to address a threat to the orderly functioning and integrity of financial markets or to the stability of the financial system in case of cross-border implication and, in particular, (ii) if no NCA has taken measures to address the threat or has taken measures that do not adequately address the threat (Article 28(2) SSR). Moreover, the SSR allows ESMA in the case of an emergency situation relating to sovereign debt or sovereign credit default swaps to resort to Article 18 ESMA Regulation and issue an emergency measure.[85]

62 The fact that these powers of ESMA can have practical importance was demonstrated in the course of the **COVID-19 pandemic** for the first time: At the peak of the first pandemic wave in spring 2020, ESMA issued a EU-wide transparency requirement for short positions if these exceeded the threshold of more than 0.1% of the share capital.[86]

6. Sanctions

63 The SSR does not contain sanctions. Rather, it requires **efficient, dissuasive and proportionate** sanctions for misconduct to be enacted by the Member States (Article 41 SSR). The SSR thus retains a well-established approach of European capital markets law as it refrains from including detailed rules on sanctions. Furthermore, the SSR does also not contain any statements on the legal consequences under civil law in the event of a violation of its provisions.

64 The enforcement of the SSR in the Member States with regard to administrative sanctions shows a great **divergence**: For example, violations in France can be punished with fines of up to € 100 million, while Estonian law provides for a maximum fine of only € 32,000. Against the background of Article 27(1) SSR and this disparate finding, it will continue to be an important task of ESMA to coordinate the activities of the national supervisory authorities and to ensure a consistent practice of intervention and sanctions.

7. The *Wirecard* Case—a Prime Example of the Pros and Cons of Short Selling

65 The policy discussions around short selling, as well as the NCA's powers of intervention with regard to short selling, were just recently illustrated in legal practice by the *Wirecard* case:[87]

---

[84] See F. Walla § 11 para. 91.
[85] See on the procedure for actions based on Article 18 ESMA Regulation F. Walla § 11 para. 92.
[86] ESMA, Opinion of 16 March 2020, ESMA70-155-9546; the measure was extended multiple time (see ESMA, Opinion of 10 June 2020, ESMA70-155-10189; ESMA, Opinion of 6 September 2020, ESMA70-155-11072).
[87] See for a summary of the case (and its accounting implications) ESMA, Fast track peer review on the application of the guidelines on the enforcement of financial information (ESMA/2014/1293) by BaFin and FREP in the context of Wirecard, Peer Review Report, 3 November 2020, ESMA42-111-5349.

Wirecard AG—a German issuer that provided online payment services—came under intense public criticism on several occasions (notably in 2002, 2016, and 2018) due to its opaque business model, its accounting practices and allegations of money laundering. In particular, a detailed research report by the research firm *Zatarra* in 2016 and in several articles published in the *Financial Times* in early 2019 accused Wirecard of a large-scale fraud scheme. On each occasion, the various press reports resulted in a rapid drop in the Wirecard shares.

Against this background, the German NCA (BaFin) banned short selling in shares of Wirecard AG on the basis of Article 20 SSR to protect Wirecard and its investors. This measure was particularly noteworthy because it was the first time in its history that BaFin had issued a short selling ban for the shares of a single issuer. BaFin's reasoning was that the price development of Wirecard shares posed a threat to financial market's stability due to their approximately 40% drop in price. Furthermore, BaFin filed a criminal complaint with the responsible public prosecutor's office against journalists from the *Financial Times* on suspicion of market manipulation. BaFin received widespread public approval for its action against 'speculators' at the time.

In retrospect, however, it seems rather doubtful whether this step by BaFin actually slowed down the decline in Wirecard's share price. In any case, with hindsight, it can be stated that BaFin acted prematurely: In April 2020, following a special audit and the subsequent refusal of the audit certificate for the 2019 annual financial statements, it became publicly known that Wirecard had fraudulently falsified its balance sheets for years, had promoted money laundering and had set up a fraud system. As a result, the Wirecard share price plummeted and it filed for insolvency in August 2020.

In line with the developments of the case, the public assessment of BaFin's intervention changed: After the fraud scheme at Wirecard came to light, BaFin was widely criticised for its intervention. This criticism was well-reasoned: The Wirecard case demonstrates that short sales can contribute to reveal severe compliance failures of issuers. Also, the case shows that short selling should not be banned in order to protect a certain issuer and its share price. Good corporate citizens must endure that the capital market may speculate against them.[88]

V. Conclusion

The experiences of the financial market crisis in the early 2000s, of the Wirecard case and the recent COVID-19 pandemic show that short selling and Credit Default Swaps always come into the focus of public (and supervisory) attention when volatility in the capital markets is high and prices have fallen sharply. When prices fall sharply (and many market participants suffer losses), public resentment is directed at those who have profited from falling prices. In such a situation, there are typically calls for more regulation of short selling and intervention against speculators.

---

[88] This opinion is shared by K. Langenbucher et al., *What are the wider supervisory implications of the Wirecard case?*, Study requested by the ECON committee, November 2020.

70 The European legislator has addressed these concerns: With the SSR, he has created a framework that is certainly not ideal in every detail, but which, taken as a whole, represents a balanced compromise between the public's need for regulation and the positive effects of short selling for the capital markets. The SSR's approach of generally permitting covered short selling, making material short selling positions transparent, and allowing for supervisory intervention in extreme cases appears appropriate. Moreover, legal and financial market practice has meanwhile adjusted its processes to this regulation.

71 Whenever the regulatory debate flares up again in the future—for instance in the context of new crises on the capital markets—the SSR's general approach should only be toughly modified in selected fields of regulation. Some directions for this can be found in ESMA's latest evaluation of the SSR.[89] The relevant decision-makers should thereby always take into account that speculation is inherent in capital market activity and not negative per se. Further regulation of short selling and CDS should in any case only happen after careful consideration of economic and empirical research.[90]

---

[89] ESMA, Review of certain aspects of the Short Selling Regulation, 21 September 2021, ESMA70-156-3914.

[90] See eg A. Bris et al., 62 J. Fin. (2007), 1029 ff.; E. Boehmer and J. Wu, 26 Review of Financial Studies (2013), 1 ff.; R. Battalio at al., Federal Reserve Bank of New York Staff Report No. 518, September 2011, 1 ff.; A. Beber and M. Pagano, 68 J. Fin. (2013), 343 ff.; M. Brenner and M. Subrahmanyam, in: V. Archarya and M. Richardson, *Restoring Financial Stability*, 269 ff.; S. Grünewald et. al., 7 International Journal of Disclosure and Regulation (2010), 108 ff.; G. Mattarocci and G. Sampagnaro, 15 Acad. Acc. Fin. Stud. J. (2011), 115 ff. On Credit Default Swaps further A. Ashcraft and J. Santos, 56 J. Mon. Econ. (2009), 514 ff.; J. Da Fonseca and P. Wang, 48 Applied Economics (2016), 1767 ff.

§ 25

Algorithmic Trading and High-Frequency Trading

Bibliography

Acquilina, Matteo et al., *Quantifying the High-Frequency Trading 'Arms Race'*, Chicago Booth Research Paper No. 20-16 (2021), available at SSRN: https://papers.ssrn.com/sol3/papers.cfm?abstract_id=3636323; Baas, Volker, *Probleme des algorithmischen Handels, Die regulatorische Einordnung der Iceberg-Order*, 20 BKR (2020), 394–397; Bell, Holly A. and Searles, Harrison, *An Analysis of Global HFT Regulation—Motivations, Market Failures, and Alternative Outcomes*, Mercatus Center, George Mason University, Working Paper No. 14–11, April 2014, available at SSRN: https://papers.ssrn.com/sol3/papers.cfm?abstract_id=2689321; Bellia, Mario et al., *High-Frequency Trading During Flash Crashes: Walk of Fame or Hall of Shame?*, SAFE Working Paper No. 270 (2020), available at SSRN: https://papers.ssrn.com/sol3/papers.cfm?abstract_id=3560238; Breckenfelder, Johannes, *Competition Among High-Frequency Traders and Market Quality*, ECB Working Paper No. 2290 (2019), available at SSRN: https://papers.ssrn.com/sol3/papers.cfm?abstract_id=3402867; Breckenfelder, Johannes, *Competition among high-frequency traders and market liquidity* (2020), available at: https://voxeu.org/article/competition-among-high-frequency-traders-and-market-liquidity; Crudele, Nicholas, *Dark Pool Regulation: Fostering Innovation and Competition While Protecting Investors*, 9 Brook. J. Corp. Fin. & Com. L. (2015), 569–590; Degryse, Hans et al., *Cross-Venue Liquidity Provision: High Frequency Trading and Ghost Liquidity*, ESMA Working Paper No. 4 (2020), available at: https://www.esma.europa.eu/sites/default/files/library/esma_wp_4_2020_hft_and_ghost_liquidity.pdf; Dolgopolov, Stanislav, *High-Frequency Trading, Order Types, and the Evolution of the Securities Market Structure: One Whistelblower's Consequences for Securities Regulation*, 1 Journal of Law, Technology & Policy (2014), 145–175; Doyle, Anna et al., *A cure for all ills?, The Commission's Proposals Must Strike a Difficult Balance between Regulatory Control and Efficient Market Functioning*, 30 IFLR (2012), 60–61; Fleckner, Andreas M., *Regulating Trading Practices*, in: Moloney, Niamh et al. (eds.), *The Oxford Handbook of Financial Regulation* (2015), 596–630; Gider, Jasmin et al., *High-Frequency Trading and Price Informativeness*, SAFE Working Paper No. 248 (2020), available at SSRN: https://papers.ssrn.com/sol3/papers.cfm?abstract_id=3349653; Gomber, Peter and Nassauer, Frank, *Neuordnung der Finanzmärkte in Europa durch MiFID II/MiFIR*, 15 ZBB (2014), 250–260; Gomber, Peter et al., *High-Frequency Trading*, SSRN Working Paper (2011), available at SSRN: http://papers.ssrn.com/sol3/papers.cfm?abstract_id=1858626; FIA/FIA Europe, *Algorithmic and High Frequency Trading—Special Report*, 18 February 2015, available at: https://www.fia.org/articles/special-report-series-part-four-algorithmic-and-high-frequency-trading; Hagströmer, Björn and Nordén, Lars, *The diversity of high-frequency traders*, SSRN Working Paper (2013), available at: http://papers.ssrn.com/sol3/papers.cfm?abstract_id=2153272&buffer_share=b063b&utm_source=buffer; Hayek, Friedrich A. von, *The Pretence of Knowledge*, Lecture to the memory of Alfred Nobel, 11 December, 1974, available at: www.nobelprize.org/nobel_prizes/economic-sciences/laureates/1974/hayek-lecture.html; Jaskulla, Ekkehard M., *Das deutsche Hochfrequenzhandelsgesetz—eine Herausforderung für Handelsteilnehmer, Börsen und Multilaterale Handelssysteme (MTF)*, 13 BKR (2013), 221–233; Jiang, Georg J. et al.,

High-Frequency Trading in the U.S. Treasury Market Around Macroeconomic News Announcements, HKIMR Working Paper No.19/2018, available at SSRN: https://papers.ssrn.com/sol3/papers.cfm?abstract_id=3233332; Kasiske, Peter, *Marktmissbräuchliche Strategien im Hochfrequenzhandel*, 68 WM (2014), 1933–1940; Kasiske, Peter, *Compliance-Risiken beim Wertpapierhandel in Dark Pools*, 15 BKR (2015), 454–459; Karmel, Roberta S., *IOSCO's Response to the Financial Crisis*, 37 J. Corp. Law (2012), 849–901; Kindermann, Jochen and Coridaß, Benedikt, *Der rechtliche Rahmen des algorithmischen Handels inklusive des Hochfrequenzhandels*, 15 ZBB (2014), 178–185; Kobbach, Jan, *Regulierung des algorithmischen Handels durch das neue Hochfrequenzhandelsgesetz: Praktische Auswirkungen und offene rechtliche Fragen*, 13 BKR (2013), 233–239; Kornpeintner, Daniel, *Die Regulierungsansätze des Hochfrequenzhandels- mit Fokus auf Reg SCI und MIFID II* (2015); Korsmo, Charles R., *High-Frequency Trading: A Regulatory Strategy*, 48 U. Rich. L. Rev. (2014), 523–609; Leis, Diego, *High Frequency Trading, Market Manipulation and Systemic Risks from an EU Perspective*, available at SSRN: http://papers.ssrn.com/sol3/papers.cfm?abstract_id=2108344; Ladley, Daniel, *The Design and Regulation of High Frequency Traders* (2019), available at SSRN: https://papers.ssrn.com/sol3/papers.cfm?abstract_id=3362328; Leuchtkafer, R., *High Frequency Trading, A bibliography of evidence-based research*, available at: https://www.treasurydirect.gov/instit/statreg/gsareg/rfi%20ommentletterleuchtkafer-2016-1.pdf; Lewis, Michael, *Flash Boys, A Wall Street Revolt* (2014); Linton, Oliver et al., *Economic impact assessments on MiFID II policy measures related to computer trading in financial markets*, Foresight, Government Office for Science, Working Paper, August 2012, available at: https://www.gov.uk/government/uploads/system/uploads/attachment_data/file/289075/12-1088-economic-impact-mifid-2-measures-computer-trading.pdf; Manahov, Viktor, *High-frequency trading order cancellations and market quality: Is stricter regulation the answer?* (2020), available at: https://onlinelibrary.wiley.com/doi/full/10.1002/ijfe.2071; Mattig, Daniel, *Kurze Leitungswege für den Handel in Milli- und Mikrosekunden—Zu den latenzminimierenden Infrastrukturen an Börsen und multilateralen Handelssystemen*, 68 WM (2014), 1940–1946; O'Connell, Kevin, *Has Regulation Affected the High Frequency Trading Market?*, 27 Cath. U. J. L. & Tech 145 (2019); O'Malley, George, *Diving into Dark Pools: An Analysis of Hidden Liquidity with Regard to the Proposed Markets in Financial Instruments Directive*, 17 Trinity C.L. Rev. (2014), 94–125; Pasquale, Frank, *Law's Acceleration of Finance: Redefining the Problem Of High-Frequency Trading*, 36 Cardozo L. Rev. (2015), 2085–2128; Patterson, Scott, *Dark Pools, The Rise of A.I. Trading Machines and the Looming Threat to Wall Street* (2012); Pistor, Katharina, *A Legal Theory of Finance*, 41 J. Comp. Econ. (2013), 315–330; Prewitt, Matt, *High-Frequency Trading: Should Regulators Do More?*, 19 Mich. Telecomm. & Tech. L. Rev. (2012), 131–161; Saliba, Pamela, *The Information Content of High Frequency Traders Aggressive Orders: Recent Evidences* (2019), available at SSRN: https://papers.ssrn.com/sol3/papers.cfm?abstract_id=3364330; Schwark, Eberhard and Zimmer, Daniel (eds.), *Kapitalmarktrechts-Kommentar*, 5th edn. (2020); Söbbing, Thomas, *Der algorithmisch gesteuerte Wertpapierhandel und die gesetzlichen Schranken für künstliche Intelligenz im digitalen Banking*, 39 ZIP (2019), 1603–1609; *Rechtsfragen künstlicher Intelligenz im Hochfrequenzhandel: Sind die Anforderungen des Hochfrequenzhandelsgesetzes (HFHG) an den algorithmisch gesteuerten Handel mit Wertpapieren ausreichend?*, InTer (2019), 64–70; Sornette, Didier and Von der Becke, Susanne, *Crashes and High Frequency Trading, An evaluation of risks posed by high-speed algorithmic trading*, Swiss Finance Institute Research Paper Series N.11-63 (2011), available at SSRN: http://ssrn.com/abstract=1976249; Vaananen, Jay, *Dark Pools & High Frequency Trading* (2015); Veil, Rüdiger and Lerch, Marcus P., *Auf dem Weg zu einem europäischen Finanzmarktrecht: die Vorschläge der Kommission zur Neuregelung der Märkte für Finanzinstrumente*, Teil I, 66 WM (2012), 1557–1565; Werner, Julian, *Hochfrequenzhandel de lege lata und möglicher Anpassungsbedarf de lege ferenda*, Bucerius Law Journal (2020), 25–31; Yoon, Mi Hyun, *Trading in a Flash: Implications of High-Frequency Trading for Securities Regulators Worldwide*, 24 Emory Int'l L. Rev. (2010), 913–948; Zaza, Kiersten, *A Fiduciary Standard as a Tool for Dark Pool Subscribers*, 18 Stan. J.L. Bus. & Fin. (2013), 319–350; Zhang, X. Frank, *High-Frequency Trading, Stock Volatility, and Price Discovery*, available at SSRN: http://papers.ssrn.com/sol3/papers.cfm?abstract_id=1691679; Zlatanov, Ivan and Weiss, Sascha, *Regulatorische Aspekte des algorithmischen Handels*, 9 RdF (2019), 290–297.

I. Introduction

Algorithmic Trading (AT) and especially High-Frequency Trading (HFT) are comparatively recent phenomena.[1] Technicalities, such as how trades are executed on stock exchanges and other trading systems, do not normally make the front page. However, the '**Flash Crash**' of 6 May 2010[2]—during which $500 billion in market capitalisation evaporated in less than five minutes before the market rebounded with almost identical momentum[3]—threw some limelight on HFT.[4] The worldwide bestseller '*Flash Boys*' by Michael Lewis[5] is a prominent example of the attention AT and particularly HFT have received in the wake of the Crash.[6]

1

At a policy level, the 'Flash Crash' has triggered an extensive discussion about how such an event could have occurred and whether new regulation is necessary to prevent similar events in the future.[7] This is in line with the goal of **revising international financial markets laws** to increase **market stability**[8] as a consequence of the severe global financial crisis of 2008–9. However, the alleged risks posed by HFT are not limited to market stability issues. They also concern investor protection. Some scholars claim that HFT firms[9] play zero-sum games of communication and information manipulation, thereby parasitically exploiting other investors.[10] The **substantial market share of HFT** in Europe[11] and

2

---

[1] Cf. A. Fleckner, *Regulating Trading Practices*, 596, 619; P. Gomber et al., *High-Frequency Trading*, 39; C. Korsmo, 48 U. Rich. L. Rev. (2014), 523, 538; D. Sornette and S. von der Becke, *Crashes and High Frequency Trading*, 4; further IOSCO, Regulatory Issues Raised by the Impact of Technological Changes on Market Integrity and Efficiency, Consultation Report, July 2011, CR02/11, p. 19, tracing them back to the year 2000. Problems arising from the technical developments at trading firms and market venues with regard to AT and HFT have not been an issue in the context of MiFID, cf. P. Gomber and F. Nassauer, 15 ZBB (2014), 250, 252. However, the search for technical advantages has always played its part in the evolution of markets, cf. J. Vaananen, *Dark Pools and High Frequency Trading*, 119, 129.
[2] Cf. IOSCO, Consultation Report, CR02/11 (fn. 1), 11 ff.; C. Korsmo, 48 U. Rich. L. Rev. (2014), 523 ff.; D. Leis, *High Frequency Trading*, 60 ff.; M. Lewis, *Flash Boys*, 81 ff. 'Flash crashes' itself are, however, not considered to be a new phenomenon, cf. D. Sornette and S. von der Becke, *Crashes and High Frequency Trading*, 3 and 10 ff.
[3] C. Korsmo, 48 U. Rich. L. Rev. (2014), 523, 524 ff.
[4] Cf. A. Fleckner, *Regulating Trading Practices*, 596, 597; IOSCO, Consultation Report, CR02/11 (fn. 1), p. 19 ff.; M. Prewitt, 19 Mich. Telecomm. & Tech. L. Rev. (2012), 131, 132. Interestingly, the official combined Securities and Exchange Commission's (SEC) and Commodity Futures Trading Commission's (CFTC) report on the Flash Crash claims that a particular large order of a mutual fund caused the turmoil, while the actions of HFT firms contributed to events that had already started before. However, the SEC's report was criticized—inter alia—for its lack of accuracy since it is only accurate to the second. The data analysis of the events of 6 May 2010 by a company called 'Nanex', which is accurate to the millisecond, clearly blames HFT for causing the flash crash, cf. J. Vaananen, *Dark Pools and High Frequency Trading*, 176 ff. further C. Korsmo, 48 U. Rich. L. Rev. (2014), 523, 575 ff. HFT may also have contributed to the technical problems with Facebook's initial public offering, cf. F. Pasquale, 36 Cardozo L. Rev. (2015), 2085, 2111; M. Prewitt, 19 Mich. Telecomm. & Tech. L. Rev. (2012), 131, 133.
[5] M. Lewis, *Flash Boys, A Wall Street Revolt* (2014).
[6] Cf. F. Pasquale, 36 Cardozo L. Rev. (2015), 2085, 2086.
[7] Cf. fn. 2 with further references.
[8] Cf. eg IOSCO, Consultation Report, CR02/11 (fn. 1), p. 6 ff., on the G20's plan to enhance the stability of financial markets. IOSCO considers HFT to be 'a key issue with respect to technology's impact on market integrity and efficiency'.
[9] HFT is not only conducted by special 'HFT boutiques' but also by proprietary trading departments of investment banks or by hedge funds, cf. C. Korsmo, 48 U. Rich. L. Rev. (2014), 523, 541.
[10] Cf. F. Pasquale, 36 Cardozo L. Rev. (2014–2015), 2085, 2124, 2127.
[11] HFT accounted for 38% of equity trading in 2010 (up from 9% in 2007), IOSCO, Consultation Report, CR02/11 (fn. 1), p. 22; further H. Bell and H. Searles, *An Analysis of Global HFT Regulation*, 6; J. Kindermann and B. Coridaß, 15 ZBB (2014), 178, 179. Cf. ESMA, Economic Report, High-frequency trading activity in EU equity markets, Number 1-2014, available at: www.esma.europa.eu/sites/default/files/library/2015/11/

the US[12] not only necessitates a better understanding of the effects caused by AT and HFT,[13] but highlights the potential impact of AT and HFT regulation on the markets.

3   Since 2005, advances in technology have **reduced transaction time** from 10.1 seconds at the New York Stock Exchange (NYSE) in 2005 to ever smaller fractions of a second today.[14] The rapid technical evolution of markets has provided benefits, such as the ability to develop automated risk controls.[15] AT and HFT both make use of technical innovations by **reducing or eliminating the role of human participation** in the initiation or execution of a trade.[16]

4   It is **important to differentiate** between the two kinds of trading because several of the risks discussed in the context of AT are unique to HFT strategies.[17] HFT firms make extensive use of algorithms[18] to analyse trade data and initiate and execute trades at minimum costs.[19] Typically, HFT firms have a high daily portfolio turnover[20] and large numbers of their orders are cancelled,[21] which is at least partially related to special order types used in HFT.[22] As such, HFT firms rely on the highest possible speed for the communication of their trade messages. HFT trading is usually proprietary trading and positions are closed at the end of the trading day.[23]

---

esma20141_-_hft_activity_in_eu_equity_markets.pdf, p. 5 ff., on the differences that occur when using different approaches to determine the size of HFT. Consequentially, market share figures of HFT require a cautious evaluation in context of the method used to determine it. Cf. further P. Gomber et al., *High-Frequency Trading*, 7; D. Kornpeintner, *Regulierungsansätze des Hochfrequenzhandels*, 4, on the differences of calculated market shares. Further D. Leis, *High Frequency Trading*, 21, on the difficulties to define the degree of HFT market adoption. In the EU, orders originating from HFT accounted for 50–70% of the quoted volumes in shares for Q2 2018 and 2019, ESMA, Consultation Paper, MiFID II/MiFIR review report on Algorithmic Trading, 18 December 2020, ESMA70-156-2368, para. 32. AT other than HFT accounted for 80% of bond trading in Q3 2019, ESMA, ibid. para. 33.

[12]   HFT accounted for 56% of US equity trading in 2010 (up from 21% in 2005), IOSCO, Consultation Report, CR02/11 (fn. 1), p. 22, with further references; cf. also H. Bell and H. Searles, *An Analysis of Global HFT Regulation*, 14 (48.5% of exchange trade volume in 2014); today, the market share is still around 50%, cf. J. Breckenfelder, Competition among high-frequency traders and market liquidity (2020); P. Gomber et al., *High-Frequency Trading*, 7 and Appendix I on HFT market sizing; J. Kindermann and B. Coridaß, 15 ZBB (2014), 178, 179; further M. Yoon, 24 Emory Int'l L. Rev. (2010), 913, 922. Cf. fn. 11 on deviations in market share figures.

[13]   P. Gomber et al., *High-Frequency Trading*, p. 9 et seq., see the drivers for the rise of AT/HFT in new market access models, trading venue's fee structures, reduction of latency and an increase in competition for and fragmentation of order flow. All these topics will be addressed in this chapter.

[14]   Today, nano seconds matter, cf. ESMA, Consultation Paper (fn. 11), para. 59; cf. also A. Fleckner, *Regulating Trading Practices*, 596, 620; cf. also IOSCO, Consultation Report, CR02/11 (fn. 1), p. 9; J. Kindermann and B. Coridaß, 15 ZBB (2014), 178, 179; C. Korsmo, 48 U. Rich. L. Rev. (2014), 523, 538; F. Pasquale, 36 Cardozo L. Rev. (2015), 2085, 2092; further K. Pistor, 41 J. Comp. Econ. (2013), 315, 326.

[15]   Cf. IOSCO, Consultation Report, CR02/11 (fn. 1), p. 9, with additional examples of possible benefits.

[16]   Cf. also J. Kindermann and B. Coridaß, 15 ZBB (2014), 178, 179, who speak of HFT as a second level of the technical evolution of trading in financial instruments. The automatisation includes the *buy side* of a trade, A. Fleckner, *Regulating Trading Practices*, 596, 620; C. Korsmo, 48 U. Rich. L. Rev. (2014), 523, 537 ff.

[17]   Cf. in more detail para. 10 ff.

[18]   IOSCO, Consultation Report, CR02/11 (fn. 1), p. 10.

[19]   IOSCO, Consultation Report, CR02/11 (fn. 1), p. 21.

[20]   According to one estimate, HFT amounts to 60 million executed transactions per day and trade unit on average. At the end of 2012, the average trade volume of a high-frequency computing centre already used to be around 250,000 transactions, cf. J. Kindermann and B. Coridaß, 15 ZBB (2014), 178, 179.

[21]   According to J. Vaananen, *Dark Pools and High Frequency Trading*, 157, the SEC communicated that 97% of all orders sent to US stock exchanges are cancelled; cf. also V. Manahov, *High-frequency trading order cancellations and market quality: Is stricter regulation the answer?* (2020).

[22]   Cf. J. Vaananen, *Dark Pools and High Frequency Trading*, 10 and 158. On the 'order-type-controversy' S. Dolgopolov, 1 Journal of Law, Technology & Policy (2014), 145, 147 ff. Cf. para. 40 on order-to-trade ratios.

[23]   Cf. ESMA, Economic Report (fn. 11), p. 5; P. Gomber et al., *High-Frequency Trading*, 15; B. Hagströmer and L. Nordén, *The diversity of high-frequency traders*, 14; IOSCO, Consultation Report, CR02/11 (fn. 1), p. 21 ff.; J. Vaananen, *Dark Pools and High Frequency Trading*, 125 ff., on the characteristics mentioned above.

II. Defining AT and HFT/Technical Aspects and Trading Strategies

1. Definitions and Important Terms

The majority of today's trading is computer-based and relies on algorithms. It is thus referred to as '**algorithmic trading**'.[24] The revised MiFID (MiFID II)[25] defines algorithmic trading in Article 4(1)(39) as

> trading in financial instruments where a computer algorithm automatically determines individual parameters of orders such as whether to initiate the order, the timing, price or quantity of the order or how to manage the order after its submission, with limited or no human intervention, and does not include any system that is only used for the purpose of routing orders to one or more trading venues[26] or for the processing of orders involving no determination of any trading parameters or for the confirmation of orders or the post-trade processing of executed transactions.

This demonstrates that AT requires **more than merely electronic trading**,[27] ie the possibility to place orders electronically ('online brokerage').[28] AT is fundamentally different as it **substitutes the human participation** of the trade decisions at least partially by an automatically operating algorithm with regard to the parameters of the trade and the decision whether to trade at all. The definition of AT is set out in more detail[29] in Article 18 of Commission Delegated Regulation (EU) 2017/565,[30] which provides that

> a system shall be considered as having no or limited human intervention where, for any order or quote generation process or any process to optimise order-execution, an automated system makes decisions at any of the stages of initiating, generating, routing or executing orders or quotes according to pre-determined parameters.

HFT is a form of appearance of AT.[31] Firms applying HFT techniques must be authorised as investment firms.[32] According to Article 4(1)(40) MiFID II **high-frequency algorithmic trading technique** means

---

[24] F. Pasquale, 36 Cardozo L. Rev. (2015), 2085, 2090.
[25] Directive 2014/65/EU of the European Parliament and of the Council of 15 May 2014 on markets in financial instruments and amending Directive 2002/92/EC and Directive 2011/61/EU, OJ 2014 L173, 12 June 2014, p. 349–496.
[26] Trading venues refers to regulated markets, MTFs or OTFs, Art. 4(1)(24) MiFID II. Cf. also para. 20 and 31.
[27] Cf. D. Leis, *High Frequency Trading*, 6 ff.; P. Gomber et al., *High-Frequency Trading*, 8 ff., on the evolution of electronic trading.
[28] Cf. ESMA, Final Report, Technical Advice to the Commission on MiFID II and MiFIR, 19 December 2014, ESMA/2014/1569, p. 342, 343 No. 3; D. Kornpeintner, *Die Regulierungsansätze des Hochfrequenzhandels*, 6; generally critical of MiFID II's definition V. Baas, 20 BKR (2020), 394, 397.
[29] ESMA has answered questions from stakeholders regarding the scope of MiFiD II's definition in its Q&A on MiFID II and MiFIR market structures topics, 6 April 2021, ESMA70-872942901-38.
[30] Commission Delegated Regulation (EU) 2017/565 of 25 April 2016 supplementing Directive 2014/65/EU of the European Parliament and of the Council as regards organisational requirements and operating conditions for investment firms and defined terms for the purposes of that Directive.
[31] Recital 61 MiFID II; German Government, Explanation of the High-frequency Trading Act, 26 November 2012, BT-Drs. 17/11631, p. 18; IOSCO, Consultation Report, CR02/11 (fn. 1), p. 21; P. Kasiske, 68 WM (2014), 1933; J. Kobbach, 13 BKR (2013), 233, 237; D. Kornpeintner, *Die Regulierungsansätze des Hochfrequenzhandels*, 8; C. Korsmo, 48 U. Rich. L. Rev. (2014), 523, 539; D. Leis, *High Frequency Trading*, 18; J. Vaananen, *Dark Pools and High Frequency Trading*, 119; for a different perspective cf. C. Kumpan, in: Schwark and Zimmer (eds.), Kapitalmarktrechts-Kommentar, § 26d BörsG para. 3 ff.
[32] Art. 2(1)(e) and (j) MIFID II.

an algorithmic trading technique characterised by:

(a) infrastructure intended to minimise network and other types of latencies, including at least one of the following facilities for algorithmic order entry: co-location, proximity hosting or high-speed direct electronic access;

(b) system-determination of order initiation, generation, routing or execution without human intervention for individual trades or orders; and

(c) high message intraday rates[33] which constitute orders, quotes or cancellations.

8   The **additional requirements for categorising** particular forms of **AT as HFT** relate to infrastructure, the complete exclusion of human intervention in the trade process,[34] and the high number of order/quote/cancellation messages. The infrastructure prerequisites are all particular means of improving the communication speed between the computers of a HFT firm and the matching engine of a trading venue.[35,36] HFT firms set up their equipment as close as possible to the relevant exchange (**proximity hosting**).[37] Sometimes they are even allowed to put their servers on the premises of the exchange, in exchange for a fee (**co-location**).[38] Some brokers provide **Direct Electronic Access**[39] **(DEA)** to the market by what is known as **Direct Market Access (DMA)** or **Sponsored Access (SA)**, which are used by HFT firms.[40] DMA is 'an arrangement through which an investment firm that is a member/participant or user of a trading platform permits specified clients […] to transmit orders electronically to the investment firm's internal electronic trading systems for automatic onward transmission under the investment firm's trading ID to a specified trading platform'.[41] SA differs from DMA in that the investment firm permits specified clients to transmit orders electronically not only to its electronic trading system, but directly to a

---

[33] Further specified in Art. 19(1) of Commission Delegated Regulation (EU) 2017/565 as the submission on average of any of the following: (a) at least two messages per second with respect to any single financial instrument traded on a trading venue; (b) at least four messages per second with respect to all financial instruments traded on a trading venue. This definition is currently under review, cf. ESMA, Consultation Paper (fn. 11), para. 38 ff.

[34] The computer programs running the trading program are also known as 'black boxes' and are secrets of the HFT firms, cf. J. Vaananen, *Dark Pools and High Frequency Trading*, 122.

[35] Trading venue/trading platform refers to a stock exchange or Alternative Trading Facilities (ATF), a.k.a. 'dark pools'. Cf. G. O'Malley, 17 Trinity C.L. Rev. (2014), 94 ff., on the nature and various forms of dark pools and applicable regulation under the MiFID and MiFID II regime. Cf. further para. 20; J. Vaananen, *Dark Pools and High Frequency Trading*, 40 ff., on different types of dark pools with examples.

[36] As usually only a fraction of the orders put into the system by HFT firms gets executed, it is more precise to refer to *communication speed* as the main goal of HFT firms rather than trade speed.

[37] Cf. D. Mattig, 68 WM (2014), 1940.

[38] A. Fleckner, *Regulating Trading Practices*, 596, 622; IOSCO, Consultation Report, CR02/11 (fn. 1), 16 ff.; D. Kornpeintner, *Die Regulierungsansätze des Hochfrequenzhandels*, 14; C. Korsmo, 48 U. Rich. L. Rev. (2014), 523, 563 ff.; M. Lewis, *Flash Boys*, 63 ff.; M. Prewitt, 19 Mich. Telecomm. & Tech. L. Rev. (2012), 131, 137 ff.; J. Vaananen, *Dark Pools and High Frequency Trading*, 121 ff. Exchanges in the US need the SEC's approval when they want to offer co-location services, cf. M. Yoon, 24 Emory Int'l L. Rev. (2010), 913, 926. As such, those services are implicitly approved of. Co-location services have been around since the late 1990s, cf. M. Prewitt, 19 Mich. Telecomm. & Tech. L. Rev. (2012), 131, 137. In the EU apparently only few trading venues offer co-location services, cf. ESMA, Consultation Paper (fn. 11), para. 185.

[39] For a definition see Art. 4(1)(41) MiFID II.

[40] Cf. ESMA/2014/1569 (fn. 28), p. 343 ff.; P. Gomber et al., *High-Frequency Trading*, 9; IOSCO, Consultation Report, CR02/11 (fn. 1), 15 ff.; R. Karmel, 37 J. Corp. Law (2012), 849, 885 ff.; M. Yoon, 24 Emory Int'l L. Rev. (2010), 913, 928 ff.

[41] ESMA, Guidelines, Systems and controls in an automated trading environment for trading platforms, investment firms and competent authorities, 24 February 2012, ESMA/2012/122, p. 4.

specified trading platform under the investment firm's trading ID, without the orders being routed through the investment firm's internal electronic trading systems beforehand.[42] DEA meets HFT firms' need to reduce latency[43] and may help a customer to avoid having to meet regulatory requirements that apply to direct market members.[44] Recently, some DMA clients have provided DMA access to their own clients (**sub-delegation**), thereby increasing the complexity of DEA regulation.[45]

The MiFID II's HFT definition requires further clarifications beyond Article 19 Commission Delegated Regulation (EU) 2017/565, which are provided by ESMA.[46] A **tremendous variety of alternative HFT definitions** can still be found in official documents and academic literature because a unified definition does not exist.[47] It is not necessary to examine all of them for the purposes of this chapter. It should be noted though that from an early stage the European Commission (Commission) used a rather wide and descriptive definition compared to MiFID II's technical approach. The Commission considers HFT to be 'trading that uses sophisticated technology to try to interpret signals from the market and, in response, executes high volume, automated trading strategies, usually either quasi market making or arbitraging, within very short time horizons. It usually involves execution of trades as principal (rather than for a client) and involves positions being closed out at the end of the day'.[48] This is a useful starting point to look at the activities intended to be captured by the regulatory regime.

9

2. Trading Strategies

(a) AT and HFT as a Technical Means for Implementing Trading Strategies

It is important to understand that **neither AT nor HFT are trading strategies** by themselves.[49] Algorithms are used by institutional investors and investment firms to determine if, when, where and in which volume a trade is to be executed. A distinction can be drawn between

10

---

[42] ESMA/2012/122 (fn. 41), p. 5; cf. further IOSCO, Consultation Report, CR02/11 (fn. 1), p. 15. SA is the fastest possible access to markets, cf. D. Leis, *High Frequency Trading*, 20, and involves higher risks than DMA, cf. ESMA, Final Report, Draft Regulatory and Implementing Technical Standards MiFID II/MiFIR, 28 September 2015, ESMA/2015/1464, p. 223.

[43] Cf. para. 10 in more detail.

[44] M. Prewitt, 19 Mich. Telecomm. & Tech. L. Rev. (2012), 131, 137.

[45] Cf. ESMA, Consultation Paper (fn. 11), para. 40 ff. and para. 67; further Art. 21(4) RTS 6, cf. para. 49 on RTS 6.

[46] Cf. para. 45 ff.

[47] Cf. IOSCO, Consultation Report, CR02/11 (fn. 1), p. 21; R. Karmel, 37 J. Corp. Law (2012), 849, 888; D. Kornpeintner, *Die Regulierungsansätze des Hochfrequenzhandels*, 7 ff.; C. Korsmo, 48 U. Rich. L. Rev. (2014), 523, 540; D. Leis, *High Frequency Trading*, 19; J. Vaananen, *Dark Pools and High Frequency Trading*, 120 ff.; M. Yoon, 24 Emory Int'l L. Rev. (2010), 913, 920 ff.; E. Jaskulla, 13 BKR (2013), 221, 227 ff., raises the question whether HFT, which is subject to permanent innovations, can be defined at all. He submits that only a descriptive definition that does not require all elements to be necessarily fulfilled at all times would be suitable. See P. Gomber et al., *High-Frequency Trading*, 13 ff., with Appendices II/III, and R. Leuchtkafer, *High Frequency Trading, A bibliography of evidence-based research*, 54 ff., on various AT and HFT definitions and related concepts.

[48] European Commission, Public Consultation, Review of Markets in Financial Instruments Directive (MiFID), 8 December 2010, available at: http://ec.europa.eu/finance/consultations/2010/mifid/docs/consultation_paper_en.pdf, p. 14 at fn. 37.

[49] Recital 61 MiFID II; cf. also P. Gomber et al., *High-Frequency Trading*, 1; IOSCO, Consultation Report, CR02/11 (fn. 1), p. 23; J. Kindermann and B. Coridaß, 15 ZBB (2014), 178; D. Leis, *High Frequency Trading*, 21; M. Prewitt, 19 Mich. Telecomm. & Tech. L. Rev. (2012), 131, 134; M. Yoon, 24 Emory Int'l L. Rev. (2010), 913, 921 (HFT as 'umbrella term' for several trading strategies using technological advantages).

agency algorithms and proprietary algorithms, those used by HFT firms falling into the proprietary category.[50] Most of the strategies that are built into algorithms can be seen as rather 'traditional';[51] however, they are executed so fast that no human can compete with the speed of a computer.[52] HFT strategies can be divided into market-making strategies and 'opportunistic' strategies, such as arbitrage and directional trading.[53] Some features are common to all HFT strategies: They are **'ultra-short-term' oriented**.[54] Further, HFT firms usually **do not hold open positions** at the end of the trading day.[55] Whichever strategy a given HFT firm uses, it will rely on the lowest possible **latency period**,[56] which is, generally speaking, the process from receiving knowledge of relevant trade information to its analysis, making a trade decision and executing it.[57] HFT firms rely on the **best technology available**, such as high-speed fibre optic cables, fast algorithm programs, DEA or co-located equipment.[58] It is not *per se* problematic that some traders have an informational edge over competitors due to their superior equipment and the resulting means of processing information faster than others. This has been a given in trading for many years[59] and may actually lead to 'technological competition', which can in turn improve the overall efficiency of the market.[60] As such, legal conclusions—especially in a regulatory context—must always take into account the particular strategies employed by the various market participants.[61] **Increased speed** has always been part of the trading evolution and is by itself **not a sufficient cause for stricter regulation**.[62]

(b) Overview of Concepts Behind Particular AT and HFT Strategies

11   It is not possible to even attempt to describe all AT and HFT strategies as there are too **many variations**, which are **changing at a great speed**.[63] Instead, this section demonstrates

---

[50] B. Hagströmer and L. Nordén, *The diversity of high-frequency traders*, 2 and 12.
[51] Cf. IOSCO, Consultation Report, CR02/11 (fn. 1), p. 23; D. Kornpeintner, *Die Regulierungsansätze des Hochfrequenzhandels*, 11; C. Korsmo, 48 U. Rich. L. Rev. (2014), 523, 542; D. Leis, *High Frequency Trading*, 18; J. Vaananen, *Dark Pools and High Frequency Trading*, 119.
[52] Cf. M. Lewis, *Flash Boys*, 9.
[53] B. Hagströmer and L. Nordén, *The diversity of high-frequency traders*, 12.
[54] B. Hagströmer and L. Nordén, *The diversity of high-frequency traders*, 2; C. Korsmo, 48 U. Rich. L. Rev. (2014), 523, 540; D. Leis, *High Frequency Trading*, 20. The average holding period is measured in seconds, cf. A. Fleckner, *Regulating Trading Practices*, 596, 620; P. Kasiske, 68 WM (2014), 1933.
[55] Cf. recital 61 MiFID II.
[56] Cf. ESMA/2014/1569 (fn. 28), p. 319. The natural limit of 'the race to zero latency' (M. Prewitt, 19 Mich. Telecomm. & Tech. L. Rev. (2012), 131, 134) is the speed of light. J. Vaananen, *Dark Pools and High Frequency Trading*, 130, contends that HFT firms are coming ever closer to reaching this limit. Then speed would be 'less of a factor in the future'. However, this is only true for HFT firms compared with their HFT competitors, not non-HFT firms. Cf. B. Hagsträmer and L. Nordén, *The diversity of high-frequency traders*, 23 ff., who contend that speed is more important for market making HFT than for other strategies. Cf. J. Vaananen, *Dark Pools and High Frequency Trading*, 209, on means for fast data transmission (fibre-optic cables, microwaves and laser beams).
[57] J. Vaananen, *Dark Pools and High Frequency Trading*, 123; further M. Lewis, *Flash Boys*, 61 ff.
[58] J. Vaananen, *Dark Pools and High Frequency Trading*, 123, 202.
[59] Cf. C. Korsmo, 48 U. Rich. L. Rev. (2014), 523, 566; cf. also P. Gomber et al., *High-Frequency Trading*, 10 and 34 ff., who mention that in traditional trading a trader could also profit from 'running faster across the trading floor'.
[60] Cf. A. Fleckner, *Regulating Trading Practices*, 596, 622; C. Korsmo, 48 U. Rich. L. Rev. (2014), 523, 560.
[61] Cf. IOSCO, Consultation Report, CR02/11 (fn. 1), p. 23. See also the references in fn. 305.
[62] Cf. P. Gomber et al., *High-Frequency Trading*, 1. Cf. also K. Pistor, 41 J. Comp. Econ. (2013), 315, 326, on how financial innovation may destabilise the financial system. Further J. Vaananen, *Dark Pools and High Frequency Trading*, 129.
[63] Cf. D. Leis, *High Frequency Trading*, p. 19 (typical lifespan of an algorithm is measured in weeks or days); further P. Gomber et al., *High-Frequency Trading*, p. 24; IOSCO, Consultation Report, CR02/11 (fn. 1), p. 10; C. Korsmo, 48 U. Rich. L. Rev. (2014), 523, 529.

some concepts on which common strategies are based. **AT trading strategies** (such as 'participation-rate' and 'time-weighted' strategies) are **often used by institutional investors** that try to keep the price impact of large orders as small as possible, for example by incrementally placing orders or splitting up an order and buying a certain amount of stock in a given time period (eg buying 50 shares every 10 minutes for 2 hours).[64] Such strategies do not necessarily require low latency and it is important to keep in mind that the 'regulatory debate' has been triggered primarily by HFT, which is only a subset of AT.[65]

HFT strategies are principally about **exploiting the reduced latency period**.[66] However, being faster than competitors is not a strategy by itself,[67] though it will allow HFT firms to be among the first to react to, and trade on the basis of, relevant information. Such information may result from 'real' news that is eg distributed via newspapers' websites and 'read' by algorithms, which then transform them into a trade decision ('**information-driven strategy**').[68] The desire to reduce latency time goes to such an extent that some HFT firms even pay news services for presenting news in an 'algorithm-friendly' way, for placing news reports on servers in locations close to the HFT firm prior to their release, or to get 'early access' (of a few milliseconds) to such reports.[69] Besides this 'outside information', the knowledge of trade information (eg orders placed by other market participants) can be equally relevant for market movements.[70] Therefore, HFT firms employ several methods of detecting large-scale orders[71] (**liquidity detection**)[72]—which are usually hidden on the market—to trade using the short-term momentum ('**momentum strategy**') caused by those orders.[73]

12

---

[64] Cf. P. Gomber et al., *High-Frequency Trading*, 21 ff., on AT strategies in more detail.
[65] Cf. para. 7.
[66] Cf. para. 10.
[67] Similar A. Fleckner, *Regulating Trading Practices*, 596, 620.
[68] Cf. D. Kornpeintner, *Die Regulierungsansätze des Hochfrequenzhandels*, 15; M. Prewitt, 19 Mich. Telecomm. & Tech. L. Rev. (2012), 131, 135 ff.; further P. Gomber et al., *High-Frequency Trading*, 23 ff.; B. Hagströmer and L. Nordén, *The diversity of high-frequency traders*, 16.
[69] J. Vaananen, *Dark Pools and High Frequency Trading*, 153 and 203; further A. Fleckner, *Regulating Trading Practices*, 596, 622; cf. F. Pasquale, 36 Cardozo L. Rev. (2015), 2085, 2091 ff. on how such early access allows certain traders to make use of potentially material but not yet public information and therefore poses questions relating to the prohibition of insider dealing or at least the rationale behind it. Cf. also P. Kasiske, 68 WM (2014), 1933, 1938 ff.; D. Mattig, 68 WM (2014), 1940 ff., with further references; J. Vaananen, *Dark Pools and High Frequency Trading*, 150.
[70] It is therefore not surprising that the sequence of the publication of order/trade confirmations sent to individuals and respective public disclosure has become a regulatory issue, cf. ESMA, Consultation Paper (fn. 11), para. 350 ff.
[71] This is called 'pinging' or 'sniffing'. By sending out small orders the algorithm can determine whether there are larger (hidden) orders available. M. Lewis, *Flash Boys*, 74, even claims that by using so called 'latency tables' HFT firms can identify particular brokers (see also P. Kasiske, 68 WM (2014), 1933, 1937). With this knowledge, the HFT firm can try to trade ahead of the trader who initiated the hidden order, thereby making a profit (cf. J. Vaananen, *Dark Pools and High Frequency Trading*, 138 ff.; further P. Kasiske, 68 WM (2014), 1933, 1937 ff.; D. Kornpeintner, *Die Regulierungsansätze des Hochfrequenzhandels*, 16; C. Korsmo, 48 U. Rich. L. Rev. (2014), 523, 558; F. Pasquale, 36 Cardozo L. Rev. (2015), 2085, 2092 and 2105 ff.; M. Prewitt, 19 Mich. Telecomm. & Tech. L. Rev. (2012), 131, 137). It is important though that the technique described above requires the HFT firm to take a risk. This is different from 'flash orders', cf. para. 13.
[72] P. Gomber et al., *High-Frequency Trading*, 28 ff.; M. Prewitt, 19 Mich. Telecomm. & Tech. L. Rev. (2012), 131, 135 ff.
[73] Cf. P. Gomber et al., *High-Frequency Trading*, 30; F. Pasquale, 36 Cardozo L. Rev. (2015), 2085, 2092; M. Prewitt, 19 Mich. Telecomm. & Tech. L. Rev. (2012), 131, 135.

HFT firms aim at closing their position before the trend changes again.[74] This all happens within fractions of a second.[75] A variation of the momentum strategy is called '**momentum ignition**', which means that HFT firms try to trigger other algorithmic traders to begin trading by putting a high quantity of orders in the order book and cancelling them almost immediately afterwards, thereby simulating 'real' trading activity.[76] In doing so, HFT firms try to exploit these self-induced price movements.[77]

13   As HFT traders can utilise their super-fast equipment, they are able to take advantage of the time that elapses between price movements and adjusted quotes from market makers[78] ('**latency arbitrage**').[79] Also, HFT firms that pay for and use **direct data feeds** from exchanges, receive relevant trade data[80] directly from the exchange and are able to process it a fraction of a second before traders using consolidated data feeds.[81] As a consequence, latency arbitrage has similarities with momentum ignition: HFT firms know which way prices are headed before the 'public'.[82] Further, informational edges may be achieved by '**flash orders**'. If an order reaches a trading platform and cannot be executed,[83] it is sometimes shown to paying members of the trading platform before being rerouted to a different venue and put on consolidated tape. This provides the recipient of the flashed order with information about order flow earlier than other market participants and gives them—for fractions of

---

[74] J. Vaananen, *Dark Pools and High Frequency Trading*, 202; cf. also D. Leis, *High Frequency Trading*, 21 ff.; IOSCO, Consultation Report, CR02/11 (fn. 1), p. 24; C. Korsmo, 48 U. Rich. L. Rev. (2014), 523, 546 ff., in general on directional strategies.

[75] Cf. IOSCO, Consultation Report, CR02/11 (fn. 1), p. 22; further German Government, Explanation of the High-frequency Trading Act (fn. 31), p. 1.

[76] Cf. P. Kasiske, 68 WM (2014), 1933, 1936; C. Korsmo, 48 U. Rich. L. Rev. (2014), 523, 548 ff. Momentum strategies use special order types, see J. Vaananen, *Dark Pools and High Frequency Trading*, 105 ff., 209 (cf. ibid., p. 93 ff. on standard order types); further on order types used by HFT firms A. Fleckner, *Regulating Trading Practices*, 596, 621; M. Lewis, *Flash Boys*, 168 ff.

[77] J. Vaananen, *Dark Pools and High Frequency Trading*, 203 ff.; cf. further D. Kornpeintner, *Die Regulierungsansätze des Hochfrequenzhandels*, 18.

[78] Cf. P. Gomber et al., *High-Frequency Trading*, 16 ff., on market making in the context of HFT. See R. Veil, § 9 para. 8 and J. Vaananen, *Dark Pools and High Frequency Trading*, 32 ff., on market making in general.

[79] Cf. C. Korsmo, 48 U. Rich. L. Rev. (2014), 523, 546; F. Pasquale, 36 Cardozo L. Rev. (2015), 2085, 2093; M. Prewitt, 19 Mich. Telecomm. & Tech. L. Rev. (2012), 131, 136; further P. Gomber et al., *High-Frequency Trading*, 27 ff.; IOSCO, Consultation Report, CR02/11 (fn. 1), p. 23 f.; D. Leis, *High Frequency Trading*, 22 ff.; M. Yoon, 24 Emory Int'l L. Rev. (2010), 913, 924 ff., on arbitrage strategies in general. M. Aquilina et al., *Quantifying the High-Frequency Trading 'Arms Race': A Simple New Methodology and Estimates*, Chicago Booth Paper No. 20-16, claim that eliminating latency arbitrage would reduce the market's cost of liquidity by 17%.

[80] Such as the National Best Bid and Offer (NBBO) in the US, cf. the references in fn. 84.

[81] Cf. F. Pasquale, 36 Cardozo L. Rev. (2015), 2085, 2093; J. Vaananen, *Dark Pools and High Frequency Trading*, 151 ff.; cf. also fn. 70. The asymmetry of private and public data feeds is currently under review, cf. ESMA, Consultation Paper (fn. 11), para. 350 ff.

[82] C. Korsmo, 48 U. Rich. L. Rev. (2014), 523, 564 ff.; J. Vaananen, *Dark Pools and High Frequency Trading*, 202 ff.; cf. further D. Kornpeintner, *Die Regulierungsansätze des Hochfrequenzhandels*, 15 ff.; cf. M. Yoon, 24 Emory Int'l L. Rev. (2010), 913, 931 ff., on the difficulties to determine who is meant by the term 'public'.

[83] This may be because the National Best Bid and Offer (NBBO), which is protected by Reg. NMS in the US, is not available at the particular trading venue. Cf. on NBBO and Reg. NMS P. Gomber et al., *High-Frequency Trading*, 39 ff.; C. Korsmo, 48 U. Rich. L. Rev. (2014), 523, 536 ff.; D. Leis, *High Frequency Trading*, 11 ff.; further N. Crudele, 9 Brook J. Corp. Fin. & Com. L. (2015), 569, 577 ff.; M. Lewis, *Flash Boys*, 96 ff.; J. Vaananen, *Dark Pools and High Frequency Trading*, 68 ff.; M. Yoon, 24 Emory Int'l L. Rev. (2010), 913, 917 ff.; K. Zaza, 18 Stan. J.L. Bus. & Fin. (2013), 319, 326 ff. As a similar rule does not apply in Europe, flash orders are especially a problem of US markets. The European execution regime is rather principle based, cf. D. Leis, *High Frequency Trading*, 15 ff., 17.

a second—the possibility to execute the trade in accordance with price protection rules.[84] Other arbitrage strategies ('**cross-market arbitrage**' and '**statistical arbitrage**') are based on utilising short-term (ie fractions of a second) price discrepancies, eg in the same or related securities at different stock exchanges and trading venues[85] by buying the stock at the lower price at venue A and selling it at the higher price at venue B.[86] Sometimes this goes hand in hand with sending huge amounts of orders and immediately cancelling them to overload the computer systems of a given exchange ('**quote stuffing**'), thereby creating the differences that are then turned into a profit by arbitrage.[87]

The majority of HFT firms[88] employ '**market-making strategies**', which—as the name suggests—fulfil the same function as designated market makers.[89] The difference between the two lies in the general absence of an obligation on the part of HFT firms to constantly quote bids and offers.[90] The principle behind a market making strategy is to turn over

14

---

[84] Cf. P. Gomber et al., *High-Frequency Trading*, 42; C. Korsmo, 48 U. Rich. L. Rev. (2014), 523, 561 ff.; M. Lewis, *Flash Boys*, 44 ff.; M. Prewitt, 19 Mich. Telecomm. & Tech. L. Rev. (2012), 131, 138; J. Vaananen, *Dark Pools and High Frequency Trading*, 141; M. Yoon, 24 Emory Int'l L. Rev. (2010), 913, 929 ff. In 2009 the SEC proposed to ban flash orders. Consequentially, most exchanges stopped offering the functionality, such as eg Direct Edge did in 2011, cf. http://www.wsj.com/articles/SB10001424052748703409304576166930877474292.

[85] Cf. B. Hagströmer and L. Nordén, *The diversity of high-frequency traders*, 26. Price differences may also occur between derivatives and their underlyings or exchange-traded-funds (ETFs) and their constituent securities, M. Prewitt, 19 Mich. Telecomm. & Tech. L. Rev. (2012), 131, 136.

[86] Cf. D. Kornpeintner, *Die Regulierungsansätze des Hochfrequenzhandels*, 13 ff.; M. Prewitt, 19 Mich. Telecomm. & Tech. L. Rev. (2012), 131, 136; M. Yoon, 24 Emory Int'l L. Rev. (2010), 913, 924 ff. As markets have become more fragmented, such price differences occur on a regular basis, even though only for a short amount of time. Market fragmentation was one of the intended consequences of the implementation of MiFID, P. Gomber et al., *High-Frequency Trading*, 11; P. Gomber and F. Nassauer, 15 ZBB (2014), 250, 251 ff.; cf. also ESMA, Economic Report (fn. 11), p. 5; IOSCO, Consultation Report, CR02/11 (fn. 1), p. 19 at fn. 19; G. O'Malley, 17 Trinity C.L. Rev. (2014), 94, 96 ff. and 110 ff.; M. Prewitt, 19 Mich. Telecomm. & Tech. L. Rev. (2012), 131, 147; M. Yoon, 24 Emory Int'l L. Rev. (2010), 913, 939. This is a good example of how the legal environment influences the market structure and practices. Cf. on market fragmentation J. Vaananen, *Dark Pools and High Frequency Trading*, 210; IOSCO, Consultation Report, CR02/11 (fn. 1), p. 13 ff. Reg. NMS had similar effects on market fragmentation in the US, cf. M. Lewis, *Flash Boys*, 15 ff.

[87] Cf. P. Kasiske, 68 WM (2014), 1933, 1935; C. Korsmo, 48 U. Rich. L. Rev. (2014), 523, 575 ff.; F. Pasquale, 36 Cardozo L. Rev. (2015), 2085, 2100; M. Prewitt, 19 Mich. Telecomm. & Tech. L. Rev. (2012), 131, 147 ff.; J. Vaananen, *Dark Pools and High Frequency Trading*, 158 ff. D. Kornpeintner, *Die Regulierungsansätze des Hochfrequenzhandels*, 17, is of the opinion that HFT traders do not benefit from quote stuffing as they would be slowed down as well. P. Kasiske, 68 WM (2014), 1933, 1935, contends that quote stuffing may also be used to disturb other HFT firms.

[88] 71,5% in 2011 and 62,8% in 2012 of the trading volume were represented by market making HFT firms. More than 80% of HFT limit order submissions resulted from market making. Cf. B. Hagströmer and L. Nordén, *The diversity of high-frequency traders*, 3 and 22 on those figures.

[89] Cf. IOSCO, Consultation Report, CR02/11 (fn. 1), p. 23; C. Korsmo, 48 U. Rich. L. Rev. (2014), 523, 543 ff.; D. Leis, *High Frequency Trading*, 21 ff.; M. Prewitt, 19 Mich. Telecomm. & Tech. L. Rev. (2012), 131, 135. See also the references in fn. 78 on market making. It should be pointed out that HFT firms often post their bids and offers across various markets, cf. O. Linton et al., *Economic impact assessments on MiFID II policy measures related to computer trading in financial markets*, 19.

[90] Cf. M. Prewitt, 19 Mich. Telecomm. & Tech. L. Rev. (2012), 131, 135; J. Vaananen, *Dark Pools and High Frequency Trading*, 199 ff. The market making of HFT firms is often also referred to as 'scalping', cf. J. Vaananen, *Dark Pools and High Frequency Trading*, 133 ff., with detailed examples; further S. Dolgopolov, 1 Journal of Law, Technology & Policy (2014), 145, 151. S. Dolgopolov (ibid., p. 167) contends that HFT market making is predatory in its nature as it aims to 'step ahead' of other traders; further N. Hirschey, *Do High-Frequency Traders Anticipate Buying and Selling Pressure?*, January 2020 (SSRN); cf. para. 37 on market making-arrangements.

acquired financial instruments quickly at a small profit and repeat this over and over again.[91] The trader is at a risk when the market moves in a direction not foreseen or if another trader gets in front of the market-making HFT firm in the order book. Another opportunity for HFT firms to make money is similar to, and may be combined with, market making: earning **liquidity rebates** from trading platforms.[92] To understand this strategy, one must realise that trading platforms are for-profit corporations.[93] They make money by charging fees for executed trades.[94] As such, it is in their interest to have high liquidity (in the sense of the ability to find buyers/sellers who are willing to trade at or close to the market price[95]) available at their trading venue to demonstrate to investors that they will be able to execute desired trades at the venue.[96] HFT firms get paid for providing 'extra' liquidity by quoting bids and offers, so in effect the trading platform owners share their execution fee with the HFT firm when an offer/bid is matched.[97] Different from a pure market-making strategy, the HFT trader does not depend on selling higher than the purchase price as long as the rebate is large enough. Another strategy uses the dependence of the price formation process at dark pools on displayed markets ('lit markets').[98] Some HFT firms place orders in lit markets to move the 'mid-price'[99]—which is eg used in dark pools to determine a price for a given stock—in a desired direction.[100] Right after the order is put into the order book of the lit market, the HFT trader executes their desired trade in the dark pool, thereby profiting from the shift in the mid-price. Finally, the lit-market order is cancelled. These three steps happen almost simultaneously.[101]

---

[91] Cf. D. Kornpeintner, *Die Regulierungsansätze des Hochfrequenzhandels*, 12 ff. (also on rebate driven strategies); J. Vaananen, *Dark Pools and High Frequency Trading*, 113.

[92] C. Korsmo, 48 U. Rich. L. Rev. (2014), 523, 544; P. Gomber et al., *High-Frequency Trading*, 25 ff., speak of 'spread driven' market making and 'rebate driven' market making as two subsets of an electronic liquidity provision strategy. Further M. Prewitt, 19 Mich. Telecomm. & Tech. L. Rev. (2012), 131, 135; J. Vaananen, *Dark Pools and High Frequency Trading*, 108 ff.; M. Yoon, 24 Emory Int'l L. Rev. (2010), 913, 923 ff.

[93] Cf. IOSCO, Consultation Report, CR02/11 (fn. 1), p. 19 at fn. 20. See A. Fleckner, *Regulating Trading Practices*, 596, 602 and R. Karmel, 37 J. Corp. Law (2012), 849, 892, on the demutualisation of exchanges.

[94] J. Vaananen, *Dark Pools and High Frequency Trading*, 208. Further, 'network effects' increase when more orders are executed at a given venue, attracting further orders, cf. A. Fleckner, *Regulating Trading Practices*, 596, 600.

[95] M. Prewitt, 19 Mich. Telecomm. & Tech. L. Rev. (2012), 131, 139. Limit-orders, which are put into the order book of a trading platform, are supplying liquidity, while market-orders, which are executed at the best available price (thereby crossing the bid-offer-spread), take liquidity away. Cf. fn. 76 with references on order types.

[96] With regard to risks associated with HFT, it is therefore not certain whether exchange operators have strong economic interests to protect the integrity of trading at their exchanges to increase the trading volume and profits as is contended by C. Korsmo, 48 U. Rich. L. Rev. (2014), 523, 531. Cf. also S. Dolgopolov, 1 Journal of Law, Technology & Policy (2014), 145, 161; A. Fleckner, *Regulating Trading Practices*, 596, 602 and 610; P. Kasiske, 15 BKR (2015), 454, 456 ff.; S. Patterson, *Dark Pools*, 43. Generally sceptical whether self-regulation can be a suitable option with regard to HFT and the finance sector F. Pasquale, 36 Cardozo L. Rev. (2015), 2085, 2099 ff.

[97] However, some HFT firms get paid to take liquidity from trading platforms, which means taking limit orders (which is an order to buy or sell a financial instrument at its specified price limit or better and for a specified size, Art. 4(1)(14) MiFID II) off the order book with market-orders or corresponding limit orders, cf. J. Vaananen, *Dark Pools and High Frequency Trading*, 200; cf. also S. Patterson, *Dark Pools*, 42 ff., on the importance of the 'maker-taker pricing model' for HFT firms.

[98] Cf. para. 20; A. Fleckner, *Regulating Trading Practices*, 596, 614; P. Kasiske, 15 BKR (2015), 454; J. Vaananen, *Dark Pools and High Frequency Trading*, 64.

[99] Cf. G. O'Malley, 17 Trinity C.L. Rev. (2014), 94, 105. Mid-price refers to the midpoint of the quoted best bid and offer prices, cf. P. Kasiske, 15 BKR (2015), 454.

[100] Cf. J. Vaananen, *Dark Pools and High Frequency Trading*, 204, for an example.

[101] J. Vaananen, *Dark Pools and High Frequency Trading*, 142 ff., 204.

III. Potential Risks and Benefits of AT and HFT

In a free society and market economy, it is principally the **regulator's burden to prove potential risks and damages** of activities that are to be (stricter) regulated. However, it must be taken into account that the current financial markets structure has not evolved in a spontaneous order[102] but is the result of how **finance is legally constructed**.[103] Nevertheless, market participants can legitimately expect that the regulator will not wilfully change the legal landscape without good cause.[104] Therefore, this section lays out potential risks of AT and HFT and subsequently demonstrates possible benefits. Both aspects need to be assessed when evaluating regulatory measures. This is particularly difficult in the case of HFT, as the empirical evidence on the topic is itself controversial.[105] Unsurprisingly, AT and HFT regulation has been among the most contentious areas in the financial markets law revision process[106] and continuously poses challenges for the regulator.[107]

1. Potential Risks of AT and HFT

(a) Systemic Risk and Market Stability

Some scholars, regulators, and legislators fear that AT and HFT impose **systematic risks on global securities markets**.[108] As the Flash Crash has shown, disruptions in one particular market cannot normally be confined to that market as modern financial markets are intertwined and interdependent (cross-market propagation).[109] AT and HFT involve very little or no human intervention, so systemic risk may arise from what are known as

---

[102] Cf. F. Pasquale, 36 Cardozo L. Rev. (2015), 2085, 2095.
[103] This assertion is the basis of the Legal Theory of Finance (LTF), K. Pistor, 41 J. Comp. Econ. (2013), 315. Cf. also with regard to HFT IOSCO, Consultation Report, CR02/11 (fn. 1), p. 19; F. Pasquale, 36 Cardozo L. Rev. (2015), 2085, 2087 ff.; J. Vaananen, *Dark Pools and High Frequency Trading*, 13 and 211.
[104] Cf. also C. Korsmo, 48 U. Rich. L. Rev. (2014), 523, 530.
[105] Cf. IOSCO, Consultation Report, CR02/11 (fn. 1), p. 24 ('mixed results'); J. Kindermann and B. Coridaß, 15 ZBB (2014), 178, 179; see also ESMA, Economic Report (fn. 11), p. 4, where it is stated that further research is needed regarding the actual contribution of HFT to liquidity and the potential risks and benefits of HFT in general. Further A. Fleckner, *Regulating Trading Practices*, 596, 620 ff.; B. Hagströmer and L. Nordén, *The diversity of high-frequency traders*, 35; C. Korsmo, 48 U. Rich. L. Rev. (2014), 523, 528 ff. See also P. Gomber et al., *High-Frequency Trading*, 32 ff. and Appendix IV, for an academic literature overview. See also D. Sornette and S. von der Becke, *Crashes and High Frequency Trading*, 5 ff., on the value of liquidity in the context of a HFT environment.
[106] Cf. FIA/FIA Europe, *Algorithmic and High Frequency Trading—Special Report*, 1; D. Leis, *High Frequency Trading*, 25.
[107] Cf. ESMA, Consultation Paper (fn. 11) for a detailed analysis of the effects of the current regulatory regime and recent phenomena which may need to be specifically addressed in the future.
[108] D. Leis, *High Frequency Trading*, 56 ff.; D. Sornette and S. von der Becke, *Crashes and High Frequency Trading*, 16 ff.; M. Yoon, 24 Emory Int'l L. Rev. (2010), 913, 914, each with further references.
[109] Cf. M. Prewitt, 19 Mich. Telecomm. & Tech. L. Rev. (2012), 131, 146; further IOSCO, Consultation Report, CR02/11 (fn. 1), p. 11; R. Karmel, 37 J. Corp. Law (2012), 849, 884; D. Leis, *High Frequency Trading*, 58; J. Vaananen, *Dark Pools and High Frequency Trading*, 171 ff., with reference to the joint report of the SEC and CFTC on the Flash Crash (extensively on the report ibid p. 170 ff.). However, it is pointed out that the interdependency of markets in Europe is not comparable to that in the US, cf. J. Kindermann and B. Coridaß, 15 ZBB (2014), 178, 179. On contractual cross-references in finance which may trigger chain reactions K. Pistor, 41 J. Comp. Econ. (2013), 315, 318.

'**rogue algorithms**'.[110] A prime example is the case of *Knight Capital*, a financial service firm that lost $440 million in only a few minutes on 1 August 2012 when an old trading algorithm accidentally sent out thousands of orders per second.[111] Such incidents may be linked to programming errors[112] or the fact that the design of the algorithm does not take into account all relevant data for the situations in which it is supposed to be used.[113] Given that, to a large extent, HFT firms trade on the information revealed by other trades,[114] it is very likely that the behaviour of a rogue algorithm (or a typical 'fat finger order' initiated by a human trader[115]) triggers other algorithms, which in turn cause further algorithms to trade on that information. Such a **cascade effect** (or **feedback loop**[116]) could lead to **disruptions in different markets**[117] and poses operational risks when unintended orders accumulate.

17 The potential for disastrous results is further increased when HFT firms have direct access to markets, especially when their sponsors do not ensure that all applicable compliance standards, such as risk thresholds, are met by the HFT firm.[118] In this context, it is relevant that HFT firms often operate with high leverage.[119] Further, the large order volumes and cancellations transmitted by HFT firms increase **operational risks** as the trading systems may not be able to cope with the data volume.[120]

(b) Market Quality and Market Integrity

18 Several studies have come to the conclusion that HFT increases **market volatility**.[121] This may result from particular HFT strategies such as 'quote stuffing'.[122] Others point out that volatility issues relate to the fact that HFT firms often use market-making strategies.[123]

---

[110] Cf. IOSCO, Consultation Report, CR02/11 (fn. 1), p. 29; C. Korsmo, 48 U. Rich. L. Rev. (2014), 523, 528 and 567 ff.; D. Leis, *High Frequency Trading*, 59; cf. also ESMA, Consultation Paper (fn. 11), para. 155 ('The testing of algorithms is paramount to the efficiency of the markets.').

[111] ESMA, Economic Report (fn. 11), p. 5; D. Kornpeintner, *Die Regulierungsansätze des Hochfrequenzhandels*, 23; C. Korsmo, 48 U. Rich. L. Rev. (2014), 523, 569 ff.; M. Prewitt, 19 Mich. Telecomm. & Tech. L. Rev. (2012), 131, 133; J. Vaananen, *Dark Pools and High Frequency Trading*, 166.

[112] Programming is the part of AT and HFT that still -for now- requires human participation, cf. para. 71.

[113] Cf. J. Vaananen, *Dark Pools and High Frequency Trading*, 166.

[114] Cf. para. 12.

[115] Cf. P. Gomber et al., *High-Frequency Trading*, 55; R. Karmel, 37 J. Corp. Law (2012), 849, 888; C. Korsmo, 48 U. Rich. L. Rev. (2014), 523, 527; J. Vaananen, *Dark Pools and High Frequency Trading*, 164.

[116] J. Kindermann and B. Coridaß, 15 ZBB (2014), 178, with further references; F. Pasquale, 36 Cardozo L. Rev. (2015), 2085, 2100; cf. also O. Linton et al., *Economic impact assessments on MiFID II policy measures related to computer trading in financial markets*, 12.

[117] IOSCO, Consultation Report, CR02/11 (fn. 1), p. 10 ff. and 29 ('transmission of shocks').

[118] M. Yoon, 24 Emory Int'l L. Rev. (2010), 913, 928 ff.

[119] S. Patterson, *Dark Pools*, 40.

[120] Cf. also D. Sornette and S. von der Becke, *Crashes and High Frequency Trading*, 13, on operation risks associated with HFT.

[121] C. Korsmo, 48 U. Rich. L. Rev. (2014), 523, 528 ff. and 577 ff.; M. Prewitt, 19 Mich. Telecomm. & Tech. L. Rev. (2012), 131, 141 ff.; J. Breckenfelder, *Competition among high-frequency traders, and market quality*, ECB Working Paper Series No 2290/June 2019; further B. Hagströmer and L. Nordén, *The diversity of high-frequency traders*, 4; M. Lewis, *Flash Boys*, 98 and 110 ff. explaining that HFT firms benefit from volatility. Cf. R. Leuchtkafer, *High Frequency Trading, A bibliography of evidence-based research*, 1 ff. for a research overview on volatility and market quality as well as p. 6 ff. for a bibliography containing studies with relevant findings with regard to volatility.

[122] Cf. J. Vaananen, *Dark Pools and High Frequency Trading*, 178 ff. on a Nanex study that sees the cause for the Flash Crash of 2010 in HFT quote stuffing; cf. para. 10 ff. on trading strategies.

[123] Market making is one of the most typical HFT strategies, cf. ESMA/2014/1569 (fn. 28), p. 336 No. 60, 62 with further references.

However, as they are generally not bound by the obligations of designated market makers to continuously perform market making, they act as 'informed' proprietary traders.[124] This relates to the question as to how HFT firms influence **market liquidity**.[125] Regardless of whether HFT firms actually provide liquidity,[126] it is claimed that HFT firms take liquidity in times when markets are under stress.[127] Liquidity shortages in times of stress can increase market volatility, especially in combination with the cascade effects mentioned above.

HFT trading raises concerns with regard to **price discovery**. Some fear that HFT decreases the market's ability to incorporate information properly.[128] This worry is based on the fact that HFT firms only hold their financial assets for a very short time.[129] The HFT strategies described above[130] are generally independent from the fundamental values of a given financial instrument, so fundamentals are not normally significant for HFT firms' order decisions. Therefore, HFT orders do not necessarily transform new information into prices[131] and if they do, they may lead to overreactions to a change in fundamentals.[132] However, arbitrage strategies, at least, can be beneficial to price discovery.[133] Even so, some scholars point out that HFT firms possibly predict price movements for 'only tens of a second' faster than other (non-high-frequency) traders, and that such other traders would also have traded on this information. If this is true, the improvement of the price discovery process by HFT firms may be of little social benefit.[134] HFT might actually be detrimental to price discovery if traders who wanted to trade on fundamental information that is not solely related to prior orders/price differences were discouraged from market participation.[135]

19

HFT could have detrimental effects on **market transparency**.[136] Markets today are highly fragmented.[137] Non-HFT market participants who may fear being exploited by HFT

20

---

[124] Cf. the summarised key findings of studies by Chae/Wang and Chung/Chuwonganant at R. Leuchtkafer, *High Frequency Trading, A bibliography of evidence-based research*, 10; on market making-arrangements para. 37.

[125] A market is liquid when an investor can sell/buy any asset for other assets or cash at will, cf. K. Pistor, 41 J. Comp. Econ. (2013), 315, 316; M. Prewitt, 19 Mich. Telecomm. & Tech. L. Rev. (2012), 131, 139.

[126] Cf. para. 23.

[127] Cf. M. Bellia et al., *High-Frequency Trading During Flash Crashes: Walk of Fame or Hall of Shame?*, SAFE Working Paper No. 270; IOSCO, Consultation Report, CR02/11 (fn. 1), p. 27; M. Prewitt, 19 Mich. Telecomm. & Tech. L. Rev. (2012), 131, 140 ff.; D. Sornette and S. von der Becke, *Crashes and High Frequency Trading*, 5 ff. M. Lewis, *Flash Boys*, 40 claims that the liquidity visible on the stock market's ticker tape is an illusion. See further D. Leis, *High Frequency Trading*, 26; J. Vaananen, *Dark Pools and High Frequency Trading*, 30 on 'phantom liquidity'.

[128] M. Prewitt, 19 Mich. Telecomm. & Tech. L. Rev. (2012), 131, 143 ff., with further references.

[129] Cf. IOSCO, Consultation Report, CR02/11 (fn. 1), p. 27; M. Yoon, 24 Emory Int'l L. Rev. (2010), 913, 921. Cf. also para. 10.

[130] However, it is important to keep in mind that different strategies may have different effects, as HFT trading is not a strategy by itself, cf. para. 10.

[131] Cf. C. Korsmo, 48 U. Rich. L. Rev. (2014), 523, 571 ff.; M. Prewitt, 19 Mich. Telecomm. & Tech. L. Rev. (2012), 131, 144, with further references on HFT's effects on price discovery.

[132] Cf. X. Zhang, *High-Frequency Trading, Stock Volatility, and Price Discovery*, 26.

[133] Cf. M. Prewitt, 19 Mich. Telecomm. & Tech. L. Rev. (2012), 131, 144. Cf. para. 13 on arbitrage strategies.

[134] M. Prewitt, 19 Mich. Telecomm. & Tech. L. Rev. (2012), 131, 146 and 161, with further references; see also H. Bell and H. Searles, *An Analysis of Global HFT Regulation*, 38; M. Lewis, *Flash Boys*, 265 ff.; D. Sornette and S. von der Becke, *Crashes and High Frequency Trading*, 7.

[135] IOSCO, Consultation Report, CR02/11 (fn. 1), p. 12; M. Prewitt, 19 Mich. Telecomm. & Tech. L. Rev. (2012), 131, 146, with further references; D. Sornette and S. von der Becke, *Crashes and High Frequency Trading*, 6; J. Gider et al., *High-Frequency Trading and Price Informativeness*.

[136] Cf. J. Vaananen, *Dark Pools and High Frequency Trading*, 212.

[137] Cf. A. Fleckner, *Regulating Trading Practices*, 596, 626 ff.; IOSCO, Consultation Report, CR02/11 (fn. 1), p. 13 ff., 24 ff. The markets are fragmented with regard to liquidity as well as information.

on 'lit markets'[138] foster this development as they can choose to trade on **'dark pools'** (ie Alternative Trading Facilities [ATFs] such as Multilateral or Organised Trading Facilities [MTFs and OTFs[139]]) that provide no pre-trade data.[140,141] It is unclear whether such an 'escape from the lit markets' actually helps, as many dark pools allow HFT firms to trade at their venue and non-high-frequency traders may find themselves at an even greater informational disadvantage when trading at such venues.[142] In any case, as dark pool orders do not appear in the order books of lit markets, a higher proportion of dark pool trading leads to greater difficulties in assessing market depth.[143]

21 HFT is associated with various **predatory practices** that affect actual and perceived **market fairness**, among them strategies with names such as quote stuffing, smoking, spoofing and layering.[144] All of them rely on exploiting the technical edge HFT firms have over other traders and the trading platforms themselves by placing super-fast orders and cancellations to move prices or hinder price adjustments.[145] They constitute **market abuse** and, depending

---

[138] Cf. G. O'Malley, 17 Trinity C.L. Rev. (2014), 94, 104 ff.

[139] Defined in Art. 4(1)(22) and (23) MiFID II. Cf. R. Veil, § 7 para. 16 and 19; further G. O'Malley, 17 Trinity C.L. Rev. (2014), 94, 114 ff. and R. Veil and M. Lerch, 66 WM (2012), 1557, 1562 ff., on the introduction of this new category of a trading facility.

[140] Cf. recital 62(1) MiFID II; N. Crudele, 9 Brook J. Corp. Fin. & Com. L. (2015), 569, 571; P. Gomber et al., *High-Frequency Trading*, 12; P. Gomber and F. Nassauer, 15 ZBB (2014), 250, 252; R. Karmel, 37 J. Corp. Law (2012), 849, 894; P. Kasiske, 15 BKR (2015), 454; C. Korsmo, 48 U. Rich. L. Rev. (2014), 523, 535. On the effects of MiFID II on dark pools see G. O'Malley, 17 Trinity C.L. Rev. (2014), 94, 113 ff.; R. Veil and M. Lerch, 66 WM (2012), 1557, 1563 ff. See N. Crudele, 9 Brook J. Corp. Fin. & Com. L. (2015), 569 ff., on dark pool regulation in more detail.

[141] Cf. N. Crudele, 9 Brook J. Corp. Fin. & Com. L. (2015), 569 and 575; P. Kasiske, 15 BKR (2015), 454, 455; M. Lewis, *Flash Boys*, 113 ff.; F. Pasquale, 36 Cardozo L. Rev. (2015), 2085, 2096 and 2104 ff.; K. Zaza, 18 Stan. J.L. Bus. & Fin. (2013), 319, 322. Cf. A. Fleckner, *Regulating Trading Practices*, 596, 616 ff. on pre- and post-trade data's relevance for the price formation process. See also fn. 35.

[142] Cf. D. Kornpeintner, *Die Regulierungsansätze des Hochfrequenzhandels*, 23; G. O'Malley, 17 Trinity C.L. Rev. (2014), 94, 103 ff. and 106 ff. and K. Zaza, 18 Stan. J.L. Bus. & Fin. (2013), 319, 331 ff., on practices used to exploit investors and information asymmetry in dark pools. Some HFT firms even operate their own dark pools, cf. P. Kasiske, 15 BKR (2015), 454, 456; further IOSCO, Consultation Report, CR02/11 (fn. 1), p. 14, on the use of actionable 'indications of interests (IOIs)' which raise fairness issues, as some members are provided with information that other traders do not receive. See K. Zaza, 18 Stan. J.L. Bus. & Fin. (2013), 319, 327 ff. on the use of IOIs in dark pools.

[143] Market depth is the number of financial instruments on offer on both sides of the trading book, cf. J. Vaananen, *Dark Pools and High Frequency Trading*, 31 and 127.

[144] Quote stuffing is explained in para. 13. Smoking means posting 'generously priced limit orders with the intention of inducing a flow of slow marketable orders.' The HFT firms then cancel their generously priced orders 'before they execute and trade with the incoming marketable orders on more advantageous terms', M. Prewitt, 19 Mich. Telecomm. & Tech. L. Rev. (2012), 131, 148. Spoofing refers to using displayed limit orders to reduce prices, while layering involves layering the order book with multiple bids and offers at different prices and sizes with cancellation rates above 90%, cf. IOSCO, Consultation Report, CR02/11 (fn. 1), p. 28; P. Kasiske, 68 WM (2014), 1933, 1935 ff.; F. Pasquale, 36 Cardozo L. Rev. (2015), 2085, 2100 ff. and 2107 ff.; S. Patterson, *Dark Pools*, 37; M. Prewitt, 19 Mich. Telecomm. & Tech. L. Rev. (2012), 131, 147 ff. See C. Korsmo, 48 U. Rich. L. Rev. (2014), 523, 555, for an example case of layering. His argument at p. 558 ff., that predatory practices are not entirely bad as they also drive the evolution of defensive mechanisms, is at least dubious (cf. also S. Patterson, *Dark Pools*, 31). However, it is true that from a systemic perspective 'parasitic pressure' forces market participants to consistently improve their own algorithms to avoid exploitation by HFT which—as a side effect—can improve the resilience of the market. P. Kasiske, 68 WM (2014), 1933, 1936, contends that layering may also be used for non-abusive reasons. D. Leis, *High Frequency Trading*, 22 and 36 points out that market making strategies imply a high order-to-trade ratio; of the same opinion B. Hagströmer and L. Nordén, *The diversity of high-frequency traders*, 38.

[145] C. Korsmo, 48 U. Rich. L. Rev. (2014), 523, 557, speaks of 'parasitic' trading which is purely designed to prey on others without any benefits to liquidity or price discovery.

on the particular strategy, amount to prohibited **market manipulation**.[146] *C. Korsmo* points out that parties potentially injured by HFT market manipulation are most likely sophisticated traders themselves, because only they were able to potentially trade on HFT orders that are subsequently cancelled.[147] Other investors would randomly benefit or suffer from manipulations. While this may be true, it is important to stress that the perceived image of a rigged market may have the general effect of prompting market participants to reduce or halt their own market activities.[148]

The aforementioned flash orders are linked to **front running** or order anticipation.[149] Front running is considered to be a severe impairment of fair market practices when conducted by brokers.[150] Further, it is contended that flash orders could create a **'two-tier' market** and circumvent the price-time-priority principle that determines which orders are matched in the market.[151] Non-high-frequency traders may therefore suffer from worse prices at which their orders are executed when HFT firms are active in the market.[152] Even when HFT firms do not use the aforementioned practices, some perceive their superior trading capabilities to be an unfair advantage[153] with regard to the opportunities that HFT firms have to step ahead of other traders, to flip out of 'toxic' trades and converse orders in order to earn rebates and to (unnecessarily) step in between customer-to-customer order matching.[154]

22

---

[146] Cf. F. Pasquale, 36 Cardozo L. Rev. (2015), 2085, 2109; M. Prewitt, 19 Mich. Telecomm. & Tech. L. Rev. (2012), 131, 148 ff.; cf. also German Government, Explanation of the High-frequency Trading Act (fn. 31), p. 2; C. Korsmo, 48 U. Rich. L. Rev. (2014), 523, 548 and 551 ff.; Kumpan, in: Schwark and Zimmer, *Kapitalmarktrechts-Kommentar*, § 26d BörsG para. 11 ff. Cf. extensively on HFT market manipulation D. Leis, *High Frequency Trading*, 36 ff. and 46 ff. Cf. R. Leuchtkafer, *High Frequency Trading, A bibliography of evidence-based research*, 2, for a research overview on manipulation and p. 6 ff. for a bibliography containing studies with relevant findings with regard to market manipulation.

[147] Cf. C. Korsmo, 48 U. Rich. L. Rev. (2014), 523, 557.

[148] Cf. C. Korsmo, 48 U. Rich. L. Rev. (2014), 523, 574.

[149] Front-running means trading ahead of the order of another trader. On front-running and flash orders C. Korsmo, 48 U. Rich. L. Rev. (2014), 523, 546 ff.; 558; M. Yoon, 24 Emory Int'l L. Rev. (2010), 913, 934; further M. Lewis, *Flash Boys*, 50; J. Vaananen, *Dark Pools and High Frequency Trading*, 144 ff. and 149 ff.; on flash-orders cf. para. 13.

[150] M. Yoon, 24 Emory Int'l L. Rev. (2010), 913, 934; cf. further C. Korsmo, 48 U. Rich. L. Rev. (2014), 546 ff., 558; F. Pasquale, 36 Cardozo L. Rev. (2015), 2085, 2099 and 2103 ff. See P. Kasiske, 15 BKR (2015), 454, 455 ff.; P. Kasiske, 68 WM (2014), 1933, 1937 on 'electronic front-running'.

[151] Cf. M. Prewitt, 19 Mich. Telecomm. & Tech. L. Rev. (2012), 131, 138. Price-time priority means that orders coming into the market are first prioritised by price and then by time, J. Vaananen, *Dark Pools and High Frequency Trading*, 35, 94 ff. Further on the concern that HFT may lead to a two-tiered market R. Karmel, 37 J. Corp. Law (2012), 849, 890; M. Lewis, *Flash Boys*, 69 ('class system, rooted in speed'). It should be kept in mind that HFT firms make use of the price-time-priority principle by being fractions of a second faster than non-HFT investors. F. Pasquale, 36 Cardozo L. Rev. (2015), 2085, 2094, points out that there is 'no inherent virtue in being able to measure the time that a trade is placed and submitted in […] quadrillionths of a second.' Cf. ibid., p. 2119, on alternatives. Cf. S. Dolgopolov, 1 Journal of Law, Technology & Policy (2014), 145, 157, on 'queue jumping'.

[152] So called 'slippage' or 'implementation shortfall', cf. J. Vaananen, *Dark Pools and High Frequency Trading*, 159 ff.

[153] Cf. IOSCO, Consultation Report, CR02/11 (fn. 1), p. 27; P. Kasiske, 68 WM (2014), 1933 ff.; C. Korsmo, 48 U. Rich. L. Rev. (2014), 523, 560; D. Leis, *High Frequency Trading*, 28.

[154] Cf. S. Dolgopolov, 1 Journal of Law, Technology & Policy (2014), 145, 149 ff. and M. Lewis, *Flash Boys*, 169 ff., on those aspects and their connection to special order types.

2. Potential Benefits of AT and HFT

(a) Increased Liquidity and Superior Intermediation

23 A positive feature often associated with HFT is **better market liquidity** as HFT firms deepen the pool of potential buyers and sellers.[155] In general, AT is well-suited to intermediate large orders by breaking them down into smaller pieces that can be traded at, or closer to, the current market price at a given time. No human could perform such services faster.[156]

(b) Increased Market Efficiency and Market Quality

24 The evolution of electronic and algorithmic trade practices has **increased the pace** of the trading process.[157] It is claimed that AT and HFT have led to **reduced transaction costs** for investors as trading platforms compete for order flow by lowering costs, amongst other things. HFT firms have taken up the role of market makers, which has reduced the bid-offer spread.[158] Some contend that HFT **decreases volatility** in the short term, at least under normal market conditions.[159] This is consistent with the liquidity provision assumption from above.[160] Further, HFT may **improve price discovery**, eg via cross-market arbitrage strategies that detect and eliminate price discrepancies faster than any human trader could.[161]

---

[155] Cf. H. Bell and H. Searles, *An Analysis of Global HFT Regulation*, 4 and 32; P. Gomber et al., *High-Frequency Trading*, 2, 32 ff.; B. Hagströmer and L. Nordén, *The diversity of high-frequency traders*, 4; IOSCO, Consultation Report, CR02/11 (fn. 1), p. 10; D. Kornpeintner, *Die Regulierungsansätze des Hochfrequenzhandels*, 19; D. Leis, *High Frequency Trading*, 26; M. Lewis, *Flash Boys*, 106 ff.; M. Yoon, 24 Emory Int'l L. Rev. (2010), 913, 936, all with further references. Cf. further R. Leuchtkafer, *High Frequency Trading, A bibliography of evidence-based research*, 6 ff., for a bibliography of studies with key findings which pertain to liquidity. G. Jiang et al., High-Frequency Trading in the U.S. Treasury Market around Macroeconomic News Announcements, HKIMR Working Paper No. 19/2018, find a negative impact of HFT on liquidity; similar J. Breckenfelder, *Competition among high-frequency traders, and market quality*, ECB Working Paper Series No 2290/June 2019; further H. Degryse et al., Cross-Venue Liquidity Provision: High Frequency Trading and Ghost Liquidity, ESMA Working Paper 4, 2020, on so called 'Ghost Liquidity'.

[156] M. Prewitt, 19 Mich. Telecomm. & Tech. L. Rev. (2012), 131, 139.

[157] Cf. H. Bell and H. Searles, *An Analysis of Global HFT Regulation*, 31; C. Korsmo, 48 U. Rich. L. Rev. (2014), 523, 532 ff.; D. Leis, *High Frequency Trading*, 26.

[158] Cf. H. Bell and H. Searles, *An Analysis of Global HFT Regulation*, 4 and 32; P. Gomber et al., *High-Frequency Trading*, 2, 6; IOSCO, Consultation Report, CR02/11 (fn. 1), p. 25; D. Kornpeintner, *Die Regulierungsansätze des Hochfrequenzhandels*, 20; C. Korsmo, 48 U. Rich. L. Rev. (2014), 523, 549 ff.; D. Leis, *High Frequency Trading*, 26; M. Yoon, 24 Emory Int'l L. Rev. (2010), 913, 935 ff., 937, all with further references. Cf. R. Leuchtkafer, *High Frequency Trading, A bibliography of evidence-based research*, 4 ff. for a research overview on investor costs and p. 6 ff. for a bibliography containing studies with relevant findings with regard to investor costs.

[159] Cf. H. Bell and H. Searles, *An Analysis of Global HFT Regulation*, 4; P. Gomber et al., *High-Frequency Trading*, 32 ff.; B. Hagströmer and L. Nordén, *The diversity of high-frequency traders*, 4 ff. and 38; D. Kornpeintner, *Die Regulierungsansätze des Hochfrequenzhandels*, 20 with further references; D. Leis, *High Frequency Trading*, 26; cf. also IOSCO, Consultation Report, CR02/11 (fn. 1), p. 26; C. Korsmo, 48 U. Rich. L. Rev. (2014), 523, 577; M. Prewitt, 19 Mich. Telecomm. & Tech. L. Rev. (2012), 131, 142 ff.

[160] See para. 23; cf. M. Prewitt, 19 Mich. Telecomm. & Tech. L. Rev. (2012), 131, 142 ff.

[161] H. Bell and H. Searles, *An Analysis of Global HFT Regulation*, 32; P. Gomber et al., *High-Frequency Trading*, 2; D. Kornpeintner, *Die Regulierungsansätze des Hochfrequenzhandels*, 15 ff., with further references; M. Prewitt, 19 Mich. Telecomm. & Tech. L. Rev. (2012), 131, 144; cf. also IOSCO, CR02/11 (fn. 1), p. 10, 25 with further references.

3. Risk-Benefit Assessment and Consequences

Regulators now find themselves in a **difficult position**.[162] The comparison of purported risks and benefits of AT and HFT shows that the findings (at least) partially contradict each other. Furthermore, the results from diverse studies on HFT are often controversial as they do not differentiate between different HFT strategies, which may be due to the problems with distinguishing between strategies in research datasets.[163] This makes it even more difficult to draw conclusions from existing research. In addition, it is necessary to **distinguish** between '**normal market circumstances**' and '**markets under stress**', as studies have shown that particular functions (such as liquidity provision) or influences associated with HFT (eg on market volatility) depend on market conditions prevalent at a particular time.[164] If, for example, HFT provides liquidity under regular market conditions but adds to downward spirals by taking liquidity away when markets are under stress, thereby ceasing to perform market making, regulators must assess whether the 'extra liquidity' in good times outweighs the risks of high volume market crashes. Reduced liquidity may simply be a price that has to be paid in exchange for higher market resilience.

In summary, various empirical studies support the claim that HFT adds liquidity and leads to a decrease in volatility under normal market circumstances.[165] The question of whether and to what extent investors benefit from lower transaction costs is controversial.[166] The effect of HFT on price discovery depends on the strategy used and may be positive or negative. There is strong evidence that HFT takes liquidity out of the market and increases volatility when markets are under stress. This may cause flash crashes; in fact, 'mini flash crashes' are frequently happening already.[167] Due to potential cascade effects, the fact that human intervention inevitably comes too late in the event an automated trading process does not run as intended, in combination with cross-market propagation, it is likely that HFT in sum[168] poses systemic risks.[169] Further, several HFT strategies discussed above amount to illegal practices, such as market manipulation or front-running, and distort the price formation process. The ultra-fast speed of HFT and a lack of information about algorithms cause significant oversight problems.[170] This setup appeared to be a **sufficient basis for regulatory measures** aimed at reducing systemic risks and containing illegal acts.[171] From

---

[162] Cf. C. Korsmo, 48 U. Rich. L. Rev. (2014), 523, 529; D. Leis, *High Frequency Trading*, 59; further J. Kobbach, 13 BKR (2013), 233, 234, with respect to the German High-frequency Trading Act (see para. 58).
[163] Cf. B. Hagströmer and L. Nordén, *The diversity of high-frequency traders*, 19; M. Prewitt, 19 Mich. Telecomm. & Tech. L. Rev. (2012), 131, 145.
[164] Cf. IOSCO, Consultation Report, CR02/11 (fn. 1), p. 12; on the difficulty to determine disorderly trading conditions cf. ESMA, Consultation Paper (fn. 11), para. 113 ff. in the context of algorithm testing.
[165] However, even under normal circumstances HFT firms may take liquidity out of the market if the strategy followed demands it, cf. J. Vaananen, *Dark Pools and High Frequency Trading*, 123 ff.
[166] Cf. S. Patterson, *Dark Pools*, 56 ff., who contends that HFT liquidity is costly for regular investors.
[167] D. Sornette and S. von der Becke, *Crashes and High Frequency Trading*, 12 ff.; further M. Lewis, *Flash Boys*, 202. Cf. J. Vaananen, *Dark Pools and High Frequency Trading*, 163 ff. extensively on flash crashes.
[168] Cf. para. 10 on the necessity to differentiate between strategies.
[169] Cf. K. Pistor, 41 J. Comp. Econ. (2013), 315, 320 ff., on how the tolerance of an unstable financial system affects the 'elasticity' of the law in situations when financial meltdowns need to be avoided.
[170] Cf. para. 27.
[171] Cf. also A. Fleckner, *Regulating Trading Practices*, 596, 603 ff.; J. Kindermann and B. Coridaß, 15 ZBB (2014), 178, 179; D. Leis, *High Frequency Trading*, 60. P. Gomber et al., *High-Frequency Trading*, 50 ff., stress that it is

the perspective of regulators and legislators it was not a feasible option to ignore the evidence-based purported risks and to wait for more conclusive research, especially since the purported social benefits of HFT are themselves controversial.[172] However, as there is also evidence for beneficial influences of HFT and considering the fact that further automation of the trading process is just another step of the evolution of trading, a **strict ban** of AT and HFT was not and is **not a suitable** option.[173]

27 When discussing regulatory responses to the potential risks of AT and HFT, one has to keep in mind that **several** of the **risks** discussed above are **not new** and do not exclusively arise in connection with AT and HFT. They are therefore already regulated, eg market manipulation has long been prohibited.[174] If illegal practices pose a substantial problem with regard to AT and HFT, for example, because manipulative trading is hard to detect,[175] the necessary regulatory response must be to **improve enforcement** of existing laws.[176] As enforcement problems likely also result from a lack of precise data,[177] improved enforcement may still necessitate new regulation that ensures that the regulatory bodies are provided with the information needed to perform their oversight functions properly. And indeed, the flow of comparable information between market participants, trade venues, national Competent Authorities (CAs) and ESMA is mentioned in various contexts in ESMA's consultation on AT.[178]

28 Risks that arise from the exclusion of human participation in the trading process, combined with scarcely possible human intervention in cases of unintended automated trading, require some form of **ex ante controls** of the techniques in question ('prevention of rogue algorithms') as well as automated interventions when there is a (potential) crisis ('**circuit breakers**').[179] However, AT and HFT have accurately been described as a

---

surprising that despite the lack of sufficient data, the necessity to regulate HFT has been treated as a given by regulators. H. Bell and H. Searles, *An Analysis of Global HFT Regulation*, 46, contend that there is only 'little evidence' that additional regulatory intervention is necessary.

[172] This argument is sometimes linked to the huge investments in the trading infrastructure made by HFT firms, cf. M. Prewitt, 19 Mich. Telecomm. & Tech. L. Rev. (2012), 131, 159. For example, Spread Networks laid a cable between New York and Chicago for $200 million to reduce latency by less than a second, cf. F. Pasquale, 36 Cardozo L. Rev. (2015), 2085, 2093 ff.

[173] Cf. also A. Fleckner, *Regulating Trading Practices*, 596, 622 ff., also on regulatory competition as a desirable consequence of lower level- and self-regulation; J. Kindermann and B. Coridaß, 15 ZBB (2014), 178, 185.

[174] Cf. C. Korsmo, 48 U. Rich. L. Rev. (2014), 523, 551 ff.; S. Patterson, *Dark Pools*, 63. The revised European market abuse regime explicitly mentions 'the fact that trading in financial instruments is increasingly automated' and therefore 'provides examples of specific abusive strategies that may be carried out by any available means of trading including *algorithmic and high-frequency trading*' (emphasis added), recital 38 MAR. Orders (including cancellations), which are at least likely to disrupt or delay the functioning of a trading system, are at least likely to make it more difficult for other persons to identify genuine orders, or are at least likely to create false or misleading signals about supply and demand of a financial instrument, constitute market manipulation, Art. 12(2)(c)(i)–(iii) MAR. This list is not to be understood as being exhaustive, recital 38 MAR. Cf. R. Veil § 15 para. 49 on market manipulation; further M. Prewitt, 19 Mich. Telecomm. & Tech. L. Rev. (2012), 131, 156.

[175] Cf. C. Korsmo, 48 U. Rich. L. Rev. (2014), 523, 557; D. Leis, *High Frequency Trading*, 36.

[176] Cf. A. Fleckner, *Regulating Trading Practices*, 596, 622.

[177] Cf. P. Gomber et al., *High-Frequency Trading*, 1; IOSCO, Consultation Report, CR02/11 (fn. 1), p. 22, 24. See ESMA, Economic Report (fn. 11), p. 19 ff., for an overview of available HFT datasets.

[178] ESMA, Consultation Paper (fn. 11), e.g. para. 73, 85, 88 ff.

[179] Cf. recital 64 MiFID II; further C. Korsmo, 48 U. Rich. L. Rev. (2014), 523, 531. Circuit breakers can appear in various forms, e.g. as trading halts or so called 'limit-up/limit-down' mechanisms that restrict the speed at which the price of a financial instrument can fluctuate, cf. M. Prewitt, 19 Mich. Telecomm. & Tech. L. Rev. (2012), 131, 151 ff., 153.; further R. Karmel, 37 J. Corp. Law (2012), 849, 899; O. Linton et al., *Economic impact assessments*

moving target from a regulatory perspective, since HFT firms are 'protean in nature'.[180] This calls not only for a **dynamic regulatory approach**[181] that is able to quickly adapt to changes in market practices, but also for incentives for market participants to comply with applicable law. Oversight and enforcement will necessarily remain one of the main challenges for supervisory bodies regardless of the information provided to them. A 'traditional' way of strengthening compliance is to foster and clarify the liability of firms and traders performing AT and HFT and firms that provide market access to them.[182]

Finally, the aim of any regulation in the field of AT and HFT has to be to eliminate discriminatory informational advantages and restore and ensure a **level playing field**.[183] Beyond that, regulatory action is not necessary where the activity of AT and HFT firms is legal and does not pose systemic risks, eg when they exploit publicly available information and trade on its basis,[184] even if this turns out to be detrimental for slower institutional investors. It is not the purpose of market regulation to ensure that certain traders do not suffer from 'better' algorithms or equipment used by other traders.[185] Regulators and legislators must strike a balance to **cope with the risks** laid out above **without jeopardising** the potential **benefits** of new technical developments, while also avoiding one-sided market interventions.[186] The regulatory debate also has political implications, as HFT may shift resources away from long-term and retail investors to short-term oriented sophisticated investors,[187] which may be an unwanted development.[188]

29

---

on MiFID II policy measures related to computer trading in financial markets, 9; cf. with more details ESMA, Consultation Paper (fn. 11), para. 166 ff. and ESMA, Guidelines, Calibration of circuit breakers and publication of trading halts under MiFID II, 6 April 2017, ESMA70-872942901-63.

[180] Cf. C. Korsmo, 48 U. Rich. L. Rev. (2014), 523, 529; further J. Vaananen, *Dark Pools and High Frequency Trading*, 211.

[181] Cf. C. Korsmo, 48 U. Rich. L. Rev. (2014), 523, 529.

[182] Cf. C. Korsmo, 48 U. Rich. L. Rev. (2014), 523, 531.

[183] Cf. ESMA/2015/1464 (fn. 42), p. 210 No. 11; ESMA, Consultation Paper (fn. 11), para. 53 ff.; A. Fleckner, *Regulating Trading Practices*, 622; D. Leis, *High Frequency Trading*, 53; cf. G. O'Malley, 17 Trinity C.L. Rev. (2014), 94, 120 ff., on the attempt of MiFID II to level the playing field between different market participants in the European securities markets. This does not mean that market participants should not be able to have an informational edge, e.g. due to better technology, cf. para. 67. Levelling the playing field has become the focus when looking at third-country firms from outside the EU, especially since Brexit, cf. ESMA, Consultation Paper (fn. 11), para. 64.

[184] Cf. also M. Yoon, 24 Emory Int'l L. Rev. (2010), 913, 914.

[185] Cf. C. Korsmo, 48 U. Rich. L. Rev. (2014), 523, 560.

[186] Cf. C. Korsmo, 48 U. Rich. L. Rev. (2014), 523, 529. This is particularly true as sometimes it may be even unclear who benefits from particular developments and related regulatory responses, cf. ESMA, Consultation Paper (fn. 11), para. 346 on a response by a market participant in the context of so called 'asymmetric speedbumps'.

[187] Cf. C. Korsmo, 48 U. Rich. L. Rev. (2014), 523, 565; D. Leis, *High Frequency Trading*, 59; F. Pasquale, 36 Cardozo L. Rev. (2015), 2085, 2086 ff. A. Fleckner, *Regulating Trading Practices*, 596, 620 (at fn. 96) points out that only a small fraction of outstanding shares is traded at all, with most shares being held by long-term investors.

[188] Cf. H. Bell and H. Searles, *An Analysis of Global HFT Regulation*, 11 and 43 ff. However, even if non-HFT (long-term) investors did indeed suffer from worse prices because of HFT, their trades still decide how capital is ultimately allocated, which F. Pasquale, 36 Cardozo L. Rev. (2015), 2085, 2117 ff., seems to ignore. It is particularly dangerous to critique HFT on the basis of how a 'good capital allocation' would look like, were it not for the existence of HFT. Instrumentalising regulation to achieve such a pre-determined and desired outcome will likely suffer from—what Hayek called—'a pretence of knowledge'. Cf. also H. Bell and H. Searles, *An Analysis of Global HFT Regulation*, 44 and 47; F. Hayek, *The Pretence of Knowledge*. Cf. the Economist, 5–11 December 2015, 13 and 22 ff., on perceived 'short-termism' and whether this should be seen as a threat to capitalism.

IV. Regulatory Measures with Regard to AT and HFT

1. European Approach

30 This section sets out the development of the European law from a non-specific regulatory regime with respect to AT and HFT under MiFID and the market abuse directive (MAD), supplemented by guidelines issued by ESMA in 2012, to MiFID II and a market abuse regulation (MAR). The latter include several provisions that are directly aimed at the regulation of risks that may arise from AT and HFT. Regulatory Technical Standards (RTS) and Delegated Acts specify the new regime that is explicitly based on ESMA's guidelines.[189]

(a) MiFID, MAD and ESMA Guidelines

31 The regulatory regime as laid out in MiFID and MAD did not include specific provisions regarding AT and HFT. However, one latency-reducing measure—known as '**naked**' or '**unfiltered**' **market access**—where clients' orders do not pass the pre-trade controls of the investment firm providing DMA/SA, had been **prohibited** under MiFID.[190] Further, ESMA had issued Guidelines in accordance with Article 16 ESMA Regulation on 'Systems and controls in an automated trading environment for trading platforms, investment firms and competent authorities' in February 2012[191] (**ESMA Guidelines**).[192] Their purpose was to ensure the uniform and consistent application of MiFID and MAD as they apply to the systems and controls that trading platforms and investment firms must have in place in an automated trading environment. They also contained rules in relation to the provision of DMA/SA.[193] The ESMA Guidelines covered the operation of electronic trading systems by Regulated Markets[194] (RMs) or MTFs and the use of electronic trading systems (including trading algorithms)[195] by an investment firm for dealing on own account or for the execution of client orders, as well as the provision of DMA/SA by an investment firm[196] as part of the execution of client orders.[197]

---

[189] Recital 63 MiFID II.

[190] ESMA/2012/122 (fn. 41), 24 February 2012, p. 22. From a systemic perspective, 'naked access' would circumvent not only risk controls but potentially also capital requirements, thereby increasing counterparty risk, which is the risk that a party will not be able to fulfil contractual obligations to pay money/transfer a financial instrument, cf. C. Korsmo, 48 U. Rich. L. Rev. (2014), 523, 531; M. Prewitt, 19 Mich. Telecomm. & Tech. L. Rev. (2012), 131, 137.

[191] ESMA/2012/122 (fn. 41).

[192] The ESMA Guidelines have been withdrawn by the ESMA Board of Supervisors on 26 September 2018 as the subject matter is now fully incorporated into MiFID II, MAR und delegated acts. Cf. R. Veil, § 5 para. 22–26 on the soft law nature and legal effects of ESMA Guidelines. D. Kornpeintner, *Die Regulierungsansätze des Hochfrequenzhandels*, 39 ff., describes the ESMA Guidelines in more detail.

[193] ESMA/2012/122 (fn. 41), p. 6.

[194] For a definition see Art. 4(1)(21) MiFID II, cf. R. Veil, § 7 para. 11.

[195] Guidelines 1 and 2 ESMA Guidelines. ESMA defined trading algorithms as 'computer software operating on the basis of key parameters set by an investment firm or client of an investment firm that generates orders to be submitted to trading platforms automatically in response to market information', or generally speaking, 'electronic systems which automatically generate orders', ESMA/2012/122 (fn. 41), 4, 5.

[196] 'Investment firm' refers to investment firms when executing orders on behalf of clients and/or dealing on own account in an automated trading environment. Should the investment firm have been operating an MTF, it was covered by the guidelines for trading platforms, ESMA/2012/122 (fn. 41), 3.

[197] ESMA/2012/122 (fn. 41), p. 3.

The ESMA Guidelines aimed at ensuring the continuity and regularity in the performance of automated markets and the compliance of investment firms with obligations under MiFID, other applicable law, and the rules of the trading platforms.[198] **Specific rules** related to monitoring, algo-testing[199] (ie testing a trading algorithm before deploying it), the promotion of fair and orderly trading, record keeping and risk management, amongst others. Further, they included measures aimed at the prevention of market abuse, eg by requiring trading systems to have sufficient capacity to deal with high-frequency order generation and being able to trace transactions. Further guidelines covered staff qualification and requirements for RMs/MTFs whose participants provide DMA/SA, and for investment firms that provide DMA/SA. They included provisions on due diligence, pre-trade controls and the possibility to halt trading by specific customers. It was stressed that the investment firm providing DMA/SA is responsible for the trading of DMA/SA clients.

32

(b) Level 1 Regime: MiFID II

Since many market participants use algorithmic trading, and because trading technology has significantly evolved, the Commission decided to specifically regulate risks arising from AT and HFT.[200] The main part of this regulation is laid out in MiFID II. Additionally, the market abuse regime contains some examples of HFT strategies that constitute market manipulation.[201] The Commission recognises that new business models have evolved that facilitate HFT, such as co-location and DMA/SA, which have increased not only the speed and capacity of the trading process, but also its complexity. The **Commission sees the benefits** of new trading technology in wider market participation, increased liquidity, narrower spreads, reduced short-term volatility and the means of obtaining better execution of client orders. Related **risks are identified** as the potential overloading of the system, duplicative or erroneous orders or other malfunctioning that may cause a disorderly market. AT may lead to overreaction to market events and exacerbate volatility. Further, certain forms of AT and HFT constitute behaviour prohibited under MAR.[202]

33

The EU's regulatory response to these perceived risks is a **combination of measures and risk controls** directed at AT and HFT firms and investment firms that provide DMA/SA, as well as measures directed at the trading platforms that are accessed by such firms.[203] Infringements of various provisions regarding AT and HFT are subject to **sanctions**.[204]

34

---

[198] Guidelines 1(1), 2(1) ESMA Guidelines.
[199] Cf. D. Kornpeintner, *Die Regulierungsansätze des Hochfrequenzhandels*, 62 ff.
[200] Cf. recitals 59, 61 MiFID II; cf. P. Gomber et al., *High-Frequency Trading*, 48 ff. and D. Leis, *High Frequency Trading*, 68 ff. on the 'Swinburne Report' on Regulation of Trading in Financial Instruments of the Committee on Economic and Monetary Affairs, which preceded the MiFID review and covered issues related to AT and HFT.
[201] Cf. para. 21 and 27.
[202] Cf. recital 62(1) and (2) MiFID II on the aforementioned aspects; further para. 21 and fn. 174.
[203] Recitals 63, 64 MiFID II.
[204] Art. 70(3)(a)(v)–(vi), (xxviii)–(xxxix) MiFID II; cf. D. Mattig, WM (2014), 1940, 1945; on sanctions in capital markets law cf. R. Veil § 12 para. 12 ff.

(aa) Provisions Concerning AT and HFT Firms and Investment Firms that Provide DMA/SA

35　**MiFID II introduces a mix** of organisational requirements, rules on co-operation with supervisory bodies, measures to stabilise liquidity provision and measures to reduce risk resulting from DEA. In the context of AT and HFT techniques definitions,[205] MiFID II stipulates that possible exemptions from the application of the directive for persons dealing on own account in financial instruments are not applicable when those persons apply a high-frequency algorithmic trading technique.[206] Consequentially, they need to be authorised and follow MiFID II's provisions even when performing proprietary trading.[207] Article 17(1) MiFID II lays out several **organisational requirements** for investment firms that engage in AT. They must have in place effective systems and risk controls suitable to the business they operate to ensure their trading systems are resilient and have sufficient capacity, are subject to appropriate trading thresholds and limits, and prevent the sending of erroneous orders or the system otherwise functioning in a way that may create or contribute to a disorderly market. Also, they must have in place effective systems and risk controls to ensure trading systems cannot be used for any purpose that is contrary to MAR or rules of the trading venue to which they are connected. Further, they must have in place business continuity arrangements to deal with any failure of their trading systems and ensure that their systems are fully tested and properly monitored.

36　A firm that engages in AT must **notify the CAs**[208] of its home Member State and of the trading venue at which the firm trades.[209] The CA of the home Member State can request from the AT firm a description of the nature of its AT strategies, details of the trading parameters or limits to which the system is subject, the key compliance and risk controls and details of the testing of its system on a regular or ad hoc basis. Such information must be communicated to the CA of the trading venue upon request. Investment firms that engage in HFT must store in an approved form accurate and time sequenced records of all its placed orders, including cancellations, executed orders and quotations on trading venues and make them available to the CA upon request.

37　Due to the importance of liquidity provision for the orderly and efficient functioning of markets,[210] MiFID II stipulates **additional provisions for AT and HFT firms** that pursue a **market-making strategy**.[211] Taking into account the liquidity, scale and nature of the specific market and the characteristics of the instrument traded, the firm must carry out

---

[205] Cf. para. 5 ff.
[206] Art. 2(1)(d)(iii), (e), (j) MiFID II; cf. also recitals 18, 20, 50 MiFID II.
[207] Cf. recital 63 MiFID II, also on possible exemptions for HFT firms already regulated under Union law regulating the financial sector. In principle, all HFT firms are to be authorised, cf. recital 63 MiFID II; ESMA/2014/1569 (fn. 28), 318, cf. also ESMA ibid., 324 No. 25. Critically on registration requirements for HFT firms C. Korsmo, 48 U. Rich. L. Rev. (2014), 523, 601 ff.
[208] As defined in Art. 4(1)(26) MiFID II.
[209] Art. 17(2) subsec. 1 MiFID II. For definitions of the terms competent authority, home member state and trading venue cf. Art. 4(1)(24), (26), (55) MiFID II.
[210] Recital 113 MiFID II.
[211] The term market making strategy is to be determined with regard to the context and purpose of MiFID II and may therefore differ from the definition of market making activities under Art. 2(1)(k) Regulation (EU) No. 236/2012 of the European Parliament and of the Council of 14 March 2012 on short selling and certain aspects of credit default swaps, OJ 2012 L86, 24 March 2012, 1–24, cf. recital 60 MiFID II.

market making continuously during a specified proportion of the trading venue's trading hours, except under exceptional circumstances, with the result of liquidity being provided on a predictable basis to the trading venue. Further, the firm must enter into a binding written agreement with the trading venue that shall at least specify the obligation to continuously carry out market making and have in place effective systems and controls to ensure the fulfilment of the obligations under the written agreement. A market-making strategy is pursued when the investment firm, as a member or participant of one or more trading venues, when dealing on own account, posts firm, simultaneous two-way quotes of comparable size and at competitive prices relating to one or more financial instruments on a single trading venue or across different trading venues, with the result of providing liquidity on a regular and frequent basis to the overall market.[212]

Investment firms that provide DMA/SA to a trading venue must have in place effective systems and controls that ensure a proper assessment and review of the suitability of clients using the service, that clients are prevented from exceeding appropriate pre-set trading and credit thresholds, that trading by clients is properly monitored and that risk controls prevent trading that may create risk for the investment firm itself or that could create or contribute to a disorderly market or could be prohibited under MAR or rules of the trading venue. DEA without such controls ('naked access') is prohibited.[213] Investment firms that provide DMA/SA are responsible for ensuring that clients using that service comply with the requirements of MiFID II and the rules of the trading venue, which is to be monitored by the investment firms. The rights and obligations of such a service are to be laid out in a binding written agreement between the investment firm and its client. Investment firms providing DMA/SA services must notify the CA of the home Member State and of the trading venue. The CA of the home Member State may require on a regular or ad hoc basis a description of the systems and controls and pass this information on to the CA of the trading venue upon request. The investment firm must keep records in relation to those matters.[214]

38

Details of the organisational requirements are laid down in Article 17(1)–(6) MiFID II. Circumstances under which investment firms must enter into a market-making agreement, the exceptional circumstances when continued market making is not required and the content of the approved form for the recorded trade information **are to be specified by RTS**.[215]

39

(bb) Provisions Concerning Trade Venues with Particular Relevance for AT and HFT

A **regulated market** (RM) is required to have in place effective systems, procedures and arrangements that, amongst other things, ensure the resilience of its trading system, and have sufficient capacity to deal with peak order and message volumes, and that reject orders that exceed pre-determined volume and price thresholds or are clearly erroneous. It must be able to temporarily halt or constrain trading if there is a significant price movement in a financial instrument and be able to cancel, vary or correct transactions

40

---

[212] Cf. Art. 17(3)(a)–(c) and (4) MiFID II on these various aspects.
[213] Art. 17(5) subsec. 1 MiFID II. Cf. also recital 66 MiFID II.
[214] Cf. Art. 17(5) subsec. 2–6 MiFID II.
[215] Art. 17(7) MiFID II; they were to be developed by ESMA and endorsed by the Commission, cf. para. 48 ff.

('**circuit breakers**').[216] Further, RMs must have **written agreements** with all investment firms pursuing market-making strategies on the RM (which includes AT firms that are not designated market makers),[217] which specify incentives in terms of rebates for the provision of liquidity, amongst other things. RMs must have schemes in place to ensure that a sufficient number of investment firms participate in such agreements. The RM must **monitor** and **enforce compliance** by investment firms that are part to the agreement, inform the CA about its content, and provide additional information upon request. Further, RMs must have in place effective systems, procedures and arrangements, including requiring members or participants to carry out appropriate **testing of algorithms** and provide environments to facilitate such testing, to ensure that AT systems cannot create or contribute to disorderly trading conditions[218] on the market, and to manage any disorderly trading conditions that do arise from such AT systems, including systems to limit the ratio of unexecuted orders-to-transactions (**OTR**) that may be entered into the system by members/participants.

41   RMs must be able to **slow down** the **flow of orders** if there is a risk of its system capacity being reached and to limit and **enforce** the **minimum tick size**[219] that may be executed on the market. Imposing minimum price ticks makes it harder for a trader to step in front of another trader by offering a fractionally better price. Also, certain HFT strategies may be harder to implement with higher ticks.[220] RMs must have the ability to distinguish and, if necessary, to **stop** orders or **trading by** a person using **DMA** separately from other orders or trading by the member or participant.[221]

---

[216] Cf. Art. 48(1), (4)–(5) MiFID II on these requirements. Circuit breakers can provide 'cooling-off periods' and may resolve uncertainty in the market, cf. O. Linton et al., *Economic impact assessments on MiFID II policy measures related to computer trading in financial markets*, 10 ff. RMs must report the parameters they use to determine whether trading needs to be halted to the relevant CA in a consistent and comparable manner. The CA in turn reports to ESMA. In the case that trading is halted at a material RM in terms of liquidity, the CA has to be notified to co-ordinate market wide responses such as halting trading at other venues, cf. Art. 48(5) subsec. 2 MiFID II. ESMA is supposed to develop guidelines on the appropriate calibration of trading halts, Art. 48(13) MiFID II (cf. fn. 179). See also D. Leis, *High Frequency Trading*, 75.

[217] Art. 48(2)(a), (3) subsec. 1 MiFID II. A market maker is defined in Art. 4(1)(7) MiFID II as a person who holds himself out on the financial markets on a continuous basis as being willing to deal on own account by buying and selling financial instruments against that person's proprietary capital at prices defined by that person. Cf. para. 14 with further references on HFT market making.

[218] Cf. ESMA, Consultation Paper (fn. 11), para. 114 ff. on ESMA's proposal to include a clear definition in Level 1 regulation.

[219] Specified in Art. 49 MiFID II; cf. also Commission Delegated Regulation (EU) 2017/588 of 14 July 2016 supplementing Directive 2014/65/EU of the European Parliament and of the Council with regard to regulatory technical standards on the tick size regime for shares, depositary receipts and exchange-traded funds (RTS11). A 'tick' is to be understood as the minimum price movement by which an instrument's price can move, IOSCO, Consultation Report, CR02/11 (fn. 1), p. 17. Tick size regulation is an indirect form of HFT regulation as it reduces the possibilities for HFT firms to 'jump the queue' by making use of the smallest possible price increments. This comes at the cost of foregoing possible spread reductions. Cf. O. Linton et al., *Economic impact assessments on MiFID II policy measures related to computer trading in financial markets*, 14 ff. Special order types are used to facilitate queue jumping, cf. S. Dolgopolov, 1 Journal of Law, Technology & Policy (2014), 145, 149 ff.

[220] IOSCO, Consultation Report, CR02/11 (fn. 1), p. 17; cf. also J. Vaananen, *Dark Pools and High Frequency Trading*, 71 on Rule 612 of Reg. NMS. This comes at a cost, as lower tick sizes benefit investors by lower trading costs and tightened spreads. Cf. also H. Bell and H. Searles, *An Analysis of Global HFT Regulation*, 41 on a study (with quite opposite implications) that suggests that deregulating tick sizes would take the 'speed advantage' away from HFT firms, as speed competition is contended to be a consequence of failed price competition.

[221] Art. 48(6), (7) subsec. 2 MiFID II. The member or participant of the trading platform remains responsible for orders and trades used by DEA clients, cf. Art. 48(7) subsec. 1 MiFID II.

RMs must have transparent, fair and non-discriminatory **rules on co-location**.[222] An   42
RM's **fee structure**,[223] including execution fees and rebates, must be transparent, fair and
non-discriminatory and must not create incentives to place, modify or cancel orders or to
execute transactions in a way that contributes to disorderly trading conditions or market
abuse. Rebates may also be granted to investment firms in exchange for market-making
obligations. It is up to the Member States whether they allow RMs to impose higher fees for
placing orders that are subsequently cancelled and to impose a higher fee on participants
placing a high ratio of cancelled orders to executed orders and on HFT firms in order to
reflect the additional burden on system capacity. RMs must be able to identify, by means
of **flagging**, members or participants, orders generated by AT, the different algorithms used
for the creation of orders, and the relevant person initiating those orders and present this
information to the CA upon request.[224]

ESMA is supposed to develop RTS specifying, amongst other things, the ratio of unexecuted   43
orders to transactions, the requirements on co-location,[225] and the requirements to ensure
appropriate testing of algorithms including HFT.[226]

The obligations laid out in **Articles 48–49 MiFID II also apply to** investment firms oper-   44
ating an **MTF or OTF**.[227] They too must have in place all the necessary effective systems,
procedures, and arrangements to comply with those provisions.

(c) Level 2: ESMA's Technical Advice and Regulatory Technical Standards

(aa) Technical Advice

On 23 April 2014, ESMA received a formal request from the Commission to provide   45
Technical Advice (TA) to assist the Commission on the possible content of the Delegated
Acts required by several provisions of MiFID II and the markets in financial instruments
regulation (MiFIR). ESMA provided this TA on 19 December 2014.[228] After a **public
discussion and consultation** process, ESMA recommended several clarifications regarding
AT. ESMA is of the opinion that while automated trading decisions and the optimisation
of order execution processes can be distinguished, both are included in the definition of
AT.[229] It is sufficient to qualify trading as AT if the system makes independent decisions at
any stage of the trading process, which includes initiation, generation, routing or execution of orders.[230] However, if the system only determines the venue where the order should

---

[222] Art. 48(8) MiFID II. This refers to access to and usage of co-location services, cf. D. Mattig, 68 WM (2014), 1940, 1944. It should be noted that proximity hosting (cf. para. 8) is not covered by MiFID II, critically ibid., p. 1945.
[223] Cf. IOSCO, Consultation Report, CR02/11 (fn. 1), p. 17 ff., on different pricing approaches.
[224] Cf. Art. 48(9) subsec. 1 and 3, 10 MiFID II on those aspects, further recital 67 MiFID II.
[225] ESMA was only supposed to further specify the requirements to ensure that co-location services are fair and non-discriminatory, critical D. Mattig, 68 WM (2014), 1940, 1944. However, Art. 2 of ESMA's RTS10 (cf. para. 57) also covers transparency aspects.
[226] Art. 48(12)(b), (d), (g) MiFID II; cf. para. 48 ff. on RTS.
[227] Art 18(5) MiFID II; cf. para. 20; further G. O'Malley, 17 Trinity C.L. Rev. (2014), 94, 114 ff.; R. Veil and M. Lerch, 66 WM (2012), 1557, 1562 ff., on the introduction of this new category of a trading venue.
[228] ESMA/2014/1569 (fn. 28).
[229] ESMA/2014/1569 (fn. 28), p. 338 No. 1. i.
[230] ESMA/2014/1569 (fn. 28), p. 338 No. 1 ii. ESMA notes that 'orders' encompasses quotes as well.

be submitted without changing any other parameters of the order ('**Automated Order Routers—AORs**'), this would be **out of scope of AT**.[231] AORs must be distinguished from **Smart Order Routers** ('**SORs**'), which determine other parameters, eg by slicing an order into 'child orders'[232] or by determining the time when the order is to be submitted. SORs fall **within the definition of AT**.[233]

46   With respect to HFT, **ESMA did not recommend a specific proxy** that should be used to identify whether an algorithmic trading technique is characterised by high message intraday rates.[234] Instead, it suggested three possible solutions the Commission could follow, which include an absolute threshold per instrument ('2 messages per second'), an absolute threshold per trading venue and per instrument ('2 messages per second with respect to any single instrument or 4 messages per second with respect to all instruments across a trading venue') and a relative threshold (a participant uses HFT where the median daily lifetime of its modified or cancelled orders falls under a threshold below the median daily lifetime of all the modified or cancelled orders submitted to a trading venue).[235] Objections had been raised to each of the proposed proxies in the consultation process,[236] which may explain why ESMA did not want to choose one particular option to propose to the Commission.[237]

47   However, ESMA pointed out that the **identification of HFT should be focused on liquid instruments**[238] at least until 3 March 2019[239] and should consider market making strategies in the calculations.[240] Finally, ESMA recommended to **only** consider **proprietary trading** order flow for HFT identification and to give investment firms the option of **challenging a classification** as HFT firm,[241] while noting that a **binary approach** should be adopted.[242] This means that an investment firm is considered to be an HFT firm even if HFT strategies are only used partially or by only a part of the firm. This classification pertains to all trading venues in the EU.[243] Overall, regarding MiFID II's purpose of imposing the aforementioned

---

[231] ESMA/2014/1569 (fn. 28), p. 324, 338 No. 1 iii.
[232] Cf. IOSCO, Consultation Report, CR02/11 (fn. 1), 26; further P. Gomber et al., *High-Frequency Trading*, 19 ff.
[233] Cf. ESMA/2014/1569 (fn. 28), 324. Cf. M. Lewis, *Flash Boys*, 74 ff., on ways how orders sent by automated routers may be exploited by HFT firms.
[234] Cf. Art. 4(1)(40)(c) MiFID II.
[235] ESMA/2014/1569 (fn. 28), 338 ff. No. 2 i–iii.
[236] Cf. ESMA/2014/1569 (fn. 28), 324 ff.; further FIA/FIA Europe, *Algorithmic and High Frequency Trading—Special Report*, p. 3 ff.; J. Vaananen, *Dark Pools and High Frequency Trading*, 142.
[237] Cf. ESMA/2014/1569 (fn. 28), p. 320 ff. In the consultation with regard to options 1 and 2, a majority preferred option 1.
[238] ESMA/2014/1569 (fn. 28), 339 No. 4 i; 'liquid' refers to the definition in Art. 2(1)(17) MiFIR. Cf. also FIA/FIA Europe, *Algorithmic and High Frequency Trading—Special Report*, p. 6. HFT adoption depends much on the degree of liquidity of a given instrument as the possibility to enter and leave the market quickly is crucial for most HFT strategies, cf. IOSCO, Consultation Report, CR02/11 (fn. 1), 22 ff., 25.
[239] This is until when the Commission was supposed to present a report to the European Parliament and the Council on the impact of requirements regarding algorithmic trading including high-frequency trading, Art. 90(1)(c) MiFID II.
[240] ESMA/2014/1569 (fn. 28), 339 No. 4 ii-iii.
[241] ESMA/2014/1569 (fn. 28), 339 No. 5. Investment firms may use the data recorded under Art. 25 MiFIR to determine the level of messaging activity which is attributable to proprietary trading. Cf. also FIA/FIA Europe, *Algorithmic and High Frequency Trading—Special Report*, 5 ff.
[242] ESMA/2014/1569 (fn. 28), 337 No. 67.
[243] Cf. ESMA/2014/1569 (fn. 28), 320 No. 10. This proposal was criticised by a majority of respondents in the consultation process, cf. ibid., 336 ff. However, when particular segments of a trade venue do not enable AT, the RTS do not apply to those segments, cf. ESMA/2015/1464 (fn. 42), 208 No. 4.

requirements on all HFT firms, ESMA was of the view that the **definition should be** sufficiently **broad and dynamic** to cope with further developments.[244]

(bb) Regulatory Technical Standards

ESMA had proposed several sets of RTS regarding AT and HFT to be adopted by the Commission. To ensure consistency with MiFID II and legal certainty, they generally **apply from 3 January 2018**. For the purposes of this chapter, it is sufficient to refer to the most important provisions and concepts developed in the relevant sets of RTS.

One set (**RTS6**) specifies the **organisational requirements of investment firms** engaged in AT, providing direct electronic access and acting as general clearing members.[245] Amongst other things, the detailed requirements in RTS6 pertain to organisational requirements such as governance, role of the compliance function, staffing, and IT outsourcing (Articles 1–4 RTS6). In support of the resilience of trading systems, RTS6 lay out rules on the testing and deployment of trading algorithms and systems, including provisions on post-deployment management, such as annual self-assessments and stress testing (Articles 5–10 RTS6). Material changes to the production environment relating to AT require review by a designated responsible party (Article 11 RTS6). AT firms are required to know the responsible algorithm/trader for each order and to have the ability to cancel unexecuted orders at all trading venues and orders at individual trading venues or originating from a particular trader, trading desk or client in case of an emergency ('**kill functionality**'; Article 12 RTS6). Further details are laid out on **detection** of potential **market manipulation** (Article 13 RTS6), and on business continuity arrangements to deal with disruptive incidents and timely resumption of AT (Article 14 RTS6). AT firms must apply pre-trade controls with regard to price collars, maximum order value and volume, as well as a maximum messaging limit (Article 15 RTS6). They are to be supplemented by post-trade controls that continuously assess and monitor the market risk and credit risk of the investment firm in terms of effective exposure (Article 17 RTS6). Further, during the hours in which AT firms send orders to a trading venue, they must **monitor** their algorithms **in real time** by the trader in charge and by an independent risk function (Article 16 RTS6).

RTS6 also contain **provisions on DEA**. As a general rule, the DEA provider remains responsible for trading carried out in its name. DEA providers must also apply pre-trade and post-trade controls, as well as real-time monitoring. All clients' orders must pass through the DEA provider's pre-trade controls (no 'naked access'; Articles 19–20 RTS6). DEA providers' systems must meet certain conditions, eg they must be able to automatically block or cancel orders from individuals or from a DEA client under certain conditions (Article 21 RTS6). Prospective DEA clients must undergo a **due diligence process** by the DEA provider, the results of which must be re-assessed on an annual basis as well as the adequacy of the provider's clients' risk systems and controls (Articles 22–23 RTS6). HFT firms must **record the details of each order** and keep the records for five years (Article 28 RTS6).

---

[244] ESMA/2014/1569 (fn. 28), 318 ff., 324; cf. also ESMA, Consultation Paper (fn. 11), para. 8.
[245] Cf. para. 35; Commission Delegated Regulation (EU) 2017/589 of 19 July 2016 supplementing Directive 2014/65/EU of the European Parliament and of the Council with regard to regulatory technical standards specifying the organisational requirements of investment firms engaged in algorithmic trading.

51   **RTS7** cover **organisational requirements of RMs, MTFs and OTFs** enabling or allowing AT through their systems.[246] As risks arising from AT can be present in any trading model supported by electronic means, RTS7 apply to all possible trading venues.[247] **In line with** the provisions regarding investment firms (**RTS6**), RTS7 provide regulation on governance arrangements, the role of the compliance function, staffing requirements and outsourcing (Recital 4 RTS7; Articles 1–6 RTS7). With respect to the aforementioned aspects, RTS7 require trading venues to self-assess compliance with Article 48 MiFID II and keep the self-assessment records for at least five years.[248] Further, detailed governance requirements are stipulated in relation to the analysis of technical, risk and compliance issues, lines of accountability, communication of information, segregation of functions as well as the areas for which senior management shall bear responsibility.[249] Article 4 RTS7 describes the role of the compliance function within the governance scheme and stipulates that compliance staff must have access to the trading venue's 'kill function' or to persons who can use that function as well as to persons responsible for the AT system. Article 5 RTS7 provides necessary qualifications of staff managing AT systems and trade algorithms with regard to knowledge, skills, and initial and ongoing training.

52   **Chapter II of RTS7** prescribes measures that trading venues have to implement with regard to their **capacity and resilience.** They must perform due diligence and risk-based assessments of their customers with regard to pre-trade controls, qualification of staff, conformance testing, the kill functionality and the provision of DEA (Article 7 RTS7). Trading venues must have the option to **penalise non-compliant members**, eg by suspending access to the venue and terminating their membership (cf. Article 7(5) RTS7). On the one hand, RTS7 further require trading venues to **test their trading systems** before deploying or updating them and, on the other hand, they have to **require** their own **members** to perform **conformance testing** prior to the deployment or substantial update of access to the trading venue's system, the member's trading system, trading algorithm or trading strategy (Articles 8–9 RTS7). For this purpose, trading venues are to **provide a testing environment** to their members.[250] However, they are not required to validate test results.[251]

53   Trading venues should be able to **cope with** at least **twice the historical peak** of messages per second and ensure that they can cope with rising message flow without material degradation of their systems performance (Article 11(1), (4) RTS7). Further resilience- and capacity-related provisions cover real-time monitoring obligations, periodic reviews of the system's performance, which include stress tests, and the requirement for business continuity arrangements and their periodic review.[252] To prevent capacity breaches and disorderly

---

[246] Cf. para. 40 ff.; Commission Delegated Regulation (EU) 2017/584 of 14 July 2016 supplementing Directive 2014/65/EU of the European Parliament and of the Council with regard to regulatory technical standards specifying organisational requirements of trading venues.

[247] Recital (3), Art. 1(1) RTS7. According to Art. 1(2) RTS7 a trading venue allows/enables AT, if order submission or matching is facilitated by electronic means.

[248] Art. 2(1) and (2) RTS7. The elements to be considered in the self-assessment are listed in the Annex of RTS7 and refer to nature, scale and complexity issues.

[249] Art. 3(1)(a)–(d), (2)(a)–(c) RTS7. They include, inter alia, the aforementioned self-assessment process and responses to material shortcomings detected in monitoring activities.

[250] The criteria those environments must meet are laid out in Art. 9(4), 10(3) RTS7.

[251] Art. 10(2) RTS7.

[252] Art. 12–13; Art. 14(3); Art. 15–17 RTS7.

trading, trading venues must have in place arrangements with respect to limits per member on the number of orders sent per second ('**throttle limits**'), mechanisms to manage volatility (such as automatically halting and containing trading) and pre-trade controls.[253] The powers that trading venues must possess to act in certain cases include a '**kill functionality**' to cancel unexecuted orders submitted by a member or SA client, eg when the order book is corrupted by erroneous duplicated orders (Article 18(2)(c) RTS7). Article 20 RTS7 lays out the specifics for mandatory pre-trade controls and optional post-trade controls by trading venues. RTS7 (cf. Article 21 RTS7) require trading venues permitting DEA to **make** their **rules on DEA public**. They must at least cover the standards laid out for organisational requirements of investment firms engaged in AT. Firms accessing the market through SA must meet the same pre-trade risk limits and controls as the members of the trading venue (Article 22 (1) RTS7).

RTS8 focus on **market-making agreements and market-making schemes**, which **apply to all trading venues**.[254] They aim to introduce an element of predictability to the apparent liquidity in the order book and incentivise firms to pursue market-making strategies, especially under stressed market conditions.[255] Members, participants or clients who have signed a market-making agreement must meet a minimum set of requirements in terms of presence, size and spread in all cases (Recital 9 RTS8). Article 1 RTS8 stipulates when an investment firm must enter into such an agreement[256] with the trading venue. This is the case when it posts firm, simultaneous two-way quotes of comparable size and competitive prices when dealing on its own account in at least one financial instrument on one trading venue for at least 50% of the daily trading hours of continuous trading at the relevant trading venue, excluding opening and closing auctions, for half of the trading day over a one-month period.[257] The **liquidity provision obligation** following from the market-making agreement **does not apply in exceptional circumstances**, such as extreme volatility or under disorderly trading conditions. Exceptional circumstances are to be identified and made public by the relevant trade venue (Articles 3 ff. RTS8).

54

Market-making schemes are **necessary only when** liquid shares and liquid Exchange Traded Funds (ETFs), options and futures directly related to them, as well as liquid equity index futures and liquid equity index options are traded through a **continuous auction order booking system**.[258] Market-making schemes must describe incentives for pursuing such a strategy; however, trading venues are only required to **provide incentives under stressed market conditions** (Article 6 RTS8). The market-making scheme must be fair and non-discriminatory and must not limit the number of participants. However, incentives may be reserved for firms meeting certain thresholds. Trading venues are supposed to **publish** the names of the **firms** that have signed market-making agreements and the relevant financial instruments that they cover (Article 7 RTS8).

55

---

[253] Cf. Art. 19(1); Art. 18(1) RTS7.
[254] Cf. para. 37, 40; Commission Delegated Regulation (EU) 2017/578 of 13 June 2016 supplementing Directive 2014/65/EU of the European Parliament and of the Council on markets in financial instruments with regard to regulatory technical standards specifying the requirements on market making agreements and schemes.
[255] Cf. recital 1, 8 RTS8.
[256] The minimum content is listed in Art. 2 RTS8.
[257] The elements of the definition are further specified in Art. 1(3) RTS8.
[258] Art. 5(1) RTS8. Cf. D. Leis, *High Frequency Trading*, 3 ff. on order- and quote-driven execution systems. Cf. Art. 5(2) RTS8 for a definition.

56 **RTS9** pertain to **OTRs**.[259] Their purpose is to ensure that AT systems cannot create or contribute to **disorderly trading conditions**, and to **avoid excessive volatility** in particular financial instruments at all trading platforms (cf. Recitals 1, 4 RTS9). Trading venues are therefore required to calculate the OTR effectively entered into the system by each of their members and participants and for every financial instrument traded under electronic continuous auction order books, quote-driven or hybrid trading system.[260]

57 **RTS10** are designed to ensure **co-location and trading venues' fee structures** are fair and non-discriminatory.[261] They cover all types of co-location services, whether provided by trading venues or managed by third parties (Recital 3, Article 1 RTS10). Trading venues are required to **publish** their **co-location policies** with information on specific details (such as 'cooling' or 'cable length'; cf. Article 2 RTS10). Those services are to be provided in a fair and non-discriminatory manner within the limits of space, power, cooling or similar facilities available, and for those who have signed up for particular services under the same conditions (Article 1(1), (2) RTS10). Trading venues must **publish** their **fee structures**, including information on incentives and rebates.[262] The fee structure must not include provisions that lower fees for a particular period (including already executed trades) if a given threshold is reached ('**cliff edge**').[263]

(d) Action Taken by Selected Member States/Gold Plating

58 AT and HFT have not only been scrutinised at the European level. Some **Member States** have taken action towards **regulation of AT and HFT** or discussed such action at a national level. A prominent example is **Germany**, where a law on high-frequency trading (Hochfrequenzhandelsgesetz) has been enacted.[264] This law includes licensing requirements, a reporting regime and an OTR requirement.[265] **France** has imposed a tax on modified or cancelled orders exceeding 80% of all orders transmitted in a month, when HFT firms transmit, modify or cancel the order within 500 ms.[266]

---

[259] Cf. para. 40; Commission Delegated Regulation (EU) 2017/566 of 18 May 2016 supplementing Directive 2014/65/EU of the European Parliament and of the Council on markets in financial instruments with regard to regulatory technical standards for the ratio of unexecuted orders to transactions in order to prevent disorderly trading conditions.

[260] Art. 2 RTS9. The RTS provide further definitions and the necessary methodology for this calculation, Art. 1 and 3 and Annex RTS9. Cf. D. Leis, *High Frequency Trading*, 3 ff. on order- and quote-driven execution systems.

[261] Cf. para. 42; Commission Delegated Regulation of 6 June 2016 supplementing Directive 2014/65/EU of the European Parliament and of the Council on markets in financial instruments with regard to regulatory technical standards on requirements to ensure fair and non-discriminatory co-location services and fee structures.

[262] Art. 3(1) RTS10. Further criteria are laid out in Art. 3(2) RTS10. Cf. P. Gomber et al., *High-Frequency Trading*, 9 ff., 26, on asymmetric fee structures as an incentive for liquidity provision.

[263] Art. 5 RTS10; cf. ESMA, Consultation Paper (fn. 11), para. 190.

[264] Cf. J. Kindermann and B. Coridaß, 15 ZBB (2014), 178, 180; P. Gomber and F. Nassauer, 15 ZBB (2014), 250, 257 also on the similarities with the European regime.

[265] E. Jaskulla, 13 BKR (2013), 221 ff.; J. Kindermann and B. Coridaß, 15 ZBB (2014), 178, 180 ff.; J. Kobbach, 13 BKR (2013), 233 ff.; cf. para. 40 on OTR.

[266] Cf. H. Bell and H. Searles, *An Analysis of Global HFT Regulation*, 13 with additional references; further R. Karmel, 37 J. Corp. Law (2012), 849, 898 ff.

As the regulation laid out in MiFID II is to be understood as maximum harmonisation,[267] there is generally **not much leeway for 'gold plating'**[268] at Member State level.[269] However, other regulation, such as a Financial Transaction Tax (FTT), may significantly influence the business models of AT and HFT firms.[270] With respect to achieving a level playing field[271] and the targeted harmonisation of capital markets law in the EU, **Member States should refrain** as much as possible **from** further **'solo actions'**.[272]

(e) Assessment of the European Union Regime

The European regulatory approach subjects AT and HFT firms to a **differentiated system** that encompasses various solutions to perceived risks of AT and HFT. An outright ban of HFT would not have been justified.[273] It is therefore to be appreciated that the **EU refrained from** taking **measures** that would have most likely **eliminated HFT** activity in the EU, such as introducing a minimum holding period for offers.[274] Such regulation would have jeopardised the benefits that HFT provides, at least under normal market conditions.[275]

The European regime puts **special emphasis on** potential **systemic risks**. As the 'human factor' is reduced or eliminated in AT and HFT, it focuses in particular on various non-human aspects that may lead to disorderly markets. One possible cause for disruptions lies with the trade systems of the trading platforms. The European regulation is aimed at boosting their resilience by a mix of technical requirements (with regard to capacity), reducing the likelihood of an overload (eg by implementing thresholds and using maximum OTRs),[276] and requirements for an intensive testing of the systems. Further requirements, such as having in place business continuity arrangements, real-time monitoring and 'kill functions' are intended to keep the impact of possible disruptions at a minimum. Requiring **automated responses to possible disruptions** of the market appears to be a **reasonable response** to

---

[267] R. Veil and M. Lerch, 66 WM (2012), 1557, 1559; following this opinion D. Mattig, 68 WM (2014), 1940, 1945; on the concept of maximum harmonisation cf. R. Veil, § 3 para. 22.

[268] Cf. D. Mattig, 68 WM (2014), 1940, 1946; in general R. Veil, § 3 para. 21.

[269] MiFID II allows for different rules in different member states with regard to particular AT and HFT provisions, such as whether trade venues are allowed to impose higher fees on cancelled orders, cf. para. 42.

[270] Cf. H. Bell and H. Searles, *An Analysis of Global HFT Regulation*, 7 ('wipe out HFTs' operation in EU markets'); R. Karmel, 37 J. Corp. Law (2012), 849, 899 ('would make HFT impossible'); C. Korsmo, 48 U. Rich. L. Rev. (2014), 523, 587; F. Pasquale, 36 Cardozo L. Rev. (2015), 2085, 2089. See also A. Fleckner, *Regulating Trading Practices*, 596, 618, who mentions that the introduction of such a tax may lead to higher leverage ratios. Cf. Korajczyk/Murphy, Do High-Frequency Traders Improve your Implementation Shortfall?, on an economic analysis of the consequences of a 'HFT tax' in Canada.

[271] Cf. ESMA, Consultation Paper (fn. 11), para. 51 ff. regarding third-country firms; further H. Bell and H. Searles, *An Analysis of Global HFT Regulation*, 7; G. O'Malley, 17 Trinity C.L. Rev. (2014), 94, 120 ff.; further P. Gomber and F. Nassauer, 15 ZBB (2014), 250, 253.

[272] Cf. also E. Jaskulla, 13 BKR (2013), 221, 223, with respect to the criticism of the German High-frequency Trading Act on the basis that a solution on the European level would have been preferable. Cf. also on this issue J. Kindermann and B. Coridaß, 15 ZBB (2014), 178, 184; J. Kobbach, 13 BKR (2013), 233, 234 and 237.

[273] Cf. para. 26.

[274] The European Parliament wanted to introduce a 'minimum resting time' of 500 ms, cf. P. Gomber and F. Nassauer, 15 ZBB (2014), 250, 257 ff.; J. Kindermann and B. Coridaß, 15 ZBB (2014), 178, 180; J. Vaananen, *Dark Pools and High Frequency Trading*, 73. This was critically seen by C. Korsmo, 48 U. Rich. L. Rev. (2014), 523, 602 ff. A similar proposal has also been rejected in Australia, cf. H. Bell and H. Searles, *An Analysis of Global HFT Regulation*, 23.

[275] Cf. para. 23 ff.

[276] As OTRs are supposed to provide a more predictable order book, they may also be seen as an instrument to improve investor confidence, cf. O. Linton et al., *Economic impact assessments on MiFID II policy measures related to computer trading in financial markets*, 24.

risks arising in an automated trading environment.[277] However, the question of whether the provisions concerning cross-market co-ordination (eg regarding circuit breakers) are practicable needs to be regularly evaluated.[278]

62   One important feature of the new European regime is that it **addresses** both **market venues and investment firms performing AT and HFT** with similar provisions.[279] This underscores that the legislator takes possible systemic risks seriously.[280] While the provisions directed at investment firms aim at preventing potentially disruptive orders entering a given trade venue, the rules directed at the trade venue act as a safeguard and are supposed to prevent disruptive practices from entering the market.[281] This comes at an **additional cost**, as both investment firms and trading venues have to implement the regulatory requirements. Trading venues and investment firms must also work together with regard to the testing of algorithms because trading platforms have to provide the necessary testing environments.

63   Several provisions of MiFID II and the applicable Level 2 measures require **self-assessments** of market participants and trading venues to calibrate the parameters of necessary schemes and arrangements. As such, the European regime utilises the knowledge of those who should know their own businesses best. The knowledge and experience of market participants and trading venues have also been taken into account by ESMA when drafting RTS and when considering potential changes to existing regulation.[282] Many provisions have been amended during the consultation process due to points raised by the participants. Further, the regulatory regime **transfers** some part of the **monitoring and enforcement functions to the trading platforms**. Amongst other things, they are required to perform due diligence on their customers and make sure that DEA providers' clients are subjected to the same rules deemed adequate for members/participants of a given market.[283] This may be seen as a 'staggered' oversight system with the CAs at the top, relying on required notifications and additional information that are provided upon request. Record-keeping obligations as well as flagging of AT and HFT orders **ensure that CAs and ESMA have sufficient data** to perform in depth ex post inquiries.[284]

64   Due to the risks arising from the reduced/eliminated human intervention, the European regime requires 'real time monitoring' and immediate actions when disruptive incidents occur. A public oversight body alone would not be able to perform such a task at all trading venues at the same time.[285] As such, the **regulatory structure** that partially relies on

---

[277] ESMA/2015/1464 (fn. 42), 202 No. 46.

[278] Cf. O. Linton et al., *Economic impact assessments on MiFID II policy measures related to computer trading in financial markets*, 12 ff.; see para. 40 on circuit breakers; cf. generally ESMA, Consultation Paper (fn. 11), para. 78 ff. on the exchange of information.

[279] As such, even non-MiFID-firms will be subject to the new regime as far as trading venues are required to implement certain measures and make sure that their participants/members comply with particular obligations, cf. also J. Kobbach, 13 BKR (2013), 233, 238, with respect to the German High-frequency Trading Act.

[280] When DEA is involved, a 'third layer' of measures and risk controls is introduced by the regulation at the DEA provider's level, cf. also recital 62(2) MiFID II.

[281] Cf. ESMA/2015/1464 (fn. 42), p. 201 No. 40.

[282] Cf. ESMA, Consultation Paper (fn. 11).

[283] Cf. S. Dolgopolov, 1 Journal of Law, Technology & Policy (2014), 145, 156 at fn. 62, with examples of some Reg. NMS provisions that require trading venues to regulate their members.

[284] Cf. also German Government, Explanation of the High-frequency Trading Act (fn. 31), 15.

[285] Cf. IOSCO, Consultation Report, CR02/11 (fn. 1), 12 ff., on the increased complexity of surveillance for CAs.

supervision of market participants by the trading venues appears to be a **feasible way to ensure comprehensive market supervision**. As the relevant risks associated with AT and HFT justify regulation,[286] the chosen setup imposes the costs of the new regulatory requirements on the trading platforms and investment firms performing AT and HFT, which appears to be rational from a public perspective. However, it must be considered that **trading platforms** profit from trades executed by HFT firms and, as such, may find themselves in a **conflict of interests** when they are responsible for the enforcement of regulatory measures directed at HFT.

As traditional market makers have been 'elbowed out' to a significant extent by HFT firms,[287] **liquidity provision obligations** appear to be **consequential measures** to ensure market-making services are still consistently provided for. It still **remains to be seen whether incentives** lead a **sufficient number of HFT firms to enter into written market-making agreements**[288] and if they prevent liquidity from evaporating when markets are under stress.[289] After all, obligations to provide liquidity would not be necessary if liquidity provision would be profitable and relatively riskless, which is precisely not the case in times of markets under stress.[290] However, as trading platforms—and not the HFT market makers themselves—get to determine when exceptional circumstances are present in the market, which suspend market making obligations, this new provision does—at least in theory—hinder HFT firms pursuing market-making strategies from leaving the market at will.

65

The European regime **strengthens compliance** features at investment firms and market venues and emphasises the qualification of staff. This is especially important with regard to predatory market practices. Various **transparency requirements**, such as published policies of trading platforms' fee structures, rules on DEA, and flagging of orders generated by an algorithm, may help to identify practices that are illegal or at least considered to be unfair.[291] This is important, as some of the practices discussed above distort the price formation process, which is a 'key mechanism' to achieve market integrity.[292] CAs can ask investment firms to explain dubious strategies. However, with strategies and algorithms changing fast and often, it will remain a significant **challenge to enforce** the **applicable law**, eg rules on

66

---

[286] Cf. para. 26.
[287] Cf. C. Korsmo, 48 U. Rich. L. Rev. (2014), 523, 578 ff.; cf. also O. Linton et al., *Economic impact assessments on MiFID II policy measures related to computer trading in financial markets*, 18; ESMA, Consultation Paper (fn. 11), para. 293.
[288] Cf. para. 37, 40 and 55; O. Linton et al., *Economic impact assessments on MiFID II policy measures related to computer trading in financial markets*, 21. See S. Dolgopolov, 1 Journal of Law, Technology & Policy (2014), 145, 166 ff. on trading obligations and privileges of market makers. For example, increased tick sizes make market making more profitable, cf. B. Hagströmer and L. Nordén, *The diversity of high-frequency traders*, 5 and 39.
[289] M. Prewitt, 19 Mich. Telecomm. & Tech. L. Rev. (2012), 131, 154, points out that HFT firms might rather pay a fine than to risk disastrous trades. See also S. Dolgopolov, 1 Journal of Law, Technology & Policy (2014), 145, 169; D. Leis, *High Frequency Trading*, 74.
[290] O. Linton et al., *Economic impact assessments on MiFID II policy measures related to computer trading in financial markets*, 19; cf. also D. Leis, *High Frequency Trading*, 74, pointing out that liquidity provision obligations directly affect the business model of HFT firms.
[291] Cf. recital 67 MiFID II; see also P. Gomber et al., *High-Frequency Trading*, 36. Cf. S. Dolgopolov, 1 Journal of Law, Technology & Policy (2014), 145, 150, on informational asymmetry with regard to order types. However, there are also some 'market responses' to the discussed 'fairness issues', eg IEX, an American trading venue, advertises that predatory HFT practices are supposedly not possible at their platform, ibid., p. 153; cf. ESMA, Consultation Paper (fn. 11), para. 330 on IEX's use of speedbumps.
[292] A. Fleckner, *Regulating Trading Practices*, 596, 600 ff.

abusive practices under MAR, and **may** even **require** costly **additional resources and staffing** at the supervisory bodies.[293] This may also be a reason why MiFID II makes use of some 'blunt' measures basically aimed at slowing down messaging speed, catching abusive and beneficial strategies alike,[294] such as OTRs that need to be observed.[295]

67 With regard to fair market practices, the regulation rightly focuses on **establishing a level playing field** among groups of market participants signing up for particular services.[296] With fractions of a second making a significant difference in today's trading environment, it is understandable that even the regulator worries about details such as 'equal cooling' or 'cable length'. Nonetheless, especially with respect to the continuing evolution of trading practices, it is **neither possible nor desirable** to try to exhaustively **regulate every** possible **detail** that may be influential. From that point of view, establishing the applicable principle, ie non-discrimination, at European level would have been sufficient.[297] Further details could have been left to local regulators and the trading venues.[298] Establishing a level playing field is not to be misunderstood as ensuring that all market participants act at the same speed in practice. As long as everyone willing to sign up for latency-reducing services (such as co-location) or who wants to provide liquidity to earn rebates, is able to enter into relevant agreements with market venues, the market set-up is to be considered **fair from a procedural perspective**.[299] The proposed requirements for fair and non-discriminatory fee structures and access to market services laid out by the regulation are sufficient from that point of view.[300] A level playing field in absolute terms would only benefit incumbent traders who cannot keep up with the evolution of the market infrastructure.[301]

68 HFT is not a strategy by itself.[302] Therefore, a **binary approach**[303] to determine if investment firms are to be considered as HFT firms appears to be **too broad**.[304] However, the difficulties with determining what falls under HFT, combined with the challenges for an effective oversight system, justify such a **simplifying strategy** to achieve legal certainty and to support regulators in detecting illegal behaviour.[305]

---

[293] Cf. also IOSCO, Consultation Report, CR02/11 (fn. 1), 28 ff.; further C. Korsmo, 48 U. Rich. L. Rev. (2014), 523, 605 ff.; D. Leis, *High Frequency Trading*, 49; O. Linton et al., *Economic impact assessments on MiFID II policy measures related to computer trading in financial markets*, 7; F. Pasquale, 36 Cardozo L. Rev. (2015), 2085, 2113 ff.

[294] Cf. O. Linton et al., *Economic impact assessments on MiFID II policy measures related to computer trading in financial markets*, 26 ff.

[295] Cf. H. Bell and H. Searles, *An Analysis of Global HFT Regulation*, 42; D. Leis, *High Frequency Trading*, 75; O. Linton et al., *Economic impact assessments on MiFID II policy measures related to computer trading in financial markets*, 24 ff.

[296] Cf. ESMA/2015/1464 (fn. 42), 242 No. 6; also P. Gomber et al., *High-Frequency Trading*, 3.

[297] Cf. A. Fleckner, *Regulating Trading Practices*, 596, 609 ff.; further D. Leis, *High Frequency Trading*, 53.

[298] Generally of the same opinion A. Fleckner, *Regulating Trading Practices*, 596, 608 and 611 ff.

[299] Cf. also H. Bell and H. Searles, *An Analysis of Global HFT Regulation*, 35 with further references; ESMA/2015/1464 (fn. 42), 247 No. 22; J. Vaananen, *Dark Pools and High Frequency Trading*, 208.

[300] Of course, such services will still only be used by market participants with the necessary resources and sophistication, C. Korsmo, 48 U. Rich. L. Rev. (2014), 523, 564.

[301] Cf. H. Bell and H. Searles, *An Analysis of Global HFT Regulation*, 35.

[302] Cf. para. 10.

[303] Cf. para. 47.

[304] Cf. also P. Gomber et al., *High-Frequency Trading*, 1, 2, 30 ff. (regulatory discussion should focus on strategies rather than HFT as such; assessment of HFT has to take a functional rather than institutional approach); further A. Fleckner, *Regulating Trading Practices*, 596, 621; B. Hagströmer and L. Nordén, *The diversity of high-frequency traders*, 24; D. Leis, *High Frequency Trading*, 27.

[305] Cf. M. Prewitt, 19 Mich. Telecomm. & Tech. L. Rev. (2012), 131, 147, 149 and 155 ff.; further F. Pasquale, 36 Cardozo L. Rev. (2015), 2085, 2101. 'Whistleblowing' may prove particularly useful in the context of HFT as a case from New York showed, in which a former *Barclays* employee provided authorities with several key emails used to

Member States should make use of the possibility to allow market venues to **charge higher** 69
prices for cancelled orders.[306] Such a policy by a trading venue would communicate to the
market that certain strategies are not wanted at that venue. As some claim that investors are
being exploited by HFT, trade venues preventing HFT could, in theory, be at a **competitive
advantage** from the perspective of investors with a critical attitude towards HFT, whose
willingness to trade might otherwise be reduced.[307] Adjusting the fees with regard to order
cancellation is superior to a FTT, at least when the reason for implementing the tax is to
contain HFT and not to generate income. Such a tax would likely be inflexible and levied
on all market participants. In contrast, adjustments of fee structures would allow trading
venues to specifically 'charge' those participants that put an additional burden on the system's capacity.[308]

The **European regime is comprehensive** and, at least to some extent, very **detailed**. 70
However, as the effects, especially of HFT, with regard to market quality are still controversial, the regulation rightly refrains from implementing measures that would have stifling
effects such as a minimum resting time.[309] **ESMA** plays an important **coordinating role**.[310]
Further, with many important details of the regulatory setup being specified in RTS, ESMA
has a key role in the **dynamic development** of further regulatory measures or changes when
they appear necessary.[311] In this dynamic approach, new market phenomena need to be
reviewed if they relate to AT and HFT, which is currently the case for mechanisms deployed
called 'speedbumps' and the issue of the sequence of publication between order/trade confirmations sent to individual participants and the public.[312] ESMA's extensive outreach to
market participants seems to be the right approach to calibrate further regulation, while
taking the needs and expertise of all stakeholders into account. Even if the regulatory regime
turned out to be not as strict as was sometimes demanded, the **cost factor** for the regulated
subjects is **significant**.[313] As such, strict regulation should likely negatively affect the market

---

prove 'fraud and deceit' in one of *Barclay's* dark pools, cf. P. Kasiske, 15 BKR (2015), 454, 456; F. Pasquale ibid., 2104 ff.; further S. Dolgopolov, 1 Journal of Law, Technology & Policy (2014), 145 ff.; D. Leis, *High Frequency Trading*, 55, on whistleblowing in the context of the market abuse regulation.

[306] The German High-frequency Trading Act even requires exchanges to do so, cf. German Government, Explanation of the High-frequency Trading Act (fn. 31), 12. This was criticised by the Bundesbank, Deutsche Bundesbank, Stellungnahme zum Entwurf eines Hochfrequenzhandelsgesetz, 10 January 2013, at No. 2.1. Cf. also C. Korsmo, 48 U. Rich. L. Rev. (2014), 523, 577.

[307] Cf. IOSCO, Consultation Report, CR02/11 (fn. 1), 12; further M. Prewitt, 19 Mich. Telecomm. & Tech. L. Rev. (2012), 131, 147. Cf. also fn. 291 on IEX, a trading platform that advertises protection against predatory trade practices which are supposedly not possible at IEX.

[308] Cf. recital 65 MiFID II; cf. also C. Korsmo, 48 U. Rich. L. Rev. (2014), 523, 574 ff.

[309] M. Prewitt, 19 Mich. Telecomm. & Tech. L. Rev. (2012), 131, 158, would have supported the introduction of a resting rule to make market abuse more difficult. This would have jeopardised the potential benefits of HFT. Cf. O. Linton et al., *Economic impact assessments on MiFID II policy measures related to computer trading in financial markets*, 21 ff., on potential risks and benefits of minimum resting times.

[310] Cf. recital 63 MiFID II. It should be noted that several provisions have been amended in the consultation process (see ESMA/2015/1464 (fn. 42), 194 ff.), which should be an encouraging incentive for market participants to participate in further consultations, knowing that their arguments will be heard.

[311] Cf. recitals 66, 68 MiFID II; further ESMA, Consultation Paper (fn. 11).

[312] ESMA, Consultation Paper (fn. 11), para. 4; 318 ff.; cf. P. Saliba, The information content of high frequency traders aggressive orders: recent evidences, for an economic study explaining the perceived necessity of speed bumps to reduce aggressive HFT behaviour.

[313] It should further be noted that profits in HFT had already declined sharply since 2009 (from $5 bn in 2009 to $1.5 bn in 2012 and $1.0 bn in 2014), cf. C. Korsmo, 48 U. Rich. L. Rev. (2014), 523, 541 and J. Vaananen, *Dark Pools and High Frequency Trading*, 130.

share of HFT and its profitability.[314] Further, other jurisdictions especially in the Asian region,[315] actively tried to attract HFT firms, which may lead to **regulatory arbitrage**.[316] An unintended consequence of overly burdensome regulation may therefore be a reduction of liquidity under normal market conditions.[317]

71 Overall, the European legislation sets out **provisions with respect to all major concerns** that have been raised with regard to AT and HFT. As mentioned above, the task for the EU remains the regulation of a moving target. It will therefore be necessary to examine the effects of the new regime very closely and to **remain open to new research results**, eg on the effects of HFT (and its regulation) on liquidity and volatility.[318] Where necessary, the regulation needs to be adjusted, eg to avoid downsides resulting from over-regulating AT and HFT.[319] This may especially be the case when various **policy measures interact** with each other and lead to **unforeseen consequences**.[320] Data provided by market participants and trading platforms will help CAs and ESMA to stay up to date and develop a deeper understanding of the markets,[321] which is necessary to further develop and adjust the applicable law.[322] Further, CAs will themselves likely rely on legal technology—eg algorithms screening AT algorithms used by investment firms—to perform their oversight function.[323] This will be increasingly necessary as 'Big Data' and Artificial Intelligence increase the share of purely machine-to-machine interactions in the trading environment.[324]

72 Since the introduction of the European regulatory regime, the markets have not suffered major crises or experienced events that would justify questioning the European approach as a whole.[325] Of course, the question remains whether this is to be attributed to appropriate regulation or whether it is merely an issue of time when the weaknesses of current regulation will be revealed. In any event, without clear evidence supporting the latter, stricter regulation would generally not be justified. At the same time, the efficiency of current regulation may be enhanced by strengthening enforcement, eg by further harmonisation of the European sanctions regime.[326]

---

[314] Cf. H. Bell and H. Searles, *An Analysis of Global HFT Regulation*, 8 ff., 13, on the effects of Germany's regulation and the introduction of a FTT in France on HFT; with more detail K. O'Connell, 27 Cath. U. J. L. & Tech 145 (2019), 145, 170 ff.
[315] H. Bell and H. Searles, *An Analysis of Global HFT Regulation*, 18 ff., 39.
[316] Cf. M. Yoon, 24 Emory Int'l L. Rev. (2010), 913, 940 ff.; see also D. Leis, *High Frequency Trading*, 77; F. Pasquale, 36 Cardozo L. Rev. (2015), 2085, 2112.
[317] Cf. ESMA/2015/1464 (fn. 42), 230 No. 21.
[318] Cf. also A. Doyle et al., 30 IFLR (2011–2012), 60, 61.
[319] Cf. on the risk of over-regulation C. Korsmo, 48 U. Rich. L. Rev. (2014), 523, 589.
[320] Cf. O. Linton et al., *Economic impact assessments on MiFID II policy measures related to computer trading in financial markets*, 27 ff.; further B. Hagströmer and L. Nordén, *The diversity of high-frequency traders*, 39.
[321] Cf. P. Gomber et al., *High-Frequency Trading*, 2 ('regulators need a full picture'); further C. Korsmo, 48 U. Rich. L. Rev. (2014), 523, 530; D. Sornette and S. von der Becke, *Crashes and High Frequency Trading*, 20.
[322] Cf. recital 68 MiFID II with regard to new abusive market practices.
[323] Cf. I. Zlatanov and S. Weiss, 9 RdF (2019), 290, 296.
[324] Cf. Bafin, Big Data trifft auf künstliche Intelligenz, Study 2018, p. 139; T. Söbbing, 39 ZIP (2019), 1603, 1605 and InTeR (2019), 64 on legal questions resulting from Artificial Intelligence used in HFT.
[325] Disruptions did occur though, cf. ESMA, Consultation Paper (fn. 11), para. 218 ff.
[326] Cf. ESMA, Final Report, Technical Advice to the Commission on the application of administrative and criminal sanctions under MiFID II/MiFIR, 29 March 2021, ESMA35-43-2430; J. Werner, Bucerius Law Journal (2020), 25, 31 ff.

2. Some Thoughts on HFT Regulation in Other Jurisdictions

It is not the purpose of this chapter to give an extensive overview on how other jurisdictions have approached the regulatory challenge[327] posed by AT and HFT. Still, it should be noted that particularly **countries in the Asian region** have been actively **trying to attract HFT**. Accordingly, their regulation had been less restrictive compared to the regulation introduced by the EU.[328] In contrast, the **US has** basically **identified the same risks** that have led to the European regime. Potential areas of regulation that have been discussed and at least partially implemented in the US include pre- and post-trade controls, mandatory registration and standardised reporting, standardisation of order types, testing of algorithms, the use of circuit breakers and the prohibition of certain strategies. Exchanges must ensure that their systems have sufficient capacity and resiliency to maintain the operational capability of fair and orderly markets. The appropriateness of these policy responses is currently under discussion.[329] As regulatory arbitrage may appear on a global scale,[330] closer collaboration between the US and the EU—who in principle share a similar view of AT and HFT—should be possible. However, differences in each of their market structures may necessitate different regulatory responses.

73

V. Conclusion

AT is a natural evolution of financial markets. HFT is still a rather young phenomenon that poses particular problems, even when 'traditional' trading strategies are used. The EU has enacted a comprehensive regulatory regime with regard to AT and HFT that encompasses all major concerns that have been raised in connection with AT and HFT in the regulatory debate. The European regime closes existing 'oversight gaps' and supports better enforcement of existing laws. As the effects of AT and especially HFT for market quality and market integrity are still controversial, the EU should remain prepared to adapt its legislation, should new research and experiences expose unintended and unforeseen consequences of the regulatory regime.[331]

74

AT and HFT are interesting and challenging fields for legal scholars for several reasons. Potential problems are at least partially rooted in the structure of the market system. The consequential interdependencies, eg with respect to the existence and regulation of dark pools,[332] must always be considered when discussing the regulation of HFT. Further, AT and

75

---

[327] Cf. para. 25.
[328] Cf. fn. 315.
[329] ESMA, Consultation Paper (fn. 11), Annex III-C, 107 ff. On the aforementioned policy measures in the US, especially SEC Regulation Systems, Compliance and Integrity (Reg. SCI), cf. H. Bell and H. Searles, *An Analysis of Global HFT Regulation*, 14 ff. Further D. Kornpeintner, *Die Regulierungsansätze des Hochfrequenzhandels*, 26 ff.; C. Korsmo, 48 U. Rich. L. Rev. (2014), 523, 581 ff.; D. Leis, *High Frequency Trading*, 66 ff.; M. Prewitt, 19 Mich. Telecomm. & Tech. L. Rev. (2012), 131, 149 ff.; see also P. Gomber et al., *High-Frequency Trading*, 39 ff.; ESMA, Consultation Paper (fn. 11), Annex III-C, 107 ff.
[330] Cf. para. 70.
[331] Cf. D. Ladley, The Design and Regulation of High Frequency Traders, who claims the majority of HFT regulations to be ineffective, however, OTRs to be promising.
[332] Cf. G. O'Malley, 17 Trinity C.L. Rev. (2014), 94, 123 ff.

HFT are international phenomena. Given that different countries have chosen to treat AT and HFT differently,[333] it is a worthwhile exercise to evaluate the consequences of various regulatory approaches. The uncertainties with respect to the economic effects of AT and HFT and the resulting problems for calibrating an adequate regulatory regime demonstrate that capital markets law relies on interdisciplinary scholarship.[334]

---

[333] The European approach is quite consistent with IOSCO's recommendations, cf. C. Korsmo, 48 U. Rich. L. Rev. (2014), 523, 586.
[334] Cf. R. Veil, § 6 para. 20–38.

6
Intermediaries

§ 26
Financial Analysts

Bibliography

Achleitner, Ann-Kristin and Bassen, Alexander (eds.), *Investor Relations am Neuen Markt* (2001); Akerlof, George A., *The Market for 'Lemons': Quality Uncertainty and the Market Mechanism*, 84 Q. J. Econ. (1970), 488–500; Agrawal, Anup and Chen, Mark A., *Do Analyst Conflicts Matter? Evidence from Stock Recommendations*, 51 JLE (2008), 503–553; Barber, Brad M. and Odean, Terrance, *All That Glitters: The Effect of Attention and News on the Buying Behavior of Individual and Institutional Investors*, 21 Rev. Fin. Studies (2008), 785–818; Bernhardt, Dan/Campello, Murillo/Kutsoati, Edward, *'Who herds?'*, 80 J. Fin. Econ. (2006), 657–675; Brown, Lawrence D./Call, Andrew C./Clement, Michael B./Sharp, Nathan Y., *Inside the 'Black Box' of Sell-Side Financial Analysts*, 53 Journal of Accounting Research (2015), 1–47; Chen, Qi and Jiang, Wei, *Analysts' Weighing of Public and Private Information*, 19 Rev. Fin. Studies (2006), 319–355; Choi, Stephen J., *A Framework for the Regulation of Securities Markets Intermediaries*, 45 BBLJ (2003), 45–82; Choi, Stephen J. and Fisch, Jill E., *How to Fix Wall Street: A Voucher Financing Proposal for Securities Intermediaries*, 113 Yale Law J. (2003), 269–346; Coffee, John C., *Gatekeepers, The Professions and Corporate Governance* (2006); Coffee, John C., *Market Failure and the Case for a Mandatory Disclosure System*, 70 Virginia L. Rev. (1984), 717–753; Dechow, Patricia M./Hutton, Amy P./Sloan, Richard G., *The Relation between Analysts' Forecasts of Long-Term Earnings Growth and Stock Price Performance Following Equity Offerings*, 17 CAR (2000), 1–32; Fisch, Jill E., *Regulatory Responses to Investor Irrationality: The Case of the Research Analyst*, 10 Lewis & Clark L. Rev. (2006), 57–83; Fisch, Jill E., *Does Analysts Independence Sell Investors Short?*, 55 UCLA L. Rev. (2007), 39–96; Fisch, Jill E. and Sale, Hillary A., *Securities Analyst as Agent: Rethinking the Regulation of Analysts*, 88 Iowa Law Review (2003), 1035–1098; Forum Group on Financial Analysts, *Best practices in an integrated European financial market* (2003), available at: https://euroirp.com/wp-content/uploads/2016/10/EU_Forum_Group_Report_04-09-03.pdf; Humpe, Andreas and Zakrewski, Mario, *Analystenempfehlungen: Guter oder schlechter Ratgeber für Investoren? Eine Untersuchung für den deutschen Aktienmarkt*, Corporate Finance (2015), 251–258; Kämmerer, Jörn A. and Veil, Rüdiger, *Analyse von Finanzinstrumenten (§ 34b WpHG) und journalistische Selbstregulierung*, BKR (2005), 379–387; Leyens, Patrick, *Informationsintermediäre des Kapitalmarkts* (2017); Malmendier, Ulrike and Shanthikumar, Devin M., *Are Small Investors Naive about Incentives?*, 85 J. Fin. Econ. (2007), 457–489; Meyer, Andreas, *Haftung für Research Reports und Wohlverhaltensregeln für Analysten*, AG (2003), 610–622; Michaely, Roni and Womack, Kent L., *Conflict of Interest and the Credibility of Underwriter Analyst Recommendations*, 12 Rev. Fin. Studies (1999), 653–686; Mülbert, Peter O., *Empfiehlt es sich, im Interesse des Anlegerschutzes und zur Förderung des Finanzplatzes Deutschland das Kapitalmarkt- und Börsenrecht neu zu regeln?*, JZ (2002), 826–837; Naffziger, Fred and Fox, Mark, *A need for balance in the regulation of analysts' conflicts*, 15 International Company and Commercial Law Review (2004), 320–324; Pixa, Constantin D. and Vöglte, Markus, *Der Einfluss von Sell-Side Research auf den Aktienkurs*, Corporate Finance (2015), 242–250; Porak, Victor, *Kapitalmarktkommunikation* (2002); van Rooij, Maarten/Lusardi, Annamaria/Alessie, Rob, *Financial Literacy and Stock Market Participation*, 101 J. Fin. Econ. (2011), 449–472; Schilder, Jörg, *Die Verhaltenspflichten von Finanzanalysten nach dem Wertpapierhandelsgesetz* (2005); Seibt, Christoph, *Finanzanalysten im Blickfeld von Aktien- und*

Kapitalmarktrecht, ZGR (2006), 501–539; Spindler, Gerald, *Finanzanalyse vs. Finanzberichterstattung: Journalisten und das AnSVG*, NZG (2004), 1138–1147; Stout, Lynn A., *Are Stock Markets Costly Casinos? Disagreement, Market Failure and Securities Regulation*, 81 Va. L. Rev. (1995), 611–712; Teigelack, Lars, *Finanzanalysen und Behavioral Finance* (2009).

I. Introduction

1   Financial analysts[1] are **information intermediaries** charged with the task of helping to overcome negative effects resulting from an asymmetric distribution of information on capital markets.[2] Not only investors and issuers, but also the public benefits from this. Financial analysts help **investors** to **filter relevant information** from the flood of information publicly available and to translate the available information into an investment decision (**transformation**).[3] Financial analysts obtain information from a number of sources, such as press releases, company reports, ad hoc notifications and other publications. Additionally they gain important insights through their contact with the issuers' management and attendance of analysts' conferences. Whilst financial analysts must not obtain inside information from management,[4] meetings with an issuer's top personnel can nevertheless help assess management's credibility. Surveyed about principal information sources, analysts have declared personal contact with management to be the most important source of information.[5] Financial analysts further monitor an issuer's profits, thereby helping to prevent unlawful transfers of profits from the issuer to management (principal–agent conflict), and management performance as a whole.[6]

2   Issuers also benefit from the work of financial analysts, because the supply of information to investors **reduces an issuer's costs of capital**: the better investors are informed about an issuer, the higher the price they will pay for an investment; uncertainty, on the other hand, has a negative effect on investment decisions (discount). Additionally, financial analysts can distribute information to a large number of investors.[7] It is therefore more effective for an issuer to inform a limited number of analysts than attempt to distribute information to all investors.[8]

---

[1] ESMA, Final Report, ESMA's technical advice on possible delegated acts concerning the Market Abuse Regulation, 3 February 2015, ESMA/2015/224, para. 326 ff. reserves the term 'financial analysts' for a specific subset of relevant persons defined under the old Implementing Directive 2003/125/EC. The terminology changes under the new regime, cf. below para. 28–30.
[2] J.E. Fisch, 55 UCLA L. Rev. (2007), 39, 46; A.-K. Achleitner and A. Bassen, *Investor Relations am Neuen Markt*, 47–48.
[3] J.E. Fisch, 55 UCLA L. Rev. (2007), 39, 47.
[4] On the prohibition to disclose information under the MAR see R. Veil § 14 para. 77 ff.
[5] Cf. L.D. Brown/A. Call/M.B. Clement/N.Y. Sharp, *Inside the Black Box of Sell-Side Financial Analysts*; V. Porak, *Kapitalmarktkommunikation*, 139 ff., 147 ff.
[6] A.-K. Achleitner and A. Bassen, *Investor Relations am Neuen Markt*, 48 ff.; T.M.J. Möllers, in: Hirte and Möllers (eds.), *Kölner Kommentar zum WpHG*, § 34b para. 3.
[7] J.E. Fisch, 55 UCLA L. Rev. (2007), 39, 45; Forum Group, *Best Practices in an Integrated European Financial Market*, 13; N. Moloney, *EU Securities and Financial Markets Regulation*, 682 ff.; on a similar phenomenon with regard to private investors see B.M. Barber and T. Odean, 21 Rev. Fin. Studies (2008), 785.
[8] J.C. Coffee, 70 Virginia L. Rev. (1984), 717, 724.

Financial analysts further **help** to **improve** the **proper functioning of capital markets**. Lower transaction costs enhance operational efficiency, and a clearer distinction between 'good and bad' companies improves the markets' allocative efficiency. Financial analysts also increase informational efficiency of the markets by ensuring that new information is reflected in the prices of securities as soon as possible.[9] The proper functioning of the markets is in the public interest, as companies and states require financing and citizens increasingly rely on publicly traded securities in saving for retirement.

The activities of financial analysts require regulation due to the severe consequences of incorrect research. Poor intermediary performance by analysts can increase the risk for investors to (partly) lose their invested capital. Although capital is merely redistributed, investors who have lost the bulk of their financial means will be dependent on the social security system[10] or could require other costly government intervention.

Flawed research may furthermore severely undermine investor confidence. Capital markets trade in expectancies instead of tangible goods, which is only possible if market participants can rely on fair procedures and mechanisms.[11] Financial analysts are regarded as reliable and fair appraisers of the financial markets (so-called **gatekeepers**). If investors can no longer rely on information being processed correctly by financial analysts, investors might withdraw from the market, reducing liquidity and possibly causing market failure in the long run.

A negative assessment of a financial instrument by an analyst can raise an issuer's cost of capital and thus even considerably affect the share price.[12] A report containing an incorrect negative assessment of an issuer can cause considerable damage to the company, as it has to pay higher interests.

Incorrect research can also harm the markets' allocative efficiency and thus dampen investment activities of 'good' companies as their financing will also be impaired. Private pension plans also rely heavily on the correct functioning of the capital markets. This poses a risk for social security systems that would not be able to cover fully capital requirements of investors after their retirement. States also depend on proper functional capital markets in order to be able to finance public debts.

II. Foundations

1. Types of Financial Analysts

Financial analysts are typically divided into three categories. **Buy-side analysts** primarily work for investors. They are usually employees of institutional investors such as funds,

---

[9] J.E. Fisch, 55 UCLA L. Rev. (2007), 39, 48; on informational efficiency see R. Veil § 2 para. 29 and H. Brinckmann § 16 para. 7–9.
[10] L.A. Stout, 81 Va. L. Rev. (1995), 611, 620 ff.
[11] Recital 2 MAR.
[12] Cf. references in J.E. Fisch, 10 Lewis & Clark L. Rev. (2006), 57, 65 and C.D. Pixa and M. Vögtle, Corporate Finance (2015), 242, 243 and their own study of recommendations regarding the German DAX30 companies beginning on page 244; more references and another study of the German market provided by A. Humpe and M. Zakrewski, Corporate Finance (2015), 251 ff.

insurances or investment consulting firms and analyse their clients' portfolios to enhance performance. Reports will generally not be made public as the institutional investor will only want to use the results for its own means.[13]

9 **Sell-side analysts** work for the sellers of securities, usually banks providing services to institutional investors. In addition to other services (eg corporate finance), these institutions offer financial analysis to improve customer satisfaction. In practice, *sell-side analysts* will typically first provide reports to their own clients, before informing the bank's general business unit of the results. In a third step, research results are made public via the Internet, newspapers or financial journals.[14]

10 **Independent financial analysts** maintain no ongoing relationship with any market participants. They sell their reports individually or as a subscription to any interested person.

2. Methods of Financial Analysis

11 Two methods have emerged for analysing stocks and other securities. **Fundamental analysis** is an established method for assessing the value of stocks.[15] It claims that the share price is determined by internal company data and external (macroeconomic and industry-specific) information. This so-called intrinsic value is determined on the basis of the profit that can be expected for the future (on the basis of past profits as well as the company's plans and prospects, adjusted, when required, for extraordinary income and losses). If the fundamental value differs from the stock market value, the share is either fundamentally undervalued or overvalued, so that it is worth buying or selling.

12 Internal company data is information on annual financial statements; it relates to the capital structure, considers the development of market shares and the company's competitive position, relates to technological developments and takes into account the export dependency of the business. The overall economic environment is determined in particular by economic and growth forecasts as well as developments on the product and credit markets.[16] Fundamental analysis operates with numerous key figures. The most important ones are (i) the price/earnings ratio (P/E ratio), which expresses how often the company's earnings are included in the current price of a share of the company, (ii) the price/book ratio (P/B ratio), which indicates the ratio of an individual share to equity, (iii) the price/sales ratio (P/S ratio) and (iv) the price/cash flow ratio, which, unlike the P/S ratio, is not substance-oriented but liquidity-oriented and is determined by dividing the share price by the cash flow per share (derived from the cash flow statement). Also worth mentioning are (v) the return on assets (ROA), which indicates how efficiently equity is used, and (vi) the equity ratio, which expresses the ratio of equity to total assets. The (vii) market-to-revenue ratio indicates how often revenue is included in market capitalisation (stock market value of all shares).

13 **Technical analysis** (also known as chart analysis) takes a different approach. It does not operate with fundamental data, but infers future price movements from the

---

[13] J.C. Coffee, *Gatekeepers*, 247, 249; Forum Group, *Best Practices in an Integrated European Financial Market*, 18; IOSCO, Report on Analyst Conflicts of Interest, September 2003, 3.
[14] J.C. Coffee, *Gatekeepers*, 248.
[15] G. Franke and H. Hax, *Finanzwirtschaft des Unternehmens und Kapitalmarkt*, 439; L. Perridon et al. (eds.), *Finanzwirtschaft der Unternehmung*, 229.
[16] G. Franke and H. Hax, *Finanzwirtschaft des Unternehmens und Kapitalmarkt*, 439.

historical price trend.¹⁷ Unlike fundamental analysis, technical analysis takes into account the fact that share prices are also influenced by rumour and (irrational) trading activities.

Technical analysis is based on the assumption that prices develop in trends for assessable periods and that certain price developments and price patterns repeat themselves because patterns of human behaviour repeat themselves in recurring situations.¹⁸ Therefore, the previous course of prices should be able to be used for a forecast. The details seem like the recipes of a secret science. For example, it is said to constitute a buy signal when the current price crosses the (adjusting) average price from below.¹⁹ A 'head and shoulders pattern' is supposed to indicate that a trend is losing strength and that a reversal may occur either in the short or medium term.

III. Regulatory Concepts

The production and dissemination of financial research is **regulated by two regimes**: First, the **MAR regime** (Article 20, Article 3(34) and (35) MAR and Delegated Regulation (EU) No. 2016/958²⁰) provides specific rules to those providing and disseminating investment recommendations (market conduct of financial analysts). Second, investment firms and firms preparing investment research are to establish organisational procedures. These **MiFID II** requirements aim to ensure that investment research be produced with due care and without any conflict of interests.

1. Market Conduct

The **MAR**, as the MAD 2003 before it, aims to strengthen the integrity of European capital markets.²¹ The MAD 2003 rules were the European legislature's response to numerous cases of misconduct by financial analysts from the 1990s to the beginning of the twenty-first century: banks had published incorrect research to the benefit of their clients in order to receive more investment banking business (ie capital increases, initial public offerings, M&A transactions). In other cases, the incentive for the publication of incorrect reports resulted from analysts' salaries being linked to the turnover of the investment banking division.²² The **lack of objectiveness** of the reports **reduced market participants' confidence** in financial analysts.

Examples: *Henry Blodget* publicly touted stocks, even though he was personally convinced of the opposite development, in order to generate income from investment banking. However, he only

---

[17] L. Perridon et al. (eds.), *Finanzwirtschaft der Unternehmung*, 231.
[18] L. Perridon et al. (eds.), *Finanzwirtschaft der Unternehmung*, 231.
[19] F. Schäfer, in: Schäfer et al. (eds.), *Handbuch der Vermögensverwaltung*, § 4 para. 5.
[20] Commission Delegated Regulation (EU) No. 2016/958 of 9 March 2016 supplementing Regulation (EU) No. 596/2014 of the European Parliament and of the Council with regard to regulatory technical standards for the technical arrangements for objective presentation of investment recommendations or other information recommending or suggesting an investment strategy and for disclosure of particular interests or indications of conflicts of interest, OJ L160, 17 June 2016, p. 15–22.
[21] Recital 2 MAR; see R. Veil § 13 para. 1–3.
[22] For a comprehensive account of the so-called 'analyst scandals' see J.E. Fisch, 10 Lewis & Clark L. Rev. (2006) 57, 60 ff.; conflicts of interest are decribed at IOSCO, Analyst Conflicts of Interest (fn. 18), 8 ff.; for a detailed history of the EU regime cf. N. Moloney, *EU Securities and Financial Markets Regulation*, 685 ff.

shared this opinion with a few of his employer's clients.[23] *Jack Grubman*, who was investigated by the SEC for numerous transactions, caused an even bigger stir. One example was the valuation of AT&T's stock, which he changed so that his children would be admitted to a certain prestigious school in New York City and to promote his employer's investment banking.[24]

18   Article 20(1) MAR obligates 'persons who produce or disseminate investment recommendations or other information recommending or suggesting an investment strategy '[to] take reasonable care to ensure that such **information** is **objectively presented** and to **disclose** their **interests** or indicate conflicts of interest concerning the financial instruments to which that information relates'. This general rule and the definitions of 'information recommending or suggesting an investment strategy' and 'investment recommendations' are the only Level 1 measures with regard to financial analysts. Commission Delegated Regulation 2016/958 puts further elements into more specific terms, such as the categories of persons to whom the MAR applies, the terms 'objectively presented' and the circumstances that may lead to disclosure obligations.[25]

19   In addition, the general rules of market abuse law apply. The analysts' access to information is limited by the prohibition of unauthorised disclosure of inside information.[26] When making a recommendation, an analyst must also observe the prohibition of information-based market manipulation.[27] Furthermore, the issue of scalping[28] is particularly relevant with regard to financial analysts because controlling the price through one's own statements requires two things. First, the scalper must ensure that his statement is perceived by as many investors as possible. The best way to achieve this is through television appearances or on the Internet. Secondly, he must ensure that he gets investors to react to the information. In other words, he must have sufficient authority so that his statements are believed to be well-founded and true. Financial analysts typically fulfill both characteristics.

2. Organisational Requirements

20   Companies that prepare and disseminate financial analyses are required to take organisational measures to ensure that they operate free of conflicts of interest. For investment firms, these requirements arise from MiFID II and the Implementing Regulation (EU) 2017/565, which provides further details. There is a set of organisational requirements for **investment firms** that, be it on their own responsibility or on the responsibility of a member of their group, prepare **financial analyses**[29] that are subsequently to be disseminated, or are likely to be disseminated, among the investment firm's clients or to the public, or have those

---

[23] Described in the SEC's lawsuit against Blodget at para. 33 ff.; cf. http://www.sec.gov/litigation/complaints/comp18115b.htm.
[24] Lawsuit of the SEC against Grubman, para. 7 f.; cf. http://www.sec.gov/litigation/complaints/comp18111b.htm.
[25] The Commission has adopted ESMA's Regulatory Technical Standards through Commission Delegated Regulation (EU) No. 2016/958.
[26] Cf. Art. 10(1) MAR. See below para. 75–77.
[27] Cf. Art. 12(1)(c) MAR. See below para. 65–68.
[28] Cf. Art. 12(2)(d) MAR. See below para. 72–73.
[29] Cf. Art. 36 Regulation (EU) 2017/565.

financial analyses prepared for them. Those investment firms must ensure that procedures and measures are in place to manage conflicts of interest with respect to the financial analysts involved in preparing these analyses.[30] They must also comply with a plentitude of other organisational requirements. For example, they are to ensure that relevant persons involved in the preparation of financial analyses do not accept inducements from persons who have a material interest in the subject matter of those financial analyses.[31]

IV. Investment Recommendations

1. Objectives

The recitals of the MAR do not specify the purpose of the different provision of Article 20 MAR. Recital 1 of Regulation 2016/958 of the European Commission merely states that harmonised standards for investment recommendations are a necessary tool for information to be presented objectively, clearly and accurately as well as for the disclosure of interests and conflicts of interest. Furthermore, the Commission states that the standards are necessary with regard to fairness, honesty and market transparency. This implies that investors trust that investment recommendations are prepared in an appropriate manner and free of conflicts of interest. The MAR regime protects this trust in the diligence and neutrality of persons making investment recommendations in order to ensure the **proper functioning** of **markets**.[32]

21

2. Scope

Not much has changed compared to the MAD 2003 regime with regard to the analyst-specific provisions.[33] Commission Delegated Regulation (EU) No. 2016/958 essentially covers two different areas:[34] (i) **production** of **research**, ie objective (formerly 'fair') presentation and disclosure (especially conflicts of interest) in Chapter II, and (ii) **dissemination** of **third-party research** in Chapter III. Commission Delegated Regulation (EU) No. 2016/958 works from general to specific in both areas. General rules apply to all persons producing research and additional rules apply to persons whom the market is said to trust more because of their expertise ('experts').

22

(a) Material Scope

The definitions of '**investment recommendations**' and '**information recommending or suggesting an investment strategy**' have been moved from Level 2 to Level 1.[35] The MAR

23

---

[30] Cf. Art. 37(1) in conjunction with Art. 34(3) Regulation (EU) 2017/565.
[31] Cf. Art. 37(2)(d) Regulation (EU) 2017/565.
[32] K. Rothenhöfer, in: Meyer et al. (eds.), *Handbuch Marktmissbrauchsrecht*, § 21 para. 2.
[33] Cf. N. Moloney, *EU Securities and Financial Markets Regulation*, 694 ff.
[34] ESMA/2015/224 (fn. 1), para. 325.
[35] The definitions used to be in Art. 1(3) and 1(4) of Implementing Directive 2003/125/EC and are now in Art. 3(1)(34) and Art. 3(1)(35) MAR.

defines 'investment recommendations' in Article 3(1)(35) as 'information recommending or suggesting an investment strategy, explicitly or implicitly, concerning one or several financial instruments or the issuers, including any opinion as to the present or future value or price of such instruments,' intended for distribution channels or for the public.' Article 3(1)(34) MAR defines the term 'information recommending or suggesting an investment strategy' as information that 'directly or indirectly, expresses a particular investment proposal in respect of a financial instrument or an issuer'. The terms 'financial instrument' and 'issuer' are defined separately.[36] No written report is needed; oral recommendations, eg on television or on the radio, can also meet the criteria.[37]

24 **Information** is understood to mean facts and opinions as well as comments. Financial instruments are defined in the MAR as shares, debt instruments and derivatives. ESMA has clarified that any note that meets the aforementioned definitions is within the scope of the regulation. It is not relevant whether a note is labelled as objective or independent within the meaning of MiFID II.[38]

25 Investment recommendations must be intended for distribution channels or for the public to fall under the MAR regime.[39] ESMA holds the opinion that this can also mean that an investment recommendation is distributed to clients or to a specific segment of clients. Whenever a 'large number of persons' have access to the recommendation, ESMA considers the recommendation to be covered by the MAR.[40] This is not the case if the information is given with an investment recommendation in a consultation. In this case, investment advice is provided and the rules of MiFID II apply.

26 Under the old MAD 2003 regime, a recommendation of a certain investment strategy could either be explicit (eg 'buy', 'hold' or 'sell' recommendations) or implicit (by reference to a price target or otherwise).[41] The MAR fails to define the terms 'directly' or 'indirectly' in relation to a recommendation but it can be assumed that they carry the same meaning as the MAD 2003 terms.

27 The **intensity** of **regulation** depends on the **person producing the recommendation**. Recommendations by 'an independent analyst, an investment firm, a credit institution, any other person whose main business is to produce recommendations or a natural person working for them under a contract of employment or otherwise' are subject to the provisions of the MAR, whether expressed directly or indirectly. Information produced by other persons is only subject to the MAR and Commission Delegated Regulation (EU) No. 2016/958 if a direct recommendation is issued.[42] European law makes this distinction

---

[36] 'Financial instrument' is defined in Art. 3(1)(1) MAR with reference to point (15) in Art. 4(1) MiFID II; 'issuer' is defined in Art. 3(21) MAR.
[37] Art. 6(4) Commission Delegated Regulation (EU) No. 2016/958; ESMA/2015/224 (fn. 1), para. 389.
[38] ESMA/2015/224 (fn. 1), para. 328.
[39] Art. 3(1)(35) MAR.
[40] ESMA/2015/224 (fn. 1), para. 340 ff.
[41] Art. 3(1)(34)(i) MAR; on the terms *credit institution* and *investment firm* see Art. 3(1)(3) MAR with reference to point (1) of Art. 4(1) of Regulation (EU) No. 575/2013 (CRR IV) and Art. 3(2) MAR with reference to point (1) of Art. 4(1) of MiFID II.
[42] Art. 3(1)(34)(i) and (ii) MAR.

because the first group (referred to as 'qualified persons') enjoys a certain reputation on the market and the legislature assumes that investors place greater confidence in their recommendations, even when only given indirectly.

(b) Personal Scope

The MAR and Commission Delegated Regulation (EU) No. 2016/958 differentiate between **general requirements** applicable to **any person** mentioned in Article 3(1)(34)(i) and (ii) MAR and **additional requirements** that only apply to a certain sub-group of these persons.[43] This concept resembles the 'relevant person' concept used by old Implementing Directive 2003/125/EC.

28

The first sub-group consists of all qualified persons and the so-called experts. The term 'expert' is new and includes any person 'referred to in Article 3(1)(34)(ii) MAR who repeatedly proposes investment decisions in respect of financial instruments and who (i) presents himself as having financial expertise or experience; or (ii) puts forward his recommendation in such a way that other persons would reasonably believe he has financial expertise or experience.'[44] The Commission wanted to promote a risk-based approach because recommendations from qualified persons and experts pose a greater risk to market integrity and investor protection. Other persons are only subject to the general requirements. The Commission explains this distinction with reasons of proportionality.[45] As a result, private individuals offering investment recommendations in Internet chat rooms will in most cases not be subject to the regulation.[46]

29

Special rules apply to **journalists**. First, the provisions of Commission Delegated Regulation (EU) No. 2016/958 do not apply to journalists if they are subject to equivalent regulation in a Member State, including equivalent appropriate self-regulation, if this regulation achieves similar effects as Commission Delegated Regulation (EU) No. 2016/958.[47] Second, where research is produced or disseminated 'for the purpose of journalism or other form of expression in the media' the information disseminated 'shall be assessed taking into account the freedom of the press [...] and the rules and codes governing the journalist profession' unless the person at issue somehow profits from the dissemination or intends to mislead the market with the dissemination.[48]

30

3. Production of Research

Rules on the production of recommendations include requirements for the objective presentation of recommendations and several disclosure obligations, most notably with regard to interests and conflicts of interest.

31

---

[43] Art. 3 and 5 Commission Delegated Regulation (EU) No. 2016/958 contain general requirements whereas Art. 4 and 6 contain additional requirements.
[44] Art. 1(a) Commission Delegated Regulation (EU) No. 2016/958.
[45] Recital 2 Commission Delegated Regulation (EU) No. 2016/958 and ESMA/2015/224 (fn. 1), para. 333 ff.
[46] The behaviour may, however, constitute market manipulation, cf. R. Veil § 15 para. 19 ff.
[47] Art. 20(3)(4) MAR.
[48] Art. 21 MAR.

(a) Objective Presentation of Investment Recommendations

(aa) General Requirements

32 All persons who produce recommendations must ensure an objective presentation of investment recommendations.[49] The aim is to make the **research results comprehensible** for investors in order to prevent them from being misled. No change to the old MAD regime was intended.[50] The guiding principle—in line with the other rules of MAR—is that of the **reasonable investor**. Neither the European legislator nor the Commission have declared that the addressee of an investment recommendation is, like a consumer, easily misled and acts without any knowledge of the market.

33 Objective presentation requires that:

— facts are clearly distinguished from interpretations, estimates, opinions and other forms of non-factual information;
— all substantially material sources of information are clearly and prominently indicated;
— all sources of information are reliable or, where there is any doubt as to whether a source is reliable, this is clearly indicated;
— all projections, forecasts and price targets are clearly labelled as such and the material assumptions made in producing or using them are indicated; and
— the date and time at which the production of the recommendation was completed is clearly and prominently indicated.[51]

34 The national supervisory authority can further request the persons who produce recommendations to substantiate any recommendation.[52] In other words, the supervisory authority can demand an explanation for a certain recommendation if it retrospectively proves to be 'incorrect'. This provision is not without criticism, because it encourages typical 'herd behaviour' among financial analysts. The more an individual analyst deviates from the recommendations of other analysts, the higher the need to justify his recommendation as 'reasonable'. This could encourage financial analysts to lean towards the recommendations of others rather than presenting a diverging prognosis.[53]

(bb) Special Requirements for Qualified Persons and Experts

35 Additional obligations exist for qualified persons and experts'.[54] ESMA considers that these persons will typically reach a larger audience and that their messages are often likely to immediately impact the market.[55] Therefore, stricter regulation is in place to enhance investor protection.

---

[49] Art. 3 Commission Delegated Regulation (EU) No. 2016/958.
[50] ESMA/2015/224 (fn. 1), para. 351.
[51] Art. 3(1)(a)–(e) Commission Delegated Regulation (EU) No. 2016/958.
[52] Art. 3(3) Commission Delegated Regulation (EU) No. 2016/958.
[53] On this 'herd behaviour' in financial analysts see D. Bernhardt et al., 80 J. Fin. Econ. (2006), 657 ff.; Q. Chen and W. Jiang, 19 Rev. Fin. Stud. (2006), 319 ff.; J.C. Coffee, *Gatekeepers*, 252 ff.
[54] Art. 4 of Commission Delegated Regulation (EU) No. 2016/958.
[55] ESMA/2015/224 (fn. 1), para. 342.

These persons must indicate whether the recommendation has been disclosed to the issuer to which it relates (directly or indirectly) and has been amended following this disclosure before its dissemination.[56] It is to be ensured that investors are informed if the issuer had the possibility to influence the wording of the research results as this can be an indication that the issuer's interests played too important a role in the financial analyst's decision making process.

Qualified persons and experts must further inform their audience about '**any basis** of **valuation** or **methodology** and the **underlying assumptions** used to either evaluate a financial instrument or an issuer, or to set a price target for a financial instrument.'[57] Consequently, they must declare whether the recommendation is based on fundamental analysis or technical analysis (see para. 11–14).[58] There is no need to publish a proprietary model but the report must indicate where 'material information' about a proprietary model is available.[59] ESMA considers it a best practice for qualified persons and experts to achieve a certain degree of cross-recommendation consistency. This means that recommendations by the 'same person for companies that belong to the same industry or [...] country should exhibit some consistent common factors.'[60]

Qualified persons and experts must also disclose the '**meaning of any recommendation** made, such as buy, sell or hold, and the length of time of the investment to which the recommendation relates and indicate any appropriate risk warning, which including a sensitivity analysis of the relevant assumptions.[61] Investors are to make their own assessment, without having to have to rely solely on the financial analyst's recommendation, although only institutional investors will usually have the necessary expertise.[62] The significance of the recommendation is also to be made clear to the investors. During the New Economy boom in the late 1990s, some analysts issued 'hold' recommendations, which in informed circles were correctly understood as 'sell' recommendations. To prevent retail investors from being at a disadvantage, recommendations must be presented in detail, for example by describing which expectations can be deduced from certain price developments of a certain security (eg *strong buy* in cases of +15% within six months).

Finally, qualified persons and experts must include several other pieces of information, such as 'a reference to the planned frequency of updates to the recommendation',[63] information on any differences in recommendation within the past 12 months for the same financial instrument or issuer[64] and a list of all recommendations from the past 12 months.[65]

---

[56] Art. 4(1)(a) Commission Delegated Regulation (EU) No. 2016/958.
[57] Art. 4(1)(b) Commission Delegated Regulation (EU) No. 2016/958; ESMA/2015/224 (fn. 1), para. 361.
[58] M. Foerster, in: Habersack et al. (eds.), *Handbuch Kapitalmarktinformation*, § 23 para. 89; K. Rothenhöfer, in: Meyer et al. (eds.), *Handbuch Marktmissbrauchsrecht*, § 23 para. 14.
[59] Art. 4(1)(d) Commission Delegated Regulation (EU) No. 2016/958.
[60] ESMA/2015/224 (fn. 1), para. 362.
[61] Art. 4(1)(e) Commission Delegated Regulation (EU) No. 2016/958.
[62] On the total lack of financial knowledge of private investors see M. van Rooij et al., *Financial Literacy and Stock Market Participation*, 11 ff.; IOSCO, Analyst Conflicts of Interest, p. 17 also mentions investor education as a tool for understanding and discounting for analyst conflicts of interest.
[63] Art. 4(1)(f) Commission Delegated Regulation (EU) No. 2016/958.
[64] Art. 4(1)(h) Commission Delegated Regulation (EU) No. 2016/958.
[65] Art. 4(1)(i) Commission Delegated Regulation (EU) No. 2016/958.

(b) Disclosure Obligations

40 The disclosure obligations refer to the **identity** of the **issuer** of the recommendation and to information on the **interests and possible conflicts of interest**. The MAR maintains the MAD's underlying concept of not attempting to prohibit certain behaviour but rather informing market participants thereof, leaving them to decide freely whether a recommendation was influenced by certain interests or conflicts of interest.

(aa) Identity of the Producer of Investment Recommendations

41 The identity of the producer of investment recommendations, his conduct of business rules and the identity of his competent authority are considered valuable information for investors.[66] Persons who produce recommendations must therefore disclose 'clearly and prominently their identity' and certain information about the 'identity of the other person(s) responsible for the production of the recommendation.'[67] This other information includes the name and job title of all natural persons involved in the production of the recommendation and, if any, the name of the legal person that the natural person is acting under contract for.[68]

42 Investment firms and credit institutions must additionally disclose the identity of the relevant competent authority.[69] Where the person who produces recommendations is neither an investment firm nor a credit institution, but is subject to self-regulatory standards or codes of conduct, the person must disclose those standards or codes.[70] The aim of these provisions is to enable persons who produce recommendations to develop a reputation by making the results of their prior recommendations public.

(bb) Conflicts of Interest

(1) General Provisions

43 All persons who produce recommendations must **disclose** 'all **relationships** and **circumstances** that may **reasonably** be **expected** to **impair** the **objectivity** of the **recommendation**, which may include where these persons or any natural person working for them [...] who was involved in producing the recommendation have an interest or a conflict of interest concerning any financial instrument or issuer to which the recommendation, directly or indirectly, relates'.[71] The wording is broader than that of Article 5(1) of the old MAD 2003 regime (Implementing Directive 2003/125/EC), which only mandated disclosure of 'significant financial' interests or conflicts. As under the old MAD 2003 regime, the terms 'interest' and 'conflict of interests' are not defined.

---

[66] Recital 3 Commission Delegated Regulation (EU) No. 2016/958; Forum Group, *Best Practices in an Integrated European Financial Market*, p. 7.
[67] Art. 2(1) Commission Delegated Regulation (EU) No. 2016/958.
[68] Art. 2(1)(a), (b) of Commission Delegated Regulation (EU) No. 2016/958.
[69] Art. 2(2) Commission Delegated Regulation (EU) No. 2016/958.
[70] Art. 2(3) Commission Delegated Regulation (EU) No. 2016/958.
[71] Art. 5(1) Commission Delegated Regulation (EU) No. 2016/958.

Natural persons producing recommendations must also disclose circumstances regarding the persons closely associated with the producer.[72] Furthermore, legal persons must disclose interests or conflicts of interest of persons belonging to the same group[73] that are known or (potentially) accessible to anyone producing the recommendation or to anyone with access to the recommendation.[74]

In other words, recommendations that are possibly influenced by interests or conflicts of interest of the person producing the recommendation are not prohibited; market participants are, however, to be informed of this fact to be able to decide on the objectivity of the recommendation themselves.[75]

The Level 2 Regulation does not provide any specific requirements on the **manner** of **disclosure**. Judicial literature suggests that the interests and conflicts of interest be disclosed with sufficient specificity to enable the addressee of the recommendation to form an informed opinion about the nature and extent of the interests and conflict of interest.[76]

(2) Additional Requirements for Qualified Persons and Experts

Recommendations produced by qualified persons and experts must contain certain information on their interests and conflicts of interest, which the European legislature deemed particularly likely to influence the objectiveness of the recommendation.[77]

The recipient of the recommendation must be informed about **major shareholdings** between the **relevant person** or any related legal person on the one hand and the **issuer** on the other hand. Under the former MAD 2003, this encompassed all cases in which the relevant person or any related legal person held more than 5% of the total issued share capital of the issuer or vice versa.[78] Commission Delegated Regulation (EU) No. 2016/958 significantly lowers the threshold and establishes 'uniform disclosure criteria'.[79]

> The 'uniform disclosure criteria' refer to net long and short positions: Qualified persons and experts must disclose whether they own 'a net long or short position exceeding [...] 0.5% of the total issued share capital of the issuer' and make 'a statement to this effect specifying whether the net position is long or short.' The calculation of the net position follows the Short Selling Regulation (SSR) to ease the administrative burden on market participants.[80] Example: If an analyst holds 0.2% shares and has entered into contracts for difference (total return swap) that give him synthetic access to 0.4%

---

[72] Art. 5(3) Commission Delegated Regulation (EU) No. 2016/958; Art. 3(1)(26) MAR defines the term 'person closely associated'.
[73] As defined in Art. 1(b) Commission Delegated Regulation (EU) No. 2016/958 with reference to Art. 2(11) of Directive 2013/34/EU (Accounting Directive).
[74] Art. 5(2)(a), (b) Commission Delegated Regulation (EU) No. 2016/958.
[75] Recitals 5, 6 Commission Delegated Regulation (EU) No. 2016/958.
[76] K. Rothenhöfer, in: Meyer et al. (eds.), *Handbuch Marktmissbrauchsrecht*, § 22 para. 36; cf. also recital 6 Commission Delegated Regulation (EU) 2016/958.
[77] Art. 6 Commission Delegated Regulation (EU) No. 2016/958.
[78] Art. 6(1)(a) Implementing Directive 2003/125/EC. Many firms prohibited their analysts from holding shares in the issuers they cover; also see IOSCO, Statement of Principles for Addressing Sell-Side Securities Analyst Conflicts of Interest, September 2003, p. 4.
[79] ESMA/2015/224 (fn. 1), para. 374.
[80] Art. 6(1)(a) Commission Delegated Regulation (EU) No. 2016/958; ESMA/2015/224 (fn. 1), para. 378.

of the shares, he has financial interests (net short position of 0.6%) that require him to disclose his position. Only the fact that the threshold has been crossed and in which direction (long or short) needs to be disclosed. No disclosure is mandated for the exact size of the net position. Where positions do not reach or cross the threshold of 0.5%, they could, however, still lead to interests or a conflict of interest to be disclosed under the general disclosure obligations.[81]

50 Qualified persons and experts must further disclose whether the **issuer** they cover **owns more** than **5%** of the total issued **share capital** of the qualified person or expert.[82] Qualified persons and experts must also disclose their position (or that of any person belonging to the same group) as **market maker** or liquidity provider in the financial instruments of the issuer.[83] Similarly, they must disclose, if, over the previous 12 months, they or any person belonging to the same group have acted as lead manager or co-lead manager of any publicly disclosed offer of the issuer's financial instruments.[84] Empirical studies have shown that analysts of an underwriter tend to assess new stock issues more positively than analysts entirely uninvolved in the transaction.[85] Underwriters will always aim to place newly issued financial instruments in their entirety and negative research is likely to impede this aim.[86]

51 Disclosure is also required if the **person** producing the **recommendation** or any person belonging to the same group is 'party to any other **agreement** with the **issuer** relating to the provision of **investment banking services**, provided that this would not entail the disclosure of any confidential commercial information and that the agreement has been in effect over the previous 12 months or has given rise during the same period to the payment of a compensation or to the promise to get a compensation paid'.[87] Reports on preferential treatment of clients of an analyst's own investment banking division are numerous. An analyst of Lehman Brothers, for example, is said to have been instructed in a number of e-mails by his superior that the stock price target of US$ 50 was to be upheld out of consideration for the investment banking department, in spite of the share price having dropped from US$ 32 to US$ 4.[88]

52 Analysts must further disclose any agreements with the issuer relating to the production of the recommendation.[89] Smaller companies usually pay analysts for coverage, wanting to draw attention to themselves, as institutional investors in particular will usually place their investments according to the number of analysts monitoring the respective financial instruments.[90]

---

[81] ESMA/2015/224 (fn. 1), para. 377 ff.
[82] Art. 6(1)(b) Commission Delegated Regulation (EU) No. 2016/958.
[83] Art. 6(1)(c)(i) Commission Delegated Regulation (EU) No. 2016/958.
[84] Art. 6(1)(c)(ii) Commission Delegated Regulation (EU) No. 2016/958.
[85] P.M. Dechow et al., 17 CAR (2000), 1 ff.; R. Michaely and K.L. Womack, 12 Rev. Fin. Studies (1999), 653; evidence is mixed, however, cf. J.E. Fisch, 55 UCLA L. Rev. (2007), 39, 62.
[86] Cf. J.E. Fisch, 55 UCLA L. Rev. (2007), 39, 57.
[87] Art. 6(1)(d)(iii) Commission Delegated Regulation (EU) No. 2016/958.
[88] J.E. Fisch, 10 Lewis & Clark L. Rev. (2006), 57, 63; cf. N. Moloney, *EU Securities and Financial Markets Regulation*, 683 ff. for a description of categories of business-driven conflicts of interest.
[89] Art. 6(1)(d)(iv) of Commission Delegated Regulation (EU) No. 2016/958.
[90] B.M. Barber and T. Odean, 21 Rev. Fin. Studies (2008), 785 ff. and J.E. Fisch, 55 UCLA L. Rev. (2007), 39, 46.

(3) Additional Requirements for Investment Firms, Credit Institutions and other Persons

Investment Firms, credit institutions or persons working for them shall also disclose a description of their internal arrangements and information barriers for the prevention and avoidance of conflicts of interest.[91] Again, the addressee is the reasonable investor. 53

> The link of **financial analysts' remuneration to investment banking results** has been strongly criticised since 2002. Commission Delegated Regulation (EU) No. 2016/958 does not prohibit the remuneration from being tied to investment banking transactions, but requires disclosure of any such connections.[92] In addition, the Level 2 Regulation requires disclosure of 'information on the price and date of acquisition of shares where natural persons working for [an investment firm or a credit institution] and who were involved in producing the recommendation, receive or purchase the shares of the issuer to which the recommendation, directly or indirectly, relates prior to a public offering of such shares'.[93] Commission Delegated Regulation (EU) 2016/958 itself does not prohibit trading in the covered instruments,[94] yet most firms will have included a prohibition to this effect in their internal rules of conduct. 54

Commission Delegated Regulation (EU) No. 2016/958 further assumes that issuers to whom the investment firm, a credit institution or a person working for them offers material investment banking services will usually be assessed more positively. Hence, disclosure is required, 'on a quarterly basis, [for] the proportion of all recommendations that are 'buy', 'hold', 'sell' or equivalent terms, over the previous 12 months, and the proportion of issuers corresponding to each of these categories to which it has supplied material investment banking services over the previous 12 months'.[95] This transparency is a two-edged sword: investors are likely to assume that all clients, for which the analysing company issues recommendations, also receive material investment banking services. The European legislature has, in other words, deemed the situation a risk to transparency, although in some cases the disclosure obligation may lead to more confusion than helpful advice, and investors may have been able to make a more valid assessment themselves. 55

4. ## Dissemination of Investment Recommendations Produced by Third Parties

The distribution of recommendations to third parties entails the risk that the recipient may evaluate the recommendation incorrectly and be misled. The European legislature therefore adopted a regulatory approach similar to the one pursued regarding the provisions on the compilation of recommendations. The **disclosure requirements** are, however, **less strict** for the **dissemination** of a recommendation, because the disseminator cannot have influenced the results due to a conflict of interests. Only if the disseminator made considerable changes to the recommendation prior to the dissemination are additional disclosure obligations required, in order to enable market participants to assess the nature of the alterations.[96] 56

---

[91] Art. 6(2)(a) Commission Delegated Regulation (EU) No. 2016/958.
[92] Art. 6(2)(b) Commission Delegated Regulation (EU) No. 2016/958.
[93] Art. 6(2)(c) Commission Delegated Regulation (EU) No. 2016/958.
[94] Art. 25(2)(a) Implementing Directive 2006/73/EC prohibits persons subject to MiFID from trading in covered instruments.
[95] Art. 6(4) Implementing Directive 2003/125/EC.
[96] Recital 8 Commission Delegated Regulation (EU) No. 2016/958.

57 Pursuant to Article 8 of Commission Delegated Regulation (EU) No. 2016/958, 'persons who disseminate recommendations produced by a third party shall disclose their identity and the date and time at which the recommendation is first disseminated'.[97]

58 The MAR regime further contains provisions ensuring that whenever a **recommendation produced by a third party** is **substantially altered** the substantial alteration is clearly indicated in detail.[98] Persons disseminating a substantially altered recommendation must further meet the requirements laid down in Articles 2–5 of Commission Delegated Regulation (EU) No. 2016/958 'to the extent of the substantial alteration'. In particular, they must also include a reference to the place where recipients can access the information according to Articles 2–6 with regard to the producer of the recommendation.[99]

59 These requirements are intended to give the recipient of the substantially altered information access to the identity of the person producing it, to the recommendation itself and to the disclosure of the producer's interests or conflicts of interest, because substantial alterations could be based on the personal interests of the disseminator. The investor must be informed of this possibility in order to be able to evaluate and assess the existence of possible conflicts of interests and to be able to adapt his investment decision accordingly.

60 In some cases, the recommendation may be disseminated as an **extract or summary**. This regularly happens on websites when the host of the site provides a summarised overview of recommendations sorted by issuer or producer. Persons disseminating an extract or a summary must 'ensure that the extract or summary is clear and not misleading, identify it as a summary or an extract and include a clear identification of the source' of the recommendation.[100] The extract or summary must also contain the information according to Articles 2–6 of Commission Delegated Regulation (EU) No. 2016/958 with regard to the producer of the recommendation or contain a reference to a place where this information is stored.[101]

61 If the producer and the disseminator belong to the same group, the disseminator can be exempted from the requirements of Commission Delegated Regulation (EU) No. 2016/958 applicable to disseminators. The exemption requires that the disseminator has no discretion in selecting the recommendations but merely serves as a distribution channel.[102]

5. Principle of Proportionality—Non-written Recommendations

62 Measures affecting an individual's rights must always be in proportion to their aim.[103] This principle of proportionality can be found in numerous areas of European financial markets law. Commission Delegated Regulation (EU) No. 2016/958 adapts several requirements in order to maintain proportionality for non-written recommendations. In particular, the Level 2 Regulation allows for certain information to be replaced by a reference to a place

---

[97] Art. 8(1)(a), (c) Commission Delegated Regulation (EU) No. 2016/958.
[98] Art. 10(1) Commission Delegated Regulation (EU) No. 2016/958.
[99] Art. 10(2) Commission Delegated Regulation (EU) No. 2016/958.
[100] Art. 9(1) Commission Delegated Regulation (EU) No. 2016/958.
[101] Art. 9(2) Commission Delegated Regulation (EU) No. 2016/958.
[102] ESMA/2015/224 (fn. 1), para. 397.
[103] ECJ of 3 December 1998, Case C-368/96 (*Generics*) [1998] ECR I-7967, para. 66–67.

where the required information can 'directly and easily be accessed free of charge by the public.' This is allowed where the disclosure of the information at issue is disproportionate in relation to the length or form of the recommendation, including in the case of non-written recommendations.[104] Commission Delegated Regulation (EU) No. 2016/958 does, however, not indicate the adaption necessary to maintain proportionality. This assessment is left to a case-by-case analysis.[105]

6. Sanctions

Member States shall, in accordance with national law, provide for competent authorities to have the power to take **appropriate administrative sanctions** and other administrative measures for infringements of Article 20(1) MAR.[106] Member States shall further ensure that the competent authorities have the power to impose at least the types of administrative sanctions spelled out in Article 30(2) MAR. With regard to administrative pecuniary sanctions the regulation obliges Member States to an 'at least up to' approach. Member States must introduce maximum administrative pecuniary sanctions of at least three times the profits gained or losses avoided because of the infringement where profits/losses can be determined.[107] For natural persons, Member States must further introduce maximum administrative pecuniary sanctions of at least € 500,000 (€ 1 million for legal persons).[108] Member States have the discretion to provide for additional sanctions and higher amounts of monetary sanctions.[109]

63

The MAR is **silent on private enforcement** of Article 20(1) MAR. It is therefore exclusively a matter of national private law in the Member States whether investors can claim damages on account of an erroneous financial analysis. Tort law is the most relevant legal basis. However, court decisions are rare,[110] thus little is known about the effectiveness of private enforcement in Europe.

64

V. Relevance of the General Rules of Conduct for Financial Analysts

1. Market Manipulation

(a) Information-Based Manipulation

Information-based manipulation is the 'dissemination of information through the media, including the internet, or by any other means which gives, or is likely to give, false or

65

---

[104] Art. 3(2), 4(2), 6(4) and 10(2) Commission Delegated Regulation (EU) No. 2016/958.
[105] ESMA/2015/224 (fn. 1), para. 387.
[106] Art. 30(1)(a) MAR.
[107] Art. 30(2)(h) MAR.
[108] Art. 30(2)(j)(iii).
[109] Art. 30(3) MAR.
[110] In France the question of a civil law liability arose in the case *LVMH v. Morgan Stanley*. The claim was based on Art. 1382 Code Civil.

misleading signals as to the supply or demand for, or price of, a financial instrument [...], or is likely to secure the price of one or several financial instruments [...] at an abnormal or artificial level, including the dissemination of rumours, where the person who made the dissemination knew, or ought to have known, that the information was false or misleading'.[111] This prohibition is of great practical relevance for financial analysts who can only fulfil their function as information intermediaries by disseminating the information they have acquired.[112] If their recommendation gives false or misleading signals regarding the analysed financial instrument, the financial analyst breaches the prohibition of market manipulation.

66 Incorrect **facts** in the reporting part of the analysis, ie information on actual circumstances that does not reflect reality, are the most obvious instances of a 'false signal'. The analyst must, for example, ensure that the information provided on the company's trading volume and debts is correct.

67 The question whether the **recommendation** to 'hold', 'buy' or 'sell' can itself constitute a **'false signal'** is not clarified by the MAR. Legal literature is predominantly of the opinion that a recommendation constitutes a value judgement that is false if it is based on facts but cannot be plausibly deduced from these.[113] If the recommendation does not contain any factual elements, a false signal is given, if the recommendation is evidentially unsubstantiated. Based on this understanding and assuming the responsible persons acted intentionally, the recommendations to acquire Enron shares, even after Enron had to restate its financial statements in October 2001,[114] can (retrospectively) be regarded as evidentially unjustifiable.

68 Identifying **misleading signals** proves more difficult. Any approach to a definition must be based on the premise that this can only mean a correct statement of facts, because the presentation of incorrect facts is already covered by the term 'false'. Misleading signals are therefore true circumstances that nevertheless give a wrong impression. If the descriptive part of the recommendation, for example, provides extensive positive information on the issuer, whilst the existence of negative information is only indicated vaguely, this is likely to mislead the investor. Incomplete information can also give a wrong impression and must therefore be regarded as misleading.

(b) Fictitious Devices or Any Other Form of Deception or Contrivance

69 The MAR further defines a 'transaction, [...] order to trade or any other means, which affects or is likely to affect the price of one or several financial instruments [...], which employs fictitious devices or any other form of deception or contrivance' as market manipulation.[115] The provision is to prevent any transactions that affect price stability and therefore cannot be accepted if the functioning of the markets is to be ensured. Annex I to the MAR lists circumstances that may indicate a market manipulation. An indication of manipulative behaviour included in the list especially for analysts, are **'orders to trade [...] given**

---

[111] Art. 12(1)(c) MAR; in more detail R. Veil § 15 para. 19 ff.
[112] See para. 1–5.
[113] See R. Veil § 15 para. 21.
[114] For a description of the Enron recommendations see J.C. Coffee, *Gatekeepers*, 30.
[115] Art. 12(1)(b) MAR.

or **transactions** [...] undertaken by persons before or after the same persons or persons linked to them produce or disseminate investment recommendations which are **erroneous** or **biased** or demonstrably influenced by material interest'.[116] The provision is thus only applicable with regard to specific transactions and to the behaviour of persons who personally produce investment recommendations or are linked to such persons.[117]

The term *erroneous* in the sense of Annex I B(b) to the MAR refers to any recommendation that cannot be justified or is based on incorrect facts without causing false or misleading signals regarding the financial instrument. The recommendation would otherwise have to be treated as an information-based manipulation. Any investment recommendation that has not been compiled with the necessary expertise, care and diligence, or is incomplete for other reasons, must be considered erroneous under this definition. The meaning of the term 'biased' is equally difficult to determine, because the directive is silent as to the cause of the bias. Legal literature generally interprets the term as referring to financial recommendations that are neither incorrect nor erroneous but still mislead investors as to the real situation. 70

The MAR does not define when a recommendation is demonstrably influenced by material interest. The question can only be answered on a case-by-case basis. The provision applies to situations in which the analyst holds shares of the respective company. This situation, however, can also be seen as a form of *scalping*. If the rules on scalping are not applicable due to correct disclosure of the financial instruments the analyst holds, the behaviour may still fall within the scope of this provision. 71

(c) Scalping

Market manipulation also includes 'taking advantage of occasional or regular access to the traditional or electronic media by voicing an opinion about a financial instrument [...] (or indirectly about its issuer) while having previously taken positions on that financial instrument [...] and profiting subsequently from the impact of the opinions voiced on the price of that instrument [...], without having simultaneously disclosed that conflict of interest to the public in a proper and effective way'.[118] This behaviour, called *scalping*, is particularly relevant with regard to financial analysts. A scalper must ensure that as many investors as possible take his opinion into account and must possess sufficient authority for his opinion to be regarded as well-founded and truthful. At least qualified persons and experts meet both requirements.[119] 72

During the New Economy boom in Germany, a number of television programmes offered investment advice to potential investors. An anchorman advertised shares that he had personally acquired and convinced investors to follow suit by predicting high profits. His aim was to subsequently sell the instrument at a profit following the rise in the market price due to his recommendation.[120] The case was presented to the BGH, and the court held that 73

---

[116] Annex I B(b) MAR.
[117] The regulation contains no definition of when a person is 'linked' to another person. This is probably a result of copying out the wording of Implementing Directive 2003/125/EC. One can assume that 'linked to' means 'closely associated' as defined in Art. 3(1)(26) MAR.
[118] Art. 12(2)(d) MAR; see also R. Veil § 15 para. 50.
[119] See above para. 19.
[120] Cf. BGH of 6.11.2003 – 1 StR 24/03, BGHSt 48, 375.

scalping constitutes a form of market manipulation. The BGH ruled out insider trading because facts created by the insider, such as the acquisition of shares and a recommendation based on the intention of achieving a better sale price, did not fall under the definition of 'precise information', as required by the former Directive. This approach was confirmed by the MAD 2003 which also considered scalping a form of market manipulation.[121]

(d) Effects of Commission Delegated Regulation (EU) No. 2016/958 on the Prohibition of Market Manipulation

74 Recommendations published in conformity with the provisions of Commission Delegated Regulation (EU) No. 2016/958 cannot constitute false or misleading information with regard to the objective presentation of investment recommendations and the disclosure of conflicts of interest. The aim of Commission Delegated Regulation (EU) No. 2016/958 is to prevent investors from being misled.[122] If a market participant abides by these rules, it cannot be accused of having misled the public. If, however, a market participant is found to have breached the Implementing Directive's provisions, this can also constitute a breach of the rules against market manipulation.

2. Prohibition of Insider Dealings

75 Persons who produce investment recommendations must ensure they comply with the rules on insider dealings when producing or disseminating research. **Investment recommendations** can only be considered **inside information**, however, **if they are not based on publicly available information.**[123] If confidential information was also taken into account in the financial analysis, it must be determined for each case individually whether the report itself also constitutes inside information.

76 Using inside information by acquiring or disposing of financial instruments[124] is also prohibited for persons who produce recommendations. If qualified persons within the meaning of Article 3(1)(34) MAR obtain inside information when producing a recommendation they become primary insiders.[125] The decision to 'hold' a financial instrument is not affected by this prohibition, pursuant to the wording of the MAR. Should the person producing recommendations have planned to dispose of the shares and then abstained from doing so due to the inside information it acquired when compiling the recommendation, this behaviour usually does not constitute a breach of the provisions on insider dealings.[126]

77 The prohibition regarding the disclosure of inside information can also become relevant for persons producing recommendations. These persons may not disclose inside information that has become known to them in their recommendation. By doing so, the person would

---

[121] See Art. 1(1)(c) indent 3 MAD.
[122] Recital 1 Commission Delegated Regulation (EU) 2016/958.
[123] Recital 28 MAR.
[124] Art. 8(1) sentence 1 MAR.
[125] Art. 8(4)(c) MAR.
[126] Cancelling or amending an order may also violate the prohibition according to Art. 8(1) sentence 2 MAR.

pass on the information to a third party, ie the recipient of the investment recommendation. The person producing the recommendation must further take into account the rules prohibiting the recommendation of the financial instruments or the inducement of others.[127]

3. Research as an Inducement under MiFID II

In the past, it was common for banks to provide investors (funds, asset managers, private investors) with research on an issuer as part of asset management and other services. However, research was only free at first glance. Investors ultimately paid for the analyses through order execution costs (dealing commissions). This has changed since 2016 due to MiFID II, under which investment research is considered as an inducement.

Under the MiFID II regime, Member States shall require that 'when providing portfolio management the **investment firm** shall **not accept** and retain fees, commissions or any monetary or non-monetary **benefits** paid or provided by any third party or a person acting on behalf of a third party in relation to the provision of the service to clients.'[128] This does not apply to 'minor non-monetary benefits that are capable of enhancing the quality of service provided to a client and are of a scale and nature such that they could not be judged to impair compliance with the investment firm's duty to act in the best interest of the client.' Member States must require these minor non-monetary benefits to be clearly disclosed.

Member States must further ensure that investment firms are regarded as non-compliant with Article 23 or Article 24(1) 'where they pay or are paid any fee or commission, or provide or are provided with any non-monetary benefit in connection with the provision of an investment service or ancillary service, to or by any party except the client or a person on behalf of the client, other than where the payment or benefit (i) is designed to enhance the quality of the relevant service to the client; and (ii) does not impair compliance with the firm's duty to act honestly, fairly and professionally in accordance with the best interest of its clients.'[129]

Member States must further ensure that if a payment or benefit meets these requirements—and is thus allowed by MiFID II—'the existence, nature and amount of the payment or benefit [...], or, where the amount cannot be ascertained, the method of calculating that amount, must be clearly disclosed to the client, in a manner that is comprehensive, accurate and understandable, prior to the provision of the relevant investment or ancillary service. Where applicable, the investment firm shall also inform the client on mechanisms for transferring to the client the fee, commission, monetary or non-monetary benefit received in relation to the provision of the investment or ancillary service.'

In other words, investment firms may only make or receive payments and give or receive benefits that are designed to **enhance the quality** of the relevant service and that do **not lead to a conflict of interest** between the investment firm and its client. Payments or benefits that pass this test must be disclosed to the client prior to providing the service, either by their

---

[127] Cf. R. Veil § 14 para. 90.
[128] Art. 24(8) MiFID II.
[129] Art. 24(9) MiFID II.

specific amount or at least by the method of calculation as well as the method of transferring the payment/benefit to the client.

83 This classification of research leaves asset managers with the option to use their own funds to pay for research or attempt to increase their management fees, thus indirectly passing on the cost of research to their clients. Alternatively, asset managers can establish a separate 'research payment account' with their clients` consent and use this account to pay for research. The research payment account must be funded by specific research charges that the clients pay and must not be linked to transaction volume of the client.

84 The prohibition on inducements is of practical relevance above all in the case of fee-based investment advice and financial portfolio management.[130] The exceptions normally do not apply. Unsurprisingly, investment firms are reluctant to pay for research when SMEs are involved. Research for SMEs has therefore declined significantly since MiFID II. This is a serious problem for the issuers' research coverage because the liquidity of the shares suffers as a result.

VI. Conclusion

85 The regime for investment research introduced in 2003 has proven its worth. In reforming market abuse law, the European legislature thus limited itself to regulating individual aspects (objective presentation of the investment recommendation and disclosure of conflicts of interest) more strictly. It has retained the conceptual basis of regulating conflicts of interest through transparency rather than through prohibitions. No scandals have come to light that would have given cause for a different fundamental approach. However, a key issue has not yet been clarified: Are investors able to properly assess disclosed conflicts of interest? The regime requires persons making investment recommendations to disclose the *existence* of financial interests and potential conflicts of interest. However, the reasonable investor does not learn how *substantial* these interests or conflicts of interest are. Finally, liability of analysts under private law remains an essentially unexplored topic in Europe.

86 The stricter regime for inducements introduced by MiFID II is causing major problems. The number of people who provide financial research (sell-side) has declined sharply. Research coverage is also down, with the consequence of lower liquidity of the shares of the companies concerned (especially SMEs). These developments give reason to readjust the MiFID II regime for inducements. Less stringent rules should apply to SMEs!

---

[130] Cf. J. Koch and R. Harnos, in: Schwark and Zimmer (eds.), *Kapitalmarkrechts-Kommentar*, § 70 WpHG para. 23.

§ 27

Rating Agencies

Bibliography

Alexander, Kern, *The Risk of Ratings in Bank Capital Regulation*, 25 EBLR (2014), 295–313; Blaurock, Uwe, *Verantwortlichkeit von Ratingagenturen—Steuerung durch Privat- oder -Aufsichtsrecht?*, 36 ZGR (2007), 603–653; Cash, Daniel, *The Role of Credit Rating Agencies in Responsible Finance* (2008); Coffee, John C., *Ratings Reform: The Good, the Bad, and the Ugly*, 1 Harv. Bus. L. Rev. (2011), 231–278; Deipenbrock, Gudula, *Was ihr wollt oder der Widerspenstigen Zähmung? Aktuelle Entwicklungen der Regulierung von Ratingagenturen im Wertpapierbereich*, 39 BB (2005), 2085–2090; Deipenbrock, Gudula, *Aktuelle Rechtsfragen zur Regulierung des Ratingwesens*, 6 WM (2005), 261–268; Deipenbrock, Gudula, *Das europäische Modell einer Regulierung von Ratingagenturen—aktuelle praxisrelevante Rechtsfragen und Entwicklungen*, 9 RIW (2010), 612–618; Dichev, Ilia D. and Piotroski, Joseph D., *The Long-Run Stock Returns Following Bond Ratings Changes*, 56 J. Fin. (2001), 173–203; Dutta, Anatol, *Die neuen Haftungsregeln für Ratingagenturen in der Europäischen Union: Zwischen Sachrechtsvereinheitlichung und europäischem Entscheidungseinklang*, 37 WM (2013), 1729–1736; Eilers, Stephan et al. (eds.), *Unternehmensfinanzierung* (2014); Flannery, Mark J. et al., *Credit Default Swap Spreads as Viable Substitutes for Credit Ratings*, 158 U. Pa. L. Rev. (2010), 2085–2123; Haar, Brigitte, *Haftung für fehlerhafte Ratings von Lehman-Zertifikaten—Ein neuer Baustein für ein verbessertes Regulierungsdesign im Ratingsektor?*, 33 NZG (2010), 1281–1285; Habersack, Mathias, *Rechtsfragen des Emittenten-Ratings*, 02-03 ZHR (2005), 185–211; IOSCO, *Statement of Principles Regarding the Activities of Credit Rating Agencies*, September 2003; IOSCO, *Code of Conduct Fundamentals for Credit Rating Agencies*, December 2004; Johnston, Andrew, *Corporate Governance Is the Problem not the Solution: A Critical Appraisal of the European Regulation of Credit Rating Agencies*, 11 J. Corp. L. Stud. (2011), 395–441; Jones, Rachel, *The Need for a Negligence Standard of Care for Credit Rating Agencies*, 1 Wm. & Mary Bus. L. Rev. (2010), 201–231; Lesquene-Roth, Caroline and van Wayenberge, Arnaud, in: Chiti, Edoardo and Vesperini, Giulio (eds.), *The Administrative Architecture of Financial Integration*, (2015), 243 ff.; Lerch, Marcus P., *Ratingagenturen im Visier des europäischen Gesetzgebers*, 10 BKR (2010), 402–408; Leyens, Patrick C., *Intermediary Independence: Auditors, Financial Analysts and Rating Agencies*, 11 J. Corp. L. Stud. (2011), 33–66; Manns, Jeffrey, *Downgrading Rating Agency Reform*, 81 Geo. Wash. L. Rev. (2013), 749–812; Möllers, Thomas M.J., *Regulierung von Ratingagenturen*, 18 JZ (2009), 861–871; Partnoy, Frank, *How and Why Credit Rating Agencies Are Not Like Other Gatekeepers*, in: Fuchita, Yasuyuki and Litan, Robert E. (eds.), *Financial Gatekeepers: Can They Protect Investors?* (2006), 59–99; Partnoy, Frank, *The Siskel and Ebert of Financial Markets: Two Thumbs Down for the Credit Rating Agencies*, 77 Wash. U. L. Q. (1999), 619–714; Rhee, Robert J., *A Critique of Proposals to Reform the Credit Rating Industry (with a Comment on Future Reform)*, 32 Banking & Fin. Serv. Pol'y Rep. (2013), 14–24; Schroeter, Ulrich G., *Ratings—Bonitätsbeurteilungen durch Dritte im System des Finanzmarkt-, Gesellschafts- und Vertragsrechts* (2014); Seibt, Christoph H., *Regulierung und Haftung von Ratingagenturen*, in: Bachmann, Gregor et al. (eds.), *Steuerungsfunktionen des Haftungsrechts im Gesellschafts- und -Kapitalmarktrecht* (2007), 191–213; Stemper, Marthe-Marie, *Rechtliche Rahmenbedingungen des Ratings* (2010); Stumpp, Maximilian, *Nachhaltigkeitsratingagenturen* (2021); Teigelack, Lars, *Finanzanalysen und Behavioral Finance* (2009); Tönningsen, Gerrit, *Die Regulierung von Ratingagenturen*, 6 ZBB 2011, 460–471; Vasella, David, *Die Haftung von Ratingagenturen* (2011); Vassalou, Maria and Xing, Yuhang, *Default Risks in Equity Returns*, 59 J. Fin. (2004), 831–868; Wimmer, Veronika, *Auswirkungen des Art. 35a der Verordnung (EU) Nr. 462/2013 auf die zivilrechtliche Haftung von Ratingagenturen* (2017); Wittenberg, Tim, *Regulatory Evolution of the EU Credit Rating Agency Framework*, 16 EBOR (2015), 559–709.

I. Foundations

1. The Role of Credit Rating Agencies

1 Primarily, credit rating agencies have an intermediary function vis-à-vis investors. **Rating agencies assess** the **creditworthiness** of **issuers**. Ideally, this enables investors to make a well-founded investment decision by eliminating or at least reducing the informational asymmetries between the investor and the issuer, be it a company, be it a country or local authority.[1] The assessment usually consists of a certain combination of letters, such as AAA, AA+ (Standard & Poor's) or Aaa, Aa1 (Moody's).[2]

2 Rating agencies further act as so-called *gatekeepers* for the issuers offering equity or debt capital.[3] They give issuers access to capital markets and regulate market access. In some markets, stock exchange rules explicitly require a rating, whereas in other segments market participants expect issuers to have a positive rating. A positive rating reduces the issuer's costs of capital,[4] whereas an issuer with a negative rating will have to pay considerable interest in order to be able to place bonds on the market.

3 Ratings also fulfil a **regulatory function**. Some jurisdictions employ ratings as a means to directly or indirectly regulate financial products or market participants. According to the third Basel Accord (Basel III), for example, a bank may rely on an external rating to **calculate** its **risk-weighted exposure** amount.[5] According to Article 113(1) CRR, the application of risk weights shall be based on the exposure class to which the exposure is assigned and its credit quality. Credit quality may be determined to the credit assessments of ECAIs or the credit assessment of export credit agencies.[6] The **investment policies** of institutional investors furthermore prescribe that investments are only to be made in securities with an investment-grade rating or even the highest possible rating. The European legislature recognised the immense relevance of the regulatory dependencies, aiming to put an end to it by 2020, but has not yet achieved this.[7]

---

[1] On the similar functions of financial analysts see R. Veil § 26 para. 2.
[2] Fitch and Standard & Poor's employ the same letter designations. Cf. C. Kumpan and R. Grütze, in: Lehmann and Kumpan (eds.), *European Financial Services Law*, Art. 3 CRAR para. 11.
[3] Cf. C. Kumpan and R. Grütze, in: Lehmann and Kumpan (eds.), *European Financial Services Law*, Art. 3 CRAR para 18.
[4] Cf. U. Blaurock, 36 ZGR (2007), 603, 609; M. Lerch, 10 BKR (2010), 402, 403.
[5] Cf. K. Alexander, 25 EBLR (2014), 295–313.
[6] In Europe, Basel III is implemented by the CRR and CRD IV. Cf. on the approaches to credit risk Art. 107 ff. CRR.
[7] See para. 57.

Sustainability rating agencies must be distinguished from credit rating agencies. The business model of these agencies consists primarily of assessing the **environmental** sustainability of companies for investors (issuer rating). They also develop sustainability indices for investors and for providers of financial products. These indices comprise companies or financial stocks that are considered to be particularly sustainable. In addition, the agencies also assess the **social** sustainability of companies and consider **governance** aspects. The sustainability rating agencies have therefore evolved into **ESG agencies**. Their business model differs from that of credit rating agencies. ESG agencies typically conclude contracts with investors (*investor-pays model*). The most important agencies are Vigeo Eiris, Sustainalytics, ISS and MSCI.[8] Some of these ESG agencies also offer other services, such as credit rating or consulting. So far, there is no specific regulation in EU supervisory law for ESG agencies.[9] However, ESG agencies are obliged under civil law to provide their clients (also called subscribers) with neutral, objective and competent ratings. If they violate these obligations, they may be liable to pay damages under national civil law.[10]

2. Effects of a Rating

An essential difference exists on rating markets between financial instruments with a so-called investment-grade rating and papers with a non-investment-grade rating.[11] Both categories contain numerous sub-categories, in the investment-grade from 'Highest Quality' via 'High Quality' and 'Upper Medium Grade' to 'Medium Grade', in the non-investment-grade from 'Lower Medium Grade' via 'Low Grade', 'Poor Quality', 'Most Speculative' and 'No interest paid or bankruptcy petition filed' to 'In Default'. Bonds with non-investment grade are often named junk bonds or high-yield bonds. The distinction between both forms is not gradual, but rather abrupt, so that the development from a lower-investment-grade rating to a 'good' junk rating will usually not merely cause slight changes to the costs of capital. Rather, there is a '**cliff**'[12] between an **investment-grade rating** and a **non-investment-grade rating**, the costs of borrowed capital being disproportionately high in the latter case. For the issuer, a junk rating also has the effect that the *covenants*, ie the contractual rules of conduct it must fulfil when borrowing funds, are far stricter. Economic studies have shown that even downgrades of debt instruments also negatively influence the issuer's equity returns. The studies have not as yet been able to determine, however, whether this is a result of the rating itself or rather of the underlying information.[13] In practice, the terms of high-yield-bonds often contain clauses according to which a change in the rating has certain consequences,

---

[8] D. Cash, *The Role of Credit Rating Agencies in Responsible Finance*, 31 ff.
[9] Detailed analysis by M. Stumpp, *Nachhaltigkeitsratingagenturen*, passim.
[10] M. Stumpp, *Nachhaltigkeitsratingagenturen*, Part 3 § 7.
[11] An investment grade starts at Standard & Poor's with AAA and ends with BBB, at Moodys's it starts with Aaa and ends with Baa. A rating for a non-investment grade starts at Standard & Poor's with BB and ends with D, at Moody's it starts with Ba and ends with C.
[12] The European legislature meanwhile refers to the term 'cliff effect', cf. Commission, Proposal for a Regulation of the European Parliament and of the Council amending Regulation (EC) No. 1060/2009 on credit rating agencies, 15 November 2011, COM (2011) 747 final, p. 4.
[13] Cf. I. Dichev and J. Piotroski, 56 J. Fin. (2001), 173–203; M. Vassalou and Y. Xing, 59 J. Fin. (2004), 831, 833.

such as a change in the interest rate or stricter covenants.[14] A further possibility is that a due diligence process prior to an equity transaction may be less intense for an issuer who has received an investment-grade rating than for an issuer who has received a non-investment-grade rating.[15]

3. Market Structure and Remuneration

6   The market for rating agencies is characterised by **oligopolistic structures**. The three largest rating agencies active worldwide—Standard & Poor's, Moody's and Fitch—have a total market share between 85 and 95%[16] and have **systematic importance** in financial markets.[17] European rating agencies have no significant relevance compared to these three rating agencies (for example Euler Hermes Rating 0.25 %, Feri EuroRating Services approx. 0.75 %, Creditreform Rating approx. 0.5 %, DBRS Ratings Limited approx. 1.3 %).

7   Rating agencies usually act on behalf of the issuers, the contracting entity usually being companies or countries (sovereign rating) and being responsible for the remuneration (*issuer pays*-model).[18] With regard to sovereign ratings, rating agencies partly supply ratings without an order to do so. The *issuer pays*-model results in considerable conflicts of interest for rating agencies, which may be inclined to submit positive ratings with regard to their customers' solvency.[19] The conflicts of interest can be mitigated by reputation mechanisms. However, the problem is certainly not solved by the fact that the business model of rating agencies is based on the assumption that they must have a good reputation in order to be mandated by issuers and therefore have an incentive to work carefully and independently. The conflicts of interest are even exacerbated if the rating agency provides additional services for the issuer.

8   The financial crisis and the sovereign debt crisis in Europe have led to discussions, whether a European rating agency should be established as competition for the large United States rating agencies.[20] Various models were deliberated on, inter alia, the concept of an independent foundation, financed with public funds and an agency financed by investors. The latter would have put an end to the *issuer pays*-model of the three large rating agencies.[21] The European rating agency would have had no incentive to obtain orders from issuers by submitting exaggerated ratings. The project, which was initiated by *Markus Krall*, a former senior advisor at Roland Berger, however, remained unsuccessful due to a lack of financial commitment by investors.

---

[14] Cf. U. Blaurock, 36 ZGR (2007), 603, 611 (rating triggers).
[15] L. Krämer and B. Gillessen, in: Marsch-Barner and Schäfer (eds.), *Handbuch börsennotierte AG*, § 10 para. 71.
[16] European Commission, Study on the State of the Credit Rating Market, Final Report, Markt/2014/257/F4/ST/OP, p. 25.
[17] C. Kumpan and R. Grütze, in: Lehmann and Kumpan, *European Financial Services Law*, Art. 3 CRAR para. 19.
[18] Cf. M. Foerster, in: Habersack et al. (eds.), *Handbuch der Kapitalmarktinformation*, § 24 para. 5: leading agencies achieve 80% of their revenue through issuer payments.
[19] Cf. M. Foerster, in: Habersack et al. (eds.), *Handbuch der Kapitalmarktinformation*, § 25 para. 5.
[20] On the attempts to open the oligopolistic market and on the limits of reputational mechanisms, cf. T. Möllers, 18 JZ (2009), 861, 863; M. Lerch, 10 BKR (2010), 402, 407.
[21] On the discussion about an *investor pays*-model see European Commission, Study on the State of the Credit Rating Market, Final Report, Markt/2014/257/F4/ST/OP, p. 114–117; T. Möllers, 18 JZ (2009), 861, 866; G. Tönningsen 6 ZBB (2011), 469 ff.

4. Development of Regulation in Europe

The importance of rating agencies can be underlined with the following quote of the journalist and award-winner of the Pulitzer Prize, *Thomas Friedman*: 'There are only two superpowers left in the world, the United States and Moody's Rating Service. The United States can destroy everyone by dropping bombs, and Moody's can destroy everyone by downgrading their bonds. And I am not sure who is more powerful.'[22]

However, for a long time, rating agencies were not subject to specific regulation, the IOSCO Code[23] being a voluntary[24] but, in the eyes of regulators, politicians and academics, sufficient regulatory measure.[25] There was the general understanding, that rating agencies had sufficient incentives for acting diligently, in particular no longer being able to win clients on the market, should they lose their reputation.[26] The MAD 2003 therefore was not applicable to rating agencies and even spectacular cases and the Asian crisis did not lead the European legislature to make any regulatory changes.

The crash of Enron, WorldCom and Parmalat led to the criticism that the ratings for these companies had not adapted quickly enough to the changes in the market.[27] Only during the financial crisis did the focus change, the excellent ratings for certain financial products and the slow speed at which ratings were adapted to changes in the markets becoming the centre of attention for the critics when it became apparent that these had been two of the causes of the financial crisis.[28] Rating agencies had not properly assessed the risk of the securitised subprime loans. Issuers further purported that the ratings assigned by the agencies were often too negative, attributing this to the lack of transparency with regard to the criteria of the rating procedure. The regulation on rating agencies is one of the reactions to this criticism.

5. Legal Sources

The Rating Regulation (hereinafter **CRAR**),[29] enacted by the European Parliament and Council in September 2009 (CRAR-I), is largely based on the Commission's draft proposal

---

[22] *Thomas Friedman* in an interview with *David Gergen* dated 13 February 1996 on NewsHour, PBS.
[23] Cf. IOSCO, Statement of Principles Regarding the Activities of Credit Rating Agencies, September 2003 and IOSCO, Code of Conduct Fundaments for Credit Rating Agencies, December 2004.
[24] More details on the IOSCO principles in G. Deipenbrock, 39 BB (2005), 2085 ff.
[25] Cf. C. Seibt, in: Bachmann et al. (eds.), *Steuerungsfunktionen des Haftungsrechts*, 191, 198; M. Habersack, 02-03 ZHR 169 (2005), 185, 190 ff. holds the opposite opinion.
[26] On the limits of the self-regulatory forces on the rating market see M.-M. Stemper, *Rechtliche Rahmenbedingungen des Ratings*, 96 ff.
[27] Cf. G. Deipenbrock, 6 WM (2005), 261, 263; summarising the Enron and Parmalat cases U. Blaurock, 36 ZGR (2007), 603, 613.
[28] Cf. G. Deipenbrock, 9 RIW (2010), 612; T. Möllers, 18 JZ (2009), 861; see also Commission, Proposal for a Regulation of the European Parliament and of the Council on Credit Rating Agencies, 12 November 2008, COM (2008) 704 final, p. 2.
[29] Regulation (EC) No. 1060/2009 of the European Parliament and of the Council of 16 September 2009 on credit rating agencies, OJ L302, 17 November 2009, p. 1. The CRAR entered into force on 7 December 2009.

of November 2008.[30] It was amended in May 2011 (CRAR-II),[31] in order to adapt the supervisory structures to the newly founded ESMA. The Member States are now no longer responsible for the supervision of rating agencies, the amendments by the CRAR-II now conferring the right to supervision and to impose sanctions on ESMA. The (for now) last amendments to the regulation were carried out in 2013 (CRAR-III)[32] and refer to the question of when and how rating agencies are permitted to evaluate sovereign debts and the financial situation of privately owned companies. The legislature further implemented a civil liability of rating agencies for incorrect ratings.

13 The Level 1 act is supplemented by numerous **Delegated Acts** by the Commission (level 2): No. 272/2010,[33] No. 446/2012,[34] No. 447/2012,[35] No. 448/2012,[36] No. 449/2012[37] and No. 946/2012.[38] In addition, ESMA has issued **Guidelines** (primarily addressed to rating agencies) and **Q&A papers**. The Interactive Single Rulebook, which is available on the ESMA website, indicates the CRAR rules on which ESMA's Level 3 measures have been issued.[39]

14 The Commission has further enacted a number of decisions on the **recognition** of the **legal** and **supervisory framework** of **other countries** as **equivalent** to the requirements of the European regulation. This is particularly the case with regard to the regulation in the United States, Canada, Australia and Japan.[40]

15 Rating agencies must further comply with the (not harmonised) general rules of civil law. Whilst they merely present their opinion on the issuer's creditworthiness and the rating

---

[30] Commission, Proposal for a Regulation of the European Parliament and of the Council on Credit Rating Agencies, 12 November 2008, COM (2008) 704 final (fn. 35).

[31] Regulation (EU) No. 513/2011 of the European Parliament and of the Council of 11 May 2011 amending Regulation (EC) No. 1060/2009 on credit rating agencies, OJ L145, 31 May 2011, p. 30–56.

[32] Regulation (EU) No. 462/2013 of 21 May 2013 amending Regulation (EC) No. 1060/2009 on credit rating agencies, OJ L145, 31 May 2013, p. 1–33.

[33] Commission Delegated Regulation (EU) No. 272/2012 of 7 February 2012 supplementing Regulation (EC) No. 1060/2009 of the European Parliament and of the Council with regard to fees charges by the European Securities and Markets Authority to credit rating agencies, OJ L90, 28 March 2012, p. 6.

[34] Commission Delegated Regulation (EU) No. 446/2012 of 21 March 2012 supplementing Regulation (EC) No. 1060/2009 of the European Parliament and of the Council with regard to regulatory technical standards on the content and format of ratings data periodic reporting to be submitted to the European Securities and Markets Authority by credit rating agencies, OJ L140, 30 May 2012, p. 2.

[35] Commission Delegated Regulation (EU) No. 447/2012 of 21 March 2012 supplementing Regulation (EC) No. 1060/2009 of the European Parliament and of the Council on credit rating agencies by laying down regulatory technical standards for the assessment of compliance of credit rating methodologies, OJ L140, 30 May 2012, p. 14.

[36] Commission Delegated Regulation (EU) No. 448/2012 of 21 March 2012 supplementing Regulation (EC) No. 1060/2009 of the European Parliament and of the Council with regard to regulatory technical standards for the presentation of the information that credit rating agencies shall make available in a central repository established by the European Securities and Markets Authority, OJ L140, 30 May 2012, p. 17.

[37] Commission Delegated Regulation (EU) No. 449/2012 of 21 March 2012 supplementing Regulation (EC) No. 1060/2009 of the European Parliament and of the Council with regard to regulatory technical standards on information for registration and certification of credit rating agencies, OJ L140, 30 May 2012, p. 32.

[38] Commission Delegated Regulation (EU) No. 946/2012 of July 2012 supplementing Regulation (EC) No. 1060/2009 of the European Parliament and of the Council with regard to rules of procedure on fines imposed to credit rating agencies by the European Securities and Markets Authority, including rules on the right of defence and temporal provisions, OJ L282, 16 October 2012, p. 23.

[39] Https://www.esma.europa.eu/databases-library/interactive-single-rulebook/crar.

[40] Cf. for further information the Commission's website https://ec.europa.eu/info/sites/info/files/business_economy_euro/banking_and_finance/documents/cra-regulation-equivalence-decisions_en.pdf.

must thus be regarded as a prognosis,[41] this does not hinder the application of Member States' national tort laws to rating situations. They also have a contractual relationship with the issuer in the case of a solicited rating.

II. Scope of Application and Regulatory Aims

1. Foundations

The CRAR constitutes the first specific regulation for rating agencies in Europe. It is directly applicable in the Member States[42] and needs therefore not be implemented into national law. Subsequently, the central provisions of the CRAR will be described in more detail, whilst the general provisions of capital markets law, which are also applicable, will not be presented in detail. It is sufficient to make clear that the distribution of information—especially from the issuer to the rating agency—may constitute a violation of the prohibition to disclose inside information.[43] The rating itself may also be classed as inside information. The issuer will then be confronted with the question whether it is obliged to disclose the rating without delay, as required by Article 17(1) MAR.[44]

16

The Rating Regulation is divided into four parts: (1) Subject matter, scope and definitions; (2) Issuing of credit ratings; (3) Surveillance of credit rating activities; (4) Penalties, committee procedure, reporting, transitional and final provisions. For the sake of clarity, the Rating Regulation further contains two annexes, both of which are part of the regulation and as such directly applicable in the Member States. Annex I on 'Independence and avoidance of conflicts of interest', divided into five parts (A–E), and Annex III with a 'list of infringements' subject to sanctions imposed by ESMA are the most important.

17

2. Aims

The CRAR 'introduces a common regulatory approach in order to enhance the **integrity, transparency, responsibility**, good **governance** and **reliability** of **credit rating** activities, contributing to the quality of credit ratings issued in the Community, thereby contributing to the smooth functioning of the internal market while achieving a high level of consumer and investor protection.'[45]

18

The CRAR does not only list investor protection, but also consumer protection as its regulatory aim.[46] This comes as a surprise considering that, unlike investment firms, rating

19

---

[41] Cf. C. Kumpan and R. Grütze, in: Lehmann and Kumpan (eds.), *European Financial Services Law*, Art. 3 CRAR para. 9; M. Habersack, 02-03 ZHR 169 (2005), 185, 200.
[42] On the legal nature of regulations see R. Veil § 3 para. 15–17.
[43] On the prohibitions under insider law see R. Veil § 14 para. 65 ff.
[44] On the term 'inside information' see R. Veil § 14 para. 19 ff. and on the legal nature of a rating as inside information subject to disclosure obligations see R. Veil § 19 para. 35.
[45] Cf. Art. 1 sentence 1 CRAR.
[46] On this regulatory approach see R. Veil § 2 para. 11.

agencies do not normally communicate directly with individual investors, but rather operate for the capital market as a whole. Whether the approach taken in Article 1 CRAR, especially the reference to investor and consumer protection, implies that the regulatory aim is the protection of individual financial interests if investors remain unclear.

20 The regulation's approach to lay down 'conditions for the issuing of credit ratings and rules on the organisation and conduct of credit rating agencies to promote their independence and the avoidance of conflicts of interest,'[47] indicates that the Member States are not permitted to enact stricter rules. The CRAR is rather to be understood as **fully harmonising legislative act**.

3. Scope of Application

21 The Rating Regulation only applies to rating agencies registered in the European Union. This does not necessarily require the company's headquarters to be in the European Union. It is sufficient for the rating agency to have established a branch in the EU.[48]

22 Any **rating** which has been **disclosed** publicly or **distributed** by subscription falls within the scope of the regulation.[49] The CRAR has, however, exempted a number of cases from its scope of application. These primarily include private credit ratings that are provided exclusively to the person who ordered them, credit scoring systems, credit ratings produced by export credit rating agencies and certain credit ratings produced by central banks.[50]

23 CRAR-II extends some of the Rating Regulation's provisions on conflicts of interest, accuracy and transparency to **rating outlooks**, ie the agency's opinion on the likely prospects of a rating. The reason for this is that outlooks are considered as relevant as the ratings themselves.[51]

4. Concepts and Definitions

24 The CRAR contains various terms that require clarification. Similar to the other European legislative acts, the Rating Regulation provides a number of definitions, such as for the terms 'credit rating', 'credit rating activities' and 'structured finance instrument'. They are to be dealt with in more detail, because these terms determine the area of application of the requirements of the CRAR.

25 A '**credit rating**' is defined as an 'opinion regarding the creditworthiness of an entity, a debt or financial obligation, debt security, preferred share or other financial instrument, or of an issuer of such an [instrument], issued using an established and defined ranking system of rating categories'.[52] The term 'entity' means any legal entity, regardless of its legal nature or the nature of its economic activity.[53]

---

[47] Cf. Art. 1 CRAR.
[48] The CRAR is further relevant with regard to agencies from third countries, see below para. 55 ff.
[49] Art. 2(1) CRAR.
[50] Art. 2(2) CRAR.
[51] Cf. recital 4 COM(2011) 747 final (fn. 12).
[52] Art. 3(1)(a) CRAR.
[53] M. Foerster, in: Habersack et al. (eds.), *Handbuch der Kapitalmarktinformation*, § 24 para. 14, with reference to the English, French and Spanish version of the regulation.

The definition explicitly does not apply to investment recommendations and financial analyses as 26
defined in Article 3(1)(35) MAR,[54] as well as recommendations or proposals for an investment strategy
as defined in Article 3(1)(34) MAR, since these are governed by the rules of conduct of the MAR.[55]
Finally, pursuant to Article 3(2)(b) CRAR, investment research is also excluded from the scope of application of the CRAR, as it is subject to the requirements of the MiFID II regime.[56] What is meant by a
financial analysis and a marketing communication is defined in Article 36(1) Regulation (EU) 2017/565.

A rating is characterised by the fact that an assessment of the creditworthiness of an issuer of secu- 27
rities is made on the basis of information.[57] It can therefore be qualified as an information-based
judgement.[58] The question of whether a rating can be wrong (a 'too good' or 'too bad' rating) is not
yet clear. It becomes particularly relevant with regard to the question whether a rating agency may
be liable to pay damages to an investor or the issuer. This question is, with the exception of Article
35a CRAR, subject to the national law of the Member States.[59]

The term '**credit rating activities**' refers to 'data and information analysis and the evalua- 28
tion, approval, issuing and review of credit ratings'.[60] As most provisions of the CRAR only
apply to agencies, the term '**credit rating agencies**' is also defined in this context, as 'a legal
person whose occupation includes the issuing of credit ratings on a professional basis'.[61]

The CRAR places particular emphasis on '**structured finance instruments**', which were 29
regarded as one of the causes of the financial crisis. A 'structured finance instrument'
means 'a financial instrument or other assets resulting from a securitisation transaction or
scheme'.[62] Some of the CRAR's provisions distinguish between ratings for structured financial instruments and other types of financial instruments. The reason for this is that the
rating of structured financial instruments causes specific problems, not only with regard
to the rating methods employed, for example, but also with regard to the interests of the
market participants involved in the rating procedure.[63]

III. Regulatory Strategies

1. Overview

As a rule, rating agencies receive remuneration from the issuer for the rating they pro- 30
vide (**issuer pays-model**). It is therefore issuers and not investors that pay for ratings.

---

[54] Art. 3(2)(a), (b) CRAR.
[55] M. Foerster, in: Habersack et al. (eds.), *Handbuch der Kapitalmarktinformation*, § 24 para. 15.
[56] M. Foerster, in: Habersack et al. (eds.), *Handbuch der Kapitalmarktinformation*, § 24 para. 15.
[57] C. Kumpan and R. Grütze, in: Lehmann and Kumpan (eds.), *European Financial Services Law*, Art. 3 CRAR para. 9.
[58] M. Foerster, in: Habersack et al. (eds.), *Handbuch der Kapitalmarktinformation*, § 24 para. 19; similar Habersack, 02-03 ZHR (2005), 185, 195 ff.
[59] See para. 77.
[60] Cf. Art. 3(1)(o) CRAR.
[61] Cf. Art. 3(1)(b) CRAR.
[62] Art. 3(1)(l) CRAR. The Regulation (EU) 2017/2402 (SR) referred to by the CRAR defines securitisation as 'a transaction or scheme, whereby the credit risk associated with an exposure or a pool of exposures is tranched, having all of the characteristics' as set out in Art. 2 (1)(a)-(d).
[63] See also below para. 41, 52.

The European legislature accepted this concept[64] and introduced a number of disclosure obligations rather than a prohibition in order to achieve the regulatory aims mentioned above.[65] This is to achieve full effectiveness of the reputational market mechanisms. At the same time, these measures are to enable new market participants to enter the market. The obligations can be divided into five categories. Firstly, the CRAR subjects credit ratings to certain conditions and introduces rules on the organisation and conduct of credit rating agencies, which promote their independence and prevent conflicts of interest.[66] The CRAR further aims to achieve an improved quality of the ratings available on the market. Additionally, it establishes transparency requirements and provides for a registration requirement for all credit rating agencies. Finally, the CRAR regulates the problem that financial market regulation often refers to ratings, so that ratings gain enormous importance (so-called over-reliance).

2. Avoidance of Conflicts of Interest

(a) Independence of Credit Rating Agencies

31   Conflicts of interest of intermediaries are one of the most pressing problems of capital market regulation.[67] The European legislature has addressed this problem by providing a number of rules of conduct. The provisions are built around a provision of a principles-based nature, requiring rating agencies to 'take all necessary steps to ensure that the **issuing of a credit rating is not affected** by any existing or potential **conflict of interest** or business relationship involving the credit rating agency issuing the credit rating, its managers, rating analysts, employees, any other natural person whose services are placed at the disposal or under the control of the credit rating agency, or any person directly or indirectly linked to it by control'.[68] Compliance with this rule is ensured by the organisational and operational requirements rating agencies must fulfil, which are listed in Annex I sections A and B.[69] This approach is the result of the occurrences during the financial crisis, when rating agencies orientated themselves towards the issuers instead of fulfilling their function as a neutral third party.[70]

32   The organisational requirements provided for in Annex I Section A are similar to those of banking regulation and the regulation of investment firms.[71] It is a principle-based regulation. The rules are characterised by the fact that a regulatory objective is specified ('business interest does not impair the independence or accuracy of the credit rating activities') and the measures a rating agency must take to achieve the objectives ('credit rating agency shall be organised in a way')[72] are only specified in abstract terms.[73] This regulatory strategy

---

[64] Cf. M. Lerch, 10 BKR (2010), 402, 406; G. Tönningsen, 6 ZBB (2011), 460, 466.
[65] Recital 10 CRAR-I; confirmed by recital 7 and 7a CRAR-III.
[66] Art. 1 CRAR.
[67] Cf. P. Leyens, 11 J. Corp. L. Stud. (2011), 33, 59–63; T. Wittenberg, 16 EBOR (2015), 669, 677, 688–692.
[68] Art. 6(1) CRAR.
[69] Art. 6(2) CRAR.
[70] CESR, CESR's Second Report to the European Commission on the compliance of credit rating agencies with the IOSCO Code and the role of credit rating agencies in structured finance, May 2008, CESR/08-277, para. 96.
[71] On the organizational requirements for investment firms M. Wundenberg § 33 para. 20 ff.
[72] Cf. Annex I Section A para. 2 CRAR.
[73] See in more detail M. Wundenberg, § 33 para. 21.

is best suited to take into account that rating agencies are affected by conflicts of interest in different ways. For some CRAs, their business model poses a major risk that they do not carry out their rating activities independently. This is less the case for other agencies. The principle-based regulation allows each agency to set up a risk-adequate organisation. Nevertheless, legislature cannot avoid specifying the basic principle in more detail. Section A of the CRAR therefore contains requirements for **governance** (especially for the members of the management and supervisory bodies) and **compliance**.

A rating agency is obliged to establish and maintain a permanent and effective **compliance function** which operates independently. The compliance function is required to monitor and report on compliance of the credit rating agency and its employees with the credit rating agency's obligations.[74] It does not necessarily have to be a separate department. In the case of a small rating agency, it may be sufficient for an employee to take over the compliance function. 33

In order to enable the compliance function to discharge its responsibilities properly and independently, the respective credit rating agency must ensure that the compliance function has the necessary authority, resources, expertise and access to all relevant information. The rating agency must further appoint a **compliance officer** responsible for the compliance function. The compliance officer must ensure that any conflicts of interest relating to the persons placed at the disposal of the compliance function are properly identified and eliminated. It must provide regular reports to senior management and the independent members of the administrative or supervisory board on his work.[75] The compliance requirements listed in the CRAR correspond with those of the MiFID II.[76] 34

It is doubtful what is meant by a compliance function acting independently. One could understand the regulatory requirement to mean that the management of the rating agency has no right to issue instructions to the compliance function, in particular to the compliance officer. This would, however, be in contradiction to corporate law, which assumes that the management has the right to issue instructions to the employees of the company. The preferred interpretation is therefore that independence only means that the compliance function and its representative must be financially independent and must be granted rights so that they can perform their duties within the company.[77] 35

The CRAR further contains requirements on the **internal control** of a credit rating agency: A credit rating agency shall have sound administrative and accounting procedures, internal control mechanisms, effective procedures for risk assessment, and effective control and safeguard arrangements for information processing system.[78] 36

The operational requirements laid down in section B provide operational requirements to avoid conflicts of interest: 'A credit rating agency shall identify, eliminate, or manage and disclose, clearly and prominently, any actual or potential conflicts of interest that may influence the analyses and judgments of its rating analysts, employees, or any other natural person whose services are placed at the disposal or under the control of the credit rating agency and who are directly involved in credit rating activities and persons approving credit ratings and rating outlooks.'[79] This principle is put into more concrete terms by numerous 37

---

[74] Annex I sec. A para. 5 CRAR.
[75] Cf. Annex I sec. A para. 6 CRAR.
[76] See in more detail M. Wundenberg § 33 para. 37 ff.
[77] Cf. Annex I sec. A para. 6 CRAR.
[78] Annex I sec. A para. 4 CRAR.
[79] Annex I sec. B para. 1 CRAR.

requirements, such as the obligation to keep records and the prohibition to provide consultancy or advisory services to the rated entity. In addition, the CRAR requires a credit rating agency to design its reporting and communication channels to ensure the independence of its rating analysts and employees. Ensuring the independence of rating agencies can be classified as a key obligation for rating agencies.[80]

38   In particular, the **prohibition** to provide certain consultancy or **advisory services**[81] is a reaction to grievances that led to the financial crisis. Rating agencies had advised companies how to structure complex financial instruments. In order to prevent a loss of business the rating agencies had then supplied the financial products with ratings or had issued an AAA rating, although this rating was not objectively justifiable as the products did not provide the necessary security against credit default risks.[82] An instant-messenger communication by Standard & Poor's, for example, contained the following announcement: 'We rate every deal. It could be structured by cows and we would rate it.'[83]

39   The reforms in 2013 (CRAR-III) introduced a **rotation mechanism** for certain types of ratings. An issuer can generally not be bound to a certain rating agency for more than four years for ratings of *re-securitisations*'.[84] Conflicts of interest are to be prevented through the future **shareholding structure** of the agencies, Article 6a CRAR laying down certain restrictions for persons with regard to rating agencies that hold 5% or more of the capital or voting rights.[85] For example, they may not hold 5% or more of the capital of another credit rating agency or be a member of the administrative or supervisory board of another credit rating agency. The massive restrictions on the freedom of investment are justified by the serious consequences of conflicts of interest of rating agencies. The CRAR **prohibits ratings** entirely under **certain circumstances**, ie if the agency stands in a close relationship to the rated company. Such a relationship is to be assumed, for example, if the credit rating agency or an employee directly or indirectly owns financial instruments of the rated entity or if a member of the credit rating agency simultaneously holds a seat on the administrative or supervisory board of the rated entity. If a credit rating already exists, these circumstances obligate the credit rating agency to disclose immediately that the credit rating is potentially affected by this fact.[86]

40   To enable the supervisory authority to verify a rating, the rating agencies are required to keep records on the identity of the rating analysts participating in the determination of the credit rating and the methods employed for the rating information as to whether the credit rating was solicited or unsolicited, and the date on which the credit rating action was taken. The records must be stored on the premises of the registered credit rating agency for at least five years.[87]

---

[80] U. Schroeter, *Ratings*, 734.
[81] Annex I sec. B para. 4, 5 CRAR.
[82] This conflict of interests was already mentioned in CESR, CESR's Second Report to the European Commission on the compliance of credit rating agencies with the IOSCO Code and the role of credit rating agencies in structured finance, May 2008, CESR/08–277, para. 96.
[83] US Senate, Exhibits, Hearing on Wall Street and the Financial Crisis: The Role of Credit Rating Agencies, 23 April 2010, Exhibit 30a, p. 132.
[84] Art. 6b CRAR.
[85] Art. 6a CRAR.
[86] Annex I sec. B para. 3 CRAR.
[87] Annex I sec. B para. 7 CRAR.

(b) Persons Involved in the Rating Procedure

The CRAR aims to prevent persons involved in the rating procedures from being misguided by monetary incentives. The **compensation** and evaluation of performance of these individuals **may not** therefore be **contingent** to the amount of **revenue** that the **credit rating agency** derives **from** the **rated entities** or related third parties.[88] These persons are therefore also prohibited from initiating or participating in negotiations regarding fees or payments with any rated entity.[89] The large variety of structured financial instruments entails the problem that issuers will have a number of subsequent transactions to offer to the rating agencies. Unlike a regular rating, this can give the credit rating agency the incentive to award a positive rating in order to be awarded the subsequent rating deals.[90]

41

This pressure on the rating agencies to submit positive ratings becomes apparent in an e-mail of August 2004 by Standard & Poor's: 'We just lost a huge Mizuho RMBS deal to Moody's due to a huge difference in the required credit support level. [...] Losing one or even several deals due to criteria issues [...] is so significant it may have an impact in the future deals.'[91]

42

Rating agencies are further required to establish an appropriate so-called '**gradual rotation mechanism**' with regard to the rating analysts and persons approving credit ratings, in order to prevent any close personal ties developing between the individual rating analysts and the rated entity.[92] The latest Commission proposal combines this mechanism to the agency rotation mechanism in order to prevent a lead analyst from taking client files when switching to another agency.[93]

43

Behavioural finance[94] additionally purports that a rotation mechanism can also prevent rating from being distorted without intent, simply because the analyst has gained a so-called *inside view*. An *inside view* is the tendency no longer to place problems into general categories, being fixated on the specific case. Insiders run the risk of overestimating the chances of success of the project by ignoring the statistical success rate.[95] According to this theory, a rating analyst may therefore be in danger of overrating a company simply because it has spent so much time assessing it. The problems associated with *inside views* thus justify a gradual rotation mechanism.

44

3. Improvement of the Quality of Ratings

After the financial crisis, critics of rating agencies particularly pointed out the deficiencies in the rating methods, ie ratings not being adjusted to the altered market situation soon enough.[96] Additionally, the models applied for the compositions of ratings were said not to adequately reflect the risks of newly structured financial products.

45

---

[88] Art. 7(5) CRAR.
[89] Art. 7(2) CRAR.
[90] CESR's Second Report to the European Commission on the compliance of credit rating agencies with the IOSCO Code and The role of credit rating agencies in structured finance, CESR/08-277, Mai 2008, CESR/08–277 para. 99.
[91] US Senate Hearing, Exhibit 2 (fn. 83), p. 44.
[92] Art. 7(4) CRAR.
[93] COM (2011) 747 final (fn. 12), p. 9.
[94] See R. Veil § 6 para. 20 ff.
[95] Cf. L. Teigelack, *Finanzanalysen und Behavioral Finance*, 96–97.
[96] Cf. recital 10 CRAR.

46   The CRAR took this criticism into account and introduced new provisions on the methods, models and general assumptions on which a rating is based, aiming to improve the quality of ratings available on the market. As investors often rely solely on ratings, it must be ensured that these provide as much information as possible.[97] A credit rating agency must therefore use '**rating methodologies** that are **rigorous, systematic, continuous** and subject to validation based on historical experience, including back-testing'.[98] The CRAR thereby wants to prevent rating methods from being applied for products to which they are not suited due to a lack of experience with such products in the past.[99]

47   ESMA had to decide on the interpretation of Article 8(3) CRAR in the case of Scope Ratings GmbH. ESMA stated the following facts: 'The 2015 Covered Bond Methodology was applied by Scope Ratings GmbH for issuing ratings to 17 covered bond programmes, which amounted to a total of 622 ratings. The cover pool was only analysed in two of these covered bond programmes. On the contrary, the ratings issued in September and November 2015 did not comprise the type of analysis of the cover pool which was foreseen by the 2015 Covered Bond Methodology.'[100] According to ESMA, Article 8(3) CRAR requires that a rating agency not only applies a systematic methodology but also applies it systematically, ie to all covered bonds. Article 5(1) of the Delegated Regulation EU No. 447/2012 supports this interpretation: 'A credit rating agency shall use a credit rating methodology and its associated analytical models, key credit rating assumptions and criteria that are applied systematically in the formulation of all credit ratings in a given asset class or market segment unless there is an objective reason for diverging from it.'[101]

48   Credit rating agencies are further obliged to disclose the methodologies, models and key rating assumptions used and to monitor and review their credit ratings and methodologies on an ongoing basis and at least annually.[102] If the methods, models or general assumptions change, the agency must take certain actions in order to ensure that the rating is adapted as soon as possible. The credit rating agency must therefore immediately disclose the likely scope of credit ratings to be affected, review the affected credit ratings as soon as possible and no later than six months after the change, place the ratings under observation in the meantime and re-rate all credit ratings affected by such changes.[103]

49   In the past, delays in adapting the rating were primarily caused by lack of staff and resources and the fear of displeasing investment banks and investors by downgrading their products.[104] Moody's explicitly admitted to re-rating only selectively: 'Moody's does not re-evaluate every outstanding affected rating. [...] This decision to selectively review certain ratings is made due to resource constraints.' Standard & Poor's adopted a similar approach: '[W]e don't have the model or resource capacity to do so, nor do we all believe that even if we did have the capability, it would be the responsible thing to do to the market.'[105]

---

[97] COM (2008) 704 final (fn. 28), p. 9.
[98] Art. 8(3) CRAR.
[99] Cf. US Senate Hearing (fn. 83), p. 7.
[100] ESMA, Decision of the Board of Supervisors to adopt supervisory measures and impose fines in respect of infringements committed by Scope Ratings GmbH (Scope), ESMA41-35677, Decision 2020/1, 28 May 2020, para. 10.
[101] The Board of Appeal of the ESAs dismissed Scope Ratings GmbH's appeal in decision 2020-D-03 of 28.12.2020.
[102] Art. 8(1), (5) CRAR. Pursuant to recital 23 CRAR-I credit rating agencies must review credit ratings at least annually.
[103] Art. 8(6) CRAR.
[104] US Senate Hearing (fn. 83), p. 8–9.
[105] US Senate Hearing, Exhibit 1e (fn. 83), p. 33–34.

4. Disclosure Obligations

(a) Disclosure and Presentation of Credit Ratings

The provisions on the disclosure and presentation of credit ratings aim to protect investors from misunderstanding the relevance of a rating.[106] The financial crisis has revealed that investors have tended to rely blindly on the results of ratings, especially where the complexity of structured financial instruments allowed them no assessment of their own.[107] Rating agencies are now obliged to adhere to the requirements listed in Annex I Section D CRAR, which sets out general and specific rules for ratings of structured finance instruments and for sovereign ratings.[108]   50

First, it is essential that ratings and rating outlooks clearly state the **name** and **function** of the **lead rating analyst** for a particular rating activity and the name and position of the person primarily responsible for approving the credit rating or rating outlook.[109] Furthermore, a rating agency must disclose sources and methodology.[110] Disclosure of **material sources** and **any communication** with the **issuer** should also help to ensure that conflicts of interest do not become relevant. Of particular interest to investors is that the methodology used must also be disclosed and the assumptions, parameters, limitations and uncertainties associated with the methodologies used in ratings must be explained.[111] This makes it easier for investors to understand whether a rating has been properly produced. Literature does, however, criticise the fact that rating agencies are not obliged to disclose the confidential information that the issuer has disclosed to them during the rating process.[112]   51

When a credit rating agency issues a credit rating for a **structured finance instrument**, it must ensure with an additional symbol that the rating category attributed to the structured finance instrument can be clearly distinguished from rating categories used for any other entities, financial instruments or financial obligations.[113] The credit rating agency is further obliged to disclose all credit ratings, as well as any decision to discontinue a credit rating in a timely manner.[114]   52

Finally, the CRAR further contains additional disclosure obligations for **unsolicited credit ratings**.[115] A rating agency must disclose its policies and procedures for unsolicited ratings. It must also state whether the rated company was involved in the rating process.   53

(b) Transparency Report

A credit rating agency is obliged to publish certain information on an annual basis, no later than three months after the end of each financial year by way of a transparency report as   54

---

[106] Seen critically by M. Lerch, 10 BKR (2010), 402, 406.
[107] CESR/08–277, May 2008, (fn. 70), para. 103, 105.
[108] Art. 10(2) CRAR.
[109] Annex I sec. D No. 1 para. 2 lit. b), 2a CRAR.
[110] Annex I sec. D No. 1 para. 2 CRAR.
[111] Annex I sec. D No. 1 para. 2 lit b), 2a CRAR.
[112] U. Schroeter, *Ratings*, 740.
[113] Art. 10(3) CRAR; cf. T. Möllers, 18 JZ (2009), 861, 868–869.
[114] Art. 10(1) CRAR.
[115] Art. 10(4), (5) CRAR.

described in Annex I Section E(III). This report must, for example, contain information on the agency's rotation policy, statistics on the internal allocation of its staff to ratings and financial information on the revenue of the credit rating agency. The report must remain available on the website of the agency for at least five years.[116]

5. Registration

55 If a credit rating agency is a legal person established in the EU, Article 14(1) CRAR requires it to apply for registration for the purposes of Article 2(1). **Registration** is thus a **prerequisite** for rating agencies to be permitted to **issue ratings** in the EU, disclose them publicly or distribute them by subscription.[117] The registration is carried out by **ESMA**. **Agencies** from **third countries** are not subject to the registration obligation. The European legislature does not have the power to introduce such a general registration obligation for agencies incorporated outside the EU, although a general applicability of the CRARS's provisions appears desirable. In order to achieve this, a regulatory 'trick' was necessary: credit institutions, investment firms and other firms listed in Article 4(1) CRAR are only permitted to use credit ratings for supervisory purposes if they are issued by credit rating agencies with their legal seat in the EU and registered in accordance with the CRAR.[118] Agencies from third countries are therefore indirectly 'forced' to register in the European Union if they wish to offer their services on the internal market.[119] The CRAR further imposes the obligation on an issuer to include information in a securities prospectus on whether or not a credit rating was issued by a credit rating agency established in the Community and registered under the CRAR.[120]

56 The application for registration must be submitted to ESMA in any of the official languages of the institutions of the Union.[121] ESMA then has 20 working days to assess whether the application is complete.[122] Within a further 45 working days, ESMA must then examine the application for registration of the credit rating agency. The examination period may be extended by 15 working days.[123] At the end of the (extended) examination period ESMA must adopt a fully reasoned decision to register or refuse registration which takes effect on the fifth working day following its decision.[124] A regularly updated list of all the credit rating agencies registered in accordance with the regulation can be found on ESMA's website.[125] In October 2021 the list comprised 48 rating agencies.

---

[116] Art. 12 CRAR; requirements are tightened under the Commission proposal, cf. COM(2011) 747 final, (fn. 17), p. 9.
[117] Art. 14(2) CRAR.
[118] Art. 4(1) CRAR.
[119] However, ratings from third countries can be used for supervisory means, provided they were compiled under similarly strict conditions as laid down in the CRAR. Cf. recital 13 and Art. 4(3) CRAR. See in more detail G. Deipenbrock, 9 RIW (2010), 612, 614–615.
[120] Recital 5 and Art. 4(1) CRAR.
[121] Art. 15(1), (3) CRAR.
[122] Art. 15(4) CRAR.
[123] Art. 16(1), (2) CRAR.
[124] Art. 16(3), (4) CRAR.
[125] Art. 18(3) CRAR; available at: www.esma.europa.eu/supervision/credit-rating-agencies/risk.

Once a rating agency is registered, it can only lose this registration if ESMA withdraws it. ESMA can take this action if the credit rating agency waives the registration, has provided no credit ratings for the preceding six months, has obtained the registration by making false statements or by any other irregular means, no longer meets the conditions under which it was registered, or has continually and seriously infringed upon the regulation's provisions on rating activities.[126] A revocation by ESMA enters into force immediately. The credit rating may, however, continue to be used during a transitional period of ten working days from the date of ESMA's decision if there are credit ratings of the same financial instrument or entity issued by other credit rating agencies or three months if no other ratings of the financial instrument or entity exist.[127] The two different transitional periods are to ensure that the market is not without access to information.[128] If other ratings exist, investors can refer to other sources and a long transitional period is not necessary.

6. The Problem of Over-Reliance

The CRAR-III further addressed the over-reliance on ratings and problems related to 'so-called' sovereign ratings, ie ratings of a state, a regional or local authority or of a debt instrument of one of these issuers.[129] The European legislature identified over-reliance—or 'mechanistical' reliance—by certain financial institutions as a substantial problem. One of the objectives of the last reform of the CRAR in 2013 was therefore to reduce over-reliance on credit ratings by financial institutions and other market participants. Similar to the regulation in the United States, financial institutions should avoid entering into contracts where they solely or mechanistically rely on credit ratings and should avoid using them in contracts as the only parameter to assess the creditworthiness of investments or to decide whether to invest or divest.[130] To this end, several provisions were introduced into European law. Firstly, **financial institutions** and other entities are to **make** their **own credit risk assessment** and are not to solely or mechanically rely on credit ratings for assessing creditworthiness of an entity or financial instrument. NCAs in charge of supervising financial institutions are to monitor the adequacy of their credit risk assessment processes, assess the use of contractual references to credit ratings and encourage the financial institutions to mitigate the impact of such references, with a view to reducing sole and mechanistic reliance on credit ratings.[131]

Secondly, the Commission was required to review whether references to credit ratings in European law trigger or have the potential to trigger sole or mechanistic reliance on credit ratings by the competent authorities, entities (credit institutions etc.) or other financial market participants with to the aim of deleting all references to credit ratings in European law for regulatory purposes by 1 January 2020, provided that appropriate alternatives to credit risk assessment have been identified and implemented.[132] On 6 February 2014, the

---

[126] Art. 20(1)(a)–(d) CRAR.
[127] Art. 20(3), 24(4)(a), (b) CRAR.
[128] COM (2008) 704 final, (fn. 28), p. 3.
[129] The term is defined in Art. 3(1)(v) CRAR.
[130] Cf. Art. 5a(1) CRAR.
[131] Cf. Art. 5a(2) CRAR.
[132] Cf. Art. 5c CRAR.

ESAs published their 'Final Report on mechanistic references to credit ratings in the ESAs' guidelines and recommendations'. The Report defines the terms 'sole and mechanistic reliance' as follows: 'It is considered that there is sole or mechanistic reliance on credit ratings (or credit rating outlooks) when an action or omission is the consequence of any type of rule based on credit ratings (or credit rating outlooks) without any discretion.'[133]

60 However, since **no adequate substitutes for ratings** exist, it appears unlikely that the European legislature removes references to credit ratings.[134] European financial markets law is still based on the assumption that credit rating agencies are best placed to assess the creditworthiness of issuers. This is mainly due to the fact that rating agencies have the necessary expertise. In addition, ratings are easy to comprehend, made available to the public free of charge and are regularly updated and adjusted.[135] This explains the difficulties to develop alternatives to credit ratings and reduce over-reliance. In particular, internal ratings are generally not adequate substitute for ratings. Firstly, it is doubtful whether persons evaluating the creditworthiness of issuers or financial instruments have the relevant expertise. Secondly, an internal rating always gives rise to massive conflicts of interests.

61 In contrast, systemic risks deriving from investment policies[136] and contractual references might be countered by different approaches. As for investment policies, regulators should make clear that managers have to make their own investment decisions; a rating is only one aspect amongst many others to be taken into account by the manager. With regard to contractual references, disclosure obligations could be strengthened.

IV. Supervision and Sanctions

1. Foundations

62 It was not until the outset of the financial crisis that the European legislature replaced the IOSCO Codes' self-regulatory approach with supervision of rating agencies by public authorities. The supervision is meanwhile being carried out solely by ESMA. The NCAs are now only responsible for supervising that the credit institutions only make use of ratings by registered agencies for regulatory purposes,[137] whilst **ESMA is responsible** for all

---

[133] EBA, EIOPA and ESMA, Final Report on mechanistic references to credit ratings in the ESAs' guidelines and recommendations, 6 February 2014, JC 2014 004, para. 26.

[134] Cf. also ESMA, Technical Advice on reducing sole and mechanistic reliance on external credit rating, 30 September 2015, ESMA/2015/1471, para 131: 'The process to reduce reliance on ratings in a European context can therefore be said to be at an early stage, with some work done on agreeing high level principles and goals but more to be done in terms of mitigating mechanistic reliance and proposing alternatives'.

[135] Cf. U. Schroeter, *Ratings*, 481–484.

[136] Contractual references to credit ratings are widely used by market participants. On the one hand, they are provided in investment guidelines/policies of institutional investors. In order to obtain as high a return as possible and as a consequence a higher remuneration, fund managers might take inappropriate risks. The purpose of contractual references is therefore to limit the fund manager's investment discretion. Typically, investment policies require an 'investment-grade' as minimum rating; other degrees of rating can hardly be observed. Once this threshold is reached, fund managers must sell the bonds or other financial instruments of the respective issuer. The consequences of such forced sales are severe: Massive negative exchange rates have been empirically proven.

[137] Art. 25a(1) CRAR.

other aspects of the **supervision** of **rating agencies**—granting it more general and extensive powers than in most other areas of capital markets law.[138] European supervision otherwise only exists for trade repositories and securitisation registers.

ESMA is however, not permitted to influence the content of a rating.[139] Measures taken by ESMA may be addressed to rating agencies, any persons involved in rating activities, third parties to whom the credit rating agencies have outsourced certain functions or activities, the rated issuers and any third parties related to them, or any person related or connected to credit rating agencies or credit rating activities. ESMA may require any of these persons to provide all the information necessary in order for the authority to carry out its duties.[140] Officials and other persons authorised by ESMA are further empowered to (a) examine any records, data, procedures and any other material relevant to the execution of their tasks; (b) take or obtain certified copies of or extracts from such records, data, procedures and other material; (c) request oral or written explanations on facts or documents related to the subject matter and purpose of the inspection; (d) interview any other natural or legal person; (e) request records of telephone and data traffic.[141]

ESMA is also permitted to conduct all necessary onsite inspections.[142] The individuals conducting the inspections act on the basis of a special power of attorney issued by ESMA after notifying the competent national authority of the affected Member State.[143] ESMA may impose penalties in order to compel a person to submit to an onsite inspection.[144]

2. Procedure

The supervisory measures laid down in the Rating Regulation are subject to detailed procedural rules which also require ESMA's Board of Supervisors (BoS) to give the persons subject to the proceedings the opportunity to be heard.[145] If ESMA finds that there are serious indications of the possible existence of facts liable to constitute an infringement of the Rating Regulation it is obliged to appoint an independent investigating officer.[146] The investigating officer must then investigate the alleged infringements and submit a complete file with his findings to ESMA's BoS,[147] notifying the persons subject to investigation of this process.[148]

The BoS must then determine whether the respective person actually committed an infringement of the provisions of the Rating Regulation on the basis of the information

---

[138] C. Lesquene-Roth and A. van Wayenberge, in: Chiti and Vesperini (eds.), *The Administrative Architecture of Financial Integration*, 243, 263:'ESMA is now a key actor of the sector'.
[139] Art. 23 CRAR.
[140] Art. 23a(1) CRAR.
[141] Art. 23b(1) CRAR.
[142] Art. 23c(1) CRAR.
[143] Art. 23c(2), (4) CRAR.
[144] Art. 36b CRAR.
[145] Art. 25 CRAR.
[146] Art. 23e(1) CRAR.
[147] Art. 23e(2) CRAR.
[148] Art. 23e(4) CRAR.

submitted by the investigating officer. Should this be the case the BoS will impose a supervisory measure.[149] The wording of Article 24(1) Rating Regulation indicates that the BoS is not permitted to abstain from imposing a supervisory measure. It is rather obliged to impose at least one of the measures listed and is also permitted to take more than one decision.[150] If the rating agency has breached one of the regulation's provisions intentionally or negligently, the BoS will impose a fine.[151] This decision is also not at the discretion of the authority but rather the inevitable consequence of an infringement.

3. Administrative Measures and Sanctions

67 ESMA has the competence to impose administrative measures and sanctions. Annex III CRAR takes account of the constitutional principle common in some Member States that prohibits provisions interfering with fundamental rights from being formulated vaguely. It explicitly lists certain obligations, the infringement of which allows ESMA to impose administrative measures and fines. The list distinguishes between infringements related to conflicts of interest, organisational or operational requirements, infringements related to obstacles to the supervisory activities and infringements related to disclosure provisions.

68 If ESMA finds that a rating agency has committed an infringement of an obligation listed in Annex III, it can take one or more of the following decisions:

(a) withdraw the registration of the credit rating agency;
(b) temporarily prohibit the credit rating agency from issuing credit ratings with effect throughout the European Union, until the infringement has been brought to an end;
(c) suspend the use of the credit ratings issued by the credit rating agency for regulatory purposes with effect throughout the Union, until the infringement has been brought to an end;
(d) require the credit rating agency to bring the infringement to an end;
(e) issue public notices.[152]

69 The BoS shall consider the nature and gravity of the violation on the basis of certain criteria. These include, but are not limited to, the duration and frequency of the violation and whether the violation was committed intentionally or negligently.[153] According to the legislature, the withdrawal of registration is the 'last resort' if a credit rating agency has seriously or repeatedly violated the provisions of the CRAR.[154]

70 Pursuant to Article 36a CRAR, ESMA may impose a **maximum fine of € 750,000** for infringements of the obligations listed in Annex III. The fines must be proportionate to the seriousness of the infringement. The fines are divided into different categories with specific limits applying to each category. ESMA applies a two-stage procedure in order to determine the height of a fine, firstly determining a basic amount at which the fine should be set before

---

[149] Art. 23e(5) CRAR.
[150] Art. 24(1) CRAR.
[151] Art. 36a(1) CRAR.
[152] Art. 24(1)(a)–(e) CRAR.
[153] Cf. Art. 24(2) CRAR.
[154] Cf. recital 25 sentence 1 CRAR-II.

adapting this with the help of certain aggravating or mitigating factors. The basic amount is determined on the basis of the annual turnover in the preceding business year.

> *Examples*: a) In the case of **Scope Ratings** GmbH (see para. 46), ESMA imposed a fine of € 640,000 for several legal infringements. b) On 21 July 2016, ESMA imposed a fine of € 1.38 million on **Fitch Ratings** Limited (Fitch) for a series of negligent breaches of the CRA-Regulation, publishing the decision of the ESMA Board of Supervisors BoS and a Public Notice in relation to this action.[155] One of the findings of the BoS was that Fitch did not meet the requirement set out in the CRA Regulation that a CRA must, at least 12 hours prior to its publication of a credit rating for a rated entity, inform the entity of the rating and of the principal grounds on which the rating is based, Fitch thus having committed the infringement specified at Annex III, Section III, point 7 of the CRA Regulation.

71

4. Criminal Measures

The CRAR does not contain any criminal law measures for breaches of the CRAR's provisions. The Member States may therefore decide independently whether they want to provide criminal sanctions. The prosecution of these crimes is then a matter for the respective Member State, ESMA not having any powers in this respect.[156]

72

V. Private Enforcement

1. Relevance

The liability of credit rating agencies towards issuers and investors was for a long time not of any particular practical relevance. This changed in the course of the financial crisis, the most spectacular known case since then certainly being the United States Ministry of Justice's lawsuit against Standard & Poor's from 2013 over a total amount of US$ 5 billion, based on the allegation of an over-positive assessment of structured finance products. Investors also filed lawsuits against the large rating agencies in the United States. In total, Standard & Poor's and Moody's together with the investment bank Morgan Stanley are assumed to have paid a total settlement sum of about US$ 225 million to the respective investors.

73

2. National Laws

A rating agency can be liable for damages towards the **issuer**. This depends on whether the rating agency was acting on behalf of the issuer (solicited rating) or without any such order from the issuer (unsolicited rating). In the first case, the issuer can claim damages or an injunction on a contractual basis. Without a contract, the issuer may be able to claim

74

---

[155] Cf. ESMA, Public Note, 21 July 2016, ESMA/2016/1159.
[156] Art. 24(2) CRAR.

75 In case of a **solicited rating**, there is a contractual relationship between the rating agency and the issuer, so that contractual claims for damages and injunctive relief may exist in the event of breaches of duties. Furthermore, the issuer may withdraw from the contract, demand a reduction in the compensation or claim damages. The rules of the CRAR can be taken into account to assess which duties of care exist. This could be considered, for example, for the question of how extensive the information basis for a rating should be. The damage that an issuer suffers can consist in particular in higher capital costs due to a rating that is too poor.

76 In case of an **unsolicited rating**, only claims of damages under tort law are conceivable. Furthermore, an issuer may have claims for injunctive relief against the rating agency.

77 Rating agencies may also be held liable by **investors** who relied on the rating when making their investment decision. There will generally be no contractual relationship in this regard, restricting possible claims to a tort law basis.

78 A central problem of all liability regimes concerns the question under which conditions a rating can be incorrect. As a starting point, it will have to be acknowledged that a rating is an opinion about the solvency of an issuer (see para. 26).[157] However, this does not exclude civil liability. Even if a rating agency has discretion in the assessment of the creditworthiness of an issuer,[158] a rating may be incorrect if it is unreasonable, ie if a rating agency draws conclusions on the basis of the available information that are not methodologically plausible or if the rating was issued on the basis of insufficient or incorrect information.

3. Liability under European Law

79 When it was adopted in 2009, the CRAR did not contain any provisions on liability under private law towards issuers or investors. At that time, the European legislature left it to the Member States to regulate this issue.[159] Only one year later, however, the European Commission raised the question of whether a uniform civil liability regime under European law was desirable.[160] The European legislature implemented the civil liability in Union law in 2013 with the CRAR-III.

80 The European legislature argued that ratings would have a considerable influence on investment decisions and on the financial attractiveness of an issuer.[161] The rating agencies would therefore have a special obligation towards investors and issuers. If there were no contractual relationship between the rating agency and the investor or, in the case of an unsolicited rating, an issuer, they would not always be able to hold the agency responsible. But even in the case of a solicited rating, an issuer could have difficulties in enforcing the civil liability

---

[157] This is also reflected in the regulatory definition: 'credit rating', Art. 3(1)(a) CRAR.
[158] M. Foerster, in: Habersack et al. (eds.), *Handbuch Kapitalmarktinformation*, § 24 para. 20.
[159] Recital 69 CRAR-I.
[160] Public Consultation on Credit Rating Agencies, 5.11.2010, p. 24, available at https://ec.europa.eu/finance/consultations/2010/cra/ docs/cpaper_en.pdf.
[161] Recital 24 CRAR-II.

§ 27   Rating Agencies   543

of a rating agency. Thus, the CRAR-III introduced a civil liability framework based on the reasoning that ratings can have a substantial effect on investment decisions.

According to Article 35a CRAR, investors or issuers may claim damages from a rating agency if the rating agency has committed, intentionally or with gross negligence, any of the infringements listed in Annex III and this had an impact on the credit rating. This provision assigns the burden of proof for a violation of law and the effect of the violation on the published rating to the investor. However, the national courts should take into account that an investor and an issuer do not have access to the relevant information.[162] 81

> The first prerequisite for a claim for damages is that the credit rating agency has committed one of the infringements listed in Annex III. Annex III distinguishes between (i) breaches related to conflicts of interest, organisational or operational requirements, (ii) breaches related to supervisory activities and (iii) breaches related to disclosure requirements. It follows that incorrect rating methods and practices also constitute a breach of duty.[163] As a large number of supervisory duties are subject to liability for damages, Article 35a CRAR aims not only to provide for compensation, but also has a preventive function.[164] 82

> Furthermore, an infringement must have had an 'impact on a rating'. This means that a rating must be incorrect, which has to be assessed from an *ex ante* point of view. Thus, the rating must have been deficient when it was issued or published.[165] The violation must also be the causal factor for the incorrect rating. This is hardly conceivable for some infringements listed in Annex III.[166] 83

A liability under Article 35 CRAR further requires that the investor reasonably relied on the rating for a decision to invest into, hold onto or divest from a financial instrument covered by the rating. There is therefore no liability if the rating agency assesses the creditworthiness of an *issuer*.[167] Under Article 35a CRAR, an investor is only protected with regard to the rating of a *financial instrument*. Proof of the impact of the rating on the transaction decision must be provided by the investor. The proposal by the Commission contained a reversal of the burden of proof to the advantage of the investor. This has not been implemented in the legislative process. Article 35a(2) CRAR states that it is the responsibility of the investor to provide accurate and detailed information showing that the credit rating agency has infringed the CRAR and that this infringement has had an impact on the credit rating issued. The legislator was well aware of the problem of the burden of proof. Article 35a(2) CRAR further stipulates: 'What constitutes accurate and detailed information shall be assessed by the competent national court, taking into consideration that the investor or issuer may not have access to information which is purely within the sphere of the credit rating agency.'[168] 84

The introduction of a civil law liability for rating agencies was a considerable challenge for the European legislature, as there is no European concept of civil law liability into which the 85

---

[162] Cf. Art. 35a(4) CRAR.
[163] Annex III sec. 1 para. 42-49 CRAR-III; V. Wimmer, *Auswirkungen des Art. 35a der Verordnung (EU) Nr. 462/2017*, 140–145.
[164] U. Schroeter, *Ratings*, 841; V. Wimmer, *Auswirkungen des Art. 35a der Verordnung (EU) Nr. 462/2017*, 131.
[165] U. Schroeter, *Ratings*, 797.
[166] V. Wimmer, *Auswirkungen des Art. 35a der Verordnung (EU) Nr. 462/2017*, 153.
[167] OLG Düsseldorf v. 8.2.2018 – I-6 U 50/17, ZIP 2018, 427.
[168] On the difficulties regarding causation in general see D. Vasella, *Die Haftung von Ratingagenturen*, 175 ff. and with regard to Art. 35a (4) CRAR T. Wittenberg, 16 EBOR (2015), 669, 703.

liability of credit rating agencies could have been integrated. Two approaches were therefore in debate: The European legislature could have regulated all relevant aspects of civil law damage claims directly in the CRAR or alternatively refer to the national laws in this regard. It opted for the second (easier) approach. Terms such as 'damage', 'intention', 'gross negligence', 'reasonably relied', 'due care', impact', 'reasonable' and 'proportionate' which are referred to in Article 35a CRAR but are not defined, should be interpreted and applied in accordance with the applicable national law as determined by the relevant rules of private international law.[169]

86 The new liability concept is thus androgynous: The legal basis can be found in European law, and certain preconditions for the claim are also determined at a European level. The responsibility for the interpretation of these requirements lies with the ECJ in the last instance. At the same time other preconditions of the claim for damages are subject to national laws and the interpretation of and application by the national courts in the Members States. The CRAR does not define how the statute of liability is to be determined. This requires a qualification of the rules on liability, whereby it appears favourable to qualify them as rules under tort law with the result that the statute of liability is to be determined on the basis of the Rome-II Regulation.[170] Pursuant to Article 4(1) Rome-II Regulation, the law applicable to a non-contractual obligation arising out of a tort/delict should be the law of the country in which the damage occurred.

87 Contractual claims of investors or issuers exist parallel to the new liability concept of the CRAR.[171] This must also apply with regard to claims under national tort laws. The European legislator's aim was to improve the situation for investors and issuers. It would therefore not be convincing to see Article 35a CRAR as lex specialis toward national legal foundations for claims under tort law.

VI. Conclusion

88 The CRAR accepts the *issuer pays* model and endeavours to combat the resulting conflicts of interest and to reduce over-reliance on ratings. The complex and detailed regime has proven its efficiency. However, the problem of 'over-reliance' on credit ratings remains unsolved.

89 The CRAR furthermore marks a new era in European capital markets law. The supervisory powers lie with ESMA, which is also empowered to take administrative measures against rating agencies and to impose sanctions. The experiences are positive. ESMA has sanctioned violations of essential regulatory requirements regarding the transparency of the rating procedure and made these violations public. These measures strengthen confidence in effective supervision of rating agencies. However, there is a need for reform of the sanctions. The level of fines is much lower than in other areas of European capital markets law.

---

[169] Cf. Art. 35a(5a) CRAR.
[170] Cf. A. Dutta, 37 WM (2013), 1729, 1731; C. Kumpan and R. Grütze, in: Lehmann and Kumpan (eds.), *European Financial Services Law*, Art. 35a CRAR para. 20.
[171] Cf. recital 24 CRAR-III; seen critically by A. Dutta, 37 WM (2013), 1729, 1735.

The civil liability of rating agencies towards issuers and investors, as introduced in 2013, also 90
marks a new era in European capital markets law. It cannot as yet be said how effective this
European regime is. There are, however, some doubts in this regard, the central issues with
regard to investor claims not having been solved. The reference to the national laws also
does not appear convincing.

§ 28

Proxy Advisors

Bibliography

Augustin, Gerald, *(Selbst-)Regulierung von institutionellen Stimmrechtsberatern auf europäischer Ebene*, 8 ÖBA (2014), 583–590; Dörrwächter, Jan, *Stimmrechts- und Vergütungsberatung – Interessenkonflikte und Unabhängigkeit*, 12 AG (2017), 409–415; Fleischer, Holger, *Proxy Advisors in Europe: Reform Proposals and Regulatory Strategies*, 9 ECL (2012), 12–20; Fleischer, Holger, *Zur Rolle und Regulierung von Stimmrechtsberatern (Proxy Advisors) im deutschen und europäischen Aktien- und Kapitalmarktrecht*, 1 AG (2012), 2–11; Gallego Córcoles, Ascensión, *Proxy Advisors in the Voting Process: Some Considerations for Future Regulation in Europe*, 1 ECFR (2016), 106–156; Hell, Patrick, *Stimmrechtsberater in der modernen Corporate Governance*, 1 ZGR (2021), 50–85; Klöhn, Lars and Schwarz, Patrick, *Die Regulierung institutioneller Stimmrechtsberater*, 4 ZIP 2012, 149–158; Langenbucher, Katja, *Stimmrechtsberater*, in: Krieger, Gerd et al. (eds.), Festschrift für Michael Hoffmann-Becking zum 70. Geburtstag (2013), 733–745; Schneider, Uwe H. and Anzinger, Heribert, *Institutionelle Stimmrechtsberatung und Stimmrechtsvertretung—, A quiet guru's enourmous clout'*, 3 NZG (2007), 88–96; Schneider, Uwe H., *Praxis und Regulierung von Stimmrechtsberatern. Eine nicht bewältigte systematische Herausforderung*, in: VGR, Gesellschaftsrecht in der Diskussion 2019 (2020), 1–11; Torggler, Ulrich, *Proxy Advisors and Disclosure of Conflicts of Interests*, in: Tountopoulos, Vassilios and Veil, Rüdiger (eds.), *Transparency of Stock Corporations in Europe* (2019), 143–154; Velte, Patrick, *Regulierung von Stimmrechtsberatern nach ARUG II*, 24 AG (2019), 893–898; Zetsche, Dirk and Preiner, Christina, *Der Verhaltenskodex für Stimmberater zwischen Vertrags- und -Wettbewerbsrecht. Zur Einordnung der Best Practice Principles für Shareholder Voting Research & Analysis*, 19 AG (2014), 685–697.

I. Introduction

Compared to financial analysts and rating agencies, proxy advisors are a relatively young type of information intermediaries. Their business model consists of giving shareholders **recommendations** on the **exercise** of **voting rights** attached to shares in listed companies and, as the case may be, also exercising voting rights for the shareholders on their behalf. This is of particular interest to institutional investors (asset managers; asset management companies of funds; sovereign wealth funds; pension funds; etc.) who hold a large number of shareholdings worldwide. It would be disproportionately costly for these investors to evaluate the agenda items of the companies' ordinary general meetings, some of which deal with highly complex issues (such as remuneration systems). This is well illustrated by the example of the Norwegian sovereign wealth fund, which has shareholdings in more than 9,000 listed companies.[1]

1

---

[1] Cf. the information on the website www.nbim.no: 9.123 companies in 73 countries (as of 15 September 2021).

2   The **market** of **proxy advisors** is characterised by duopolistic structures.[2] The market leader is Institutional Shareholder Services (ISS) with a market share of approximately 70%. In addition to advising institutional investors on voting rights, ISS also provides various consulting services for companies. These so-called corporate advisory services mainly concern the remuneration of board members. Besides ISS, only Glass Lewis (GL) has a relevant market share. GL is not said to provide any services for issuers apart from advice on exercise of voting rights.

3   Proxy advisors make it easier for shareholders to exercise their voting rights at general meetings. Against the background of low attendance at general meetings due to rational apathy (disproportionate information costs) of shareholders, this is a useful service for investors. Nevertheless, academics, policymakers and practitioners have discussed intensively since the 2010s whether proxy advisors should be subject to a specific regulation. Firstly, they address the enormous impact of proxy advisors, especially in companies without blockholders or a high proportion of institutional investors.[3] Critics argue that institutional investors often blindly follow the voting recommendations of proxy advisors. In particular, this would be true for passive investors.[4] They point out in this context that share ownership and decision-making power fall apart.[5] Secondly, voting advice is often too schematic, does not sufficiently take into account national specificities of the governance structure and is based on methodologically dubious assessments. Thirdly, proxy advisors are subject to massive conflicts of interest. This is said to apply in particular to those advisors who advise investors and issuers simultaneously.[6]

II. Regulatory Concepts

4   The regulatory debate in Europe was initially dominated by the perception that market failure could not be identified. ESMA saw no need for a specific legally binding regime. Instead, policymakers and academics considered the self-regulation initiated by ESMA in the form of a code of conduct (Best Practice Principles for Providers of Shareholder Voting Research & Analysis)[7] to be sufficient. The restraint can be explained firstly by the fact that, unlike rating agencies, proxy advisors are not systemically relevant. Misconduct does not threaten to affect financial stability. Secondly, no similar scandals were observed as was the case with financial analysts at the beginning of the 2000s. Nevertheless, the European legislature finally introduced a set of harmonising rules. The Shareholder Rights Directive II (SRD II)[8] recognises the positive role of proxy advisors in helping to reduce the cost of analysing corporate information. Nevertheless, it requires Member States to provide for a

---

[2] Cf. in more detail L. Klöhn and P. Schwarz, 4 ZIP (2012), 149, 150.
[3] P. Velte, 24 AG (2019), 893, 895.
[4] Cf. J. Dörrwächter, 12 AG (2017), 409 (regarding rejected remuneration schemes).
[5] H. Fleischer, 1 AG (2012), 2, 4; pointedly formulated U. Schneider, in: *VGR*, 1, 6.
[6] H. Fleischer, 1 AG (2012), 2, 4 f.
[7] Best Practice Principle Group, Best Practice Principles for Providers of Shareholder Voting Research & Analysis, March 2014; Review and Update July 2019.
[8] Directive (EU) 2017/828 of the European Parliament and of the Council of 17 May 2017 amending Directive 2007/36/EC as regards the encouragement of long-term shareholder engagement, OJ L 132, 20 May 2017, p. 1 ff. (SRD II).

minimum set of rules, as many institutional investors and asset managers with highly diversified portfolios would increasingly rely on recommendations from proxy advisors.[9]

1. Transparency

The SRD II does not introduce regulatory requirements for an objective service free of conflicts of interest, but maintains the self-regulatory approach of a code of conduct for proxy advisors. Furthermore, it provides for a disclosure obligation on certain aspects of proxy advisory services and of actual or potential conflicts of interest.

The **disclosure obligation** regarding the **code of best practices** provides for a **comply-or-explain mechanism**. Member States must ensure that proxy advisors publicly refer to a code of conduct that they apply and report on the application of the code of conduct. If they do not apply a code of conduct, they must provide a clear and reasoned explanation as to why this is the case. If proxy advisors deviate from individual recommendations, they must explain this.[10]

> Which code of conduct a proxy advisor applies is left to the proxy advisors. The SRD II also does not specify any minimum requirements for the code of conduct. Theoretically, a proxy advisor can draw up its own code and refer to this 'more closely specified' code. However, in practice codes developed by an individual proxy advisor do not play a role. Instead, advisors commit to the code drawn up by the BPP Group (see para. 4).

> The BPP Group's **Best Practice Principles** are based on the idea that investors need access to information that makes it easier for them to exercise their rights and responsibilities.[11] The BPP Group has developed three best practice principles. The first principle deals with 'Service Quality', the second with 'Conflicts-of-Interest Avoidance or Management' and the third with 'Communications Policy'. The three principles are explained in more detail in the 'Guidance on Applying the Principles'. They are quite rich in content. Therefore, the criticism being meaningless does not convince.[12] A privately created body—the 'BBP Oversight Committee'—has the task of monitoring compliance with the principles by the signatories (the voting advisors).

Proxy advisors are also obliged to **inform** their clients about the **accuracy** and **reliability** of their **activities**.[13] They have to comply with this obligation on an annual basis. This requirement reflects criticisms regarding the quality of advice on the exercise of voting rights. The disclosure obligation has a regulatory function.[14] The information made publicly available on the website of the proxy advisor concerns in particular the methods and models used, the qualifications of the staff and the characteristics of the proxy policy pursued.

The European legislature addresses the issue of conflicts of interest (see para. 3) through transparency rather than prohibitions. A proxy advisor must identify actual or potential **conflicts of interest** or business relationships that could affect the preparation of its research, advice and voting recommendations. Clients shall be promptly informed of such

---

[9] Recital 25 SRD II.
[10] Cf. Art. 3j(1) SRD II.
[11] See on the responsibility of institutional investors R. Veil § 22 para. 28 ff.
[12] Exaggerated criticism by U. Schneider, in: *VGR*, 1, 6 ('meagre principles'); convincing U. Torggler, in: Tountopoulos and Veil, *Transparency of Stock Corporations in Europe*, 143, 150.
[13] Cf. Art. 3j(2) SRD II.
[14] See on the regulatory function of disclosure obligations R. Veil § 2 para. 39.

conflicts and the steps taken by the proxy advisor to eliminate or mitigate or address them.[15] Similar to financial analysts, a prohibition would disproportionately infringe the professional freedom of proxy advisors.[16] However, it is not convincing that the concept of actual or potential conflicts of interest is not defined.

2. Liability under Private Law

11 Questions of private enforcement are not subject to European legislation and are therefore determined by the applicable national law. This will be briefly explained by way of example for Germany. Proxy advisors are liable to pay damages to their client pursuant to §§ 675, 280 BGB. A breach of contractual obligations may primarily lie in an improper analysis resulting in a recommendation, which the investor may reasonably follow. As a rule, however, an investor is not likely to have recoverable losses if, on the basis of erroneous advice, he exercises his right to vote, for example, on the appointment of the members of the supervisory board, the distribution of the balance sheet profit or the remuneration system.[17] This applies in particular in the case of violations of the disclosure obligations regarding conflicts of interest, which may also give rise to contractual duties of disclosure.

12 Another question is whether the proxy advisor may be liable to pay damages to the company. Such liability may only arise if there is a contractual relationship between the proxy advisor and the issuer and the proxy advisor provides deficient advice to the issuer on corporate governance issues. In this case, a claim according to §§ 675, 280 BGB can be considered. However, the issuer is unlikely to suffer any losses subject to compensation under private law.

3. Public Enforcement

13 The NCAs are not competent for ensuring compliance with the rules (code of conduct; disclosure obligations). It is conceivable, however, that false information could constitute market manipulation (Article 12 MAR), subject to supervision by the NCAs. The BBP Group has established the BBP Oversight Committee to monitor compliance with the Best Practice Principles (see para. 8).

14 Violations of the disclosure requirements may be sanctioned, provided national law provides for administrative sanctions. However, European law does not stipulate any requirements in this regard.

III. Conclusion

15 The legal situation, consisting of *soft law* and statutory disclosure obligations, appears sufficient at present to ensure that proxy advisors provide services that are in line with the

---

[15] Cf. Art. 3j(3) SRD II.
[16] Dissenting opinion U. Schneider, in: *VGR*, 1, 6; P. Velte, 24 AG (2019), 893, 897; sceptical L. Klöhn and P. Schwarz, 4 ZIP (2012), 149, 156.
[17] Cf. D. Illhardt, in: Schmidt and Lutter, *AktG*, § 134d para. 25.

interests of their clients. The conflicts resulting from the simultaneous activity for contractual partners with diverging interests (institutional investors; management of the company) do not justify a prohibition of advisory services. The approach of countering conflicts of interest through disclosure obligations is also pursued in other areas of European capital markets law. Admittedly, it will make sense to define the standards of the code of conduct in more detail.[18] Moreover, the much-lamented influence of proxy advisors on the exercise of voting rights by institutional investors is best countered by market forces. The problem remains, however, that there is no competition between the proxy advisors. Instead, further concentration can be observed.

Private liability is not expected to contribute to the proper conduct of proxy advisors. It will therefore have to be evaluated in the future whether the self-regulatory approach of the Best Practice Principles works or should be replaced by a regime supervised by national authorities.[19] It will then also have to be taken into account that the business models of advisors are evolving and increasingly include aspects of ESG investment.[20]

---

[18] Cf. U. Torggler, in: Tountopoulos and Veil, *Transparency of Stock Corporations in Europe*, 143, 151.
[19] In contrast, U. Torggler, in: Tountopoulos and Veil, *Transparency of Stock Corporations in Europe*, 143, 154, argues for a strengthening of liability under private law.
[20] See on sustainability rating agencies R. Veil § 27 para. 4.

7
Investment Firms

§ 29

Foundations

Bibliography

Colaert, Veerle, *Investor Protection in the Capital Markets Union*, in: Busch, Danny et al. (eds.), *Capital Markets Union in Europe* (2018), ch. 16; Kalss, Susanne, *Civil Law Protection of Investors in Austria—A Situation Report from Amidst a Wave of Investor Lawsuits*, 13 EBOR (2012), 211–236; Moloney, Niamh, *The Investor Model Underlying the EU's Investor Protection Regime: Consumers or Investors?*, 13 EBOR (2012), 169–193; Mülbert, Peter O., *Auswirkungen der MiFID-Rechtsakte für Vertriebsvergütungen im Effektengeschäft der Kreditinstitute*, ZHR 172 (2008), 170–209; Mülbert, Peter O., *Anlegerschutz und Finanzmarktregulierung – Grundlagen*, ZHR 177 (2013), 160–211; Veil, Rüdiger and Lerch, Marcus P., *Auf dem Weg zu einem Europäischen Finanzmarktrecht: die Vorschläge der Kommission zur Neuregelung der Märkte für Finanzinstrumente*, 33 WM (2012), 1557–1565 (Part I) and 34 WM (2012), 1605–1613 (Part II).

I. Introduction

Investors usually carry out the acquisition and sale of securities with the assistance of banks and other investment firms. For three decades, the EU has pursued the goal of protecting investors who use investment services. The legal framework has grown tremendously during this time. There are many reasons for this. Securities investment is of paramount importance to retail investors, who are increasingly relying on it to provide for their old age. Traditional investments are practically out of the question in a zero-interest environment. Retail investors have a special need for protection because they are often unable to assess the quality of the financial product. They therefore depend on investment services being provided in a way that is in their best interest. Experience shows that this is not always the case. In addition, increasingly complex financial products pose a threat to financial stability.[1] Finally, legal harmonisation for 27 Member States means that the rules are becoming more detailed.

Regulatory strategies have become more diverse over the past three decades. Directive 93/22/EEC was limited to requiring investment firms to be authorised by the supervisory authority before the commencement of business. It also provided for rules of conduct that ensured investor protection primarily through information. These rules went into impressive detail in 2004 (with MiFID I replacing Directive 93/22/EEC) and 2014 (with MiFID II replacing MiFID I and the PRIIPs Regulation being adopted). The information model, which has

---

[1] Cf. recital 37 Directive 2014/65/EU of the European Parliament and of the Council of 15 May 2014 on markets in financial instruments and amending Directive 2002/92/EC and Directive 2011/61/EU (MiFID II).

only been successful to a limited extent, is now also supplemented by product governance requirements and product intervention measures.

3   The European legislature implemented reforms regarding this 'cornerstone of financial market integration in Europe' in order to comply with the resolutions passed at the G20 summit in Pittsburgh on 24/25 September 2009 on effective responses to the causes of the financial crisis. The crisis had disclosed weaknesses in the regulation of financial instruments other than shares. Furthermore, financial innovations and the increasing complexity of financial instruments had shown that investor protection needed to be improved. Reforms were also necessary due to the fact that the strongly competitive environment had led to new challenges. Other provisions of MiFID I were outdated due to market and technological developments.[2]

4   The market for investment firms is competitive. The EBA found that, in 2015, there were more than 6,500 investment firms in Europe. However, half of these were from the United Kingdom. With Brexit, the number of authorised firms has therefore decreased significantly. The range of services investment firms typically offer is wide. Investment brokerage, investment advice and asset management are the most important.[3]

II. Legal Framework

1. Supervisory Law

5   The legal foundations for financial services supplied by investment firms are largely supervisory law. Compliance with these rules is supervised by the NCAs, and infringements are subsequently also sanctioned by the NCAs, eg by way of fines. The supervisory provisions themselves are meanwhile to be found more or less entirely at a European level (maximum harmonisation). Supervisory law for investment firms consists of three regimes. The MiFID II regime – in the form of a directive (**MiFID II**)[4] and a regulation (**MiFIR**)[5] as well as numerous Level 2 and 3 measures – provides requirements for the authorisation and activities of investment firms. The body of rules and regulations is enormous: It comprises legal texts of more than 7,000 pages!

(a) The MiFID II Regime

6   **MiFIR** establishes uniform requirements in relation to (i) the disclosure of trade data to the public, (ii) the reporting of transactions to the NCAs, (iii) the trading of derivatives

---

[2] Cf. Commission, Explanatory Memorandum on the Proposal for a revision of MiFID, 20 October 2011, COM (2011) 656 final, p. 2.

[3] Cf. EBA, Report on Investment Firms, EBA/Op/2015/20, p. 97.

[4] Directive 2014/65/EU of the European Parliament and of the Council of 15 May 2014 on markets in financial instruments and amending Directive 2002/92/EC and Directive 2011/61/EU, OJ L 173, 12 June 2014, p. 349–496.

[5] Regulation (EU) No 600/2014 of the European Parliament and of the Council of 15 May 2014 on markets in financial instruments and amending Regulation (EU) No 648/2012, OJ L 173, 12 June 2014, p. 84–148.

on organised venues, (iv) non-discriminatory access to clearing and to trading in benchmarks, (v) product intervention powers of the NCAs and the ESAs, and (vi) the provision of investment services by third-country firms.[6] MiFIR is a regulation and therefore directly applicable in the Member States. The European legislator has adopted a regulation instead of a directive because this is a more suitable form of action to transfer direct supervisory powers to ESMA and EBA. A regulation is furthermore better able to prevent supervisory arbitrage and ensure uniform competitive conditions.

MiFID II establishes requirements in relation to (i) the authorisation and operating conditions for investment firms, (ii) the provision of investment services by third-country firms, (iii) the authorisation and operation of regulated markets, (iv) the authorisation and operation of data reporting services and (v) supervision, cooperation and enforcement by NCAs.[7]

7

The MiFID II regime (consisting of the MiFIR and MiFID II) applies to investment firms. An **investment firm** is a legal person that provides one or more investment services to third parties and/or performs one or more investment activities on a professional basis in the ordinary course of its business or profession. **Investment services** and activities means any service and activity listed in Section A of Annex I that relates to a financial instrument,[8] namely (1) the reception and transmission of orders, (2) the execution of orders on behalf of clients, (3) dealing on own account, (4) portfolio management, (5) investment advice, (6) the underwriting of financial instruments, (7) the placement of financial instruments, (8) the operation of an MTF, and (9) the operation of an OTF.

8

(b) PRIIPs

The second regime consists of the **PRIIPs Regulation**,[9] which concerns so-called packaged investment products and insurance investment products. The regulation has a 'cross-sectoral approach' because it covers not only traditional financial products but also insurance-linked products.[10] The products offer a maturity value or a surrender value that is fully or partially exposed, directly or indirectly, to market fluctuations. The regime applies to so-called PRIIP manufacturers and persons who advise on or sell PRIIPs. These may be investment firms but also other market participants.

9

The regulatory approach of the PRIIPS Regulation is to require **disclosure**: a basic information sheet (also known as a key information document or KID) must be prepared and made available at the time of the advice or sale. It is intended to enable investors, especially inexperienced and uninformed ones, to understand a (complex!) financial product. For this reason, the regulation provides for detailed requirements regarding the form and content of a basic information sheet. This information document – also referred to as a 'short document' – must be precise, honest and clear and must not be misleading.[11]

10

---

[6] Cf. Art. 1(1) MiFIR.
[7] Cf. Art. 1(2) MiFID II.
[8] Cf. Art. 4(1) no. 2 MiFID II.
[9] Regulation (EU) No 1286/2014 of the European Parliament and of the Council of 26 November 2014 on key information documents for packaged retail and insurance-based investment products, OJ L 352, 9 December 2014, p. 1–23.
[10] Cf. V. Colaert, in: Busch et al. (eds.), *Capital Markets Union in Europe*, para. 16.25 and 16.84 (who welcomes this approach in principle).
[11] Cf. Art. 6(1) and (4) PRIIPs Regulation.

(c) IFR/IFD Regime

11   The third regime concerns **prudential supervision** of investment firms. Regulation (EU) 2019/2033 (**IFR**) sets out uniform prudential requirements for authorised and supervised investment firms, compliance with which is supervised by national authorities under Directive (EU) 2019/2034 (**IFD**). Large investment firms are subject to the rules of Regulation (EU) 648/2012 (Capital Adequacy Regulation or **CRR**). The IFR regime has its focus on the risks arising from the business activities of investment firms.

12   Investment firms do not accept client funds as deposits and do not grant loans. Their risk profile differs significantly from the risk profile of banks. The **capital requirements** of the IFR/IFD regime are designed to address the firm, client and market risks specific to investment firms. Furthermore, the regime limits concentration risks and counteracts liquidity risks. The new regime is intended to be risk-sensitive. As the supervisory framework is designed to be risk-based, it is not the specific investment service that is the decisive factor, but rather the risk profile that is to be assessed in each individual case on the basis of abstract criteria (so-called K-factors).

13   In addition to initial capital, the IFR/IFD regime also regulates governance aspects that supplement those of MiFID II/CRD IV.[12] Investment firms are subject to a differentiated system of **solvency supervision**, which also includes requirements for internal governance and places obligations on the management board with regard to the company's risk management system and the remuneration policies.

2. Enforcement Mechanisms

14   **Supervisory law** is traditionally enforced by means of administrative law and criminal law. MiFID II and the IFR/IFD regime impose detailed requirements on Member States as to the minimum powers of the national supervisory authorities. They must also ensure that national supervisory authorities can impose fines. In this respect they contain minimum harmonising rules.

15   Additionally, private law applies to financial services, investment advice being rendered on the basis of a contract between the investment firm and the client. The contract determines the mutual rights and obligations. The supervisory authorities are generally not permitted to file claims with regard to clients' rights. Such claims must be asserted by the clients themselves before the national courts. As of yet, the European legislature has not harmonised this field of law. In particular, MiFID II does not contain rules concerning contractual terms and obligations. The legal relationships under private law are therefore determined by the applicable national regimes. They are of paramount importance in practice. Whether the prudential rules also determine the contractual obligations is a fundamental question that is treated differently in the different Member States.[13]

---

[12] See M. Wundenberg § 34.
[13] See R. Veil § 30 para. 61 ff.

§ 30

Investment Services

Bibliography

Balzer, Peter, *Vermögensverwaltung durch Kreditinstitute* (1999); Balzer, Peter, in: Derleder et al. (eds.), *Deutsches und Europäisches Kapitalmarktrecht*, 129–173; Benicke, Christoph, *Vermögensverwaltung* (2007); Colaert, Veerle, *Investor Protection in the Capital Markets Union*, in: Busch, Danny et al. (eds.), *Capital Markets Union in Europe*, 2018, ch. 16; Forschner, Julius, *Wechselwirkungen von Aufsichtsrecht und Zivilrecht* (2013); Freitag, Robert, *Überfällige Konvergenz von privatem und öffentlichem Recht der Anlageberatung*, 6 ZBB (2014), 357–365; Grigoleit, Hans Christoph, *Anlegerschutz – Produktinformation und Produktverbote*, ZHR 177 (2013), 264–309; Herbst, Jonathan and Lovegrove, Simon, *A Practitioner's Guide to MiFID II*, 3rd edn. (2018); Kalss, Susanne, *Civil Law Protection of Investors in Austria – A Situation Report from A midst a Wave of Investor Lawsuits*, 13 EBOR (2012), 211–236; Köndgen, Johannes, *Wie viel Aufklärung braucht ein Wertpapierkunde*, 4 ZBB (1996), 361–365; Kumpan, Christoph and Hellgardt, Alexander, *Haftung der Wertpapierfirma nach Umsetzung der EU-Richtlinie über Märkte für Finanzinstrumente (MiFID)*, 32 DB (2006), 1714–1720; Lang, Norbert, *Doppelnorm im Recht der Finanzdienstleistungen*, 4 ZBB (2004), 289–295; Lang, Volker, *Einmal mehr: zur Schutzgesetzeigenschaft der Verhaltenspflichten der §§ 63 ff. WpHG unter dem Regime von MiFID II*, ZBB 2021, 47–57; Leisch, Franz C., *Informationspflichten nach § 31 WpHG* (2004); Lerch, Marcus P., *Anlageberater als Finanzintermediäre* (2015); Möllers, Thomas M. J., *Effizienz als Maßstab des Kapitalmarktrechts*, AcP 208 (2008), 1–36; Moloney, Niamh, *The Investor Model Underlying the EU's Investor Protection Regime: Consumers or Investors?*, 13 EBOR (2012), 169–193; Mülbert, Peter O., *Anlegerschutz und Finanzmarktregulierung – Grundlage*, ZHR 177 (2013), 160–211; Nelson, Paul, *Capital Markets Law and Compliance* (2008); Perrone, Andrea and Valente, Stefano, *Against all odds: Investor Protection in Italy and the Role of Courts*, 13 EBOR (2012), 31–44; Sethe, Rolf, *Anlegerschutz im Recht der Vermögensverwaltung* (2005); van Kampen, Charlotte, *Der Anlageberatungsvertrag* (2020); Veil, Rüdiger, *Vermögensverwaltung und Anlageberatung im neuen Wertpapierhandelsrecht – eine behutsame Reform der Wohlverhaltensregeln?*, 1 ZBB (2008), 34–42; Veil, Rüdiger, *Anlageberatung im Zeitalter der MiFID – Inhalt und Konzeption der Pflichten und Grundlagen einer zivilrechtlichen Haftung*, 39 WM (2007), 1821–1827; Vogel, Christian, *Vom Anlegerschutz zum Verbraucherschutz: Informationspflichten im europäischen Kapitalmarkt-, Anlegerschutz und Verbraucherschutzrecht* (2005); Walker, George and Purves, Robert, *Financial Services Law* (2018); Walla, Fabian, *The Swedish Capital Markets from a European Perspective*, 22 EBLR (2011), 211–221; Wallinga, Marnix Wibo, *EU investor protection regulation and private law. A comparative analysis of the interplay between MiFID & MiFID II and liability for investment losses* (2018). Q.v. the bibliographical references in § 29.

I. Introduction

Many investors lack an overview of financial products as well as the knowledge necessary to assess the (increasingly complex) financial products that may be suitable for them.[1]

---

[1] Cf. P. Balzer, *Vermögensverwaltung durch Kreditinstitute*, 14.

Investors also have different levels of risk tolerance. They are increasingly dependent on personal recommendations. As a result, they typically use a variety of services when buying or selling securities. An investor may let another person manage his assets (**asset management**); he may obtain advice on the sale and acquisition of financial products (**investment advice**) or on potential contractual partners (**investment brokerage**). In addition, investors are not authorised to close the respective deals.[2] A securities dealer purchases the securities in his own name but for the account of the investor (**commission**). The securities dealer may also acquire the securities for his own account (**proprietary trading**) to then resell them to the investor.

2 The legal framework governing investment services has grown tremendously over the past three decades. This section will cover the regulatory concept of the MiFID II regime in more detail. The focus will be on the requirements for investment firms when manufacturing financial instruments and providing certain investment services, such as investment advice and portfolio management. In addition, this section will examine the obligations under civil law relating to investment advice and asset management.

II. Regulatory Concept of the MiFID II Regime

1. Overview

3 MiFID II applies to investment firms, market operators, data provision services and third-country companies that provide investment services or carry out investment activities through a company branch in the EU.[3] The conditions for the admission and the operation of investment firms, as well as the admission and operation of regulated markets will be discussed in more detail hereinafter.[4]

2. Investment Firms

4 A key condition for the performing of investment services as a regular professional or commercial activity is the prior authorisation by the national supervisory authority.[5] MiFID II stipulates that any such activity is prohibited unless permission is granted. This approval requirement is meant to ensure investor protection and the stability of the financial system.[6]

5 Approval may be granted when the investment firm meets the corporate governance requirements of MiFID II (in particular with regard to the **management body**)[7] and has

---

[2] At the stock exchanges, investors cannot conduct equity transactions themselves. To enter into a transaction they must mandate someone who is authorised to participate in exchange trading. The details are laid down in the Member States' stock exchange laws.
[3] Cf. Art. 1(1) MiFID II.
[4] Cf. Art. 1(2)(a) and (c) MiFID II.
[5] Cf. Art. 5(1) MiFID II; cf. also M. Lehmann, in: Lehmann/Kumpan (eds.), European Financial Services Law, Art. 5 MiFID II para. 2: 'core principle'.
[6] Cf. recital 37 MiFID II.
[7] Cf. Art. 9 ff. MiFID II. See M. Wundenberg § 34.

sufficient **initial capital**.[8] Furthermore, the investment firm must comply with a wide range of **organisational requirements**[9] ensuring that conflicts resulting from the firm's various activities do not affect the interests of the clients.[10]

According to its Annex I, Section A, MiFID II defines **investment services** as (1) the reception and transmission of orders in relation to one or more financial instruments; (2) the execution of orders on behalf of clients; (3) dealing on own account; (4) portfolio management; (5) investment advice; (6) the underwriting of financial instruments and/or placing of financial instruments on a firm commitment basis; (7) the placing of financial instruments without a firm commitment basis; (8) the operation of an MTF; and (9) the operation of an OTF. An investment firm that provides one or more investment services for third parties in the course of its regular professional or commercial activity must comply with the **rules of conduct** of MiFID II provided for in Chapter II when providing these services. 6

In Section B of its Annex I, MiFID II also lists **ancillary securities services**. These are services that are typically related to investment services.[11] In particular, it covers (1) the safekeeping and administration of financial instruments for the account of clients, (2) the granting of credits or loans to an investor to allow him to carry out a transaction in one or more financial instruments, (3) advising companies on capital structure etc., (4) foreign exchange services, (5) investment research and financial analysis and (6) services related to underwriting. When providing these ancillary services, the investment firm must also comply with the MiFID II **rules of conduct**. However, a company does not become an investment firm solely by providing ancillary investment services. 7

3. Market Operators (Regulated Market)

With the notion of a market operator, MiFID II covers people who manage and/or operate the business of a regulated market.[12] A regulated market, like an MTF or OTF, is a trading venue within the meaning of MiFID II.[13] While the operation of an MTF or OTF is covered in MiFID II as an investment service, MiFID II governs regulated markets through an independent regime,[14] which provides for similar regulatory concepts as the regime for investment services. For example, a regulated market requires authorisation.[15] The market operator's management body must comply with certain governance[16] and organisational requirements.[17] Only the aspect of capital resources is regulated relatively liberally.[18] 8

---

[8] Cf. Art. 15 MiFID II.
[9] Cf. Art. 16 MiFID II and Art. 25 ff. IFD.
[10] Cf. recital 56 MiFID II.
[11] Cf. C. Kumpan, in: Schwark and Zimmer (eds.), *Kapitalmarktrechts-Kommentar*, § 2 WpHG para. 167.
[12] Cf. Art. 4(1) no. 18 MiFID II; in more detail M. Lehmann, in: Lehmann/Kumpan (eds.), European Financial Services Law, Art. 1 MiFID II para. 9.
[13] See R. Veil § 7 para. 11.
[14] Cf. Title III MiFID II.
[15] Cf. Art. 44 MiFID II.
[16] Cf. Art. 45 MiFID II.
[17] Cf. Art. 47 MiFID II.
[18] Cf. Art. 47(1)(f) MiFID II with the requirement for the admission to listing to continuously have sufficient financial resources.

4. Supervision and Sanctions

9   Compliance with the rules of conduct is supervised by national authorities (NCAs). That is why the rules of conduct are also referred to as supervisory law. MiFID II requires that the authorities have certain powers, in particular the right to inspect documents of all kinds, to request information and to carry out on-site investigations.[19]

10 MiFID II requires the Member States to ensure that administrative sanctions and measures can be imposed in the event of violations of MiFID II.[20] The Member States have to ensure that the authorities consider certain circumstances when exercising their powers, such as the severity and duration of the violation, the degree of responsibility of the person responsible and the person's financial capacity.[21] In addition, the competent authorities must be allowed to immediately make public the decisions imposing an administrative sanction or measure.[22]

III. General Rules of Conduct for Investment Firms

11 MiFID II provides for a specifically tailored regime of obligations when investment firms provide investment services. The rules of conduct take into account the characteristic legal relationships in the various types of investment services. There is a different potential for conflicts with investment advice than there is with asset management. In the case of investment advice, the client makes an investment decision himself, whereas in the case of asset management, the decision is made by the manager. The fiduciary relationship between client and asset manager requires a different regulatory approach. Nevertheless, it makes sense to provide certain basic rules of conduct for all investment services as well as ancillary services. It makes sense generally to stipulate that an investment firm must act carefully and deal appropriately with conflicts of interest.

1. Due Diligence Obligations

12 An investment firm must respect general principles when providing investment and ancillary services. It must act **honestly, in good faith** and **professionally in the best possible interests of its clients**.[23] This principle determines the relationship between an investment firm and a client.[24] It is similar with the duties under private law, however, subject to supervision by a public authority. In contrast to civil law, supervisory law does not allow to waive or restrict due diligence obligations.

13 'Honest and in good faith' not only means that an investment company must not commit any pecuniary crimes directly directed at the client's assets,[25] but it must be guided by the model of a prudent businessman who not only strives for profit but also shares a trusting

---

[19] Cf. Art. 69(2)(a)–(u) MiFID II.
[20] Cf. Art. 70 MiFID II.
[21] Cf. Art. 72 MiFID II.
[22] Cf. Art. 71 MiFID II.
[23] Cf. Art. 24(1) MiFID II.
[24] Cf. K. Rothenhöfer, in: Schwark and Zimmer (eds.), *Kapitalmarkrechts-Kommentar*, § 63 WpHG para. 6.
[25] Cf. K. Rothenhöfer, in: Schwark and Zimmer (eds.), *Kapitalmarkrechts-Kommentar*, § 63 WpHG para. 11.

and loyal relationship with his client.[26] The requirement of professional activity implies that an investment firm must have the necessary expertise,[27] in particular with regard to the financial instruments that are the subject of the investment service.

An investment firm must act in the best interests of its client. This does not exclude the investment firm from pursuing its own profit interests.[28] An investment firm can therefore of course ask to be remunerated for its services. But it must ensure that risks for the clients are minimised. The level 1 principles are put into more concrete terms in Articles 58, 64, 65 and 67–69 Delegated Regulation (EU) 2017/565.   14

A central issue when executing orders are the costs and the conditions of the transaction. According to Article 27(1) MiFID II, investment firms shall 'take all sufficient steps to obtain, when executing orders, the best possible result for their clients taking into account price, costs, speed, likelihood of execution and settlement, size, nature or any other consideration relevant to the execution of the order.' According to Article 64 Delegated Regulation (EU) 2017/565, these factors are to be determined on the basis of the following criteria: the characteristics of the client including his categorisation as retail or professional; the characteristics of the client order; the characteristics of the financial instruments; the characteristics of the execution venues. However, an investment firm must not ignore the client's ideas; instructions from the clients take priority.[29]   15

The point of reference for the best possible interest is the specific, individual client, rather than an average client. With regard to the client's interest, a variable standard applies.[30] This means that the duty to safeguard interests precisely prohibits an investment firm from disregarding ideas expressed by the customer, even if they are objectively unreasonable.[31] A client does not waive the investment firm's duty to safeguard his interests by insisting on making objectively unreasonable investments. Nevertheless, the client's statements are legally relevant for the firm. The investment firm is obliged to act in accordance with the objectively unreasonable ideas of the client. This is consistent with the fact that the client can choose between a higher and a lower level of protection by opting for a specific client category defined by the asset manager.[32]   16

2. Obligations in Cases of Conflict of Interest

The European legislator has based the rules concerning conflicts of interest on the fact that the increasing range of activities that many investment firms carry out at once has increased the potential for conflicts of interest between these different activities and the clients' interests.[33] Article 23(1) MiFID II describes the relationships in which such conflicts can occur: Conflicts of interest can arise between the investment firm—including its management, employees and contractually bound agents, or other persons who are directly or   17

---

[26] Cf. I. Koller, in: Assmann et al. (eds.), *Kommentar zum Wertpapierhandelsrecht*, § 63 para. 17; K. Rothenhöfer, in: Schwark and Zimmer (eds.), *Kapitalmarkrechts-Kommentar*, § 63 WpHG para. 10.
[27] Cf. K. Rothenhöfer, in: Schwark and Zimmer (eds.), *Kapitalmarkrechts-Kommentar*, § 63 WpHG para. 15.
[28] Cf. I. Koller, in: Assmann et al. (eds.), *Kommentar zum Wertpapierhandelsrecht*, § 63 para. 20.
[29] Cf. Art. 27(1) sentence 2 MiFID and Art. 64(2) Delegated Regulation (EU) 2017/565.
[30] Cf. A. Fuchs, in: Fuchs (ed.), *WpHG*, § 31 para. 35.
[31] Cf. K. Rothenhöfer, in: Schwark and Zimmer (eds.), *Kapitalmarkrechts-Kommentar*, § 63 WpHG para. 35.
[32] Cf. A. Fuchs, in: Fuchs (ed.), *WpHG*, § 31 para. 35.
[33] Cf. recital 56 sentence 1 MiFID II.

indirectly connected to the investment firm—and the firm's clients, as well as between the clients themselves.

18 The exact characteristics of a conflict of interest are not defined by law. In general, it can be stated that there is a conflict of interest when two (or more) parties pursue certain goals, but it is not possible for both parties to do so in full.[34] The MiFID II regime only covers those conflicts that are related to investment services or ancillary services.

19 Conflicts of interest between the client and the investment firm are of a structural nature, especially if the investment firm is a universal bank. The client's interest in executing the order in accordance with his interests may be impaired if the investment firm wants to execute the order itself, ie, from its own portfolio (proprietary trading). It is also in blatant contrast to the client's interests if the investment firm, with knowledge of the customer order, first purchases or sells securities itself (so-called *front running*). It is also problematic if an investment company manufactures securities itself (in-house financial products) and pursues its own sales interest, to which an interest in remuneration is added (hidden benefits).[35]

20 As mentioned, conflicts of interest can also arise between different clients of the same investment firm. It is in the client's interests that his order be carried out on the most favourable terms and at the lowest possible cost. The order of a single client can affect the price formation, so that the following order will be executed at less favourable prices.

21 The MiFID II regime seeks to counter the investment firm's conflicts of interest with **organisational requirements** and **rules of conduct** (two pillars).[36] The first pillar pursues the goal of proactively preventing the occurrence of (avoidable) conflicts of interest and ensuring that the investment firm deals appropriately with the conflicts that do arise. The organisational rules consist primarily of the requirement to take precautions for appropriate measures that prevent conflicts of interest from harming clients' interests.[37] The second pillar of rules of conduct refers to the relationship between the investment firm on the one hand, and the client on the other. It aims to minimise the client's risk exposure by stipulating that conflicts of interest be disclosed.[38] The client should be able to recognise the investment firm's conflict of interest and assess whether and to what extent it may affect the firm's service. Transparency therefore enables the client to make an appropriate investment decision.

IV. Product Approval Process (Product Governance)

1. Overview

22 With MiFID II, the European legislator has introduced a new regulatory approach to achieve a high level of investor protection.[39] The organisational requirements for investment firms,

---

[34] Cf. I. Koller, in: Assmann et al. (eds.), *Kommentar zum Wertpapierhandelsrecht*, § 80 para. 14; K. Rothenhöfer, in: Schwark and Zimmer (eds.), *Kapitalmarkrechts-Kommentar*, § 63 WpHG para. 42.
[35] Cf. K. Rothenhöfer, in: Schwark and Zimmer (eds.), *Kapitalmarkrechts-Kommentar*, § 63 WpHG para. 46; Lerch, Anlageberater als Finanzintermediäre, passim.
[36] Cf. K. Rothenhöfer, in: Schwark and Zimmer (eds.), *Kapitalmarkrechts-Kommentar*, § 63 WpHG para. 38.
[37] Cf. Art. 18(3) MiFID II. See M. Wundenberg § 33 para. 14.
[38] Cf. Art. 23(2) and (3) MiFID II.
[39] Cf. Art. 4(1) no. 2 in conjunction with Annex 1 Section A MiFID II.

also referred to as product governance, are intended to improve investor protection with regard to investment advice as well as advice-free investment services. The rules are intended to have a preventive effect.[40]

The MiFID II approach is twofold. Firstly, investment firms that manufacture financial instruments must ensure that these products are manufactured in such a way that they meet the needs of a specific target market of end customers within the respective customer category (**organisational requirements** for the **manufacturer**). Secondly, investment firms shall take appropriate measures to ensure that the financial instruments are sold to the identified target market and regularly review the identification of the target market and the performance of the products offered (**organisational requirements** for the **sale** of financial products). The main objective of these principles is to ensure that an investment firm avoids conflicts of interest. 23

> The principles provided for in MiFID II are specified in the Commission Delegated Directive (EU) 2017/593 of April 7, 2016.[41] Article 9 of this Directive regulates in detail the product monitoring obligations for investment firms that design financial instruments, and Article 10 deals with the distributors' product monitoring obligations. The new regulations of the MiFID II regime (Article 16(3) and 24(2) MiFID II and Article 9 and 10 of the Commission Delegated Directive of April 7, 2016) are not directly applicable. Member States must introduce corresponding provisions in their national laws. 24

> ESMA has also issued guidelines to ensure that the rules are applied uniformly.[42] The guidelines are not legally binding. In practice, however, they play an important role, especially considering NCAs have declared that they will apply the guidelines. 25

2. Scope

The rules concerning product governance apply to financial instruments, ie, transferable securities (stocks and bonds), money market instruments, shares in collective investment schemes, options, futures, swaps and other derivative contracts, derivative instruments for the transfer of credit risk and financial speculations on differences.[43] The personal scope includes investment firms[44] that are registered as investment firms under national law. 26

3. Manufacturers

An investment firm that designs financial instruments to sell to clients must maintain, operate and review a **process** for the **approval** of any **financial instrument** and of significant adjustments to existing financial instruments before the instrument can be marketed or 27

---

[40] Cf. I. Koller, in: Assmann et al. (eds.), *Kommentar zum Wertpapierhandelsrecht*, § 80 para. 129; D. Zetzsche, in: Lehmann/Kumpan (eds.), European Financial Services Law, Art. 16 MiFID II para. 17.
[41] Commission Delegated Directive (EU) 2017/593 of April 7 2016 supplementing Directive 2014/65/EU of the European Parliament and of the Council with regard to safeguarding of financial instruments and funds belonging to clients, product governance obligations and the rules applicable to the provision or reception of fees, commissions or any monetary or non-monetary benefits, C(2016) 2031 final.
[42] Cf. ESMA, Guidelines on MiFID II Product Governance Requirements, 5 February 2018, ESMA35-43-620 EN.
[43] Cf. Art. 4(1) no. 15 in conjunction with Annex 1 Section C MiFID II.
[44] Cf. Art. 4(1) no. 2 in conjunction with Annex 1 Section A MiFID II.

distributed to clients.[45] This obligation is closely related to the obligation under Article 24(2) MiFID II, according to which investment firms that design financial instruments to sell to clients must ensure that these financial instruments are designed in such a way that they **meet** the **needs** of a specific **target market** of **end customers** within the respective customer type, that the distribution strategy is compatible with the specific target market and that reasonable steps are taken to ensure that the financial instrument is sold to the specific target market. It is of central importance that a target market for end customers is defined for each financial instrument in the product approval process. In particular, all relevant risks for the target market must be assessed.[46]

28 As a rule, manufacturers have no direct customer contact and therefore determine the target market based on their theoretical knowledge and experience with the product. ESMA recommends taking five 'categories' into account.[47] A manufacturer should determine (i) what type of customer the product is targeting, (ii) what knowledge and experience the target clients should have, (iii) the clients' financial loss-bearing capacity, (iv) their risk tolerance and (v) goals and needs.

29 The product approval process is an internal process of the investment firm. The NCA is not involved in the process. However, the NCA monitors whether an investment firm complies with the regulatory requirements. The principle-based requirements of MiFID II are specified in more detail in Article 9 Delegated Directive 2017/593. The extensive regime need not be considered in detail. Only the most relevant requirements for the product approval process will be highlighted.

30 Firstly, an investment firm's processes and measures must ensure that the design of financial instruments meets the requirements for the proper handling of conflicts of interest, including remuneration. Investment firms that design financial instruments must ensure in particular that the design of the financial instrument, including its characteristics, does not have a negative impact on end customers and does not lead to problems with market integrity by enabling the company to reduce its own risks or positions in the underlying assets of the product and/or to dispose of it in case the investment firm already holds the underlying assets for its own account.[48]

31 Financial products can compromise the proper functioning or the stability of the financial markets. Therefore, before deciding to proceed with the launch of a specific product on the market, investment firms are required to check whether the financial investment may represent a threat.[49]

32 The greatest challenge lies in **determining** the **target market**, since it is particularly unclear how exactly it must be determined. MiFID II does not contain any specific requirements in this regard. The Level 2 guideline requires investment firms 'to identify at a sufficiently granular level the potential target market for each financial instrument and specify the type(s) of client for whose needs, characteristics and objectives, including any sustainability related objectives, the financial instrument is compatible. As part of this process, the firm shall identify any group(s) of clients for whose needs, characteristics and objectives the financial instrument is not compatible, except where financial instruments consider sustainability factors. Where investment firms collaborate to manufacture

---

[45] Cf. Art. 16(3) subsec. 2 MiFID II. Manufacturing encompasses the creation, development, issuance and/or design of financial instruments, cf. Art. 9(1) subsec. 1 Delegated Directive 2017/593.

[46] Cf. Art. 16(3) subsec. 3 MiFID II.

[47] Cf. ESMA, Guidelines on MiFID II Product Governance Requirements, 5 February 2018, ESMA35-43-620 EN, para. 18.

[48] Cf. Art. 9(2) Delegated Directive 2017/593.

[49] Cf. Art. 9(4) Delegated Directive 2017/593.

a financial instrument, only one target market needs to be identified.'⁵⁰ Union law acknowledges the principle of **proportionality**. Thus, in the case of a plain vanilla instrument (such as a share or a bond) the target market definition can be relatively simple.⁵¹

However, the Member States must require investment firms to identify the respective potential target market with sufficient precision and to indicate the type(s) of clients for whose needs, characteristics and objectives the financial instrument is suitable.⁵² For simpler, more common products, the target market may be determined in less detail, while for complex or less common products, the target market should be determined in more detail.⁵³ 33

An investment firm must also follow certain rules for carrying out product approval, including a **scenario analysis** of the financial instruments that is intended to assess the risk of poor results as well as under what circumstances these results may occur.⁵⁴ 34

A final key point is the question of who should be responsible for the approval process within an investment firm. On the one hand, Article 9(7) of the Commission Delegated Directive 2017/593 provides that **the compliance function** monitors the development and regular review of the product monitoring precautions to avoid any risk that the company does not comply with the provisions set out in this article. Second, the management body of the investment firm must exercise effective control over the firm's product governance process.⁵⁵ This is in line with the general compliance requirements under MiFID II.⁵⁶ 35

4. Distributors

The rules on product governance also apply to the sale of financial instruments. The investment firm must develop a sales strategy that is consistent with the identified target market.⁵⁷ In addition, the investment firm must take reasonable steps to ensure that the financial instrument is distributed to the identified target market. 36

The principles are specified in the Level 2 Directive. The obligation to define the target market for the respective financial instrument is of pivotal importance, even if the target market was not defined by the manufacturer.⁵⁸ Investment firms must ensure that they receive adequate and reliable information from manufacturers to ensure that the products are distributed in accordance with the characteristics, objectives and needs of the target market. The investment firms use the information obtained from the manufacturers as well as information about their own clients to determine the target market and distribution strategy. Naturally, when an investment firm acts as both a manufacturer and a trader, only one target market assessment is required.⁵⁹ 37

---

⁵⁰ Cf. Art. 9(9) Delegated Directive 2017/593, amended by Commission Delegated Directive 2021/1269 of 21 April 2021 amending Delegated Directive (EU) 2017/593 as regards the integration of sustainability factors into the product governance obligations.
⁵¹ Cf. D. Zetzsche, in: Lehmann/Kumpan (eds.), European Financial Services Law, Art. 16 MiFID II para. 24.
⁵² Cf. Art. 9(9) Delegated Directive 2017/593.
⁵³ Cf. recital 19 Delegated Directive 2017/593.
⁵⁴ Cf. Art. 9(10) Delegated Directive 2017/593.
⁵⁵ Cf. Art. 9(6) Delegated Directive 2017/593.
⁵⁶ See M. Wundenberg § 33 para. 31–88.
⁵⁷ Cf. Art. 16(3) subsec. 3 MiFID II.
⁵⁸ Cf. Art. 10(1) subsec. 2 Delegated Directive 2017/593.
⁵⁹ Cf. Art. 10(2) subsec. 3 Delegated Directive 2017/593.

38 Investment firms must take compliance measures to ensure that these requirements are met.[60] Finally, they are obliged to regularly review and update their governance arrangements to ensure that they remain robust and fit for their purpose, and take appropriate actions if necessary.[61]

39 In essence, the product governance regime aims to ensure that financial products are only sold within their respective target market. However, there is no legal obligation to do so.[62] In individual cases, it can even make sense to sell a **financial product** to a **customer** who is **outside the target market**. According to portfolio theory,[63] it may be appropriate for this customer to purchase a particularly risky product. The ESMA guidelines (see para. 30) recognise this: 'When providing investment advice adopting a portfolio approach and portfolio management to the client, the distributor can use products for diversification and hedging purposes. In this context, products can be sold outside of the product target market, if the portfolio as a whole or the combination of a financial instrument with its hedge is suitable for the client' (para. 52 ESMA guidelines).

V. Investment Advice

1. Terminology

40 MiFID II understands investment advice to be 'the provision of **personal recommendations** to a **client**, either upon its request or at the initiative of the investment firm, in respect of one or more **transactions** relating to **financial instruments**.'[64] To substantiate, Article 9 Delegated Regulation (EU) 2017/565[65] stipulates that a personal recommendation is a 'recommendation that is made to a person in his capacity as an investor or potential investor, or in his capacity as an agent for an investor or potential investor. That recommendation shall be presented as suitable for that person, or shall be based on a consideration of the circumstances of that person.' In addition, it must 'take one of the following sets of steps: (a) to buy, sell, subscribe for, exchange, redeem, hold or underwrite a particular financial instrument; (b) to exercise or not to exercise any right conferred by a particular financial instrument to buy, sell, subscribe for, exchange, or redeem a financial instrument.' Finally, Article 9 stipulates that a recommendation will not be regarded as a personal recommendation if it is exclusively issued to the public. As a result, advice given in a newspaper, journal, magazine, web article, television or radio does not constitute investment advice within the meaning of MiFID II. Tips in stock market information services and stock market letters also usually do not constitute investment advice.[66]

41 Investment advice is traditionally provided in discussions between employees of an investment firm and the client. The digitisation of business life has meanwhile also produced other forms of

---

[60] Cf. Art. 10(3) Delegated Directive 2017/593.
[61] Cf. Art. 10(4) Delegated Directive 2017/593.
[62] I. Koller, in: Assmann et al. (eds.), *Kommentar zum Wertpapierhandelsrecht*, § 80 para. 149.
[63] See R. Veil § 9 para. 17.
[64] Cf. Art. 4(1) no. 4 MiFID II.
[65] This Regulation was amended by Commission Delegated Regulation (EU) 2021/1253 of 21 April 2021 amending Delegated Regulation (EU) 2017/565 as regards the integration of sustainability factors, risks and preferences into certain organisational requirements and operating conditions for investment firms, OJ L 277 of 2.8.2021, p. 1.
[66] Cf. H.-D. Assmann, in: Assmann et al. (eds.), *Kommentar zum Wertpapierhandelsrecht*, § 2 para. 176.

investment advice (so-called **robo advice**), which, for investors, can be a cost-effective alternative to traditional investment advice. These other forms of investment advice are partially or fully automated systems that function entirely or largely without human interaction. Recommendations are made on the basis of an algorithm that takes into account the client's information, in particular about his investment objectives. This has the advantage of a higher degree of rationality than traditional investment advice given by a human. Digital advice on capital investments does not take place in a legal vacuum. The MiFID II regime is technology-neutral and therefore also applies to digital investment advice.[67]

Investment advice is to be distinguished from **investment brokerage** in particular. This investment service consists of the receipt and transmission of orders relating to one or more financial instruments.[68] This is done by bringing two or more investors together, which enables a business deal to be concluded between these investors.[69] Investment brokerage is provided by anyone who, as a 'messenger', forwards the investor's declaration of intent, which is aimed at the acquisition or sale of financial instruments, to the person with whom the investor wishes to conclude such a deal.[70] The activity must go beyond simply providing evidence of the opportunity to conclude transactions in financial instruments. Cases in which the service is limited to establishing contact between the investor and a seller of financial instruments are not considered investment brokerage.[71] However, in these cases, there is also no advice given, eg about the investment goals and the risk-bearing capacity of the investor, which is characteristic of investment advice.[72] 42

MiFID II differentiates according to whether the investment advice is provided independently or not. **Independent investment advice** is also called fee-based independent investment advice because the consultant demands remuneration from the client (on the basis of a contract). This regime reflects mis-selling problems observed in all European countries under the MiFID I regime.[73] Thus, strict requirements apply. In particular, the investment firm is not permitted to accept or retain any fees, commissions or other monetary or non-monetary benefits from a third party or a person acting on behalf of a third party for the provision of the service to the clients.[74] Payments are made solely by the customer. If the advice is not classified as independent fee-based investment advice, the investment firm can indirectly financially benefit 'through the recommended financial products' by receiving financial inducements from the issuer of the product. 43

2. Rules of Conduct

MiFID II recognises that investment recommendations are of paramount importance to investors and that investment decisions have become complex.[75] It therefore aims to improve client protection through information (so-called information model). The term '**client**' 44

---

[67] Cf. BaFin, Robo Advice, 19 February 2020.
[68] Cf. Annex I Section A no. 1 MiFID II.
[69] Cf. recital 44 MiFID II.
[70] Cf. BaFin, Notes on Investment Advice (Merkblatt zur Anlageberatung) of 17 May 2011, last amended on 18 February 2019.
[71] Cf. BaFin, Notes on Investment Advice (Merkblatt zur Anlageberatung) of 17 May 2011, last amended on 18 February 2019; H.-D. Assmann, in: Assmann et al. (eds.), *Kommentar zum Wertpapierhandelsrecht*, § 2 para. 127.
[72] Cf. H.-D. Assmann, in: Assmann et al. (eds.), *Kommentar zum Wertpapierhandelsrecht*, § 2 para. 129.
[73] Cf. M. Brenncke, in: Lehmann/Kumpan (eds.), *European Financial Services Law*, Art. 24 MiFID II para. 31.
[74] Cf. Art. 24(7)(b) MiFID II.
[75] Cf. recital 70 MiFID II.

means 'any natural or legal person to whom an investment firm provides investment or ancillary services'.[76] This can be either a **professional client** or a **retail investor**.[77] Because of the disparate nature of the multitude of investors, the categories remain vague. This is not to say, however, that the requirements for investment advice are the same with regard to all kinds of investors. The question of whether a financial instrument is suitable for a client depends on the customer's goals and his knowledge, ie it is taken into account when investors are inexperienced and risk-averse.[78] The following paragraphs will deal only with obligations that apply to investment firms providing investment advice to retail investors, taking into account that European legislation has aligned the requirements for investment firms with the **idea of sustainability**. First, Delegated Regulation (EU) No. 2021/1253 incorporates sustainability factors, risks and preferences into organisational requirements and conditions for the performance of the activities of investment firms. Second, the disclosure obligations provided for financial advisors in Regulation (EU) 2019/2088 (SFDR) also become relevant. However, the transparency of sustainability risk policies (Article 3), transparency of adverse sustainability impacts at entity level (Article 4), transparency of remuneration policies in relation to the integration of sustainability risks (Article 5) and the transparency of the integration of sustainability risks (Article 6) are not considered in detail below.

(a) Exploration

45   An investment firm is first required to obtain **information** (i) about the client's **knowledge** and **experience** of dealing in certain types of financial instruments or investment services, (ii) about the client's **financial situation**, including his ability to bear losses, and (iii) about his **investment objectives**,[79] including his risk tolerance, so as to enable the investment firm to recommend to the client the services and products that are suitable for the client and, in particular, correspond to his risk tolerance and ability to bear losses. This is also referred to with the words *'know your customer'*.[80]

46   The general requirements of Art. 25(2) MiFID II are specified in the Delegated Regulation 2017/565.[81] For example, information about the client's financial situation includes information about the origin and amount of the client's regular income, assets, investments and real estate as well as regular financial obligations. With regard to the client's investment objectives, information must be obtained about the period in which the client intends to hold the investment, the client's risk preferences, risk profile and the purpose of the investment. Finally, a client must be asked whether he wants to take **sustainability factors** into consideration in the selection process of financial instruments. This implies, among other things, investing a minimum amount in environmentally sustainable investments.

(b) Information

47   An investment firm must provide its clients with 'all relevant information'.[82] Information requirements have increased steadily over the course of almost three decades. The latest

---

[76] Cf. Art. 4(1) no. 9 MiFID II.
[77] Cf. Art. 4(1) no. 10 and 11 MiFID II.
[78] Cf., with regard to MiFID I, N. Moloney, 13 EBOR (2012), 169, 179 ff.
[79] See also R. Veil § 23 on the different investment objectives.
[80] Cf. P. Nelson, *Capital Markets Law and Compliance*, para. 14.52.
[81] Cf. Art. 54(2), (5) and (7), Art. 55(1) Regulation 2017/565.
[82] Cf. recital 72 MiFID II.

reform, realised through MiFID II, takes particular account of the fact that financial instruments are highly complex products and that their design is subject to continuous innovation.[83] The regulatory requirements also take into account that investors often have difficulties understanding financial products. **Comprehensibility** is therefore an essential requirement of MiFID II. Furthermore, the rules endeavour to counter the problem of *information overload*[84] by simply limiting the maximum amount of information documents.

The current regime consists of three pillars. The first pillar concerns **general mandatory information** that an investment firm must provide before or when providing investment services. The information relates to the investment firm itself as well as its services, the financial instruments and proposed investment strategies, execution venues and costs as well as ancillary costs. Clients should reasonably understand the types of financial instruments or investment services offered to or requested by them, as well as their respective risks, and be able to make their investment decisions on that basis. The information can also be made available in standardised form. It must be presented in such a way that it can be **understood** by an **average member** of the **group** to whom it is **directed** or by whom it is likely to be received.[85] 48

The second pillar of the information model is specifically tailored to investment advice and requires an investment firm to **disclose** the **nature** and **content** of the **investment advice**. An investment firm that provides investment advice must inform the client comprehensively and well in advance about (i) whether the investment advice is provided independently or not (see para. 43), (ii) whether the investment advice is based on an extensive or rather limited analysis of various types of financial instruments; and (iii) whether the investment firm will regularly provide the client with a suitability assessment concerning the recommended financial instruments. The details of the disclosure obligation are covered by Article 52 Delegated Regulation 2017/562. The information now also includes **sustainability factors**, which are taken into consideration in the selection process of financial instruments.[86] 49

Finally, investment advice must contain **product-specific information**. This is done either by means of a key information sheet (to be drawn up in accordance with the provisions of the PRIIPS Regulation) or by means of a 'short and easily understandable information sheet' or other type of **information document**.[87] An information sheet must contain the essential information about the respective financial instrument, so that the client can assess the type of instrument, how it works, the associated risks, the prospects for returns and capital repayment under different market conditions, as well as the costs associated with the investment, and is able to compare all this to the characteristics of other financial instruments. For non-complex instruments, the maximum size of an information sheet is two A4 pages. 50

---

[83] Cf. recital 79 MiFID II.
[84] See R. Veil § 6 para. 32.
[85] Cf. Art. 44(2)(d) Regulation 2017/565.
[86] 'Sustainability factors' mean environmental, social and employee matters, respect for human rights, anti-corruption and anti-bribery matters. Cf. Art. 2(9) Delegated Regulation (EU) 2017/565 in connection with Art. 2, point (22) Regulation (EU) 2019/2088 (SFDR).
[87] Cf. ESMA, Guidelines on MiFID II Product Governance Requirements, 5 February 2018, ESMA35-43-620 EN, para 52.

(c) Assessment of Suitability

51 The so-called *suitability doctrine* is at the heart of MiFID II's client protection regime: an investment firm may recommend to its client only those financial instruments and investment services that are suitable for the client based on the information obtained. The details of this process-based regime[88] can be found in Articles 54 and 55 of the Delegated Regulation 2017/565. Looking at the comprehensive and detailed set of rules, it becomes clear what outstanding importance the legislature attaches to suitability testing. The focus is on the individual investor being advised by the investment firm, not on the average customer! For example, a derivative may be suitable for a commercially savvy attorney; it is not, however, for a risk-averse pensioner who wants to invest the money for the long term.

52 A transaction is **suitable** for a client if it (i) **corresponds** to the **investment objectives** of the client in question, also with regard to his willingness to take risks and any **sustainability preferences**, (ii) it is designed in such a way that any **investment risks** associated with the transaction are **financially acceptable** considering the client's investment objectives, and (iii) it is such that the client has the necessary experience and knowledge in order to **understand** the **risks** involved in the transaction or in the management of his portfolio.[89] The suitability test does not require an investment firm to recommend the most suitable financial instrument.[90] The target market determined by the manufacturer or distributor (see para. 27) does not set any limits to the recommendation.[91] However, an investment firm has a special duty of care when it recommends a product to a client who is not included in the product's target market.[92] If an investment firm cannot obtain the necessary information about the client (see para. 45), it must not recommend any investment services or financial instruments to the client (**supervisory prohibition**).[93]

53 An investment firm must provide its retail client with a **statement** on the **suitability** of the financial instrument. It may not make a recommendation if the instruments are not suitable for the client. However, an investment firm shall not recommend financial instruments or decide to trade such instruments as meeting a client's or potential client's **sustainability preferences** when those financial instruments do not meet those preferences.[94] A 'brown' product may therefore be recommended to a client interested in 'green' investments, but the investment firm may not describe it as 'green'. The purpose is to prevent greenwashing.

(d) Execution Only

54 Under certain conditions MiFID II allows an investment firm to not obtain any information from its client.[95] This applies to companies whose investment services only consist of the **execution** of **client orders** or the **receipt** and **transmission** of **client orders** (also referred to as *execution only*). Essentially, this concerns financial transactions on a commission basis,

---

[88] Cf. M. *Brenncke*, in: Lehmann/Kumpan, European Financial Services Law, Art. 25 MiFID II para. 5.
[89] Cf. Art. 54(2)(a)–(c) Regulation 2017/562.
[90] Cf. *Brenncke*, in: Lehmann/Kumpan, European Financial Services Law, Art. 25 MiFID II para. 12.
[91] Cf. Art. 54(2)(a)–(c) Regulation 2017/562.
[92] Cf. I. Koller, in: Assmann et al. (eds.), *Kommentar zum Wertpapierhandelsrecht*, § 64 para. 41; M. Brenncke, in: Lehmann/Kumpan (eds.), European Financial Services Law, Art. 24 MiFID II para. 14.
[93] Cf. Art. 54(8) Regulation 2017/562.
[94] Cf. Art. 54(10) Regulation 2017/562, as amended by Delegated Regulation 2021/1253.
[95] Cf. Art. 25(4) MiFID II.

proprietary trading, contract brokerage and investment brokerage. Naturally, this privilege is limited to transactions involving only **non-complex financial instruments**.[96] It is also a prerequisite that the service is provided at the request of the client, that the client is informed about the absence of a suitability assessment, and that the firm complies with the rules on conflicts of interest.[97]

3. Obligations under Private Law

MiFID II does not specify any requirements for legal relationships under private law. In particular, it does not make any explicit statement on the civil liability of an investment firm due to incorrect investment advice. In the absence of a European regulation, it is up to the national legal systems of the individual Member States to determine the contractual consequences of a violation of the rules of conduct.[98] This is a central issue, however: It is indispensable for effective investor protection that investors are compensated for incorrect information they are given.[99] Private enforcement not only has a compensatory but also a preventive function.[100]

The legal situation in Europe has so far only been researched in part. Comparative research on English, French, Italian, Dutch and Swedish law shows that the basis for claims lies in contract law and tort law.[101] There are different answers to the question of the relationship between supervisory and civil law, called 'hybridisation of judicial reasoning' by M.W. Wallinga.[102] This will be discussed below using German law as an example.

The starting point for the legal development in Germany is the famous **Bond decision** of the Federal Court of Justice made in 1993.[103] The Court not only commented on the conditions under which a contract between an investment advisor and a client is concluded, but also set out the obligations an investment advisor has towards his client.

Facts: The plaintiffs had been investing their savings (approx. DM 55,000) with the defendant Volksbank for more than 20 years in secure forms of investment (fixed-term deposits, savings balances, federal savings notes). After an amount of over DM 20,000 had become due, a consultation took place about the reinvestment of this amount. The investment advisor presented the plaintiffs with a list of offers from their investment programme, which listed, inter alia, the DM bond of the Australian Bond Finance Ltd. Before taking up this investment recommendation, the defendant had informed itself that the bond had been admitted to official trading on the Frankfurt Stock Exchange shortly beforehand on the basis of a prospectus containing an audit opinion, and had obtained the listing prospectus. The Australian Ratings Agency had already rated the bond 'BB' (speculative

---

[96] Cf. Art. 25(4)(a) MiFID II in conjunction with Art. 57 Regulation 2017/565.
[97] Cf. Art. 25(4)(b)-(d) MiFID II.
[98] Cf., with regard to MiFID I, ECJ of 30 May 2013, Case C-604/11, ZIP (2013), 1417, 1419, para. 57 (Juzgado de Primera Instancia n° 12 de Madrid).
[99] Cf. P. Mülbert, ZHR 177 (2013), 160, 194.
[100] Cf. C. Kumpan and A. Hellgardt, DB (2006), 1714.
[101] Cf. A. Perrone and S. Valente, 13 EBOR (2012), 31, 33; M.W. Wallinga, *EU investor protection regulation and private law*, passim; F. Walla, 22 EBLR (2011), 211, 218–219, with regard to Swedish law.
[102] M.W. Wallinga, *EU investor protection regulation and private law*, 393: 'The hybridisation of judicial reasoning as a result of the complementarity model demonstrates the integration of EU investor protection regulation into national private law'.
[103] BGH of 6. 7. 1993 – XI ZR 12/93, BGHZ 123, 126.

with below-average coverage) in June 1988 and 'B' (highly speculative with low capital coverage) in December 1988. After the bond's listing on the stock exchange, it was rated 'CCC', indicating the risk of the issuer's bankruptcy. On the basis of the adviser's recommendation, the plaintiffs bought the bond with a nominal value of DM 20,000 from the defendant.

59 The BGH ruled that an advisory contract had been concluded between the investors and Volksbank: 'If a prospective investor approaches a bank or a bank's investment advisor approaches a client in order to be advised or advise on the investment of a sum of money, this constitutes an offer to conclude an investment advisory contract that is tacitly accepted by starting the consultation.'

60 Advice from a bank or an investment advisor must, firstly, be based on whether the intended investment transaction is intended to serve as a safe investment or whether it is speculative in nature. With this objective in mind, the recommended investment must be tailored to the personal circumstances of the client, ie **'investor-appropriate'**.[104] Secondly, the advice must be **'instrument-specific'**. This means that concerning the object of the investment, the advice must relate to those properties and risks that are or can be of material importance for the respective investment decision. A distinction must be made between general risks (economic situation, development of the stock market) and the special risks that result from the individual circumstances of the investment object (price, interest rate and currency risk). The advice given by the bank must be correct and thorough, comprehensible and complete.[105]

61 In the *Bond* decision, the BGH ruled that the defendant had violated its obligations in several ways: First, the defendant's investment advisor's response to the question of the bond's price risk had been misleading. The risk of the proposed investment was the issuer's possible bankruptcy. Such bankruptcy would not only have resulted in the loss of interest payments but also in a decline in the bond issue's market value. Second, the recommendation to buy the bond issue was not 'investor-appropriate'. The defendant had known from their long-term business relationship that the plaintiffs had invested their savings exclusively in secure forms of investment and had so far avoided any risk of loss. They had no experience in corporate bonds. Knowing these circumstances, recommending to buy foreign corporate bonds using a substantial part of the savings, and without a thorough investigation into the creditworthiness of the foreign issuer, was a breach of a duty.[106]

62 The BGH has outlined and further developed advisory obligations in numerous rulings. The *Lehman* decisions represent a milestone. According to the rulings, an investment advisor has to inform customers about the **general issuer risk**:[107] When selling index certificates, the advisory bank is obliged to inform the investor that he will lose all of the invested capital in the event of the issuer's insolvency, even if there is no specific indication of an impending insolvency. However, according to the BGH, if the bank has properly provided information about the general issuer risk, no further information is required.

63 The principles of contractual obligations developed by the BGH in the *Bond* judgment must be specified in more detail in each individual case. In supervisory law, legislature has already regulated a variety of aspects of investor client protection with differentiated obligations. The question therefore arises as to whether the supervisory rules of conduct can be

---

[104] BGH of 6. 7. 1993 – XI ZR 12/93, BGHZ 123, 126, 129.
[105] BGH of 6. 7. 1993 – XI ZR 12/93, BGHZ 123, 126, 129.
[106] BGH of 6. 7. 1993 – XI ZR 12/93, BGHZ 123, 126, 129 f.
[107] BGH of 27. 9. 2011 – XI ZR 182/10, BGHZ 191, 119, 125 ff.

applied to determine the contractual obligations. This question is highly controversial because when regulating the obligations, the European legislator did not have legal consequences in private law in mind, but rather developed those obligations as behavioural standards that are monitored by a supervisory authority. Nevertheless, some advocate that the supervisory rules are **dual in nature**, that is, those exact rules also apply when it comes to contractual relationships.[108] Others assign at least some kind of impact on private law to the supervisory obligations,[109] in the sense that they indirectly affect the contractual duties of the investment advisor (also called spill-over effect—*Ausstrahlungswirkung*).

The BGH is opposed to the application of supervisory law in private law.[110] The court recognises that the supervisory regulations 'can be of importance for the content and scope of (pre-)contractual information and advice obligations.'[111] However, according to the BGH, the rules are 'exclusively of a public law nature and therefore do not affect the civil law obligation relationship between the investment services company and the client.' According to the BGH, the responsibility lies with the BaFin, which supervises investment firms. The provisions of supervisory law 'cannot justify an independent obligation under the law of obligations to inform the defendant about the profit margin achieved by a securities transaction, not even through a spill-over. The supervisory rules of conduct [...], insofar as their objective is investor protection, can be of importance for the content and scope of (pre-)contractual information and advice obligations. However, their scope of protection under private law does not go beyond those (pre-)contractual obligations.'[112]

VI. Asset Management

1. Terminology

Asset management is characterised by the fact that a (natural or legal) person manages assets that are economically not attributed to the person, but to a third party.[113] The asset manager is therefore involved in the asset investment affairs of another person. In this respect, he looks after the interests of the other person. He has a certain freedom of action.

MiFID II understands portfolio management as 'the **management** of **portfolios** on a **client-by-client basis** with a **margin of discretion** within the scope of the **client's mandate**, provided that these portfolios contain one or more financial instruments.'[114] The regulatory

---

[108] Cf. J. Köndgen, ZBB (1996), 361 f.; N. Lang, ZBB (2004), 289, 295; F. Leisch, *Informationspflichten nach § 31 WpHG*, 85; C. Benicke, *Wertpapiervermögensverwaltung*, 461 ff.; T. Möllers, in: *Kölner Kommentar zum WpHG*, § 31 para. 6 f.
[109] Cf. I. Koller, in: Assmann et al. (eds.), *Kommentar zum Wertpapierhandelsrecht*, § 64 para. 9; R. Sethe, *Anlegerschutz im Recht der Vermögensverwaltung* (2005), 748 ff.
[110] This applies to the XIth Civil Chamber; the issue is handled differently by the IIIrd Civil Chamber. According to J. Forschner, *Wechselwirkungen von Aufsichtsrecht und Zivilrecht*, 203, the two Civil Chambers must therefore call the Grand Senate pursuant to § 132 GVG.
[111] Cf. BGH of 19. 6. 2006 – XI ZR 56/05, WM (2007), 487, 489.
[112] Cf. BGH of 17. 9. 2013 – XI ZR 332/12, NZG (2013), 1226, 1228 para. 20.
[113] F. Schäfer et al., in: Schäfer et al. (eds.), *Handbuch der Vermögensverwaltung*, § 1 para. 8.
[114] Art. 4 (1) no. 8 MiFID II.

term is broad. It covers both trust management as well as administration by way of power of attorney.

67 Trust management (widespread in the Anglo-Saxon region) indicates that the asset manager acquires the securities as property and holds them in trust for the benefit of his clients. The (external) legal power of the asset manager is limited (internally) by the trust agreement. By means of indirect representation, the trustee manages assets that are legally his own but economically the client's.[115] Clients have a contractual right to the proper administration and transfer of the managed assets.[116]

68 In contrast, power of attorney is mainly used in German-speaking countries. The asset manager acts in the name of and for the account of a third party, so that the investor becomes the owner of the securities and other assets.[117] However, the asset manager can also be authorised to dispose of the entrusted assets in his own name.[118]

69 The asset management contract can entitle the asset manager to dispose of the investor's custody account. It is then necessary to make a separate agreement granting the asset manager *in rem* power of disposition.[119] In this case, the asset manager requires a bank power of attorney.

70 The MiFID II regime is not limited to traditional asset management, but also applies to **digital asset management** (MiFID II technology neutrality).[120] Digital asset management indicates that the service is provided on the basis of an algorithm that offers the client a solution based on prior data entry.[121] The agreed upon strategy is implemented in the client's investment portfolio using algorithms. The proposals for a change in composition of the portfolio are also based on an algorithm. The European Commission has rightly made it clear that the investment firm is responsible for the use of the software.[122]

2. Rules of Conduct

71 The obligations for an investment firm are essentially the same as those for investment advice. An investment firm must obtain the relevant **information** about its clients and provide the clients with general (see para. 48) and specific information (see para. 50). Transactions that are carried out in the context of financial portfolio management must, as with investment advice (see para. 51), be suitable for the customer (so-called **suitability assessment**).

72 The European legislature has strengthened the regime for **inducements** (fees, commissions and any monetary or non-monetary benefits paid or provided by any third party)

---

[115] F. Möslein, in: Langenbucher et al. (eds.), *Bankrechts-Handbuch*, ch. 34 para. 11.
[116] F. Schäfer et al., in: Schäfer et al. (eds.), *Handbuch der Vermögensverwaltung*, § 1 para. 43.
[117] F. Schäfer et al., in: Schäfer et al. (eds.), *Handbuch der Vermögensverwaltung*, § 1 para. 53; F. Möslein, in: Langenbucher et al. (eds.), *Bankrechts-Handbuch*, ch. 34 para. 10.
[118] F. Schäfer et al., in: Schäfer et al. (eds.), *Handbuch der Vermögensverwaltung*, § 1 para. 53.
[119] F. Schäfer et al., in: Schäfer et al. (eds.), *Handbuch der Vermögensverwaltung*, § 1 para. 55; F. Möslein, in: Langenbucher et al. (eds.), *Bankrechts-Handbuch*, ch. 34 para. 10.
[120] Cf. U. Schäfer, in: Assmann et al. (eds.), *Handbuch des Kapitalanlagerechts*, § 23 para. 20.
[121] Cf. M. Brenncke, in: Lehmann/Kumpan, *European Financial Services Law*, Art. 24 MiFID II para. 38.
[122] Cf. Art. 54(1) subsec. 2 Delegated Regulation (EU) 2017/565: 'Where […] portfolio management services are provided in whole or in part through an automated or semi-automated system, the responsibility to undertake the suitability assessment shall lie with the investment firm providing the service and shall not be reduced by the use of an electronic system in making the […] decision to trade.'

taking into account mis-selling practices and poor quality of investment services.[123] Under MiFID II, particularly strict requirements apply to inducements. An investment firm may not accept or retain any inducements from third parties in connection with financial portfolio management. Only minor non-monetary benefits are permitted (*de minimis* exception), provided that they are (i) suitable for improving the quality of the investment service provided to the client, (ii) reasonable and proportionate in terms of their scope and (iii) unambiguously disclosed to the client.

The asset manager has a certain amount of discretion. It therefore makes sense that the client should be regularly informed about how the asset manager has invested the money. The asset manager is therefore obliged to report regularly on the development of the portfolio. At the heart of the **reporting requirement** is a periodic list that includes a fair and balanced review of the measures taken and the performance of the portfolio during the regular reporting period of three months.[124] In addition, the asset manager must inform his client immediately if a loss threshold of 10% of the portfolio is exceeded.[125]

VII. Conclusion

The European regime of investment services has now reached a proud age of 30 years. It is characterised by a tremendous depth of detail concerning the rules of conduct. This is due to the objective of creating a uniform legal framework within the EU. This entails considerable regulatory costs for investment firms. In view of the outstanding importance of securities investments for EU citizens' pensions provisions, it was inevitable to create a dense network of rules of conduct that takes into account the information deficits of investors and the various conflicts of interest of investment firms. The complexity of the regulatory levels is of course in need of improvement. The numerous information obligations and other prudential requirements originate from MiFID II, the provisions of which have been implemented in the national legal systems, but are specified in a European regulation (2017/562). This is an unnecessarily complex legal situation.

Despite the far-reaching supervisory regulations, the EU is far from having a uniform legal framework. This is mainly due to the fact that the European legal acts do not cover the legal relationships under private law. European legal research on private law obligations in investment advice, asset management and other securities services is still in its early stages. For the time being, we only know that fundamental issues are treated very differently.[126] This applies, for example, to the question of whether the supervisory rules of conduct affect private law obligations or are even directly applicable in private law. In view of this level of knowledge, it should come as no surprise that the discussion about harmonising private law governing investment services is still in its infancy.

Over the past 30 years, the content of the rules of conduct under supervisory law has also evolved. The idea remains that investors are able to draw appropriate conclusions for an

---

[123] Cf. Art. 60 Regulation 2017/562.
[124] Cf. Art. 60 Regulation 2017/562.
[125] Cf. Art. 62(1) Regulation 2017/562.
[126] Impressive analyses by M.W. Wallinga, *EU investor protection regulation and private law*.

investment decision from the information provided.[127] However, MiFID II and PRIIPS Regulation now recognise that the majority of investors have no relevant financial knowledge and tend to behave irrationally. The matter has therefore developed into a kind of consumer protection law[128] that operates with paternalistic concepts. The information model complemented by product governance rules is supplemented by product intervention powers of the supervisory authorities, which can be exercised if investor protection cannot be established through information.

77 These developments reflect extensive experience with poor investment advice. Jurisprudence clearly shows that advisors repeatedly recommend unsuitable securities to their clients. It remains to be seen whether the increasing digitisation of investment advice and asset management will help clients invest more appropriately and be less exposed to harmful conflicts of interest.

---

[127] Cf. V. Colaert, in: Busch et al. (eds.), *Capital Markets Union in Europe*, para. 16.77.
[128] Cf. C. Vogel, *Vom Anlegerschutz zum Verbraucherschutz*, passim.

§ 31

Product Intervention

Bibliography

Bußalb, Jean-Pierre, *Produktintervention und Vermögensanlagen*, 12 WM (2017), 553–558; Colaert, Veerle, *The MiFID and PRIIPs Product Intervention Regime: In Need of Intervention?*, 1 ECFR (2020), 99–124; Ehlers, Jan H., *Das Produktinterventionsrecht der BaFin nach § 4b WpHG*, 9 WM (2017), 420–427; Ferran, Eilís, *Regulatory Lessons from the Payment Protection Insurance Mis-selling Scandal in the UK*, 13 EBOR (2012), 247–270; Gläßner, Anne, *Die Beschränkung des Vertriebs von Finanzprodukten* (2017); Kerssenbrock, Rupert H. Graf, *Die Regulierung komplexer Finanzinstrumente: MiFID II/MiFIR und Behavioral Finance* (2018); Klingenbrunn, Daniel, *Produktverbote zur Gewährleistung von Finanzmarktstabilität* (2018); Moloney, Niamh, *The Investor Model Underlying the EU's Investor Protection Regime: Consumers or Investors?*, 13 EBOR (2012), 169–193; Mülbert, Peter O., *Anlegerschutz und Finanzmarktregulierung*, ZHR 177 (2013), 160–211; Schäfer, Frank A., *Überblick über die Produktinterventionsrechte deutscher und europäischer Finanzmarktaufsichtsbehörden*, in: Festschrift Reinhard Marsch-Barner (2018), 471–482; Veil, Rüdiger, *Regulierung von Finanzprodukten – Abschied vom Leitbild des verständigen Anlegers?*, in: Bumke, Christian and Röthel, Anne (eds.), *Autonomie im Recht* (2017), 185–200; Veil, Rüdiger, *Produktintervention im Finanzdienstleistungsrecht. Systematik, Dogmatik und Grundsatzfragen der neuen Aufsichtsbefugnisse*, in: Bankrechtliche Vereinigung (ed.), Bankrechtstag 2017 (2018), 159–176; Zerey, Jean-Claude (ed.), *Finanzderivate*, 4th edn. (2016).

I. Introduction

The financial crisis of 2007/08 revealed that the MiFID information model[1] had reached its limits and that further regulatory approaches were necessary in order to achieve effective investor protection and guarantee the stability of the financial system.[2] This insight is also based on the findings of behavioural finance[3] and initially led to individual Member States granting their supervisory authorities product intervention powers. 1

The first spectacular case of a ban on the sale of financial instruments concerned contingent convertible bonds (CoCos). This type of financial instrument is designed in a similar way to traditional convertible bonds.[4] These are bonds whose nominal value is written down or converted into equity capital in certain circumstances (so-called trigger events), eg if the issuer no longer meets certain balance sheet ratios following losses.[5] Investors may therefore 2

---

[1] See R. Veil § 30 para. 46.
[2] Cf. E. Ferran, 13 EBOR (2012), 247, 265–267; N. Moloney, 13 EBOR (2012), 169, 181–183.
[3] Cf. R. Veil, *Regulierung von Finanzprodukten – Abschied vom Leitbild des verständigen Anlegers?*, in: Bumke and Röthel (eds.), *Autonomie im Recht*, 185, 190 ff.
[4] See R. Veil § 8 para. 18.
[5] A distinction is made between book value-based, market value-based and discretionary trigger events. In more detail R. Kerssenbrock, *Die Regulierung komplexer Finanzinstrumente*, 11 ff.

receive shares in the issuer rather than getting their capital back.[6] In the case of CoCos, the exchange from debt to equity takes place automatically, namely upon the occurrence of the circumstances specified in the bond terms and conditions. The creditor becomes a shareholder of the company, usually in a near-bankruptcy crisis of the company.

3   *Example*: The FCA found that banks had issued CoCos worth about $ 70 billion between 2009 and 2013.[7] The agency also estimated that the European market for CoCos would grow to more than € 150 billion by 2020. The FCA was therefore concerned that banks would increasingly issue CoCos to meet Tier 1 capital requirements. This would lead to an increase in CoCos being issued to retail clients of banks. According to the FCA, retail clients are particularly worthy of protection because of the complexity and risk structure of CoCos.[8] The FCA also complained that irrational investor behaviour was imminent. In view of low returns on conventional financial products, it was likely that investors who were previously only familiar with cash savings would be tempted by the high interest rates offered by CoCos.[9]

4   In other Member States, the authorities were given similar powers, and similar measures were taken to protect investors from complex financial products. Against this background, it is not surprising that the European legislator introduced uniform rules across the EU by way of reforming its legislation on investment services. According to the European legislator, seizing product intervention powers should be the last resort for supervisory authorities.[10]

II. Legal Sources

5   The Markets in Financial Instruments Regulation (**MiFIR**) provides for a 'mechanism for prohibiting or restricting the marketing, distribution and sale of any financial instrument or structured deposit giving rise to serious concerns regarding investor protection, orderly functioning and integrity of financial markets, or commodities markets, or the stability of the whole or part of the financial system.'[11] At its core is the power of product intervention by national supervisors.[12] ESMA and EBA have powers of temporary intervention.[13] These are subsidiary powers of intervention because they presuppose that the competent national authority has not taken measures to address the threat or that the measures taken do not address the threat.[14] Finally, under Article 16 PRIIPS Regulation,[15] EIOPA may prohibit

---

[6] Vgl. T. Danz et al., in: Zerey (ed.), *Finanzderivate*, § 41 para. 37.
[7] Cf. FCA, Temporary product intervention rules – restrictions in relation to the retail distribution of contingent convertible instruments, August 2014, para. 35–37.
[8] Similarly ESMA, Statement: Potential Risks Associated with Investing in Contingent Convertible Instruments v. 31.7.2014, ESMA/2014/944, para. 6.
[9] Cf. FCA, Temporary product intervention rules – restrictions in relation to the retail distribution of contingent convertible instruments, August 2014, para. 14–25.
[10] Commission Staff Working Paper: Impact Assesment of the MiFID II and MiFIR, 20.11.2011, SEC (2011) 1226 final, p. 45; cf. also ESMA, Consultation Paper MiFID II/MiFIR, 22 May 2014, ESMA/2014/549, p. 167; consenting A. Gläßner, *Die Beschränkung des Vertriebs von Finanzprodukten*, 304 ('ultima ratio').
[11] Recital 29 subsec. 1 sentence 1 MiFIR.
[12] Art. 42 MiFIR.
[13] Art. 40 and 41 MiFIR.
[14] Art. 40 (2)(c) and Art. 41(2)(c) MiFIR.
[15] Regulation (EU) No 1286/2014 of the European Parliament and of the Council of 26 November 2014 on key information documents for packaged retail and insurance-based investment products (PRIIPs), OJ L 352, 9 December 2014, p. 1–23.

or restrict the marketing, distribution or sale of certain insurance investment products or insurance investment products.

The Level 1 provisions provide for principle-based requirements for product intervention. To ensure that the powers are exercised as uniformly as possible in the EU, the European Commission has specified the MiFIR requirements in a Level 2 Regulation. The **Delegated Regulation (EU) 2017/567**[16] provides, in its Articles 19–21, criteria and factors to be taken into account by ESMA, EBA and national authorities when determining whether there are investor protection concerns or a threat to the orderly functioning and integrity of financial or commodity markets or to the stability of the financial system.

III. Product Intervention Pursuant to Article 42 MiFIR

1. Premises

An NCA has the power to prohibit or restrict the **marketing** and **distribution** of **financial instruments** and structured deposits as well as certain types of **financial activities** and **practices**. 'Financial activities and practices' refers in particular to sales and distribution practices.[17] The scope of the intervention powers pursuant to Article 42 MiFIR is conceivably broad in view of potential circumvention strategies trough financial innovation.[18] It therefore makes sense that the NCA can also take action against financial activities and practices. This, of course, raises the question of how these terms are to be interpreted.[19] The preferred interpretation is that a financial activity or practice must be related to a financial instrument or structured deposit.

The NCA may prohibit or restrict distribution of financial products for reasons of **investor protection** or to ensure the **functioning of markets** or **financial stability**. Article 41(2)(a)(i) MiFIR requires that a financial instrument raises '*significant* investor protection concerns or poses a threat to the orderly functioning and integrity of financial markets or commodity markets.' In its Delegated Regulation (EU) 2017/567, the European Commission has set out criteria and factors to be taken into account by national authorities when determining whether there are significant investor protection concerns or whether the orderly functioning and integrity of financial markets or commodity markets or the stability of the financial system are at risk. Article 21 provides for 22 factors and criteria, such as the **degree** of **complexity**, the **extent** of potential **adverse effects**, the **type of clients involved**, and the **level of transparency of the financial instrument**. The catalogue of factors and criteria is

---

[16] Commission Delegated Regulation (EU) 2017/567 of 18 May 2016 supplementing Regulation (EU) No 600/2014 of the European Parliament and of the Council with regard to definitions, transparency, portfolio compression and supervisory measures on product intervention and positions, OJ L 87, 31 March 2017, p. 90–116.
[17] Cf. J.-P. Bußalb, WM (2017), 553, 554.
[18] Still, ESMA is in favour of extending the rules to investment companies. Cf. ESMA, Opinion on the Impact of the exclusion of fund management companies from the scope of the MiFIR Intervention Powers, 12 January 2017, ESMA50-1215332076-23.
[19] Cf. J. Ehlers, WM (2017), 420, 422.

non-exhaustive. This can be justified by the fact that the supervisory authorities should be able to intervene when new financial instruments emerge.[20]

9   The level 2 regime regulates in detail how the factors and criteria are to be assessed. For example, with respect to the degree of complexity, it is provided that the following factors and criteria are to be taken into account: (i) the nature of the underlying or reference assets and the level of transparency in relation to the underlying or reference assets; (ii) the level of transparency in relation to costs and fees; (iii) the complexity of the calculation of performance, taking into account whether the return depends on the performance of one or more underlying or reference assets; (iv) the nature and extent of possible risks; (v) whether the product or service is bundled with other products or services; (vi) the complexity of the terms and conditions.

2. Legal Consequences

10 The NCA may **prohibit** or **restrict** the **marketing** and **distribution** of financial instruments and structured deposits and types of financial activity and practice. This power is subject to the proviso that 'existing regulatory requirements under Union law [...] do not sufficiently address the risks [...] and the issue would *not* be better addressed by improved supervision or enforcement of existing requirements' (**subsidiarity**).[21] 'Existing requirements' are in particular the supervisory rules on product governance[22] and the rules on conduct for investment firms, such as the suitability doctrine.[23]

11 Finally, the **measure** must be **proportionate**, taking into account the nature of the risks identified, the level of knowledge of investors or market participants, and the likely effect of the measure on investors and market participants.[24] The interests of the providers of a financial instrument are not explicitly mentioned. However, a NCA must take them into account because a ban or restriction interferes with the providers' fundamental right to property.

12 Measures that are less intrusive than a ban include, in particular, the issuance of a warning by the respective authority. Other measures include improved transparency of product features and risks (facilitating an investment decision) and voluntary sales restrictions that reduce the likelihood of the financial instruments being sold to retail investors (eg raising the minimum investment amount).

13 The NCA may also impose a **prohibition** as a **precautionary** measure before a financial instrument is marketed, distributed or sold to clients. It can therefore also take preventive action in order to ensure investor protection or the financial stability of markets. However, the European legislator did not intend to introduce a requirement of 'product approval' or any approval procedure in the sense of a financial MOT.[25]

---

[20] Cf. ESMA, Consultation Paper MiFID II/MiFIR, 22 May 2014, ESMA/2014/549, p. 167 ('intervention powers are dynamic enough to enable NCAs [...] to deal with a range of different exceptional situations').
[21] Art. 42(2)(b) MiFIR.
[22] See R. Veil § 30 para. 22.
[23] See R. Veil § 30 para. 50.
[24] Art. 42(2)(c) MiFIR.
[25] Cf. also recital 29 subsec. 2 MiFIR; in more detail R. Veil, *Produktintervention im Finanzdienstleistungsrecht. Systematik, Dogmatik und Grundsatzfragen der neuen Aufsichtsbefugnisse*, in: Bankrechtliche Vereinigung (ed.), Bankrechtstag 2017, 159, 176 ff.

IV. Conclusion

The EU product intervention regime shows impressively that consumer protection has found its way into financial services law.[26] Its aim is to protect even the most inexperienced and irrational investor. This development is to be welcomed because of the weaknesses of the disclosure regime under MiFID II and the outstanding importance of capital investment for retail clients.

The product intervention regime has weaknesses, as financial products are treated unequally. A supervisory authority can prohibit the sale of a particularly complex product but at the same time choose to not prevent the sale of a no-less-complex product because it does not see the risk that this product will be offered to a large number of private investors. Finally, the product intervention regime carries the risk that investors will not inform themselves about financial products or will not do so adequately. Investors might assume that in the absence of prohibition or distribution restrictions, the financial products offered are understandable and do not pose (disproportionate) risks. This could lead to a situation where private investors do not carry out an independent examination and have the idea that the competent authority reacts to all risks of a financial product with adequate restrictions and prohibitions.

Nevertheless, the product intervention regime is an important step forward in realising a high level of investor protection. The first years have shown that the authorities' powers of intervention do not have an inhibiting effect on innovation. Moreover, in the few cases in which the authorities did intervene, there was a need for action because of the risk profiles and (resulting from an innovation process)[27] complexity of the financial products.[28] Paternalistic intervention by the authorities was necessary to protect the interests of consumers. But product bans also serve financial market stability. This becomes particularly relevant for financial products that are based on regulatory arbitrage and are therefore irrelevant for corporate finance.[29]

---

[26] P. Mülbert, ZHR 177 (2013), 160, 180 ff.
[27] Cf. D. Klingenbrunn, *Produktverbote zur Gewährleistung von Finanzmarktstabilität*, 269.
[28] Cf. D. Klingenbrunn, *Produktverbote zur Gewährleistung von Finanzmarktstabilität*, 269.
[29] Cf. V. Colaert, ECFR (2020), 99, 120.

§ 32

Foundations of Compliance

Bibliography

Arndorfer, Isabella and Minto, Andrea, *The 'four lines of defence model' for financial institutions*, Occasional Paper, Financial Stability Institute, December 2015; Bazley, Stuart and Haynes, Andrew, *Financial Services Authority and Risk-based Compliance*, 2nd ed. (2009); Buff, Herbert G., *Compliance: Führungsrolle durch den Verwaltungsrat* (2000); Casper, Matthias, *Rechtliche Grundlagen und aktuelle Entwicklungen der Compliance am Beispiel des Kapitalmarktrechts*, in: Hadding, Walther et al. (eds.), *Verbraucherschutz im Kreditgeschäft, Compliance in der Kreditwirtschaft, Bankrechtstag 2008*, 139–177; Chiu, Iris H.-Y., *Regulating (From) the Inside* (2015); Dreher, Meinrad, *Ausstrahlungen des Aufsichtsrechts auf das Aktienrecht*, 2–3 ZGR (2010), 496–542; Edwards, Jonathan and Wolfe, Simon, *The Compliance Function in Banks*, 12 J. Fin. Reg. & Comp. (2004), 216–224; Eisele, Dieter, *Insiderrecht und Compliance*, 23 WM (1993), 1021–1026; Kalss, Susanne, *Amtshaftung und Compliance als Instrumente zur Durchsetzung kapitalmarktrechtlicher Regelungen—Diskutiert am Beispiel Österreich*, in: Möllers, Thomas M.J. (ed.), *Vielfalt und Einheit: wirtschaftliche und rechtliche Rahmenbedingungen von Standardbildung* (2008), 81–105; Griffith, Sean J., *Corporate Governance in an Era of Compliance*, 57 William & Mary Law Review (2016), 2075–2140; Klein, Peter, *Anwendbarkeit und Umsetzung von Risikomanagementsystemen auf Compliance-Risiken im Unternehmen* (2008); Küting, Karlheinz and Busch, Julia, *Zum Wirrwarr der Überwachungsbegriffe*, 26 DB (2009), 1361–1367; Lösler, Thomas, *Compliance im Wertpapierdienstleistungskonzern* (2003); Lucius, Otto et al. (eds.), *Compliance im Finanzdienstleistungsbereich* (2010); Marekfia, Wolfgang and Nissen, Volker, *Strategisches GRC-Management*, in: Nissen, Volker, *Forschungsberichte zur Unternehmensberatung*, Working Paper (2009); Menzies, Christof, *Sarbanes-Oxley und Corporate Compliance* (2006); Mills, Annie, *Essential Strategies for Financial Services Compliance* (2008); Miller, Geoffrey P., *The Law of Governance, Risk Management, and Compliance* (2014); Miller, Geoffrey P., *The compliance function: an overview*, SSRN Working Paper (2014), available at SSRN: http://papers.ssrn.com/sol3/papers.cfm?abstract_id=2527621; Miller, Geoffrey P., *The Role of Risk Management and Compliance in Banking Integration*, SSRN Working Paper (2014), available at SSRN: http://papers.ssrn.com/sol3/papers.cfm?abstract_id=2527222; Morton, Jeffrey C., *The Development of a Compliance Culture*, 6 J. Invest. Comp. (2005), 59–66; Racz, Nicolas, Weippl, Edgar and Seufert, Andreas, *A Frame of Reference for Research of Integrated Governance, Risk & Compliance (GRC)*, in: Decker, Bart De and Schaumüller-Bichl, Ingrid (eds.), *Communications and Multimedia Security*, 106–117, available at: http://grc-resource.com/resources/racz_al_frame_reference_grc_cms2010.pdf; Schneider, Uwe H., *Compliance als Aufgabe der Unternehmensleitung*, 15 ZIP (2003), 645–650; Securities Industry Association, *The Role of Compliance*, 6 J. Invest. Comp. (2005), 4–22; Spindler, Gerald, *Compliance in der multinationalen Bankengruppe*, 20 WM (2008), 905–918; Taylor, Chris, *The evolution of compliance*, 6 J. Invest. Comp. (2005), 54–58; Walker, Rebecca, *International corporate compliance programmes*, 3 Int'l J. Discl. & Gov. (2006), 70–81; Weiss, Ulrich, *Compliance-Funktion in einer deutschen Universalbank*, Die Bank (1993), 136–139; Wild, Robert J., *Designing an Effective Securities Compliance Program*, Corporate Compliance Series, Vol. 10, looseleaf (2010–2011).

I. Compliance

1   'Compliance' is one of today's most prominently discussed legal concepts.[1] A uniform understanding of the term has not yet been achieved.[2] Based on the general meaning of the word, compliance (to comply with) means conforming to a rule.[3] It has, however, been acknowledged by legal practitioners and academics alike that the concept reaches farther than merely describing the obligation to act in accordance with the law, also encompassing the organisational provisions, policies and procedures that aim to prevent or expose breaches of law.[4] Elements of this so-called **compliance organisation** include, inter alia:

   (i)   internal compliance policies that contain basic principles to be followed by management and staff;
   (ii) informational barriers ('Chinese walls') which regulate the flow of confidential information within a company;
   (iii) whistleblowing and reporting systems for exposing and reporting violations of law;
   (iv) compliance-training programmes; and
   (v)   compliance-monitoring and surveillance systems that monitor whether applicable laws and the internal rules of the company are applied correctly.[5]

2   In more simple terms, 'compliance' describes the efforts institutions undertake to ensure that the firm and its employees do not violate applicable rules and regulations.[6] In addition to this functional meaning of compliance, the concept is also used in an organisational sense, describing an independent department of a company's organisation, responsible for any compliance-related tasks.[7] This 'compliance department' thus fulfils executive functions within the compliance organisation.[8] Finally, 'compliance' may refer to a regulatory **enforcement strategy** whereby the internal control systems are utilised by the regulators to ensure that the supervised firms obey applicable rules and regulations.[9]

---

[1] Cf. S. Kalss, in: Möllers (ed.), *Vielfalt und Einheit*, 81, 98 (one of the most important terms of company law); from a US-law perspective G.P. Miller, *The Law of Governance, Risk Management, and Compliance*, 137 ff. and S. Griffith, 57 William & Mary Law Review (2016), 2075 (arguing that compliance is the 'new corporate governance').

[2] Countless attempts have been made to define the term. For an overview of the approaches taken in Anglo-American and Continental-European law see A. Mills, *Financial Services Compliance*, 16–18; H. Buff, *Compliance: Führungsrolle durch den Verwaltungsrat*, 10 ff.; G. Miller, *The Law of Governance, Risk Management, and Compliance*, 137.

[3] A. Mills, *Financial Services Compliance*, 16–18; C. Hauschka et al., in: Hauschka et al. (eds.), *Corporate Compliance*, § 1 para. 2; U. Schneider, 15 ZIP (2003), 645, 646.

[4] Cf. A. Mills, *Financial Services Compliance*, 16–18; R. Walker, 3 Int'l J. Discl. & Gov. (2006), 70, 71; Casper, in: Hadding et al. (eds.), *Bankrechtliche Vereinigung, Bankrechtstag 2008*, 139, 141–142.

[5] Cf. R. Wild, in: *Corporate Compliance Series*, § 3.1 ff.; D. Eisele, in: Schimanski et al. (eds.), *Bankrechts-Handbuch*, § 109 para. 125 ff.; see generally C. Hauschka et al. (eds.), *Corporate Compliance*, §§ 1, 17 ff. and 48.

[6] G. Miller, *The compliance function*, 1.

[7] K. Küting and J. Busch, 26 DB (2009), 1361, 1364.

[8] Securities Industry Association, 6 J. Invest. Comp. (2005), 4 ff. ('compliance departement'); M. Casper, in: Hadding et al. (eds.), *Bankrechtliche Vereinigung, Bankrechtstag 2008*, 139, 145. See also G. Spindler, 20 WM (2008), 905, 907 (horizontal control bodies in companies). US-American legal literature in particular understands compliance in a very broad sense, which also includes the ethical dimension of business. Compliance is therefore understood as the 'moral DNA' of a company. Cf. J. Morton, 6 J. Invest. Comp (2005), 59; R. Walker, 3 Int'l J. Discl. & Gov. (2006), 70.

[9] See below para. 4 and G. Miller, *The Law of Governance, Risk Management, and Compliance*, 130 ('form of privatised law enforcement').

II. Relationship between Compliance, Risk Management and Other Internal Control Functions

The relationship between compliance and the other internal control functions of a company, such as risk management, has not yet been fully examined. At first, the distinction appears straightforward: while compliance aims to ensure conformity with legal requirements, risk management systematically identifies, assesses, monitors, controls and mitigates material risks that are likely to affect the company. Both areas, however, overlap to the extent that the risk of noncompliance with legal requirements also constitutes an operational risk that is covered by risk management. Compliance should therefore be regarded as an element of **qualitative risk management**.[10] Conversely, the fact that the requirements for the organisation of the company's risk management have become subject to supervisory law which makes them relevant to the compliance department of the supervised company, which is in turn responsible for ensuring compliance with the risk-management provisions.[11] The relationship between compliance and risk management can therefore be described as follows: compliance constitutes an element of qualitative risk management, which must control and mitigate compliance risks. At the same time, however, compliance also constitutes an indispensable prerequisite for risk management, as the compliance function monitors the effectiveness of the risk management systems and ensures abidance with the regulatory requirements.[12]

The close functional and conceptual relationship between both elements of internal control has led to the understanding that compliance and risk management constitute one uniform organisational task for the company: based on the **governance, risk and compliance (GRC) model** developed in business practice, the areas concerning governance, risk management and compliance are increasingly implemented in the organisation of firms in an integrated way.[13]

---

[10] Basel Committee on Banking Supervision, Compliance and the Compliance Function in Banks, April 2005, available at: www.bis.org/publ/bcbs113.pdf, Principle 10 ('core risk management function'). This coincides with the understanding of numerous national supervisory authorities. Cf. BaFin, Rundschreiben (circular) 05/2018 (WA)—Mindestanforderungen an die Compliance-Funktion und die weiteren Verhaltens-, Organisations- und Transparenzpflichten nach §§ 63 ff. WpHG für Wertpapierdienstleistungsunternehmen (MaComp), 19 April 2018, AT 3.2 (Germany); CSSF Circular 04/155, The Compliance Function, September 2004, para. 9 (Luxembourg); Board of Governors of the Federal Reserve System, Compliance Risk Management Programs, October 2008 (USA); FSA, Managing Compliance Risk in Major Investment Banks—Good Practices, July 2007 (UK); Rundschreiben der eidg. Bankenkommission, Überwachung und interne Kontrolle (circular), September 2006, para. 100 ff. (Switzerland). Cf. also ESMA, Guidelines on Certain Aspects of the MiFID II Compliance Function Requirements, 6 April 2021, ESMA35-36-1952, guideline 1, para. 14 ('ESMA Guidelines'); MIFID II also follows a risk-oriented approach to compliance, see below M. Wundenberg § 33 para. 15.

[11] M. Dreher, 2-3 ZGR (2010), 496, 537.

[12] Compliance and risk management stand in a symbiotic relationship to one another: an effective risk management is not possible without an effective compliance organisation, whilst compliance at the same time requires a fully operational risk management. Cf. P. Klein, *Risikomanagementsysteme*, 102. From a US-law perspective G. Miller, *The Law of Governance, Risk Management, and Compliance*, 532 (substantial overlap between risk management and compliance).

[13] Cf. N. Racz et al., *Integrated Governance, Risk & Compliance*, 106–117; C. Menzies (ed.), *Corporate Compliance*, 63–77; W. Marekfia and V. Nissen, *Strategisches GRC-Management*, 9 ff. Technically this can be achieved through standardised IT systems, such as those offered by SAP (business objects GRC solutions).

The supervisory authorities confirm this close connection between compliance and risk management,[14] the latter also termed as 'compliance in a broader sense'.[15]

5   The relationship between the different control functions within a firm (in particular compliance, risk management and internal audit) is often described by the '**three lines of defence**' model.[16] According to this model, the business units serve as a 'first' line of defence, whereby the control functions performed by compliance and risk management constitute the 'second' line of defence. The internal audit function is charged with the 'third' line of defence, conducting risk-based and general audits and reviews. While the three lines of defence model has proven to be a very useful tool to conceptualise the interaction of the respective control and governance functions, it may not fully reflect the governance requirements applicable under supervisory law, in particular after the enactment of the CRD IV/MiFID II regime.[17] Firstly, the traditional three lines of defence model does not expressly mention the pivotal role of the board with regard to compliance and risk management obligations.[18] Secondly, the 'three lines of defence' model does not expressly acknowledge the important role that supervisory authorities play in ensuring compliance with the governance (as well as other regulatory) requirements, constituting an additional 'fourth' line of defence.[19] In July 2020, a revised version of the three lines of defence model was published (now referred to as '**three lines model**').[20] The revised model explicitly follows a principles-based approach and puts a stronger emphasis on the responsibilities of board members and senior management as well as external stakeholders.[21]

III. Developments and Legal Foundations

6   In Anglo-American countries, banks began developing compliance organisations in the 1960s.[22] In continental Europe investment firms have also been setting up compliance

---

[14] Cf. Banca d'Italia, Supervisory Regulations, The Compliance Function, July 2007, p. 6 (interaction with other corporate functions). See now also ESMA, MiFID II Compliance Guidelines (fn. 10), guideline 10.

[15] BaFin, Rundschreiben (circular) 05/2018—MaComp (fn. 10), BT 1.1 para. 5. At an organisational level, compliance and risk management should generally be separated. See below M. Wundenberg § 33 para. 27–30.

[16] The 'three lines of defense model' was conceptualised in 2008–2010 by the Federation of European Risk Management Associations (FERMA) and the European Confederation of Institutes of International Auditing (ECIIA). The model was developed to provide guidance on Art. 41 of the 8th EU-Directive (Directive 2006/43/EC); cf. ECIIA/FERMA, Monitoring the effectiveness of internal control, internal audit and risk management systems, September 2010 (available at: https://www.iia.nl/SiteFiles/ECIIA%20FERMA.pdf). It was developed in more detail in an influential paper of the Institute of Internal Auditors (IIA), The three lines of defense in effective risk management and control, January 2013 (available at: https://na.theiia.org/standards-guidance/Public%20Documents/PP%20The%20Three%20Lines%20of%20Defense%20in%20Effective%20Risk%20Management%20and%20Control.pdf).

[17] Cf. M. Wundenberg § 34 on corporate governance.

[18] The CRD IV/MiFID II framework recognises – in line with the general requirements under general corporate law – that the board has the ultimate responsibility of compliance und risk management.

[19] For a critical assessment of the 'three lines of defence' model see I. Arndorfer and A. Minto, *The 'four lines of defence model' for financial institutions*, December 2015.

[20] IIA, The IIA's Three Lines Model: An update on the Three Lines of Defense, July 2020 (available at: https://na.theiia.org/about-ia/PublicDocuments/Three-Lines-Model-Updated.pdf).

[21] Cf. on principles-based approaches to regulation M. Wundenberg § 33 para. 6 et seq.

[22] On the development of the compliance concept in the US see Securities Industry Association, 6 J. Invest. Comp. (2005), 4 ff. and G. Miller, *The Law of Governance, Risk Management, and Compliance*, 138 ff. (highlighting that certain elements of the compliance function may be traced back as early as the Interstate Commerce Act of 1887); on the UK see C. Taylor, 6 J. Invest. Comp. (2005), 54 ff.

programmes for decades.²³ The implementation of compliance programmes was generally optional and based on self-regulation initiatives, aimed at **preventing insider dealings**.²⁴ Only gradually did compliance become affected by the European Union's efforts to harmonise the law. This development began with the legally non-binding Commission Recommendations of 25 July 1977 concerning a European code of conduct relating to transactions in transferrable securities which contained general principles on investment advice, the management of conflicts of interest, and controlling the flow of information in a company.²⁵ The Investment Services Directive,²⁶ enacted on 10 May 1993, was the first European legislative act to contain minimum binding organisational requirements for investment firms in order to ensure investor protection. Subsequently, the recommendations and supervisory principles of the **Basel Committee on Banking Supervision** (hereafter the 'Basel Committee') triggered further developments. The ten organisational principles published in the Basel Committee's policy paper 'Compliance and the Compliance Function in Banks',²⁷ based on Principle 14 of the 'Core Principles for Effective Supervision'²⁸ of September 1997, lay down the most relevant aspects that banks and banking groups must take into account when setting up a compliance organisation.²⁹ The final version of these principles was enacted in April 2005 and has enlarged the focus of compliance in a crucial way: the Basel Committee does not only regard compliance as essential for preventing insider dealings and reacting to conflicts of interest but also as an element of general **legal risk management**.³⁰ Although not legally binding, the recommendations of the Basel Committee have effectively become the primary standards of banking practice and as such have had a decisive influence on European legal developments.³¹

The Markets in Financial Instruments Directive (**MiFID**), 2004/39/EC, has achieved a comprehensive harmonisation of the organisational requirements that have to be taken into account by investment firms. This framework directive, however, only contained general principles, which were put into more concrete terms on the second level of the Lamfalussy Process³² by Directive 2006/73/EC³³ (denoted 'Organisational Requirements Directive' or 'implementing directive' hereafter).³⁴ These legislative acts introduced compliance, risk management and internal audit functions at a European level for the first time. The European provisions reflect a regulatory trend (now carried forward by the **MiFID II**

7

---

²³ On the origin of compliance in Germany see D. Eisele, 23 WM (1993), 1021; U. Weiss, *Die Bank*, 136; on the developments in Austria see B. Bauer and K. Muther-Pradler, in: Lucius et al. (eds.), *Compliance im Finanzdienstleistungsbereich*, 36 ff.
²⁴ Cf. Securities Industry Association, 6 J. Invest. Comp. (2005), 4; T. Lösler, *Compliance im Wertpapierdienstleistungskonzern*, 15 ff.
²⁵ Commission Recommendation No. 77/534/EEC concerning a European Code of Conduct relating to transactions in transferable securities, OJ L212, 20 August 1977, p. 37–43.
²⁶ Council Directive 93/22/EEC of 10 May 1993 on investment services in the securities field, OJ L141, 11 June 1993, p. 27–46. See R. Veil § 1 para. 12.
²⁷ Basel Committee on Banking Supervision, Compliance and the Compliance Function in Banks, October 2003—consultation paper and April 2005—final (fn. 10).
²⁸ Equivalent to Principle 26 of the 'Core Principles' as of 2012.
²⁹ For details see J. Edwards and S. Wolfe, 12 J. Fin. Reg. & Comp. (2004), 216 ff.
³⁰ On these legal developments see S. Bazley and A. Haynes, *Risk-based Compliance*, 173–174.
³¹ D. Gebauer and S. Niermann, in: C. Hauschka et al. (eds.), *Corporate Compliance*, § 48 para. 14.
³² See F. Walla § 4 para. 4–36.
³³ Commission Directive 2006/73/EC of 10 August 2006 implementing Directive 2004/39/EC of the European Parliament and of the Council as regards organisational requirements and operating conditions for investment firms and defined terms for the purposes of that Directive, OJ L241, 2 September 2006, p. 26–58.
³⁴ The implementing directive was preceded by 'technical standards' published by CESR in January 2005.

framework and the respective **Delegated Regulations**) that has also become apparent in other areas of supervisory law: to require the supervised firms to develop comprehensive systems of internal control in order to ensure **investor protection** and increase the supervisory requirements for the management and control of the firms.[35]

8   Compliance has grown even more important in the course of the **financial crisis**, during which serious shortcomings regarding internal control systems and governance arrangements became apparent.[36] The reports on the causes of the financial crisis indicate that these deficits and weaknesses in corporate governance led to a loss of investor confidence, thus weakening the stability of the financial system. These findings have prompted calls for more stringent supervisory governance requirements for financial service providers and have highlighted the importance of compliance and risk management.[37] As a result, the European Securities and Markets Authority (ESMA) has published guidelines that aim to increase the effectiveness of the compliance function and emphasised the importance of an effective compliance system in its MiFID II implementation advice.[38] The loss of millions of Euros suffered by the Société Général due to the speculative transactions of the trader Jérome Kerviel is a good example of the risks resulting from weak internal control structures. Compliance failings and weak corporate governance arrangements have also contributed to the manipulation of Libor and Euribor rates.[39] It is to be expected that the recent collapse of the German payment provider **Wirecard** resulting from apparent fraudulent activities will lead to further discussions on the role of effective internal control functions.

---

[35] Similar developments took place in insurance supervision, Art. 41 ff. of the Solvency-II Directive 2009/138/EC list requirements (consisting of risk management, compliance, internal audit and actuarial functions) for governance systems of (re-)insurance companies. See also M. Wundenberg § 34 (corporate governance).

[36] Cf. The High-Level Group on Financial Supervision in the EU (de Larosière Group), Report, 25 February 2009 (de Larosière Report), available at: http://ec.europa.eu/internal_market/finances/docs/de_larosiere_report_en.pdf, para. 13 ff., 23 ff., 122 ff. and 236; Commission, Green Paper of the European Commission on Corporate governance in financial institutions and remuneration policies, 2 June 2010, COM(2010) 284 final, p. 2.

[37] COM(2010) 284 final (fn. 35). On risk management see also the declaration of the Summit of Financial Markets and the World Economy of the Group of Twenty meeting of 15 November 2008, para. 2 and 8.

[38] ESMA/2012/388 - now updated by the ESMA MiFID II Compliance Guidelines (fn. 10); ESMA, Final Report, ESMA's Technical Advice to the Commission on MIFID II and MiFIR, 19 December 2014, ESMA/2014/1569, p. 14 ff.

[39] See M. Wundenberg § 33 para 82 as well as § 35 para. 5 ff.

§ 33

Compliance Requirements

Bibliography

Abegglen, Sandro, *Wissenszurechnung bei der juristischen Person und im Konzern, bei Banken und Versicherungen* (2004); Alexander, Kern, *Principles v. Rules in Financial Regulation*, 10 EBOR (2009), 163–173; Andrés, Anna M., *La regulación de las 'murallas chinas': una técnica de prevención de conflictos de interés en el mercado de valores español*, 81 RDBB (2001), 49–86; Baglieri, Maria R., *Conflicts of Interest and Duty: A Persistent Threat—The Italian Legislation*, 31 Company Lawyer (2010), 186–189; Bauer, Barbara and Muther-Prader, Katharina, *Gesetzliche und aufsichtsrechtliche Anforderungen an Compliance*, in: Lucius, Otto et al. (eds.), *Compliance im Finanzdienstleistungsbereich* (2010), 36–66; Bazley, Stuart and Haynes, Andrew, *Financial Services Authority Regulation and Risk-Based Compliance* (2006); Benicke, Christoph, *Wertpapiervermögensverwaltung* (2006); Black, Julia, *Regulatory Styles and Supervisory Strategies*, in: Niamh Moloney et al. (eds.), *Oxford Handbook of Financial Regulation* (2015), 217–253; Black, Julia, *Forms and Paradoxes of Principles-Based Regulation*, 3 CMLJ (2008), 425–457; Black, Julia, *The Rise, Fall and Fate of Principles Based Regulation*, SSRN Working Paper (2010), available at: http://papers.ssrn.com/sol3/papers.cfm?abstract_id=1267722; Biegelman, Martin T., *Building a World-Class Compliance-Program* (2008); Boardman, Nigel and Crosthwait, John, *A Practitioners Guide to FSA Regulation of Investment Banking* (2002); Buck-Heeb, Petra, *Insiderwissen, Interessenkonflikte und Chinese Walls bei Banken*, in: Grundmann, Stefan et al. (eds.), *Festschrift für Klaus J. Hopt*, Vol. I (2010), 1647–1670; Buisson, Françoise, *La transposition de la directive européenne Marchés d'Instruments Financiers (MIF) en droit français*, 2 RTDF (2007), 6–17; Casper, Matthias, *Der Compliancebeauftragte*, in: Georg Bitter et al. (eds.), *Festschrift für Karsten Schmidt* (2009), 199–216; Chiu, Iris H.-Y., *Regulating (From) the Inside* (2015); Coglianese, Cary and Lazer, David, *Management-Based Regulation*, 37 Law & Soc'y Rev. (2003), 691–730; Coglianese, Cary and Mendelson, Evan, *Meta-Regulation and Self-Regulation*, in: Baldwin, Robert et al. (eds.), *The Oxford Handbook of Regulation* (2010), 146–168; Ford, Cristie L., *New Governance, Compliance, and Principles-Based Securities Regulation*, 45 Am. Bus. Law J. (2008), 1–60; Fulconis-Tielens, Adréane, *Responsable conformité, une nouvelle fonction devenue clé*, Revue Banque (November 2008), 28; Früh, Andreas, *Legal & Compliance—Abgrenzung oder Annäherung (am Beispiel einer Bank)*, 4 CCZ (2010), 121–126; Gabbi, Giampaolo et al., *Managing Compliance Risk after MiFID*, SSRN Working Paper (2012), available at: http://papers.ssrn.com/sol3/papers.cfm?abstract_id=2028860; Gallo, Manuela, *The Compliance Function and the Evolution of Internal Structure of Italian Banking Intermediaries*, Studi e Note di Economia (2009), 325–353; Gray, Joanna, *Is it Time to Highlight the Limits of Risk-Based Financial Regulation?*, 4 CMLJ (2009), 50–62; Harm, Julian A., *Compliance in Wertpapierdienstleistungsunternehmen und Emittenten von Finanzinstrumenten* (2008); Hollander, Charles and Salzedo, Simon, *Conflicts of Interest & Chinese Walls*, 2nd ed. (2004); Hopt, Klaus J., *Prävention und Repression von Interessenkonflikten*, in: Susanne Kalss et al. (eds.), *Festschrift für Peter Doralt* (2004), 213–234; Illing, Diana and Umnuß, Karsten, *Die arbeitsrechtliche Stellung des Compliance Managers—insbesondere Weisungsunterworfenheit und Reportingpflichten*, 1 CCZ (2009), 1–8; Jarvis, Kit, *Does the Fiduciary Bell*

Toll?, 3 J. Financ. Crime (2007), 192–195; Jochnick, Kerstin and Jansson, Per, *MiFID—ettstegpåvägenmot en europeiskvärdepappersmarknad*, ERT (2007), 741–757; Jost, Oliver, *Compliance in Banken* (2010); Kittelberger, Ralf, *Einführung einer neuen Berichtspflicht für Wertpapierdienstleistungsunternehmen und deren Folgen* (2005); Kloepfer Pelèse, Martine, *Analyse financière produite et diffusée par un PSI: les précisions apportées par l'AMF. (Sanct. AMF, 1re sect., 8 janv. 2009, Société Euroland finance)*, Bull. Joly Bourse (2009), 204–210; Lippe, Donovan, *Compliance in Banken und Bankkonzernen* (2011); Lipton, Martin and Mazur, Robert B., *The Chinese Wall Solution of the Conflict Problem of Securities Firms*, 50 NYU L. Rev. (1975), 459–511; Lösler, Thomas, *Das moderne Verständnis von Compliance im Finanzmarktrecht*, 3 NZG (2005), 104–108; Lösler, Thomas, *Spannungen zwischen der Effizienz der internen Compliance und möglichen Reporting- Pflichten des Compliance Officers*, 15 WM (2007), 676–683; Lösler, Thomas, *Zur Rolle und Stellung des Compliance-Beauftragten*, 24 WM (2008), 1098–1104; Lösler, Thomas, *Die Mindestanforderungen an Compliance und die weiteren Verhaltens-, Organisations- und Transparenzpflichten nach §§ 31 ff. WpHG (MaComp)*, 41 WM (2010), 1917–1923; McVea, Harry, *Financial Conglomerates and the Chinese Wall* (1993); Miller, Geoffrey P., *The Law of Governance, Risk Management, and Compliance* (2014); Miller, Geoffrey P., *The compliance function: an overview*, SSRN Working Paper (2014), available at: http://papers.ssrn.com/sol3/papers.cfm?abstract_id=2527621; Miller, Geoffrey Parsons, *The Role of Risk Management and Compliance in Banking Integration*, SSRN Working Paper (2014), available at: http://papers.ssrn.com/sol3/papers.cfm?abstract_id=2527222; Moloney, Niamh, *Financial Services and Markets*, in: Baldwin, Robert et al. (eds.), *The Oxford Handbook of Regulation* (2010), 437–461; Mwenda, Kenneth K., *Banking Supervision and Systemic Bank Restructuring* (2000); Nelson, Paul, *Capital markets law and compliance* (2008); Newton, Andrew, *The Handbook of Compliance* (1998); Niermann, Stephan, *Die Compliance-Organisation im Zeitalter der MaComp*, 5 ZBB (2010), 400–427; Oelkers, Janine, *Compliance in Banken*, in: Lucius, Otto et al. (eds.), *Compliance im Finanzdienstleistungsbereich* (2010), 36–66; Poser, Norman, *Chinese Wall or Emperor's New Clothes? Regulating Conflicts of Interest of Securities Firms in the US and the UK*, 9 Mich. YBI Legal Stud. (1988), 91–103; Renz, Hartmut and Stahlke, Karsten, *Wird die Watch-List bei Kreditinstituten durch das Insiderverzeichnis abgelöst?*, ZfgK (2006), 353–355; Preuße, Thomas and Zingel, Frank, *Wertpapierdienstleistungs-Verhaltens- und Organisationsverordnung* (2015); Rodewald, Jörg and Unger, Ulrike, *Kommunikation und Krisenmanagement im Gefüge der Corporate Compliance-Organisation*, 31 BB (2007), 1629–1635; Röh, Lars, *Compliance nach der MiFID—zwischen höherer Effizienz und mehr Bürokratie*, 9 BB (2008), 398–410; Rönnau, Thomas and Schneider, Frédéric, *Der Compliance-Beauftragte als strafrechtlicher Garant*, 2 ZIP (2010), 53–61; Sandmann, Daniel, *Der Compliance-Bericht im Wertpapierdienstleistungsunternehmen*, 3 CCZ (2008), 104–107; Scharpf, Marcus A., *Corporate Governance Compliance und Chinese Walls* (2000); Schlicht, Manuela, *Compliance nach Umsetzung der MiFID-Richtlinie*, 12 BKR (2006), 469–475; SDA Bocconi, *The Evolution of Compliance Function and Compliance Risk in Investement Services*, SSRN Working Paper (2009), available at: http://papers.ssrn.com/sol3/papers.cfm?abstract_id=1446759; Skinner, Chris, *The Future of Investing* (2007); Spindler, Gerald, *Compliance in der multinationalen Bankengruppe*, 20 WM (2008), 905–918; Taylor, Chris, *The Evolution of Compliance*, 6 J. Invest. Comp. (2005), 54–58; Tuch, Andrew T., *Financial Conglomerates and Informational Barriers*, 39 J. Corp. Law (2014), 102–153; Veil, Rüdiger, *Compliance-Organisation in Wertpapierdienstleistungsunternehmen im Zeitalter der MiFID*, 24 WM (2008), 1093–1098; Walsh, John H., *Right the First Time: Regulation, Quality, and Preventive Compliance in the Securities Industry*, Colum. Bus. L. Rev. (1997), 165–240; Wolf, Stefan, *Der Wandel der spanischen Finanzmärkte durch neue europarechtliche Entwicklungen* (2008); Wundenberg, Malte, *Compliance und die prinzipiengeleitete Aufsicht über Bankengruppen* (2012). Cf. further the bibliography in § 32.

I. Regulatory Concepts in European Law

1. Overview

The **MiFID** requires Member States to ensure that investment firms comply with the fundamental organisational requirements set out in Article 16 MiFID II.[1] The European provisions are, however, drafted in a rather abstract fashion: Article 13(2) MiFID II, for example, merely requires investment firms to 'establish adequate policies and procedures sufficient to ensure compliance of the firm including its managers, employees and tied agents with its obligations under the provisions of this Directive as well as appropriate rules governing personal transactions by such persons'. Article 16(3) MiFID II proves to be equally vague, demanding that investment firms maintain and operate effective organisational and administrative arrangements with a view to taking all reasonable steps designed to prevent conflicts of interest as defined in Article 23 MIFID II from adversely affecting the interests of its clients.[2]

The organisational requirements were initially more concretely defined in Article 5 ff. of the **Organisational Requirements Directive**,[3] which was enacted as an implementing directive to the MiFID I and had to be implemented by the respective Member States. Under the MiFID II regime the Organisational Requirements Directive was replaced by the Delegated Regulation EU 2017/565 in the Level 2 legislation process ('**Delegated Regulation**').[4] Unlike the former Organisational Requirements Directive the Delegated Regulation is directly binding in all Member States. As a result, the organisational requirements of investment firms are now to a large extent shaped by European law.

The Delegated Regulation puts the general organisational principles of the MiFID II into more concrete terms as follows: Article 21 defines the term 'general organisational requirements'. Articles 22–24 set forth the requirements regarding internal control structures, Article 22 referring to compliance, Article 23 dealing with risk management and Article 24 pertaining to internal audit. All of these organisational provisions must be seen in connection with the requirements regarding the management of conflicts of interests as laid down in Articles 33 ff. According to these provisions, investment firms shall 'establish, implement and maintain an effective conflicts of interest policy set out in writing and appropriate to the size and organisation of the firm and the nature, scale and complexity of its business'.[5]

---

[1] The MiFID defines the term 'investment firm' as any legal person—and under certain conditions undertakings which are not legal persons—whose regular occupation or business is the provision of one or more investment services to third parties and/or the performance of one or more investment activities on a professional basis; cf. Art. 4(1)(1) MiFID II.
[2] More specific requirements can be found in Art. 16(3)(2–6) MiFID II regarding, inter alia, the product approval process (cf. R. Veil § 30 para. 2–10). Furthermore, specific organisational requirements now also apply to investment firms which engage in algorithmic trading (Art. 17 MiFID II), cf. M. Lerch § 25 para. 35, 49, 51. Art. 73(2) MiFID II furthermore introduced the obligation to implement whistleblowing procedures.
[3] Commission Directive 2006/73/EC of 10 August 2006 implementing Directive 2004/39/EC of the European Parliament and of the Council as regards organisational requirements and operating conditions for investment firms and defined terms for the purposes of that Directive, OJ L241, 2 September 2006, p. 26–58.
[4] Commission Delegated Regulation (EU) 2017/565 of 25 April 2016 supplementing Directive 2014/65/EU of the European Parliament and of the Council as regards organisational requirements and operating conditions for investment firms and defined terms for the purposes of that Directive.
[5] Art. 34(1) Delegated Regulation.

4   The regulatory provisions regarding the compliance function have been specified in more detail in guidelines published by ESMA which have been updated in April 2021('**ESMA Guidelines**').[6] The purpose of these guidelines (issued under Article 16 ESMA regulations)[7] is to promote greater convergence in the interpretation of the European compliance requirements by both market participants and national supervisory authorities. Even though the ESMA Guidelines are technically not binding, they have proven to be of great importance for legal practice. The competent authorities of all Member States have stated that they intend to comply with the ESMA Guidelines.[8]

5   This section will place particular emphasis on the organisational requirements for compliance in investment firms, as described in Article 16(2) MiFID II in conjunction with Article 22 of the Delegated Regulation.

2. Principles-based Approach to Regulation

6   The requirements contained in the MiFID II and the Delegated Regulation are based on vague legal criteria, as is typical of an approach to regulation that is commonly described as **principles-based regulation** in Anglo-American law.[9] While this concept has its origins in the United Kingdom's capital markets law,[10] elements of principles-based regulation can also be found in EU law. According to the European Commission, the reliance on 'clear principles' constitutes one of the main political considerations that guided the drafting of the initial Organisational Requirements Directive.[11] This approach to regulation—which generally continues under the MiFID II compliance regime[12]—has been described by the Commission as follows:

> The Level 1 Directive and its implementing directive introduce a modern and comprehensive regime governing organisational and operating requirements for investment firms. The implementing directive covers all facets of an investment firm's organisation and introduces a high level of investor protection in the areas concerned with the relationship between investment firms and their clients. It has relied mainly on a *principles-based approach establishing clear standards and objectives that investment firms need to attain rather than prescribing specific and detailed rules*. The advantage of this approach is that it provides the flexibility needed when regulating a diverse universe of entities and activities while also imposing a significant degree of responsibility on all the actors concerned.[13]

---

[6] ESMA, Guidelines on Certain Aspects of the MiFID II Compliance Function Requirements, 6 April 2021, ESMA35-36-1952.

[7] See for details R. Veil § 5 para. 22 ff.

[8] ESMA, Guidelines compliance table, Guidelines on Certain Aspects of the MiFID Compliance Function Requirements', 24 April 2014, ESMA/2013/923 (regarding the initial version of the ESMA-Guidelines).

[9] See in the context of the MiFID C. Skinner, *The Future of Investing*, 85; N. Moloney, *EC Securities and Financial Markets Regulation*, 369 ff. and passim; N. Moloney, in: Baldwin et al. (eds.), *Oxford Handbook of Regulation*, 437, 447–449. In general on principles-based regulation see in detail M. Wundenberg, *Compliance und die prinzipiengeleitete Aufsicht über Bankengruppen*, 34–116 examining the characteristics of principles-based regulation and the theoretical distinction between rules and principles in banking supervisory law.

[10] See R. Veil and M. Wundenberg, *Englisches Kapitalmarktrecht*, 9–13.

[11] Cf. Commission, Working Document, Explanatory Note, 13 May 2005, ESC/18/2005.

[12] N. Moloney, *EU Securities and Financial Markets Regulation*, 367. In other fields (such as client classification requirements) MiFID II follows a more prescriptive (rules-based) approach.

[13] Commission, Background Note, Draft, Commission Directive implementing Directive 2004/39/EC.

The principles-based approach to regulation taken by the European lawmaker has two 7
main characteristics. Firstly, the regulation is primarily based on **high-level regulatory
objectives**[14] that are drafted in a rather general way, and do not provide any detailed and
prescriptive rules. Secondly, the regulation aims to be sufficiently flexible in allowing the
investment firms to achieve the regulatory objectives through the means they consider most
appropriate regarding the size and the nature of their business.[15]

The principles-based approach taken by the European lawmaker has two aims. Firstly, the 8
regulatory regime is supposed to be flexible enough to take into account the wide variety
of investment firms with regard to their size, structure and the nature of their business.[16]
Regulatory solutions following a 'one-size-fits-all' approach are deemed inadequate for
catering to different needs resulting from a heterogeneous corporate landscape. To this end,
the Delegated Regulation has incorporated a number of 'proportionality clauses' in order
to ensure that the organisational requirements are aligned with the individual risk situation
of the individual investment firm.[17] Secondly, the focus on the regulatory outcomes is to
ensure a high level of investor protection.

The principles-based approach becomes visible both at the level of rule-making and the 9
level of rule enforcement.[18] On the level of **rule-making** the principles-based approach is
characterised by a regulatory regime that relies mainly on outcome-based standards with
a high level of generality. As opposed to detailed and prescriptive behavioural-based rules,
principles generally focus on the regulatory aim and only vaguely outline the behavioural
and organisational requirements necessary to achieve this aim. The provisions on compliance
management of investment firms examined in this chapter can be seen as a typical
example of principles-based rule-making, being drafted as qualitative regulatory objectives,
complemented by a general organisational requirement: Article 16(2) MiFID II, for example,
requires that investment firms establish 'adequate policies and procedures' (organisational
requirement) sufficient to ensure compliance of the firm, including its managers,
employees and tied agents, with its obligations under the provisions of this Directive as well
as appropriate rules governing personal transactions by such persons (regulatory objective).
The regulatory objectives are put into more concrete terms by the supervisory authorities in
cooperation with market participants, enabling a continual adaptation of the organisational
principles to the latest market developments. On the level of **rule enforcement** principles-
based regulation can thus be seen as a regulatory regime in which the market rules are not
unilaterally dictated by the legislator but are developed step-by-step in cooperation with
supervisory authorities and market participants.[19]

According to the Commission, the principles-based approach to regulation has a consider- 10
able impact on the responsibilities of national supervisory authorities as well as investment

---

[14] Cf. ibid.; Commission (fn. 13), No. 3.1 ('general compliance objectives', 'regulatory objectives').
[15] Cf. Commission (fn. 13), No. 3.1.
[16] Recital 33 of the Delegated Regulation. See also R. Veil, 24 WM (2008), 1093, 1095.
[17] Art. 22(1)(2) and (4) (Compliance); Art. 23(2) (Risk Management); Art. 24 (Internal audit) of the Delegated Regulation.
[18] For a more detailed analysis of the characteristics of principles-based regulation and the theoretical distinction between rules and principles in banking supervisory law see M. Wundenberg, *Compliance und die prinzipiengeleitete Aufsicht über Bankengruppen*, 35–116.
[19] Cf. J. Black, 3 CMLJ (2008), 425, 434 ff.; C. Ford, 45 Am. Bus. Law J. (2008), 1 ff. (principles-based regulation as a form of new governance); M. Wundenberg, *Compliance und die prinzipiengeleitete Aufsicht über Bankengruppen*, 34–72. See below para.10 –11.

firms: it imposes the **responsibility** on the investment firm and its **senior management** to monitor the firm's own activities and to determine whether these comply with the principles set out in the MiFID and the implementing directive. The national supervisory authorities need to acquire the operational expertise required in order to guide the industry and to enforce the provisions effectively.[20] The Commission therefore expected the national supervisory authorities to issue guidance pertaining to the applicability and interpretation of the general organisational requirements, thus mitigating any legal uncertainty associated with the principles-based approach.[21] As noted above, ESMA has recently updated its 'Guidelines on Certain Aspects of the MiFID II Compliance Function Requirements', which aim to clarify the application of the MiFID II compliance requirements and to promote greater convergence in the interpretation of these rules.[22] The competent authorities of all Member States have implemented the ESMA Guidelines in their national supervisory practice.[23]

11   In legal literature, the principles-based approach to regulation has proved to be **controversial**. A disadvantage of this approach is the fact that it can lead to increased legal uncertainty and unpredictability for market participants. Principles-based regulation further places high demands on the competent national authorities which must supervise the investment firms and ensure abidance with the principles. The experience gained during the financial crisis has further raised doubts regarding the effectiveness of this regulatory approach.[24] The ensuing discussion on the merits and the perils of principles-based regulation has shown that an **effective enforcement** of the principles can only be ensured if the principles are accompanied by adequate sanctioning powers of the supervisory authorities. There have been concerns whether an effective supervision can be guaranteed, especially in Member States with no experience with the principles-based approach to regulation.[25] Against this backdrop, it is noteworthy that the administrative sanctioning powers of the national authorities have been strengthened under the new MiFID II regime.[26] Furthermore, the attempts made by ESMA to promote greater convergence in the interpretation and supervision of the compliance requirements by publishing the ESMA Guidelines are to be welcomed.[27]

3. Regulatory Aim

12   The compliance obligations laid down in Article 16(2) MiFID II in conjunction with Article 22 Delegated Regulation have two regulatory aims. On the one hand they aim to **protect investment firms** from potential civil and administrative sanctions as well

---

[20] Cf. Commission, Background Note (fn. 13), sec. 2.1.
[21] Recital 12 of the former Organisational Requirements Directive. The responsibility to provide guidance has now been conferred to ESMA, see above para. 4.
[22] ESMA35-36-1952 (fn. 6).
[23] Cf. para. 4 above and fn. 8. In addition, the competent supervisory authorities of many member states have issued additional guidelines on the compliance and risk management requirements, cf. the overview in the second edition of this chapter (§ 33 para. 11).
[24] Seen critically by J. Gray, 4 CMLJ (2009), 50 ff.; K. Alexander, 10 EBOR (2009), 163 ff. See also J. Black, *The Rise, Fall and Fate of Principles Based Regulation*. For a discussion of the impact of the financial crisis on principles-based regulation see J. Black, in: Moloney et al. (eds.), *Oxford Handbook of Financial Regulation*, 217. 226 ff.
[25] As pointed out by N. Moloney, *EC Securities and Financial Markets Regulation*, 374.
[26] See below para. 79–87.
[27] ESMA35-36-1952 (fn. 6).

as reputational damages that may result from a violation of MiFID rules. On the other hand the compliance obligations also aim to ensure **investor protection** and the efficient **functioning of the capital markets:**[28] the compliance requirements are supposed to ensure that the rules designed to protect investors are effectively applied and do not remain 'law in the books'.[29] By harmonising the organisational requirements of investment firms in the European Union, illegal practices are supposed to be prevented, thereby increasing investor confidence and market efficiency.[30] Both regulatory aims (protection of the investment firm and investor protection) must be kept in mind when interpreting the directives' provisions.[31]

Regulating and supervising the internal organisation of investment firms is a typical characteristic of the regulatory concept described as '**management- based-regulation**' (sometimes also referred to as 'meta-based regulation') in Anglo-American law.[32] This regulatory strategy 'combines' internal control mechanisms with instruments of public supervision. The investment firms are required to organise and monitor their company in a way that fulfils certain regulatory objectives. The internal control systems are thereby utilised for supervisory means (ie in this case preventing breaches of the law), in order to increase investor protection and market efficiency. The European requirements regarding compliance and risk management can thus be understood as an **internal enforcement strategy**[33] that complements the traditional mechanisms of private and public enforcement.[34]

II. Regulatory Objectives and Scope of Compliance Obligations

1. Mitigation of Compliance Risk and Risk-Based Approach

The regulatory objective laid down in Article 16(2) MiFID II to ensure compliance of investment firms with their obligations under the provision of the MiFID is put into more concrete terms by Article 22 Delegated Regulation in three ways. Firstly, investment firms shall 'establish, implement and maintain adequate policies and procedures designed to detect any

---

[28] Improving investor protection is one of the MiFID's key aims. See Recitals 5, 7, 39, 45, 57, 58, 87, 133 and 144 of MiFID II.
[29] Securities and Markets Stakeholder Group, Advice on Guidelines on Certain Aspects of the MiFID Compliance Function Requirements, 15 February 2012, ESMA/2012/SMSG/12, p. 1. See also FSA, Organisational Systems and Controls, May 2006, CP 06/9, para. 1.1: 'Confidence in the [...] financial markets depends on firms organising and controlling their affairs responsibly and effectively.'
[30] Cf. A. Fuchs, in: Fuchs (ed.), *Kommentar zum WpHG*, § 33 para. 3.
[31] The dual regulatory objective of the compliance obligations can give rise to interpretational difficulties regarding the responsibilities of the compliance staff and senior management. See in the context of the legal status of the compliance officer below para. 42–45.
[32] Cf. C. Coglianese and D. Lazer, 37 Law & Soc'y Rev. (2003), 691 ff. On meta-based regulation see C. Coglianese and E. Mendelson, in: Baldwin et. al (eds.), *Oxford Handbook of Regulation*, 146 ff., J. Black, in: Moloney et al. (eds.), *Oxford Handbook of Financial Regulation*, 217 ff. See also in the context of risk management and compliance I. Chiu, *Regulating from the Inside*, 14 ff. and passim.
[33] On compliance as a concept of internal law enforcement J. Walsh, 165 Colum. Bus. L. Rev. (1997), 165 ff. See also G. Miller, *The Compliance Function*, 1 (form of 'internalised law enforcement').
[34] On this aspect in the concept of 'qualitative banking supervision' see M. Wundenberg, *Compliance und die prinzipiengeleitete Aufsicht über Bankengruppen*, 82–83.

risk of failure by the firm to comply with its obligations under [the MiFID II], as well as the associated risks'. Secondly, investment firms shall further put in place adequate 'measures and procedures' designed to minimise such risks. Finally, those procedures implemented by the investment firms shall 'enable the competent authorities to exercise their powers effectively'.

15 Article 22 Delegated Regulation reflects the **risk-based approach** to compliance[35] taken by European law: the overall aim is to minimise the risk of violations of applicable law by identifying, evaluating and monitoring compliance risks and taking adequate measures in order to manage these risks.[36] In fact, the **risk-based approach** has now expressly been hardwired into the MiFID II regime, requiring the compliance function to 'establish a risk-based monitoring programme that takes into consideration all areas of the investment firm's investment services'.[37] The responsibility for this obligation lies with the senior management.[38] This risk-based approach is also expressly recognized in the (updated) ESMA Guidelines.[39]

16 The risk-based approach to regulation has far-reaching consequences for the structure of the compliance organisation: the investment firm and its **senior management** must identify the areas of risk that are particularly relevant for the specific business of the firm by way of **self-assessment**.[40] In line with this risk-based approach ESMA argues that the compliance function shall 'conduct a risk assessment to ensure that compliance risks are comprehensively monitored'.[41] As a result of the MiFID's risk-orientated approach the specific organisational measures that have to be implemented are not the same for all investment firms but depend on the respective risk situation of the investment firm. This is explicitly recognised in Article 22(1) subsec. 2 Delegated Regulation, which states that investment firms shall take into account the nature, scale and complexity of the business of the firm, and the nature and range of investment services and activities undertaken in the course of that business. This provision reflects the **principle of proportionality**, which is central to the MiFID.

17 The **principle of proportionality** is a common feature in today's international financial markets regulation. It can also be found in similar forms in insurance and banking

---

[35] This approach is based on the work of the Basel Committee on Banking Supervision. For more details on the development of a 'risk-based compliance' see S. Bazley and A. Haynes, *Financial Services Authority Regulation and Risk-Based Compliance*, 173 ff. and passim. For a general discussion of 'risk-based' approaches to regulation and supervision see J. Black, in: Moloney et al. (eds.), *The Oxford Handbook of Financial Regulation*, 217, 221 ff.

[36] According to the Basel Committee on Banking Supervision, Compliance and Compliance Function in Banks, April 2005, available at: www.bis.org/publ/bcbs113, para. 3 the compliance risk can be defined as the 'risk of legal or regulatory sanctions, material financial loss, or loss to reputation a bank may suffer as a result of its failure to comply with laws, regulations, rules, related self-regulatory organisation standards, and codes of conduct applicable to its banking activities'.

[37] Art. 22(2)(2)(1) Delegated Regulation. The monitoring program shall establish priorities determined by the compliance risk assessment ensuring that compliance risk is comprehensively monitored (Art. 22(2)(2)(2) Delegated Regulation).

[38] Art. 25 Delegated Regulation. The overall responsibility of the senior management for compliance is internationally accepted. Cf. Basel Committee, Compliance (fn. 36), principle 2. In this chapter, the term 'senior management' is used in a functional manner, referring to the managers responsible for the day-to-day management. Depending on the national governance regime, such managers may be members of the management body. See also the chapter on Corporate Governance (§ 34).

[39] ESMA35-36-1952 (fn. 6), guideline 2, para. 21.

[40] For details see S. Gebauer and S. Niermann, in: Hauschka et al. (eds.), *Corporate Compliance*, § 48 para. 40 ff.; M. Schlicht, 12 BKR (2006), 469, 470 with examples from legal practice. On risk assessment see R. Wild, in: *Corporate Compliance Series*, § 2.13 ff. From a US perspective G. Miller, *The Role of Risk Management and Compliance in Banking Integration*, 17 ff.

[41] ESMA35-36-1952 (fn. 6), guideline 1, para. 14.

supervision law.⁴² With regard to the compliance organisation the principle of proportionality entails that the procedures and instruments applied by investment firms to monitor and manage compliance risk can differ greatly. As a general rule, larger investment firms with a diverse product portfolio will be subject to stricter organisational requirements than smaller financial institutions which offer less complex financial services.⁴³ European law thus provides a **flexible organisational framework** which takes the individual risk structure of the investment firm into account.⁴⁴ It is the task of the investment firm's senior management to determine the most suitable structure of the compliance organisation, taking into consideration the specific compliance risks faced by the investment firm.⁴⁵ The principle of proportionality is visible in the numerous opening clauses of MiFID II: an investment firm is, for example, not required to comply with Article 22(3)(d) or (e) Delegated Regulation if in view of the nature, scale and complexity of its business, and the nature and range of investment services and activities, it is able to demonstrate that the organisational requirements are disproportionate and its compliance function is effective without these additional requirements.⁴⁶ Even in these cases, however, the appointment of a compliance officer and the implementation of a compliance function must be ensured.

2. Scope of the Compliance Obligations

The wording of the MiFID II seems to imply that the investment firms are only required to ensure compliance with their obligations under the provisions of the MiFID II.⁴⁷ Yet systematically the obligation must reach farther, also including at a minimum the prevention of insider dealings by employees of the investment firm.⁴⁸ However, a legal obligation to prevent non-compliance with any and all applicable rules cannot be derived from the European provisions.

Some Member States follow a far more comprehensive approach regarding the scope of the compliance requirements. For example, prior to Brexit taking effect the **United Kingdom's** capital markets law clarified that the compliance obligations refer to the entire

---

⁴² EBA Banking Stakeholder Group, Proportionality in Banking Regulation, June 2014 (available at: https://eba.europa.eu/sites/default/documents/files/documents/10180/807776/de9b6372-c2c6-4be4-ac1f-49f4e80f9a66/European%20Banking%20Authority%20Banking%20Stakeholder%20Group-%20Position%20paper%20on%20proportionality.pdf?retry=1). For more details on the 'double proportionality' principle in banking supervision see M. Wundenberg, *Compliance und die prinzipiengeleitete Aufsicht über Bankengruppen*, 83–91.
⁴³ CESR, Advice on Possible Implementing Measures of the Directive 2004/39/EC on Markets in Financial Instruments, Consultation Paper, June 2004, CESR/04–261b, p. 11. For an overview of the factors that can be taken into account in deciding which organisational measures are proportionate see ESMA35-36-1952 (fn. 6), guideline 9, para. 62 ff.
⁴⁴ See above para. 8.
⁴⁵ Cf. ESMA35-36-1952 (fn. 6), guideline 9, para. 62: 'Firms should decide which measures, including organisational measures and the level of resources, are best suited to ensuring the effectiveness of the compliance function in the firm's particular circumstances.'
⁴⁶ See for details ibid., guideline 9, para. 59–65.
⁴⁷ Art. 16(2) MiFID II ('ensure compliance with […] laid down in paragraphs 2 to 10 of this Article and in Article 17 [MiFID II]'; Art. 22(1) and 25(1) Delegated Regulation ('comply with its obligations under [MiFID II]').
⁴⁸ Art. 29 Delegated Regulation. For more details on the supervision of employee transactions see D. Eisele and A. Faust, in: Schimansky et al. (eds.), *Bankrechts-Handbuch*, § 109 para. 130 ff.

'regulatory system' (ie, not only to the MiFID II regime).[49] The **German**[50] law also has a more extensive understanding of compliance than the MiFID. The Basel Committee's recommendations and supervisory standards also understand compliance as referring to all applicable laws and regulations.[51] The guidelines issued by **ESMA** offer a potentially more narrow interpretation of the scope of compliance obligations, stating that the compliance risk assessment should consider the applicable obligations 'under MiFID and the national implementing rules'.[52]

III. Elements of a Compliance Organisation

20 The European law distinguishes between 'principles, measures and procedures' designed to detect and minimise compliance risks and the establishment of a permanent and effective 'compliance function' by investment firms operating independently (see below 1). The Delegated Regulation requires investment firms to appoint a compliance officer, who is responsible for the compliance function and compliance reports (see below 2). Another core element of the compliance organisation are informational barriers ('Chinese walls') that restrict the flow of information within the investment firm (see below 3).

1. Compliance Function

21 In line with the Basel Committee's recommendations,[53] Article 22(2) Delegated Regulation requires investment firms to establish and maintain a permanent and effective compliance function which operates independently. As to be expected from a principles-based approach to regulation, the term 'compliance function' is not further defined in the Delegated Regulation.[54] European law thus does not prescribe a certain form of organisation; the Delegated Regulation only formulates three **abstract regulatory objectives** of the compliance function (independence, effectiveness, permanence).[55]

(a) Requirements

(aa) Independence

22 In order to discharge its responsibilities effectively, it is a necessary prerequisite that the compliance function holds a position in the organisational structure that ensures that the

---

[49] SYSC 6.1.1. FCA Handbook.

[50] § 80(1) WpHG. For a more detailed analysis of the scope of the compliance obligations in the respective Member States please refer to the first edition, § 35 para. 28.

[51] Basel Committee on Banking Supervision, Core Principles for Effective Banking Supervision, September 2012, available at: www.bis.org/publ/bcbs230.pdf, principle 26; Basel Committee, Compliance (fn. 36), para. 3–5.

[52] ESMA35-36-1952 (fn. 6), guideline 1, para. 16.

[53] Basel Committee, Compliance (fn. 36), Principles 5 ff.

[54] Commission, Background Note (fn. 13), sec. 3.2 (regarding MiFID). See also Basel Committee, Compliance (fn. 36), para. 6; IOSCO, Compliance Function at Market Intermediaries, Final Report, March 2006, available at: www.iosco.org/library/pubdocs/pdf/IOSCOPD214.pdf, p. 2. A more general definition can be found in Recital 31 Solvency II Directive (2009/138/EC), which refers to the compliance function as the administrative capacity undertaking particular governance tasks.

[55] Cf. ESMA35-36-1952 (fn. 6), guidelines 7, 8 and 9. See also above para. 6 ff. and 25 ff.

compliance officer and other compliance staff act independently when performing their tasks.[56] This legal principle of independence involves a number of different aspects: as a general rule, persons involved in compliance tasks must perform their monitoring and advisory functions objectively and free from any conflicts of interest. The provisions of the Delegated Regulation highlight two cases in which the principle of independence assumes particular relevance: Firstly, the relevant persons involved in the compliance function are not permitted to be involved in the performance of the services or activities they monitor.[57] This rule refers to the general prohibition of self-monitoring (**operational independence**). Secondly, the Delegated Regulation purports **financial independence** of the compliance function. The method of determining the remuneration of the relevant persons involved in the compliance function must not compromise their objectivity.[58]

(1) Operational and Financial Independence

The prohibition of self-monitoring entails that the compliance function must be held separate from the operational business units in order to prevent influence from being exercised on the compliance staff.[59] This does not, however, mean that the compliance function cannot be personally involved in the respective business activities of the investment firm, as an effective management of legal risks requires active cooperation between the control functions and the operative business units.[60] This becomes particularly clear with regard to the development of **new financial products**, for which it can be helpful, and often even advisable, to include compliance staff in the product approval process in order to identify legal risks at an early stage in the distribution process.[61] 23

The requirement of financial independence restricts the possibilities of a **performance-based remuneration** for compliance staff. The remuneration structure must ensure that the compliance staff's salary does not depend on the results of the monitored business units, thereby prohibiting any remuneration concepts that provide financial incentives to cover up breaches of law in order to increase the operative profits and thereby the compliance staff's own salary.[62] Performance-based remuneration is therefore only permitted if it is constructed as a long-term incentive and focuses on the company's profits as a whole.[63] 24

Both the (former) **CESR** and national supervisory authorities address this problem regarding the remuneration of compliance staff. The CESR stated that 'the independence of compliance function personnel may be undermined if their remuneration is related to the 25

---

[56] Ibid., guideline 8, para. 59–6159. The importance of the principle of independence is emphasised in nearly all statements and has meanwhile been internationally recognised as an essential criterion of an effective compliance organisation. Cf. Basel Committee, Compliance (fn. 36), Principle 5; IOSCO, Compliance (fn. 54), topic 3; Board of Governors of the Federal Reserve System, Compliance Risk Management, 16 October 2008, SR 08-8, sec. 2.

[57] Art. 22(3)(d) of the Delegated Regulation.

[58] Art. 22(3)(e) of the Delegated Regulation. On the compliance officer's independence from the management and in disciplinarian questions see below para. 43 ff.

[59] Cf. ESMA35-36-1952 (fn. 6), guideline 8, para. 59–61.

[60] T. Lösler, 3 NZG (2005), 104, 107–108.

[61] Cf. ESMA35-36-1952 (fn. 6), guideline 4, para. 38; Basel Committee, Compliance (fn. 36), Principle 7, para. 37; BaFin, Rundschreiben (circular) 05/2018—MaComp, 19.4.2018 (last amended 10.8.2021), BT 1.2.4 para. 3. For details regarding the new product process requirements under MiFID II cf. R. Veil § 30 para. 22–39.

[62] M. Casper, in: Casper (ed.), *Bankrechtstag 2008*, 139, 149.

[63] Cf. ibid. Similarly Basel Committee, Compliance (fn. 36), Principle 5, para. 29: 'remuneration related to the financial performance of the bank as a whole should generally be acceptable'. In more detail G. Spindler, 20 WM (2008), 905, 910.

financial performance of the business line for which they exercise compliance responsibilities. However, it should generally be acceptable to relate their remuneration to the financial performance of the investment firm as a whole.'[64] The **British** FSA (now FCA)[65] and the **German** BaFin[66] come to a similar conclusion. The **Austrian** FMA recommends a performance-orientated remuneration following qualitative and not quantitative criteria.[67]

26 The principles of operational and financial independence cannot be applied without exception. According to the Delegated Regulation investment firms are not obliged to comply with the obligations laid down in Article 22(3) (d) and (e) of the Delegated Regulation if they are able to demonstrate that, in view of the nature, scale and complexity of their business, and the nature and range of investment services and activities, the requirements under those points are not proportionate.[68] The investment firm can, however, only rely on this exemption if the senior management can ensure that the company's compliance function continues to be effective.[69] ESMA has provided guidelines regarding the criteria which should be taken into account by the investment firm and its senior management in this regard.[70]

(2) Organisational Independence

27 The principle of independence further entails that the compliance function must be organisationally independent from the operative business units, constituting an independent part of the corporate structure. This follows from the principle of a **separation of functions**. Investment firms, however, have a large margin of appreciation with regard to the organisational approach they take in order to fulfil this requirement[71] and therefore do not necessarily need to introduce a separate **compliance department**.[72] The degree to which the compliance function must be organised independently depends on the nature, scale and complexity of the company's business. National supervisory practice generally regards an independent organisational unit as necessary provided the staff has regular access to inside and other confidential information.[73]

28 In this context the question if (and under which circumstances) the compliance function can be combined with other internal control functions, such as risk management or internal audit, assumes particular importance.[74],[75] The Delegated Regulation only contains explicit rules on

[64] CESR, CESR's Technical Advice on Possible Implementing Measures of the Directive 2004/39/EC on Markets in Financial Instruments, CESR/05-024c, January 2005, p. 12.
[65] FSA, Organisational Systems and Controls, November 2006, PS 06/13, para. 4.8.
[66] BaFin, Rundschreiben (circular) 05/2018—MaComp (fn. 61), BT 1.3.3.4 para. 6.
[67] FMA, Organisationsrundschreiben WAG 2018, September 2018, para. 56.
[68] In that case, the investment firm is responsible to assess whether the effectiveness of the compliance function is compromised (Art. 22(4) sentence 2 Delegated Regulation).
[69] See above para. 16 ff.
[70] ESMA/35-36-1952 (fn. 6), guideline 9 para. 60.
[71] See above para. 6 ff.
[72] Commission, Background Note (fn. 13), sec. 3.2: '[T]hese functions [Compliance, risk management and internal audit] may be embedded in the organisation of the firm in different ways. These differences reflect the nature of these functions as well as the need for proportionality.'
[73] BaFin, Rundschreiben (circular) 05/2018—MaComp (fn. 61), BT 1.3.3.4, para. 1.
[74] ESMA/35-36-1952 (fn. 6), guideline 10. Business practice offers a number of possible structures. Cf. Gabbi et al., *Managing Compliance Risk after MiFID*, 5–10; J. Oelkers, *Compliance in Banken*, in: Lucius et al. (eds.), *Compliance im Finanzdienstleistungsbereich*, 131, 152 ff. (Austria); M. Gallo, *Compliance Function*, 325 ff. (Italy); M. Biegelman, *Compliance Program*, 178 (USA); S. Scholz-Fröhling, in: Preuße and Zingel (eds.), WpDVerOV, § 12 (Germany).
[75] For a discussion of different models of a compliance organisation I. Chiu, *Regulating (From) the Inside*, 54 ff.

the relationship between the compliance function and the **internal audit function**. Pursuant to Article 24 Delegated Regulation investment firms must establish and maintain an internal audit function which is separate and independent from the other functions and activities of the investment firm and fulfils the responsibilities listed in Article 24(a)–(c) of the Delegated Regulation. The internal audit must thus not only be independent from the other control functions of the investment firms but must rather also be organised separately as an independent department. The reason for this is that the internal audit is charged with the oversight of the adequacy and effectiveness of the investment firm's compliance function.[76] This requires the internal audit to be organisationally separated from the other business units.[77]

Whether compliance and **risk management** also require strict organisational separation appears less clear.[78] The legislative records indicate that European law takes a rather flexible and principles-based approach to this issue: while the principle of independence supports the argument that the compliance function should generally not be an organisational component of risk management, this distinction is less strict than it is the case with regard to the internal audit function. It should be kept in mind that the responsibility of the compliance function also includes the task of monitoring compliance with the rules on risk management and that effective oversight always requires sufficient organisational independence of the controlling body from the controlled instances. At the same time, Recital 37 of the Delegated Regulation recognises that the fact that risk management and compliance functions are performed by the same person does not necessarily jeopardise the independent functioning of each control function. In this regard, the organisational independence is thus subject to and restricted by the principle of proportionality.[79] In the case of larger firms, an organisational separation of the control functions is typically advisable.

29

This interpretation is in line with the ESMA Guidelines: In the updated Guidelines ESMA emphasises that the investment firms should 'favour an organisation where control functions are properly separated'.[80] According to **ESMA** the combination of the compliance function with other control functions (such as risk management) may be acceptable if this does not compromise the effectiveness and independence of the compliance function and if this is appropriately documented. The **German** BaFin stated that the compliance function may be combined with other control units, such as departments responsible for money-laundering prevention or risk control, but that internal audit must remain separate at all times.[81] The **Austrian** FMA underlines the fact that the compliance staff must be restricted to fulfilling compliance duties and should at no time be permitted to take over other duties or advise clients. The simultaneous assignment of an employee to the risk management function and the legal department is generally accepted.[82]

30

---

[76] Art. 24(a) Delegated Regulation. Cf. ESMA/35-36-1952 (fn. 6), guideline 10, para. 69.
[77] According to the ESMA Guidelines the separation of compliance and internal audit may, however, be disproportionate for very small investment firms.
[78] The connection of the compliance function to the risk management function is particularly common in Anglo-American banks and investment firms. Cf. C. Taylor, 6 J. Invest. Comp. (2005), 54, 58. On the functional relationship between both functions see M. Wundenberg § 32 para. 3–5.
[79] For more details see the Swedish report on implementation, One Year with MiFID, April 2009, p. 8–9. On the relationship of the compliance function with the legal department see A. Früh, 4 CCZ (2010), 121 ff.; T. Lösler, 41 WM (2010), 1917, 1920; S. Niermann, 5 ZBB (2010),400, 422.
[80] ESMA/35-36-1952 (fn. 6), guideline 10 para. 69.
[81] BaFin, Rundschreiben (circular) 05/2018—MaComp (fn. 61), BT 1.3.3.2 para. 1 and 2.
[82] FMA, Organisationsrundschreiben WAG 2018 (fn. 67), para. 76.

(bb) Permanence and Effectiveness

31   The compliance function must be established on a permanent basis and must be institutionalised in the company's organisation by appropriate measures.[83] Although not explicitly provided by European law, the principles of '**permanence**' typically entails that the status and authority of the compliance function is documented in writing.[84]

32   The elements of an '**effective**' compliance function[85] are further specified by Article 22(3)(a) of the Delegated Regulation. According to this provision the compliance function must have the necessary authority, resources, expertise and access to all relevant information.[86] National supervisory practice further demands that the compliance staff is to be supplied with all relevant information and documents, and has unrestricted access to the premises, records and data processing systems as well as to any further information necessary for the performance of compliance tasks.[87] According to the Austrian Standard Compliance Code, withholding information constitutes a serious offence for company employees and calls for disciplinary action.[88]

(b) Responsibilities

33   Legal literature traditionally distinguished between advisory and informational responsibilities of the compliance function and responsibilities regarding quality control.[89] Since the enactment of the MiFID the responsibility towards investor protection must also be considered a priority.[90] The Delegated Regulation places particular emphasis on two responsibilities of the compliance function: (i) the more repressive measures of monitoring and assessing the adequacy and effectiveness of the procedures designed to mitigate compliance risk;[91] and (ii) advisory and assisting responsibilities with more preventive effects.[92]

(aa) Monitoring and Assessment

34   The compliance function monitors and assesses the adequacy and effectiveness of the measures, policies and procedures put in place by the investment firm in order to minimise compliance risks as well as the actions taken to address any deficiencies in the firm's compliance with its obligations.[93] These monitoring and assessment responsibilities are to ensure that, with the help of senior management, all relevant legal risks can be identified and any

---

[83] ESMA/35-36-1952 (fn. 6), guideline 7, para. 55; L. Röh, 9 BB (2008), 398, 403.
[84] ESMA/35-36-1952 (fn. 6), guideline 7, para. 55; Basel Committee, Compliance (fn. 36), Principle 5, para. 22 ff.; Banca d'Italia, Compliance Function, July 2007, p. 5: 'formalize the function's status and authority' (repealed).
[85] For an economic analysis of an effective compliance program see G.P. Miller, *An Economic Analysis of Effective Compliance Programs* (2014).
[86] See for details ESMA35-36-1952 (fn. 6), guideline 5, para. 43 ff.
[87] BaFin, Rundschreiben (circular) 05/2018—MaComp (fn. 61), BT 1.3.1.2 para. 1. See also Basel Committee, Compliance (fn. 36), Principle 5, para. 30 ff. For details on the compliance officer's informational rights and right to issue instructions see below para. 47–49.
[88] Standard Compliance Code, Grundsätze ordnungsgemäßer Compliance, No. 6; T. Lösler, 3 NZG (2005), 104 ff.
[89] Cf. Standard Compliance Code, Grundsätze ordnungsgemäßer Compliance, No. 2. In detail T. Lösler, 3 NZG (2005), 104 ff.
[90] See above para. 12.
[91] Art. 22(2)(a) Delegated Regulation.
[92] Art. 22(2)(b) Delegated Regulation.
[93] Art. 22(2)(a) Delegated Regulation. On the compliance function's responsibilities concerning monitoring and control see ESMA35-36-1952 (fn. 6), guideline 2. A. Newton, *Compliance*, 143 ff.; S. Gebauer and S. Niermann, in: Hauschka et al. (eds.), *Corporate Compliance*, § 48 para. 22 ff.

shortcomings of the compliance function can be determined. As a general principle, the monitoring responsibility is comprehensive: it applies both to the organisational measures and procedures taken by senior management in order to prevent legal risks, as well as to the day-to-day business carried out by the operative staff, although the latter cannot be directly deduced from the provision's wording.[94] However, this does not prevent the compliance function (following a risk-based approach) from establishing **priorities** determined by the investment firm's compliance risk assessment ensuring that compliance risks are adequately monitored.[95] The aim of compliance monitoring is to ensure that the firm's employees abide by the internal organisational principles and internal rules. If the compliance function identifies weaknesses in the principles and procedures developed by the investment firm, it must make suggestions on how to improve the compliance organisation and submit a report to the senior management thereon.[96] The compliance function must further determine and manage **conflicts of interest** and monitor the flow of inside information.[97] The Delegated Regulation clarifies that the monitoring obligations also refer to the general client-handling process.[98]

The importance of an effective compliance (monitoring) system as well as the management of conflicts of interests has become apparent in relation to the (alleged) **Libor-benchmark** manipulations. The conflicts of interests resulted from the fact that, on the one hand, panel banks contributed to the calculation of the Libor benchmark by making submissions while those banks had, on the other hand, a self-interest in the development of the Libor interest rate.[99] According to the decisions of the FSA/FCA in the United Kingdom[100] relating to manipulations of Libor submissions there had been significant shortcomings in the compliance systems of the involved institutions in this regard. On 6 June 2016, the European Parliament and Council adopted a **Regulation on Benchmarks** (Regulation (EU) No. 2016/2011) which took effect on 1 January 2018.[101]

35

(bb) Advice and Assistance

The compliance function is further tasked with advising and assisting the relevant persons responsible for carrying out investment services and activities to comply with the firm's obligations under the MiFID II.[102] This advisory role of the compliance function is becoming increasingly important in legal practice.[103] It reflects the MiFID's understanding of the compliance function as an essential element of the investment firm's value chain.[104]

36

---

[94] See also J. Harm, *Compliance*, 44.
[95] This is now expressly recognised in Art. 22(2)(2)(2) Delegated Regulation.
[96] See below para. 50 ff.
[97] See below (in the context of the establishment of Chinese walls) para. 59 ff.
[98] Art. 22(2)(d) Delegated Regulation.
[99] See below para. 82 and §§ 35 and 36 (Regulation of Benchmarks).
[100] See below para. 82.
[101] Cf. chapters §§ 35 and 36 (Regulation of Benchmarks).
[102] Art. 22(2)(b) Delegated Regulation.
[103] K. Rothenhöfer, in: Kümpel and Wittig (eds.), *Bank- und Kapitalmarktrecht*, para. 3.375.
[104] On the development of the compliance function from an internal control body, acting repressively, to a central management function essential to the value chain see C. Taylor, 6 J. Invest. Comp. (2005), 54, 58: 'genuinely strategic, forward facing management function that rightly has the ear of the board and the senior management'; A. Newton, *Compliance*, 72 ff.; SDA Bocconi, *Evolution of Compliance Function*, 5 (empirical evidence). See also G. Miller, *The Role of Risk Management and Compliance in Banking Integration*, 17: 'dramatic change' of the compliance function.

The compliance function can give advice and assistance in three ways.[105] It advises senior management and staff on the interpretation and application of statutes and internal guidelines. It further trains staff to recognise and understand regulatory requirements, thereby reducing the risk of 'accidental' offences resulting from a lack of knowledge regarding applicable legal requirements.[106] Finally, it compiles compliance handbooks and codes of conduct that give guidance to the staff in the operative units in their day-to-day business.

2. Compliance Officer

37 A novel concept introduced by the MiFID I Regime is the obligation to appoint a compliance officer, responsible for the compliance function and compliance reports.[107] The legal status, responsibilities and powers of the compliance officer are only outlined roughly in the MiFID II regime. It thus comes as no surprise that with regard to the status of the compliance officer significant differences in the legal practice of the Member States exist.

(a) Appointment

(aa) Registration and Qualification Requirements

38 Pursuant to Article 22(3)(b) Delegated Regulation the compliance officer must be appointed and replaced by the investment firm.[108] The Delegated Regulation does not require a registration or a supervisory assessment of the potential compliance officer's qualifications, the regulation merely stating that the 'relevant persons for the compliance function'—a term that also includes the compliance officer—must have the necessary expertise.[109]

39 Based on recommendations of the Basel Committee,[110] the supervisory practice in the Member States usually requires investment firms to **inform** the supervisory authorities of **any change** in the person of the compliance officer. This procedure is recommendable as the compliance officer often coordinates the exchange of information between the senior management, the staff and the supervisory authorities, and therefore functions as a contact person for the supervisory authorities. The details of the notification, registration and approval obligations regarding compliance officers (if any) vary between the Member States.

40 In its updated guidelines, ESMA recognises that different regulatory approaches may be implemented at national level in the Member States in order to demonstrate the necessary

---

[105] ESMA35-36-1952 (fn. 6), guideline 4, para. 31 ff. Cf. also D. Lippe, *Compliance*, 176 ff.; A. Fuchs, in: Fuchs (ed.), *Kommentar zum WpHG*, § 33 para. 72–73; K. Rothenhöfer, in: Kümpel and Wittig (eds.), *Bank- und Kapitalmarktrecht*, para. 3.371 ff.

[106] For details on 'compliance training' see A. Newton, *Compliance*, 113 ff. and ESMA35-36-1952 (fn. 6), guideline 4, para. 33.

[107] The compliance requirements under capital markets law are more extensive than those under insurance and banking supervision. Neither the CRD IV directive nor the Solvency II framework directive contain the legal obligation to introduce the concept of compliance officers. Only the Basel Committee, Compliance (fn. 36), Principle 5, para. 24 ff. recommends the appointment of a so-called 'head of compliance'—a concept that has recently also been introduced for rating agencies. See R. Veil § 27 para. 39.

[108] This organisational requirement is binding and not subject to the principle of proportionality, cf. Art. 22(4) Delegated Regulation which only refers to Art. 22(3)(d) or (e) *e contrario*.

[109] See above para. 32.

[110] Basel Committee, Compliance (fn. 36), Principle 5, para. 27.

level of knowledge and experience of the compliance officer.[111] While some competent authorities formally approve the appointment of the compliance officer after an assessment procedure, in other jurisdictions it remains the responsibility of the senior management to assess the compliance officer's qualifications. In **Germany** investment firms are required to inform BaFin of the appointment or dismissal of a compliance officer[112] and to demonstrate that the compliance officer has the required professional expertise.[113] The supervisory authority's powers in **France** have traditionally been far more extensive: Compliance officers (*responsable de la conformité*) must be registered with the AMF and must obtain administrative permission to exercise their profession (*carte professionnelle*) which will only be granted if they first pass an oral suitability test.[114] In the **United Kingdom**, it is an established principle of financial supervision that so-called approved persons with special responsibilities within a company must acquire separate permission before they are permitted to exercise so-called 'controlled functions',[115] ie particularly important functions within an investment firm.[116] This also applies to the position of the compliance officer.[117] The permission is granted if the person passes the *fit and proper test*, ie if the compliance officer is regarded as being able to exercise her responsibilities with honesty and integrity as well as with competence and capability. Both in the United Kingdom and in France the appointment of a compliance officer is thus subject to a comprehensive ex-ante assessment by the competent authorities. This reflects a regulatory trend in European law not only to subject the investment firm itself and its senior management to capital market supervision, but also the members of the second management tier.[118]

(bb) Appointment of Members of Senior Management as Compliance Officers

The European provisions do not state whether a member of the senior management can be appointed as a compliance officer. The former CESR's technical advice, which was published to prepare the implementing measures under MiFID, allows members of senior management to simultaneously be appointed as compliance officers.[119] In Germany, BaFin also assumes that members of the management board can also become compliance officers, provided the specific risk situation of the company does not require a full-time compliance officer.[120] In the light of the prohibition of self-monitoring this combination of positions must, however, be seen critically.[121] Especially with regard to larger investment firms, 41

---

[111] Cf. ESMA/35-36-1952, Guideline 6, para. 49.
[112] § 87 WpHG.
[113] § 3 Abs. 1 and 2 WpHGMaAnzV.
[114] See the referenced stated in the 2nd edition of this chapter.
[115] A list of 'controlled functions' can be found in SUP 10.4.5 FCA Handbook.
[116] Sec. 59 FSMA and SUP 10A FCA Handbook. Cf. S. Bazley and A. Haynes, *Financial Services Authority Regulation and Risk-Based Compliance*, para. 1.7.; P. Nelson, *Compliance*, para. 5.3.1 ff.
[117] S. Bazley and A. Haynes, *Financial Services Authority Regulation and Risk-Based Compliance*, para. 1.7. Cf. SUP 10.7.8 FCA Handbook ('compliance oversight person').
[118] On the underlying regulatory concept of 'management-based regulation' see above para. 13. In the context of the governance requirements (key function holders) cf. M. Wundenberg § 34 para. 8, 15.
[119] CESR/05-024c (fn. 64), p. 15, Box 2 No. 9a and Commission, Background Note (fn. 13), sec. 3.2. The ESMA Guidelines do not seem to address this issue.
[120] BaFin, Rundschreiben (circular) 05/2018—MaComp (fn. 61), BT 1.3.3.1 para. 4.
[121] In detail: J. Harm, *Compliance*, 65–66. According to the Basel Committee, Compliance (fn. 36), Principle 5, para. 26, the head of compliance who is at the same time part of the senior management should not have direct business line responsibilities.

appointing managing directors simultaneously as compliance officers should be avoided in order to prevent conflicts of interest.[122]

(b) Legal Status

42 The compliance officer has an important position in the company: in order to ensure that she can act effectively the compliance officer should have a high position in the company's hierarchy and be able to **report directly** to the senior management.[123] It is thus generally recommended that the compliance officer is placed at the top of the organisation under the direct authority of the senior management.[124] Furthermore, the principle of independence that applies to both the compliance function and the compliance officer requires that the compliance officer is **not subject to instructions** or otherwise influenced by other units of the investment firm.[125]

(aa) Independence Towards Senior Management

43 A number of legal issues relate to the question of independence of the compliance officer towards the senior management. While the fact that measures adopted by the senior management are also subject to the compliance officer's monitoring activities, indicating that the compliance officer should also be independent from the senior management,[126] Article 25 Delegated Regulation assign the final right and obligation to ensure compliance to senior management.[127] This leads to **considerable tension** between the principle of independence of the compliance officer on the one hand and the corporate and supervisory principle of an overall compliance responsibility of senior management on the other. The legal literature is thus embroiled in an intense debate on the legal nature and the status of the compliance officer, centring around the question whether this officer is bound to instructions by the management or is independent thereof.[128]

44 The discussion can be led back to the dual regulatory aim of the European compliance regime addressed above.[129] The MiFID's concept of a compliance officer requires her to deal with conflicting interests:[130] as an employee of an investment firm she is obliged to act in the interest of the company. At the same time, the compliance officer's responsibility to monitor legal compliance of the firm is in the public interest.[131] So far, the legal literature

---

[122] Cf. J. Harm, *Compliance*, 65–66.
[123] Art. 22(2)(c) Delegated Regulation; see also CESR/05-024c (fn. 64), p. 15, Box 2 No. 9a: 'direct reporting line'; Basel Committee, Compliance (fn. 36), Principle 5, para. 24 ff.
[124] Cf. Austrian Standard Compliance Code, Grundsätze ordnungsgemäßer Compliance, para. 5 and 6; Gabbi et al., *Managing Compliance Risk after MiFID*, 5; R. Veil, 24 WM (2008), 1093, 1097; T. Lösler, 24 WM (2008), 1098, 1102–1103.
[125] BaFin, Rundschreiben (circular) 05/2018—MaComp (fn. 61), BT 1.3.3 para. 1.
[126] Cf. ESMA35-36-1952 (fn. 6), guideline 8, para. 5, which clarifies that the tasks performed by the compliance function should be 'carried out independently from senior management'.
[127] See above para. 15.
[128] Cf. R. Veil, 24 WM (2008), 1093 ff. on the one hand and T. Lösler, WM (2008), 1098 ff. and M. Casper, *Der Compliancebeauftragte*, in: Bitter et al. (eds.), *FS für Karsten Schmidt*, 199 ff. on the other. See also J. Harm, *Compliance*, 64 ff.
[129] See above para. 12–13.
[130] Cf. R. Veil, 24 WM (2008), 1093, 1096 ff.
[131] See above para. 12.

has placed a greater emphasis on the first aspect, understanding the compliance officer as a 'man/woman of the company'.[132],[133] The enactment of MiFID has, however, brought a change in the responsibilities of the compliance officer: the fact that one of the main regulatory objectives of the directive is to promote investor protection indicates that the compliance officer can now also be understood as an advocate of public interest (ie, ensuring compliance with applicable regulations).[134] In this respect, the compliance officer is charged with specific responsibilities within the company.[135] The compliance officer's legal status is increasingly becoming comparable to that of a *Betriebsbeauftragter*, ie company representative, in German law who is independent in terms of performing her duties (even in many regards from the management board).[136]

The national supervisory authorities appear to follow the understanding that the compliance officer is bound by instructions given by the management,[137] her independence being nonetheless ensured by a number of additional measures. The **German** BaFin, for example, does not only require to notify BaFin when a compliance officer is dismissed, but also to document whenever the senior management overrules the compliance officer's evaluations and recommendations.[138] This is in line with the ESMA Guidelines.[139] Such actions must be mentioned in the compliance report.[140] In practice this leads to a strengthening of the compliance officer's position. The **Austrian** financial supervision provides for an even farther-reaching concept of independence, having explicitly opposed the concept of the compliance officer being bound by managerial instructions.[141] In general, there is a regulatory trend to strengthen the position of the compliance officer vis-à-vis the management board.

45

(bb) Disciplinarian Independence and Protection against Dismissal

The independence from instructions must be distinguished from the disciplinary independence of compliance officers.[142] This concept relates to the protection of the compliance officer against 'abusive' dismissals or other sanctions which would jeopardise the compliance

46

---

[132] T. Lösler, in: Hellner and Steuer (eds.), *Bankrecht und Bankpraxis*, para. 7/814.
[133] Cf. T. Lösler, 24 WM (2008), 1098 ff. and M. Casper, *Der Compliancebeauftragte*, in: Bitter et al. (eds.), *FS für Karsten Schmidt*, 199 ff.
[134] See above para. 13–19.
[135] See para. 47 ff.
[136] Summarising the concept of a compliance officer under German law, T. Lösler, in: Hellner and Steuer (eds.), *Bankrecht und Bankpraxis*, para. 7/814. For more details on this complex question R. Veil, 24 WM (2008), 1093, 1096 ff. and J. Harm, *Compliance*, 67 ff.
[137] Cf. BaFin, Rundschreiben (circular) 05/2018—(MaComp), 19.4.2018, BT 1.1 para. 1. In the most recent version of the MaComp it is emphasised that the compliance function performs its tasks independently also vis-à-vis the senior management. This does not, however, seem to preclude the senior management from issuing instructions towards the compliance officer (or other personnel of the compliance function), cf. BT 1.3.3 para. 1 sentence 2 MaComp (fn. 61).
[138] Ibid., BT 1.3.3 para. 2.
[139] ESMA35-36-1952 (fn. 6), Guideline 8, para. 61. ESMA initially proposed that senior management shall only be allowed to issue 'general instructions' to compliance staff and shall otherwise not interfere with the compliance function's day-to-day activities. As this may have been incompatible with the ultimate compliance responsibility of senior management, this sentence has been deleted in the final guidelines.
[140] On the compliance report see below para. 50 ff.
[141] FMA, Rundschreiben (circular) betreffend die organisatorischen Anforderungen des Wertpapieraufsichtsgesetzes, May 2007, p. 9. However, the most recent version of the circular (fn. 67) is less clear in this regard.
[142] The terminology is not yet uniform. Cf. T. Lösler, in: Hellner and Steuer, *Bankrecht und Bankpraxis*, para. 7/833.

officer's independence. Whether the compliance officer should generally be protected from the risk of **dismissal** has been much debated in the legal literature.[143] European law does not expressly require this form of protection under its MiFID II regime. However, the Delegated Regulation specifies that the compliance officer can only be replaced by the 'management body', thereby protecting her from dismissals from members of the business units.[144] In Germany, BaFin suggests that a compliance officer should be appointed for at least 24 months in order to ensure independence, recommending a 12-month period of notice.[145]

(c) Responsibilities and Powers

(aa) Right to Issue Instructions and Obtain Information

47   The compliance officer's powers can be divided into investigative powers on the one hand and intervention powers on the other: just like other members of the compliance staff, a compliance officer must be granted unrestricted **access to all information** necessary in order to fulfil her compliance duties,[146] and furthermore must be permitted **to report directly to senior management**.[147] The ESMA Guidelines state that the compliance officer should also be able to **attend meetings** of senior management or the supervisory function.[148]

48   The principle of effectiveness further requires compliance officers to have authority to terminate critical transactions at a very early stage.[149] BaFin, for example, allows compliance officers to intervene in the process of signing and approving new products.[150] The European provisions do not, however, require that compliance officers be given the right to issue instructions and remedy infringements personally. This can be deduced *e contrario* from Article 22(2)(a) and (3)(b)/(c) Delegated Regulation, which require that the compliance function monitors and assesses the adequacy and effectiveness of the measures and procedures of the investment firm, and reports its findings to senior management. The compliance function is not, however, required to take the necessary corrective measures. The European understanding of the compliance officer is thus that she monitors legal risks and reports those risks to the senior management and in certain cases to the supervisory authority.[151] Depending on the size and the risk structure of the investment firm, the compliance officer may have to be granted independent investigative powers and the right to issue instructions in certain cases, in order to ensure an effective management of compliance risks and thereby a sufficient level of investor protection.[152]

---

[143] On this discussion see R. Veil, 24 WM (2008), 1093, 1997–1998; M. Casper, *Der Compliancebeauftragte*, in: Bitter et al. (eds.), *FS für Karsten Schmidt*, 199, 210–211; D. Illing and K. Umnuß, 1 CCZ (2009), p. 1, 6 ff.; J. Rodewald and U. Unger, 31 BB (2007), 1629, 1633 requires the compliance officer to be protected from dismissal *de lege ferenda*.
[144] Art. 22(3)(b) Delegated Regulation.
[145] BaFin, Rundschreiben (circular) 05/2018—MaComp (fn. 61), BT 1.3.3.4 para. 4. Similarly Standard Compliance Code, Grundsätze ordnungsgemäßer Compliance, No. 5.
[146] Art. 22(3)(c) Delegated Regulation. See above para. 33.
[147] The Delegated Regulation expressly provides that Compliance Officer reports to the management body, cf. Art.22(2)(c) Delegated Regulation.
[148] ESMA35-36-1952 (fn. 6), Guideline 5, para. 47.
[149] R. Veil, 24 WM (2008), 1093, 1098.
[150] BaFin, Rundschreiben (circular) 05/2018—MaComp (fn. 61), BT 1.2.4 para. 3. For the product approval process requirements pursuant to Art. 16(3) subsec. 2 MiFID II see R. Veil § 20 para. 2–10.
[151] More details in M. Casper, in: Casper (ed.), *Bankrechtstag 2008*, 139, 158 ff.
[152] On this compliance risk assessment by the senior management see above para. 14 ff.

The exact nature of the compliance officer's investigative powers and right to issue instructions is a matter of national company law. Due to the fact that the overall responsibility for the compliance organisation lies with the **senior management**, it must ultimately also decide how to prevent and sanction infringements of law. *De lege ferenda* and based on MiFID's aim to enhance investor protection, however, it seems recommendable to further strengthen the legal status of the compliance officer and to equip her legally with an independent **right to issue instructions** and to intervene personally in specific cases. Such instruction rights seem particularly important in cases in which the senior management, to which the compliance officer must report, is personally involved in any violation of the law.

(bb) Compliance Reporting

(1) Internal Reporting

The compliance officer must submit reports to the senior management and—if existent— to the supervisory function[153] at regular intervals.[154] The European law does not prescribe details on the specific content and format of the report, merely stating that the reports should be submitted on a frequent basis, at least annually, and in writing. However, the general information which should be covered in the compliance reports are outlined in the (updated) ESMA Guidelines.[155] According to those guidelines, the mandatory compliance reports should, inter alia, contain (i) general information on the compliance function's structure, (ii) the manner of monitoring and reviewing of compliance relevant aspects by the compliance function, (iii) a summary of major compliance findings as well as (iv) a summary of the action taken in order to ensure compliance.

This **mandatory compliance report** has three aims. The first aim is to ensure that the members of the management body receive the information required in order to assess that the investment firm is complying with applicable regulations and that necessary measures are taken in order to rectify any deficiencies identified by the compliance function.[156] The second aim of the compliance report is to provide a written basis for the compliance officer to make suggestions to senior management—and if existent to the supervisory function— on possible measures to improve compliance management.[157] While the compliance officer's suggestions and recommendations are not binding for senior management, the management will nevertheless have to examine them closely and will often follow these recommendations.[158] In some Member States the compliance report also aims to support the supervisory tasks of the competent authorities.[159]

The compliance reports should be synchronised with the reports submitted by the risk management and the internal audit function as the three areas overlap.[160] The volume and

---

[153] Art. 22(1)(c) in conjunction with Art. 25(2) and (3) Delegated Regulation.
[154] Art. 22(3)(c), 25(2) and 25(3) Delegated Regulation.
[155] ESMA35-36-1952 (fn. 6), guideline 3, para. 27 ff.
[156] See also K. Muther-Pradler and M. Ortner, in: Brandl and Saria (eds.), *Praxiskommentar zum Wertpapieraufsichtsgesetz*, § 18 para. 33. Cf. D. Sandmann, 3 CCZ (2008), 104.
[157] In more detail J. Harm, *Compliance*, 76 ff.
[158] As mentioned above, ESMA guidelines suggest that any deviations from important recommendations or assessments issued by the compliance function must be documented. See ESMA35-36-1952 (fn. 6), guideline 8, para. 58.
[159] Cf. the references in the previous edition of this chapter (para 61 fn. 210).
[160] Cf. para. 27 ff.

frequency of the reports depend on the individual risk situation. In general, annual reports will be regarded as insufficient to supply the management with all necessary information in larger companies, quarterly reports having become most common in practice.[161]

53　The regular reports must be distinguished from so-called **ad hoc reports** that must be submitted by the compliance function directly to the management body where significant compliance failures are detected.[162] If the violation is less severe it will generally be sufficient to inform only the next higher level in the company.[163]

(2) External Reports

54　A controversial issue relates to the question of whether a compliance officer is obliged to inform external bodies, such as supervisory authorities, of legal violations (so-called **external reports**). The regulatory aim to promote an effective capital market supervision as well as the principle of investor protection seem to support this idea. A disadvantage of this obligation would be that the reputation of the investment firm may suffer and it would no longer be able to sanction the violation internally.

55　The 'Standards for Investor Protection' published by CESR in July 2002 contemplated an external reporting requirement in cases of 'serious breaches of conduct of business rules'.[164] As opposed to this, the current European regime does, as a general rule, not require that potential compliance breaches are reported to supervisory authorities unless this is specifically required by mandatory law.[165]

56　The **United Kingdom** introduced external reporting obligations on the basis of the duty of firms to cooperate with the regulator, as described in Principle 11 of the FCA Handbook. The FCA has defined this obligation more concretely, stating that any significant breach of a supervisory rule by an investment firm or one of its employees must be reported to the respective authority.[166] In **Germany** the concept of external reports is controversial.[167] The legal literature largely assumes that there is no legal basis for such an obligation.[168] As mentioned above, the competent authorities in the Member States may request compliance reports from the companies' compliance officers based on national law.[169]

---

[161] See the empirical data in: Gallo, *Compliance Function*, 325 ff. (Italy); J. Oelkers, *Compliance in Banken*, in: Lucius et al. (eds.), *Compliance im Finanzdienstleistungsbereich*, 130, 174 ff. (Austria).

[162] Art. 22(3)(b) Delegated Regulation.

[163] For details see M. Casper, in: Casper (ed.), *Bankrechtstag 2008*, 139, 158 ff.

[164] CESR, A European Regime of Investor Protection—The Professional and the Counterparty Regimes, July 2002, CESR/02-098b, para. 11.

[165] See para. 58 below.

[166] SUP 15.3.11 FCA Handbook. Cf. S. Bazley and A. Haynes, *Financial Services Authority Regulation and Risk-Based Compliance*, 386 ff. For a discussion of reporting obligations under the new conduct rules see I. Chiu, *Regulating (From) the Inside*, 241 ff.

[167] Cf. R. Kittelberger, *Einführung einer neuen Berichtspflicht für Wertpapierdienstleistungsunternehmen und deren Folgen*; T. Lösler, 15 WM (2007), 676 ff.; M. Casper, *Der Compliancebeauftragte*, in: Bitter et al. (eds.), *FS für Karsten Schmidt*, 199, 211.

[168] For banking supervision the 'Mindestanforderungen an das Risikomanagement' (MaRisk—minimum requirements for risk management) contain a reporting duty of the internal audit function towards the supervisory authority should 'severe violations' by the management become apparent. Cf. BaFin, Rundschreiben (circular) 10/2021 (BA), August 2021, BT 2.4. para. 5.

[169] See para. 51 (France, Luxembourg, Germany).

As a general note, external reporting obligations (resulting from settlement agreements with prosecutors or regulatory authorities) are also well established in **US law:** Settlement agreements often contain provisions according to which violations of law (as well as potentially other improper conduct) have to be reported to the authorities (or a compliance monitor committee implemented by the settlement agreement).[170]

Mandatory reporting requirements may arise in specific circumstances. For example, notification obligations for potential breaches of the rules on insider dealings or market manipulation can be found in Article 16(3) MAR. Furthermore, a firm may be required to disclosure a potential breach of legal requirements pursuant to Article 17 MAR under the ad-hoc regime if such breach would constitute inside information. Reporting obligations may also arise in the case of breaches of data protection requirements as well as certain anti-money laundering provisions.

3. Informational Barriers ('Chinese Walls')

Informational barriers or 'Chinese walls' are an essential element of the compliance system for several decades.[171] The term refers to any internal policies and procedures that restrict the flow of information within the investment firm and prevent information which is confidential to one department from being passed freely to other departments.[172] Chinese walls follow two closely connected aims: the restricted flow of information aims to reduce **conflicts of interest** between the investment firm and the client or between two clients of the investment firm. Chinese walls are further supposed to safeguard inside or other **confidential information** from being traded or disseminated. The establishment of areas of confidentiality helps to ensure that inside information is only disseminated to other employees of the investment firm if this is permitted pursuant to Article 10(1) MAR and thus cannot be used to the detriment of clients.[173]

The concept of Chinese walls originated in **US capital markets law**[174] where it was first developed in a settlement made between the supervisory authority SEC and the brokerage firm **Merrill Lynch, Pierce, Fenner & Smith, Inc.,**[175] on the basis of the following facts (abridged):

> Merrill Lynch obtained inside information on the economic situation (negative profit expectations) of the aircraft manufacturer Douglas Aircraft in the course of its work as lead manager for

---

[170] Cf. the deferred prosecution agreement with the Royal Bank of Scotland (under xi.—reports to the Commission), available at: www.justice.gov/sites/default/files/criminal-vns/legacy/2013/03/22/2013-02-rbs-dpa.pdf.

[171] Also termed 'screens', 'firewalls' or 'insulation walls' in Anglo-American law. Cf. K. Hopt, in: Kalss et al. (eds.), *FS für Peter Doralt*, 213, 214. For a (critical) assessment of the effectiveness of informational barriers from a US-American perspective see A. Tuch, 39 J. Corp. Law (2014), 102 ff.

[172] See also the definition offered by The Law Commission, Great Britain, Fiduciary Duties and Regulatory Rules, Consultation Paper No. 124, 138: 'Procedures for restricting flow of information within a firm to ensure that information which is confidential to one department is not improperly communicated [...] to any other department within the conglomerate.'

[173] T. Lösler, in: Hellner and Steuer, *Bankrecht und Bankpraxis*, para. 7/8432. On the requirements for a dissemination of inside information see R. Veil § 14 para. 69–76.

[174] On the legal developments in Anglo-American law see H. McVea, *Financial Conglomerates*, 171 and passim; N. Poser, 9 Mich. YBI Legal Stud. (1988), 91.

[175] *In re Merrill Lynch, Pierce, Fenner& Smith, Inc.* [1968], 43 SEC 933. In detail N. Poser, 9 Mich. YBI Legal Stud. (1988), p. 91, 105–106.

the issuance of bonds. The 'Underwriting Division' passed this information on to the investment department of the brokerage firm, which then informed selected customers of the negative profit expectations of the issuer. The SEC regarded this behaviour as a breach of inside information rules. Without confirming this legal assessment, Merrill Lynch committed itself to restricting the internal flow of information and thus preventing the abuse of inside information by taking certain organisational measures.[176]

62   In the **United Kingdom** Chinese walls have been used to manage conflicts of interest since the 1970s.[177] Based on the experience in the Anglo-American jurisdictions, Chinese walls have also become a common feature in continental European banks and investment firms.[178]

(a) Legal Foundations

63   In the Recitals to the former MAD, Chinese walls were explicitly mentioned as a preventive measure to tackle market abuse.[179] As opposed to this, the MiFID/MiFID II and its implementing legislation do not make any explicit reference to the establishment of Chinese walls. Nonetheless it can be deducted from the European law that investment firms are required to control their internal flow of information through organisational arrangements: the Delegated Regulation requires the investment firms to 'establish, implement and maintain systems and procedures that are adequate to safeguard the security, integrity and confidentiality of information, taking into account the nature of the information in question'.[180] This general principle is put into more concrete terms in Article 34(3)(a) Delegated Regulation with regard to the management of conflicts of interest without, however, describing in more detail how the control of the information flow should be organised.[181]

(b) Elements

64   Firms use a combination of different measures in order to control the internal flow of confidential information effectively. Based on the concept of the 'reinforced Chinese wall'[182] the restriction of the flow of information by means of informational barriers is supplemented by trading restrictions and further measures designed to prevent conflicts of interest and insider trading.[183] Chinese walls usually consist of the following elements.

---

[176] The organisational measures are described in a 'Statement of Policy', imprinted in H. McVea, *Financial Conglomerates*, Appendix II.

[177] The Law Commission's recommendations on the 'Fiduciary Duties and Regulatory Rules' of 1992 (fn. 172) play an important role in the development of the Chinese wall concept in the UK.

[178] On the legal developments in Germany see D. Eisele and A. Faust, in: Schimansky et al. (eds.), *Bankrechts-Handbuch*, § 109 para. 125 ff.; on Swiss law see S. Abegglen, *Wissenszurechnung bei der juristischen Person*, 363 ff.; on the legal developments in Spain see A. Andrés, 81 RDBB (2001), 49 ff.

[179] Recital 24 MAD. See now also Art. 9(1)(a) MAR.

[180] Art. 21(2) Delegated Regulation.

[181] This is based on a deliberate decision by the legislator: the first CESR Consultation Paper of June 2004 suggested the establishment of informational barriers between proprietary trading, portfolio management and corporate governance, CESR/04-261b, Box 6 No. 7 and 8. This was criticised in the course of the consultation procedure, CESR consequentially introducing more flexible requirements regarding the control of the flow of information in the final version. This regulatory approach is reflected in the final version of the Organisational Requirements Directive, the term 'informational barrier' having been replaced by a less stringent definition in Art. 22(3)(2)(a)/ Art. 34(3)(a) Delegated Regulation.

[182] Cf. M. Lipton and R. Mazur, 50 N.Y.U. L. Rev. (1975), 459 ff.

[183] D. Eisele and A. Faust, in: Schimansky et al. (eds.), *Bankrechts-Handbuch*, § 109 para. 135a ff.

(aa) Segregation of Confidential Areas

Confidential areas are those departments of a company that are continually or temporarily in the possession of inside information or other compliance-relevant information.[184] In investment firms this may include, inter alia, the underwriting division, the credit department or the department responsible for mergers and acquisitions.[185] Any such areas must be segregated from the other departments of the company by effective measures, ensuring that confidential information remains within this segregated area unless dissemination is necessary for operational reasons.[186] Depending on the size of a company, segregation is possible on a number of levels: the departments can be **separated physically**, for example, by situating them on different floors or in separate buildings. Further possible measures include the restriction of communication and access to databases.[187] Employees must undergo training in order to be sensitised regarding the importance of a restricted flow of information (**'mental' Chinese wall**). Further measures become necessary if an employee is removed from one confidential area to another (**'personal' Chinese wall**).[188]

65

The dissemination of confidential information cannot be prohibited without exception as the establishment of informational barriers may conflict with the economic aim of efficient company communication and can even endanger the clients' interest.[189] A **'wall crossing'**, ie exceptions from the informational barriers, must therefore be permitted if necessary to ensure the aims of capital market law or to fulfil a legal obligation.[190] A cross-departmental flow of information is, however, always subject to strict requirements and follows the **'need-to-know'** principle, only allowing the dissemination of information if absolutely necessary and only to the extent of absolute necessity.[191]

66

The restrictions on the flow of information further depend on the nature of the information involved: inside information as defined by the MAR may only be passed on to other employees under the conditions of Article 10(1) MAR, ie 'in the normal exercise of an employment, a profession or duties'.[192] As opposed to this, publicly known information may be passed on without restriction, unless other legal provisions state otherwise, for example for reasons of data protection. 'Confidential' information stands between these two extremes, the lack of price relevance preventing it from being classed as inside information, but its disclosure still constituting a potential risk to the clients' interests.[193] Whether 'wall crossings' are

67

---

[184] Cf. § 3 No. 3 ECV 2007. Any information that may cause a conflict of interests can be described as 'compliance-relevant'.
[185] A. Meyer and U. Paetzel, in: Hirte and Möllers (eds.), *Kölner Kommentar zum WpHG*, § 33 para. 70.
[186] T. Lösler, in: Hellner and Steuer (eds.), *Bankrecht und Bankpraxis*, para. 7/843.
[187] Cf. M. Kloepfer Pelèse, Bull. Joly Bourse (2009), 204, 210.
[188] Law Commission, Fiduciary Duties (fn. 172), 156 ff. Cf. C. Hollander and S. Salzedo, *Conflicts of Interest & Chinese Walls*, para. 13–22; D. Eisele and A. Faust, in: H. Schimansky et al. (eds.), *Bankrechts-Handbuch*, § 109 para. 142d.
[189] C.f. H. McVea, *Financial Conglomerates*, 201 ff.; T. Lösler, in: Hellner and Steuer, *Bankrecht und Bankpraxis*, para. 7/843.
[190] An effective risk management may require that inside information is passed on to the risk control function immediately. Cf. M. Jahn and N. Welter, in: Jost (ed.), *Compliance in Banken*, 175, 180 ff. with further examples.
[191] Cf. C. Hollander and S. Salzedo, *Conflicts of Interest & Chinese Walls*, para. 13–22; A. Meyer and U. Paetzel, in: Hirte and Möllers (eds.), *Kölner Kommentar zum WpHG*, § 33 para. 72–73. The requirements for 'wall crossing' remain unclear: P. Buck-Heeb, *Insiderwissen, Interessenkonflikte und Chinese Walls bei Banken*, in: Grundmann et al. (eds.), *FS für Klaus J. Hopt*, 1647, 1666 attempts to define these requirements more concretely.
[192] See R. Veil § 14 para. 69–76.
[193] BaFin, Rundschreiben (circular) 05/2018—MaComp (fn. 61), AT 6.1. lists the knowledge of customer orders that are used to the clients disadvantage through proprietary transactions as an example.

permitted in these cases must be determined for each case individually, based on a consideration of the conflicting interests.[194]

68   Some Member States have introduced provisions on the requirements for 'wall crossings'. The **German** BaFin allows crossings, provided they are necessary for the investment firm to fulfil its obligations. BaFin argues that if an investment firm is active in a number of different business segments, it may be necessary to disclose confidential information to staff members of other business areas, especially in complex business transactions.[195] In **Austria**, the ECV of 2007 takes a similar stance in its principles regarding the disclosure of inside information.[196]

69   Any cross-departmental dissemination of information must be documented and monitored by the compliance function. The compliance officer holds a position above—or 'on'—the wall, and acts as a 'clearing house' for any compliance relevant information.[197]

(bb)   Watch Lists and Restricted Lists

70   A '**watch list**'[198] is a highly confidential and regularly updated list of financial instruments on which the investment firm holds compliance-relevant information.[199] The list can then be used by the compliance function in order to examine proprietary, customer and employee tradings for possible insider dealings and conflicts of interest.[200]

71   The business activities of an investment firm are not affected by the fact that certain instruments are included in the watch list. These financial instruments can continue to be recommended to investors and still be acquired or sold by the firm in the course of its proprietary trading activities. However, if the watch list reveals gaps in the Chinese wall or gives rise to the suspicion that inside information is being used abusively, the compliance officer may terminate the respective transactions.[201] The watch list can only fulfil its aim if employees notify the compliance officer of compliance-relevant information.[202]

---

[194] K. Rothenhöfer, in: Kümpel and Wittig (eds.), *Bank- und Kapitalmarktrecht*, para. 3.346–347.
[195] BaFin, Rundschreiben (circular) 05/2018—MaComp (fn. 61), AT 6.2. para. 3(b).
[196] § 6(2) ECV 2007.
[197] The importance of the compliance function for the supervision of the internal flow of information is emphasised in the SEC's paper Broker-Dealer Policies and Procedures Designed to Segment the Flow and Prevent the Misuse of Material Nonpublic Information, March 1990, available at www.sec.gov/divisions/marketreg/brokerdealerpolicies.pdf, p. 23. See also D. Eisele and A. Faust, in: Schimansky et al. (eds.), *Bankrechts-Handbuch*, § 109 para. 36 ff.
[198] On the relationship between watch lists and the insider lists as required by Art. 18 MAR and the former Art. 5 Commission Directive 2004/72/EC of 29 April 2004 implementing Directive 2003/6/EC of the European Parliament and of the Council as regards accepted market practices, the definition of inside information in relation to derivatives on commodities, the drawing up of lists of insiders, the notification of managers' transactions and the notification of suspicious transactions, OJ L162, 30 April 2004, p. 70–75 see H. Renz and K. Stahlke, ZfgK (2006), 353.
[199] See SEC, Broker-Dealer Policies (May 1990), p. 4 ff. (USA); Law Commission, Fiduciary Duties (fn. 172), p. 159 ff. (UK); BaFin, Rundschreiben (circular) 05/2018—MaComp (fn. 61), AT 6.2. para. 3(c) (Germany); Standard Compliance Code of 2008, Modul 2: Insider Dealings and Market Manipulation, No. 5.2.1.2 (Austria).
[200] T. Lösler, in: Hellner and Steuer (eds.), *Bankrecht und Bankpraxis*, para. 7/815.
[201] D. Eisele and A. Faust, in: Schimansky et al. (eds.), *Bankrechts-Handbuch*, § 109 para. 150 ff. This particularly applies, if the compliance officer has been awarded the power to personally take remedial measures. See above para. 58–59.
[202] BaFin, Rundschreiben (circular) 05/2018—MaComp (fn. 61), AT 6.2 para. 3(c).

Most investment firms have additionally introduced a so-called '**restricted list**' which— 72
unlike the watch list—is freely accessible to all company employees.[203] Proprietary and third-party trading and the recommendation of financial instruments in this list is prohibited.[204] Investment firms may, however, with the authorisation of the compliance officer, make exceptions to these prohibitions.[205]

Restricted lists first became relevant in US law. In the case of *Slade v. Shearson, Hammill &* 73
Co.[206] a brokerage house (Shearson, Hammill & Co.) had obtained inside information on the negative economic developments of a certain issuer (Tidal Marine International Corp.) but had nonetheless recommended the company's shares to clients. Shearson argued that the securities department had not known about the inside information due to the existing areas of confidentiality. In an *amicus curiae* brief the SEC recommended diffusing the conflict between the issuer and his clients by introducing restricted lists.[207]

Taking into account the far-reaching effects, the restricted list should only contain finan- 74
cial instruments on which an investment firm has inside information that is likely to have a considerable effect on the share price if it becomes public.[208] The inclusion of financial instruments in the restricted list should therefore be seen as an *ultima ratio* measure for situations in which the conflict of interests cannot be mitigated solely by the restriction of the internal information flow.[209]

(c) Legal Effects

The legal effects of Chinese walls have been a subject of controversy in the legal literature, 75
primarily with regard to the question as to whether effectively established confidential areas protect the firms under civil law and criminal law from the accusation of having participated in **insider dealings**. Another question that remains unanswered is whether the implementation of informational barriers is sufficient to prevent an **attribution of knowledge** within the company.

These questions have been addressed in the **United Kingdom**. When a firm establishes 76
and maintains a Chinese wall it may withhold the information and also permit persons employed in the respective part of its business to withhold the information from those employed in other areas.[210] Information may also be withheld between different parts

---

[203] In legal practice there are a number of different restricted lists. The Standard Compliance Code of 2008, Modul 2: Insider Dealings and Market Manipulation, No. 5.2.1.2 distinguishes between selective lists (only applicable for certain departments) and comprehensive lists (applicable to all company employees). Cf. A. Meyer and U. Paetzel, in: Hirte and Möllers (eds.), *Kölner Kommentar WpHG*, § 33 para. 77.
[204] BaFin, Rundschreiben (circular) 05/2018—MaComp (fn. 61), AT 6.2 para. 3(c).
[205] Restricted lists are therefore also described as prohibitions subject to the possibility of authorisation. Cf. D. Eisele and A. Faust, in: Schimansky et al. (eds.), *Bankrechts-Handbuch*, § 109 para. 151.
[206] 517 F.2d 398 (2d Cir. 1974).
[207] Cf. L. Loss and J. Seligman, *Fundamentals of Securities Regulation*, 1008 ff. and C. Benicke, *Wertpapiervermögensverwaltung*, 753 ff.
[208] Cf. I. Koller, in: Assmann and Schneider (eds.), *Kommentar zum WpHG*, § 33 para. 11 (possibility of a suspension of quotation); K. Rothenhöfer, in: Kümpel and Wittig (eds.), *Bank- und Kapitalmarktrecht*, para. 3.361 (immediate and considerable price change).
[209] The restricted list as a means to prevent insider dealings is seen critically, for example by H. McVea, *Financial Conglomerates*, 231–232 and D. Eisele and A. Faust, in: Schimansky et al. (eds.), *Bankrechts-Handbuch*, § 109 para. 154.
[210] SYSC 10.2.2 FCA Handbook. In detail C. Hollander and S. Salzedo, *Conflicts of Interest & Chinese Walls*, para. 13–01 ff. and R. Veil and M. Wundenberg, *Englisches Kapitalmarktrecht*, 145–146.

of a business within the same group.[211] If the flow of information has been effectively restricted by the use of Chinese walls, this generally provides a defence against proceedings brought under sections 89–91 Financial Services Act 2012 on the basis of an alleged market manipulation.[212] The Handbook also contains detailed provisions on the effects of Chinese walls on an attribution of knowledge. Generally an investment firm will not be assumed to have acted knowingly if none of the relevant individuals involved on behalf of the firm acted with that knowledge as a result of established Chinese walls.[213]

77 Whilst the FCA's provisions provide a very far-reaching protection against supervisory sanctions, it is as yet unclear whether they also constitute a defence against a **common law** claim for breach of fiduciary duties.[214] Case law appears to be limited regarding a civil law acknowledgement of Chinese walls,[215] an attribution of knowledge not generally being prevented and liability not automatically being excluded by the establishment of Chinese walls.[216] In line with the prevailing view, the same applies with regard to **German** law.[217]

78 The legal effects of Chinese walls are now also addressed in the Market Abuse Regulation ('MAR'): Article 9(1)(a) MAR provides that for purposes of insider dealing and of unlawful disclosure of inside information a legal person shall not have 'used' information where that legal person has 'established, implemented and maintained adequate and effective internal arrangements and procedures that effectively ensure that neither the natural person who has made the decision on its behalf to acquire or dispose of financial instruments to which the information relates, nor another person who may have had an influence on that decision, was in possession of insider information'.[218]

IV. Sanctions

79 The MiFID II framework has introduced a comprehensive **public sanctioning regime**: Member States must now provide that the competent national authorities have the power to impose, inter alia, maximum administrative fines of at least € 5,000,000 or up to 10% of the total turnover (as well as the other measures mentioned in Article 70(1) MiFID II) in case the compliance obligations pursuant to Article 16(1) MiFID II have been violated.[219]

---

[211] SYSC 10.2.2(2) FCA Handbook which, however, only refers to the COBS section of the FCA Handbook (rules of conduct).
[212] SYSC 10.2.3(1) (G) FCA Handbook.
[213] SYSC 10.2.4 and 10.2.5 (G) FCA Handbook. SYSC 10.2.4. only states this explicitly with regard to the rules of conduct laid down in the COBS and CASS sections of the Handbook. SYSC 10.2.5 is merely a guidance that, however, appears to prevent an attribution of knowledge for all regulated areas.
[214] For an overview of this complex issue see C. Hollander and S. Salzedo, *Conflicts of Interest & Chinese Walls*, para. 13–07 ff.; H. McVea, *Financial Conglomerates*, 135 ff. and passim; Law Commission, Fiduciary Duties (fn. 172), p. 152 ff. See also K. Jarvis, 3 J. Financ. Crime (2007), 192–195.
[215] Cf. House of Lords judgment in the case *Prince Jefri Bolkiah v. KPMG* [1999] 1 All ER 517.
[216] See K. Mwenda, *Banking Supervision*, 88: 'Law courts have usually taken the view that Chinese Walls do not afford a solution to the attribution of knowledge'; C. Hollander and S. Salzedo, *Conflicts of Interest & Chinese Walls*, para. 13–08 ff. Seen restrictively by the Law Commission, Fiduciary Duties (fn. 172), p. 152 ff.
[217] Cf. P. Buck-Heeb, *Insiderwissen, Interessenkonflikte und Chinese Walls*, in: Grundmann, et al. (eds.), *FS für Klaus J. Hopt*, 1647, 1656 ff.
[218] See also R. Veil § 14 para. 73.
[219] Art. 70(3) and (6) MiFID II.

1. Sanctions against Investment Firms

The Member States have developed different enforcement strategies for the compliance requirements.[220] All approaches centre on administrative enforcement by way of investigative and remedial measures and the power to impose administrative fines. The administrative enforcement of the organisational obligations is, however, implemented in different ways. In Germany, the former § 33 WpHG (now § 80 WpHG) did initially not impose any fines for breaches of the organisational obligations, relying on the general regulatory powers of BaFin to remedy infringements of supervisory law.[221] It has now been clarified by the German lawmaker that breaches of organisational requirements can lead to, inter alia, administrative fines.[222] In the United Kingdom violations of organisational requirements can in principle be sanctioned with unlimited fines.[223]

80

In the **United Kingdom** the (former) FSA has repeatedly sanctioned failings in the internal governance and control systems, a landmark decision being the case of *Carr Sheppards Crosthwaite Ltd.* (**CSC**), which occurred before MiFID was implemented.[224] CSC, a subsidiary 100% owned by Investec plc, was specialised in asset management for private clients. The parent company had identified deficits in the internal control systems during an internal audit and had informed the FSA thereof. The FSA regarded CSC's compliance system as insufficient and imposed a fine of £ 500,000. The FSA criticised the fact that the subsidiary's compliance department did not introduce a direct reporting line to the parent undertaking and that the compliance handbooks were incomplete. More recently the FSA imposed a considerable fine (£ 5.25 million) against the insurance company Aon Ltd. on the grounds that the company had not taken adequate measures in order to prevent corruption and bribery.[225]

81

Alleged compliance failings have also been at the heart of several decisions relating to manipulations of the **Libor** interest rate benchmark: In the landmark decision against **Barclays Bank plc**[226] Barclays was found to have manipulated submissions which formed part of Libor (the estimated interest rate at which banks can borrow funds from other banks in the London interbank market) between 2005 and 2009. According to the FSA, Barclays failed to conduct its business with due skill, care and diligence when considering issues raised internally in relation to its Libor submissions. Libor issues were escalated to Barclays' compliance function on three occasions during 2007 and 2008. In each case the compliance staff failed (according to the findings of the FSA) to assess and address these issues effectively. Due to these compliance failings (and other breaches of law) the FSA fined Barclays

82

---

[220] For an overview of the Member States' supervisory powers and possible sanctions regarding the obligations laid down in MiFID see CESR, Supervisory Powers, Supervisory Practices, Administrative and Criminal Sanctioning Regimes of Member States in Relation to the Markets in Financial Instruments Directive (MiFID), February 2009, CESR/08-220.
[221] Cf. A. Fuchs, in: A. Fuchs (ed.), *Kommentar zum WpHG*, § 33 para. 6.
[222] Cf. § 120(8)(97–109) WpHG.
[223] On the enforcement practice of the FSA see Financial Services Decision Digest, p. 273 ff.
[224] FSA, Final Notice, 19 May 2004.
[225] FSA, Final Notice, 6 January 2009.
[226] FSA, Final Notice, 27 June 2012.

£ 59.6 million. For similar reasons, fines were imposed on UBS,[227] RBS,[228] Rabobank[229] and Deutsche Bank.[230]

83   Sanctions under **civil law** against the investment firm do not as yet appear to play a significant role in sanctioning breaches of compliance obligations; in fact, civil law sanctions have been expressly ruled out by some Member States.[231] However, civil liability plays an increasingly important role regarding the sanctions targeted at the senior management of the investment firm (see below).

2. Sanctions against the Senior Management and the Compliance Officer

84   The enforcement measures that can be taken against investment firms must be distinguished from measures addressed directly to senior management or to the compliance officer. This concept of a direct supervisory responsibility of senior management or the compliance officer is known, for example, in the United Kingdom[232] and—in principle—in Germany.[233] The breach of compliance obligations can further constitute a breach of internal duties of care, leading to damage claims for the investment firm against the management.[234] In the United Kingdom fines and other supervisory measures can be directed against both senior management and the compliance officer.[235]

85   In **Germany** the Bundesgerichtshof (BGH, German Federal Court of Justice) decision of 17 July 2009 has led to a controversial discussion on the criminal liability of compliance officers.[236] The 5th Strafsenat (criminal division) purported in an obiter dictum that the compliance officer will generally have a special responsibility as required by § 13(1) StGB (German Criminal Code) (so-called *Garantenstellung*, ie guarantor duty) to prevent employees of an investment firm from committing crimes related to the company's business. According to the BGH this constituted the necessary consequence of the compliance officers' obligation to prevent violations of legal provisions (particularly criminal offences).[237] The legal literature has strongly criticised the BGH's ruling.[238] Whether the compliance

---

[227] FSA, Final Notice, 27 June 2012, para. 17–18 and 162–184. Interestingly, the fine was imposed solely on the basis of the FSA Principles (Principles 2, 3 and 5) and not on the basis of MiFID rules.
[228] FSA, Final Notice, 6 February 2013.
[229] FCA, Final Notice, 29 October 2013.
[230] FCA, Final Notice, 23 April 2015.
[231] In the United Kingdom liability is excluded in SYSC Sch. 5.4 FCA Handbook (and in sec. 138D FSMA with regard to private damage claims). In Germany it is assumed that violations of compliance obligations (§ 80 WpHG) do not give rise to a private cause of action, cf. l.Koller in Assmann/Schneider/Mülbert, WpHG, § 80 WpHG para. 1
[232] Sec. 66 FSMA.
[233] This applies to investment firms that are credit and financial service institutions in the sense of the KWG, cf. § 25a(1)(2) KWG. Breaches of the organisational obligations can lead to warnings or a dismissal of the management, cf. § 36 KWG.
[234] More details on this topic in German law in M. Wundenberg, *Compliance und die prinzipiengeleitete Aufsicht über Bankengruppen*, 132–136 and passim.
[235] Compliance officers are 'approved persons' and as such must adhere to the FCA Handbook's 'Statements of Principles', cf. APER 2.1A.3 (P), especially Principle 5, see above para. 40. For details on the FCA's sanctioning powers towards approved persons see FCA, Enforcement Guide, January 2016, para. 7.1. ff and passim.
[236] BGHSt 54, p. 44, 50.
[237] BGHSt 54, p. 44, 50.
[238] Cf. T. Rönnau and F. Schneider, 2 ZIP (2010), 53 ff.

officer is to be regarded as criminally responsible for preventing breaches of law based on his *Garantenstellung* therefore appears doubtful.

In a controversially discussed decision, the German District Court Munich I addressed the management board's obligation for compliance (Siemens/Neubürger decision).[239] The District Court Munich I ruled that members of the management board can be liable for civil damages not only in cases of direct involvement in misconduct, but also for failing to implement adequate systems and controls to prevent violations of law by employees of the company.

In the **United Kingdom**, the accountability of senior management for compliance failings has been subject of the FSA decision against *John Pottage*. The (former) FSA alleged that Pottage (who was in a controlling function of UBS Wealth Management Ltd.) failed 'to take reasonable steps to identify and remediate the serious flaws in the design and operational effectiveness of the governance and risk management framework', issuing a fine of £ 100,000 for breaching APER Statement of Principle 7. However, this decision was overruled by the Upper Tribunal, which concluded that there was insufficient evidence to support the case, indicating that an approved person will only be in breach of the Principles where it is 'personally culpable, and not simply because a regulatory failure has occurred in an area of business for which it is responsible'.[240,241]

V. Conclusion

MiFID II and the Delegated Regulation have introduced a comprehensive regime regarding compliance, risk management and internal audit in investment firms.

The European provisions reflect a regulatory trend that has also become apparent in other areas of supervisory law, namely to require supervised firms as well as their senior management to develop systems of internal control and governance arrangements in order to enhance investor protection and market efficiency. The European legislator opted for a principles-based approach to regulation, granting investment firms a large margin of appreciation regarding the implementation of the regulatory requirements. The European provisions do, however, explicitly require the establishment of an independent compliance function and the appointment of a compliance officer.

The European provisions are based on the Basel Committee on Banking Supervision's principles concerning the development of a risk-orientated compliance organisation and are an important contribution to the harmonisation of the organisational obligations of investment firms. Nevertheless differences in the legal practice of the Member States still exist, especially regarding the legal status of the compliance officer and the supervisory authorities' sanctioning powers. Against this backdrop, the attempts made by ESMA to promote greater convergence in the interpretation of the organisational principles laid down in the

---

[239] LG München I, 10.12.2013 – 5 HK O 1387/10.
[240] *John Pottage v. FSA*, FS/2010/0033 at para. 148.
[241] For a discussion of further enforcement actions against internal control individuals in the UK see I. Chiu, *Regulating (From) the Inside*, 242 ff.

MiFID II regime, as well as the supervision of these principles by the competent national authorities, must be welcomed.

91 The compliance obligations under the new MiFID II framework are generally in line with those established under the former MiFID I regime. However, as a key difference to the former regime the level 2 legislation has now been implemented by way of a regulation which is directly binding in all Member States. As a result, the organisational requirements are now to a large extent shaped by directly applicable European law.

§ 34

Governance

Bibliography

Baums, Theodor, *Unabhängige Aufsichtsratsmitglieder*, 180 ZHR (2016), 697–707; Bazley, Stuart and Haynes, Andrew, *Financial Services Authority and Risk-based Compliance*, 2nd edn. (2009); Binder, Jens-Hinrich, *Governance of Investment Firms under MiFID II*, in: Busch, Danny and Ferrarini, Guido (eds.), *Regulation of the EU Financial Markets MiFID II and MiFIR* (2017), Part II. 3; Binder, Jens-Hinrich, *Organisationspflichten und das Finanzdienstleistungs-Unternehmensrecht: Bestandsaufnahme, Probleme, Konsequenzen*, 44 ZGR (2015), 667–708; Cadbury, Adrian, *Report of the Committee on the Financial Aspects of Corporate Governance* (1992); Chiu, Iris H.-Y., *Corporate Governance and Risk Management in Banks and Financial Institutions*, in: Chiu, Iris H.-Y. and McKee, Michael (eds.), *The Law on Corporate Governance in Banks* (2015), 169–195; Chiu, Iris H.-Y., *Regulating (From) The Inside* (2015); Enriques, Luca and Zetzsche, Dirk, *Quack Corporate Governance, Round III? Bank Board Regulation Under the New European Capital Requirement Directive*, 16 Theoretical Inquiries in Law (2015), 211–244; Jayaraman, Narayanan et al., *Does Combining the CEO and Chair Roles Cause Poor Firm Governance?*, SSRN Working Paper (2015), available at SSRN: http://papers.ssrn.com/sol3/papers.cfm?abstract_id=2690281&download=yes; Jungmann, Carsten, *The Effectiveness of Corporate Governance in One-Tier and Two-Tier Board Systems*, 3 ECFR (2006), 426–474; Hopt, Klaus J., *Better Governance of Financial Institutions*, SSRN Working Paper (2013), available at SSRN: https://ssrn.com/abstract=1918851; Hopt, Klaus J., *Corporate Governance after the Financial Crisis*, in: E. Wymeersch et al. (eds.), *Financial Regulation and Supervision* (2012), 337–367; Hopt, Klaus J., *The German Law of and Experience with the Supervisory Board*, SSRN Working Paper (2016), available at SSRN: https://ssrn.com/abstract=2722702; Hopt, Klaus J. and Wohlmannstetter, Gottfried (eds.), *Handbuch Corporate Governance* (2011); Kokkinis, Andreas, *A Primer on Corporate Governance in Banks and Financial Institutions: Are Banks Special?*, in: Chiu, Iris H.-Y. and McKee, Michael (eds.), *The Law on Corporate Governance in Banks* (2015), 1–41; Miller, Geoffrey P., *The Law of Governance, Risk Management and Compliance* (2014); Mülbert, Peter O. and Wilhelm, Alexander, *CRD IV Framework for Banks' Corporate Governance*, in: Busch, Danny and Ferrarini, Guido (eds.), *European Banking Union*, 2nd edn. (2020), 223–280; Verse, Dirk A., *§ 21: Besonderheiten des Aufsichtsrats in Kreditinstituten und Versicherungsunternehmen*, in: Lutter, Marcus et al. (eds.), *Rechte und Pflichten des Aufsichtsrats*, 7th edn. (2020); Raschauer, Nicolas, *Geplante EBA- und ESMA-Leitlinien für Fit & Proper rechtswidrig?*, Zeitschrift für Finanzmarktrecht (2017), 420 ff.; Schneider, Uwe. H. and Schneider, Sven H., *Der Aufsichtsrat der Kreditinstitute zwischen gesellschaftsrechtlichen Vorgaben und aufsichtsrechtlichen Anforderungen*, 45 ZGR (2016), 41–47; Spindler, Gerald and Stilz, Eberhard (eds.), *Aktiengesetz*, 4th edn. (2019); Staake, Marco, *Arbeitnehmervertreter als unabhängige Aufsichtsratsmitglieder?*, 19 NZG 2016, 853–857; Veil, Rüdiger, *Europäische Kapitalmarktunion*, 43 ZGR (2014), 544–607; Veil, Rüdiger and Wundenberg, Malte, *Englisches Kapitalmarktrecht* (2010); Winter, Jaap W., *The Financial Crisis: Does Good Corporate Governance Matter and How to Achieve It?*, in: E. Wymeersch et al. (eds.), *Financial Regulation and Supervision* (2012), 368–388; Wundenberg, Malte, *Perspektiven der privaten Rechtsdurchsetzung im europäischen Kapitalmarktrecht*, 44 ZGR (2015), 125–160; Wundenberg, Malte, *Fit and Proper Assessments of Board Members of Banks and Investment Firms: A European Perspective*, 33 JIBLR (2018), 191–199; Wundenberg, Malte, *Compliance und die prinzipiengeleitete Aufsicht über Bankengruppen* (2012).

I. Introduction

1   Corporate Governance, like Compliance, is 'en vogue'.[1] The traditional definition of this term refers to the relationship between the company's senior management, its board of directors, its shareholders and other stakeholders, such as employees and their representatives.[2] Corporate governance provides the structure through which the objectives of the company are set, and the arrangements by which the company is directed and controlled.[3]

2   The regulation and supervision of the internal governance of banks and investment firms has emerged gradually. Traditionally, governance related issues have been addressed by the general (national) **corporate laws** as well as by non-binding codices and guidelines.[4],[5] Over time, the internal governance of financial institutions has more and more become a focus of **supervisory law**. Of pivotal importance have been the guidelines published by the Basel Committee for Banking Supervision ('**Basel Committee**'), in particular the principles for 'enhancing corporate governance' initially published in September 1999 and then revised in 2010 and 2015, respectively.[6] On a European level, the Capital Requirement Directive has introduced certain governance requirements for banks.[7] And as discussed in detail in the previous chapters, MiFID I has harmonised the regime regarding compliance, risk management and internal audit of investment firms.

---

[1] G. Miller, *The Law of Governance, Risk Management, and Compliance*, 1.

[2] Cf. the definition used by the Commission, Green Paper, Corporate Governance in financial institutions and remuneration policies, COM(2010) 284 final, p. 3, which itself draws on the definition used in the '**OECD principles**', G20/OECD Principles of Corporate Governance, 2015, available at: http://dx.doi.org/10.1787/9789264236882-en, 9. 'Corporate Governance', as used in this chapter, refers to the 'internal' governance (vis-à-vis the external corporate governance by auditors and rating agencies).

[3] There have been countless attempts to define this term. According to a classic definition corporate governance is 'the system by which companies are directed and controlled', A. Cadbury, *Report of the Committee on the Financial Aspect of Corporate Governance*, para. 2.5. See also the definition used by the Basel Committee on Banking Supervision, Corporate governance principles for banks, July 2015, available at: www.bis.org/bcbs/publ/d328.pdf, 3: 'Corporate governance determines the allocation of authority and responsibilities by which the business and affairs of a bank are carried out by its board and senior management'. According to G. Miller, *The Law of Governance, Risk Management, and Compliance*, 1 the term governance refers to the 'processes by which decisions relative to risk management and compliance are made within an organization'. See for an overview of the corporate governance discussion K. Hopt, in: Wymeersch et al. (eds.), *Financial Regulation and Supervision, Corporate Governance of Banks after the Financial Crisis*, para. 11.01. Cf. for the relationship between governance, risk management and compliance also M. Wundenberg § 32 para. 3.

[4] The United Kingdom has, however, recognised for long the need to regulate and supervise the internal governance mechanisms of firms. Cf. M. Wundenberg § 40 para. 33 as well as R. Veil and M. Wundenberg, *Englisches Kapitalmarktrecht*, 141 ff.

[5] Cf. for Germany the German Corporate Governance Code, available at: www.dcgk.de/en/home.html, and for the United Kingdom the UK Corporate Governance Code, available at: www.frc.org.uk/Our-Work/Codes-Standards/Corporate-governance/UK-Corporate-Governance-Code.aspx.

[6] Basel Committee, Corporate governance principles (fn. 3). For a more comprehensive analysis of the role of the Basel Committee in the development of governance-based regulation M. Wundenberg, *Compliance und die prinzipiengeleitete Aufsicht über Bankengruppen*, 16 ff.

[7] See in particular Art. 22, 123 and 124 of the Directive 2006/48/EC of the European Parliament and of the Council of 14 June 2006 relating to the taking up and pursuit of the business of credit institutions (recast), OJ L 177, 30 June 2006, p. 1–200 '(**CRD I**). For an analysis of these provisions, in particular in the context of the so-called 'pillar 2' requirements under the international capital framework (Basel II/III), M. Wundenberg, *Compliance und die prinzipiengeleitete Aufsicht über Bankengruppen*, 16 ff.

However, it was not until the enactment of the so-called **CRD IV/CRR regime** in the **banking sector** which came into effect in January 2014 that the European legislator has introduced a comprehensive governance framework for banks.[8] The CRD/CRR regime has in the meanwhile been amended by the **CRD V/CRR II** framework.[9] The **MiFID II framework** incorporates key governance requirements of the CRD IV relating to, in particular, the composition and the obligations of the board (as discussed in more detail below) into the legal regime for investment firms.[10] This chapter focuses on the governance requirements of investment firms pursuant to Article 9 MiFID II in conjunction with the respective provisions of the CRD (Article 88 and Article 91 CRD IV, as amended by CRD V).[11]

II. 'Governance-based' Regulation of Investment Firms

The recent governance reforms relating to banks and investment firms have been enacted as a response to the **financial crisis**. According to the recitals of MiFID II, weaknesses in corporate governance in financial institutions, including the absence of effective checks and balances, have been a contributory factor to the financial crisis.[12] In the light of perceived governance failures, the European lawmaker aims to strengthen the role of management bodies (ie the board) in order to avoid excessive and imprudent risk taking.

The MiFID II Directive describes the **regulatory aim** as follows:

> There is agreement among regulatory bodies at international level that weaknesses in corporate governance in a number of financial institutions, including the absence of effective checks and balances within them, have been a contributory factor to the financial crisis. Excessive and imprudent risk taking may lead to the failure of individual financial institutions and systemic problems in Member States and globally. Incorrect conduct of firms providing services to clients may lead to investor detriment and loss of investor confidence. In order to address the potentially detrimental effect of those weaknesses in corporate governance arrangements, Directive 2004/39/EC should be supplemented by more detailed principles and minimum standards. Those principles and standards should apply taking into account the nature, scale and complexity of investment firms.

---

[8] Consisting of the Directive 2013/36/EU of the European Parliament and of the Council of 26 June 2013 on access to the activity of credit institutions and the prudential supervision of credit institutions and investment firms, amending Directive 2002/87/EC and repealing Directives 2006/48/EC and 2006/49/EC, OJ L 176, 27 June 2013, p. 338–435 (**CRD IV**) and the Regulation (EU) No. 575/2013 of the European Parliament and of the Council of 26 June 2013 on prudential requirements for credit institutions and investment firms and amending Regulation (EU) No. 648/2012, OJ L 176, 27 June 2013, p.1–337 (**CRR**).

[9] Directive (EU) 2019/878 of the European Parliament and of the Council of 20 May 2019 amending Directive 2013/36/EU as regards exempted entities, financial holding companies, mixed financial holding companies, remuneration, supervisory measures and powers and capital conservation measures (**CRD V**). Regulation (EU) 2019/876 of the European Parliament and of the Council of 20 May 2019 amending Regulation (EU) No 575/2013 as regards the leverage ratio, the net stable funding ratio, requirements for own funds and eligible liabilities, counterparty credit risk, market risk, exposures to central counterparties, exposures to collective investment undertakings, large exposures, reporting and disclosure requirements, and Regulation (EU) No 648/2012 (**CRR II**).

[10] Art. 9 of MiFID II which requires that competent authorities granting the authorisation shall ensure that investment firms and their management bodies comply with Art. 88 and Art. 91 CRD IV. See also N. Moloney, *EU Securities and Financial Markets Regulation*, 357: 'roots of the 2014 MiFID II governance reform are in the reforms made to governance in the banking sector'.

[11] In the following, all reference to Articles in the CRD refer to the CRD IV as amended by CRD V.

[12] Recital 5 MiFID II.

The European lawmaker concludes that it is, therefore, necessary 'to strengthen the role of management bodies of investment firms, regulated markets and data reporting services providers in ensuring sound and prudent management of the firms, the promotion of the integrity of the market and the interest of investors'.[13]

6   Based on the recitals, the governance requirements have two **regulatory aims**: On the one hand, the provisions shall reduce 'excessive risk taking' and prevent failures of individual firms (which may pose **systemic risks**).[14] On the other hand, the governance regime shall ensure the 'integrity of the market' as well as the '**interest of investors**'. This regulatory aim goes clearly beyond the traditional approach of corporate governance in general corporate law, which primarily focuses on principle-agent problems between the shareholders and the management as well as the protection of the shareholders' interests.[15]

7   As discussed in the previous chapters, the regulation of the internal governance of investment firms is part of a regulatory strategy that can be described as '**management-based**' or '**governance-based**' **regulation** which combines internal governance mechanisms with instruments of public supervision.[16] From a practical perspective, the new provisions have a significant impact on the board members' duties and obligations. The reason being that the governance requirements under CRD IV/MiFID II may (in part) be stricter than those already applicable under general corporate law and that compliance with these requirements is supervised by the competent authorities.[17]

III. Regulatory Framework

1. Overview

8   The core governance requirements of investment firms are outlined in Article 9 MiFID II in conjunction with Articles 88 and 91 of the CRD IV (as amended by the CRD V). Article 9(1) MiFID II provides that the competent authorities shall ensure that investment firms and their management bodies comply with the governance requirements applicable to credit institutions pursuant to Article 88 and Article 91 CRD IV, thereby incorporating the prudential banking governance requirements into the MiFID II framework. Article 9(3) and (4) MiFID II then supplements the general governance provisions of the CRD IV by additional governance requirements designed to address specific issues related to the provision of investment services.

---

[13] Recital 53 MiFID II.
[14] That MiFID II expressly recognises systemic stability considerations as a driver for reform is remarkable. See for a detailed analysis of the underlying policy considerations J.-H. Binder, in: Busch and Ferrarini (eds.), *Regulation of EU Financial Markets: MiFID II*, 3.
[15] There is an elaborate body of legal literature which analyses the particularities of banks' corporate governance. See eg K. Hopt, in: Wymeersch et al. (eds.), *Financial Regulation and Supervision, Corporate Governance of Banks after the Financial Crisis*, para. 11.01 ff. with further references; A. Kokkinis, in: Chiu and Donavan (eds.), *Corporate Governance in Banks*, para. 1.01 ff.
[16] See for details M. Wundenberg § 33 para. 13.
[17] See below under para. 42. The governance requirements under CRD IV/MiFID II supplement and overlap with the requirements under general corporate law. This can result in difficulties relating to the coordination of the general corporate law and supervisory law requirements.

These governance requirements are drafted in a rather abstract fashion. Article 9 MiFID therefore provides that the content of these requirements shall be specified in more detail by guidelines adopted jointly by ESMA/EBA.[18] On 28 September 2017 the ESMA and the EBA published their final report on the assessment of the suitability of members of the management body and key function holders under Directive 2013/36/EU (CRD IV) and Directive 2014/65/EU (MiFID II) (**Joint Guidelines**).[19] Earlier that year, the European Central Bank (ECB) issued its final guide to fit and proper assessments for banks' executive and non-executive members of the management board (**ECB Guide**).[20] On 31 July 2020 the ESMA and EBA have launched a consultation to revise the Joint Guidelines.[21] The revised Joint Guidelines were adopted on 2 July 2021 and will apply from 31 December 2021 (**Revised Joint Guidelines**).[22]

9

In broad terms, the governance requirements under MiFID II (in conjunction with the respective provision in the CRD IV/V as well as the Joint Guidelines) address the following issues: (i) the general board structure as well as the composition of the board (see below under 2.), (ii) the personal requirements to be met by board members (see below under 3.), (iii) provisions relating to the board members' duties (see below under 4.) as well procedural aspects (see below under 5.).[23]

10

The European lawmaker has introduced a new prudential regime for investment firms which took effect on 26 June 2021 (**IFR/IFD-regime**).[24] Initially both credit institutions as well as investment firms were subject to the prudential requirements set out in the CRD/CRR framework. Now smaller investment are subject to a revised prudential regime (which includes a revised version of the governance requirements).[25] However, the MIFID/MiFIR provisions remain applicable for all investment firms. As a result, the governance

11

---

[18] Art. 9(1)(2) MiFID II in conjunction with Art. 91(12) CRD IV.
[19] ESMA/EBA, *Joint ESMA and EBA Guidelines on the assessment of the suitability of members of the management body and key function holders under Directive 2013/36/EU and Directive 2014/65/EU*, Final Report, EBA/GL/2017/12/ESMA71-99-598, 26 September 2017 ('Joint Guidelines'). On the same day, EBA has published its final report of its *Guidelines on internal governance under Directive 2013/36/EU*, EBA/GL/2017/11 ('Guidelines on Internal Governance'). The final guidelines have been published in all languages of the Members States in March 2018 (EBA/GL/2017/12).
[20] ECB, *Guide to fit and proper assessments*, May 2017 ('ECB Guide').
[21] ESMA/EBA, *Consultation Paper on draft joint ESMA and EBA Guidelines on the assessment of the suitability of members of the management body and key function holders under Directive 2013/36/EU and Directive 2014/65/EU*, EBA/GL/2020/19 and ESMA-43-2464.
[22] ESMA/EBA, *Final report on joint ESMA and EBA Guidelines on the assessment of the suitability of members of the management body and key function holders under Directive 2013/36/EU and Directive 2014/65*, EBA/GL/2021/06.
[23] In addition to the requirements outlined below, Art. 92 CRD IV as well as Art. 9(3)(c) MiFID II contain provisions relating to the remuneration policies. See for an analysis of remuneration requirements under the CRD IV/V regime M. Wundenberg, *Europäisches Bankenaufsichtsrecht*, § 12 para. 65 ff.; P. Mülbert and A. Wilhelm, in: Busch and Ferrarini (eds.), *European Banking Union*, § 6.23 ff.
[24] Consisting of Directive (EU) 2019/2034 of the European Parliament and of the Council of 27 November 2019 on the prudential supervision of investment firms and amending Directives 2002/87/EC, 2009/65/EC, 2011/61/EU, 2013/36/EU, 2014/59/EU and 2014/65/EU (IFD) and Regulation (EU) 2019/2033 of the European Parliament and of the Council of 27 November 2019 on the prudential requirements of investment firms and amending Regulations (EU) No 1093/2010, (EU) No 575/2013, (EU) No 600/2014 and (EU) No 806/2014 (IFR).
[25] The IFD/IFR introduce a new classification system for investment firms, based on their activities, systemic importance and size. 'Class 1' firms will remain subject to the prudential CRD/CRR requirements. 'Class 2' and 'Class 3' firms will be subject to the revised IFD/IFR prudential framework. Larger and interconnected firms ('Class 2') are subject to more stringent requirements than smaller and less inter-connected firms ('Class 3').

requirements pursuant to Article 9 MiFID (in conjunction with Articles 88 and 91 CRD) will arguably continue to apply to all investment firms. The revised IFR/IFD-regime is beyond the scope of this chapter.

2. Board Structure and Composition

(a) One-tier vs. Two-tier Board Structures

12   Like banks, investment firms are subject to rather intrusive requirements relating to the organisational structure of the 'management body'.[26] According to the recitals, MIFID II intends to embrace all existing governance structures used in the Member States without advocating any particular structure.[27]

13   As a general rule, two board structures[28] can be distinguished: In a **one-tier** board model followed by the United Kingdom and many other countries worldwide, the management and supervisory functions are exercised within a single board of directors. In **two-tier** systems followed by, inter alia, Germany, France, Italy and the Netherlands[29] the board is separated into a management board and a supervisory board (the latter responsible for overseeing and monitoring the management board).[30]

14   In the light of the existence of different board structures across Europe, the definition **'management body'** follows a **functional approach** referring to the 'body or bodies of an investment firm [...] which are empowered to set the entity's strategy, objectives and overall direction, and which oversee and monitor management decision-making and include persons who effectively direct the business of the entity'.[31] With few exceptions, the European provisions address obligations on the 'management body' without specifying which of the two bodies of the board (eg the management board and/or the supervisory board) is to be targeted in a two-tier structure. Against this background, the European legislator concedes that where the CRD IV or MiFID II make reference to the 'management body' and, pursuant to national law, the managerial and supervisory functions of the management body are assigned to different bodies, the Member State shall identify the bodies or members of the management body responsible in accordance with its national law.[32] The Member States are, therefore, free to determine the pertinent bodies (the management board and/

---

[26] See for details J.-H. Binder, in: Busch and Ferrarini (eds.), *Regulation of EU Financial Markets: MiFID II*, 14.

[27] See recital 5 of MiFID II: 'Different governance structures are used across the member states. In most cases a unitary or dual structure is used. The definitions used intended to embrace all existing structures without advocating any particular structure. They are purely functional for purpose of setting out rules aiming to achieve a particular outcome irrespective of the national company law applicable to the institution in each member state. The definitions should not interfere with the general allocation of competences in accordance with national company law.'

[28] For a detailed analysis of the differences between one-tier and two-tier board models see C. Jungmann, 3 ECFR (2006), 426 ff.

[29] The two-tier systems also exist in Poland, Italy and the Netherlands as well as other non-European countries including China. French law leaves corporations with the choice to either opt for a unitary or for a two-tier board system. See K. Hopt, *The German Law of and Experience with the Supervisory Board*, 2.

[30] 'Hybrid' forms of governance also exist. Some states such as Switzerland and Belgium generally follow a one-tier system, but require a two-tier board for banking institutions. See K. Hopt, in: Wymeersch et al. (eds.), *Financial Regulation and Supervision, Corporate Governance of Banks after the Financial Crisis*, para. 11.42.

[31] Art. 4(1)(36) MiFID II.

[32] Art. 4(1)(36) MiFID II; Art. 3(2) CRD IV.

or supervisory board) that must comply with the respective requirements under the MiFID II/CRD IV governance regime.[33] Despite the contemplated 'neutral' approach regarding the applicable board structure, the provisions of MiFID II and CRD IV appear to be conceptually based on a single board structure; this results in a number of inconsistencies which are highlighted below.[34]

(b) Separation of Functions; Establishment of Board Committees for 'Significant' Firms

According to Article 88(1)(e) CRD IV, the chairman of the management board in its supervisory function of an institution must not exercise simultaneously the functions of a chief executive officer within the same institution, unless justified by the institution and authorised by competent authorities. This **separation of the CEO and the chairman**, which is in line with OECD's principles of corporate governance[35] as well as the guidelines of the Basel Committee,[36] aims to ensure an appropriate balance of power and increase accountability of the board members.[37]

As another important feature of the MiFID II/CRD IV framework, Member States are required to ensure that firms which are **'significant'** in terms of their size, internal organisation and the nature, scope and complexity of their business comply with certain additional governance requirements. These additional requirements include, in particular, the establishment of committees within the board (that is a risk committee, a nomination committee as well as a remuneration committee).[38]

The establishment of specialised board committees (composed of non-executive board members) has already been considered to be 'good practice' in many Member States prior to implementation of the CRD IV and has been recommended by the Basel Committee.[39] The tasks and responsibilities of the respective committees are specified in a rather descriptive manner: The **nomination committee** shall, among other things, (i) identify and recommend candidates to fill management board vacancies, and (ii) assess the composition and performance as well as the skills and experience of the board members;[40] the **risk committee** is responsible for advising the board on the institution's overall risk appetite and strategy;[41] and the **remuneration committee** is responsible for the preparation of decisions relating to remuneration.[42] Institutions are furthermore required to implement an **audit**

---

[33] Cf. P. Mülbert and A. Wilhelm, in: Busch and Ferrarini (eds.), *European Banking Union*, § 6.47.
[34] This has been observed by P. Mülbert and A. Wilhelm, in: Busch and Ferrarini (eds.), *European Banking Union*, § 6.46 ff. referring to, inter alia, inconsistencies with regard to the definition 'senior management' in the CRD IV Directive.
[35] OECD Principles (fn. 2), 51.
[36] Basel Committee, Corporate governance principles (fn. 3), Principle 3 para. 62.
[37] However, this provision has been criticised in legal literature. See in particular L. Enriques and D. Zetzsche, 16 Theoretical Inquiries in Law (2015), 232 ff. For an empirical assessment of the combination of the CEO and the chairman of the board see N. Jayaraman et al., *Combining the CEO and Chair Roles*, arguing that there is no evidence that combining the CEO-chair positions hurts shareholder interests.
[38] Cf. Art. 76(3), 88(2) and 95(1) CRD IV. However, only Art. 88(2) CRD IV (nomination committee) is expressly referred to in Art. 9(1) MiFID II.
[39] Basel Committee, Corporate governance principles (fn. 3), Principle 3 para. 63 ff. outlining the tasks of the committees in more detail.
[40] Art. 88(2)(a)–(d) CRD IV.
[41] Art. 76(3) CRD IV. See also Basel Committee, Corporate governance principles (fn. 3), Principle 3 para. 71.
[42] Art. 95(2) CRD IV. See also Basel Committee, Corporate governance principles (fn. 3), Principle 3 para. 76 (compensation committee).

committee which is responsible for, inter alia, monitoring the effectiveness of the company's financial reporting process as well as the internal control systems.[43] The competent authorities may allow 'non-significant' institutions to combine the risk committee and the audit committee in a single committee.[44]

18 Neither CRD IV nor MiFID II specify which firms are to be considered 'significant'. As a result, the Member States have discretion in defining the applicable threshold determining which institutions are subject to the more stringent governance regime. In **Germany**, institutions are considered significant if the total balance sum exceeds € 15 billion or if they are subject to direct supervision of the ECB pursuant to Article 6(4) of the Regulation (EU) No. 1024/2013.[45] In the **United Kingdom** a more nuanced concept has been introduced (prior to Brexit entering into effect): An institution is considered 'significant' if at least one of the following requirements is fulfilled: (i) its total assets exceeds £ 530 million; (ii) its total liabilities exceeds £ 380 million; (iii) the annual fees and commission income it receives in relation to the regulated activities carried on by the firm exceeds £ 160 million in the 12 month period immediately preceding the date the firm carries out the assessment on a rolling basis; (iv) the client money that it receives or holds exceeds £ 425 million; or (v) the assets belonging to its clients that it holds in the course of, or connected with, its regulated activities exceeds £ 7.8 billion.[46]

(c) Diversity Requirements

19 As a controversial feature[47] of the MiFID II/CRD IV regime, the European legislator has addressed the topic of **board diversity**: According to Article 91(10) CRD, the Member States or the competent authorities shall require the institutions and their respective nominations committees[48] to engage a broad set of qualities and competences when recruiting members to the management body and to put in place for that purpose a 'diversity' policy. The diversity requirements are aimed to prevent 'groupthink'.[49] This is based on the assumption that more diverse composed boards lead to a more prudent management and oversight

---

[43] This follows from Art. 41 of Directive 2006/43/EC of the European Parliament and of the Council of 17 May 2006 on statutory audits of annual accounts and consolidated accounts, amending Council Directives 78/660/EEC and 83/349/EEC and repealing Council Directive 84/253/EEC, OJ L 157, 17 May 2016, p. 87–107 (applying to 'public interest' entities) as well as the EBA Guidance on Internal Governance, 27 September 2011, available at: www.eba.europa.eu/documents/10180/103861/EBA-BS-2011-116-final-EBA-Guidelines-on-Internal-Governance-%282%29_1.pdf, para. 14(9) ff.

[44] Art. 76(3)(4) CRD IV. See in this context also the European Central Bank, ECB Guide on options and discretions available in Union law, March 2016, ch. 9 para. 3 relating to 'significant' credit institutions subject to ECB supervision pursuant to Art. 6 of the Council Regulation (EU) No. 1024/2013 of 15 October 2013 conferring specific tasks on the European Central Bank concerning policies relating to the prudential supervision of credit institutions, OJ L 287, 29 October 2013, p. 63–89 ('SSM Regulation').

[45] Cf. § 1(3c) KWG (German Banking Act-*Kreditwesengesetz*).

[46] IFPRU 1.2.2 of the FCA Handbook.

[47] For a critical analysis of diversity requirements see L. Enriques and D. Zetzsche, 16 Theoretical Inquiries in Law (2015), 232 ff. focusing on gender equality; J.-H. Binder, in: Busch and Ferrarini (eds.), *Regulation of EU Financial Markets: MiFID II*, 24, each with further references to the empirical literature. See also I. Chiu, *Regulating (From) the Inside*, 190 ff.

[48] See above under para. 17.

[49] Recital 53 MiFID II: 'To avoid group thinking and facilitate independent opinions and critical challenge, management bodies should therefore be sufficiently diverse as regards age, gender, geographic provenance and educational and professional background to present a variety of views and experiences'.

of the firm, thereby avoiding excessive risk taking.[50] While the diversity requirements are commonly understood as an instrument to promote gender justice, 'diversity' as defined by CRD IV/MiFID II is a multidimensional (albeit also rather elusive) concept, referring to the age, gender, geographic provenance and educational and professional background of the board members.[51]

The Joint Guidelines specify the criteria which shall be referenced in the institution's diversity policy. These include the (i) educational and professional background, (ii) gender, (iii) age, and, for institutions that are active internationally and if permissible under the laws of the respective member state, (iv) geographical provenance.[52] In case of 'significant institutions' the diversity policy should include, in the view of ESMA/EBA, a quantitative target for the representation of the underrepresented gender and specify an appropriate timeframe within which the target should be met (and how it will be met).[53] In their Revised Guidelines, ESMA/EBA particularly emphasise the importance of gender equality, stating that the institutions should aim at an appropriate representation of all genders within the management body and ensure that the principle of equal opportunities is respected when selecting members of the management body.[54] If adopted in the Member States, such gender equality requirement will likely have a significant impact on the composition of the board (in particular in Member States which follow a two-tier system since the equality principle would also apply to the composition of the management board). 20

(d) Independent Board Members

As one of the most controversial aspects, the Joint Guidelines require that significant CRD institutions[55] and listed CRD institutions include a sufficient number of fully independent members in the management body in its supervisory function.[56] CRD institutions that are neither significant nor listed should in the view of ESMA/EBA have at least one independent member within the management body in its supervisory function.[57] Exemptions are foreseen for CRD institutions that are wholly owned by a CRD institution as well as for non-significant investment firms.[58] 21

In view of ESMA/EBA, a board member can be regarded to be 'independent' if he or she does not have any present or recent past relationships or links of any nature with the CRD institution or its management that could influence the member's objective and balanced 22

---

[50] The importance of 'diversity' is also stressed by the Basel Committee. See Basel Committee, Corporate governance principles (fn. 3), para. 13. For a critical assessment of this assumption see the references in fn. 47 above.
[51] Recital 53 MiFID II.
[52] Joint Guidelines (fn. 19), para. 105 and Revised Joint Guidelines (fn. 22), para. 103. Cf. also recital (60) CRD IV and recital (53) MiFID II.
[53] Joint Guidelines (fn. 19), para. 105 and Revised Joint Guidelines (fn. 22), para. 106. In the view of ESMA/EBA, the target should be defined for the management body collectively, but may be broken down into the management and supervisory functions where a sufficient management body exists. In all other institutions, in particular with a management body of fewer than five members, the target may be expressed in a qualitative way.
[54] Revised Joint Guidelines (fn. 23), para. 102.
[55] CRD institutions currently refer to credit institutions as well as investment firms defined in Art. 4(1)(1) and (2) CRR with effect as of 26 June 2021.
[56] Joint Guidelines (fn. 19), para. 88 ff and Revised Joint Guidelines (fn. 22), para. 88.
[57] Joint Guidelines (fn. 19), para. 89 and Revised Joint Guidelines (fn. 22), para. 88 (b).
[58] Joint Guidelines (fn. 19), para. 89(b)(i) and (ii) and Revised Joint Guidelines (fn. 22), para. 88 (b)(i) and (ii).

judgement and reduce the member's ability to take decisions independently.[59] It is presumed that a board member is not regarded as 'being independent' if such member is employed by any entity within the scope of consolidation.

23 This independence requirement, which has been criticised[60] by various stakeholders in the consultation process, is problematic for a number of reasons: *Firstly*, neither CRD IV/V nor MiFID II contain any provisions concerning the notion of 'independence' of any members of the management body. Hence, ESMA/EBA seem to have exceeded their mandate to issue guidelines in this regard.[61] *Secondly*, the requirement to have a sufficient number of fully independent members of the management body in its supervisory function goes well beyond the concept of 'independence' as introduced by Article 39 of the Directive 2006/43/EC (as amended by Directive 2014/56/EC). Pursuant to this provision, the European Member States shall ensure that each credit institution is required to have an audit committee in which the majority of members and the chairperson shall be independent of the respective institution. However, where all members of the audit committee are members of the administrative or supervisory body, ie, where the audit committee is a (sub-)committee of the management body in its supervisory function of the respective credit institution, Article 39(5) of Directive 2006/43/EC allows Member States to exempt such audit committee from the independent requirements.

24 Against this background, it should be the (sole) responsibility of the national legislators to impose stricter independence requirements for the management bodies of institutions than those set out in Directive 2006/43/EC.[62],[63] Arguably, the requirement to include a sufficient

---

[59] Joint Guidelines (fn. 19), para. 81 and Revised Joint Guidelines (fn. 22), para. 80. This concept of 'being independent' must be distinguished from the notion of 'independence of mind' (as discussed in more detail below). The former refers to a 'structural' requirement that must, in the view of ESMA/EBA, be fulfilled for a *certain* number of members of the management board in its supervisory function (ie which have no employment or other relationship with the respective institution). In contrast, the concept of 'independence of mind' applies to *all* members of the management body, and relates to a 'pattern of behavior' which includes the ability to make sound, objective and independent decisions (see below under 'Personal Requirements').

[60] Cf. the summary of the responses received from the stakeholder on p. 113 of the Joint Guidelines.

[61] This was implicitly recognised by ESMA/EBA in the cost-benefit analysis of the initial Consultation Paper dated 28 October 2016 (EBA/CP/2016/17), p. 76: 'not expressly covered under the mandate mentioned in Art. 91(12) CRD IV'. In the response to the comments received from stakeholders, ESMA/EBA have taken the view that having a sufficient number of independent members within the management body is part of robust governance arrangements pursuant to Art. 74(1), (3) CRD IV (cf. Joint Guidelines (fn. 19), p. 113).

[62] Cf. in this context also N. Raschauer, Zeitschrift für Finanzmarktrecht (2017), 420. In Germany, with effect as of 17 March 2016, the legislator has repealed the explicit legal requirement to have sufficient number of independent members of the supervisory board, as the separation between the management board and the supervisory board (as it is inherent in a two-tier board model) already warrants a high degree of 'independence' of the supervisory board. Cf. the legislative materials published in connection with the Audit Reform Act (*Abschlussprüfungsreformgesetz*), BT-Drucks. 18/7219, 56. Cf. for details M. Staake, 19 NZG (2016), 853. The recommendation to have independent supervisory board members is, however, mentioned in the German Corporate Governance Code (cf. fn. 5).

[63] The independence requirement has, however, been recognized by various international standard setters, eg Basel Committee on Banking Supervision, *Corporate governance principles for banks*, July 2015, para. 47. In Germany, the German Corporate Governance Code also recommends that the supervisory board shall include what it considers to be an appropriate number of independent members (see 5.4.2. of the German Corporate Governance Code). Furthermore, the requirement to have an independent member of the supervisory board is foreseen for external management companies of investment funds pursuant to Sec. 18(3) of the German Capital Investment Code (KAGB).

number of fully independent members should therefore only apply to institutions located in jurisdictions which have implemented an independence requirement in their national statutory laws.[64] The German Federal Financial Supervisory Authority (BaFin) stated that it does not intent to comply with the requirement to appoint independent directors as German law does not contain such obligation.[65]

As an additional topic, the Joint Guidelines raise questions regarding the definition of the independence criterion, in particular with regard to **employee representatives**.[66] In the final version of the Joint Guidelines it has been clarified that the aforementioned presumption[67] shall not apply to employees not belonging to the senior management and which have been 'elected to the supervisory function in the context of a system of employees' representation and national law provides for adequate protection against abusive dismissal and other forms of unfair treatment'.[68] Against this background, employee representatives should, as a general rule, qualify as 'independent' board members.[69]

25

3. Personal Requirements of the Board Members

(a) Fit and Properness

Members of the management body shall at all times be of 'sufficiently good repute and possess sufficient knowledge, skills and experience to perform their duties' and commit sufficient time to perform their functions.[70] At board level, Article 91(7) CRD IV requires the management body in its entirety to 'possess adequate collective knowledge, skill and experience to be able to understand the institution's activities, including the main risks'. To this end, institutions shall devote adequate human and financial resources to induction and training of members of the management body.[71] The specific requirements relating to the

26

---

[64] This interpretation is also supported by the ECB Guide, which clarify that 'specific formal independence criteria' (only) need to be observed if required by 'national substantive law', cf. ECB Guide (fn. 20), para. 4.3. (p. 17).

[65] BaFin Journal, October 2017, 9.

[66] On the question whether employee representatives can be considered 'independent' cf. T. Baums, 180 ZHR (2016), 697, 703 ff.; M. Staake, 19 NZG (2016), 853.

[67] Ie that a board member is not regarded as 'being independent' if such member is employed by any entity within the scope of consolidation.

[68] Joint Guidelines (fn. 19), para. 91(e)(i) and (ii) and Revised Joint Guidelines (fn. 22), para. 89 (e)(i) and (ii). This corresponds with Annex ii No. 1(b) of the Commission Recommendation 2005/162/EC.

[69] In apparent contradiction to this clarification in the Joint Guidelines, ESMA/EBA state in their analysis of the responses received in the consultation process from stakeholders that 'members representing employees should not be counted towards the required sufficient number of independent members', cf. Joint Guidelines (fn. 19), 114 (second column, analysis to comments received from stakeholders under para. 124). In German legal literature it is disputed whether employee representatives qualify as independent members of the supervisory board within the meaning of Section 100(5) of the German Stock Corporation Act (as applicable prior to the implementation of the Audit Reform Act, cf. fn. 62) and 5.4.2. of the 5.4.2. of the German Corporate Governance Code. Cf. for further references T. Baums, 180 ZHR (2016), 697, 703 ff.; M. Staake, 19 NZG (2016), 853, 855.

[70] Art. 91(1) CRD IV and Art. 9(4) MiFID II. Special requirements with regard to non-executive board members must be fulfilled by specific committee members (such as the financial expert on the audit committee and the remuneration and risk expert on the remuneration committee).

[71] Art. 91(9) CRD IV. As a consequence, the approach to provide advanced training of board members becomes increasingly professionalised.

fitness (ie personal qualification, experience) and **properness** (ie personal reliability) have been specified in the guidelines and regulations published by the NCA.[72]

27 Ensuring the fitness and properness of board members has been on the regulatory agenda for a considerable time. However, in the light of the financial crisis the personal requirements have substantially increased, in particular with regard to the professional qualification and expertise of board members.[73] As a result, the appointment of board members of banks and investment firms is increasingly scrutinised by the competent authorities.

28 The required knowledge, skill and experience of the members of the management body are specified in the Joint Guidelines in a rather broad, *principles-based* fashion. As a general rule, ESMA/EBA expect that all members of the management body should have an up-to-date understanding of the business of the institution and it risks, at a level commensurate with their responsibilities.[74] This also includes an understanding of those areas for which an individual board member is not individually responsible (but is merely collectively accountable).[75]

29 In order to assess the skills of the members of the management body, the Joint Guidelines provide a very comprehensive (although non-exhaustive) list of relevant skills that should be taken into account by the institution for the suitability assessment. This list includes a set of a total of 16 attributes, including more elusive criteria such as 'authenticity', 'loyalty', 'strategic acumen', 'teamwork' or 'sense of responsibility'.[76]

30 With regard to the required practical experience, the Joint Guidelines do not state fixed thresholds of practical experience in which required experience can be assumed.[77]

(b) Limitation of Directorships

31 Of significant importance are the restrictions for significant institutions (see above) on the numbers of permitted board mandates. This obligation must be seen in connection with the general requirement to commit **sufficient time** to perform their functions.[78]

---

[72] Cf. for Germany the guidelines published by BaFin, Merkblatt zu den Geschäftsleitern gemäß KWG, ZAG und KAG (management board), 4 January 2016 (as amended on 29 December 2020), available at: https://www.bafin.de/SharedDocs/Veroeffentlichungen/DE/Merkblatt/mb_geschaeftsleiter_KWG_ZAG_KAGB.html, and BaFin, Merkblatt zu den Mitgliedern von Verwaltungs- und Aufsichtsorganen gem. KWG und KAGB, 4 January 2016 (as amended on 29 December 2019), available at: https://www.bafin.de/SharedDocs/Veroeffentlichungen/DE/Merkblatt/mb_verwaltungs-aufsichtsorgane_KWG_KAGB.html. Cf. for the United Kingdom the FIT section of the FCA Handbook (Fit and Proper Test for Approved Person). For the far-reaching approved person regime in the United Kingdom, applying not only to board members but also to other 'controlled functions', see M. Wundenberg § 33 para. 40.

[73] Traditionally, there has been a focus on the 'properness' of board members, eg absence of criminal records or insolvency proceedings of previously managed undertakings. As a result of the financial crisis, the assessment of the 'fitness' of the board members has gained importance. See in this respect OECD, Corporate Governance and the Financial Crisis: Key Findings and Main Messages, June 2009, available at: www.oecd.org/corporate/ca/corporategovernanceprinciples/43056196.pdf, 45.

[74] Joint Guidelines (fn. 19), para. 58 and Revised Joint Guidelines (fn. 22), para. 56.

[75] Joint Guidelines (fn. 19), para. 58 and Revised Joint Guidelines (fn. 22), para. 56.

[76] Joint Guidelines (fn. 19), Annex II.

[77] In contrast, the ECB Guide, applicable for credit institutions under the direct supervision of the ECB, follow a so-called '*two-stage approach*' ECB Guide (fn. 20), para. 4.1 (p. 11 ff.). Cf. for details M. Wundenberg, 33 JIBLR (2018), 191, 197.

[78] Art. 91(2)(2) CRD IV in conjunction with Art. 9(1) MiFID II.

Members of the management board shall not hold more than (i) **one executive directorship** and **two non-executive directorships** or (ii) **four non-executive directorships**.[79] When granting authorisation, competent authorities may authorise members of the management body to hold one additional non-executive directorship.[80] Directorships held within the same group count as a single directorship.[81]

The provisions of the CRD relating to the limitations of directorships have raised a number of questions relating to the scope of these requirements, in particular in two-tier board regimes. The Joint Guidelines now clarify that the 'group privilege' is to be understood in a rather broad way: *Firstly*, the Joint Guidelines specify that the accounting scope of consolidation should be used for purpose of defining the 'group'.[82] This approach is, as a general rule, broader than eg the (former) approach taken by the German legislator, where in principle only mandates held within a regulatory consolidated group could be taken into account for the group exemption (which is narrower that the accounting group).[83] *Secondly*, when the members of the management board hold both executive and non-executive directorships within a 'group', such mandates shall count as *one* executive directorship (eg not as both one executive and one non-executive directorship). With regard to sanctions in case of non-compliance with the requirements relating to the limitations of directorships, see below.[84]

(c) Collective Suitability

The MiFID II/CRD IV-regime requires that the overall composition of the management body shall reflect an adequately broad range of experiences. The management body shall possess adequate collective knowledge, skills and experience to be able to understand the institution's activities, including the main risks.[85]

In order to assess the collective competence of members of the management body, the European authorities have prepared a very detailed and granular template matrix which is intended to serve as 'self-assessment tool' for institutions to periodically assess the collective suitability of its members of the management body'.[86]

This approach appears problematic for a number of reasons: Firstly, the information required for the suitability assessment according to the template matrix appear to be overly descriptive and burdensome, in particular for smaller institutions. While the use of the template is not supposed to be mandatory and may be adapted to specific circumstances,

---

[79] Competent authorities may authorise members of the management board to hold one additional non-executive directorship than allowed in accordance with Art. 91(3) CRD IV.

[80] Art. 9(2) MiFID II; see also Art. 91(6) CRD IV.

[81] Art. 91(4)(a) CRD IV. The same applies to (i) directorships held within institutions which are members of the same institutional protection scheme provided that the conditions set out on Art. 113(7) are fulfilled as well as (ii) undertakings in which the institution holds a qualifying holding, cf. Art. 91(4)(b) CRD IV. See for the interpretation of Art. 91(4)(b)(ii) CRD IV the response of EBA to Q&A 2014_1595, 13 November 2015, available at: www.eba.europa.eu/single-rule-book-qa/-/qna/view/publicId/2014_1595.

[82] Cf. the definition of 'group' on p. 20 of the Joint Guidelines.

[83] In the course of the implementation of the CRD V the definition has been amended and now refers to a group within the meaning of Article 4(1)(138) CRR.

[84] Para. 54 below.

[85] Art. 91(7) CRD IV (as amended by the CRD V).

[86] Joint Guidelines (fn. 19), Annex II.

ESMA/EBA nonetheless emphasize that the outcome of the matrix can be requested by the competent authorities for their (external) suitability assessments. Secondly, concerns have been raised that the use of the matrix may reduce the assessment of collective suitability to a mechanical 'tick the box exercise', thereby contradicting the legislative purpose of the suitability requirements.

4. Board Members' Duties

37 CRD IV and MiFID II lay out, albeit in a rather complex and partly duplicative manner,[87] a comprehensive set of **duties of board members** of banks and investment firms: Member States shall ensure that the management body defines, oversees and is accountable for the implementation of the governance arrangements that ensure effective and prudent management of the firm, including the segregation of duties and the prevention of conflicts of interest.[88] With regard to investment firms, Article 9(3) MiFID II adds that the management body must exercise these functions 'in a manner that promotes the **integrity of the market** and the **interest of the client**'.

38 These principles are specified by Article 88(1)(2) CRD which requires the management body to (i) approve and oversee the implementation of the institution's strategic objectives, risk strategy and internal governance; (ii) ensure the 'integrity of the accounting and financial reporting systems'; (iii) oversee the process of disclosure and communications; and (iv) effectively oversee the senior management.[89]

39 'Without prejudice' to the aforementioned requirements, Article 9(3)(2) MiFID II specifies the obligations of the management body of investment firms further, adding that the governance arrangements shall ensure that the management body define, approve and oversee: (i) the organisation of the firm for the provision of investment services and activities and ancillary services, including the skills, knowledge and expertise required by personnel, the resources, the procedures and the arrangements for the provision of services and activities, taking into account the nature, scale and complexity of its business and all the requirements the firm has to comply with; (ii) a policy as to services, activities, products and operations offered or provided, in accordance with the risk tolerance of the firm and the characteristics and needs of the clients of the firm to whom they will be offered or provided, including carrying out appropriate stress testing, where appropriate; and (iii) a remuneration policy of persons involved in the provision of services to clients aiming to encourage responsible business conduct, fair treatment of clients as well as avoiding conflicts of interest in the relationships with clients. The management body shall furthermore monitor and periodically assess the adequacy and the implementation of the firm's strategic objectives in the provision of investment services and activities and ancillary services, the effectiveness of

---

[87] As pointed out by J.-H. Binder, in: Busch and Ferrarini (eds.), *Regulation of EU Financial Markets: MiFID II and MiFIR*, 18.

[88] Art. 88(1) CRD IV, referred to in Art. 9(1) MiFID II, as well as the identical wording contained in Art. 9(3) MiFID II.

[89] As pointed out by P. Mülbert and A. Wilhelm, in: Busch and Ferrarini (eds.), *European Banking Union*, § 6.51 the group of persons covered by the definition of 'senior management' appears to be smaller in two-tier board systems than in one-tier systems and cover only members of the management board (but not executives below board level).

the investment firm's governance arrangements and the adequacy of the policies relating to the provision of services to clients and take appropriate steps to address any deficiencies.[90]

Finally, Article 91(8) CRD IV requires that each member of the management body shall act with honesty, integrity and '**independence of mind**' to effectively assess and challenge the decisions of the senior management where necessary and to effectively oversee and monitor management decision making, thereby defining a **standard of care** for the execution of board duties.[91] 40

This notion of independence of mind, as understood by ESMA/EBA, relates to a 'pattern of behavior' which includes the ability to make sound, objective and independent decisions and to withstand '**groupthink**'.[92] The independence of mind of board members can be affected by conflicts of interest. The Joint Guidelines specify situations which may result in material conflicts of interest. These include, *inter alia*, conflicts of interest resulting from personal, professional, financial or political relationships with the other board members, the supervised entities or significant shareholders.[93] 41

The approach of CRD IV and MiFID II to harmonise board members' duties is remarkable for a number of reasons: Firstly, while broadly in line with the general principles under national corporate law, these governance requirements are part of regulatory law; compliance with the board management duties is, therefore, **supervised by the competent authorities** and breaches of the governance requirements can trigger administrative fines as well as other sanctions.[94] Secondly, the legislative aim of the regulatory provisions on directors' duties differs from those under general corporate law: While the corporate law requirements primarily aim to protect the interests of the firm as well as their shareholders, the CRD IV/MiFID II governance regime focuses on **broader public interest** concerns, taking investor protection and the integrity of the markets (as well as systemic risk concerns[95]) 42

---

[90] Art. 9(3)(3) MiFID. The members of the management body shall furthermore have adequate access to information and documents which are needed to oversee and monitor management decision-making.

[91] See also J.-H. Binder, in: Busch and Ferrarini (eds.), *Regulation of EU Financial Markets: MiFID II and MiFIR*, 23. For a critical assessment see L. Enriques and D. Zetzsche, 16 Theoretical Inquiries in Law (2015), 218, 228. As noted above (fn. 89) the persons covered by the definition of 'senior management' appear to differ in one-tier and two-tier board structures.

[92] Cf. Joint Guidelines (fn. 19), para 80 and 82 and Revised Joint Guidelines (fn. 22), para. 79 and 81. Understood literally, the notion of 'independence of mind' (like the requirement to act with 'honesty and integrity') refers to a specific skill or trait of character of the respective board members. In fact, the Joint Guidelines foresee that the institutions shall assess whether the members of the management body have the required '*courage, conviction and strength*' to challenge the proposed decision of other members of the management body. For a critical assessment of the perceived 'over-emphasis of board members' character', P. Mülbert and A. Wilhelm, in: Busch and Ferrarini (eds.), *European Banking Union*, para. 6.79 ff.

[93] Joint Guidelines (fn. 19), para. 84 and Revised Joint Guidelines (fn. 22), para. 83; ECB Guide (fn. 20), para. 4.3 (p. 15). Situations where a material conflict of interest is presumed to exist are summarised in Table 1 of the ECB Guide. In case of a material conflict of interest, the institution must, in the view of the ECB, perform (i) a detailed assessment of the particular situation and (ii) decide which preventive/mitigating measures will be implemented. The supervised entity will be required to explain to the complement authority in a 'conflict of interest statement' how the conflict of interest in being prevented, mitigated and managed.

[94] See also K. Hopt, in: Wymeersch et al. (eds.), *Financial Regulation and Supervision, Corporate Governance of Banks after the Financial Crisis*, para. 11.50: 'most important enforcement dimension that is lacking for corporate governance of firms generally'. For the sanctioning regime see below para. 50 ff.

[95] The extent to which MiFID II aims to reduce systemic risks is debated in legal literature. For a detailed assessment see J.-H. Binder, in: Busch and Ferrarini (eds.), *Regulation of EU Financial Markets: MiFID II and MiFIR*, 13 and passim.

into account.[96,97] Thirdly, the MiFID II/CRD IV requirements may possibly also have an impact on the civil liability of board members (in particular if the regulatory governance requirements are stricter than their corporate law counterparts).[98]

5. Procedural Aspects

43 The assessment procedures regarding the **assessment of the fit-and properness** of the members of the management body of the respective national competent authorities have so far not been harmonized by European law.[99] As a result, the administrative practices vary significantly among the European member states. The differences relate, among other things, to the timing of the assessment (*ex-ante* vs. *ex-post* assessments), the personal scope (assessment only of board members *vis-à-vis* suitability assessments also for certain key function holders), the decision-making periods as well as the methods used for the assessment process (eg the use of interviews[100] as an assessment tool).[101] In order to promote greater consistency of the supervisory practices, the Joint Guidelines specify various aspects of the assessment process. These relate to both the internal assessment conducted by the respective institutions as well as the external assessment conducted by the competent authorities.

(a) Assessment by the Institution

44 The prime responsibility for the assessment of the individual and collective suitability of the members of the management body lies with the institution.[102] Such **'internal' assessments** shall be conducted when material changes to the composition of the management body occur, eg in case of an appointment of a new board member. In addition, ESMA/EBA expect that the individual and collective suitability is monitored by the institutions on an ongoing basis, which includes at least annual re-assessments in case of significant institutions.[103]

45 As a controversial issue, the Joint Guidelines specify a number of notification requirements in connection with the internal assessment procedure which are not foreseen in

---

[96] This raises the question to which extent board members must take the 'interest of clients' or the 'integrity of the market' into account, in particular in cases where such broader public interests are not aligned (or even collide) with the interests of the investment firm.

[97] See above para. 4 ff. Art. 9(3) MiFID II expressly provides that members of the management body must exercise their functions 'in a manner that promotes the integrity of the market and the interest of the client' which clearly extends the traditional doctrine which focuses on board members' duties toward the company as well as their shareholders.

[98] See below para. 53.

[99] For significant credit institutions under the direct supervision of the ECB Art. 93ff. of the Regulation (EU) No 468/2014 (SSM Framework Regulation) apply. Furthermore, the European Commission has published a proposal of a so-called 'banking package' on 27 October 2021 which contemplates, inter alia, a further harmonisation of the fit-and-proper assessments.

[100] Both the Joint Guidelines as well as the ECB Guide contemplate that interviews may be used as an assessment tool. Cf. Joint Guidelines (fn. 19), para. 182 and Revised Joint Guidelines, (fn. 22). para. 183 (for significant institutions, for other institutions on the basis of a 'risk-based approach'); ECB Guide (fn. 20), para. 5 (new appointment of CEO or chairman positions for the top-level / largest bank in the group).

[101] For an overview see the Impact Assessment of the Joint Guidelines (fn. 20), 78 ff.

[102] This is now expressly emphasized in Art. 91(1) CRD (as amended by CRD V). See also Joint Guidelines (fn. 19), para. 24 ff. and 49 ff. and Revised Joint Guidelines (fn. 22), para. 22 ff. and 47 ff.

[103] Cf. in particular para. 24 ff., 135 ff. and 155 of the Joint Guidelines (fn. 19).

the CRD IV or MiFID II and which have proven to be difficult to implement in practice. For example, the Joint Guidelines state that the results of the internal suitability assessments shall be reported to the competent authorities.[104] In a similar fashion, institutions are expected to inform the authorities without delay in case the institution reaches the conclusion that either a board member individually or the management body as a whole collectively is not suitable.[105] These notification obligations go beyond what is required by CRD IV and MiFID II and should therefore only apply if foreseen by national law.

(b) Assessment by Competent Authorities

The initial draft of the Joint Guidelines aimed for a far-reaching harmonization of the competent authorities' assessment procedures. In particular, it was proposed that the suitability assessments are conducted by the competent authorities on an *ex-ante* basis prior to the appointment of a member of the management body and, for significant institutions, the heads of internal control functions and the CFO even if they are not members of the management body.

46

As a reaction to various criticism received from stakeholders in the consultation process, the Joint Guidelines were changed to allow for a neutral approach regarding the assessment of the members of the management body. While a higher level of harmonization regarding the administrative assessment processes was considered to be desirable, ESMA/EBA concluded that such a harmonization could not be achieved under their current mandate.[106] It therefore remains in the discretion of the European member state to decide whether the suitability of the members of the management board shall be assessed on the basis of an *ex-ante* or an *ex-post* approach.

47

Controversially, however, ESMA/EBA have retained the requirement of a formal suitability assessment of the heads of the internal control functions and the CFO, where they are not part of the management body, for significant CRD-institutions.[107] Institutions are expected to notify the competent authority at the latest within two weeks of the appointment of an individual for such functions.

48

The extension of the formal suitability regime to such **key functions holders** (ie the heads of the internal control functions and the CFO, even if they are not members of the management body) appears problematic: While in some jurisdictions such as the United Kingdom[108] it is a well-established practice that fit and proper requirements also relate to certain individuals below board level, in other European jurisdictions such as Germany a formal suitability assessment by the authorities is in principle only foreseen for members of the management board or the supervisory board.[109] Furthermore, neither the CRD IV

49

---

[104] Joint Guidelines (fn. 19), para. 144 and 162 and Revised Joint Guidelines (fn. 22), para. 143 and 163.
[105] Joint Guidelines (fn. 19), para. 161 and Revised Joint Guidelines (fn. 22), para. 162.
[106] Joint Guidelines (fn. 19), 118 and Revised Joint Guidelines (fn. 22), para. 117.
[107] Joint Guidelines (fn. 19), 118 and Revised Joint Guidelines (fn. 22), para. 117. This shall apply to (i) significant consolidating CRD-institutions, (ii) significant CRD-institutions that are part of a group, where the consolidating CRD-institution is not a significant institution or (iii) significant institutions that are not part of a group.
[108] Cf. ia APER and FIT section of the FCA handbook. On the new accountability framework I. Chiu, *Regulating (From) the Inside*, 239 ff.; M. Wundenberg § 33 para. 40.
[109] However, certain notification and suitability requirements may apply to specific individuals below board level such as *ia* the compliance officer and the AML-officer. Furthermore, the German BaFin requires that it will be informed about personal changes of *ia* the head of the internal risk management function.

nor MiFID II contain any provisions that would require the member states to implement an administrative assessment of such key function holders. Arguably, these requirements should only apply if foreseen by national law. The proposal published by the European Commission in October 2021 contemplates that a formal assessment requirement will be introduced for heads of internal control functions.

IV. Sanctions

1. Administrative Sanctions

50 In the light of the experiences of the financial crisis, the (administrative) sanctioning regime under the reformed MiFID II/CRD IV framework has been strengthened considerably.[110] Both MiFID II and CRD IV devote an entire section to the designation of supervisory and enforcement powers of the competent authorities.[111]

51 In case of infringements of governance requirements pursuant to Article 9 MiFID II in conjunction with Article 88 and 91 CRD IV, Member States shall ensure that competent authorities may impose maximum administrative fines of at least up to ten per cent of their total annual net turnover with regard to legal entities or € 5,000,000 with regard to natural persons.[112] Administrative sanctions can in principle be directed toward both the **board members** as well as the **investment firm**.[113]

52 With regard to the sanctions vis-à-vis the **board members**, MiFID II requires that the competent authorities have the power to require the removal of board members of investment firms.[114] With regard to the sanctions vis-à-vis the **investment firm**, infringements of the governance requirements can lead in principle, as an ultima ratio measure, to a revocation of the authorisation of the investment firm.[115]

2. Civil Sanctions

53 The administrative enforcement measures taken against the investment firm and/or board members must be distinguished from the civil liability of the board members. While neither MiFID II nor CRD IV address issues of civil liability, the provisions in the directives may nonetheless have an impact on the civil law responsibilities of the board members. For example, in some Member States such as Germany it is an established principle that infringements of regulatory requirements also constitute a breach of fiduciary duties of

---

[110] See for the underlying policy rationale the High-Level Group on Financial Supervision in the EU (de Larosière Group), Report, 25 February 2009 ('de Larosière Report'), available at: http://ec.europa.eu/internal_market/finances/docs/de_larosiere_report_en.pdf, para. 83ff. The harmonisation of the sanctioning regime does not, however, extent to the private enforcement. See M. Wundenberg, 44 ZGR (2015), 124 ff.
[111] Art. 64–72 CRD IV; Art. 56–78 MiFID II.
[112] Art. 70(3)(a)(ii), (6)(f) and (g) MiFID II.
[113] See also in the context of compliance M. Wundenberg § 33 para. 80 ff.
[114] Art. 69(2)(u) MiFID II.
[115] Art. 9(1)(c) MiFID II.

the board members vis-à-vis the investment firm.[116] Such breach of fiduciary duties can, in turn, give rise to damage claims of the firm against the board members.[117]

Whether infringements of personal requirements of board members, in particular the limitations of directorships,[118] have any impact on the validity of the appointment of the board members is a question of national law.[119] However, the European provisions seem to imply that violations of the provisions relating to the limitations of directorships have no effect on the validity of the appointment of the board members.[120]

V. Conclusions

As a response to the financial crisis, MiFID II has introduced a comprehensive regime relating to the corporate governance of investment firms. The governance reforms, which have their roots in the recent reforms in the field of banking law (CRD IV/V), have a significant impact on the duties and obligations of the board members of investment firms.

The MiFID II governance requirements lay out far-reaching obligations relating to, inter alia, the duties and obligations of the members of the board of investment firms as well as the general board structure. They complement the obligations relating to compliance, risk management and internal audit already addressed in the MiFID I regime.[121]

The MiFID II governance obligations are drafted in an abstract fashion. The various notions of suitability have been put into a more concrete form by the Joint Guidelines issued by ESMA/EBA. The attempt of the European authorities to achieve a greater consistency of the supervisory practices within the EU is to be welcomed. However, the Joint Guidelines prove in many respects to be overly prescriptive and burdensome, in particular for smaller institutions. Furthermore, they contain a number of requirements (such as the obligation to include a sufficient number of fully independent board members as well as suitability assessments for key function holders) that go well beyond what is required under the CRD IV/MiFID II regime (and have, therefore, not been adopted by some of the national competent authorities). Arguably, these requirements shall only apply if foreseen by national statutory law. A further harmonisation of the current governance framework would arguably require a more robust legal basis, and could only be achieved by means of a binding legal instrument (ie either a directive or regulation). The European Commission has in the meantime published a proposal in October 2021 (banking package) which aims for a further harmonisation of the regulatory governance regime.

---

[116] So called external legality principle (*externe Legalitätspflicht*). See H. Fleischer, in: Spindler and Stilz (eds.), *Aktiengesetz*, § 93 para. 28 ff.

[117] Further issues relate to the question whether the governance provisions of the CRD IV/MiFID II have an impact on the applicability of the 'business judgment rule' which is recognised in various Member States. See P. Mülbert and A. Wilhelm, in: Busch and Ferrarini (eds.), *European Banking Union*, § 6.62 ff.

[118] See above para. 31 ff.

[119] This issue has been discussed in Germany. See for example M. Lutter et al. (eds.), *Rechte und Pflichten des Aufsichtsrats*, § 21 para. 1501. There are strong arguments that support the view that board mandates held in violation of the limitations of directorships are, from a German law perspective, neither void nor revocable. See ibid.

[120] This is supported by the fact that the competent authorities shall have the power to request the removal of board members, implying the board membership itself is valid, even if the personal eligibility requirements are not fulfilled.

[121] See M. Wundenberg §§ 32 and 33.

8

Regulation of Benchmarks

§ 35

Foundations

Bibliography

Abrantes-Metz, Rosa M. et al., *Libor manipulation?*, 36 Journal of Banking and Finance (2012), 136–150; Abrantes-Metz, Rosa M. et al., *Revolution in Manipulation Law: The New CFTC Rules and the Urgent Need for Economic and Empirical Analyses*, 15 U. Pa. J. Bus. L. (2012), 357–418; Awrey, Dan, *Hardwired Conflicts: The Big Bang Protocol, Libor and the Paradox of Private Ordering*, SSRN Working Paper (2013), available at SSRN: http://ssrn.com/abstract=2262712; Bainbridge, Stephen M., *Reforming Libor: Wheatley versus the Alternatives*, SSRN Working Paper (2013), available at SSRN: http://ssrn.com/abstract=2209970; Chiu, Iris H.-Y., *Regulating Financial Benchmarks by 'Proprietisation': A Critical Discussion*, SSRN Working Paper (2015), available at SSRN: http://ssrn.com/abstract=2686585; Click, Christopher J., *Death of a Benchmark: The Fall of LIBOR and the Rise of Alternative Rates in the United States*, 22 North Carolina Banking Institute (2018), 283–307; de Jager, Phillip et al., *JIBAR Manipulation?*, SSRN Working Paper (2013), available at SSRN: http://ssrn.com/abstract=2224597; Fleischer, Holger and Bueren, Eckart, *Die Libor-Manipulation zwischen Kapitalmarkt- und Kartellrecht*, 65 DB (2012), 2561–2568; Fletcher, Gina-Gail S., *Benchmark Regulation*, SSRN Working Paper (2016), available at SSRN: http://ssrn.com/abstract=2776731; Gütte, Kristina L., *Regulierung finanzieller Referenzwerte* (2020); Hull, John C., *Options, Futures and Other Derivatives*, 8th edn. (2012); Rauterberg, Gabriel and Verstein, Andrew, *Index Theory: The Law, Promise and Failure of Financial Indices*, 30 Yale J. on Reg. (2013), 1–62; Sajnovits, Alexander, *Financial-Benchmarks* (2018); Säcker, Franz J. et al. (eds.), *Münchener Kommentar zum BGB*, 8th edn. (2020); Spindler, Gerald, *Der Vorschlag einer EU-Verordnung zu Indizes bei Finanzinstrumenten (Benchmark-VO)*, 27 ZBB (2015), 165–176; Verstein, Andrew, *Benchmark Manipulation*, 56 Boston College Law Review (2015), 215–272.

I. Introduction

An **index** can be defined as a measure that is calculated according to a pre-determined methodology from a set of underlying data. If it serves as a reference price for other financial instruments or contracts it is referred to as a **benchmark**.[1]

Benchmarks have become an essential feature of today's financial markets. They play an important role in the determination of the prices of many different kinds of financial

---

[1] See for the definitions in the context of the Benchmark Regulation below (M. Wundenberg § 36 para. 6).

instruments and financial contracts.[2] In the legal and economic debate, the focus lies on interest rate benchmarks such as Libor (*London Interbank Offered Rate*) (which is about to phase out, as discussed below) and Euribor (*Euro Interbank Offered Rate*). They are used, inter alia, as reference rates for derivative instruments (such as interest swap agreements) as well as a wide range of retail products such as mortgages and student loans. It is estimated that financial products with an overall outstanding value of more than US$ 360 trillion have been linked to Libor.[3] Against this background, the Libor has been called 'the most important number of the world'.[4]

3 **Libor** was originally published by Thomson Reuters for the British Banking Association (BBA) at 11 am each business day for a number of different maturities and currencies. Since 2014 Libor is administered by Intercontinental Exchange Inc. (ICE). Libor is based on the submissions of the contributing banks (the so-called 'reference-panel'). The panel banks submit the interest rate at which they expect that they could borrow (unsecured) funds for a given currency and maturity.[5] The submission process was so far not necessarily based on actual transactions and involved estimates and assessments.[6] The Libor rate is determined as a trimmed arithmetic mean of the banks' submissions under exclusion of the highest and the lowest 25%. In November 2020 the administrator of the Libor (ICE) announced that it plans to **cease the publication** of the respective Libor rates on 31 December 2021 and 30 June 2023, respectively.[7] **Euribor** is the European equivalent of Libor. Euribor is defined as the rate at which Euro interbank term deposits are being offered within the EU and EFTA by one 'prime bank' at 11 am Brussels time.[8] The highest and lowest 15% of the quotes are not taken into account in the calculation.[9] As is the case with regard to Libor, the calculation of Euribor was so far not necessarily based on actual transactions and involved assessments.[10] Benchmarks further play an important role in the commodities markets (see for example the reference prices of the information provider **Platts** for crude oil).[11]

---

[2] Cf. for an overview: Commission, Proposal for a Regulation of the European Parliament and the Council on indices used as benchmarks in financial instruments and financial contracts, Impact Assessment, 18 September 2013, SWD(2013) 337 final, p. 84 ff. and p. 128 ff.; in legal literature, see G. Rauterberg and A. Verstein, 30 Yale J. on Reg. (2013), 1; G.-G. Fletcher, *Benchmark Regulation*, 1.

[3] Wheatley Review of LIBOR, Final Report, available at: www.gov.uk/government/uploads/system/uploads/attachment_data/file/191762/wheatley_review_libor_finalreport_280912.pdf, para. C.7. This is the equivalent of one hundred times (!) the annual economic output of Germany. In total, financial instruments with a value of up to US$ 1,015 trillion are allegedly connected to the interest rate indices, cf. SWD(2013) 337 final (fn. 2), p. 78.

[4] Libor: The World's Most Important Number, MoneyWeek, 10 October 2008.

[5] The question to be answered by the panel-banks is: 'At which rate could you borrow funds, were you to do so by asking for and then accepting inter-bank offers in a reasonable market size just prior to 11 a.m.?' Cf. Calculating ICE Libor, available at www.theice.com/iba/libor.

[6] The methodology to calculate Libor is subject to reform. See ICE Benchmark Administration Limited, Roadmap for ICR Libor, 18 March 2016, available at: www.theice.com/publicdocs/ICE_LIBOR_Roadmap0316.pdf; FSB, Progress in Reforming Major Interest Rate Benchmarks, 9 July 2015, available at: www.fsb.org/wp-content/uploads/OSSG-interest-rate-benchmarks-progress-report-July-2015.pdf, 8 ff.

[7] The announcements are available at: https://www.theice.com/iba/libor. For a detailed analysis of the rise and demise of Libor cf. J. Click, 22 North Carolina Banking Institute (2018), 283–397.

[8] EMMI, Euribor Code of Conduct, 1 October 2013 (as revised on 1 October 2015), available at: www.emmi-benchmarks.eu/assets/files/Code%20of%20conduct/D2712I-2014-Euribor%20Code%20of%20Conduct%2001Oct2013%20-%20Revised%20in%201%20Oct2015_final.pdf, 2.

[9] EMMI, Euribor Code of Conduct (fn. 8), C.2.3 para. 2.

[10] Like Libor, the submission and calculation process of Euribor is subject to reform. Cf. EMMI, The Path Forward to Transaction-Based Euribor, 21 June 2016, available at: www.emmi-benchmarks.eu/assets/files/D0273B-2016%20The%20path%20forward%20to%20Transaction-based%20Euribor.pdf; EMMI, Consultative Position Paper on the Evolution of Euribor, 30 October 2015, available at: www.emmi-benchmarks.eu/assets/files/Euribor_Paper.pdf.

[11] IOSCO, Principles for Oil Price Reporting Agencies, Final Report, 5 October 2012, available at: www.iosco.org/library/pubdocs/pdf/IOSCOPD391.pdf.

II. Legal Background and Regulatory Initiatives

The importance of financial benchmarks has for a long time been ignored by both academics and the legislator. Until recently, a specific governmental regulation did not exist,[12] the area rather being subject to self-regulation.

It was only in the course of the uncovering of alleged manipulations of the Libor- and Euribor reference rates by a number of major banks ('**Libor-Scandal**') that the legislator began to focus on the regulation of benchmarks. In many parts of the world, supervisory authorities initiated investigations into manipulations of interest rate and other (derivatives and commodities) benchmarks.[13] In total, a fine of US$ 2.5 billion was imposed against the British Barclays Bank, the Swiss UBS and the Scottish RBS for alleged manipulations of Libor and Euribor.[14] Additionally, administrative fines were imposed on Rabobank[15] and Deutsche Bank.[16]

Example: An illustrative example of the factual background of the alleged manipulations is the decision of the FSA (since April 2013: FCA) against **Barclays Bank**[17] dated 27 June 2012. The decision rests essentially on two allegations: *Firstly*, according to the findings of the FSA, Barclays made inappropriate submissions following requests by derivative traders of Barclays (and potentially other banks).[18] As Barclays (like many other banks) invested in interest rate derivatives, the derivative traders profited, depending on their trading position, from a rising or falling Libor rate.[19] *Secondly*, the FSA asserted that during the financial crisis Barclays made incorrect—too low—submissions in order to avoid negative media coverage.[20] Based on these findings, the FSA imposed a fine in an amount of £ 59.6 million on Barclays.[21]

---

[12] Certain European directives and regulations had already addressed specific aspects of this topic, cf. examples listed under No. 1.2 of the Explanatory Memorandum on the Benchmark Regulation.

[13] On the developments in Asia see Monetary Authority of Singapore, Proposed Regulatory Framework for Financial Benchmarks, June 2013, available at: www.mas.gov.sg; Hong Kong Association of Banks, Review of Hong Kong Interbank Offered Rate, November 2012, available at: www.tma.org.hk; see also the ruling of the Japan Financial Services Agency (JFSA) against RBS Securities Japan Ltd. of 12 April 2013, available at: www.fsa.go.jp/en/news/2013/20130412.html; with regard to the United Kingdom see FSA Final Notices dating 27 June 2012 (*Barclays*), 19 December 2012 (*UBS*) and 6 February 2013 (*RBS*), all of which are available at: www.fsa.gov.uk/static/pubs/final; on the developments in the US see US CFTC Order dating 27 June 2012 (*Barclays*) and 19 December 2012 (*UBS*), both available at: www.cftc.gov; see also the non-prosecution agreement between the US Department of Justice and Barclays of 26 June 2012, available at: www.justice.gov/iso/opa/resources/3372012710173354698 22.pdf; on the developments in South Africa see P. de Jager et al., *Signs of JIBAR Manipulation*.

[14] Joint Committee Report on Risk and Vulnerabilities in the EU Financial System, March 2013, 20 fn. 1 (available at: www.eba.europa.eu). See also M. Wundenberg § 33 para. 82.

[15] FCA, Final Notice, 29 October 2013.

[16] FCA, Final Notice, 23 April 2015.

[17] FSA, Final Notice, 27 June 2012. See also M. Wundenberg § 33 para. 82.

[18] FSA, Final Notice, 27 June 2012, para. 8 and para. 53 ff.

[19] This highlighted the conflicts of interest inherent in the submission process. The conflicts of interest resulted from the fact that, on the one hand, panel banks contributed to the calculation of the Libor benchmark by making submissions while those banks had, on the other hand, a self-interest in the development of the Libor interest rate. See in the context of conflict of interest management also M. Wundenberg § 33 para. 35. On the functioning of interest rate derivatives see H. Fleischer and E. Bueren, 65 DB (2012), 2561, 2562.

[20] Low submissions were interpreted by the market participants as a signal for a strong economic position of that banks, see below para. 14.

[21] See M. Wundenberg § 33 para. 82.

7   As a response to the alleged manipulations of Libor and Euribor reference rates, legislators and international standard-setters have initiated various initiatives to reform the benchmark setting process.[22] In the United Kingdom, a report commissioned by the HM Treasury (**Wheatley Review**)[23] made a number of suggestions for a reform of Libor which have in the meanwhile been enacted.[24] At a European level, ESMA/EBA—in close cooperation with the European Commission[25] and IOSCO[26]—have published **Principles for the Benchmarks-Setting Process in the EU**.[27] Furthermore, on 25 July 2012 the European Commission adopted 'amended proposals for a Regulation and for a Directive to prohibit and criminalise manipulation of benchmarks'. This proposal on the **prohibition of benchmark manipulations** has been incorporated in Article 12(1) MAR and Article 5(2)(d) CRIM-MAD.

8   Based on EBA/ESMA's recommendations and after an extensive consultation with market participants, the European Commission published on 18 September 2013 a proposal for a 'Regulation on indices used as benchmarks in financial instruments and financial contracts' (subsequently '**Commission Proposal**').[28] On 24 November 2015, the European Parliament and the Council reached a preliminary political agreement on a compromise text of the Benchmark Regulation, an agreement that was confirmed on 9 December 2015 by the Permanent Representatives Committee of the Council of the European Union. On 6 June 2016, the final text of a **Regulation of Benchmarks**[29] (subsequently '**Benchmark Regulation**') was adopted.

9   With the Benchmark Regulation which entered into effect on 1 January 2018, the European lawmaker has introduced a comprehensive regime governing the entire benchmark setting process for the first time. It has in the meanwhile been specified in more detail by the Level 2 implementing legislation as well as Q&As published by ESMA.[30] Since its adaption, the Benchmark Regulation has been amended several times (most recently in February 2021).[31]

---

[22] Cf. overview of international developments by FSB, Reforming Major Interest Rate Benchmarks (fn. 6); A. Verstein, 56 Boston College Law Review (2015), 215, 250 ff. (comparing the US-American and European regulatory approach).
[23] Wheatley Review (fn. 3).
[24] The Financial Services and Markets Act 2000 (Regulated Activities) (Amendment) Order 2013; HM Treasury, Implementing the Wheatley Review, draft secondary legislation, November 2012; FSA, The regulation and supervision of benchmarks, March 2013, PS 13/6.
[25] Commission, Consultation Document on the Regulation of Indices, 5 September 2012, available at: http://ec.europa.eu/finance/consultations/2012/benchmarks/docs/consultation-document_en.pdf.
[26] IOSCO, Principles for Financial Benchmarks, Final Report, July 2013, available at: www.iosco.org/library/pubdocs/pdf/IOSCOPD415.pdf.
[27] ESMA/EBA, Principles for Benchmarks-Setting Process in the EU, Final Report, 6 June 2013, ESMA/2013/658.
[28] Commission, Proposal for a Regulation of the European Parliament and of the Council on indices used as benchmarks in financial instruments and financial contracts, 18 September 2013, COM(2013) 641 final.
[29] Regulation (EU) No. 2016/1011 of the European Parliament and of the Council of 8 June 2016 on indices used as benchmarks in financial instruments and financial contracts or to measure the performance of investment funds and amending Directives 2008/48/EC and 2014/17/EU and Regulation (EU) No. 596/2014, OJ L 171, 29 June 2016, p. 1–65.
[30] Available at: https://www.esma.europa.eu/policy-rules/benchmarks.
[31] Cf the following amendment Regulations: (i) Regulation (EU) 2019/2089 of the European Parliament and of the Council of 27 November 2019 amending Regulation (EU) 2016/1011 as regards EU Climate Transition Benchmarks, EU Paris-aligned Benchmarks and sustainability-related disclosures for benchmarks; (ii) Art. 5 of the Regulation (EU) 2019/2175 of the European Parliament and of the Council of 18 December 2019 (ESAs-Review); (iii) Regulation (EU) 2021/168 of the European Parliament and of the Council of 10 February 2021 amending Regulation (EU) 2016/1011 as regards the exemption of certain third-country spot foreign exchange benchmarks and the designation of replacements for certain benchmarks in cessation, and amending Regulation (EU) No 648/2012.

III. Functions of Benchmarks

Four different functions of financial benchmarks can be distinguished: 10

Firstly, as mentioned above, benchmarks are used by market participants as reference rates 11
to determine the price of, or payment obligations under, financial instruments and contracts (**reference function**).

There is a particular need to refer to accepted benchmarks with regard to long-term contracts, such as mortgage loans. Instead of having to determine the interest rate for the entire term of the contract in advance, the parties to the contract can link the interest rate to an accepted reference value, such as Libor or Euribor.[32] Benchmarks further play an important role in the pricing of derivative financial instruments.[33] 12

Secondly, benchmarks play an important role with regard to investment decisions (**investment function**). For example, benchmarks are used in the context of asset management to evaluate the performance of asset managers (*performance benchmarks*).[34] They further constitute the basis for so-called 'index funds' that attempt to track a key benchmark, such as a stock market index (DAX-30, FTSE 100, S&P 500, Euro Stoxx 50), as closely as possible. In recent years following the adoption of the Paris Agreement furthermore various types of benchmarks have emerged which are supposed to measure the carbon footprint of investment portfolios. 13

Thirdly, benchmarks are essential for the processing of information on the capital markets (**information function**). For example, during the financial crisis an increase of the Libor rate was seen as an indication for an increased vulnerability of the banking sector. In turn, low submissions of a participating panel bank were interpreted as an indication of a strong economic position of that panel bank. In this respect the Libor was regarded as a 'barometer'[35] measuring the health of the entire banking system. 14

> The former vice-governor of the Bank of England, *Paul Tucker*, describes this as follows: '[W]hat is important from quite early in the crisis, from the summer of 2007 onwards, is that LIBOR became increasingly used as a *summary statistic* of what was going on in the market. [...] [E]verybody rather slipped into the habit of using LIBOR as a kind of portmanteau term for money market conditions, bank funding conditions, actual submissions [...].'[36] 15

---

[32] See also G. Rauterberg and A. Verstein, 30 Yale J. on Reg. (2013), 1, 8 ff.
[33] Derivatives are financial instruments that derive their value from the performance of an underlying entity (underlying). The underlying can be, *inter alia*, an asset or an index such as Libor. One example of derivatives that may use interest rate benchmarks as the underlying are interest-swaps. In this case the parties 'swap' fixed interest payments (ie 5%) for variable payments (ie the respective 3-month Libor). For details see J. Hull, *Options, Futures, and other Derivatives*, 200 ff. and passim.
[34] The performance goals of asset managers can, for example, be defined as a percentage surcharge on a predetermined reference price, such as Libor/Euribor or other benchmarks.
[35] This expression is used by ICE, Roadmap for ICR Libor (fn. 6), para. 1.3.
[36] House of Commons, Treasury Committee, Fixing LIBOR: some preliminary findings, 18 August 2012, available at: www.publications.parliament.uk/pa/cm201213/cmselect/cmtreasy/481/481.pdf, para. 41.

16   Finally and *fourthly*, benchmarks are used by the legislator and authorities for regulatory purposes (**regulatory function**). The Swiss National Bank for example, for a long time implemented its monetary policy by fixing a target range for the three-month Swiss franc Libor.[37] In Germany, according to § 675g(3) BGB payment service providers are only permitted to change interest rates for loans (such as overdraft interest rates) without prior notice to the borrower if the changes are based on reference interest rates (such as the three month Euribor rate).[38]

---

[37] Cf. Information on the homepage of the Swiss National Bank, available at: https://www.snb.ch/en/iabout/monpol/id/qas_gp_ums_1#t2 (as of 13 June 2019, the SNB policy rate replaced the target range for the three-month Swiss franc Libor).

[38] M. Casper, in: Säcker et al. (eds.), *Münchener Kommentar zum BGB*, § 675g para. 15.

§ 36

Market Supervision and Organisational Requirements

Bibliography

Cf. § 35.

I. Regulatory Concept of the Benchmark Regulation

1. Regulatory Aim and Structure

The overriding **aim** of the Benchmark Regulation is laid out in the introductory *subject matter*: It aims to provide a common framework to ensure the accuracy and integrity of indices used as benchmarks in financial instruments and financial contracts, or to measure the performance of investment funds.[1] The Regulation intends to thereby contribute to the proper functioning of the internal market whilst achieving a high level of consumer and investor protection.[2] Furthermore it aims to reduce **systemic risks**.[3]   1

To this end, the Benchmark Regulation combines a number of regulatory strategies: *Firstly*, it introduces governance requirements for benchmark administrators which intend to improve the governance and controls over the benchmark process and to ensure that administrators avoid conflicts of interest. *Secondly*, it aims to improve the quality of input data and methodologies used by the administrator in the determination of the benchmark. *Thirdly*, it lays out internal control and compliance requirements for the contributors of the benchmark (such as panel banks that submit data to the benchmark administrators). *Finally*, it intends to protect consumers and investors by introducing, *inter alia*, transparency and licensing requirements.[4]   2

The regulation is divided into eight sections (titles). These relate to the (1) subject matter, scope and definitions, Articles 1–3; (2) benchmark integrity and reliability, Articles 4–16; (3) requirements for different types of benchmarks (eg interest rate and commodity   3

---

[1] Art. 1(1) Benchmark Regulation.
[2] Art. 1(2) Benchmark Regulation.
[3] Cf. Commission, Proposal for a Regulation of the European Parliament and of the Council on indices used as benchmarks in financial instruments and financial contracts, 18 September 2013, COM(2013) 641 final, p. 70 (Legislative Financial Statements).
[4] Cf. COM(2013) 641 final (fn. 3), p. 2 ff. (Explanatory Memorandum No. 1.1.).

benchmark), Articles 17–26; (4) transparency and consumer protection, Articles 27–28, (5) the use of benchmarks in the European Union (third-country benchmarks), Articles 29–33 (6) authorisation, registration and supervision of administrators, Articles 34–48; (7) delegated and implementing acts, Articles 49–50 as well as (8) transitional provisions (Articles 51–59).

4   The Benchmark Regulation is directly applicable in the Member States and does not require implementation into the national laws.[5] It follows the concept of **maximum harmonisation**,[6] aiming to prevent the Member States from adopting diverging approaches to the regulation of benchmarks.[7]

2. Scope and Definitions

5   The Benchmark Regulation is designed to cover a **broad range** of benchmarks and activities; it applies to the *provision* of benchmarks, the *contribution* of input data as well as the *use* of a benchmark within the European Union.[8] As a general rule, all types of benchmarks published in the European Union fall within the scope of the Benchmark Regulation,[9] ie not only interest rate benchmarks such as Libor or Euribor but also numerous other reference rates such as indices relating to commodities and electricity markets or share indices (Dax 30, Euro Stoxx 50, etc.).[10],[11]

6   A **benchmark** is defined as (i) an index by **reference** to which the **amount payable** under a financial instrument[12] or a financial contract[13] or the value of a financial instrument is determined or (ii) an index that is used to **measure the performance** of an investment fund.[14]

---

[5] On the legal nature of regulations see R. Veil § 3 para. 15.

[6] Cf. the terminology employed by the Commission in COM(2013) 641 final (fn. 3), p. 6 (Explanatory Memorandum No. 3.3): 'The cross border nature of many benchmarks creates a need for *maximum harmonisation* of these requirements' (emphasis added). See also recital 7 ('obligations to be applied in a uniform manner'). On this see R. Veil § 3 para. 22.

[7] Cf. COM(2013) 641 final (fn. 3), p. 6 ff. (Explanatory Memorandum No. 3.3). See also recital 4 and 7 of the Benchmark Regulation.

[8] Art. 2(1) Benchmark Regulation.

[9] Art. 2(1) Benchmark Regulation.

[10] Benchmarks calculated on the basis of non-economic numbers or values such as weather-parameters are also included in the scope of the regulation, cf. recital 9 Benchmark Regulation. Art. 2(2) Benchmark Regulation, however, excludes certain benchmarks, such as reference prices submitted by Members of the European System of Central Banks, from the scope of the Regulation, as these are already subject to control by public authorities, cf. recital 14 Benchmark Regulation.

[11] Furthermore, the provision of single reference prices of financial instruments as defined in Annex I Section C of Directive 2014/65/EU are excluded, see Art. 2(2)(d) and recital 18. As the policy rationale the recitals state that 'where a single price or value is used as a reference to a financial instrument [...] there is no calculation, input data or discretion.' Whether this reason is, in fact, justified, appears questionable (critically in this context A. Verstein, 56 Boston College Law Review (2015), 215, 265).

[12] Cf. Art. 3(1)(16) Benchmark Regulation.

[13] Cf. Art. 3(1)(18) Benchmark Regulation (consumer credit agreement within the meaning of Art. 3(c) Directive 2008/48/EC and Art. 4(3) Directive 2014/17/EU).

[14] Art. 3(1)(3) Benchmark Regulation. For a critical analysis of this definition see A. Verstein, 56 Boston College Law Review (2015), 215, 265 arguing that the definition of 'benchmark' is under-inclusive, as benchmarks are hardwired in more contracts than those listed in the Benchmark Regulation (mentioning employment contracts as an example).

In this context, an **index** is defined as any figure (i) that is published or made available to the public;[15] (ii) that is regularly determined, entirely or partially, by the application of a formula or 'any other method of calculation', or by an 'assessment' (iii) where this determination is made on the basis of the value of one or more underlying assets, or prices, including estimated prices, or 'other values'.[16] It is not required that the benchmark administrator[17] intends market participants to make use of the index as a benchmark.[18]

> Similar definitions can be found in the Principles published by ESMA/EBA and IOSCO.[19] However, the definition in the Benchmark Regulation goes beyond the definition in Article 3(1)(29) MAR (prohibition of benchmark manipulation) as well as the definition used by IOSCO insofar as it also includes indices which are used as performance indicators for investment funds (eg not to determine payment obligations or prices of financial instruments). Such benchmarks are often used in the context of asset management.[20]

7

Taking into account the multiple areas in which benchmarks are used, the broad scope of the Benchmark Regulation is to be welcomed. Whilst an initial proposal for a Benchmark Regulation required the benchmark to be determined by a 'formula' or on the basis of underlying assets, it is now sufficient that the benchmark administrator determines the benchmark by way of 'any other method of calculation', or by an 'assessment',[21] thereby acknowledging that the benchmark may be calculated on the basis of personal assessments by the administrator rather than by a formula.[22]

8

The **personal scope** of the Benchmark Regulation relates primarily to the so-called **benchmark administrator**, ie the natural or legal person that has control over the provision of a benchmark.[23] The Benchmark Regulation further refers to the market participants that contribute input data to the administrators, such as banks. These persons are named **contributors**.[24] Finally, it imposes restrictions on (supervised) entities that '**use**' benchmarks provided by administrators located in the European Union.[25]

9

---

[15] Cf. on this aspect ESMA, Discussion Paper, Benchmarks Regulation, 15 February 2016, ESMA/2016/288, p. 9 ff.
[16] Art. 3(1)(1) Benchmark Regulation.
[17] See below para. 9.
[18] However, the Regulation is not applicable to an index provider where that index provider is unaware and could not reasonably be aware that the index is used as a reference rate (see Art. 2(2)(h) Benchmark Regulation).
[19] ESMA/EBA, Final Report, Principles for Benchmark-Setting Processes in the EU, 6 June 2013, ESMA/2013/658, p. 4; IOSCO, Principles for Financial Benchmarks, Final Report, July 2013, available at: www.iosco.org/library/pubdocs/pdf/IOSCOPD415.pdf, p. 35.
[20] See M. Wundenberg § 35 para. 13.
[21] See above para. 6.
[22] The reference prices of the information provider *Platts* with regard to commodity trading can be seen as an example of such benchmarks which are based on (subjective) assessment. Cf. also IOSCO, Principles for Oil Price Reporting Agencies, Final Report, 5 October 2012, available at: www.iosco.org/library/pubdocs/pdf/IOSCOPD391.pdf. The definition adopted by IOSCO, Principles for Financial Benchmarks (fn. 19), p. 35 ('another method of calculation') goes in the same direction.
[23] Art. 3(1)(6) Benchmark Regulation.
[24] Art. 3(1)(9) Benchmark Regulation. The natural person employed by the contributor for the purpose of contributing input data is named 'submitter', cf. Art. 3(1)(11) Benchmark Regulation.
[25] The 'use of benchmarks' is defined in Art. 3(1)(7) of the Benchmark Regulation.

3. Concepts

10 While broad in scope, the Regulation pursues a flexible, **'risk-based' approach** based on the principle of proportionality: As a general rule, the provisions of the Regulation relate to all types of benchmarks.[26] With regard to certain benchmarks, however, which are considered to be 'critical' for the market integrity and investor protection, additional requirements are imposed to ensure the integrity and robustness of such benchmarks.[27] In turn, the Regulation provides for certain exemptions from the requirements of the Regulation with regard to other, less critical benchmarks which are subject to a less stringent regime. From a 'vertical' perspective the Regulation distinguishes between three types of benchmarks: *critical*, *significant* and *non-significant* benchmarks.

11 A **critical benchmark** is defined[28] as a benchmark which satisfies **at least one** of the following conditions: (i) it is used as a reference for financial instruments or financial contracts or for the determination of the performance of investment funds having a total value of at least € 500 billion (quantitative threshold), or (ii) it is based on submissions by contributors the majority of whom are located in one EU Member State and is recognised as critical in that Member State by the relevant competent authority, or (iii) (a) it is used as a reference for financial instruments or financial contracts or for the determination of the performance of investment funds having a total value of at least € 400 billion (quantitative threshold), (b) there are no or few market-led substitutes (qualitative criterion) and (c) cessation of the benchmark would have significant and adverse consequences not only for consumers but also for the financing of households and corporations in one or more EU Member States (qualitative criterion). Under certain conditions, the relevant competent authorities may agree to recognise the benchmark as critical even if the quantitative threshold (€ 400 billion) is not met.[29] To date, five benchmarks have been qualified as 'critical benchmarks' by the European lawmaker.[30]

12 A **significant benchmark** is a benchmark which does not satisfy all of the criteria necessary for it to be a critical benchmark, but (i) is used as a reference for financial instruments or financial contracts or for the determination of the performance of investment funds having a total average value of at least € 50 billion over a period of six months; or (ii) has no or very few market-led substitutes and its absence would have significant and adverse consequences not only for consumers but also for the financing of households and corporations in one or more EU Member States.[31] A **non-significant benchmark** is a benchmark which does not fulfil the necessary criteria for it to be a critical benchmark or a significant benchmark.[32]

13 The classification as 'critical', 'significant' or 'non-significant' is important to determine the obligations that apply to benchmark administrators and contributors: With regard to 'critical' benchmarks, additional obligations relating to, inter alia, a mandatory administration and mandatory contributions must be complied with (cf. Articles 20–23 Benchmark Regulation). With regard to 'non-significant' benchmarks, the administrator may choose

---

[26] See para. 5.
[27] See recital 35.
[28] Art. 20(1) Benchmark Regulation.
[29] Art. 20(1)(b) and (3) Benchmark Regulation.
[30] Annex of the Commission Implementing Regulation (EU) No. 2016/1368, as amended by the Regulation (EU) 2019/482 of 22 March 2019 (Euribor, Eonia, Libor, Stibor, Wibor).
[31] Art. 3(1)(27) and Art. 24 Benchmark Regulation.
[32] Art. 26 Benchmark Regulation.

not to apply certain Articles of the Regulation provided that it is clearly stated in the compliance statement why it is appropriate not to comply with those provisions ('**comply-or-explain**' mechanism).[33] With regard to 'significant benchmarks' certain exemptions apply to certain provisions if the application of those provisions would be disproportionate (and the decision not to apply these requirements is disclosed in the compliance statement).[34] However, the competent authority may require changes to ensure compliance with the Regulation (option of '**regulatory override**').[35]

Additionally, the Benchmark Regulation differentiates '*horizontally*' between different types of benchmarks depending on the nature of the underlying assets and data. In particular, the Regulation provides sector-specific requirements for **interest rate**[36] and **commodity**[37] benchmarks.[38] Furthermore, certain exemptions apply to so-called '**regulated-data benchmarks**' which use only input data from specific sources.[39] Finally, specific requirements have been enacted for **climate benchmarks** (see below).

The respective provisions that apply for different types of benchmarks are summarised in **Annex 1** below. The complex regulatory concept can be illustrated as follows:[40]

General Requirements
Non-significant benchmarks: Certain exemptions available ('comply-or-explain') (Art. 26)
Significant benchmarks (Art. 24–25); Certain exemptions apply with option of 'regulatory override'
Regulated-data benchmarks: Certain exemptions apply (Art. 17)

Specific requirements for interest rate benchmarks (eg Libor, Euribor): Art. 18 and Annex I	Specific requirements for commodity benchmarks (eg Platts): Art. 19 and Annex II	Specific requirements for EU climate transition benchmarks and EU–Paris aligned Benchmarks: Chapter 3A and Annex III

Critical benchmarks (Art. 13–14)

Regulatory Concepts of the EU Benchmark Regulation

---

[33] Art. 26(1) and (3) Benchmark Regulation.
[34] Art. 25(1) Benchmark Regulation.
[35] Art. 25(3) Benchmark Regulation.
[36] Art. 18 in conjunction with Annex I Benchmark Regulation. According to Art. 18(2) Benchmark Regulation the exemptions for 'significant' and 'non-significant' benchmarks are not available for interest rate benchmarks.
[37] Art. 19 in conjunction with Annex II Benchmark Regulation. According to Art. 19(2) Benchmark Regulation the exemptions for 'significant' and 'non-significant' benchmarks are also not available for commodity benchmarks. Where the commodity benchmark is a 'critical' benchmark and the underlying asset is gold, silver or platinum, the requirements of Title II of the Benchmark Regulation shall apply instead of Annex II.
[38] See above para. 3.
[39] Art. 17 Benchmark Regulation.
[40] For details see below (Annex I).

16   The **'risk-based' approach** taken by the European lawmaker is to be welcomed. It takes into account that the degree of risk related to a failure of a benchmark and the potential conflicts of interest that may arise in the benchmark setting process differ substantially. For example, the risk of conflicts of interest is particularly high when the submitted data and/or the calculation of the benchmarks depends on **subjective evaluations and assessments** of market participants—as it was the case with regard to Libor and Euribor.[41] On the other hand, the risk of conflicts of interest is reduced when the benchmark is based on publicly available and empirically confirmable market data (eg share indices). Finally, the 'systemic' impact of the failure of a benchmark[42] (ie the impact on the financial stability and real economy) depends on how widely it is used as a reference rate by market participants and whether market-substitutes are available.

4. Legal Requirements

(a) Governance Requirements Relating to the Benchmark Administrator

17   Benchmark administrators[43] must have in place **'robust governance arrangements'** which include a clear organisational structure with well-defined, transparent and consistent roles and responsibilities for all persons involved in the provision of the benchmark.[44] Administrators are further required to take adequate steps to identify and manage conflicts of interest between themselves, the contributors and the users of the benchmark, and to ensure that, where any **judgment or discretion** in the benchmark determination process is required, such judgment or discretion is independently and honestly exercised.[45] Furthermore, a permanent and effective **oversight function**[46] must be established.[47] The Benchmark Regulation further requires administrators to establish an effective **internal control framework** that ensures that their benchmarks are provided and published or are made available in accordance with the provisions of the Regulation.[48]

18   The organisational requirements are put into more concrete terms in Article 4 ff. Benchmark Regulation and also in regulatory technical standards.[49] The requirements are generally in

---

[41] For a comprehensive analysis of the 'subjectiveness' of indices and benchmarks see G. Rauterberg and A. Verstein, 30 Yale J. on Reg. (2013), 15 ff.
[42] See in this context also recital 9 of the Benchmark Regulation.
[43] See para. 9 above.
[44] Art. 4(1) Benchmark Regulation.
[45] Art. 4(1)(2) Benchmark Regulation. If discretion or judgement is required in the benchmark setting process, it is to be exercised 'independently and honestly', cf. Art. 4(1)(2) Benchmark Regulation.
[46] Art. 5(1) Benchmark Regulation. National regulators have the power to require the benchmark administrator to establish an *'independent'* oversight function (see para. 18 below).
[47] The requirements relating to the oversight functions are put into more concrete terms in Art. 5 Benchmark Regulation. For interest rate benchmarks Annex I (3) Benchmark Regulation provides that the administrator is required to establish an *independent oversight committee*.
[48] Art. 6 Benchmark Regulation.
[49] Commission Delegated Regulation (EU) 2018/1637 of 13 July 2018 supplementing Regulation (EU) 2016/1011 of the European Parliament and of the Council with regard to regulatory technical standards for the procedures and characteristics of the oversight function.

line with the recommendations of the *Wheatley-Review*[50] and the principles laid out in the ESMA/EBA[51] and IOSCO[52] reports and focus on the management of conflict of interest. The competent authorities are granted the power to establish an 'independent' oversight function (with balanced stakeholder representation) if conflicts of interest cannot be adequately mitigated and, as an *ultima ratio* measure, to direct the cessation of the benchmark (Article 4(3) and (4) Benchmark Regulation). The governance and control requirements include, inter alia, (i) general governance and conflict of interest requirements (Article 4); (ii) obligations relating to the introduction of an *oversight function* (Article 5), (iii) internal control requirements (*control framework*, Article 6) and (iv) accountability and record-keeping requirements (Article 7 and 8 Benchmark Regulation).

The aforementioned governance requirements will in the future further be specified by Regulatory Technical Standards (RTS). In the course of the so-called ESAs Review ESMA has been mandated to develop RTS in order to ensure that the governance arrangements of benchmark administrators are sufficiently robust.[53]

(b) Input Data and Calculation Methodology

The integrity of a benchmark depends on the accuracy of the input data provided by the contributors as well as the methodology used for its calculation.[54] Based on the recommendations of the *Wheatley-Review*[55] and the ESMA/EBA[56] and IOSCO[57] principles, the Benchmark Regulation aims to reduce the **degree of discretion** involved in the benchmark calculation process. If available and appropriate, benchmarks are supposed to be based on verifiable **transaction data**.[58] Details are specified in a Delegated Regulation.[59]

The requirement that benchmarks should primarily be based on actual transaction data can be seen as a reaction to the '**Libor scandal**'.[60] In practice, however, this requirement may be

---

[50] Wheatley Review of LIBOR, Final Report, available at: https://www.gov.uk/government/publications/the-wheatley-review, para. 3.17 ff.
[51] ESMA/2013/658 (fn. 19), p. 35 ff.
[52] IOSCO, Principles for Financial Benchmarks (fn. 19), Principles 1–5.
[53] Art. 4(9) Benchmark Regulation (as amended by the Regulation (EU) 2019/2175). In the meanwhile, the respective RTS have been adopted. Cf. the Commission Delegated Regulation (EU) 2021/1350 of 6 May 2021 supplementing Regulation (EU) 2016/1011 of the European Parliament and of the Council with regard to regulatory technical standards specifying the requirements to ensure that an administrator's governance arrangements are sufficiently robust.
[54] See in this context recital 27 and 30 Benchmark Regulation.
[55] Wheatley Review (fn. 50), para. 5.1 ff. (on reforms of Libor).
[56] ESMA/2013/658 (fn. 19), para. 35 ff.
[57] IOSCO, Principles for Financial Benchmarks (fn. 19), Principles 6–10.
[58] Art. 11(1)(a) Benchmark Regulation. Cf. also recital 26 Benchmark Regulation and Commission, Proposal for a Regulation of the European Parliament and the Council on indices used as benchmarks in financial instruments and financial contracts, Impact Assessment, 18 September 2013, SWD (2013) 337 final, p. 26 ff. for the underlying policy considerations.
[59] Commission Delegated Regulation (EU) 2018/1638 of 13 July 2018 supplementing Regulation (EU) 2016/1011 of the European Parliament and of the Council with regard to regulatory technical standards specifying further how to ensure that input data is appropriate and verifiable, and the internal oversight and verification procedures of a contributor that the administrator of a critical or significant benchmark has to ensure are in place where the input data is contributed from a front office function.
[60] See above M. Wundenberg § 35 para. 3 ff. As described, both Libor and Euribor at least in the past depended to a large extent on the subjective assessment of market participants.

difficult to implement. It requires the existence of a sufficiently liquid market, which may not necessarily exist—as the experience during the financial crisis has shown with regard to interbank reference interest rates. Against this background, the Regulation acknowledges that if transaction data is not appropriate to represent accurately and reliably the market or economic reality that the benchmark intends to measure, input data which is not transaction data may be used, including estimated prices, quotes or other values. Specific requirements apply for **interest rate benchmarks**[61] (such as Libor and Euribor) and for **commodity benchmarks**.[62]

22 The Benchmark Regulation further provides that where a benchmark is based on input data from contributors, the administrator shall, where appropriate, obtain the input data from a representative group (panel) of market participants.[63] With regard to critical benchmarks additional requirements apply. In this case a competent authority has the power to (temporarily) require supervised entities to contribute input data to the administrator in order to ensure the representativeness of the benchmark (**mandatory contributions**).[64] The competent authority is further permitted to (temporarily) compel an administrator to continue to publish a critical benchmark.[65]

23 The provisions relating to mandatory contribution requirements can be seen as a regulatory response to the observation in the aftermath of the 'Libor scandal' where banks withdrew from the Libor and Euribor panels after accusations of alleged manipulations emerged. The 'mandatory contribution' requirements are based on the policy rationale that important ('critical') benchmarks such as Libor and Euribor are vital for the functioning of the financial markets (and the economy as a whole), thereby constituting a 'public good'.[66] At the same time, the power of the supervisory authorities to require mandatory contributions (albeit only for a temporary time period) can be seen critically as benchmark submission is a voluntary activity and contributors may face sanctions if the submitted data prove to be incorrect.

24 The administrator is required to establish adequate systems and controls to ensure the integrity of input data and to **report** to the competent authority any conduct that may involve manipulation of the benchmark.[67] It must further develop a **code of conduct** that specifies the contributors' responsibilities with respect to the contribution of input data.[68]

---

[61] Art. 18 in conjunction with Annex I (1) and (2) Benchmark Regulation. If no transaction data is available, interest rate reference rates may also be based on indicative quotes or expert judgments, cf. Annex I(1)(d).

[62] Art. 19 in conjunction with Annex II(1) ff. Benchmark Regulation.

[63] Art. 11(1)(d) Benchmark Regulation.

[64] Art. 23(6) Benchmark Regulation. Such mandatory contributions may, however, only be ordered for a certain period of time (not exceeding 12 months). Furthermore, the mandatory contribution requirements only apply to 'supervised entities'.

[65] See for details Art. 21(3) Benchmark Regulation.

[66] European Central Bank, European Commission's Public Consultation on the Regulation of Indices Eurosystem's Response, November 2012. In economic terms, public goods are goods that are both 'non-excludable' and 'non-rivalrous' (ie individuals cannot be effectively excluded from use and the use by one individual does not reduce availability to others). Benchmarks may qualify as 'public goods' in an economic sense if market participants may use such benchmarks without the consent of the benchmark administrator (ie if market-participants can make reference to a benchmark without infringing IP-rights). See for a discussion of the 'free-rider' problem associated with public goods G. Rauterberg and A. Verstein, 30 Yale J. on Reg. (2013), 36 and passim (proposing to strengthen the administrators IP rights).

[67] Art. 14 Benchmark Regulation. See for the external reporting in the context of compliance requirements for investment firms M. Wundenberg § 33 para. 84.

[68] Art. 15 Benchmark Regulation. The obligation to compile a code of conduct does not exist for 'regulated-data benchmarks', cf. Art. 17 Benchmark Regulation.

The requirements relating to the administrator's code of conduct are specified in Article 15   25
Benchmark Regulation as well as in a Delegated Regulation.[69] The rationale behind the
benchmark methodology must be disclosed in the **benchmark statement** of the administrator
(Article 27 Benchmark Regulation). The benchmark statement shall enable users to understand the risks related to a specific benchmark. It is seen as a tool to ensure market transparency and consumer protection.[70] The benchmark statement must contain, inter alia,
a description of the criteria and procedures used to determine the benchmark and must
identify the elements in relation to which discretion may be exercised.[71] Details are specified
in a Delegated Regulation.[72]

(c) Governance and Control Requirements for Contributors

Based on the ESMA/EBA[73] principles, the Benchmark Regulation lays out comprehensive   26
governance and control requirements for (supervised) contributors, ie the market participants that provide input data to administrators.[74] The organisational principles are broadly
in line with those applicable to investment firms,[75] such as the requirement to implement
measures for the management of conflicts of interest (eg the establishment of Chinese
walls).[76] With regard to interest rate benchmarks this is put into more concrete terms,
requiring that the submitters[77] shall work in locations physically separated from interest
rate derivatives traders.[78]

These organisational requirements, however, only apply to 'supervised' contributors such   27
as credit firms within the meaning of the CRR-Regulation or MiFID II investment firms.[79]
Other companies not subject to financial supervision must comply with the requirements
laid out in the administrator's code of conduct.[80]

The Benchmark Regulation requires administrators to develop a **code of conduct**[81] for each   28
benchmark clearly specifying contributors' responsibilities with respect to the contribution

---

[69] Commission Delegated Regulation (EU) 2018/1639 of 13 July 2018 supplementing Regulation (EU) 2016/1011 of the European Parliament and of the Council with regard to regulatory technical standards specifying further the elements of the code of conduct to be developed by administrators of benchmarks that are based on input data from contributors.

[70] Cf. title 4 of the Benchmark Regulation 'Transparency and Consumer Protection'. Details regarding the benchmark statement are laid down in Art. 27 Benchmark Regulation.

[71] Art. 27(2) Benchmark Regulation.

[72] Commission Delegated Regulation (EU) 2018/1643 of 13 July 2018 supplementing Regulation (EU) 2016/1011 of the European Parliament and of the Council with regard to regulatory technical standards specifying further the contents of, and cases where updates are required to, the benchmark statement to be published by the administrator of a benchmark.

[73] ESMA/2013/658 (fn. 19), p. 38 ff.

[74] Art. 16 Benchmark Regulation.

[75] See in more detail M. Wundenberg § 33.

[76] Art. 16(2)(c) Benchmark Regulation. On Chinese Walls see also M. Wundenberg § 33 para. 59 ff. Furthermore, the submitters must take into consideration how to remove incentives, created by remuneration policies, to manipulate a benchmark.

[77] A submitter is defined as a natural person employed by the contributor for the purpose of contributing input data (Art. 3(11)(11) Benchmark Regulation).

[78] Annex I (7)(d)(2) Benchmark Regulation. See in this context the decision of the former FSA (now FCA) against the Barclays Bank (M. Wundenberg § 33 para. 82).

[79] Cf. the definition in Art. 3(1)(17) Benchmark Regulation.

[80] On the code of conduct see para. 28 below. Cf. also SWD(2013) 337 final (fn. 58), p. 21 ff.

[81] A code of conduct is only required where a benchmark is based on contribution from contributors, cf. Art. 15(1) Benchmark Regulation ('input data from contributors').

of input data.[82] The European legislature thereby implements one of the recommendations of the *Wheatley-Review*.[83] The **legal nature** of the code of conduct and its impact on the contractual rights and obligations of the administrator and the contributors is not addressed in the Benchmark -Regulation.[84]

29 The elements which are required to be addressed in the code of conduct are specified in considerable detail.[85] By obliging the administrator to develop such code of conduct (and by specifying its content) the European lawmaker 'indirectly' regulates the compliance and control requirements of the contributors. From a regulatory perspective, this obligation constitutes an example of 'regulated' self-regulation.[86] With regard to 'critical' benchmarks, the competent authorities have under certain conditions the power to require the administrator to change the code of conduct.[87] This power of the competent authorities can be seen critically, as it affects the internal relationship between the submitters and contributors.[88,89]

(d) Investor Protection (Assessment Obligations)

30 Another key element of the Benchmark Regulation are provisions relating to transparency and consumer protection,[90] including the obligation of the administrator to publish a **benchmark statement** (as described above).[91]

31 The initial Commission Proposal required supervised entities to obtain the necessary information regarding the consumer's knowledge and experience with regard to the benchmark ('**assessment of suitability**') before it enters into a financial contract with a consumer that makes reference to a benchmark.[92] This concept was based on the suitability and 'know your customer-obligations' of investment firms in relation to giving investment advice.[93] The final text of the Benchmark Regulation does not contain such assessment of suitability obligations. Supervised entities are, however, subject to certain **restrictions on use** of benchmarks (as outlined below).

---

[82] Art. 15 Benchmark Regulation.
[83] Wheatley Review (fn. 50), para. 4.14 ff.
[84] The Commission Proposal initially required administrators and contributors to sign the code of conduct which was then legally binding for all parties (Art. 9(2) of the Commission Proposal), cf. fn. 3.
[85] Cf. Art. 15(2) Benchmark Regulation as well as Commission Delegated Regulation (EU) 2018/1639 of 13 July 2018.
[86] Cf. in this context now also K. Gütte, *Regulierung finanzieller Referenzwerte*, 338 ff.
[87] The wording of the Benchmark Regulation now clarifies that the supervisory authorities have no direct powers to amend the content of the code of conduct themselves (ie the changes must rather be implemented by the administrator), cf. Art. 23(6)(e) Benchmark Regulation.
[88] It must further be taken into account that too detailed requirements in the code of conduct may deter market participants from contributing data for the determination of a benchmark, cf. ESMA/2016/288 (fn. 15), p. 48, para. 147: 'There is a balance to be found between ensuring a sufficiently detailed code—as a useful guideline for contribution—and the risk of a benchmark becoming non-representative by introducing demanding requirements which may cause unsupervised contributors to cease voluntarily contributing to that benchmark'.
[89] As mentioned above, the Commission Proposal originally required administrators and contributors to sign the code of conduct which was then legally binding for all parties (Art. 9(2) of the Commission Proposal). This concept is no longer contained in the final text version of the Benchmark Regulation. The Regulation clarifies, however, that the administrator must be convinced that the contributors abide by the code of conduct.
[90] Title 4 of the Benchmark Regulation refers to *consumer protection*. Whether this is to be distinguished from the aim of *investor protection* laid down in Art. 1 Benchmark Regulation appears unclear. In the context of the Rating Regulation see R. Veil § 27 para. 18.
[91] See above para. 25.
[92] Art. 18 of the Commission Proposal for a Benchmark Regulation, COM(2013) 641 final (fn. 3).
[93] Cf. R. Veil § 30 para. 45.

(e) ESG Disclosure Requirements; Specific Requirements for Climate Benchmarks

As part of its efforts to facilitate the transition to a more sustainable economy, the European lawmaker amended the Benchmark Regulation in order to promote sustainability goals.[94] As a first measure, specific **disclosure requirements** regarding Environmental, Social and Governance (ESG) factors have been introduced. Benchmark administrators are now required to publish an explanation of how the key elements of the methodology of the benchmark reflect ESG factors for each benchmark.[95] In a similar fashion, the benchmark statement issued by the administrator must contain explanations of how ESG factors are reflected in each benchmark of the benchmark provider.[96]

As a second measure, the European lawmaker introduced specific requirements for two types of sustainability benchmarks, namely EU Climate Transition Benchmarks as well as EU Paris-Aligned Benchmarks.[97] The **EU Climate Transition Benchmark** is defined as a benchmark that is labelled as an EU Climate Transition Benchmark where the underlying assets are selected, weighted or excluded in such a manner that the resulting benchmark portfolio is on a decarbonisation trajectory and is also constructed in accordance with the minimum standards laid down in the delegated acts.[98] The '**EU Paris-aligned Benchmark**' refers to a 'benchmark that is labelled as an EU Paris-aligned Benchmark where the underlying assets are selected in such a manner that the resulting benchmark portfolio's GHG emissions are aligned with the long-term global warming target of the Paris Climate Agreement and is also constructed in accordance with the minimum standards laid down in the delegated acts'.[99] While both benchmarks are focussed on decarbonisation, they differ in the thresholds that apply (ie, the second benchmark is aligned to the Paris Agreement goal to limit the increase in global average temperatures to well below 2°C above pre-industrial levels).

For both types of benchmarks, specific requirements regarding, inter alia, the methodology that are used for their calculations apply.[100] Details are specified in Delegated Regulations.[101]

---

[94] Those requirements have been introduced by the Regulation (EU) 2019/2089 of the European Parliament and of the Council of 27 November 2019 amending Regulation (EU) 2016/1011 as regards EU Climate Transition Benchmarks, EU Paris-aligned Benchmarks and sustainability-related disclosures for benchmarks.
[95] Art. 13(1)(d) Benchmark Regulation. Exception apply for interest rate and foreign exchange benchmarks.
[96] Art. 27(2a) Benchmark Regulation.
[97] Those requirements have been introduced by the Regulation (EU) 2019/2089 of the European Parliament and of the Council of 27 November 2019 amending Regulation (EU) 2016/1011 as regards EU Climate Transition Benchmarks, EU Paris-aligned Benchmarks and sustainability-related disclosures for benchmarks.
[98] Art. 3(1)(23a) Benchmark Regulation.
[99] Art. 3(1)(23b) Benchmark Regulation.
[100] Art. 19a–19c Benchmark Regulation in conjunction with Annex III.
[101] Commission Delegated Regulation (EU) 2020/1816 of 17 July 2020 supplementing Regulation (EU) 2016/1011 of the European Parliament and of the Council as regards the explanation in the benchmark statement of how environmental, social and governance factors are reflected in each benchmark provided and published; Commission Delegated Regulation (EU) 2020/1817 of 17 July 2020 supplementing Regulation (EU) 2016/1011 of the European Parliament and of the Council as regards the minimum content of the explanation on how environmental, social and governance factors are reflected in the benchmark methodology; Commission Delegated Regulation (EU) 2020/1818 of 17 July 2020 supplementing Regulation (EU) 2016/1011 of the European Parliament and of the Council as regards minimum standards for EU Climate Transition Benchmarks and EU Paris-aligned Benchmarks.

(f) Power to Replace References in Contracts

35 In February 2021, the Benchmark regime was amended in order to address the impact of the anticipated discontinuation of the Libor benchmark.[102] In order to avoid a significant disruption in the functioning of the financial markets in the EU, a new Chapter 4a was included in the Benchmark Regulation. The new provision grants the European Commission the power to designate a mandatory replacement benchmark and to replace under certain conditions all references in contracts and financial instruments to the benchmark that has ceased.[103] Similar powers are granted to the national competent authority in the Member States (NCAs) where a majority of contributors to a relevant benchmark are located.[104] In principle, the aforementioned powers not only apply to 'critical' benchmarks such as Libor, but also to other benchmarks if their cessation would significantly disrupt the functioning of financial markets in the Union.[105]

36 Under the requirements specified in the Benchmark Regulation, the references in contracts and financial instruments are replaced by **operation of law** if those contracts do not contain a suitable fall-back provision.[106] This is remarkable: The Commission and, as the case may be, the NCAs now have the authority to unilaterally amend financial contracts negotiated by private parties. However, the replacement regime is only foreseen as a 'fall-back' solution. It does not apply where the parties of the respective contract have agreed to apply a different replacement for the respective benchmark.[107]

5. Restrictions on Use and Third-Country Benchmarks

37 Supervised entities will be prohibited from **'using'** indices as benchmarks unless the benchmark is provided by an administrator located in the European Union and is included in ESMA's register for that purpose (see for the registration and authorisation requirements below). The 'use' of benchmarks includes, inter alia, the issuance of a financial instrument which references an index or a combination of indices.[108] Supervised entities that use benchmarks are also required to maintain robust written contingency plans setting out the actions that they would take in the event a benchmark materially changes or ceases to be provided.

38 The restrictions on use may lead to considerable challenges with regard to the use of benchmarks of **non EU-administrators**.[109] Third country benchmarks are only qualified for use (and for registration in ESMA's register) if one of the following three requirements is fulfilled: (i) The Commission has adopted an **equivalence** decision and the further equivalence

---

[102] Regulation (EU) 2021/168 of the European Parliament and of the Council of 10 February 2021 amending Regulation (EU) 2016/1011 as regards the exemption of certain third-country spot foreign exchange benchmarks and the designation of replacements for certain benchmarks in cessation, and amending Regulation (EU) No 648/2012.
[103] Art. 23b Benchmark Regulation.
[104] Art. 23c Benchmark Regulation.
[105] Art. 23b(1) Benchmark Regulation.
[106] Art. 23b(3) and (4), Art. 23c(3) and (4) Benchmark Regulation.
[107] Art. 23b(11), 23c(4) Benchmark Regulation.
[108] Cf. the definition of 'use of benchmarks' in Art. 3(7) Benchmark Regulation.
[109] The Benchmark Regulation contains, however, certain grandfathering provisions. See in particular Art. 51(5) Benchmark Regulation.

requirements pursuant to Article 30 Benchmark are fulfilled, (ii) until the equivalence decision has been adopted the administrator has been '**recognised**' by the competent authority pursuant to Article 32 Benchmark Regulation or (iii) an administrator or any other supervised entity has been authorised by the competent authority to endorse the benchmarks pursuant to Article 33 Benchmark Regulation. To date, the Commission has adopted equivalence decisions regarding the legal framework of Australia[110] as well as Singapore.[111,112]

The third-country benchmark regime has particular relevance in the light of the decision of the UK to leave the EU (**Brexit**). As Brexit has taken effect, UK benchmark administrators qualify as third country administrators. ESMA clarified that during a transitional period foreseen in the Benchmark Regulation third country benchmarks could still be used by supervised entities in the European Union. In the absence of an equivalence decision by the European Commission, UK administrators would have until the end of the transitional period to apply for recognition or endorsement in the EU.[113] In the course of the amendment of the Benchmark Regulation in February 2021, the transitional date was extended from 1 January 2021 to 31 December 2023. The European Commission has furthermore been granted the power to extend that period by a maximum of two years (ie to 31 December 2025).[114]

6. Authorisation, Supervision and Sanctions

The Benchmark Regulation contains detailed rules regarding the supervisory and enforcement powers of the competent authorities as well as authorisation or registration requirements of the benchmark administrators. Unlike a prior proposal, the adopted text of the Benchmark Regulation does not, however, contain any provisions on the liability under civil law.

(a) Authorisation and Registration

The (EU) administrator[115] of a benchmark is required to apply to the competent authority of the Member State in which the administrator is located for authorisation or registration.[116] The procedure is laid out in Article 34 Benchmark Regulation. The authorised or registered administrators will be listed in a public register maintained by ESMA.[117]

---

[110] Commission Implementing Decision (EU) 2019/1274 of 29 July 2019 on the equivalence of the legal and supervisory framework applicable to benchmarks in Australia in accordance with Regulation (EU) 2016/1011 of the European Parliament and of the Council.
[111] Commission Implementing Decision (EU) 2019/1275 of 29 July 2019 on the equivalence of the legal and supervisory framework applicable to benchmarks in Singapore in accordance with Regulation (EU) 2016/1011 of the European Parliament and of the Council.
[112] The equivalence decisions are available at: https://www.esma.europa.eu/policy-activities/benchmarks/equivalence.
[113] ESMA, Public statement: Impact of Brexit on the Benchmark Regulation, 1.10.2020, ESMA80-187-610.
[114] Art. 54(6) as amended by the Regulation (EU) 2021/168 of the European Parliament and of the Council of 10 February 2021 amending Regulation (EU) 2016/1011 as regards the exemption of certain third-country spot foreign exchange benchmarks and the designation of replacements for certain benchmarks in cessation, and amending Regulation (EU) No 648/2012.
[115] For third-country administrators see above under para. 37–39.
[116] Art. 34(1) Benchmark Regulation.
[117] Art. 36(1) Benchmark Regulation.

42 An '**authorisation**' is required for non-supervised administrators (unless they provide only non-significant benchmarks) as well as for supervised entities that provide critical benchmarks. In turn, only a '**registration**' is required for supervised entities that provide non-critical benchmarks as well as for non-supervised administrators which provide only non-significant benchmarks.[118] According to recital 48 of the Benchmark Regulation, compared to registration, 'authorisation requires a more extensive assessment of the administrator's application'. However, registered and authorised administrators are subject to the same supervisory regime. The authorisation or registration may be withdrawn or suspended under the conditions listed in Article 35 Benchmark Regulation (in particular in cases of serious and repeated infringements of the provision of the Regulation).

(b) Supervisory Powers and Sanctions

(aa) Supervisory Powers of the National Supervisory Authorities

43 The supervisory powers of the national competent supervisory authorities are laid down in Article 41 Benchmark Regulation. In order to fulfil their duties under the Regulation, the competent national supervisory authorities are granted comprehensive supervisory and investigatory powers, including the right to carry out on-site investigations. They shall further have the power to impose appropriate administrative sanctions and other administrative measures. These include, inter alia, the following measures and sanctions: (i) ordering the administrator or supervised entity to cease any practice which infringes the Regulation; (ii) ordering a disgorgement of profits; (iii) publishing a public warning which indicates the person responsible and the nature of the infringement; (iv) withdrawing or suspending the authorisation or registration of the administrator and (v) (temporarily) banning any natural person, who is held responsible for such an infringement, from exercising management functions in administrators or supervised contributors. Additionally, the supervisory authorities may impose administrative fines.[119]

44 The minimum amount of such fines is determined in Article 42(2)(g) and (h) Benchmark Regulation. For most offences, the maximum administrative pecuniary sanctions must amount to at least € 500,000 for natural persons and for legal persons the higher of either € 1 million or 10% of the total annual turnover.[120] Alternatively, the Benchmark Regulation also allows administrative fines of up to three times the amount of the profits gained or losses avoided because of the infringement where those can be determined.[121]

(bb) ESMA's Role

45 In an initial proposal of the Regulation, the European Commission proposed to provide ESMA with direct supervisory powers with regard to critical benchmarks. In particular, it

---

[118] Art. 34(1)(1) Benchmark Regulation. See also the clarifications in recital 48 Benchmark Regulation. The details relating to the authorisation/registration procedure will be specified by technical standards. Cf. ESMA, consultation Paper. Draft technical standards under the Benchmarks Regulation, ESMA/2016/1406, 29 September 2016, p. 118 ff.
[119] Cf. for details Art. 42 Benchmark Regulation.
[120] This applies with regard to infringements of Art. 4, 5, 6, 7, 8, 9, 10, points (a), (b), (c) and (e) of Art. 11(1), Art. 11(2) and (3), and Art. 12, 13, 14, 15, 16, 21, 23, 24, 25, 26, 27, 28, 29 and 34 Benchmark Regulation.
[121] Art. 42(2)(f) Benchmark Regulation.

§ 36 *Market Supervision and Organisational Requirements* 665

was contemplated that ESMA should be responsible for both imposing sanctions in cases of infringements of the provision of the Benchmark Regulation as well as for the authorisation process of the administrators.[122]

The Benchmark Regulation adopted in 2016 did not grant ESMA such direct supervisory powers. Rather, the supervisory and enforcement competencies remain principally with the national competent authorities. With regard to critical benchmarks, however, the Regulation provides for the establishment of so-called **colleges of competent authorities**.[123] The college shall comprise the competent authority of the administrator, ESMA and the competent authorities of the supervised contributors.[124] Competent authorities of other Member States shall also have the right to become a member of such a college under the conditions set out in Article 46 para. 3 Benchmark Regulation.[125]

46

The establishment of the colleges aims to contribute to a harmonised application of rules under the Benchmark Regulation and to the convergence of the national supervisory practices between the different authorities and the convergence of national supervisory practices.[126] For this purpose, the colleges shall establish written arrangements and coordinate their decision-making processes.[127] If the national supervisory authorities fail to reach an agreement, the Benchmark Regulation requires ESMA to mediate between the authorities involved.[128] ESMA has, therefore, so far primarily a coordination role between the competent authorities.[129]

47

According to the legislative materials, the European legislator initially refrained from granting ESMA direct supervisory powers as this would have required additional resources and the supervision by the national authorities was considered to be more effective.[130] The initial proposal of direct supervision of benchmark administrators by ESMA also faced severe political opposition by some Member States (in particular the United Kingdom).

48

In the course of the recent ESAs Review, ESMA has been awarded **direct supervisory responsibilities** for critical benchmarks with effect as of 1 January 2022.[131] In addition, ESMA will also be responsible for the recognition of third-country benchmarks.[132] These developments constitute a remarkable **shift in the regulatory policy** of the European

49

---

[122] See for a similar approach with regard to regulation of rating agencies R. Veil § 27 para. 62 ff.
[123] Art. 46 Benchmark Regulation. On supervisory colleges in general see Art. 21 ESMA Regulation.
[124] Art. 46(2) Benchmark Regulation.
[125] However, this requires that the cessation of the benchmark would have a significant adverse impact on the financial stability, or the orderly functioning of markets, or consumers, or the real economy of these Member States.
[126] Cf. recital 62 Benchmark Regulation.
[127] Art. 46(6) Benchmark Regulation.
[128] See in this context recital 62 Benchmark Regulation ('key element'). Cf. in this context Art. 46(4) Benchmark Regulation in conjunction with Art. 21 para. 4 ESMA Regulation and Art. 46 para. 7 and 10 Benchmark Regulation.
[129] In the context of short selling see F. Walla § 24 para. 61.
[130] Cf. SWD(2013) 337 final (fn. 58), p. 43.
[131] Regulation (EU) 2019/2175 of the European Parliament and of the Council of 18 December 2019 amending Regulation (EU) No 1093/2010 establishing a European Supervisory Authority (European Banking Authority), Regulation (EU) No 1094/2010 establishing a European Supervisory Authority (European Insurance and Occupational Pensions Authority), Regulation (EU) No 1095/2010 establishing a European Supervisory Authority (European Securities and Markets Authority), Regulation (EU) No 600/2014 on markets in financial instruments, Regulation (EU) 2016/1011 on indices used as benchmarks in financial instruments and financial contracts or to measure the performance of investment funds, and Regulation (EU) 2015/847 on information accompanying transfers of funds.
[132] Cf. Art. 40 Benchmark Regulation (as amended by the Regulation (EU) 2019/2175).

regime. Already in the second edition of this chapter it was argued that in the light of the global nature of 'critical benchmarks' a national approach to supervision may not be sufficient to ensure an efficient oversight over those benchmarks. Against this background, the new approach is generally to be welcomed. However, the shift to a more European supervision of the benchmark regime requires that ESMA will be equipped with adequate resources to perform its tasks. It will remain to be seen how the new supervisory regime will work in practice.

(cc) Civil Law Liability

50   Both institutional and private investors have filed numerous claims against banks and other market participants based on alleged manipulations of the Libor and Euribor benchmarks.[133] However, the assertion of claims under civil law has proven to be extremely complex.

51   Against this background, an initial European Commission's proposal for a Benchmark Regulation contained a provision on civil liability. As opposed to this, the Commission Proposal from September 2013 as well as the final text of the Benchmark Regulation does not address the issue of liability of administrators and/or submitters under civil law. Whether the administrators and/or contributors are subject to civil liability in cases of infringements of the provisions of the Regulation (or in cases of benchmark manipulations) must therefore be determined on the basis of the respective national legislation, such as tort law.

52   It was to be expected that the initial proposal to introduce a statutory civil law liability in the Benchmark Regulation would be discussed controversially. While the national regimes appear to impose high hurdles for the assertion of civil law claims related to (alleged) benchmark manipulations or other related misconduct, there are strong arguments against the introduction of such a statutory civil law liability. In particular, administrators and contributors would be confronted with potential liability vis-à-vis a vast number of benchmark users which would, in turn, reduce the willingness of the administrators and contributors to participate in the benchmark setting process. Against this background the European lawmakers' decision to refrain from introducing a statutory liability must be welcomed.[134]

II. Conclusion

53   Benchmarks have become an essential feature of today's financial markets. Reference rates such as Libor and Euribor play an important role in the determination of the price of many financial instruments and contracts worldwide. The alleged manipulations of Libor/Euribor reference rates as well as foreign exchange and commodity benchmarks have

---

[133] See for an overview the report published in the Economist on 5 January 2013: The Libor scandal: Year of the lawyer, available at: www.economist.com/news/finance-and-economics/21569053-banks-face-another-punishing-year-fines-and-lawsuits-year-lawyer.

[134] For an analysis of the impact of benchmark manipulations under German tort law cf. A. Sajnovits, *Financial-Benchmarks*, 285–339 (arguing that civil cause of action exists under narrow circumstances); K. Gütte, *Regulierung finanzieller Referenzwerte*, 400–408.

§ 36 Market Supervision and Organisational Requirements

severely affected the confidence of market participants in the accuracy and integrity of such benchmarks.

Against this background, the European lawmaker has introduced a comprehensive regime governing the entire benchmark setting process. The aim of the Benchmark Regulation is to reduce the risk of manipulation of benchmarks and other misconduct by addressing conflicts of interest, the internal governance as well as the use of discretion in the benchmark determination process. For this purpose, the Benchmark Regulation imposes detailed governance and control requirements for benchmark administrators and contributors and introduces a new authorisation/registration regime. 54

With the adoption of the Benchmark Regulation the European legislator has broken new ground. The European provisions build on (but also go beyond) the principles published by IOSCO[135] as well as by ESMA/EBA.[136] In the legislative process, the Council and the European Parliament took the opportunity to address certain inconsistencies in the initial proposal of the European Commission, in particular with regard to the initially proposed 'suitability' obligations of the contributors,[137] the enforcement and supervisory powers of the authorities[138] as well as the definition of 'critical' benchmarks in the Benchmark Regulation.[139] 55

Since the initial enactment of the Benchmark Regulation the regime has been subject to substantial reforms. In particular, ESMA has been awarded direct supervisory powers over certain 'critical' benchmarks. This reflects a significant policy shift since so far the supervision of benchmarks largely relied on the national authorities. 56

---

[135] IOSCO, Principles for Financial Benchmarks (fn. 19); IOSCO, Principles for Oil Price Reporting Agencies (fn. 22). See also the latest implementation report of the IOSCO, Second Review of the Implementation of IOSCO's Principles for Financial Benchmarks by Administrators of Euribor, Libor and Tibor, February 2016, available at: www.iosco.org/library/pubdocs/pdf/IOSCOPD526.pdf.
[136] ESMA/2013/658 (fn. 19).
[137] See para. 31 above.
[138] See para. 40 ff. above.
[139] Cf. the previous German version (M. Wundenberg § 31 para. 45).

Annex 1. Overview of the Application of the Benchmark Regulation on Different Benchmarks

Provision	Subject Matter	Exemptions and/or modifications for specific types of Benchmarks					
		Interest Rate Benchmarks (Annex 1 applies generally in addition to the requirements of Title II)	Commodity Benchmarks (Annex 2 applies generally instead of the requirements of Title II)	Significant Benchmarks[140]	Non-significant Benchmarks[141]	Regulated Data Benchmarks	Critical Benchmarks (additional requirements pursuant to Chapter 4 apply)
Title II: Benchmark Integrity and Reliability							
Chapter 1: Governance and control of Administrators							
Article 4	Governance and Conflict of Interest Requirements		In part modified by Annex 2	Articles 4(2) and 4(7) (c), (d), (e)	Articles 4(2), 4(7) (c), (d), (e) and 4(8)		
Article 5	Oversight Function Requirements	Articles 5(4) and 5(5) (substituted by Annex 1(3))			Articles 5(2), 5(3) and 5(4)		
Article 6	Control Framework Requirements				Articles 6(1), 6(3) and 6(5)		
Article 7	Accountability Framework Requirements				Article 7(2)		

[140] Exemption only applies if administrator considers that the application of the respective provisions would be disproportionate. 'Comply or explain' mechanisms (compliance statement) applies. The competent authority may decide that respective provisions must nonetheless be complied with ('regulatory override').
[141] 'Comply or explain' mechanisms (compliance statement) applies.

§ 36 Market Supervision and Organisational Requirements

					Article 8(1)(a)[142]
Article 8	Record Keeping Requirements				
Article 9	Complaints Handling Mechanisms				
Article 10	Outsourcing				
Chapter 2: Input Data, Methodology and Reporting of Infringement					
Article 11	Input Data	Article 11(1)(a) and (c) modified / substituted by Annex 1(1) Article 11(1)(a) and Article 11(4) modified / substituted by Annex 1(2)	In part modified by Annex 2	Article 11(3)(b)	Articles 11(1)(b), 11(2)(b) and (c) and 11(3)	Articles 11(1)(d) and (e), 11(2) and 11(3)
Article 12	Methodology				
Article 13	Transparency of Methodology			Article 13(2)	
Article 14	Reporting of Infringements			Article 14(2)	Articles 14(1) and 14(2)

(continued)

[142] Exempt only with regard to input data that are contributed entirely and directly as specified in Art. 3(1)(24).

Annex 1. Overview of the Application of the Benchmark Regulation on Different Benchmarks (*Continued*)

Provision	Subject Matter	Exemptions and/or modifications for specific types of Benchmarks					
		Interest Rate Benchmarks (Annex 1 applies generally in addition to the requirements of Title II)	Commodity Benchmarks (Annex 2 applies generally instead of the requirements of Title II)	Significant Benchmarks	Non-significant Benchmarks	Regulated Data Benchmarks	Critical Benchmarks (additional requirements pursuant to Chapter 4 apply)
Chapter 3: Code of Conduct and Requirements for Contributors							
Article 15	Code of Conduct		Entire Article (provisions of Annex 2 apply)	Article 15(2)	Article 15(2)	Entire Article	
Article 16	Governance and Controls Requirements for Supervised Contributors	Article 16(5) does not apply. Article 16 supplemented by Annex(1)(5) et seq.	Entire Article (provisions of Annex 2 apply)		Articles 16(2) and 16(3)	Entire Article	
Title IV: Transparency and Consumer Protection							
Article 27	Benchmark Statement						
Article 28	Cessation of a Benchmark						

9

Takeover Law

§ 37

Foundations

Bibliography

Armour, John, *Enforcement Strategies in UK Corporate Governance: A Roadmap and Empirical Assessment*, in: Pacces, Alessio M. (ed.), *The law and economics of corporate governance: changing perspectives* (2010), 213–258; Baums, Theodor and Thoma, Georg F., *Takeover Laws in Europe* (2003); Cramer, Carsten, *Change of Control-Klauseln im deutschen Unternehmensrecht* (2009); Edwards, Vanessa, *The Directive on Takeover Bids—Not Worth the Paper it's Written on?*, 1 ECFR (2004), 416–439; Fleischer, Holger and Kalss, Susanne, *Das neue Wertpapiererwerbs- und Übernahmegesetz* (2002); Hirte, Heribert, *The Takeover Directive—A Mini-Directive on the Structure of the Corporation: Is it a Trojan Horse?*, 2 ECFR (2005), 1–19; Hopt, Klaus J. and Wymeersch, Eddy, *European Takeovers: Law and Practice*, 1992; Hopt, Klaus J., *Europäisches Übernahmerecht* (2014); Kalss, Susanne, *The Austrian Law on Public Offers and Takeovers*, 1 EBOR (2000), 479–506; Maul, Silja and Kouloridas, Athanasios, *The Takeover Bids Directive*, 5 GLJ (2004), 355–366; Maul, Silja and Muffat-Jeandet, Danièle, *Die EU-Übernahmerichtlinie—Inhalt und Umsetzung in nationales Recht*, AG (2004), 221–234 and 306–318; McCahery, Joseph A. and Vermeulen, Erik P.M., *The Case Against Reform of the Takeover Bids Directive*, 22 EBLR (2011), 541–557; Nussbaum, Matthias, *Abfindungen und Anerkennungsprämien für Vorstandsmitglieder deutscher Aktiengesellschaften. 'Goldene Handschläge' und 'Fallschirme'* (2009); Sailer, Viola, *Offenlegung von Change of Control-Klauseln im Jahresabschluss*, AG (2006), 913–927; Seibt, Christoph H. and Heiser, Kristian J., *Analyse des Übernahmerichtlinie-Umsetzungsgesetzes (Regierungsentwurf)*, AG (2006), 301–320; Stohlmeier, Thomas, *German Public Takeover Law*, Bilingual Edition with an Introduction to the Law, 3rd ed. (2015); Wooldridge, Frank, *The Recent Directive on Takeover-Bids*, 15 EBLR (2000), 147–158; Wright, Crisp et al., *A Practitioner's Guide to the City Code on Takeovers and Mergers* (2018/19).

I. Legal Sources

A takeover bid consists of a person or a **legal entity**—the 'offeror'—**making a public offer** to the **holders** of the **securities** of a **company**—the 'target'—to acquire all or some of those securities for a price determined by the offeror and usually exceeding the current stock price. It has the aim of acquiring the majority of a company's shares, thus gaining control over the target company. The offer can be friendly or hostile, the latter consisting of an offer that is submitted against the will or without the knowledge of the target company's managing board. 1

At a European level, attempts to regulate takeover law began early but failed at this stage to come to any result. A Commission proposal from 1989 on a directive on takeover bids, did not obtain the approval of all Member States due to diverging regulatory conceptions and interests. The Commission's amended proposal, submitted to the Council in November 2

1997, took these diverging concepts into account, and led to the publication of a Common Position by the Council in June 2000. The European Parliament's objections resulted in a joint draft by the Conciliation Committee, published on 5 June 2001. This, however, was not accepted by the European Parliament.

3   A new draft proposal for a directive presented in October 2002 threatened to fail once again due to the diverging regulatory conceptions of some Member States. A political agreement could, however, finally be achieved thanks to the compromises regarding the obligation of neutrality for the managing board and the handling of defensive tactics against public takeovers (poison pills)[1] presented by Portugal and the **Takeover Directive (TOD)** was finally enacted on 30 April 2004.

4   The TOD coordinates the laws, regulations, administrative provisions, codes of practice and other arrangements of the Member States on takeover bids. Its scope of application is restricted to offers for securities of companies whose securities are admitted to trading on a regulated market in one or more Member States and which are governed by the laws of a Member State.[2] The TOD does not apply to offers for the acquisition of securities on MTFs.[3]

5   The TOD is a **framework directive**,[4] merely laying down the central elements of takeover proceedings, but permitting the Member States to develop their own, more specific rules on certain aspects. This can, for example, be seen with regard to the rules on mandatory bids: the TOD contains no rules on how an offeree gains control over the target company, leaving the Member States to decide.[5] Other aspects, however, such as the procedure of a takeover and its supervision by the national authorities,[6] are described in great detail in the directive. The TOD also contains specific provisions for the board of the offeree company[7] and exceptions from restrictions on takeover bids,[8] leaving the Member States little room for deviation in the implementation.

6   It is not possible to describe the implementation of the TOD in all European countries. It shall be sufficient to have a closer look at the legal foundations in Germany (where BaFin carries out supervision as a government agency)[9] and the United Kingdom (where supervision is carried out by the Takeover Panel).[10] The United Kingdom has left the EU. However, European takeover law is significantly influenced by the rules in the UK. Therefore, the UK regime will continue to be dealt with in this book. In **Germany** the legislator implemented

---

[1] Such defensive tactics can result from the national company laws of some Member States, such as multiple-voting shares permitted in France and Sweden, but prohibited in Germany.

[2] Cf. Art. 1(1) TOD.

[3] On the term MTF see R. Veil § 7 para. 4.

[4] The proposals for a directive submitted in 1989 and 1990 aimed to fully regulate all aspects. Not until 1996 did the European Commission follow the doubts of some Member States and restrict its proposal to some framework provisions.

[5] See R. Veil § 39 para. 6.

[6] Any association or private body empowered by national law or the national authorities can act as supervisory body. Cf. Art. 4(1) sentence 2 TOD.

[7] Cf. Art. 9 TOD.

[8] Cf. Art. 11 and 12 TOD.

[9] This is the case in most European countries, such as France, Italy, Poland, Spain, etc.

[10] Supervision carried out by the UK Takeover Panel is described as the commission model. On the governance-based approach see J. Armour, *Enforcement Strategies in UK Corporate Governance: A Roadmap and Empirical Assessment*, in: Pacces (ed.), *The law and economics of corporate governance: changing perspectives* (2010), 213–258. Supervision by a commission is also provided in Austria and Sweden.

the TOD in the *Wertpapiererwerbs- und -übernahmegesetz* (WpÜG—Securities Acquisition and Takeover Act). The German Federal Ministry of Finance has enacted a number of supplementary regulations, clarifying questions relating to the applicability of the WpÜG and other technical questions. In the **United Kingdom** the respective legislation can be found in the Companies Act 2006 and in the City Code on Takeovers and Mergers (City Code).

A reform of the TOD is currently unlikely. Between 2010 and 2012 the Commission reviewed the TOD and reached the conclusion 'that, generally, the regime created by the TOD is working satisfactorily'. Whilst it identified individual topics that 'could be clarified on EU level in order to provide more legal certainty to international investors',[11] it could not make out a concrete need for action.

II. Implications of Takeover Bids

The legal implications of public takeover bids are ambivalent. On the one hand, it is necessary that mismanaged companies, which are less successful and thus listed under value on the stock exchange, can be taken over, so that the management can be replaced. A '**market for corporate control**' disciplines the governing bodies of a company, the risk of a takeover ensuring that the management sets its own interests aside and follows a strategy that maximises the company's value. Additionally, from a shareholder's perspective, the opportunity to sell shares above the stock exchange price is of interest.

On the other hand, a takeover bid might lead the management of a company to take certain measures that may be detrimental to the company from a long-term perspective. Furthermore cash offers require a viable financing concept. This can lead to large debts which the offeror will in general subsequently attempt to shift to the target company. Additionally, there are numerous examples showing that one of the incentives of the management of a company to take over another company was to increase its own reputation and remuneration in a larger 'corporate empire'.

Despite such risks, however, it cannot be the aim in a market economy to suppress or prevent such a market for corporate control. The respective provisions must rather ensure an adequate **shareholder protection**. This is therefore the central aim of the TOD: 'It is necessary to protect the interests of holders of the securities of companies [...] when those companies are the subject of takeover-bids or of changes of control'.[12] It further aims to achieve a 'community-wide clarity and transparency in respect of legal issues to be settled in the event of takeover-bids and to prevent patterns of corporate restructuring within the community from being distorted by arbitrary differences in governance and management cultures'.[13]

---

[11] Report from the Commission to the European Parliament, the Council, the European Economic and Social Committee and the Committee of the Regions, Application of Directive 2004/25/EC on takeover bids, 28 June 2012, COM(2012) 347 final, para. 21–23.
[12] Cf. Recital 2 TOD.
[13] Cf. Recital 3 TOD.

III. Administration and Supervision

11   The TOD requires the Member States to designate the authority competent to supervise bids.[14] The Member States may either establish 'public authorities' or 'private bodies recognised by national law' or by public authorities expressly empowered for that purpose by national law.[15]

12   The **United Kingdom** has opted for the latter, Sec. 943 and 944 Companies Act 2006 granting the Takeover Panel the power to issue rules on this matter. Section 945 Companies Act 2006 additionally permits the Takeover Panel to rule on the construction and applicability of the City Code in case of disputes. Pursuant to Sec. 942 Companies Act the Takeover Panel, may do anything that it considers necessary or expedient for the purposes of, or in connection with, its functions. It is thus solely the Takeover Panel (and neither the FCA nor the Bank of England) that is responsible for the supervision of takeover proceedings in the United Kingdom.

13   In **Germany**, the WpÜG assigns the responsibility for the supervision of takeover bids to the BaFin, a public authority.[16] The BaFin is responsible for counteracting any grievances that may impair the proper execution of procedures or have severe detrimental effects on the securities market supervision of grievances. It may issue any orders suitable and necessary to resolve or prevent the respective grievances.

IV. Disclosure of Defensive Structures and Mechanisms

14   One of the key aims of the European legislature was to reinforce the freedom to deal in the securities of companies and the freedom to exercise voting rights. Following the recommendations of the High Level Group of Company Law Experts,[17] the Takeover Directive (TOD) requires that the Member States introduce provisions obliging companies to make their defensive structures and mechanisms transparent.[18] This **obligation** is to **enable potential offerees** to **assess** the target and **possible barriers** to **takeover bids**.[19]

15   The rules on transparency only apply to companies[20] whose securities are all or partly admitted to trading on the regulated market[21] of one or more Member States.[22] However, Member States are free to apply takeover law to companies whose shares are listed on a MTF.[23]

---

[14] Cf. Art. 4(1) TOD.
[15] Cf. Art. 4(1) sentence 2 TOD.
[16] Cf. § 4(1) WpÜG.
[17] Cf. Report of the High Level Group of Company Law Experts on Issues Related to Takeover Bids (so-called Winter Group), 10 January 2002, p. 6 and 25–26.
[18] Cf. Art. 10 and Recital 18 TOD.
[19] Cf. P. Kajüter, in: Schmidt (ed.), *Münchener Kommentar zum HGB*, § 289a para. 3.
[20] The company must be subject to the law of a Member State. Cf. Art. 1(1) TOD and Recital 1.
[21] On the concept of a regulated market see R. Veil § 7 para. 11–15.
[22] Cf. Art. 10(1) in conjunction with Art. 1(1) TOD.
[23] In the UK the Takeover Code applies to AIM quoted companies incorporated in the UK, Channel Islands or Isle of Man, if the company is considerd by the Takover Panel to be 'centrally managed and controlled' in the UK, Channel Islands or Isle of Man.

Unlike the Level 1 directives and regulations under capital markets law,[24] the TOD restricts its understanding of securities to transferrable securities carrying voting rights in a company,[25] ie shares. The TOD does not distinguish between small and larger companies—this being seen critically considering the costs involved. It cannot be determined as yet, however, whether the TOD will be amended to exclude small and medium-sized enterprises (SME) from its scope of application.[26]

When giving an overview of the information a company must disclose, it is not necessary to mention the national implementing laws separately, as the directive's provisions are so precise that they cover all possible cases in which a public takeover may be affected. No noteworthy leeway is given to the Member States for gold plating. The TOD also defines exactly which medium must be used for publication and which additional information is required: the information must be published in the company's annual reports.[27] Furthermore the board of directors must present an explanatory report on the information published to the annual general meeting of shareholders.[28]

1. Structure of the Capital

The annual report must contain information on the structure of the capital, including securities which are not admitted to trading on a regulated market. An offeror must be capable of gaining insight into the company's financing.[29] Companies that offer different classes of shares—eg non-voting shares or shares with a priority over common stock in the payment of dividends—must also include an indication of the different classes of shares and, for each class of shares, the rights and obligations attaching to it and the percentage of total share capital that it represents.

2. Transfer of Shares

Companies must further provide information regarding the restrictions on the transfer of their securities. The TOD lists a number of examples for this, such as **limitations** on the **holding of securities** or the **need** to **obtain** the **approval of the company** or other holders of securities. Not all Member States have the same types of restrictions. Some, such as Germany, permit no limitations on the holding of securities under company law. Italy and the Netherlands, on the other hand, provide the possibility to introduce limitations on the percentage of shares that may be held in the company's articles of association.[30] Where such limitations exist the company must provide information thereon in its annual

---

[24] See R. Veil § 1 para. 19 ff.
[25] Cf. Art. 2(1)(e) TOD.
[26] The European Commission raised this issue for discussion (cf. Consultation document on the modernisation of the Directive 2004/109/EC on the harmonisation of transparency requirements in relation to information about issuers whose securities are admitted to trading on a regulated market, 27 May 2010, p. 5), but did not come back to it (cf. Report from the Commission to the European Parliament, the Council, the European Economic and Social Committee and the Committee of the Regions, Application of Directive 2004/25/EC on takeover bids, 28 June 2012, COM(2012) 347 final).
[27] Cf. Art. 10(2) TOD; on the management report see H. Brinckmann § 18 para. 39.
[28] Cf. Art. 10(3) TOD.
[29] Cf. S. Maul and D. Muffat-Jeandet, AG (2004), 306, 308.
[30] Cf. ibid.

report. Limitations requiring the approval of the company for the transfer of securities are of the greatest relevance in legal practice. In Germany this primarily affects registered shares. Such limitations can impede takeovers[31] and must therefore be disclosed. The aim of the disclosure obligation is to require the company to disclose the conditions that must be met in order for approval to be declared and whether the management or the general shareholders' meeting is responsible for the approval.

3. Significant Shareholdings

19   Companies must further publish information on all significant direct or indirect shareholdings, for example in the form of **pyramid financial schemes** and **cross-shareholdings**. To put the concept of a significant shareholding into more concrete terms, the TOD makes reference to Article 85 of Directive 2001/34/EC, which laid down disclosure requirements regarding major shareholding prior to the enactment of the Transparency Directive (TD) in 2004.[32] According to this former provision, notification obligations ensued if an investor's voting rights reached or exceeded 10%.[33] The annual report of a listed company must therefore only contain information on shareholdings exceeding 10% of the company's capital; indirect holdings must be added to direct holdings in accordance with the provisions on the disclosure of major shareholdings.[34]

20   *Example*: A shareholder has 5% of a company's shares; a subsidiary holds another 3% and further 3% are held by a trustee of the shareholder. In such a scenario the company must publish the total of 11% of the company's shares held by this shareholder in its annual report. It can do so due to the fact that on exceeding a threshold of 10% of the company's shares the shareholder must notify the company of this fact.[35]

21   With the enactment of the TD in 2004 the European legislature undertook fundamental reforms to the regime of disclosure of major shareholdings. It reduced the lowest threshold from 10% to 5%, in order to increase market efficiency. A holding of 5% can be sufficient for exerting considerable influence on a listed company if the shares are mainly free floating. It would be advisable to apply these amendments in securities law to takeover law *de lege ferenda* and also introduce disclosure obligations for major shareholdings from a threshold of 5% onwards in the TD.

4. Holders of Special Rights

22   In its annual report a company must further publish information on holders of any securities with special control rights by name and a description of those rights. Special rights

---

[31] Whether the management or supervisory board may make use of provisions requiring approval in order to prevent a takeover is an entirely different question. This question must be answered under consideration of the management and administrative board's obligation not to take any measures that may prevent a takeover bid (cf. Art. 9 TOD). Preventing a pending takeover will only rarely be in the interest of the company, thus generally prohibiting a refusal to consent.

[32] See R. Veil § 1 para. 19.

[33] Cf. Art. 85(1) in conjunction with Art. 89(1) Directive 2001/34/EC.

[34] Cf. H.-J. Kirsch et al., in: *Beck'sches Handbuch der Rechnungslegung*, Chapter B 510 Content of the management report, para. 213.

[35] See R. Veil § 20 para. 23.

usually refer to the power to name members of the management, administrative or supervisory board. Whether such special rights exist must be determined according to the national law of the respective Member State. In Germany, for example, rights to appoint may only be granted with respect to a certain percentage of the shareholder representatives in the supervisory board.[36] Other special rights cannot be granted due to the fact that the German Stock Corporation Act is conclusive in this respect.[37] Other Member States have introduced different forms of special rights, such a **right to veto**,[38] **multiple voting rights**, common especially in France and Sweden.

5. System of Control for Employee Share Schemes

A company must further make public which system of control exists for any employee share scheme where the control rights are not exercised directly by the employees. Such an indirect influence is usually only possible if the voting rights can be separated from the shares under company law,[39] which is not permitted in a number of Member States. Other possible cases are that the employees hold shares through investment companies[40] or if they jointly hold shares and their voting rights are exercised by a shared proxy.[41]

23

6. Voting Rights

The obligation to publish information on all restrictions on voting rights is a centre-piece of transparency regarding defensive structures and mechanisms envisaged by the companies. The TOD lists examples of restrictions, such as '**limitations** of the **voting rights** of **holders** of a given percentage or number of votes, deadlines for exercising voting rights, or systems whereby, with the company's cooperation, the financial rights attaching to securities are separated from the holding of securities'.[42] Limitations depending on the percentage of number of voting rights held are of varying popularity in the Member States,[43] being prohibited, for example, for listed companies in Germany.[44]

24

'Systems whereby, with the company's cooperation, the financial rights attaching to securities are separated from the holding of securities' must also be made public. This particularly applies to the Dutch certification system.[45]

25

---

[36] A maximum of one third of the members of the supervisory board may be appointed from the pool of shareholders. Cf. § 101(2) AktG.
[37] Cf. § 23(5) AktG.
[38] Cf. S. Maul and D. Muffat-Jeandet, AG (2004), 306, 308.
[39] Cf. H.-J. Kirsch et al., in: *Beck'sches Handbuch der Rechnungslegung*, Chapter B 510 Content of the management report, para. 216.
[40] Cf. C.H. Seibt and K.J. Heiser, AG (2006), 301, 316.
[41] Cf. H.-J. Kirsch et al., in: *Beck'sches Handbuch der Rechnungslegung*, Chapter B 510 Content of the management report, para. 217.
[42] Cf. Art. 10(1)(f) TOD.
[43] Cf. S. Maul and D. Muffat-Jeandet, AG (2004), 306, 309.
[44] Cf. § 134(1) sentence 2 AktG.
[45] On this see S. Maul and D. Muffat-Jeandet, AG (2004), 306, 309.

7. Agreements between Shareholders

26 Any agreements between shareholders which are known to the company and may result in restrictions on the transfer of securities and/or voting rights must also be made public. This includes **agreements** between the shareholders on **how voting rights are to be exercised**,[46] a form of agreement particularly common in companies in which one or more families hold shares.[47]

27 Numerous jurisdictions do not allow the company to have knowledge of these agreements, most shareholders aiming to keep them secret—an interest that is respected in most European jurisdictions. In Germany, for example, the issuer has the right to demand proof of a shareholder's holding in the company,[48] not, however, the right to demand submission of the agreement.[49] If the company does not have any knowledge of the agreement the shareholder need not inform it thereof, unlike in Italy, where a legal obligation to make public agreements between shareholders exists and the agreement will not become effective until it has been made public.

8. Appointment and Replacement of Board Members

28 The annual report must further contain information on the company rules governing the appointment and replacement of board members and the amendment of the articles of association. The reason for this is that an investor may have an interest in replacing the management after a successful takeover, for example, if it follows different strategic aims from the former management. Especially in companies with a two-tier system (board of directors and supervisory board) it can be very difficult for an offeror to replace the management, making it essential to be informed of the legal basis for this in the respective company before the takeover.[50]

29 Generally, it is sufficient if the annual report makes reference to the respective legal provisions. However, the articles of association may contain special provisions on their amendment, for example requiring a higher rate of approval for resolutions (such as 9/10 instead of 3/4 of the represented share capital). In these cases, the articles of association must also be listed in the annual report.[51]

9. Issue and Buyback of Shares

30 A company is also obliged to make public information on the powers of board members to issue and buy back shares. Whilst it need not provide information on the general rights

---

[46] Cf. P. Kajüter, in: Schmidt (ed.), *Münchener Kommentar zum HGB*, § 289a para. 9.
[47] Cf. H.-J. Kirsch et al., in: *Beck'sches Handbuch der Rechnungslegung*, Chapter B 510 Content of the management report, para. 210.
[48] The issuer's right to be informed of major shareholdings as described in § 42 WpHG refers to 'notified shares' under the regime of disclosure of major shareholdings (harmonised in the EU under the Transparency Directive).
[49] Cf. C. Dolff, *Der Rechtsverlust gem. § 28 WpHG aus der Perspektive eines Emittenten* (2011).
[50] Cf. S. Maul and D. Muffat-Jeandet, AG (2009), 306, 309.
[51] Cf. H.-J. Kirsch et al., in: *Beck'sches Handbuch der Rechnungslegung*, Chapter B 510 Content of the management report, para. 219; P. Kajüter, in: Schmidt (ed.), *Münchener Kommentar zum HGB*, § 289a para. 18; S. Maul and D. Muffat-Jeandet, AG (2009), 306, 309.

and obligations of the board members, it must describe the powers conveyed to the management or the administrative board by the articles of association or in resolutions of the general meeting.[52]

It must further inform the public whether the board members are permitted to use authorised capital, issue convertible or participating bonds or acquire the company's shares. Any of these measures could cause the takeover to become more expensive for the offeror, the issue of new shares causing a dilution of the offeror's stocks.

31

10. Change of Control Clauses

European takeover law also requires that the company makes public **any significant agreements** to which the **company** is a **party** and which **take effect, alter** or **terminate upon a change of control of the company** following a takeover bid, and the effects thereof. Such change-of-control clauses can impede or even prevent a company takeover.[53] It is especially important for an offeror to receive information on the possible economic effects resulting from an agreement.[54] The disclosure obligation refers to loan agreements and employment contracts,[55] but exempts any agreements the disclosure of which would be seriously prejudicial to the company.[56] This exception does not, however, apply to cases in which the company is specifically obliged to disclose such information on the basis of other legal requirements.

32

This provision refers to agreements to which the company is party, and therefore does not involve any transparency regarding the contracts that terminate or may be rescinded in subsidiaries due to the takeover.[57] A further problem is the fact that an offeror will not receive any information on agreements with change of control clauses newly concluded during the current fiscal year, as the TOD contains no obligation to keep the information in the annual report up to date.[58]

33

11. Compensation Agreements

The annual report must finally also contain information on the agreements between the company and its board members (**golden parachutes**) or employees (**tin parachutes**) providing compensation if they resign or are made redundant without valid reason or if their employment ceases due to a takeover bid.[59] Such agreements can also hinder a takeover and must therefore be disclosed. The company must further publish the height of the

34

---

[52] Cf. H.-J. Kirsch et al., in: *Beck'sches Handbuch der Rechnungslegung*, Chapter B 510 Content of the management report, para. 219.
[53] Cf. C. Cramer, *Change of Control-Klauseln im deutschen Unternehmensrecht*, 110 ff.
[54] Cf. H.-J. Kirsch et al., in: *Beck'sches Handbuch der Rechnungslegung*, Chapter B 510 Content of the management report, para. 221.
[55] Cf. S. Maul and D. Muffat-Jeandet, AG (2004), 306, 309.
[56] Examples in: C. Cramer, *Change of Control-Klauseln im deutschen Unternehmensrecht*, 289 ff.
[57] Cf. ibid, 294–295.
[58] Seen critically by ibid., 295.
[59] See M. Nussbaum, *Abfindungen und Anerkennungsprämien für Vorstandsmitglieder deutscher Aktiengesellschaften*, 31 ff. and 150 ff., on the admissablilty of such clauses under takeover law.

compensation and the persons benefiting from it, including their position in the company.[60] Otherwise the aim of the provision would not be fulfilled.

12. Conclusion

35 The TOD lays down various disclosure obligations that help to give a potential offeror an idea of the defensive structures and mechanisms in listed companies. These obligations are based on the aim of achieving a functioning market for corporate control, an aim that has been largely achieved. It must be conceded, however, that numerous aspects are in need of reform. One could, for example, discuss whether it has become necessary to require a general disclosure of all agreements between shareholders, following the example of Italy and Spain. Need for action most certainly exists with regard to transparency of change of control clauses. The European provisions allow far too much leeway, enabling disclosure evasion.

---

[60] Cf. H.-J. Kirsch et al., in: *Beck'sches Handbuch der Rechnungslegung*, Chapter B 510 Content of the management report, para. 233; V. Sailer, AG (2006), 913, 921; C.H. Seibt and K.J. Heiser, AG (2006), 301, 316.

§ 38

Public Takeovers

Bibliography

Hamann, Uwe, *Die Angebotsunterlage nach dem WpÜG—Ein praxisorientierter Überblick*, ZIP (2001), 2249–2257; Maul, Silja and Kouloridas, Athanasios, *The Takeover Bids Directive*, 5 GLJ (2004), 355–366; Maul, Silja and Muffat-Jeandet, Danièle, *Die EU-Übernahmerichtlinie–Inhalt und Umsetzung in nationales Recht*, AG (2004), 221–234 and 306–318; McCahery, Joseph A. and Vermeulen, Erik P.M., *The Case Against Reform of the Takeover Bids Directive*, 22 EBLR (2011), 541–557; Ventoruzzo, Marco, *Takeover Regulation as a Wolf in Sheep's Clothing: Taking UK Rules to Continental Europe*, 11 U. Pa. J. Bus. L. (2008–2009), 135–174; Wooldridge, Frank, *The Recent Directive on Takeover-Bids*, 15 EBLR (2000), 147–158.

I. Introduction

Before submitting an acquisition or takeover bid, the bidder usually conducts a **due diligence** of the target company. It is provided with all relevant documents by the board of directors of the target company in order to be able to assess the business and legal risks of the target company. On the one hand, the board of the target company is not obliged to facilitate the due diligence. On the other hand, it is not prohibited to do so. It acts in accordance with its duty if it gives a prospective buyer insight into the business circumstances. However, as a matter of principle the board of directors is not allowed to pass on business secrets. In addition, the board members must observe the prohibition on disclosing inside information.[1] Another question is whether the management of the target company is obliged to conduct due diligence before making an offer. It has to be answered according to the applicable national company law (of the bidder). It has to be taken into account that there may be good reasons to refrain from doing so and to make a takeover bid that has not been coordinated with the management of the target company (so-called hostile takeover bid). 1

It is common practice for the bidder to enter into agreements with the target company in advance of the decision to make a bid. These agreements may be **business combination agreements** which deal with the future reorganisation of the target company and the composition of the management bodies. The limits of the legality of such agreements are to be determined in accordance with the general provisions of company law. Break fee agreements are also common. The purpose of these is that the bidder can demand reimbursement 2

---

[1] See R. Veil § 14 para. 77.

of costs from the target company if the negotiations on a takeover are broken off or fail. Depending on the terms of the agreement, however, they can also take on a punitive character and sanction the termination of negotiations by the board of the target company. The TOD does not provide any rules in this regard. The Takeover Code of the United Kingdom generally prohibits such agreements (cf. Rule 21.2). In Germany, the admissibility of the contractual agreement is determined on the basis of the provisions of the German Stock Corporation Act (in particular §§ 57, 71a (1), 76, 93). To the extent that the bidder does not hold a stake in the target company, a reimbursement of costs by the target company in the event of a breakdown of negotiations is not considered a violation of the rules on capital maintenance. For the management board of the target company, it may be a prudent business decision to promise the bidder a reimbursement of costs.

II. Types of Bids

3   The TOD distinguishes between different types of bids. '**Takeover bid**' or '**bid**' refers to a public offer (other than by the offeree company itself) made to the holders of the securities of a company to acquire all or some of those securities, whether mandatory or voluntary, which follows or has as its objective the acquisition of control of the offeree company.[2] '**Securities**' in the sense of the directive are only transferrable securities carrying voting rights in a company,[3] ie shares. Shares to which no voting rights are attached do not fall within the scope of the directive.[4] The Member States are, however, not prevented from extending the scope of application of the TOD in their national implementing takeover laws.[5]

4   The TOD applies to bids that refer to a certain percentage of shares (ie 10%) and to bids referring to all shares, the latter being called a takeover bid. Should the offeror have gained control of the company following a voluntary bid, ie by enlarging his percentage of shares from 15% to 40% by way of a public offer, the TOD requires him to make a bid to all holders of the offeree company's securities,[6] the only exception being for cases in which control was acquired following a voluntary bid made to all the holders of securities for their entire holdings.[7]

III. Decision to Launch a Bid

5   Member States have to ensure that a **decision** to make a bid is **made public** without delay and that the supervisory authority is informed of the bid.[8] This requirement is based on the

---

[2] Cf. Art. 2(1)(a) TOD.
[3] Cf. Art. 2(1)(e) TOD.
[4] Cf. S. Maul and D. Muffat-Jeandet, AG (2004), 221, 225–226.
[5] Cf. Recital 11 TOD.
[6] Cf. S. Maul and D. Muffat-Jeandet, AG (2004), 221, 225.
[7] Cf. Art. 5(2) TOD.
[8] Cf. Art. 6(1) TOD.

European legislature's aim to reduce the possibilities for insider dealings.[9] The concept of this disclosure obligation is thus part of the obligation to disclose inside information as laid down in the MAR.

The TOD does not contain any provisions on the necessity to **finance** a takeover bid. It only requires that an offeror must announce a bid only after ensuring that he can fulfil in full any cash consideration, if such is offered, and after taking all reasonable measures to secure the implementation of any other type of consideration.[10] The national legislatures of the Member States have therefore determined that the offeror must take the necessary measures to ensure that at the time at which the claim for consideration falls due, it has the necessary means at its disposal for performing the offer in full. The TOD does not provide for specific rules on the price with regard to takeover bids (cf. para. 11). Only the general principle that the shareholders of the target company are to be treated equally applies.[11] Consideration may consist of a cash payment (**cash offer**) or liquid shares admitted to trading on an organised market and conferring voting rights (**exchange offer**). If the shareholders of the target company are to be offered cash, a bank must confirm that the offeror has taken the necessary measures.

IV. Offer Document

The Member States must ensure that an offeror draws up and makes public in good time an offer document containing the information necessary to enable the holders of the offeree company's securities—including shares—to reach a properly informed decision on the bid.[12] The offer document constitutes the offer to acquire securities as required under civil law.[13] Its necessary content is described in the TOD in detail[14] and includes the terms of the offer and the identity of the offeror.

Whilst the details of the offer document need not be examined any closer, it is important to know that the **offeror** must also give **information** on his **intentions** with regard to the future business of the offeree company. The TOD puts the offeror's obligation to make his intentions regarding the future business of the offeree company public into more concrete terms, requiring that the offeror also provides information on his **strategic plans** for the company and the likely repercussions for employment and companies' places of business.[15]

Before the offered document is made public the offeror shall communicate it to the supervisory authority for examination.[16] The Member States can determine that the publication of the offer document is subject to the prior approval by the supervisory authority. In this

---

[9] Cf. Recital 12 TOD.
[10] Cf. Art. 3(1)(e) TOD.
[11] Cf. Art. 3(1)(a) TOD.
[12] Cf. Art. 6(2) TOD.
[13] Cf. W. Renner, in: W. Haarmann and M. Schüppen (eds.), *Frankfurter Kommentar zum WpÜG*, § 11 para. 13; G.F. Thoma, in: T. Baums and G.F. Thoma (eds.), *Kommentar zum WpÜG*, § 11 para. 6.
[14] Cf. Art. 6(3) TOD.
[15] Cf. Art. 6(3)(i) TOD.
[16] Cf. Art. 6(2) sentence 2 TOD.

case, the offer document may not be made public until the supervisory authority has explicitly agreed to its publication or a certain time frame has elapsed without the supervisory authority prohibiting the publication.

10   As soon as the bid has been made public, the boards of the offeree company and the offeror shall inform the representatives of their respective employees or, where there are no such representatives, the employees themselves.[17]

11   The TOD does not contain any provisions on the consideration for takeover bids, merely determining in cases of **mandatory bids** that the **price** must be **equitable**.[18] In case of a takeover bid, the offeror can therefore at its discretion offer **cash** or **liquid shares** admitted to trading on a regulated market and conferring voting rights. The fact that the TOD does not contain any provisions on the type of consideration means, however, that the Member States are free to lay down their own rules in this regard, requiring, for example, cash payments in certain cases. A reason for such a provision could be the aim of ensuring an equal treatment of shareholders. In the case of a takeover bid, there is, of course, no particular need to provide specifications for the price, because the bidder typically has an incentive to offer a reasonable price. Otherwise, the shareholders of the target company will not accept the offer.

12   The board of the offeree company provides a document setting out its opinion on the bid and the reasons on which this is based in order to supply the shareholders with all information necessary in order to decide on the acceptance of the offer (**statement on the offer**). In particular, the document must contain the type and amount of the consideration, the expected implications of a successful offer, the strategy and aim the offeror pursues with the takeover bid and, provided members of the managing or supervisory board are also shareholders of the target company, information as to whether they intend to accept the offer.[19]

13   Member States shall determine that the time allowed for the acceptance of a bid may be neither less than two weeks nor more than ten weeks from the date of publication of the offered document.[20] This **limitation** of the **time frame** takes into account the fact that a takeover situation has negative effects on the target company. Under certain circumstances it can, however, be appropriate to provide a longer time period for the acceptance of a bid. Therefore, Member States may determine that the period of ten weeks may be extended under the condition that the offeror gives at least two weeks' notice of his/her intention to close the bid.[21] The aim of this is to enable small shareholders to accept a takeover bid when it becomes apparent that the takeover will be successful. Finally, Member States may provide for rules changing the period of acceptance in specific cases.[22] Some Member States have made use of this possibility for cases in which the offeror changes the offer. The shareholders then have a certain time frame in which they can decide to accept the offer. An extension of the acceptance period is also possible in case of a competing bid.

---

[17] Cf. Art. 6(1) sentence 2 TOD.
[18] Cf. Art. 5(4) TOD.
[19] Cf. Art. 9(5) TOD.
[20] Cf. Art. 7(1) TOD.
[21] Cf. Art. 7(1) sentence 2 TOD.
[22] Cf. Art. 7(2) TOD.

§ 39

Mandatory Bid

Bibliography

Agstner, Peter and Mascheroni, Davide M., *Breach of the Mandatory Bid Rule: Minority Shareholders' Protection in the Public vs. Private Enforcement Debate*, ECFR (2020), 726–759; Baj, Claude, *Action de concert et dépôt obligatoire d'une offre publique d'achat: deux réflexions à la lumière de l'affaire Eiffage*, 3 RDBF (2008), 8–9; Baj, Claude, *L'action de concert dans l'affaire Eiffage: les aspects débattus*, 3 RDBF (2008), 10–17; Baums, Theodor, *Low Balling, Creeping in und deutsches Übernahmerecht*, ZIP (2010), 2374–2390; Biard, Jean-François, *Action de concert et non-conformité d'une offre publique*, 5 RDBF (2008), 67–73; Bolle, Caroline, *A Comparative Overview of the Mandatory Bid Rule in Belgium, France, Germany and the United Kingdom* (2008); Bonneau, Thierry and Pietrancosta, Alain, *Acting in concert in French Capital Markets and Takeover Law*, 1 RTDF (2013), 37–43; Brellochs, Michael, *Konzernrechtliche Beherrschung und übernahmerechtliche Kontrolle*, NZG (2012), 1010–1019; Cahn, Andreas, *Der Kontrollbegriff des WpÜG*, in: Mülbert, Peter O., Kiem, Roger and Wittig, Arne (eds.), *10 Jahre WpÜG*, ZHR Beiheft 76 (2011), 77–107; Crawshay, Charles M., *Mandatory Bids in UK*, in: Veil, Rüdiger (ed.), *Übernahmerecht in Praxis und Wissenschaft* (2009), 83–92; Fleischer, Holger, *Finanzinvestoren im ordnungspolitischen Gesamtgefüge von Aktien-, Bankaufsichts- und Kapitalmarktrecht*, ZGR (2008), 185–224; Hopt, Klaus J., *European Takeover Reform of 2012/2013—Time to Re-examine the Mandatory Bid*, 15 EBOR (2014), 143–190; Kalss, Susanne, *Creeping-in und Beteiligungspublizität nach österreichischem Recht*, in: Kämmerer Axel and Veil, Rüdiger (eds.), *Übernahme- und Kapitalmarktrecht in der Reformdiskussion*, 2013, 139–162; Krause, Hartmut, *Stakebuilding im Kapitalmarkt- und Übernahmerecht*, in: Kämmerer Axel and Veil, Rüdiger (eds.), *Übernahme- und Kapitalmarktrecht in der Reformdiskussion* (2013), 163–197; Le Nabasque, Hervé, *Annotation to CA Paris, 1re ch., sect. H., 2 April 2008, Sté Sacyr Vallehermoso c/Sté Eiffage*, 3 RDBF (2008), 54–55; Strunk, Klaus-Jürgen/Holst, Raven/Salomon, Heike, *Aktuelle Entwicklungen im Übernahmerecht*, in: Veil, Rüdiger (ed.), *Übernahmerecht in Praxis und Wissenschaft* (2009), 1–42; Tountopoulos, Vassilios, *Anlegerschutz bei unterlassenem Pflichtangebot nach europäischem Kapitalmarktrecht*, WM (2014), 337–346; Veil, Rüdiger, *Acting in Concert in Capital Markets and Takeover Law—Need for a Further Harmonisation in Europe?*, 1 RTDF (2013), 33–37; Winner, Martin, *Active Shareholders and European Takeover Regulation*, ECFR (2014), 364–392.

I. Introduction

An investor can gain control over the target company without having made a takeover bid. In such cases, the Member States are required to maintain shareholder protection under the Takeover Directive (TOD), by ensuring that the offeror is required to make a bid addressed to all minority shareholders for all their holdings at an equitable price as a means of protection. 1

2   The obligation to make such a bid when having gained control is discussed controversially in literature. One main point of criticism is that the mandatory bid makes public takeovers more costly and thus weakens the market for corporate control. However, there are strong reasons for this rule. The mandatory bid's primary **aim** is one under company law: the TOD assumes that it is necessary to **protect minority shareholders**.[1] The mandatory bid can thus be understood as a special concept of company law, protecting shareholders in cases in which the company is to become part of a group and faces the danger of tunnelling (transfer of assets and profits for the benefit of the mother company). The preventative measure of a mandatory bid is not seen as unnecessary solely on account that the target company is protected from detrimental influence by the controlling company under the national company laws of the Member States.

3   The mandatory offer can, furthermore, also be understood as an element of capital markets law: the target company's shareholders based their decision to invest in the company on the fact that the company had no major shareholder who could considerably influence the future of the company. The mandatory offer thus improves the proper functioning of the capital markets by increasing investor confidence in the fact that the company had no controlling shareholder at the time of their decision and thus was independent. Finally, the rules on mandatory bids can be justified by the fact that they prevent inefficient takeovers.[2]

II. Prerequisites

4   When, as a **result** of an **acquisition of shares**, a natural or legal person holds **securities** in a company which, added to any existing holdings of those securities, directly or indirectly **give** him a **specified percentage** of **voting rights** and thus **control** of that company, the person must make a mandatory bid to all shareholders for their shares.[3] Securities are to be understood as **shares** in the company.

5   *Example*: A shareholder is in possession of 10% of a company's shares and acquires a further 25%. Assuming the threshold for control lies at 30%, this shareholder has then obtained a percentage of voting rights giving it control of the company, and is therefore obliged to make a bid for the additional 65%.

6   It is relevant to determine where '**control**' of a company begins. The European legislature left this question open: the percentage of voting rights required for control of a company and the calculation of this percentage must be determined under the national laws of the Member State in which the company has its seat.[4]

The Member States have introduced very different thresholds regarding the concept of control.[5] Some Member States introduced thresholds as high as 40% (Lithuania and the

---

[1] Cf. Art. 5(1) TOD.
[2] In more detail K.J. Hopt, 15 EBOR (2014), 143, 166–171.
[3] Cf. Art. 5(1) TOD.
[4] Cf. Art. 5(3) TOD.
[5] Cf. Commission Staff Working Document, Report on the implementation of the Directive on Takeover Bids, 21 February 2007, SEC(2007) 268, Annex 2, p. 13–14.

Czech Republic), 50% (Latvia and Malta) or even 66% (Poland). In most Member States, such as Austria, Belgium, Cyprus, Finland, France, Germany, Ireland, Italy, the Netherlands and Spain, and in other European countries, such as the United Kingdom, the threshold lies at 30% of all voting rights. Other Member States, such as Luxembourg, Slovakia and Switzerland have opted for a threshold of 33.33%. Hungary and Slovenia only require 25% of the voting rights for control of the company.

The **mandatory bid** must be addressed **to all shareholders** of the target company. This means that partial bids are inadmissible. The purpose is to protect all shareholders. 7

The TOD stipulates several **requirements** for the **price**. Article 5(4) subsec. 1 sentence 1 TOD provides for a **pre-acquisition rule**. 'The highest price paid for the same securities by the offeror, or by persons acting in concert with him/her, over a period, to be determined by Member States, of not less than six months and not more than 12 before the bid [...] shall be regarded as the equitable price.' In addition, the bidder has to consider the **parallel acquisition rule**, laid down in Article 5(4) subsec. 1 sentence 2 TOD: 'If, after the bid has been made public and before the offer closes for acceptance, the offeror or any person acting in concert with him/her purchases securities at a price higher than the offer price, the offeror shall increase his/her offer so that it is not less than the highest price paid for the securities so acquired.' Finally, Member States may authorise their supervisory authorities to adjust the price in certain circumstances.[6] By way of example, the TOD mentions cases where the highest price was set by agreement between the purchaser and a seller, where the market prices of the securities in question have been manipulated, where market prices in general or certain market prices in particular have been affected by exceptional occurrences, or in order to enable a firm in difficulty to be rescued. According to the concept of the TOD, Member States may determine the conditions under which the maximum price may be adjusted upwards or downwards and the criteria to be used in these cases, such as market value, break-up value or other objective valuation criteria generally used in financial analysis. The European courts have already dealt with these rules, which are implemented very differently in the Member States, on several occasions.[7] 8

III. Exemptions from the Mandatory Bid

The TOD does not state whether the term 'control' is to be defined in a formal or material way by the Member States. Most opted for a formal definition of control which does not require an actual controlling influence of voting rights for the assumption of control (**formal concept**). Whilst this concept has the advantage of legal certainty, its results are not always convincing. If, for example, shareholder A has acquired 32% of a company's shares and the company has a further major shareholder, holding 55% of all shares and all other shares are in free float, shareholder A will not be able to take any control at the general 9

---

[6] Cf. Art. 5 (4) subsec. 2 TOD.
[7] EFTA of 10.12.2010 – E-1/10 (Periscopus AS/Oslo Bors AS and Erika Must AS), [2009–2010] EFTA Ct. Rep. 198; ECJ of 20.7.2017 – C-206/16 (Marco Tronchetti Provera SpA/Consob); ECJ of 10.12.2020 – C-735/19 (Euromin Holdings (Cyprus) Ltd/Finanšu un kapitāla tirgus komisija).

shareholder meeting. In such cases, the mandatory bid rule is not really justified. The share package of 32% does not give the holder any possibility to exercise control. Takeover law must therefore provide the possibility for a shareholder to be exempted from the obligation to give a bid. The TOD has determined that this is a matter for the national laws of the Member States who can decide independently whether and under which conditions an offeror can be exempted from making a mandatory bid.[8] The differing national provisions play an important role in the legal practice of takeovers.[9] Member States following a formal concept of control have had to introduce further-reaching exemptions than those Member States adopting a material approach to the concept of control.[10]

10 The rules on the exemption from a mandatory bid vary between the different Member States. Whilst some Member States provide for an automatic **exemption *ex lege*** if certain conditions are fulfilled, other Member States grant the **supervisory authorities** the power **to decide** on an **exemption**, albeit only with a limited discretion for this decision, specific conditions pre-determining when an exemption from the mandatory bid is to be granted.[11]

11 Determining 'control' on the basis of fixed percentages has the advantage of legal certainty. It has the disadvantage, however, that cases in which an acquisition of shares below this threshold already enables an investor to influence important personnel decisions allowing him to follow his strategic aims, cannot be covered. This can especially be the case when the attendance rate at the general shareholder meeting of the target company is low.

12 *Example*: Shareholder A has acquired 28% of the shares. If the company does not have any other major shareholder, all other shares being in free float, and if—as is regularly the case—only 30% of these shares are represented at the general shareholder meeting of the company, this allows A to assert himself against 21.6% of the voting shares in all agenda items for which the resolution is passed with a simple majority of votes, ie in particular with regard to the appointment of members of the board of directors in a company with a single-tier management or respectively members of the supervisory board in a company with a dual-tier management system.

13 The disadvantage of the formal definition of the term control is much criticised.[12] It is argued that control can be exercised even below the threshold. Certain takeovers have shown that provisions preventing circumvention are necessary. Nevertheless, the more compelling reasons speak in favour of a formal definition of control. It is necessary for it to be clearly defined whether the obligations resulting from a takeover situation exist in a certain case. Whether takeover law applies to a specific case should be determinable on the basis of legally certain rules.[13] Should it become apparent that the current approach indeed does not provide sufficient shareholder protection, it would be preferable to simply reduce

---

[8] Cf. Art. 4(5) sentence 2 in conjunction with Art. 4(2)(e) TOD; P.O. Mülbert, NZG (2004), 633, 641.
[9] Cf. on the legal practice of takeovers in Germany K.-J. Strunk et al. (eds.), in: Veil (ed.), *Übernahmerecht in Praxis und Wissenschaft*, 1, 23; on the legal practice in England C.M. Crawshay, in: Veil (ed.), *Übernahmerecht in Praxis and Wissenschaft*, 83, 89.
[10] The Commission concluded further investigation on how minority shareholders are protected when a national derogation to the mandatory bid rule applies. Cf. Commission, Report on the Application of Directive 2004/25/EC on takeover bids, 28 June 2012, COM(2012) 347 final, p. 10.
[11] Cf. the study compiled for the European Commission by Marccus Partners, The Takeover Bids Directive Assessment Report, p. 139 ff.
[12] Cf. A. Cahn, in: Mülbert et al. (eds.), *10 Jahre WpÜG*, ZHR Beiheft 76 (2011), 77, 97.
[13] Cf. M. Brellochs, NZG (2012), 1010.

the threshold from which onward control over a company is assumed, for example to 25% of the voting rights.

IV. Creeping-in

Some jurisdictions have introduced second thresholds at 50% of the voting rights. The main reason for such an additional threshold is to prevent the rules regarding mandatory bids from being circumvented. This was the case particularly through so-called *low ball offers*, in which the offeror obtains a share package just below the control threshold before at a later point in time with a favourable share price either exceeding the threshold by acquiring a few additional shares and thereby triggering the obligation to make a mandatory bid, or by submitting a voluntary takeover bid.[14] In both cases the offeror only has to acquire a few shares. Some Member States, such as France and Austria, reacted to these methods by extending the rules on mandatory bid,[15] following the example of the United Kingdom where offerors must make mandatory bids for every additional acquisition of shares after the 30% threshold.[16] The European Commission announced that it planned to take the necessary measures in order to prevent the circumventive practices developing in the EU.[17] As yet, however, no such measures have been proposed.

V. Gaining Control by Acting in Concert

1. Legal Foundations

The Transparency Directive (TD) contains detailed provisions concerning the attribution of voting rights in order to determine disclosure obligations. It particularly contains rules on the attribution of voting rights in corporate groups, attached to shares held in trust or held by persons acting in concert.[18]

The TOD, however, leaves these questions to the discretion of the Member States,[19] only requiring that a mandatory offer must be made as soon as the acquisition of shares—by the person himself or by persons acting in concert with him—leads to a total sum of voting rights sufficient for him to take control of the company.[20] In this context, 'persons acting in concert' are defined by the TOD as any **natural** or **legal person** who **cooperates** with the **offeror** or the offeree company on the **basis** of an **agreement**, either express or tacit, either

---

[14] The cases *Porsche/VW* (2006/2007) and *ACS/Hochtief* (2007) were particularly spectacular.
[15] Cf. S. Kalss, in: Kämmerer and Veil (eds.), *Übernahme- und Kapitalmarktrecht in der Reformdiskussion*, 139, 154 f.; H. Merkt, in: Veil (ed.), *Übernahmerecht in Praxis und Wissenschaft*, 53, 71 ff.
[16] Cf. C. Crawshay, in: Veil (ed.), *Übernahmerecht in Praxis und Wissenschaft*, 83, 85.
[17] COM(2012) 347 final (fn. 10), p. 10.
[18] Thus stakebuilding is revealed at an early stage. See R. Veil § 20 para. 41 ff.
[19] Cf. Art. 5(3) TOD.
[20] Cf. Art. 5(1) TOD.

oral or written, **aimed** either at **acquiring control** of the offeree company or at **frustrating the successful outcome** of a **bid**.[21]

17   The Member States are thus not entirely free in their understanding of the term 'acting in concert': a mandatory bid must be made even when control has only been gained through an 'acting in concert',[22] and an agreement on the acquisition of shares may also lead to the obligation to make a mandatory bid.[23] Whilst France[24] and Austria[25] adhere strictly to this understanding, Germany has introduced its own definition of 'acting in concert'.[26]

2. Legal Practice in the Member States

18   The Member States' experience with acting in concert varies considerably. This is mainly due to the fact that neither the TD nor the TOD gives a precise definition of the concept, only minimum requirements regarding implementation, thus permitting Member States to exceed these and introduce stricter rules.

19   It therefore comes as no surprise that national concepts of acting in concert differ greatly. A description of all the national rules on takeover law would go beyond the scope of this book.[27] We shall rather depict the problems encountered by the supervisory authorities and courts in legal practice on the basis of two cases, when determining whether shareholders are acting in concert. Both also show the difficulties of regulating the concept of acting in concert at a European level.

(a) Sacyr/Eiffage (France)

20   *Facts (abridged)*:[28] The Spanish company Sacyr had first acquired shares in the French company Eiffage in December 2005 and had subsequently attempted to merge the two companies. At Eiffage's general meeting in April 2007, the chair of the general meeting denied Sacyr's voting rights and those of 88 other Spanish shareholders due to the fact that they had failed to disclose that they had exceeded one of the thresholds by acting in concert. On 19 April 2007 Sacyr made an exchange offer for shares of Eiffage. At this time Sacyr held 33.32% of Eiffage's nominal capital and 29.61% of all voting rights. The AMF declared the public exchange offer to be illegal and required Sacyr to make a mandatory bid for Eiffage and another mandatory bid for the Eiffage-subsidiary Autoroutes Paris-Rhin-Rhône (APRR) which constituted one of the main assets of Eiffage.

21   The case of *Sacyr/Eiffage* shows how difficult it is in legal practice to determine when shareholders are acting in concert and must therefore be obliged to make a mandatory bid. The AMF reasoned that Sacyr, acting in concert with at least six other shareholders, had exceeded the threshold of holding one-third of Eiffage's capital and had acquired more

---

[21] Cf. Art. 2(1) TOD.
[22] Cf. P.O. Mülbert, NZG (2004), 633, 642.
[23] Cf. P.O. Mülbert, NZG (2004), 633, 642; H. Fleischer, ZGR (2008), 185, 198–199.
[24] Cf. the famous case *Gecina*: CA Paris, 1re ch., 24 Juin 2008, no. 07–21.048, *Société Gecina*, with annotations by T. Bonneau, Dr. soc. Oct. 2008, 39 ff.; F. Martin Laprade, Rev. soc. (2008), 644 ff.; H. Le Nabasque, Bull. Joly Soc. (2008), 135 ff.; published in J.-F. Biard, RDBF (2008), 67, 70 ff.
[25] Cf. § 1(6) ÜbG.
[26] Cf. § 30(2) WpÜG.
[27] See for a detailed analysis C. Bolle, *A Comparative Overview of the Mandatory Bid Rule* (2008).
[28] CA Paris, 1re ch., sect. H, 2 Avril 2008, no. 2007/11675, *Sacyr Vallehermoso SA et autres c/ Eiffage SA*, Dr. soc. Oct. 2008, 35 ff. Summarised by J. Baj, RDBF (2008), 8–9.

than 5% of its nominal capital within the last 12 months. This resulted in an obligation to make a mandatory bid with an optional cash offer, the minimum price corresponding at least with the highest share price paid by Sacyr and the other persons acting in concert within the last 12 months.[29]

The court subsequently entrusted with the case also came to the conclusion that the shareholders had made an agreement to act in concert at the extraordinary general meeting in April 2007 with the aim of achieving a reorganisation of the administrative board that would allow Sacyr to merge the two companies.[30] Neither the AMF nor the court could prove that such an agreement had actually been reached. They based their decision solely on circumstantial evidence, the most relevant elements being:

— Sacyr's request to appoint its own representatives to the administrative board was dismissed at the general meeting on 19 April 2006. Sacyr had not yet achieved this aim by April 2007.
— According to its declaration of intent of 5 April 2006[31] based on Article L. 233-7 C. com., Sacyr intended neither to take control of Eiffage nor to make a public offer. This was repeated only a few days before the draft exchange offer was submitted.
— Between 19 April 2006 and 23 March 2007 Sacyr acquired about 2.2 million shares of Eiffage (a quarter of these within the last four days), thereby increasing its shareholding to 33.32%.
— Sacyr wanted to be introduced to the shareholders that were to support Sacyr's request to nominate five representatives of the administrative board at the general meeting on 19 April 2006. Sacyr asked its bank for the necessary contact information.
— The six other persons acting in concert all acquired shares in Eiffage between June 2006 and March 2007, all remaining below the 1% threshold. If they had reached this threshold, they would have been legally obliged to disclose their shareholdings under Eiffage's articles of association.
— Two of these companies temporarily exceeded the 1% threshold without complying with their notification obligations, before quickly reducing their shares to below 1% once again.
— The management and/or shareholders of five of the companies acting in concert with Sacyr had a personal, financial or business interest in Sacyr. Their company purposes were entirely different to Sacyr's.

Even in countries where acting in concert does not require a legally binding agreement between the shareholders, it can be difficult to prove concerted action. In 2005,[32] for example, the German BaFin was not able to prove that several institutional investors around the British TCI The Children's Investment Fund Management were acting in concert. BaFin therefore could not require them to make a mandatory bid to the other shareholders of Deutsche Börse AG.[33]

---

[29] A mandatory bid would have been double as expensive for *Sacyr*.
[30] The court agreed with the AMF that the exchange offer was illegal, however, reversing the obligation to make a mandatory bid on the basis of a procedural error, as the AMF had omitted to hear the other parties acting in concert. The court avoided using the term *action de concert*, rather speaking of a *démarche collective organisée*. Seen critically by H. Le Nabasque, RDBF (2008), 54–55.
[31] On this disclosure obligation see R. Veil § 20 para. 129–132.
[32] German takeover law defines acting in concert as any behaviour of the offeror concerning the target company that has been adjusted on the basis of an agreement or in any other way (cf. § 30(2) WpÜG). A concerted action 'in another way' is defined as any legally non-binding agreement or concerted behaviour without the intention to thereby be legally bound.
[33] Cf. BaFin, Press Release, 19 October 2005: 'However, the statements provided by the parties involved did not provide sufficient proof that the fund companies coordinated their efforts to exert influence on Deutsche Börse's management and supervisory boards.'

(b) WMF (Germany)

24 *Facts (abridged):*[34] In 1993, a former major shareholder (G) of a listed stock corporation sold some of his shares to three financial investors. Ten years later G and the financial investors agreed to vote unanimously at the upcoming general meeting for certain candidates at the election of the shareholder representatives for the supervisory board. Despite this agreement they could not agree on a chairman for the board of directors: G wanted to elect his representative M, whilst the financial investors wanted to vote for A. Shortly before the general meeting, the financial investors informed G that they expected him to vote for A and would not accept an abstention from the vote. G, as requested by the investors, succumbed and the shareholder representatives for the supervisory board were elected in the general meeting according to the plan. The supervisory board then nominated A as its chairman and M as second deputy chairman. G later claimed interest payments from one of the financial investors and argued the voting rights of the other financial investors had to be attributed to this investor due to concerted action, subsequent to which the defendant had gained control of the company.

25 The case of *WMF* depicts clearly how difficult it is to draw the line between influence on the management and supervisory board that is not relevant under takeover law and actual control over the company. In a principle-establishing judgment the BGH ruled on a number of interpretational aspects.[35] Firstly, the court ruled that the motivation behind an agreement played no role for the question as to whether the parties had acted in concert. Concerted action can therefore also be assumed if the behaviour is the result of a struggle for power between two or more major shareholders. In the case at hand, it was therefore not only the financial investors who had acted in concert but also the financial investors with the former major shareholder (G). According to the wording of the provision, this rule of German takeover law, however, only applies to agreements that refer to the exercise of voting rights attached to shares of the target company, ie only to voting rights at the general meeting.[36]

26 Supervisory board votes are therefore not subject to the rules on acting in concert. The BGH justified this interpretation with the wording of the statute. The provision could also not be applied analogously to this case. Capital markets law provisions are generally not applicable by analogy. The violation of the provisions on mandatory offers is subject to fines. They are thus to be understood as a part of criminal law, which under the German constitution is subject to a strict prohibition of analogies to the detriment of the respective person.[37] The BGH also did not see the necessity to class agreements regarding the vote for a chair and deputy chair of the supervisory board as concerted acts: all members of the supervisory board are bound by the company's best interests. They are free from taking any orders and it would therefore be inappropriate to treat them as shareholder representatives.[38]

3. Attempts to Further Harmonise the Concept

27 The interpretation by the French and German courts proves how difficult it is to define the concept of acting in concert at a European level. Strict rules may even be counterproductive

---

[34] BGH of 18.9.2006 – II ZR 137/05, BGHZ 169, 98.
[35] The attribution of voting rights on the basis of an *acting in concert* is based on § 30(2) WpÜG.
[36] Cf. BGH of 18.9.2006 – II ZR 137/05, BGHZ 169, 98, 105 para. 17.
[37] Cf. BGH of 18.9.2006 – II ZR 137/05, BGHZ 169, 98, 106 para. 17.
[38] Cf. BGH of 18.9.2006 – II ZR 137/05, BGHZ 169, 98, 106 para. 18.

as effective corporate governance has an interest in having active shareholders that clearly describe their interests to the management. The notion of acting in concert must also take into account the underlying concepts of company law. The provisions under company law regarding the rights and duties of board members and members of the administrative board have not been harmonised at a European level. It is therefore essential to determine the rights and obligations of these persons according to the respective Member State's law before any conclusions can be drawn regarding the concept of acting in concert.

For institutional investors it is important to be able to determine a possible acting in concert and the resulting obligation to make a mandatory bid with legal certainty. This was acknowledged by the European Commission in its Report on the application of the TOD.[39] Its action plan on European company law and corporate governance states that 'effective, sustainable shareholder engagement is one of the cornerstones of listed companies' corporate governance model'.[40] Furthermore the Commission concluded that if clarification on the concept of acting in concert were not provided, 'shareholders may avoid cooperation, which in turn could undermine the potential for long-term engaged share ownership under which shareholders effectively hold the board accountable for its actions.'

28

A uniform understanding of acting in concert should, however, not be achieved through further harmonisation but rather through guidelines to be provided by ESMA. **ESMA** has thus published a **public statement** on '**information on shareholder cooperation and acting in concert under the Takeover Bids Directive**'.[41] Whilst this statement is not legally binding, it does prove helpful to institutional investors in as far as it contains a 'white list' of activities, such as 'entering into discussions with each other about possible matters to be raised with the company's board' will 'not, *in and of itself*, lead to a conclusion that the shareholders are acting in concert.'

29

VI. Conclusion

Whether the obligation to make a mandatory bid is really legitimate can clearly be disputed—especially in cases where investors are very effectively protected by company law—as is the case in the US[42] and in Germany.[43] Nevertheless, a mandatory offer is still justified in these jurisdictions, too, fulfilling an essential function under capital markets law.[44]

30

It seems acceptable that the TOD does not contain a precise threshold at which control of the company is taken—the national provisions to this respect only differ marginally.

31

---

[39] COM(2012) 347 final (fn. 10), p. 9.
[40] Cf. Communication from the Commission to the European Parliament, the Council, the European Economic and Social Committee and the Committee of the Regions, European company law and corporate governance—a modern legal framework for more engaged shareholders and sustainable companies, 12 December 2012, COM(2012) 740 final, p. 8.
[41] ESMA, Public statement, Information on shareholder cooperation and acting in concert under the Takeover Bids Directive, 1st update, 20 June 2014, ESMA/2014/677.
[42] Cf. K.J. Hopt, 15 EBOR (2014), 143, 170, regarding the US, where the acquirer of a controlling block shareholding needs the authorisation of the company's board for certain transactions for a period of three to five years.
[43] In Germany shareholders of a stock corporation are protected under the provisions of group law (§§ 291–324 AktG).
[44] US-American law does, however, not provide a mandatory bid rule.

As opposed to this, the fact that the TOD does not define precisely how the voting rights held by the respective person are to be calculated must be viewed critically. It would be recommendable to determine this at a European level, whilst at the same time possibly even amending the respective provisions in the TOD. The so-called *creeping-in* phenomenon is also subject to very different rules in the Member States. It would be desirable that Europe achieves a uniform solution in this respect. This is also true with regard to the situation of acting in concert. It is recommendable to develop a uniform definition of this concept and ensure a uniform application across the EU. ESMA's information on shareholder cooperation and acting in concert is only a first step.[45]

---

[45] See in more detail R. Veil, 1 RTDF (2013), 33, 35–37; M. Winner, ECFR (2014), 364, 387–392.

§ 40

Defence against Takeover Bids

Bibliography
Bainbridge, Stephen M, *Director Primacy in Corporate Takeovers*, Delaware Journal of Corporate Law (2006), 769–863; Bebchuk, Lucian A, Coates IV, John C. and Subramanian, Guhan, *The Powerful Antitakeover Force of Staggered Boards: Theory, Evidence, and Policy*, Stanford Law Review (2002), 887–951; Goergen, Marc, Martynova, Marina and Renneboog, Luc, *Corporate Governance Convergence: Evidence From Takeover Regulation Reforms in Europe*, Oxford Review of Economic Policy (2005), 243–268; Hill, Jennifer G., *Takeovers, Poison Pills and Protectionism in Comparative Corporate Governance*, in: Grundmann, Stefan et al. (eds.), *Festschrift für Klaus J. Hopt zum 70. Geburtstag* (2010), 795–815; Hopt, Klaus, *Europäisches Übernahmerecht* (2013); Pisani, Hervé, *Public Tender Offers in France. The Sanofi–Aventi Case*, in: Veil, Rüdiger/Drinkuth, Henrik (eds.), *Reformbedarf im Übernahmerecht* (2015), 85–94; Veil, Rüdiger, *Die Übernahmerichtlinie und ihre Auswirkungen auf das nationale Übernahmerecht*, in: Veil, Rüdiger/Drinkuth, Henrik (eds.), *Reformbedarf im Übernahmerecht* (2015), 95–112; Ventoruzzo, Marco, *Empowering Shareholders in Dirctors' Elections: A Revolution in the Making*, European Company and Financial Law Review (2011), 105–144; Wymeersch, Eddy, *Shareholder(s) matter(s)*, in: Grundmann, Stefan et al. (eds.), *Festschrift für Klaus J. Hopt zum 70. Geburtstag* (2010), Volume 1, 1565–1592.

I. Board Members

The board of the target company may be inclined to prevent the takeover bid because the bidder wants to replace the board after a successful takeover. It is therefore of key importance whether the board is also empowered to take defensive measures. Numerous strategies and measures come into consideration. There are no concerns if the board of directors searches for a **competing offer**, the white knight. If another investor is willing to take over the company, this can only be advantageous for the shareholders of the target company, because they are given another opportunity to sell their shares. It is more difficult to assess whether the board of the target company may make it more difficult for the bidder to obtain the necessary controlling majority or whether it may take measures that result in the takeover becoming more expensive. For example, in the case of crown jewels defensive, the attractiveness of the company for a bidder is reduced by selling or spinning off those parts of the company or assets with synergy potential that are of interest to a bidder. 1

The European legislator pursues the goal of effectively protecting shareholders. This is already expressed in recital 16 TOD: 'In order to prevent operations which could frustrate a bid, the powers of the board of an offeree company to engage in operations of an exceptional nature should be limited, without unduly hindering the offeree company in carrying on its 2 normal business activities.' In this sense, Article 3(1)(c) TOD stipulates that 'the **board** of an **offeree company** must **act** in the **interests** of the **company** as a whole and must not deny the holders of securities the opportunity to decide on the merits of the bid.'

3   Internationally, different approaches can be identified as to what powers and duties the board has in takeover bids. On the one hand, it is conceivable to subject the board to a strict neutrality requirement. On the other hand, it is possible to grant the board far-reaching discretion to take defensive measures. European law has opted for the first approach. The TOD provides for a prohibition of the target company's board of directors from preventing a takeover bid: 'The **board** of the offeree company shall obtain the **prior authorisation** of the **general meeting** of shareholders given for this purpose before **taking any action**, other than seeking alternative bids, which may result in the **frustration** of the **bid** and in particular before issuing any shares which may result in a lasting impediment to the offeror's acquiring control of the offeree company.'[1] It follows that the board of directors may not take any defensive measures without the consent of the shareholders. As no other exceptions are provided for, the board of directors is strictly bound to neutrality.[2] A crown jewel defence would therefore be in breach of the board's duties. The same applies to the issue of new shares to the other shareholders. This measure would dilute the bidder's shareholding. However, it is an inadmissible measure under European takeover law! In addition, strict requirements also apply to measures taken by the board of directors prior to the takeover bid: 'As regards decisions taken before the [offer] and not yet partly or fully implemented, the general meeting of shareholders shall approve or confirm any decision which does not form part of the normal course of the company's business and the implementation of which may result in the frustration of the bid.'[3]

4   This high level of shareholder protection is diluted by the fact that Member States have the power to provide for other rules.[4] However, in the case of an opt-out, Member States are obliged to give companies the option of subjecting themselves to the regime of the TOD. They must give companies which have their registered offices within their territories the choice to apply Article 9(2) and (3) TOD (opt-in). The company's decision is made by the general meeting in accordance with the law of the state in which the company has its registered office, and in accordance with the regulations on amendments to the articles of association.

5   Member States have largely made use of their power not to apply the strict regime of the TOD. European law therefore plays no role in practice. Instead, the admissibility of defensive measures is assessed according to the specific and general rules of the Member States (stock corporation and takeover law). In Germany, for example, the board has more discretion to take defensive measures. Firstly, the board is allowed to take actions that would also have been taken by a prudent manager of a company that is not affected by a takeover bid. Secondly, the board of directors is permitted, with the consent of the supervisory board, to take actions which could frustrate the success of the offer. However, the divergent rules in the 27 Member States cannot be explored in depth here.

---

[1] Cf. Art. 9(2) TOD.
[2] K. Hopt, *Europäisches Übernahmerecht*, 81; R. Veil, in: Veil and Drinkuth (eds.), *Reformbedarf im Übernahmerecht*, 95, 97.
[3] Cf. Art. 9(3) TOD.
[4] Cf. Art. 12(1) TOD.

The Member States are obliged to prescribe the disclosure of an **opinion** by the board of the 6
target company on **the takeover bid**: 'The board of the offeree company shall draw up and
make public a document setting out its opinion of the bid and the reasons on which it is
based, including its views on the effects of implementation of the bid on all the company's
interests and specifically employment, and on the offeror's strategic plans for the offeree
company and their likely repercussions on employment and the locations of the company's
places of business […]. The board of the offeree company shall at the same time communicate that opinion to the representatives of its employees or, where there are no such representatives, to the employees themselves. Where the board of the offeree company receives in
good time a separate opinion from the representatives of its employees on the effects of the
bid on employment, that opinion shall be appended to the document.'

This obligation helps to ensure that the shareholders of the target company can make an 7
informed decision about the offer. On the other hand, it is an opportunity for the board to
draw attention to the weaknesses of the offer, especially with regard to the appropriateness
of the price. In practice, the statement plays a very important role.

II. Breakthrough

A takeover bid can be made more difficult or even impossible by numerous rules under 8
company law. The TOD therefore stipulates that various **takeover impediments**, such as
multiple voting rights or **restrictions** on the **transferability of registered shares**, do **not
apply** to the offer phase and the period after a takeover.[5] Such restrictions provided for in
the articles of association of the offeree company shall not apply vis-à-vis the offeror during the time allowed for acceptance of the bid. However, Member States do have the right
not to require companies having their registered office in their territory to apply the rules
on the breakthrough of certain takeover barriers (opt-out).[6] The European legislatures has
justified this regulatory option with 'existing differences in Member States' company law
mechanisms and structures.'[7]

The approach of giving companies the choice to subject themselves to the strict rules of the 9
TOD is not suitable for creating a uniform regime for the market for corporate control. The
incentive for the shareholders of the target company to declare the European breakthrough
rules applicable results primarily from the expectation that the capital market will reward
this. However, submission to the standards of the TOD can also be interpreted by market participants as a signal that the company sees itself as a potential takeover candidate.
Moreover, it cannot be ruled out that in companies with controlling shareholders the incentives are not strong enough.

---

[5] Cf. Art. 11 TOD.
[6] Cf. Art. 12(1) TOD.
[7] Cf. Recital 21 TOD.

BIBLIOGRAPHY

Alcock, Alistair et al. (eds.), *Gore-Browne on Companies*, looseleaf, as of July 2016.
Annunziata, Filippo, *La disciplina del mercato mobiliare*, 10th edn. (2020).
Assmann, Heinz-Dieter, Schneider, Uwe H. and Mülbert, Peter O. (eds.), *Wertpapierhandelsrecht, Kommentar*, 7th edn. (2019).
Assmann, Heinz-Dieter and Schütze, Rolf A. (eds.), *Handbuch des Kapitalanlagerechts*, 5th edn. (2020).
Baetge, Jörg et al., *Bilanzen*, 15th edn. (2019).
Bagge, James et al. (eds.), *Financial Services Decision Digest: FSA Final Notices and FSMT Decisions* (2007).
Baumbach, Adolf and Hopt, Klaus J., *Handelsgesetzbuch, Kommentar*, 40th edn. (2021).
Baums, Theodor and Thoma, Georg F. (eds.), *Kommentar zum WpÜG*, looseleaf, as of August 2012.
Bieber, Roland et al., *Die Europäische Union*, 14th edn. (2020).
Birds, John and Boyle, A.J., *Boyle & Birds' Company Law*, 10th edn. (2019).
Blair, Michael/Walker, George/Purves, Robert (eds.), *Financial Services Law*, 4th edn. (2018).
Bonneau, Thierry and Drumond, France, *Droit des marchés financiers*, 3rd edn. (2010).
Brandl, Ernst and Saria, Gerhard (eds.), *Praxiskommentar zum Wertpapieraufsichtsgesetz*, 2nd edn. (2010).
Brealey, Richard/Myers, Stewart/Allen, Franklin, *Principles of Corporate Finance*, 13th edn. (2019).
Buck-Heeb, Petra, *Kapitalmarktrecht*, 11th edn. (2020).
Callies, Christian and Ruffert, Matthias (eds.), *Das Verfassungsrecht der Europäischen Union mit Europäischer Grundrechtecharta—Kommentar*, 5th edn. (2016).
Campbell, Dennis (ed.), *International Securities Law and Regulation* 2nd edn. (2015).
Carlson, Laura, *Fundamentals of Swedish Law*, 3rd edn. (2019).
Claussen, Carsten P., *Bank- und Börsenrecht*, 5th edn. (2014).
Claussen, Carsten P./Scherrer, Gerhard, *Kölner Kommentar zum Rechnungslegungsrecht (§§ 238–342e HGB)*, (2010).
Coffee, John C., Jr. and Seligman, Joel, *Securities Regulation*, 9th edn. (2003).
Conac, Pierre-Henri/Gelter, Martin (eds.), *Global Securities Litigation and Enforcement* (2019).
Costi, Renzo, *Il mercato mobiliare*, 11th edn. (2018).
Couret, Alain and Le Nabasque, Hervé, *Droit financier*, 3rd edn. (2019).
Cox, James D. and Hazen, Thomas L., *Corporations*, 3rd edn. (2011).
Dauses, Manfred A. (ed.), *Handbuch des EU-Wirtschaftsrechts*, looseleaf, as of February 2021.
Davies, Paul L. and Worthington, Sarah, *Gower and Davies' principles of modern company law*, 11th edn. (2021).
Edwards, Vanessa, *EC Company Law* (1999).
Eidenmüller, Horst (ed.), *Ausländische Kapitalgesellschaften im deutschen Recht*, 2nd edn. (2010).
Eilers, Stephan et al. (eds.), *Unternehmensfinanzierung*, 2nd edn. (2014).
Emde, Ernst Thomas/Dornseifer, Frank/Dreibus, Alexandra (eds.), *KAGB Kommentar*, 2nd edn. (2019).
Ferran, Eilís, *Company Law and Corporate Finance* (1999).
Fleischer, Holger (ed.), *Handbuch des Vorstandsrechts* (2006).
Franke, Günter and Hax, Herbert, *Finanzwirtschaft des Unternehmens und Kapitalmarkt*, 6th edn. (2009).

French, Derek et al., Mayson, *French & Ryan on Company Law*, 37th edn. (2021).
Fuchs, Andreas (ed.), *Kommentar zum WpHG* 2nd edn. (2016).
Goette, Wulf and Habersack, Mathias (eds.), *Münchener Kommentar zum Aktiengesetz*, Vol. 1, 5th edn. (2019); Vol. 6, 5th edn. (2021).
Grabitz, Eberhard and Hilf, Meinhard (eds.), *Das Recht der Europäischen Union*, Vol. 3, looseleaf, as of August 2020.
Groß, Wolfgang (ed.), *Kapitalmarktrecht—Kommentar zum Börsengesetz, zur Börsen-zulassungs-Verordnung, zum Wertpapierprospektgesetz*, 7th edn. (2020).
Gruber, Michael (ed.), *BörseG 2018/MAR Kommentar* (2020).
Grundmann, Stefan (ed.), *Bankvertragsrecht, Band 2 (Investmentbanking), 7. Teil: Organisationsanforderungen an Marktteilnehmer und Marktinfrastruktur* (2020).
Grunewald, Barbara and Schlitt, Michael, *Einführung in das Kapitalmarktrecht*, 4th edn. (2020).
Gullifer, Louise and Payne, Jennifer, *Corporate Finance Law*, 3rd edn. (2020).
Haarmann, Wilhelm and Schüppen, Matthias (eds.), *Frankfurter Kommentar zum WpÜG*, 4th edn. (2014).
Habersack, Mathias and Verse, Dirk A., *Europäisches Gesellschaftsrecht*, 5th edn. (2019).
Habersack, Mathias et al. (eds.), *Unternehmensfinanzierung am Kapitalmarkt*, 4th edn. (2019).
Habersack, Mathias et al. (eds.), *Handbuch der Kapitalmarktinformation*, 3rd edn. (2020).
Haratsch, Andreas et al., *Europarecht*, 12th edn. (2020).
Hauschka, Christoph E. et al. (eds.), *Corporate Compliance: Handbuch der Haftungsvermeidung im Unternehmen*, 3rd edn. (2016).
Haynes, Andrew, *Financial Services Law Guide*, 5th edn. (2021).
Hazen, Thomas L., *The Law of Securities Regulation*, 8th edn. (2020).
Heinze, Stephan, *Europäisches Kapitalmarktrecht, Recht des Primärmarktes* (1999).
Hellner, Thorwald and Steuer, Stephan (eds.), *Bankrecht und Bankpraxis*, looseleaf, as of May 2021.
Hernández Sainz, Esther, *El abuso de información privilegiada en los mercados de valores* (2007).
Hess, Burkhard et al. (eds.), *Kölner Kommentar zum KapMuG*, 2nd edn. (2014).
Hirte, Heribert and Möllers, Thomas M.J. (eds.), *Kölner Kommentar zum WpHG*, 2nd edn. (2014).
Hirte, Heribert and von Bülow, Christoph (eds.), *Kölner Kommentar zum WpÜG*, 2nd edn. (2010).
Hopt, Klaus J., *Der Kapitalanlegerschutz im Recht der Banken* (1975).
Hopt, Klaus J./Seibt, Christoph H. (eds.), *Schuldverschreibungsrecht* (2017).
Hopt, Klaus J. and Voigt, Hans-Christoph (eds.), *Prospekt- und Kapitalmarktinformationshaftung—Recht und Reform in der Europäischen Union, der Schweiz und den USA* (2005).
Horspool, Margot and Humphreys, Matthew, *European Union Law*, 10th edn. (2018).
Jordan, Kelly, *International Capital Markets*, 1st edn. (2014).
Kalss, Susannne et al., *Kapitalmarktrecht I*, 2nd edn. (2015).
Kalss, Susanne/Oppitz, Martin/Torggler, Ulrich/Winner, Martin (eds.), *BörseG 2018 / MAR Kommentar* (2019).
Klöhn, Lars (Hrsg.), *Marktmissbrauchsverordnung (MAR), Kommentar* (2018).
Kümpel, Siegfried et al. (eds.), *Kapitalmarktrecht*, looseleaf, as of December 2019.
Kümpel, Siegfried and Veil, Rüdiger, *Wertpapierhandelsgesetz*, 2nd edn. (2006).
Kümpel, Siegfried and Wittig, Arne (eds.), *Bank- und Kapitalmarktrecht*, 5th edn. (2019).
Langenbucher, Katja, *Aktien- und Kapitalmarktrecht*, 4th edn. (2018).
Langenbucher, Katja (ed.), *Europäisches Privat- und Wirtschaftsrecht*, 4th edn. (2017).
Lenenbach, Markus, *Kapitalmarktrecht und kapitalmarktrelevantes Gesellschaftsrecht*, 2nd edn. (2010).
Lenz, Carl-Otto and Borchardt, Klaus-Dieter (eds.), *EU-Verträge: Kommentar nach dem Vertrag von Lissabon*, 6th edn. (2012).
Lomnicka, Eva and Powell, John L. (eds.), *Encyclopedia of Financial Services Law*, looseleaf, as of April 2021.
Lord Millett et al. (eds.), *Gore-Browne on Companies*, looseleaf, as of May 2021.

Loss, Louis and Seligman, Joel, *Securities Regulation*, Vol. 1, 6th edn. (2019).
Loss, Louis and Seligman, Joel, *Fundamentals of Security Regulation*, 7th edn. (2018).
Lutter, Marcus et al., *Rechte und Pflichten des Aufsichtsrats*, 6th edn. (2014).
Lycke, Johan, Lexino Lagkommentar på Internet, *Lag* (2007:528) *om värdepappersmarkna-den* (2013).
Lycke, Johan/Afrell, Lars, Lexino Lagkommentar på Internet, Lag (1991:980) *om handel med finansiella instrument* (2013).
MacNeil, Iain, G., *An Introduction to the Law on Financial Investment*, 2nd edn. (2012).
Markowitz, Harry, *Portfolio Selection* (1952).
Markowitz, Harry, *Portfolio Selection, Efficient Diversification* (1991).
Marsch-Barner, Reinhard and Schäfer, Frank A. (eds.), *Handbuch börsennotierte AG*, 4th edn. (2017).
Mathijsen, Petrus S.R.F., *A Guide to European Union Law*, 11th edn. (2013).
Menéndez, Aurelio, *Lecciones de Derecho Mercantil*, 18th edn. (2020).
Merkt, Hanno and Göthel, Stephan R., *US-amerikanisches-Gesellschaftsrecht*, 3rd edn. (2013).
Meyer, Andreas/Veil, Rüdiger/Rönnau, Thomas (eds.), *Handbuch zum Marktmissbrauchsrecht* (2018).
Moloney, Niamh, *EC Securities and Financial Markets Regulation*, 3rd edn. (2014).
Morse, Geoffrey (ed.), *Palmer's Company Law*, looseleaf, as of July 2016.
Oppermann, Thomas et al., *Europarecht*, 9th edn. (2021).
Panasar, Raj and Boeckman, Philip, *European Securities Law*, 3rd edn. (2021).
Park, Tido (ed.), *Kapitalmarktstrafrecht*, 5th edn. (2019).
Perridon, Louis/Steiner, Manfred/Rathgeber, Andreas W., *Finanzwirtschaft der Unternehmung*, 17th edn. (2017).
Raiser, Thomas and Veil, Rüdiger, *Recht der Kapitalgesellschaften*, 6th edn. (2015).
Rechtschaffen, Alan N., *Capital Markets, Derivatives and the Law*, 3rd edn. (2019).
Richter, Rudolf and Furubotn, Eirik G., *Neue Institutionenökonomie*, 4th edn. (2010).
Riesenhuber, K. (ed.), *Europäischen Methodenlehre—Grundfragen der Methoden des Europäischen Privatrechts*, 3rd edn. (2015).
Samuelsson, Per et al., *Lagen om marknadsmissbruk och lagen om anmälningsskylighet—En kommentar* (2005).
Schäfer, Frank A. and Hamann, Uwe (eds.), *Kapitalmarktgesetze, Kommentar*, looseleaf, as of January 2013.
Schäfer, Frank A./Hamann, Uwe (eds.), *Kapitalmarktgesetze, Kommentar*, 2nd edn., April 2012.
Schimansky, Herbert et al. (eds.), *Bankrechts-Handbuch*, 5th edn. (2017).
Schmidt, K. (ed.), *Münchener Kommentar zum Handelsgesetzbuch*, Vol. 3, 4th edn. (2019); Vol. 5, 4th edn. (2018).
Schmidt, Karsten and Lutter, Marcus (eds.), *Aktiengesetz—Kommentar*, 4th edn. (2020).
Schmidt, Reinhard H./Terberger, Eva, *Grundzüge der Investitions- und Finanzierungstheorie*, 3rd edn. (1996).
Schroeter, Ulrich G., *Ratings—Bonitätsbeurteilungen duch Dritte im System des Finanzmarkt-, Gesellschafts- und Vertragsrechts* (2014).
Schulze, Rainer et al. (eds.), *Europarecht, Handbuch für die deutsche Rechtspraxis*, 4th edn. (2020).
Schwark, Eberhard and Zimmer, Daniel (eds.), *Kapitalmarktrechtskommentar*, 5th edn. (2020).
Schwarze, Jürgen (ed.), *EU-Kommentar*, 4th edn. (2019).
Sealy, Len and Worthington, Sarah, *Cases and Materials in Company Law*, 11th edn. (2016).
Steiner, Josephine and Woods, Lorna, *EU Law*, 14th edn. (2020).
Streinz, Rudolf (ed.), *EUV/EGV: Vertrag über die Europäische Union und Vertrag zur Gründung der Europäischen Gemeinschaft, Kommentar*, 3rd edn. (2018).
Streinz, Rudolf et al., *Der Vertrag von Lissabon zur Reform der EU*, 3rd edn. (2010).
Swan, Edward J. and Virgo, John, *Market Abuse Regulation*, 3rd edn. (2019).
Tapia Hermida, Alberto J., *Derecho del Mercado de Valores*, 2nd edn. (2003).
Valette, Jean-Paul, *Droit de la régulation des marchés financiers* (2005).

Veil, Rüdiger (ed.), *Europäisches Kapitslmarktrecht*, 2nd edn. (2014).
Veil, Rüdiger and Koch, Philipp, *Französisches Kapitalmarktrecht* (2010).
Veil, Rüdiger and Walla, Fabian, *Schwedisches Kapitalmarktrecht* (2010).
Veil, Rüdiger and Wundenberg, Malte, *Englisches Kapitalmarktrecht* (2010).
Von der Groeben, Hans and Schwarze, Jürgen (eds.), *Kommentar zum Vertrag über die Europäische Union und zur Gründung der Europäischen Gemeinschaft*, 7th edn. (2015).
Walker, George and Purves, Robert (eds.), Financial Services Law, 4th edn. (2018).
Weber, Stefan, *Kapitalmarktrecht* (1999).
Werlauff, Erik, *EU Company Law, Common Business Law of 28 Member States*, 3rd edn. (2017).
Winternitz, Christian P. and Aigner, Lukas, *Wertpapieraufsichtsgesetz* (2007).
Wöhe, Günter/Döring, Ulrich/Brösel, Gerrit, *Einführung in die Allgemeine Betriebswirtschaftslehre*, 27th edn. (2020).
Wundenberg, Malte, *Europäisches Bankenaufsichtsrecht. Grundfragen des Single Rulebooks für Kreditinstitute in Europa* (2022).
Zerey, Jean-Claude (ed.), *Finanzderivate*, 4th edn. (2016).
Zib, Christian et al. (eds.), *Kapitalmarktgesetz Kommentar* (2008).
Zöllner, Wolfgang and Noack, Ulrich (eds.), *Kölner Kommentar zum Aktiengesetz*, Vol. 6, 3rd edn. (2016).
Zunzunegui, Fernando, *Derecho del Mercado Financiero*, 3rd edn. (2005).
Guidelines, reports and other CESR and ESMA documents cited in this book are available at: www.esma.europa.eu.

SUBJECT INDEX

The numbers in bold type refer to §, the numbers in normal type refer to para.

Accepted market practice 9 7; 15 4, 37
Access to Markets
   Banking Syndicate 7 37
   Book-building procedure 7 38
   Underwriting Agreement 7 37
Accounting Law 6 11; 18 26; 18 35; 18 45
Acquisition of Own Shares by a Company 15 57
Acting in Concert
   Acquisition of shares 20 62; 39 17
   Agreement 20 47; 20 50; 20 68
   Attribution to the trustee 20 83
   Elements 20 47; 20 52; 20 60; 20 65; 39 16
   Exercise of voting rights 20 49; 20 60; 39 25
   In another manner 20 58
   Interpretation 39 16
   Lasting common policy 20 48
   Legal ground for attribution 20 51
   Pooling agreements 20 56; 20 64
   Problems of evidence 39 22; 39 25
   Reciprocal attribution 20 51; 20 5
   Sanctions 20 67
Ad hoc Disclosure
   Administrative sanctions 19 74
   Aims of regulation 19 16
   Civil liability 19 80
   Conscious decision by the issuer 19 66
   Corporate Groups 19 26; 19 46
   Criminal sanctions 19 78
   Delay in disclosure *see* Delay in Disclosure
   Disclosure to third parties 19 72
   European legal sources 19 16
   Home Member State rule 19 25
   Inside information *see* Inside Information
   Member State legal sources 19 22
   Obligation to disclose 19 24
   Offsetting of information 19 37
   Publication procedure 19 41
   Regulatory goals 19 1
   Relation to periodic disclosure 19 20
   Relation to takeover disclosure 19 35
   Relation to transparency of major shareholdings and financial instruments 19 21
   Relevance in practice 19 10
   Sanctions 19 74
   Sanctions in practice 19 79

Administrative Fines 6 5; 11 11; 11 36
Adverse Selection 16 6
Agency Costs 16 20
AIFM 5 13; 9 20; 22 28; 23 20
Algorithmic Trading 25 5
   Automated order routers 25 45
   Benefits 25 23
   Direct electronic access 25 8
   Direct market access 25 8
   Flash crash 25 1
   High-frequency trading 25 7
   Market manipulation 15 49
   Regulation 15 13; 25 30
   Risks 25 2; 25 16
   Smart order routers 25 45
   Sponsored access 25 8
   Trading strategies 25 11
Alongside Purchases 14 75
Alternative Investment Market 15 1; 20 14
AMF 11 29
   Avis 5 52
   Instructions 5 52
   Recommendations 5 52
   Règlement général 5 52
Ancillary Stabilisation 15 69
Annual Financial Report 18 22; 18 32
   Annual financial statement 18 32
   Balance sheet oath 18 33
   Disclosure procedures 18 58
   Information 18 35
   Management report 18 32; 18 42
Annual Financial Statement 18 32
Attribution of Voting Rights *see also* **Transparency of Major Shareholdings and Financial Instruments; Mandatory Offer**
   Acting in concert *see* Acting in Concert
   By any other means 20 44
   Cash-settled equity swaps 20 87
   Collateral 20 72
   Concept 20 41
   In a corporate group 20 75; *see also* Attribution of Voting Rights in a Corporate Group
   Life interest 20 74
   Misleading 20 45
   On behalf of another person 20 83

Subject Index

Proxy **20** 88
Regulatory concept **20** 41
Securities lending agreement **20** 85
Transfer of voting rights **20** 70
Treuhand **20** 83
Trust **20** 83
Attribution of Voting Rights in a Corporate Group
Definition of corporate group **20** 77
Deposited shares **20** 81
Dominant influence **20** 78
Legal foundations **20** 75
Reform needs **20** 80
Autorité des Marchés Financiers *see* **AMF**
Availability Bias **6** 29; **15** 30
BaFin
Bulletins **5** 54
Foundation **11** 22
Issuer guideline **5** 54; **19** 53;
Newsletters **5** 54
Statements **5** 54
Balance Sheet Oath **18** 33; **18** 42
Base Prospectus *see* **Prospectus**
Basel Committee on Banking Supervision
Compliance and the compliance function in banks **32** 5
Core Principles for Effective Supervision **32** 5
Behavioural Finance-Research **6** 21; **6** 30; **6** 34; **15** 30; **16** 31; **27** 44
Benchmark
Administrator **36** 9
Authorisation **36** 42
Civil law liability **36** 40
Commodity benchmark **36** 21
Code of conduct **36** 24
Conflicts of interest **33** 35
Contributor **36** 9
Critical **36** 11
Definition **35** 1; **36** 6
Euribor **35** 2
Function **35** 10
Input data **36** 19
Integrity **36** 19
Interest-rate benchmark **36** 20
Investor protection **36** 30
Libor **35** 2
Libor scandal **33** 82; **35** 5; **36** 21
Manipulation; **33** 35; **35** 7
Market manipulation **15** 4; **15** 22; **15** 42
Non-significant **36** 12
Principles for the Benchmarks-Setting Process in the EU **35** 7
Public good **36** 23
Registration **36** 42
Regulation **1** 49; **5** 9; **36** 10
Risk-based approach **36** 10
Significant **36** 12
Supervision **36** 43
Third-country **36** 37
Wheatley Review **35** 7
Beneficiary **8** 25; **20** 74
Better Regulation **1** 30

Block Trades **15** 67
Board of Appeal ESAs **5** 27; **11** 67, 72, 102
Bonds
Definition **8** 16
High-yield bonds **27** 5
Junk bonds **27** 5
Maturity **8** 17
Rights **8** 17
Term **8** 19
Bookbuilding **15** 69
Bounded Rationality **6** 22
Bundesanstalt für Finanzdienstleistungsaufsicht *see* **BaFin**
Buy-back Programme **15** 57
Admissibility **15** 58
Aim **15** 58
Conditions **15** 61
Disclosure obligations **15** 60
Restrictions **15** 62
Call Option **8** 21; **20** 100
Capital Maintenance **6** 17; **17** 92; **19** 87
Capital Market Efficiency **2** 7; **16** 4
Capital Markets *see also* **Securities Markets**
Destabilisation **24** 12
Liquidity **15** 1
Capital Markets Law
Aims **2** 6
Definition **2** 1
Definition of capital market **7** 1
Dual nature **6** 6
Interpretation of European law **5** 14
Interpretation of national law **5** 18
Legal nature **6** 4
Legal sources **5** 2
Legal sources Austria **5** 49
Legal sources France **5** 51
Legal sources Germany **5** 53
Legal sources Italy **5** 57
Legal sources Spain **5** 59
Legal sources Sweden **5** 61
Legal sources United Kingdom **5** 63
National law **4** 40; **5** 48
Need to regulate insider dealings **13** 1
Regulatory strategies **2** 25
Capital Markets Union **1** 1; **1** 50; **1** 59; **1** 61; **5** 19; **18** 50
Cash Markets *see* **Securities Markets**
Cash-Settled Equity Swaps **8** 26; **15** 47; **20** 87; **20** 92
CCP **1** 48; **8** 23
Central Counterparty **7** 4
Certification System **40** 12
CESR **1** 18; **1** 23; **1** 34; **1** 40; **5** 27
Guidelines **5** 27; **14** 47; **14** 52; **14** 105; **15** 59
Indirect legal effect **5** 21; **5** 27
Change of Control Clause **39** 19
Cheapest Cost Avoider **2** 10; **2** 36
Chinese Walls **33** 59
Aims **33** 59
Attribution of knowledge **33** 75
Compliance officer **33** 69

Subject Index

Compliance-relevant information 33 65; 33 69; 33 71
  Design 33 65
  Elements 33 64
  'Need-to-know' principle 33 66
  Legal effects 33 75
  Legal foundations 33 63
  Origins 33 60
  Protection from liability 33 77
  Reinforced Chinese walls 33 64
  Restricted list 33 72
  Segregation of confidential areas 33 65
  Wall crossing 33 66
  Watch list 27 45; 33 70
Circuit breaker 24 57; 25 28, 40, 61, 71
Civil Liability *see also* **Informational Liability**
  Ad hoc disclosure 19 80
  Benchmark regulation 36 57
  Board members 34 44
  Damages 12 1
  Directors' dealings 21 28
  Financial analysts 26 64
  Financial reporting 18 75
  Insider dealing 14 117
  Market manipulation 15 91
  Prospectus disclosure 17 73
  Rating agencies 27 73
Class Action 12 23; 12 28; 17 54; 17 95
Clearing 8 23
Closed or Prohibited Periods 15 61; 21 20
CNMV 5 23; 11 25
Code of Conduct
  Benchmark administrator 36 24; 36 28
  Best Practice Principles for Providers of Shareholder Voting Research & Analysis 28 4
  Proxy advisors 28 4
  Stewardship Code 22 29
Codification 1 64; 14 118
Collateral 20 72
Comisión Nacional del Mercado de Valores *see* **CNMV**
Comitology Procedure 1 18; 4 1
Commissione Nazionale per le Società e la Borsa *see* **Consob**
Company Organisation
  Compliance *see* Compliance
  Internal audit *see* Internal Audit
  Investor protection 32 5; 33 11
  Risk management *see* Risk Management
Comparative Law 6 1
Compliance
  Advice and assistance 33 36
  Aim 33 12
  Chinese walls 33 65; *see also* Chinese Walls
  Code of conduct 33 36
  Compliance department 32 2; 33 32; *see also* Compliance Function
  Compliance function 33 21; *see also* Compliance Function
  Compliance 'in a broader sense' 32 3

Compliance obligation *see* Compliance Obligation
Compliance officer 33 37; *see also* Compliance Officer
Compliance organisation *see* Compliance Organisation
Compliance policies 32 1
Compliance report 33 50; *see also* Compliance Reporting
Compliance risk *see* Compliance Risk
Compliance-relevant information 33 65; 33 69; 33 71
Confidential areas 33 75; *see also* Chinese Walls
Conflicts of interest management 26 20; 32 5; 33 1; 33 22; 33 34; 33 59; 33 63
Definition 32 1
Development of new financial products 33 23
Developments 32 5
Documentation 33 31; 33 45
Enforcement strategy 33 11
Financial crisis 32 7
GRC model 32 3
Independence 33 22; 33 43; *see also* Compliance Function
Investment firms 32 5; 33 1
Legal foundations 32 5
Organisational concept 32 1; *see also* Compliance Organisation
Prevention of insider dealings 14 13; 32 5; 33 18; 33 59; 33 63; *see also* Insider Dealings
Principles-based regulation 33 6; *see also* Principles-based Regulation
Prohibition to provide consultancy services 27 38
Rating agencies 27 31
Reform 32 7
Regulatory concepts 33 1; 33 6
Relation to internal audit function 33 28
Relation to risk management 32 2; 33 29
Responsibility of the senior management 33 43
Restricted list 33 72
Risk-based approach 32 3; 32 5; 33 15
Sanctions 33 79; 33 84
Self-regulation initiatives 32 5
Société Générale 32 7
Standard Compliance Code 33 32
Watch list 27 45; 33 70
Compliance Function
  Access to information 33 32
  Advice and assistance 33 36
  Assessment 33 34
  Concept 33 36
  Conflicts of interest management 33 34; 33 59
  Connection to organisational and staff units 33 36
  Effectiveness 33 32
  Financial analysts 26 20
  Independence, financial 33 22
  Independence, operational 33 22
  Independence, organisational 33 27
  Instruments 33 70
  Investment firms 33 21

Involvement in operational business units **33** 23; **33** 28; **33** 34
Monitoring **33** 34
Permanence **33** 31
Prohibition of self-monitoring **33** 22
Rating agencies **27** 33
Relation to internal audit function **33** 28
Relation to risk management **32** 2; **33** 29
Remuneration **33** 24
Reporting obligation **33** 34; **33** 50; *see also* Compliance Reporting
Requirements **33** 22
Responsibilities **33** 33
Right to intervene **33** 47; **33** 48
Sanctions **33** 79

Compliance Obligation
Prevention of insider dealings **14** 13; **32** 5; **33** 18; **33** 59; **33** 63; *see also* Insider Dealings
Scope **33** 18

Compliance Officer
Access to information **33** 47
Administrative permission to exercise **33** 40
Appointment **33** 38
Approved person **33** 40
Company representative **33** 44
Conflicting interests **33** 44
Criminal liability **33** 85
Direct reporting **33** 42; **33** 47; *see also* Compliance Reporting
Dismissal **33** 40; **33** 46
Fit and proper test **33** 40
Independence, disciplinarian **33** 46
Independence, operational **33** 43
Independence towards the management **33** 43
Legal status **33** 42
Liability **33** 84
Obligation to pass on information **33** 48
Powers **33** 47
Protection against dismissal **33** 46
Qualification requirements **33** 38
Rating agencies **27** 34
Registration requirements **33** 39
Responsibilities **33** 47
Right to intervene **33** 48
Right to issue instructions **33** 48
Right to make suggestions **33** 51
Sanctions **33** 84

Compliance Organisation
Aims **33** 14
Elements **32** 1; **33** 20
Independence **33** 27; **33** 29
Margin of appreciation **33** 27
Principle of proportionality **33** 16; **33** 17; **33** 29
Principles-based approach **32** 5; **33** 21; **33** 29; **33** 98
Risk-orientated **32** 2; **33** 15

Compliance Reporting
Ad hoc reports **33** 53
Aims **33** 51
Compliance report **33** 45; **33** 50

External reporting **33** 54
Internal reports **33** 50

Compliance Risk
Definition **33** 15
Firm-specific risk profile **33** 16
Risk analysis **33** 16

Condensed Balance Sheet **18** 45
Condensed Profit and Loss Account **18** 45
Condensed Set of Financial Statements **18** 42
Confidentiality Obligation **19** 61
Conflicts of Interests Management *see* Compliance
Consob
Comunicazione **5** 58
Supervisory body **11** 25

Consolidated Accounts **18** 35; **18** 36; **18** 43
Consumer Protection **27** 18; **27** 30
Contracts for Difference **20** 93; **20** 94; **20** 99
Controlled Functions **33** 40
Corporate Governance **19** 58; **23** 1; **32** 3; **32** 7; *see also* Governance
Corporate Governance Statement **23** 5

Corporate Law **6** 13
Costs
Agency costs **16** 20
Costs of acquisition **16** 16
Costs of processing **16** 16
Costs of verification **16** 16
Proprietary costs **16** 21

Costs of Capital **26** 2; **26** 6; **27** 2
Credence Products *see* Securities
Credit Default Swaps
Effects **24** 8
ESMA powers **24** 57
Prohibition **1** 47; **24** 45

Credit Rating Agencies *see* Rating Agencies
Creeping In **20** 4; **20** 92; **39** 14
CRIM-MAD **3** 12; **5** 5; **8** 2; **13** 10; **14** 116
Crowdfunding **1** 57; **2** 3; **7** 20; **17** 15
Cryptoassets
Blockchain **10** 2
Currency token **10** 6
Distributed ledger technology **10** 2
DLT pilot regime **10** 27
Key **10** 5; **10** 11
Initial Coin Offering (ICO) **10** 12
Investment token **10** 7
Markets in Cryptoassets (MiCa) **10** 30
Smart contract **10** 5
Trading platforms **10** 17
Utility token **10** 8

Damages *see* Civil Liability
De Larosière Report **1** 36
Debt Securities **8** 16
Exercise of rights **22** 19

Delay in Disclosure **19** 44
Board member retirement **19** 7
Confidentiality **19** 61
Confidentiality leak **19** 64
Duty to instruct **19** 63
ESMA guidance **19** 68; **19** 51

Subject Index

Impending developments 19 52
Information to the competent authority 19 45
Legal sources 19 16
Legitimate interests 19 51
Liquidity support facilities 19 71
Misleading the public 19 59
Multi-stage decision-making processes 19 58
Negotiations 19 51
Period 19 46
Practical relevance 19 10
Delisting 7 42
Derivates *see* **Financial Instruments**
Derivatives Market 1 48; 7 3; 7 4; 8 21
Directive
    Consultations 1 40
    Direct effect 3 20
    Framework directive 1 18; 1 20; 1 25; 1 26; 3 6;
        3 18; 5 2
    Gold plating *see* Gold Plating
    Harmonisation 3 21
    Implementing measures 1 24; 1 25; 1 27; 4 14
    Interpretation 5 18
    Legal effects 3 20
    Margin of appreciation 3 18
    Member States' autonomy 4 14
    Revision 1 40
    Transposition 3 18
Directors' Dealings
    Aims 21 2
    Civil liability 21 28
    Closed period 21 20
    Disclosure requirements 21 12
    Disgorgement of profits 21 26
    Empirical studies 21 5
    Fines 21 25
    Harmonisation 21 9
    Member State legal sources 21 7
    Noise trading 21 4
    Persons discharging managerial
        responsibilities 21 12
    Publication procedure 21 19
    Relation to ad hoc disclosure 21 10
    Scope of application 21 12
    Source of information 21 2
    Sources of law 21 1; 21 3; 21 7
    Supervision 21 24
    Transactions subject to the notification
        requirement 21 15
Disclosure
    Ad hoc disclosure 19 2
    Austrian Financial Reporting Enforcement
        Panel 18 67
    Control of decisions 16 30
    Development in Europe 16 36
    Directors' dealings 21 1
    European Electronic Access Point 16 48; 18 61
    Ongoing 16 37; 19 3; 20 1; 21 1
    Financial Enforcement Panel 18 67
    Financial instruments *see* Financial Instruments
        Transparency

    Financial reports 16 37; 18 1
    Functions 2 25
    General meeting's rights 22 1
    Inside information 19 2
    Intentions of an investor *see* Intentions
    Issuer 16 24
    Major shareholdings 20 1
    Market exit 16 37
    Minimal framework 16 1
    Need for regulation 16 3; 16 24
    Offer document 17 1
    Periodic 16 37; 18 1
    Prospectus disclosure 16 37; 17 1; *see also*
        Prospectus Disclosure
    Segré report 16 1
    System 16 36
    Voting rights *see* Transparency of Major
        Shareholdings and Financial Instruments
Disclosure Philosophy 16 1
Disgorgement 12 16, 21; 21 26
Dissemination of Information 16 46; 16 47; 18 58
Dodd-Frank Act 1 33
Dominant Market Position 15 45
Due Diligence 14 69; 25 50; 27 5
EC Treaty 3 2
ECB
    Direct supervision 11 31
    ESRB 11 58
    SSM *see* SSM
ECJ
    Interpretation 5 28
    Preliminary ruling 5 18
Economic Analysis 6 20
EEC Treaty 3 2
Effet Utile *see* **Interpretation**
Efficiency
    Allocational 2 8; 16 5; 16 32
    Institutional 2 7; 16 13; 16 32
    Operational 2 10; 16 15
Efficient Capital Market Hypothesis (ECMH) 2 29;
    6 3; 16 7; 16 10; 16 29; 17 2
EGESC 4 16
Enforcement 2 48; 12 5; 12 8
    Effects of ESMA standards 11 106
    Harmonisation 3 21; 13 12
    Intensity 11 40; 12 10
    Internal 33 13
    Member States 3 12; 11 11; 11 35; 12 5; 12 13
    Private enforcement 12 8; 12 23; 30 54;
    Public enforcement 12 5; 12 12
    Strategies 12 1; 32 2
Equal Treatment 2 13; 21 23; 22 17
    Shareholders 22 17; 38 11
European Single Access Point 16 49
ESC 4 2
ESG
    Benchmark 36 32
    Disclosure requirements *see* Sustainability
    ESG criteria 8 29
    ESG investments 23 8

Financial products 8 27
Fundamental value-related information 14 56
Green Bonds 8 28
Greenwashing 8 30
Label for ecologically and/or socially
    sustainability 8 29
Non-financial reporting *see* Sustainability
Rating Agency *see* Sustainability
Taxonomy regulation *see* Sustainability
ESMA 1 37; 11 66
    Board of Appeal 11 67; 11 72; 11 102
    Board of Supervisors 11 67
    Budget autonomy 11 74
    Chairperson 11 68
    Comply or explain mechanism 4 26
    Executive director 11 69
    Guidelines 4 24; 5 2; 11 97; 13 5
    Implementing technical standards 4 19; 5 38; 13 5
    Independence 11 73
    Internal organisation 11 67
    Liability 11 104
    Management board 11 67; 11 70
    Micro-prudential supervision 11 59
    Powers in cases of disagreements 11 85
    Powers in emergency situations 11 84
    Powers of intervention 11 59; 11 75; 11 89; 27 62
    Prohibitions 11 91
    Questions & answers 4 33; 5 2; 13 7; 17 14
    Recommendations 4 24; 5 2; 5 22
    Regulatory technical standards 4 16; 5 38; 13 5
    Right to initiate investigations 11 79
    Seat 11 66
    Securities and Markets Stakeholders Group 11 71
    Supervision of market participants 11 89
    Supervision of credit rating agencies 1 39; 11 93
    Supervision of trade repositories 11 92
    Technical advice 4 17; 5 38
    Warnings 11 91
Event Study 19 12; 20 6
EU
    Legal acts 3 13; 5 1
    Legislative instruments 3 13
    Member State 3 3
    Treaty 3 2
Euribor *see* **Benchmark**
European Financial Stability Facility *see* **EFSF**
European Market Infrastructure Regulation *see* **EMIR**
European System of Financial Supervision *see*
    Supervision
European Systemic Risk Board *see* **Supervision**
Exchange Market 7 3
Exchange Traded Funds 2 21; 25 55
Expert Group of the European Securities Committee
    see **EGESC**
Explanatory Notes 18 44
Exploration 30 45
Fairness 6 24; 15 45; 25 21
FCA 11 30
    Approved person 5 33; 33 40
    Code of Practice for Approved Persons APER 5 66

Control of Information Rules 33 64
Evidential rules 5 67
Guidance 5 67
Handbook 5 66
Principles for Business PRIN 5 66
Rules 5 67
Safe Harbour Rules 5 72
Supervisory authority 11 52
Financial Analysis
    Alteration 26 56
    Conflicts of interests 26 18; 26 40; 26 43; 26 53
    Disclosure obligations 26 40
    Dissemination 26 56
    Extract 26 60
    Forecast 26 14
    Incorrect 26 66
    Information 26 1; 26 18; 26 24
    Market manipulation 26 65
    Non-written recommendations 26 62
    Presentation 26 22; 26 32
    Production 26 15; 26 22; 26 31
    Projections 26 33
    Recommendation 26 18; 26 21
    Sanctions 26 63
    Scope of application 26 22
    Summary 26 60
    Value judgement 26 67
Financial Analysts
    Aims 26 1
    Categories 26 8
    Conferences 26 1
    Damages 26 64
    Dependency 26 10; 26 43
    European legal sources 26 15
    Fines 26 63
    Functions 26 1
    Incentive 26 16
    Information intermediaries 26 1
    Inside information 26 1; 26 19; 26 75
    Investment banking 26 16; 26 51; 26 55
    Investment firms 26 20; 26 53; 26 80; 26 82
    Journalists 26 30
    Organisational obligations 26 20
    Prohibition to undertake personal
        transactions 26 69
    Self-regulation 26 30
Financial Conduct Authority *see* **FCA**
Financial Crisis 1 33; 7 4; 11 4; 11 28; 12 10
    Compliance 32 7; 33 11
    Corporate governance 34 4; 34 27
    Credit-rating agencies 1 38; 27 8; 27 11;
        27 31; 27 45
    Derivatives 1 48
    Financial stability 2 15
    Principles-based regulation 33 13
    Sanctions 34 51
    Short selling 1 47; 2 15; 24 19
    Structured finance instruments 27 29
Financial Instruments
    Concept 8 2

Subject Index

Contracts for difference 8 2; **20** 94
Derivatives 1 48; 7 3; 8 3; 8 21; **15** 53; **24** 8
Futures 8 24
Forwards 8 24
Repos 8 24
Securities *see* Securities
Stock loans 8 24
Structured 27 27; **27** 50
Swaps 8 24; **15** 10; **24** 2
Financial Instruments Transparency
    Cash-settled equity swaps 15 47; **20** 87; **20** 92
    Disclosure requirements **20** 90
    Fines **20** 121
    Notification requirements **20** 98
    Reform **20** 92
    Sanctions **20** 115
    Thresholds **20** 102
Financial Investor 9 13; **20** 8; **20** 59
Financial Market Participant 1 22; **5** 22; **8** 28; **23** 10
Financial Market Supervision 11 21
Financial Reporting
    Criminal and administrative sanctions **18** 77
    European legal sources **18** 22
    Financial accounting information **18** 7
    Formats 18 5; **18** 82
    Liability **18** 75
    Relation to ad hoc disclosure **19** 20
Financial Services Action Plan 1 13; 1 17; **1** 20; **1** 30; **4** 2; **18** 4
Financial Services and Markets Act 2000 *see* **FSMA**
Financial Services Authority *see* **FSA**
Financial Stability 2 15; **10** 24; **11** 58, 66, 83, 90; **19** 49, 69; **23** 19; **24** 19, 24, 52; **25** 2, 24; **29** 1, 4; **31** 5, 8
Finansinspektionen *see* **FI**
Finanzmarktaufsicht *see* **FMA**
Fines 2 47; **6** 5; **11** 11; **11** 16; **11** 93; **12** 1; **12** 7; **12** 17; **17** 71; **19** 75; **33** 79; **34** 52
Fitch 9 1; **27** 6; **27** 71
Flash Crash 25 1; **25** 16; **25** 26
Flipping **15** 64
FMA
    Circulars 5 50
    Supervisory authority **11** 22
Forecasts 14 14; **15** 21; **26** 22
Framework Directive *see* **Directive**
Framing 6 26; **6** 37
Framing Effect **15** 30
Frankfurt Stock Exchange 7 10; **7** 14; **7** 26; **7** 43; **18** 57
Fraud 2 2; **18** 71; **24** 65
Fraud on the Market Theory 2 34; **16** 10; **19** 85; **19** 96
Freedom of Establishment **3** 4
Frontrunning 14 32; **25** 22; **30** 19
FSA 11 21; **11** 30
FSMA 5 69; **19** 96
Fundamental value 2 32; **5** 43; **14** 56; **19** 55; **25** 19; **26** 11
Futures 7 3; **8** 21; **8** 24; **20** 99; **23** 16; **30** 26

Gatekeeper 26 5; **27** 2
General Disposition towards Acquisition *see* **Prospectus Liability**
Gold Plating 3 21; **20** 30; **25** 58
Golden Parachutes **37** 34
Governance Investment Firms
    Board structure **34** 12
    Diversity **34** 19
    Duties board members **34** 38
    Independence **34** 21
    Risk management **29** 13
GRC Model **32** 3
Green Paper
    Financial Services Policy (2005) 1 30
Greenshoe Option 15 69; **15** 71
Guidelines
    AMF **5** 23
    BaFin 5 23; **11** 17
    CESR *see* CESR
    ESMA *see* ESMA
    FMA **5** 50
    FCA **5** 67
Half-yearly Financial Report 18 3; **18** 42
    Auditing **18** 47
    Condensed balance sheet **18** 45
    Condensed profit and loss account **18** 45
    Disclosure **18** 55
    Explanatory notes **18** 44
    Half-Yearly Report Directive 16 40; **18** 3
Harmonisation
    Definition **3** 21
    ESMA 4 3; **4** 17; **11** 97
    Financial reporting 5 6; **18** 5
    Hybrid concepts **3** 26
    Insider dealing 1 11; **14** 6
    Investment services **1** 12
    Market abuse 1 21; **13** 4
    Maximum harmonisation 3 17; **3** 22; **3** 23
    Minimum harmonisation 1 6; **3** 21
    Prospectus law 1 6; **1** 10
    Sanctions 2 47; **3** 12; **6** 5; **11** 14; **11** 16; **12** 1
    Short selling **24** 21
    Stock Exchange rules **1** 8
    Takeover law **1** 28
    Transparency of major shareholdings and financial instruments 1 27; **20** 8
    Transparency requirements **1** 26
Hedge Funds 9 13; **23** 5, 18, 24
Hedging 24 7; **24** 46
Heuristics **6** 22
High-Frequency Trading *see* **Algorithmic Trading**
Hindsight Bias **6** 27
Home Member State Rule 11 43; **17** 14; **19** 22; **20** 13; **25** 36
Homo Oeconomicus 6 3; **6** 20; **6** 32
Implementing Technical Standards *see* **ESMA**
Improper Matched Orders **15** 35
Individual Accounts 18 35; **18** 43
Information
    Analysis **26** 1

Financial accounting information 18 7; 18 35; 18 43
Investment services 30 46
Internal company data 16 23; 16 25; 26 11
Officially appointed mechanisms 16 45; 18 58
Prognosis 18 8
Public goods 16 22
Information Costs 2 31; 16 16
Information Intermediaries see **Financial Analysts**
Information Overload 2 36; 16 31; 17 49; 21 31; 30 46
Informational Asymmetries 2 26; 15 1; 16 5; 16 18; 16 25; 22 2; 27 1
Informational Efficiency 16 7; 16 12; 16 15; 19 3; 19 80
Informational Liability
Capital maintenance 19 87
Causation 19 85; 19 91
Claimable damages 19 86; 19 98
Directors' dealings 21 28
Intent, negligence and recklessness 19 90
Members of the management board 19 83
Public policy and immorality 19 83
Restitution 19 86
Special provisions 19 88; 19 98
Torts 17 75; 19 80; 19 98; 20 126
Transparency of major shareholdings and financial instruments 20 118
Inside Information
Board member retirement 14 21
Decision to make a bid 5 32
Definition 14 11; 14 19; 14 32
Derivatives on commodities 14 32
Disclosure obligation 19 9
Economic data 19 33
Financial instruments 14 36
Front running 14 32
Future circumstances 14 41; 19 40
Individual step in a multi-stage process 14 23; 14 25
Interpretation 14 19
Legal foundations 14 9
Market data 19 33
Multi-stage processes 14 23; 19 30; 19 58
Offsetting 19 37
Precise information 14 36; 14 41
Price relevance 14 53
Probability/magnitude formula 14 28; 14 42
Rating 19 35; 27 16
Reference to an issuer 14 50
Rumours 14 47; 19 64
Scalping 14 40; 15 50; 26 72
Sensitive 14 81
Squeeze-out 19 35
Subprime-based instruments 14 55; 19 91
Takeover offer 19 35
Inside View 27 44
Insider 9 22; 14 10; 26 75
Insider Dealings
Chinese walls 14 13
Civil liability 14 117
Compliance 14 13; 32 5; 33 18; see also Compliance
Duty to inform 14 104
Exemptions 14 93
Interpretation of prohibitions 14 65
Notification obligation 14 106
Prohibition to disclose to another person 14 10; 14 77; 26 77
Prohibition to engage or attempt to engage in insider dealing 14 10; 14 66; 26 76
Prohibition to recommend or induce 14 10; 14 90
Regulation in the USA 14 1
Sanctions 13 3; 13 10; 13 12; 14 8; 14 111
Supervision 14 96
Insider Lists 14 100
Insider Supervision 14 104; 14 108
Insolvency Law 6 11
Interim Financial Report 18 44; 21 6; 21 20
Interim Management Report 18 42; 18 46
Interim Management Statements 18 5; 18 51; 18 54; 18 57
Internal Audit 32 5; 33 3; 33 28; 33 30
Internal Control 22 6; 32 2; 33 13; 33 28; 33 81; 36 17
Internal Market 1 1; 1 7; 1 20; 1 53; 3 9
Interpretation
Conform with the directive 5 18
Contextual 5 30
Dual 6 9
ECJ 5 18; 5 29; 5 45
Effet utile 5 45
Historical 5 37
Principles 5 28
Prohibition to draw an analogy 6 8
Teleological 5 40
Textual 5 29
Investment
Magic triangle 23 1
Speculation 23 6
Investment Advice
Definition 30 40
Suitability 30 50
Investment Firms
Board structure 34 12
Compliance see Compliance
Conflicts of interest 30 17
Exploration and assessment of suitability 30 45; 30 50
Independent advice 30 43
Inducements 30 77
Information obligations 30 46
Investment advisory services see Investment Advisory Services
Organisational requirements 33 1
Sanctions 30 10
Supervision 30 9
Investment Funds 7 8; 9 13; 23 20
Investment Restrictions
Institutional 23 20
Private 23 14

Subject Index

Investment Services Directive   5 3; 32 5
Investor
   Confidence   1 9; 2 8; 2 43; 5 41; 14 4; 14 17;
      15 30; 16 13; 19 85
   Definition   9 13
   Individual investor protection   16 27
   Institutional   7 7; 9 13; 9 26; 22 28; 23 20; 26 8
   Notification requirements   20 1; 20 18; 20 20
   Private   7 8; 9 13; 15 30; 19 9
   Professional   9 13; 17 21; 18 7; 23 15
   Protection   1 9; 2 7; 2 11; 6 31; 9 20; 10 33; 12 23;
      14 117; 16 27; 17 30; 20 1; 30 22; 36 30
   Qualified   9 27; 17 3
   Rational apathy   12 23; 28 3
   Reasonable   2 4; 6 31; 14 45; 14 53; 14 56; 15 31;
      16 28; 17 50
   Retail   9 28; 17 3; 23 17; 29 1
IOSCO Code   27 10; 27 62
Issue of Shares
   By the issuer   7 6
   Through securities underwriting   7 7
Issuer
   Definition   9 10; 18 29
   Market participant   9 11
Issuer Guideline see **BaFin**
Journalists   15 8; 24 65; 26 30; 27 9
Know Your Customer   30 45; 36 31
Lamfalussy
   Committee   1 16; 1 34
   Lamfalussy II   4 4
   Level 1   4 5
   Level 2   4 14
   Level 3   4 24
   Level 4   4 7
   Process   1 18; 1 20; 4 1; 4 4
   Report   1 16; 1 64
Legal Instruments   3 13
Legal Nature see **Capital Markets Law**
Legal Risk Management   32 5
Lehman Brothers insolvency   1 48
Level Playing Field   3 22; 3 24; 5 1; 25 29
Leverage   8 22
Libor see **Benchmark**
Liquidity   9 5; 9 22; 15 1; 16 14; 23 1; 25 12
London Stock Exchange   7 9; 9 4
Loss of Rights see **Sanctions; Supervision;
   Transparency of Major Shareholdings and
   Financial Instruments**
Management Report   18 18; 18 20; 18 37; 22 4
Management-based Regulation   33 13
Mandatory Bid   39 1
   Acting in concert   39 15
   Change of control requirement   39 6
   Concept   39 1
   Control thresholds   39 6
   Creeping-in   39 14; 39 31
   Exemption   39 9
   Formal definition of control   39 9; 39 13
   Legal foundations   39 15
   Material definition of control   39 9
   Price   39 8

   Reform needs   39 14
   Regulatory aims   39 2
MAD   1 21; 4 7; 12 8; 13 1; 14 5
MAR   1 42; 5 5; 11 3; 13 2; 14 7; 17 8; 21 3
Market Abuse Directive see **MAD**
Market Abuse Directive on Criminal Sanctions see
   CRIM-MAD
Market Abuse Regulation see **MAR**
Market Efficiency   1 24; 2 28; 8 25; 14 1; 16 4; 17 1;
   19 14; 25 24; 33 13
Market Failure   2 26; 16 5; 16 17; 26 5
Market for Lemons   2 26; 16 5
Market Maker   9 8; 14 2; 20 33; 24 1; 25 13; 25 18;
   25 65; 26 450
Market Manipulation
   Accepted market practice   15 4; 15 37
   Access to information   15 77
   Ad hoc disclosure   15 65
   Civil liability   15 89
   Core definition   15 4; 15 14; 15 53; 15 92
   Criminal offence   15 83
   Data traffic   15 77
   Dominant market position   15 45
   European legal sources   15 3
   Instances of manipulative behaviour   15 14
   Fines   15 15; 15 79; 15 83; 15 88
   High-frequency trading   25 21
   Imprisonment   15 86
   Information-based   15 1; 15 13; 15 17; 26 65
   Journalists   15 8
   Legitimate reason   15 37
   National legal sources   15 7
   Need for regulation   15 1
   Other forms   15 40; 26 69
   Reform needs   15 93
   Regulatory aims   15 3
   Safe harbour rules   15 56
   Sanctioning requirements   15 79
   Scalping   14 40; 15 50; 26 72
   Scope of application   15 8
   Signals   15 13; 15 19; 15 32; 15 83
   Supervision   15 74
   Trading suspension   15 77
   Transaction-based   15 1; 15 13; 15 32
Market Sounding   14 86
Markets in Financial Instruments Directive see
   MiFID
Markets in Financial Instruments Regulation see
   MiFIR
Marking the Close   15 35; 15 48
Medium Term Notes   17 29
Memorandum of Understanding (MoU)   11 49;
   14 99
Meta-based Regulation   33 13
MiFID   I 20; 1 25; 1 44; 3 18; 4 6; 5 2
MiFIR   1 44; 2 17; 3 25; 5 3; 7 4; 29 5; 31 7
Money Market   7 3
Moody's   9 1; 27 1; 27 9; 27 48; 27 73
Moral Hazard   16 6
MTF   7 16
Multilateral Trading Facility see **Trading Venue**

Naming and Shaming 11 14; 12 1; 12 22; 14 115;
  15 81; 19 76
Netting 8 23
New Economy 15 51; 26 38; 26 73
No Comment Policy 19 65
Noise Trading 2 32; 9 22; 21 4
Offer
  Disclosure obligation 19 35
  Primary market 7 5
  Public offer 17 18
Officially Appointed Mechanism 16 45; 18 59
Open Market 15 1; 20 14
Opening Clause 33 17
Options 7 3; 8 21; 20 100
Organisational Obligations
  Financial analysts 26 20
  Investment firms 32 1; 33 1
OTC Derivatives 1 45; 7 4
OTF 7 19
Overconfidence 6 23; 15 30
Pension Funds 7 8; 9 13; 23 20
Periodic Disclosure
  Enforcement 18 63
  European legal sources 18 22
  National legal sources 18 31
  Reform needs 18 81
  Sanctions 18 74
Pooling Agreements 20 56
Portfolio Management 26 84; 29 8; 30 6, 39, 65
Portfolio Theory 9 17; 30 39; 33 17
PRA 11 30
Price Formation 2 32; 15 2; 25 66
PRIIPS-Regulation 6 37
Primary Markets *see* **Securities Markets**
Principle of Proportionality 26 62; 33 16; 33 17;
  36 10
  As a characteristic of financial markets
    regulation 33 17
Principles-based Regulation
  Advantages 33 6
  Aims 33 8
  Concept 33 6
  Disadvantages 33 11
  Enforcement 33 9
  Evaluation 33 11
  High-level standards 33 6
  Impact 33 10
  Interpretation 33 10
  Legal certainty 33 11
  Legal structure 33 9; 33 10
  MiFID 33 6
  Minimum Requirements for the Compliance
    Function (MaComp) 33 11
  Rulemaking 33 9
  United Kingdom 33 6
Private Enforcement *see* **Enforcement**
Private Equity Companies 9 15
Product Governance
  Consumer protection 30 14
  Distribution strategy 30 9
  Distributor 30 8

  ESMA powers 31 5
  Manufacturer 30 27
  NCA powers 31 7; 30 8
  Organisational requirements for the
    manufacturer 30 23
  Product Intervention 31 1
  Requirements for the distribution of financial
    products 30 23
  Scope 30 26
Prognosis 18 8; 26 32
Prohibition of Insider Dealings
  Interpretation 14 24
Projections *see* **Prognosis**
Proprietary-costs 16 21
Prospect Theory 6 25
Prospectus
  Admission 17 5
  Approval 17 27; 17 54
  Base prospectus 17 26; 17 28
  Building block 17 35
  Content 17 41
  Deposit 17 17
  Format 17 26
  Frequent issuer 17 27
  High-risk investment 17 77
  Key investor information 17 10; 17 42; 17 44
  Language 17 52
  Legal foundations 17 5
  Material aspect 17 78
  Private placement 17 19; 17 22
  Prognoses 17 82; 17 83
  Public offer 17 16; 17 18
  Publication 17 58
  Reference 17 51
  Risk factors 17 46
  Schedule 17 36; 17 41
  Security 17 78
  Separate documents 17 26
  Shares 17 24
  Single document 17 26
  Single European passport 17 59
  Summary 17 42
  Supervision 17 68
  Supplement 17 62
  Universal Registration Document 17 27
  Update 17 62
  Warnings 17 44
  Withdrawal 17 63
Prospectus Directive 1 24; 1 41; 1 52; 16 40; 17 10;
  17 71
Prospectus Disclosure 1 10; 17 1
  European legal sources 17 10
  Exemptions 17 21
  Key investor information 17 10; 17 42; 17 44
  National legal sources 17 15
  Obligation 17 5
  Sanctions 17 71
Prospectus Liability
  Banks 17 86
  Capital maintenance 17 92
  Causation 17 87

Subject Index

Claimant 17 84
Deficiency of the prospectus 17 76
Director 17 86
Expert 17 86
General disposition towards acquisition 17 88
Issuer 17 85
Legal consequences 17 90
Major shareholder 17 86
Opposing party 17 85
Reform needs 17 96
Responsibility 17 89
Specific performance 17 91
Prospectus Regulation 1 24; 1 52; 5 4; 17 1; 17 11; 17 16; 17 68; 17 76
Proxy Advisors
  Best Practice Principles for Providers of Shareholder Voting Research and Analysis 28 4
  Communication 28 8
  Competition 28 15
  Conflicts of interest 28 5; 28 10
  Criticism 28 9
  Definition 28 1
  Regulatory concepts 28 4
  Influence 28 15
  Liability 28 11
  Self-binding code of conduct 28 4; 28 5
Prudential Regulation Authority *see* PRA
Public Law 6 2; 6 4
Put Option 8 21
Pyramid Financial Scheme 37 19
Quarterly Financial Report 18 5; 18 22; 18 50; 18 53
  Abolition in the TD 18 22; 18 54; 18 56
  Concept 18 49; 18 54
  Content 18 53; 18 57
  Controversy 18 48
  National rules 18 55
Question & Answers (Q&A) 5 25; 11 33
Rating
  Assessment 27 1
  Creditworthiness 27 1; 27 25
  Criminal sanctions 27 72
  Definition 27 24
  Disclosure 27 50
  Effects 27 5
  Functions 27 1
  Incorrect 27 12; 27 78; 27 82
  Investment-grade 27 5
  Methods 27 46
  Models 27 46
  Non-investment-grade 27 5
  Over-reliance 27 30; 27 58
  Presentation 27 50
  Prohibition 27 38
  Quality 27 45
  Regulation 27 40, 53, 74
  Solicited 27 73
  Sustainability 27 4
  Symbols 27 52
  Transparency report 27 54
  Unsolicited 27 53; 27 74

Rating Activities 27 28
Rating Agencies
  Administrative sanctions 27 67
  Civil liability 27 73
  Conflicts of interests 27 7; 27 31
  Definition 27 28
  ESMA 27 12; 27 47; 27 56; 27 62; 27 65; 27 67
  Functions 27 1
  Gatekeeper 27 2
  Independence 27 31
  Issuer-pays model 27 7; 27 30; 27 88
  Oligopoly 27 6
  Organisational requirements 27 32
  Prohibition to provide consultancy services 27 38
  Registration 27 55
  Regulation 1 32; 1 37; 27 12
  Rotation mechanism 27 39; 27 43; 27 44
  Shareholding structure 27 39
  Supervision 27 62
Recommendations *see* ESMA
Regulated Information 16 39; 16 41; 16 42
Regulated Information Service 18 60
Regulated Market
  Definition 7 2; 7 11
  List 7 14
  Segments 7 15
  Scope of application 13 15
  Requirements 7 13
Regulation
  Definition 3 15
  Legal effects 3 15
  Legal foundations 3 15
Regulation on Credit Rating Agencies 1 38; 3 10; 5 8; 27 12; 27 16; 27 18; 27 21; 27 80
Regulation on OTC Derivatives 1 48
Regulations on the European Supervisory Authorities 5 11
Regulatory Technical Standards *see* ESMA
Related Party Transactions 22 33
Relevant Information Not Generally Available 4 13; 14 19
Reporting Thresholds *see* Transparency of Major Shareholdings and Financial Instruments
Representativeness 6 29
Research Reports 24 15; 26 8
Restricted List 33 72; *see also* Chinese Walls
Right to Appoint 22 15; 22 33
Risks
  Agency 1 55
  Aversity 5 26; 30 44
  Business 8 3; 9 18
  Concentration 1 55
  Credit 1 38, 48; 8 22; 14 55; 24 43; 27 3; 30 26
  Currency 8 3; 9 18; 30 59
  Cyber 10 28
  Default 1 55; 8 23; 27 38
  Diversification 9 19; 23 18
  Factors 17 34, 41, 46
  Financial investments 23 1
  Interest rate 9 18; 30 59
  Issuer 30 61; *see also* default and credit risk

Legal   17 48; 30 6; 31 23, 34, 48
Liquidity   1 55
Market risk   23 3
Noise trading   21 4
Operational   1 55; 25 16
Political   9 18
Price   8 26
Regulatory arbitrage   3 12; 19 65
Settlement failures   24 11
Sustainability (ESG)   1 60; 2 22; 8 29; 14 55; 16 34; 17 48; 23 11
Systematic   9 18
Systemic   1 36, 47; 8 23; 11 28; 19 65; 25 16, 26; 34 6, 41; 36 1
Tolerance   30 1, 28, 50; 34 40
Underlying asset   8 22; 27 11
Unsystematic   9 18
Risk Management see also **Compliance; Compliance Function**
GRC model   32 3
Qualitative risk management   32 2
Relation to Compliance   32 2; 33 29
Rumours   14 47; 15 18; 15 19; 15 29; 19 64; 26 65
Safe Harbour Provision   5 24; 5 72; 15 56
Salience   6 29
Sanctions
Administrative   12 1; 12 4; 12 12; 12 16
Benchmark   36 43
Civil   12 1; 12 3; 12 8
Compliance   33 79
Corporate governance   34 51
Criminal   12 1; 12 5; 12 10; 12 13
Directors' dealings   21 25
Disclosure of inside information   19 74
Disclosure of major holdings   20 121
Effective   12 12; 12 23;
Financial analysts   26 63
Fines see Fines
Forfeiture of profits see Forfeiture of profits
Harmonisation   12 12; 12 25
Insider dealing   14 111
Investment advisory services   30 10
Loss of rights   12 1; 12 8
Market manipulation   15 79
Naming and shaming see Naming and Shaming
Periodic disclosure   18 74
Pre-crisis era   12 5
Prospectus disclosure   17 71
Rating agencies   27 67
Short sales   24 63
Trading suspension see Trading Suspension
Reforms   12 10
Requirements   12 5; 12 8
Sanctioning activity   11 39
Types   12 1
Sarbanes-Oxley-Act   18 27
Scalping   14 40; 15 50; 24 13; 26 72
Secondary Markets see **Securities Markets**
Securities
Admission   5 4; 16 40; 17 4; 17 5; 17 16; 17 20

Bonds see Bonds
Concept   8 4
Credence products   17 2
Disclosure of rights   22 18
Non-equity   7 21; 17 28
Public offer   17 18
Share see Share
Securitisation   1 54; 5 10; 9 11; 23 17; 27 29; 27 39
Securities Markets
Cash markets   7 1
Liquidity   1 8
Primary markets   7 5; 9 1
Regulation   2 6
Secondary markets   7 8; 9 1
Segments   7 15
Spot transactions   8 21
Stock exchanges   7 9
Supply and demand   2 9; 7 1
Segré Report   1 2; 18 3
Self-regulation   5 2; 18 56; 12 1; 14 3; 26 30; 26 42; 27 62; 28 5; 35 4; 36 29
Separation of Functions   33 27; 34 15
Settlement   7 23; 10 28
Period   7 1
Short selling   24 27
Share
Buy-back   14 93; 15 57
Classes   22 17; 37 17
Definition   8 11
Deposition   20 81
Disclosure of changes in rights   22 18
Employees   37 23
Exercise of rights   20 17; 20 20
Non-par value share   8 13
Par value share   8 13
Preferred stock   8 13; 20 25
Registered share   8 14
Restrictions on voting rights   37 24
Special rights   37 22
Transferability   8 14; 37 18
Trust   20 83
Shareholders' Agreement   37 26
Short Selling   24 4
Covered   24 5
Criticism   24 11
Destabilising the financial system   24 19
Disclosure obligations   24 32
Economic intention   24 7
ESMA   24 21; 24 61
Leverage   9 15
Liquidity   24 9
Locate agreement   24 28
Market manipulation   24 13
Naked   24 6
Positive effects   24 9
Prohibitions   24 27
Regulation   1 47; 24 20; 24 26
Rules on sovereign credit default swap agreements   24 43
Short position   24 32

Supervision 11 99; 24 49
 Thresholds 24 32
 Types 24 5
 Uncovered 24 6; 24 11; 24 26
Regulation on Short Selling and Credit Default
 Swaps 2 17; 5 7; 24 20
Signal Theory 16 21
Single European Passport *see* Prospectus;
 Supervision
Single Rulebook 1 17; 4 21; 5 2; 12 17; 13 5; 13 9;
 14 9; 27 13
Single Supervisory Mechanism *see* SSM
SME Growth Markets *see* Trading Venue
Social Responsible Investment (SRI) *see* ESG
Sovereign Credit Defaults Swaps 24 43
Sovereign Debt Instruments 24 19; 24 29; 24 31;
 24 37; 24 43
Sovereign Wealth Funds 9 13; 9 16
Spoofing 15 35; 25 21
SSM 11 31; 11 33; 11 61
Stabilisation Activities 15 64
 Ancillary 15 71
 Disclosure obligations 15 69
 Legitimacy 15 64
 Period 15 68
 Scope of application 15 66
Stakebuilding 14 40; 14 76; 20 7
Standard & Poor's 9 1; 27 1; 27 6; 27 38; 27 42;
 27 49; 27 73
Standard Compliance Code 33 32; *see also* Compliance
Stock Exchange
 Admission 9 1
 Bodies 7 10
 Concept 7 9
 Management 7 10;
 Open market *see* Open Market
 Operating institution 7 10
 Supervisory authority 7 13
Stock Lending Agreements 20 85
Stock Price
 Determination 7 10; 7 38
 Publication 7 10
Structured Finance Instruments 27 29; 27 50
Subprime Crisis 19 91
Suitability 30 50; 30 70; 31 10; 34 35; 34 43; 36 31
Supervision
 Authorities 1 8; 2 15
 Capital markets 11 1
 Competition between institutions 11 52
 Convergence in Europe 4 29; 11 97; 14 110
 Cooperation in Europe 1 18; 1 31; 11 43
 Cooperation with third countries 11 48
 Delegation to other entities 11 5
 EBA 1 34; 11 25; 11 59; 11 59
 EIOPA 1 34; 11 25; 11 59; 11 59
 ESMA *see* ESMA
 ESME 1 40
 European 1 34; 11 54
 European System of Financial Supervision
  (ESFS) 1 36; 2 15; 11 54

European Systemic Risk Board (ESRB) 11 58
 Fines 11 10
 Function 2 48
 General clauses 11 7; 11 10
 Home country control 1 8
 Hybrid models 11 27
 Institutional concepts 11 2; 11 18; 11 32
 Integrated supervision 11 21
 Internal organisation 11 34
 Liability of supervisory authorities 11 38
 Loss of rights 11 15
 Macro-prudential 1 36; 11 58
 Micro-prudential 1 36; 11 59
 Minimum powers 11 7
 National supervisory authorities 1 18; 1 31; 1 34;
  11 1; 11 21; 11 22; 11 25; 11 27; 11 29;
  11 30; 14 109
 Path dependence 11 32
 Peer reviews 11 76; 14 110
 Prudential supervision 11 20; 11 28
 Sanctioning activity 11 39
 Sanctions 11 14; 11 16
 Sectoral supervision 11 19; 11 25
 Single Bank Resolution Fund 11 64
 Single European passport 11 45; 11 50; 17 59
 Single Supervisory Mechanism 11 61
 Single Resolution Mechanism 11 61
 Supervisory convergence 11 97
 Suspension of trading 15 77
 Twin peaks model 11 28
Supervisory Board 6 15; 19 58; 34 13
Sustainability
 Action Plan Financing Sustainable Growth 1 63;
  16 33; 18 19
 CSR Directive 2 23; 2 41; 18 16
 Dimensions 2 21
 Disclosure requirements 2 22; 2 41; 16 33;
  18 18; 23 10
 Greenwashing 8 31
 Non-financial reporting 18 11
 Rating Agency 27 4
 Sustainable corporate governance 22 11
 Sustainable finance 1 59; 2 24; 18 25
 Sustainability report *see* Non-Financial Reporting
 Sustainability screened ETF 8 29
 Taxonomy Regulation 1 59; 2 22; 16 34
Swaps 8 24; 20 87
 Credit default swaps *see* Credit Default Swaps
 Cash-settled equity swaps *see* Cash-settled
  Equity Swaps
Systematic Internaliser 7 32
Takeover Directive 1 28; 5 32; 37 3
Takeover Disclosure
 Aims 37 10; 37 14
 Change of control clauses 37 32
 Compensation agreements 37 34
 Control of employee shares 37 23
 Decision to launch a bid 38 5
 Legal foundations 37 1
 Loan agreements 37 32

Market for corporate control 37 35
Medium of publication 37 16
Offer document 38 7
Reform needs 37 35
Replacing the management 37 28
Restrictions on voting rights 37 24
Scope of application 37 15
Secrecy interest 37 17
Share buy-back 37 30
Share issue 37 30
Shareholders' agreements 37 26
Significant shareholdings 37 19
Special rights 37 22
Structure of the capital 37 17
Transfer of shares 37 18
Takeovers
Legal sources 37 1
Mandatory bid *see* Mandatory Bid
Takeover Directive 37 3
Transparency *see* Takeover Disclosure
Types 38 3
Voluntary bid 38 4
Taxonomy *see* **Sustainability**
Technical Advice *see* **ESMA**
Testo Unico della Finanza (TUF) 5 62
TEU 3 3
TFEU 3 3
Thresholds *see* **Financial Instruments Transparency; Mandatory Bid; Short Selling; Transparency of Major Shareholdings and Financial Instruments**
Tin Parachutes 37 34
Trading Suspension 12 16; 14 98; 15 77
Trading Venue 7 1
Multilateral trading facilities (MTF) 7 2; 7 16; 14 7
Organised trading facilities (OTF) 7 19
Regulated markets® 7 2
SME growth markets 7 23; 17 9; 17 20; 17 65;
Systematic internalisers (SI) 7 32
Transaction Cost Theory 16 24
Transparency 2 25; 16 4; 19 5; *see also* Disclosure
Transparency Directive 1 26; 3 6; 3 10; 3 26; 5 6; 18 4; 20 1; 20 12
Transparency of Major Shareholdings and Financial Instruments
Acquisition 20 24
Aims 20 1

Attribution of voting rights 20 13; 20 41; 20 102; *see also* Attribution of Voting Rights
Disposal 20 24
European legal sources 20 12
Exemptions 20 32
Financial instruments *see* Financial Instruments
Fines 20 123
Home Member State 20 15
Information 20 18
Loss of rights 6 7; 20 67; 20 116; 20 123
Market maker 20 33
Maximum harmonisation 20 9
Minimum harmonisation 20 8
Notification 20 98
Notification obligation 20 23
Order to notify 20 117
Power to require information 20 117
Preference shares 20 25
Proportion of voting rights 20 31
Publication 20 39
Reform needs 20 129
Relation to further disclosure requirements 20 20
Reporting thresholds 20 1; 20 23; 20 26
Sanctions 20 121; 20 464
Scope of application 20 14
Stricter regulation 20 8; 20 10; 20 55; 20 130
Supervision 20 117
Time limit 20 37
Voting rights 20 1
True and Fair View 18 27; 18 32
UCITS 1 8; 5 13; 8 30; 9 16; 22 28; 23 10, 20
Underlying 2 26; 8 21
Unification 1 1; 1 33; 1 53; 3 5; 3 18; 11 107; 14 8; 14 118; 19 22
Volatility 16 13; 16 14; 24 11; 25 18; 25 24; 25 25
Voting Rights
Exercised by proxy 20 81; 20 88
Transfer 20 70
Wall Crossing 14 88; 33 66
Wash Sales 15 35
Watch List 33 70; *see also* Chinese Walls
Whistleblowing 12 14; 14 106; 15 76
White Paper
Completing the Internal Market (1985) 1 7
Financial Services Policy (2005) 1 30
Writer of an Option 8 25

INDEX OF NATIONAL LAWS

Abbreviation / Title	Full National Title	Translated Title	Country
ABGB	Allgemeines Bürgerliches Gesetzbuch	Austrian General Civil Code	Austria
ABL	Aktiebolagslag (SFS 2005:551)	Swedish Stock Corporation Act	Sweden
AktG	Aktiengesetz	German Stock Corporations Act	Germany
AnsFUG	Gesetz zur Stärkung des Anlegerschutzes und Verbesserung der Funktionsfähigkeit des Kapitalmarktes	Act to Strengthen Investor Protection and Improve the Functioning of Capital Markets	Germany
AnSVG	Anlegerschutzverbesserungsgesetz	German Investor Protection Improvement Act	Germany
AO	Abgabenordnung	German Act on the Administrative Procedures in Taxation	Germany
APER	Code of Practice of Approved Persons (FCA Handbook)		UK
årsredovisningslag	årsredovisningslag	Swedish Accounts Act	Sweden
BEHV–EBK	Verordnung der Eidgenössischen Finanzmarktaufsicht über die Börsen und den Effektenhandel	Swiss Regulation on Stock Exchanges and Securities Trading	Switzerland
Beteiligungsfondsgesetz	Beteiligungsfondsgesetz	Austrian Equity Participation Funds Act	Austria
BGB	Bürgerliches Gesetzbuch	German Civil Code	Germany
BilMoG	Gesetz zur Modernisierung des Bilanzrechts	German Accounting Law Modernisation Act	Germany
BörseG	Börsengesetz	Austrian Stock Exchange Act	Austria
BörsG	Börsengesetz	German Stock Exchange Act	Germany

Index of National Laws

Abbreviation / Title	Full National Title	Translated Title	Country
BörsO FWB	Börsenordnung für die Frankfurter Wertpapierbörse	German Exchange Rules for the Frankfurter Wertpapierbörse	Germany
BörsZulVO	Börsenzulassungs-Verordnung	German Stock Exchange Admission Regulation	Germany
BrB	Brottsbalk (SFS 1995:1554)	Swedish Criminal Code	Sweden
C. com.	Code de commerce	French Commercial Code	France
C. mon. fin.	Code monétaire et financier	French Monetary and Financial Code	France
CASS	Client Asset Sourcebook (FCA Handbook)		UK
Cc	Code Civil	French Civil Code	France
CC	Código Civil	Spanish Civil Code	Spain
CJA	Criminal Justice Act 1993		UK
COBS	Conduct of Business Sourcebook (FCA Handbook)		UK
Codice Civil	Codice Civil	Italian Civil Code	Italy
Companies Act 2006	Companies Act 2006		UK
Company Act 1980	Company Act 1980		UK
Consiglio Nazionale degli Ordini dei Giornalisti	Consiglio Nazionale degli Ordini dei Giornalisti	The Italian National Council's Regulation of Journalists	Italy
CP	Código Penal	Spanish Criminal Code	Spain
Criminal Justice Act 1993 (Commencement No. 5) Order (SI 1994/242)	Criminal Justice Act 1993 (Commencement No. 5) Order (SI 1994/242)		
DepotG	Depotgesetz	Custody Act	Germany
DTR	Disclosure Rules and Transparency Rules (FCA Handbook)		UK
ECV	Emittenten-Compliance-Verordnung of 2007	Austrian Issuer Compliance Regulation	Austria
Finansinspektionen's regulation FFFS 2007:16	Finansinspektionen's regulation FFFS 2007:16	Shwedish MaComp	Sweden
Finanzmarktaufsichtsgesetz	Finanzmarktaufsichtsgesetz	Austrian Financial Market Supervision Act	Austria

Index of National Laws

Abbreviation / Title	Full National Title	Translated Title	Country
FinDAG	Gesetz über die Bundesanstalt für Finanzdienstleistungsaufsicht	German Law on the Financial Services Supervisory Authority	Germany
FISG	Finanzmarktintegritätsstärkungsgesetz	Financial Market Integrity Strengthening Act	Germany
FMABG	Finanzmarktaufsichtsbehördengesetz	Austrian Financial Markets Supervisory Authorities Act	Austria
FRUG	Finanzmarktrichtlinie- Umsetzungsgesetz	German Financial Market Directive Implementation Act	Germany
FCA Handbook	FCA's Handbook of Rules and Guidance		UK
FSMA 2000	Financial Services and Markets Act 2000		UK
Gesetz zur Stärkung des Anlegerschutzes und Verbesserung der Funktionsfähigkeit des Kapitalmarktes	Gesetz zur Stärkung des Anlegerschutzes und Verbesserung der Funktionsfähigkeit des Kapitalmarktes	German Investor Protection Enhancement and Improvement of the Functioning of the Capital Markets Act	Germany
GG	Grundgesetz	German Constitution	Germany
Grundsätze ordnungsmäßer Compliance	Grundsätze ordnungsmäßer Compliance	Austrian Standard Compliance Code	Austria
HGB	Handelsgesetzbuch	German Commercial Code	Germany
Investment Recommendations (Media) Regulations 2005	Investment Recommendations (Media) Regulations 2005		UK
Investmentfondsgesetz	Investmentfondsgesetz	Austrian Investmentfund Act	Austria
KAGB	Kapitalanlagegesetzbuch	Investment Act	Germany
KapInHaG	Kapitalmarktinformationshaftungsgesetz	German Capital Markets Information Liability Act	Germany
KapMuG	Gesetz über Musterverfahren in kapitalmarktrechtlichen Streitigkeiten	German Capital Markets Model Case Act	Germany
KMG	Kapitalmarktgesetz	Austrian Capital Market Act	Austria

Abbreviation / Title	Full National Title	Translated Title	Country
KuMaKV	Verordnung zur Konkretisierung des Verbots der Kurs- und Marktpreismanipulation	German Regulation for the Implementation of the Prohibition on Market and Price Manipulation	Germany
KWG	Gesetz über das Kreditwesen	German Banking Act	Germany
lag om anmälningsskyldighet vissa innehav av finansiella instrument	lag om anmälningsskyldighet vissa innehav av finansiella instrument	Swedish Act on the Disclosure of Ownership regarding Certain Financial Instruments	Sweden
lag om börs- och clearingverksamhet (SFS 1992:543)	lag om börs- och clearingverksamhet (SFS 1992:543)	Swedish Act on Stock Markets and Clearing	Sweden
lag om investeringsfonds (SFS 2004:46)	lag om investeringsfonds (SFS 2004:46)	Swedish Investment Fund Act	Sweden
lag om offentliga uppköpserbjudanden på aktiemarknaden (SFS 2000:1087)	lag om offentliga uppköpserbjudanden på aktiemarknaden (SFS 2000:1087)	Swedish Takeover Act	Sweden
lag om straff för marknadsmissbruk vid handel med finansiella instrument (SFS 2005:377)	lag om straff för marknadsmissbruk vid handel med finansiella instrument (SFS 2005:377)	Swedish Market Abuse Act	Sweden
lag om värdepappersrörelse (SFS 1991:981)	lag om värdepappersrörelse (SFS 1991:981)	Swedish Act on securities transactions	Sweden
lag omgrupprättegång (SFS 2002:599)	lag omgrupprättegång (SFS 2002:599)	Swedish Group Proceedings Act	Sweden
LHF	lag om handel med finansiella instrument (SFS 1991:980)	Swedish Act on the trading in Financial Instruments	Sweden
LMV	Ley 24/1988, de 28 de julio, del Mercado de Valores	Spanish Securities Market Act	Spain
LSA	Ley de Sociedades Anónimas	Spanish Stock Corporation Act	Spain
LVM	lag om värdepappersmarknadenv (SFS 2007:528)	Swedish Securities Market Act	Sweden
MaComp	Mindestanforderungen an Compliance	BaFin's Minimum Requirements for Compliance	Germany
MaKonV	Verordnung zur Konkretisierung des Verbotes der Marktmanipulation	German Implementing Regulation on the Prohibition of Market Manipulation	Germany

Abbreviation / Title	Full National Title	Translated Title	Country
MAR	Code of Market Conduct (FCA Handbook)		UK
MaRisk	Mindestanforderungen an das Risikomanagement	German Minimum Requirements for Risk Management	Germany
MVSV	Mindestinhalts-, Veröffentlichungs- und Sprachenverordnung	Austrian Ordinance on Minimum Contents, Publication and Language	Austria
öAktG	Österreichisches Aktiengesetz	Austrian Stock Corporation Act	Austria
öUWG	Unlauterer-Wettbewerbs-Gesetz	Austrian Act against Unfair Practices	Austria
OWiG	Gesetz über Ordnungswidrigkeiten	German Administrative Offenses Act	Germany
PRIN	Principles for Businesses (FCA Handbook)		UK
RD	Real Decreto	Spanish Royal Decree (Regulation)	Spain
RD 1310/2005	Real Decreto 1310/2005, de 4 de noviembre, por el que se desarrolla parcialmente la Ley 24/1988, de 28 de julio, del Mercado de Valores, en materia de admisión a negociación de valores en mercados secundarios oficiales, de ofertas públicas de venta o suscripción y del folleto exigible a tales efectos	Spanish Royal Decree (Regulation) on Prospectuses	Spain
RD 1333/2005	Real Decreto 1333/2005, de 11 de noviembre, por el que se desarrolla la Ley 24/1988, de 28 de julio, del Mercado de Valores, en materia de abuso de mercado	Spanish Royal Decree (Regulation) on Market Abuse	Spain
RD 1362/2007	Real Decreto 1362/2007, de 19 de octubre, por el que se desarrolla la Ley 24/1988, de 28 de julio, del Mercado de Valores, en relación con los requisitos de transparencia relativos a la información sobre los emisores cuyos valores estén admitidos a negociación en un mercado secundario oficial o en otro mercado regulado de la Unión Europea	Spanish Royal Decree (Regulation) on Transparency on Capital Markets	Spain
RD 217/2008	Real Decreto 217/2008, de 15 de febrero, sobre el régimen jurídico de las empresas de servicios de inversión y de las demás entidades que prestan servicios de inversión y por el que se modifica parcialmente el Reglamento de la Ley 35/2003, de 4 de noviembre, de Instituciones de Inversión Colectiva, aprobado por el Real Decreto 1309/2005, de 4 de noviembre	Spanish Royal Decree (Regulation) on Investment Firms	Spain

Abbreviation / Title	Full National Title	Translated Title	Country
RD 1066/2007	Real Decreto 1066/2007, de 27 de julio, sobre el régimen de las ofertas públicas de adquisición de valores	Spanish Royal Decree (Regulation) on Takeovers	Spain
RE	Regolamento Emittenti	Italian Issuers' Regulation	Italy
	Real Decreto-ley 5/2005, de 11 de marzo, de reformas urgentes para el impulso a la productividad y para la mejora de la contratación pública	Spanish Royal Decree-Act (Regulation) on urgent reforms to increase productivity and to improve public procurement	Spain
Regolamento Congiunto	Regolamento Congiunto	Italian Compliance Regulation	Italy
Regolamento Intermediari	Regolamento Intermediari	Italian Regulation on Intermediaries	Italy
Regolamento Mercati	Regolamento Mercati	Italien Financial Markets Regulation	Italy
Regulation FFFS 2005:9	Regulation FFFS 2005:9	Swedish Regulations and general guidelines regarding investment recommendations directed to the general public and the management of conflicts of interest	Sweden
RG AMF	Règlement général Autorité des Marchés Financiers	General Regulations of the French Stock Market Authority	France
RRM	Reglamento del Registro Mercantil	Spanish regulation on Company Registries	Spain
SchVG	Schuldverschreibungsgesetz	German Bond Act	Germany
SEC Rules	SEC Rules		USA
Securities Exchange Act 1934	Securities Exchange Act 1934		USA
SFS	Svensk författningssamling	Swedish law gazette	Sweden
StGB	Strafgesetzbuch	German Criminal Code	Germany
SYSC	Senior Management Arrangements, Systems and Controls (FCA Handbook)		UK

Index of National Laws

Abbreviation / Title	Full National Title	Translated Title	Country
Takeover Code	Takeover Code		UK
TUF	Testo Unico della Finanza	Italian Consolidated Laws on Finance	Italy
TUG	Transparenzrichtlinie-Umsetzungsgesetz	German Implementing Act on the Transparency Directive	Germany
UmwG	Umwandlungsgesetz	Transformation Act	Germany
ÜbG	Übernahmegesetz	Austrian Takeover Act	Austria
VAG	Versicherungsaufsichgesetz	German Law on Insurance Supervision	Germany
VMV	Veröffentlichungs- und Meldeverordnung	Austrian Disclosure and Notification Regulation	Austria
vædipapirhandelslov	vædipapirhandelslov	Danish Securities Trading Act	Denmark
WAG	Werpapieraufsichtsgesetz	Austrian Securities Supervision Act	Austria
WpAV	Verordnung zur Konkretisierung von Anzeige-, Mitteilungs- und Veröffentlichungspflichten nach dem Wertpapierhandelsgesetz	German Regulation on Disclosure of Securities Trading and Insider Dealings	Germany
WpDVerOV	Verordnung zur Konkretisierung der Verhaltensregeln und Organisationsanforderungen für Wertpapierdienstleistungsunternehmen	German Regulation Implementing the Rules of Conduct and Organisational Requirements for Investment Service Companies	Germany
WpHG	Gesetz über den Wertpapierhandel	German Securities Trading Act	Germany
WpHMV	Verordnung über die Meldepflichten beim Handel mit Wertpapieren und Derivaten	German Regulation on the Notification Obligations when Trading with Securities and Derivatives	Germany
WpPG	Wertpapierprospektgesetz	German Securities Prospectus Act	Germany

Abbreviation / Title	Full National Title	Translated Title	Country
WpÜG	Wertpapiererwerbs- und -Übernahmegesetz	German Securities Acquisition and Takeover Act	Germany
WpÜGAngebVO	Verordnung über den Inhalt der Angebotsunterlage, die Gegenleistung bei Übernahmeangeboten und Pflichtangeboten und die Befreiung von der Verpflichtung zur Veröffentlichung und zur Abgabe eines Angebots	German WpÜG Offer Ordinance	Germany
ZPO	Zivilprozessordnung	German Civil Procedure Code	Germany

INDEX OF NATIONAL LAWS BY COUNTRY

Austria

National Title	Translated Title	Abbreviation
Allgemeines Bürgerliches Gesetzbuch	Austrian General Civil Code	ABGB
Alternative Investmentfonds Manager-Gesetz		AIFMG
Beteiligungsfondsgesetz	Austrian Equity Participation Funds Act	
Börsengesetz	Austrian Stock Exchange Act	BörseG
Emittenten-Compliance-Verordnung of 2007	Austrian Issuer Compliance Regulation	ECV
Finanzmarktaufsichtsbehördengesetz	Austrian Financial Market Supervisory Authorities Act	FMABG
Finanzmarktaufsichtsgesetz	Austrian Financial Market Supervision Act	
Grundsätze ordnungsmäßer Compliance	Austrian Standard Compliance Code	
Investmentfondsgesetz	Austrian Investment Fund Act	
Kapitalmarktgesetz	Austrian Capital Market Act	KMG
Kuratorengesetz	Austrian Bond Act	
Mindestinhalts-, Veröffentlichungs- und Sprachenverordnung	Austrian Ordinance on Minimum Contents, Publication and Language	MVSV
Österreichisches Aktiengesetz	Austrian Stock Corporation Act	öAktG
Übernahmegesetz	Austrian Takeover Act	ÜbG
Unlauterer-Wettbewerbs-Gesetz	Austrian Act against Unfair Practices	öUWG
Veröffentlichungs- und Meldeverordnung	Austrian Disclosure and Notification Regulation	VMV
Werpapieraufsichtsgesetz	Austrian Securities Supervision Act	WAG

Denmark

National Title	Translated Title	Abbreviation
vædipapirhandelslov	Danish Securities Trading Act	

France

National Title	Translated Title	Abbreviation
Code Civil	French Civil Code	Cc
Code de commerce	French Commercial Code	C. com.
Code monétaire et financier	French Monetary and Financial Code	C. mon. fin.
Règlement général Autorité des Marchés Financiers	General Regulations of the French Stock Market Authority	RG AMF

Germany

National Title	Translated Title	Abbreviation
Abgabenverordnung	German Act on the Administrative Procedures in Taxation	AO
Aktiengesetz	German Stock Corporations Act	AktG
Gesetz zur Stärkung des Anlegerschut-zes und Verbesserung der Funktions-fähigkeit des Kapitalmarktes	Act to Strengthen Investor Protection and Improve the Functioning of Capital Markets	AnsFUG
Anlegerschutzverbesserungsgesetz	German Investor Protection Improvement Act	AnSVG
Börsengesetz	German Stock Exchange Act	BörsG
Börsenordnung für die Frankfurter Wertpapierbörse	German Exchange Rules for the Frankfurter Wertpapierbörse	BörsO FWB
Börsenzulassungs-Verordnung	German Stock Exchange Admission Regulation	BörsZulVO
Bürgerliches Gesetzbuch	German Civil Code	BGB
Depotgesetz	Custody Act	DepotG
Finanzmarktintegritätsstärkungsgesetz	Financial Market Integrity Strengthening Act	FISG
Finanzmarktrichtlinie-Umsetzungsgesetz	German Financial Market Directive Implementation Act	FRUG
Gesetz über das Kreditwesen	German Banking Act	KWG
Gesetz über den Wertpapierhandel	German Securities Trading Act	WpHG
Gesetz über die Bundesanstalt für Finanzdienstleistungsaufsicht	German Law on the Financial Services Supervisory Authority	FinDAG
Gesetz über Musterverfahren in kapitalmarktrechtlichen Streitigkeiten	German Capital Markets Model Case Act	KapMuG
Gesetz über Ordnungswidrigkeiten	German Administrative Offenses Act	OWiG
Gesetz zur Modernisierung des Bilanzrechts	German Accounting Law Modernisation Act	BilMoG
Gesetz zur Stärkung des Anlegerschutzes und Verbesserung der Funktionsfähigkeit des Kapitalmarktes	German Investor Protection Enhancement and Improvement of the Functioning of the Capital Markets Act	
Gesetz zur Vorbeugung gegen missbräuchliche Wertpapier- und Derivategeschäfte	Act on the Prevention of Improper Securities and Derivatives Transactions	
Grundgesetz	German Constitution	GG
Handelsgesetzbuch	German Commercial Code	HGB

Kapitalanlagegesetzbuch	Investment Act	KAG
Kapitalmarktinformationshaftungsgesetz	German Capital Markets Information Liability Act	KapInHaG
Mindestanforderungen an Compliance	BaFin's Minimum Requirements for Compliance	MaComp
Mindestanforderungen an das Risikomanagement	German Minimum Requirements for Risk Management	MaRisk
Schuldverschreibungsgesetz	Bond Act	SchVG
Strafgesetzbuch	German Criminal Code	StGB
Transparenzrichtlinie-Umsetzungsgesetz	German Implenting Act on the Transparency Directive	TUG
Umwandlungsgesetz	Transformation Act	UmwG
Verordnung über den Inhalt der Angebotsunterlage, die Gegenleistung bei Übernahmeangeboten und Pflichtangeboten und die Befreiung von der Verpflichtung zur Veröffentlichung und zur Abgabe eines Angebots	German WpÜG Offer Ordinance	WpÜGAngebVO
Verordnung über die Meldepflichten beim Handel mit Wertpapieren und Derivaten	German Regulation on the Notification Obligations when Trading with Securities and Derivatives	WpHMV
Verordnung zur Konkretisierung der Verhaltensregeln und Organisationsanforderungen für Wertpapierdienstleistungsunternehmen	German Regulation Implementing the Rules of Conduct and Organisational Requirements for Investment Service Companies	WpDVerOV
Versicherungsaufsichgesetz	German Law on Insurance Supervision	VAG
Verordnung zur Konkretisierung von Anzeige-, Mitteilungs- und Veröffentlichungspflichten sowie der Pflicht zur Führung von Insiderverzeichnissen nach dem Wertpapierhandelsgesetz		WpAV
Wertpapiererwerbs- und -Übernahmegesetz	German Securities Acquisition and Takeover Act	WpÜG
Wertpapierprospektgesetz	German Securities Prospectus Act	WpPG
Zivilprozessordnung	German Civil Procedure Code	ZPO

Greece

National Title	Translated Title	Abbreviation
Law No. 4514/2018	Transposition of MiFID II	FEK A 14
Law No. 3556/2007	Transposition of the TD	FEK A 91
Law No. 3461/2006	Transposition of the TOD	FEK A 106
Law No. 3371/2005	Listing Act	FEK A 178
Law No. 4443/2016	Transposition of the CRIM-MAD	FEK A 232
Law No. 3401/2005	Prospectus Law	

Italy

National Title	Translated Title	Abbreviation
Codice Civil	Italian Civil Code	
Consiglio Nazionale degli Ordini dei Giornalisti	The Italian National Council's Regulation of Journalists	
Regolamento Congiunto	Italian Compliance Regulation	
Regolamento Emittenti	Italian Issuers' Regulation	RE
Regolamento Intermediari	Italian Regulation on Intermediaries	
Regolamento Mercati	Italien Financial Markets Regulation	
Testo Unico della Finanza	Italian Consolidated Laws on Finance	TUF

Spain

National Title	Translated Title	Abbreviation
Código Civil	Spanish Civil Code	CC
Código Penal	Spanish Criminal Code	CP
Ley 24/1988, de 28 de julio, del Mercado de Valores	Spanish Securities Market Act	LMV
Ley de Sociedades Anónimas	Spanish Stock Corporation Act	LSA
Real Decreto	Spanish Royal Decree (Regulation)	RD
Real Decreto 1066/2007, de 27 de julio, sobre el régimen de las ofertas públicas de adquisición de valores	Spanish Royal Decree (Regulation) on Takeovers	RD 1066/2007
Real Decreto 1362/2007, de 19 de octubre, por el que se desarrolla la Ley 24/1988, de 28 de julio, del Mercado de Valores, en relación con los requisitos de transparencia relativos a la información sobre los emisores cuyos valores estén admitidos a negociación en un mercado secundario oficial o en otro mercado regulado de la Unión Europea	Spanish Royal Decree (Regulation) on Transparency on Capital Markets	RD 1362/2007
Reglamento del Registro Mercantil	Spanish regulation on Company Registries	RRM

Sweden

National Title	Translated Title	Abbreviation
Aktiebolagslag (SFS 2005:551)	Swedish Stock Corporation Act	ABL
lag om börs- och clearingverksamhet (SFS 1992:543)	Swedish Act on Stock Markets and Clearing (no longer in force)	
lag om handel med finansiella instrument (SFS 1991:980)	Swedish Act on the trading with Financial Instruments	LHF
lag om offentliga uppköpserbjudanden på aktiemarknaden (SFS 2006:451)	Swedish Takeover Act	
lag om straff för marknadsmissbruk vid handel med finansiella instrument (SFS 2005:377)	Swedish Market Abuse Act	

lag om värdepappersmarknadenv (SFS 2007:528)	Swedish Securities Market Act	LVM
lag om värdepappersrörelse (SFS 1991:981)	Swedish Act on Securities Transactions	
Svensk förtattningssamling	Swedish Law Gazette	SFS

United Kingdom

National Title	Translated Title	Abbreviation
Code of Conduct (FCA Handbook)		COCON
Code of Practice of Approved Persons (FCA Handbook)		APER
Companies Act 2006		
Conduct of Business Sourcebook (FCA Handbook)		COBS
Disclosure Rules and Transparency Rules (FCA Handbook)		DTR
Financial Services and Markets Act 2000		FSMA 2000
FCA's Handbook of Rules and Guidance		FCA Handbook
Handbook of the Prudential Regulation Authority		PRA Handbook
Listing Rules (FCA Handbook)		LR
Principles for Businesses (FCA Handbook)		PRIN
Prospectus Regulation Rules sourcebook (FCA Handbook)		PRR
The Market Abuse (Amendment) (EU Exit) Regulations 2019		
The Official Listing of Securities, Prospectus and Transparency (Amendment etc.) (EU Exit) Regulations 2019		

USA

National Title	Translated Title	Abbreviation
SEC Rules		
Securities Exchange Act 1934		SEA
Securities Act 1933		SA

INDEX OF EUROPEAN LAWS

Title	Subject	Abbreviation
Treaty on the Functioning of the European Union		TFEU
Directives (Level 1)		
Directive (EU) No. 2011/61	Alternative Investment Fund Managers	AIFMD
Directive (EU) No. 2014/57	Criminal sanctions for market abuse	CRIM-MAD
Directive (EU) No. 2019/2034	Investment Firm Directive	IFD
Directive (EC) No. 2003/6	Market abuse (no longer in force)	MAD 2003
Directive (EU) No. 2014/65	Markets in financial instruments	MiFID II
Directive (EC) No. 2007/36	Shareholder rights	SRD
Directive (EU) No. 2017/828	Shareholder rights	SRD II
Directive (EC) No. 2004/109	Transparency requirements	TD
Directive (EC) No. 2004/25	Takeover bids	TOD
Directive (EC) No. 2009/65	Undertakings for collective investment in transferable securities (UCITS)	UCITS
Regulations (Level 1)		
Regulation (EU) No. 2016/1011	Benchmarks	BR
Regulation (EC) No. 1060/2009	Credit rating agencies	CRAR
Regulation (EU) No. 462/2013	Credit rating agencies	CRAR III
Regulation (EU) No. 1093/2010	European Banking Authority	EBA
Regulation (EU) No. 2020/1503	European Crowdfunding Service Providers	ECSP
Regulation (EU) No. 1094/2010	European Insurance and Occupational Pensions Authority	EIOPA
Regulation (EU) No. 1095/2010	European Securities and Markets Authority	ESMA
Regulation (EU) No. 2020/852	Framework to facilitate sustainable investment	SFTaxR
Regulation (EC) No. 1606/2002	International accounting standards	IAS
Regulation (EU) No. 2019/2033	Investment Firm Regulation	IFR

Regulation (EU) No. 1286/2014	Key information documents for packaged retail and insurance-based investment products	PRIIPS
Regulation (EU) No. 596/2014	Market abuse	MAR
Regulation (EU) No. 600/2014	Markets in financial instruments	MiFIR
Regulation (EU) No. 2017/1129	Prospectus to be published when securities are offered to the public or admitted to trading on a regulated market	PR
Regulation (EU) No. 2017/2402	Securitisations	SR
Regulation (EU) No. 236/2012	Short selling and certain aspects of credit default swaps	SSR
Regulation (EU) No. 2019/2088	Sustainability-related disclosures in the financial services sector	SFDR

INDEX OF SUPERVISORY AND COURT RULINGS

The numbers in bold type direct to main reference.

Case	Authority	Subject(s)	Reference
Barclays Bank Plc	FSA	Compliance failings regarding manipulated submission of Libor and Euribor rates	§ 33 para. 82, **§ 35 para. 6**
Basic Inc. v. Levinson	US Supreme Court	Semi-strong form of ECMH; presumption of reliance on misrepresentations	**§ 2 para. 34**, § 16 para. 10, § 19 para. 85
Bond	BGH	Investment advice and suitability doctrine under civil law	**§ 30 para. 57**
BuM/WestLB	BGH	Prospectus liability for incorrect information; liability relating to prognoses	**§ 17 para. 77**, 79, 83
Carr Sheppards Crosthwaite	FSA	Fine as a sanction for insufficient compliance systems	§ 33 para. 81
CoCos	FCA	Prohibition of distribution of CoCos	§ 31 para. 3
Comroad	BGH	Liability for disclosure of false inside information	§ 19 para. 84
Continental/Schaeffler	BaFin	Transparency of major shareholdings and takeover law; disclosure obligations and attribution of voting rights in cases of cash settled equity swaps	§ 20 para. 93
Daimler/Geltl	ECJ/BGH/OLG Stuttgart	Definition of inside information; prerequisites for the adhoc disclosure obligation; delay in disclosure; civil liability	§ 5 para. 42, 44, **§ 14 para. 21**, § 19 para. 63
EM.TV	BGH	Liability for disclosure of false inside information	§ 19 para. 84
Fitch Ratings Limited	ESMA	Administrative sanctions; infringements of CRA-Regulation	§ 27 para. 71
Georgakis	ECJ	Definition of inside information; prerequisites for the prohibition of the use of inside information	§ 14 para. 51
Grøngaard/Bang	ECJ	Insider regulation; definition of inside information; prerequisites for the prohibition of disclosing inside information to other persons	§ 6 para. 16, **§ 14 para. 80**
IKB	BGH/OLG Düsseldorf	Definition of inside information; liability for omitted disclosure	**§ 14 para. 55**, § 19 para. 90

IKB	LG Düsseldorf	Market manipulation through false information about necessary depreciation as a consequence of the subprime crisis	§ 15 para. 27
Infomatec	BGH	Liability for disclosure of false inside information; market manipulation	§ 19 para. 82
John Pottage	FSA/Upper Tribunal	Responsibility of senior management for compliance failings	§ 33 para. 87
Hirmann	ECJ	Liability of issuers; Restitution and capital maintenance requirements	§ 17 para. 93
Lafonta	ECJ	Definition of inside information; determination of likely direction of price change	§ 14 para. 48
Merrill Lynch, Pierce, Fenner & Smith	SEC	Compliance; requirements for compliance organisation; Chinese walls	§ 33 para. 61
Mohammed	FSA Tribunal	Definition of inside information; rumours	§ 14 para. 46
Munoz	ECJ	Private liability and *effet utile*	§ 5 para. 46
Opel	BGH	Scalping as a form of market manipulation	§ 15 para. 51, **§ 26 para. 73**
Porsche/VW	OLG Stuttgart/LG Braunschweig	Accusation of information-based market manipulation; accusation of market manipulation by securing a dominant market position	**§ 15 para. 17**, 44 § 19 para. 117
Pottage	FSA	Aper Statement Principle 7, compliance requirements	§ 33 para. 87
Sacyr/Eiffage	Cour d'appel Paris	Prerequisites of a takeover offer; attribution of voting rights because of *acting in concert*	§ 39 para. 22
Scope Ratings	ESMA/BoA	Rating Methodologies	§ 27 para. 47, 71
Slade v. Shearson, Hammill & Co.	SEC	Compliance; restricted list as element of compliance organisation	§ 33 para. 73
Spector	ECJ	Insider regulation; prerequisites for the prohibition of the use of inside information	§ 5 para. 19, 36, 49, **§ 14 para. 70**
VW Dieselgate	LG Stuttgart	Disclosure of insider information, definition of inside information; requirement of precise information	§ 19 para. 27, 31
Wirecard	BaFin	Market manipulation, fraudulent financial reporting, short selling	§ 18 para. 72, **§ 24 para. 65**
WMF	BGH	Takeover law; attribution of voting rights because of *acting in concert*	§ 39 para. 24
Wolfson Microelectronics	FSA	Obligation to disclose inside information; offsetting of information	§ 19 para. 38
	BGH	Transparency of major shareholdings; attribution of voting rights in case of stock lending agreements	§ 20 para. 86
	BGH	Transparency of major shareholdings; attribution of voting rights in case of trusts	§ 20 para. 84